MW00413288

SECOND EDITION

Chaucer's Poetry

AN ANTHOLOGY FOR THE MODERN READER

Selected and Edited by
E. T. DONALDSON
INDIANA UNIVERSITY

Scott, Foresman and Company
Glenview, Illinois

Dallas, Tex. Oakland, N.J. Palo Alto, Cal.
Tucker, Ga. London, England

Library of Congress Cataloging in Publication Data

Chauncer, Geoffrey, d. 1400.
Chaucer's poetry.

Reprint. Originally published: 2nd ed. New York : Wiley, c1975.
Bibliography: p.
I. Donaldson, E. Talbot (Ethelbert Talbot), 1910– II. Title.
PR1855 1984 821'.1 82-20444
ISBN 0-673-15667-2

1011121314-DOC-00999897

PREFACE

When this anthology was first conceived—more than twenty-five years ago—its title was to be *The Best of Chaucer.* But as the editorial work proceeded it became clear that a title which suggested that the editor was skimming the cream off a pail of milk was grossly misleading; with Chaucer the normal proportions of cream and milk are reversed, so that the best of Chaucer is most of Chaucer. The popularity and wide use of the first edition, which did contain most of Chaucer's poetry, has encouraged the editor and his publishers to bring out a second edition that contains still more: all the *Canterbury Tales* written in verse. If even this enlarged volume does not have all of the best, it surely has God's plenty, which I offer gratefully to the many users of the first edition who have asked for more.

Chaucer may be legitimately treated as little more than a distinguished representative of the culture of the Middle Ages. But Chaucer is a great poet whose poetry is as valid and as exciting today as it was in the fourteenth century; to the student of literature, indeed, it is far more important than the fourteenth century. This has seemed, both to the publishers and to me, the chief justification for presenting a new edition of the major part of his poetry—one that focuses on the poetry as the important thing and that provides critical and historical apparatus as an aid to experiencing, rather than a justification for reading, the poetry. The purpose of this book, then, is to make the pleasure of Chaucer as accessible as possible. The assumption under which I have worked is that, in reading poetry, understanding is dependent on pleasure and will diminish proportionately as pleasure does.

The principal hindrance to a full enjoyment of Chaucer is the fourteenth-century English in which he wrote. The apparent strangeness of his ideas is largely the result of readers' discomfort with his language, so that increased ease in reading causes much of this sense of strangeness to vanish. Yet the time it takes to master Chaucer's Middle English is so considerable that it is surely worthwhile to lighten the burden for the reader coming to Chaucer for the first time.

In this edition, the text of Chaucer's poetry has been reproduced in a spelling that is designed to improve the reader's recognition of recurrent words, and has been thoroughly glossed as well. The spelling system offers the greatest readability that is possible without sacrificing either the phonological values or the general appearance of Middle English orthography. The spelling of the manuscripts has been given internal consistency in this book, so that an individual word—one not subject to inflectional alteration—will generally (for oversights occur) be spelled in the same way. In order to make comprehension easier, a word still current has been given the Middle English form closest to that of the Modern English word. (For detailed discussion, see pages 1008–9.)

It has seemed essential, however, to preserve phonological values. Even though it is possible to read Chaucer with some pleasure in a phonological vacuum, poetry is by definition a matter of sound as well as of sense, and to ignore the sound is to cut oneself off from a whole dimension of pleasure. Therefore I have tried never to put down a combination of letters that would have been entirely strange to Chaucer. To preserve the appearance of Middle English spelling has seemed less imperative. Since Chaucer heard rather than saw his own poetry, the visual image we have of it is little more than a historical accident —we possess no autograph to show what Chaucer's spelling was. Nevertheless, I have been reluctant to sacrifice the visual image that scholars have of Middle English. Historically we have become readers of rather than listeners to poetry, and the visual image has become part of our poetic experience. I have tried to adhere to most of the known conventions of Middle English spelling, although my system may not be that of any actual medieval English scribe.

The punctuation is my own. In the process of supplying it I have been struck, like previous editors, by how little Chaucer's highly colloquial style is adapted to the formality of modern punctuation—one might as well try to punctuate the literal transcription of an informal conversation. One common Chaucerian construction in particular seems foreign to modern written English and to its system of punctuation—this is the use of a single statement both as the consequence of a preceding idea and the introduction to a following one. My desire to suggest the intermediary function of such statements accounts for the large number of dashes and colons in the text.

In the glossing at the foot of the page, clarity has been the chief aim. If any given gloss does not represent a reader's idea of the *mot juste,* it will in any case direct him toward a more exact meaning. Certain very common Middle English words which have come down to us with their idiomatic meanings somewhat altered have not been glossed. My assumption is that in these cases Chaucer's exact sense is readily deducible from the modern sense. For instance, in Middle English both children and adults "play," but in Modern English only children do; I have been reluctant to make Chaucer's characters "sport" or "jest" or—worse—"enjoy recreation" or "take it easy," trusting the reader to understand that what they are doing is not necessarily childish. Despite these omissions—which are generally remedied by the Glossary at the back of the book—the glossing at the bottom of the page is thorough and full.

All the texts printed here are the result of a fresh consultation of the manuscripts printed by the Chaucer Society. For the *Canterbury Tales* I have followed the lead of Manly and Rickert by using Hengwrt as my base; for *Troilus* I have adhered to Corpus; for the minor poems I have usually followed the manuscripts traditionally considered the best, except in a few cases where I have experimented. Chaucer has been too well edited to yield many major discoveries, but in a number of lines, which the scholar will recognize, I have adopted a reading I consider superior to the one generally accepted.

In the criticism my desire has been to suggest and to stimulate. "Definitive" criticism of Chaucer is obviously an impossibility. For each poem I have given some essential general information and such critical commentary as seems to me fresh and valid. The length of the discussions is in no way proportional to the length of the poems. Where Chaucer's meaning and art seem to me entirely apparent—as, for instance, in the links of the *Canterbury Tales*—I have denied myself the pleasure of saying again in prose what he has said in poetry. I have also neglected certain topics traditional to Chaucer criticism. For instance, I have said little about Chaucer's dramatic technique in the *Canterbury Tales,* which is superb but has been well treated elsewhere many times. Again, I have not restated Kittredge's ingenious framework for the Marriage Group. This omission does not mean that I think that either this idea or other traditional ones I have slighted are wrong—although sometimes I do—but is a result of my desire to emphasize values in Chaucer's poetry that have hitherto received less notice or stress and yet are as important as those that have received their full share of critical consideration.

Minor pieces of essential historical information have been included within the glosses. Major historical matters, such as the answer to the question, "What is a pardoner?" have been treated in the discussions of individual poems. In accordance with the aim of the edition to make history serve Chaucer's poetry rather than be served by it, the historical background has received less attention than it generally does. Even historical considerations must not be permitted to detract from the reader's enjoyment of great poetry.

It follows that in my criticism I have been reluctant to invoke historical data from outside the poem to explain what is in it: the criticism is in general based firmly on the text. I have therefore eschewed the historical approach used both by the great Chaucerians of the earlier part of this century and by those scholars who have recently been reading Chaucer primarily as an exponent of medieval Christianity. The fact that the difference between what these two historical approaches have attained is absolute—if Chaucer means what the older Chaucerians thought he meant he cannot possibly mean what these newer Chaucerians think he means—has encouraged me to rely on the poems as the principal source of their meaning.

The critical commentaries are at the back of the book. I suggest that the reader read the poems first. Ultimately, it is what Chaucer wrote that matters.

I should like to repeat my thanks for the help given me by Mrs. Alice Augusta Miskimin and Miss Mara R. Maizitis in preparing the first edition. For help in preparing the second, I am enormously grateful to the many users of the first edition who have communicated with me in order to point out errors in the text or glosses or to express appreciation or disapproval of what I have written. I believe, as stated above, that there neither is nor ever will be a "definitive" Chaucer criticism, and my remarks were and are intended to provoke thought rather than to settle issues. That the study of Chaucer is being carried on today in a most lively fashion in our colleges and universities is, I believe, partly due to the first edition of this book, and I hope that the second will contribute to the continuation of this activity. For that is my intent.

E. T. DONALDSON

Bloomington, Indiana
March, 1975

CONTENTS

Part I
POETRY

Part II

COMMENTARY

Part I
POETRY

Table of

ME Vowel Sound	ME Spelling
a (short)	*a* in s*a*t
a (long)	*a, aa* in n*a*me, c*aa*s
e (short)	*e* in s*e*t
e (short final)	*e* in nam*e*
ę (long open)	*e, ee* in m*e*te, h*ee*th
e (long close)	*e, ee, ie* in b*e,* sw*ee*te, gr*ie*f
i (short)	*i, y* in w*i*t, ph*y*sik
i (long)	*i, y* in wh*i*t, merc*y*
o (short)	*o* in g*o*d
ǫ (long open)	*o, oo* in g*o,* m*o*ne, *oo*th
o (long close)	*o, oo* in d*o,* r*oo*te
u (short)	*u, o* in f*u*l, s*o*ne, l*o*ve
u (long)	*ou, ow* in ab*ou*te, f*ow*l
u (long)	*u* in vert*u*

ME Diphthongs

ai, ay, ei, ey are sounded like the *ay* in ModE *day,* or better, between that sound and the sound of *ai* in ModE *aisle.*

au, aw are sounded like the *ou* in ModE *house.*

eu, ew are generally sounded like the *ew* in ModE *few*; the commonest exceptions are ME *fewe, lewed, shewe, shrewe,* where the sound is that of ME short *e* plus *u.*

oi, oy are sounded like *oy* in ModE *toy.*

ou, ow in words whose ModE descendants do *not* have the sound of *ou* in ModE *house* (see Long *u* above) are sounded like the *aw* of *law* plus a *u*-glide: this sound occurs in the combination *ought* (*thought, broughte,* etc.), in words rhyming with *knowe, lowe,* etc., and in *soule, trouthe, routhe, slouthe.*

Pronunciation

ME Pronunciation	ModE Spelling
o in American h*o*t	*a* in s*a*t
a in ModE f*a*ther *	*a* in n*a*me, c*a*se
e in ModE s*e*t	*e* in s*e*t
a in ModE sof*a*	*e* (silent) in nam*e*
e in ModE th*e*re	*ea* in m*ea*t, h*ea*th
ea in ModE br*ea*k	*e, ee, ie* in b*e*, sw*ee*t, gr*ie*f
i in ModE w*i*t	*i, y* in w*i*t, ph*y*sic
i in ModE mach*i*ne	*i, y* in wh*i*te, merc*y*
o in ModE g*o*d †	*o* in g*o*d
oa in ModE br*oa*d	*o, oa* in g*o*, m*oa*n, *oa*th
o in ModE t*o*e	*o, oo* in d*o*, r*oo*t
u in ModE f*u*ll	*u, o* in f*u*ll, s*o*n, l*o*ve (note ModE *u* for ME *o*: sonne, s*u*n)
oo in ModE sp*oo*n	*ou, ow* in ab*ou*t, f*ow*l (note the diphthongs *ou, ow,* below)
ew in ModE f*ew*	*u* in virt*u*e

* But fronted toward the *a* in c*a*t.
† But rounded as in British speech toward the *aw* in l*aw*.

ME Consonants

ME consonants are in general pronounced as in ModE. Initial *g, k,* and *w* are sounded: *gnawe, knight, write.* The combination *gh* is sounded like German *ch.*

The Canterbury Tales

THE GENERAL PROLOGUE

Whan that April with his showres soote°
The droughte of March hath perced to the roote,
And bathed every veine in swich licour,°
Of which vertu° engendred is the flowr;
Whan Zephyrus° eek with his sweete breeth
Inspired hath in every holt and heeth°
The tendre croppes, and the yonge sonne°
Hath in the Ram his halve cours yronne,
And smale fowles maken melodye
That sleepen al the night with open yë—
So priketh hem Nature in hir corages°—
Thanne longen folk to goon on pilgrimages,
And palmeres° for to seeken straunge strondes
To ferne halwes, couthe° in sondry londes;
And specially from every shires ende
Of Engelond to Canterbury they wende,

1. **his,** its; **soote,** sweet. 3. **veine,** i.e., in plants; **licour,** liquid. 4. **Of . . . vertu,** i.e., by the power of which. 5. **Zephyrus,** the west wind. 6. **holt,** grove; **heeth,** field. 7. **croppes,** shoots; **yonge sonne,** the sun is young because it is still in Aries, the Ram, which is the first sign of the zodiac in the solar year. 11. **corages,** hearts. 13. **palmeres,** palmers, wide-ranging pilgrims. 14. **ferme halwes,** far-off shrines; **couthe,** known.

The holy blisful martyr° for to seeke
That hem hath holpen° whan that they were seke.
  Bifel that in that seson on a day,
In Southwerk° at the Tabard as I lay,
Redy to wenden on my pilgrimage
To Canterbury with ful devout corage,
At night was come into that hostelrye
Wel nine and twenty in a compaignye
Of sondry folk, by aventure° yfalle
In felaweshipe, and pilgrimes were they alle
That toward Canterbury wolden ride.
The chambres and the stables weren wide,
And wel we weren esed° at the beste.
And shortly, whan the sonne was to reste,°
So hadde I spoken with hem everichoon
That I was of hir felaweshipe anoon,
And made forward° erly for to rise,
To take oure way ther as I you devise.
  But nathelees, whil I have time and space,°
Er that I ferther in this tale pace,°
Me thinketh it accordant to resoun
To telle you al the condicioun
Of eech of hem, so as it seemed me,
And whiche they were, and of what degree,
And eek in what array that they were inne:
And at a knight thanne wol I first biginne.
  A Knight ther was, and that a worthy man,
That fro the time that he first bigan
To riden out, he loved chivalrye,
Trouthe and honour, freedom° and curteisye.
Ful worthy was he in his lordes werre,°
And therto hadde he riden, no man ferre,°

17. martyr, St. Thomas à Becket, murdered in Canterbury Cathedral in 1170. **18. holpen,** helped; **seke,** sick. **20. Southwerk,** Southwark, site of the Tabard Inn, was then a suburb of London, south of the Thames. **25. aventure,** chance. **29. esed,** accommodated. **30. to reste,** i.e., had set. **33. made forward,** i.e., (we) made an agreement. **35. space,** i.e., opportunity. **36. pace,** pass. **46. Trouthe,** integrity; **freedom,** generosity of spirit. **47. werre,** war. **48. ferre,** further.

As wel in Cristendom as hethenesse,°
And° evere honoured for his worthinesse.
At Alisandre° he was whan it was wonne;
Ful ofte time he hadde the boord bigonne°
Aboven alle nacions in Pruce;
In Lettou had he reised,° and in Ruce,
No Cristen man so ofte of his degree;
In Gernade at the sege eek hadde he be
Of Algezir, and riden in Belmarye;
At Lyeis was he, and at Satalye,
Whan they were wonne; and in the Grete See
At many a noble arivee° hadde he be.
At mortal batailes° hadde he been fifteene,
And foughten for oure faith at Tramissene°
In listes thries, and ay slain his fo.
This ilke° worthy Knight hadde been also
Somtime with the lord of Palatye°
Again° another hethen in Turkye;
And everemore he hadde a soverein pris.°
And though that he were worthy,° he was wis,
And of his port° as meeke as is a maide.
He nevere yit no vilainye° ne saide
In al his lif unto no manere wight:
He was a verray, parfit,° gentil knight.
But for to tellen you of his array,
His hors° were goode, but he was nat gay.
Of fustian he wered a gipoun°
Al bismotered with his haubergeoun,°

49. **hethenesse,** i.e., heathen lands. 50. **And,** i.e., and he was. 51. **ff. Alisandre,** Alexandria: **Pruce,** Prussia; **Lettou,** Lithuania; **Ruce,** Russia; **Gernade,** Granada: **Algezir,** Algeciras; **Belmarye,** Ben-marin; **Lyeis,** Ayas; **Satalye,** Antalya; **Grete See,** i.e., the Mediterranean. 52. **boord bigonne,** sat in the seat of honor at military feasts. 54. **reised,** campaigned. 60. **arivee,** military landing. 61. **mortal batailes,** tournaments fought to the death. 62. **Tramissene,** Tlemcen. 64. **ilke,** same. 65. **Palatye,** Balat. 66. **Again,** against: alliances of convenience were often made between Christians and pagans. 67. **pris,** reputation. 68. **worthy,** i.e., a valiant knight. 69. **port,** demeanor. 70. **vilainye,** rudeness. 72. **verray,** true; **parfit,** perfect. 74. **hors,** horses. 75. **fustian,** thick cloth; **gipoun,** tunic worn under the coat of mail. 76. **bismotered with,** rust-stained from; **haubergeoun,** hauberk, coat of mail.

For he was late come from his viage,°
And wente for to doon his pilgrimage.
  With him ther was his sone, a yong Squier,
A lovere and a lusty bacheler,°
With lokkes crulle° as they were laid in presse.
Of twenty yeer of age he was, I gesse.
Of his stature he was of evene° lengthe,
And wonderly delivere,° and of greet strengthe.
And he hadde been som time in chivachye°
In Flandres, in Artois, and Picardye,
And born him wel as of so litel space,°
In hope to stonden in his lady° grace.
  Embrouded was he as it were a mede,°
Al ful of fresshe flowres, white and rede;
Singing he was, or floiting,° al the day:
He was as fressh as is the month of May.
Short was his gowne, with sleeves longe and wide.
Wel coude he sitte on hors, and faire ride;
He coude songes make, and wel endite,°
Juste and eek daunce, and wel portraye° and write.
So hote he loved that by nightertale°
He slepte namore than dooth a nightingale.
Curteis he was, lowely,° and servisable,
And carf° biforn his fader at the table.
  A Yeman hadde he° and servants namo
At that time, for him liste ride so;
And he was clad in cote and hood of greene.
A sheef of pecok arwes, bright and keene,
Under his belt he bar ful thriftily;°
Wel coude he dresse his takel yemanly:°

77. **viage,** expedition. 80. **bacheler,** young knight still in the service of an older one. 81. **crulle,** curly. 83. **evene,** moderate. 84. **delivere,** agile. 85. **in chivachye,** on cavalry expeditions. 87. **as . . . space,** i.e., considering the little time he had been in service. 88. **lady,** lady's. 89. **Embrouded,** embroidered; **mede,** meadow. 91. **floiting,** whistling. 95. **endite,** compose verse. 96. **Juste,** joust; **portraye,** sketch. 97. **hote,** hotly; **by nightertale,** at night. 99. **lowely,** humble. 100. **carf,** carved. 101. **he** i.e., the Knight. 102. **him liste,** it pleased him to. 103. **he,** i.e., the Yeoman. 105. **bar,** bore; **thriftily,** properly. 106. **dresse,** tend to; **takel,** gear; **yemanly,** in a workmanlike way.

His arwes drouped nought with fetheres lowe.
And in his hand he bar a mighty bowe.
A not-heed° hadde he with a brown visage.
Of wodecraft wel coude° he al the usage.
Upon his arm he bar a gay bracer,°
And by his side a swerd and a bokeler,°
And on that other side a gay daggere,
Harneised° wel and sharp as point of spere;
A Cristophre on his brest of silver sheene;°
An horn he bar, the baudrik° was of greene.
A forster° was he soothly, as I gesse.
  Ther was also a Nonne, a Prioresse,
That of hir smiling was ful simple and coy.°
Hir gretteste ooth was but by Sainte Loy!°
And she was cleped° Madame Eglantine.
Ful wel she soong the service divine,
Entuned in hir nose ful semely;°
And Frenssh she spak ful faire and fetisly,°
After the scole of Stratford at the Bowe°—
For Frenssh of Paris was to hire unknowe.
At mete wel ytaught was she withalle:°
She leet no morsel from hir lippes falle,
Ne wette hir fingres in hir sauce deepe;
Wel coude she carye a morsel, and wel keepe°
That no drope ne fille° upon hir brest.
In curteisye was set ful muchel hir lest.°
Hir over-lippe wiped she so clene
That in hir coppe ther was no ferthing° seene
Of grece,° whan she dronken hadde hir draughte;
Ful semely after hir mete she raughte.°

109. **not-heed,** close-cut head. 110. **coude,** knew. 111. **bracer,** wrist-guard for archers. 112. **bokeler,** buckler, a small shield. 114. **Harneised,** mounted. 115. **Cristophre,** St. Christopher medal; **sheene,** bright. 116. **baudrik,** baldric, supporting strap. 117. **forster,** forester. 119. **simple . . . coy,** sincere and mild. 120. **Loy,** Eloi. 121. **cleped,** named. 123. **Entuned,** chanted; **semely,** in a seemly manner. 124. **fetisly,** elegantly. 125. **Stratford at the Bowe,** a suburb of London, site of a convent. 127. **mete,** meals; **withalle,** besides. 130. **keepe,** take care. 131. **fille,** should fall. 132. Her chief delight lay in good manners. 134. **coppe,** cup; **ferthing,** bit. 135. **grece,** grease. 136. **raughte,** reached.

And sikerly she was of greet disport,°
And ful plesant, and amiable of port,°
And pained hire to countrefete cheere°
Of court, and to been estatlich° of manere,
And to been holden digne° of reverence.
But, for to speken of hir conscience,
She was so charitable and so pitous
She wolde weepe if that she saw a mous
Caught in a trappe, if it were deed° or bledde.
Of° smale houndes hadde she that she fedde
With rosted flessh, or milk and wastelbreed;°
But sore wepte she if oon of hem were deed,
Or if men smoot it with a yerde° smerte;
And al was conscience and tendre herte.
Ful semely hir wimpel pinched° was,
Hir nose tretis,° hir yën greye as glas,
Hir mouth ful smal, and therto softe and reed°—
But sikerly she hadde a fair forheed:
It was almost a spanne brood, I trowe,°
For hardily,° she was nat undergrowe.
Ful fetis° was hir cloke, as I was war;
Of smal° coral aboute hir arm she bar
A paire of bedes, gauded al with greene,°
And theron heeng a brooch of gold ful sheene,°
On which ther was first writen a crowned *A*,°
And after, *Amor vincit omnia*.°
  Another Nonne with hire hadde she
That was hir chapelaine,° and preestes three.

137. sikerly, certainly; **disport,** good cheer. **138. port,** mien. **139.** And she took pains to imitate the behavior. **140. estatlich,** dignified. **141. holden digne,** considered worthy. **145. deed,** dead. **146. Of,** i.e., some. **147. wastelbreed,** bread of good quality. **149. men,** someone; **yerde,** rod. **151. wimpel,** headdress; **pinched,** pleated. **152. tretis,** well-proportioned. **153. reed,** red. **155. spanne,** handsbreadth; **brood,** broad; **trowe,** believe. **156. hardily,** assuredly. **157. fetis,** becoming. **158. smal,** dainty. **159. paire,** string, i.e., a rosary; **gauded . . . greene,** provided with green beads to mark certain prayers. **160. heeng,** hung; **sheene,** bright. **161. crowned A,** an A with an ornamental crown on it. **162. Amor . . . omnia,** Love conquers all. **164. chapelaine,** secretary.

A Monk ther was, a fair for the maistrye,°
An outridere that loved venerye,°
A manly man, to been an abbot able.°
Ful many a daintee hors hadde he in stable,
And whan he rood, men mighte his bridel heere
Ginglen° in a whistling wind as clere
And eek as loude as dooth the chapel belle
Ther as this lord was kepere of the celle.°
The rule of Saint Maure or of Saint Beneit,°
By cause that it was old and somdeel strait°—
This ilke Monk leet olde thinges pace,°
And heeld after the newe world the space.°
He yaf nought of that text a pulled hen°
That saith that hunteres been nought holy men,
Ne that a monk, whan he is recchelees,°
Is likned til a fissh that is waterlees—
This is to sayn, a monk out of his cloistre;
But thilke text heeld he nat worth an oystre.
And I saide his opinion was good:
What sholde he studye and make himselven wood°
Upon a book in cloistre alway to poure,
Or swinke° with his handes and laboure,
As Austin bit?° How shal the world be served?
Lat Austin have his swink to him reserved!
Therfore he was a prikasour° aright.
Grehoundes he hadde as swift as fowl in flight.
Of priking° and of hunting for the hare
Was al his lust,° for no cost wolde he spare.
I sawgh his sleeves purfiled° at the hand

165. a fair . . . maistrye, a superlatively fine one. **166. outridere,** a monk charged with supervising property distant from the monastery; **venerye,** hunting. **167. able,** worthy. **170. Ginglen,** jingle. **172. kepere . . . celle,** keeper of an outlying cell of the monastery. **173. Maure, Beneit,** St. Maurus and St. Benedict, authors of monastic rules. **174. strait,** strict. **175. pace,** pass away. **176. space,** course. **177.** He didn't give a plucked hen for that text. **179. recchelees,** reckless, careless of rule. **184. What,** why; **wood,** crazy. **186. swinke,** work. **187. Austin,** St. Augustine, who wrote that monks should perform manual labor; **bit,** bids. **189. prikasour,** hard rider. **191. priking,** riding. **192. lust,** pleasure. **193. purfiled,** fur-lined.

With gris° and that the fineste of a land;
And for to festne his hood under his chin
He hadde of gold wrought a ful curious° pin:
A love-knotte in the grettere° ende ther was.
His heed was balled,° that shoon as any glas,
And eek his face, as he hadde been anoint:
He was a lord ful fat and in good point;°
His yën steepe,° and rolling in his heed,
That stemed as a furnais of a leed;°
His bootes souple, his hors in greet estat°—
Now certainly he was a fair prelat.°
He was nat pale as a forpined° gost:
A fat swan loved he best of any rost.
His palfrey° was as brown as is a berye.
 A Frere ther was, a wantoune and a merye,
A limitour,° a ful solempne man.
In alle the ordres foure is noon that can°
So muche of daliaunce° and fair langage:
He hadde maad ful many a mariage
Of yonge wommen at his owene cost;
Unto his ordre he was a noble post.°
Ful wel biloved and familier was he
With frankelains° over al in his contree,
And with worthy wommen of the town—
For he hadde power of confessioun,
As saide himself, more than a curat,°
For of his ordre he was licenciat.°
Ful swetely herde he confessioun,
And plesant was his absolucioun.
He was an esy man to yive penaunce

194. gris, grey fur. **196. curious,** of careful workmanship. **197. grettere,** greater. **198. balled,** bald. **200. in . . . point,** in good shape, plump. **201. steepe,** protruding. **202.** That glowed like a furnace with a pot in it. **203. souple,** supple; **estat,** condition. **204. prelat,** prelate, important churchman. **205. forpined,** wasted away. **207. palfrey,** saddle horse. **209. limitour,** friar granted exclusive begging rights in a certain area. **210. can,** knows. **211. daliaunce,** flirtation. **214. post,** i.e., pillar. **216. frankelains,** franklins, men of substance. **219. curat,** parish priest. **220. of,** by; **licenciat,** licensed to hear confessions.

Ther as he wiste to have a good pitaunce;°
For unto a poore ordre for to yive
Is signe that a man is wel yshrive;°
For if he yaf, he dorste make avaunt°
He wiste that a man was repentaunt;
For many a man so hard is of his herte
He may nat weepe though him sore smerte:°
Therfore, in stede of weeping and prayeres,
Men mote yive silver to the poore freres.
  His tipet was ay farsed° ful of knives
And pinnes, for to yiven faire wives;
And certainly he hadde a merye note;
Wel coude he singe and playen on a rote;°
Of yeddinges he bar outrely the pris.°
His nekke whit was as the flowr-de-lis;°
Therto he strong was as a champioun.°
He knew the tavernes wel in every town,
And every hostiler and tappestere,°
Bet than a lazar or a beggestere.°
For unto swich a worthy man as he
Accorded nat, as by his facultee,°
To have with sike° lazars aquaintaunce:
It is nat honeste, it may nought avaunce,°
For to delen with no swich poraile,°
But al with riche, and selleres of vitaile;°
And over al ther as profit sholde arise,
Curteis he was, and lowely of servise.
Ther was no man nowher so vertuous:°
He was the beste beggere in his hous.
And yaf a certain ferme for the graunt:°

224. wiste to have, knew he would have; **pitaunce,** donation. **226. yshrive,** shriven, absolved. **227. make avaunt,** boast. **230. him . . . smerte,** he is sorely grieved. **233. tipet,** scarf; **farsed,** packed. **236. rote,** fiddle. **237.** He absolutely took the prize for ballads. **238. flowr-de-lis,** lily. **239. champioun,** experienced fighter. **241. hostiler . . . tappestere,** innkeeper and barmaid. **242. lazar,** leper; **beggestere,** female beggar. **244.** It was not suitable, because of his position. **245. sike,** sick. **246. honeste,** dignified; **avaunce,** profit. **247. poraile,** poor people. **248. vitaile,** foodstuffs. **251. vertuous,** efficient. **253.** And he paid a certain rent for the privilege of begging.

Noon of his bretheren cam ther in his haunt.°
For though a widwe hadde nought a sho,
So plesant was his *In principio*°
Yit wolde he have a ferthing er he wente;
His purchas was wel bettre than his rente.°
And rage he coude as it were right a whelpe;°
In love-dayes° ther coude he muchel helpe,
For ther he was nat lik a cloisterer,
With a thredbare cope, as is a poore scoler,
But he was lik a maister° or a pope.
Of double worstede was his semicope,°
And rounded as a belle out of the presse.°
Somwhat he lipsed for his wantounesse°
To make his Englissh sweete upon his tonge;
And in his harping, whan that he hadde songe,
His yën twinkled in his heed aright
As doon the sterres° in the frosty night.
This worthy limitour was cleped Huberd.
  A Marchant was ther with a forked beerd,
In motlee,° and hye on hors he sat,
Upon his heed a Flandrissh° bevere hat,
His bootes clasped faire and fetisly.°
His resons° he spak ful solempnely,
Souning° alway th'encrees of his winning.
He wolde the see were kept for any thing°
Bitwixen Middelburgh and Orewelle.°
Wel coude he in eschaunge sheeldes° selle.
This worthy man ful wel his wit bisette:°

254. **haunt,** assigned territory. 256. **In principio,** the Friar's salutation, John i:1. 258. **purchas,** money got by begging; **rente,** payment for territorial rights. 259. **rage,** flirt wantonly; **as . . . whelpe,** as if he were a puppy. 260. **love-dayes,** days appointed for the settlement of lawsuits out of court. 263. **maister,** a man of recognized learning. 264. **semicope,** short robe. 265. **presse,** bell-mould. 266. **lipsed,** lisped; **wantounesse,** affectation. 270. **sterres,** stars. 273. **motlee,** cloth of mixed color. 274. **Flandrissh,** Flemish. 275. **fetisly,** elegantly. 276. **resons,** opinions. 277. **Souning,** sounding. 278. **kept . . . thing,** guarded at all costs. 279. Trade in wool with the continent was carried on between Orwell in Suffolk and Middelburgh in the Netherlands. 280. **sheeldes,** shields, French coins: i.e., he could speculate profitably in foreign exchange. 281. **bisette,** employed.

Ther wiste no wight that he was in dette,
So estatly was he of his governaunce,
With his bargaines, and with his chevissaunce.
Forsoothe he was a worthy man withalle;
But, sooth to sayn, I noot how men him calle.
  A Clerk ther was of Oxenforde also
That unto logik hadde longe ygo.
As lene was his hors as is a rake,
And he was nought right fat, I undertake,
But looked holwe, and therto sobrely.
Ful thredbare was his overeste courtepy,
For he hadde geten him yit no benefice,
Ne was so worldly for to have office.
For him was levere have at his beddes heed
Twenty bookes, clad in blak or reed,
Of Aristotle and his philosophye,
Than robes riche, or fithele, or gay sautrye.
But al be that he was a philosophre
Yit hadde he but litel gold in cofre;
But al that he mighte of his freendes hente,
On bookes and on lerning he it spente,
And bisily gan for the soules praye
Of hem that yaf him wherwith to scoleye.
Of studye took he most cure and most heede.
Nought oo word spak he more than was neede,
And that was said in forme and reverence,
And short and quik, and ful of heigh sentence:
Souning in moral vertu was his speeche,
And gladly wolde he lerne, and gladly teche.
  A Sergeant of the Lawe, war and wis,

282. **wiste,** knew. 283. **estatly,** dignified; **governaunce,** the management of his affairs. 284. **bargaines,** bargainings; **chevissaunce,** borrowing. 286. **noot,** don't know. 292. **overeste courtepy,** outer cloak. 293. **benefice,** ecclesiastical living. 294. **office,** secular employment. 295. **him . . . levere,** he would rather. 298. **fithele,** fiddle; **sautrye,** psaltery, a kind of harp. 299. **philosophre,** there is a pun on a secondary sense of the word, i.e., alchemist. 301. **hente,** take. 304. **scoleye,** study. 305. **cure,** care. 307. **in forme,** with decorum. 308. **quick,** lively; **heigh sentence,** elevated thought. 309. **Souning,** resounding.

That often hadde been at the Parvis°
Ther was also, ful riche of excellence.
Discreet he was, and of greet reverence—
He seemed swich, his wordes weren so wise.
Justice he was ful often in assise°
By patente and by plein° commissioun.
For his science° and for his heigh renown
Of fees and robes hadde he many oon.
So greet a purchasour° was nowher noon;
Al was fee simple° to him in effect—
His purchasing mighte nat been infect.°
Nowher so bisy a man as he ther nas;
And yit he seemed bisier than he was.
In termes hadde he caas and doomes° alle
That from the time of King William° were falle.
Therto he coude endite and make a thing,°
Ther coude no wight pinchen° at his writing;
And every statut coude he plein by rote.°
He rood but hoomly in a medlee° cote,
Girt with a ceint of silk, with barres° smale.
Of his array telle I no lenger tale.
  A Frankelain was in his compaignye:
Whit was his beerd as is the dayesye;°
Of his complexion he was sanguin.°
Wel loved he by the morwe a sop in win.°
To liven in delit was evere his wone,°
For he was Epicurus owene sone,

312. **Parvis,** the "Paradise," a meeting place for lawyers. 316. **assise,** circuit courts. 317. **patente,** official warrant; **plein,** full. 318. **science,** knowledge. 320. **purchasour,** speculator in land. 321. **fee simple,** owned outright without legal impediments. 322. **infect,** invalidated on a legal technicality. 325. **In termes,** i.e., by heart; **caas and doomes,** lawcases and decisions. 326. **William,** i.e., the Conqueror. 327. **endite . . . thing,** compose and draw up a deed. 328. **pinchen,** cavil. 329. **coude,** knew; **plein,** entire; **by rote,** by heart. 330. **hoomly,** unpretentiously; **medlee,** of mixed color. 331. **ceint,** belt; **barres,** transverse stripes. 334. **dayesye,** daisy. 335. **complexion . . . sanguin,** referring to the blood-dominated temperament of the Franklin as well as to his red face. 336. **by . . . morwe,** in the morning; **sop . . . win,** bread soaked in wine. 337. **delit,** i.e., sensual delight; **wone,** custom.

That heeld opinion that plein°delit
Was verray felicitee parfit.
An housholdere and that a greet was he:
Saint Julian°he was in his contree.
His breed, his ale, was always after oon;°
A bettre envined°man was nevere noon.
Withouten bake mete was nevere his hous,
Of fissh and flessh, and that so plentevous°
It snewed°in his hous of mete and drinke,
Of alle daintees that men coude thinke.
After the sondry sesons of the yeer
So chaunged he his mete and his soper.°
Ful many a fat partrich hadde he in mewe,°
And many a breem, and many a luce in stewe.°
Wo was his cook but if his sauce were
Poinant°and sharp, and redy al his gere.
His table dormant in his halle alway
Stood redy covered al the longe day.°
At sessions ther was he lord and sire.°
Ful ofte time he was Knight of the Shire.°
An anlaas and a gipser°al of silk
Heeng at his girdel, whit as morne°milk.
A shirreve hadde he been, and countour.°
Was nowher swich a worthy vavasour.°
  An Haberdasshere and a Carpenter,
A Webbe, a Dyere, and a Tapicer°—
And they were clothed alle in oo liveree°

339. **plein,** full. 342. **Julian,** patron saint of hospitality. 343. **after oon,** of the same high quality. 344. **envined,** wine-stocked. 346. **plentevous,** plenteous. 347. **snewed,** snowed. 350. **mete . . . soper,** dinner and supper. 351. **mewe,** cage. 352. **breem,** carp; **luce,** pike; **stewe,** fishpond. 354. **Poinant,** pungent. 355–56. Tables were usually dismounted when not in use, but the Franklin kept his mounted and set (covered), hence dormant. 357. i.e., sessions of the justices of the peace. 358. **Knight of the Shire,** county representative in Parliament. 359. **anlaas,** dagger; **gipser,** purse. 360. **Heeng,** hung; **girdel,** belt; **morne,** morning. 361. **shirreve,** sheriff; **countour,** auditor of county finances. 362. **vavasour,** member of an upper, but not aristocratic, feudal class. 364. **Webbe,** weaver; **Tapicer,** tapestry-maker. 365. **oo liveree,** one livery, i.e., the same uniform.

Of a solempne and a greet fraternitee.°
Ful fresshe and newe hir gere apiked° was;
Hir knives were chaped° nought with bras,
But al with silver; wrought ful clene and weel
Hir girdles and hir pouches everydeel.
Wel seemed eech of hem a fair burgeis°
To sitten in a yeldehalle° on a dais.
Everich, for the wisdom that he can,°
Was shaply° for to been an alderman.
For catel hadde they ynough and rente,°
And eek hir wives wolde it wel assente—
And elles certain were they to blame:
It is ful fair to been ycleped "Madame,"
And goon to vigilies al bifore,°
And have a mantel royalliche ybore.
  A Cook they hadde with hem for the nones,°
To boile the chiknes with the marybones,°
And powdre-marchant tart and galingale.°
Wel coude he knowe° a draughte of London ale.
He coude roste, and seethe,° and broile, and frye,
Maken mortreux,° and wel bake a pie.
But greet harm was it, as it thoughte me,
That on his shine a mormal° hadde he.
For blankmanger,° that made he with the beste.
  A Shipman was ther, woning° fer by weste—
For ought I woot, he was of Dertemouthe.°
He rood upon a rouncy° as he couthe,
In a gowne of falding° to the knee.
A daggere hanging on a laas° hadde he

366. **fraternitee,** parish gild, a partly religious, partly social fraternity. 367. **apiked,** polished. 368. **chaped,** mounted. 371. **burgeis,** burgher. 372. **yeldehalle,** gildhall. 373. **can,** was capable of. 374. **shaply,** suitable. 375. **catel,** property; **rente,** income. 379. **vigilies,** feasts held on the eve of saints' days; **al bifore,** i.e., at the head of the procession. 381. **for the nones,** for the occasion. 382. **marybones,** marrowbones. 383. **powdre-marchant, galingale,** flavoring materials. 384. **knowe,** recognize. 385. **seethe,** boil. 386. **mortreux,** stews. 388. **mormal,** ulcer. 389. **blankmanger,** an elaborate stew. 390. **woning,** dwelling. 391. **Dertemouthe,** Dartmouth, a port in the southwest. 392. **rouncy,** large nag. 393. **falding,** heavy wool. 394. **laas,** strap.

Aboute his nekke, under his arm adown.
The hote somer hadde maad his hewe al brown;
And certainly he was a good felawe.
Ful many a draughte of win hadde he drawe
Fro Burdeuxward, whil that the chapman sleep.°
Of nice conscience took he no keep;°
If that he faught and hadde the hyer hand,
By water he sente hem hoom to every land.
But of his craft, to rekene wel his tides,
His stremes and his daungers° him bisides,
His herberwe and his moone, his lodemenage,°
Ther was noon swich from Hulle to Cartage.°
Hardy he was and wis to undertake;
With many a tempest hadde his beerd been shake;
He knew alle the havenes° as they were
Fro Gotlond to the Cape of Finistere,°
And every crike in Britaine° and in Spaine.
His barge ycleped was the Maudelaine.°
  With us ther was a Doctour of Physik:
In al this world ne was ther noon him lik
To speken of physik and of surgerye.
For he was grounded in astronomye,°
He kepte his pacient a ful greet deel
In houres by his magik naturel.°
Wel coude he fortunen the ascendent
Of his images for his pacient.°
He knew the cause of every maladye,
Were it of hoot or cold or moiste or drye,°

399. **Fro Burdeuxward,** i.e., while carrying wine from Bordeaux in France; **chapman sleep,** merchant slept. **400. nice,** fastidious; **keep,** heed. **404. stremes,** currents; **daungers,** hazards. **405. herberwe,** anchorage; **lodemenage,** pilotage. **406. Hulle,** Hull, in Yorkshire; **Cartage,** Mediterranean port, Cartagena. **409. havenes,** harbors. **410. Gotlond,** Gotland, island in the Baltic; **Finistere,** Finisterre, the "land's end" of western Spain. **411. crike,** inlet; **Britaine,** Brittany. **412. Maudelaine,** Magdalene. **416. For,** because; **astronomye,** astrology. **417–18.** He tended his patient closely at the hours dictated by his knowledge of astrology. **419–20. fortunen . . . images,** assign the propitious time, according to the position of the stars, for using talismanic images. **422.** Diseases were thought to be caused by a disturbance of one or another of the four bodily humors, each of which, like the four elements, was a compound of two of the elementary qualities men-

And where engendred and of what humour:
He was a verray parfit praktisour.°
The cause yknowe, and of his harm the roote,
Anoon he yaf the sike man his boote.°
  Ful redy hadde he his apothecaries
To senden him drogges and his letuaries,°
For eech of hem made other for to winne:
Hir frendshipe was nought newe to biginne.
Wel knew he the olde Esculapius,°
And Deiscorides and eek Rufus,
Olde Ipocras, Hali, and Galien,
Serapion, Razis, and Avicen,
Averrois, Damascien, and Constantin,
Bernard, and Gatesden, and Gilbertin.
Of his diete mesurable° was he,
For it was of no superfluitee,
But of greet norissing and digestible.
His studye was but litel on the Bible.
In sanguin and in pers° he clad was al,
Lined with taffata and with sendal;°
And yit he was but esy of dispence;°
He kepte that he wan in pestilence.
For gold in physik is a cordial,°
Therfore he loved gold in special.
  A good Wif was ther of biside Bathe,
But she was somdeel deef, and that was scathe.°

---

tioned: the melancholy humor, seated in the black bile, was, like earth, cold and dry; the sanguine, seated in the blood, like air hot and moist; the choleric, seated in the yellow bile, like fire hot and dry; the phlegmatic, seated in the phlegm, like water, cold and moist. **424. verray,** true; **parfit,** perfect; **praktisour,** practitioner. **426. boote,** remedy. **428. drogges,** drugs; **letuaries,** medicines. **431.** The Doctor is familiar with the treatises that the Middle Ages attributed to the "great names" of medical history: the purely legendary Greek demigod Aesculapius; the Greeks Dioscorides, Rufus, Hippocrates, Galen, and Serapion; the Persians Hali and Rhazes; the Arabians Avicenna and Averroes; and the Christians John (?) of Damascus, Constantine Afer, the Scotsman Bernard Gordon, and the Englishmen John of Gatesden and Gilbert, the former an earlier contemporary of Chaucer. **437. mesurable,** moderate. **441. sanguin,** blood-red; **pers,** blue. **442. sendal,** silk. **443. dispence,** expenditure. **445. For,** because; **cordial,** stimulant. **448. scathe,** a pity.

Of cloth-making she hadde swich an haunt,°
She passed hem of Ypres and of Gaunt.°
In al the parissh wif ne was ther noon
That to the offring° bifore hire sholde goon,
And if ther dide, certain so wroth° was she
That she was out of alle charitee.
Hir coverchiefs ful fine were of ground°—
I dorste swere they weyeden° ten pound
That on a Sonday weren upon hir heed.
Hir hosen weren of fin scarlet reed,
Ful straite yteyd, and shoes ful moiste° and newe.
Bold was hir face and fair and reed° of hewe.
She was a worthy womman al hir live:
Housbondes at chirche dore she hadde five,
Withouten other compaignye in youthe—
But therof needeth nought to speke as nouthe.°
And thries hadde she been at Jerusalem;
She hadde passed many a straunge streem;
At Rome she hadde been, and at Boloigne,
In Galice at Saint Jame, and at Coloigne:°
She coude° muchel of wandring by the waye.
Gat-toothed° was she, soothly for to saye.
Upon an amblere° esily she sat,
Ywimpled° wel, and on hir heed an hat
As brood as is a bokeler or a targe,°
A foot-mantel° aboute hir hipes large,
And on hir feet a paire of spores° sharpe.
In felaweshipe wel coude she laughe and carpe:°
Of remedies of love she knew parchaunce,°

449. **haunt,** practice. 450. **passed,** surpassed; **Gaunt,** Ghent, like **Ypres,** a Flemish cloth-making center. 452. **offring,** the offering in church, when the congregation brought its gifts forward. 453. **wroth,** angry. 455. **ground,** the basic material that receives the pattern. 456. **weyeden,** weighed. 459. **straite yteyd,** tightly laced; **moiste,** unworn. 460. **reed,** red. 464. **nouthe,** now. 467–68. Rome, Boulogne in France, St. James of Compostella in Galicia, Spain, and Cologne in Germany were the sites of shrines much visited by pilgrims. 469. **coude,** knew. 470. **Gat-toothed,** gap-toothed. 471. **amblere,** horse with an easy gait. 472. **Ywimpled,** veiled. 473. **bokeler, targe,** small shields. 474. **foot-mantel,** riding-skirt. 475. **spores,** spurs. 476. **carpe,** talk. 477. **parchaunce,** as it happened.

For she coude of that art the olde daunce.°
  A good man was ther of religioun,
And was a poore Person° of a town,
But riche he was of holy thought and werk.
He was also a lerned man, a clerk,
That Cristes gospel trewely wolde preche;
His parisshens° devoutly wolde he teche.
Benigne he was, and wonder° diligent,
And in adversitee ful pacient,
And swich he was preved ofte sithes.°
Ful loth were him to cursen for his tithes,°
But rather wolde he yiven, out of doute,
Unto his poore parisshens aboute
Of his offring and eek of his substaunce:°
He coude in litel thing have suffisaunce.°
Wid was his parissh, and houses fer asonder,
But he ne lafte° nought for rain ne thonder,
In siknesse nor in meschief, to visite
The ferreste in his parissh, muche and lite,°
Upon his feet, and in his hand a staf.
This noble ensample° to his sheep he yaf
That first he wroughte,° and afterward he taughte.
Out of the Gospel he tho wordes caughte,
And this figure he added eek therto:
That if gold ruste, what shal iren do?
For if a preest be foul, on whom we truste,
No wonder is a lewed° man to ruste.
And shame it is, if a preest take keep,°
A shiten° shepherde and a clene sheep.
Wel oughte a preest ensample for to yive
By his clennesse how that his sheep sholde live.

478. i.e., She knew all the tricks of that trade. **480. Person,** parson. **484. parisshens,** parishioners. **485. wonder,** wonderfully. **487. preved,** proved; **sithes,** times. **488.** He would be most reluctant to invoke excommunication in order to collect his tithes. **491. substaunce,** property. **492. suffisaunce,** sufficiency. **494. lafte,** left, ceased. **496. ferreste,** farthest; **muche . . . lite,** great and small. **498. ensample,** example. **499. wroughte,** i.e., practised what he preached. **504. lewed,** uneducated. **505. keep,** heed. **506. shiten,** befouled.

He sette nought his benefice° to hire
And leet° his sheep encombred in the mire
And ran to London, unto Sainte Poules,°
To seeken him a chaunterye for soules,
Or with a bretherhede to been withholde,°
But dwelte at hoom and kepte wel his folde,
So that the wolf ne made it nought miscarye:
He was a shepherde and nought a mercenarye.
And though he holy were and vertuous,
He was to sinful men nought despitous,°
Ne of his speeche daungerous ne digne,°
But in his teching discreet and benigne,
To drawen folk to hevene by fairnesse
By good ensample°—this was his bisinesse.
But it were any persone obstinat,
What so he were, of heigh or lowe estat,
Him wolde he snibben sharply for the nones:°
A bettre preest I trowe° ther nowher noon is.
He waited after° no pompe and reverence,
Ne maked him a spiced conscience,°
But Cristes lore° and his Apostles twelve
He taughte, but first he folwed it himselve.
  With him ther was a Plowman, was his brother,
That hadde ylad of dong ful many a fother.°
A trewe swinkere° and a good was he,
Living in pees° and parfit charitee.
God loved he best with al his hoole° herte
At alle times, though him gamed or smerte,°

509. **benefice,** i.e., parish: a priest might rent his parish to another and take a more profitable position. 510. **leet,** i.e., he did not leave. 511. St. Paul's in London had many chantries, i.e., foundations that employed priests for the sole duty of saying masses for the souls of certain persons. 513. Or to be employed by a brotherhood; i.e., to take a lucrative and fairly easy position with a parish gild. 518. **despitous,** scornful. 519. **daungerous . . . digne,** disdainful nor haughty. 522. **ensample,** example. 525. **snibben,** scold; **for . . . nones,** on any occasion. 526. **trowe,** believe. 527. **waited after,** i.e., expected. 528. Nor did he assume an overfastidious conscience. 529. **lore,** teaching. 532. **ylad,** carried; **dong,** dung; **fother,** load. 533. **swinkere,** worker. 534. **pees,** peace. 535. **hoole,** whole. 536. **him . . . smerte,** he was pleased or grieved.

And thanne his neighebor right as himselve.
He wolde thresshe, and therto dike° and delve,
For Cristes sake, for every poore wight,
Withouten hire, if it laye in his might.
His tithes payed he ful faire and wel,
Bothe of his propre swink and his catel.°
In a tabard he rood upon a mere.°
  Ther was also a Reeve and a Millere,
A Somnour,° and a Pardoner also,
A Manciple,° and myself—ther were namo.
  The Millere was a stout carl° for the nones.
Ful big he was of brawn° and eek of bones—
That preved° wel, for overal ther he cam
At wrastling he wolde have alway the ram.°
He was short-shuldred, brood, a thikke knarre.°
Ther was no dore that he nolde heve of harre,°
Or breke it at a renning with his heed.°
His beerd as any sowe or fox was reed,°
And therto brood, as though it were a spade;
Upon the cop right of his nose he hade
A werte,° and theron stood a tuft of heres,
Rede as the bristles of a sowes eres;
His nosethirles° blake were and wide.
A swerd and a bokeler bar° he by his side.
His mouth as greet was as a greet furnais.°
He was a janglere and a Goliardais,°
And that was most of sinne and harlotries.°
Wel coude he stelen corn and tollen thries°—

538. **dike,** dig ditches. 542. **propre swink,** own work; **catel,** property. 543. **tabard,** short coat; **mere,** mare. 545. **Somnour,** summoner. 546. **Manciple,** steward. 547. **carl,** fellow. 548. **brawn,** muscle. 549. **preved,** proved, i.e., was evident. 550. A ram was frequently offered as a prize in wrestling. 551. **brood,** broad; **knarre,** bully. 552. **nolde . . . harre,** would not heave off hinge. 553. **renning,** running; **heed,** head. 554. **reed,** red. 556. **cop,** ridge. 557. **werte,** wart. 559. **nosethirles,** nostrils. 560. **bokeler,** shield; **bar,** bore. 561. **furnais,** furnace. 562. **janglere,** chatterer; **Goliardais,** Goliard, teller of tall stories. 563. **harlotries,** obscenities. 564. **tollen thries,** take toll thrice, deduct from the grain far more than the lawful percentage.

And yit he hadde a thombe° of gold, pardee.
A whit cote and a blew hood wered° he.
A baggepipe wel coude he blowe and soune,
And therwithal he broughte us out of towne.
  A gentil Manciple was ther of a temple,°
Of which achatours° mighte take exemple
For to been wise in bying of vitaile;°
For wheither that he paide or took by taile,°
Algate he waited so in his achat°
That he was ay biforn and in good stat.°
  Now is nat that of God a ful fair grace
That swich a lewed mannes wit shal pace°
The wisdom of an heep of lerned men?
Of maistres hadde he mo than thries ten
That weren of lawe expert and curious,°
Of whiche ther were a dozeine in that hous
Worthy to been stiwardes of rente° and lond
Of any lord that is in Engelond,
To make him live by his propre good°
In honour dettelees but if he were wood,°
Or live as scarsly as him list° desire,
And able for to helpen al a shire
In any caas that mighte falle° or happe,
And yit this Manciple sette hir aller cappe!°
  The Reeve was a sclendre colerik° man;
His beerd was shave as neigh as evere he can;
His heer was by his eres ful round yshorn;
His top was dokked° lik a preest biforn;
Ful longe were his legges and ful lene,

565. thombe, thumb: the narrator seems to be disproving the adage that an honest miller has a golden thumb. **566. wered,** wore. **569. temple,** community of lawyers. **570. achatours,** purchasers of food. **571. vitaile,** victuals. **572. by taile,** by talley, i.e., on credit. **573. Algate,** always; **waited,** was on the watch; **achat,** purchasing. **574. biforn,** i.e., ahead of the game; **stat,** financial condition. **576. lewed,** ignorant; **pace,** surpass. **579. curious,** cunning. **581. rente,** income. **583. propre good,** own money. **584. but if,** unless; **wood,** insane. **585. scarsly,** parsimoniously; **list,** it pleases. **587. caas,** event; **falle,** befall. **588. sette . . . cappe,** made fools of them all. **589. colerik,** i.e., dominated by yellow bile. **592. dokked,** cut short: the clergy wore the head partially shaved.

Ylik a staf, ther was no calf yseene.
Wel coude he keepe a gerner and a binne—
Ther was noon auditour coude on him winne.
Wel wiste he by the droughte and by the rain
The yeelding of his seed and of his grain.
His lordes sheep, his neet, his dayerye,
His swin, his hors, his stoor, and his pultrye
Was hoolly in this Reeves governinge,
And by his covenant yaf the rekeninge,
Sin that his lord was twenty yeer of age.
Ther coude no man bringe him in arrerage.
Ther nas baillif, hierde, nor other hine,
That he ne knew his sleighte and his covine—
They were adrad of him as of the deeth.
His woning was ful faire upon an heeth;
With greene trees shadwed was his place.
He coude bettre than his lord purchace.
Ful riche he was astored prively.
His lord wel coude he plesen subtilly,
To yive and lene him of his owene good,
And have a thank, and yit a cote and hood.
In youthe he hadde lerned a good mister:
He was a wel good wrighte, a carpenter.
This Reeve sat upon a ful good stot
That was a pomely grey and highte Scot.
A long surcote of pers upon he hade,
And by his side he bar a rusty blade.
Of Northfolk was this Reeve of which I telle,
Biside a town men clepen Baldeswelle.

594. **yseene,** visible. 595. **keepe,** guard; **gerner,** granary. 596. **on . . . winne,** i.e., find him in default. 597. **wiste,** knew. 599. **neet,** cattle. 600. **stoor,** stock. 601. **hoolly,** wholly. 602. **by . . . covenant,** according to his contract; **yaf,** i.e., he gave. 604. **bringe . . . arrerage,** convict him of being in arrears financially. 605. **bailiff,** i.e., foreman; **hierde,** shepherd; **hine,** farm laborer. 606. **covine,** conspiracy. 607. **adrad,** afraid; **deeth,** pestilence. 608. **woning,** dwelling; **heeth,** meadow. 610. **purchace,** acquire possessions. 611. **astored,** stocked; **prively,** secretly. 613. **lene,** lend. 615. **mister,** occupation. 617. **stot,** stallion. 618. **pomely,** dappled; **highte,** was named. 619. **surcote,** overcoat; **pers,** blue; **upon . . . hade,** he had on. 620. **bar,** bore. 622. **Baldeswelle,** Bawdswell.

Tukked he was as is a frere aboute,
And evere he rood the hindreste of oure route.
  A Somnour was ther with us in that place
That hadde a fir-reed cherubinnes face,
For saucefleem he was, with yën narwe,
And hoot he was, and lecherous as a sparwe,
With scaled browes blake and piled beerd:
Of his visage children were aferd.
Ther nas quiksilver, litarge, ne brimstoon,
Boras, ceruce, ne oile of tartre noon,
Ne oinement that wolde clense and bite,
That him mighte helpen of his whelkes white,
Nor of the knobbes sitting on his cheekes.
Wel loved he garlek, oinons, and eek leekes,
And for to drinke strong win reed as blood.
Thanne wolde he speke and crye as he were wood;
And whan that he wel dronken hadde the win,
Thanne wolde he speke no word but Latin:
A fewe termes hadde he, two or three,
That he hadde lerned out of som decree;
No wonder is—he herde it al the day,
And eek ye knowe wel how that a jay
Can clepen "Watte" as wel as can the Pope—
But whoso coude in other thing him grope,
Thanne hadde he spent all his philosophye;
Ay *Questio quid juris* wolde he crye.
  He was a gentil harlot and a kinde;
A bettre felawe sholde men nought finde:
He wolde suffre, for a quart of win,

623. Tukked, with clothing tucked up. **624. hindreste,** hindmost; **route,** group. **626. fir-reed,** fire-red; **cherubinnes,** cherub's, often pictured in art with a red face. **627. saucefleem,** pimply. **628. hoot,** hot; **sparwe,** sparrow. **629. scaled,** scabby; **piled,** uneven, partly hairless. **630. aferd,** afraid. **631. litarge,** lead ointment; **brimstoon,** sulfur. **632. Boras,** borax; **ceruce,** white lead; **oile of tartre,** an acid solution. **634. whelkes,** blotches. **635. knobbes,** lumps. **638. wood,** mad. **644. jay,** parrot. **645. clepen,** call out. **646. grope,** examine. **647. philosophye,** i.e., learning. **648. Questio . . . juris,** a phrase frequently used in ecclesiastical courts. **649. harlot,** rascal.

A good felawe to have his concubin
A twelfmonth, and excusen him at the fulle;
Ful prively a finch eek coude he pulle.°
And if he foond° owher a good felawe
He wolde techen him to have noon awe
In swich caas of the Ercedekenes curs,°
But if° a mannes soule were in his purs,
For in his purs he sholde ypunisshed be.
"Purs is the Ercedekenes helle," saide he.
  But wel I woot he lied right in deede:
Of cursing° oughte eech gilty man him drede,
For curs wol slee right as assoiling° savith—
And also war him of a *significavit*.°
  In daunger hadde he at his owene gise°
The yonge girles of the diocise,
And knew hir conseil, and was al hir reed.°
A gerland hadde he set upon his heed
As greet as it were for an ale-stake;°
A bokeler hadde he maad him of a cake.
  With him ther rood a gentil Pardoner
Of Rouncival, his freend and his compeer,°
That straight was comen fro the Court of Rome.
Ful loude he soong,° "Com hider, love, to me."
This Somnour bar to him a stif burdoun:°
Was nevere trompe° of half so greet a soun.
  This Pardoner hadde heer as yelow as wex,
But smoothe it heeng as dooth a strike of flex;°

654. "To pull a finch" is to have carnal dealings with a woman. 655. **foond,** found; **owher,** anywhere. 657. **Ercedekenes,** Archdeacon's; **curs,** sentence of excommunication. 658. **But if,** unless. 662. **cursing,** excommunication. 663. **slee,** slay; **assoiling,** absolution. 664. And also one should be careful of a *Significavit,* the writ which transferred the guilty offender from the ecclesiastical to the civil arm for punishment. 665. **In daunger,** under his domination; **gise,** i.e., disposal. 667. **conseil,** secrets; **al . . . reed,** their chief source of advice. 669. **ale-stake:** a tavern was signalized by a pole, rather like a modern flagpole, projecting from its front wall; on this hung a garland or "bush." 672. **Rouncival,** Roncesvalles in Spain, site of a hospital with a branch in London; **compeer,** comrade. 674. **soong,** sang. 675. **bar,** i.e., provided; **burdoun,** vocal accompaniment. 676. **trompe,** trumpet. 678. **heeng,** hung; **strike,** hank; **flex,** flax.

By ounces° heenge his lokkes that he hadde,
And therwith he his shuldres overspradde;°
But thinne it lay, by colpons,° oon by oon;
But hood for jolitee wered° he noon,
For it was trussed up in his walet:°
Him thoughte he rood al of the newe jet.°
Dischevelee° save his cappe he rood al bare.
Swiche glaring yën hadde he as an hare.
A vernicle° hadde he sowed upon his cappe,
His walet biforn him in his lappe,
Bretful of pardon, comen from Rome al hoot.°
A vois he hadde as smal as hath a goot;°
No beerd hadde he, ne nevere sholde have;
As smoothe it was as it were late yshave:
I trowe° he were a gelding or a mare.
But of his craft, fro Berwik into Ware,°
Ne was ther swich another pardoner;
For in his male he hadde a pilwe-beer°
Which that he saide was Oure Lady veil;
He saide he hadde a gobet° of the sail
That Sainte Peter hadde whan that he wente
Upon the see, til Jesu Crist him hente.°
He hadde a crois of laton,° ful of stones,
And in a glas he hadde pigges bones,
But with thise relikes whan that he foond°
A poore person° dwelling upon lond,
Upon a day he gat him more moneye
Than that the person gat° in monthes twaye;
And thus with feined flaterye and japes°
He made the person and the peple his apes.°

679. **ounces,** i.e., thin strands. 680. **overspradde,** overspread. 681. **colpons,** strands. 682. **jolitee,** i.e., nonchalance; **wered,** wore. 683. **walet,** pack. 684. **jet,** fashion. 685. **Dischevelee,** with hair down. 687. **vernicle,** portrait of Christ's face as it was impressed on St. Veronica's handkerchief. 689. **Bretful,** brimful; **hoot,** hot. 690. **smal,** fine; **goot,** goat. 693. **trowe,** believe. 694. **Berwik, Ware,** ? towns south and north of London. 696. **male,** bag; **pilwe-beer,** pillowcase. 698. **gobet,** piece. 700. **hente,** seized. 701. **crois,** cross; **laton,** brassy metal. 703. **foond,** found. 704. **person,** parson. 705. **gat,** got. 707. **feined,** false; **japes,** tricks. 708. **apes,** i.e., dupes.

But trewely to tellen at the laste,
He was in chirche a noble ecclesiaste;
Wel coude he rede a lesson and a storye,
But alderbest he soong an offertorye,
For wel he wiste whan that song was songe,
He moste preche and wel affile his tonge
To winne silver, as he ful wel coude—
Therfore he soong the merierly and loude.
  Now have I told you soothly in a clause
Th'estaat, th'array, the nombre, and eek the cause
Why that assembled was this compaignye
In Southwerk at this gentil hostelrye
That highte the Tabard, faste by the Belle;
But now is time to you for to telle
How that we baren us that ilke night
Whan we were in that hostelrye alight;
And after wol I telle of oure viage,
And al the remenant of oure pilgrimage.
  But first I praye you of youre curteisye
That ye n'arette it nought my vilainye
Though that I plainly speke in this matere
To telle you hir wordes and hir cheere,
Ne though I speke hir wordes proprely;
For this ye knowen also wel as I:
Who so shal telle a tale after a man
He moot reherce, as neigh as evere he can,
Everich a word, if it be in his charge,
Al speke he nevere so rudeliche and large,
Or elles he moot telle his tale untrewe,
Or feine thing, or finde wordes newe;
He may nought spare although he were his brother:

711. storye, liturgical narrative. **712. alderbest,** best of all. **713. wiste,** knew. **714. affile,** sharpen. **716. merierly,** more merrily. **717. clause,** i.e., short space. **721. Belle,** another Southwark tavern. **723. baren us,** bore ourselves; **ilke,** same. **725. viage,** trip. **728. arette it,** charge it to; **vilainye,** lack of decorum. **730. cheere,** behavior. **731. proprely,** accurately. **734. moot,** must. **735. charge,** responsibility. **736. Al . . . he,** although he speak; **large,** broadly. **738. feine,** falsify; **finde,** devise. **739. spare,** i.e., spare any one.

He moot as wel saye oo word as another.
Crist spak himself ful brode in Holy Writ,
And wel ye woot no vilainye is it;
Eek Plato saith, who so can him rede,
The wordes mote be cosin to the deede.
Also I praye you to foryive it me
Al° have I nat set folk in hir degree
Here in this tale as that they sholde stonde:
My wit is short, ye may wel understonde.
Greet cheere made oure Host us everichoon,
And to the soper sette he us anoon.
He served us with vitaile° at the beste.
Strong was the win, and wel to drinke us leste.°
A semely man oure Hoste was withalle
For to been a marchal° in an halle;
A large man he was, with yën steepe;°
A fairer burgeis was ther noon in Chepe°—
Bold of his speeche, and wis, and wel ytaught,
And of manhood him lakkede right naught.
Eek therto he was right a merye man,
And after soper playen he bigan,
And spak of mirthe amonges othere thinges—
Whan that we hadde maad oure rekeninges—
And saide thus, "Now, lordinges, trewely,
Ye been to me right welcome, hertely.°
For by my trouthe, if that I shal nat lie,
I sawgh nat this yeer so merye a compaignye
At ones in this herberwe° as is now.
Fain wolde I doon you mirthe, wiste I° how.
And of a mirthe I am right now bithought,
To doon you ese, and it shal coste nought.
Ye goon to Canterbury—God you speede;
The blisful martyr quite you youre meede.°

746. **Al,** although. 751. **vitaile,** food. 752. **leste,** it pleased. 754. **marchal,** marshal, one who was in charge of feasts. 755. **steepe,** prominent. 756. **burgeis,** burgher; **Chepe,** Cheapside, bourgeois center of London. 764. **hertely,** heartily. 767. **herberwe,** inn. 768. **Fain,** gladly; **wiste I,** if I knew. 772. **quite . . . meede,** pay you your reward.

And wel I woot as ye goon by the waye
Ye shapen you to talen° and to playe,
For trewely, confort ne mirthe is noon
To ride by the waye domb as stoon;°
And therfore wol I maken you disport
As I saide erst,° and doon you som confort;
And if you liketh alle, by oon assent,
For to stonden at my juggement,
And for to werken as I shal you saye,
Tomorwe whan ye riden by the waye—
Now by my fader soule that is deed,
But ye be merye I wol yive you myn heed!°
Holde up youre handes withouten more speeche."
  Oure conseil was nat longe for to seeche;°
Us thoughte it was nat worth to make it wis,°
And graunted him withouten more avis,°
And bade him saye his voirdit as him leste.°
  "Lordinges," quod he, "now herkneth for the beste;
But taketh it nought, I praye you, in desdain.
This is the point, to speken short and plain,
That eech of you, to shorte with oure waye
In this viage, shal tellen tales twaye—
To Canterburyward, I mene it so,
And hoomward he shal tellen othere two,
Of aventures that whilom° have bifalle;
And which of you that bereth him best of alle—
That is to sayn, that telleth in this cas
Tales of best sentence and most solas°—
Shal have a soper at oure aller cost,°
Here in this place, sitting by this post,
Whan that we come again fro Canterbury.
And for to make you the more mury°

774. **shapen you,** intend; **talen,** converse. 776. **stoon,** stone. 778. **erst,** before. 784. **But,** unless; **heed,** head. 786. **seeche,** seek. 787. We didn't think it worthwhile to make an issue of it. 788. **avis,** deliberation. 789. **voirdit,** verdict; **leste,** it pleased. 797. **whilom,** once upon a time. 800. **sentence,** purport; **solas,** delight. 801. **oure . . . cost,** the cost of us all. 804. **mury,** merry.

I wol myself goodly° with you ride—
Right at myn owene cost—and be youre gide.
And who so wol my juggement withsaye°
Shal paye al that we spende by the waye.
And if ye vouche sauf that it be so,
Telle me anoon, withouten wordes mo,
And I wol erly shape me° therfore."
  This thing was graunted and oure othes swore
With ful glad herte, and prayden° him also
That he wolde vouche sauf for to do so,
And that he wolde been oure governour,
And of oure tales juge and reportour,°
And sette a soper at a certain pris,°
And we wol ruled been at his devis,°
In heigh and lowe; and thus by oon assent
We been accorded to his juggement.
And therupon the win was fet° anoon;
We dronken and to reste wente eechoon
Withouten any lenger taryinge.
  Amorwe° whan that day bigan to springe
Up roos oure Host and was oure aller cok,°
And gadred us togidres in a flok,
And forth we riden, a litel more than pas,°
Unto the watering of Saint Thomas;
And ther oure Host bigan his hors arreste,°
And saide, "Lordes, herkneth if you leste:°
  Ye woot youre forward and it you recorde:°
If evensong and morwesong° accorde,
Lat see now who shal telle the firste tale.
As evere mote I drinken win or ale,
Who so be rebel to my juggement
Shal paye for al that by the way is spent.

805. **goodly,** kindly. 807. **withsaye,** contradict. 811. **shape me,** prepare myself. 813. **prayden,** i.e., we prayed. 816. **reportour,** i.e., accountant. 817. **pris,** price. 818. **devis,** disposal. 821. **fet,** fetched. 824. **Amorwe,** in the morning. 825. **oure . . . cok,** rooster for us all. 827. **pas,** a step. 829. **arreste,** halt. 830. **leste,** it please. 831. **forward,** agreement; **you recorde,** recall. 832. **morwesong,** morningsong.

Now draweth cut er that we ferrer twinne:°
He which that hath the shorteste shal biginne.
  Sire Knight," quod he, "my maister and my lord,
Now draweth cut, for that is myn accord.°
Cometh neer," quod he, "my lady Prioresse,
And ye, sire Clerk, lat be youre shamefastnesse—
Ne studieth nought. Lay hand to, every man!"
  Anoon to drawen every wight bigan,
And shortly for to tellen as it was,
Were it by aventure, or sort, or cas,°
The soothe is this, the cut fil° to the Knight;
Of which ful blithe and glad was every wight,
And telle he moste° his tale, as was resoun,
By forward and by composicioun,°
As ye han herd. What needeth wordes mo?
And whan this goode man sawgh that it was so,
As he that wis was and obedient
To keepe his forward by his free assent,
He saide, "Sin I shal biginne the game,
What, welcome be the cut, in Goddes name!
Now lat us ride, and herkneth what I saye."
And with that word we riden forth oure waye,
And he bigan with right a merye cheere°
His tale anoon, and saide as ye may heere.

THE KNIGHT'S TALE

PART ONE

Whilom,° as olde stories tellen us,
Ther was a duc that highte° Theseus:
Of Atthenes he was lord and governour,

837. **cut,** lots; **ferrer twinne,** further part. 840. **accord,** wish. 846. Whether it was luck, fate, or chance. 847. **fil,** fell. 849. **moste,** must. 850. **forward,** agreement; **composicioun,** treaty. 859. **cheere,** countenance.
1. **Whilom,** once upon a time. 2. **highte,** was named.

And in his time swich a conquerour
That gretter was ther noon under the sonne.
Ful many a riche contree hadde he wonne;
What with his wisdom and his chivalrye,
He conquered al the regne of Femenye,
That whilom was ycleped Scythia,
And weddede the queene Ipolyta,
And broughte hire hoom with him in his contree,
With muchel glorye and greet solempnitee,
And eek hir yonge suster Emelye.
And thus with victorye and melodye
Lete I this noble Duc to Atthenes ride,
And al his host in armes him biside.
  And certes, if it nere too long to heere,
I wolde have told you fully the manere
How wonnen was the regne of Femenye
By Theseus and by his chivalrye,
And of the grete bataile for the nones
Bitwixen Atthenes and Amazones,
And how asseged was Ipolyta,
The faire hardy queene of Scythia,
And of the feeste that was at hir weddinge,
And of the tempest at hir hoom-cominge.
But al that thing I moot as now forbere:
I have, God woot, a large feeld to ere,
And waike been the oxen in my plough;
The remenant of the tale is long ynough.
I wol nat letten eek noon of this route—
Lat every felawe telle his tale aboute,
And lat see now who shal the soper winne.
And ther I lefte I wol ayain biginne.
  This Duc of whom I make mencioun,
Whan he was come almost to the town

5. **gretter,** greater. 8. **regne,** kingdom; **Femenye,** Feminia, the land of the Amazons. 10. **Ipolyta,** Hippolyta. 13. **Emelye,** Emily or Amelia. 21. **for the nones,** on the occasion. 23. **asseged,** besieged. 27. **moot,** must. 28. **ere,** plow. 29. **waike,** weak. 31. **letten,** hinder; **route,** group. 32. **aboute,** i.e., in turn.

In al his wele° and in his moste pride,
He was war° as he caste his yë aside
Wher that ther kneeled in the hye waye
A compaignye of ladies, twaye and twaye,
Eech after other, clad in clothes blake.
But swich a cry and swich a wo they make
That in this world nis creature livinge
That herde swich another waymentinge;°
And of this cry they nolde nevere stenten°
Til they the reines of his bridel henten.°
"What folk been ye that at myn home-cominge
Perturben so my feeste with cryinge?"
Quod Theseus. "Have ye so greet envye
Of myn honour, that thus complaine and crye?
Or who hath you misboden° or offended?
And telleth me if it may been amended,
And why that ye been clothed thus in blak?"
The eldeste lady of hem alle spak,
Whan she hadde swouned with a deedly cheere,°
That it was routhe° for to seen and heere.
She saide, "Lord to whom Fortune hath yiven
Victorye, and as a conquerour to liven,
Nought greveth us youre glorye and youre honour,
But we biseeken mercy and socour:
Have mercy on oure wo and oure distresse;
Som drope of pitee, thurgh thy gentilesse,°
Upon us wrecched wommen lat thou falle,
For certes, lord, ther nis noon of us alle
That she ne hath been a duchesse or a queene;
Now be we caitives,° as it is wel seene,
Thanked be Fortune and hir false wheel,°
That noon estaat assureth to been weel.°

37. wele, pomp. **38. war,** aware. **44. waymentinge,** lamentation. **45. stenten,** cease. **46. henten,** grasped. **51. misboden,** injured. **55. swouned,** swooned; **cheere,** countenance. **56. routhe,** pity. **62. gentilesse,** gentleness. **66. caitives,** wretches. **67.** The Goddess Fortune was thought of as turning a great wheel on which men rode to the heights or depths. **68.** Who guarantees that no class will be well-off.

Now certes, lord, to abiden youre presence,
Here in this temple of the Goddesse Clemence°
We have been waiting al this fourtenight.
Now help us, lord, sith it is in thy might.
  I, wrecche, which that weepe and waile thus,
Was whilom wif to King Cappaneus°
That starf°at Thebes—cursed be the day!
And alle we that been in this array
And maken al this lamentacioun,
We losten alle oure housbondes at that town,
Whil that the sege theraboute lay.
And yet now the olde Creon, wailaway,°
That lord is now of Thebes the citee,
Fulfild°of ire and of iniquitee,
He for despit°and for his tyrannye,
To doon the dede°bodies vilainye
Of alle oure lordes whiche that been slawe,°
Hath alle the bodies on an heep ydrawe,
And wol nat suffren hem by noon assent
Neither to been yburied nor ybrent,°
But maketh houndes ete hem in despit."
And with that word, withouten more respit,°
They fillen gruf°and criden pitously,
"Have on us wrecched wommen som mercy,
And lat oure sorwe sinken in thyn herte."
  This gentil Duc down from his courser sterte°
With herte pitous whan he herde hem speke.
Him thoughte that his herte wolde breke
Whan he sawgh hem so pitous and so mat,°
That whilom weren of so greet estat;
And in his armes he hem alle up hente,°

70. Clemence, Mercy. **74 ff.** After the disastrous ending of the expedition of the Seven against Thebes (see *T. C.*, V, 1464 ff. and note), the city was seized by Creon, who through impious tyranny refused to permit the survivors of the late besiegers to bury their dead. **75. starf,** died. **80. wailaway,** alas. **82. Fulfild,** filled full. **83. despit,** malice. **84. dede,** dead. **85. slawe,** slain. **88. ybrent,** burned. **90. respit,** delay. **91. fillen,** fell; **gruf,** prone. **94. sterte,** leapt. **97. mat,** overcome. **99. hente,** took.

And hem conforteth in ful good entente,
And swoor his ooth, as he was trewe knight,
He wolde doon so ferforthly° his might
Upon the tyrant Creon hem to wreke,°
That al the peple of Greece sholde speke
How Creon was of Theseus yserved,°
As he that hadde his deeth ful wel deserved.
And right anoon withouten more abood°
His baner he desplayeth° and forth rood
To Thebesward, and al his host biside:
No neer° Atthenes wolde he go nor ride,
Ne take his ese fully half a day,
But onward on his way that night he lay,
And sente anoon Ipolyta the queene,
And Emelye hir yonge suster sheene,°
Unto the town of Atthenes to dwelle,
And forth he rit:° ther nis namore to telle.
  The rede statue of Mars with spere and targe°
So shineth in his white baner large
That alle the feeldes glitren up and down;
And by his baner born was his penoun°
Of gold ful riche, in which ther was ybete°
The Minotaur, which that he wan° in Crete.
  Thus rit this Duc, thus rit this conquerour,
And in his host of chivalrye the flowr,
Til that he cam to Thebes and alighte
Faire in a feeld ther as he thoughte° fighte.
  But shortly for to speken of this thing,
With Creon which that was of Thebes king
He faught, and slow° him manly as a knight
In plain° bataile, and putte the folk to flight;
And by assaut° he wan the citee after,

102. so ferforthly, to such an extent. **103. wreke,** avenge. **105. yserved,** treated. **107. abood,** delay. **108. desplayeth,** unfolds. **110. neer,** nearer; **go,** walk. **114. sheene,** bright, fair. **116. rit,** rides. **117. targe,** shield. **120. penoun,** pennon. **121. ybete,** inlaid. **122. wan,** won; the exploit took place in Theseus' youth. **126. thoughte,** intended to. **129. slow,** slew. **130. plain,** open. **131. assaut,** assault.

And rente adown bothe wal and sparre° and rafter,
And to the ladies he restored again
The bones of hir freendes that were slain,
To doon obsequies as was tho the gise.°
But it were al too long for to devise
The grete clamour and the waymentinge°
That the ladies made at the brenninge°
Of the bodies, and the grete honour
That Theseus, the noble conquerour,
Dooth to the ladies whan they from him wente:
But shortly for to telle is myn entente.
  Whan that this worthy Duc, this Theseus,
Hath Creon slain and wonne Thebes thus,
Stille in that feeld he took al night his reste,
And dide with al the contree as him leste.°
  To ransake in the taas° of bodies dede,
Hem for to strepe of harneis and of weede,°
The pilours diden bisinesse and cure,°
After the bataile and disconfiture.°
And so bifel that in the taas they founde,
Thurgh-girt° with many a grevous bloody wounde,
Two yonge knightes, ligging by and by,°
Bothe in oon armes° wrought ful richely;
Of whiche two Arcita highte° that oon,
And that other knight highte Palamon.
Nat fully quik ne fully deed° they were;
But by hir cote-armures and by hir gere°
The heraudes° knewe hem best in special
As they that weren of the blood royal
Of Thebes, and of sustren° two yborn.

132. **sparre,** beam. 135. **gise,** fashion. 137. **waymentinge,** lamentation. 138. **brenninge,** burning. 146. **leste,** pleased. 147. **taas,** piles. 148. **strepe,** strip; **harneis . . . weede,** armor and clothing. 149. **pilours,** plunderers; **diden . . . cure,** i.e., performed their business carefully. 150. **disconfiture,** defeat. 152. **Thurgh-girt,** pierced through. 153. **ligging,** lying; **by and by,** side by side. 154. **in . . . armes,** with the same coats of arms. 155. **highte,** was named. 157. **deed,** dead. 158. **cote-armures,** coats of arms; **gere,** armor. 159. **heraudes,** heralds. 161. **sustren,** sisters.

Out of the taas the pilours han hem torn,
And han hem caried softe unto the tente
Of Theseus, and he ful soone hem sente
To Atthenes to dwellen in prisoun
Perpetuelly: he nolde no raunsoun.°
And whan this worthy Duc hath thus ydoon,
He took his host and hoom he rit° anoon,
With laurer° corowned as a conquerour.
And ther he liveth in joye and in honour
Terme of his lif.° What needeth wordes mo?
And in a towr, in anguissh and in wo,
Dwellen this Palamon and eek Arcite
For everemore: ther may no gold hem quite.°
This passeth yeer by yeer and day by day,
Til it fil ones in a morwe° of May
That Emelye, that fairer was to seene
Than is the lilye upon his stalke greene,
And fressher than the May with flowres newe—
For with the rose colour stroof° hir hewe:
I noot° which was the fairer of hem two—
Er it were day, as was hir wone° to do,
She was arisen and al redy dight;°
For May wol have no slogardye° anight:
The seson priketh every gentil herte,
And maketh it out of his sleep to sterte,
And saith, "Aris and do thyn observaunce."°
This maketh Emelye have remembraunce
To doon honour to May and for to rise.
Yclothed was she fresshe to devise;
Hir yelow heer was broided° in a tresse
Bihinde hir bak a yerde long, I gesse,
And in the gardin at the sonne upriste°

166. **raunsoun,** ransom. 168. **rit,** rides. 169. **laurer,** laurel. 171. **Terme . . . lif,** i.e., as long as he lives. 174. **quite,** redeem. 176. **fil,** befell; **morwe,** morning. 180. **stroof,** strove. 181. **noot,** know not. 182. **wone,** custom. 183. **dight,** dressed. 184. **slogardye,** laziness. 187. **observaunce,** rite. 191. **broided,** braided. 193. **upriste,** rise.

She walketh up and down, and as hire liste
She gadreth flowres party° white and rede
To make a subtil gerland for hir hede,°
And as an angel hevenisshly she soong.°
  The grete towr that was so thikke and strong,
Which of the castel was the chief dongeoun,°
Ther as the knightes weren in prisoun—
Of whiche I tolde you and tellen shal—
Was evene joinant° to the gardin wal
Ther as this Emelye hadde hir playinge.°
Bright was the sonne and cleer in that morninge,
And Palamon, this woful prisoner,
As was his wone° by leve of his gailer,
Was risen and romed in a chambre an heigh,
In which he al the noble citee seigh,°
And eek the gardin, ful of braunches greene,
Ther as the fresshe Emelye the sheene
Was in hir walk and romed up and down.
This sorweful prisoner, this Palamoun,
Gooth in the chambre roming to and fro,
And to himself complaining of his wo.
That he was born ful ofte he saide allas.
And so bifel, by aventure or cas,°
That thurgh a windowe thikke of° many a barre
Of iren greet and square as any sparre,°
He caste his yë upon Emelya,
And therwithal he bleinte° and cride "A!"
As though he stongen° were unto the herte.
  And with that cry Arcite anoon up sterte
And saide, "Cosin myn, what aileth thee
That art so pale and deedly° on to see?
Why cridestou? Who hath thee doon offence?
For Goddes love, taak al in pacience

195. **party,** variegated. 196. **hede,** head. 197. **soong,** sang. 199. **dongeoun,** strong-tower. 202. **evene joinant,** directly adjacent. 203. **playinge,** i.e., recreation. 206. **wone,** custom. 208. **seigh,** saw. 216. **cas,** chance. 217. **thikke of,** i.e., provided with. 218. **square,** strong; **sparre,** beam. 220. **bleinte,** flinched. 221. **stongen,** pierced. 224. **deedly,** deadly.

Oure prison, for it may noon other be—
Fortune hath yiven us this adversitee:
Som wikke aspect or disposicioun°
Of Saturne, by som constellacioun,°
Hath yiven us this, although we hadde it sworn.
So stood the hevene whan that we were born.
We mote endure it: this is the short and plain."
  This Palamon answerde and saide again,
"Cosin, forsoothe of this opinioun
Thou hast a vain imaginacioun.
This prison caused me nought for to crye,
But I was hurt right now thurghout myn yë
Into myn herte, that wol my bane° be.
The fairnesse of that lady that I see
Yond in the gardin romen to and fro
Is cause of al my crying and my wo:
I noot wher° she be womman or goddesse,
But Venus is it soothly as I gesse."
And therwithal on knees down he fil°
And saide, "Venus, if it be thy wil
You° in this gardin thus to transfigure
Bifore me, sorweful, wrecched creature,
Out of this prison help that we may scape.°
And if so be my destinee be shape
By eterne° word to dien in prisoun,
Of oure linage have som compassioun,
That is so lowe ybrought by tyrannye."
  And with that word Arcite gan espye
Wher as this lady romed to and fro,
And with that sighte hir beautee hurte him so
That if that Palamon was wounded sore,
Arcite is hurt as muche as he or more;
And with a sik° he saide pitously,

229. **wikke aspect,** i.e., evil astrological aspect; **disposicioun,** planetary position. 230. **constellacioun,** arrangement of planets. 231. **it,** i.e., the opposite. 239. **bane,** destruction. 243. **noot wher,** know not whether. 245. **fil,** fell. 247. **you,** yourself. 249. **scape,** escape. 251. **eterne,** eternal. 259. **sik,** sigh.

"The fresshe beautee sleeth me sodeinly
Of hire that rometh in the yonder place,
And but I have hir mercy and hir grace,
That I may seen hire at the leeste waye,
I nam but deed: ther nis namore to saye."
  This Palamon, whan he tho wordes herde,
Despitously he looked and answerde,
"Wheither saistou this in ernest or in play?"
  "Nay," quod Arcite, "in ernest, by my fay.
God help me so, me list ful yvele playe."
  This Palamon gan knitte his browes twaye.
"It were to thee," quod he, "no greet honour
For to be fals, ne for to be traitour
To me, that am thy cosin and thy brother,
Ysworn ful deepe, and eech of us til other,
That nevere, for to dien in the paine,
Til that the deeth departe shal us twaine,
Neither of us in love to hindre other,
Ne in noon other caas, my leve brother,
But that thou sholdest trewely forthren me
In every caas, and I shal forthren thee:
This was thyn ooth as myn also, certain.
I woot right wel thou darst it nat withsayn.
Thus artou of my conseil, out of doute,
And now thou woldest falsly been aboute
To love my lady whom I love and serve,
And evere shal til that myn herte sterve.
Now certes, false Arcite, thou shalt nat so:
I loved hire first and tolde thee my wo,
As to my conseil and my brother, sworn
To forthre me as I have told biforn.
For which thou art ybounden as a knight

260. sleeth, slays. **263. at . . . waye,** at least. **264. I . . . deed,** I'm no better than dead. **266. Despitously,** angrily. **267. Wheither saistou,** do you say. **268. fay,** faith. **269. me . . . playe,** I feel little like joking. **273. brother,** i.e., sworn friend. **275. in . . . paine,** in torture. **276. departe,** divide. **279. forthren,** further. **282. withsayn,** deny. **283. of . . . conseil,** i.e., a sharer of my secrets. **286. sterve,** die.

To helpe me if it laye in thy might,
Or elles artou fals, I dar wel sayn."
  This Arcite ful proudly spak again:
"Thou shalt," quod he, "be rather° fals than I,
And thou art fals, I telle thee outrely:°
For paramour° I loved hire first er thou.
What wiltou sayn? Thou wistest° nat yet now
Wheither she be a womman or goddesse.
Thyn is affeccion of holinesse,
And myn is love as to a creature,
For which I tolde thee myn aventure,
As to my cosin and my brother sworn.
I pose° that thou lovedest hire biforn:
Woostou nat wel the olde clerkes sawe
That 'Who shal yive a lovere any lawe?'
Love is a gretter lawe, by my pan,°
Than may be yive to any erthely man,
And therfore positif° lawe and swich decree
Is broke alday° for love in eech degree.
A man moot needes love, maugree his heed;°
He may nat fleen it though he sholde be deed,
Al be she° maide, widwe, or elles wif.
And eek it is nat likly al thy lif
To stonden in hir grace. Namore shal I,
For wel thou woost thyselve verraily
That thou and I be dampned° to prisoun
Perpetuelly—us gaineth° no raunsoun.
We strive as dide the houndes for the boon:°
They foughte al day, and yet hir part was noon:
Ther cam a kite° whil that they were so wrothe
That bar away the boon bitwixe hem bothe.
And therfore, at the kinges court, my brother,
Eech man for himself: ther is noon other.

295. rather, sooner. **296. outrely,** plainly. **297. paramour,** with earthly love. **298. wistest,** knew. **304. pose,** assume for argument's sake. **306. pan,** skull. **309. positif,** arbitrary, man-made. **310. alday,** constantly. **311. maugree,** despite; **heed,** head. **313. Al be she,** whether she is. **317. dampned,** condemned. **318. gaineth,** avails. **319. boon,** bone. **321. kite,** hawk.

Love if thee list, for I love and ay shal;
And soothly, leve° brother, this is al:
Here in this prison mote we endure,
And everich° of us take his aventure."
  Greet was the strif and long bitwixe hem twaye,
If that I hadde leiser° for to saye,
But to th'effect: it happed on a day—
To telle it you as shortly as I may—
A worthy duc that highte Perotheus,°
That felawe° was unto Duc Theseus
Sin thilke day that they were children lite,°
Was come to Atthenes his felawe to visite,
And for to playe, as he was wont to do,
For in this world he loved no man so.
And he loved him as tendrely again;
So wel they loved, as olde bookes sayn,
That whan that oon was deed, soothly to telle,
His felawe wente and soughte him down in helle:
But of that storye list me nought to write.
Duc Perotheus loved wel Arcite,
And hadde him knowe at Thebes yeer by yere,
And finally, at requeste and prayere
Of Perotheus, withouten any raunsoun
Duc Theseus him leet out of prisoun,
Freely to goon wher that him liste overal,
In swich a gise° as I you tellen shal.
This was the forward,° plainly for t'endite,
Bitwixe Theseus and him Arcite:
That if so were that Arcite were yfounde
Evere in his lif, by day or night or stounde,°
In any contree of this Theseus,
And he were caught, it was accorded° thus,
That with a swerd he sholde lese° his heed:
Ther nas noon other remedye ne reed,°

326. leve, dear. **328. everich,** each. **330. leiser,** leisure. **333. Perotheus,** Pirithous. **334. felawe,** companion. **335. lite,** little. **350. gise,** manner. **351. forward,** agreement. **354. stounde,** moment. **356. accorded,** agreed. **357. lese,** lose. **358. reed,** plan, i.e., way out.

But taketh his leve, and hoomward he him spedde.
Lat him be war: his nekke lith to wedde.
  How greet a sorwe suffreth now Arcite!
The deeth he feeleth thurgh his herte smite.
He weepeth, waileth, crieth pitously;
To sleen himself he waiteth privély;
He saide, "Allas the day that I was born!
Now is my prison worse than biforn.
Now is me shape eternally to dwelle
Nought in purgatorye, but in helle.
Allas that evere knew I Perotheus,
For elles hadde I dwelled with Theseus,
Yfettred in his prison everemo.
Thanne hadde I been in blisse and nat in wo.
Only the sighte of hire whom that I serve—
Though that I nevere hir grace may deserve—
Wolde have suffised right ynough for me.
  O dere cosin Palamon," quod he,
"Thyn is the victorye of this aventure:
Ful blisfully in prison maistou dure.
In prison? Nay, certes, but in Paradis!
Wel hath Fortune yturned thee the dis.
That hast the sighte of hire, and I th'absence.
For possible is, sin thou hast hir presence,
And art a knight, a worthy and an able,
That by som caas, sin Fortune is chaungeable,
Thou maist to thy desir som time attaine;
But I, that am exiled, and bareine
Of alle grace, and in so greet despair
That ther nis erthe, water, fir, ne air,
Ne creature that of hem maked is,
That may me helpe or do confort in this,
Wel oughte I sterve in wanhope and distresse.
Farwel my lif, my lust, and my gladnesse!

360. **lith to wedde,** lies as a pledge. 364. **sleen,** slay; **waiteth,** waits his time. 367. **is . . . shape,** am I destined. 378. **dure,** remain. 380. **dis,** dice. 384. **caas,** chance. 386. **bareine,** barren. 391. **sterve,** die; **wanhope,** despair. 392. **lust,** delight.

Allas, why plainen° folk so in commune
On purveyance° of God, or of Fortune,
That yiveth hem ful ofte in many a gise°
Wel bettre than they can hemself devise?
Som man desireth for to have richesse
That cause is of his mordre° or greet siknesse;
And som man wolde out of his prison fain,°
That in his hous of his meinee° is slain.
Infinite harmes been in this matere:
We woot nat what thing that we prayen here.
We fare as he that dronke is as a mous.
A dronke man woot wel he hath an hous,
But he noot which the righte way is thider,°
And to a dronke man the way is slider.°
And certes in this world so faren we.
We seeken faste after felicitee,
But we goon wrong ful ofte, trewely.
Thus may we saye alle, and nameliche° I,
That wende° and hadde a greet opinioun
That if I mighte scapen fro prisoun,
Thanne hadde I been in joye and parfit hele,°
Ther now I am exiled fro my wele;°
Sin that I may nat seen you, Emelye,
I nam but deed: ther nis no remedye."
Upon that other side Palamon,
Whan that he wiste Arcite was agoon,°
Swich sorwe he maketh that the grete towr
Resouneth of his yowling and clamour.
The pure fettres of his shines° grete
Were of his bittre salte teres wete.
"Allas," quod he, "Arcita, cosin myn,
Of al oure strif, God woot, the fruit° is thyn.

393. **plainen,** complain. 394. **purveyance,** providence. 395. **gise,** way. 398. **mordre,** murder. 399. **out,** i.e., get out; **fain,** gladly. 400. **meinee,** household retainers. 405. **noot,** knows not; **thider,** thither. 406. **slider,** slippery. 410. **nameliche,** particularly. 411. **wende,** supposed. 413. **hele,** welfare. 414. **wele,** happiness. 418. **agoon,** gone away. 421. **pure,** very; **shines,** shins. 424. **fruit,** i.e., better part.

Thou walkest now in Thebes at thy large,
And of my wo thou yivest litel charge.°
Thou maist, sin thou hast wisdom and manhede,°
Assemblen al the folk of oure kinrede,°
And make a werre° so sharpe on this citee
That by som aventure or som tretee°
Thou maist have hire to lady and to wif,
For whom that I moste needes lese° my lif.
For as by way of possibilitee,
Sith thou art at thy large, of prison free,
And art a lord, greet is thyn avantage,
More than is myn, that sterve° here in a cage;
For I moot weepe and waile whil I live
With al the wo that prison may me yive,
And eek with paine that love me yiveth also,
That doubleth al my torment and my wo."
Therwith the fir of jalousye up sterte
Within his brest, and hente° him by the herte
So woodly° that he lik was to biholde
The boxtree or the asshen° dede and colde.
  Thanne saide he, "O cruel goddes that governe
This world with binding of youre word eterne,
And writen in the table of adamaunt
Youre parlement° and youre eterne graunt,
What is mankinde more unto you holde°
Than is the sheep that rouketh° in the folde?
For slain is man right as another beest,
And dwelleth eek in prison and arrest,
And hath siknesse and greet adversitee,
And ofte times giltelees, pardee.
  What governance is in this prescience°
That giltelees tormenteth innocence?
And yet encreesseth this al my penaunce,°

426. **yivest . . . charge,** care very little. 427. **manhede,** manhood. 428. **kinrede,** kindred. 429. **werre,** war. 430. **tretee,** treaty. 432. **lese,** lose. 436. **sterve,** die. 442. **hente,** seized. 443. **woodly,** madly. 444. **asshen,** ashes. 448. **parlement,** i.e., decisions. 449. **What,** in what way; **holde,** obligated. 450. **rouketh,** cowers. 455. **governance,** i.e., reasonable management; **prescience,** providence. 457. **penaunce,** suffering.

That man is bounden to his observaunce,°
For Goddes sake, to letten° of his wille,
Ther as a beest may al his lust fulfille.
And whan a beest is deed it hath no paine,
But man after his deeth moot weepe and plaine,°
Though in this world he have care and wo.
Withouten doute, it may stonden so.
The answere of this lete° I to divines,
But wel I woot that in this world greet pine° is.
Allas, I see a serpent or a thief,
That many° a trewe man hath doon meschief,
Goon at his large and where him list may turne,
But I moot been in prison thurgh Saturne,°
And eek thurgh Juno, jalous and eek wood,°
That hath destroyed wel neigh al the blood
Of Thebes, with his waste walles wide.
And Venus sleeth° me on that other side
For jalousye and fere of him Arcite."
  Now wol I stinte° of Palamon a lite,
And lete him in his prison stille dwelle,
And of Arcita forth I wol you telle.
  The somer passeth and the nightes longe
Encreessen double wise the paines stronge
Bothe of the lovere and the prisoner.
I noot which hath the sorwefuller mister:°
For soothly for to sayn, this Palamoun
Perpetuelly is dampned° to prisoun,
In chaines and in fettres to been deed;
And Arcite is exiled upon his heed°
For everemo as out of that contree,
Ne neveremo ne shal his lady see.

458. **observaunce,** rule of conduct. 459. **letten,** restrain himself. 462. **plaine,** lament. 465. **lete,** leave. 466. **pine,** suffering. 468. **many,** i.e., to many. **470 ff.** Saturn is not the pagan god but the baleful planet; Juno, on the other hand, is the queen of the pagan gods who was angry at Thebes because of its connection with several of her husband Jupiter's mistresses. 471. **wood,** furious. 474. **sleeth,** slays. 476. **stinte,** cease. 482. **noot,** know not; **mister,** occupation. 484. **dampned,** condemned. 486. **upon his heed,** on pain of losing his head.

You loveres axe I now this questioun:
Who hath the worse, Arcite or Palamoun?
That oon may seen his lady day by day,
But in prison moot he dwelle alway;
That other where him list may ride or go,
But seen his lady shal he neveremo.
Now deemeth as you liste, ye that can,
For I wol telle forth as I bigan.

PART TWO

Whan that Arcite to Thebes comen was,
Ful ofte a day he swelte and saide allas,
For seen his lady shal he neveremo;
And shortly to concluden al his wo,
So muchel sorwe hadde nevere creature
That is or shal whil that the world may dure.
His sleep, his mete, his drinke is him biraft,
That lene he weex and drye as is a shaft;
His yën holwe and grisly to biholde;
His hewe falow and pale as asshen colde;
And solitarye he was and evere allone,
And wailing al the night, making his mone;
And if he herde song or instrument,
Thanne wolde he weepe, he mighte nat be stent;
So fieble eek were his spirits and so lowe,
And chaunged so that no man coude knowe
His speeche nor his vois, though men it herde;
And in his gere for al the world he ferde
Nat only lik the loveres maladye
Of hereos, but rather lik manie,
Engendred of humour malencolik,
Bifore in his celle fantastik;

489. **axe,** ask. 495. **deemeth,** judge. 498. **swelte,** swooned. 502. **shal,** i.e., shall be; **dure,** last. 503. **biraft,** i.e., lost to. 504. **weex,** grew; **shaft,** spear-handle. 506. **falow,** yellowish. 510. **stent,** stopped. 514. **gere,** wild mood; **ferde,** behaved. 516. **hereos,** a disease caused by love, Eros; **manie,** mania. 517–18. Caused by the humor of melancholy (black bile), and taking effect in the forward cell of his brain, where the imagination operates.

And shortly, turned was al up-so-down°
Bothe habit° and eek disposicioun
Of him, this woful lovere daun° Arcite.
What° sholde I al day of his wo endite?
Whan he endured hadde a yeer or two
This cruel torment and this paine and wo
At Thebes in his contree, as I saide,
Upon a night in sleep as he him laide
Him thoughte how that the winged god Mercurye
Biforn him stood, and bad him to be murye:
His sleepy yerde° in hande he bar uprighte;
An hat he wered° upon his heres brighte;
Arrayed was this god, as he took keep,°
As he was whan that Argus took his sleep;°
And saide him thus, "To Atthenes shaltou wende:
Ther is thee shapen° of thy wo an ende."
And with that word Arcite wook and sterte;°
"Now trewely, how sore that me smerte,"°
Quod he, "to Atthenes right now wol I fare.
Ne for the drede of deeth shal I nat spare°
To see my lady that I love and serve:
In hir presence I recche nat to sterve."°
And with that word he caughte a greet mirour,
And sawgh that chaunged was al his colour,
And saw his visage in another kinde,
And right anoon it ran him in his minde
That sith his face was so disfigured
Of maladye the which he hadde endured,
He mighte wel, if that he bar him lowe,°
Live in Atthenes everemore unknowe,
And seen his lady wel neigh day by day.
And right anoon he chaunged his array,

519. **up-so-down,** upside down. 520. **habit,** behavior. 521. **daun,** lord. 522. **What,** why. 529. **sleepy yerde,** sleep-inducing rod. 530. **wered,** wore. 531. **he,** i.e., Arcite; **keep,** heed. 532. Even many-eyed Argus had been put to sleep by Mercury. 534. **shapen,** destined. 535. **wook,** woke; **sterte,** leapt up. 536. **how . . . smerte,** no matter how much it hurts me. 538. **spare,** hesitate. 540. **recche . . . sterve,** care not if I die. 547. **bar . . . lowe,** behaved humbly.

And cladde him as a poore laborer,
And al allone, save only a squier
That knew his privetee and al his cas,°
Which was disgised poorely as he was,
To Atthenes is he goon the nexte° way.
And to the court he wente upon a day,
And at the gate he profreth his servise,
To drugge and drawe what so men wol devise.
  And shortly of this matere for to sayn,
He fil in office° with a chamberlain,
The which that dwelling was with Emelye—
For he was wis, and coude soone espye
Of every servant which that serveth here.°
Wel coude he hewen wode and water bere,
For he was yong and mighty for the nones,°
And therto he was strong and big of bones,
To doon what any wight can him devise.
A yeer or two he was in this servise,
Page of the chambre of Emelye the brighte,
And Philostrate° he saide that he highte.
  But half so wel-biloved a man as he
Ne was ther nevere in court of his degree:
He was so gentil of condicioun
That thurghout al the court was his renown;
They saiden that it were a charitee
That Theseus wolde enhauncen his degree,°
And putten him in worshipful servise,
Ther as he mighte his vertu exercise.
And thus withinne a while his name is spronge°—
Bothe of his deedes and his goode tonge—
That Theseus hath taken him so neer,
That of his chambre he made him a squier,
And yaf him gold to maintene his degree;
And eek men broughte him out of his contree,

553. **privetee,** private affairs; **cas,** fortune. 555. **nexte,** i.e., by the nearest. 558. **drugge . . . drawe,** fetch and carry. 560. **fil in office,** entered employment. 563. **here,** her. 565. **the nones,** i.e., any purpose. 570. **Philostrate,** i.e., "prostrated by love." 576. **enhauncen,** improve; **degree,** station. 579. **is spronge,** has become known.

Fro yeer to yeer, ful prively his rente°–
But honestly and slyly° he it spente
That no man wondred how that he it hadde.
And three yeer in this wise his lif he ladde,°
And bar him° so in pees and eek in werre,
Ther was no man that Theseus hath derre.°
And in this blisse lete° I now Arcite,
And speke I wol of Palamon a lite.°
  In derknesse and horrible and strong prisoun
This seven yeer hath seten° Palamoun,
Forpined,° what for wo and for distresse;
Who feeleth double soor° and hevinesse
But Palamon, that love distraineth° so
That wood° out of his wit he gooth for wo?
And eek therto he is a prisoner,
Perpetuelly, nat only for a yeer.
Who coude ryme in Englissh proprely
His martyrdom? Forsoothe, it am nought I.
Therfore I passe as lightly° as I may.
  It fil° that in the seventhe yeer, of May
The thridde night, as olde bookes sayn,
That al this storye tellen more plein,°
Were it by aventure or destinee–
As whan a thing is shapen° it shal be–
That soone after the midnight, Palamoun,
By helping of a freend, brak° his prisoun,
And fleeth the citee, faste as he may go,
For he hadde yive his gailer drinke so,
Of a clarree° maad of a certain win
With nercotikes and opie of Thebes fin,°
That al that night, though that men wolde him shake,
The gailer sleep,° he mighte nought awake.

585. **rente,** income. 586. **honestly,** honorably; **slyly,** wisely. 588. **ladde,** led. 589. **bar him,** bore himself. 590. **hath derre,** holds dearer. 591. **lete,** leave. 592. **lite,** little. 594. **seten,** sat. 595. **Forpined,** wasted away. 596. **soor,** sore. 597. **distraineth,** afflicts. 598. **wood,** mad. 603. **lightly,** quickly. 604. **fil,** befell. 606. **plein,** full. 608. **shapen,** destined. 610. **brak,** broke. 613. **clarree,** wine punch. 614. **opie . . . fin,** pure Theban opium. 616. **sleep,** slept.

And thus he fleeth as faste as evere he may:
The night was short and faste by° the day,
That needes cost° he moste himselven hide;
And til a grove faste ther biside
With dredful° foot thanne stalketh Palamoun,
For shortly, this was his opinioun:
That in that grove he wolde him hide al day,
And in the night thanne wolde he take his way
To Thebesward,° his freendes for to praye
On Theseus to helpe him to werreye;°
And shortly, outher he wolde lese° his lif,
Or winnen Emelye unto his wif:
This is th'effect and his entente plain.
Now wol I turne to Arcite again,
That litel wiste° how neigh that was his care,
Til that Fortune hadde brought him in the snare.
The bisy larke, messager of day,
Salueth° in hir song the morwe grey,
And firy Phebus riseth up so bright
That al the orient laugheth of the light,
And with his stremes dryeth in the greves°
The silver dropes hanging on the leves;
And Arcita, that in the court royal
With Theseus is squier principal,
Is risen and looketh on the merye day,
And for to doon his observance to May—
Remembring on the point of his desir—
He on a courser startling° as the fir
Is riden into the feeldes him to playe,
Out of the court were it a mile or twaye;
And to the grove of which that I you tolde
By aventure his way he gan to holde,
To maken him a gerland of the greves,
Were it of wodebinde or hawethorn leves.

618. **faste by,** close to. 619. **needes cost,** at any cost. 621. **dredful,** fearful. 625. **To Thebesward,** toward Thebes. 626. **werreye,** make war. 627. **outher,** either; **lese,** lose. 631. **wiste,** knew. 634. **Salueth,** salutes. 637. **stremes,** beams; **greves,** foliage. 644. **startling,** prancing.

And loude he soong ayain the sonne sheene,
"May, with alle thy flowres and thy greene,
Welcome be thou, faire fresshe May,
In hope that I som greene gete may."
And from his courser with a lusty herte
Into the grove ful hastily he sterte,
And in a path he rometh up and down,
Ther as by aventure this Palamoun
Was in a bussh, that no man mighte him see,
For sore afered of his deeth was he.
No thing ne knew he that it was Arcite—
God woot he wolde have trowed it ful lite:
But sooth is said, go sithen many yeres,
That feeld hath yën and the wode hath eres;
It is ful fair a man to bere him evene,
For alday meeteth men at unset stevene.
Ful litel woot Arcite of his felawe
That was so neigh to herknen al his sawe,
For in the bussh he sitteth now ful stille.
 Whan that Arcite hadde romed al his fille,
And songen al the roundel lustily,
Into a studye he fil sodeinly,
As doon thise loveres in hir quainte geres—
Now in the crop, now down in the breres;
Now up, now down, as boket in a welle;
Right as the Friday, soothly for to telle,
Now it shineth, now it raineth faste,
Right so can gery Venus overcaste
The hertes of hir folk; right as hir day
Is gereful, right so chaungeth she array:
Selde is the Friday al the wike ylike.
 Whan that Arcite hadde songe he gan to sike,

651. **ayain,** i.e., to greet; **sheene,** bright. 662. **trowed,** believed; **lite,** little. 663. **go . . . yeres,** many years ago. 665–66. It is a good thing for a man to behave coolly, For one constantly keeps appointments one has not made. 668. **sawe,** speech. 673. **geres,** moods. 674. **crop,** treetop; **breres,** briars, underbrush. 675. **boket,** bucket. 676. **Right,** just. 678. **gery,** moody. 680. **gereful,** changeful. 681. **Selde,** seldom; **al . . . ylike,** like the rest of the week. 682. **songe,** sung; **sike,** sigh.

And sette him down withouten any more.
"Allas," quod he, "that day that I was bore!°
How longe, Juno, thurgh thy crueltee
Woltou werreyen° Thebes the citee?
Allas, ybrought is to confusioun
The blood royal of Cadme and Amphioun°—
Of Cadmus, which that was the firste man
That Thebes builte or first the town bigan,
And of the citee first was crowned king.
Of his linage am I and his ofspring,
By verray° line, as of the stock royal.
And now I am so caitif and so thral,°
That he that is my mortal enemy,
I serve him as his squier poorely;
And yet dooth Juno me wel more shame,
For I dar nought biknowe° myn owene name,
But ther as I was wont to highte Arcite,
Now highte I Philostrate, nought worth a mite.
  Allas, thou felle Mars! Allas, Juno!
Thus hath youre ire oure linage al fordo,°
Save only me and wrecched Palamoun,
That Theseus martyreth in prisoun.
And over al this, to sleen me outrely,°
Love hath his firy dart so brenningly°
Ystiked thurgh my trewe careful herte,
That shapen was my deeth erst than my sherte.°
Ye sleen me with youre yën, Emelye!
Ye been the cause wherfore that I die!
Of al the remenant of myn other care
Ne sette I nought the mountance of a tare,°
So that I coude doon ought to youre pleasaunce."
And with that word he fil down in a traunce,
A longe time, and afterward up sterte.

684. bore, born. **686. werreyen,** make war on. **688.** Cadmus and Amphion were founders of Thebes. **693. verray,** true. **694. caitif,** wretched; **thral,** servile. **698. biknowe,** acknowledge. **702. fordo,** ruined. **705. sleen,** slay; **outrely,** entirely. **706. brenningly,** burningly. **708. shapen,** destined; **erst . . . sherte,** i.e., before my shirt was cut out. **712.** I don't hold at as much value as a weed.

This Palamon, that thoughte that thurgh his herte
He felte a cold swerd sodeinliche glide,
For ire he quook,° no lenger wolde he bide;
And whan that he hadde herd Arcites tale,
As he were wood, with face deed° and pale,
He sterte him up out of the busshes thikke,
And saide, "Arcite, false traitour wikke,°
Now artou hent,° that lovest my lady so,
For whom that I have al this paine and wo—
And art my blood and to my conseil° sworn,
As I ful ofte have told thee herbiforn—
And hast bijaped° here Duc Theseus,
And falsly chaunged hast thy name thus.
I wol be deed or elles thou shalt die:
Thou shalt nought love my lady Emelye,
But I wol love hire only and namo,°
For I am Palamon thy mortal fo,
And though that I no wepne° have in this place,
But out of prison am astert° by grace,
I drede nought that outher° thou shalt die,
Or thou ne shalt nat loven Emelye:
Chees° which thou wolt, or thou shalt nought asterte."
This Arcite with ful despitous° herte,
Whan he him knew and hadde his tale herd,
As fiers as leon pulled out his swerd,
And saide thus, "By God that sitteth above,
Nere it° that thou art sik and wood for love,
And eek that thou no wepne hast in this place,
Thou sholdest nevere out of this grove pace°
That thou ne sholdest dien of myn hond;
For I defye the suretee° and the bond
Which that thou saist that I have maad to thee.
What, verray fool, think wel that love is free,

718. quook, quaked. **720. wood,** mad; **deed,** dead. **722. wikke,** wicked. **723. hent,** caught. **725. conseil,** secrets. **727. bijaped,** tricked. **731. namo,** i.e., no one else shall love her. **733. wepne,** weapon. **734. astert,** escaped. **735. drede,** doubt; **outher,** either. **737. Chees,** choose. **738. despitous,** cruel. **742. Nere it,** were it not. **744. pace,** pass. **746. suretee,** contract.

And I wol love hire, maugree° al thy might.
But for as muche as thou art a worthy knight,
And wilnest to darreine° hire by bataile,
Have here my trouthe, tomorwe I nil nat faile,
Withouten witing° of any other wight,
That here I wol be founden as a knight,
And bringen harneis° right ynough for thee—
And chees the beste, and leef° the worste for me!
And mete and drinke this night wol I bringe
Ynough for thee, and clothes for thy beddinge.
And if so be that thou my lady winne
And slee° me in this wode ther I am inne,
Thou maist wel have thy lady as for me."
This Palamon answerde, "I graunte it thee."
And thus they been departed til amorwe,°
Whan eech of hem hadde laid his faith to borwe.°
O Cupide, out of alle charitee!
O regne, that wolde no felawe have to thee!
Ful sooth is said that love ne lordshipe
Wol nought, his thankes,° have no felaweshipe:
Wel finden that Arcite and Palamoun.
Arcite is riden anoon unto the town,
And on the morwe er it were dayes light,
Ful prively two harneis hath he dight,°
Bothe suffisant and meete to darreine°
The bataile in the feeld bitwixe hem twaine;
And on his hors, allone as he was born,
He carieth al this harneis him biforn;
And in the grove at time and place yset
This Arcite and this Palamon been met.
To chaungen gan the colour in hir face,
Right as the hunteres in the regne of Trace,°
That stondeth at the gappe° with a spere,

749. maugree, despite. **751. wilnest,** desire; **darreine,** settle claim to. **753. witing,** knowledge. **755. harneis,** armor. **756. leef,** leave. **760. slee,** slay. **763. departed,** separated; **amorwe,** morning. **764. to borwe,** in pledge. **768. his thankes,** willingly. **772. dight,** prepared. **773. suffisant . . . meete,** adequate and proper; **darreine,** settle. **780. regne,** realm; **Trace,** Thrace. **781. gappe,** i.e., in a hedge.

Whan hunted is the leon or the bere,°
And hereth him come russhing in the greves,°
And breketh bothe boughes and the leves,
And thinketh, "Here cometh my mortal enemy!
Withoute faile he moot° be deed or I,
For outher° I moot sleen him at the gappe,
Or he moot slee me if that me mishappe."
So ferden° they in chaunging of hir hewe.
  As fer as everich of hem other knewe,°
Ther nas no "good day" ne no saluinge,
But straight, withouten word or rehercinge,°
Everich of hem heelp° for to armen other,
As freendly as he were his owene brother;
And after that with sharpe speres stronge
They foinen° eech at other wonder longe:
Thou mightest weene° that this Palamoun
In his fighting were a wood leoun,
And as a cruel tigre was Arcite;
As wilde bores gonnen they to smite,
That frothen whit as foom, for ire wood;°
Up to the ancle foughte they in hir blood.
And in this wise I lete° hem fighting dwelle,
And forth I wol of Theseus you telle.
  The destinee, ministre° general,
That executeth in the world overal
The purveyance° that God hath seen biforn,
So strong it is that, though the world hadde sworn
The contrarye of a thing by ye or nay,°
Yet som time it shal fallen° on a day,
That falleth nat eft° withinne a thousand yeer:
For certainly, oure appetites° heer,
Be it of werre, or pees, or hate, or love,

782. **bere,** bear. 783. **greves,** thickets. 786. **moot,** must. 787. **outher,** either. 789. **ferden,** acted. 790. i.e., despite their close acquaintance. 792. **rehercinge,** i.e., repetition of the agreement. 793. **heelp,** helped. 796. **foinen,** thrust. 797. **weene,** suppose. 801. **wood,** mad. 803. **lete,** leave. 805. **ministre,** agent. 807. **purveyance,** providence. 809. **by . . . nay,** by yes or no, i.e., categorically. 810. **fallen,** happen. 811. **eft,** again. 812. **appetites,** desires.

Al is this ruled by the sighte above.
This mene I now by mighty Theseus,
That for to hunten is so desirous,
And namely at the grete hert in May,
That in his bed ther daweth him no day
That he nis clad and redy for to ride,
With hunte and horn and houndes him biside;
For in his hunting hath he swich delit
That it is al his joye and appetit
To been himself the grete hertes bane,
For after Mars he serveth now Diane.
Cleer was the day, as I have told er this,
And Theseus, with alle joye and blis,
With his Ipolyta the faire queene,
And Emelye clothed al in greene,
On hunting be they riden royally.
And to the grove that stood ful faste by,
In which ther was an hert, as men him tolde,
Duc Theseus the straighte way hath holde;
And to the launde he rideth him ful right,
For thider was the hert wont have his flight,
And over a brook, and so forth on his waye:
This Duc wol han a cours at him or twaye,
With houndes swiche as that him list comaunde.
And whan this Duc was come unto the launde,
Under the sonne he looketh, and anoon
He was war of Arcite and Palamon,
That foughten breme as it were boles two.
The brighte swerdes wente to and fro
So hidously, that with the leeste strook
It seemed as it wolde felle an ook,
But what they were no thing he ne woot.
This Duc his courser with the spores smoot,
And at a stert he was bitwixe hem two,

817. **namely,** especially; **hert,** hart. 818. **daweth him,** dawns on him. 820. **hunte,** huntsman. 823. **bane,** destroyer. 833. **launde,** glade. 836. **cours,** chase with hounds. 839. **Under . . . sonne,** i.e., between the sun and the horizon. 841. **breme,** fierce; **boles,** bulls. 846. **spores,** spurs. 847. **at a stert,** with a lunge.

And pulled out a swerd, and cried, "Ho!
Namore, up paine of lesing of youre heed!
By mighty Mars, he shal anoon be deed
That smiteth any strook that I may seen!
But telleth me what mister men ye been,
That been so hardy for to fighten heer,
Withouten juge or other officer,
As it were in a listes royally?"
  This Palamon answerde hastily,
And saide, "Sire, what needeth wordes mo?
We have the deeth deserved bothe two:
Two woful wrecches been we, two caitives,
That been encombred of oure owene lives;
And as thou art a rightful lord and juge,
Ne yif us neither mercy ne refuge.
But slee me first, for sainte charitee,
But slee my felawe eek as wel as me.
Or slee him first, for though thou knowest it lite,
This is thy mortal fo, this is Arcite,
That fro thy land is banisshed on his heed,
For which he hath deserved to be deed;
For this is he that cam unto thy gate,
And saide that he highte Philostrate—
Thus hath he japed thee ful many a yeer,
And thou hast maked him thy chief squier;
And this is he that loveth Emelye:
For sith the day is come that I shal die,
I make pleinly my confessioun
That I am thilke woful Palamoun,
That hath thy prison broken wikkedly.
I am thy mortal fo, and it am I
That loveth so hote Emelye the brighte,
That I wol dien present in hir sighte:
Wherfore I axe deeth and my juwise—

849. **up,** upon; **lesing,** losing. 852. **mister,** kind of. 860. **encombred of,** burdened by. 862. **yif,** give; **refuge,** safety. 863. **slee,** slay. 865. **lite,** little. 867. **on . . . heed,** i.e., on pain of death. 871. **japed,** tricked. 876. **thilke,** that same. 881. **axe,** ask; **juwise,** punishment.

But slee my felawe in the same wise,
For bothe have we deserved to be slain."
  This worthy Duc answerde anoon again,
And saide, "This is a short conclusioun.°
Youre owene mouth by youre confessioun
Hath dampned you, and I wol it recorde:°
It needeth nought to pine you with the corde;°
Ye shul be deed, by mighty Mars the rede!"
  The queene anoon for verray wommanhede
Gan for to weepe, and so dide Emelye,
And alle the ladies in the compaignye;
Greet pitee was it, as it thoughte hem alle,
That evere swich a chaunce sholde falle,
For gentil men they were of greet estat,
And no thing but for love was this debat;
And sawe hir bloody woundes wide and sore,
And alle criden, bothe lasse and more,°
"Have mercy, lord, upon us wommen alle."
And on hir bare knees adown they falle,
And wolde have kist his feet ther as he stood,
Til at the laste aslaked was his mood°—
For pitee renneth° soone in gentil herte—
And though he first for ire quook and sterte,°
He hath considered shortly, in a clause,°
The trespas° of hem bothe, and eek the cause,
And although that his ire hir gilt accused,°
Yet in his reson he hem bothe excused.
As thus: he thoughte wel that every man
Wol helpe himself in love if that he can,
And eek delivere himself out of prisoun;
And eek his herte hadde compassioun
On wommen, for they weepen evere in oon.°
And in his gentil herte he thoughte anoon,
And softe unto himself he saide, "Fy

885. **conclusioun,** demonstration. 887. **dampned,** damned; **recorde,** remember. 888. **pine,** torture; **corde,** rope. 898. **lasse and more,** small and great. 902. **aslaked,** softened; **mood,** anger. 903. **renneth,** runs, surges. 904. **quook . . . sterte,** quaked and trembled. 905. **clause,** i.e., brief consideration. 906. **trespas,** wrong doing. 907. **accused,** blamed. 913. **in oon,** continuously.

Upon a lord that wol have no mercy,
But be a leon bothe in word and deede
To hem that been in repentance and drede,
As wel as to a proud despitous° man
That wol maintene that° he first bigan.
That lord hath litel of discrecioun°
That in swich caas can no divisioun,°
But weyeth pride and humblesse after oon." °
And shortly, whan his ire is thus agoon,°
He gan to looken up with yën lighte,
And spak thise same wordes al on highte:°
"The God of Love, a, benedicite,°
How mighty and how greet a lord is he!
Agains his might ther gaineth° none obstacles:
He may be cleped° a god for his miracles,
For he can maken at his owene gise°
Of everich herte as that him list° devise.
Lo, here this Arcite and this Palamoun,
That quitly° were out of my prisoun,
And mighte have lived in Thebes royally,
And witen° I am hir mortal enemy,
And that hir deeth lith° in my might also—
And yet hath love, maugree° hir yën two,
Brought hem hider bothe for to die.
Now looketh, is nat that an heigh folye?
Who may been a fool, but if° he love?
Bihold, for Goddes sake that sit° above,
See how they bleede. Be they nought wel arrayed?
Thus hath hir lord the God of Love ypayed
Hir wages and hir fees for hir servise!
And yet they weenen° for to be ful wise,
That serven love, for ought that may bifalle.

919. despitous, malicious. **920. that,** what. **921. discrecioun,** power to make distinctions. **922. can . . . divisioun,** recognizes no distinction. **923. weyeth,** weighs; **after oon,** in the same way. **924. agoon,** passed away. **926. on highte,** aloud. **927. benedicite,** bless us. **929. gaineth,** avail. **930. cleped,** called. **931. gise,** desire. **932. as . . . list,** whatever he pleases to. **934. quitly,** freely. **936. witen,** know. **937. lith,** lies. **938. maugree,** despite. **941. but if,** unless. **942. sit,** sits. **946. weenen,** suppose themselves.

But this is yet the beste game of alle,
That she for whom they have this jolitee
Can hem therfore as muche thank° as me:
She woot namore of al this hote fare,°
By God, than woot a cokkou of an hare.
But al moot been assayed, hoot° and cold;
A man moot been a fool, or yong or old;
I woot it by myself ful yore agoon,
For in my time a servant° was I oon;
And therfore, sin I knowe of Loves paine,
And woot how sore it can a man distraine,°
As he that hath been caught ofte in his las,°
I you foryive al hoolly° this trespas,
At requeste of the queene that kneeleth here,
And eek of Emelye my suster dere;
And ye shal bothe anoon unto me swere
That neveremo ye shal my contree dere,°
Ne make werre upon me, night nor day,
But been my freendes in al that ye may.
I you foryive this trespas everydeel."
And they him sworen his axing° faire and weel,
And him of lordshipe and of mercy prayde;
And he hem graunteth grace, and thanne he saide:
"To speke of royal linage and richesse,
Though that she were a queene or a princesse,
Eech of you bothe is worthy, doutelees,
To wedden whan time is, but, nathelees–
I speke as for my suster Emelye
For whom ye have this strif and jalousye–
Ye woot yourself she may nat wedden two
Atones, though ye fighten everemo:
That oon of you, al be him loth or lief,°
He moot go pipen in an ivy leef.°
This is to sayn, she may nat now have bothe,

950. Can, shows; **thank,** gratitude. **951. fare,** behavior. **953. hoot,** hot. **956. servant,** i.e., lover. **958. distraine,** afflict. **959. las,** snare. **960. hoolly,** wholly. **964. dere,** harm. **968. axing,** request. **979. al . . . lief,** whether he like it or not. **980.** i.e., he must get along without her.

Al be ye nevere so jalous ne so wrothe.
And forthy I you putte in this degree,
That eech of you shal have his destinee
As him is shape; and herkneth in what wise;
Lo, heere youre ende of that I shal devise:
  My wil is this, for plat conclusioun,
Withouten any replicacioun—
If that you liketh, take it for the beste:
That everich of you shal goon where him leste,
Freely, withouten raunson or daunger,
And this day fifty wikes, fer ne neer,
Everich of you shal bringe an hundred knightes,
Armed for listes up at alle rightes,
Al redy to darreine hire by bataile;
And this bihote I you withouten faile,
Upon my trouthe and as I am a knight,
That wheither of you bothe that hath might—
This is to sayn, that wheither he or thou
May with his hundred as I spak of now
Sleen his contrarye, or out of listes drive—
Thanne shal I yive Emelye to wive
To whom that Fortune yiveth so fair a grace.
The listes shal I maken in this place,
And God so wisly on my soule rewe,
As I shal evene juge been and trewe.
Ye shal noon other ende with me maken,
That oon of you ne shal be deed or taken.
And if you thinketh this is wel ysaid,
Saye youre avis, and holdeth you apaid.
This is youre ende and youre conclusioun."
  Who looketh lightly now but Palamoun?

982. **Al,** although. 983. **forthy,** therefore; **degree,** condition. 985. **As . . . shape,** as it is fated for him. 987. **plat,** flat. 988. **replicacioun,** answering back. 990. **him leste,** he may desire. 991. **raunson,** ransom. 992. **fer . . . neer,** neither a longer nor a shorter time. 995. **darreine hire,** settle claim to her. 996. **bihote,** promise. 998. **wheither,** whichever. 1001. **Sleen,** slay; **contrarye,** opponent. 1005. **wisly,** surely; **rewe,** have mercy. 1006. **evene,** impartial. 1007. **ende,** agreement. 1008. **deed,** dead. 1010. **avis,** opinion; **apaid,** content.

Who springeth up for joye but Arcite?
Who coude telle, or who coude it endite,
The joye that is maked in the place,
Whan Thesus hath doon so fair a grace?
But down on knees wente every manere wight,
And thanken him with al hir herte and might,
And namely the Thebans ofte sithe.°
And thus with good hope and with herte blithe
They take hir leve, and hoomward gonne they ride
To Thebes with his olde walles wide.

PART THREE

I trowe° men wolde deeme it necligence
If I foryete to tellen the dispence°
Of Theseus, that gooth so bisily
To maken up the listes royally,
That swich a noble theatre as it was
I dar wel sayen in this world ther nas.
The circuit a mile was aboute,
Walled of stoon and diched al withoute;
Round was the shap in manere of compas,
Ful of degrees, the heighte of sixty pas,°
That whan a man was set on oo degree
He letted° nought his felawe for to see.
  Eestward ther stood a gate of marbel whit;
Westward right swich another in the opposit;
And shortly to concluden, swich a place
Was noon in erthe as in so litel a space;°
For in the land ther was no crafty° man
That geometrye or ars-metrike can,°
Ne portrayour, ne kervere° of images,
That Theseus ne yaf him mete and wages,
The theatre for to maken and devise.

1019. **namely,** especially; **sithe,** times. 1023. **trowe,** believe. 1024. **dispence,** expenditure. 1032. **degrees,** steps; **pas,** yards. 1034. **letted,** prevented. 1038. **space,** time. 1039. **crafty,** skilled. 1040. **ars-metrike,** arithmetic; **can,** knows. 1041. **portrayour,** artist; **kervere,** carver.

And for to doon his rite and sacrifise,
He eestward hath upon the gate above,
In worshipe of Venus, goddesse of love,
Doon maad an auter° and an oratorye;
And on the westward gate in memorye
Of Mars, he maked hath right swich another,
That coste largely of gold a fother;°
And northward in a touret° on the wal,
Of alabastre whit and reed° coral,
An oratorye riche for to see,
In worshipe of Diane of chastitee,
Hath Theseus doon wrought° in noble wise.
  But yet hadde I forgeten to devise
The noble kerving° and the portraitures,
The shap, the countenance,° and the figures,
That weren in thise oratories three.
  First, in the temple of Venus maistou see,
Wrought on the wal, ful pitous to biholde,
The broken sleepes and the sikes° colde,
The sacred teres and the waymentinge,°
The firy strokes of the desiringe
That Loves servants in this lif enduren;
The othes that hir covenants assuren;°
Plesance and Hope, Desir, Foolhardinesse,
Beautee and Youthe, Bawderye,° Richesse,
Charmes and Force, Lesinges,° Flaterye,
Dispence, Bisinesse,° and Jalousye,
That wered° of yelowe goldes a gerland,
And a cokkou° sitting on hir hand;
Feestes, instruments, caroles,° daunces,
Lust and array, and alle the circumstaunces
Of love, which that I rekened and rekene shal,

1047. **Doon maad,** had made; **auter,** altar. 1050. **fother,** load. 1051. **touret,** turret. 1052. **reed,** red. 1055. **doon wrought,** had built. 1057. **kerving,** sculpture. 1058. **countenance,** appearance. 1062. **sikes,** sighs. 1063. **waymentinge,** lamenting. 1066. **assuren,** bind. 1068. **Bawderye,** pimping. 1069. **Lesinges,** lies. 1070. **Dispence,** expenditure; **Bisinesse,** assiduousness. 1071. **wered,** wore. 1072. **cokkou,** cuckoo. 1073. **caroles,** dances with song.

By ordre weren painted on the wal,
And mo than I can make of mencioun.
For soothly al the Mount of Citheroun,°
Ther Venus hath hir principal dwellinge,
Was shewed on the wal in portrayinge,
With al the gardin and the lustinesse—
Nat was foryeten the porter Idelnesse,°
Ne Narcisus the faire of yore agoon,
Ne yet the folye of king Salomon,°
Ne yet the grete strengthe of Ercules,
Th'enchantements of Medea and Circes,
Ne of Turnus with the hardy fiers corage,°
The riche Cresus, caitif in servage.°
  Thus may ye seen that wisdom ne richesse,
Beautee ne sleighte,° strengthe, hardinesse,
Ne may with Venus maken champartye,°
For as hire list, the world thanne may she gie.°
Lo, alle thise folk so caught were in hir las°
Til they for wo ful ofte saide allas.
Suffiseth here ensamples oon or two,
And though I coude rekene a thousand mo.
  The statue of Venus, glorious for to see,
Was naked, fleting° in the large see,
And fro the navele down al covered was
With wawes° greene and brighte as any glas;
A citole° in hir right hand hadde she,
And on hir heed, ful semely for to see,
A rose gerland fressh and wel smellinge;
Above hir heed hir douves flikeringe.
Biforn hire stood hir sone Cupido;

1078. Citheroun, Cithaeron, erroneously supposed to be sacred to Venus, Cytherea. **1082 f.** Idleness is gatekeeper of the garden of Love in the *Romance of the Rose*; the pool in which Narcissus saw and loved his own image is in the same garden. **1084 ff.** Solomon, Hercules, Croesus, and Aeneas' opponent Turnus are all types of the man fooled by Love; Medea and Circe were typical enchantresses. **1087. corage,** heart. **1088. caitif,** prisoner; **servage,** slavery. **1090. sleighte,** cleverness. **1091. champartye,** division of power. **1092. gie,** guide. **1093. las,** net. **1098. fleting,** floating. **1100. wawes,** waves. **1101. citole,** cithara.

Upon his shuldres winges hadde he two,
And blind he was, as it is ofte seene;
A bowe he bar, and arwes brighte and keene.
  Why sholde I nat as wel eek telle you al
The portraiture that was upon the wal
Withinne the temple of mighty Mars the rede?
Al painted was the wal in lengthe and brede
Lik to the eestres of the grisly place
That highte the grete temple of Mars in Trace,
In thilke colde frosty regioun
Ther as Mars hath his soverein mansioun.
  First on the wal was painted a forest,
In which ther dwelleth neither man ne beest,
With knotty knarry bareine trees olde
Of stubbes sharpe and hidouse to biholde,
In which ther ran a rumbel in a swough,
As though a storm sholde bresten every bough;
And downward on an hil under a bente
Ther stood the temple of Mars armipotente,
Wrought al of burned steel, of which the entree
Was long and strait and gastly for to see,
And therout cam a rage and swich a veze
That it made al the gate for to reze.
The northren light in at the dores shoon,
For window on the wal ne was ther noon
Thurgh which men mighten any light discerne;
The dore was al of adamant eterne,
Yclenched overthwart and endelong
With iren tough; and for to make it strong
Every piler the temple to sustene
Was tonne-greet, of iren bright and sheene.
  Ther sawgh I first the derke imagininge

1111. rede, red. **1112. brede,** breadth. **1113. eestres,** interior parts. **1114. Trace,** Thrace. **1119. knarry,** gnarled; **bareine,** barren. **1120. stubbes,** stumps. **1121. rumbel . . . swough,** i.e., a murmuring, sighing sound. **1122. bresten,** break. **1123. bente,** cliff. **1124. armipotente,** powerful in arms. **1125. burned,** burnished. **1126. strait,** narrow. **1127. rage,** roar; **veze,** blast. **1128. reze,** shake. **1129. shoon,** shone. **1133.** Braced crosswise and lengthwise. **1136. tonne-greet,** as big as a cask; **sheene,** shiny.

Of Felonye, and al the compassinge,°
The cruel Ire, reed as any gleede,°
The pike-purs,° and eek the pale Drede,
The smilere with the knif under the cloke,
The shipne brenning° with the blake smoke,
The treson of the mordring° in the bed,
The open Werre, with woundes al bibled,°
Contek with bloody knif and sharp manace°—
Al ful of chirking° was that sory place.
  The sleere° of himself yet sawgh I ther:
His herte blood hath bathed al his heer;
The nail ydriven in the shode° anight;
The colde Deeth, with mouth gaping upright.
Amiddes of the temple sat Meschaunce,
With disconfort° and sory countenaunce.
  Yet sawgh I Woodnesse,° laughing in his rage;
Armed Complainte, Outhees,° and fiers Outrage;
The caroine in the bussh with throte ycorve;°
A thousand slain and nought of qualm ystorve;°
The tyrant with the preye by force yraft;°
The town destroyed, ther was no thing laft.
  Yet sawgh I brent the shippes hoppesteres;°
The hunte strangled with° the wilde beres;
The sowe freten° the child right in the cradel;
The cook yscald for al his longe ladel.
  Nought was forgeten by the infortune of Marte°
The cartere overriden with his carte—
Under the wheel ful lowe he lay adown;
Ther were also of Martes divisioun°

1138. **compassinge,** plotting. 1139. **reed,** red; **gleede,** live coal. 1140. **pike-purs,** cutpurse. 1142. **shipne,** dairy; **brenning,** burning. 1143. **mordring,** murdering. 1144. **bibled,** blood-smeared. 1145. **Contek,** strife; **manace,** threat. 1146. **chirking,** croaking. 1147. **sleere,** slayer. 1149. **shode,** crown of the head. 1152. **disconfort,** defeated. 1153. **Woodnesse,** madness. 1154. **Outhees,** outcry. 1155. **caroine,** dead body; **ycorve,** cut. 1156. **of . . . ystorve,** dead of pestilence. 1157. **yraft,** removed. 1159. **brent,** burnt; **hoppesteres,** tossing. 1160. **hunte,** huntsman; **with,** by. 1161. **freten,** eat. 1163. **infortune,** evil influence; **Marte,** Mars. 1166. All who worked with edged tools were of Mars's division, i.e., under his planet.

The barbour and the bocher° and the smith
That forgeth sharpes swerdes on his stith.°
  And al above depainted in a towr
Sawgh I Conquest, sitting in greet honour,
With the sharpe swerd over his heed
Hanging by a subtil twines threed.
  Depainted was the slaughtre of Julius,°
Of grete Nero, and of Antonius:°
Al be that thilke time they were unborn,
Yet was hir deeth depainted therbiforn,
By manacing of Mars, right by figure;°
So was it shewed in that portraiture,
As is depainted in the sterres° above
Who shal be slain, or elles deed for love.
Suffiseth oon ensample in stories olde:
I may nat rekene hem alle though I wolde.
  The statue of Mars upon a carte stood
Armed, and looked grim as he were wood;°
And over his heed ther shinen two figures
Of sterres, that been cleped° in scriptures
That oon Puella, that other Rubeus;°
This god of armes was arrayed thus:
A wolf ther stood bifore him at his feet,
With yën rede, and of a man he eet°—
With subtil pencel was depaint this storye
In redoubting° of Mars and of his glorye.
  Now to the temple of Diane the chaste
As shortly as I can I wol me haste,
To telle you al the descripsioun.
Depainted been the walles up and down
Of hunting and of shamefast chastitee.
Ther saw I how woful Calistopee,°

1167. bocher, butcher. **1168. stith,** forge. **1173. Julius,** i.e., Caesar. **1174. Antonius,** Mark Antony. **1177. manacing,** threat; **by figure,** in likeness. **1179. sterres,** stars. **1184. wood,** insane. **1186. cleped,** called. **1187.** Puella and Rubeus are not actually stars, but constellation-like patterns of dots belonging to the science of geomancy. **1190. eet,** ate. **1192. redouting,** awe. **1198. Calistopee,** Callisto, seduced by Jupiter, was changed by her angry mistress Diana into a bear, and subsequently by Jupiter into the constellation Ursa Major (not the North Star).

Whan that Diane agreved was with here,°
Was turned fro a womman til a bere,
And after was she maad the Lode-Sterre:°
Thus was it painted—I can saye you no ferre.°
Hir sone is eek a sterre, as men may see.
Ther saw I Dane° turned til a tree—
I mene nat the goddesse Diane,
But Penneus doughter, which that highte Dane.
  Ther saw I Attheon an hert° ymaked,
For vengeance that he saw Diane al naked;
I sawgh how that his houndes have him caught
And freten° him, for that they knewe him naught.
  Yet painted was a litel ferther moor°
How Atthalante° hunted the wilde boor,
And Meleagre, and many another mo,
For which Diane wroughte him care and wo.
Ther saw I many another wonder storye,
The whiche me list nat drawen to memorye.°
  This goddesse on an hert ful hye seet,°
With smale houndes al aboute hir feet;
And undernethe hir feet she hadde a moone:
Waxing it was, and sholde wanie soone;
In gaudee° greene hir statue clothed was,
With bowe in hande and arwes in a cas;°
Hir yën caste she ful lowe adown
Ther Pluto hath his derke regioun;°
A womman travailing° was hire biforn,
But for hir child so longe was unborn,
Ful pitously Lucina° gan she calle,
And saide, "Help, for thou maist best of alle."

1199. **agreved,** angry; **here,** her. 1201. **Lode-Sterre,** North Star. 1202. **ferre,** further. 1204. **Dane,** Daphne, daughter of Peneus, saved from Apollo's passion by being turned into a laurel tree. 1207. **Attheon,** Actaeon; **hert,** hart. 1210. **freten,** eaten. 1211. **moor,** i.e., on. 1212. **Atthalante,** Atalanta, the huntress to whom Meleager presented the head of the Calydonian boar. 1216. Which I don't wish to mention. 1217. **hert,** hart; **seet,** sat. 1221. **gaudee,** yellowish. 1222. **cas,** case. 1224. Pluto was god of the underworld, and his queen Proserpina was sometimes considered an aspect of Diana. 1225. **travailing,** in labor. 1227. **Lucina,** goddess of childbirth, one of the manifestations of Diana.

Wel coude he painte lifly° that it wroughte;
With many a florin he the hewes boughte.
  Now been thise listes maad, and Theseus,
That at his grete cost arrayed thus
The temples and the theatre everydeel,
Whan it was doon him liked° wonder weel.
But stinte° I wol of Theseus a lite,
And speke of Palamon and of Arcite.
  The day approcheth of hir returninge,
That everich sholde an hundred knightes bringe
The bataile to darreine,° as I you tolde.
And til Atthenes, hir covenant for to holde,
Hath everich of hem brought an hundred knightes,
Wel armed for the werre at alle rightes,
And sikerly ther trowed° many a man
That nevere sithen that the world bigan,
As for to speke of knighthood of hir hand,°
As fer as God hath maked see and land
Nas of so fewe so noble a compaignye;
For every wight that loved chivalrye,
And wolde, his thankes, han a passant° name,
Hath prayed that he mighte been of that game;
And wel was him that therto chosen was,
For if ther fille tomorwe swich a cas,°
Ye knowen wel that every lusty knight
That loveth paramours° and hath his might,
Were it in Engelond or elleswhere,
They wolde, hir thankes, wilnen° to be there.
To fighten for a lady, benedicite,°
It were a lusty sighte for to see.
  And right so ferden° they with Palamon:
With him ther wenten knightes many oon;
Som wol been armed in an haubergeoun,°

1229. lifly, i.e., realistically. **1234. him liked,** it pleased him. **1235. stinte,** cease. **1239. darreine,** settle. **1243. sikerly,** certainly; **trowed,** believed. **1245. of . . . hand,** with respect to their valor. **1249. his thankes,** willingly; **passant,** excellent. **1252. fille,** happened; **cas,** event. **1254. paramours,** i.e., women. **1256. wilnen,** desire. **1257. benedicite,** bless me. **1259. ferden,** behaved. **1261. Som,** one; **haubergeoun,** coat of mail.

And in a brestplate and in a light gipoun;°
And som wol have a paire° plates large;
And som wol have a Pruce sheeld or a targe;°
Som wol been armed on his legges weel,°
And have an ax, and som a mace of steel—
Ther nis no newe gise that it nas° old.
Armed were they as I have you told,
Everich after his opinioun.
  Ther maistou seen coming with Palamoun
Lygurge himself, the grete king of Trace:°
Blak was his beerd and manly was his face;
The cercles° of his yën in his heed,
They gloweden bitwixen yelow and reed;
And like a griffon looked he aboute,
With kempe heres on his browes stoute;°
His limes grete, his brawnes° harde and stronge,
His shuldres brode, his armes rounde and longe;
And as the gise was in his contree,
Ful hye upon a chaar° of gold stood he,
With foure white boles° in the trais;
In stede of cote-armure over his harneis,°
With nailes yelowe and brighte as any gold
He hadde a beres skin, col-blak for old;
His longe heer was kembd° behinde his bak:
As any ravenes fethere it shoon° for blak;
A wrethe of gold, arm-greet, of huge wighte,°
Upon his heed, and ful of stones brighte,
Of fine rubies and of diamaunts;
Aboute his chaar ther wente white alaunts,°
Twenty and mo, as grete as any steer,
To hunten at the leon and the deer,

1262. **gipoun,** tunic. 1263. **paire,** pair of. 1264. **Pruce,** Prussian; **targe,** light shield. 1265. **weel,** well. 1267. **gise,** fashion; **nas,** was not. 1271. **Trace,** Thrace. 1273. **cercles,** i.e., pupils. 1276. **kempe,** coarse; **stoute,** prominent. 1277. **limes,** limbs; **brawnes,** muscles. 1280. **chaar,** chariot. 1281. **boles,** bulls; **trais,** traces. 1282. **cote-armure,** coat of arms; **harneis,** battle dress. 1285. **kembd,** combed. 1286. **shoon,** shone. 1287. **arm-greet,** as thick as an arm; **wighte,** weight. 1290. **alaunts,** wolf-hounds.

And folwed him with mosel° faste ybounde,
Colered of gold and turrettes° filed rounde;
An hundred lordes hadde he in his route,°
Armed ful wel, with hertes sterne and stoute.
  With Arcita, in stories as men finde,
The grete Emetrius, the king of Inde,
Upon a steede-bay° trapped in steel,
Covered in cloth of gold, diapred° weel,
Cam riding lik the god of armes Mars;
His cote-armure was of cloth of Tars,°
Couched with perles° white and rounde and grete;
His sadel was of brend gold newe ybete;°
A mantelet upon his shulder hanginge,
Bretful° of rubies rede as fir sparklinge;
His crispe heer like ringes was yronne,°
And that was yelow and glitred as the sonne;
His nose was heigh, his yën bright citrin,°
His lippes rounde, his colour was sanguin;
A fewe fraknes in his face yspreind,°
Bitwixen yelow and somdeel blak ymeind;°
And as a leon he his looking caste;°
Of five and twenty yeer his age I caste;
His beerd was wel bigonne for to springe;
His vois was a trompe° thonderinge;
Upon his heed he wered of laurer° greene
A gerland fressh and lusty for to seene;
Upon his hand he bar for his deduit°
An egle tame, as any lilye whit;
An hundred lordes hadde he with him there,
Al armed, save hir hedes, in al hir gere,
Ful richely in alle manere thinges:

1293. mosel, muzzle. **1294. Colered,** collared; **turrettes,** leash-rings. **1295. route,** company. **1299. steede-bay,** brown warhorse. **1300. diapred,** patterned with crisscrosses. **1302. Tars,** Tarsus. **1303. Couched,** set; **perles,** pearls. **1304. brend,** burnished; **ybete,** hammered. **1306. Bretful,** crammed full. **1307. yronne,** i.e., curled. **1309. citrin,** citron. **1311. fraknes,** freckles; **yspreind,** sprinkled. **1312. ymeind,** mingled. **1314. caste,** estimate. **1316. trompe,** trumpet. **1317. wered,** wore; **laurer,** laurel. **1319. bar,** bore; **deduit,** delight.

For trusteth wel that dukes, erles, kinges,
Were gadred° in this noble compaignye,
For love and for encrees of chivalrye;
Aboute this king ther ran on every part
Ful many a tame leon and leopart.
  And in this wise thise lordes alle and some°
Been on the Sonday to the citee come
Aboute prime,° and in the town alight.
  This Theseus, this Duc, this worthy knight,
Whan he hadde brought hem into his citee,
And inned hem, everich at° his degree,
He feesteth hem and dooth so greet labour
To esen hem° and doon hem al honour,
That yet men weenen° that no mannes wit,
Of noon estaat, ne coude amenden° it.
  The minstralcye, the service at the feeste,
The grete yiftes to the meeste° and leeste,
The riche array of Theseus palais,
Ne who sat first or last upon the dais,
What ladies fairest been and most daunselinge,°
Or which of hem can daunce best and singe,
Ne who most feelingly speketh of love,
What hawkes sitten on the perche above,
What houndes liggen° on the floor adown—
Of al this make I now no mencioun,
But al th'effect: that thinketh me the beste.
Now comth the point, and herkneth if you leste.°
  The Sonday night, er day bigan to springe,
Whan Palamon the larke herde singe—
Although it nere nat day by houres two
Yet soong the larke, and Palamon right tho,°
With holy herte and with an heigh corage,°
He roos° to wenden on his pilgrimage,
Unto the blisful Cytherea benigne—

1325. **gadred,** gathered. 1329. **alle . . . some,** one and all. 1331. **prime,** 9 A.M. 1334. **inned,** lodged; **at,** according to. 1336. **esen hem,** put them at ease. 1337. **weenen,** suppose. 1338. **amenden,** improve on. 1340. **meeste,** most. 1343. **daunselinge,** charming. 1347 **liggen,** lie. 1350. **leste,** it please. 1354. **soong,** sang; **tho,** then. 1355. **corage,** spirit. 1356. **roos,** arose.

I mene Venus honourable and digne;°
And in hir hour he walketh forth a pas°
Unto the listes ther hir temple was,
And down he kneeleth, and with humble cheere
And herte soor, he saide as ye shal heere:
"Faireste of faire, O lady myn Venus,
Doughter of Jove and spouse to Vulcanus,
Thou gladere° of the Mount of Citheron,
For thilke love thou haddest to Adon,°
Have pitee of my bittre teres smerte,
And taak myn humble prayere at thyn herte.
Allas, I ne have no langage to telle
Th'effectes ne the torments of myn helle.
Myn herte may mine harmes nat biwraye;°
I am so confus that I can nought saye
But mercy, lady bright, that knowest wele
My thought and seest what harmes that I feele.
Considere al this, and rewe° upon my soor,
As wisly° as I shal for everemoor,
Emforth° my might, thy trewe servant be,
And holden werre° alway with chastitee.
That make I myn avow, so ye me helpe.
I keepe nought of armes for to yelpe,°
Ne I ne axe° nought tomorwe to have victorye,
Ne renown in this caas, ne vaine glorye
Of pris° of armes blowen up and down;
But I wolde have fully possessioun
Of Emelye, and die in thy servise.

1358. digne, reverend. **1359.** Night and day were divided into twelve hours, which were assigned in rotating order to the seven "planets," Saturn, Jupiter, Mars, the Sun, Venus, Mercury, the Moon; the first daylight hour of each day of the week belonged to the planet with which the day was associated: on Sunday the Sun had the first, eighth, fifteenth, and twenty-second hours, Venus the second, ninth, sixteenth and twenty-third (when Palamon prays to her); on Monday Diana (the Moon goddess) had the first hour (when Emily prays to her) and Mars the fourth (when Arcite prays to him). **1365. gladere,** gladdener. **1366. Adon,** Adonis, Venus' lover, whom she was unable to save from the fatal bite of a wild boar. **1371. biwraye,** disclose. **1375. rewe,** have pity. **1376. wisly,** surely. **1377. Emforth,** to the extent of. **1378. werre,** war. **1380. keepe,** care; **yelpe,** boast. **1381. axe,** ask. **1383. pris,** reputation.

Find thou the manere how and in what wise:
I recche nat but° it may bettre be
To have victorye of hem, or they of me,
So that I have my lady in mine armes.
For though so be that Mars is god of armes,
Youre vertu° is so greet in hevene above
That, if you list,° I shal wel have my love.
  Thy temple wol I worshipe everemo,
And on thyn auter,° wher I ride or go,
I wol doon sacrifice and fires bete.°
And if ye wol nought so, my lady sweete,
Thanne praye I thee tomorwe with a spere
That Arcita me thurgh the herte bere°—
Thanne rekke° I nought, whan I have lost my lif,
Though that Arcita winne hire to his wif.
This is th'effect and ende of my prayere:
Yif° me my love, thou blisful lady dere."
  Whan the orison was doon of Palamon,
His sacrifice he dide, and that anoon,
Ful pitously, with alle circumstaunces,°
Al telle I° nat as now his observaunces.
But at the laste the statue of Venus shook,
And made a signe wherby that he took
That his prayere accepted was that day,
For though the signe shewed a delay,
Yet wiste he wel that graunted was his boone,
And with glad herte he wente him hoom ful soone.
  The thridde hour inequal that° Palamon
Bigan to Venus temple for to goon,
Up roos the sonne, and up roos Emelye,
And to the temple of Diane gan hie.°

1387. recche, care; **but,** i.e., whether. **1391. vertu,** power. **1392. you list,** it pleases. **1394. auter,** altar. **1395. bete,** make. **1398. bere,** i.e., pierce. **1399. rekke,** care. **1402. Yif,** give. **1405. circumstaunces,** details. **1406. Al . . . I,** although I tell. **1413. that,** i.e., after. Emily's prayer takes place on the *third* hour after Palamon's because medieval counting included both the first and last item in a series. The hour is *unequal* because except at the equinox daylight and darkness are not of equal duration so that the twelve daylight hours are not of the same length as the twelve hours of darkness. **1416. hie,** hasten.

Hir maidens that she thider with hire ladde,°
Ful redily with them the fir they hadde,
Th'encens, the clothes, and the remenant al,
That to the sacrifice longen shal°—
The hornes ful of meeth, as was the gise:°
Ther lakked nought to doon hir sacrifise.
  Smoking° the temple, ful of clothes faire,
This Emelye with herte debonaire°
Hir body wessh° with water of a welle.
But how she dide hir rite I dar nat telle,
But° it be any thing in general—
And yet it were a game to heeren al:
To him that meneth wel it nere no charge,°
But it is good a man be at his large.°
  Hir brighte heer was kembed untressed° al;
A corowne of a greene ook cerial°
Upon hir heed was set, ful fair and meete;°
Two fires on the auter gan she bete,°
And dide hir thinges as men may biholde
In Stace° of Thebes and thise bookes olde.
Whan kindled was the fir, with pitous cheere°
Unto Diane she spak as ye may heere:
  "O chaste goddesse of the wodes greene,
To whom bothe hevene and erthe and see is seene;°
Queene of the regne° of Pluto, derk and lowe;
Goddesse of maidens, that my herte hast knowe
Ful many a yeer, and woost° what I desire,
As keep me fro thy vengeance and thyn ire,
That Attheon aboughte° cruelly.
Chaste goddesse, wel woostou that I
Desire to been a maiden al my lif,

1417. ladde, led. **1420. longen shal,** ought to belong. **1421. meeth,** mead; **gise,** fashion. **1423. Smoking,** i.e., censing. **1424. debonaire,** humble. **1425. wessh,** washed. **1427. But,** unless. **1429. charge,** burden. **1430.** ? But it's a good thing for a man to be free to omit what he wants. **1431. kembed,** combed; **untressed,** unbraided. **1432. cerial,** evergreen. **1433. meete,** fitting. **1434. bete,** make. **1436. Stace,** Statius, author of the *Thebaid,* one of Chaucer's lesser sources for this tale. **1437. cheere,** countenance. **1440. seene,** visible. **1441. regne,** kingdom. **1443. woost,** know. **1445. Attheon,** Actaeon: see l. 1207 above; **aboughte,** paid for.

Ne nevere wol I be no love ne wif.
I am, thou woost, yet of thy compaignye,
A maide, and love hunting and venerye,
And for to walken in the wodes wilde,
And nought to been a wif and be with childe.
Nought wol I knowe compaignye of man.
Now help me lady, sith ye may and can,
For tho three formes that thou hast in thee.
And Palamon, that hath swich love to me,
And eek Arcite, that loveth me so sore,
This grace I praye thee withoute more:
As sende love and pees bitwixe hem two,
And fro me turn away hir hertes so
That al hir hote love and hir desir,
And al hir bisy torment and hir fir,
Be queint or turned in another place.
And if so be thou wolt nought do me grace,
Or if my destinee be shape so
That I shal needes have oon of hem two,
As sende me him that most desireth me.
Bihold, goddesse of clene chastitee,
The bittre teres that on my cheekes falle.
Sin thou art maide and kepere of us alle,
My maidenhood thou keepe and wel conserve,
And whil I live, a maide I wol thee serve."
  The fires brenne upon the auter clere,
Whil Emelye was thus in hir prayere;
But sodeinly she sawgh a sighte quainte:
For right anoon oon of the fires queinte,
And quiked again, and after that anoon
That other fir was queint and al agoon,
And as it queinte it made a whistelinge,
As doon thise wete brondes in hir brenninge,

1450. venerye, hunting. **1452. with childe,** pregnant. **1455. three formes:** Luna of the Moon, Diana of the Woods, Proserpina of the Underworld. **1459. pees,** peace. **1462. bisy,** anxious. **1463. queint,** quenched. **1470. kepere,** guardian. **1473. brenne,** burn; **auter,** altar; **clere,** brightly. **1476. queinte,** went out. **1477. quiked,** blazed up. **1478. agoon,** vanished. **1480. brenninge,** burning.

And at the brondes ende out ran anoon
As it were bloody dropes many oon.
For which so sore agast was Emelye
That she was wel neigh mad, and gan to crye,
For she ne wiste what it signified;
But only for the fere thus hath she cried,
And weep that it was pitee for to heere.
  And therwithal Diane gan appere,
With bowe in hand, right as an hunteresse,
And saide, "Doughter, stint thyn hevinesse:
Among the goddes hye it is affermed,
And by eterne word writen and confermed,
Thou shalt be wedded unto oon of tho
That han for thee so muche care and wo;
But unto which of hem I may nought telle.
Farwel, for I ne may no lenger dwelle.
The fires whiche that on myn auter brenne
Shul thee declaren er that thou go henne
Thyn aventure of love as in this caas."
And with that word the arwes in the caas
Of the goddesse clateren faste and ringe,
And forth she wente, and made a vanisshinge.
For which this Emelye astoned was,
And saide, "What amounteth this, allas?
I putte me in thy proteccioun,
Diane, and in thy disposicioun."
And hoom she gooth anoon the nexte waye.
This is th'effect: ther nis namore to saye.
  The nexte houre of Mars folwinge this,
Arcite unto the temple walked is
Of fierse Mars, to doon his sacrifise,
With alle the rites of his payen wise;
With pitous herte and heigh devocioun,
Right thus to Mars he saide his orisoun:
  "O stronge god, that in the regnes colde

1487. weep, wept. **1490. stint,** cease. **1494. han,** have. **1498. henne,** hence. **1503. astoned,** astonished. **1504. What,** i.e., to what. **1506. disposicioun,** disposal. **1507. nexte,** nearest. **1512. payen,** pagan. **1515. regnes,** kingdoms.

Of Trace honoured art and lord yholde,°
And hast in every regne and every land
Of armes al the bridel° in thyn hand,
And hem fortunest as thee list° devise,
Accepte of me my pitous sacrifise.
If so be that my youthe may deserve,
And that my might be worthy for to serve
Thy godhede, that I may be oon of thine,
Thanne praye I thee to rewe upon my pine,°
For thilke paine and thilke° hote fir
In which thou whilom brendest° for desir
Whan that thou usedest° the beautee
Of faire, yonge, fresshe Venus free,°
And haddest hire in armes at thy wille—
Although thee ones on a time misfille,°
Whan Vulcanus hadde caught thee in his las,°
And foond thee ligging° by his wife, allas!
For thilke sorwe that was in thyn herte,
Have routhe° as wel upon my paines smerte:
I am yong and unconning° as thou woost,
And as I trowe, with love offended° most
That evere was any lives° creature;
For she that dooth° me al this wo endure
Ne reccheth nevere wher I sinke or flete;°
And wel I woot er she me mercy hete,°
I moot with strengthe winne hire in the place;
And wel I woot withouten help or grace
Of thee ne may my strengthe nought availe:
Thanne help me, lord, tomorwe in my bataile,
For thilke fir that whilom brende thee,

1516. **Trace,** Thrace; **yholde,** held, considered. 1518. **bridel,** i.e., management. 1519. **fortunest,** assign fortunes to; **list,** it pleases. 1524. **rewe,** have pity; **pine,** suffering. 1525. **thilke,** that same. 1526. **brendest,** burned. 1527. **usedest,** enjoyed. 1528. **free,** noble. 1530. **misfille,** misfortune occurred. 1531. **las,** net: Vulcan was Venus' husband, and once trapped his wife and her lover in the manner described. 1532. **foond,** found; **ligging,** lying. 1534. **routhe,** pity. 1535. **unconning,** unskilled. 1536. **trowe,** believe; **offended,** injured. 1537. **lives,** living. 1538. **dooth,** makes. 1539. **reccheth,** cares; **wher,** whether; **fleete,** float. 1540. **hete,** promise.

As wel as thilke fir now brenneth° me;
And do° that I tomorwe may have victorye:
Myn be the travaile, and thyn be the glorye.
Thy soverein temple wol I most honouren
Of any place, and alway most labouren
In thy plesance and in thy craftes stronge;
And in thy temple I wol my baner honge,°
And alle the armes of my compaignye,
And everemo until that day I die
Eterne fir I wol bifore thee finde;°
And eek to this avow I wol me binde:
My beerd, myn heer, that hangeth long adown,
That nevere yet ne felte offensioun°
Of rasour nor of shere,° I wol thee yive,
And been thy trewe servant whil I live.
Now lord, have routhe upon my sorwes sore:
Yif me the victorye—I axe° thee namore."
 The prayere stint° of Arcita the stronge,
The ringes on the temple dore that honge
And eek the dores clatereden ful faste,
Of which Arcita somwhat him agaste;°
The fires brende upon the auter brighte
That it gan al the temple for to lighte;
A sweete smel anoon the ground up yaf;
And Arcita anoon his hand up haf,°
And more encens° into the fir he caste,
With othere rites mo, and at the laste
The statue of Mars bigan his hauberk° ringe,
And with that soun he herde a murmuringe,
Ful lowe and dim, and saide thus, "Victorye."
For which he yaf to Mars honour and glorye.
 And thus with joye and hope wel to fare
Arcite anoon unto his in° is fare,
As fain° as fowl is of the brighte sonne.

1546. **brenneth,** burns. 1547. **do,** cause. 1552. **honge,** hang. 1555. **finde,** provide. 1558. **offensioun,** injury. 1559. **rasour,** razor; **shere,** shears. 1562. **Yif,** give; **axe,** ask. 1563. **stint,** having ended. 1566. **him agaste,** was afraid. 1570. **haf,** lifted. 1571. **encens,** incense. 1573. **hauberk,** coat of mail. 1578. **in,** lodging. 1579. **fain,** glad.

And right anoon swich strif ther is bigonne
For thilke graunting in the hevene above
Bitwixe Venus, the goddesse of love,
And Mars, the sterne god armipotente,°
That Juppiter was bisy it to stente,°
Til that the pale Saturnus the colde,°
That knew so manye of aventures olde,
Foond in his olde experience an art
That he ful soone hath plesed every part:
As sooth is said, elde° hath greet avantage;
In elde is bothe wisdom and usage;°
Men may the olde atrenne and nat atrede.°
Saturne anoon, to stinten strif and drede,°
Al be it that it is again his kinde,°
Of al this strif he can remedye finde.
"My dere doughter Venus," quod Saturne,
"My cours,° that hath so wide for to turne,
Hath more power than woot any man:
Myn is the drenching° in the see so wan;
Myn is the prison in the derke cote;°
Myn is the strangling and hanging by the throte;
The murmur and the cherles rebellinge;°
The groining° and the privee empoisoninge;
I do vengeance and plein correccioun°
Whil I dwelle in the signe of the leoun;°
Myn is the ruine° of the hye halles,
The falling of the towres and of the walles
Upon the minour° or the carpenter;
I slow° Sampson, shaking the piler;

1583. armipotente, powerful in arms. **1584. stente,** stop. **1585. colde,** throughout this section the word also signifies fatal, baleful. **1587. Foond,** found. **1589. elde,** old age. **1590. usage,** experience. **1591. atrenne,** outrun; **atrede,** outsmart. **1592. stinten,** put an end to; **drede,** doubt. **1593.** Although it is contrary to his nature: Saturn was considered the most malign of the planets. **1596. cours,** orbit. **1598. Myn,** resulting from my influence; **drenching,** drowning. **1599. prison,** imprisonment; **cote,** hut. **1601. murmur,** grumbling; **cherles rebellinge,** revolt of the lower classes. **1602. groining,** complaining. **1603. plein correccioun,** full chastisement. **1604. signe . . . leoun,** the sign of the Lion is one of the astrological "houses." **1605. ruine,** collapse. **1607. minour,** miner. **1608. slow,** slew.

And mine be the maladies colde,
The derke tresons, and the castes° olde;
My looking is the fader of pestilence:
Now weep namore, I shal doon diligence
That Palamon, that is thyn owene knight,
Shal have his lady as thou hast him hight.°
Though Mars shal helpe his knight, yet nathelees,
Bitwixe you ther moot be som time pees,°
Al be ye nought of oo complexioun°—
That causeth alday swich divisioun.
I am thyn aiel,° redy at thy wille;
Weep now namore: I wol thy lust° fulfille."
  Now wol I stinten° of the goddes above,
Of Mars and of Venus, goddesse of love,
And telle you as plainly as I can
The grete effect for which that I bigan.

PART FOUR

  Greet was the feeste in Atthenes that day,
And eek the lusty seson of that May
Made every wight to been in swich pleasaunce
That al that Monday justen° they and daunce,
And spenden it in Venus heigh servise;
But by the cause that° they sholde rise
Erly for to seen the grete fight,
Unto hir reste wente they at night.
And on the morwe whan the day gan springe,
Of hors and harneis noise and clateringe
Ther was in hostelries al aboute;
And to the palais rood ther many a route°
Of lordes upon steedes and palfreys:
Ther maistou seen devising° of harneis,

1610. **castes,** conspiracies. 1614. **hight,** promised. 1616. **pees,** peace. 1617. **oo complexioun,** i.e., the same humor or temperament. 1619. **aiel,** grandfather. 1620. **lust,** desire. 1621. **stinten,** cease. 1628. **justen,** joust. 1630. **by . . . that,** because. 1636. **rood,** rode; **route,** group. 1638. **devising,** preparation.

So uncouth and so riche, and wrought so weel°
Of goldsmithrye, of brouding,° and of steel;
The sheeldes brighte, testers and trappures;°
Gold-hewen helmes, hauberkes, cote-armures;
Lordes in parements on hir courseres;°
Knightes of retenue° and eek squieres
Nailing the speres and helmes bokelinge;°
Gigging of sheeldes, with lainers° lacinge—
Ther as neede is they were no thing idel;
The fomy steedes on the golden bridel
Gnawing; and faste the armurers also
With file and hamer priking° to and fro;
Yemen on foote and communes° many oon,
With shorte staves, thikke as they may goon;
Pipes, trompes, nakers,° clariouns,
That in the bataile blowen bloody souns;
The palais ful of peples up and down—
Here three, ther ten, holding her questioun,°
Divining° of thise Thebans knightes two.
Some saide thus, some saiden it shal be so;
Some heelden with him with the blake beerd,
Some with the balled, some with the thikke-herd;°
Some saide he looked grimme, and he wolde fighte—
"He hath a sparth of twenty pound of wighte."°
Thus was the halle ful of divininge
Longe after that the sonne gan to springe.
The grete Theseus, that of his sleep awaked
With minstralcye and noise that was maked,
Heeld yet the chambres of his palais riche,
Til that the Theban knightes, bothe yliche°
Honoured, weren into the palais fet.°

1639. uncouth, strange; **weel,** well. **1640. brouding,** embroidery. **1641. testers,** head armor; **trappures,** horse armor. **1643. parements,** robes of state; **courseres,** chargers. **1644. of retenue,** in service. **1645. bokelinge,** buckling. **1646. Gigging,** attaching; **lainers,** straps. **1650. priking,** riding. **1651. Yemen,** yeomen; **communes,** common soldiers. **1653. trompes, clariouns,** trumpets; **nakers,** kettledrums. **1656. questioun,** discussion. **1657. Divining,** conjecturing. **1660. thikke-herd,** thick-haired. **1662. sparth,** battle axe; **wighte,** weight. **1668. yliche,** alike. **1669. fet,** fetched.

Duc Theseus is at a window set,
Arrayed right as he were a god in trone;°
The peple preesseth° thiderward ful soone,
Him for to seen and doon heigh reverence,
And eek to herkne his heeste and his sentence.°
An heraud on a scaffold made an "Oo!"°
Til al the noise of the peple was ydo;°
And whan he sawgh the peple of noise al stille,
Thus shewed he the mighty Dukes wille:
"The lord hath of his heigh discrecioun
Considered that it were destruccioun
To gentil blood to fighten in the gise°
Of mortal bataile now in this emprise;°
Wherfore, to shapen° that they shal nought die,
He wol his firste purpos modifye:
No man therfore, up° paine of los of lif,
No manere shot,° ne polax, ne short knif,
Into the listes sende or thider bringe;
Ne short-swerd for to stoke° with point bitinge,
No man ne drawe ne bere it by his side;
Ne no man shal unto his felawe ride
But oo cours with a sharpe ygrounde spere—
Foine if him list on foote himself to were;°
And he that is at meschief shal be take,°
And nought slain, but be brought unto the stake
That shal been ordained° on either side;
But thider he shal by force, and ther abide;
And if so falle the chieftain be take,
On outher side, or elles sleen his make,°
No lenger shal the tourneyinge laste.
God speede you: go forth and lay on faste.
With long swerd and with mace fighteth youre fille.
Go now youre way. This is the lordes wille."

1671. **trone,** throne. 1672. **preesseth,** press. 1674. **heeste,** command; **sentence,** judgment. 1675. **Oo,** i.e., hear ye. 1676. **ydo,** done. 1681. **gise,** manner. 1682. **emprise,** enterprise. 1683. **shapen,** bring it about. 1685. **up,** upon. 1686. **shot,** missile. 1688. **stoke,** stab. 1692. **Foine,** parry; **were,** defend. 1693. **at meschief,** in trouble; **take,** taken prisoner. 1695. **ordained,** placed. 1698. **outher,** either; **sleen,** slay; **make,** mate.

The vois of peple touchede the hevene,
So loude cride they with merye stevene,
"God save swich a lord that is so good:
He wilneth no destruccion of blood."
Up goon the trompes and the melodye,
And to the listes rit the compaignye,
By ordinance, thurghout the citee large,
Hanged with cloth of gold and nought with sarge.
Ful lik a lord this noble Duc gan ride,
Thise two Thebans upon either side;
And after rood the queene and Emelye,
And after that another compaignye
Of oon and other after hir degree;
And thus they passen thurghout the citee,
And to the listes come they bitime—
It nas nat of the day yet fully prime.
Whan set was Theseus ful riche and hye,
Ipolyta the queene and Emelye,
And othere ladies in degrees aboute,
Unto the setes preesseth al the route,
And westward thurgh the gates under Marte
Arcite and eek the hundred of his parte,
With baner reed, is entred right anoon.
And in that selve moment Palamon
Is under Venus eestward in the place,
With baner whit and hardy cheere and face.
In al the world, to seeken up and down,
So evene withouten variacioun
Ther nere swiche compaignies twaye;
For ther was noon so wis that coude saye
That any hadde of other avantage,
Of worthinesse, ne of estaat ne age,
So evene were they chosen for to gesse;

1704. stevene, voice. **1706. wilneth,** desires. **1707. trompes,** trumpets. **1708. rit,** rides. **1709. By ordinance,** in order. **1710. sarge,** serge, generally used for hangings. **1715. after,** according to. **1717. bitime,** early. **1718. prime,** 9 A.M. **1722. route,** mob. **1723. Marte,** Mars. **1725. reed,** red. **1726. selve,** same. **1728. cheere,** countenance. **1730. variacioun,** difference. **1735. for . . . gesse,** i.e., at a rough estimate.

And in two renges faire they hem dresse.°
  Whan that hir names rad° were everichoon,
That in hir nombre gile was ther noon,
Tho were the gates shet° and cried was loude,
"Do now youre devoir,° yonge knightes proude!"
  The heraudes lefte hir priking° up and down;
Now ringen trompes loude and clarioun;
Ther is namore to sayn, but west and eest
In goon the speres ful sadly in the arrest;°
In gooth the sharpe spore° into the side;
Ther seen men who can juste° and who can ride;
Ther shiveren shaftes upon sheeldes thikke;
He feeleth thurgh the herte-spoon° the prikke;
Up springeth speres twenty foot on highte;
Out goon the swerdes as the silver brighte;
The helmes they tohewen and toshrede;°
Out brest the blood with sterne° stremes rede;
With mighty maces the bones they tobreste;°
He thurgh the thikkeste of the throng gan threste;°
Ther stomblen steedes stronge, and down gooth al;
He rolleth under foot as dooth a bal;
He foineth on his feet with his tronchoun;°
And he him hurtleth with his hors adown;
He thurgh the body is hurt and sithen take,
Maugree his heed,° and brought unto the stake:
As forward° was, right ther he moste abide;
Another lad° is on that other side.
  And som time dooth° hem Theseus to reste,
Hem to refresshe and drinken if hem leste.°
Ful ofte aday have thise Thebanes two
Togidre ymet and wrought his felawe wo:

1736. **renges,** rings; **hem dresse,** take their positions. **1737. rad,** read. 1739. **shet,** shut. 1740. **devoir,** duty, i.e., your best. **1741. priking,** riding. 1744. **sadly,** firmly; **arrest,** spear rest. 1745. **spore,** spur. 1746. **juste,** joust. 1748. **herte-spoon,** breastbone. 1751. **tohewen, toshrede,** cut to pieces. 1752. **brest,** bursts; **sterne,** violent. 1753. **tobreste,** break to bits. 1754. **threste,** thrust. 1757. **foineth,** parries; **tronchoun,** truncheon, spear shaft. 1760. **Maugree . . . heed,** i.e., despite anything he could do. 1761. **forward,** agreement. 1762. **lad,** led off. 1763. **dooth,** causes. 1764. **leste,** it please.

Unhorsed hath eech other of hem tweye.°
Ther nas no tigre in the vale of Galgopheye,°
Whan that hir whelpe is stole whan it is lite,
So cruel on the hunte° as is Arcite,
For jalous herte, upon this Palamoun;
Ne in Belmarye ther nis so fel° leoun,
That hunted is or for his hunger wood,°
Ne of his preye desireth so the blood,
As Palamon to sleen° his fo Arcite.
The jalous strokes on hir helmes bite:
Out renneth° blood on bothe hir sides rede.
  Som time an ende ther is of every deede:
For er the sonne unto the reste wente,
The stronge king Emetrius gan hente°
This Palamon as he faught with Arcite,
And made his swerd deepe in his flessh to bite,
And by the force of twenty is he take,
Unyolden, and ydrawen° to the stake;
And in the rescous° of this Palamoun,
The stronge king Lygurge is born adown,
And king Emetrius, for al his strengthe,
Is born out of his sadel a swerdes lengthe,
So hitte him Palamon er he were take.
But al for nought, he was brought to the stake:
His hardy herte mighte him helpe naught;
He moste abide whan that he was caught,
By force and eek by composicioun.°
  Who sorweth now but woful Palamoun,
That moot namore goon again to fighte?
And whan that Theseus hadde seen this sighte,
Unto the folk that foughten thus eechoon
He cride, "Ho, namore, for it is doon!
I wol be trewe juge and nat partye:°

1767. tweye, twice. **1768. Galgopheye,** this and Benmarin (see l. 1772) were probably associated with the wild beasts mentioned. **1770. hunte,** hunter. **1772. fel,** cruel. **1773. wood,** raging. **1775. sleen,** slay. **1777. renneth,** runs. **1780. hente,** seize. **1784. Unyolden,** unyielded; **ydrawen,** dragged. **1785. rescous,** attempt at rescue. **1793. composicioun,** contract. **1799. partye,** partial.

Arcite of Thebes shal have Emelye,
That by his fortune hath hire faire ywonne."
Anoon ther is a noise of peple bigonne,
For joye of this, so loud and heigh withalle,
It seemed that the listes sholde falle.
  What can now faire Venus doon above?
What saith she now? What dooth this queene of love?—
But weepeth so for wanting° of hir wille,
Til that hir teres in the listes fille.°
She saide, "I am ashamed, doutelees."
  Saturnus saide, "Doughter, hold thy pees!°
Mars hath his wil: his knight hath al his boone,
And, by myn heed, thou shalt been esed° soone."
  The trompours° with the loude mynstralcye,
The heraudes that ful loude yelle and crye,
Been in hir wele° for joye of daun Arcite—
But herkneth me, and stinteth° noise a lite,
Which° a miracle ther bifel anoon:
  This fierse Arcite hath of° his helm ydoon,
And on a courser for to shewe his face,
He priketh endelong° the large place,
Looking upward upon this Emelye,
And she again him caste a freendly yë—
For wommen, as to speken in commune,
They folwen al the favour of Fortune—
And she was al his cheere as in his herte.
Out of the ground a furye infernal sterte,°
From Pluto sent at requeste of Saturne,
For which his hors for fere gan to turne
And leep aside, and foundred° as he leep;
And er that Arcite may taken keep,°
He pighte him on the pomel of his heed,°

1807. **wanting**, lacking. 1808. **fille**, fell. 1810. **pees**, peace. 1812. **heed**, head; **esed**, made happy. 1813. **trompours**, trumpeters. 1815. **wele**, gladness. 1816. **stinteth**, stop. 1817. **Which**, what. 1818. **of**, off. 1820. **endelong**, from end to end of. 1826. **sterte**, started up. 1829. **leep**, leapt; **foundred**, stumbled. 1830. **keep**, heed. 1831. Apparently Arcite was thrown against an ornamental knob (pommel) on the saddlebow and then pitched off the horse so that he fell beside its head.

That in the place he lay as he were deed,
His brest tobrosten with his sadel bowe.
As blak he lay as any cole or crowe,
So was the blood yronnen in his face.
Anoon he was yborn out of the place,
With herte soor, to Theseus palais.
Tho was he corven out of his harneis,
And in a bed ybrought ful faire and blive—
For he was yet in memorye and alive,
And alway crying after Emelye.
  Duc Theseus with all his compaignye
Is comen hoom to Atthenes his citee
With alle blisse and greet solempnitee;
Al be it that this aventure was falle,
He sholde nought disconforten hem alle.
  Men saide eek that Arcite shal nat die;
"He shal been heled of his maladye."
And of another thing they were as fain:
That of hem alle was ther noon yslain,
Al were they sore yhurt, and namely oon,
That with a spere was thirled the brest-boon.
  To othere woundes and to broken armes
Some hadden salves and some hadden charmes;
Fermacies of herbes and eek save
They dronken, for they wolde hir limes have;
For which this noble Duc, as he wel can,
Conforteth and honoureth every man,
And made revel al the longe night
Unto the straunge lordes, as was right.
  Ne ther was holden no disconfitinge,
But as a justes or a tourneyinge,
For soothly ther was no disconfiture—

1833. **tobrosten,** broken open; **with,** by. 1838. **corven,** cut; **harneis,** battledress. 1839. **blive,** quickly. 1846. **disconforten,** inconvenience. 1849. **fain,** glad. 1851. **Al . . . they,** although they were; **namely,** especially. 1852. **thirled,** pierced. 1855. **Fermacies,** medicines; **save,** herb-drink. 1856. **limes have,** i.e., preserve their limbs. 1860. **straunge,** foreign. 1861. Nor was there considered to be any question of a bad defeat. 1862. **justes,** jousting. 1863. **disconfiture,** rout.

For falling nis nat but an aventure,
Ne to been lad by force unto the stake,
Unyolden, and with twenty knightes take,
A persone allone, withouten mo,
And haried forth by armes, foot and to,
And eek his steede driven forth with staves,
With footmen, bothe yeman and eek knaves—
It nas aretted him no vilainye:
Ther may no man clepe it cowardye.
  For which anoon Duc Theseus leet crye,
To stinten alle rancour and envye,
The gree as wel of oo side as of other,
And either side ylik as otheres brother;
And yaf hem yiftes after hir degree,
And fully heeld a feeste dayes three,
And convoyed the kinges worthily
Out of his town a journee largely.
And hoom wente every man the righte way;
Ther was namore but "Farewel, have good day."
Of this bataile I wol namore endite,
But speke of Palamon and of Arcite.
  Swelleth the brest of Arcite, and the soor
Encreesseth at his herte more and moor;
The clothered blood, for any leechecraft,
Corrupteth and is in his bouk ylaft,
That neither veine-blood, ne ventusinge,
Ne drinke of herbes may been his helpinge:
The vertu expulsif or animal
Fro thilke vertu cleped natural
Ne may the venim voiden ne expelle;

1865. **lad,** led. 1866. **Unyolden,** unyielded. 1867. **A,** one. 1868. **to,** toe. 1870. **With,** by; **knaves,** servants. 1871. No dishonor was charged to him. 1872. **cowardye,** cowardice. 1873. **leet crye,** caused to be announced. 1874. **stinten,** put an end to. 1875. **gree,** victory. 1880. **journee,** day's journey; **largely,** fully. 1881. **righte,** direct. 1886. **Encreesseth,** increases. 1887. **clothered,** clotted; **for,** despite; **leechecraft,** medical attention. 1888. **bouk,** body; **ylaft,** left. 1889. Neither bleeding nor cupping. 1891–92. The "animal" power (virtue) of the body was thought to expel from the system poisons noxious to the "natural" power.

The pipes° of his longes gan to swelle,
And every lacerte° in his brest adown
Is shent° with venim and corrupcioun;
Him gaineth° neither, for to gete his lif,
Vomit upward, ne downward laxatif;
Al is tobrosten° thilke regioun;
Nature hath no dominacioun,
And certainly, ther Nature wol nat wirche,°
Farewel, physik:° go bere the man to chirche.
This al and som,° that Arcita moot die.
For which he sendeth after Emelye,
And Palamon that was his cosin dere;
Thanne saide he thus, as ye shal after heere:
"Nat may the woful spirit in myn herte
Declare a point of alle my sorwes smerte
To you, my lady, that I love most;
But I biquethe the service of my gost°
To you aboven every creature
Sin that my lif may no lenger dure.°
Allas the wo, allas the paines stronge
That I for you have suffred, and so longe;
Allas the deeth, allas myn Emelye;
Allas, departing° of oure compaignye;
Allas, myn hertes queene, allas, my wif,
Myn hertes lady, endere of my lif!
What is this world? What axeth men° to have?—
Now with his love, now in his colde grave,
Allone withouten any compaignye.
Farewel, my sweete fo, myn Emelye,
And softe take me in youre armes twaye,
For love of God, and herkneth what I saye:
I have heer with my cosin Palamon
Had strif and rancour many a day agoon
For love of you, and for my jalousye;

1894. pipes, tubes. **1895. lacerte,** muscle. **1896. shent,** infected. **1897. Him gaineth,** there avails him. **1899. tobrosten,** shattered. **1901. wirche,** work. **1902. physik,** medicine. **1903. This . . . som,** i.e., this is the whole story. **1910. gost,** spirit. **1912. dure,** last. **1916. departing,** separating. **1919. axeth men,** does one ask.

And Juppiter so wis my soule gie,°
To speken of a servant° proprely,
With circumstances alle trewely,
That is to sayn, trouthe,° honour, knighthede,
Wisdom, humblesse, estaat, and heigh kinrede,°
Freedom and al that longeth to that art,°
So Juppiter have of my soule part,
As in this world right now ne knowe I noon
So worthy to been loved as Palamon,
That serveth you, and wol doon al his lif;
And if that evere ye shal been a wif,
Foryet nat Palamon, the gentil man."
And with that word his speeche faile gan,
For from his feet up to his brest was come
The cold of deeth that hadde him overcome;
And yet more over,° for in his armes two
The vital strengthe is lost and al ago:
Only° the intellect withoute moor,
That dwelled in his herte sik and soor,
Gan failen whan the herte felte deeth:
Dusked his yën two and failed breeth;
But on his lady yet caste he his yë.
His laste word was, "Mercy, Emelye."
His spirit chaunged hous and wente ther,
As I cam nevere, I can nat tellen wher;
Therfore I stinte—I nam no divinistre:°
Of soules finde I nat in this registre,
Ne me ne list° thilke opinions to telle
Of hem though that they writen wher they dwelle.
Arcite is cold, ther Mars his soule gie.°
Now wol I speken forth of Emelye.
  Shrighte° Emelye and howleth Palamon,
And Theseus his suster took anoon

1928. **wis,** surely; **gie,** guide. 1929. **servant,** i.e., lover. 1931. **trouthe,** integrity. 1932. **kinrede,** kindred. 1933. **Freedom,** magnanimity; **longeth,** pertains; **art,** profession. 1943. **more over,** i.e., that is not all. 1945. **Only,** construe with *whan* (l. 1947). 1953. **stinte,** leave off; **divinistre,** theologian. 1955. **list,** it pleases. 1957. **ther,** i.e., may; **gie,** guide. 1959. **Shrighte,** shrieked.

Swouning, and bar hire fro the corps away.
What helpeth it to tarien forth the day
To tellen how she weep bothe eve and morwe?
For in swich caas wommen have swich sorwe,
Whan that hir housbondes been from hem ago,
That for the more part they sorwen so,
Or elles fallen in swich a maladye,
That at the laste certainly they die.
  Infinite been the sorwes and the teres
Of olde folk and folk of tendre yeres
In al the town for deeth of this Theban;
For him ther weepeth bothe child and man;
So greet weeping was ther noon, certain,
Whan Ector was ybrought al fresshe yslain
To Troye. Allas, the pitee that was ther—
Cracching of cheekes, renting eek of heer;
"Why woldestou be deed," thise wommen crye,
"And haddest gold ynough, and Emelye?"
  No man mighte gladen Theseus
Saving his olde fader Egeus,
That knew this worldes transmutacioun,
As he hadde seen it chaungen, bothe up and down,
Joye after wo, and wo after gladnesse,
And shewed hem ensample and liknesse:
  "Right as ther died nevere man," quod he,
"That he ne lived in erthe in som degree,
Right so ther lived nevere man," he saide,
"In al this world that som time he ne deide.
This world nis but a thurghfare ful of wo,
And we been pilgrimes passing to and fro:
Deeth is an ende of every worldly soor."
And overal this yet saide he muchel moor
To this effect, ful wisely to enhorte
The peple that they sholde hem reconforte.

1963. weep, wept. **1974. Ector,** Hector, the Trojan hero, slain by Achilles. **1976. Cracching,** scratching; **renting,** tearing. **1977. deed,** dead. **1984. ensample . . . liknesse,** i.e., precedents and analogies. **1993. enhorte,** exhort. **1994. hem reconforte,** take comfort.

Duc Theseus with all his bisy cure
Caste now wher that the sepulture
Of good Arcite may best ymaked be,
And eek most honourable in his degree;
And at the laste he took conclusioun
That ther as first Arcite and Palamoun
Hadden for love the bataile hem bitweene,
That in the selve grove, swoote and greene,
Ther as he hadde his amorouse desires,
His complainte, and for love his hote fires,
He wolde make a fir in which the office
Funeral he mighte al accomplice;
And leet anoon comande to hakke and hewe
The okes olde, and layen hem on a rewe,
In colpons, wel arrayed for to brenne.
His officers with swifte feet they renne
And ride anoon at his comandement,
And after this Duc Theseus hath ysent
After a beere, and it al overspradde
With cloth of gold, the richeste that he hadde;
And of the same suite he cladde Arcite;
Upon his handes two his gloves white,
Eek on his heed a crowne of laurer greene,
And in his hand a swerd ful bright and keene;
He laide him, bare the visage, on the beere.
Therwith he weep that pitee was to heere;
And for the peple sholde seen him alle,
Whan it was day he broughte him to the halle,
That roreth of the crying and the soun.
Tho cam this woful Theban Palamoun,
With flotery beerd and ruggy asshy heres,
In clothes blake, ydropped al with teres,

1995. cure, care. **1996. Caste,** planned; **sepulture,** burial, i.e., funeral. **2002. selve,** same; **swoote,** sweet. **2005 f. office Funeral,** funeral rites. **2007. leet comande,** caused commands to be issued. **2008. rewe,** row. **2009. in colpons,** i.e., at intervals; **brenne,** burn. **2010. renne,** run. **2013. beere,** bier; **overspradde,** overspread. **2015. suite,** material. **2017. laurer,** laurel. **2020. weep,** wept. **2025. flotery,** fluttering; **ruggy,** wild; **asshy,** ash-sprinkled.

And passing othere° of weeping, Emelye,
The rewefulleste° of al the compaignye.
In as muche as the service sholde be
The more noble and riche in his° degree,
Duc Theseus leet forth three steedes bringe,°
That trapped weren in steel al gliteringe,
And covered with the armes of daun Arcite;
Upon thise steedes grete and white
Ther seten folk of which oon bar° his sheeld;
Another his spere upon his handes heeld;°
The thridde bar with him his bowe Turkeis°—
Of brend gold was the caas and eek the harneis;°
And riden forth a paas with sorweful cheere°
Toward the grove, as ye shal after heere.
The nobleste of the Greekes that ther were
Upon hir shuldres carieden the beere,
With slak° paas, and yën rede and wete,
Thurghout the citee by the maister° streete,
That sprad° was al with blak; and wonder hye
Right of the same is the streete ywrye.°
Upon the right hand wente olde Egeus,
And on that other side Duc Theseus,
With vessels in hir hand of gold ful fin,
Al ful of hony, milk, and blood, and win,
Eek Palamon with ful greet compaignye;
And after that cam woful Emelye,
With fir in hande, as was that time the gise,°
To do the office° of funeral servise.
  Heigh labour and ful greet apparailinge°
Was at the service and the fir-makinge,
That with his greene top the hevene raughte,°

2027. **passing,** surpassing; **othere,** others. 2028. **rewefulleste,** most filled with sorrow. 2030. **his,** its. 2031. **leet bringe,** had brought. 2035. **seten,** sat; **bar,** bore. 2036. **heeld,** held. 2037. **Turkeis,** Turkish. 2038. **brend,** burnished; **harneis,** straps. 2039. **paas,** short distance; **cheere,** countenance. 2043. **slak,** slow. 2044. **maister,** i.e., main. 2045. **sprad,** spread. 2046. **ywrye,** covered, hung. 2053. **gise,** fashion. 2054. **office,** duty. 2055. **apparailinge,** preparation. 2057. **raughte,** reached.

And twenty fadme° of brede° the armes° straughte°—
This is to sayn, the boughes were so brode;
Of stree° first ther was laid ful many a lode.
But how the fir was maked upon highte,
Ne eek the names how the trees highte—
As ook, firre, birch, asp,° alder, holm, popler,
Wilow, elm, plane, assh, box, chestain,° linde,° laurer,
Mapel, thorn, beech, hasel, ew,° whippeltree—
How they were feld shal nat been told for me;
Ne how the goddes° ronnen° up and down,
Disherited of hir habitacioun,
In which they woneden° in reste and pees—
Nymphes, faunes, and amadrydes;°
Ne how the beestes and the briddes alle
Fledden forfered° whan the wode was falle;°
Ne how the ground agast was of the light,
That was nat wont to seen the sonne bright;
Ne how the fir was couched° first with stree,°
And thanne with drye stikkes cloven a-three,
And thanne with greene wode and spicerye,°
And thanne with cloth of gold and with perrye,°
And gerlandes hanging with ful many a flowr;
The myrre, th'encens with al so greet savour;°
Ne how Arcite lay among al this,
Ne what richesse aboute the body is,
Ne how that Emelye, as was the gise,
Putte in the fir of funeral servise,
Ne how she swouned whan men made the fir,
Ne what she spak, ne what was hir desir,
Ne what jewels men in the fire caste,
Whan that the fir was greet and brente faste;
Ne how some caste hir sheeld and some hir spere,

2058. **fadme,** fathoms; **brede,** breadth; **armes,** i.e., of the fire; **straughte,** stretched. 2060. **stree,** straw. 2063. **asp,** aspen. 2064. **chestain,** chestnut; **linde,** linden. 2065. **ew,** yew. 2067. **goddes,** i.e., tree spirits; **ronnen,** ran. 2069. **woneden,** dwelled. 2070. **amadrydes,** hamadryads. 2072. **forfered,** terrified; **falle,** felled. 2075. **couched,** laid; **stree,** straw. 2077. **spicerye,** various spices. 2078. **perrye,** jewels. 2080. **savour,** smell.

And of hir vestiments whiche that they were,
And coppes fulle of milk and win and blood
Into the fir that brente as it were wood;
Ne how the Greekes with an huge route
Thries riden al the fir aboute,
Upon the left hand, with a loud shoutinge,
And thries with hir speres clateringe,
And thries how the ladies gonne crye;
And how that lad was hoomward Emelye,
Ne how Arcite is brent to asshen colde;
Ne how that lichewake was yholde
Al thilke night; ne how the Greekes playe
The wake-playes, ne keepe I nought to saye—
Who wrastleth best naked with oile anoint,
Ne who that bar him best in no disjoint;
I wol nat tellen alle how they goon
Hoom til Atthenes whan the play is doon,
But shortly to the point thanne wol I wende,
And maken of my longe tale an ende.
  By proces and by lengthe of certain yeres,
Al stinted is the moorning and the teres
Of Greekes by oon general assent.
Thanne seemed me ther was a parlement
At Atthenes, upon a certain points and cas;
Among the whiche points yspoken was
To have with certain contrees alliaunce,
And have fully of Thebans obeisaunce:
For which this noble Theseus anoon
Leet senden after gentil Palamon,
Unwist of him what was the cause and why;
But in his blake clothes sorwefully
He cam at his comandement in hie.
Tho sente Theseus for Emelye.

2091. coppes, cups. **2092. wood,** raging. **2093. route,** company. **2098. lad,** led. **2100. lichewake,** the funeral wake. **2102. wake-playes,** funeral games; **keepe,** care. **2104. bar,** bore; **no disjoint,** any predicament. **2109. proces,** course of time. **2110. stinted,** ended. **2113. certain,** certain number of; **cas,** affairs. **2119. Unwist of,** unknown to. **2121. hie,** haste.

Whan they were set, and hust was al the place,
And Theseus abiden hath a space
Er any word cam from his wise brest,
His yën sette he ther as was his lest,
And with a sad visage he siked stille,
And after that right thus he saide his wille:
"The Firste Mevere of the cause above,
Whan he first made the faire chaine of love,
Greet was th'effect, and heigh was his entente—
Wel wiste he why and what therof he mente:
For with that faire chaine of love he boond
The fir, the air, the water, and the lond
In certain boundes that they may nat flee.
That same Prince and that Mevere," quod he,
"Hath stablissed in this wrecched world adown
Certaine dayes and duracioun
To al that is engendred in this place,
Over the whiche day they may nat pace,
Al mowe they yet tho dayes wel abregge.
Ther needeth noon auctoritee to allegge,
For it is preved by experience,
But that me list declaren my sentence.
Thanne may men by this ordre wel discerne
That thilke Mevere stable is and eterne;
Wel may men knowe, but it be a fool,
That every part deriveth from his hool;
For Nature hath nat taken his biginning
Of no partye, or cantel of a thing,
But of a thing that parfit is and stable,
Descending so til it be corrumpable;
And therfore for his wise purveyaunce
He hath so wel biset his ordinaunce

2123. **hust,** hushed. 2126. **sette,** i.e., fixed; **lest,** pleasure. 2127. **sad,** sober; **siked,** sighed; **stille,** quietly. 2129. **Firste Mevere,** First Mover, God. 2133. **boond,** bound. 2137. **stablissed,** established. 2140. **pace,** pass. 2141. **Al . . . they,** although they can; **abregge,** shorten. 2142. **allegge,** adduce. 2143. **preved,** proved. 2144. **sentence,** sentiments. 2148. **hool,** whole. 2150. **partye,** i.e., mere part; **cantel,** portion. 2152. **corrumpable,** capable of corruption. 2153. **purveyaunce,** providence. 2154. **biset,** limited; **ordinaunce,** scheme.

That speces of thinges and progressiouns°
Shullen enduren by successiouns,
And nought eterne, withouten any lie.
This maistou understonde and seen at yë.
  Lo, the ook that hath so long a norissinge°
Fro the time that it first biginneth springe,
And hath so long a life, as ye may see,
Yet at the laste wasted is the tree;
Considereth eek how that the harde stoon
Under oure foot on which we ride and goon,
Yet wasteth it as it lith° by the waye;
The brode river som time wexeth dreye;°
The grete townes see we wane and wende;°
Thanne see ye that al this thing hath ende.
Of man and womman see we wel also
That needeth° in oon of thise termes two—
This is to sayn, in youthe or elles age—
He moot be deed, the king as shal a page,
Som in his bed, som° in the deepe see,
Som in the large feeld, as ye may see.
Ther helpeth nought: al gooth that ilke° waye.
Thanne may I sayn that al this thing moot deye.
What maketh this but Juppiter the king,
That is Prince and cause of alle thing,
Converting al unto his propre welle,°
From which he° is derived, sooth to telle?
And heeragains no creature on live,
Of no degree, availeth for to strive.
  Thanne is it wisdom, as it thinketh me,
To maken vertu of necessitee,
And take it wel that we may nat eschue,°
And nameliche° that to us alle is due;

2155. speces, varieties; **progressiouns,** ? things growing. **2159. norissinge,** i.e., period of growth. **2165. lith,** lies. **2166. wexeth dreye,** grows dry. **2167. wende,** pass away. **2170. That needeth,** whom it is necessary: the conclusion "to die" is postponed until l. 2172, by which time the syntax has been altered. **2173. som,** one. **2175. ilke,** same. **2179. his,** its; **welle,** source. **2180. he,** it. **2185. that,** what; **eschue,** eschew. **2186. nameliche,** particularly.

And who so gruccheth ought,° he dooth folye,
And rebel is to him that al may gie.°
And certainly a man hath most honour
To dien in his excellence and flowr,
Whan he is siker° of his goode name:
Thanne hath he doon his freend ne him no shame,
And gladder oughte his freend been of his deeth
Whan with honour yolden° is up his breeth,
Than whan his name appalled° is for age,
For al forgeten is his vasselage.°
Thanne is it best, as for a worthy fame,
To dien whan that he is best of name.
  The contrarye of al this is wilfulnesse:
Why grucchen we, why have we hevinesse,
That goode Arcite, of chivalrye flowr,
Departed is with duetee° and with honour
Out of this foule prison of this lif?
Why gruccheth here his cosin and his wif
Of his welfare that loveth him so weel?°
Can he hem thank?°—nay, God woot, neveradeel—
That bothe his soule and eek hemself offende.°
And yet they mowe hir lustes nat amende.°
  What may I conclude of this longe serie,°
But after wo I rede° us to be merye,
And thanken Juppiter of al his grace,
And, er we departen from this place,
I rede that we make of sorwes two
Oo parfit joye, lasting everemo;
And looketh now wher most sorwe is herinne,
Ther wol I first amenden and biginne.
  Suster," quod he, "this is my ful assent,°
With al th'avis° heer of my parlement:

2187. **gruccheth,** grumbles; **ought,** at all. 2188. **gie,** guide. 2191. **siker,** sure. 2194. **yolden,** yielded. 2195. **appalled,** faded. 2196. **vasselage,** prowess. 2202. **duetee,** duty. 2205. **weel,** well. 2206. **Can . . . thank,** does he show them gratitude. 2207. **offende,** injure. 2208. **mowe,** can; **hir . . . amende,** i.e., come no nearer to achieving their desires. 2209. **serie,** series of arguments. 2210. **rede,** advise. 2217. **assent,** desire. 2218. **avis,** advice.

That gentil Palamon, youre owene knight,
That serveth you with wil and herte and might,
And evere hath doon sin ye first him knewe,
That ye shal of youre grace upon him rewe,°
And taken him for housbonde and for lord:
Lene me youre hand, for this is oure accord.°
Lat see now of youre wommanly pitee.
He is a kinges brother sone, pardee,
And though he were a poore bacheler,
Sin he hath served you so many a yeer,
And had for you so greet adversitee,
It moste been considered, leveth° me:
For gentil mercy oughte to passen° right."
  Thanne saide he thus to Palamon the knight,
"I trowe° ther needeth litel sermoning
To make you assente to this thing.
Come neer and taketh youre lady by the hond."
Bitwixe hem was maad anoon the bond
That highte matrimoigne° or mariage,
By al the conseil and the baronage.
And thus with alle blisse and melodye
Hath Palamon ywedded Emelye;
And God, that al this wide world hath wrought,
Sende him his love that hath it dere abought;°
For now is Palamon in alle wele,°
Living in blisse, in richesse, and in hele;°
And Emelye him loveth so tendrely,
And he serveth hire so gentilly,
That nevere was ther no word hem bitweene
Of jalousye or any other teene.°
Thus endeth Palamon and Emelye,
And God save al this faire compaignye.

Amen

2222. rewe, have pity. **2224. Lene,** give; **accord,** wish. **2230. leveth,** believe. **2231. passen,** go beyond. **2233. trowe,** believe. **2237. matrimoigne,** matrimony. **2342. dere abought,** paid for it dearly. **2343. wele,** happiness. **2344. hele,** health. **2348. teene,** vexation.

THE MILLER'S TALE

The Introduction

Whan that the Knight hadde thus his tale ytold,
In al the route° nas ther yong ne old
That he ne saide it was a noble storye,
And worthy for to drawen° to memorye,
And namely the gentils° everichoon.
  Oure Hoste lough and swoor, "So mote I goon,°
This gooth aright: unbokeled is the male.°
Lat see now who shal telle another tale.
For trewely the game is wel bigonne.
Now telleth ye, sire Monk, if that ye conne,°
Somwhat to quite° with the Knightes tale."
  The Millere, that for dronken° was al pale,
So that unnethe° upon his hors he sat,
He nolde avalen° neither hood ne hat,
Ne abiden no man for his curteisye,
But in Pilates vois° he gan to crye,
And swoor, "By armes° and by blood and bones,
I can° a noble tale for the nones,
With which I wol now quite the Knightes tale."
  Oure Hoste sawgh that he was dronke of ale,
And saide, "Abide, Robin, leve° brother,
Som bettre man shal telle us first another.
Abide, and lat us werken thriftily." °
  "By Goddes soule," quod he, "that wol nat I,
For I wol speke or elles go my way."
  Oure Host answerde, "Tel on, a devele way!°
Thou art a fool; thy wit is overcome."

2. **route,** group. 4. **drawen,** recall. 5. **namely,** especially; **gentils,** gentle folk. 6. **lough,** laughed; **So . . . goon,** so might I walk. 7. **male,** pouch. 10. **conne,** can. 11. **quite,** repay. 12. **dronken,** i.e., drunkenness. 13. **unnethe,** with difficulty. 14. **avalen,** doff. 16. **Pilates vois,** the harsh voice traditionally associated with Pontius Pilate in the mystery plays. 17. **By armes,** i.e., by God's arms. 18. **can,** know. 21. **leve,** dear. 23. **thriftily,** with propriety. 26. **a . . . way,** i.e., in the devil's name.

"Now herkneth," quod the Millere, "alle and some.°
But first I make a protestacioun°
That I am dronke: I knowe it by my soun.°
And therfore if that I mis°speke or saye,
Wite it° the ale of Southwerk, I you praye;
For I wol telle a legende and a lif
Bothe of a carpenter and of his wif,
How that a clerk hath set the wrightes° cappe."
The Reeve answerde and saide, "Stint thy clappe!°
Lat be thy lewed dronken harlotrye.°
It is a sinne and eek a greet folye
To apairen° any man or him defame,
And eek to bringen wives in swich fame.°
Thou maist ynough of othere thinges sayn."
This dronken Millere spak ful soone again,
And saide, "Leve° brother Osewold,
Who hath no wif, he is no cokewold.°
But I saye nat therfore that thou art oon.
Ther ben ful goode wives many oon,
And evere a thousand goode ayains oon badde.
That knowestou wel thyself but if thou madde.°
Why artou angry with my tale now?
I have a wif, pardee, as wel as thou,
Yet nolde I, for the oxen in my plough,
Take upon me more than ynough
As deemen of myself that I were oon:
I wol bileve wel that I am noon.
An housbonde shal nought been inquisitif
Of Goddes privetee,° nor of his wif.
So he may finde Goddes foison° there,
Of the remenant needeth nought enquere."°
What sholde I more sayn but this Millere

28. **alle and some,** each and every one. 29. **protestacioun,** public affirmation. 30. **soun,** tone of voice. 31. **mis,** amiss. 32. **Wite it,** blame it on. 35. To set a cap is to make a fool of; **wrightes,** carpenter's. 36. **Stint,** stop; **clappe,** chatter. 37. **lewed,** ignorant; **harlotrye,** obscenity. 39. **apairen,** injure. 40. **fame,** report. 43. **leve,** dear. 44. **cokewold,** cuckold. 48. **madde,** rave. 56. **privetee,** secrets. 57. **So,** provided that; **foison,** plenty. 58. **enquere,** inquire.

He nolde his wordes for no man forbere,
But tolde his cherles tale in his manere.
M'athinketh° that I shal reherce it here,
And therfore every gentil wight I praye,
Deemeth nought, for Goddes love, that I saye
Of yvel entente, but for° I moot reherse
Hir tales alle, be they bet° or werse,
Or elles falsen° som of my matere.
And therfore, whoso list it nought yheere
Turne over the leef, and chese° another tale,
For he shal finde ynowe,° grete and smale,
Of storial thing that toucheth gentilesse,°
And eek moralitee and holinesse:
Blameth nought me if that ye chese amis.
The Millere is a cherl, ye knowe wel this,
So was the Reeve eek, and othere mo,
And harlotrye° they tolden bothe two.
Aviseth you,° and putte me out of blame:
And eek men shal nought maken ernest of game.

The Tale

Whilom° ther was dwelling at Oxenforde
A riche gnof that gestes heeld to boorde,°
And of his craft he was a carpenter.
With him ther was dwelling a poore scoler,
Hadde lerned art, but al his fantasye°
Was turned for to lere° astrologye,
And coude a certain of conclusiouns,
To deemen by interrogaciouns,°

63. **M'athinketh,** I regret. 65. **for,** because. 66. **bet,** better. 67. **falsen,** falsify. 69. **chese,** choose. 70. **ynowe,** enough. 71. **storial,** historical, i.e., true; **gentilesse,** gentility. 76. **harlotrye,** ribaldry. 77. **Aviseth you,** take heed.

1. **Whilom,** once upon a time. 2. **gnof,** boor; **gestes . . . boorde,** i.e., took in boarders. 5. **Hadde . . . art,** who had completed the first stage of university education, the trivium; **fantasye,** i.e., intellectual interest. 6. **lere,** learn. 7–8. And he knew a number of propositions by which to judge in astrological analyses.

If that men axed him in certain houres
Whan that men sholde have droughte or elles showres,
Or if men axed° him what shal bifalle
Of every thing—I may nat rekene hem alle.
  This clerk was cleped hende° Nicholas.
Of derne love he coude, and of solas,°
And therto he was sly and ful privee,°
And lik a maide meeke for to see.
A chambre hadde he in that hostelrye
Allone, withouten any compaignye,°
Ful fetisly ydight with herbes swoote,°
And he himself as sweete as is the roote
Of licoris or any setewale.°
His Almageste° and bookes grete and smale,
His astrelabye, longing for° his art,
His augrim stones,° layen faire apart
On shelves couched° at his beddes heed;
His presse ycovered with a falding reed;°
And al above ther lay a gay sautrye,°
On which he made a-nightes melodye
So swetely that al the chambre roong,°
And *Angelus ad Virginem*° he soong,
And after that he soong the *Kinges Note*:°
Ful often blessed was his merye throte.
And thus this sweete clerk his time spente
After° his freendes finding and his rente.
  This carpenter hadde wedded newe° a wif
Which that he loved more than his lif.
Of eighteteene yeer she was of age;
Jalous he was, and heeld hire narwe in cage,

11. axed, asked. **13. cleped,** called; **hende,** handy, sly, attractive. **14. derne,** secret; **solas,** i.e., pleasurable practices. **15. privee,** secretive. **18.** Cf. Knight's Tale, l. 1921. **19. fetisly ydight,** elegantly furnished; **swoote,** sweet. **21. setewale,** setwall, a spice. **22. Almageste,** an astronomical treatise by Ptolemy. **23. astrelabye,** astrolabe, an astronomical instrument; **longing for,** belonging to. **24. augrim stones,** counters used in arithmetic. **25. couched,** set. **26. presse,** storage chest; **falding,** coarse wool; **reed,** red. **27. sautrye,** psaltery. **29. roong,** rang. **30. Angelus . . . Virginem,** the Angel's Address to the Virgin. **31. Kinges Note,** a (popular ?) song. **34. After,** in accordance with; **finding,** provision; **rente,** income. **35. newe,** lately.

For she was wilde and yong, and he was old,
And deemed himself been lik a cokewold.°
He knew nat Caton,° for his wit was rude,
That bad men° sholde wedde his similitude:
Men sholde wedden after hir estat,°
For youthe and elde is often at debat.
But sith that he was fallen in the snare,
He moste endure, as other folk, his care.
   Fair was this yonge wif, and therwithal
As any wesele hir body gent and smal.°
A ceint she wered, barred° al of silk;
A barmcloth° as whit as morne milk
Upon hir lendes, ful of many a gore;°
Whit was hir smok, and broiden° al bifore
And eek bihinde, on hir coler° aboute,
Of° col-blak silk, withinne and eek withoute;
The tapes of hir white voluper°
Were of the same suite of° hir coler;
Hir filet brood° of silk and set ful hye;
And sikerly she hadde a likerous° yë;
Ful smale ypulled° were hir browes two,
And tho were bent, and blake as any slo.°
She was ful more blisful on to see
Than is the newe perejonette° tree,
And softer than the wolle is of a wether;°
And by hir girdel heeng° a purs of lether,
Tasseled with silk and perled with latoun.°
In al this world, to seeken up and down,

40. i.e., And suspected of himself that he was a potential cuckold. **41. Caton,** Dionysius Cato, the supposed author of a book of maxims used in elementary education. **42. bad,** commanded that; **men,** one. **43. estat,** condition. **48. wesele,** weasel; **gent . . . smal,** slender and delicate. **49. ceint,** belt; **wered,** wore; **barred,** with transverse stripes. **50. barmcloth,** apron. **51. lendes,** loins; **gore,** strip of cloth. **52. smok,** undergarment; **broiden,** embroidered. **53. coler,** collar. **54. Of,** with. **55. tapes,** ribbons; **voluper,** cap. **56. suite of,** i.e., pattern as. **57. filet,** headband; **brood,** broad. **58. sikerly,** certainly; **likerous,** wanton. **59. smale,** delicately; **ypulled,** plucked. **60. bent,** arching; **slo,** sloeberry. **62. perejonette,** pear. **63. wolle,** wool; **wether,** ram. **64. girdel,** belt; **heeng,** hung. **65. perled . . . latoun,** i.e., with brassy spangles on it.

Ther nis no man so wis that coude thenche°
So gay a popelote° or swich a wenche.
Ful brighter was the shining of hir hewe
Than in the Towr the noble° yforged newe.
But of hir song, it was as loud and yerne°
As any swalwe sitting on a berne.°
Therto she coude skippe and make game°
As any kide or calf folwing his dame.
Hir mouth was sweete as bragot or the meeth,°
Or hoord of apples laid in hay or heeth.°
Winsing she was as is a joly° colt,
Long as a mast, and upright as a bolt.°
A brooch she bar upon hir lowe coler
As brood as is the boos of a bokeler;°
Hir shoes were laced on hir legges hye.
She was a primerole, a piggesnye,°
For any lord to leggen° in his bedde,
Or yet for any good yeman to wedde.
  Now sire, and eft° sire, so bifel the cas
That on a day this hende Nicholas
Fil with this yonge wif to rage° and playe,
Whil that hir housbonde was at Oseneye°
(As clerkes been ful subtil and ful quainte),°
And prively he caughte hire by the queinte,°
And saide, "Ywis, but if ich° have my wille,
For derne love of thee, lemman, I spille,"°
And heeld hire harde by the haunche-bones,
And saide, "Lemman,° love me al atones,
Or I wol dien, also° God me save."
And she sproong as a colt dooth in a trave,°
And with hir heed she wried° faste away;

67. **thenche,** imagine. 68. **popelote,** doll. 70. **Towr,** Tower of London; **noble,** gold coin. 71. **yerne,** lively. 72. **berne,** barn. 73. **make game,** play. 75. **bragot, meeth,** honey-drinks. 76. **heeth,** heather. 77. **Winsing,** skittish; **joly,** high-spirited. 78. **upright,** straight; **bolt,** arrow. 80. **boos,** boss; **bokeler,** shield. 82. **primerole,** cowslip; **piggesnye,** pig's eye. 83. **leggen,** lay. 85. **eft,** again. 87. **Fil,** happened; **rage,** flirt. 88. **Oseneye,** town near Oxford. 89. **quainte,** clever. 90. **queinte,** pudendum. 91. **ich,** I. 92. **derne,** secret; **spille,** die. 94. **Lemman,** mistress. 95. **also,** so. 96. **sproong,** sprang; **trave,** frame for a restive horse. 97. **wried,** twisted.

She saide, "I wol nat kisse thee, by my fay.°
Why, lat be," quod she, "lat be, Nicholas!
Or I wol crye 'Out, harrow, and allas!'
Do way youre handes, for your curteisye!"
  This Nicholas gan mercy for to crye,
And spak so faire, and profred him° so faste,
That she hir love him graunted atte laste,
And swoor hir ooth by Saint Thomas of Kent
That she wolde been at his comandement,
Whan that she may hir leiser° wel espye.
"Myn housbonde is so ful of jalousye
That but ye waite° wel and been privee,
I woot right wel I nam but deed," quod she.
"Ye moste been ful derne as in this cas."
  "Nay, therof care thee nought," quod Nicholas.
"A clerk hadde litherly biset his while,°
But if he coude a carpenter bigile."
And thus they been accorded and ysworn
To waite° a time, as I have told biforn.
Whan Nicholas hadde doon this everydeel,
And thakked hire upon the lendes° weel,
He kiste hire sweete, and taketh his sautrye,
And playeth faste, and maketh melodye.
  Thanne fil° it thus, that to the parissh chirche,
Cristes owene werkes for to wirche,°
This goode wif wente on an haliday:°
Hir forheed shoon as bright as any day,
So was it wasshen whan she leet° hir werk.
  Now was ther of that chirche a parissh clerk,
The which that was ycleped° Absolon:
Crul° was his heer, and as the gold it shoon,
And strouted as a fanne° large and brode;

98. **fay,** faith. 103. **profred him,** i.e., pushed himself. 107. **leiser,** i.e., opportunity. 109. **waite,** be on guard. 113. **litherly biset,** poorly employed; **while,** time. 116. **waite,** watch for. 118. **thakked,** patted; **lendes,** loins. 121. **fil,** befell. 122. **wirche,** perform. 123. **haliday,** holy day. 125. **leet,** left. 127. **ycleped,** called. 128. **Crul,** curly. 129. **strouted,** spread out; **fanne,** wide-mouthed basket for separating grain from chaff.

Ful straight and evene lay his joly shode.
His rode was reed, his yën greye as goos.
With Poules window corven on his shoos,
In hoses rede he wente fetisly.
Yclad he was ful smale and proprely,
Al in a kirtel of a light waget—
Ful faire and thikke been the pointes set—
And therupon he hadde a gay surplis,
As whit as is the blosme upon the ris.
A merye child he was, so God me save.
Wel coude he laten blood, and clippe, and shave,
And maken a chartre of land, or acquitaunce;
In twenty manere coude he trippe and daunce
After the scole of Oxenforde tho,
And with his legges casten to and fro,
And playen songes on a smal rubible;
Therto he soong somtime a loud quinible,
And as wel coude he playe on a giterne:
In al the town nas brewhous ne taverne
That he ne visited with his solas,
Ther any gailard tappestere was.
But sooth to sayn, he was somdeel squaimous
Of farting, and of speeche daungerous.
  This Absolon, that joly was and gay,
Gooth with a cencer on the haliday,
Cencing the wives of the parissh faste,
And many a lovely look on hem he caste,
And namely on this carpenteres wif:
To looke on hire him thoughte a merye lif.

130. **shode,** parting of the hair. 131. **rode,** complexion; **goos,** goose. 132. **Poules window,** St. Paul's window, intricate tooled designs; **corven,** cut. 133. **hoses,** stockings; **fetisly,** elegantly. 134. **smale,** finely. 135. **kirtel,** tunic; **waget,** light blue. 136. **pointes,** laces for fastening the tunic and holding up the hose. 137. **surplis,** surplice. 138. **ris,** bough. 139. **child,** lad. 140. **laten,** let. 141. **acquitaunce,** legal release. 144. **casten,** prance. 145. **rubible,** fiddle. 146. **quinible,** part requiring a very high voice. 147. **giterne,** guitar. 149. **solas,** entertainment. 150. **gailard tappestere,** gay barmaid. 151. **squaimous,** squeamish. 152. **daungerous,** fastidious. 153. **joly,** pretty, amorous. 154. **cencer,** incense-burner. 157. **namely,** especially.

She was so propre and sweete and likerous,
I dar wel sayn, if she hadde been a mous,
And he a cat, he wolde hire hente anoon.
This parissh clerk, this joly Absolon,
Hath in his herte swich a love-longinge
That of no wif ne took he noon offringe—
For curteisye he saide he wolde noon.
The moone, whan it was night, ful brighte shoon,
And Absolon his giterne hath ytake—
For paramours he thoughte for to wake—
And forth he gooth, jolif and amorous,
Til he cam to the carpenteres hous,
A litel after cokkes hadde ycrowe,
And dressed him up by a shot-windowe
That was upon the carpenteres wal.
He singeth in his vois gentil and smal,
"Now dere lady, if thy wille be,
I praye you that ye wol rewe on me,"
Ful wel accordant to his giterninge.
This carpenter awook and herde him singe,
And spak unto his wif, and saide anoon,
"What, Alison, heerestou nought Absolon
That chaunteth thus under oure bowres wal?"
And she answerde hir housbonde therwithal,
"Yis, God woot, John, I heere it everydeel."
  This passeth forth. What wol ye bet than weel?
Fro day to day this joly Absolon
So woweth hire that him is wo-bigoon:
He waketh al the night and al the day;
He kembed his lokkes brode and made him gay;
He woweth hire by menes and brocage,

159. **propre,** neat; **likerous,** wanton, appetizing. 161. **hente,** pounce on. 163. **love-longing,** love-sickness. 166. **shoon,** shone. 167. **giterne,** guitar. 168. **paramours,** love. 169. **jolif,** pretty. 172. **dressed . . . up,** took his position; **shot-windowe,** hinged window. 174. **smal,** dainty. 176. **rewe,** have pity. 177. **accordant to,** in harmony with; **giterninge,** guitar-playing. 181. **bowres,** bedroom's. 184. **bet,** better; **weel,** well. 186. **woweth,** woos. 188. **kembed,** combed; **brode,** i.e., wide-spreading. 189. **menes,** intermediaries; **brocage,** mediation.

And swoor he wolde been hir owene page;°
He singeth, brokking° as a nightingale;
He sente hire piment, meeth,° and spiced ale,
And wafres piping hoot out of the gleede;°
And for she was of towne, he profred meede—
For som folk wol be wonnen for richesse,
And som for strokes,° and som for gentilesse.
Somtime to shewe his lightnesse and maistrye,°
He playeth Herodes upon a scaffold° hye.
But what availeth him as in this cas?
She loveth so this hende Nicholas
That Absolon may blowe the bukkes horn;°
He ne hadde for his labour but a scorn.
And thus she maketh Absolon hir ape,°
And al his ernest turneth til a jape.°
Ful sooth is this proverbe, it is no lie;
Men saith right thus: "Alway the nye slye°
Maketh the ferre leve to be loth."°
For though that Absolon be wood° or wroth,
By cause that he fer was from hir sighte,
This nye° Nicholas stood in his lighte.
  Now beer° thee wel, thou hende Nicholas,
For Absolon may waile and singe allas.
  And so bifel it on a Saterday
This carpenter was goon til Oseney,
And hende Nicholas and Alisoun
Accorded been to this conclusioun,
That Nicholas shal shapen hem a wile°
This sely° jalous housbonde to bigile,
And if so be this game wente aright,

190. **page,** personal servant. 191. **brokking,** trilling. 192. **piment,** spiced wine; **meeth,** mead. 193. **wafres,** pastries; **gleede,** coals. 194. **for . . . towne,** since she was a town woman; **meede,** bribe. 196. **strokes,** blows. 197. **lightnesse,** facility; **maistrye,** virtuosity. 198. **Herodes,** Herod, a role traditionally played as a bully in the mystery plays; **scaffold,** platform, stage. 201. To blow the buck's horn is to go without reward. 203. To make some one an ape is to make a fool of him. 204. **jape,** joke. 206. **nye slye,** the sly man at hand. 207. **ferre leve,** distant dear one; **loth,** hated. 208. **wood,** furious. 210. **nye,** near-by. 211. **beer,** bear. 217. **shapen,** arrange; **wile,** trick. 218. **sely,** "poor innocent."

She sholden sleepen in his arm al night—
For this was his desir and hire° also.
And right anoon, withouten wordes mo,
This Nicholas no lenger wolde tarye,
But dooth ful softe unto his chambre carye
Bothe mete and drinke for a day or twaye,
And to hir housbonde bad hire for to saye,
If that he axed after Nicholas,
She sholde saye she niste° wher he was—
Of al that day she sawgh him nought with yë:
She trowed° that he was in maladye,
For for no cry hir maide coude him calle,
He nolde answere for no thing that mighte falle.°
  This passeth forth al thilke° Saterday
That Nicholas stille in his chambre lay,
And eet, and sleep, or dide what him leste,°
Til Sonday that the sonne gooth to reste.
  This sely carpenter hath greet mervaile
Of Nicholas, or what thing mighte him aile,
And saide, "I am adrad,° by Saint Thomas,
It stondeth nat aright with Nicholas.
God shilde° that he deide sodeinly!
This world is now ful tikel,° sikerly:
I sawgh today a corps yborn to chirche
That now a Monday last I sawgh him wirche.°
Go up," quod he unto his knave° anoon,
"Clepe at his dore or knokke with a stoon.°
Looke how it is and tel me boldely."
  This knave gooth him up ful sturdily,
And at the chambre dore whil that he stood
He cride and knokked as that he were wood,°
"What? How? What do ye, maister Nicholay?
How may ye sleepen al the longe day?".
But al for nought: he herde nat a word.

221. **hire,** hers. 228. **niste,** didn't know. 230. **trowed,** believed. 232. **falle,** happen. 233. **thilke,** this. 235. **eet . . . sleep,** ate and slept; **him leste,** he wanted. 239. **adrad,** afraid. 241. **shilde,** forbid. 242. **tikel,** changeable. 244. **a,** on; **wirche,** work. 245. **knave,** manservant. 246. **Clepe,** call; **stoon,** stone. 250. **wood,** mad.

An hole he foond ful lowe upon a boord,
Ther as the cat was wont in for to creepe,
And at that hole he looked in ful deepe,
And atte laste he hadde of him a sighte.
  This Nicholas sat evere caping uprighte
As he hadde kiked on the newe moone.
Adown he gooth and tolde his maister soone
In what array he saw this ilke man.
  This carpenter to blessen him bigan,
And saide, "Help us, Sainte Frideswide!
A man woot litel what him shal bitide.
This man is falle, with his astromye,
In som woodnesse or in som agonye.
I thoughte ay wel how that it sholde be:
Men sholde nought knowe of Goddes privetee.
Ye, blessed be alway a lewed man
That nought but only his bileve can.
So ferde another clerk with astromye:
He walked in the feeldes for to prye
Upon the sterres, what ther sholde bifalle,
Til he was in a marle-pit yfalle—
He saw nat that. But yet, by Saint Thomas,
Me reweth sore for hende Nicholas.
He shal be rated of his studying,
If that I may, by Jesus, hevene king!
Get me a staf that I may underspore,
Whil that thou, Robin, hevest up the dore.
He shal out of his studying, as I gesse."
And to the chambre dore he gan him dresse.
His knave was a strong carl for the nones,
And by the haspe he haaf it up atones:

258. **caping,** gaping. 259. **kiked,** gazed. 261. **array,** condition; **ilke,** same. 262. **blessen him,** cross himself. 265. **astromye,** illiterate form of **astronomye.** 266. **woodnesse,** madness. 269. **lewed,** ignorant. 270. **bileve,** creed; **can,** knows. 271. **ferde,** fared. 273. **sterres,** stars. 274. **marle-pit,** pit from which a fertilizing clay is dug. 276. **Me . . . for,** I sorely pity. 277. **rated of,** scolded for. 279. **underspore,** pry up. 280. **hevest,** heave. 281. **shal,** i.e., shall come. 282. **gan . . . dresse,** took his stand. 283. **carl,** fellow; **nones,** purpose. 284. **haaf,** heaved.

Into the floor the dore fil° anoon.
This Nicholas sat ay as stille as stoon,
And evere caped up into the air.
This carpenter wende° he were in despair,
And hente° him by the shuldres mightily,
And shook him harde, and cride spitously,°
"What, Nicholay, what, how! What! Looke adown!
Awaak and thenk on Cristes passioun!°
I crouche thee from elves and fro wightes."°
Therwith the nightspel° saide he anoonrightes
On foure halves of the hous aboute,
And on the thresshfold° on the dore withoute:
"Jesu Crist and Sainte Benedight,°
Blesse this hous from every wikked wight!
For nightes nerye the White Pater Noster.°
Where wentestou, thou Sainte Petres soster?"°
And at the laste this hende Nicholas
Gan for to sike° sore, and saide, "Allas,
Shal al the world be lost eftsoones° now?"
  This carpenter answerde, "What saistou?
What, thenk on God as we doon, men that swinke."°
  This Nicholas answerde, "Fecche me drinke,
And after wol I speke in privetee
Of certain thing that toucheth me and thee.
I wol telle it noon other man, certain."
  This carpenter gooth down and comth again,
And broughte of mighty ale a large quart,
And whan that eech of hem hadde dronke his part,
This Nicholas his dore faste shette,°
And down the carpenter by him he sette,
And saide, "John, myn hoste lief° and dere,
Thou shalt upon thy trouthe° swere me here

285. **Into,** on; **fil,** fell. 288. **wende,** thought. 289. **hente,** seized. 290. **spitously,** roughly. 292. **passioun,** i.e., the crucifixion. 293. **crouche,** make the sign of the cross on; **wightes,** wicked creatures. 294. **nightspel,** night-charm. 296. **thresshfold,** threshold. 297. **Benedight,** Benedict. 299. **nerye,** defend (us); **the . . . Noster,** the White Lord's Prayer: this personification was considered a powerful beneficent spirit. 300. **soster,** sister. 302. **sike,** sigh. 303. **eftsoones,** a second time. 305. **swinke,** work. 313. **shette,** shut. 315. **lief,** beloved. 316. **trouthe,** word of honor.

That to no wight thou shalt this conseil wraye;
For it is Cristes conseil that I saye,
And if thou telle it man, thou art forlore,
For this vengeance thou shalt have therfore,
That if thou wraye me, thou shalt be wood."
"Nay, Crist forbede it, for his holy blood,"
Quod tho this sely man. "I nam no labbe,
And though I saye, I nam nat lief to gabbe.
Say what thou wilt, I shal it nevere telle
To child ne wif, by him that harwed helle."
"Now John," quod Nicholas, "I wol nought lie.
I have yfounde in myn astrologye,
As I have looked in the moone bright,
That now a Monday next, at quarter night,
Shal falle a rain, and that so wilde and wood,
That half so greet was nevere Noees flood.
This world," he saide, "in lasse than an hour
Shal al be dreint, so hidous is the showr.
Thus shal mankinde drenche and lese hir lif."
This carpenter answerde, "Allas, my wif!
And shal she drenche? Allas, myn Alisoun!"
For sorwe of this he fil almost adown,
And saide, "Is there no remedye in this cas?"
"Why yis, for Gode," quod hende Nicholas,
"If thou wolt werken after lore and reed—
Thou maist nought werken after thyn owene heed;
For thus saith Salomon that was ful trewe,
'Werk al by conseil and thou shalt nought rewe.'
And if thou werken wolt by good conseil,
I undertake, withouten mast or sail,
Yet shal I save hire and thee and me.

317. conseil, secret; **wraye,** disclose. **319. man,** to any one; **forlore,** lost. **321. be wood,** go mad. **323. sely,** innocent; **labbe;** blabbermouth. **324.** And though I say it myself, I don't like to gossip. **326. him . . . helle,** him that despoiled hell, i.e., Christ. **330. quarter night,** i.e., shortly before dawn. **331. wood,** furious. **332. Noees,** Noah's. **333. lasse,** less. **334. dreint,** drowned. **335. drenche,** drown; **lese,** lose. **338. fil almost,** almost fell. **340. for,** i.e., by. **341. werken after,** act according to; **lore . . . reed,** learning and advice. **342. heed,** head. **344. rewe,** be sorry.

Hastou nat herd how saved was Noee
Whan that Oure Lord hadde warned him biforn
That al the world with water sholde be lorn?"°
"Yis," quod this carpenter, "ful yore ago."
"Hastou nat herd," quod Nicholas, "also
The sorwe of Noee with his felaweshipe?
Er that he mighte gete his wif to shipe,
Him hadde levere,° I dar wel undertake,
At thilke time than alle his wetheres° blake
That she hadde had a ship hirself allone.
And therfore woostou° what is best to doone?
This axeth haste, and of an hastif° thing
Men may nought preche or maken tarying.
Anoon go gete us faste into this in°
A kneeding trough or elles a kimelin°
For eech of us, but looke that they be large,°
In whiche we mowen swimme as in a barge,°
And han therinne vitaile suffisaunt°
But for a day—fy° on the remenaunt!
The water shal aslake° and goon away
Aboute prime° upon the nexte day.
But Robin may nat wite° of this, thy knave,
Ne eek thy maide Gille I may nat save.
Axe nought why, for though thou axe me,
I wol nought tellen Goddes privetee.
Suffiseth thee, but if thy wittes madde,°
To han° as greet a grace as Noee hadde.
Thy wif shal I wel saven, out of doute.
Go now thy way, and speed thee heraboute.
But whan thou hast for hire° and thee and me
Ygeten us thise kneeding-tubbes three,

350. **lorn,** lost. 355. **Him . . . levere,** he had rather. 356. **wetheres,** rams: i.e., he'd have given all the rams he had. 357. Noah's wife's reluctance to board the Ark is a traditional comic theme in the mystery plays. 358. **woostou,** do you know. 359. **axeth,** requires; **hastif,** urgent. 361. **in,** lodging. 362. **kimelin,** brewing-tub. 363. **large,** wide. 364. **mowen,** can; **swimme,** float; **barge,** vessel. 365. **vitaile suffisaunt,** sufficient victuals. 366. **fy,** fie. 367. **aslake,** diminish. 368. **prime,** 9 A.M. 369. **wite,** know. 373. **madde,** go mad. 374. **han,** have. 377. **hire,** her.

Thanne shaltou hangen hem in the roof ful hye,
That no man of oure purveyance° espye.
And whan thou thus hast doon as I have said,
And hast oure vitaile faire in hem ylaid,
And eek an ax to smite the corde atwo,
Whan that the water comth that we may go,
And broke an hole an heigh° upon the gable
Unto the gardinward,° over the stable,
That we may freely passen forth oure way,
Whan that the grete showr is goon away,
Thanne shaltou swimme as merye, I undertake,
As dooth the white doke° after hir drake.
Thanne wol I clepe,° 'How, Alison? How, John?
Be merye, for the flood wol passe anoon.'
And thou wolt sayn, 'Hail, maister Nicholay!
Good morwe, I see thee wel, for it is day!'
And thanne shal we be lordes al oure lif
Of al the world, as Noee and his wif.
But of oo thing I warne thee ful right:
Be wel avised on that ilke night
That we been entred into shippes boord
That noon of us ne speke nought a word,
Ne clepe, ne crye, but been in his prayere,
For it is Goddes owene heeste dere.°
Thy wif and thou mote hange fer atwinne,°
For that bitwixe you shal be no sinne—
Namore in looking than ther shal in deede.
This ordinance is said: go, God thee speede.
Tomorwe at night whan men been alle asleepe,
Into oure kneeding-tubbes wol we creepe,
And sitten there, abiding Goddes grace.
Go now thy way, I have no lenger space°
To make of this no lenger sermoning.
Men sayn thus: 'Send the wise and say no thing.'

380. purveyance, foresight. **385. an heigh,** on high. **386. Unto . . . gardinward,** toward the garden. **390. doke,** duck. **391. clepe,** call. **402. heeste dere,** precious command. **403. fer atwinne,** far apart. **410. space,** time.

Thou art so wis it needeth thee nat teche:
Go save oure lif, and that I thee biseeche."
This sely carpenter gooth forth his way:
Ful ofte he saide allas and wailaway,
And to his wif he tolde his privetee,
And she was war, and knew it bet° than he,
What al this quainte cast was for to saye.°
But nathelees she ferde° as she wolde deye,
And saide, "Allas, go forth thy way anoon.
Help us to scape,° or we been dede eechoon.
I am thy trewe verray wedded wif:
Go, dere spouse, and help to save oure lif."
Lo, which a greet thing is affeccioun!°
Men may dien of imaginacioun,
So deepe° may impression be take.
This sely carpenter biginneth quake;
Him thinketh verrailiche° that he may see
Noees flood come walwing° as the see
To drenchen° Alison, his hony dere.
He weepeth, waileth, maketh sory cheere;
He siketh with ful many a sory swough,°
And gooth and geteth him a kneeding-trough,
And after a tubbe and a kimelin,
And prively he sente hem to his in,°
And heeng° hem in the roof in privetee;
His° owene hand he made laddres three,
To climben by the ronges and the stalkes°
Unto the tubbes hanging in the balkes,°
And hem vitailed,° bothe trough and tubbe,
With breed and cheese and good ale in a jubbe,°
Suffising right ynough as for a day.
But er that he hadde maad al this array,

418. **war,** aware; **bet,** better. 419. **cast,** trick; **saye,** mean. 420. **ferde,** acted. 422. **scape,** escape. 425. **affeccioun,** emotion. 427. **deepe,** deeply. 429. **verrailiche,** truly. 430. **walwing,** rolling. 431. **drenchen,** drown. 433. **siketh,** sighs; **swough,** breath. 436. **in,** dwelling. 437. **heeng,** hung. 438. **His,** i.e., with his. 439. **ronges,** rungs; **stalkes,** uprights. 440. **balkes,** rafters. 441. **vitailed,** victualed. 442. **jubbe,** jug.

He sente his knave, and eek his wenche also,
Upon his neede° to London for to go.
And on the Monday whan it drow to° nighte,
He shette° his dore withouten candel-lighte,
And dressed° alle thing as it sholde be,
And shortly up they clomben° alle three.
They seten stille wel a furlong way.°
"Now, Pater Noster, clum,"° saide Nicholay,
And "Clum" quod John, and "Clum" saide Alisoun.
This carpenter saide his devocioun,
And stille he sit° and biddeth his prayere,
Awaiting on the rain, if he it heere.°
The dede sleep, for wery bisinesse,
Fil° on this carpenter right as I gesse
Aboute corfew time,° or litel more.
For travailing of his gost° he groneth sore,
And eft he routeth,° for his heed mislay.
Down of the laddre stalketh Nicholay,
And Alison ful softe adown she spedde:
Withouten wordes mo they goon to bedde
Ther as the carpenter is wont to lie.
Ther was the revel and the melodye,
And thus lith° Alison and Nicholas
In bisinesse of mirthe and of solas,
Til that the belle of Laudes° gan to ringe,
And freres in the chauncel° gonne singe.
This parissh clerk, this amorous Absolon,
That is for love alway so wo-bigoon,
Upon the Monday was at Oseneye,
With compaignye him to disporte and playe,
And axed upon caas a cloisterer°

446. Upon his neede, on an errand for John. **447. drow to,** drew toward. **448. shette,** shut. **449. dressed,** arranged. **450. clomben,** climbed. **451. seten,** sat; **a . . . way,** the time it takes to go a furlong. **452. clum,** ? hush. **455. sit,** sits. **456. heere,** might hear. **458. Fil,** fell. **459. corfew time,** probably about 8 P.M. **460. travailing,** affliction; **gost,** spirit. **461. eft,** then; **routeth,** snores. **467. lith,** lies. **469. Laudes,** the first church service of the day. **470. chauncel,** chancel. **475. upon caas,** by chance; **cloisterer,** member of the religious order.

Ful prively after John the carpenter;
And he drow him apart out of the chirche,
And saide, "I noot: I sawgh him here nought wirche°
Sith Saterday. I trowe that he be went
For timber ther oure abbot hath him sent.
For he is wont for timber for to go,
And dwellen atte grange° a day or two.
Or elles he is at his hous, certain.
Where that he be I can nought soothly sayn."
  This Absolon ful jolif was and light,°
And thoughte, "Now is time to wake al night,
For sikerly,° I sawgh him nought stiringe
Aboute his dore sin day bigan to springe.
So mote° I thrive, I shal at cokkes crowe
Ful prively knokken at his windowe
That stant ful lowe upon his bowres° wal.
To Alison now wol I tellen al
My love-longing,° for yet I shal nat misse
That at the leeste way° I shal hire kisse.
Som manere confort shal I have, parfay.°
My mouth hath icched al this longe day:
That is a signe of kissing at the leeste.
Al night me mette° eek I was at a feeste.
Therfore I wol go sleepe an hour or twaye,
And al the night thanne wol I wake and playe."
  Whan that the firste cok hath crowe, anoon
Up rist° this joly lovere Absolon,
And him arrayeth gay at point devis.°
But first he cheweth grain° and licoris,
To smellen sweete, er he hadde kembd° his heer.
Under his tonge a trewe-love he beer,°

478. **noot**, don't know; **wirche**, work. 482. **grange**, the outlying farm. 485. **jolif . . . light**, amorous and gay. 487. **sikerly**, certainly. 489. **mote**, may. 491. **stant**, stands; **bowres**, bower's, bedroom's. 493. **love-longing**, love-sickness. 494. **leeste way**, i.e., least. 495. **parfay**, in faith. 498. **me mette**, I dreamed. 502. **rist**, rises. 503. **at . . . devis**, to perfection. 504. **grain**, grain of Paradise, a spice. 505. **kembd**, combed. 506. **trewe-love**, sprig of a clover-like plant; **beer**, bore.

For therby wende he to be gracious.°
He rometh° to the carpenteres hous,
And stille he stant° under the shot-windowe—
Unto his brest it raughte,° it was so lowe—
And ofte he cougheth with a semisoun.°
"What do ye, hony-comb, sweete Alisoun,
My faire brid,° my sweete cinamome?
Awaketh, lemman° myn, and speketh to me.
Wel litel thinken ye upon my wo
That for your love I swete° ther I go.
No wonder is though that I swelte° and swete:
I moorne as dooth a lamb after the tete.°
Ywis, lemman, I have swich love-longinge,
That lik a turtle° trewe is my moorninge:
I may nat ete namore than a maide."
  "Go fro the windowe, Jakke fool," she saide.
"As help me God, it wol nat be com-pa-me.°
I love another, and elles I were to blame,
Wel bet° than thee, by Jesu, Absolon.
Go forth thy way or I wol caste a stoon,
And lat me sleepe, a twenty devele way."°
  "Allas," quod Absolon, "and wailaway,
That trewe love was evere so yvele biset.°
Thanne kis me, sin that it may be no bet,
For Jesus love and for the love of me."
  "Woltou thanne go thy way therwith?" quod she.
  "Ye, certes, lemman," quod this Absolon.
  "Thanne maak thee redy," quod she. "I come anoon."
And unto Nicholas she saide stille,
"Now hust,° and thou shalt laughen al thy fille."
  This Absolon down sette him on his knees,
And saide, "I am a lord at alle degrees,°
For after this I hope ther cometh more.

507. **wende,** supposed; **gracious,** pleasing. 508. **rometh,** strolls. 509. **stant,** stands. 510. **raughte,** reached. 511. **semisoun,** small sound. 513. **brid,** bird or bride. 514. **lemman,** mistress. 516. **swete,** sweat. 517. **swelte,** melt. 518. **tete,** tit. 520. **turtle,** dove. 523. **com-pa-me,** come-kiss-me. 525. **bet,** better. 527. **a . . . way,** in the name of twenty devils. 529. **yvele biset,** ill-used. 536. **hust,** hush. 538. **at . . . degrees,** in every way.

Lemman, thy grace, and sweete brid, thyn ore!"
The windowe she undooth, and that in haste.
"Have do," quod she, "com of and speed thee faste,
Lest that oure neighebores thee espye."
This Absolon gan wipe his mouth ful drye:
Derk was the night as pich or as the cole,
And at the windowe out she putte hir hole,
And Absolon, him fil no bet ne wers,
But with his mouth he kiste hir naked ers,
Ful savourly, er he were war of this.
Abak he sterte, and thoughte it was amis,
For wel he wiste a womman hath no beerd.
He felte a thing al rough and longe yherd,
And saide, "Fy, allas, what have I do?"
"Teehee," quod she, and clapte the windowe to.
And Absolon gooth forth a sory pas.
"A beerd, a beerd!" quod hende Nicholas,
"By Goddes corpus, this gooth faire and weel."
This sely Absolon herde everydeel,
And on his lippe he gan for anger bite,
And to himself he saide, "I shal thee quite."
Who rubbeth now, who froteth now his lippes
With dust, with sond, with straw, with cloth, with chippes,
But Absolon, that saith ful ofte allas?
"My soule bitake I unto Satanas,
But me were levere than all this town," quod he,
"Of this despit awroken for to be.
Allas," quod he, "allas I ne hadde ybleint!"
His hote love was cold and al yqueint,
For fro that time that he hadde kist hir ers
Of paramours he sette nought a kers,
For he was heled of his maladye.

540. **ore,** mercy. 547. **him fil,** it befell him; **bet . . . wers,** better or worse. 549. **savourly,** with relish. 550. **sterte,** started. 552. **yherd,** haired. 555. **a . . . pas,** i.e., walking sadly. 557. **corpus,** body. 560. **quite,** repay. 561. **froteth,** wipes. 562. **sond,** sand. 564. **bitake,** commit; **Satanas,** Satan. 565. **me . . . levere,** I had rather. 566. **despit,** insult; **awroken,** avenged. 567. **ybleint,** turned aside. 568. **yqueint,** quenched. 570. He didn't care a piece of cress for woman's love.

Ful ofte paramours he gan defye,
And weep as dooth a child that is ybete.
A softe paas he wente over the streete
Until a smith men clepen daun Gervais,
That in his forge smithed plough harneis:
He sharpeth shaar and cultour bisily.
This Absolon knokketh al esily,
And saide, "Undo, Gervais, and that anoon."
"What, who artou?" "It am I, Absolon."
"What, Absolon? What, Cristes sweete tree!
Why rise ye so rathe? Ey, benedicite,
What aileth you? Som gay girl, God it woot,
Hath brought you thus upon the viritoot.
By Sainte Note, ye woot wel what I mene."
This Absolon ne roughte nat a bene
Of al his play. No word again he yaf:
He hadde more tow on his distaf
Than Gervais knew, and saide, "Freend so dere,
This hote cultour in the chimenee here,
As lene it me: I have therwith to doone.
I wol bringe it thee again ful soone."
Gervais answerde, "Certes, were it gold,
Or in a poke nobles alle untold,
Thou sholdest have, as I am trewe smith.
Ey, Cristes fo, what wol ye do therwith?"
"Therof," quod Absolon, "be as be may.
I shal wel telle it thee another day,"
And caughte the cultour by the colde stele.
Ful softe out at the dore he gan to stele,
And wente unto the carpenteres wal:
He cougheth first and knokketh therwithal

572. **defye,** renounce. 573. **weep,** wept. 574. **softe pass,** i.e., quiet walk. 575. **Until,** to. 576. **harneis,** equipment. 577. **sharpeth,** sharpens; **shaar,** plowshare; **cultour,** coulter, the turf-cutter on a plow. 578. **esily,** quietly. 582. **rathe,** early; **benedicite,** bless me. 584. **viritoot,** i.e., prowl. 586. **ne . . . bene,** didn't care a bean. 588. **more . . . distaf,** i.e., more on his mind. 590. **chiminee,** fireplace. 591. **As lene,** i.e., please lend. 594. **poke,** bag; **nobles,** gold coins; **untold,** uncounted. 596. **fo,** foe, i.e., Satan. 599. stele, handle.

Upon the windowe, right as he dide er.°
  This Alison answerde, "Who is ther
That knokketh so? I warante° it a thief."
  "Why, nay," quod he, "God woot, my sweete lief,°
I am thyn Absolon, my dereling.
Of gold," quod he, "I have thee brought a ring—
My moder yaf it me, so God me save;
Ful fin it is and therto wel ygrave:°
This wol I yiven thee if thou me kisse."
  This Nicholas was risen for to pisse,
And thoughte he wolde amenden al the jape:°
He sholde kisse his ers er that he scape.
And up the windowe dide he hastily,
And out his ers he putteth prively,
Over the buttok to the haunche-boon.
  And therwith spak this clerk, this Absolon,
"Speek, sweete brid, I noot nought wher thou art."
This Nicholas anoon leet flee° a fart
As greet as it hadde been a thonder-dent°
That with the strook he was almost yblent,°
And he was redy with his iren hoot,°
And Nicholas amidde the ers he smoot:°
Of gooth the skin an hande-brede° aboute;
The hote cultour brende so his toute°
That for the smert he wende for to° die;
As he were wood° for wo he gan to crye,
"Help! Water! Water! Help, for Goddes herte!"
  This carpenter out of his slomber sterte,
And herde oon cryen "Water!" as he were wood,
And thoughte, "Allas, now cometh Noweles° flood!"
He sette him up withoute wordes mo,
And with his ax he smoot the corde atwo,

603. **er,** before. 605. **warante,** i.e., wager. 606. **lief,** dear. 610. **ygrave,** engraved. 613. **amenden,** improve on; **jape,** joke. 620. **leet flee,** let fly. 621. **thonder-dent,** thunderbolt. 622. **yblent,** blinded. 623. **hoot,** hot. 624. **smoot,** smote. 625. **hande-brede,** handsbreadth. 626. **toute,** buttocks. 627. **wende . . . to,** thought he would. 628. **wood,** crazy. 632. **Noweles,** John confuses Noah and Nowel.

And down gooth al: he foond neither to selle
Ne breed ne ale til he cam to the celle,°
Upon the floor, and ther aswoune° he lay.
  Up sterte hire° Alison and Nicholay,
And criden "Out" and "Harrow" in the streete.
The neighebores, bothe smale and grete,
In ronnen for to gauren° on this man
That aswoune lay bothe pale and wan,
For with the fal he brosten° hadde his arm;
But stonde he moste unto his owene harm,
For whan he spak he was anoon bore down°
With° hende Nicholas and Alisoun:
They tolden every man that he was wood—
He was agast so of Noweles flood,
Thurgh fantasye, that of his vanitee°
He hadde ybought him kneeding-tubbes three,
And hadde hem hanged in the roof above,
And that he prayed hem, for Goddes love,
To sitten in the roof, *par compaignye*.°
  The folk gan laughen at his fantasye.
Into the roof they kiken and they cape,°
And turned al his harm unto a jape,°
For what so that this carpenter answerde,
It was for nought: no man his reson herde;
With othes grete he was so sworn adown,
That he was holden wood° in al the town,
For every clerk anoonright heeld with other:
They saide, "The man was wood, my leve brother,"
And every wight gan laughen at this strif.°
Thus swived° was the carpenteres wif
For al his keeping° and his jalousye,
And Absolon hath kist hir nether° yë,

635–36. **he . . . celle,** he found time to sell neither bread nor ale until he arrived at the foundation. 637. **aswoune,** in a faint. 638. **sterte hire,** started. 641. **gauren,** gape. 643. **brosten,** broken. 645. **bore down,** refuted. 646. **With,** by. 649. **vanitee,** folly. 653. **par compaignye,** for company's sake. 655. **kiken . . . cape,** peer and gape. 656. **jape,** joke. 660. **holden wood,** considered mad. 663. **strif,** fuss. 664. **swived,** slept with. 665. **keeping,** guarding. 666. **nether,** lower.

And Nicholas is scalded in the toute:
This tale is doon, and God save al the route!

THE REEVE'S TALE

The Introduction

Whan folk hadde laughen at this nice cas°
Of Absolon and hende Nicholas,
Diverse folk diversely they saide,
But for the more part they loughe and playde;°
Ne at his tale I sawgh no man him greve,
But it were only Osewold the Reeve:
By cause he was of carpenteres craft
A litel ire is in his herte ylaft.°
He gan to grucche° and blamed it a lite.
"So theek," quod he, "ful wel coude I thee quite°
With blering of a proud milleres yë,°
If that me liste speke of ribaudye;°
But ik° am old; me list not playe for age:
Gras time is doon, my fodder is now forage;
This white top writeth° mine olde yeres;
Myn herte is also mouled° as mine heres,
But if ik fare as dooth an open-ers:°
That ilke fruit is evere lenger the wers,°
Til it be roten in mullok or in stree.°
We olde men, I drede, so fare we—
Til we be roten can we nought be ripe;
We hoppe° alway whil that the world wol pipe,

1. **nice cas,** foolish incident. 4. **loughe,** laughed; **playde,** i.e., enjoyed themselves. 5. **him greve,** become angry. 8. **ylaft,** left. 9. **grucche,** pout. 10. **So theek,** so might I thrive; **quite,** pay back. 11. To blear an eye is to trick. 12. **me liste,** I wanted to; **ribaudye,** ribaldry. 13. **ik,** I (northern form). 14. **forage,** dry winter food. 15. **writeth,** i.e., indicates. 16. **also,** as; **mouled,** moulded. 17. **But if,** unless; **open-ers,** medlar, a kind of fruit. 18. **evere . . . wers,** always worse and worse. 19. **mullok,** pile of refuse; **stree,** straw. 22. **hoppe,** dance.

For in oure wil ther stiketh evere a nail,°
To have an hoor heed and a greene tail,
As hath a leek; for though oure might be goon,
Oure wil desireth folye evere in oon.°
For whan we may nought doon, thanne wol we speke.
Yit in oure asshen olde is fir yreke.°
Foure gleedes° have we whiche I shal devise:
Avaunting, lying, anger, coveitise.°
Thise foure sparkles longen unto elde.°
Oure olde limes mowe wel been unweelde,°
But wil ne shal nought failen, that is sooth.
And yit I have alway a coltes tooth;°
As many a yeer as it is passed henne°
Sin that my tappe of lif bigan to renne°—
For sikerly, whan ik was bore,° anoon
Deeth drow the tappe of lif and leet° it goon,
And evere sith hath so the tappe yronne,
Til that almost al empty is the tonne:°
The streem of life now droppeth on the chimbe;°
The sely tonge may wel ringe and chimbe°
Of wrecchednesse that passed is ful yore:°
With olde folk save dotage is namore."°
  Whan that oure Host hadde herd this sermoning,
He gan to speke as lordly as a king.
He saide, "What amounteth al this wit?
What, shal we speke al day of Holy Writ?
The devel made a reeve for to preche,
Or of a soutere a shipman or a leeche.°
Say forth thy tale, and tarye nought the time:
Lo, Depeford, and it is halfway prime;°

23. i.e., We're always goaded by a desire. **26. in oon,** continually. **28. yreke,** raked, banked. **29. gleedes,** hot coals. **30. Avaunting,** boasting; **coveitise,** avarice. **31. longen,** belong; **elde,** old age. **32. limes,** limbs; **unweelde,** weak. **34. a . . . tooth,** youthful desires. **35. henne,** hence. **36. renne,** run. **37. bore,** born. **38. drow,** drew; **leet,** let. **40. tonne,** tun. **41. chimbe,** cask-rim. **42. sely,** silly; **chimbe,** chime. **43. yore,** long ago. **44. save . . . namore,** there is nothing left but senility. **50. soutere,** shoemaker; **leeche,** doctor. **52. Depeford,** Deptford, a town close to London; **halfway prime,** 7:30 A.M.

Lo, Grenewich, ther many a shrewe is inne;°
It were al time thy tale to biginne."
"Now, sires," quod this Osewold the Reeve,
"I praye you alle that ye nought you greve
Though I answere and somdeel sette his houve,°
For leveful is with force force of-shouve.°
This dronken Millere hath ytold us heer
How that bigiled was a carpenter—
Paraventure° in scorn, for I am oon.
And by youre leve, I shal him quite anoon;
Right in his cherles termes wol I speke;
I praye to God his nekke mote tobreke°—
He can wel in myn yë seen a stalke,°
But in his owene he can nought seen a balke."°

The Tale

At Trumpington, nat fer fro Cantebrigge,°
Ther gooth a brook and over that a brigge,°
Upon the whiche brook ther stant a melle;°
And this is verray sooth that I you telle.
A millere was ther dwelling many a day—
As any pecok he was proud and gay:
Pipen he coude, and fisshe, and nettes bete,°
And turne coppes, and wel wrastle and shete;°
And by his belt he bar a long panade,°
And of a swerd ful trenchant was the blade;
A joly poppere° bar he in his pouche—
Ther was no man for peril dorste him touche;

53. Lo, Greenwich, where many rascals live: Chaucer lived there for a time. 57. **sette . . . houve,** adjust his cap, i.e., pay back the Miller. 58. For it is legal to repel force with force. 61. **Paraventure,** perhaps. 64. **mote tobreke,** may break. 65. **stalke,** mote. 66. **balke,** beam.

N. B. In the glosses of this tale an asterisk is used to designate northernisms in the speech of the two clerks. 1. **Cantebrigge,** Cambridge. 2. **brigge,** bridge. 3. **stant,** stands; **melle,** mill. 7. **Pipen,** play a bagpipe; **bete,** repair. 8. **turne coppes,** drink bottoms up; **shete,** shoot. 9. **panade,** cutlass. 11. **joly poppere,** short dagger.

A Sheffeld thwitel° bar he in his hose.
Round was his face, and camuse° was his nose;
As piled° as an ape was his skulle.
He was a market-betere atte fulle:°
Ther dorste no wight hand upon him legge°
That he ne swoor he sholde anoon abegge.°
A thief he was forsoothe of corn and mele,
And that a sly, and usant for to stele.°
His name was hoten deinous° Simekin.
A wif he hadde, comen of noble kin:
The person° of the town hir fader was.
With hire° he yaf ful many a panne of bras;
For that Simekin sholde in his blood allye,°
She was yfostred° in a nonnerye,
For Simekin wolde no wif, as he saide,
But she were wel ynorissed° and a maide,
To saven his estaat of yemanrye.°
And she was proud and pert as is a pie.°
A ful fair sighte was it upon hem two:
On halidayes biforn hire wolde he go
With his tipet° wounden aboute his heed,
And she cam after in a gite of reed,°
And Simekin hadde hosen of the same.
Ther dorste no wight clepen hire but "Dame."
Was noon so hardy that wente by the waye
That with hire dorste rage° or ones playe,
But if he wolde be slain of Simekin,
With panade, or with knif or boidekin,°
For jalous folk been perilous everemo—
Algate they wolde hir wives wenden° so.
And eek, for she was somdeel smoterlich,°

13. thwitel, knife. **14. camuse,** stubby. **15. piled,** bald. **16.** He was a fine street-loafer. **17. legge,** lay. **18. abegge,** pay for it. **20. usant . . . stele,** one who made a practice of stealing. **21. hoten,** called; **deinous,** haughty. **23. person,** parson. **24. With hire,** i.e., as her dowry. **25. allye,** i.e., marry her. **26. yfostered,** educated. **28. ynorissed,** brought up. **29.** To maintain the dignity of his status as a small landowner. **30. pert,** uppish; **pie,** magpie. **33. tipet,** scarf. **34. gite,** dress; **reed,** red. **38. rage,** flirt. **40. boidekin,** dagger. **42. Algate,** at any rate; **wenden,** thought. **43. smoterlich,** perhaps suggesting a wanton appearance belying her haughty manner.

She was as digne as water in a dich,°
And ful of hoker and of bisemare:°
Hire thoughte that a lady sholde hire spare,°
What for hir kinrede and hir nortelrye°
That she hadde lerned in the nonnerye.
A doughter hadde they bitwixe hem two
Of twenty yeer, withouten any mo,
Saving a child that wäs of half yeer age;
In cradel it lay and was a propre page.°
This wenche thikke and wel ygrowen was,
With camuse nose, and yën greye as glas,
With buttokes brode, and brestes rounde and hye,
But right fair was hir heer,° I wol nat lie.
The person of the town, for she was fair,
In purpos was to maken hire his heir
Bothe of his catel and his mesuage,°
And straunge he made it° of hir mariage;
His purpos was for to bistowe hire hye
Into som worthy blood of auncetrye,°
For holy chirches good moot been dispended°
On holy chirches blood that is descended:
Therfore he wolde his holy blood honoure,
Though that he holy chirche sholde devoure.
Greet sokne° hath this millere out of doute
With whete and malt of al the land aboute;
And nameliche° ther was a greet collegge—
Men clepeth the Soler Halle of Cantebregge—
Ther was hir whete and eek hir malt ygrounde.
And on a day it happed in a stounde°
Sik lay the manciple on a maladye:
Men wenden wisly° that he sholde die,
For which this millere stal° bothe mele and corn

44. **digne,** scornful, hence repellent; **water . . . dich,** i.e., stagnant water. 45. **hoker,** scorn; **bisemare,** mockery. 46. **hire spare,** i.e., hold herself aloof. 47. **kinrede,** kindred; **nortelrye,** education. 52. **page,** lad. 56. **heer,** hair. 59. **catel,** money; **mesuage,** land. 60. **straunge . . . it,** he made an issue. 62. **auncetrye,** ancestry. 63. **moot,** must; **dispended,** spent. 67. **sokne,** toll from grinding grain. 69. **nameliche,** especially. 72. **stounde,** time. 74. **wenden,** thought; **wisly,** surely. 75. **stal,** stole.

An hundred time more than biforn—
For therbiforn he stal but curteisly,
But now he was a thief outrageously;
For which the wardein chidde and made fare,°
But therof sette the millere nought a tare:°
He craked boost,° and swoor it was nought so.
  Thanne were ther yonge poore scolers two
That dwelten in the halle of which I saye:
Testif they were, and lusty° for to playe,
And only for hir mirthe and reverye°
Upon the wardein bisily they crye
To yive hem leve but a litel stounde°
To go to mille and seen hir corn ygrounde,
And hardily they dorste laye° hir nekke
The millere sholde nought stelen hem half a pekke
Of corn by sleighte, ne by force hem reve;°
And atte laste the wardein yaf hem leve.
John highte that oon, and Alain highte that other:
Of oon town were they born that highte Strother,
Fer in the north—I can nought telle where.
This Alain maketh redy al his gere,
And on a hors the sak he caste anoon;
Forth gooth Alain the clerk and also John,
With good swerd and with bokeler° by his side.
John knew the waye—him needede no gide—
And at the mille the sak adown he laith.
  Alain spak first: "Al hail, Simond, in faith.
How fares thy faire doughter and thy wif?"
  "Alain, welcome!" quod Simekin, "by my lif.
And John also! How now, what do ye heer?"
  "By God," quod John, "Simond, neede has na peer.°
Him boes serve himself that has na swain,°
Or elles he is a fool, as clerkes sayn.

79. wardein, warden of the college; **chidde,** chided; **fare,** fuss. **80. sette,** i.e., cared; **tare,** weed. **81. craked boost,** made loud threats. **84. Testif,** headstrong; **lusty,** eager. **85. reverye,** wantonness. **87. stounde,** time. **89. hardily,** confidently; **laye,** bet. **91. reve,** rob. **99. bokeler,** shield. **106. *na,** no; **peer,** equal. **107. *Him boes,** it behooves him; ***na swain,** no servant.

Oure manciple, I hope° he wil be deed,
Swa werkes ay the wanges° in his heed.
And therfore is I° come, and eek Alain,
To grinde oure corn and carye it haam° again.
I praye you, speed us heithen° that ye may."
"It shal be doon," quod Simekin, "by my fay.°
What wol ye doon whil that it is in hande?"°
"By God, right by the hoper wil I stande,"
Quod John, "and see howgates the corn gaas° in.
Yit saw I nevere, by my fader kin,
How that the hoper wagges til and fra."°
Alain answerde, "Johan, wiltou swa?°
Thanne wil I be binethe, by my crown,
And see how that the mele falles down
Into the trough. That sal° be my disport.
For John, in faith, I may been of youre sort:
I is as ille° a millere as ar ye."
This millere smiled of hir nicetee,°
And thoughte, "Al this nis doon but for a wile.
They weene that no man may hem bigile,
But by my thrift, yet shal I blere hir yë,°
For al the sleighte in hir phislophye.°
The more quainte crekes° that they make,
The more wol I stele whan I take:
In stede of flour yet wol I yive hem bren.°
The gretteste clerkes been nought the wisest men,
As whilom to the wolf thus spak the mare.°
Of al hir art counte I nought a tare."°
Out at the dore he gooth ful prively,
Whan that he sawgh his time softely:

109. ***hope,** expect. **110.** ***Swa,** so; ***werkes,** ache; ***wanges,** molar teeth. **111.** ***is I,** am I. **112.** ***haam,** home. **113.** ***heithen,** hence; **that,** i.e., as much as. **114. fay,** faith. **115. in hande,** on hand, i.e., being done. **117.** ***howgates,** how; ***gaas,** goes. **119. wagges,** rocks; ***til . . . fra,** to and fro. **120.** ***swa,** so. **123.** ***sal,** shall. **125.** ***ille,** bad. **126. nicetee,** foolishness. **129. blere . . . yë,** blear their eye, trick them. **130. sleighte,** trickery; **phislophye,** illiterate form of **philosophye. 131. quainte crekes,** cute tricks. **133. bren,** husks. **135.** The mare lured the wolf into examining her hind foot, whereupon she kicked him. **136.** i.e., I don't care a hang for all her tricks.

He looketh up and down til he hath founde
The clerkes hors ther as it stood ybounde
Bihinde the mille, under a leefseel.°
And to the hors he gooth him faire and weel;°
He strepeth° of the bridel right anoon,
And whan the hors was laus,° he ginneth goon
Toward the fen ther wilde mares renne,°
And forth with "Weehee," thurgh thikke and thenne.°
The millere gooth ayain—no word he saide—
But dooth his note° and with the clerkes playde,
Til that hir corn was faire and wel ygrounde.
And whan the mele is sakked and ybounde,
This John gooth out and fint° his hors away,
And gan to crye "Harrow and wailaway!
Oure hors is lost! Alain, for Goddes banes,°
Step on thy feet! Com of, man, al atanes!°
Allas, oure wardein has his palfrey lorn!"
  This Alain al forgat bothe mele and corn:
Al was out of his minde his housbondrye.°
"What, whilk way is he gaan?"° he gan to crye.
  The wif cam leping inward with a ren;°
She saide, "Allas, youre hors gooth to the fen
With wilde mares, as faste as he may go.
Unthank come on his hand that boond° him so,
And he that bettre sholde have knit° the reine."
  "Allas," quod John, "Alain, for Cristes paine,
Lay down thy swerd, and I wil myn alswa.°
I is ful wight, God waat, as is a raa.°
By Goddes herte, he sal nat scape us bathe.°
Why ne had thou pit the capil in the lathe?°
Ilhail, by God, Alain, thou is a fonne."°

141. **leefseel,** arbor. 142. **weel,** well, softly. 143. **strepeth,** strips. 144. **laus,** loose. 145. **renne,** run. 146. **thenne,** thin. 148. **note,** business. 151. **fint,** finds. 153. ***banes,** bones. 154. **Step . . . feet,** get moving; ***atanes,** at once. 157. **housbondrye,** domestic economy. 158. ***whilk,** which; ***gaan,** gone. 159. **ren,** run. 162. **Unthank come,** no thanks be; **boond,** bound. 163. **knit,** tied. 165. ***alswa,** also. 166. ***is; wight,** quick; ***waat,** knows; ***raa,** roe. 167. ***bathe,** both. 168. ***pit,** put; **capil,** horse; ***lathe,** barn. 169. ***Ilhail,** bad luck; ***fonne,** fool.

Thise sely clerks han ful faste yronne
Toward the fen, bothe Alain and eek John;
And whan the millere sawgh that they were goon,
He half a busshel of hir flour hath take,
And bad his wif go kneede it in a cake.
He saide, "I trowe the clerkes were aferd:
Yet can a millere make a clerkes beerd
For al his art. Ye, lat hem goon hir waye.
Lo, wher he gooth! Ye, lat the children playe.
They gete him nought so lightly, by my crown."
Thise sely clerkes rennen up and down
With "Keep! Keep! Stand! Stand! Jossa! Warderere!
Gaa whistle thou, and I sal keepe him here."
But shortly, til that it was verray night,
They coude nought, though they dide al hir might,
Hir capil cacche, he ran alway so faste,
Til in a dich they caughte him at the laste.
Wery and weet, as beest is in the rain,
Comth sely John, and with him comth Alain.
"Allas," quod John, "the day that I was born:
Now ar we driven til hething and til scorn;
Oure corn is stoln, men wil us fooles calle,
Bathe the wardein and oure felawes alle,
And namely the millere, wailaway."
Thus plaineth John as he gooth by the way
Toward the mille, and Bayard in his hond.
The millere sitting by the fir he foond,
For it was night, and ferther mighte they nought.
But for the love of God they han bisought
Of herberwe and of ese, as for hir peny.
The millere saide again, "If ther be eny,

170. **sely,** "poor innocent." 174. **bad,** bade. 175. **trowe,** believe; **aferd,** suspicious. 176. To make some one's beard is to get the better of him. 177. **art,** education. 178, **he,** i.e., the horse. 179. **lightly,** easily. 180. **rennen,** run. 181. **Keep,** look out; **Jossa,** down; **Warderere,** watch out behind. 182. ***Gaa,** go; **sal keepe,** shall watch for. 187. **weet,** wet. 190. ***til,** to; ***hething,** shame. 192. ***Bathe,** both. 193. **namely,** especially. 194. **plaineth,** complains. 195. **Bayard,** i.e., the horse. 196. **foond,** found. 199. **herberwe,** lodging; **as . . . peny,** at a price. 200. **eny,** any.

Swich as it is yet shal ye have youre part;
Myn hous is strait,° but ye han lerned art:
Ye can by argumentes make a place
A mile brood° of twenty feet of space.
Lat see now if this place may suffise,
Or make it roum with speeche as is youre gise."°
"Now Simond," saide this John, "by Saint Cutberd,
Ay is thou mirye, and that is faire answerd.
I have herd saye men sal taa° of two thinges,
Swilk° as he findes, or taa swilk as he bringes;
But specially I praye thee, hoste dere,
Get us som mete and drinke and make us cheere,
And we wol payen trewely atte° fulle:
With empty hand men may none hawkes tulle.°
Lo, here oure silver, redy for to spende."
This Millere into town his doughter sende°
For ale and breed, and rosted hem a goos,
And boond° hir hors, it sholde namore go loos,
And in his owene chambre hem made a bed,
With sheetes and with chalons° faire yspred,
Nought from his owene bed ten foot or twelve.
His doughter hadde a bed al by hirselve
Right in the same chambre by and by.°
It mighte be no bet, and cause why?—
Ther was no roumer herberwe° in the place.
They soupen and they speken hem to solace,°
And drinken evere strong ale at the beste.
Aboute midnight wente they to reste.
Wel hath this millere vernisshed his heed:°
Ful pale he was for dronke, and nought reed;°
He yexeth° and he speketh thurgh the nose,

202. **strait,** limited. 204. **brood,** broad. 206. **roum,** roomy; **gise,** custom. 209. ***sal taa,** shall take. 210. ***Swilk,** such. 213. **atte,** at the. 214. **tulle,** lure. 216. **into town,** to the village; **sende,** sent. 218. **boond,** bound. 220. **chalons,** blankets. 223. **by . . . by,** side by side. 225. **roumer herberwe,** roomier lodging. 226. **soupen,** sup; **speken . . . solace,** chat pleasantly. 229. To varnish one's head is to drink largely. 230. **for dronke,** for drunkenness; **reed,** red. 231. **yexeth,** hiccoughs.

As he were on the quakke or on the pose.°
To bedde he gooth, and with him gooth his wif—
As any jay she light was and jolif,
So was hir joly whistle wel ywet.
The cradel at hir beddes feet is set
To rokken, and to yive the child to souke.°
And whan that dronken al was in the crouke,°
To bedde wente the doughter right anoon.
To bedde gooth Alain and also John.
Ther nas namore: hem needed no dwale.°
This millere hath so wisely bibbed° ale
That as an hors he fnorteth° in his sleep,
Ne of his tail bihinde he took no keep.°
His wif bar him a burdon,° a ful strong:
Men mighten hir routing° heeren a furlong;
The wenche routeth eek, *par compaignye*.°
Alain the clerk, that herde this melodye,
He poked John and saide, "Sleepestou?
Herd thou evere slik a sang° er now?
Lo, swilk a complin is ymel° hem alle!
A wilde fir upon their bodies falle!
Wha herkned evere swilk a ferly° thing?
Ye, they sal have the flowr of ille ending.°
This lange night ther tides° me na reste.
But yit, na fors,° al sal be for the beste:
For John," saide he, "als° evere mote I thrive,
If that I may, yon wenche wil I swive.°
Som esement has lawe shapen° us:
For John, ther is a lawe that says thus,
That gif a man in a° point be agreved,

232. As if he were hoarse or had a cold in the head. **237. souke,** suck. **238. crouke,** crock. **241. dwale,** sleeping potion. **242. bibbed,** quaffed. **243. fnorteth,** snorts. **244. keep,** heed. **245. bar . . . burdon,** provided him an accompaniment. **246. routing,** snoring. **247. par compaignye,** for the sake of companionship. **250. *slik a sang,** such a song. **251. *swilk,** such; **complin,** evening service; ***ymel,** among. **253. *ferly,** wonderful. **254. *the . . . ending,** the best part of a bad end. **255. *lange,** long; **tides,** i.e., comes to. **256. fors,** matter. **257. als,** as. **258. swive,** sleep with. **259. esement,** recompense; **shapen,** decreed. **261. *gif,** if; **a,** one.

That in another he sal be releved.
Oure corn is stoln soothly, it is no nay,
And we han had an ille fit today,
And sin I sal have naan amendement
Again my los, I wil have esement.
By Goddes saule, it sal naan other be."
  This John answerde, "Alain, avise thee:
The millere is a perilous man," he saide,
"And if that he out of his sleep abraide,
He mighte doon us bathe a vilainye."
  Alain answerde, "I counte him nought a flye."
And up he rist, and by the wenche he crepte.
This wenche lay uprighte and faste slepte,
Til he so neigh was er she mighte espye
That it hadde been too late for to crye;
And shortly for to sayn, they were at oon.
Now, play, Alain, for I wol speke of John.
  This John lith stille a furlong way or two,
And to himself he maketh routhe and wo.
"Allas," quod he, "this is a wikked jape.
Now may I sayn that I is but an ape.
Yit has my felawe somwhat for his harm:
He has the milleres doughter in his arm.
He auntred him, and has his needes sped,
And I lie as a draf-sak in my bed.
And whan this jape is tald another day,
I sal be halden a daf, a cokenay.
I wil arise and auntre it, by my faith:
Unhardy is unsely, thus men saith."
  And up he roos, and softely he wente

263. it . . . nay, there's no use denying the fact. **264. *ille fit,** bad time. **265. *naan,** no; **amendement,** amends. **267. *saule,** soul. **268. avise thee,** take thought. **270. abraide,** start up. **271. *bathe,** both. **272. I . . . nought,** I don't consider him as much as. **273. rist,** rises. **274. uprighte,** supine. **279. lith,** lies; **a furlong,** i.e., the time it takes to go a furlong. **280. routhe,** pity. **281. jape,** joke. **282. ape,** i.e., dupe. **285. auntred him,** ventured; **has . . . sped,** has succeeded. **286. draf-sak,** bag of chaff. **287. *tald,** told. **288. *halden . . . daf,** held a fool; **cokenay,** sissy. **289. *auntre it,** take a chance. **290. Unhardy . . . unsely,** the timorous is unlucky.

Unto the cradel, and in his hand it hente,
And bar it softe unto his beddes feet:
Soone after this the wif hir routing leet,
And gan awake, and wente hire out to pisse,
And cam again, and gan hir cradel misse,
And groped heer and ther, but she foond noon.
"Allas," quod she, "I hadde almost misgoon;
I hadde almost goon to the clerkes bed—
Ey, benedicite, thanne hadde I foule ysped!"
And forth she gooth til she the cradel foond;
She gropeth alway ferther with hir hond,
And foond the bed, and thoughte nought but good,
By cause that the cradel by it stood,
And niste wher she was, for it was derk,
But faire and wel she creep into the clerk,
And lith ful stille, and wolde have caught a sleep.
Withinne a while this John the clerk up leep,
And on this goode wif he laith on sore.
So merye a fit ne hadde she nat ful yore:
He priketh harde and deepe as he were mad.
This joly lif han thise two clerkes lad
Til that the thridde cok bigan to singe.
  Alain weex wery in the daweninge,
For he hadde swonken al the longe night,
And saide, "Farwel, Malin, sweete wight.
The day is come, I may no lenger bide,
But everemo, wherso I go or ride,
I is thyn awen clerk, so have I seel."
  "Now dere lemman," quod she, "go, farweel.
But er thou go, oo thing I wol thee telle:
Whan that thou wendest hoomward by the melle,
Right at the entree of the dore bihinde
Thou shalt a cake of half a busshel finde,
That was ymaked of thyn owene mele,

292. **hente,** took. 294. **routing,** snoring; **leet,** left off. 297. **foond,** found. 300. **benedicite,** bless me. 305. **niste,** knew not. 306. **creep,** crept. 308. **leep,** leapt. 310. **fit,** bout; **ful yore,** since long ago. 312. **lad,** led. 314. **weex,** waxed, grew. 315. **swonken,** labored. 319. ***awen,** own; ***seel,** salvation. 320. **lemman,** lover. 322. **melle,** mill.

Which that I heelp my sire° for to stele.
And goode lemman, God thee save and keepe."
And with that word almost she gan to weepe.
  Alain up rist and thoughte, "Er that it dawe,°
I will go creepen in by my felawe,"
And foond° the cradel with his hand anoon.
"By God," thoughte he, "al wrang° I have misgoon.
Myn heed is toty of my swink° tonight:
That maketh me that I go nought aright.
I woot wel by the cradel I have misgo—
Here lith° the millere and his wif also."
And forth he gooth a twenty devele way°
Unto the bed ther as the millere lay.
He wende have cropen° by his felawe John,
And by the millere in he creep° anoon,
And caughte him by the nekke, and softe he spak.
He saide, "Thou John, thou swines-heed, awak,
For Cristes saule,° and heer a noble game;
For by that lord that called is Saint Jame,
As I have thries in this shorte night
Swived the milleres doughter bolt upright,
Whil thou hast as a coward been agast."
  "Ye, false harlot," quod the millere, "hast?°
A, false traitour, false clerk," quod he,
"Thou shalt be deed,° by Goddes dignitee—
Who dorste be so bold to disparage°
My doughter, that is come of swich linage?"
And by the throte-bolle° he caughte Alain,
And he hente him despitously° again,
And on the nose he smoot him with his fest°—
Down ran the bloody streem upon his brest.
And on the floor, with nose and mouth tobroke,°

326. **heelp,** helped; **sire,** father. 329. **rist,** rises; **dawe,** dawn come. 331. **foond,** found. 332. ***wrang,** wrong. 333. **heed,** head; **toty,** dizzy; **swink,** work. 336. **lith,** lies. 337. **a . . . way,** the way of twenty devils. 339. **wende . . . cropen,** thought to have crept. 340. **creep,** crept. 343. ***saule,** soul. 348. **harlot,** ribald; **hast,** have you. 350. **deed,** dead. 351. **disparage,** disgrace. 353. **throte-bolle,** Adam's apple. 354. **hente,** seized; **despitously,** roughly. 355. **fest,** fist. 357. **tobroke,** broken.

They walwen° as doon two pigges in a poke,
And up they goon and down again anoon,
Til that the millere sporned on a stoon,°
And down he fil bakward upon his wif
That wiste no thing of this nice° strif,
For she was falle asleepe a litel wight°
With John the clerk that waked hadde al night;
And with the fal out of hir sleep she braide.°
"Help, holy crois of Bromeholm!"° she saide.
"*In manus tuas,*° Lord, to thee I calle!
Awaak, Simond, the feend is on me falle!
Myn herte is broken. Help! I nam but deed:
Ther lith oon up my wombe° and up myn heed.
Help, Simekin, for the false clerkes fighte."
  This John sterte up as faste as evere he mighte,
And graspeth° by the walles to and fro
To finde a staf, and she sterte up also,
And knew the eestres bet° than dide this John,
And by the wal a staf she foond anoon,
And sawgh a litel shimering of a lighte—
For at an hole in shoon the moone brighte—
And by that lighte she sawgh hem bothe two,
But sikerly she niste° who was who,
But as she sawgh a whit thing in hir yë,
And whan she gan this white thing espye,
She wende the clerk hadde wered a voluper,°
And with the staf she drow ay neer and neer,°
And wende han hit this Alain atte fulle,°
And smoot the millere on the piled° skulle
That down he gooth and cride, "Harrow, I die."
Thise clerkes bete him wel and lete him lie,

358. **walwen,** roll about. 360. **sporned,** tripped; **stoon,** stone pot. 362. **nice,** foolish. 363. **wight,** while. 365. **braide,** started. 366. **Bromeholm,** Bromholm Priory possessed a famous cross. 367. **In . . . tuas,** into thy hands. 370. **lith,** lies; **up,** upon; **wombe,** stomach. 373. **graspeth,** gropes. 375. **eestres,** interior arrangements; **bet,** better. 380. **niste,** didn't know. 383. **wende,** thought; **voluper,** nightcap. 384. **drow,** drew; **neer,** nearer. 385. **wende han,** thought to have; **atte fulle,** squarely. 386. **piled,** bald.

And greithen° hem and tooke hir hors anoon,
And eek hir mele, and on hir way they goon,
And at the mille yit they took hir cake,
Of half a busshel flour ful wel ybake.
  Thus is this proude millere wel ybete,
And hath ylost the grinding of the whete,
And payed for the soper everydeel
Of Alain and of John that bete him weel.
His wife is swived and his doughter als.°
Lo, which° it is a millere to be fals!
And therfore this proverbe is said ful sooth:
Him thar nat weene° wel that yvele dooth:
A gilour° shal himself bigiled be.
And God, that sitteth heigh in majestee,
Save al this compaignye, grete and smale:
Thus have I quit° the Millere in my tale.

THE COOK'S TALE

The Introduction

The Cook of London, whil the Reeve spak,
For joye him thoughte he clawed him on the bak.°
"Haha," quod he, "for Cristes passioun,
This millere hadde a sharp conclusioun
Upon his argument of herbergage.°
Wel saide Salomon in his langage,
'Ne bring nat every man into thyn hous.'
For herberwing° by nighte is perilous;
Wel oughte a man avised for to be
Whom that he broughte into his privetee.

389. greithen, dress. **397. als,** also. **398. which,** what a thing. **400. thar,** need; **weene,** expect. **401. gilour,** beguiler, cheat. **404. quit,** repaid.
2. Because of the joy he felt it seemed as if the Reeve were scratching his back. **4–5.** The Cook is mocking the miller's mockery of the clerks' training in logic; see ll. 206–7 above; **herbergage,** lodging. **8. herberwing,** taking in lodgers.

I praye to God, so yive me sorwe and care
If evere, sith I highte° Hogge of Ware,
Herde I a millere bettre yset awerk:°
He hadde a jape° of malice in the derk.
But God forbede that we stinten° here;
And therfore, if ye vouche sauf to heere
A tale of me, that am a poore man,
I wol you telle as wel as evere I can
A litel jape that fil° in oure citee."
Oure Host answerde and saide, "I graunte it thee.
Now tel on, Roger, looke that it be good.
For many a pastee hastou laten blood,°
And many a Jakke of Dovere° hastou sold
That hath been twies hoot° and twies cold.
Of many a pilgrim hastou Cristes curs,
For of thy percely° yet they fare the wors,
That they han eten with thy stubbel° goos,
For in thy shoppe is many a flye loos.
Now tel on, gentil Roger by thy name.
But yet I praye thee, be nat wroth for game:
A man may saye ful sooth in game and play."
"Thou saist ful sooth," quod Roger, "by my fay.°
But 'Sooth play, quaad play,'° as the Fleming saith;
And therfore, Herry Bailly, by thy faith,
Be thou nat wroth er we departen° heer
Though that my tale be of an hostiler;°
But nathelees I wol nat telle it yit,
But er we parte, ywis, thou shalt be quit."°
And therwithal he lough° and made cheere,
And saide his tale as ye shal after heere.

12. **highte,** was named. 13. **yset awerk,** put to work. 14. **jape,** joke. 15. **stinten,** stop. 19. **fil,** happened. 22. i.e., For you've taken the filling out of many a tart. 23. **Jakke of Dovere,** a kind of tart. 24. **hoot,** hot. 26. **percely,** parsley. 27. **stubbel,** stubble-fed. 32. **fay,** faith. 33. **Sooth . . . play,** true joke, bad joke. 35. **departen,** separate. 36. **hostiler,** inn-keeper. 38. **quit,** paid back. 39. **lough,** laughed.

The Tale

A prentis whilom° dwelled in oure citee
And of a craft of vitailers° was he.
Gaillard he was as goldfinch in the shawe,°
Brown as a berye—a propre short felawe,
With lokkes blake ykembd ful fetisly;°
Dauncen he coude so wel and jolily
That he was cleped° Perkin Revelour.
He was as ful of love and paramour°
As is the hive ful of hony sweete:
Wel was the wenche with him mighte meete.
At every bridale° wolde he singe and hoppe;
He loved bet° the taverne than the shoppe,
For whan ther any riding was in Chepe°
Out of the shoppe thider wolde he lepe:
Til that he hadde al the sighte ysein°
And daunced wel, he wolde nat come again;
And gadered him a meinee° of his sort
To hoppe and singe and maken swich disport,
And there they setten stevene° for to meete
To playen at the dis° in swich a streete.
For in the towne nas ther no prentis
That fairer coude caste a paire of dis
Than Perkin coude, and therto he was free°
Of his dispense—in place of privetee:°
That foond his maister wel in his chaffare,°
For ofte time he foond his box ful bare.
For sikerly a prentis revelour°
That haunteth dis, riot, or paramour°—

1. **whilom,** once. 2. **vitailers,** victualers. 3. **Gaillard,** merry; **shawe,** wood. 5. **ykembd,** combed; **fetisly,** neatly. 7. **cleped,** called. 8. **paramour,** sexiness. 11. **bridale,** wedding feast. 12. **bet,** better. 13. **Chepe,** Cheapside, one of London's busiest and gayest streets. 15. **ysein,** seen. 17. **meinee,** company. 19. **setten stevene,** made an appointment. 20. **dis,** dice. 23. **free,** generous. 24. **dispense,** expenditure; **privetee,** privacy. 25. **foond,** found; **chaffare,** merchandise. 27. **sikerly,** certainly; **revelour,** party-loving. 28. Who practices dice, rowdy behavior, or wenching.

His maister shal it in his shoppe abye,°
Al haue he° no part of the minstralcye.
For thefte and riot, they been convertible,°
Al conne he playe on giterne or ribible;°
Revel and trouthe, as in a lowe degree,°
They been ful wrothe alday,° as men may see.
This joly prentis with his maister bood°
Til he were neigh out of his prentishood,°
Al were he snibbed° bothe erly and late,
And som time lad with revel to Newgate;°
But atte laste his maister him bithoughte,
Upon a day whan he his paper° soughte,
Of a proverbe that saith this same word,
"Wel bet° is roten apple out of hoord
Than that it rotte al the remenaunt";°
So fareth it by a riotous servaunt:
It is ful lasse harm to lete him pace°
Than he shende° alle the servants in the place.
Therfore his maister yaf him acquitaunce°
And bad him go, with sorwe and with meschaunce.
And thus this joly prentis hadde his leve;
Now lat him riote al the night, or leve.°
And for ther nis no theef withoute a louke°
That helpeth him to wasten and to souke°
Of that he bribe° can or borwe may,
Anoon he sente his bed and his array°
Unto a compeer° of his owene sort
That loved dis and revel and disport,

29. **abye,** pay for. 30. **Al . . . he,** although he have. 31. **convertible,** interchangeable. 32. Even though one can play a guitar or a fiddle. 33. **trouthe,** integrity; **lowe degree,** lower-class person. 34. **ful . . . alday,** constantly at odds. 35. **bood,** remained. 36. **neigh,** nearly; **prentishood,** apprenticeship. 37. **Al . . . snibbed,** although he was scolded. 38. **lad,** led; **Newgate,** a prison to which criminals were taken escorted by musicians and onlookers. 40. **paper,** either the contract of apprenticeship or, possibly, the account book. 42. **bet,** better. 43. **remenant,** remainder. 45. **lasse,** less; **pace,** pass. 46. **shende,** ruin. 47. **acquitaunce,** a release. 50. **leve,** leave off, i.e., do what he wants. 51. **for** because; **louke,** accomplice. 52. **souke,** suck, i.e., "bleed." 53. **bribe,** steal. 54. **array,** possessions. 55. **compeer,** co-equal.

And hadde a wif that heeld for countenaunce°
A shoppe, and swived for hir sustenaunce.°

(Unfinished)

THE MAN OF LAW'S TALE

The Introduction

Oure Hoste saw wel that the brighte sonne
The ark of his artificial day° hath ronne
The ferthe° part, and half an hour and more,
And though he were nat deepe ystert in lore,°
He wiste it was the eightetethe° day
Of April, that is messager to May,
And saw wel that the shadwe of every tree
Was as in lengthe the same quantitee
That was the body erect that caused it;
And therfore by the shadwe he took his wit°
That Phebus,° which that shoon so clere and brighte,
Degrees was five and fourty clombe° on highte,
And for that day, as in that latitude,
It was ten at the clokke, he gan conclude;
And sodeinly he plighte° his hors aboute:
"Lordinges," quod he, "I warne you al this route,°
The ferthe party° of this day is goon:
Now for the love of God and of Saint John,
Leseth no time as ferforth as ye may.°
Lordinges, the time it wasteth night and day,

57. **countenance,** i.e., appearance's sake. **58. swived,** i.e., practiced prostitution; **sustenaunce,** livelihood.

2. **artificial day,** i.e., the actual sunlight hours, as contrasted with the natural day of twenty-four hours. **3. ferthe,** fourth. **4. deepe . . . lore,** i.e., had not got far in learning. **5. eightetethe,** eighteenth. **10. took . . . wit,** deduced. **11. Phebus,** the sun. **12. was clombe,** had climbed. **15. plighte,** pulled. **16. route,** company. **17. ferthe party,** fourth part. **19. Leseth,** lose; **as . . . as,** in so far as.

And steleth from us, what prively sleepinge,
And what thurgh necligence in oure wakinge,
As dooth the streem that turneth nevere again,
Descending fro the montaigne into plain.
Wel can Senek° and many a philosophre
Biwailen time more than gold in coffre,
'For los of catel° may recovered be,
But los of time shendeth° us,' quod he.
It wol nat come again withouten drede°
Namore than wol Malkins maidenhede,
Whan she hath lost it in hir wantounesse.
Lat us nat moulen° thus in idelnesse.
  Sire Man of Lawe," quod he, "so have ye blis,
Telle us a tale anoon, as forward° is.
Ye been submitted thurgh youre free assent
To stonden in this caas at my juggement.
Acquiteth you now of youre biheeste:°
Thanne have ye doon youre devoir° atte leeste."
  "Hoste," quod he, "depardieux,° ich assente;
To breken forward is nat myn entente:
Biheeste is dette, and I wol holde fain°
Al my biheeste. I can no bettre sayn.
For swich lawe as man yiveth another wight,
He sholde himself usen° it by right.
Thus wol° oure text. But nathelees, certain,
I can right now no thrifty° tale sayn
That Chaucer, though he can but lewedly
On metres and on riming craftily,
Hath said hem in swich Englissh as he can,°
Of olde time, as knoweth many a man.
And if he have nat said hem, leve° brother,
In oo book, he hath said hem in another.

25. **Senek,** Seneca. 27. **catel,** property. 28. **shendeth,** ruins. 29. **drede,** doubt. 32. **moulen,** mould. 34. **forward,** agreement. 37. **biheeste,** promise. 38. **devoir,** duty. 39. **depardieux,** by the gods. 41. **fain,** gladly. 44. **usen,** i.e., be obedient to. 45. **wol,** i.e., will say. 46. **thrifty,** proper. 47–49. Which Chaucer, even though he knows little about meter and artful riming, has not told in such English as he knows. 51. **leve,** dear.

For he hath told of loveres up and down
Mo than Ovide° made of mencioun
In his Episteles that been ful olde.
What sholde I tellen hem, sin they been tolde?
In youthe he made of Ceys and Alcyone,°
And sithen hath he spoke of everichone,
Thise noble wives and thise loveres eke,
Whoso that wole his large volume seeke
Cleped the Saintes Legende of Cupide.°
Ther maistou seen the large woundes wide
Of Lucrece and of Babylan Thisbee,°
The swerd of Dido for the false Enee,
The tree of Phyllis for hir Demophon,
The plainte° of Dianire and of Hermion,
Of Adriane° and of Ysiphilee—
The bareine ile stonding in the see;
The dreinte° Leandre for his Erro,
The teres of Elaine, and eek the wo
Of Brixseide, and of thee, Ladomia;
The crueltee of thee, queene Medea—
The litel children hanging by the hals°
For thy Jason, that was of love so fals.
O Ypermistra, Penelopee, Alceste,
Youre wifhood he comendeth with the beste.
But certainly no word ne writeth he

54. Ovide, Ovid, whose poetic Epistles (the *Heroides*) recount the sad stories of most of the ladies mentioned below. **57. Ceys and Alcyone.** The story of Ceyx and Alcyone is told by Chaucer in the *Book of the Duchess* (see below). **61. Saintes . . . Cupide,** i.e., *Legend of Good Woman*. **63 ff.** These ladies committed suicide: Lucrece after her rape by Tarquin; Babylonian Thisbe after her lover Pyramus had killed himself; Dido in Virgil's *Aeneid* when Aeneas abandoned her; Phyllis when deserted by Demophon; Dejanira after accidentally causing Hercules' death. The other ladies were notable—and often had sad or violent experiences—because of their great love for their men: Hermione, Ariadne, Hypsipyle, Helen, Briseis, Laodamia, Medea (who slew her children as part of her complicated revenge on her lover Jason), Hypermnestra, Penelope, and Alceste. Leander (l. 69) drowned while swimming the Hellespont to visit his mistress Hero. **66. plainte,** complaint. **67.** Ariadne was left by Theseus on a barren island. **69. dreinte,** drowned. **73. hals,** neck.

Of thilke wikke ensample° of Canacee,
That loved hir owene brother sinfully:
Of swiche cursed stories I saye 'Fy!'
Or elles of Tyro Appollonius°—
How that the cursed king Antiochus
Birafte° his doughter of hir maidenhede;
That is so horrible a tale for to rede—
Whan he hire threw upon the pavement.
And therfore he of ful avisement°
Nolde nevere write in noon of his sermouns
Of swiche unkinde° abhominaciouns,
Ne I wol noon reherce if that I may.
  But of my tale how shal I doon this day?
Me were loth° be likned, doutelees,
To muses that been cleped Pierides°—
Metamorphosios woot° what I mene.
But nathelees, I recche° nought a bene
Though I come after him with hawe bake:°
I speke in prose, and lat him rymes make."
And with that word he with a sobre cheere
Bigan his tale, as ye shal after heere.

78. wikke, wicked; **ensample,** example: the story of Canace is told in Gower's *Confessio Amantis.* **81. Tyro Appollonius,** Gower also tells the story of Apollonius of Tyre, but does not include the horrible detail mentioned below. **83. Birafte,** deprived. **86. he,** i.e., Chaucer; **of . . . avisement,** with deliberate intent. **88. unkinde,** unnatural. **91. Me . . . loth,** I should be reluctant to. **92. Pierides,** frequenters of the Pierian spring, legendary source of artistic inspiration. **93. Metamorphosios,** Ovid's *Metamorphoses;* **woot,** knows. **94. recche,** care. **95. hawe bake,** baked haws, simple food.

The Prologue

O hateful harm, condicion of poverte,
With thirst, with cold, with hunger so confounded
To axen help thee shameth in thyn herte;
If thou noon axe, with neede artou so wounded
That verray° neede unwrappeth al thy wounde hid:
Maugree thyn heed, thou most for indigence
Or stele or begge or borwe thy dispence.°

Thou blamest Crist, and saist ful bittrely
He misdeparteth° richesse temporal.
Thy neighebore thou witest° sinfully
And saist thou hast too lite° and he hath al.
"Parfay." saistou, "som time he rekene shal,
Whan that his tail shal brennen in the gleede,°
For he nought helpeth needeful in hir neede."

Herke what is the sentence° of the wise:
"Bet is to dien than have indigence."
"Thy selve° neighebore wol thee despise
If thou be poore: farewel thy reverence!"
Yit of the wise man taak this sentence:
"Alle the dayes of poore men been wikke."°
Be war, therfore, er thou come to that prikke.°

If thou be poore, thy brother hateth thee,
And alle thy freendes fleen from thee, allas!
O riche marchants, ful of wele° been ye!
O noble, o prudent folk, as in this cas!
Youre bagges been nought filled with *ambas as*,°

5. **verray,** i.e., alone. 6. **Maugree . . . heed,** despite your head, i.e., anything you can do about it; **most,** must; **dispence,** expenses. 9. **misdeparteth,** divides wrongly. 10. **witest,** blame. 11. **lite,** little. 13. **brennen,** burn; **gleede,** hot coal. 15. **sentence,** opinion. 17. **selve,** very. 20. **wikke,** wretched. 21. **prikke,** point. 24. **wele,** welfare. 26. **ambas as,** double one, a losing throw in dice.

But with *sis cink* that renneth for youre chaunce:°
At Cristemasse merye may ye daunce.

Ye seeken land and see for youre winninges;
As wise folk ye knowen al th'estat°
Of regnes; ye been fadres of tidinges
And tales, bothe of pees and of debat.°
I were right now of tales desolat
Nere° that a marchant, goon is many a yere,
Me taughte a tale which that ye shal heere.

The Tale

PART ONE

In Surrye whilom° dwelte a compaignye
Of chapmen riche, and therto sad° and trewe,
That widewhere senten hir spicerye°—
Clothes of gold and satins riche of hewe:°
Hir chaffare was so thrifty and so newe
That every wight hath daintee° to chaffare
With hem, and eek to sellen hem hir ware.

Now fel° it that the maistres of that sort
Han shapen hem° to Rome for to wende;
Were it for chapmanhood or for disport,
Noon other message° wolde they thider sende
But comen hemself to Rome—this is the ende;

27. **sis cink,** six and five, a winning throw; **renneth,** runs; **chaunce,** good luck. **30. estat,** condition. **32. debat,** strife. **34. Nere,** if it weren't.

1. **Surrye,** Syria; **whilom,** once. **2. chapmen,** merchants; **sad,** sober. **3. widewhere,** far and wide; **spicerye,** merchandise. **4. hewe,** hue. **5. chaffare,** merchandise; **thrifty,** of high quality; **newe,** attractive. **6. wight,** person; **daintee,** pleasure. **8. fel,** befell. **9. shapen hem,** arranged. **11. message,** messenger, agent.

And in swich place as thoughte hem° avauntage
For hir entente they take hir herbergage.°

Sojurned han thise marchants in that town
A certain time, as fel to hir plesaunce;
But so bifel that th'excellent renown
Of th'Emperoures doughter, dame Custaunce,
Reported was with every circumstaunce°
Unto thise Surrian marchants in swich wise,
Fro day to day, as I shal you devise.°

This was the commune vois of every man:
"Oure Emperour of Rome—God him see°—
A doughter hath that, sin° the world bigan,
To rekne as wel hir goodnesse as beautee,
Nas nevere swich another as is she.
I praye to God in honor hire sustene,°
And wolde she were of al Europe the queene.

In hire is heigh beautee withoute pride,
Youthe withouten greenehede° or folye;
To alle hir werkes vertu is hir gide;
Humblesse° hath slain in hire al tyrannye;
She is mirour of alle curteisye;
Hir herte is verray° chambre of holinesse,
Hir hand ministre of freedom for almesse."°

And al this vois was sooth, as God is trewe.
But now to purpos lat us turne again:
Thise marchants han doon fraught hir shippes newe,°
And whan they han this blisful maiden sein°
Hoom to Surrye been they went ful fain,°

13. thoughte hem, it seemed to them. **14. entente,** intentions; **herbergage,** lodging. **19. circumstaunce,** detail. **21. devise,** describe. **23. see,** i.e., protect. **24. sin,** since. **27. sustene,** sustain. **30. greenehede,** immaturity. **32. Humblesse,** humility. **34. verray,** true. **35. ministre . . . almesse,** agent of generosity for almsgiving. **38. han . . . fraught,** have had loaded; **newe,** again. **39. sein,** seen. **40. fain,** glad.

And doon hir needes as they han doon yore,°
And liven in wele°—I can saye you namore.

Now fel it that thise marchants stoode in grace
Of him that was the Soudan° of Surrye,
For whan they come from any straunge° place
He wolde, of his benigne curteisye,
Make hem good cheere and bisily espye
Tidinges of sondry regnes, for to lere°
The wondres that they mighte seen or heere.

Amonges othere thinges specially
Thise marchants han him told of dame Custaunce
So greet noblesse, in ernest, seriously,°
That this Soudan hath caught so greet plesaunce
To han hir figure° in his remembraunce
That al his lust and al his bisy cure°
Was for to love hire whil his lif may dure.°

Paraventure in thilke° large book
Which that men clepe° the hevene ywriten was
With sterres° whan that he his birthe took
That he for love sholde han his deeth, allas:
For in the sterres, clerer than is glas,
Is writen, God woot, whoso° coude it rede,
The deeth of every man, withouten drede.°

In sterres many a winter therbiforn
Was writen the deeth of Ector,° Achilles,
Of Pompey, Julius,° er they were born,
The strif of Thebes, and of Hercules,
Of Sampson, Turnus,° and of Socrates

41. yore, previously. **42. wele,** welfare. **44. Soudan,** sultan. **45. straunge,** foreign. **48. lere,** learn. **52. seriously,** in detail. **54. figure,** person. **55. lust,** desire; **bisy cure,** anxious care. **56. dure,** last. **57. thilke,** that same. **58. clepe,** call. **59. sterres,** stars. **62. woot,** knows; **whoso,** i.e., if any one. **63. drede,** doubt. **65. Ector,** Hector of Troy. **66. Julius,** i.e., Caesar. **68. Turnus,** Aeneas' antagonist in the latter part of the *Aeneid*.

The deeth; but mennes wittes been so dulle
That no wight can wel rede it atte fulle.

This Soudan for his privee conseil sente,
And shortly of this matere for to pace,°
He hath to hem declared his entente,
And saide hem, certain, but° he mighte have grace
To han Custance within a litel space,
He nas but deed; and charged hem in hie°
To shapen° for his lif som remedye.

Diverse men diverse thinges saiden:
They argumenten, casten° up and down;
Many a subtil reson° forth they laiden;
They speken of magic and abusioun;°
But finally, as in conclusioun,
They can nat seen in that noon avauntage,
Ne in noon other way save mariage.

Thanne sawe they therin swich difficultee
By way of reson, for to speke al plain,
By cause that ther was swich diversitee
Bitweene hir bothe lawes° that they sayn
They trowe that "no Cristen prince wolde fain°
Wedden his child under oure lawe sweete
That us was taught by Mahoun° oure prophete."

And he answerde, "Rather than I lese°
Custance, I wol be cristened doutelees:
I moot been hires, I may noon other chese.°
I praye you, hold youre arguments in pees:
Saveth my lif, and beeth nat recchelees°
To geten hire that hath my lif in cure,°
For in this wo I may nat longe endure."

72. pace, pass. **74. but,** unless. **76. nas but,** i.e., was no better than; **hie,** haste. **77. shapen,** arrange. **79. casten,** make suggestions. **80. reson,** idea. **81. abusioun,** deceit. **88. hir . . . lawes,** their two religions. **89. trowe,** believe; **fain,** gladly. **91. Mahoun,** Mohammed. **92. lese,** lose. **94. moot,** must; **chese,** choose. **96. recchelees,** negligent. **97. cure,** charge.

What needeth gretter dilatacioun?°
I saye by tretis° and embassadrye,
And by the Popes mediacioun,
And al the Chirche, and al the chivalrye,°
That in destruccioun of Maumetrye,°
And in encrees of Cristes lawe dere,
They been accorded so as ye shal heere:

How that the Soudan and his baronage
And alle his liges° sholde ycristened be;
And he shal han Custance in mariage,
And certain gold—I noot° what quantitee;
And herto founden sufficient suretee.°
This same accord was sworn on either side.
Now, faire Custance, almighty God thee gide!

Now wolde some men waiten,° as I gesse,
That I sholde tellen al the purveyaunce°
That th'Emperour, of his grete noblesse,
Hath shapen for his doughter, dame Custaunce:
Wel may men knowen that so greet ordinaunce°
May no man tellen in a litel clause°
As was arrayed for so heigh a cause.

Bisshopes been shapen with hire for to wende,
Lordes, ladies, knightes of renown,
And other folk ynowe—this is th'ende;
And notified° is thurghout the town
That every wight with greet devocioun
Sholde prayen Crist that he this mariage
Receive in gree, and speede this viage.°

The day is comen of hir departing—
I saye the woful day fatal is come

99. dilatacioun, expansion. **100. tretis,** treaty. **102. chivalrye,** i.e., knights. **103. Maumetrye,** Mohammedanism. **107. liges,** subjects. **109. noot,** don't know. **110. suretee,** bond. **113. waiten,** expect. **114. purveyaunce,** preparation. **117. ordinaunce,** preparation. **118. litel clause,** short space. **123. notified,** made known. **126. in gree,** with approval; **viage,** undertaking.

That ther may be no lenger° tarying,
But forthward they hem dresse, alle and some.°
Custance, that was with sorwe al overcome,
Ful pale arist° and dresseth hire to wende,
For wel she seeth ther nis noon other ende.

Allas, what wonder is it though she wepte,
That shal be sent to straunge nacioun
Fro freendes that so tendrely hire kepte,
And to be bounden under subjeccioun
Of oon, she knoweth nat his condicioun?
Housbondes been alle goode, and han been yore:°
That knowen wives—I dar saye you namore.

"Fader," she saide, "thy wrecched child Custaunce,
Thy yonge doughter, fostered up so softe,
And ye, my moder, my soverein° plesaunce
Over alle thing, outtaken° Crist on lofte,
Custance youre childe hire recomandeth° ofte
Unto youre grace, for I shal° to Surrye,
Ne shal I nevere seen you more with yë.

Allas, unto the Barbre° nacioun
I moste anoon, sin° that it is youre wille.
But Crist that starf° for oure redempcioun
So yive me grace his heestes° to fulfille.
I, wrecche womman, no fors though I spille:°
Wommen are born to thraldom and penaunce,°
And to been under mannes governaunce."

I trowe at Troye whan Pyrrus brak° the wal,
Or Ilion brende,° n'at Thebes the citee,

129. lenger, longer. **130.** But they prepare to set forth, one and all. **132. arist,** arises. **139. yore,** i.e., throughout the past. **143. soverein,** chief. **144. outtaken,** excepting. **145. hire recomandeth,** commends herself. **146. shal,** must go. **148. Barbre,** barbarian, i.e., pagan. **149. moste,** must go; **sin,** since. **150. starf,** died. **151. heestes,** commands. **152. fors,** matter; **spille,** am ruined. **153. thraldom,** slavery; **penaunce,** suffering. **155. trowe,** think; **Pyrrus,** Pyrrhus, who led the final Greek assault on Troy; **brak,** broke. **156. Ilion,** the supposed citadel of Troy; **brende,** burned.

N'at Rome for the harm thurgh Hanibal
That Romains hath venquisshed times three,
Nas herd swich tendre weeping for pitee
As in the chambre was for hir departinge:
But forth she moot,° wherso° she weepe or singe.

O firste meving,° cruel firmament,
With thy diurnal sweigh° that crowdest° ay°
And hurlest al from eest til occident,
That naturelly wolde holde° another way,
Thy crowding set° the hevene in swich array
At the biginning of this fierse viage°
That cruel° Mars hath slain this mariage.

Infortunat ascendent tortuous°
Of which the lord° is helplees falle, allas,
Out of his angle into the derkest hous!°
O Mars, o Atazir° as in this caas!
O fieble moone, unhappy been thy paas:°
Thou knittest thee ther thou nart nat received;°
Ther thou were wel, fro thennes artou waived.°

Imprudent Emperour of Rome, allas,
Was ther no philosophre in al thy town?
Is no time bet° than other in swich caas?
Of viage is ther noon eleccioun°—
Namely° of folk of heigh condicioun?

161. **moot,** must go; **wherso,** whether. 162. **firste meving,** the *primum mobile,* the outermost of the spheres whose motion controls that of the planets. 163. **sweigh,** force; **crowdest,** push; **ay,** ever. 165. **holde,** take. 166. **set,** sets. 167. **fierse viage,** cruel expedition. 168. **cruel,** i.e., baleful as a planetary influence. 169–75. Scholars do not agree on the exact astrological situation reflected here, though it is clear that Mars is in a most unfavorable position for Custance's voyage, and that the Moon's influence is either lacking or malign. 169. **ascendent,** the sign of the Zodiac just rising in the east at one's birth. 170. **lord,** dominant planet. 171. **angle,** quarter of the sky; **derkest hous,** least favorable location. 172. **Atazir,** planetary influence. 173. **paas,** steps, movements. 174. You enter into a planetary conjunction where your power is impaired. 175. **waived,** pushed. 178. **bet,** better. 179. **eleccioun,** choice of favorable times determined by astrological calculation. 180. **Namely,** especially.

Nat whan a roote° is of a birthe yknowe?
Allas, we been too lewed or too slowe.°

To ship is brought this woful faire maide,
Solempnely, with every circumstaunce.°
"Now Jesus Crist be with you alle," she saide.
Ther is namore, but "Farewel, faire Custaunce."
She paineth hire° to make good countenaunce,
And forth I lete hire saile in this manere,
And turne I wol again to my matere.

The moder of the Soudan, welle of vices,
Espied hath hir sones plein° entente—
How he wol lete° his olde sacrifices,
And right anoon she for hir conseil sente,
And they been come to knowen what she mente.
And whan assembled was this folk in fere,°
She sette hire down and saide as ye shal heere.

"Lordes," quod she, "ye knowen everichoon
How that my sone in point is° for to lete
The holy lawes of oure Alkaron°
Yiven by Goddes message Makomete.°
But oon avow to grete god I hete:°
The lif shal rather out of my body sterte
Than Makometes lawe out of myn herte.

What sholde us tiden of° this newe lawe
But thraldom to oure bodies and penaunce,
And afterward in helle to be drawe
For we renayed Mahoun oure creaunce?°
But lordes, wol ye maken assuraunce

181. roote, i.e., horoscope. **182. lewed,** ignorant; **slowe,** lazy. **184. Solempnely,** ceremoniously; **circumstaunce,** detail of propriety. **187. paineth hire,** takes pains. **191. plein,** full. **192. lete,** leave. **195. in fere,** together. **198. in . . . is,** is about. **199. Alkaron,** Koran. **200. message Makomete,** messenger Mohammed. **201. hete,** promise. **204. us . . . of,** come to us from. **207. For,** because; **renayed,** denied; **creaunce,** belief.

As I shal sayn, assenting to my lore,°
And I shal make us sauf° for evere more?"

They sworen and assenten every man
To live with hire and die, and by hire stonde,
And everich in the beste wise he can
To strengthen hire shal alle his freendes fonde;°
And she hath this emprise° ytake on honde
Which ye shal heeren as I shal devise,
And to hem alle she spak right in this wise:

"We shul first feine us° Cristendom to take:
Cold water shal nat greve us but a lite.°
And I shal swich a feeste and revel make
That, as I trowe, I shal the Soudan quite.°
For though his wif be cristned nevere so white,
She shal have neede to wasshe away the rede,
Though she a font-ful water with hire lede." °

O Soudanesse,° roote of iniquitee,
Virago, thou Semirame° the secounde,
O serpent under femininitee,
Lik to the serpent deepe in helle ybounde!
O feined° womman, al that may confounde
Vertu and innocence thurgh thy malice
Is bred in thee as nest of every vice!

O Satan, envious sin thilke° day
That thou were chaced from oure heritage,
Wel knowestou to wommen th'olde way:
Thou madest Eva bringe us in servage;°
Thou wolt fordoon° this Cristen mariage.

209. As, i.e., to do as; **lore,** instruction. **210. And,** if; **sauf,** safe. **214. fonde,** test out. **215. emprise,** undertaking. **218. feine us,** pretend. **219. lite,** little. **221. trowe,** think; **quite,** repay. **224. lede,** bring. **225 Soudanesse,** Sultaness. **226. Semirame,** Semiramis, founder of Babylon, who was considered in the Middle Ages a most unwomanly woman. **229. feined,** counterfeit. **232. sin,** since; **thilke,** that same. **235. servage,** bondage. **236. fordoon,** destroy.

Thyn instrument, so wailaway the while,
Makestou of wommen whan thou wolt bigile.

This Soudanesse whom I thus blame and warye
Leet prively hir conseil goon hir way.
What sholde I in this tale lenger tarye?
She rideth to the Soudan on a day
And saide him that she wolde renaye hir lay,
And Cristendom of preestes handes fonge,
Repenting hire she hethen was so longe,

Biseeking him to doon hire that honour
That she moste han the Cristen folk to feeste:
"To plesen hem I shal do my labour."
The Soudan saith, "I wol doon at youre heeste,"
And kneeling thanketh hire of that requeste;
So glad he was, he niste what to saye.
She kiste hir sone and hoom she gooth hir waye.

PART TWO

Arrived been this Cristen folk to londe
In Surrye with a greet solempne route,
And hastily this Soudan sente his sonde
First to his moder and al the regne aboute,
And saide his wif was comen, out of doute,
And prayde hire for to ride again the queene,
The honour of his regne to sustene.

Greet was the prees and riche was th'array
Of Surrians and Romains met yfere.

237. wailaway, alas. **239. warye,** curse. **240. hir(2),** their. **241. What,** why. **243. renaye,** renounce; **lay,** religion. **244. fonge,** take. **247. moste,** might. **249. heeste,** command. **251. niste,** knew not. **254. solempne,** festive; **route,** crowd. **255. sonde,** message. **257. out of,** without. **258. again,** to meet. **260. prees,** throng. **261. yfere,** together.

The moder of the Soudan, riche and gay,
Receiveth hire with al so glad a cheere
As any moder mighte hir doughter dere;
And to the nexte citee therbiside
A softe paas solempnely they ride.

Nought trowe I the triumphe of Julius,
Of which that Lucan maketh swich a boost,
Was royaler ne more curious
Than was th'assemblee of this blisful host.
But this scorpion, this wikked goost,
The Soudanesse, for al hir flateringe,
Caste under this ful mortally to stinge.

The Soudan comth himself soone after this
So royally that wonder is to telle.
He welcometh hire with alle joye and blis,
And thus in mirthe and joye I lete hem dwelle.
The fruit of this matere is that I telle.
Whan time cam, men thoughte it for the beste
That revel stinte and men go to hir reste.

The time cam this olde Soudanesse
Ordained hath this feeste of which I tolde,
And to the feeste Cristen folk hem dresse,
In general, ye, bothe yonge and olde.
Here may men feeste and royaltee biholde
And daintees mo than I can you devise:
But al too dere they boughte it er they rise.

O sodein wo that evere art successour
To worldly blisse, spreind with bitternesse!
Th'ende of the joye of oure worldly labour!

266. softe, i.e., slow. **268. Lucan,** author of the *Pharsalia,* which fails to describe any triumph celebrated by Julius Caesar, though it concerns his wars; **boost,** boast. **269. curious,** elaborate. **273. Caste,** planned. **278. that,** what. **280. stinte,** should stop. **283. hem dresse,** betake themselves. **284. In general,** in a body. **286. mo,** more. **289. spreind,** sprinkled.

Wo occupieth the fin° of oure gladnesse.
Herke this conseil for thy sikernesse:°
Upon thy glade day have this in minde,
The unwar° wo or harm that comth bihinde.

For shortly for to tellen at oo word,
The Soudan and the Cristene° everichone
Been al tohewe and stiked° at the boord,
But° it were only dame Custance allone.
This olde Soudanesse, cursed crone,
Hath with hir freendes doon this cursed deede,
For she hireself wolde al the contree lede.

Ne ther nas Surrian noon that was converted
That of the conseil of the Soudan woot,°
That he nas al tohewe er he asterted.°
And Custance han they take anoon foot-hoot°
And in a ship al sterelees,° God woot,
They han hire set, and bidde hire lerne saile
Out of Surrye againward° to Itaile.

A certain tresor that she thider ladde°
And, sooth to sayn, vitaile° greet plentee
They han hire yiven, and clothes eek she hadde;
And forth she saileth in the salte see.
O my Custance, ful of benignitee,
O emperoures yonge doughter dere,
He that is lord of fortune be thy steere!°

She blisseth hire° and with ful pitous vois
Unto the crois of Crist thus saide she:
"O clere, o weleful auter,° holy crois,

291. fin, end. **292. sikernesse,** security. **294. unwar,** unexpected. **296. Cristene,** Christians. **297. tohewe,** cut to pieces; **stiked,** stabbed. **298. But,** except. **303. woot,** knows. **304. asterted,** escaped. **305. foot-hoot,** foot-hot. **306. sterelees,** rudderless. **308. againward,** back. **309. ladde,** brought. **310. vitaile,** victuals. **315. steere,** rudder. **316. blisseth hire,** crosses herself. **318. clere,** bright; **weleful auter,** salvation-bringing altar.

Reed° of the Lambes blood ful of pitee,
That wessh° the world fro th'olde iniquitee,
Me fro the feend and fro his clawes keepe
That day that I shal drenchen° in the deepe.

Victorious tree, proteccion of trewe,°
That only worthy were for to bere
The King of Hevene with his woundes newe,°
The white Lamb that hurt was with a spere;
Flemere° of feendes out of him and here,
On which° thy limes faithfully extenden,
Me keepe, and yive me might my lif t'amenden."

Yeres and dayes fleet° this creature
Thurghout the see of Greece° unto the straite
Of Marroc,° as it was hir aventure.
O, many a sory meel now may she baite:°
After hir deeth ful often may she waite,°
Er that the wilde wawes° wol hire drive
Unto the place ther she shal arrive.°

Men mighten axen why she was nought slain
Eek at the feeste? Who mighte hir body save?
And I answere to that demande again,
Who saved Daniel in th'horrible cave
Ther every wight save he, maister and knave,°
Was with the leon frete er he asterte?°
No wight, but God that he bar° in his herte.

God liste° to shewe his wonderful miracle
In hire, for we sholde seen his mighty werkes.

319. Reed, red. **320. wessh,** washed. **322. drenchen,** drown. **323. trewe,** true persons. **325. newe,** fresh. **327. Flemere,** expeller; **328. On which,** over whom. **330. fleet,** floated. **331. see of Greece,** i.e., Mediterranean. **332. Marroc,** Morocco, i.e., Strait of Gibraltar. **333. baite,** feed on. **334. waite,** look. **335. wawes,** waves. **336. arrive,** come to land. **341. knave,** servant. **342. with,** by; **frete,** eaten; **asterte,** might escape. **343. bar,** bore. **344. liste,** pleased.

Crist which that is to every harm triacle°
By certain menes° ofte, as knowen clerkes,
Dooth thing for certain ende that ful derk is
To mannes wit, that, for oure ignoraunce,
Ne conne nat knowe his prudent purveyaunce.°

Now sith she was nat at the feeste yslawe,°
Who kepte hire fro the drenching° in the see?
Who kepte Jonas in the fisshes mawe°
Til he was spouted up at Ninevee?
Wel may men knowe it was no wight, but he
That kepte peple Ebraic° from hir drenching,
With drye feet thurghout the see passing.

Who bad the foure spirits of tempest
That power han t'anoyen° land and see,
Bothe north and south and also eest and west,
"Anoyeth neither see ne land ne tree."
Soothly, the comandour of that was he
That fro the tempest ay° this womman kepte,
As wel whan she wook as whan she slepte.

Where mighte this womman mete and drinke have
Three yeer and more? How lasteth hir vitaile?
Who fedde the Egypcian Marye° in the cave
Or in desert? No wight, but Crist, *sans faile;*°
Five thousand folk it was as greet mervaile
With looves five and fisshes two to feede:
God sente his foison° at hir grete neede.

She driveth forth into oure occian°
Thurghout oure wilde see, til at the laste

346. triacle, medicine. **347. menes,** means. **350. purveyaunce,** foresight. **351. sith,** since; **yslawe,** slain. **352. drenching,** drowning. **353. mawe,** belly. **356. Ebraic,** Hebrew. **359. anoyen,** injure. **363. ay,** always. **367. Egypcian Marye,** St. Mary of Egypt, a hermit. **368. sans faile,** without doubt. **371. foison,** plenty. **372. driveth,** drifts; **oure occian,** our ocean, i.e., the eastern Atlantic.

Under an hold that nempnen° I ne can,
Fer in Northumberland, the wawe° hire caste,
And in the sand hir ship stiked° so faste
That thennes wolde it nought of al a tide:
The wil of Crist was that she sholde abide.

The constable of the castel down is fare
The seen this wrak, and al the ship he soughte,°
And foond° this wery womman ful of care;
He foond also the tresor that she broughte.
In hir langage mercy she bisoughte
The lif out of hir body for to twinne,°
Hire to delivere of wo that she was inne.

A manere Latin corrupt was hir speeche,
But algates° therby was she understonde.
This constable, whan him liste° no lenger seeche,
This woful womman broughte he to the londe.
She kneeleth down and thanketh Goddes sonde.°
But what she was she wolde no man saye,
For foul ne fair, though that she sholde deye.

She saide she was so mazed° in the see
That she forgat her minde, by hir trouthe.
The constable hath of hire so greet pitee,
And eek his wif, that they weepen for routhe.°
She was so diligent, withouten slouthe,°
To serve and plese everich in that place
That alle hire loven that looken on hir face.

This constable and dame Hermengild his wif
Were payens,° and that contree everywhere;

374. hold, stronghold; **nempnen,** name. **375. Fer,** far; **wawe,** wave. **376. stiked,** stuck. **380. wrak,** shipwreck; **soughte,** searched. **381. foond,** found. **384. twinne,** separate. **387. algates,** in any case. **388. liste,** it pleased. **390. sonde,** sending. **393. mazed,** confused. **396. routhe,** pity. **397. slouthe,** sloth. **401. payens,** pagans.

But Hermengild loved hire right as hir lif,
And Custance hath so longe sojurned there
In orisons, with many a bittre tere,
Til Jesu hath converted thurgh his grace
Dame Hermengild, constablesse of that place.

In al that land no Cristene dorste route:
Alle Cristene folk been fled fro that contree,
Thurgh payens that conquereden al aboute
The plages of the north by land and see.
To Wales fledde the Cristianitee
Of olde Britons dwelling in this ile:
Ther was hir refut for the mene while.

But yit nere Cristene Britons so exiled
That ther nere some that in hir privetee
Honoured Crist, and hethen folk bigiled;
And neigh the castel swiche ther dwelten three:
That oon of hem was blind and mighte nat see
But it were with thilke yën of his minde
With which men seen after that they been blinde.

Bright was the sonne as in that someres day,
For which the constable and his wif also,
And Custance, hath ytake the righte way
Toward the see a furlong way or two,
To playen and to romen to and fro,
And in hir walk this blinde man they mette,
Crooked and old, with yën faste yshette.

"In name of Crist," cride this blinde Britoun,
"Dame Hermengild, yif me my sighte again."
This lady weex affrayed of the soun,
Lest that hir housbonde, shortly for to sayn,

404. orisons, prayers. **407. Cristene,** Christians; **route,** assemble. **410. plages,** regions. **413. refut,** refuge. **414. nere,** were not. **415. privetee,** privacy. **419. But,** unless; **thilke,** those. **423. righte,** direct. **425. romen,** walk. **427. yshette,** shut. **430. weex,** grew; **soun,** sound.

Wolde hire for Jesu Cristes love han slain,
Til Custance made hire bold and bad hire wirche
The wil of Crist, as doughter of his chirche.

The constable weex abasshed of that sight
And saide, "What amounteth al this fare?"
Custance answerde, "Sire, it is Cristes might
That helpeth folk out of the Feendes snare."
And so ferforth she gan oure lay declare
That she the constable, er that it was eve,
Converteth, and on Crist made him bileve.

This constable was no thing lord of this place
Of which I speke, ther he Custance foond,
But kepte it strongly, many winters space,
Under Alla, king of al Northumberlond,
That was ful wis and worthy of his hond,
Again the Scottes, as men may wel heere.
But turne I wol again to my matere:

Satan, that ever us waiteth to bigile,
Saw of Custance al hir perfeccioun
And caste anoon how he mighte quite hir while,
And made a yong knight that dwelte in that town
Love hire so hote, of foul affeccioun,
That verraily he thoughte he sholde spille
But he of hire mighte ones have his wille.

He woweth hire, but it availeth nought:
She wolde do no sinne by no waye.
And for despit he compassed in his thought
To maken hire on shameful deeth to deye.

433. **wirche,** work. 435. **weex,** grew. 436. **fare,** fuss. 438. **Feendes,** Fiend's. 439. **ferforth,** fully; **lay,** law. 443. **foond,** found. 446. **hond,** i.e., deeds. 447. **Again,** against. 449. **waiteth,** lies in wait. 451. **caste,** considered; **quite hir while,** pay her off. 453. **hote,** hotly. 454. **verraily,** truly; **spille,** die. 455. **But,** unless. 456. **woweth,** woos. 458. **despit,** revenge; **compassed,** planned.

He waiteth° whan the constable was awaye,
And prively° upon a night he crepte
In Hermengildes chambre whil she slepte.

Wery forwaked° in hir orisouns
Sleepeth Custance and Hermengild also.
This knight, thurgh Satanes temptaciouns,
Al softely is to the bed ygo
And cutte the throot of Hermengild atwo,
And laide the bloody knif by dame Custaunce,
And wente his way—ther° God yive him meschaunce!

Soone after comth this constable hoom again,
And eek Alla, that king was of that lond,
And saw his wif despitously yslain,
For which ful ofte he weep° and wrong his hond;
And in the bed the bloody knif he foond°
By dame Custance. Allas, what mighte she saye?
For verray wo hir wit was al awaye.

To King Alla was told al this meschaunce,
And eek the time, and where, and in what wise
That in a ship was founden this Custaunce,
As herbiforn that ye han herd devise.°
The kinges herte of pitee gan agrise°
Whan he saw so benigne a creature
Falle in disese° and in misaventure.

For as the lamb toward his deeth is brought,
So stant this innocent bifore the king.
This false knight, that hath this treson wrought,
Bereth hire on hand° that she hath doon this thing.
But nathelees ther was there greet moorning

460. waiteth, watches. **461. prively,** secretly. **463. Wery forwaked,** wearied from staying awake. **469. ther,** i.e., may. **473. weep,** wept. **474. foond,** found. **480. devise,** describe. **481. agrise,** tremble. **483. disese,** trouble. **487. Bereth . . . hand,** falsely accuses her.

Among the peple, and sayn they can nat gesse
That she hath doon so greet a wikkednesse,

For they han seen hire evere so vertuous,
And loving Hermengild right as hir lif:
Of this bar witnesse everich in that hous
Save he that Hermengild slow with his knif.
This gentil king hath caught a greet motif
Of this witnesse, and thoughte he wolde enquere
Depper in this, a trouthe for to lere.

Allas, Custance, thou nast no champioun,
Ne fighte canstou nought, so wailaway!
But he that starf for oure redempcioun
And boond Satan—and yit lith ther he lay—
So be thy stronge champion this day:
For but if Crist open miracle kithe
Withouten gilt thou shalt been slain as swithe.

She sette hire down on knees and thus she saide:
"Immortal God that savedest Susanne
Fro fals blame, and thou, merciful maide,
Marye I mene, doughter to Sainte Anne,
Biforn whos child angeles singe 'Osanne,'
If I be giltelees of this felonye
My sucour be, for elles shal I die."

Have ye nat seen som time a pale face,
Among a prees, of him who hath be lad
Toward his deeth, wher as him gat no grace?
And swich a colour in his face hath had,
Men mighte knowe his face that was bistad

489. gesse, imagine. **493. bar,** bore. **494. slow,** slew. **495. motif,** suspicion. **497. lere,** learn. **499. wailaway,** alas. **500. starf,** died. **501. boond,** bound; **lith,** (Satan) lies. **503. but if,** unless; **kithe,** show. **504. as swithe,** at once. **506. Susanne,** Susannah, who was unjustly accused by two old lechers of indecent conduct: see the Book of Susannah. **509. Osanne,** Hosannah. **513. prees,** crowd; **lad,** led. **516. bistad,** in grave danger.

Amonges alle the faces in that route.
So stant Custance and looketh hire aboute.

O queenes living in prosperitee,
Duchesses and ye ladies everichone,
Haveth som routhe on hir adversitee!
An emperoures doughter stant allone:
She hath no wight to whom to make hir mone.
O blood royal that stondest in this drede,
Fer be thy freendes at thy grete neede.

This Alla king hath swich compassioun—
As gentil herte is fulfild of pitee—
That from his yën ran the water down.
"Now hastily do fecche a book," quod he,
"And if this knight wol sweren how that she
This womman slow, yit wol we us avise
Whom that we wol that shal been oure justise."

A Briton book writen with Evangiles
Was fet, and on this book he swoor anoon
She gilty was; and in the menewhiles
An hand him smoot upon the nekke boon
That down he fel at ones as a stoon,
And bothe his yën broste out of his face
In sighte of everybody in that place.

A vois was herd in general audience,
And saide, "Thou hast disclaundered giltelees
The doughter of holy chirche in heigh presence:
Thus hast thou doon, and yit I holde my pees."
Of this mervaile agast was al the prees:
As mazed folk they stooden everichone
For drede of wreche, save Custance allone.

517. route, throng. **518. stant,** stands. **521. routhe,** pity. **522. stant,** stands. **525. Fer,** far off. **527. fulfild,** filled full. **529. do fecche,** have fetched. **531. us avise,** consider farther. **533. Evangiles,** Gospels. **534. fet,** fetched. **538. broste,** burst. **541. disclaundered,** slandered. **544. prees,** throng. **546. wreche,** vengeance.

Greet was the drede and eek the repentaunce
Of hem that hadden wrong suspecioun
Upon this sely° innocent Custaunce;
And for this miracle, in conclusioun,
And by Custances mediacioun,
The king and many another in that place
Converted was, thanked be Cristes grace.

This false knight was slain for his untrouthe
By juggement of Alla hastily;
And yit Custance hadde of his deeth greet routhe.°
And after this, Jesus of his mercy
Made Alla wedden ful solempnely
This holy maiden that is so bright and sheene:°
And thus hath Crist ymaad Custance a queene.

But who was woful, if I shal nat lie,
Of this wedding but Donegild and namo,°
The kinges moder, ful of tyrannye?
Hire thoughte hir cursed herte braste° atwo;
She wolde nought hir sone hadde doon so;
Hire thoughte a despit° that he sholde take
So straunge a creature unto his make.°

Me list nat of the chaf ne of the stree°
Maken so long a tale as of the corn.°
What° sholde I tellen of the royaltee
At mariages, or which cours gooth biforn,
Who bloweth in a trompe° or in an horn?
The fruit of every tale is for to saye:°
They ete and drinke and daunce and singe and playe.

They goon to bed as it was skile° and right,
For though that wives been ful holy thinges,

549. sely, "poor." **556. routhe,** pity. **559. sheene,** shining. **562. namo,** no one else. **564. braste,** would break. **566. despit,** insult. **567. straunge,** alien; **make,** mate. **568. list,** it pleases; **stree,** husks. **569. corn,** grain. **570. What,** why. **572. trompe,** trumpet. **573. fruit,** i.e., main point; **is . . . saye,** i.e., ought to be told. **575. skile,** reason.

They moste take in pacience at night
Swich manere necessaries as been plesinges
To folk that han ywedded hem with ringes,
And laye a lite hir holinesse aside
As for the time—it may noon other bitide.

On hire he gat a knave child anoon,
And to a bisshop and his constable eek
He took his wif to keepe whan he is goon
To Scotlandward, his fomen for to seeke.
Now faire Custance that is so humble and meeke
So longe is goon with childe til that stille
She halt hir chambre, abiding Goddes wille.

The time is come a knave child she ber:
Mauricius at the font-stoon they him calle.
This constable dooth forth come a messager
And wroot unto his king that cleped was Alle
How that this blisful tiding is bifalle,
And othere tidinges speedful for to saye.
He takth the lettre and forth he gooth his waye.

This messager, to doon his avauntage,
Unto the kinges moder rideth swithe,
And salueth hire ful faire in his langage:
"Madame," quod he, "ye may be glad and blithe,
And thanketh God an hundred thousand sithe:
My lady queene hath child, withouten doute,
To joye and blis of al this regne aboute.

Lo, here the lettres seled of this thing
That I moot bere with al the haste I may.

577. moste, must. **580. lite,** little. **582. gat,** begot; **knave,** boy. **584. took,** entrusted. **587. stille,** constantly. **588. halt,** holds to. **589. ber,** bore. **591. dooth,** has. **592. cleped,** called. **594. speedful,** profitable. **596. doon . . . avauntage,** suit his own interest. **597. swithe,** quickly. **598. salueth,** greets. **600. sithe,** times. **602. regne,** realm. **603. seled,** sealed. **604. moot,** must.

If ye wol ought unto youre sone the king,
I am youre servant bothe night and day."
Donegild answerde, "As now at this time, nay.
But here al night I wol thou take thy reste.
Tomorwe wol I saye thee what me leste."°

This messager drank sadly° ale and win,
And stolen were his lettres prively°
Out of his box, whil he sleep as a swin,
And countrefeted was ful subtilly
Another lettre, wrought ful sinfully,
Unto the king direct° of this matere
Fro his constable, as ye shul after heere.

The lettre spak the queene delivered was
Of so horrible a feendlich° creature
That in the castel noon so hardy was
That any while dorste there endure.
The moder was an elf,° by aventure
Ycomen, by charmes or by sorcerye,
And everich wight hateth hir compaignye.

Wo was this king whan he this lettre hadde sein,°
But to no wight he tolde his sorwes sore,
But of his owene hand he wroot again,
"Welcome the sonde° of Crist for everemore
To me that am now lerned in his lore.
Lord, welcome be thy lust° and thy plesaunce:
My lust I putte al in thyn ordinaunce.

Keepeth this child, al be it foul or fair,
And eek my wif unto° myn hoom-coming.
Crist whan him list° may sende me an heir
More agreeable than this to my liking."

605. wol, i.e., will say. **609. leste,** it please. **610. sadly,** deeply. **611. prively,** secretly. **615. direct,** addressed. **618. feendlich,** fiendish. **621. elf,** fairy, member of the otherworld. **624. sein,** seen. **627. sonde,** sending. **629. lust,** pleasure. **632. unto,** until. **633. list,** pleases.

This lettre he seleth prively weeping,
Which to the messager was take soone,
And forth he gooth: ther is namore to doone.

O messager, fulfild of dronkenesse,
Strong is thy breeth, thy limes faltren ay,
And thou biwrayest alle secrenesse;
Thy minde is lorn, thou janglest as a jay;
Thy face is turned in a newe array.
Ther dronkenesse regneth in any route,
There is no conseil hid, withouten doute.

O Donegild, I ne have noon Englissh digne
Unto thy malice and thy tyrannye,
And therfore to the Feend I thee resigne:
Lat him enditen of thy traitorye.
Fy, manissh, fy—O, nay, by God I lie:
Fy, feendlich spirit, for I dar wel telle
Though thou here walke, thy spirit is in helle.

This messager comth from the king again
And at the kinges modres court he lighte;
And she was of this messager ful fain,
And plesed him in al that evere she mighte.
He drank and wel his girdel underpighte;
He sleepeth and he fnorteth in his gise
Al night, til that the sonne gan arise.

Eft were his lettres stolen evrichoon,
And countrefeted lettres in this wise:
"The king comandeth his constable anoon,
Up paine of hanging and on heigh juwise,
That he ne sholde suffren in no wise

636. take, given. **640. biwrayest,** betray. **641. lorn,** lost; **janglest,** prate. **642. array,** condition. **643. route,** group. **644. conseil,** secret. **645. digne,** worthy. **648. enditen,** make record. **649. manissh,** i.e., unwomanly. **654. fain,** glad. **656. underpighte,** stuffed. **657. fnorteth,** snores. **659. Eft,** again. **662. Up,** upon; **juwise,** penalty.

Custance inwith° his regne for t'abide
Three dayes and a quarter of oo tide.°

But in the same ship as he hire foond,°
Hire and hir yonge sone and al hir gere
He sholde putte, and crowde° hire fro the lond,
And charge hire that she nevere eft° come there."
O my Custance, wel may thy goost have fere
And sleeping in thy dreem been in penaunce,°
When Donegild caste al this ordinaunce.°

This messager on morwe whan he wook
Unto the castel halt the nexte° way,
And to the constable he the lettre took;
And whan that he this pitous lettre sey,°
Ful ofte he saide "Allas and wailaway!"°
"Lord Crist," quod he, "how may this world endure,
So ful of sinne is many a creature?

O mighty God, if that it be thy wille,
Sith° thou art rightful juge, how may it be
That thou wolt suffren innocents to spille,°
And wikked folk regnen in prosperitee?
O goode Custance, allas, so wo is me
That I moot° be thy tormentour or deye
On shames deeth—ther is no other waye."

Weepen bothe yonge and olde in al that place
Whan that the king this cursed lettre sente.
And Custance, with a deedly pale face,
The ferthe day toward hir ship she wente.
But nathelees she takth in good entente

664. **inwith,** within. 665. **quarter . . . tide,** the first quarter of the time between high tide and low tide. 666. **foond,** found. 668. **crowde,** push. 669. **charge,** command; **eft,** again. 671. **penaunce,** anxiety. 672. **caste,** contrived; **ordinaunce,** arrangement. 674. **halt,** holds; **nexte,** nearest. 676. **sey,** saw. 677. **wailaway,** woe. 681. **Sith,** since. 682. **spille,** be ruined. 685. **moot,** must.

The wil of Crist, and kneeling on the stronde,°
She saide, "Lord, ay welcome be thy sonde.°

He that me kepte fro the false blame
Whil I was on the land amonges you,
He can me keepe from harm and eek fro shame
In salte see, although I see nat how.
As strong as evere he was he is yit now;
In him truste I, and in his moder dere,
That is to me my sail and eek my steere."°

Hir litel child lay weeping in hir arm,
And kneeling pitously to him she saide,
"Pees, litel sone, I wol do thee noon harm."
With that hir kerchief of hir heed she braide°
And over his litel yën she it laide,
And in hir arm she lulleth it ful faste,
And into hevene hir yën up she caste.

"Moder," quod she, "and maiden bright, Marye,
Sooth is that thurgh wommanes eggement°
Mankinde was lorn° and dampned ay to die,
For which thy child was on a crois yrent;°
Thy blisful yën sawe al his torment:
Thanne is ther no comparison bitweene
Thy wo and any wo man may sustene.°

Thou saw thy child yslain bifore thine yën,
And yit now liveth my litel child, parfay.
Now, lady bright, to whom alle woful cryen,
Thou glorye of wommanhood, thou faire may,°
Thou haven of refut, brighte sterre° of day,
Rewe° on my child, that of thy gentilesse
Rewest on every rewful° in distresse.

692. stronde, beach. **693. ay,** ever; **sonde,** sending. **700. steere,** rudder. **704. heed,** head; **braide,** snatched. **709. eggement,** egging. **710. lorn,** lost. **711. yrent,** torn. **714. sustene,** sustain. **718. may,** maid. **719. refut,** refuge; **sterre,** star. **720. Rewe,** have pity on. **721. rewful,** pitiful one.

O litel child, allas, what is thy gilt,
That nevere wroughtest sinne as yit, pardee?
Why wil thyn harde fader han thee spilt?°
O mercy, dere constable," quod she,
"As lat my litel child dwelle here with thee.
And if thou darst nat saven him for blame,
So kis him ones in his fadres name."

Therwith she looketh backward to the londe
And saide, "Farewel, housbonde routhelees."°
And up she rist° and walketh down the stronde
Toward the ship; hire folweth al the prees.°
And evere she prayeth hir child to holde his pees,
And takth hir leve, and with an holy entente
She blesseth hire,° and into ship she wente.

Vitailed was the ship, it is no drede,°
Abundantly for hire ful longe space,°
And othere necessaries that sholde neede°
She hadde ynowe, yheried° be Goddes grace.
For wind and weder, almighty God purchace,°
And bringe hire hoom: I can no bettre saye,
But in the see she driveth° forth hir waye.

PART THREE

Alla the king comth hoom soone after this
Unto his castel, of the which I tolde,
And axeth° where his wif and his child is.
The constable gan aboute his herte colde,°
And pleinly° al the manere he him tolde
As ye han herde—I can telle it no bettre—
And sheweth the king his seel and eek his lettre,

724. spilt, destroyed. **730. routhelees,** merciless. **731. rist,** rises. **732. prees,** crowd. **735. blesseth hire,** makes the sign of the cross. **736. Vitailed,** provisioned; **drede,** doubt. **737. space,** time. **738. neede,** be needed. **739. yheried,** praised. **740. purchace,** make provision. **742. driveth,** drifts. **745. axeth,** asks. **746. colde,** grow colde. **747. pleinly,** fully.

And saide, "Lord, as ye comanded me
Up paine of deeth, so have I doon, certain."
This messager tormented was til he
Moste biknowe and tellen, plat and plein,
Fro night to night in what place he hadde lain.
And thus by wit and subtil enqueringe
Imagined was by whom this harm gan springe.

The hand was knowe that the lettre wroot,
And al the venim of this cursed deede—
But in what wise, certainly, I noot.
Th'effect is this, that Alla, out of drede,
His moder slow—that men may plainly rede—
For that she traitor was to hir ligeaunce:
Thus endeth olde Donegild with meschaunce.

The sorwe that this Alla night and day
Maketh for his wif and for his child also
Ther is no tonge that it telle may.
But now wol I unto Custance go
That fleeteth in the see in paine and wo
Five yeer and more, as liked Cristes sonde,
Er that hir ship approched unto londe.

Under an hethen castel atte laste
Of which the name in my text nought I finde,
Custance and eek hir child the see up caste:
Almighty God that saveth al mankind
Have on Custance and on hir child som minde
That fallen is in hethen hand eftsoone
In point to spille, as I shal telle you soone.

Down from the castel comth ther many a wight
To gauren on this ship and on Custaunce.

751. Up, upon. **752. tormented,** tortured. **753.** Had to admit and tell, flatly and fully. **757. knowe,** recognized. **758. venim,** malice. **759. noot,** don't know. **760. drede,** doubt. **761. slow,** slew. **762. ligeaunce,** allegiance. **768. fleeteth,** floats. **769. liked,** pleased; **sonde,** i.e., purpose. **776. eftsoone,** again. **777. In . . . spille,** about to be ruined. **779. gauren,** gaze.

But shortly from the castel on a night
The lordes stiward—God yive him meschaunce!—
A theef that hadde renayed oure creaunce,°
Cam into ship allone, and saide he sholde
Hir lemman be, wherso° she wolde or nolde.

Wo was this wrecched womman tho° bigoon;
Hir child cride, and she cride pitously.
But blisful Marye heelp° hire right anoon,
For with hir strugling wel and mightily
The theef fel overboord al sodeinly,
And in the see he dreinte° for vengeaunce:
And thus hath Crist unwemmed° kept Custaunce.

O foule lust of luxurye,° lo thyn ende!
Nat only that that thou faintest° mannes minde,
But verraily thou wolt his body shende.°
Th'ende of thy werk, or of thy lustes blinde
Is complaining:° how many oon may men finde
That nought for werk° som time but for th'entente
To doon this sinne been outher slain or shente.°

How may this waike° womman have this strengthe
Hire to defende against this renegat?°
O Golias,° unmesurable of lengthe,
How mighte David make thee so maat?°
So yong and of armure° so desolat,
How dorste he looke upon thy dredful face?
Wel may men seen that it was but Goddes grace.

Who yaf Judith corage or hardinesse
To sleen° him Holofernes in his tente,

782. **renayed,** renounced; **creaunce,** creed. 784. **lemman,** lover; **wherso,** whether. 785. **tho,** then. 787. **heelp,** helped. 790. **dreinte,** drowned. 791. **unwemmed,** unspotted. 792. **luxurye,** lechery. 793. **faintest,** enfeeble. 794. **shende,** spoil. 796. **complaining,** lamentation. 797. **werk,** i.e., the deed. 798. **outher,** either; **shente,** ruined. 799. **waike,** weak. 800. **renegat,** renegade. 801. **Golias,** Goliath. 802. **maat,** defeated. 803. **armure,** weapons. 807. **sleen,** slay: for Judith's delivering the children of Israel by beheading the enemy general, see the Book of Judith.

And to deliveren out of wrecchednesse
The peple of God? I saye for this entente:
That right as God spirit of vigor sente
To hem and saved hem out of meschaunce,
So sente he might and vigor to Custaunce.

Forth gooth hir ship thurghout the narwe mouth
Of Jubaltare and Septe driving ay,
Som time west and som time north and south,
And som time eest, ful many a wery day,
Til Cristes moder—blessed be she ay—
Hath shapen thurgh hir endelees goodnesse
To make an ende of al hir hevinesse.

Now lat us stinte of Custance but a throwe
And speke we of the Romain Emperour,
That out of Surrye hath by lettres knowe
The slaughtre of Cristene folk and dishonour
Doon to his doughter by a fals traitour—
I mene the cursed wikked Soudanesse
That at the feeste leet slain both more and lesse.

For which this Emperour hath sent anoon
His senatour with royal ordinaunce
And othere lordes, God woot, many oon
On Surrians to taken heigh vengeaunce:
They brennen, slayn, and bringe hem to meschaunce
Ful many a day; but shortly, this is th'ende,
Hoomward to Rome they shapen hem to wende.

This senatour repaireth with victorye
To Romeward, sailing ful royally,
And mette the ship driving, as saith the storye,
In which Custance sit ful pitously.

809. saye, speak. **814. Jubaltare,** Gibraltar; **Septe,** a seven-peaked range in Morocco; **driving,** drifting. **818. shapen,** arranged. **820. stinte,** cease; **throwe,** moment. **826. leet,** caused to be. **829. woot,** knows. **831. brennen,** burn. **833. shapen hem,** plan. **837. sit,** sits.

Nothing ne knew he what she was ne why
She was in swich array, ne she nil saye
Of hir estaat, although she sholde deye.

He bringeth hire hoom to Rome and to his wif
He yaf hire and hir yonge sone also;
And with the senatour she ladde hir lif:
Thus can oure Lady bringen out of wo
Woful Custance and many another mo.
And longe time she dwelled in that place
In holy werkes evere, as was hir grace.

The senatoures wif her aunte was,
But al for that she knew hire nevere the more.
I wol no lenger taryen as in this cas,
But to King Alla, which I spak of yore,
That for his wif weepeth and siketh sore
I wol retourne, and lete I wol Custaunce
Under the senatoures governaunce.

King Alla, which that hadde his moder slain,
Upon a day fel in swich repentaunce
That, if I shortly tellen shal and plain,
To Rome he comth to receive his penaunce,
And putte him in the Popes ordinaunce
In heigh and lowe, and Jesus Crist bisoughte
Foryive his wikked werkes that he wroughte.

The fame anoon thurgh Rome town is born
How Alla king shal come in pilgrimage,
By herbergeours that wenten him biforn;
For which the senatour, as was usage,
Wente him agains, and many of his linage,

839. array, situation. **843. ladde,** led. **845. mo,** more. **849. knew hire,** recognized her, i.e., Custance. **851. yore,** earlier. **852. siketh,** sighs. **853. lete,** leave. **859. ordinaunce,** power. **864. herbergeours,** harbingers, men who went ahead to arrange lodging for eminent persons. **866. agains,** i.e., to meet; **linage,** kindred.

As wel to shewen his hye magnificence
As to doon any king a reverence.

Greet° cheere dooth this noble senatour
To King Alla, and he to him also;
Everich of hem dooth other greet honour;
And so bifel that in a day or two
This senatour is to King Alla go
To feeste, and shortly, if I shal nat lie,
Custances sone wente in his compaignye.

Some men wolde saye at requeste of Custaunce
This senatour hath lad° this child to feeste.
I may nat tellen every circumstaunce;°
Be as be may, ther was he atte leeste;
But sooth is this, that at his modres heeste°
Biforn Alla, during the metes space,°
The child stood looking in the kinges face.

This Alla king hath of this child greet wonder,
And to the senatour he saide anoon,
"Whos is that faire child that stondeth yonder?"
"I noot,"° quod he, "by God and by Saint John.
A moder he hath, but fader hath he noon
That I of woot." And shortly, in a stounde,°
He tolde Alla how that this child was founde.

"But God woot," quod this senatour also,
"So vertuous a livere in my lif
Ne saw I nevere as she, ne herde of mo°
Of worldly wommen, maide, ne of wif.
I dar wel sayn hire hadde levere a knif
Thurghout hir breest than been a womman wikke:°
Ther is no man coude bringe hire to that prikke."°

869. Greet, great. **877. lad,** led. **878. circumstaunce,** detail. **880. heeste,** command. **881. metes space,** mealtime. **886. noot,** don't know. **888. woot,** know; **stounde,** moment. **892. mo,** others. **895. wikke,** wicked. **896. prikke,** point.

Now was this child as lik unto Custaunce
As possible is a creature to be.
This Alla hath the face in remembraunce
Of dame Custance, and theron mused he
If that this childes moder were ought she—
That is, his wif; and prively he sighte,
And spedde him fro the table that he mighte.

"Parfay," thoughte he, "fantome is in myn heed.
I oughte deeme of skilful juggement
That in the salte see my wif is deed."
And afterward he made his argument,
"What woot I if that Crist hath hider sent
My wif by see, as wel as he hire sente
To my contree, fro thennes that she wente?"

And after noon hoom with the senatour
Gooth Alla for to seen this wonder chaunce.
This senatour dooth Alla greet honour,
And hastily he sente after Custaunce:
But trusteth wel, hire liste nat to daunce
Whan that she wiste wherfore was that sonde;
Unnethe upon hir feet she mighte stonde.

Whan Alla saw his wif faire he hire grette,
And weep that it was routhe for to see,
For at the firste look he on hire sette
He knew wel verraily that it was she.
And she for sorwe as domb stant as a tree,
So was hir herte shet in hir distresse,
Whan she remembred his unkindenesse.

901. ought, i.e., possibly. **902. prively,** quietly; **sighte,** sighed. **903. that,** i.e., as soon as. **904. heed,** head. **905. skilful,** reasonable, **906. deed,** dead. **912. wonder,** wonderful. **915. hire liste,** she desired. **916. wiste,** knew; **sonde,** summons. **917. Unnethe,** scarcely. **918. grette,** greeted. **919. weep,** wept; **routhe,** pity. **922. stant,** stands. **923. shet,** shut.

Twies she swouneth° in his owene sighte;
He weep and him excuseth pitously:
"Now God," quod he, "and alle his halwes° brighte
So wisly° on my soule as have mercy,
That of youre harm as giltelees am I
As is Maurice, my sone so lik youre face:
Elles the Feend me fecche out of this place."

Long was the sobbing and the bittre paine
Er that hir woful hertes mighte ceesse.
Greet was the pitee for to heere hem plaine,°
Thurgh whiche plaintes° gan hir wo encreesse.
I praye you alle my labour to releesse:
I may nat telle hir wo until tomorwe,
I am so wery for to speke of sorwe.

But finally whan that the sooth is wist°
That Alla giltelees was of hir wo,
I trowe° an hundred times been they kist,
And swich a blis is ther bitwixe hem two
That, save the joye that lasteth everemo,
There is noon lik that any creature
Hath seen, or shal whil that the world may dure.°

Tho° prayede she hir housbonde meekely,
In relief of hir longe pitous pine°
That he wolde praye hir fader specially,
That of his majestee he wolde encline
To vouche sauf som day with hem to dine.
She prayde him eek he sholde by no waye
Unto hir fader no word of hire saye.

Some men wolde sayn how that the child Maurice
Dooth this message unto this Emperour;

925. swouneth, swoons. **927. halwes,** saints. **928. wisly,** surely. **934. plaine,** complain. **935. plaintes,** complaints. **939. wist,** known. **941. trowe,** believe. **945. dure,** last. **946. Tho,** then. **947. pine,** torment.

But, as I gesse, Alla was nought so nice,°
To him that was of so soverein honour,
As he that is of Cristene folk the flowr,
Sente° any child; but it is best to deeme
He wente himself, and so it may wel seeme.

This Emperour hath graunted gentilly
To come to diner as he him bisoughte.
And wel rede I, he looked bisily
Upon this child, and on his doughter thoughte.
Alla gooth to his in° and as him oughte
Arrayed° for this feeste in every wise,
As ferforth as his conning° may suffise.

The morwe cam and Alla gan him dresse,°
And eek his wif, this Emperour to meete,
And forth they ride in joye and in gladnesse.
And whan she saw hir fader in the streete,
She lighte down and falleth him to feete.
"Fader," quod she, "youre yonge child Custaunce
Is now ful clene out of youre remembraunce.

I am youre doughter Custance," quod she,
"That whilom° ye han sent unto Surrye.
It am I, fader, that in the salte see
Was put allone and dampned for to die.
Now goode fader, mercy I you crye:
Sende me namore unto noon hethenesse,°
But thanke my lord here of his kindenesse."

Who can the pitous joye tellen al
Bitwixe hem three, sin° they be thus ymette?
But of my tale make an ende I shal:
The day gooth faste, I wol no lenger lette.°

955. nice, foolish. **958. Sente,** i.e., to send. **964. in,** lodging. **965. Arrayed,** prepared. **966. ferforth,** far; **conning,** wits. **967. dresse,** prepare. **975. whilom,** once. **979. hethenesse,** heathen land. **982. sin,** since. **984. lette,** delay.

This glade folk to diner they hem sette;
In joye and blisse at mete I lete hem dwelle
A thousandfold wel more than I can telle.

This child Maurice was sithen emperour
Maad by the Pope, and lived Cristenly:
To Cristes chirche he dide greet honour.
But I lete al this storye passen by:
Of Custance is my tale specially—
In th'olde Romain geestes may men finde
Maurices lif: I bere it nought in minde.

This King Alla, whan he his time sey,
With his Custance, his holy wif so sweete,
To Engelond been they come the righte way,
Wher as they live in joye and in quiete:
But litel while it lasteth, I you hete,
Joye of this world, for time wol nat abide;
Fro day to night it chaungeth as the tide.

Who lived evere in swich delit a day
That him ne meved outher conscience
Or ire or talent or som kinnes affray,
Envy or pride, or passion or offence?
I ne saye but for this ende this sentence:
That litel while in joye or in plesaunce
Lasteth the blis of Alla with Custaunce.

For deeth that takth of heigh and lowe his rente,
Whan passed was a yeer evene, as I gesse,
Out of this world this King Alla he hente,
For whom Custance hath ful greet hevinesse:
Now lat us prayen God his soule blesse.

988. sithen, afterward. **993. geestes,** chronicles. **995. sey,** saw. **977. righte,** direct. **999. hete,** promise. **1003. meved,** disturbed; **outher,** either. **1004. talent,** desire; **affray,** fright. **1006. sentence,** sentiment. **1011. hente,** seized.

And dame Custance, finally to saye,
Toward the town of Rome gooth hir waye.

To Rome is come this holy creature
And findeth there hir freendes hool and sounde:
Now is she scaped al hir aventure.
And whan that she hir fader hath yfounde,
Down on hir knees falleth she to grounde,
Weeping for tendrenesse; in herte blithe
She herieth God an hundred thousand sithe.

In vertu and in holy almesdeede
They liven alle and nevere asonder wende;
Til deeth departeth hem this lif they lede.
And fareth now wel, my tale is at an ende.
Now Jesu Crist, that of his might may sende
Joye after wo, governe us in his grace,
And keepe us alle that been in this place.
Amen

The Epilogue

Oure Host upon his stiropes stood anoon
And saide, "Goode men, herkneth everichoon,
This was a thrifty tale for the nones.
Sire parissh preest," quod he, "for Goddes bones,
Tel us a tale as was thy forward yore.
I see wel that ye lerned men in lore
Can muche good, by Goddes dignitee."
The Person him answerde, "Benedicite,
What aileth the man so sinfully to swere?"
Oure Host answerde, "O Jankin, be ye there?

1017. hool, hale. **1018. scaped,** escaped from. **1022. herieth,** praises; **sithe,** times. **1025. departeth,** separates.

3. thrifty, proper; **nones,** occasion. **5. forward,** agreement; **yore,** earlier. **7. Can,** know. **8. Benedicite,** bless me.

I smelle a lollere° in the wind," quod he.
"Now, goode men," quod oure Hoste, "herkneth me:
Abideth, for Goddes digne° passioun,
For we shal have a predicacioun.°
This lollere here wol prechen us somwhat."
"Nay, by my fader soule, that shal he nat,"
Saide the [Wif of Bathe],° "shal he nat preche:
He shal no gospel glosen° here ne teche.
We leven alle in the grete God," quod [she].°
"He wolde sowen som difficultee
Or sprengen cokkel in oure clene corn.°
And therfore, Host, I warne thee biforn,
My joly body shal a tale telle,
And I shal clinken you so merye a belle
That I shal waken al this compaignye.
But it shal nat been of philosophye,
Ne physlias,° ne termes quainte of lawe:
Ther is but litel Latin in my mawe."

11. lollere: the contemptuous term used by the Host was commonly applied to priests who pressed for ecclesiastical reform and were popularly suspected of heresy. **13. digne,** worthy. **14. predicacioun,** sermon. **17. Wif of Bathe,** no manuscript gives this reading; see discussion on p. 1074. **18. glosen,** gloss, explain so as to deceive. **19. leven,** believe; **she,** the manuscripts have **he.** **21. sprengen cokkel,** spread tares; **corn,** wheat. **27. physlias,** though the meaning is unknown, the word is probably an ignorant attempt on the part of the speaker to exemplify either a philosophical term or a "curious" legal term.

THE WIFE OF BATH'S PROLOGUE

Experience, though noon auctoritee
Were in this world, is right ynough for me
To speke of wo that is in mariage:
For lordinges, sith I twelf yeer was of age—
Thanked be God that is eterne on live—
Housbondes at chirche dore I have had five
(If I so ofte mighte han wedded be),
And alle were worthy men in hir degree.
But me was told, certain, nat longe agoon is,
That sith that Crist ne wente nevere but ones
To wedding in the Cane of Galilee,
That by the same ensample taughte he me
That I ne sholde wedded be but ones.
Herke eek, lo, which a sharp word for the nones,
Biside a welle, Jesus, God and man,
Spak in repreve of the Samaritan:
"Thou hast yhad five housbondes," quod he,
"And that ilke man that now hath thee
Is nat thyn housbonde." Thus saide he certain.
What that he mente therby I can nat sayn,
But that I axe why that the fifthe man
Was noon housbonde to the Samaritan?
How manye mighte she han in mariage?
Yit herde I nevere tellen in myn age
Upon this nombre diffinicioun.
Men may divine and glosen up and down,
But wel I woot, expres, withouten lie,

4. lordinges, gentlemen. **6. chirche dore,** the actual wedding ceremony was celebrated at the church door, not in the chancel. **11. Cane,** Cana. **12. ensample,** example. **14. which,** what; **for the nones,** to the purpose. **16. repreve,** reproof. **18. ilke,** same. **21. axe,** ask. **21–22.** Christ was actually referring to a sixth man who was not married to the Samaritan woman. **25. diffinicioun,** definition. **26. divine,** guess; **glosen,** interpret. **27. woot,** know; **expres,** expressly.

God bad us for to wexe° and multiplye:
That gentil text can I wel understonde.
Eek wel I woot he saide that myn housbonde
Sholde lete° fader and moder and take to me,
But of no nombre mencion made he—
Of bigamye or of octogamye:
Why sholde men thanne speke of it vilainye?
Lo, here the wise king daun° Salomon:
I trowe° he hadde wives many oon,
As wolde God it leveful° were to me
To be refresshed half so ofte as he.
Which yifte° of God hadde he for alle his wives!
No man hath swich that in this world alive is.
God woot this noble king, as to my wit,
The firste night hadde many a merye fit°
With eech of hem, so wel was him on live.
Blessed be God that I have wedded five,
Of whiche I have piked out the beste,°
Bothe of hir nether purs and of hir cheste.°
Diverse scoles maken parfit° clerkes,
And diverse practikes° in sondry werkes
Maken the werkman parfit sikerly:
Of five housbondes scoleying° am I.
Welcome the sixte whan that evere he shal!°
For sith I wol nat keepe me chast in al,
Whan myn housbonde is fro the world agoon,
Som Cristen man shal wedde me anoon.
For thanne th'Apostle saith that I am free
To wedde, a Goddes half,° where it liketh me.
He said that to be wedded is no sinne:
Bet is to be wedded than to brinne.°
What rekketh me° though folk saye vilainye

28. wexe, i.e., increase. **31. lete,** leave. **35. daun,** master. **36. trowe,** believe. **37. leveful,** permissible. **39. Which yifte,** what a gift. **42. fit,** bout. **45.** i.e., Whom I have cleaned out of everything worthwhile. **46. nether,** lower; **cheste,** moneybox. **47. parfit,** perfect. **48. practikes,** i.e., practical experiences. **50. scoleying,** schooling. **51. shal,** i.e., shall come along. **56. a . . . half,** on God's behalf. **58. Bet,** better; **brinne,** burn. **59. rekketh me,** do I care.

Of shrewed Lamech and his bigamye?°
I woot wel Abraham was an holy man,
And Jacob eek, as fer as evere I can,°
And eech of hem hadde wives mo than two,
And many another holy man also.
  Where can ye saye in any manere age
That hye God defended° mariage
By expres word? I praye you, telleth me.
Or where comanded he virginitee?
I woot as wel as ye, it is no drede,°
Th'Apostle, whan he speketh of maidenhede,°
He saide that precept therof hadde he noon:
Men may conseile a womman to be oon,°
But conseiling nis no comandement.
He putte it in oure owene juggement.
For hadde God comanded maidenhede,
Thanne hadde he dampned° wedding with the deede;
And certes, if ther were no seed ysowe,
Virginitee, thanne wherof sholde it growe?
Paul dorste nat comanden at the leeste
A thing of which his maister yaf no heeste.°
The dart° is set up for virginitee:
Cacche whoso may, who renneth° best lat see.
But this word is nought take of° every wight,
But ther as God list° yive it of his might.
I woot wel that th'Apostle was a maide,°
But nathelees, though that he wroot or saide
He wolde that every wight were swich as he,
Al nis but conseil to virginitee;
And for to been a wif he yaf me leve
Of indulgence; so nis it no repreve°
To wedde me if that my make° die,

60. **shrewed,** cursed; **Lamech,** the first man whom the Bible mentions as having two wives. 62. **can,** know. 66. **defended,** prohibited. 69. **drede,** doubt. 70. **Th'Apostle,** Paul; **maidenhede,** maidenhood. 72. **oon,** single. 76. **dampned,** condemned; **with . . . deede,** i.e., at the same time. 80. **yaf,** gave; **heeste,** command. 81. **dart,** i.e., prize in a race. 82. **renneth,** runs. 83. **take of,** understood for, i.e., applicable to. 84. **list,** it pleases. 85. **maide,** virgin. 90. **repreve,** disgrace. 91. **To . . . wedde,** for me to marry; **make,** mate.

Withouten excepcion of bigamye°—
Al were it good no womman for to touche
(He mente as in his bed or in his couche,
For peril is bothe fir and tow° t'assemble—
Ye knowe what this ensample may resemble)°.
This al and som°, he heeld virginitee
More parfit than wedding in freletee.°
(Freletee clepe I but if° that he and she
Wolde leden al hir lif in chastitee).
I graunte it wel, I have noon envye
Though maidenhede preferre bigamye:°
It liketh hem to be clene in body and gost.°
Of myn estaat ne wol I make no boost;
For wel ye knowe, a lord in his houshold
Ne hath nat every vessel al of gold:
Some been of tree,° and doon hir lord servise.
God clepeth folk to him in sondry wise,
And everich hath of God a propre yifte,
Som this, som that, as him liketh shifte.°
Virginitee is greet perfeccioun,
And continence eek with devocioun,
But Crist, that of perfeccion is welle,°
Bad nat every wight he sholde go selle
Al that he hadde and yive it to the poore,
And in swich wise folwe him and his fore:°
He spak to hem that wolde live parfitly°—
And lordinges, by youre leve, that am nat I.
I wol bistowe the flour of al myn age
In th'actes and in fruit of mariage.
  Telle me also, to what conclusioun°
Were membres maad of generacioun
And of so parfit wis a wrighte ywrought?°

92. **excepcion,** legal objection; **of,** i.e., on the score of: **bigamye** in this context refers to successive, rather than simultaneous marriages. 95. **tow,** flax. 96. **ensample,** i.e., metaphor; **resemble,** i.e., apply to. 97. **al . . . som,** is all there is to it. 98. **freletee,** fraility. 99. **clepe . . . if,** I call it unless. 102. **preferre,** excel; **bigamye,** remarriage. 103. **gost,** spirit. 107. **tree,** wood. 110. **shifte,** ordain. 113. **welle,** source. 116. **fore,** footsteps. 117. **parfitly,** perfectly. 121. **conclusioun,** end. 123. And wrought by so perfectly wise a maker.

Trusteth right wel, they were nat maad for nought.
Glose° whoso wol, and saye bothe up and down
That they were maked for purgacioun
Of urine, and oure bothe thinges smale
Was eek to knowe a femele from a male,
And for noon other cause—saye ye no?
Th'experience woot wel it is nought so.
So that the clerkes be nat with me wrothe,
I saye this, that they maked been for bothe—
That is to sayn, for office° and for ese
Of engendrure, ther we nat God displese.
Why sholde men elles in hir bookes sette
That man shal yeelde° to his wif hir dette?
Now wherwith sholde he make his payement
If he ne used his sely° instrument?
Thanne were they maad upon a creature
To purge urine, and eek for engendrure.
  But I saye nought that every wight is holde,°
That hath swich harneis° as I to you tolde,
To goon and usen hem in engendrure:
Thanne sholde men take of chastitee no cure.°
Crist was a maide° and shapen as a man,
And many a saint sith that the world bigan,
Yit lived they evere in parfit chastitee.
I nil envye no virginitee:
Lat hem be breed of pured° whete seed,
And lat us wives hote° barly breed—
And yit with barly breed, Mark telle can,
Oure Lord Jesu refresshed many a man.
In swich estaat as God hath cleped us
I wol persevere: I nam nat precious.°
In wifhood wol I use myn instrument
As freely° as my Makere hath it sent.

125. **Glose**, interpret. 133. **office**, excretion. 136. **yeelde**, i.e., pay. 138. **sely**, innocent. 141. **holde**, bound. 142. **harneis**, equipment. 144. **cure**, heed. 145. **maide**, virgin. 149. **breed**, bread; **pured**, refined. 150. **hote**, be called. 154. **precious**, fastidious. 156. **freely**, generously.

If I be daungerous,° God yive me sorwe:
Myn housbonde shal it han both eve and morwe,°
Whan that him list° come forth and paye his dette.
An housbonde wol I have, I wol nat lette,°
Which shal be bothe my dettour and my thral,°
And have his tribulacion withal
Upon his flessh whil that I am his wif.
I have the power during al my lif
Upon his propre° body, and nat he:
Right thus th'Apostle tolde it unto me,
And bad oure housbondes for to love us weel.
Al this sentence° me liketh everydeel.

AN INTERLUDE

Up sterte° the Pardoner and that anoon:
"Now dame," quod he, "by God and by Saint John,
Ye been a noble prechour in this cas.
I was aboute to wedde a wif: allas,
What sholde I bye° it on my flessh so dere?
Yit hadde I levere wedde no wif toyere."°
"Abid," quod she, "my tale is nat bigonne.
Nay, thou shalt drinken of another tonne,°
Er that I go, shal savoure wors than ale.
And whan that I have told thee forth my tale
Of tribulacion in mariage,
Of which I am expert in al myn age—
This is to saye, myself hath been the whippe—
Thanne maistou chese° wheither thou wolt sippe
Of thilke tonne that I shal abroche:°
Be war of it, er thou too neigh approche,
For I shal telle ensamples mo than ten.
'Whoso that nile° be war by othere men,

157. **daungerous,** stand-offish. 158. **morwe,** morning. 159. **him list,** he wishes to. 160. **nat lette,** make no difficulty. 161. **dettour,** debtor; **thral,** slave. 165. **propre,** own. 168. **sentence,** purport. 169. **sterte,** started. 173. **What,** why; **bye,** purchase. 174. **toyere,** this year. 176. **tonne,** tun. 182. **chese,** choose. 183. **abroche,** broach. 186. **nile,** would not.

By him shal othere men corrected be.'
Thise same wordes writeth Ptolomee:
Rede in his Almageste and take it there."°
"Dame, I wolde praye you if youre wil it were,"
Saide this Pardoner, "as ye bigan,
Telle forth youre tale; spareth for no man,
And teche us yonge men of youre practike."°
"Gladly," quod she, "sith it may you like;°
But that I praye to al this compaignye,
If that I speke after my fantasye,
As taketh nat agrief° of that I saye,
For myn entente nis but for to playe."

THE WIFE CONTINUES

Now sire, thanne wol I telle you forth my tale.
As evere mote I drinke win or ale,
I shal saye sooth: tho housbondes that I hadde,
As three of hem were goode, and two were badde.
The three men were goode, and riche, and olde;
Unnethe° mighte they the statut holde
In which they were bounden unto me—
Ye woot wel what I mene of this, pardee.
As help me God, I laughe whan I thinke
How pitously anight I made hem swinke;°
And by my fay, I tolde of it no stoor:°
They hadde me yiven hir land and hir tresor;
Me needed nat do lenger diligence
To winne hir love or doon hem reverence.
They loved me so wel, by God above,
That I ne tolde no daintee of° hir love.
A wis womman wol bisye hire evere in oon°
To gete hire love, ye, ther as she hath noon.

188–89. Ptolemy's *Almagest* contains no such aphorism, which does, however, appear in a collection ascribed to Ptolemy. **193. practike,** mode of operation. **194. like,** please. **197. agrief,** amiss. **204. Unnethe,** with difficulty. **208. swinke,** work. **209. fay,** faith; **tolde . . . stoor,** set no store by it. **214. tolde . . . of,** set no store by. **215. bisye hire,** busy herself; **in oon,** constantly.

But sith I hadde hem hoolly in myn hand,
And sith that they hadde yiven me al hir land,
What sholde I take keep° hem for to plese,
But it were for my profit and myn ese?
I sette hem so awerke, by my fay,°
That many a night they songen° wailaway.
The bacon was nat fet° for hem, I trowe,
That some men han in Essexe at Dunmowe.°
I governed hem so wel after my lawe
That eech of hem ful blisful was and fawe°
To bringe me gaye thinges fro the faire;
They were ful glade whan I spak to hem faire,
For God it woot, I chidde hem spitously.°
  Now herkneth how I bar me° proprely:
Ye wise wives, that conne understonde,
Thus sholde ye speke and bere him wrong on honde°—
For half so boldely can ther no man
Swere and lie as a woman can.
I saye nat this by wives that been wise,
But if it be whan they hem misavise.°
A wis wif, if that she can hir good,°
Shal bere him on hande the cow is wood,°
And take witnesse of hir owene maide
Of hir assent.° But herkneth how I saide:
  "Sire olde cainard,° is this thyn array?
Why is my neighebores wif so gay?
She is honoured overal ther she gooth:
I sitte at hoom; I have no thrifty° cloth.
What doostou at my neighebores hous?
Is she so fair? Artou so amorous?

219. **What,** why; **keep,** care. **221. awerke,** awork; **fay,** faith. **222. songen,** sang. **223. fet,** brought back. **224.** The Dunmow flitch is awarded to a married couple that has not quarreled for a year. **226. fawe,** glad. **229. chidde,** chided; **spitously,** cruelly. **230. bar** me, bore myself, behaved. **232. bere . . . honde,** accuse him falsely. **236. hem misavise,** make a mistake. **237. can . . . good,** knows what's good for her. **238. bere . . . hande,** persuade him; **cow . . . wood,** the chough (a bird supposed to tell husbands of their wives' infidelity) has gone crazy. **239–40. And . . . assent,** and call as a witness her maid who is on her side. **241. cainard,** sluggard. **244. thrifty,** decent.

What roune ye with oure maide, benedicite?°
Sire olde lechour, lat thy japes° be.
And if I have a gossib° or a freend,
Withouten gilt ye chiden as a feend,
If that I walke or playe unto his hous.
Thou comest hoom as dronken as a mous,
And prechest on thy bench, with yvel preef.°
Thou saist to me, it is a greet meschief
To wedde a poore womman for costage.°
And if that she be riche, of heigh parage,°
Thanne saistou that it is a tormentrye
To suffre hir pride and hir malencolye.
And if that she be fair, thou verray knave,
Thou saist that every holour° wol hire have:
She may no while in chastitee abide
That is assailed upon eech a side.
  Thou saist som folk desiren us for richesse,
Som° for oure shap, and som for oure fairnesse,
And som for she can outher° singe or daunce,
And som for gentilesse and daliaunce,°
Som for hir handes and hir armes smale—
Thus gooth al to the devel by thy tale!°
Thou saist men may nat keepe° a castel wal,
It may so longe assailed been overal.
And if that she be foul, thou saist that she
Coveiteth° every man that she may see;
For as a spaniel she wol on him lepe,
Til that she finde som man hire to chepe.°
Ne noon so grey goos gooth ther in the lake,
As, saistou, wol be withoute make;°
And saist it is an hard thing for to weelde°
A thing that no man wol, his thankes, heelde.°

247. **roune,** whisper; **benedicite,** bless me. 248. **japes,** tricks, intrigues. 249. **gossib,** confidant. 253. **with . . . preef,** (may you have) bad luck. 255. **costage,** expense. 256. **parage,** descent. 260. **holour,** whoremonger. 264ff. **som,** one. 265. **outher,** either. 266. **daliaunce,** flirtatiousness. 268. **by . . . tale,** i.e., according to your story. 269. **keepe,** i.e., keep safe. 272. **Coveiteth,** desires. 274. **chepe,** buy. 276. **make,** mate. 277. **weelde,** possess. 278. **his thankes,** willingly; **heelde,** hold.

Thus saistou, lorel,° whan thou goost to bedde,
And that no wis man needeth for to wedde,
Ne no man that entendeth° unto hevene—
With wilde thonder-dint and firy levene°
Mote thy welked nekke be tobroke!°
Thou saist that dropping° houses and eek smoke
And chiding wives maken men to flee
Out of hir owene houses: a, benedicite,°
What aileth swich an old man for to chide?
Thou saist we wives wil oure vices hide
Til we be fast,° and thanne we wol hem shewe—
Wel may that be a proverbe of a shrewe!°
Thou saist that oxen, asses, hors,° and houndes,
They been assayed at diverse stoundes;°
Bacins, lavours, er that men hem bye,
Spoones, stooles, and al swich housbondrye,°
And so be pottes, clothes, and array°—
But folk of wives maken noon assay
Til they be wedded—olde dotard shrewe!
And thanne, saistou, we wil oure vices shewe.
Thou saist also that it displeseth me
But if that thou wolt praise my beautee,
And but thou poure alway upon my face,
And clepe me 'Faire Dame' in every place,
And but thou make a feeste on thilke day
That I was born, and make me fressh and gay,
And but thou do to my norice° honour,
And to my chamberere within my bowr,°
And to my fadres folk, and his allies°—
Thus saistou, olde barel-ful of lies.
And yit of our apprentice Janekin,
For his crispe° heer, shining as gold so fin,

279. **lorel,** loafer. 281. **entendeth,** aims. 282. **thonder-dint,** thunderbolt; **levene,** lightning. 283. **Mote,** may; **welked,** withered; **tobroke,** broken. 284. **dropping,** leaking. 286. **benedicite,** bless me. 289. **fast,** i.e., married. 290. **shrewe,** villain. 291. **hors,** horses. 292. **stoundes,** times. 293. **lavours,** wash-bowls. 294. **housbondrye,** household goods. 295. **be,** are; **array,** clothing. 305. **norice,** nurse. 306. **chamberere,** chambermaid; **bowr,** bedroom. 307. **allies,** relatives by marriage. 310. **crispe,** curly.

And for he squiereth me bothe up and down,
Yit hastou caught a fals suspecioun;
I wil him nat though thou were deed° tomorwe.
  But tel me this, why hidestou with sorwe°
The keyes of thy cheste away fro me?
It is my good as wel as thyn, pardee.
What, weenestou° make an idiot of oure dame?
Now by that lord that called is Saint Jame,
Thou shalt nought bothe, though that thou were wood,°
Be maister of my body and of my good:
That oon thou shalt forgo, maugree thine yën.°
  What helpeth it of me enquere° and spyen?
I trowe thou woldest loke° me in thy cheste.
Thou sholdest saye, 'Wif, go wher thee leste.°
Taak youre disport. I nil leve° no tales:
I knowe you for a trewe wif, dame Alis.'
We love no man that taketh keep or charge°
Wher that we goon: we wol been at oure large.°
Of alle men yblessed mote he be
The wise astrologen° daun Ptolomee,
That saith this proverbe in his Almageste:
'Of alle men his wisdom is the hyeste
That rekketh° nat who hath the world in honde.'
By this proverbe thou shalt understonde,
Have thou ynough, what thar° thee rekke or care
How merily that othere folkes fare?
For certes, olde dotard, by youre leve,
Ye shal han queinte° right ynough at eve:
He is too greet a nigard that wil werne°
A man to lighte a candle at his lanterne;
He shal han nevere the lasse° lighte, pardee.

313. **wil,** want; **deed,** dead. 314. **with sorwe,** i.e., with sorrow to you. 317. **weenestou,** do you think to. 319. **wood,** furious. 321. **maugree . . . yën,** despite your eyes, i.e., anything you can do about it. 322. **enquere,** inquire. 323. **loke,** lock. 324. **leste,** it may please. 325. **leve,** believe. 327. **keep,** notice; **charge,** i.e., interest. 328. **large,** i.e., liberty. 330. **astrologen,** astronomer. 333. **rekketh,** cares. 335. **Have thou,** if you have; **thar,** need. 338. **queinte,** pudendum. 339. **werne,** refuse. 341. **lasse,** less.

Have thou ynough, thee thar nat plaine thee.°
  Thou saist also that if we make us gay
With clothing and with precious array,
That it is peril of oure chastitee,
And yit with sorwe thou moste enforce thee,°
And saye thise wordes in th'Apostles name:
'In habit maad with chastitee and shame
Ye wommen shal apparaile you,' quod he,
'And nat in tressed heer and gay perree,°
As perles ne with gold ne clothes riche.'
After thy text, ne after thy rubriche,°
I wol nat werke as muchel as a gnat.
Thou saidest this, that I was lik a cat:
For whoso wolde senge° a cattes skin,
Thanne wolde the cat wel dwellen in his in;°
And if the cattes skin be slik° and gay,
She wol nat dwelle in house half a day,
But forth she wol, er any day be dawed,°
To shewe her skin and goon a-caterwawed.°
This is to saye, if I be gay, sire shrewe,
I wol renne out, my borel° for to shewe.
Sire olde fool, what helpeth thee t'espyen?
Though thou praye Argus with his hundred yën
To be my wardecors,° as he can best,
In faith, he shal nat keepe me but me lest:°
Yit coude I make his beerd, so mote I thee.°
  Thou saidest eek that ther been thinges three,
The whiche thinges troublen al this erthe,
And that no wight may endure the ferthe.°
O leve sire shrewe, Jesu shorte° thy lif!
Yit prechestou and saist an hateful wif

342. **plaine thee,** complain. 346. **enforce thee,** i.e., strengthen your position. 350. **tressed heer,** i.e., elaborate hairdo; **perree,** jewelry. 352. **rubriche,** rubric, i.e., direction. 355. **senge,** singe. 356. **in,** lodging. 357. **slik,** sleek. 359. **be dawed,** has dawned. 360. **a-caterwawed,** caterwauling. 362. **renne,** run; **borel,** clothing. 365. **wardecors,** bodyguard. 366. **keepe,** guard; **but . . . lest,** unless I please. 367. **make . . . beerd,** i.e., deceive him; **thee,** thrive. 370. **ferthe,** fourth. 371. **leve,** dear; **shorte,** shorten.

Yrekened is for oon of thise meschaunces.
Been ther nat none othere resemblaunces
That ye may likne youre parables to,°
But if a sely° wif be oon of tho?
  Thou liknest eek wommanes love to helle,
To bareine° land ther water may nat dwelle;
Thou liknest it also to wilde fir—
The more it brenneth,° the more it hath desir
To consumen every thing that brent° wol be;
Thou saist right as wormes shende° a tree,
Right so a wif destroyeth hir housbonde—
This knowen they that been to wives bonde."°
  Lordinges, right thus, as ye han understonde,
Bar I stifly mine olde housbondes on honde°
That thus they saiden in hir dronkenesse—
And al was fals, but that I took witnesse
On Janekin and on my nece also.
O Lord, the paine I dide hem and the wo,
Ful giltelees, by Goddes sweete pine!°
For as an hors I coude bite and whine;
I coude plaine° and I was in the gilt,
Or elles often time I hadde been spilt.°
Whoso that first to mille comth first grint;°
I plained first: so was oure werre stint.°
They were ful glad to excusen hem ful blive°
Of thing of which they nevere agilte hir° live.
Of wenches wolde I beren hem on honde,
Whan that for sik they mighte unnethe° stonde,
Yit tikled I his herte for that he
Wende I hadde had of him so greet cheertee.°
I swoor that al my walking out by nighte

374–75. Isn't there something else appropriate that you can apply your metaphors to. **376. But if,** unless; **sely,** innocent. **378. bareine,** barren. **380. brenneth,** burns. **381. brent,** burned. **382. shende,** destroy. **384. bonde,** bound. **386. Bar on honde,** accused; **stifly,** rigorously. **391. pine,** suffering. **393. plaine,** complain. **394. spilt,** ruined. **395. grint,** grinds. **396. werre,** war; **stint,** brought to end. **397. blive,** quickly. **398. of which,** in which; **agilte,** offended; **hir,** i.e., in their. **400. sik,** i.e., sickness; **unnethe,** scarcely. **402. Wende,** thought; **cheertee,** affection.

Was for to espye wenches that he dighte.°
Under that colour° hadde I many a mirthe.
For al swich wit is yiven us in oure birthe:
Deceite, weeping, spinning God hath yive
To wommen kindely° whil they may live.
And thus of oo thing I avaunte me:°
At ende I hadde the bet° in eech degree,
By sleighte or force, or by som manere thing,
As by continuel murmur or grucching;°
Namely° abedde hadden they meschaunce:
Ther wolde I chide and do hem no plesaunce;
I wolde no lenger in the bed abide
If that I felte his arm over my side,
Til he hadde maad his raunson° unto me;
Thanne wolde I suffre him do his nicetee.°
And therfore every man this tale I telle:
Winne whoso may, for al is for to selle;
With empty hand men may no hawkes lure.
For winning° wolde I al his lust endure,
And make me a feined appetit—
And yit in bacon° hadde I nevere delit.
That made me that evere I wolde hem chide;
For though the Pope hadde seten° hem biside,
I wolde nought spare hem at hir owene boord.
For by my trouthe, I quitte° hem word for word.
As help me verray God omnipotent,
Though I right now sholde make my testament,
I ne owe hem nat a word that it nis quit.
I broughte it so aboute by my wit
That they moste yive it up as for the beste,
Or elles hadde we nevere been in reste;
For though he looked as a wood° leoun,
Yit sholde he faile of his conclusioun.°

404. **dighte,** had intercourse with. 405. **colour,** i.e., excuse. 408. **kindely,** naturally. 409. **avaunte me,** boast. 410. **bet,** better. 412. **murmur,** complaint; **grucching,** grumbling. 413. **Namely,** especially. 417. **raunson,** ransom. 418. **nicetee,** lust. 422. **winning,** profit. 424. **bacon,** i.e., old meat. 426. **seten,** sat. 428. **quitte,** repaid. 435. **wood,** furious. 436. **conclusioun,** object.

Thanne wolde I saye, "Goodelief, taak keep°
How mekely looketh Wilekin, oure sheep!
Com neer my spouse, lat me ba° thy cheeke—
Ye sholden be al pacient and meeke,
And han a sweete-spiced° conscience,
Sith ye so preche of Jobes pacience;
Suffreth alway, sin ye so wel can preche;
And but ye do, certain, we shal you teche
That it is fair to han a wif in pees.
Oon of us two moste bowen, doutelees,
And sith a man is more resonable
Than womman is, ye mosten been suffrable°
What aileth you to grucche° thus and grone?
Is it for ye wolde have my queinte° allone?
Why, taak it al—lo, have it everydeel.
Peter, I shrewe° you but ye love it weel.
For if I wolde selle my bele chose°
I coude walke as fressh as is a rose;
But I wol keepe it for youre owene tooth°
Ye be to blame. By God, I saye you sooth!"
Swiche manere wordes hadde we on honde.
Now wol I speke of my ferthe° housbonde.

My ferthe housbonde was a revelour—
This is to sayn, he hadde a paramour°—
And I was yong and ful of ragerye°
Stibourne and strong and joly as a pie:°
How coude I daunce to an harpe smale°
And singe, ywis, as any nightingale,
Whan I hadde dronke a draughte of sweete win.
Metellius, the foule cherl, the swin,
That with a staf birafte° his wif hir lif
For° she drank win, though I hadde been his wif,
Ne sholde nat han daunted me fro drinke;

437. Goodelief, good friend; **keep,** notice. **439. ba,** kiss. **441. sweete-spiced,** i.e., delicate. **448. suffrable,** patient. **449. grucche,** grumble. **450. queinte,** pudendum. **452. shrewe,** curse. **453. bele chose,** fair thing. **455. tooth,** taste. **458. ferthe,** fourth. **460. paramour,** mistress. **461. ragerye,** wantonness. **462. Stibourne,** untamable; **pie,** magpie. **463. smale,** gracefully. **467. birafte,** deprived. **468. For,** because.

And after win on Venus moste° I thinke,
For also siker° as cold engendreth hail,
A likerous mouth moste han a likerous° tail:
In womman vinolent° is no defence—
This knowen lechours by experience.
  But Lord Crist, whan that it remembreth me
Upon my youthe and on my jolitee,
It tikleth me aboute myn herte roote—
Unto this day it dooth myn herte boote°
That I have had my world as in my time.
But age, allas, that al wol envenime,°
Hath me biraft° my beautee and my pith—
Lat go, farewel, the devel go therwith!
The flour is goon, ther is namore to telle:
The bren° as I best can now moste I selle;
But yit to be right merye wol I fonde.°
Now wol I tellen of my ferthe housbonde.
  I saye I hadde in herte greet despit
That he of any other hadde delit,
But he was quit,° by God and by Saint Joce:
I made him of the same wode a croce°—
Nat of my body in no foul manere—
But, certainly, I made folk swich cheere
That in his owene grece I made him frye,
For angre and for verray jalousye.
By God, in erthe I was his purgatorye,
For which I hope his soule be in glorye.
For God it woot, he sat ful ofte and soong°
Whan that his sho ful bitterly him wroong.°
Ther was no wight save God and he that wiste°
In many wise how sore I him twiste.
He deide whan I cam fro Jerusalem,
And lith ygrave under the roode-beem,°

470. moste, must. **471. siker,** sure. **472. likerous,** greedy, lecherous. **473. vinolent,** bibulous. **478. boote,** good. **480. envenime,** poison. **481. me biraft,** taken away from me. **484. bren,** bran. **485. fonde,** strive. **489. quit,** paid back. **490. croce,** cross. **497. soong,** sang. **498. wroong,** wrung. **499. wiste,** knew. **502. lith,** lies; **ygrave,** buried; **roode-beem,** timber between nave and chancel.

Al is his tombe nought so curious°
As was the sepulcre of him Darius,
Which that Appelles wroughte subtilly:
It nis but wast to burye him preciously.°
Lat him fare wel, God yive his soule reste;
He is now in his grave and in his cheste.
  Now of my fifthe housbonde wol I telle—
God lete his soule nevere come in helle—
And yit he was to me the moste shrewe:°
That feele I on my ribbes al by rewe,°
And evere shal unto myn ending day.
But in oure bed he was so fressh and gay,
And therwithal so wel coude he me glose°
Whan that he wolde han my bele chose,
That though he hadde me bet on every boon,°
He coude winne again my love anoon.
I trowe I loved him best for that he
Was of his love daungerous° to me.
We wommen han, if that I shal nat lie,
In this matere a quainte fantasye:
Waite what thing we may nat lightly° have,
Therafter wol we crye al day and crave;
Forbede us thing, and that desiren we;
Preesse on us faste, and thanne wol we flee.
With daunger oute we al oure chaffare:°
Greet prees at market maketh dere ware,°
And too greet chepe is holden at litel pris.°
This knoweth every womman that is wis.
  My fifthe housbonde—God his soule blesse!—
Which that I took for love and no richesse,
He somtime was a clerk of Oxenforde,
And hadde laft° scole and wente at hoom to boorde

503. **Al,** although; **curious,** carefully wrought. 506. **preciously,** expensively. 511. **moste shrewe,** worst rascal. 512. **by rewe,** in a row. 515. **glose,** wheedle. 517. **bet,** beaten; **boon,** bone. 520. **Was daungerous,** played hard to get. 523. **Waite what,** whatever; **lightly,** easily. 527. **daunger,** coyness; **oute,** spread out; **chaffare,** merchandise. 528. **prees,** crowd; **maketh . . . ware,** makes goods expensive. 529. **too . . . chepe,** too good a bargain; **pris,** value. 534. **laft,** left.

With my gossib° dwelling in oure town—
God have hir soule!—hir name was Alisoun;
She knew myn herte and eek my privetee
Bet than oure parissh preest, as mote I thee.°
To hire biwrayed I my conseil° al,
For hadde myn housbonde pissed on a wal,
Or doon a thing that sholde han cost his lif,
To hire° and to another worthy wif,
And to my nece which that I loved weel,
I wolde han told his conseil everydeel;
And so I dide ful often, God it woot,
That made his face often reed and hoot°
For verray shame, and blamed himself for he
Hadde told to me so greet a privetee.
  And so bifel that ones in a Lente—
So often times I to my gossib wente,
For evere yit I loved to be gay,
And for to walke in March, Averil, and May,
From hous to hous, to heere sondry tales—
That Janekin clerk and my gossib dame Alis
And I myself into the feeldes wente.
Myn housbonde was at London al that Lente:
I hadde the better leiser for to playe,
And for to see, and eek for to be seye°
Of lusty folk—what wiste I wher my grace°
Was shapen° for to be, or in what place?
Therfore I made my visitaciouns
To vigilies° and to processiouns,
To preching eek, and to thise pilgrimages,
To playes of miracles and to mariages,
And wered upon my gaye scarlet gites°—
Thise wormes ne thise motthes ne thise mites,
Upon my peril, frete° hem neveradeel:

535. **gossib,** confidante. 538. **Bet,** better; **thee,** thrive. 539. **biwrayed,** disclosed; **conseil,** secrets. 542. **hire,** her. 546. **reed,** red; **hoot,** hot. 558. **seye,** seen. 559. **grace,** luck. 560. **shapen,** destined. 562. **vigilies,** feasts preceding a saint's day. 565. **wered upon,** wore; **gites,** dress. 567. **frete,** ate.

And woostou why? For they were used weel.
  Now wol I tellen forth what happed me.
I saye that in the feeldes walked we,
Til trewely we hadde swich daliaunce,°
This clerk and I, that of my purveyaunce°
I spak to him and saide him how that he,
If I were widwe, sholde wedde me.
For certainly, I saye for no bobaunce°
Yit was I nevere withouten purveyaunce
Of mariage n'of othere thinges eek:
I holde a mouses herte nought worth a leek
That hath but oon hole for to sterte° to,
And if that faile thanne is al ydo.
I bar him on hand° he hadde enchaunted me
(My dame taughte me that subtiltee);
And eek I saide I mette° of him al night:
He wolde han slain me as I lay upright,°
And al my bed was ful of verray blood—
"But yit I hope that ye shul do me good;
For blood bitokeneth gold, as me was taught."
And al was fals, I dremed of it right naught,
But as I folwed ay my dames lore°
As wel of that as of othere thinges more.
But now sire—lat me see, what shal I sayn?
Aha, by God, I have my tale again.
  Whan that my ferthe housbonde was on beere,°
I weep algate,° and made sory cheere,
As wives moten, for it is usage,°
And with my coverchief covered my visage;
But for that I was purveyed of a make,°
I wepte but smale, and that I undertake.°
  To chirche was myn housbonde born amorwe°
With neighebores that for him maden sorwe,

571. **daliaunce,** flirtation. 572. **purveyaunce,** foresight. 575. **bobaunce,** boast. 579. **sterte,** run. 581. **bar . . . hand,** pretended to him. 583. **mette,** dreamed. 584. **upright,** supine. 589. **lore,** teaching. 593. **beere,** bier. 594. **weep,** wept; **algate,** anyhow. 595. **moten,** must; **usage,** custom. 597. **purveyed,** provided; **make,** mate. 598. **undertake,** guarantee. 599. **amorwe,** in the morning.

And Janekin oure clerk was oon of tho.
As help me God, whan that I saw him go
After the beere, me thoughte he hadde a paire
Of legges and of feet so clene° and faire,
That al myn herte I yaf unto his hold.°
He was, I trowe, twenty winter old,
And I was fourty, if I shal saye sooth—
But yit I hadde alway a coltes tooth:°
Gat-toothed° was I, and that bicam me weel;
I hadde the prente of Sainte Venus seel.°
As help me God, I was a lusty oon,
And fair and riche and yong and wel-bigoon;°
And trewely, as mine housbondes tolde me,
I hadde the beste quoniam° mighte be.
For certes I am al Venerien
In feeling, and myn herte is Marcien:°
Venus me yaf my lust, my likerousnesse,°
And Mars yaf me my sturdy hardinesse.
Myn ascendent was Taur° and Mars therinne—
Allas, allas, that evere love was sinne!
I folwed ay my inclinacioun
By vertu of my constellacioun;°
That made me I coude nought withdrawe
My chambre of Venus from a good felawe.
Yit have I Martes° merk upon my face,
And also in another privee place.
For God so wis be my savacioun,°
I loved nevere by no discrecioun,
But evere folwede myn appetit,
Al were he short or long or blak or whit;
I took no keep, so that he liked° me,
How poore he was, ne eek of what degree.

604. clene, i.e., neat. **605. hold,** possession. **608. a coltes tooth,** i.e., youthful appetites. **609. Gat-toothed,** gap-toothed. **610. prente,** print, i.e., a birthmark; **seel,** seal. **612. wel-bigoon,** well-situated. **614. quoniam,** pudendum. **616. Marcien,** Martian. **617. likerousnesse,** lecherousness. **619. ascendent,** horoscope; **Taur,** Taurus. **622. constellacioun,** i.e., horoscope. **625. Martes,** Mars's. **627. wis,** surely; **savacioun,** salvation. **631. keep,** heed; **liked,** pleased.

What sholde I saye but at the monthes ende
This joly clerk Janekin that was so hende°
Hath wedded me with greet solempnitee,
And to him yaf I al the land and fee°
That evere was me yiven therbifore—
But afterward repented me ful sore:
He nolde suffre no thing of my list.°
By God, he smoot me ones on the list°
For that I rente° out of his book a leef,
That of the strook myn ere weex° al deef.
Stibourne I was as is a leonesse,
And of my tonge a verray jangleresse,°
And walke I wolde, as I hadde doon biforn,
From hous to hous, although he hadde it° sworn;
For which he often times wolde preche,
And me of olde Romain geestes° teche,
How he Simplicius Gallus lafte° his wif,
And hire forsook for terme of al his lif,
Nought but for open-heveded he hire sey°
Looking out at his dore upon a day.
Another Romain tolde he me by name
That, for his wif was at a someres° game
Withouten his witing,° he forsook hire eke;
And thanne wolde he upon his Bible seeke
That ilke proverbe of Ecclesiaste°
Where he comandeth and forbedeth faste
Man shal nat suffre his wif go roule° aboute;
Thanne wolde he saye right thus withouten doute:
"Whoso that buildeth his hous al of salwes,°
And priketh his blinde hors over the falwes,°
And suffreth his wif to go seeken halwes,°
Is worthy to be hanged on the galwes."°

634. **hende**, nice. 636. **fee**, property. 639. **list**, pleasure. 640. **smoot**, smote, struck; **list**, ear. 641. **rente**, tore. 642. **strook**, blow; **weex**, grew. 644. **jangleresse**, blabbermouth. 646. **it**, i.e., the contrary. 648. **geestes**, stories. 649. **lafte**, left. 651. Just because he saw her bare-headed. 654. **someres**, summer's. 655. **witing**, knowledge. 657. **Ecclesiaste**, Ecclesiasticus. 659. **roule**, roam. 661. **salwes**, willow sticks. 662. **priketh**, rides; **falwes**, plowed land. 663. **halwes**, shrines. 664. **galwes**, gallows.

But al for nought—I sette nought an hawe°
Of his proverbes n'of his olde sawe;
N'I wolde nat of him corrected be:
I hate him that my vices telleth me,
And so doon mo, God woot, of us than I.
This made him with me wood al outrely:°
I nolde nought forbere° him in no cas.
  Now wol I saye you sooth, by Saint Thomas,
Why that I rente° out of his book a leef,
For which he smoot me so that I was deef.
He hadde a book that gladly night and day
For his disport he wolde rede alway.
He cleped it Valerie and Theofraste,°
At which book he lough° alway ful faste;
And eek ther was somtime a clerk at Rome,
A cardinal, that highte Saint Jerome,
That made a book again Jovinian;°
In which book eek ther was Tertulan,°
Crysippus, Trotula, and Helouis,°
That was abbesse nat fer fro Paris;°
And eek the Parables° of Salomon,
Ovides Art,° and bookes many oon—
And alle thise were bounden in oo volume.
And every night and day was his custume,
Whan he hadde leiser and vacacioun
From other worldly occupacioun,
To reden in this book of wikked wives.
He knew of hem mo legendes and lives
Than been of goode wives in the Bible.

665. **sette an hawe,** rated at the value of a hawthorn berry. **670. al outrely,** entirely. **671. forbere,** submit to. **673. rente,** tore. **677. Valerie,** i.e., the *Letter of Valerius concerning Not Marrying* by Walter Map; **Theofraste,** Theophrastus' *Book concerning Marriage.* 678. **lough,** laughed. **680–81.** St. Jerome's antifeminist *Reply to Jovinian.* 682. **Tertulan,** Tertullian, author of treatises on sexual modesty. **683. Crysippus,** Chrysippus is mentioned by Jerome as an antifeminist; **Trotula,** a female doctor whose presence here is unexplained; **Helouis,** Eloise, whose love affair with the great scholar Abelard was a medieval scandal. **684.** Eloise later became abbess of a nunnery near Paris. **685. Parables,** Biblical Book of Proverbs. **686. Ovides Art,** Ovid's *Art of Love.*

For trusteth wel, it is an impossible°
That any clerk wol speke good of wives,
But if° it be of holy saintes lives,
N'of noon other womman nevere the mo—
Who painted the leon, tel me who?°
By God, if wommen hadden writen stories,
As clerkes han within hir oratories,
They wolde han writen of men more wikkednesse
Than al the merk° of Adam may redresse.
The children° of Mercurye and Venus
Been in hir werking ful contrarious:°
Mercurye loveth wisdom and science,
And Venus loveth riot and dispence;°
And for hir diverse disposicioun
Each falleth in otheres exaltacioun;°
And thus, God woot, Mercurye is desolat°
In Pisces wher Venus is exaltat,°
And Venus falleth ther Mercurye is raised:
Therfore no womman of no clerk is praised.
The clerk, whan he is old and may nought do
Of Venus werkes worth his olde sho,°
Thanne sit he down and writ° in his dotage
That wommen can nat keepe hir mariage.
But now to purpos why I tolde thee
That I was beten for a book, pardee:
Upon a night Janekin, that was oure sire,°
Redde on his book as he sat by the fire
Of Eva first, that for hir wikkednesse
Was al mankinde brought to wrecchednesse,
For which that Jesu Crist himself was slain

694. **impossible,** impossibility. 696. **But if,** unless. 698. In Aesop, the lion, on being shown a picture of a man killing a lion, asked who painted the picture: a leonine version would reverse the situation. 702. **merk,** mark, sex. 703. **children,** etc.: clerks and women, ruled by Mercury and Venus respectively. 704. **werking,** operation; **contrarious,** opposed. 706. **riot,** parties; **dispence,** expenditure. 708. Each loses its power when the other is dominant: the reference is planetary. 709. **desolat,** deprived of power. 710. **Pisces,** the Sign of the Fish; **exaltat,** dominant. 714. **sho,** shoe. 715. **sit,** sits; **writ,** writes. 719. **oure sire,** my husband.

That boughte° us with his herte blood again—
Lo, heer expres of wommen may ye finde
That womman was the los° of al mankinde.
  Tho redde he me how Sampson loste his heres:
Sleeping his lemman kitte° it with hir sheres,
Thurgh which treson loste he both his yën.
  Tho redde he me, if that I shal nat lien,
Of Ercules and of his Dianire,°
That caused him to sette himself afire.
  No thing forgat he the sorwe and wo
That Socrates hadde with his wives two—
How Xantippa caste pisse upon his heed:
This sely° man sat stille as he were deed;
He wiped his heed, namore dorste he sayn
But "Er that thonder stinte,° comth a rain."
  Of Phasipha° that was the queene of Crete—
For shrewednesse° him thoughte the tale sweete—
Fy, speek namore, it is a grisly thing
Of hir horrible lust and hir liking.°
  Of Clytermistra° for hir lecherye
That falsly made hir housbonde for to die,
He redde it with ful good devocioun.
  He tolde me eek for what occasioun
Amphiorax° at Thebes loste his lif:
Myn housbonde hadde a legende of his wif
Eriphylem, that for an ouche° of gold
Hath prively unto the Greekes told
Wher that hir housbonde hidde him in a place,
For which he hadde at Thebes sory grace.
  Of Livia tolde he me and of Lucie:°

724. boughte, redeemed. **726. los,** ruin. **728. lemman,** mistress; **kitte,** cut. **731.** Dejanira unwittingly gave Hercules a shirt that hurt him so that he committed suicide. **736. sely,** silly. **738. stinte,** stops. **739. Phasipha,** Pasiphaë, who fell in love with a bull. **740. shrewednesse,** malice. **742. liking,** pleasure. **743. Clytermistra,** Clytemnestra, who murdered Agamemnon in order to continue her relationship with her lover Aegisthus. **747. Amphiorax,** Amphiaraus, betrayed by his wife Eriphyle and forced to go to the war against Thebes. **749. ouche,** trinket. **753. Livia** murdered her husband in behalf of her lover Sejanus; **Lucie,** Lucilla, who poisoned her husband, the poet Lucretius, with a potion designed to keep him faithful.

They bothe made hir housbondes for to die,
That oon for love, that other was for hate;
Livia hir housbonde on an even late
Empoisoned hath for that she was his fo;
Lucia likerous° loved hir housbonde so
That for° he sholde alway upon hire thinke,
She yaf him swich a manere love-drinke
That he was deed er it were by the morwe.°
And thus algates° housbondes han sorwe.
  Thanne tolde he me how oon Latumius
Complained unto his felawe Arrius
That in his gardin growed swich a tree,
On which he saide how that his wives three
Hanged hemself for herte despitous.°
  "O leve° brother," quod this Arrius,
"Yif me a plante of thilke blessed tree,
And in my gardin planted shal it be."
  Of latter date of wives hath he red
That some han slain hir housbondes in hir bed
And lete hir lechour dighte° hire al the night,
Whan that the cors lay in the floor upright;°
And some han driven nailes in hir brain
Whil that they sleepe, and thus they han hem slain;
Some han hem yiven poison in hir drinke.
He spak more harm than herte may bithinke,°
And therwithal he knew of mo proverbes
Than in this world ther growen gras or herbes:
"Bet is," quod he, "thyn habitacioun
Be with a leon or a foul dragoun
Than with a womman using° for to chide."
"Bet is," quod he, "hye in the roof abide
Than with an angry wif down in the hous:
They been so wikked° and contrarious,
They haten that hir housbondes loveth ay."

758. likerous, lecherous. **759. for,** in order that. **761. was deed,** died; **by the morwe,** near morning. **762. algates,** constantly. **767. for . . . despitous,** for malice of heart. **768. leve,** dear. **773. dighte,** have intercourse with. **774. cors,** corpse; **upright,** supine. **778. bithinke,** imagine. **783. using,** accustomed. **786. wikked,** perverse.

He saide, "A womman cast° hir shame away
Whan she cast of hir smok,"° and ferthermo,
"A fair womman, but she be chast also,
Is lik a gold ring in a sowes nose."
Who wolde weene,° or who wolde suppose
The wo that in myn herte was and pine?°
And whan I sawgh he wolde nevere fine°
To reden on this cursed book al night,
Al sodeinly three leves have I plight°
Out of his book right as he redde, and eke
I with my fist so took° him on the cheeke
That in oure fir he fil° bakward adown.
And up he sterte as dooth a wood° leoun,
And with his fist he smoot me on the heed°
That in the floor I lay as I were deed.
And whan he sawgh how stille that I lay,
He was agast, and wolde have fled his way,
Til atte laste out of my swough I braide:°
"O hastou slain me, false thief?" I saide,
"And for my land thus hastou mordred° me?
Er I be deed° yit wol I kisse thee."
And neer he cam and kneeled faire adown,
And saide, "Dere suster Alisoun,
As help me God, I shal thee nevere smite.
That I have doon, it is thyself to wite.°
Foryif it me, and that I thee biseeke."
And yit eftsoones° I hitte him on the cheeke,
And saide, "Thief, thus muchel am I wreke.°
Now wol I die: I may no lenger speke."
But at the laste with muchel care and wo
We fille° accorded by us selven two.
He yaf me al the bridel° in myn hand,
To han the governance of hous and land,
And of his tonge and his hand also;

788. **cast,** casts. 789. **of,** off; **smok,** undergarment. 792. **weene,** think. 793. **pine,** suffering. 794. **fine,** end. 796. **plight,** snatched. 798. **took,** i.e., hit. 799. **fil,** fell. 800. **wood,** raging. 801. **heed,** head. 805. **swough,** swoon; **braide,** started. 807. **mordred,** murdered. 808. **deed,** dead. 812. **wite,** blame. 814. **eftsoones,** again. 815. **wreke,** avenged. 818. **fille,** i.e., became. 819. **bridel,** bridle.

And made him brenne° his book anoonright tho.
And whan that I hadde geten unto me
By maistrye al the sovereinetee,°
And that he saide, "Myn owene trewe wif,
Do as thee lust° the terme of al thy lif,
Keep thyn honour, and keep eek myn estat,"
After that day we hadde nevere debat.
God help me so, I was to him as kinde
As any wif from Denmark unto Inde,
And also trewe, and so was he to me.
I praye to God that sit° in majestee,
So blesse his soule for his mercy dere.
Now wol I saye my tale if ye wol heere.

ANOTHER INTERRUPTION

The Frere lough° whan he hadde herd al this:
"Now dame," quod he, "so have I joye or blis,
This is a long preamble of a tale."
And whan the Somnour herde the Frere gale,°
"Lo," quod the Somnour, "Goddes armes two,
A frere wol entremette him° everemo!
Lo, goode men, a flye and eek a frere
Wol falle in every dissh and eek matere.
What spekestou of preambulacioun?
What, amble or trotte or pisse or go sitte down!
Thou lettest° oure disport in this manere."
  "Ye, woltou so, sire Somnour?" quod the Frere.
"Now by my faith, I shal er that I go
Telle of a somnour swich a tale or two
That al the folk shal laughen in this place."
  "Now elles, Frere, I wol bishrewe° thy face,"
Quod this Somnour, "and I bishrewe me,
But if I telle tales two or three

822. **made**, i.e., I made; **brenne**, burn. 824. **maistrye**, skill; **sovereinetee**, dominion. 826. **lust**, it pleases. 832. **sit**, sits. 835. **lough**, laughed. 838. **gale**, exclaim. 840. **entremette him**, intrude himself. 845. **lettest**, hinder. 850. **bishrewe**, curse.

Of freres, er I come to Sidingborne,
That I shal make thyn herte for to moorne—
For wel I woot thy pacience is goon."
  Oure Hoste cride, "Pees, and that anoon!"
And saide, "Lat the womman telle hir tale:
Ye fare as folk that dronken been of ale.
Do, dame, tel forth youre tale, and that is best."
  "Al redy, sire," quod she, "right as you lest—
If I have licence of this worthy Frere."
"Yis, dame," quod he, "tel forth and I wol heere."

THE WIFE OF BATH'S TALE

In th'olde dayes of the King Arthour,
Of which that Britouns speken greet honour,
Al was this land fulfild of faïrye:
The elf-queene with hir joly compaignye
Daunced ful ofte in many a greene mede—
This was the olde opinion as I rede;
I speke of many hundred yeres ago.
But now can no man see none elves mo,
For now the grete charitee and prayeres
Of limitours, and othere holy freres,
That serchen every land and every streem,
As thikke as motes in the sonne-beem,
Blessing halles, chambres, kichenes, bowres,
Citees, burghes, castels, hye towres,
Thropes, bernes, shipnes, dayeries—
This maketh that ther been no faïries.
For ther as wont to walken was an elf

853. Sidingborne, Sittingbourne, forty miles from London. **860. lest,** it pleases.

2. Britouns, Bretons. **3. fulfild,** filled full; **fairye,** supernatural creatures. **5. mede,** meadow. **10. limitours,** friars licensed to beg in a certain territory. **14. burghes,** townships. **15. Thropes,** thorps, villages; **bernes,** barns; **shipnes,** stables.

Ther walketh now the limitour himself,
In undermeles and in morweninges,°
And saith his Matins and his holy thinges,°
As he gooth in his limitacioun.°
Wommen may go saufly° up and down:
In every bussh or under every tree
Ther is noon other incubus° but he,
And he ne wol doon hem but° dishonour.
  And so bifel it that this King Arthour
Hadde in his hous a lusty bacheler,
That on a day cam riding fro river,°
And happed that, allone as he was born,
He sawgh a maide walking him biforn;
Of which maide anoon, maugree hir heed,°
By verray force he rafte° hir maidenheed;
For which oppression° was swich clamour,
And swich pursuite° unto the King Arthour,
That dampned was this knight for to be deed°
By cours of lawe, and sholde han lost his heed—
Paraventure swich was the statut tho—
But that the queene and othere ladies mo
So longe prayeden the king of grace,
Til he his lif him graunted in the place,
And yaf him to the queene, al at hir wille,
To chese wheither she wolde him save or spille.°
The queene thanked the king with al hir might,
And after this thus spak she to the knight,
Whan that she saw hir time upon a day:
"Thou standest yit," quod she, "in swich array°
That of thy lif yit hastou no suretee.°
I graunte thee lif if thou canst tellen me

19. **undermeles,** afternoons; **morweninges,** mornings. 20. **thinges,** i.e., prayers. 21. **limitacioun,** i.e., the friar's assigned area. 22. **saufly,** safely. 24. **incubus,** a spirit that lies with mortal women. 25. **ne but,** only. 28. **river,** hawking, generally carried out on the banks of a stream. 29. **happed,** it happened. 31. **maugree hir heed,** despite her head, i.e., anything she could do. 32. **rafte,** deprived her of. 33. **oppressioun,** rape. 34. **pursuite,** petitioning. 35. **dampned,** condemned; **deed,** dead. 42. **chese,** choose; **spille,** put to death. 46. **array,** condition. 47. **suretee,** guarantee.

What thing it is that wommen most desiren:
Be war and keep thy nekke boon° from iren.
And if thou canst nat tellen me anoon,
Yit wol I yive thee leve for to goon
A twelfmonth and a day to seeche and lere°
An answere suffisant° in this matere,
And suretee wol I han er that thou pace,°
Thy body for to yeelden in this place."
  Wo was this knight, and sorwefully he siketh.°
But what, he may nat doon al as him liketh,
And atte laste he chees° him for to wende,
And come again right at the yeres ende,
With swich answere as God wolde him purveye,°
And taketh his leve and wendeth forth his waye.
He seeketh every hous and every place
Wher as he hopeth for to finde grace,
To lerne what thing wommen love most.
But he ne coude arriven in no coost°
Wher as he mighte finde in this matere
Two creatures according in fere.°
  Some saiden wommen loven best richesse;
Some saide honour, some saide jolinesse;°
Some riche array, some saiden lust° abedde,
And ofte time to be widwe and wedde.
Some saide that oure herte is most esed
Whan that we been yflatered and yplesed—
He gooth ful neigh the soothe, I wol nat lie:
A man shal winne us best with flaterye,
And with attendance and with bisinesse°
Been we ylimed,° bothe more and lesse.
  And some sayen that we loven best
For to be free, and do right as us lest,°
And that no man repreve° us of oure vice,

50. boon, bone. **53. seeche,** seek; **lere,** learn. **54. suffisant,** satisfactory. **55. pace,** pass. **57. siketh,** sighs. **59. chees,** chose. **61. purveye,** provide. **66. coost,** i.e., country. **68. according . . . fere,** agreeing together. **70. jolinesse,** wantonness. **71. lust,** pleasure. **77. bisinesse,** assiduousness. **78. ylimed,** ensnared. **80. lest,** it pleases. **81. repreve,** reprove.

But saye that we be wise and no thing nice.°
For trewely, ther is noon of us alle,
If any wight wol clawe us on the galle,°
That we nil kike for° he saith us sooth:
Assaye and he shal finde it that so dooth.
For be we nevere so vicious withinne,
We wol be holden° wise and clene of sinne.
  And some sayn that greet delit han we
For to be holden stable and eek secree,°
And in oo purpos stedefastly to dwelle,
And nat biwraye° thing that men us telle—
But that tale is nat worth a rake-stele.°
Pardee, we wommen conne no thing hele:°
Witnesse on Mida.° Wol ye heere the tale?
  Ovide, amonges othere thinges smale,
Saide Mida hadde under his longe heres,
Growing upon his heed, two asses eres,
The whiche vice° he hidde as he best mighte
Ful subtilly from every mannes sighte,
That save his wif ther wiste° of it namo.
He loved hire most and trusted hire also.
He prayed hire that to no creature
She sholde tellen of his disfigure.°
  She swoor him nay, for al this world to winne,
She nolde do that vilainye or sinne
To make hir housbonde han so foul a name:
She nolde nat telle it for hir owene shame.
But nathelees, hir thoughte that she dyde°
That she so longe sholde a conseil° hide;
Hire thoughte it swal° so sore aboute hir herte
That nedely som word hire moste asterte,°
And sith she dorste nat telle it to no man,
Down to a mareis faste° by she ran—

82. nice, foolish. **84. galle,** sore spot. **85. kike,** kick; **for,** because. **88. holden,** considered. **90. stable,** reliable; **secree,** close-mouthed. **92. biwraye,** disclose. **93. rake-stele,** rake handle. **94. hele,** conceal. **95. Mida,** Midas. **99. vice,** defect. **101. wiste,** knew. **104. disfigure,** deformity. **109. dyde,** would die. **110. conseil,** secret. **111. swal,** swelled. **112. nedely,** of necessity; **hire . . . asterte,** must escape her. **114. mareis,** marsh; **faste,** close.

Til she cam there hir herte was afire—
And as a bitore bombleth° in the mire,
She laide hir mouth unto the water down:
"Biwray me nat, thou water, with thy soun,"°
Quod she. "To thee I telle it and namo:°
Myn housbonde hath longe asses eres two.
Now is myn herte al hool;° now is it oute.
I mighte no lenger keepe it, out of doute."
Here may ye see, though we a time abide,
Yit oute it moot:° we can no conseil hide.
The remenant of the tale if ye wol heere,
Redeth Ovide, and ther ye may it lere.°
  This knight of which my tale is specially,
Whan that he sawgh he mighte nat come therby—
This is to saye what wommen loven most—
Within his brest ful sorweful was his gost,°
But hoom he gooth, he mighte nat sojurne:°
The day was come that hoomward moste° he turne.
And in his way it happed him to ride
In al this care under a forest side,
Wher as he sawgh upon a daunce go
Of ladies foure and twenty and yit mo;
Toward the whiche daunce he drow ful yerne,°
In hope that som wisdom sholde he lerne.
But certainly, er he cam fully there,
Vanisshed was this daunce, he niste° where.
No creature sawgh he that bar° lif,
Save on the greene he sawgh sitting a wif—
A fouler wight ther may no man devise.°
Again° the knight this olde wif gan rise,
And saide, "Sire knight, heer forth lith no way.°
Telle me what ye seeken, by youre fay."°

116. **bitore,** bittern, a heron; **bombleth,** makes a booming noise. 118. **Biwray,** betray; **soun,** sound. 119. **namo,** to no one else. 121. **hool,** i.e., sound. 124. **moot,** must. 126. **lere,** learn: the reeds disclosed the secret by whispering *aures asinelli*, "ass's ears." 130. **gost,** spirit. 131. **sojurne,** delay. 132. **moste,** must. 137. **drow,** drew; **yerne,** quickly. 140. **niste,** did not know. 141. **bar,** bore. 143. **devise,** imagine. 144. **Again,** i.e., to meet. 145. **lith,** lies; **way,** road. 146. **fay,** faith.

Paraventure° it may the better be:
Thise olde folk conne° muchel thing," quod she.
"My leve moder,"° quod this knight, "certain,
I nam but deed but if that I can sayn
What thing it is that wommen most desire.
Coude ye me wisse, I wolde wel quite youre hire."°
"Plight me thy trouthe here in myn hand," quod she,
"The nexte thing that I requere° thee,
Thou shalt it do, if it lie in thy might,
And I wol telle it you er it be night."
"Have heer my trouthe," quod the knight. "I graunte."
"Thanne," quod she, "I dar me wel avaunte°
Thy lif is sauf,° for I wol stande therby.
Upon my lif the queene wol saye as I.
Lat see which is the pruddeste° of hem alle
That wereth on a coverchief or a calle°
That dar saye nay of that I shal thee teche.
Lat us go forth withouten lenger speeche."
Tho rouned she a pistel° in his ere,
And bad him to be glad and have no fere.
Whan they be comen to the court, this knight
Saide he hadde holde his day as he hadde hight,°
And redy was his answere, as he saide.
Ful many a noble wif, and many a maide,
And many a widwe—for that they been wise—
The queene hirself sitting as justise,
Assembled been this answere for to heere,
And afterward this knight was bode° appere.
To every wight comanded was silence,
And that the knight sholde telle in audience°
What thing that worldly wommen loven best.
This knight ne stood nat stille as dooth a best,°
But to his question anoon answerde

147. **Paraventure,** perhaps. 148. **conne,** know. 149. **moder,** mother. 152. **wisse,** teach; **quite . . . hire,** repay your trouble. 154. **requere,** require of. 158. **avaunte,** boast. 159. **sauf,** safe. 161. **pruddeste,** proudest. 162. **wereth on,** wears; **calle,** headdress. 165. **rouned,** whispered; **pistel,** sentence. 168. **hight,** promised. 174. **bode,** bidden to. 176. **audience,** open hearing. 178. **best,** beast.

With manly vois that al the court it herde.
  "My lige° lady, generally," quod he,
"Wommen desire to have sovereinetee°
As wel over hir housbonde as hir love,
And for to been in maistrye him above.
This is youre moste desir though ye me kille.
Dooth as you list:° I am here at youre wille."
  In al the court ne was ther wif ne maide
Ne widwe that contraried° that he saide,
But saiden he was worthy han° his lif.
  And with that word up sterte° that olde wif,
Which that the knight sawgh sitting on the greene;
"Mercy," quod she, "my soverein lady queene,
Er that youre court departe, do me right.
I taughte this answere unto the knight,
For which he plighte me his trouthe there
The firste thing I wolde him requere°
He wolde it do, if it laye in his might.
Bifore the court thanne praye I thee, sire knight,"
Quod she, "that thou me take unto thy wif,
For wel thou woost that I have kept° thy lif.
If I saye fals, say nay, upon thy fay."
  This knight answerde, "Allas and wailaway,
I woot right wel that swich was my biheeste.°
For Goddes love, as chees° a newe requeste:
Taak al my good and lat my body go."
  "Nay thanne," quod she, "I shrewe° us bothe two.
For though that I be foul and old and poore,
I nolde for al the metal ne for ore
That under erthe is grave or lith° above,
But if thy wif I were and eek thy love."
  "My love," quod he. "Nay, my dampnacioun!°
Allas, that any of my nacioun°

181. **lige,** liege. 182. **sovereinetee,** dominion. 186. **list,** please. 188. **contraried,** contradicted. 189. **han,** to have. 190. **sterte,** started. 196. **requere,** require. 200. **kept,** saved. 203. **biheeste,** promise. 204. **chees,** choose. 206. **shrewe,** curse. 209. **grave,** buried; **lith,** lies. 211. **dampnacioun,** damnation. 212. **nacioun,** i.e., family.

Sholde evere so foule disparaged° be."
But al for nought, th'ende is this, that he
Constrained was: he needes moste hire wedde,
And taketh his olde wif and gooth to bedde.
  Now wolden some men saye, paraventure,
That for my necligence I do no cure°
To tellen you the joy and al th'array
That at the feeste was that ilke day.
To which thing shortly answere I shal:
I saye ther nas no joye ne feeste at al;
Ther nas but hevinesse and muche sorwe.
For prively he wedded hire on morwe,°
And al day after hidde him as an owle,
So wo was him, his wif looked so foule.
  Greet was the wo the knight hadde in his thought:
Whan he was with his wif abedde brought,
He walweth° and he turneth to and fro.
His olde wif lay smiling everemo,
And saide, "O dere housbonde, benedicite,°
Fareth° every knight thus with his wif as ye?
Is this the lawe of King Arthures hous?
Is every knight of his thus daungerous?°
I am youre owene love and youre wif;
I am she which that saved hath youre lif;
And certes yit ne dide I you nevere unright.
Why fare ye thus with me this firste night?
Ye faren like a man hadde lost his wit.
What is my gilt? For Goddes love, telle it,
And it shal been amended if I may."
  "Amended!" quod this knight. "Allas, nay, nay,
It wol nat been amended neveremo.
Thou art so lothly° and so old also,
And therto comen of so lowe a kinde,°
That litel wonder is though I walwe and winde.°

213. disparaged, disgraced. **218. do . . . cure,** do not take the trouble. **224. on morwe,** in the morning. **229. walweth,** tosses. **231. benedicite,** bless me. **232. Fareth,** behaves. **234. daungerous,** stand-offish. **244. lothly,** loathsome. **245. kinde,** race. **246. winde,** turn.

So wolde God myn herte wolde breste!"°
"Is this," quod she, "the cause of youre unreste?"
"Ye, certainly," quod he. "No wonder is."
"Now sire," quod she, "I coude amende al this,
If that me liste, er it were dayes three,
So wel ye mighte bere you° unto me.
But for ye speken of swich gentilesse
As is descended out of old richesse—
That therfore sholden ye be gentilmen—
Swich arrogance is nat worth an hen.
Looke who that is most vertuous alway,
Privee and apert,° and most entendeth ay
To do the gentil deedes that he can,
Taak him for the gretteste° gentilman.
Crist wol° we claime of him oure gentilesse,
Nat of oure eldres for hir 'old richesse.'°
For though they yive us al hir heritage,
For which we claime to been of heigh parage,°
Yit may they nat biquethe for no thing
To noon of us hir vertuous living,
That made hem gentilmen ycalled be,
And bad° us folwen hem in swich degree.
Wel can the wise poete of Florence,
That highte Dant, speken in this sentence;°
Lo, in swich manere rym is Dantes tale:
'Ful selde up riseth by his braunches° smale
Prowesse° of man, for God of his prowesse
Wol that of him we claime oure gentilesse.'
For of oure eldres may we no thing claime
But temporel thing that man may hurte and maime.
Eek every wight woot this as wel as I,
If gentilesse were planted natureelly
Unto a certain linage down the line,

247. **breste,** break. 252. **So,** provided that; **bere you,** behave. 258. **Privee . . . apert,** privately and publicly. 260. **gretteste,** greatest. 261. **wol,** desires that. 262. See Chaucer's poem on p. 707. 264. **parage,** descent. 268. **bad,** they bade. 270. **Dant,** Dante: see his *Convivio*; **sentence,** topic. 272. **selde,** seldom; **his,** its own; **braunches,** i.e., efforts. 273. **Prowesse,** excellence.

Privee and apert, thanne wolde they nevere fine°
To doon of gentilesse the faire office°—
They mighte do no vilainye or vice.
  Taak fir and beer° it in the derkeste hous
Bitwixe this and the Mount of Caucasus,
And lat men shette the dores and go thenne,°
Yit wol the fir as faire lie and brenne°
As twenty thousand men mighte it biholde:
His° office natureel ay wol it holde,
Up° peril of my lif, til that it die.
Heer may ye see wel how that genterye°
Is nat annexed to possessioun,°
Sith folk ne doon hir operacioun
Alway, as dooth the fir, lo, in his kinde.°
For God it woot, men may wel often finde
A lordes sone do shame and vilainye;
And he that wol han pris of his gentrye,°
For he was boren° of a gentil hous,
And hadde his eldres noble and vertuous,
And nil himselven do no gentil deedes,
Ne folwen his gentil auncestre that deed° is,
He nis nat gentil, be he duc or erl—
For vilaines sinful deedes maken a cherl.
Thy gentilesse nis but renomee°
Of thine auncestres for hir heigh bountee,°
Which is a straunge° thing for thy persone.
For gentilesse cometh fro God allone.
Thanne comth oure verray gentilesse of grace:
It was no thing biquethe us with oure place.
Thenketh how noble, as saith Valerius,°
Was thilke Tullius Hostilius

280. fine, cease. **281. office,** function. **283. beer,** bear. **285. shette,** shut; **thenne,** thence. **286. lie,** i.e., remain; **brenne,** burn. **288. His,** its. **289. Up,** upon. **290. genterye,** gentility. **291. annexed,** related; **possessioun,** i.e., inheritable property. **293. kinde,** nature. **296. pris of,** credit for; **gentrye,** noble birth. **297. boren,** born. **300. deed,** dead. **303. renomee,** renown. **304. bountee,** magnanimity. **305. straunge,** alien. **309. Valerius,** a Roman historian.

That out of poverte roos° to heigh noblesse.
Redeth Senek, and redeth eek Boece:°
Ther shul ye seen expres that no drede° is
That he is gentil that dooth gentil deedes.
And therfore, leve housbonde, I thus conclude:
Al were it that mine auncestres weren rude,°
Yit may the hye God—and so hope I—
Graunte me grace to liven vertuously.
Thanne am I gentil whan that I biginne
To liven vertuously and waive° sinne.
  And ther as ye of poverte me repreve,°
The hye God, on whom that we bileve,
In wilful poverte chees° to live his lif;
And certes every man, maiden, or wif
May understonde that Jesus, hevene king,
Ne wolde nat chese° a vicious living.
Glad poverte is an honeste° thing, certain;
This wol Senek and othere clerkes sayn.
Whoso that halt him paid° of his poverte,
I holde him riche al hadde he nat a sherte.°
He that coveiteth° is a poore wight,
For he wolde han that is nat in his might;
But he that nought hath, ne coveiteth° have,
Is riche, although we holde him but a knave.
Verray poverte it singeth proprely.°
Juvenal saith of poverte, 'Merily
The poore man, whan he gooth by the waye,
Biforn the theves he may singe and playe.'
Poverte is hateful good, and as I gesse,
A ful greet bringere out of bisinesse;°
A greet amendere eek of sapience
To him that taketh it in pacience;
Poverte is thing, although it seeme elenge,°

311. **poverte,** poverty. 312. **Senek,** Seneca; **Boece,** Boethius. 313. **drede,** doubt. 316. **rude,** i.e., low born. 320. **waive,** avoid. 321. **repreve,** reprove. 323. **wilful,** voluntary; **chees,** chose. 326. **chese,** choose. 327. **honeste,** honorable. 329. **halt him,** considers himself; **paid,** satisfied. 330. **sherte,** shirt. 331. **coveiteth,** i.e., suffers desires. 333. **coveiteth,** desires to. 335. **proprely,** appropriately. 340. **bisinesse,** i.e., cares. 343. **elenge,** wretched.

Possession that no wight wol chalenge;°
Poverte ful often, whan a man is lowe,
Maketh° his God and eek himself to knowe;
Poverte a spectacle is,° as thinketh me,
Thurgh which he may his verray freendes see.
And therfore, sire, sin that I nought you greve,
Of my poverte namore ye me repreve.°
  Now sire, of elde° ye repreve me:
And certes sire, though noon auctoritee
Were in no book, ye gentils of honour
Sayn that men sholde an old wight doon favour,
And clepe him fader for youre gentilesse–
And auctours° shal I finden, as I gesse.
  Now ther ye saye that I am foul and old:
Thanne drede you nought to been a cokewold,°
For filthe and elde, also mote I thee,°
Been grete wardeins° upon chastitee.
But nathelees, sin I knowe your delit,
I shal fulfille youre worldly appetit.
  Chees° now," quod she, "oon of thise thinges twaye:
To han me foul and old til that I deye
And be to you a trewe humble wif,
And nevere you displese in al my lif,
Or elles ye wol han me yong and fair,
And take youre aventure of the repair°
That shal be to youre hous by cause of me–
Or in som other place, wel may be.
Now chees youreselven wheither° that you liketh."
  This knight aviseth him and sore siketh;°
But atte laste he saide in this manere:
"My lady and my love, and wif so dere,
I putte me in youre wise governaunce:
Cheseth youreself which may be most plesaunce°

344. chalenge, claim as his property. **346. Maketh,** i.e., makes him. **347. spectacle,** pair of spectacles. **350. repreve,** reproach. **351. elde,** old age. **356. auctours,** i.e., authorities. **358. cokewold,** cuckold. **359. also . . . thee,** so may I thrive. **360. wardeins,** guardians. **363. Chees,** choose. **368. aventure,** chance; **repair,** i.e., visits. **371. wheither,** whichever. **372. aviseth him,** considers; **siketh,** sighs. **376. Cheseth,** choose; **plesaunce,** pleasure.

And most honour to you and me also.
I do no fors the wheither° of the two,
For as you liketh it suffiseth° me."
"Thanne have I gete° of you maistrye," quod she,
"Sin I may chese and governe as me lest?"°
"Ye, certes, wif," quod he. "I holde it best."
"Kisse me," quod she. "We be no lenger wrothe.
For by my trouthe, I wol be to you bothe—
This is to sayn, ye, bothe fair and good.
I praye to God that I mote sterven wood,°
But° I to you be al so good and trewe
As evere was wif sin that the world was newe.
And but I be tomorn° as fair to seene
As any lady, emperisse, or queene,
That is bitwixe the eest and eek the west,
Do with my lif and deeth right as you lest:
Caste up the curtin, looke how that it is."
And whan the knight sawgh verraily al this,
That she so fair was and so yong therto,
For joye he hente° hire in his armes two;
His herte bathed in a bath of blisse;
A thousand time arewe° he gan hire kisse,
And she obeyed him in every thing
That mighte do him plesance or liking.°
And thus they live unto hir lives ende
In parfit° joye. And Jesu Crist us sende
Housbondes meeke, yonge, and fresshe abedde—
And grace t'overbide° hem that we wedde.
And eek I praye Jesu shorte° hir lives
That nought wol be governed by hir wives,
And olde and angry nigardes of dispence°—
God sende hem soone a verray° pestilence!

378. **do . . . fors,** do not care; **the wheither,** whichever. 379. **suffiseth,** satisfies. 380. **gete,** got. 381. **lest,** it pleases. 386. **sterven wood,** die mad. 387. **But,** unless. 389. **tomorn,** tomorrow morning. 396. **hente,** took. 398. **arewe,** in a row. 400. **liking,** pleasure. 402. **parfit,** perfect. 404. **overbide,** outlive. 405. **shorte,** shorten. 407. **dispence,** expenditure. 408. **verray,** veritable.

THE FRIAR'S TALE

The Introduction

This worthy limitour, this noble Frere,
He made alway a manere louring cheere°
Upon the Somnour, but for honestee°
No vilains° word as yit to him spak he.
But atte laste he saide unto the Wif,
"Dame," quod he, "God yive you right good lif.
Ye han heer touched, also mote I thee,°
In scole matere° greet difficultee.
Ye han said muche thing right wel, I saye.
But dame, heer as we riden by the waye,
Us needeth nat to speken but of game,°
And lete° auctoritees, on Goddes name,
To preching and to scole of clergye.
But if it like° to this compaignye,
I wol you of a somnour telle a game.°
Pardee, ye may wel knowe by the name
That of a somnour may no good be said.
I praye that noon of you be yvele apaid:°
A somnour is a rennere° up and down
With mandements° for fornicacioun,
And is ybet° at every townes ende."
  Oure Host tho spak, "A, sire, ye sholde be hende°
And curteis, as a man of youre estat.
In compaignye we wol° noon debat.
Telleth youre tale and lat the Somnour be."
  "Nay," quod the Somnour, "lat him saye to me
What so him list. Whan it comth to my lot,
By God, I shal him quiten every grot.°

2. louring cheere, frowning face. **3. honestee,** dignity. **4. vilains,** vulgar. **7. also . . . thee,** so may I thrive. **8. scole matere,** scholarly topics. **11. game,** sport. **12. lete,** leave. **14. like,** please. **15. game,** joke. **18. yvele apaid,** ill pleased. **19. rennere,** runner. **20. mandements,** summonses. **21. ybet,** beaten. **22. hende,** polite. **24. wol,** want. **28. grot,** bit.

I shal him telle which a greet honour
It is to be a flatering limitour,
And of many another manere crime,
Which needeth nat rehercen for this time.
And his office I shal him telle, ywis."
Oure Host answerde, "Pees, namore of this!"
And after this he saide unto the Frere,
"Telle forth youre tale, leve maister dere."

The Tale

Whilom ther was dwelling in my contree
An erchedekne, a man of heigh degree,
That boldely dide execucioun
In punisshing of fornicacioun,
Of wicchecraft and eek of bawderye,
Of defamacion and avoutrye,
Of chirche reves and of testaments,
Of contractes and of lak of sacraments,
Of usure, and of simonye also;
But certes, lecchours dide he grettest wo:
They sholde singen if that they were hent.
And smale titheres were foule yshent
If any person wolde upon hem plaine:
Ther mighte asterte him no pecunial paine.
For smale tithes and for smal offringe
He made the peple pitously to singe.
For er the bisshop caughte hem with his hook

29. **which,** what. 33. **office,** function.

1. **Whilom,** once. 2. **erchedekne,** archdeacon. 5. **bawderye,** pimping. 6–7. Of slander and adultery, Of church thefts and of wills. 9. **usure,** usury; **simonye:** misuse of ecclesiastical perquisites by priests. 11. **hent,** caught. 12. **smale titheres,** persons who paid less than the required 10% tax to the Church; **yshent,** injured. 13. **person,** parson; **plaine,** complain. 14. No kind of pecuniary punishment might elude him (the archdeacon). 17. **hook,** crosier: the bishop's staff was hooked, like a shepherd's.

They weren in the erchedeknes book;
Thanne hadde he, thurgh his jurisdiccioun,
Power to doon on hem correccioun.
He hadde a somnour, redy to his hond—
A slyer boy nas noon in Engelond,
For subtilly he hadde his espiaile°
That taughte him wher that him mighte availe:°
He coude spare of lecchours oon or two
To techen him to foure and twenty mo.°
For though this Somnour wood° were as an hare,
To telle his harlotrye° I wol nat spare,
For we been out of his correccioun:°
They han of us no jurisdiccioun,
Ne nevere shullen, terme of hir lives.
—"Peter! so been the wommen of the stives,"°
Quod the Somnour, "yput out of my cure."°
"Pees, with meschaunce and with misaventure"—
Thus saide oure Hoost—"and lat him telle his tale.
Now telleth forth, though that the Somnour gale:°
Ne spareth nat, myn owene maister dere."—
This false theef, this somnour (quod the Frere)
Hadde alway bawdes° redy to his hond
As any hawk to lure° in Engelond.
That tolde him al the secree that they knewe,
For hir aquaintance was nat come of newe.
They weren his approwours° prively;
He took himself a greet profit therby:
His maister knew nat alway what he wan.°
Withouten mandement a lewed° man
He coude somne on paine of Cristes curs,
And they were glade for to fille his purs

23. espiaile, network of spies. **24. availe,** prove profitable. **26. To . . . him,** i.e., to learn about; **mo,** others. **27. wood,** crazy. **28. harlotrye,** dirty behavior. **29. correccioun,** i.e., power to bring to court: the orders of friars were not subject to the bishop's rule. **32. stives,** brothels, also exempted from the bishop's jurisdiction. **33. cure,** care. **36. gale,** rage. **39. bawdes,** pimps. **40. lure:** obedient hawks returned to the falconer when shown the lure. **42. of newe,** recently. **43. approwours,** agents. **45. wan,** won. **46. mandement,** official summons; **lewed,** ignorant.

And make him grete feestes atte nale.°
And right as Judas hadde purses smale
And was a theef, right swich a theef was he:
His maister hadde but half his duetee.°
He was, if I shal yiven him his laude,°
A theef, and eek a somnour, and a bawde.°
He hadde eek wenches at his retenue°
That wheither that sire Robert or sire Hewe,
Or Jakke, or Rauf, or whoso that it were
That lay by hem, they tolde it in his ere.
Thus was the wenche and he of oon assent,
And he wolde fecche a feined° mandement
And somne hem to chapitre° bothe two,
And pile° the man, and lete the wenche go.
Thanne wolde he saye, "Freend, I shal, for thy sake,
Do strike hire° out of oure lettres blake:
Thee thar namore as in this caas travaile.°
I am thy freend ther I thee may availe."°
Certain he knew of briberies mo°
Than possible is to telle in yeres two,
For in this world nis dogge for the bowe°
That can an hurt deer from an hool° yknowe
Bet° than this somnour knew a sly lecchour,
Or an avoutour, or a paramour;°
And for that was the fruit of al his rente°
Therfore on it he sette al his entente.
And so bifel that ones on a day
This somnour, evere waiting on° his prey,
Rood for to somne an old widwe, a ribibe,°

49. atte nale, at the alehouse. **52. duetee,** i.e., what was due him. **53. laude,** praise. **54. bawde,** pimp. **55. at,** in; **retenue,** following. **60. feined,** counterfeited. **61. chapitre,** i.e., chapterhouse, where the archdeacon held court. **62. pile,** pillage. **64. Do . . . hire,** have her name stricken. **65. thar,** need; **travaile,** i.e., worry: presumably thereafter the lecher could have the wench with impunity. **66. availe,** help. **67. briberies,** i.e., ways of getting money dishonestly; **mo,** more. **69. for the bowe,** i.e., hunting. **70. hool,** i.e., unhurt. **71. Bet,** better. **72. avoutour,** adulterer; **paramour,** lover. **73. fruit,** i.e., best part; **rente,** income. **76. waiting on,** watching for. **77. ribibe,** ? hag.

Feining a cause, for he wolde bribe.°
Happed° that he saw bifore him ride
A gay yeman under a forest side.
A bowe he bar,° and arwes brighte and keene;
He hadde upon a courtepy° of greene,
An hat upon his heed with frenges blake.
"Sire," quod this somnour, "hail and wel ytake."°
"Welcome," quod he, "and every good felawe.
Where ridestou under this greene shawe?"°
Saide this yeman. "Wiltou fer° today?"
This somnour him answerede and saide, "Nay:
Here faste° by," quod he, "is myn entente
To riden for to raisen up a rente°
That longeth to my lordes duetee."°
"Artou thanne a bailly?"° "Ye," quod he:
He dorste nat, for verray filthe and shame,
Saye that he was a somnour, for the name.
"Depardieux,"° quod this yeman, "dere brother:
Thou art a bailly and I am another.
I am unknowen as in this contree.
Of thyn aquaintance I wolde praye thee,
And eek of bretherhede if that thee leste.°
I have gold and silver in my cheste:
If that thee happe to comen in oure shire,
Al shal be thyn, right as thou wolt desire."
"Graunt mercy,"° quod this somnour, "by my faith."
Everich in otheres hand his trouthe° laith
For to be sworn bretheren til they deye.
In daliance° they riden forth and playe.
This somnour, which that was as ful of jangles°
As ful of venim been thise wariangles,°

78. Feining, pretending to have; **bribe,** make some money. **79. Happed,** it happened. **81. bar,** bore. **82. courtepy,** short coat. **84. ytake,** i.e., met. **86. shawe,** wood. **87. fer,** far. **89. faste,** close. **90. raisen . . . rente,** i.e., collect a bill. **91. longeth,** belongs; **duetee,** i.e., estate. **92. bailly,** bailiff, administrative agent of a large land holder. **95. Depardieux,** by God. **99. bretherhede,** i.e., sworn brotherhood; **leste,** pleased. **103. Graunt mercy,** many thanks. **104. trouthe,** pledge. **106. daliance,** conversation. **107. jangles,** chatter. **108. wariangles,** shrikes.

And evere enquering upon every thing,
"Brother," quod he, "where is now youre dwelling,
Another day if that I sholde you seeche?"
  This yeman him answerde in softe speeche:
"Brother," quod he, "fer in the north contree,
Wheras I hope som time I shal thee see.
Er we departe I shal thee so wel wisse°
That of myn hous ne shaltou nevere misse."
  "Now brother," quod this somnour, "I you praye,
Teche me whil that we riden by the waye—
Sin that ye been a bailiff as am I—
Som subtiltee, and tel me faithfully
In myn office° how that I may most winne;
And spareth nat for conscience ne sinne,
But as my brother tel me how do ye."
  "Now by my trouthe, brother dere," saide he,
As I shal tellen thee a faithful tale:
My wages been ful straite° and ful smale;
My lord is hard to me and daungerous;°
And myn office is ful laborous;
And therfore by extorcions I live.
Forsoothe, I take al that men wol me yive.
Algate° by sleighte or by violence
Fro yeer to yere I winne al my dispence.°
I can no bettre tellen, faithfully."
  "Now, certes," quod this somnour, "so fare I!
I spare nat to taken, God it woot,°
But° it be too hevy or too hoot.
What I may gete in conseil° prively—
No manere conscience of that have I.
Nere° myn extorcion I mighte nat liven,
Ne of swiche japes° wol I nat be shriven.
Stomak ne conscience ne knowe I noon:

115. departe, separate; **wisse,** teach. **121. office,** position. **126. straite,** restricted. **127. daungerous,** scornful. **131. Algate,** at any rate. **132. dispence,** expenses. **135. woot,** knows. **136. But,** unless. **137. conseil,** i.e., secret. **139. Nere,** were it not for. **140. japes,** tricks.

I shrewe thise shrifte-fadres° everichoon.
Wel be we met, by God and by Saint Jame!
But, leve° brother, tel me thanne thy name,"
Quod this somnour. In this mene while
This yeman gan a litel for to smile:
"Brother," quod he, "woltou that I thee telle?
I am a feend: my dwelling is in helle.
And here I ride aboute my purchasing°
To wite° wher men wol yive me anything;
My purchas is th'effect of al my rente.°
Looke how thou ridest for the same entente,
To winne good—thou rekkest° nevere how:
Right so fare I, for ride wolde I now
Unto the worldes ende for a preye."
"A," quod this somnour, "benedicite,° what say ye?
I wende° ye were a yeman trewely:
Ye han a mannes shap as wel as I.
Han ye a figure thanne determinat°
In helle ther ye been in youre estat?"
"Nay, certainly," quod he, "ther have we noon.
But whan us liketh we can take us oon,
Or elles make you seeme° we been shape
Som time lik a man or lik an ape,
Or lik an angel can I ride or go.
It is no wonder thing though it be so:
A lousy jogelour° can deceive thee,
And, pardee, yit can° I more craft than he."
"Why," quod this somnour, "ride ye thanne or goon
In sondry shap and nat alway in oon?"
"For we," quod he, "wol us swiche formes make
As most able° is oure preyes for to take."
"What maketh you to han al this labour?"
"Ful many a cause, leve sire somnour,"

142. shrewe, curse; **shrifte-fadres,** confessors, i.e., friars. **144. leve,** dear. **149. purchasing,** procurement. **150. wite,** learn. **151.** I.e., my whole income consists of what I can get. **153. rekkest,** care. **156. benedicite,** bless me. **157. wende,** supposed. **159. determinat,** fixed. **163. you seeme,** it seem to you. **167. jogelour,** juggler. **168. pardee,** by God; **can,** know. **172. able,** suitable.

Saide this feend, "but alle thing hath time:
The day is short, and it is passed prime,
And yit ne wan I nothing in this day.
I wol entende to winning if I may,
And nat entende oure wittes to declare.
For, brother myn, thy wit is al too bare
To understonde although I tolde hem thee.
But for thou axest why labouren we:
For som time we been Goddes instruments
And menes to doon his comandements,
Whan that him list, upon his creatures,
In divers art and in diverse figures.
Withouten him we han no might, certain,
If that him list to stonde theragain.
And som time at oure prayere han we leve
Only the body and nat the soule greve:
Witnesse on Job, whom that we diden wo.
And som time han we might of bothe two—
This is to sayn, of soule and body eke.
And som time we been suffered for to seeke
Upon a man and do his soule unreste,
And nat his body; and al is for the beste:
Whan he withstandeth oure temptacioun
It is a cause of his savacioun—
Al be it that it was nat oure entente
He sholde be sauf, but that we wolde him hente.
And som time we be servant unto man
As to the erchebisshop Saint Dunstan
And to th'Apostles servant eek was I."
"Yit tel me," quod the somnour, "faithfully:
Make ye newe bodies thus alway
Of elements?" The feend answerde, "Nay:

176. prime, about 9:00 A.M. **177. wan,** won. **178. entende,** attend. **179. declare,** show off. **182. axest,** ask. **184. menes,** means. **185. list,** it pleases. **194. suffered,** permitted. **198. savacioun,** salvation. **200. sauf,** safe; **hente,** seize. **202. erchebisshop,** archbishop: saints were often said to have controlled devils.

Som time we feine° and som time we arise
With dede bodies in ful sondry wise,
And speke as renably° and faire and wel
As to the Pythonissa° dide Samuel
(And yit wol some men saye it was nat he:
I do no fors of° youre divinitee.)
But oo thing warne I thee, I wol nat jape:°
Thou wolt algates wite° how we be shape.
Thou shalt herafterwards, my brother dere,
Come there thee needeth nat of me to lere.°
For thou shalt, by thyn owene experience,
Conne in a chayer rede of this sentence°
Bet than Virgile,° whil he was on live,
Or Dant also. Now lat us ride blive°
For I wol holde compaignye with thee
Til it be so that thou forsake me."
"Nay," quod this somnour, "that shal nat bitide:
I am a yeman, knowen is ful wide;
My trouthe wol I holde, as in this cas.
For though thou were the devel Satanas,
My trouthe wol I holde to thee, my brother,
As I am sworn, and eech of us til other,
For to be trewe brother in this cas.
And bothe we goon abouten oure purchas:°
Taak thou thy part, what that men wol thee yive,
And I shal myn—thus may we bothe live.
And if that any of us have more than other,
Lat him be trewe and parte° with his brother."
"I graunte," quod the devel, "by my fay."°
And with that word they riden forth hir way,

207. feine, counterfeit. **209. renably,** fluently. **210. Pythonissa,** pythoness: the Witch of Endor; see I Chronicles X 13 for the dead Samuel's appearance to the Witch. **212. do . . . of,** pay no heed to: contrary to the opinion of some theologians, the devil is suggesting that it was Samuel, and not a devil in his form, that appeared to the Witch of Endor. **213. jape,** joke. **214. algates,** in any case; **wite,** learn. **216. lere,** learn. **218.** Be able, in a (professorial) chair, to discourse of this matter. **219.** Virgil and Dante both tell of hell. **220. blive,** quickly. **230. purchas,** acquisitions. **234. parte,** share. **235. fay,** faith.

And right at th'entring of the townes ende
To which this somnour shoop him° for to wende,
They saw a carte that charged° was with hay
Which that a cartere droof° forth in his way:
Deep° was the way, for which the carte stood.
This cartere smoot and cride as he were wood,°
"Hait, Brok! Hait, Scot! What° spare ye for the stones?
The Feend," quod he, "you fecche, body and bones,
As ferforthly as evere were ye foled,°
So muche wo as I have with you tholed,°
The Devel have al, bothe hors and carte and hay!"
This somnour saide, "Here shul we han a play."
And neer the feend he drough° as nought ne were,
Ful prively, and rouned° in his ere:
"Herkne, my brother, herkne, by thy faith:
Heerestou nat how that the cartere saith?
Hent° it anoon, for he hath yive it thee,
Bothe hay and carte and eek his caples° three."
"Nay," quod the devel, "God woot, nevere a deel:°
It is nat his entente, trust thou me wel.
Axe him thyself if thou nat trowest° me,
Or elles stint° a while and thou shalt see."
This cartere thakketh his hors upon the croupe,°
And they bigonne drawen and to stoupe.°
"Hait now," quod he, "ther° Jesu Crist you blesse,
And al his handeswerk, bothe more and lesse.
That was wel twight, myn owene liard° boy.
I praye God save thee, and Sainte Loy.
Now is my carte out of the slough, pardee."°
"Lo, brother," quod the feend, "what tolde I thee?
Here may ye see, myn owene dere brother,

238. shoop him, was planning. **239. charged,** loaded. **240. droof,** drove. **241. Deep,** i.e., deep with mud. **242. wood,** crazy. **243. Hait,** pull; **What,** why. **245.** I.e., as surely as you were foaled. **246. tholed,** suffered. **249. drough,** drew. **250. rouned,** whispered. **253. Hent,** seize. **254. caples,** horses. **255. deel,** bit. **257. Axe,** ask; **trowest,** trust. **258. stint,** wait. **259. thakketh,** whips; **croupe,** crupper. **260. stoupe,** i.e., put their backs into it. **261. ther,** i.e., may. **263. twight,** pulled; **liard,** gray. **265. pardee,** by God.

The carl spak oo thing but he thoughte another.
Lat us go forth abouten oure viage:
Here winne I nothing upon cariage."
  Whan that they comen somwhat out of towne,
This somnour to his brother gan to roune;
"Brother," quod he, "here woneth an old rebekke
That hadde almost as lief to lese hir nekke
As for to yive a peny of hir good.
I wol han twelve pens though that she be wood,
Or I wol somne hire unto oure office.
And yit, God woot, of hire knowe I no vice.
But for thou canst nat, as in this contree,
Winne thy cost, taak here ensample of me."
  This somnour clappeth at the widwes gate.
"Com out," quod he, "thou olde viritrate:
I trowe thou hast som frere or preest with thee."
  "Who clappeth?" saide this wif. "Benedicite,
God save you, sire. What is youre sweete wille?"
  "I have," quod he, "of somonce here a bille:
Up paine of cursing looke that thou be
Tomorn bifore the erchedeknes knee
T'answere to the court of certain thinges."
  "Now Lord," quod she, "Crist Jesu, king of kinges,
So wisly helpe me as I ne may:
I have been sik and that ful many a day;
I may nat go so fer," quod she, "ne ride
But I be deed, so priketh it in my side.
May I nat axe a libel, sire somnour,
And answere there by my procuratour
To swich thing as men wol opposen me?"
  "Yis," quod this somnour, "pay anoon—lat see—

268. carl, churl; **thoughte,** intended. **269. viage,** i.e., business. **270. upon cariage,** i.e., that I can claim for my lord. **272. roune,** whisper. **273. woneth,** dwells; **rebekke,** crone. **274. lese,** lose. **276. wood,** crazy. **277. office,** i.e., court. **280. ensample,** example. **282. viritrate,** ? man-layer. **283. trowe,** think. **284. Benedicite,** bless me. **286. somonce,** summons; **bille,** writ. **287. Up,** upon; **cursing,** excommunication. **288. Tomorn,** tomorrow. **291. wisly,** surely. **293. go,** walk; **fer,** far. **294. But . . . deed,** unless I die. **295. axe,** ask; **libel,** bill of particulars. **296. procuratour,** agent.

Twelve pens to me, and I wol thee acquite.
I shal no profit han therby but lite:
My maister hath the profit and nat I.
Com of, and lat me riden hastily.
Yif me twelve pens—I may no lenger tarye."
  "Twelve pens!" quod she. "Now lady Sainte Marye,
So wisly helpe me out of care and sinne,
This wide world though that I sholde winne,
Ne have I nat twelve pens within myn hold.
Ye knowen wel that I am poore and old:
Kithe youre almesse on me, poore wrecche."
  "Nay, thanne," quod he, "the foule Feend me fecche
If I th'excuse, though thou shul be spilt."
  "Allas," quod she, "God woot I have no gilt."
  "Pay me," quod he, "or by the sweete Sainte Anne
As I wol bere away thy newe panne
For dette which thou owest me of old:
Whan that thou madest thyn housbonde cokewold
I payde at hoom for thy correcioun."
  "Thou lixt," quod she; "by my savacioun,
Ne was I nevere er now, widwe ne wif.
Somned unto youre court in al my lif.
Ne nevere I nas but of my body trewe.
Unto the Devel blak and rough of hewe
Yive I thy body and my panne also."
  And whan the devel herde hire cursen so
Upon hir knees, he saide in this manere:
"Now Mabely, myn owene moder dere,
Is this youre wil in ernest that ye saye?"
  "The Devel," quod she, "so fecche him er he deye,
And panne and al, but he wol him repente."
  "Nay, olde stot, that is nat myn entente,"
Quod this somnour, "for to repente me
For anything that I have had of thee.

300. lite, little. **305. wisly,** surely. **307. hold,** possession. **309. Kithe,** show; **almesse,** i.e., generosity. **311. spilt,** ruined. **317. hoom,** i.e., court. **318. lixt,** lie; **savacioun,** salvation. **329. but,** unless. **330. stot,** whore.

I wolde I hadde thy smok and every cloth."
"Now, brother," quod the devel, "be nat wroth:
Thy body and this panne been mine by right.
Thou shalt with me to helle yit tonight,
Wher thou shalt knowen of oure privetee°
More than a maister of divinitee."
And with that word this foule feend him hente:°
Body and soule he with the devel wente
Wher as that somnours han hir heritage.
And God, that made after his image
Mankinde, save and gide us alle and some,°
And leve° thise somnours goode men bicome.—
Lordinges, I coude han told you (quod the Frere),
Hadde I had leiser° for this Somnour here,
After the text of Crist and Paul and John,
And of oure othere doctours many oon,
Swiche paines that youre hertes mighte agrise°—
Al be it so no tonge may devise,°
Though that I mighte a thousand winter telle,
The paines of thilke cursed hous of helle.
But for to keepe us fro that cursed place,
Waketh and prayeth Jesu for his grace
So keepe us fro the temptour Satanas.
Herketh this word: beeth war as in this cas;
The leon sit in his await° alway
To slee° the innocent if that he may.
Disposeth ay youre hertes to withstonde
The Feend that you wolde maken thral and bonde.°
He may nat tempte you over youre might,
For Crist wol be youre champion and knight.
And prayeth that thise somnours hem repente
Of hir misdeedes er that the Feend hem hente.°

337. privetee, secrets. **339. hente,** seized. **343. alle and some,** each and every one. **344. leve,** let. **346. leiser,** leisure. **349. agrise,** shudder. **350. devise,** describe. **357. sit,** sits; **await,** ambush. **358. slee,** slay. **360. thral and bonde,** slave and bondman. **364. hente,** seize.

THE SUMMONER'S TALE

The Introduction

This Somnour in his stiropes hye stood:
Upon this Frere his herte was so wood°
That lik an aspen leef he quook° for ire.
  "Lordinges,"° quod he, "but oo thing I desire:
I you biseeke° that of youre curteisye,
Sin ye han herd this false Frere lie,
As suffreth me I may my tale telle.
This Frere boosteth° that he knoweth helle,
And God it woot° that it is litel wonder:
Freres and feendes been but lite asonder.°
For, pardee, ye han ofte time herd telle
How that a frere ravisshed was to helle
In spirit ones by avisioun;°
And as an angel ladde° him up and down
To shewen him the paines° that there were,
In al the place sawgh he nat a frere—
Of other folk he sawgh ynowe° in wo.
Unto this angel spak the frere tho:
  'Now sire,' quod he, 'han freres swich a grace
That noon of hem shal come to this place?'
  'Yis,' quod the angel, 'many a millioun,'
And unto Satanas he ladde him down.
'And now hath Satanas,' saith he, 'a tail
Brodder than of a carrik° is the sail.
Hold up thy tail, thou Satanas!' quod he.
'Shew forth thyn ers,° and lat the frere see
Wher is the nest of freres in this place.'
And er that half a furlong way of space,°

2. **wood,** infuriated. 3. **quook,** quaked. 4. **Lordinges,** gentlemen. 5. **biseeke,** beseech. 8. **boosteth,** boasts. 9. **woot,** knows. 10. **lite,** little; **asonder,** apart. 13. **by avisioun,** i.e., in a dream. 14. **ladde,** led. 15. **paines,** torments. 17. **ynowe,** enough. 24. **Brodder,** broader; **carrik,** ship. 26. **ers,** rump. 28. i.e., Before one could walk half a furlong.

Right so as bees out swarmen from an hive,
Out of the Develes ers ther gonne drive°
Twenty thousand freres on a route,°
And thurghout helle swarmeden aboute,
And comen again as faste as they may goon,
And in his ers they crepten everichoon:
He clapte his tail again and lay ful stille.
This frere, whan he looked hadde his fille
Upon the torments of this sory place,
His spirit God restored of his grace
Unto his body again and he awook.
But nathelees, for fere yit he quook,°
So was the Develes ers ay in his minde,
That is his heritage of verray kinde.°
God save you alle save this cursed Frere—
My prologe wol I ende in this manere."

The Tale

Lordinges, ther is in Yorkshire, as I gesse,
A mersshy contree called Holdernesse,
In which ther wente a limitour° aboute
To preche, and eek to begge, it is no doute.
  And so bifel that on a day this frere
Hadde preched at a chirche in his manere,
And specially, aboven everything,
Excited he the peple in his preching
To trentals,° and to yive, for Goddes sake,
Wherwith men mighte holy houses make,
Theras divine service is honoured—

30. drive, push. **31. on a route,** in a mob. **40. quook,** quaked. **42. heritage,** birthright; **verray kinde,** the very nature of things.

3. limitour, begging friar. **9. trentals,** series of thirty masses said for the souls of dead persons.

Nat ther as it is wasted and devoured,
Ne ther it needeth nat for to be yive,
As to possessioners that mowen live
(Thanked be God) in wele and habundaunce.
"Trentals," saide he, "delivereth from penaunce
Hir freendes soules, as wel olde as yonge—
Ye, whan that they been hastily ysonge,
Nat for to holde a preest joly and gay:
He singeth nat but oo masse in a day.
  Delivereth out," quod he, "anoon the soules:
Ful hard it is with flesshhook or with oules
To been yclawed, or to brenne or bake.
Now speede you hastily, for Cristes sake!"
And whan this frere hadde said al his entente
With *qui cum patre* forth his way he wente.
  When folk in chirche hadde yive him what hem leste,
He wente his way—no lenger wolde he reste.
With scrippe and tipped staf, ytukked hye,
In every hous he gan to poure and prye,
And beggeth mele and cheese or elles corn.
His felawe hadde a staf tipped with horn,
A paire of tables al of ivory,
And a pointel polisshed fetisly,
And wroot the names alway as he stood
Of alle folk that yaf hem any good,
Ascaunces that he wolde for hem praye.
"Yif us a busshel whete, malt, or reye,
A Goddes kechil or a trip of cheese,
Or elles what you list—we may nat chese.

14. possessioners, i.e., beneficed clergy, more specifically, chantry priests, paid to say one mass a day for the dead, and monks; **mowen,** may. **15. wele,** welfare. **18. hastily,** quickly: the Friar is suggesting that a convent of friars can do thirty masses in a very few days, while a single priest can only say one mass a day. **19. holde,** keep. **22. oules,** awls. **23. brenne,** burn. **26. qui . . . patre,** who with the Father: part of a parting blessing. **27. leste,** pleased. **29. scrippe,** bag; **ytukked,** i.e., with his frock tucked up. **30. poure,** peep. **31. corn,** grain. **33. tables,** tablets. **34. pointel,** stylus; **fetisly,** splendidly. **37. Ascaunces,** as if to suggest. **38. reye,** rye. **39. kechil,** cake: here and in l. **41. Goddes** seems to mean "small"; **trip,** piece. **40. list,** please; **chese,** choose.

A Goddes halfpeny or a masse peny,
Or yif us of youre brawn° if ye have eny.
A dagon of youre blanket, leve° dame,
Oure suster dere—lo, here I write youre name—
Bacon or boef° or swich thing as ye finde."
A sturdy harlot wente ay° hem bihinde
That was hir hostes-man and bar° a sak,
And what men yaf hem laide it on his bak.
And whan that he was out at dore, anoon
He planed away the names everichoon
That he biforn hadde writen in his tables:
He served hem with nifles° and with fables.
—"Nay, ther thou lixt°, thou Somnour," quod the Frere.
"Pees," quod oure Hoost, "for Cristes moder dere.
Tel forth thy tale and spare it nat at al."—
So thrive I (quod this Somnour), so I shal:
So longe he wente hous by hous til he
Cam til an hous ther he was wont° to be
Refresshed more than in an hundred places.
Sik lay the goode man whos that the place is:
Bedrede° upon a couche lowe he lay.
"Deus hic,"° quod he, "O Thomas, freend, good day,"
Saide this frere curteisly and softe.
"Thomas," quod he, "God yeelde° you, ful ofte
Have I upon this bench faren° ful weel;
Here have I eten many a mirye meel."
And fro the bench he droof away the cat
And laide adown his potente° and his hat,
And eek his scrippe°, and sette him softe adown.
(His felawe was go walked° into town
Forth with his knave° into that hostelrye
Wher as he shoop him° thilke night to lie.)

42. **brawn,** pork. 43. **dagon,** bit; **blanket,** ? cut of meat; **leve,** dear. 45. **boef,** beef. 46. **harlot,** ruffian; **ay,** always. 47. **hostes-man,** servant; **bar,** bore. 52. **nifles,** tricks. 53. **lixt,** lie. 58. **wont,** accustomed. 61. **Bedrede,** bed-ridden. 62. **Deus hic,** i.e., may God be here. 64. **yeelde,** repay. 65. **faren,** fared. 68. **potente,** staff. 69. **scrippe,** bag. 70. **was . . . walked,** had gone walking. 71. **knave,** servant. 72. **shoop him,** planned.

"O dere maister," quod this sike man,
"How han ye fare sith° that March bigan?
I saw you nat this fourtenight or more."
"God woot," quod he, "laboured I have ful sore;
And specially for thy savacioun
Have I said many a precious orisoun,°
And for oure othere freendes, God hem blesse.
I have today been at youre chirche at messe°
And said a sermon after my simple wit—
Nat al after° the text of Holy Writ,
For it is hard to you, as I suppose,
And therfore wol I teche you al the glose:°
Glosing° is a glorious thing, certain,
For lettre sleeth,° so as we clerkes sayn.
There have I taught hem to be charitable,
And spende hir good ther it is resonable,
And ther I saw oure dame—a, where is she?"
"Yond in the yeerd I trowe° that she be,"
Saide this man, "and she wol come anoon."
"Ey, maister, welcome be ye, by Saint John,"
Saide this wif. "How fare ye, hertely?"°
The frere ariseth up ful curteisly
And hire embraceth in his armes narwe,°
And kiste hire sweete, and chirteth° as a sparwe
With his lippes. "Dame," quod he, "right weel,
As he that is youre servant every deel,°
Thanked be God that you yaf soule and lif.
Yit saw I nat this day so fair a wif
In al the chirche, God so save me."
"Ye, God amende defautes,° sire," quod she.
"Algates welcome be ye, by my fay."°
"Graunt mercy,° dame, this have I founde alway.

74. sith, since. **78. orisoun,** prayer. **80. messe,** mass. **81, 82. after,** according to. **84. glose,** gloss, marginal interpretation. **85. Glosing,** interpreting. **86. lettre sleeth,** the letter kills: see II Corinthians III 6. **90. trowe,** think. **93. hertely,** really. **95. narwe,** closely. **96. chirteth,** chirps. **98. deel,** bit. **102. defautes,** defects. **103. Algates,** always; **fay,** faith. **104. Graunt mercy,** many thanks.

But of youre grete goodnesse, by youre leve,
I wolde praye you that ye nat you greve:
I wol with Thomas speke a litel throwe°—
Thise curats° been ful necligent and slowe
To grope tendrely a conscience
In shrifte.° In preching is my diligence
And studye in Petres wordes and in Poules.
I walke and fisshe Cristen mennes soules
To yeelden Jesu Crist his propre rente:°
To sprede his word is set al myn entente."
"Now by youre leve, o dere sire," quod she,
"Chideth him wel, for Sainte Trinitee:
He is as angry as a pissemire°
Though that he have al that he can desire;
Though I him wrye° anight and make him warm,
And on him laye my leg outher° myn arm,
He groneth lik oure boor, lith° in oure sty.
Other disport° right noon of him have I:
I may nat plese him in no manere cas."
"O Thomas, *je vous di,*° Thomas, Thomas,
This maketh the Feend! This moste° been amended.
Ire is a thing that hye God defended,°
And therof wol I speke a word or two."
"Now maister," quod the wif, "er that I go,
What wol ye dine? I wol go theraboute."
"Now, dame," quod he, "now *je vous di sans doute,*°
Have I nat of a capon but the livere,
And of youre softe breed nat but shivere,°
And after that a rosted pigges heed—
But that I nolde no beest for me were deed°—
Thanne hadde I with you hoomly suffisaunce.°

107. **throwe,** time. 108. **curats,** curates, parish priests. 110. **shrifte,** confession. 113. **rente,** income. 117. **pissemire,** ant. 119. **wrye,** cover. 120. **outher,** or. 121. **boor, lith,** boar that lies. 122. **disport,** pleasure. 124. **je . . . di,** I say to you. 125. **moste,** must. 126. **defended,** forbade. 130. **sans doute,** without doubt. 132. **shivere,** thin slice. 134. **nolde,** wouldn't want; **deed,** dead. 135. **hoomly suffisaunce,** simple sufficiency.

I am a man of° litel sustenaunce:
My spirit hath his fostering in the Bible;
My body is ay so redy and penible°
To wake that my stomak is destroyed.
I praye you, dame, ye be nat anoyed
Though I so freendly you my conseil shewe:
By God, I wolde nat telle it but a fewe."
"Now sire," quod she, "but oo word er I go:
My child is deed within thise wikes° two,
Soone after that ye wente out of this town."
"His deeth saw I by revelacioun,"
Saide this frere, "at hoom in oure dortour.°
I dar wel sayn that er that half an hour
After his deeth I saw him born to blisse
In myn avision, so God me wisse;°
So dide oure sextein and oure fermerer°
That han been trewe freres fifty yeer:
They may now—God be thanked of his lone°—
Maken hir jubilee° and walke allone.
And up I roos, and al oure covent° eke,
With many a tere trikling on my cheeke,
Withouten noise or clatering of belles—
Te deum° was oure song and nothing elles.
Save that to Crist I saide an orisoun
Thanking him of my revelacioun.
For sire and dame, trusteth me right wel:
Oure orisons been more effectuel,
And more we seen of Cristes secree thinges
Than burel folk, although they were kinges.
We live in poverte and in abstinence,
And burel folk in richesse and dispence°
Of mete and drinke, and in hir foule delit.

136. of, i.e., requiring. **137. penible,** long-suffering. **144. wikes,** weeks. **147. dortour,** dormitory. **150. avision,** vision; **wisse,** guide. **151. sextein,** sexton; **fermerer,** infirmary superintendent. **153. lone,** gift. **154. jubilee,** fiftieth anniversary: until their jubilee, friars were required always to appear in public in couples. **155. covent,** convent. **158. Te deum** (We praise) thee, O God. **166. burel,** lay; **dispence,** expenditure.

We han this worldes lust al in despit.
Lazar and Dives liveden diversly,
And divers guerdon hadde they therby.
Whoso wol praye, he moot faste and be clene,
And fatte his soule, and make his body lene.
We fare as saith th'Apostle: cloth and foode
Suffiseth us though they be nat ful goode.
The clennesse and the fasting of us freres
Maketh that Crist accepteth oure prayeres.
  Lo, Moses fourty dayes and fourty night
Fasted er that the hye God of might
Spak with him in the Mountaine of Sinai;
With empty wombe, fasting many a day,
Received he the lawe that was writen
With Goddes finger; and Elye, wel ye witen,
In Mount Oreb, er he hadde any speeche
With hye God that is oure lives leeche,
He fasted longe and was in contemplaunce.
  Aaron that hadde the temple in governaunce,
And eek the othere preestes everichoon,
Into the temple when they sholde goon
To praye for the peple and do servise,
They nolde drinken in no manere wise
No drinke which that mighte hem dronke make,
But there in abstinence praye and wake
Lest that they deiden—taak heede what I saye:
But they be sobre that for the peple praye—
War that I saye—Namore, for it suffiseth.
  Oure Lord Jesu, as Holy Writ deviseth,
Yaf us ensample of fasting and prayeres.
Therfore we mendinants, we sely freres,

168. lust, pleasure. **169. Lazar,** Lazarus: when Dives the rich man died and went to hell, he could see the poor man Lazarus lying in Abraham's bosom; see Luke XVI. **170. guerdon,** reward. **171. moot,** must. **177. Moses:** see Exodus XXXIV. **180. wombe,** belly. **182. Elye,** Elijah: see I Kings XIX; **witen,** know. **183. Oreb,** Horeb. **184. leeche,** physician. **185. contemplaunce,** contemplation. **186. Aaron:** see Leviticus X. **194. But,** unless. **195. War,** beware. **196. deviseth,** describes. **197. ensample,** example. **198. mendinants,** mendicants; **sely,** innocent.

Been wedded to poverte and continence,
To charitee, humblesse, and abstinence,
To persecucion for rightwisnesse,
To weeping, misericorde,° and clennesse.
And therfore may ye see that oure prayeres
(I speke of us, we mendinants, we freres)
Be to the hye God more acceptable
Than youres, with youre feestes at the table.
Fro Paradis first, if I shal nat lie,
Was man out chaced for his glotonye—
And chast was man in Paradis, certain.
  But herkne now, Thomas, what I shal sayn:
I ne have no text of it, as I suppose,
But I shal finde it in a manere glose,°
That specially oure sweete Lord Jesus
Spak this by freres whan he saide thus:
'Blessed be they that poore in spirit been.'°
And so forth al the Gospel may ye seen
Wher it be likker° oure professioun
Or hire° that swimmen in possessioun—
Fy on hir pompe and hir glotonye,
And for hir lewednesse° I hem defye.
  Me thinketh they been like Jovinian,°
Fat as a whale and walking as° a swan,
Al vinolent as botel in the spence;°
Hir prayere is of ful greet reverence
Whan they for soules saye the psalm of Davit:
'Lo, buf,' they saye, '*Cor meum eructavit.*'°
Who folweth Cristes gospel and his fore°
But we that humble been, and chaste, and poore—

202. misericorde, compassion. **212. glose,** marginal explanation. **215.** See Matthew V 3. **217. Wher,** whether; **likker,** liker, more applicable to. **218. hire,** theirs. **220. lewednesse,** ignorance. **221. Jovinian,** St. Jerome's antagonist, who provoked the antifeminist tract that so preoccupies the Wife of Bath: see Commentary on the *Wife of Bath's Prologue*. **222. as** (2), like. **223. vinolent,** wine-filled; **spence,** cupboard. **226. buf,** a belching sound; **Cor . . . eructavit,** my heart has belched forth: see Psalm XLIV 2 Vulgate. **227. fore,** footsteps.

Werkers of Goddes word, nat auditours?
Therfore right as an hawk up at a sours
Up springeth into th'air, right so prayeres
Of charitable and chaste bisy freres
Maken hir sours to Goddes eres two.
Thomas, Thomas, so mote I ride or go,
And by that lord that cleped is Saint Ive,
Nere thou oure brother, sholdestou nat thrive.
In oure chapitre praye we day and night
To Crist that he thee sende hele and might,
Thy body for to weelden hastily."
"God woot," quod he, "nothing therof feele I.
As helpe me Crist, as I in fewe yeres
Have spent upon diverse manere freres
Ful many a pound, yit fare I nevere the bet.
Certain, my good have I almost biset:
Farewel, my gold, for it is al ago."
The frere answerde, "O, Thomas, doost thou so?
What needeth you diverse freres seeche?
What needeth him that hath a parfit leeche
To seechen othere leeches in the town?
Youre inconstance is youre confusioun.
Holde ye thanne me or elles oure covent
To praye for you been insufficient?
Thomas, that jape nis nat worth a mite:
Youre maladye is for we have too lite.
'A, yif that covent half a quarter otes.'
'A, yif that covent foure and twenty grotes.'
'A, yif that frere a peny and lat him go.'
Nay, nay, Thomas, it may no thing be so.
What is a farthing worth parted in twelve?

230. **sours,** upward swoop. 234. **mote,** may; **go,** walk. 235. **cleped,** called. 236. **nere,** if you weren't. 237. **chapitre,** chapterhouse. 238. **hele,** health. 239. **weelden,** wield, i.e., be able to use. 240. **woot,** knows. 244. **biset,** i.e., used up. 247. **seeche,** seek. 248. **parfit,** perfect; **leeche,** doctor. 250. **inconstance,** inconstancy; **confusioun,** ruin. 251. **Holde,** consider. 253. **jape,** trick. 254. **lite,** little. 256. **grotes,** groats, small coins. 259. **parted,** divided.

Lo, eech thing that is oned in himselve
Is more strong than whan it is toscatered.
Thomas, of me thou shalt nat been yflatered:
Thou woldest han oure labour al for nought.
The hye God that al this world hath wrought
Saith that the werkman worthy is his hire;
Thomas, nought of youre tresor I desire
As for myself, but that al oure covent
To praye for you is ay so diligent,
And for to builden Cristes owene chirche.
Thomas, if ye wol lernen for to wirche,
Of building up of chirches ye may finde
If it be good in Thomas lif of Inde.
Ye lie here ful of anger and of ire
With which the Devel set youre herte afire,
And chiden here the sely innocent,
Youre wif, that is so meeke and pacient.
And therfore, Thomas, trowe me if thee leste,
Ne strive nat with thy wif as for thy beste.
And bere this word away now, by thy faith;
Touching swich thing, lo what the wise man saith:
'Within thyn hous ne be thou no leoun;
To thy subjets do noon oppressioun,
Ne make thine aquaintances nat to flee.'
And, Thomas, yit eftsoones I charge thee:
Be war from hire that in thy bosom sleepeth;
War fro the serpent that so slyly creepeth
Under the gras, and stingeth subtilly.
Be war, my sone, and herkne paciently,
That twenty thousand men han lost hir lives
For striving with hir lemmans and hir wives.

260. oned in himselve, i.e., kept in one piece. **261. toscatered,** scattered about. **268. ay,** always. **270. for to wirche,** ? so that it works upon you. **Thomas . . . Inde:** the life of St. Thomas of India, where the apostle was said to have built many churches. **274. set,** sets. **275. sely,** poor. **277. trowe,** believe; **leste,** please. **284. eftsoones,** moreover. **285. hire,** her, with a possible pun on "ire": the friar's rhetoric seems out of control, and it is not certain whether it is Thomas' wife or his ire that he is to beware of. **290. lemmans,** mistresses.

Now sith° ye han so holy meeke a wif,
What needeth you, Thomas, to maken strif?
Ther nis, ywis,° no serpent so cruel
Whan man tret° on his tail, ne half so fel,
As womman is whan she hath caught an ire.
Vengeance is thanne al that they desire.
Ire is a sinne, oon of the grete° of sevene,
Abhominable unto the God of hevene;
And to himself it is destruccioun.
This every lewed viker or persoun°
Can saye how ire engendreth homicide.
Ire is in sooth executour of pride.
I coude of ire saye so muche sorwe
My tale sholde laste til tomorwe.
And therfore praye I God bothe day and night,
An irous° man, God sende him litel might.
It is greet harm and, certes, greet pitee
To sette an irous man in heigh degree:
Whilom ther was an irous potestat,°
As saith Senek, that during his estat,°
Upon a day out riden knightes two,
And as Fortune wolde that it were so,
That oon of hem cam hoom, that other nought.
Anoon the knight bifore the juge is brought
That saide thus: 'Thou hast thy felawe slain;
For which I deeme thee to the deeth, certain.'
And to another knight comanded he:
'Go, lede him to the deeth, I charge thee.'
And happed° as they wente by the waye
Toward the place ther he sholde deye,
The knight cam which men wenden° hadde be deed.
Thanne thoughten they it were the beste reed°
To lede hem bothe to the juge again.

291. sith, since. **293. ywis,** indeed. **294. tret,** treads. **297. grete,** principal ones. **300. lewed,** ignorant; **viker,** vicar; **persoun,** parson. **306. irous,** ireful. **309. Whilom,** once; **potestat,** potentate. **310. Senek,** Seneca; **estat,** tenure of office. **319. happed,** it happened. **321. wenden,** supposed. **322. reed,** plan.

They saiden, 'Lord, the knight ne hath nat slain
His felawe: here he stondeth, hool,° alive.'
'Ye shul be deed,' quod he, 'so moot° I thrive:
This is to sayn, bothe oon and two and three.'
And to the firste knight right thus spak he:
'I dampned thee: thou most algate° be deed.
And thou also most needes lese° thyn heed,
For thou art cause why thy felawe deith.'
And to the thridde knight right thus he saith:
'Thou hast nat doon that I comanded thee.'
And thus he dide do sleen hem° alle three.
 Irous Cambyses was eek dronkelewe,°
And ay delited him to been a shrewe;°
And so bifel a lord of his meinee°
That loved vertuous moralitee
Saide on a day bitwixe hem two right thus:
'A lord is lost if he be vicious,
And dronkenesse is eek a foul record
Of any man, and namely° in a lord.
Ther is ful many an yë and many an ere
Awaiting on a lord, and he noot° where.
For Goddes love, drink more attemprely.°
Win maketh man to lesen° wrecchedly
His minde and eek his limes° everichoon.'
'The revers shaltou see,' quod he anoon,
'And preve° it by thyn owene experience
That win ne dooth to folk no swich offence.
Ther is no win bireveth me my might
Of hand ne foot, ne of myn yën-sight.'
And for despit° he drank ful muchel more,
An hundred part, than he hadde doon bifore.
And right anoon this irous cursed wrecche

325. hool, healthy. **326. moot,** may. **329. dampned,** condemned; **most,** must; **algate,** in any case. **330. lese,** lose. **334. dide . . . hem,** had them killed. **335. dronkelewe,** given to drunkenness. **336. ay,** ever; **shrewe,** wicked person. **337. meinee,** household. **341. record,** reputation; **namely,** especially. **344. Awaiting** on, watching; **noot,** knows not. **345. attemprely,** moderately. **346. lesen,** lose. **347. limes,** limbs. **349. preve,** prove. **353. despit,** scorn.

Bifore him leet this knightes sone fecche,
Comanding him he sholde bifore him stonde;
And sodeinly he took his bowe in honde,
And up the streng he pulled to his ere,
And with an arwe he slow the child right there.
'Now wheither have I a siker hand or noon?'
Quod he. 'Is al my might and minde agoon?
Hath win bireved me myn yën-sight?'
What sholde I telle th'answere of the knight?
His sone was slain, ther is namore to saye.
Beeth war, therfore, with lordes how ye playe;
Singeth *Placebo* and 'I shal if I can,'
But if it be unto a poore man:
To a poore man men sholde his vices telle,
But nat to a lord, though he sholde go to helle.
Lo, irous Cyrus, thilke Percien,
How he destroyed the river of Gysen
For that an hors of his was dreint therinne
Whan that he wente Babyloine to winne:
He made that the river was so smal
That wommen mighte wade it over al.
Lo, what saide he that so wel teche can:
'Ne be no felawe to an irous man,
Ne with no wood man walke by thy waye
Lest thee repente.' I wol no ferther saye.
Now, Thomas, leve brother, leef thyn ire.
Thou shalt me finde as just as is a squire.
Hold nat the develes knif ay at thyn herte.
Thyn anger dooth thee al too sore smerte;
But shewe to me al thy confessioun."
"Nay," quod the sike man, "by Saint Simoun,
I have be shriven this day at my curat.

356. leet, had. **360. slow,** slew. **361. siker,** sure. **367. Placebo,** I shall please: see Psalm CXIV 9 Vulgate. **368. But if,** unless. **371. Percien,** Persian. **372. Gysen,** Gyndes. **373. dreint,** drowned. **376. over al,** anywhere. **379. wood,** mad. **381. leve,** dear; **leef,** leave. **382. squire,** carpenter's square. **384. dooth,** makes. **387. at,** by; **curat,** priest.

I have him told holly al myn estat.°
Needeth namore to speke of it, saith he,
But if me list° of myn humilitee."
  "Yif me thanne of thy gold to make oure cloistre,"
Quod he, "for many a muscle° and many an oystre,
Whan othere men han been ful wel at aise,°
Hath been oure foode, oure cloistre for to raise.
And yit, God woot, unnethe the fundament°
Parfourned° is, ne of oure pavement
Nis nat a tile yit within oure wones.°
By God, we owen fourty pound for stones.
Now help, Thomas, for him that harwed° helle,
Or elles mote° we oure bookes selle,
And if you lakke oure predicacioun°
Thanne gooth the world al to destruccioun,
For whoso fro this world wolde us bireve,°
So God me save, Thomas, by youre leve,
He wolde bireve out of the world the sonne.
For who can teche and werchen as we conne?°
And that is nat of litel time," quod he,
"But sith Elye was or Elisee°
Han freres been—that finde I of record—
In charitee, ythanked be oure Lord.
Now, Thomas, help, for Sainte Charitee."
And down anoon he sette him on his knee.
  This sike man weex wel neigh wood for ire:°
He wolde that the frere hadde been afire
With his fals dissimulacioun.
"Swich thing as is in my possessioun,"
Quod he, "that may I yive and noon other.
Ye saye me thus, how that I am youre brother?"
  "Ye, certes," quod the frere, "trusteth weel:

388. holly, wholly; **estat,** condition. **390. But if,** unless; **list,** it pleases. **392. muscle,** mussel. **393. aise,** ease. **395. unnethe,** hardly; **fundament,** foundation. **396. Parfourned,** finished. **397. wones,** buildings. **399. harwed,** harried, despoiled. **400. mote,** must. **401. predicacioun,** preaching. **403. bireve,** remove. **406. conne,** can. **408.** I.e., but since the time of Elijah or Elisha. **413. wex,** grew; **wood,** crazy.

I took oure dame oure lettre with oure seel."°
"Now, wel," quod he, "and somwhat shal I yive
Unto youre holy covent whil I live;
And in thyn hand thou shalt it han anoon,
On this condicioun, and other noon:
That thou departe° it so, my dere brother,
That every frere have as muche as other.
This shaltou swere on thy professioun.
Withouten fraude or cavelacioun."°
"I swere it," quod this frere, "upon my faith."
And therwithal his hand in his he laith:
"Lo, here my faith: in me shal be no lak."°
"Now, thanne, put thyn hand down by my bak,"
Saide this man, "and grope wel bihinde:
Binethe my buttok there shaltou finde
A thing that I have hid in privetee."
"A," thoughte this frere, "that shal go with me."
And down his hand he launcheth to the clifte°
In hope for to finde there a yifte.
And whan this sike man felte this frere
Aboute his tuwel° grope there and here,
Amidde his hand he leet the frere a fart—
Ther nis no capul° drawing in a cart
That mighte han lete a fart of swich a soun.
The frere up sterte as dooth a wood° leoun.
'A, false cherl," quod he, "for Goddes bones,
This hastou for despit doon for the nones.°
Thou shalt abye° this fart if that I may!"
His meinee° which that herden this affray
Cam leping in and chaced out the frere.
And forth he gooth with a ful angry cheere,°
And fette his felawe ther as lay his stoor.°

420. I gave your wife our letter with our seal: the letter is the official appointment of Thomas as a "brother" of the friar's order. **425. departe,** divide. **428. cavelacioun,** quibbling. **431. lak,** fault. **437. launcheth,** darts; clifte, **cleft. 440. tuwel,** anus. **442. capul,** horse. **444. wood,** mad. **446. despit,** scorn; **for the nones,** i.e., for that reason only. **447. abye,** pay for. **448. meinee,** servants. **450. cheere,** face. **451. fette,** fetched; **stoor,** goods.

He looked as it were a wilde boor;
He grindeth with his teeth, so was he wroth.
A sturdy paas down to the court he gooth
Wheras ther woned° a man of greet honour,
To whom that he was alway confessour.
This worthy man was lord of that village.
The frere cam as he were in a rage
Wher as this lord sat eting at his boord.°
Unnethe° mighte the frere speke a word,
Til atte laste he saide, "God you see."
  This lord gan looke and saide, "Benedicite!°
What, frere John, what manere world is this?
I see wel that som thing ther is amis:
Ye looken as the wode° were ful of theves.
Sit down anoon, and tel me what youre grief is,
And it shal been amended if I may."
  "I have," quod he, "had a despit° today—
God yeelde° you—adown in youre village,
That in this world ther nis so poore a page
That he nolde have abhominacioun
Of that I have received in youre town.
And yit ne greveth me nothing so sore
As that this olde cherl, with lokkes hore,°
Blasphemed hath oure holy covent eke."
  "Now, maister," quod this lord, "I you biseeke—"
  "No maister, sire," quod he, "but servitour°—
Though I have had in scole that honour:
God liketh nat that 'Rabi'° men us calle
Neither in market n'in youre large halle."
  "No fors,"° quod he. "But telle me al youre grief."
"Sire," quod this frere, "an odious meschief
This day bitid° is to myn ordre and me,

455. woned, dwelt. **459. boord,** table. **460. Unnethe,** scarcely. **462. Benedicite,** bless me. **465. wode,** wood. **468. despit,** insult. **469. yeelde,** repay. **474. hore,** hoary. **477. servitour,** servant. **479. Rabi,** rabbi, master. **481. fors,** matter. **483. bitid,** happened to.

And so *per consequens* to eech degree
Of holy chirche, God amende it soone."
 "Sire," quod the lord, "ye woot what is to doone.
Distempre you nought: ye be my confessour;
Ye been the salt of th'erthe and the savour.
For Goddes love, youre pacience ye holde.
Telle me your grief." And he anoon him tolde
As ye han herde biforn—ye woot wel what.
 The lady of the hous ay stille sat
Til she herd hadde what the frere saide.
"Ey, Goddes moder," quod she, "blisful maide,
Is ther ought elles? Telle me faithfully."
 "Madame," quod he, "how thinketh you therby?"
 "How that me thinketh?" quod she, "so God me speede:
I saye a cherl hath doon a cherles deede.
What sholde I saye? God lat him nevere thee:
His sike heed is ful of vanitee;
I holde him in a manere frenesye."
 "Madame," quod he, "by God, I shal nat lie:
But I on other wise may be wreke,
I shal defame him overal wher I speke—
The false blasphemour that charged me
To parte that wol nat departed be
To every man yliche, with meschaunce."
 The lord sat stille as he were in a traunce,
And in his herte he rolled up and down,
"How hadde this cherl imaginacioun
To shewe swich a probleme to the frere?
Nevere erst er now herde I of swich matere.
I trowe the Devel putte it in his minde:
In ars-metrike shal ther no man finde
Biforn this day of swich a questioun.
Who sholde make a demonstracioun

484. per, by. **486. woot,** know; **is to,** ought to be. **487. Distempre,** disturb. **495. ought,** anything. **499. thee,** thrive. **501. frenesye,** frenzy. **503. But,** unless; **wreke,** avenged. **506. parte,** portion out; **that,** what; **departed,** divided. **512. erst,** before. **513. trowe,** think. **514. ars-metrike,** arithmetic. **515. of,** i.e., any.

That every man sholde han ylike his part
As of a soun or savour of a fart?
O, nice, proude cherl, I shrewe his face.
Lo, sires," quod the lord, "with harde grace,
Whoevere herde of swich a thing er now?
To every man ylike, telle me how?
It is an impossible, it may nat be.
Ey, nice cherl, God lat him nevere thee!
The rumbling of a fart and every soun
Nis but of air reverberacioun,
And there it wasteth lite and lite away.
Ther nis no man can deeme, by my fay,
If that it were departed equally.
What, lo, my cherl, lo, yit how shrewedly
Unto my confessour today he spak:
I holde him certainly demoniak.
Now ete youre mete and lat the cherl go playe.
Lat him go hange himself, a devel waye."
  Now stood the lordes squier at the boord
That carf his mete, and herde word by word
Of alle thing of which I have you said.
"My lord," quod he, "be ye nat yvele apaid:
I coude telle, for a gowne-cloth,
To you, sire frere, so ye be nat wroth,
How that this fart sholde evene ydeled be
Among youre covent, if it liked me."
  "Tel," quod the lord, "and thou shalt have anoon
A gowne-cloth, by God and by Saint John."
  "My lord," quod he, "whan that the weder is fair,
Withouten wind or perturbing of air,
Lat bringe a cartwheel here into this halle—
But looke that it have his spokes alle:
Twelve spokes hath a cartwheel communly.
And bringe me thanne twelve freres. Woot ye why?

519. nice, foolish; **shrewe,** curse. **524. thee,** thrive. **527. lite,** little. **528. deeme,** judge; **fay,** faith. **529. departed,** divided. **530. shrewedly,** mischievously. **532. demoniak,** possessed by a demon. **534. a. . . waye,** i.e., however he wants. **535. boord,** table. **536. carf,** carved. **538. yvele apaid,** ill-pleased. **541. ydeled,** distributed. **542. liked,** pleased. **550. Woot,** know.

For thritteene is a covent, as I gesse.
Youre confessour here, for his worthinesse,
Shal parfourne up the nombre of this covent.
Thanne shal they kneele adown by oon assent,
And t'every spokes ende in this manere
Ful sadly laye his nose shal a frere.
Youre noble confessour—ther God him save—
Shal holde his nose upright under the nave.
Thanne shal this cherl, with bely stif and tought
As any tabour, hider been ybrought,
And sette him on the wheel right of this cart,
Upon the nave, and make him lete a fart:
And ye shal seen, on peril of my lif,
By preve which that is demonstratif,
That equally the soun of it wol wende—
And eek the stink—unto the spokes ende;
Save that this worthy man, youre confessour,
By cause he is a man of greet honour,
Shal han the firste fruit, as reson is.
The noble usage of freres yit is this:
The worthy men of hem shul first be served.
And, certainly, he hath it wel deserved:
He hath today taught us so muchel good
With preching in the pulpit ther he stood,
That I may vouche sauf—I saye for me—
He hadde the firste smel of fartes three;
And so wolde al his covent, hardily,
He bereth him so faire and holily."
  The lord, the lady, and eech man, save the frere,
Saiden that Jankin spak in this matere
As wel as Euclide dide or Ptolomee.
Touching the cherl, they saide subtiltee
And heigh wit made him speke as he spak:
"He nis no fool ne no demoniak."
And Jankin hath ywonne a newe gowne.
My tale is doon: we been almost at towne.

553. parfourne, make. **556. sadly,** steadily. **557. ther,** may. **559. tought,** taut. **560. tabour,** drum. **564. preve,** proof. **577. hardily,** assuredly. **581. Euclide,** Euclid, founder of geometry; **Ptolemee,** Ptolemy, the great astronomer.

THE CLERK'S TALE

The Introduction

"Sire Clerk of Oxenforde," oure Hoste saide,
"Ye ride as coy° and stille as dooth a maide
Were newe spoused, sitting at the boord.
This day ne herde I of your tonge a word—
I trowe ye studye aboute som sophime,°
But Salomon seith 'Every thing hath time.'
For Goddes sake, as beeth of bettre cheere!
It is no time for to studyen here.
Telle us som merye tale, by youre fay;°
For what man that is entred in a play,°
He needes moot° unto the play assente—
But precheth nat, as freres doon in Lente,
To maken us for oure olde sinnes weepe—
Ne that thy tale make us nat to sleepe.
  Telle us som merye thing of aventures.
Youre termes, youre colours, and youre figures,°
Keepe hem in stoor° til so be ye endite
Heigh style, as whan that men to kinges write.
Speketh so plain at this time, we you praye,
That we may understonde what ye saye."
  This worthy Clerk benignely answerde:
"Hoste," quod he, "I am under youre yerde.°
Ye han of us as now the governaunce,
And therfore wol I do you obeisaunce°
As fer as reson axeth, hardily.°

2. **coy**, shy. 5. **sophime**, sophism. 9. **fay**, faith. 10. **play**, game. 11. **moot**, must. 16. **termes**, technical terms; **colours**, patterns of rhetoric; **figures**, i.e., of speech. 17. **stoor**, stock. 22. **yerde**, rod, rule. 24. **obeisaunce**, obedience. 25. **axeth**, i.e., requires; **hardily**, assuredly.

I wol you telle a tale which that I
Lerned at Padwe of a worthy clerk,
As preved by his wordes and his werk.
He is now deed and nailed in his cheste—
I praye to God so yive his soule reste.
  Fraunceis Petrak, the lauriat poete,
Highte this clerk, whos retorike sweete
Enlumined al Itaile of poesye,
As Linian dide of philosophye,
Or lawe, or other art particuler.
But deeth, that wol nat suffre us dwellen heer
But as it were a twinkling of an yë,
Hem bothe hath slain, and alle shul we die.
  But forth to tellen of this worthy man
That taughte me this tale, as I bigan,
I saye that first with heigh style he enditeth,
Er he the body of his tale writeth,
A prohemie in which descriveth he
Pemond and of Saluces the contree,
And speketh of Appenin, the hilles hye,
That been the boundes of West Lumbardye,
And of Mount Vesulus in special,
Wher as the Po, out of a welle smal,
Taketh his firste springing and his sours
That eestward ay encreesseth in his cours
To Emeleward, to Ferare and Venise,
The which a long thing were to devise;
And trewely, as to my juggement,
Me thinketh it a thing impertinent,
Save that he wole convoyen his matere;
But this his tale which that ye shal heere."

27. **Padwe,** Padua. 28. **preved,** was proved. 29. **deed,** dead. 31. **Petrak,** Petrarch, Italian poet and scholar, died in 1374; **lauriat,** laurel-crowned. 32. **retorike,** rhetoric. 33. **Enlumined,** illuminated; **Itaile,** Italy. 34. **Linian,** Lignaco, Italian scholar, died in 1383. 43. **prohemie,** prologue; **descriveth,** describes. 44. **Pemond,** Piedmont; **Saluces,** Saluzzo. 45. **Appenin,** the Apennine mountains. 46. **Lumbardye,** Lombardy. 47. **Vesulus,** Viso. 48. **welle,** spring. 51. Toward Emilia, toward Ferrara and Venice. 54. **impertinent,** irrelevant. 55. **convoyen,** introduce.

The Tale

PART ONE

Ther is at the weste side of Itaile,
Down at the roote of Vesulus the colde,
A lusty plaine habundant of vitaile,°
Wher many a towr and town thou maist biholde,
That founded were in time of fadres° olde,
And many another delitable° sighte,
And Saluces this noble contree highte.

A markis whilom° lord was of that land,
As were his worthy eldres him bifore;
And obeisant,° ay redy to his hand,
Were alle his liges, bothe lasse and more.°
Thus in delit he liveth and hath doon yore,°
Biloved and drad° thurgh favour of Fortune
Bothe of his lordes and of his commune.°

Therwith he was, to speke as of linage,
The gentileste yborn of Lumbardye:
A fair persone and strong and yong of age,
And ful of honour and of curteisye,
Discreet ynough his contree for to gie°—
Save in some thinges that he was to blame;
And Walter was this yonge lordes name.

I blame him thus: that he considered nought
In time coming what mighte him bitide,
But on his lust° present was al his thought,
As for to hawke and hunte on every side.
Wel neigh alle othere causes leet° he slide.

3. **vitaile,** food. 5. **fadres,** fathers. 6. **delitable,** delightful. 8. **markis,** marquis; **whilom,** once. 10. **obeisant,** obedient. 11. **liges,** vassals; **lasse . . . more,** low and high. 12. **yore,** for a long time. 13. **drad,** dreaded, held in awe. 14. **commune,** i.e., the common people. 19. **gie,** lead. 24. **lust,** pleasure. 26. **leet,** let.

And eek he nolde°—and that was worst of alle—
Wedde no wif for nought that may bifalle.

Only that point his peple bar so sore°
That flokmele° on a day they to him wente,
And oon of hem that wisest was of lore,°
Or elles that the lord best wolde assente
That he sholde telle him what his peple mente,
Or elles coude he shewe wel swich matere,
He to the markis saide as ye shal heere:

"O noble markis, your humanitee
Assureth us and yiveth us hardinesse°
As ofte as time is of necessitee
That we to you mowe° telle oure hevinesse.
Accepteth, lord, now of youre gentilesse
That we with pitous herte unto you plaine,°
And lat youre eres nat my vois desdaine.

Al have I° nought to doone in this matere
More than another man hath in this place,
Yit for as muche as ye, my lord so dere,
Han alway shewed me favour and grace,
I dar the bettre axe of you a space°
Of audience, to shewen oure requeste;
And ye, my lord, to doon right as you leste.°

For certes, lord, so wel us liketh you
And al youre werk, and evere han doon, that we
Ne couden nat us self devisen how
We mighte liven in more felicitee—
Save oo thing, lord, if it youre wille be,
That for to been a wedded man you leste:
Thanne were youre peple in soverein hertes reste.°

27. nolde, would not. **29. bar . . . sore,** took so badly. **30. flokmele,** in a flock. **31. lore,** learning. **37. hardinesse,** confidence. **39. mowe,** may. **41. plaine,** complain. **43. Al . . . I,** although I have. **47. axe,** ask; **space,** time. **49. leste,** it may please. **56. soverein,** supreme; **reste,** i.e., ease.

Boweth youre nekke under that blisful yok
Of sovereinetee,° nought of servise,
Which that men clepe spousaile° or wedlok.
And thenketh, lord, among youre thoughtes wise,
How that oure dayes passe in sondry wise:
For though we sleepe or wake or renne° or ride,
Ay fleeth the time—it nil no man abide.

And though youre greene youthe flowre as yit,
In creepeth age alway as stille as stoon;
And deeth manaceth every age, and smit°
In eech estaat, for ther escapeth noon.
And also certain as we knowe eechoon
That we shal die, as uncertain we alle
Been of that day whan deeth shal on us falle.

Accepteth thanne of us the trewe entente,°
That nevere yit refuseden youre heeste,°
And we wol, lord, if that ye wol assente,
Chese° you a wif in short time, at the leeste
Born of the gentileste and of the meeste°
Of al this land, so that it oughte seeme
Honour to God and you, as we can deeme.

Delivere us out of al this bisy° drede
And take a wif, for hye Goddes sake.
For if it so bifelle, as God forbede,
That thurgh youre deeth youre line sholde slake,°
And that a straunge° successour sholde take
Youre heritage, O, wo were us alive!
Wherfore we praye you hastily to wive."°

Hir meeke prayere and hir pitous cheere°
Made the markis herte han pitee.

58. **sovereinetee,** dominion. 59. **spousaile,** marriage. 62. **renne,** run. 66. **manaceth,** threatens; **smit,** smites. 71. **entente,** spirit. 72. **heeste,** command. 74. **Chese,** choose. 75. **meeste,** most, i.e., greatest. 78. **bisy,** i.e., haunting. 81. **slake,** fail. 82. **straunge,** foreign. 84. **wive,** marry. 85. **cheere,** behavior.

"Ye wol," quod he, "myn owene peple dere,
To that I nevere erst thoughte straine me:°
I me rejoised of my libertee
That selde° time is founde in mariage.
Ther I was free I moot been in servage.

But, nathelees, I see youre trewe entente,
And truste upon youre wit and have doon ay;
Wherfore of my free wil I wol assente
To wedde me as soone as evere I may.
But ther as ye han profred me today
To chese° me a wif, I you releesse
That chois, and praye you of that profre ceesse.

For God it woot that children ofte been
Unlik hir worthy eldres hem bifore:
Bountee comth al of God, nat of the streen°
Of which they been engendred and ybore.°
I truste in Goddes bountee, and therfore
My mariage and myn estaat and reste
I him bitake:° he may doon as him leste.

Lat me allone in chesing° of my wif:
That charge° upon my bak I wol endure.
But I praye you—and charge upon youre lif—
That what wif that I take, ye me assure
To worshipe hire whil that hir lif may dure,°
In word and werk, bothe heer and everywhere,
As she an emperoures doughter were.

And ferthermore, this shal ye swere: that ye
Again my chois shal neither grucche° ne strive.
For sith I shal forgoon my libertee
At youre requeste, as evere mote I thrive,

88. i.e., constrain me to do what I never hitherto intended. **90. selde,** seldom. **97. chese,** choose. **101. Bountee,** magnanimity; **streen,** strain. **102. ybore,** born. **105. him bitake,** entrust to him. **106. chesing,** choosing. **107. charge,** load. **110. dure,** last. **114. grucche,** grumble.

Ther as myn herte is set, ther wol I wive.
And but ye wol assente in swich manere,
I praye you speketh namore of this matere."

With hertely wil they sworen and assenten
To al this thing—ther saide no wight nay—
Biseeking him of grace, er that they wenten,
That he wolde graunten hem a certain day
Of his spousaile, as soone as evere he may:
For yit alway the peple somwhat dredde
Lest that the markis no wif wolde wedde.

He graunted hem a day swich as him leste
On which he wolde be wedded sikerly,
And saide he dide al this at hir requeste.
And they with humble entente buxomly,
Kneeling upon hir knees ful reverently,
Him thanken alle, and thus they han an ende
Of hir entente, and hoom again they wende.

And herupon he to his officers
Comandeth for the feeste to purveye,
And to his privee knightes and squiers
Swich charge yaf as him liste on hem laye;
And they to his comandement obeye,
And eech of hem dooth al his diligence
To doon unto the feeste reverence.

PART TWO

Nought fer fro thilke palais honourable
Wher as this markis shoop his mariage,
Ther stood a throop of site delitable,

120. **hertely,** sincere. 122. **Biseeking,** beseeching. 124. **spousaile,** marriage. 128. **sikerly,** certainly. 130. **entente,** heart; **buxomly,** obediently. 132. **ende,** i.e., desired effect. 133. **entente,** purpose. 135. **purveye,** provide. 142. **shoop,** was planning. 143. **throop,** village; **delitable,** delightful.

In which that poore folk of that village
Hadden hir beestes and hir herbergage,°
And of° hir labour tooken hir sustenaunce,
After that the erthe yaf° hem habundaunce.

Among thise poore folk ther dwelte a man
Which that was holden° poorest of hem alle:
But hye God somtime senden can
His grace into a litel oxes stalle.
Janicula men of that throop him calle;
A doughter hadde he, fair ynough to sighte,
And Grisildis this yonge maiden highte.

But for to speke of vertuous beautee,
Thanne was she oon° the faireste under sonne.
For pooreliche yfostred up° was she,
No likerous lust was thurgh hir herte yronne;°
Wel ofter of the welle than of the tonne°
She drank; and for she wolde vertu plese,
She knew wel labour but noon idel ese.

But though this maide tendre were of age,
Yit in the brest of hir virginitee
Ther was enclosed ripe and sad corage;°
And in greet reverence and charitee
Hir olde poore fader fostred she.
A fewe sheep, spinning, on feeld she kepte;°
She wolde nought been idel til she slepte.

And whan she hoomward cam she wolde bringe
Wortes° or othere herbes times ofte,
The whiche she shredde and seeth° for his livinge,
And made hir bed ful harde and no thing softe;

145. hebergage, dwelling. **146. of,** by. **147. After that,** according as; **yaf,** gave. **149. holden,** considered. **156. oon,** i.e., one of. **157. For,** because; **pooreliche,** in poverty; **yfostred up,** reared. **158. likerous,** lecherous; **was yronne,** had penetrated. **159. tonne,** (wine-)tun. **164. ripe,** mature; **sad,** constant; **corage,** heart. **167. spinning,** while spinning; **kepte,** tended. **170. Wortes,** edible greens. **171. shredde,** sliced; **seeth,** boiled.

And ay she kepte hir fadres lif on lofte°
With every obeisance° and diligence
That child may doon to fadres reverence.

Upon Griselde, this poore creature,
Ful ofte sithe° this markis sette his yë,
As he on hunting rood, paraventure;
And whan it fil° that he mighte hire espye,
He nought with wantoune looking of folye
His yën caste on hire, but in sad° wise
Upon hir cheere he wolde him ofte avise,°

Commending in his herte hir wommanhede,
And eek hir vertu, passing° any wight
Of so yong age, as wel in cheere° as deede.
For though the peple hath no greet insight
In vertu, he considered ful right
Hir bountee, and disposed° that he wolde
Wedde hire only, if evere he wedden sholde.

The day of wedding cam, but no wight can
Telle what womman that it sholde be.
For which merveile wondred many a man,
And saiden whan they were in privetee,
"Wol nat oure lord yit leve his vanitee?
Wol he nat wedde? Allas the while!
Why wol he thus himself and us bigile?"

But nathelees this markis hath doon make,°
Of gemmes set in gold and in asure,°
Brooches and ringes for Griseldis sake;
And of hir clothing took he the mesure
Of a maide lik to hir stature,

173. **on lofte,** i.e., from sinking. 174. **obeisance,** courtesy. 177. **sithe,** time. 179. **fil,** befell. 181. **sad,** sober. 182. **cheere,** face; **him . . . avise,** ponder. 184. **passing,** surpassing. 185. **cheere,** manner. 188. **bountee,** goodness; **disposed,** decided. 197. **doon make,** had made. 198. **asure,** lapis lazuli.

And eek of othere aornementes° alle
That unto swich a wedding sholde falle.°

The time of undren° of the same day
Approcheth that this wedding sholde be,
And al the palais put was in array,
Bothe halle and chambres, eech in his degree—
Houses of office° stuffed with plentee:
Ther maistou seen of daintevous° vitaile
That may be founde as fer as last° Itaile.

This royal markis richeliche arrayed,
Lordes and ladies in his compaignye,
The whiche that to the feeste were ypraved,°
And of his retenue the bachelrye,°
With many a soun of sondry melodye,
Unto the village of the which I tolde
In this array the righte way han holde.

Grisilde of this, God woot, ful innocent
That for hire shapen° was al this array,
To fecchen water at a welle is went,
And cometh hoom as soone as evere she may.
For wel she hadde herd said that thilke day
The markis sholde wedde, and if she mighte,
She wolde fain° han seen som of that sighte.

She thoughte, "I wol with othere maidens stonde,
That been my felawes, in oure dore and see
The markisesse, and therfore wol I fonde°
To doon at hoom as soone as it may be
The labour which that longeth° unto me;
And thanne I may at leiser hire biholde,
If she this way° unto the castel holde."

202. aornementes, adornments. **203. sholde falle,** were appropriate. **204. undren,** afternoon. **208. Houses . . . office,** storage buildings. **209. daintevous,** delicate. **210. last,** i.e., extends. **213. yprayed,** invited. **214. bachelrye,** i.e., the young knights. **219. shapen,** destined. **224. fain,** gladly. **227. markisesse,** marquise; **fonde,** try. **229. longeth,** is of concern. **231. way,** i.e., route.

And as she wolde over the thresshfold° goon,
The markis cam and gan hire for to calle,
And she sette down hir water-pot anoon
Biside the thressfold in an oxes stalle,
And down upon hir knees she gan to falle,
And with sad° countenance kneeleth stille
Til she hadde herd what was the lordes wille.

This thoughtful markis spak unto this maide
Ful sobrely, and saide in this manere:
"Wher is youre fader, O Grisildis?" he saide.
And she with reverence in humble cheere°
Answerde, "Lord, he is al redy here."
And in she gooth withouten lenger lette,°
And to the markis she hir fader fette.°

He by the hand than took this olde man,
And saide thus whan he him hadde aside:
"Janicula, I neither may ne can
Lenger the plesance of myn herte hide:
If that thou vouche sauf what so bitide,
Thy doughter wol I take er that I wende
As for my wif, unto my lives ende.

Thou lovest me, I woot it wel, certain,
And art my faithful lige man ybore,°
And al that liketh° me, I dar wel sayn,
It liketh thee, and specially therfore,
Tel me that point that I have said bifore:
If that thou wolt unto that purpos drawe°
To take me as for thy sone-in-lawe."

The sodein caas this man astonied° so
That reed he weex; abaist° and al quakinge

232. **thresshfold,** threshold. 237. **sad,** sober. 242. **cheere,** manner. 244. **lette,** delay. 245. **fette,** fetched. 254. **lige,** liege; **ybore,** born. 255. **liketh,** pleases. 258. **drawe,** i.e., assent. 260. **caas,** event; **astonied,** astonished. 261. **reed,** red; **weex,** grew; **abaist,** abashed.

He stood. Unnethe° saide he wordes mo,
But only this: "Lord," quod he, "my willinge
Is as ye wole, ne ayains youre likinge
I wol no thing. Ye be my lord so dere:
Right as you list governeth this matere."

"Yit wol I," quod this markis softely,
"That in thy chambre I and thou and she
Have a collacion.° And woostou why?
For I wol axe if it hir wille be
To be my wif and rule hire after me.
And al this shal be doon in thy presence:
I wol nought speke out of thyn audience."°

And in the chambre whil they were aboute°
Hir tretis° which as ye shal after heere,
The peple cam unto the hous withoute,
And wondred hem in how honeste° manere
And tentifly° she kepte hir fader dere;
But outrely° Grisildis wondre mighte,
For nevere erst° ne saw she swich a sighte.

No wonder is though that she were astoned°
To seen so greet a gest° come in that place:
She nevere was to swiche gestes woned,°
For which she looked with ful pale face.
But shortly forth this matere for to chace,°
Thise arn the wordes that this markis saide
To this benigne, verray, faithful maide.

"Grisilde," he saide, "ye shal wel understonde
It liketh to youre fader and to me
That I you wedde, and eek it may so stonde
As I suppose ye wol that it so be.

262. **Unnethe,** with difficulty. 269. **collacion,** consultation. 273. **audience,** hearing. 274. **aboute,** busy about. 275. **tretis,** business. 277. **honeste,** honorable. 278. **tentifly,** attentively. 279. **outrely,** above all. 280. **erst,** before. 281. **astoned,** astonished. 282. **gest,** guest. 283. **woned,** accustomed. 285. **chace,** drive.

But thise demandes axe I first," quod he,
"That sith it shal be doon in hastif° wise,
Wol ye assente or elles you avise?°

I saye this, be ye redy with good herte
To al my lust,° and that I freely may,
As me best thinketh, do° you laughe or smerte,
And nevere ye to grucche° it night ne day?
And eek whan I saye 'Ye' ne saye nat 'Nay,'
Neither by word ne frowning countenaunce:
Swere this, and here I swere oure alliaunce."

Wondring upon this word, quaking for drede,
She saide, "Lord, undigne° and unworthy
I am to thilke honour that ye me bede.°
But as ye wol yourself, right so wol I:
And here I swere that nevere willingly
In werk ne thought I nil you disobeye,
For to be deed,° though me were loth to deye."

"This is ynough, Grisilde myn," quod he.
And forth he gooth with a ful sobre cheere
Out at the dore, and after that cam she;
And to the peple he saide in this manere:
"This is my wif," quod he, "that standeth here:
Honoureth hire and loveth hire I praye
Who so me loveth. Ther is namore to saye."

And for that no thing of hir olde gere°
She sholde bringe into his hous, he bad
That wommen sholde dispoilen° hire right there;
Of which thise ladies were nought right glad
To handle hir clothes wherinne she was clad,
But nathelees this maide bright of hewe
Fro foot to heed they clothed han al newe.

293. hastif, hasty. **294. you avise,** deliberate, with the idea of refusal. **296. lust,** pleasure. **297. do,** make. **298. grucche,** grumble about. **303. undigne,** unworthy. **304. bede,** offer. **308. deed,** dead. **316. gere,** i.e., possessions. **318. dispoilen,** undress.

Hir heres han they kembd, that lay untressed°
Ful rudely, and with hir fingres smale°
A corowne on hir heed they han ydressed,°
And sette hir ful of nowches° grete and smale.
Of hir array what sholde I make a tale?
Unnethe° the peple hire knew for hir fairnesse,
Whan she translated° was in swich richesse.

This markis hath hire spoused° with a ring
Brought for the same cause, and thanne hire sette
Upon an hors snow-whit and wel ambling,
And to his palais er he lenger lette,°
With joyful peple that hire ladde° and mette,
Convoyed hire; and thus the day they spende
In revel til the sonne gan descende.

And shortly forth this tale for to chace,
I saye that to this newe markisesse
God hath swich favour sente hire of his grace
That it ne seemed nat by liklinesse°
That she was born and fed in rudenesse,
As in a cote° or in an oxes stalle,
But norissed° in an emperoures halle.

To every wight she woxen° is so dere
And worshipful, that folk ther she was bore,°
That from hir birthe knewe hire yeer by yere,
Unnethe trowed they, but dorste han swore,°
That to Janicle, of which I spak bifore,
She doughter were, for as by conjecture°
Hem thoughte she was another creature.

323. kembd, combed; **untressed,** unbraided. · **324. hir,** their; **smale,** dainty. **325. ydressed,** placed. **326. nowches,** jewels. **328. Unnethe,** scarcely. **329. translated,** transformed. **330. spoused,** married. **333. lette,** delayed. **334. ladde,** led. **340. by liklinesse,** likely. **342. cote,** cottage. **343. norissed,** brought up. **344. woxen,** grown. **345. bore,** born. **347. Unnethe,** with difficulty; **trowed,** believed; **swore,** i.e., sworn the opposite. **349. by conjecture,** i.e., judging from appearances.

For though that evere vertuous was she,
She was encreessed in swich excellence
Of thewes good, yset in heigh bountee,°
And so discreet and fair of eloquence,
So benigne and so digne° of reverence,
And coude so the peples herte embrace,
That eech hire loved that looked on hir face.

Nought only of Saluces in the town
Publissed° was the bountee of hir name,
But eek biside in many a regioun;
If oon saide wel, another saide the same;
So spradde° of hir hye bountee the fame
That men and wommen, as wel yonge as olde,
Goon to Saluce upon hire to biholde.

Thus Walter lowely—nay, but royally—
Wedded with fortunat honestetee,°
In Goddes pees° liveth ful esily
At hoom, and outward grace ynough hath he;
And for he saw that under lowe degree
Was ofte vertu hid, the peple him heelde
A prudent man, and that is seen ful selde.°

Nought only this Grisildis thurgh hir wit
Coude al the fet° of wifly humblenesse,
But eek whan that the caas required it,
The commune profit° coude she redresse:
Ther nas discord, rancour, ne hevinesse
In al that land that she ne coude apese,°
And wisely bringe hem alle in reste and ese.

Though that hir housbonde absent were, anoon,
If gentil men or othere of hir contree

353. thewes, habits, qualities; **bountee,** excellence. **355. digne,** worthy. **359. Publissed,** made known. **362. spradde,** spread. **366. honestetee,** dignity. **367. pees,** peace. **371. selde,** seldom. **373. Coude,** knew; **fet,** action. **375. commune profit,** general welfare. **377. apese,** appease.

Were wrothe, she wolde bringen hem at oon;°
So wise and ripe° wordes hadde she,
And juggements of so greet equitee,
That she from hevene sent was, as men wende,°
Peple to save and every wrong t'amende.

Nat longe time after that this Grisild
Was wedded, she a doughter hath ybore°—
Al hadde hire levere have born a knave° child.
Glad was the markis and the folk therfore,
For though a maide child come al bifore,
She may unto a knave child attaine
By liklihede, sin she nis nat bareine.°

PART THREE

Ther fil,° as it bifalleth times mo,
Whan that this child hath souked but a throwe,°
This markis in his herte longeth so
To tempte his wif, hir sadnesse° for to-knowe,
That he ne mighte out of his herte throwe
This merveilous desir his wif t'assaye:
Nedelees, God woot, he thoughte hire for t'affraye.°

He hadde assayed hire ynough bifore
And foond° hire evere good. What needed it
Hire for to tempte, and alway more and more,
Though some men praise it for a subtil wit?°
But as for me, I saye that yvele it sit°
T'assaye a wif whan that it is no neede,
And putten hire in anguissh and in drede.

381. at oon, in agreement. **382. ripe,** mature. **384. wende,** supposed. **387. ybore,** born. **388. Al . . . levere,** although she would rather; **knave,** boy. **392. liklihede,** probability; **bareine,** barren. **393. fil,** befell. **394. souked,** sucked; **throwe,** short time. **396. tempte,** test; **sadnesse,** constancy. **399. thoughte,** intended; **affraye,** frighten. **401. foond,** found. **403. wit,** idea. **404. yvele . . . sit,** it is ill-fitting.

For which this markis wroughte in this manere:
He cam allone anight ther as she lay,
With sterne face and with ful trouble cheere,°
And saide thus: "Grisilde," quod he, "that day
That I you took out of youre poore array
And putte you in estaat of heigh noblesse—
Ye have nat that forgeten, as I gesse?

I saye, Grisilde, this present dignitee
In which that I have put you, as I trowe,
Maketh you nat foryetful for to be
That I you took in poore estaat ful lowe,
For any wele ye mote yourselven knowe.°
Take heede of every word that I you saye:
Ther is no wight that heereth but we twaye.

Ye woot yourself wel how that ye cam here
Into this hous—it is nat longe ago.
And though to me that ye be lief° and dere,
Unto my gentils° be ye no thing so:
They sayn to hem it is greet shame and wo
For to be subgets° and been in servage
To thee, that born art of a smal village.

And namely sith thy doughter was ybore°
Thise wordes han they spoken, doutelees.
But I desire, as I have doon bifore,
To live my lif with hem in reste and pees.
I may nat in this caas be recchelees:°
I moot doon with thy doughter for the beste—
Nat as I wolde, but as my peple leste.°

And yit, God woot, this is ful loth° to me.
But nathelees, withouten youre witing°

409. trouble, disturbed; **cheere,** countenance. **418.** Despite any prosperity you might yourself have experience with, i.e., despite your lack of wealth. **423. lief,** beloved. **424. gentils,** nobles. **426. subgets,** subjects. **428. namely,** especially; **ybore,** born. **432. recchelees,** negligent. **434. leste,** it may please. **435. loth,** hateful. **436. witing,** knowledge.

I wol nat doon.° But this wol I," quod he,
"That ye to me assente as in this thing.
Shewe now youre pacience in youre werking°
That ye me highte° and swore in youre village,
That day that maked was oure mariage."

Whan she hadde herd al this she nought ameved°
Neither in word or cheere° or countenaunce,
For as it seemed, she was nat agreved.°
She saide, "Lord, al lith in your plesaunce;°
My child and I with hertely obeisaunce°
Been youres al, and ye mowe save or spille°
Youre owene thing: werketh after youre wille.

Ther may no thing—God so my soule save—
Liken to° you that may displesen me,
Ne I ne desire no thing for to have,
Ne drede for to lese,° save only thee.
This wil is in myn herte and ay shal be:
No lengthe of time or deeth may this deface,
Ne chaunge my corage° to another place."

Glad was this markis of hir answeringe,
But yit he feined° as he were nat so:
Al drery was his cheere° and his lookinge,
Whan that he sholde out of the chambre go.
Soone after this a furlong way° or two,
He prively hath told al his entente
Unto a man, and to his wif him sente.

A manere sergeant was this privee° man,
The which that faithful ofte he founden hadde

437. **doon,** take action. 439. **werking,** behavior. 440. **highte,** promised. 442. **ameved,** moved, i.e., appeared disturbed. 443. **cheere,** manner. 444. **agreved,** angry. 445. **lith,** lies; **plesaunce,** pleasure. 446. **hertely,** heart-felt; **obeisaunce,** obedience. 447. **mowe,** may; **spille,** ruin. 450. **liken to,** please. 452. **lese,** lose. 455. **corage,** heart. 457. **feined,** feigned. 458. **cheere,** face. 460. **a . . . way,** i.e., the time it takes to go a furlong. 463. **manere,** kind of; **privee,** secretive.

In thinges grete, and eek swich folk wel can
Doon execucion in thinges badde.
The lord knew wel that he him loved and dradde.°
And whan this sergeant wiste° his lordes wille,
Into the chambre he stalked him ful stille.

"Madame," he said, "ye mote foryive it me
Though I do thing to which I am constrained.
Ye been so wis that ful wel knowe ye
That lordes heestes mowe nat been yfeined;°
They mowe wel been biwailed or complained,
But men mote neede unto hir lust° obeye,
And so wol I; ther is namore to saye.

This child I am comanded for to take—"
And spak namore, but out the child he hente°
Despitously, and gan a cheere make°
As though he wolde han slain it er he wente.
Grisildis moot al suffre and al consente,
And as a lamb she sitteth meeke and stille,
And leet this cruel sergeant doon his wille.

Suspecious was the defame° of this man,
Suspect his face, suspect his word also,
Suspect the time in which he this bigan.
Allas, hir doughter that she loved so,
She wende° he wolde han slain it right tho.
But nathelees, she neither weep ne siked,°
Conforming hire to that the markis liked.°

But at the laste speken she bigan,
And mekely she to the sergeant prayde,
So as he was a worthy gentil man,
That she moste kisse hir child er that it deide.°

467. dradde, dreaded. **468. wiste,** knew. **473. heestes,** commands; **mowe,** may; **yfeined,** shirked. **475. lust,** desire. **478. hente,** seized. **479. Despitously,** roughly; **a cheere make,** assume a manner. **484. defame,** evil reputation. **488. wende,** thought. **489. weep . . . siked,** wept nor sighed. **490. liked,** pleased. **494. deide,** died.

And on hir barm this litel child she laide,
With ful sad face, and gan the child to blisse,°
And lulled it, and after gan it kisse.

And thus she saide in hir benigne vois,
"Farewel my child, I shal thee nevere see.
But sith I thee have marked with the crois°
Of thilke Fader—blessed mote he be—
That for us deide upon a crois of tree,°
Thy soule, litel child, I him bitake,°
For this night shaltou dien for my sake."°

I trowe that to a norice° in this cas
It hadde been hard this routhe° for to see;
Wel mighte a moder° thanne have cried allas.
But nathelees, so sad° stedefast was she
That she endured al adversitee,
And to the sergeant mekely she saide,
"Have heer again youre litel yonge maide.

Gooth now," quod she, "and dooth my lordes heeste.°
But oo thing wol I praye you of youre grace:
That but my lord forbad you, at the leeste
Burieth this litel body in som place,
That beestes ne no briddes it torace."°
But he no word wol to that purpos saye,
But took the child and wente upon his waye.

This sergeant cam unto his lord again,
And of Grisildis wordes and hir cheere°
He tolde him point for point in short and plain,
And him presenteth with his doughter dere.
Somwhat this lord hadde routhe in his manere,

495. **barm,** lap. 496. **sad,** unmoved; **blisse,** mark with the sign of the cross. 500. **crois,** cross. 502. **tree,** wood. 503. **bitake,** intrust to. 504. **sake,** fault. 505. **norice,** nurse. 506. **routhe,** pity. 507. **moder,** mother. 508. **sad,** constant. 512. **heeste,** command. 516. **torace,** tear apart. 520. **cheere,** behavior.

But nathelees his purpos heeld he stille,
As lordes doon whan they wol han hir wille.

And bad this sergeant that he prively
Sholde this child ful softe winde and wrappe,
With alle circumstances° tendrely,
And carye it in a cofre or in a lappe,°
But upon paine his heed of for to swappe,°
That no man sholde knowe of his entente,
Ne whennes° he cam, ne whider that he wente,

But at Bologne° he to his suster dere—
That ilke time of Panik° was countesse—
He sholde it take and shewe hire this matere,
Biseeking hire to doon hir bisinesse°
This child to fostre in alle gentilesse;
And whos child that it was he bad hire hide
From every wight, for ought that may bitide.

The sergeant gooth and hath fulfild this thing—
But to this markis now returne we.
For now gooth he ful faste imagining°
If by his wives cheere he mighte see,
Or by hir word aperceive, that she
Were chaunged. But he nevere hire coude finde
But evere in oon ylike sad° and kinde.

As glad, as humble, as bisy in servise
And eek in love as she was wont to be,
Was she to him in every manere wise,
Ne of hir doughter nought a word spak she:
Noon accident° for noon adversitee
Was seen in hire, ne nevere hir doughter name
Ne nempned° she, in ernest ne in game.

528. **With . . . circumstances,** in every small detail. 529. **cofre,** box; **lappe,** folded cloth. 530. **heed,** head; **swappe,** strike. 532. **whennes,** whence. 533. **Boloigne,** Bologna. 534. **Panik,** Panico. 536. **Biseeking,** beseeching; **bisinesse,** i.e., everything possible. 542. **imagining,** pondering. 546. **in oon,** continually; **sad,** stable. 551. **accident,** outward change. 553. **nempned,** named.

PART FOUR

In this estaat ther passed been four yeer
Er she with childe was, but as God wolde
A knave child she bar by this Walter,
Ful gracious and fair for to biholde.
And whan that folk it to his fader tolde,
Nat only he, but al his contree merye
Was for this child, and God they thanke and herye.

Whan it was two yeer old and fro the brest
Departed of his norice, on a day
This markis caughte yit another lest
To tempte his wif yit ofter if he may.
O, nedelees was she tempted in assay!
But wedded men ne knowe no mesure
Whan that they finde a pacient creature.

"Wif," quod this markis, "ye han herd er this
My peple sikly berth this mariage,
And namely sith my sone yboren is,
Now is it wors than evere in al oure age:
The murmur sleeth myn herte and my corage,
For to mine eres comth the vois so smerte
That it wel neigh destroyed hath myn herte.

Now saye they thus: 'Whan Walter is agoon,
Thanne shal the blood of Janicle succeede
And been oure lord, for other have we noon.'
Swiche wordes saith my peple, out of drede.
Wel oughte I of swich murmur taken heede,
For certainly, I drede swich sentence,
Though they nat plain speke in myn audience.

554. **estaat,** condition. 556. **knave,** boy; **bar,** bore. 560. **herye,** praise. 562. **Departed,** removed; **norice,** nurse. 563. **lest,** desire. 564. **tempte,** test; **ofter,** more often. 566. **mesure,** moderation. 569. **sikly berth,** bear ill. 570. **namely,** especially. 572. **murmur,** grumbling; **sleeth,** slays; **corage,** spirit. 578. **drede,** doubt. 580. **sentence,** opinion. 581. **audience,** hearing.

I wolde live in pees if that I mighte;
Wherfore I am disposed outrely,
As I his suster servede by nighte,
Right so thenke I to serve him prively.
This warne I you that ye nat sodeinly
Out of yourself for no wo sholde outraye:
Beeth pacient, and therof I you praye."

"I have," quod she, "said thus and evere shal:
I wol no thing ne nil no thing, certain,
But as you list; nought greveth me at al
Though that my doughter and my sone be slain—
At youre comandement, this is to sayn.
I have nat had no part of children twaine
But first siknesse and after wo and paine.

Ye been oure lord: dooth with youre owene thing
Right as you list; axeth no reed at me.
For as I lefte at hoom al my clothing,
Whan I first cam to you, right so," quod she,
"Lefte I my wil and al my libertee,
And took youre clothing; wherfore I you praye,
Dooth youre plesance: I wol youre lust obeye.

And certes, if I hadde prescience
Youre wil to knowe er ye youre lust me tolde,
I wolde it doon withouten necligence.
But now I woot youre lust and what ye wolde,
Al youre plesance ferm and stable I holde.
For wiste I that my deeth wolde doon you ese,
Right gladly wolde I dien, you to plese.

Deeth may nat make no comparisoun
Unto your love." And whan this markis sey

583. **outrely,** absolutely. 584. **servede,** treated. 585. **thenke,** intend. 587. Should not lose control of yourself for any sorrow. 590. **wol,** desire. 597. **axeth . . . reed,** ask no advice. 602. **lust,** desire. 603. **prescience,** foreknowledge. 608. **wiste I,** if I knew. 611. **sey,** saw.

The constance° of his wif, he caste adown
His yën two, and wondreth that she may
In pacience suffre al this array.°
And forth he gooth with drery countenaunce,
But to his herte it was ful greet plesaunce.

This ugly sergeant in the same wise
That he hir doughter caughte,° right so he—
Or worse, if men worse can devise°—
Hath hent° hir sone that ful was of beautee.
And evere in oon° so pacient was she
That she no cheere° made of hevinesse,
But kiste hir sone and after gan it blesse.°

Save this: she prayed him that if he mighte
Hir litel sone he wolde in erthe grave,°
His tendre limes, delicat to sighte,
Fro fowles and fro beestes for to save.
But she noon answere of him mighte have:
He wente his way as him no thing ne roughte,°
But to Boloigne he tendrely it broughte.

This markis wondreth evere lenger the more°
Upon hir pacience, and if that he
Ne hadde soothly knowen therbifore
That parfitly° hir children loved she,
He wolde have wend° that of som subtiltee,
And of malice or of cruel corage,°
That she hadde suffred this with sad° visage.

But wel he knew that next himself, certain,
She loved hir children best in every wise.
But now of wommen wolde I axen fain°

612. constance, constancy. **614. array,** treatment. **618. caughte,** seized. **619. devise,** imagine. **620. hent,** seized. **621. in oon,** constantly. **622. cheere,** appearance. **623. blesse,** mark with the cross. **625. grave,** bury. **629. him roughte,** he cared. **631. evere . . . more,** always more and more. **634. parfitly,** perfectly. **635. wend,** supposed. **636. corage,** heart. **637. sad,** unmoved. **640. fain,** gladly.

If thise assayes mighte nat suffise:
What coude a sturdy housbonde more devise
To preve hir wifhood and hir stedfastnesse,
And he continuing evere in sturdinesse?

But ther been folk of swich condicioun
That whan they have a certain purpos take,
They can nat stinte of hir entencioun,
But right as they were bounden to that stake,
They wol nat of that firste purpos slake:
Right so this markis fulliche hath purposed
To tempte his wif as he was first disposed.

He waiteth if by word or countenaunce
That she to him was chaunged of corage,
But nevere coude he finde variaunce:
She was ay oon in herte and in visage,
And ay the ferther that she was of age,
The more trewe, if that it were possible,
She was to him in love, and more penible.

For which it seemed thus, that of hem two
Ther nas but oo wil, for as Walter leste,
The same lust was hir plesance also.
And God be thanked, al fil for the beste.
She shewed wel for no worldly unreste
A wif, as of hirself, no thing ne sholde
Wille in effect but as hir housbonde wolde.

The sclaundre of Walter ofte and wide spradde
That of a cruel herte he wikkedly,
For he a poore womman wedded hadde,
Hath mordred bothe his children prively.

642. **sturdy,** harsh. 643. **preve,** test. 647. **stinte,** cease. 649. **slake,** desist. 652. **waiteth,** watches. 658. **penible,** painstaking. 660. **leste,** it pleased. 661. **lust,** desire. 662. **fil,** fell, i.e., turned out. 666. **sclaundre,** slander, i.e., evil report; **spradde,** spread. 668. **For,** because. 669. **mordred,** murdered.

Swich murmur was among hem communely:
No wonder is, for to the peples ere
Ther cam no word but that they mordred were.

For which, wher as his peple therbifore
Hadde loved him wel, the sclaundre of his defame°
Made hem that they him hatede therfore:
To been a mordrere is an hateful name.
But nathelees, for ernest ne for game,
He of his cruel purpos nolde stente°—
To tempte his wif was set al his entente.

Whan that his doughter twelf yeer was of age,
He to the court of Rome, in subtil wise
Enformed of his wil, sente his message,
Comanding hem swiche bulles° to devise
As to his cruel purpos may suffise—
How that the Pope, as for his peples reste,
Bad him to wedde another if him leste.

I saye, he bad they sholde countrefete
The Popes bulles, making mencioun
That he hath leve his firste wif to lete°
As by the Popes dispensacioun,
To stinte° rancour and dissencioun
Bitwixe his peple and him—thus saide the bulle,
The which they han publissed° at the fulle.

The rude peple, as it no wonder is,
Wenden° ful wel that it hadde been right so.
But whan thise tidinges cam to Grisildis,
I deeme that hir herte was ful wo;
But she, ylike sad° for everemo,
Disposed was, this humble creature,
Th'adversitee of Fortune al t'endure;

674. sclaundre . . . defame, rumor of his evil reputation. **678. stente,** cease. **683. bulles,** papal edicts. **689. lete,** leave. **691. stinte,** put an end to. **693. publissed,** made public. **695. Wenden,** thought. **698. sad,** steadfast.

Abiding evere his lust° and his plesaunce,
To whom that she was yiven herte and al,
As to hir verray worldly suffisaunce.°
But shortly if this storye I tellen shal,
This markis writen hath in special
A lettre in which he sheweth his entente,
And secreely he to Boloigne it sente.

To the Erl of Panik, which that hadde tho
Wedded his suster, prayde he specially
To bringen hoom again his children two,
In honourable estaat al openly.
But oo thing he him prayed outrely,°
That he to no wight, though men wolde enquere,°
Sholde nat tellen whos children that they were,

But saye the maiden sholde ywedded be
Unto the Markis of Saluce anoon.
And as this erl was prayed so dide he,
For at day-set° he on his way is goon
Toward Saluce, and lordes many oon
In riche array, this maiden for to gide—
Hir yonge brother riding hire biside.

Arrayed was toward hir mariage
This fresshe maide, ful of gemmes clere;°
Hir brother, which that seven yeer was of age,
Arrayed eek ful fressh in his manere.
And thus in greet noblesse and with glad cheere,
Toward Saluces shaping hir journey,
Fro day to day they riden in hir way.

PART FIVE

Among al this after his wikke usage,°
This markis yit his wif to tempte more

701. lust, desire. **703. suffisaunce,** source of happiness. **712. outrely,** i.e., emphatically. **713. enquere,** inquire. **718. day-set,** sunrise. **723. clere,** bright. **729. wikke usage,** evil custom.

To the outtreste preve of hir corage,°
Fully to han experience and lore°
If that she were as stedefast as bifore,
He on a day in open audience,°
Ful boistously,° hath said hire this sentence:

"Certes, Grisilde, I hadde ynough plesaunce
To han you to my wif for youre goodnesse,
And for youre trouthe, and for youre obeisaunce°—
Nought for your linage ne for youre richesse.
But now I knowe in verray soothfastnesse
That in greet lordshipe, if I wel avise,°
Ther is greet servitute° in sondry wise.

I may nat do as every plowman may:
My peple me constraineth for to take
Another wif, and cryen day by day;
And eek the Pope, rancour for to slake,°
Consenteth it, that dar I undertake.°
And trewely thus muche I wol you saye,
My newe wif is coming by the waye.

Be strong of herte and voide° anoon hir place,
And thilke dowere° that ye broughten me,
Taak it again—I graunte it of my grace.
Returneth to youre fadres hous," quod he.
"No man may alway han prosperitee.
With evene herte I rede° you t'endure
The strook of Fortune or of aventure."

And she again answerde in pacience:
"My lord," quod she, "I woot, and wiste alway,
How that bitwixen youre magnificence

731. outtreste, uttermost; **preve,** proof; **corage,** spirit. **732. lore,** knowledge. **734. in . . . audience,** i.e., in public. **735. boistously,** coarsely. **738. trouthe,** fidelity; **obeisaunce,** obedience. **741. avise,** consider. **742. servitute,** servitude. **746. slake,** abate. **747. undertake,** guarantee. **750. voide,** make empty. **751. thilke,** that same; **dowere,** dowry. **755. evene,** i.e., calm; **rede,** advise.

And my poverte no wight can ne may
Maken comparison, it is no nay.
I ne heeld me nevere digne in no manere
To be youre wif, no, ne youre chamberere.

And in this hous ther ye me lady made,
The hye God take I for my witnesse,
And also wisly he my soule glade,
I nevere heeld me lady ne maistresse,
But humble servant to youre worthinesse,
And evere shal whil that my lif may dure,
Aboven every worldly creature.

That ye so longe of youre benignitee
Han holden me in honour and nobleye,
Wher as I was nought worthy for to be,
That thanke I God and you, to whom I praye
Foryeelde it you. Ther is namore to saye.
Unto my fader gladly wol I wende,
And with him dwelle unto my lives ende.

Ther I was fostred as a child ful smal,
Til I be deed my lif ther wol I lede,
A widwe clene in body, herte, and al;
For sith I yaf to you my maidenhede,
And am youre trewe wif, it is no drede,
God shilde swich a lordes wif to take
Another man to housbonde or to make.

And of youre newe wif God of his grace
So graunte you wele and prosperitee—
For I wol gladly yeelden hire my place,
In which that I was blisful wont to be;
For sith it liketh you, my lord," quod she,

761. **it . . . nay,** it can't be denied. 762. **digne,** worthy. 763. **chamberere,** chambermaid. 766. **wisly,** surely; **glade,** make glad. 769. **dure,** last. 772. **nobleye,** splendor. 775. **Foryeelde,** repay. 779. **deed,** dead. 782. **drede,** doubt. 783. **shilde,** forbid. 784. **make,** mate. 786. **wele,** happiness. 787. **yeelden hire,** yield to her. 789. **liketh,** pleases.

"That whilom° weren al myn hertes reste,
That I shal goon, I wol goon whan you leste.°

But ther as ye me profre swich dowaire°
As I first broughte, it is wel in my minde
It were my wrecched clothes no thing faire,
The whiche to me were hard now for to finde—
O goode God, how gentil and how kinde
Ye seemed by youre speeche and youre visage
The day that maked was oure mariage!

But sooth is said—algate° I finde it trewe,
For in effect it preved° is on me—
Love is nought old as whan that it is newe.
But certes, lord, for noon adversitee,
To dien in this caas, it shal nat be
That evere in word or werk I shal repente
That I you yaf myn herte in hool entente.°

My lord, ye woot that in my fadres place
Ye dide me strepe out of my poore weede,°
And richely me cladden of youre grace:
To you broughte I nought elles, out of drede,°
But faith, and nakednesse, and maidenhede.
And here again youre clothing I restore,
And eek youre wedding-ring for everemore.

The remenant of youre jewels redy be
Inwith youre chambre, dar I saufly° sayn.
Naked out of my fadres hous," quod she,
"I cam, and naked moot I turne again.
Al youre plesance wol I folwen fain.°
But yit I hope it be nat youre entente
That I smoklees° out of youre palais wente.

790. whilom, once. **791. leste,** it may please. **792. dowaire,** dowry. **799. algate,** in any case. **800. preved,** proved. **805. in . . . entente,** whole-heartedly. **807. dide . . . strepe,** had me stripped; **weede,** clothing. **809. drede,** doubt. **814. Inwith,** within; **saufly,** safely. **817. fain,** gladly. **819. smoklees,** i.e., without an undergarment to cover me.

Ye coude nat doon so dishoneste° a thing
That thilke wombe in which youre children laye
Sholde biforn the peple in my walking
Be seen al bare. Wherfore I you praye,
Lat me nat like a worm go by the waye.
Remembre you, myn owene lord so dere,
I was youre wif though I unworthy were.

Wherfore in guerdon° of my maidenhede,
Which that I broughte and nought again I bere,
As voucheth sauf to yive me to my meede°
But swich a smok as I was wont to were,°
That I therwith may wrye the wombe of here°
That was youre wif. And here I take my leve
Of you, myn owene lord, lest I you greve."

"The smok," quod he, "that thou hast on thy bak,
Lat it be stille and beer° it forth with thee."
But wel unnethes° thilke word he spak,
But wente his way for routhe° and for pitee.
Biforn the folk hirselven strepeth° she,
And in hir smok, with heed and feet al bare,
Toward hir fader hous forth is she fare.°

The folk hire folwen, weeping in hir waye,
And Fortune ay they cursen as they goon.
But she fro weeping kepte hir yën dreye,°
Ne in this time word ne spak she noon.
Hir fader, that this tiding herde anoon,
Curseth the day and time that nature
Shoop him to been a lives° creature.

For out of doute this olde poore man
Was evere in suspect° of hir mariage,

820. dishoneste, dishonorable. **827. guerdon,** recompense. **829. to . . . meede,** as my reward. **830. were,** wear. **831. wrye,** cover; **here,** her. **835. beer,** bear. **836. unnethes,** with difficulty. **837. routhe,** ruth. **838. strepeth,** strips. **840. is . . . fare,** has she gone. **843. dreye,** dry. **847. Shoop,** created; **lives,** living. **849. suspect,** suspicion.

For evere he deemed sith that it bigan
That whan the lord fulfild hadde his corage,°
Him wolde thinke it were a disparage°
To his estaat so lowe for t'alighte,
And voiden° hire as soone as evere he mighte.

Agains° his doughter hastiliche gooth he,
For he by noise of folk knew hir cominge,
And with hir olde cote as it mighte be
He covered hire, ful sorwefully weepinge.
But on hir body mighte he it nat bringe,
For rude was the cloth and she more of age
By dayes fele° than at hir mariage.

Thus with hir fader for a certain space°
Dwelleth this flowr of wifly pacience,
That neither by hir wordes ne hir face,
Biforn the folk, ne eek in hir° absence,
Ne shewed she that hire° was doon offence,
Ne of hir hye estaat no remembraunce
Ne hadde she, as by hir countenaunce.

No wonder is, for in hir grete estat
Hir gost was evere in plein° humilitee:
No tendre° mouth, noon herte delicat,
No pompe, no semblant° of royaltee,
But ful of pacient benignitee,
Discreet and pridelees, ay honourable,
And to hir housbonde evere meeke and stable.

Men speke of Job, and most for his humblesse,
As clerkes whan hem list conne wel endite,
Namely° of men, but as in soothfastnesse,
Though clerkes praise wommen but a lite,°

851. **corage,** desire. 852. **Him,** to him; **thinke,** seem; **disparage,** dishonor. 854. **voiden,** get rid of. 855. **Agains,** i.e., to meet. 861. **fele,** many. 862. **space,** time. 865. **hir,** their. 866. **hire,** i.e., to her. 870. **gost,** spirit; **plein,** full. 871. **tendre,** i.e., pampered. 872. **semblant,** appearance. 878. **Namely,** especially. 879. **lite,** little.

Ther can no man in humblesse him acquite
As wommen can, ne can be half so trewe
As wommen been, but it be falle of newe.°

PART SIX

Fro Boloigne is this Erl of Panik come,
Of which the fame up sproong° to more and lesse,
And to the peples eres alle and some°
Was couth eek that a newe markisesse°
He with him broughte, in swich pompe and richesse
That nevere was ther seen with mannes yë
So noble array in al West Lumbardye.

The markis, which that shoop° and knew al this,
Er that this erl was come sente his message
For thilke sely° poore Grisildis;
And she with humble herte and glad visage,
Nat with no swollen thought in hir corage,°
Cam at his heeste,° and on hir knees hire sette,
And reverently and wisely she him grette.°

"Grisilde," quod he, "my wil is outrely°
This maiden, that shal wedded been to me,
Received be tomorwe as royally
As it possible is in my hous to be,
And eek that every wight in his degree
Have his estaat in sitting and servise
And heigh plesance, as I can best devise.

I have no wommen suffisant,° certain,
The chambres for t'arraye in ordinaunce°
After my lust, and therfore wolde I fain°

882. but . . . newe, unless it has happened recently. **884. fame,** report; **sproong,** sprang. **885. alle . . . some,** each and every one. **886. couth,** made known; **markisesse,** marquise. **890. shoop,** was arranging. **892. sely,** innocent. **894. corage,** heart. **895. heeste,** command. **896. grette,** greeted. **897. outrely,** absolutely. **904. suffisant,** competent. **905. arraye . . . ordinaunce,** put in order. **906. lust,** desire; **fain,** gladly.

That thyn were al swich manere governaunce:
Thou knowest eek of old al my plesaunce.
Though thyn array be badde and yvele-biseye,
Do thou thy devoir at the leeste waye."

"Nat only, lord, that I am glad," quod she,
"To doon youre lust, but I desire also
You for to serve and plese in my degree,
Withouten fainting, and shal everemo,
Ne nevere, for no wele ne no wo,
Ne shal the gost within myn herte stente
To love you best with al my trewe entente."

And with that word she gan the hous to dighte,
And tables for to sette, and beddes make,
And pained hire to doon al that she mighte,
Praying the chambereres, for Goddes sake,
To hasten hem and faste sweepe and shake—
And she, the moste servisable of alle,
Hath every chambre arrayed and his halle.

Abouten undren gan this erl alighte,
That with him broughte thise noble children twaye,
For which the peple ran to seen the sighte
Of hir array so richely biseye;
And thanne at erst amonges hem they saye
That Walter was no fool though that him leste
To chaunge his wif, for it was for the beste.

For she is fairer, as they deemen alle,
Than is Grisilde, and more tendre of age,
And fairer fruit bitweene hem sholde falle,
And more plesant for hir heigh linage—

907. governaunce, management. **909. array,** clothing; **yvele-biseye,** ill-appearing. **910. devoir,** duty; **at . . . waye,** in any case. **915. wele,** happiness. **916. gost,** spirit; **stente,** cease. **917. trewe entente,** sincere heart. **918. dighte,** prepare. **920. pained hire,** took pains. **921. chambereres,** chambermaids. **923. servisable,** diligent. **925. undren,** midafternoon. **928. biseye,** appearing. **929. erst,** last.

Hir brother eek so fair was of visage,
That hem to seen the peple hath caught° plesaunce,
Commending now the markis governaunce.°

"O stormy peple, unsad and evere untrewe!°
Ay undiscreet and chaunging as a vane,°
Deliting evere in rumbel° that is newe,
For lik the moone ay wexe ye and wane,
Ay ful of clapping, dere ynough a jane;°
Youre doom is fals, youre constance yvele preveth°—
A ful greet fool is he that on you leveth."°

Thus saiden sadde° folk in that citee,
Whan that the peple gazed up and down,
For they were glad right for the noveltee
To han a newe lady of hir town.
Namore of this make I now mencioun,
But to Grisilde again I wol me dresse,°
And telle hir constance and hir bisinesse.

Ful bisy was Griselde in every thing
That to the feeste was apertinent.°
Right nought was she abaist° of hir clothing,
Though it were rude and somdeel eek torent,°
But with glad cheere to the gate is went,
With other folk, to greete the markisesse,
And after that dooth forth hir bisinesse.

With so glad cheere his gestes she receiveth,
And conningly,° everich in his degree,
That no defaute° no man aperceiveth,
But ay they wondren what she mighte be

937. **caught,** taken. 938. **governaunce,** behavior. 939. **unsad,** inconstant; **untrewe,** lacking fidelity. 940. **vane,** weathervane. 941. **rumbel,** bustle. 943. **clapping,** chatter; **dere . . . jane,** i.e., not worth a cent. 944. **doom,** judgment; **constance,** constancy; **yvele preveth,** i.e., stands up badly. 945. **leveth,** trusts. 946. **sadde,** sober. 951. **dresse,** turn. 954. **apertinent,** pertinent. 955. **abaist,** abashed. 956. **torent,** torn. 961. **conningly,** skillfully. 962. **defaute,** defect.

That in so poore array was for to see,
And coude° swich honour and reverence;
And worthily they praisen hir prudence.

In al this mene while she ne stente°
This maide and eek hir brother to commende
With al hir herte in ful benigne entente,
So wel that no man coude hir pris amende.°
But at the laste, whan that thise lordes wende°
To sitten down to mete, he gan to calle
Grisilde as she was bisy in the halle.

"Grisilde," quod he, as it were in his play,
"How liketh thee my wif and hir beautee?"
"Right wel," quod she, "my lord, for in good fay,°
A fairer saw I nevere noon than she.
I praye to God yive hire prosperitee,
And so hope I that he wol to you sende
Plesance ynough unto your lives ende.

Oo thing biseeke° I you—and warne also—
That ye ne prike° with no tormentinge
This tendre maiden as ye han doon mo.°
For she is fostred in hir norissinge°
More tendrely, and to my supposinge,
She coude nat adversitee endure,
As coude a poore fostred creature."

And whan this Walter saw hir pacience,
Hir glade cheere, and no malice at al—
And he so ofte hadde doon to her offence,
And she ay sad° and constant as a wal,
Continuing evere hir innocence overal—
This sturdy markis gan his herte dresse°
To rewen° upon hir wifly stedfastnesse.

965. **coude,** i.e., showed. 967. **stente,** ceased. 970. **pris,** praise; **amende,** better. 971. **wende,** thought. 976. **fay,** faith. 981. **biseeke,** beseech. 982. **prike,** prick. 983. **mo,** others. 984. **norissinge,** bringing up. 991. **sad,** steadfast. 993. **sturdy,** cruel; **dresse,** turn. 994. **rewen,** have pity.

"This is ynough, Grisilde myn," quod he.
"Be now namore agast ne yvele apayed:
I have thy faith and thy benignitee
As wel as evere womman was assayed.
In greet estaat and pooreliche arrayed,
Now knowe I, dere wif, thy stedfastnesse"—
And hire in armes took and gan hire kesse.

And she for wonder took of it no keep;
She herde nat what thing he to hire saide;
She ferde as she hadde stert out of a sleep,
Til she out of hir mazednesse abraide.
"Grisilde," quod he, "by God that for us deide,
Thou art my wif, ne noon other I have,
Ne nevere hadde, as God my soule save.

This is thy doughter which thou hast supposed
To be my wif. That other faithfully
Shal be myn heir, as I have ay supposed.
Thou bare him in thy body trewely.
At Boloigne have I kept him prively.
Taak him again, for now maistou nat saye
That thou hast lorn noon of thy children twaye.

And folk that otherways han said of me,
I warne hem wel that I have doon this deede
For no malice ne for no crueltee,
But for t'assaye in thee thy wommanhede;
And nat to sleen my children, God forbede,
But for to keep hem prively and stille,
Til I thy purpos knewe and al thy wille."

Whan she this herde, aswoune down she falleth
For pitous joye, and after hir swouninge
She bothe hir yonge children to hire calleth,

996. **yvele apayed,** ill-pleased. **1001. kesse,** kiss. **1002. keep,** notice. **1004. ferde,** behaved; **stert,** started. **1005. mazednesse,** amazement; **abraide,** i.e., recovered. **1011. supposed,** intended. **1012. bare,** bore. **1015. lorn,** lost. **1020. sleen,** slay. **1023. aswoune,** in a swoon.

And in hir armes, pitously weepinge,
Embraceth hem, and tendrely kissinge
Ful lik a moder, with hir salte teres
She batheth bothe hir visage and hir heres.

O which° a pitous thing it was to see
Hir swouning, and hir humble vois to heere!
"Graunt mercy,° lord, God thanke it you," quod she,
"That ye han saved me my children dere.
Now rekke I nevere to been deed° right here;
Sith I stonde in your love and in youre grace
No fors of deeth ne whan my spirit pace.°

O tendre, O dere, O yonge children mine,
Youre woful moder wende stedefastly
That cruel houndes or som foul vermine
Hadde eten you; but God of his mercy—
And youre benigne fader—tendrely
Hath doon you kept"—and in that same stounde°
Al sodeinly she swapte° adown to grounde.

And in hir swough so sadly° holdeth she
Hir children two whan she gan hem t'embrace,
That with greet sleighte° and greet difficultee
The children from hir arm they gonne arace.°
O many a tere on many a pitous face
Down ran of hem that stooden hire biside—
Unnethe° aboute hire mighte they abide.

Walter hire gladeth and hir sorwe slaketh;°
She riseth up abaised° from hir traunce,
And every wight hire joye and feeste maketh°

1030. which, what. **1032. Graunt mercy,** many thanks. **1034. rekke,** care; **deed,** dead. **1036. fors,** matter; **pace,** may pass away. **1038. wende,** supposed. **1042. doon you kept,** had you kept safe; **stounde,** moment. **1043. swapte,** fell. **1044. swough,** swoon; **sadly,** firmly. **1046. greet sleighte,** i.e., much manipulation. **1047. arace,** tear away. **1050. Unnethe,** with difficulty. **1051. gladeth,** gladdens; **slaketh,** assuages. **1052. abaised,** abashed. **1053. hire . . . maketh,** shows her joy and honor.

Til she hath caught again hir countenaunce.°
Walter hire dooth so faithfully plesaunce
That it was daintee° for to seen the cheere
Bitwixe hem two, now they been met yfere.°

Thise ladies, whan that they hir time sey,°
Han taken hire and into chambre goon,
And strepen° hire out of hir rude array,
And in a cloth of gold that brighte shoon,
With a corowne of many a riche stoon
Upon hir heed, they into halle hire broughte,
And ther she was honoured as she oughte.

Thus hath this pitous day a blisful ende,
For every man and womman dooth his might
This day in mirthe and revel to dispende,
Til on the welkne shoon the sterres° light.
For more solempne° in every mannes sight
The feeste was, and gretter of costage,°
Than was the revel of hir mariage.

Ful many a yeer in heigh prosperitee
Liven thise two in concord and in reste,
And richely his doughter maried he
Unto a lord, oon of the worthieste
Of al Itaile; and thanne in pees and reste
His wives fader in his court he keepeth,
Til that the soule out of his body creepeth.

His sone succeedeth in his heritage
In reste and pees after his fader° day,
And fortunat was eek his mariage—
Al putte he nat° his wif in greet assay.

1054. Till she has composed herself again. **1056. daintee,** delight. **1057. yfere,** together. **1058. sey,** saw. **1060. strepen,** stripped. **1068. welkne,** sky; **sterres,** stars. **1069. solempne,** festive. **1070. gretter . . . costage,** of greater cost. **1080. fader,** father's. **1082. Al . . . nat,** although he did not put.

This world is nat so strong, it is no nay,
As it hath been in olde times yore.
And herkneth what this auctour saith therfore:

This storye is said, nat for that wives sholde
Folwen Grisilde as in humilitee,
For it were importable though they wolde,
But for that every wight in his degree
Sholde be constant in adversitee,
As was Grisilde. Therfore Petrak writeth
This storye, which with heigh style he enditeth.

For sith a womman was so pacient
Unto a mortal man, wel more us oughte
Receiven al in gree that God us sent.
For greet skile is he preve that he wroughte;
But he ne tempteth no man that he boughte,
As saith Saint Jame if ye his pistel rede:
He preveth folk alday, it is no drede,

And suffreth us, as for oure exercise,
With sharpe scourges of adversitee
Ful ofte to be bete in sondry wise,
Nat for to knowe oure wil—for certes he
Er we were born knew al oure freletee.
And for oure beste is al his governaunce:
Lat us thanne live in vertuous suffraunce.

But oo word, lordinges, herkneth er I go:
It were ful hard to finde nowadayes
In al a town Grisildis three or two,
For if that they were put to swiche assayes,
The gold of hem hath now so badde alayes

1083. **nay,** i.e., denial. 1088. **importable,** intolerable; **wolde,** wanted to. 1095. **in gree,** with good will; **sent,** sends. 1096. **greet . . . is,** there is good reason; **preve,** test; **that,** what. 1097. **tempteth,** i.e., tests severely, as did Walter; **boughte,** redeemed. 1098. **pistel,** Epistle. 1099. **drede,** doubt. 1100. **exercise,** training. 1102. **bete,** beaten. 1104. **freletee,** frailty. 1106. **suffraunce,** patience. 1111. **alayes,** alloys.

With bras, that though the coine be fair at yë,°
It wolde rather breste atwo than plye.°

For which, heer for the Wives love of Bathe—
Whos lif and al hir secte God maintene°
In heigh maistrye, or elles were it scathe°—
I wol with lusty herte, fressh and greene,
Saye you a song to glade° you, I weene.
And lat us stinte of° ernestful° matere.
Herkneth my song that saith in this manere:

THE CLERK'S ENVOY

Grisilde is deed and eek hir pacience,
And bothe atones buried in Itaile,
For which I crye in open audience:
No wedded man so hardy be t'assaile
His wives pacience in trust to finde
Grisildis, for in certain he shal faile.

O noble wives, ful of heigh prudence,
Lat noon humilitee youre tonge naile,
Ne lat no clerk have cause or diligence
To write of you a storye of swich merveile°
As of Grisildis, pacient and kinde,
Lest Chichevache you swolwe in hir entraile.°

Folweth Ekko that holdeth no silence,
But evere answereth at the countretaile;°
Beeth nat bidaffed° for youre innocence,
But sharply take on you the governaile;°
Emprenteth° wel this lesson in youre minde
For commune profit, sith it may availe.

1112. **at yë,** to look at. 1113. **rather,** sooner; **breste,** break; **plye,** bend. 1115. **secte,** sex; **maintene,** maintain. 1116. **maistrye,** control; **scathe,** a shame. 1118. **glade,** cheer. 1119. **stinte of,** put an end to; **ernestful,** serious. 1130. **merveile,** marvelousness. 1132. **Chichevache,** a fabled cow that feeds on patient wives; **swolwe,** swallow; **entraile,** stomach. 1134. **at . . . countretaile,** in immediate reply. 1135. **bidaffed,** made a fool of. 1136. **governaile,** control. 1137. **Emprenteth,** imprint.

Ye archewives, stondeth at defence,
Sin ye be strong as is a greet camaile;°
Ne suffreth nat that men you doon offence;
And sclendre wives, fieble as in bataile,
Beeth egre° as is a tigre yond in Inde:
Ay clappeth° as a mille, I you conseile.

Ne drede hem nat, dooth hem no reverence,
For though thyn housbonde armed be in maile,
The arwes of thy crabbed eloquence
Shal perce his brest and eek his aventaile;°
In jalousye I rede° eek thou him binde,
And thou shalt make him couche° as dooth a quaile.

If thou be fair, ther folk been in presence°
Shew thou thy visage and thyn aparaile;°
If thou be foul, be free of thy dispence;°
To gete thee freendes ay do thy travaile;°
Be ay of cheere as light as leef on linde;°
And lat him care and weepe and wringe and waile.

THE HOST'S COMMENT

This worthy Clerk whan ended was his tale,
Oure Hoste saide and swoor, "By Goddes bones,
Me were levere° than a barel ale
My wif at hoom hadde herd this legende ones.
This is a gentil tale for the nones,
As to my purpos, wiste ye° my wille—
But thing that wol nat be, lat it be stille."

1140. camaile, camel. **1143. egre,** fierce. **1144. clappeth,** chatter. **1148. aventaile,** mouthpiece of a helmet. **1149. rede,** advise. **1150. couche,** cower. **1151. in presence,** gathered together. **1152. aparaile,** clothing. **1153. dispence,** expenditure. **1154. travaile,** i.e., best. **1155. cheere,** behavior; **linde,** linden tree. **1159. Me . . . levere,** I had rather. **1162. wiste ye,** if you knew.

THE MERCHANT'S TALE

The Introduction

"Weeping and wailing, care and other sorwe°
I knowe ynough, on even and amorwe,"°
Quod the Marchant, "and so doon othere mo
That wedded been. I trowe° that it be so,
For wel I woot it fareth so with me.
I have a wif, the worste that may be:
For though the feend to hire ycoupled were,
She wolde him overmacche, I dar wel swere.
What sholde I you reherce in special
Hir heigh malice? She is a shrewe at al.°
Ther is a long and large difference
Bitwixe Grisildis grete pacience
And of my wif the passing° crueltee.
Were I unbounden, also moote I thee,°
I wolde nevere eft° comen in the snare.
We wedded men live in sorwe and care—
Assaye whoso wole and he shal finde
I saye sooth, by Saint Thomas of Inde,
As for the more part—I saye nat alle:
God shilde° that it sholde so bifalle.
  A, goode sire Host, I have ywedded be
Thise monthes two, and more nat, pardee,
And yit I trowe he that al his live
Wiflees hath been, though that men wolde him rive°
Unto the herte, ne coude in no manere
Tellen so muchel sorwe as I now here
Coude tellen of my wives cursednesse."°
  "Now," quod oure Host, "Marchant, so God you blesse,

1. See l. 1156 of the *Clerk's Tale*. 2. **on . . . amorwe,** evening and morning. 4. **trowe,** believe. 10. **at al,** in every respect. 13. **passing,** surpassing. 14. **unbounden,** unwed; **thee,** thrive. 15. **eft,** again. 20. **shilde,** forbid. 24. **rive,** pierce. 27. **cursednesse,** wickedness.

Sin ye so muchel knowen of that art,
Ful hertely I praye you telle us part."
"Gladly," quod he, "but of myn owene sore
For sory herte I telle may namore."

The Tale

Whilom ther was dwelling in Lumbardye°
A worthy knight that born was of Pavie,°
In which he lived in greet prosperitee;
And sixty yeer a wiflees man was he,
And folwed ay his bodily delit
On wommen ther as was his appetit,
As doon thise fooles that been seculer.°
And whan that he was passed sixty yeer—
Were it for holinesse or for dotage
I can nat saye—but swich a greet corage°
Hadde this knight to been a wedded man,
That day and night he dooth al that he can
T'espyen where he mighte wedded be,
Praying oure Lord to graunten him that he
Mighte ones knowe of thilke blisful lif
That is bitwixe an housbonde and his wif,
And for to live under that holy bond
With which that first God man and womman boond.°
"Noon other lif," saide he, "is worth a bene,°
For wedlok is so esy and so clene
That in this world it is a Paradis."
Thus saide this olde knight that was so wis.
And certainly, as sooth as God is king,
To take a wif, it is a glorious thing,
And namely° whan a man is old and hoor:
Thanne is a wif the fruit of his tresor;°

1. **Whilom,** once upon a time; **Lumbardye,** Lombardy. 2. **Pavie,** Pavia. 7. **seculer,** not in clerical orders. 10. **corage,** desire. 18. **boond,** bound. 19. **bene,** bean. 25. **namely,** especially. 26. **fruit,** best part; **tresor,** treasure.

Thanne sholde he take a yong wif and a fair,
On which he mighte engendren him an heir,
And lede his lif in joye and in solas,°
Wher as thise bacheleres singe allas,
Whan that they finde any adversitee
In love, which nis but childissh vanitee.
And trewely, it sit° wel to be so
That bacheleres have ofte paine and wo:
On brotel° ground they builde, and brotelnesse
They finde whan they weene sikernesse;°
They live but as a brid° or as a beest
In libertee and under noon arrest,°
Ther as a wedded man in his estat
Liveth a lif blisful and ordinat°
Under this yok of mariage ybounde:
Wel may his herte in joye and blisse habounde.°
For who can be so buxom° as a wif?
Who is so trewe and eek so ententif°
To keepe him, sik and hool, as is his make?°
For wele° or wo she wol him nat forsake.
She nis nat wery him to love and serve,
Though that he lie bedrede til he sterve.°
And yit some clerkes sayn it is nat so,
Of whiche he Theofraste° is oon of tho—
What fors though Theofraste liste° lie?
  "Ne taak no wif," quod he, "for housbondrye°
As for to spare in houshold thy dispence.°
A trewe servant dooth more diligence
Thy good to keepe than thyn owene wif,
For she wol claime half part al hir lif.
And if thou be sik, so God me save,

29. **solas,** delight. 33. **sit,** suits. 35. **brotel,** brittle. 36. **weene,** expect; **sikernesse,** security. 37. **brid,** bird. 38. **arrest,** control. 40. **ordinat,** regulated. 42. **habounde,** abound. 43. **buxom,** obedient. 44. **ententif,** attentive. 45. **keepe,** watch over; **hool,** whole, healthy; **make,** mate. 46. **wele,** happiness. 48. **bedrede,** bedridden; **sterve,** die. 50. **Theofraste,** Theophrastus, author of an antifeminist tract preserved in St. Jerome's *Against Jovinian.* 51. **fors,** matter; **liste,** it please. 52. **housbondrye,** economy. 53. **dispence,** expenses.

Thy verray freendes or a trewe knave
Wol keepe thee bet than she that waiteth ay
After thy good, and hath do many a day.
And if thou take a wif [unto thyn hold,
Ful lightly maistou been a cokewold."]
  This sentence and an hundred thinges worse
Writeth this man, ther God his bones curse!
But take no keep of al swich vanitee:
Defye Theofraste and herke me.
  A wif is Goddes yifte verraily;
Alle othere manere yiftes hardily,
As landes, rentes, pasture, or commune,
Or moebles, alle been yiftes of Fortune,
That passen as a shadwe upon a wal.
But drede nat, if plainly speke I shal,
A wif wol laste and in thyn hous endure
Wel lenger than thee list, paraventure.
  Mariage is a ful greet sacrament.
He which that hath no wif I holde him shent.
He liveth helplees and al desolat—
I speke of folk in seculer estat.
  And herke why I saye nat this for nought
That womman is for mannes help ywrought:
The hye God, whan he hadde Adam maked
And sawgh him allone, bely-naked,
God of his grete goodnesse saide than,
"Lat us now make an help unto this man
Lik to himself." And thanne he made him Eve.
Heer may ye see, and heerby may ye preve
That wif is mannes help and his confort,
His Paradis terrestre and his disport.
So buxom and so vertuous is she
They moste needes live in unitee:

58. knave, servant. **59. bet,** better; **waiteth,** lies in wait. **61–62.** The bracketed words are a scribe's attempt to complete a couplet either left unfinished by Chaucer or censored out of his text. **62. lightly,** easily; **cokewold,** cuckold. **63. sentence,** sentiment. **64. ther,** i.e., may. **65. keep,** heed. **68. hardily,** certainly. **69. rentes,** incomes; **commune,** pasturage rights. **70. moebles,** furniture. **76. shent,** ruined. **86. preve,** prove. **88. terrestre,** terrestrial. **89. buxom,** obedient.

Oo flessh they been, and oo flessh, as I gesse,
Hath but oon herte in wele and in distresse.
  A wif, a, Sainte Marye, benedicite,
How mighte a man han any adversitee
That hath a wif? Certes, I can nat saye.
The blisse which that is bitwixe hem twaye,
Ther may no tonge telle or herte thinke.
If he be poore, she helpeth him to swinke.
She keepeth his good and wasteth neveradeel.
Al that hir housbonde lust hire liketh weel.
She saith nat ones "Nay" whan he saith "Ye."
"Do this," saith he. "Al redy, sire," saith she.
  O blisful ordre of wedlok precious,
Thou art so merye and eek so vertuous,
And so commended and appreved eek,
That any man that halt him worth a leek
Upon his bare knees oughte al his lif
Thanken his God that him hath sent a wif,
Or elles praye to God him for to sende
A wif to laste unto his lives ende:
For thanne his lif is set in sikernesse.
He may nat be deceived, as I gesse,
So that he werke after his wives reed;
Thanne may he boldely keepen up his heed,
They been so trewe and therwithal so wise;
For which, if thou wolt werken as the wise,
Do alway so as wommen wol thee rede.
Lo how that Jacob, as thise clerkes rede,
By good conseil of his moder Rebekke
Boond the kides skin aboute his nekke,
For which his fadres benison he wan.
  Lo Judith, as the storye eek telle can,
By good conseil she Goddes peple kepte,

92. **wele,** happiness. 93. **benedicite,** bless me. 98. **swinke,** work. 100. **lust,** desires; **liketh,** pleases. 105. **appreved,** approved. 106. **halt . . . leek,** considers himself worth a leek. 111. **sikernesse,** security. 113. **reed,** advice. 114. **heed,** head. 117. **rede,** advise. 118. **rede,** relate; see Genesis XXV. 120. **Boond,** bound; **kides,** kid's. 121. **benisoun,** blessing; **wan,** won. 123. **kepte,** saved; see the Book of Judith.

And slow him Olofernus° whil he slepte.
Lo Abigail by good conseil how she°
Saved her housbonde Nabal whan that he
Sholde han been slain. And looke Ester° also
By good conseil delivered out of wo
The peple of God, and made him Mardochee°
Of Assuere enhaunced° for to be.
Ther is nothing in gree° superlatif,
As saith Senek,° above an humble wif.
Suffre thy wives tonge, as Caton bit.°
She shal comande and thou shalt suffren it,
And yit she wol obeye of curteisye.
A wif is kepere of thyn housbondrye:°
Wel may the sike man biwaile and weepe
Ther as ther is no wif the hous to keepe.
I warne thee, if wisely thou wolt wirche,°
Love wel thy wif as Crist loved his chirche;
If thou lovest thyself thou lovest thy wif:
No man hateth his flessh, but in his lif
He fostreth it, and therfore bidde I thee,
Cherisse thy wif or thou shalt nevere thee.°
Housbonde and wif, what so men jape° or playe,
Of worldly folk holden the siker° waye.
They been so knit° ther may noon harm bitide,
And namely° upon the wives side.—
For which this Januarye of whom I tolde
Considered hath inwith° his dayes olde
The lusty lif, the vertuous quiete
That is in mariage hony sweete,
And for his freendes on a day he sente
To tellen hem th'effect of his entente.
With face sad° this tale he hath hem told:

124. slow, slew; **Olofernus,** Holofernes. **125.** See I Samuel XXV. **127. Ester,** see the Book of Esther. **129. Mardochee,** Mordecai. **130. Assuere,** Ahasuerus; **enhaunced,** exalted. **131. gree,** degree. **132. Senek,** Seneca. **133. Caton,** the Cato Book, a school primer; **bit,** bids. **136. kepere,** guardian; **housbondrye,** household. **139. wirche,** work. **144. thee,** prosper. **145. jape,** joke. **146. siker,** sure. **147. knit,** joined together. **148. namely,** especially. **150. inwith,** within. **155. sad,** sober.

He saide, "Freendes, I am hoor and old,
And almost, God woot, on my pittes brinke:°
Upon my soule somwhat moste° I thinke.
I have my body folily dispended°—
Blessed be God that it shal been amended.
For I wol be, certain, a wedded man,
And that anoon, in al the haste I can,
Unto som maide fair and tendre of age.
I praye you shapeth° for my mariage
Al sodeinly, for I wol nat abide;
And I wol fonde° t'espyen on my side
To whom I may be wedded hastily.
But for as muche as ye been mo than I,
Ye shullen rather° swich a thing espyen
Than I, and wher me best were to allyen.
  But oo thing warne I you, my freendes dere:
I wol noon old wif han in no manere;
She shal nat passe sixteen yeer certain—
Old fissh and yong flessh wol I have fain.°
Bet is," quod he, "a pik° than a pikerel,
And bet than old boef is the tendre veel:°
I wol no womman thritty yeer of age—
It is but bene-straw and greet forage.°
And eek thise olde widwes, God it woot,
They conne so muche craft on Wades boot,°
So muchel broken harm whan that hem leste,°
That with hem sholde I nevere live in reste.
For sondry scoles maketh subtile clerkes:
Womman of manye scoles half a clerk is.
But certainly a yong thing may men gie,°

157. pittes brinke, grave's edge. **158. moste,** must. **159. folily,** foolishly; **dispended,** expended. **164. shapeth,** arrange. **166. fonde,** try. **169. rather,** sooner. **174. fain,** gladly. **175. Bet,** better; **pik,** a pike was considered to be an old pickerel. **176. boef,** beef; **veel,** veal. **178. bene-straw,** beanstraw, dried beanstems; **greet forage,** coarse winter fodder. **180.** They have so much skill in Wade's boat: Wade was a legendary hero, but his relevance here is not known. **181. broken harm,** traffic in injuries; **hem leste,** they feel like it. **184.** Women are part-time students in many schools. **185. gie,** guide.

Right as men may warm wex with handes plye.
Wherfore I saye you plainly in a clause,
I wol noon old wif han right for this cause:
For if so were I hadde swich meschaunce
That I in hire ne coude han no plesaunce,
Thanne sholde I lede my lif in avoutrye,
And go straight to the devel whan I die;
Ne children sholde I none upon hire geten,
Yit me were levere houndes hadde me eten
Than that myn heritage sholde falle
In straunge hand; and this I telle you alle:
I dote nat, I woot the cause why
Men sholde wedde, and ferthermore woot I
Ther speketh many a man of mariage
That woot namore of it than woot my page
For whiche causes man sholde take a wif:
If he ne may nat live chast his lif,
Take him a wif with greet devocioun,
By cause of leveful procreacioun
Of children, to th'honour of God above,
And nat only for paramour or love;
And for they sholde lecherye eschue,
And yeelde hir dette whan that it is due;
Or for that eech of hem sholde helpen other
In meschief, as a suster shal the brother,
And live in chastitee ful holily—
But sires, by youre leve, that am nat I.
For God be thanked, I dar make avaunt,
I feele my limes stark and suffisaunt
To do al that a man bilongeth to.
I woot myself best what I may do.
  Though I be hoor, I fare as dooth a tree
That blosmeth er the fruit ywoxen be,
And blosmy tree nis neither drye ne deed:

186. **plye,** mold. 191. **avoutrye,** adultery. 196. **straunge,** i.e., unlineal. 204. **leveful,** lawful. 206. **paramour,** bodily love. 207. **eschue,** eschew. 208. **yeelde,** i.e., pay. 213. **avaunt,** boast. 214. **limes,** limbs; **stark,** strong; **suffisaunt,** competent. 218. **ywoxen,** grown. 219. **deed,** dead.

I feele me nowher hoor but on myn heed;
Myn herte and alle my limes been as greene
As laurer thurgh the yeer is for to seene.
And sin that ye han herd al myn entente,
I praye you to my wil ye wol assente."
  Diverse men diversely him tolde
Of mariage manye ensamples olde:
Some blamed it, some praised it, certain;
But at the laste, shortly for to sayn,
As alday falleth altercacioun
Bitwixe freendes in disputisoun,
Ther fil a strif bitwixe his bretheren two,
Of whiche that oon was cleped Placebo;
Justinus soothly called was that other.
  Placebo saide, "O Januarye brother,
Ful litel neede hadde ye, my lord so dere,
Conseil to axe of any that is here,
But that ye been so ful of sapience
That you ne liketh, for youre heigh prudence,
To waiven fro the word of Salomon;
This word saide he unto us everichoon:
'Werk alle thing by conseil,' thus saide he,
'And thanne shaltou nat repenten thee.'
But though that Salomon spak swich a word,
Myn owene dere brother and my lord,
So wisly God my soule bringe at reste,
I holde youre owene conseil is the beste.
For brother myn, of me take this motif:
I have now been a court-man al my lif,
And God it woot, though I unworthy be,
I have stonden in ful greet degree
Abouten lordes in ful greet estat,
Yit hadde I nevere with noon of hem debat;
I nevere hem contraried, trewely;

221. **limes,** limbs. 222. **laurer,** laurel. 226. **ensamples,** illustrative stories. 229. **alday,** constantly. 230. **disputisoun,** argument. 231. **fil,** occurred. 236. **axe,** ask. 237. **But,** except. 239. **waiven,** depart. 245. **wisly,** surely. 247. **motif,** proposition. 253. **contraried,** contradicted.

I woot wel that my lord can° more than I;
What that he saith, I hold it ferm° and stable;
I saye the same or elles thing semblable.°
A ful greet fool is any conseilour
That serveth any lord of heigh honour
That dar presume or elles thenken° it
That his conseil sholde passe° his lordes wit.
Nay, lordes be no fooles, by my fay.°
Ye han yourselven shewed heer today
So heigh sentence° so holily and weel,
That I consente and conferme everydeel
Youre wordes alle and youre opinioun.
By God, ther nis no man in al this town,
Ne in Itaile, coude bet° han ysaid.
Crist halt him of this conseil wel apaid.°
And trewely it is an heigh corage°
Of any man that stapen° is in age
To take a yong wif! By my fader kin,
Youre herte hangeth on a joly pin!
Dooth now in this matere right as you leste,
For finally, I holde it for the beste."
Justinus that ay stille sat and herde,
Right in this wise he to Placebo answerde:
"Now, brother myn, be pacient I praye,
Sin ye han said, and herkneth what I saye:
Senek° amonges othere wordes wise
Saith that a man oughte him right wel avise°
To whom he yiveth his land or his catel;°
And sin I oughte avisen me right wel
To whom I yive my good away fro me,
Wel muchel more I oughte avised be
To whom I yive my body for alway.
I warne you wel, it is no childes play

254. **can,** knows. 255. **ferm,** firm. 256. **semblable,** similar. 259. **thenken,** imagine. 260. **passe,** be superior to. 261. **fay,** faith. 263. **sentence,** sentiments. 267. **Itaile,** Italy; **bet,** better. 268. **halt him,** considers himself; **apaid,** pleased. 269. **corage,** spirit. 270. **stapen,** advanced. 279. **Senek,** Seneca. 280. **him avise,** consider. 281. **catel,** property.

To taken a wif withouten avisement.
Men moste enquere—this is myn assent—
Wher she be wis, or sobre, or dronkelewe,
Or proud, or elles otherways a shrewe,
A chidestere, or wastour of thy good,
Or riche, or poore, or elles mannissh wood—
Al be it so that no man finden shal
Noon in this world that trotteth hool in al,
Ne man ne beest swich as men coude devise.
But nathelees, it oughte ynough suffise
With any wif, if so were that she hadde
Mo goode thewes than hir vices badde.
And al this axeth leiser for t'enquere.
For God it woot, I have wept many a tere
Ful prively sin that I hadde a wif:
Praise whoso wol a wedded mannes lif,
Certain I finde in it but cost and care,
And observances of alle blisses bare.
And yit, God woot, my neighebores aboute,
And namely of wommen many a route,
Sayn that I have the moste stedefast wif,
And eek the mekeste oon that bereth lif—
But I woot best where wringeth me my sho.
Ye mowe for me right as you liketh do.
Aviseth you—ye been a man of age—
How that ye entren into mariage,
And namely with a yong wif and a fair.
By him that made water, erthe, and air,
The yongeste man that is in al this route
Is bisy ynough to bringen it aboute
To han his wif allone. Trusteth me,
Ye shul nat plesen hire fully yeres three—

287. **avisement,** deliberation. 288. **enquere,** inquire; **assent,** opinion. 289. **Wher,** whether; **dronkelewe,** given to drunkenness. 291. **chidestere,** chider. 292. **mannissh wood,** ? unfemininely inclined to rage. 294. **trotteth,** trots, i.e., appears; **hool,** whole. 295. **devise,** imagine. 298. **thewes,** characteristics. 299. **axeth,** requires. 304. **observances,** duties. 306. **namely,** especially; **route,** group. 308. **mekeste,** meekest. 309. **wringeth,** pinches; **sho,** shoe. 310. **mowe,** may.

This is to sayn, to doon hire ful plesaunce:
A wif axeth ful many an observaunce.°
I praye you that ye be nat yvele apaid."°
"Wel," quod this Januarye, "and hastou said?
Straw for thy Senek and for thy proverbes!
I counte nat a panier° ful of herbes
Of scole-termes.° Wiser men than thou,
As thou hast herd, assenteden right now
To my purpos. Placebo, what saye ye?"
"I saye it is a cursed man," quod he,
"That letteth matrimoigne, sikerly."°
And with that word they risen sodeinly,
And been assented fully that he sholde
Be wedded whan him liste and wher° he wolde.
Heigh fantasye and curious bisinesse°
Fro day to day gan in the soule impresse°
Of Januarye aboute his mariage:
Many fair shap and many a fair visage
Ther passeth thurgh his herte night by night;
As whoso tooke a mirour polisshed bright,
And sette it in a commune market-place,
Thanne sholde he see ful many a figure pace°
By his mirour; and in the same wise
Gan Januarye inwith° his thought devise
Of maidens whiche that dwelten him biside.
He wiste nat wher that he mighte abide:°
For if that oon have beautee in hir face,
Another stant° so in the peples grace
For hir sadnesse° and hir benignitee,
That of the peple grettest vois° hath she;
And some were riche and hadden badde name.

320. **observaunce,** little ritual. 321. **yvele apaid,** ill-pleased. 324. **counte,** value; **panier,** basket. 325. **scole-terms,** school-terms, i.e., subtle arguments. 329. **letteth,** hinders; **matrimoigne,** matrimony; **sikerly,** certainly. 332. **wher,** i.e., to whom. 333. **fantasye,** imagining; **curious,** careful; **bisinesse,** attentiveness. 334. **in . . . impresse,** i.e., took hold upon the spirit. 340. **pace,** pass. 342. **inwith,** within. 344. **wiste,** knew; **abide,** settle. 346. **stant,** stands. 347. **sadnesse,** constancy. 348. **grettest vois,** i.e., loudest acclaim.

But nathelees, bitwixe ernest and game,
He atte laste appointed him on° oon,
And leet alle othere° from his herte goon,
And chees hire of his owene auctoritee°—
For Love is blind alday° and may nat see.
And whan that he was in his bed ybrought,
He portrayde in his herte and in his thought
Hir fresshe beautee and hir age tendre,
Hir middel smal, hir armes longe and sclendre,
Hir wise governance, hir gentilesse,°
Hir wommanly bering and hir sadnesse.°
And whan that he on hire was condescended,°
Him thoughte his chois mighte nat been amended;°
For whan that he himself concluded° hadde,
Him thoughte eech other mannes wit so badde,
That impossible it were to replye°
Again his chois: this was his fantasye.
  His freendes sente he to at his instaunce,
And prayed hem to doon him that plesaunce
That hastily they wolden to him come:
He wolde abregge hir labour alle and some;°
Needeth namore for him to go ne ride;
He was appointed° ther he wolde abide.
  Placebo cam and eek his freendes soone,
And alderfirst he bad° hem alle a boone,
That noon of hem none argumentes make
Again the purpos which that he hath take,
Which purpos was plesant to God, saide he,
And verray ground of his prosperitee.
  He saide ther was a maiden in the town
Which that of beautee hadde greet renown;
Al were it so she were of smal degree,°

351. **appointed him on,** determined upon. 352. **leet,** let; **othere,** others. 353. **chees,** chose; **auctoritee,** authority. 354. **alday,** always. 359. **governance,** behavior; **gentilesse,** gentility. 360. **sadnesse,** constancy. 361. **condescended,** settled. 362. **amended,** improved upon. 363. **concluded,** come to a decision. 365. **replye,** i.e., to object. 370. **abregge,** shorten; **alle . . . some,** each and every one of them. 372. **appointed,** determined. 374. **alderfirst,** first of all; **bad,** prayed. 381. **Al,** although; **degree,** social rank.

Suffiseth him hir youthe and hir beautee;
Which maide he saide he wolde han to his wif,
To lede in ese and holinesse his lif,
And thanked God that he mighte han hire al,
That no wight his blisse parten shal;
And prayde hem to labouren in this neede,
And shapen that he faile not to speede.
For thanne he saide his spirit was at ese.
"Thanne is," quod he, "no thing may me displese.
Save oo thing priketh in my conscience,
The which I wol reherce in youre presence.
I have," quod he, "herd said ful yore ago
Ther may no man han parfite blisses two—
This is to saye, in erthe and eek in hevene.
For though he keepe him fro the sinnes sevene,
And eek from every braunche of thilke tree,
Yit is ther so parfit felicitee
And so greet ese and lust in mariage,
That evere I am agast now in myn age
That I shal lede now so merye a lif,
So delicat, withouten wo and strif,
That I shal han myn hevene in erthe here.
For sith that verray hevene is bought so dere
With tribulaciouns and greet penaunce,
How sholde I thanne, that live in swich plesaunce
As alle wedded men doon with hir wives,
Come to the blisse ther Crist eterne on live is?
This is my drede, and ye, my bretheren twaye,
Assoileth me this question, I praye."
Justinus, which that hated his folye,
Answerde anoonright in his japerye;
And for he wolde his longe tale abregge,
He wolde noon auctoritee allegge,
But saide, "Sire, so ther be noon obstacle

385. Her youth and beauty are enough for him. **386. parten,** share. **388. shapen,** arrange; **speede,** attain his end. **393. yore,** i.e., long. **394. parfite,** perfect. **397. braunche,** the seven deadly sins were divided into branches and subbranches. **399. lust,** pleasure. **402. delicat,** delightful. **410. Assoileth,** resolve. **412. japerye,** joking. **413. abregge,** shorten. **414. allegge,** adduce.

Other than this, God of his heigh miracle
And of his mercy may so for you wirche,°
That er ye have youre right° of holy chirche,
Ye may repente of wedded mannes lif,
In which ye sayn ther is no wo ne strif.
And elles God forbede but° he sente
A wedded man him grace to repente
Wel ofte rather than a sengle° man.
And therfore, sire, the beste reed I can:°
Despaire you nought, but have in youre memorye
Paraunter° she may be youre purgatorye;
She may be Goddes mene° and Goddes whippe!
Thanne shal youre soule up to hevene skippe
Swifter than dooth an arwe out of a bowe.
I hope to God heerafter shul ye knowe
That ther nis noon so greet felicitee
In mariage, ne nevere mo shal be,
That you shal lette° of youre savacioun,
So that ye use, as skile° is and resoun,
The lustes of youre wif attemprely,°
And that ye plese hire nat too amorously,
And that ye keepe you eek from other sinne.
My tale is doon, for my wit is thinne.
Beeth nat agast heerof, my brother dere,
But lat us waden° out of this matere.
The Wif of Bathe, if ye han understonde,
Of mariage which ye han on honde
Declared hath ful wel in litel space.
Fareth now wel. God have you in his grace."
  And with that word this Justin and his brother
Han take hir leve and eech of hem of other,
For whan they saw that it moste needes be,
They wroughten so by sly and wis tretee°
That she, this maiden which that Mayus highte,

417. wirche, work. **418. right,** due, i.e., burial. **421. but,** unless. **423. rather,** sooner; **sengle,** single. **424. reed,** advice; **can,** am capable of. **426. Paraunter,** perhaps. **427. mene,** means, i.e., agent. **433. lette,** hinder. **434. skile,** reason. **435. lustes,** pleasures; **attemprely,** moderately. **440. waden,** move. **448. sly,** clever; **tretee,** negotiation.

As hastily as evere that she mighte,
Shal wedded be unto this Januarye.
  I trowe it were too longe you to tarye
If I you tolde of every scrit° and bond
By which that she was feffed in° his lond,
Or for to herknen of hir riche array;
But finally ycomen is that day
That to the chirche bothe be they went
For to receive the holy sacrament.
  Forth comth the preest with stole aboute his nekke,
And bad hire be lik Sarra° and Rebekke
In wisdom and in trouthe° of mariage,
And saide his orisons as is usage,
And croucheth° hem, and bad God sholde hem blesse,
And made al siker° ynough with holinesse.
  Thus been they wedded with solempnitee,
And at the laste sitteth he and she
With other worthy folk upon the dais.
Al ful of joye and blisse is the palais,
And ful of instruments and of vitaile,°
The moste daintevous° of al Itaile.
Biforn hem stoode instruments of swich soun,°
That Orpheus n'of Thebes Amphioun°
Ne maden nevere swich a melodye.
At every cours thanne cam loud minstralcye,
That nevere tromped Joab° for to heere,
Ne he Theodamas° yit half so clere
At Thebes whan the citee was in doute.
Bacus the win hem shenketh° al aboute,
And Venus laugheth upon every wight,
For Januarye was bicome hir knight,

453. **scrit,** writ. 454. **feffed in,** endowed with. 460. **Sarra,** Sarah. 461. **trouthe,** fidelity. 463. **croucheth,** signs with the cross. 464. **siker,** secure. 469. **instruments,** i.e., provisions; **vitaile,** foodstuffs. 470. **daintevous,** tasty. 471. **soun,** sound. 472. **Orpheus, Amphioun,** legendary musicians of ancient Greece. 475. **Joab,** King David's officer, who on several occasions controlled the people with his trumpet. 476. **Theodamas,** a Theban seer whose auguries were announced with a trumpet. 478. **Bacus,** Bacchus; **shenketh,** pours.

And wolde bothe assayen his corage
In libertee and eek in mariage;
And with hir firbrand in hir hand aboute
Daunceth bifore the bride and al the route.
And certainly, I dar right wel saye this:
Ymeneus° that God of Wedding is
Sawgh nevere his lif so merye a wedded man.
Hold thou thy pees, thou poete Marcian,°
That writest us that ilke wedding murye
Of hire Philologye and him Mercurye,
And of the songes that the Muses songe°—
Too smal is bothe thy penne and eek thy tonge
For to descriven° of this mariage.
Whan tendre youthe hath wedded stouping° age,
Ther is swich mirthe that it may nat be writen;
Assayeth it yourself, thanne may ye witen°
If that I lie or noon in this matere.
  Mayus, that sit with so benigne a cheere°
Hire to biholde it seemed faïrye°—
Queene Ester looked nevere with swich an yë
On Assuer, so meeke a look hath she—
I may you nat devise al hir beautee,
But thus muche of hir beautee telle I may,
That she was lik the brighte morwe of May,
Fulfild° of alle beautee and plesaunce.
  This Januarye is ravisshed in a traunce
At every time he looked on hir face,
But in his herte he gan hire to manace°
That he that night in armes wolde hire straine°
Harder than evere Paris dide Elaine.°
But nathelees yit hadde he greet pitee
That thilke night offenden hire moste° he,
And thoughte, "Allas, O tendre creature,

486. **Ymeneus,** Hymen. 488. **Marcian,** Martianus Capella, author of a medieval Latin poem which describes the wedding of Philology and Mercury. 491. **songe,** sang. 493. **descriven,** describe. 494. **stouping,** stooping. 496. **witen,** learn. 498. **sit,** sits; **cheere,** expression. 499. **fairye,** magic. 505. **Fulfild,** filled full. 508. **manace,** menace. 509. **straine,** constrain. 510. **Elaine,** Helen of Troy. 512. **moste,** must.

Now wolde God ye mighte wel endure
Al my corage, it is so sharp and keene:
I am agast ye shul it nat sustene—
But God forbede that I dide al my might!
Now wolde God that it were woxen night,
And that the night wolde lasten everemo.
I wolde that al this peple were ago."
And finally he dooth al his labour,
As he best mighte, saving his honour,
To haste hem fro the mete in subtil wise.
The time cam that reson was to rise,
And after that men daunce and drinken faste,
And spices al aboute the hous they caste.
And ful of joye and blis is every man—
Al but a squier highte Damian,
Which carf biforn the knight ful many a day:
He was so ravisshed on his lady May
That for the verray paine he was neigh wood;
Almost he swelte and swouned ther he stood,
So sore hath Venus hurt him with hir brand,
As that she bar it dauncing in hir hand.
And to his bed he wente him hastily.
Namore of him at this time speke I,
But ther I lete him weepe ynough and plaine,
Til fresshe May wol rewen on his paine.
O perilous fir that in the bedstraw breedeth!
O familier fo that his service bedeth!
O servant traitour, false hoomly hewe,
Lik to the naddre in bosom, sly, untrewe!
God shilde us alle from youre aquaintaunce!
O Januarye, dronken in plesaunce
In mariage, see how thy Damian,
Thyn owene squier and thy boren man,

515. **corage,** spirit, but with the added sense of sexual prowess. 516. **sustene,** sustain. 518. **woxen,** grown. 529. **carf,** carved. 531. **wood,** mad. 532. **swelte,** fainted. 537. **plaine,** complain. 538. **rewen,** have pity. 539. **breedeth,** i.e., starts. 540. **bedeth,** offers. 541. **hoomly,** domestic; **hewe,** servant. 542. **naddre,** adder; **untrewe,** treacherous. 543. **shilde,** defend. 546. **boren,** born.

Entendeth for to do thee vilainye!
God graunte thee thyn hoomly fo espye,
For in this world nis worse pestilence
Than hoomly fo alday in thy presence.
  Parfourned hath the sonne his ark diurne:°
No lenger may the body of him sojurne
On th'orisonte° as in that latitude;
Night with his mantel that is derk and rude
Gan oversprede th'hemisperye° aboute,
For which departed is this lusty route,°
For Januarye with thank on every side.
Hoom to hir houses lustily they ride,
Wher as they doon hir thinges as hem leste,
And whan they sawgh hir time go to reste.
  Soone after that this hastif° Januarye
Wol go to bedde—he wol no lenger tarye.
He drinketh ipocras, clarree and vernage°
Of spices hote t'encreessen° his corage,
And many a letuarye hadde he ful fin,°
Swich as the cursed monk daun Constantin°
Hath writen in his book *De Coitu:*
To eten hem alle he nas no thing eschu.°
And to his privee freendes thus saide he:
"For Goddes love, as soone as it may be,
Lat voiden° al this hous in curteis wise."
And they han doon right as he wol devise.
Men drinken and the travers° drawe anoon.
The bride was brought abedde as stille as stoon.
And whan the bed was with the preest yblessed,
Out of the chambre hath every wight him dressed.°
And Januarye hath faste in armes take
His fresshe May, his Paradis, his make;°

551. **ark diurne**, diurnal arc. 553. **orisonte**, horizon. 555. **hemisperye**, hemisphere. 556. **route**, company. 561. **hastif**, impatient. 563. **ipocras . . . vernage**, wine-drinks thought to be aphrodisiac. 564. **encreessen**, increase. 565. **letuarye**, medicine; **fin**, pure. 566. **Constantin**, Constantinus Afer, author of a treatise on copulation. 568. **eschu**, averse. 571. **voiden**, empty. 573. **travers**, curtains. 576. **dressed**, turned. 578. **make**, mate.

He lulleth hire, he kisseth hire ful ofte—
With thikke bristles of his beerd unsofte,
Lik to the skin of houndfissh, sharpe as brere,°
For he was shave al newe in his manere—
He rubbeth hire aboute hir tendre face,
And saide thus, "Allas, I moot trespace°
To you, my spouse, and you greetly offende
Er time come that I wol down descende.
But nathelees, considereth this," quod he,
"Ther nis no werkman, whatsoevere he be,
That may bothe werke wel and hastily.
This wol be doon at leiser parfitly.°
It is no fors° how longe that we playe:
In trewe wedlok coupled be we twaye,
And blessed be the yok that we been inne,
For in oure actes we mowe° do no sinne;
A man may do no sinne with his wif,
Ne hurte himselven with his owene knif;
For we han leve to playe us by the lawe."
Thus laboureth he til that the day gan dawe,°
And thanne he taketh a sop in fin clarree,°
And upright in his bed thanne sitteth he;
And after that he soong° ful loude and clere,
And kiste his wif and made wantoune cheere:
He was al coltissh, ful of ragerye,°
And ful of jargon as a flekked pie.°
The slakke skin aboute his nekke shaketh
Whil that he soong, so chaunteth he and craketh.°
But God woot what that May thoughte in hir herte
Whan she him saw up sitting in his sherte,°
In his night-cappe and with his nekke lene—
She praiseth nat his playing worth a bene.°

581. houndfissh, dogfish; **brere,** briar. **584. trespace,** do injury. **590. parfitly,** perfectly. **591. fors,** matter. **594. mowe,** may. **598. dawe,** dawn. **599. sop . . . clarree,** bread soaked in fine wine. **601. soong,** sang. **603. coltissh,** frisky; **ragerye,** flirtatiousness. **604. pie,** magpie. **606. craketh,** caws. **608. sherte,** shirt. **610. bene,** bean.

Thanne saide he thus, "My reste wol I take.
Now day is come I may no lenger wake."
And down he laide his heed and sleep til prime,
And afterward whan that he saw his time
Up riseth Januarye. But fresshe May
Heeld hir chambre unto the fourthe day,
As usage is of wives for the beste,
For every labour som time moot han reste,
Or elles longe may he nat endure—
This is to sayn, no lives creature,
Be it fissh or brid or beest or man.
  Now wol I speke of woful Damian
That languissheth for love, as ye shal heere.
Therfore I speke to him in this manere:
  I saye, "O sely Damian, allas,
Answere to my demande as in this cas:
How shaltou to thy lady fresshe May
Telle thy wo? She wol alway saye nay.
Eek if thou speke, she wol thy wo biwraye.
God be thyn help, I can no bettre saye."
  This sike Damian in Venus fir
So brenneth that he dieth for desir,
For which he putte his life in aventure:
No lenger mighte he in this wise endure,
But prively a penner gan he borwe,
And in a lettre wroot he al his sorwe,
In manere of a complainte or a lay,
Unto his faire fresshe lady May;
And in a purs of silk heeng on his sherte
He hath it put and laid it at his herte.
  The moone, that at noon was thilke day
That Januarye hath wedded fresshe May
In two of Taur, was into Cancre gliden,

613. **sleep,** slept; **prime,** 9 A.M. 620. **lives,** living. 621. **brid,** bird. 625. **sely,** silly. 629. **biwraye,** disclose. 632. **brenneth,** burns. 633. **putte . . . aventure,** risked his life. 635. **penner,** pencase. 639. **heeng,** that hung. 643. **two,** i.e., degrees; **Taur,** the Sign of the Bull; **Cancre,** the Sign of the Crab.

So longe hath Mayus in hir chambre abiden,
As custume is unto thise nobles alle:
A bride shal nat eten in the halle
Til dayes foure, or three dayes atte leeste,
Ypassed been—thanne lat hire go to feeste.
The fourthe day compleet fro noon to noon,
Whan that the hye masse was ydoon,
In halle sit this Januarye and May,
As fressh as is the brighte someres day.
And so bifel how that this goode man
Remembred him upon this Damian,
And saide, "Sainte Marye, how may it be
That Damian entendeth nat to me?
Is he ay sik, or how may this bitide?"
His squiers whiche that stooden ther biside
Excused him by cause of his siknesse,
Which letted him to doon his bisinesse:
Noon other cause mighte make him tarye.
"That me forthinketh," quod this Januarye.
"He is a gentil squier, by my trouthe.
If that he deide, it were harm and routhe.
He is as wis, discreet, and eek secree,
As any man I woot of his degree,
And therto manly and eek servisable,
And for to be a thrifty man right able.
But after mete as soone as evere I may,
I wol myself visite him, and eek May,
To do him al the confort that I can."
And for that word him blessed every man
That of his bountee and his gentilesse
He wolde so conforten in siknesse
His squier—for it was a gentil deede.
"Dame," quod this Januarye, "take good heede:
At after-mete ye with your wommen alle,
Whan ye han been in chambre out of this halle,

651. **sit,** sits. 656. **entendeth,** attends. 660. **letted,** prevented. 662. **me forthinketh,** I regret. 664. **routhe,** pity. 668. **thrifty,** proper. 673. **bountee,** goodness; **gentilesse,** courtesy. 677. **after-mete,** after dinner.

That alle ye go to this Damian.
Dooth him disport—he is a gentil man—
And telleth him that I wol him visite,
Have I no thing but rested me a lite.°
And speede you faste, for I wol abide
Til that ye sleepe faste by my side."
And with that word he gan to him to calle
A squier that was marchal° of his halle,
And tolde him certain thinges what he wolde.
  This fresshe May hath straight hir way yholde
With alle hir wommen unto Damian:
Down by his beddes side sit° she than,
Conforting him as goodly as she may.
  This Damian, whan that his time he sey,°
In secree wise his purs and eek his bille,°
In which that he ywriten hadde his wille,
Hath put into hir hand withoute more,
Save that he siketh° wonder deepe and sore,
And softely to hire right thus saide he:
"Mercy, and that ye nat discovere° me,
For I am deed if that this thing be kid."°
The purs hath she inwith° hir bosom hid,
And wente hir way—ye gete namore of me.
But unto Januarye ycomen is she,
That on his beddes side sit ful softe,
And taketh hire and kisseth hire ful ofte,
And laide him down to sleepe and that anoon.
She feined hire° as that she moste goon
Ther as ye woot that every wight moot neede,
And whan she of this bille hath taken heede,
She rente it al to cloutes° at the laste,
And in the privee softely it caste.
  Who studieth now but faire fresshe May?

682. After I've rested just a little. **686. marchal,** marshal, major domo. **690. sit,** sits. **692. sey,** saw. **693. bille,** letter. **696. siketh,** sighs. **698. discovere,** betray. **699. kid,** made known. **700. inwith,** within. **706. feined hire,** pretended. **709. rente,** tore; **cloutes,** shreds.

Adown by olde Januarye she lay,
That sleep° til that the coughe hath him awaked.
Anoon he prayde hire strepen° hire al naked;
He wolde of hire, he saide, han som plesaunce;
He saide hir clothes dide him encombraunce.
And she obeyeth, be hire lief° or loth.
But lest that precious° folk be with me wroth,
How that he wroughte I dar nat to you telle—
Or wheither hire thoughte° Paradis or helle.
But here I lete hem werken in hir wise
Til evensong roong° and that they moste arise.
  Were it by destinee or aventure,°
Were it by influence° or by nature,
Or constellacion that in swich estat
The hevene stood that time fortunat
As for to putte a bille of Venus werkes°—
For alle thing hath time, as sayn thise clerkes—
To any womman for to gete hir love,
I can nat saye, but grete God above,
That knoweth that noon act is causelees,
He deeme° of al, for I wol holde my pees.
  But sooth is this: how that this fresshe May
Hath taken swich impression that day
Of pitee on this sike Damian,
That from hir herte she ne drive can
The remembrance° for to doon him ese.
"Certain," thoughte she, "whom that this thing displese
I rekke° nat. For here I him assure
To love him best of any creature,
Though he namore hadde than his sherte."
Lo, pitee renneth° soone in gentil herte!
  Here may ye see how excellent franchise°

713. sleep, slept. **714. strepen,** strip. **717. lief,** agreeable. **718. precious,** fastidious. **720. thoughte,** it seemed. **722. roong,** rang. **723. aventure,** accident. **724. influence,** i.e., occult interference. **727. putte . . . bille,** present a petition; **werkes,** works. **732. He deeme,** let him judge. **737. remembrance,** memorandum. **739. rekke,** care. **742. renneth,** runs. **743. franchise,** generosity.

In wommen is whan they hem narwe avise.
Som tyrant is, as ther be many oon,
That hath an herte as hard as is a stoon,
Which wolde han lete him sterven in the place,
Wel rather than han graunted him hir grace,
And hem rejoisen in hir cruel pride,
And rekke nat to been an homicide.
  This gentil May, fulfilled of pitee,
Right of hir hand a lettre maked she,
In which she graunteth him hir verray grace:
Ther lakketh nought only but day and place
Wher that she mighte unto his lust suffise;
For it shal be right as he wol devise.
And when she saw hir time upon a day
To visite this Damian gooth May,
And subtilly this lettre down she threste
Under his pilwe: rede it if him leste.
She taketh him by the hand and harde him twiste,
So secreely that no wight of it wiste,
And bad him be al hool, and forth she wente
To Januarye whan that he for hire sente.
  Up riseth Damian the nexte morwe:
Al passed was his siknesse and his sorwe.
He kembeth him, he preineth him and piketh,
He dooth al that his lady lust and liketh.
And eek to Januarye he gooth as lowe
As evere dide a dogge for the bowe.
He is so plesant unto every man—
For craft is al, whoso that do it can—
That every wight is fain to speke him good.
And fully in his lady grace he stood.
Thus lete I Damian aboute his neede,

744. hem . . . avise, consider closely. **747. sterven,** die. **750. rekke nat,** do not scruple. **751. fulfilled,** filled full. **752. Right . . . hir,** in her own. **755. suffise,** satisfy. **759. threste,** thrust. **761. twiste,** twisted. **762. wiste,** knew. **763. be hool,** i.e., get well. **765. morwe,** morning. **767. kembeth,** combs; **preineth,** preens; **piketh,** cleans. **768. lust,** pleases. **769. lowe,** humbly. **770.** The image is of a well-trained hunting dog. **773. fain,** glad. **775. lete,** leave.

And in my tale forth I wol proceede.
Some clerkes holden that felicitee
Stant in delit,° and therfore certain he,
This noble Januarye, with al his might
In honeste wise as longeth° to a knight,
Shoop° him to live ful deliciously:
His housing, his array as honestly
To his degree was maked as a kinges.
Amonges othere of his honeste thinges,
He made a gardin walled al of stoon—
So fair a gardin woot I nowher noon,
For out of doute I verraily suppose
That he that wroot the *Romance of the Rose*°
Ne coude of it the beautee wel devise;
Ne Priapus ne mighte nat suffise—
Though he be god of gardins—for to telle
The beautee of the gardin, and the welle°
That stood under a laurer° alway greene.
Ful ofte time he Pluto and his queene
Proserpina and al hir fairye°
Disporten hem and maken melodye
Aboute that welle, and daunced, as men tolde.
This noble knight, this Januarye the olde,
Swich daintee° hath in it to walke and playe,
That he wol no wight suffre bere the keye,
Save he himself; for of the smale wiket°
He bar alway of silver a cliket,°
With which whan that him leste he it unshette.°
And whan he wolde paye his wif hir dette
In somer seson, thider wolde he go,
And May his wif, and no wight but they two.
And thinges whiche that were nat doon abedde,
He in the gardin parfourned hem and spedde.

778. **Stant,** stands; **delit,** material delight. 780. **honeste,** honorable; **longeth,** befits. 781. **Shoop,** arranged. 788. **Romance of the Rose,** Guillaume de Lorris' French allegory, set in the garden of love. 792. **welle,** spring. 793. **laurer,** laurel. 795. **fairye,** fairies. 799. **daintee,** delight. 801. **wiket,** wicket-gate. 802. **cliket,** latch-key. 803. **unshette,** unlocked.

And in this wise many a merye day
Lived this Januarye and fresshe May.
But worldly joye may nat alway dure°
To Januarye, ne to no creature.
  O sodein hap,° O thou Fortune unstable,
Lik to the scorpion so deceivable,°
That flaterest with thyn heed° whan thou wolt stinge,
Thy tail is deeth thurgh thyn enveniminge!°
O brotel joye, O sweete venim quainte!°
O monstre, that so subtilly canst painte
Thy yiftes under hewe of stedfastnesse,
That thou deceivest bothe more and lesse,
Why hastou Januarye thus deceived,
That haddest him for thy fulle freend received?
And now thou hast biraft° him bothe his yën,
For sorwe of which desireth he to dien.
Allas, this noble Januarye free,°
Amidde his lust° and his prosperitee,
Is woxen° blind, and that al sodeinly.
He weepeth and he waileth pitously,
And therwithal the fir of jalousye,
Lest that his wif sholde falle in som folye,
So brente his herte that he wolde fain°
That som man bothe hire and him hadde slain;
For neither after his deeth ne in his lif,
Ne wolde he that she were love ne wif,
But evere live as widwe in clothes blake,
Soul as the turtle that hath lost hir make.°
But atte laste, after a month or twaye,
His sorwe gan assuage, sooth to saye,
For whan he wiste° it may noon other be,
He paciently took his adversitee—

811. **dure,** continue. 813. **sodein,** unanticipated; **hap,** chance. 814. **deceivable,** deceitful. 815. **heed,** head. 816. **enveniminge,** poisoning: the scorpion was popularly supposed to ingratiate its victim with its head before stinging with its tail. 817. **brotel,** brittle; **venim,** poison; **quainte,** curious. 823. **biraft,** deprived of. 825. **free,** generous. 826. **lust,** heart's desire. 827. **woxen,** grown. 831. **brente,** burned; **fain,** gladly. 836. **Soul,** sole; **turtle,** turtle dove; **make,** mate. 839. **wiste,** knew.

Save out of doute he may nat forgoon
That he nas jalous everemore in oon.°
Which jalousye it was so outrageous
That neither in halle ne in noon other hous,
Ne in noon other place neverthemo,
He nolde suffre hire for to ride or go,
But if that he hadde hand on hire alway:
For which ful ofte weepeth fresshe May,
That loveth Damian so benignely
That she moot outher° dien sodeinly,
Or elles she moot han him as hire leste.
She waiteth° whan hir herte wolde breste.
  Upon that other side Damian
Bicomen is the sorwefulleste man
That evere was, for neither night ne day
Ne mighte he speke a word to fresshe May,
As to his purpos of no swich matere,
But if that Januarye moste it heere,
That hadde an hand upon hire evermo;
But nathelees, by writing to and fro,
And privee signes, wiste° what she mente,
And she knew eek the fin° of his entente.
  O Januarye, what mighte it thee availe
Though thou mightest see as fer as shippes saile?
For as good is blind deceived be,
As be deceived whan a man may see.
Lo Argus, which that hadde an hundred yën,
For al that evere he coude poure° or pryen,
Yit was he blent,° and God woot so been mo
That weenen wisly° that it be nat so.
Passe over is an ese,° and saye namore.
  This fresshe May that I spak of so yore,°
In warm wex hath emprinted the cliket°
That Januarye bar of that smale wiket,

842. in oon, constantly. **850. outher,** either. **852. waiteth,** i.e., anticipates the time. **861. wiste,** i.e., he knew. **862. fin,** end. **868. poure,** gaze. **869. blent,** blinded, deceived. **870. wisly,** surely. **871. ese,** relief. **872. yore,** long ago. **873. wex,** wax; **clicket,** key.

By which into his gardin ofte he wente;
And Damian that knew al hir entente
The cliket countrefeted° prively—
Ther nis namore to saye, but hastily
Som wonder by this cliket shal bitide,
Which ye shal heeren if ye wol abide.
  O noble Ovide, sooth saistou, God woot,
What sleighte it is, though it be long and hoot,°
That he° nil finde it out in som manere!
By Pyramus and Thisbee may men lere:°
Though they were kept ful longe straite° overal,
They been accorded rouning° thurgh a wal,
Ther no wight coude han founde out swich a sleighte.
But now to purpos: er that dayes eighte
Were passed of the month of Juin, bifil°
That Januarye hath caught so greet a wil—
Thurgh egging of his wif—him for to playe
In his gardin, and no wight but they twaye,
That in a morwe unto his May saith he,
"Ris up, my wif, my love, my lady free;
The turtles vois is herd, my douve° sweete;
The winter is goon with alle his raines wete.
Com forth now with thine yën columbin:°
How fairer been thy brestes than is win!
The garden is enclosed al aboute:
Com forth, my white spouse! out of doute,
Thou hast me wounded in myn herte. O wif,
No spot of thee ne knew I al my lif.
Com forth and lat us taken oure disport—
I chees° thee for my wif and my confort."
  Swiche olde lewed° wordes used he.
On Damian a signe made she
That he sholde go biforn with his cliket.

877. **countrefeted,** i.e., duplicated. 882. **sleighte,** trick; **hoot,** i.e., perilous. 883. **he,** i.e., Love. 884. **lere,** learn. 885. **straite,** strictly. 886. **rouning,** whispering: the story of Pyramus and Thisbe is in Ovid's *Metamorphoses.* 889. **Juin,** June; **bifil,** it happened. 895. **turtles,** turtle-dove's; **douve,** dove. 897. **columbin,** dove-like. 904. **chees,** chose. 905. **lewed,** unskilful: the words are a paraphrase of a passage in the Song of Solomon.

This Damian thanne hath opened the wiket,
And in he sterte,° and that in swich manere
That no wight mighte it see neither yheere,
And stille he sit° under a bussh anoon.
  This Januarye, as blind as is a stoon,
With Mayus in his hand and no wight mo,
Into his fresshe gardin is ago,°
And clapte to° the wiket sodeinly.
"Now wif," quod he, "here nis but thou and I,
That art the creature that I best love,
For by that Lord that sit in hevene above,
Levere ich hadde to dien on a knif
Than thee offende, trewe dere wif.
For Goddes sake, thenk how I thee chees,°
Nought for no coveitise,° doutelees,
But only for the love I hadde to thee.
And though that I be old and may nat see,
Beeth to me trewe, and I wol telle why.
Three thinges, certes, shal ye winne therby:
First, love of Crist, and to yourself honour,
And al myn heritage, town and towr°—
I yive it you: maketh chartres as you leste.
This shal be doon tomorwe er sonne reste,
So wisly° God my soule bringe in blisse.
I praye you first in covenant ye me kisse,
And though that I be jalous, wite° me nought:
Ye been so deepe emprinted in my thought,
That whan that I considere youre beautee,
And therwithal the unlikly elde° of me,
I may nought, certes, though I sholde die,
Forbere to been out of youre compaignye
For verray love. This is withouten doute.
Now kis me, wif, and lat us rome aboute."
  This fresshe May, whan she thise wordes herde,

909. **sterte,** went. 911. **sit,** sits. 914. **is ago,** has gone. 915. **clapte to,** slammed shut. 921. **chees,** chose. 922. **coveitise,** avarice. 928. **towr,** i.e., castle. 931. **wisly,** surely. 933. **wite,** blame. 936. **unlikly,** unsuitable; **elde,** old age.

Benignely to Januarye answerde,
But first and forward° she bigan to weepe.
"I have," quod she, "a soule for to keepe°
As wel as ye, and also myn honour,
And of my wifhood thilke tendre flowr,
Which that I have assured° in youre hond,
Whan that the preest to you my body boond;°
Wherfore I wol answere in this manere,
By the leve of you, my lord so dere:
I praye to God that nevere dawe° the day
That I ne sterve as foule° as womman may,
If evere I do unto my kin that shame,
Or elles I empaire° so my name
That I be fals; and if I do that lak,°
Do strepe me,° and putte me in a sak,
And in the nexte river do me drenche:°
I am a gentil womman and no wenche.
Why speke ye thus? But men been evere untrewe,
And wommen have repreve° of you ay newe.
Ye han noon other countenance, I leve,°
But speke to us of untrust and repreve."
  And with that word she saw wher Damian
Sat in the bussh, and coughen she bigan,
And with hir finger signes made she
That Damian sholde climbe upon a tree
That charged was with fruit; and up he wente,
For verraily he knew al hir entente,
And every signe that she coude make,
Wel bet than Januarye, hir owene make,°
For in a lettre she hadde told him al
Of this matere how he werken shal.
And thus I lete him sitte on the pirye,°
And Januarye and May roming mirye.

943. **forward,** foremost. 944. **keepe,** save. 947. **assured,** pledged. 948. **boond,** bound. 951. **dawe,** dawn. 952. **sterve,** die; **foule,** shamefully. 954. **empaire,** impair. 955. **lak,** crime. 956. **Do . . . me,** have me stripped. 957. **nexte,** nearest; **do . . . drenche,** have me drowned. 960. **repreve,** reproof. 961. **countenance,** i.e., way of covering your own fault; **leve,** believe. 970. **bet,** better; **make,** mate. 973. **pirye,** peartree.

Bright was the day and blew the firmament.
Phebus hath of gold his stremes down sent
To gladen every flowr with his warmnesse.
He was that time in Geminis, as I gesse,
But litel fro his declinacioun
Of Cancer, Joves exaltacioun.
And so bifel that brighte morwetide
That in that gardin in the ferther side
Pluto, that is king of fairye,
And many a lady in his compaignye,
Folwing his wif, the queene Proserpina
Which that he ravisshed out of Etna
Whil that she gadred flowres in the mede—
In Claudian ye may the stories rede
How in his grisly carte he hire fette—
This king of fairye thanne adown him sette
Upon a bench of turves fressh and greene,
And right anoon thus saide he to his queene.
"My wif," quod he, "ther may no wight saye nay:
Th'experience so preveth every day
The treson which that womman dooth to man.
Ten hundred thousand tales tellen I can
Notable of youre untrouthe and brotelnesse.
O Salomon, wis and richest of richesse,
Fulfild of sapience and of worldly glorye,
Ful worthy been thy wordes to memorye
To every wight that wit and reson can—
Thus praiseth he yit the bountee of man:
'Amonges a thousand men yit foond I oon,
But of wommen alle foond I noon.'
Thus saith the king that knoweth youre wikkednesse.

975. blew, blue. **976. stremes,** beams. **978. Geminis,** the Sign of the Twins. **979. declinacioun,** i.e., position upon entering. **980. Cancer,** the Sign of the Crab; **Joves exaltacioun,** Jupiter's position of dominant influence. **981. morwetide,** morningtime. **988. Claudian,** author of the late Latin poem, *The Rape of Proserpine,* which describes the seizure by the gloomy king of the underworld of the fair young girl. **989. fette,** fetched. **994. preveth,** proves. **997. untrouthe,** infidelity; **brotelnesse,** fickleness. **1001. can,** recognizes. **1002. bountee,** goodness. **1003. foond,** found.

And Jesus filius Syrak,° as I gesse,
Ne speketh of you but selde° reverence—
A wilde fir and corrupt pestilence
So falle upon youre bodies yit tonight!
Ne see ye nought this honourable knight?
By cause, allas, that he is blind and old,
His owene man shal make him cokewold.°
Lo wher he sit,° the lechour in the tree!
Now wol I graunten of my majestee
Unto this olde, blinde, worthy knight
That he shal have ayain his yën-sight,
Whan that his wif wolde doon him vilainye.
Thanne shal he knowen al hir harlotrye,
Bothe in repreve° of hire and othere mo."
"Ye shal?" quod Proserpine. "Wol ye so?
Now by my modres sires° soule I swere
That I shal yiven hire suffisant° answere,
And alle wommen after for hir sake,
That though they be in any gilt ytake,
With face bold they shul hemself excuse,
And bere hem down that wolde hem accuse:
For lak of answere noon of hem shal dien.
Al° hadde men seen a thing with bothe his yën,
Yit shal we wommen visagen it hardily,°
And weepe and swere and chide subtilly,
So that ye men shul been as lewed° as gees—
What rekketh me of youre auctoritees?°
I woot wel that this Jew, this Salomon,
Foond of us wommen folies many oon,
But though that he ne foond no good womman,
Yit hath ther founde many another man
Wommen ful trewe, ful goode and vertuous.
Witnesse on hem that dwelte in Cristes hous:

1006. Jesus . . . Syrak, Jesus, son of Sirak, supposed author of the Book of Ecclesiasticus. **1007. selde,** seldom. **1012. cokewold,** cuckold. **1013. sit,** sits. **1019. repreve,** reproof. **1021. modres sires,** mother's father's. **1022. suffisant,** satisfactory. **1028. Al,** although. **1029. visagen,** face out; **hardily,** confidently. **1031. lewed,** stupid. **1032. rekketh me,** do I care; **auctoritees,** authorities.

With martyrdom they preved hir constaunce.°
The Romain geestes° eek maken remembraunce
Of many a verray, trewe wif also.
But sire, ne be nat wroth, al be it so,
Though that he saide he foond no good womman,
I praye you, take the sentence° of the man:
He mente thus, that in soverein bountee°
Nis noon but God, but neither he ne she.
Ey, for verray God that nis but oon,
What make ye so muche of Salomon?
What though he made a temple, Goddes hous?
What though he were riche and glorious?
So made he eek a temple of false goddes:
How mighte he do a thing that more forbode° is?
Pardee, as faire as ye his name emplastre,°
He was a lechour and an idolastre,°
And in his elde° he verray God forsook.
And if God ne hadde, as saith the book,
Yspared him for his fadres sake, he sholde
Have lost his regne rather than he wolde.°
I sette° right nought of al the vilainye
That ye of wommen write a boterflye.°
I am a womman, needes moot I speke,
Or elles swelle til myn herte breke.
For sithen he saide that we been jangleresses,°
As evere hool I moote brouke° my tresses,
I shal nat spare for no curteisye
To speke him harm that wolde° us vilainye."
"Dame," quod this Pluto, "be no lenger wroth.
I yive it up. But sith I swoor myn ooth
That I wolde graunten him his sighte ayain,
My word shal stonde, I warne you certain.

1039. **constaunce,** constancy. **1040. geestes,** stories, the *Gesta Romanorum.* **1044. sentence,** meaning. **1045. soverein bountee,** paramount excellence. **1052. forbode,** forbidden. **1053. emplastre,** whitewash. **1054. idolastre,** idolator. **1055. elde,** old age. **1058. rather,** sooner; **wolde,** wanted. **1059. sette,** i.e., care. **1060. boterflye,** butterfly. **1063. jangleresses,** idle talkers. **1064. hool,** i.e., in health; **brouke,** enjoy. **1066. wolde,** i.e., wished on.

I am a king: it sit° me nought to lie."
  "And I," quod she, "a queene of fairye:
Hir answere shal she have, I undertake.
Lat us namore wordes heerof make.
Forsoothe, I wol no lenger you contrarye."°
  Now lat us turne again to Januarye
That in the gardin with his faire May
Singeth ful merier than the papenjay,°
"You love I best, and shal, and other noon."
So longe aboute the aleyes° is he goon
Til he was come ayains thilke pirye,°
Wher as this Damian sitteth ful mirye
On heigh among the fresshe leves greene.
  This fresshe May, that is so bright and sheene,°
Gan for to sike° and saide, "Allas, my side!
Now sire," quod she, "for ought that may bitide,
I moste han of the peres° that I see,
Or I moot die, so sore longeth me°
To eten of the smale peres greene.
Help for hir love that is of hevene queene!
I telle you wel, a womman in my plit°
May han to fruit so greet an appetit
That she may dien but° she of it have."
  "Allas," quod he, "that I ne hadde heer a knave°
That coude climbe! Allas, allas," quod he,
"For I am blind!" "Ye, sire, no fors,"° quod she.
"But wolde ye vouche sauf, for Goddes sake,
The pirye inwith° youre armes for to take—
For wel I woot that ye mistruste me—
Thanne sholde I climbe wel ynough," quod she,
"So I my foot mighte sette upon youre bak."
  "Certes," quod he, "theron shal be no lak,°
Mighte I you helpen with myn herte blood."

1071. sit, suits. **1075. contrarye,** contradict. **1078. papenjay,** parrot. **1080. aleyes,** garden paths. **1081. thilke,** that same; **pirye,** peartree. **1084. sheene,** shining. **1085. sike,** sigh. **1087. peres,** pears. **1088. longeth me,** I long. **1091. plit,** condition. **1093. but,** unless. **1094. knave,** servant. **1096. fors,** matter. **1098. inwith,** within. **1102. lak,** fault.

He stoupeth° down, and on his bak she stood,
And caughte hire by a twiste,° and up she gooth.
Ladies, I praye you that ye be nat wroth:
I can nat glose,° I am a rude man.
And sodeinly anoon this Damian
Gan pullen up the smok and in he throong.°
  And whan that Pluto sawgh this grete wrong,
To Januarye he yaf again his sighte,
And made him see as wel as evere he mighte;
And whan that he hadde caught his sighte again,
Ne was ther nevere man of thing so fain.°
But on his wif his thought was everemo:
Unto the tree he caste his yën two,
And sawgh that Damian his wif had dressed°
In swich manere it may nat been expressed,
But if° I wolde speken uncurteisly,
And up he yaf a roring and a cry,
As dooth the moder whan the child shal die.
"Out! Help! Allas! Harrow!" he gan to crye.
"O stronge lady store,° what doostou?"
  And she answerde, "Sire, what aileth you?
Have pacience and reson in youre minde.
I have you holpe° on bothe youre yën blinde.
Up° peril of my soule, I shal nat lien,
As me was taught, to hele° with youre yën
Was no thing bet° to make you to see
Than strugle with a man upon a tree:
God woot I dide it in ful good entente."
  "Strugle!" quod he. "Ye, algate° in it wente!
God yive you bothe on shames deeth to dien!
He swived° thee: I saw it with mine yën,
And elles be I hanged by the hals."°
  "Thanne is," quod she, "my medicine al fals.

1104. stoupeth, stoops. **1105. twiste,** twig. **1107. glose,** speak circumspectly. **1109. throong,** pressed. **1114. fain,** glad. **1117. dressed,** placed. **1119. But if,** unless. **1123. stronge,** flagrant; **store,** crude. **1126. holpe,** helped. **1127. Up,** upon. **1128. hele,** heal. **1129. bet,** better. **1132. algate,** at any rate. **1134. swived,** copulated with. **1135. hals,** neck.

For certainly if that ye mighte see,
Ye wolde nat sayn thise wordes unto me.
Ye han som glimsing and no parfit° sighte."
  "I see," quod he, "as wel as evere I mighte,
Thanked be God, with bothe mine yën two,
And by my trouthe, me thoughte he dide thee so."
  "Ye maze, maze,° goode sire," quod she.
"This thank have I for I have maad you see.
Allas," quod she, "that evere I was so kinde!"
  "Now dame," quod he, "lat al passe out of minde.
Com down, my lief,° and if I have missaid,
God help me so as I am yvele apaid.°
But by my fader soule, I wende have sein°
How that this Damian hadde by thee lain,
And that thy smok hadde lain upon thy brest."
  "Ye, sire," quod she, "ye may weene as you lest.
But sire, a man that waketh out of his sleep
He may nat sodeinly wel taken keep°
Upon a thing, ne seen it parfitly,
Til that he be adawed° verraily;
Right so a man that longe hath blind ybe
Ne may nat sodeinly so wel ysee,
First whan his sighte is newe come again,
As he that hath a day or two ysein.°
Til that youre sighte ysatled° be a while,
Ther may ful many a sighte you bigile.
Beeth war, I praye you, for, by hevene king,
Ful many a man weeneth to see a thing
And it is al another than it seemeth:
He that misconceiveth, he misdeemeth."°
And with that word she leep° down fro the tree.
  This Januarye, who is glad but he?
He kisseth hire and clippeth° hire ful ofte,

1139. glimsing, glimpsing; **parfit,** perfect. **1143. maze,** are dazed. **1147. lief,** dear. **1148. yvele apaid,** ill-pleased. **1149. wende . . . sein,** thought I saw. **1154. keep,** notice. **1156. adawed,** wakened. **1160. ysein,** seen. **1161. ysatled,** settled. **1166. misdeemeth,** misjudges. **1167. leep,** leapt. **1169. clippeth,** hugs.

And on hir wombe he stroketh hire ful softe,
And to his palais hoom he hath hire lad.°
Now goode men, I praye you to be glad.
Thus endeth here my tale of Januarye.
God blesse us and his moder, Sainte Marye.

THE SQUIRE'S TALE

The Introduction

"Ey, Goddes mercy," saide oure Hoste tho,
"Now swich a wif I praye God keepe me fro.
Lo whiche sleightes° and subtilitees
In wommen been, for ay as bisy as bees
Been they us sely° men for to deceive,
And from a sooth evere wol they waive.°
By this Marchantes tale it preveth° weel.
But, doutelees, as trewe as any steel
I have a wif, though that she poore be;
But of hir tonge a labbing° shrewe is she,
And yit she hath an heep of vices mo—
Therof no fors,° lat alle swiche thinges go.
But wite ye what? In conseil° be it said,
Me reweth sore I am unto hire teyd°—
For and° I sholde rekenen every vice
Which that she hath, ywis, I were too nice.°
And cause why? it sholde reported be,
And told to hire of some of this meinee.°
Of whom? it needeth nat for to declare,
Sin wommen connen oute swich chaffare.°
And eek my wit suffiseth nat therto
To tellen al; wherfore my tale is do.

1171. lad, led.

3. whiche, what; **sleightes,** tricks. **5. sely,** innocent. **6. waive,** depart. **7. preveth,** i.e., is proved. **10. labbing,** blabbing. **12. fors,** matter. **13. wite,** know; **conseil,** secrecy. **14. Me reweth,** I regret; **teyd,** tied. **15. and,** if. **16. nice,** foolish. **18. meinee,** group. **20.** i.e., Since women know how to bring into the open matters of this sort.

Squier, com neer, if it youre wille be,
And say somwhat of love, for certes ye
Connen° theron as muche as any man."
"Nay, sire," quod he, "but I wol saye as I can
With hertly° wil, for I wol nat rebelle
Again youre lust—a tale wol I telle.
Have me excused if I speke amis:
My wil is good, and lo, my tale is this."

The Tale

PART ONE

At Sarray° in the land of Tartarye
Ther dwelte a king that werreyed° Russie,
Thurgh which ther deide many a doughty man.
This noble king was cleped° Cambiuskan,
Which in his time was of so greet renown
That ther nas nowher in no regioun
So excellent a lord in alle thing:
Him lakked nought that longed° to a king.
As of the secte° of which that he was born
He kepte his lay° to which that he was sworn.
And therto he was hardy, wis, and riche,°
Pitous and just, and evere more yliche°
Sooth° of his word, benigne and honorable,
Of his corage as any centre° stable,
Young, fressh, and strong; in armes desirous°

25. **Connen,** know. 27. **hertly,** hearty. 28. **lust,** desire.

1. **Sarray,** Sarai, in what is now southwest Russia. 2. **werreyed,** made war on. 4. **cleped,** called. 8. **longed,** was appropriate to. 9. **secte,** religion. 10. **lay,** law. 11. **riche,** splendid. 12. **Pitous,** merciful; **yliche,** alike. 13. **sooth,** true. 14. **corage,** heart; **centre,** axis of a circle. 15. **desirous,** eager.

As any bacheler of al his hous.
A fair persone he was, and fortunat,
And kepte alway so wel royal estat
That ther was nowher swich another man.
  This noble king, this Tartre Cambiuskan,
Hadde two sones on Elfeta his wif,
Of whiche the eldeste highte Algarsif;
That other sone was cleped Cambalo.
A doughter hadde this worthy king also
That yongest was, and highte Canacee:
But for to telle you al hir beautee
It lith nat in my tonge, n'in my conning:
I dar nat undertake so heigh a thing;
Myn Englissh eek is insufficient;
It moste been a rhetor excellent
That coude his colours longing for that art,
If he sholde hire descriven every part;
I am noon swich, I moot speke as I can.
  And so bifel that when this Cambiuskan
Hath twenty winter born his diademe,
As he was wont fro yeer to yere, I deeme,
He leet the feeste of his nativitee
Doon cryen thurghout Sarray his citee,
The laste Ides of March after the yeer.
Phebus the sonne ful jolif was and cleer
For he was neigh his exaltacioun
In Martes face, and in his mansioun,
In Aries, the colerik, hote signe.

16. **bacheler,** young knight. 22. **highte,** was named. 27. **lith,** lies; **conning,** skill. 30. **moste,** must; **rhetor,** rhetorician. 31. **coude,** knew; **colours,** i.e., rhetorical figures; **longing for,** appropriate to. 32. **descriven,** describe. 33. **moot,** must. 35. **diademe,** crown. 36. **wont,** accustomed; **deeme,** think. 37. **leet,** caused. 38. **Doon cryen,** to be announced. 39. **laste . . . March,** March fifteenth: since there is only one ides in a month, it is unclear what the Squire means by the last; **after . . . yeer,** according to some medieval reckoning, the new year began on March fifteenth. 40. **jolif,** cheerful; **cleer,** bright. 41. **exaltacioun,** position of strongest planetary influence. 42–43. **Aries,** the sign of the Ram, is also a mansion of the planet Mars in which Mars's influence is especially strong; the first ten degrees of Aries are the face of Mars; **colerik,** fiery.

Ful lusty° was the weder and benigne,
For which the fowles again the sonne sheene°—
What for the seson and the yonge greene—
Ful loude songen hir affeccions:°
Hem seemed han geten hem proteccions°
Again the swerd° of winter, keene and cold.
  This Cambiuskan of which I have you told
In royal vestiment sit° on his dais
With diademe, ful hye in his palais,
And halt° his feeste solempne and so riche
That in this world ne was ther noon it liche,°
Of which if I shal tellen al th'array,
Thanne wolde it occupye a someres day;
And eek it needeth nat for to devise°
At every cours the ordre of hir servise:
I wol nat tellen of hir straunge sewes,°
Ne of hir swannes, ne of hir heronsewes.°
Eek in that land, as tellen knightes olde,
Ther is som mete that is ful daintee holde°
That in this land men recche of° it but smal.
Ther is no man that may reporten al:
I wol nat taryen you, for it is prime;°
And for it is no fruit,° but los of time,
Unto my firste° I wol have my recours:
And so bifel that after the thridde cours,
Whil that this king sit thus in his nobleye°
Herkning his minstrales hir thinges playe
Biforn him at the boord° deliciously,
In at the halle dore al sodeinly
Ther cam a knight upon a steede of bras,
And in his hand a brood° mirour of glas;

44. **lusty,** enjoyable. 45. **again,** i.e., in; **sheene,** shining. 47. **affecciouns,** good feeling. 48. They seemed to have got protections. 49. **Again,** against; **swerd,** sword. 51. **sit,** sits. 53. **halt,** holds. 54. **liche,** like. 57. **devise,** describe. 59. **sewes,** dishes. 60. **heronsewes,** servings of young heron. 62. **daintee,** tasty; **holde,** considered. 63. **recche of,** care for. 65. **prime,** mid-morning. 66. **fruit,** profit. 67. **firste,** i.e., first topic. 69. **sit,** sits; **nobleye,** splendor. 71. **boord,** table. 74. **brood,** broad.

Upon his thombe he hadde of gold a ring,
And by his side a naked swerd hanging;
And up he rideth to the hye boord:
In al the halle ne was ther spoke a word
For merveile of this knight, him to biholde;
Ful bisily they waiten, yonge and olde.
This straunge knight that cam thus sodeinly,
Al armed, save his heed, ful richely,
Salueth king and queene and lordes alle
By ordre as they seten in the halle,
With so heigh reverence and obeisaunces,
As wel in speeche as in his countenaunces,
That Gawain, with his olde curteisye,
Though he were come again out of fairye,
Ne coude him nat amende with a word.
And after this, biforn the hye boord
He with a manly vois saide his message,
After the forme used in his langage,
Withouten vice of syllable or of lettre;
And for his tale sholde seeme the bettre,
Accordant to his wordes was his cheere,
As techeth art of speeche hem that it lere.
Al be that I can nat soune his style,
Ne can nat climben over so heigh a stile,
Yit saye I this: as to commune entente,
Thus muche amounteth al that evere he mente,
If it so be that I have it in minde:
He saide, "The king of Arabe and of Inde,
My lige lord, on this solempne day
Salueth you as he best can and may,
And sendeth you, in honour of youre feeste,

80. bisily, anxiously; **waiten,** watch. **81. straunge,** foreign. **82. heed,** head. **83. Salueth,** greets. **85. obeisaunces,** bows. **86. countenaunces,** gestures. **87. Gawain,** the Arthurian knight famed for his good manners. **88. fairye,** fairyland. **89. amende,** improve on. **93. vice,** fault. **94. tale,** speech. **95. Accordant** to, in accord with; **cheere,** expression. **96. lere,** learn. **97. soune,** express. **99. commune entente,** general purport. **100.** I.e., this is the whole of what he had to say. **103. lige,** liege. **104. Salueth,** greets.

By me, that am al redy at youre heeste,°
This steede of bras, that esily and wel
Can in the space of oo day naturel—
This is to sayn, in foure and twenty houres—
Wherso you list,° in droughte or elles showres,
Beren youre body into every place
To which youre herte wilneth for to pace°
Withouten wem° of you, thurgh foul or fair;
Or if you list° to flye as hye in th'air
As dooth an egle whan him list to sore,
This same steede shal bere you evere more
Withouten harm til ye be ther you leste,°
Though that ye sleepen on his bak or reste,
And turne again with writhing° of a pin:
He that it wroughte coude many a gin;°
He waited many a constellacioun°
Er he hadde doon this operacioun,
And knew ful many a seel° and many a bond.
  This mirour eek that I have in myn hond
Hath swich a might that men may in it see
Whan ther shal fallen any adversitee
Unto youre regne,° or to youreself also,
And openly who is youre freend or fo.
  And over al this, if any lady bright
Hath set hir herte on any manere wight,°
If he be fals she shal his traison see,
His newe love, and al his subtiltee,
So openly that ther shal nothing hide;
Wherfore again this lusty° someres tide
This mirour and this ring that ye may see
He hath sent to my lady Canacee,
Youre excellente doughter that is here.
  The vertu° of the ring—if ye wol heere—

106. heeste, command. **110. list,** please. **112. wilneth,** wishes; **pace,** pass. **113. wem,** hurt. **114. list,** pleases. **117. leste,** please. **119. again,** i.e., back; **writhing,** twisting. **120. gin,** trick. **121. waited,** watched for; **constellacioun,** (favorable) planetary formation. **123. seel,** seal: seals and bonds are often associated with magic. **127. regne,** realm. **130. wight,** creature. **134. again,** i.e., in view of; **lusty,** pleasant. **138. vertu,** power.

Is this: that if hire list° it for to were
Upon hir thombe or in hir purs it bere,
Ther nis no fowl that fleeth° under the hevene
That she ne shal wel understonde his stevene°
And knowe his mening openly and plain,
And answere him in his langage again;
And every gras that groweth upon roote
She shal eek knowe, and whom it wol do boote,°
Al° be his woundes nevere so deepe and wide.
  This naked swerd that hangeth by my side
Swich vertu hath that what man so ye smite,
Thurghout his armure it wol kerve° and bite,
Were it as thikke as is a braunched ook.
And what man that is wounded with the strook
Shal nevere be hool til that you liste° of grace
To stroke him with the platte in thilke° place
Ther he is hurt: this is as muche to sayn,
Ye mote° with the platte swerd again
Stroke him in the wounde, and it wol close.
This is a verray sooth, withouten glose;°
It faileth nat whiles it is in youre hold."
  And whan this knight hath thus his tale ytold,
He rideth out of halle, and down he lighte.
His steede, which that shoon as sonne brighte,
Stant° in the court as stille as any stoon.
This knight is to his chambre lad° anoon
And is unarmed, and to mete° yset.
  The presents been ful royalliche yfet°—
This is to sayn, the swerd and the mirour—
And born anoon into the hye towr
With certain officers ordained° therfore;
And unto Canacee the ring is bore,°

139. list, pleases. **141. fleeth,** flies. **142. stevene,** voice, i.e., words. **146. do boote,** help. **147. Al,** although. **150. kerve,** carve. **153. hool,** whole; **liste,** it please. **154. platte,** flat; **thilke,** that same. **156. mote,** must. **158. glose,** deception. **163. Stant,** stands. **164. lad,** led. **165. mete,** i.e., dinner. **166. yfet,** fetched. **169. With,** by; **ordained,** appointed. **170. bore,** borne.

Solempnely, ther she sit at the table.
But sikerly, withouten any fable,
The hors of bras, that may nat be remued:
It stant as it were to the ground yglued;
Ther may no man out of the place it drive
For noon engin of windas or polive;
And cause why? for they can nat the craft.
And therfore in the place they han it laft
Til that the knight hath taught hem the manere
To voiden him, as ye shul after heere.
  Greet was the prees that swarmeth to and fro
To gauren on this hors that stondeth so,
For it so heigh was, and so brood and long,
So wel proporcioned for to been strong,
Right as it were a steede of Lombardye;
Therwith so horsly and so quik of yë
As it a gentil Poilais courser were.
For certes fro his tail unto his ere
Nature ne art ne coude him nat amende
In no degree, as al the peple wende.
But everemore hir moste wonder was
How that it coude goon and was of bras:
It was a fairye, as the peple seemed.
Diverse folk diversely han deemed:
As manye hedes, as manye wittes ther been.
They murmured as dooth a swarm of been,
And maden skiles after hir fantasies,
Rehersing of thise olde poetries,
And saiden it was lik the Pegasee,
The hors that hadde winges for to flee,

171. Solempnely, ceremoniously. **172. sikerly,** certainly; **fable,** lie. **173. remued,** moved. **176. For,** i.e., with; **windas,** windlass; **polive,** pulley. **177. can,** know. **178. laft,** left. **180. voiden,** remove. **181. prees,** crowd. **182. gauren,** gaze. **183. brood,** broad. **186. quik,** lively. **187. Poilais,** Apulian. **190. wende,** thought. **192. goon,** move. **193. fairye,** i.e., something enchanted; **seemed,** it seemed. **196. been,** bees. **197. skiles,** explanations; **after,** according to. **199. Pegasee,** Pegasus, the winged horse of Greek legend.

Or elles it was the Greekes hors Sinoun
That broughte Troye to destruccioun,
As men in thise olde geestes rede.
  "Myn herte," quod oon, "is evere more in drede:
I trowe some men of armes been therinne
That shapen hem this citee for to winne.
It were right good that al swich thing were knowe."
  Another rouned to his felawe lowe
And saide, "He lieth, for it is rather lik
An apparence ymaad by som magik,
As jogelours playen at thise feestes grete."
Of sondry doutes thus they jangle and trete,
As lewed peple deemeth communly
Of thinges that been maad more subtilly
Than they can in hir lewednesse comprehende:
They deemen gladly to the baddere ende.
  And some of hem wondren on the mirour
That born was up unto the maister towr,
How men mighte in it swiche thinges see.
  Another answerde and saide, "It mighte wel be
Naturelly, by composiciouns
Of angles and of slye reflecciouns,"
And saide that in Rome was swich oon.
They speke of Alocen and Vitulon,
Of Aristotle, that writen in hir lives
Of quainte mirours and of perspectives,
As knowen they that han hir bookes herd.
  And other folk han wondred on the swerd
That wolde percen thurghout every thing,
And felle in speeche of Telophus the king,
And of Achilles for his quainte spere:

201. Greekes . . . Sinoun, the horse of the Greek Sinon, i.e., the Trojan horse. **202. geestes,** stories. **203. trowe,** believe. **206. shapen hem,** are preparing. **208. rouned,** whispered. **210. apparence,** illusion. **211. jogelours,** jugglers, prestidigitators. **213. lewed,** ignorant. **218. maister,** highest. **221. composiciouns,** combinations. **222. slye,** ingenious. **224. Alocen,** Alhazen; **Vitulon,** Vitello: the former wrote a work on optics translated by the latter. **226. quainte,** curious; **perspectives,** magnifying glasses. **230.** Telephus was wounded by Achilles' spear and cured by its rust. **231. quainte,** curious.

For he coude with it bothe hele and dere°
Right in swich wise as men may with the swerd
Of which right now ye han youreselven herd.
They speke of medicines therwithal,
And speke of sondry harding° of metal,
And how and whan it sholde yharded be—
Which is unknowe, algates° unto me.
  Tho° speke they of Canacees ring,
And saiden alle that swich a wonder thing
Of craft of ringes herde they nevere noon,
Save that he Moises and King Salomon
Hadde a name of conning° in swich art.
Thus sayn the peple, and drawen hem apart.
  But nathelees, some saiden that it was
Wonder to maken of fern asshen° glas,
And yit is glas nat lik asshen of fern;
But for they han knowen it so fern,°
Therfore ceesseth hir jangling and hir wonder.
  As sore wondren some on cause of thonder,
On ebbe and flood,° on gossomer and on mist,
And alle thing til that the cause is wist.°
Thus janglen they and deemen and devise°
Til that the king gan from the boord arise.
  Phebus hath laft the angle meridional,°
And yit ascending was the beest royal,°
The gentil leon with his Aldiran,
Whan that this Tartre king Cambiuskan
Roos fro his boord ther as he sat ful hye:
Biforn him gooth the loude minstralcye
Til he cam to his chambre of parements,°
Ther as ther sounen diverse instruments

232. hele, heal; **dere,** harm. **236. sondry harding,** various ways of hardening. **238. algates,** at any rate. **239. Tho,** then. **243. name of conning,** reputation for skill. **246. asshen,** ashes. **248. so fern,** for such a long time. **251. flood,** i.e., floodtide. **252. wist,** known. **253. devise,** conjecture. **255.** I.e., the sun has left the tenth mansion, making the time after noon. **256. beest royal:** the royal beast is the constellation Leo, which rises with the star Aldiran. **261. parements,** cloth-hangings: these hung in the audience room of the palace.

That it is lik an hevene for to heere.
Now dauncen lusty Venus children dere,
For in the Fissh hir lady sat ful hye°
And looketh on hem with a freendly ÿe.
  This noble king is set upon his trone;°
This straunge° knight is brought to him ful soone,
And on the daunce he gooth with Canacee.
Here is the revel and the jolitee
That is nat able a dul man to devise:°
He moste° han knowe Love and his servise
And been a feestlich° man as fressh as May
That sholde you devisen° swich array.
  Who coude telle you the forme of daunces,
So uncouthe,° and swiche fresshe countenaunces,
Swich subtil looking and dissimulinges°
For drede of jalous mennes aperceivinges?°
No man but Launcelot, and he is deed.
Therfore I passe of al this lustiheed:°
I saye namore; but in this jolinesse
I lete hem, til men to the soper dresse.°
  The stiward bit the spices for to hie°
And eek the win in al this melodye.
The usshers° and the squiers been ygoon;
The spices and the win is come anoon;
They ete and drinke, and whan this hadde an ende,
Unto the temple, as reson was, they wende.
  The service doon, they soupen al by day.°
What needeth you rehercen hir array?
Eech man woot° wel that at a kinges feeste
Hath plentee to the moste° and to the leeste,
And daintees mo° than been in my knowing.

265. Venus is at its greatest influence in Pisces, the Fishes. **267. trone,** throne. **268. straunge,** stranger. **271. devise,** describe. **272. moste,** must. **273. feestlich,** festive. **274. devisen,** describe. **276. uncouthe,** strange. **277. dissimulinges,** dissimulations. **278. aperceivinges,** noticing. **280. lustiheed,** gaiety. **282. lete,** leave; **dresse,** prepare. **283. bit,** bids; **hie,** hasten. **285. usshers,** waiters. **289. by day,** day long. **291. woot,** knows. **292. moste,** greatest. **293. mo,** more.

At after soper gooth this noble king
To seen this hors of bras with al a route
Of lordes and of ladies him aboute.
Swich wondring was ther on this hors of bras
That, sin the grete sege of Troye was,
Ther as men wondreden on an hors also,
Ne was ther swich a wondring as was tho.
But finally the king axeth this knight
The vertu of this courser and the might,
And prayed him to telle his governaunce.
This hors anoon bigan to trippe and daunce,
Whan that this knight laide hand upon his reine,
And saide, "Sire, ther is namore to sayne,
But whan you list to riden anywhere,
Ye moten trille a pin, stant in his ere,
Which I shal telle you bitwixe us two.
Ye mote nempne him to what place also
Or to what contree that you list to ride,
And when ye come ther as you list abide,
Bid him descende and trille another pin—
For therin lith th'effect of al the gin—
And he wol down descende and doon youre wille,
And in that place he wol abiden stille
Though al the world the contrarye had yswore:
He shal nat thennes be ydrawe n'ybore.
Or if you liste bidde him thennes goon
Trille this pin, and he wol vanisshe anoon
Out of the sighte of every manere wight,
And come again, be it by day or night,
Whan that you list to clepen him again
In swich a gise as I shal to you sayn
Bitwixen you and me, and that ful soone.
Ride whan you list, ther is namore to doon."

295. route, crowd. **298. sin,** since. **300. tho,** then. **301. axeth,** asks. **302. vertu,** property. **303. his governaunce,** i.e., how to manage him. **307. list,** it pleases. **308. moten,** must; **trille,** turn; **stant,** (that) stands. **310. nempne,** name to. **314. lith,** lies; **effect,** operation; **gin,** device. **318. ydrawe n'ybore,** dragged nor carried. **323. clepen,** call. **324. gise,** way.

Enformed whan the king was of that knight,
And hath conceived in his wit aright
The manere and the forme of al this thing,
Ful glad and blithe this noble doughty king
Repaireth to his revel as biforn.
The bridel is unto the towr yborn
And kept among his jewels leve and dere;
The hors vanisshed, I noot in what manere,
Out of hir sighte; ye gete namore of me,
But thus I lete, in lust and jolitee,
This Cambiuskan his lordes festeyinge
Til wel neigh the day bigan to springe.

PART TWO

The norice of digestioun, the Sleep,
Gan on hem winke and bad hem take keep
That muche drinke and labour wol have reste,
And with a galping mouth hem alle he keste
And saide that it was time to lie adown,
For Blood was in his dominacioun:
"Cherissheth Blood, Natures freend," quod he.
They thanken him, galping, by two, by three,
And every wight gan drawe him to his reste
As Sleep hem bad—they take it for the beste.
Hir dremes shul nat now been told for me:
Ful were hir hedes of fumositee
That causeth dreem of which ther nis no charge.
They sleepen til that it was prime large,
The moste part, but it were Canacee:
She was ful mesurable, as wommen be,

327. of, by. **328. conceived,** comprehended. **331. Repaireth,** returns. **333. leve,** precious. **334. noot,** don't know. **336. lete,** leave; **lust,** pleasure. **337. festeyinge,** feasting. **339. norice,** nurse. **340. keep,** heed. **342. galping,** yawning; **keste,** kissed. **344.** Blood supposedly dominated the body at night. **348. bad,** bade. **349. for,** i.e., by. **350. fumositee,** fumes from alcohol. **351. of . . . charge,** i.e., which has no importance. **352. prime large,** late morning. **353. but it were,** except for. **354. mesurable,** temperate.

For of hir fader hadde she take leve
To goon to reste soone after it was eve;
Hire liste nat appalled° for to be,
Nor on the morwe unfeestlich for to see;°
And slepte hir firste sleep, and thanne awook,
For swich a joye she in hir herte took
Bothe of hir quainte° ring and hir mirour
That twenty time she chaunged hir colour,
And in hir sleep, right for impressioun°
Of hir mirour, she hadde a visioun.°
Wherfore, er that the sonne gan up glide,
She clepte upon hir maistresse° hire biside
And saide that hire liste° for to rise.
  Thise olde wommen that been gladly wise,
As is hir maistresse, answerde hire anoon
And saide, "Madame, whider wol ye goon
Thus erly, for the folk been alle on reste?"
"I wol," quod she, "arise, for me leste°
No lenger° for to sleepe, and walke aboute."
  Hir maistresse clepeth wommen a greet route°
And up they risen, wel a ten or twelve.
Up riseth fresshe Canacee hireselve
As rody° and bright as dooth the yonge sonne
That in the Ram is foure degrees up ronne;°
Noon hyer was he whan she redy was.
And forth she walketh esily a pas,°
Arrayed—after the lusty seson soote°—
Lightly, for to playe and walke on foote,
Nat but with five or sixe of hir meinee,°

357. **liste,** it pleased; **appalled,** made pale. 358. **unfeestlich,** jaded; **see,** i.e., appear. 361. **quainte,** curious. 363. **impressioun,** strong memory. 364. **visioun,** prophetic dream. 366. **clepte,** called; **maistresse,** governess. 367. **liste,** it pleased. 372. **leste,** it would please.. 373. **lenger,** longer. 374. **route,** group. 377. **rody,** brightly complexioned. 378. It is the sixteenth of March, four degrees (or days) after the sun has entered Aries, the Ram, the first Sign of the Zodiac. 379. The sun was no higher than four degrees from the horizon: it was about 6:00 A.M. 380. **a pas,** at a footpace. 381. **after,** in accordance with; **lusty,** pleasant; **soote,** sweet. 383. **meinee,** company.

And in a trench forth in the park gooth she.
  The vapour which that fro the erthe glood
Made the sonne to seeme rody and brood,
But nathelees it was so fair a sighte
That it made al hir hertes for to lighte,
What for the seson and the morweninge,
And for the fowles that she herde singe—
For right anoon she wiste what they mente
Right by hir song, and knew al hir entente.
  The knotte why that every tale is told,
If it be taried til that lust be cold
Of hem that han it after herkned yore,
The savour passeth evere the lenger the more
For fulsomnesse of his prolixitee;
And by this same reson, thinketh me,
I sholde to the knotte condescende
And maken of hir walking soone an ende.
  Amidde a tree for drye as whit as chalk,
As Canacee was playing in hir walk,
Ther sat a faucon over hir heed ful hye
That with a pitous vois so gan to crye
That al the wode resouned of hir cry.
Ybeten hadde she hireself so pitously
With bothe hir winges til the rede blood
Ran endelong the tree ther as she stood;
And evere in oon she cride alway and shrighte,
And with hir beek hireselven so she prighte
That ther nis tigre ne noon so cruel beest
That dwelleth outher in wode or in forest
That nolde han wept if that he weepe coude
For sorwe of hire, she shrighte alway so loude.

384. **trench,** wooded path. 385. **glood,** glided, arose. 386. **rody,** ruddy; **brood,** broad. 389. **morweninge,** morning. 391. **wiste,** knew. 392. **Right,** just. 393. **knotte,** main point. 394. **lust,** desire. 395. **after . . . yore,** been listening for it for a long time. 396. **the . . . more,** more and more. 397. Because of the tediousness of its length. 399. **condescende,** settle down. 401. **drye,** dryness. 406. **Ybeten,** beaten. 408. **endelong,** down along. 409. **in oon,** alike; **shrighte,** shrieked. 410. **prighte,** pricked. 412. **outher,** either.

For ther nas nevere no man yit on live—
If that I coude a faucon wel descrive—
That herde of swich another of fairnesse,
As wel of plumage as of gentilesse
Of shap, of al that mighte yrekened be.
A faucon pergrin thanne seemed she
Of fremde land, and evere more as she stood
She swouned now and now for lak of blood,
Til wel neigh is she fallen fro that tree.
  This faire kinges doughter Canacee
That on hir finger bar the quainte ring
Thurgh which she understood wel every thing
That any fowl may in his ledene sayn,
And coude answere him in his ledene again,
Hath understonden what this faucon saide,
And wel neigh for the routhe almost she deide.
And to the tree she gooth ful hastily
And on this faucon looketh pitously,
And heeld hir lappe abrood, for wel she wiste
The faucon moste fallen fro the twiste
Whan that it swouneth next for lak of blood.
A longe while to waiten hire she stood,
Til at the laste she spak in this manere
Unto the hawk, as ye shul after heere:
  "What is the cause, if it be for to telle,
That ye been in this furial pine of helle?"
Quod Canacee unto this hawk above.
"Is this for sorwe of deeth, or los of love?
For as I trowe thise been causes two
That causen most a gentil herte wo.
Of other harm it needeth nat to speke,
For ye youreself upon youself you wreke,

416. descrive, describe. **420. faucon peregrin,** pilgrim falcon, a type of falcon much used in hawking. **421. fremde,** foreign. **427. ledene,** language. **430. routhe,** pity. **433. lappe abrood,** i.e., skirt out; **wiste,** knew. **434. moste,** must; **twiste,** branch. **440. furial pine,** fury's torment. **443. trowe,** believe. **446. you wreke,** avenge yourself.

Which preveth wel that outher ire or drede
Moot been encheson of youre cruel deede,
Sin that I see noon other wight you chace.
For love of God, as dooth youreselven grace,
Or what may been youre help, for west ne eest
Ne saw I nevere er now no brid ne beest
That ferde with himself so pitously.
Ye sleen me with youre sorwe, verraily:
I have of you so greet compassioun.
For Goddes love, com fro the tree adown.
And as I am a kinges doughter trewe,
If that I verraily the cause knewe
Of youre disese, if it laye in my might,
I wolde amende it er that it were night,
As wisly helpe me grete God of Kinde.
And herbes shal I right ynowe finde
To hele with youre hurtes hastily."
   Tho shrighte this faucon yit more pitously
Than evere she dide, and fel to ground anoon,
And lith aswoune deed, and lik a stoon,
Til Canacee hath in hir lappe hire take
Unto the time she gan of swoune awake.
   And after that she of swough gan abraide
Right in hir hawkes ledene thus she saide:
"That pitee renneth soone in gentil herte,
Feeling his similitude in paines smerte,
Is preved alday, as men may it see
As wel by work as by auctoritee;
For gentil herte kitheth gentilesse.
I see wel that ye han of my distresse
Compassioun, my faire Canacee,

447. preveth, proves; **outher,** either. **448. Moot,** must; **encheson,** cause. **449. Sin,** since. **453. ferde,** behaved. **454. sleen,** slay; **verraily,** truly. **461. wisly,** surely; **Kinde,** nature. **462. ynowe,** enough. **464. shrighte,** shrieked. **466. lith,** lies; **aswoune deed,** in a dead faint. **469. swough,** swooning; **abraide,** come out. **470. ledene,** language. **471. renneth,** i.e., wells up. **472. his,** its. **473. preved,** proved; **alday,** constantly. **474. by work,** i.e., in practice; **auctoritee,** i.e., books. **475. kitheth,** makes known.

Of verray wommanly benignitee
That Nature in youre principles hath set.
But for noon hope for to fare the bet,
But for t'obeye unto youre herte free,
And for to maken othere ywar by me
(As by the whelpe chasted is the leoun),
Right for that cause and that conclusioun,
Whil that I have a leiser and a space,
Myn harm I wol confessen er I pace."
 And evere whil that oon hir sorwe tolde
That other weep as she to water wolde,
Til that the faucon bad hire to be stille,
And with a sik right thus she saide hir wille:
 "Ther I was bred—allas, that ilke day!—
And fostered in a roche of marbel gray
So tendrely that nothing ailed me,
I niste nat what was adversitee,
Til I coude flee ful hye under the sky.
Tho dwelte a tercelet me faste by
That seemed welle of alle gentilesse:
Al were he ful of traison and falsnesse,
It was so wrapped under humble cheere,
And under hewe of trouthe, in swich manere,
Under plesance and under bisy paine,
That no wight wolde han wend he coude feine,
So deepe in grain he dyed his colours:
Right as a serpent hit him under flowres
Til he may see his time for to bite,
Right so this god of loves ypocrite
Dooth so his cerimonies and obeisaunces,

478. verray, true. **479. principles,** innate tendencies. **480. bet,** better. **481. free,** generous. **482. ywar,** wary. **483.** It was believed that if a lion saw a dog being beaten he would draw a lesson concerning his own behavior. **485. leiser,** leisure. **486. pace,** pass. **488. wolde,** i.e., would turn. **490. sik,** sigh. **491. bred,** hatched. **492. roche,** cliff. **494. niste,** didn't know. **495. flee,** fly. **496. Tho,** then; **tercelet,** male falcon. **497. welle,** fountain. **498. Al,** although. **499. cheere,** appearance. **500. hewe,** hue. **501. bisy paine,** assiduousness. **502. wend,** supposed; **feine,** dissemble. **504. hit,** hides. **507. obeisaunces,** acts of homage.

And keepeth in semblaunt° alle his observaunces
That sounen into° gentilesse of love;
As on a tombe is al the faire° above,
And under is the corps, swich as ye woot,°
Swich was this ypocrite bothe cold and hoot.
And in this wise he served° his entente
That, save the Feend, noon wiste° what he mente,
Til he so longe hadde wopen° and complained,
And many a yeer his service to me feined,°
Til that myn herte—too pitous and too nice,°
Al innocent of his crowned° malice,
Forfered of his deeth,° as thoughte me—
Upon his othes and his suretee,°
Graunted him love, on this condicioun:
That everemo myn honour and renown
Were saved, bothe privee and apert;°
This is to sayn, that after° his desert
I yaf him al myn herte and my thought—
God woot, and he, that otherwise nought°—
And took his herte in chaunge of myn for ay.°
But sooth is said, goon sithen° many a day,
A trewe wight and a theef thinketh nat oon.°
And whan he saw the thing so fer° ygoon
That I hadde graunted him fully my love
In swich a gise as I have said above,
And yiven him my trewe herte as free°
As he swoor he yaf his herte to me,
Anoon this tigre, ful of doublenesse,
Fel on his knees with so devout humblesse,
With so heigh reverence and, as by his cheere,°

508. semblaunt, outward appearance. **509. sounen into,** are appropriate for. **510. faire,** fair part. **511. woot,** know. **513. served,** i.e., furthered. **514. Feend,** Devil; **wiste,** knew. **515. wopen,** wept. **516. feined,** pretended. **517. nice,** foolish. **518. crowned,** i.e., consummate. **519. For . . . deeth,** afraid that he would die (for love). **520. suretee,** solemn assurance. **523.** Should be preserved, both privately and publicly. **524. after,** according to. **526. woot,** knows; **that . . . nought,** i.e., in no other way (did I give my heart). **527. ay,** ever. **528. sithen,** since. **529. oon,** the same. **530. fer,** far. **533. free,** freely. **537. cheere,** appearance.

So lik a gentil lovere of manere,
So ravisshed—as it seemed—for the joye,
That nevere Jason ne Paris of Troye—
Jason, certes, ne noon other man
Sin Lameth was that alderfirst bigan
To loven two, as writen folk biforn—
Ne nevere sin the firste man was born
No coude man by twenty thousand part
Countrefete the sophimes of his art,
Ne were worthy unbokele his galoche,
Ther doublenesse of feining sholde approche,
Ne so coude thanke a wight as he dide me.
His manere was an hevene for to see
Til any womman, were she nevere so wis,
So painted he and kembde at point devis
As wel his wordes as his countenauce.
And I so loved him for his obeisaunce,
And for the trouthe I deemed in his herte,
That if so were that any thing him smerte,
Al were it nevere so litel, and I it wiste,
Me thoughte I felte deeth myn herte twiste.
And shortly, so ferforth this thing is went
That my wil was his willes instrument—
This is to sayn, my wil obeyed his wil
In alle thing, as fer as reson fil,
Keeping the boundes of my worshipe evere.
Ne nevere hadde I thing so lief ne levere
As him, God woot, ne nevere shal namo.
This laste lenger than a yeer or two
That I supposed of him nought but good.

540. Jason abandoned both Hypsipyle and Medea; Paris abandoned Oenone for Helen. **542. Sin,** since; **Lameth,** Lamech, the first biblical figure to have two wives; **alderfirst,** first of all. **545–46.** No man could duplicate the twenty-thousandth part of the deceits of his art. **547. unbokele . . . galoche,** unbuckle his boot. **548. feining,** pretense; **approche,** i.e., be the issue. **551. Til,** to. **552. kembde,** combed; **at . . . devis,** carefully. **556. smerte,** smarted. **557. Al,** although; **and,** if; **wiste,** knew. **559. ferforth,** far. **562. reson fil,** i.e., it accorded to reason. **563. worshipe,** honor. **564. lief ne levere,** dear nor dearer. **565. woot,** knows; **namo,** no more. **566. laste,** lasted.

But finally, thus at the laste it stood
That Fortune wolde that he moste twinne°
Out of that place which that I was inne.
Wher° me was wo, that is no questioun;
I can nat make of it descripcioun.
For oo° thing dar I telle boldely:
I knowe what is the paine of deeth therby,
Swich harm I felte for he ne mighte bleve.°
So on a day of me he took his leve
So sorwefully, that I wende verraily°
That he hadde feeled as muche harm as I,
Whan that I herde him speke and saw his hewe.°
But natheless I thoughte he was so trewe
And eek that he repaire° sholde again
Within a litel while, sooth to sayn;
And reson wolde eek that he moste° go
For his honour, as ofte happeth so,
That I made vertu of necessitee
And took it wel, sin° that it moste be.
As I best mighte, I hidde from him my sorwe,
And took him by the hand, Saint John to borwe,°
And saide thus: 'Lo, I am youres al.
Beeth swich as I to you have been and shal.'
What he answerde it needeth nat reherse:
Who can sayn bet° than he? who can doon werse?
Whan he hath al wel said, thanne hath he doon.
Therfore bihoveth hire° a ful long spoon
That shal ete with a feend:° thus herde I saye.
So at the laste he moste forth his waye,
And forth he fleeth° til he cam ther him leste.
Whan it cam him to purpos for to reste,
I trowe° he hadde thilke text in minde

569. moste, must; **twinne,** go away. **571. Wher,** whether. **573. oo,** one. **575. bleve,** remain. **577. wende,** supposed; **verraily,** truly. **579. hewe,** hue. **581. repaire,** return. **583. wolde,** wished, i.e., urged; **moste,** must. **586. sin,** since. **588. Saint . . . borwe,** i.e., making a pledge by St. John. **592. bet,** better. **594. bihoveth hire,** she needs. **595. feend,** devil. **597. fleeth,** flies. **599. trowe,** think.

That alle thing, repairing to his kinde,°
Gladeth himself: thus sayn men; as I gesse,
Men loven of propre kinde° newfangelnesse
As briddes° doon that men in cages feede:
For though thou night and day take of hem heede,
And strawe hir cages faire and softe as silk,
And yive hem sugre, hony, breed, and milk,
Yit right anoon as that his dore is uppe°
He with his feet wol spurne° down his cuppe,
And to the wode he wol, and wormes ete,
So newefangel° been they of hir mete,
And loven novelries° of propre kinde—
No gentilesse of blood may hem binde.
  So ferde° this tercelet, allas the day!
Though he were gentil born and fressh and gay,
And goodlich for to seen, and humble and free,°
He saw upon a time a kite flee,°
And sodeinly he loved this kite so
That al his love is clene fro me ago,
And hath his trouthe falsed in this wise.
Thus hath this kite my love in hir servise,
And I am lorn° withouten remedye."
And with that word this faucon gan to crye
And swouned eft in Canacees barm.°
  Greet was the sorwe for the hawkes harm
That Canacee and alle hir wommen made.
They niste° how they mighte the faucon glade;
But Canacee hoom bereth hire in hir lappe,
And softely in plastres gan hire wrappe
Ther as she with hir beek hadde hurt hireselve.
Now can nat Canacee but herbes delve°

600. repairing, returning; **his kinde,** its nature. **602. propre kinde,** their very nature. **603. briddes,** birds. **607. uppe,** i.e., open. **608. spurne,** kick. **610. newefangel,** novelty-loving. **611. novelries,** novelties. **613. ferde,** behaved. **615. free,** noble. **616. kite,** a lower species of hawk, known for its rapaciousness; **flee,** fly. **621. lorn,** lost. **623. eft,** again; **barm,** lap. **626. niste,** didn't know. **630.** Now Canacee knows how to dig herbs (through the power of her ring).

Out of the ground, and maken saves newe°
Of herbes preciouse and fine of hewe.°
To helen with this hawk fro day to night
She dooth hir bisinesse and al hir might.
And by hir beddes heed she made a mewe°
And covered it with veluettes blewe°
In signe of trouthe that is in wommen seene;
And al withoute the mewe is painted greene,°
In which were painted alle thise false fowles,
As been thise tidives,° tercelets and owls
Right for despit were painted hem biside,
And pies° on hem for to crye and chide.
  Thus lete° I Canacee hir hawk keeping:
I wol namore as now speke of hir ring
Til it come eft° to purpos for to sayn
How that this faucon gat hir love again,
Repentant, as the storye telleth us,
By mediacion of Cambalus,
The kinges sone, of which I you tolde.
But hennesforth I wol my process° holde
To speke of aventures and of batailes,
That nevere yit was herd so grete mervailes.
  First wol I telle you of Cambiuskan
That in his time many a citee wan;°
And after wol I speke of Algarsif,
How that he wan Theodora to his wif—
For whom ful ofte in greet peril he was
Ne hadde he been holpen° by the steede of bras;
And after wol I speke of Cambalo
That fought in listes with the bretheren two
For Canacee, er that he mighte hire winne.
And ther I lefte I wol ayain biginne.

631. saves, salves; **newe,** strange. **632. hewe,** hue. **635. heed,** head; **mewe,** coop. **636. veluettes,** velvets; **blewe,** blue (symbolizing fidelity). **638. greene:** green symbolizes infidelity. **640. tidives:** the tidif was a bird (of unknown species) famed for its loose behavior. **642. pies,** magpies, known for their constant scolding. **643. lete,** leave. **645. eft,** again. **650. proces,** story. **654. wan,** won. **658. Ne . . . he,** had he not; **holpen,** helped.

PART THREE

Appollo whirleth up his chaar° so hye
Til that the god Mercurius hous the slye°—

(Here the tale stops or is stopped.)

THE FRANKLIN'S TALE

The Introduction

"In faith, Squier, thou hast thee wel yquit°
And gentilly. I praise wel thy wit,"
Quod the Frankelain. "Considering thy youthe,
So feelingly thou spekest, sire, I allowe° thee:
As to my doom° ther is noon that is heer
Of eloquence that shal be thy peer,
If that thou live. God yive thee good chaunce,
And in vertu sende thee continuaunce,
For of thy speeche I have greet daintee.°
I have a sone, and by the Trinitee,
I hadde levere than twenty pound worth land,
Though it right now were fallen° in myn hand,
He were a man of swich discrecioun
As that ye been. Fy on possessioun
But if° a man be vertuous withal!
I have my sone snibbed° and yit shal
For he to vertu listeth nat entende,°
But for to playe at dees and to dispende,°

663. chaar, chariot. **664.** Till the house (astrological mansion) of the sly god Mercury.

1. yquit, acquitted. **4. allowe,** praise. **5. doom,** judgment. **9. daintee,** delight. **12. fallen,** i.e., delivered. **15. But if,** unless. **16. snibbed,** scolded. **17. entende,** attend. **18. dees,** dice; **dispende,** spend money.

And lese° al that he hath is his usage.
And he hath levere talken with a page
Than to commune with any gentil wight,
Where he mighte lerne gentilesse° aright."
"Straw for youre gentilesse!" quod oure Host.
"What, Frankelain, pardee sire, wel thou woost
That eech of you moot tellen atte leeste
A tale or two, or breken his biheeste."°
"That knowe I wel, sire," quod the Frankelain.
"I praye you, haveth me nat in desdain,
Though to this man I speke a word or two."
"Tel on thy tale withouten wordes mo."
"Gladly, sire Host," quod he, "I wol obeye
Unto youre wil. Now herkneth what I saye.
I wol you nat contrarien° in no wise
As fer as that my wittes wol suffise.
I praye to God that it may plesen you:
Thanne woot I wel that it is good ynow."°

The Prologue

Thise olde gentil Britons° in hir dayes
Of diverse aventures maden layes,
Rymeyed° in hir firste Briton tonge;
Whiche layes with hir instruments they songe,°
Or elles redden° hem for hir plesaunce;
And oon of hem have I in remembraunce,
Which I shal sayn with good wil as I can.
But sires, by cause I am a burel° man,
At my biginning first I you biseeche
Have me excused of my rude speeche.
I lerned nevere retorike,° certain:
Thing that I speke it moot be bare and plain;

19. lese, lose. **22. gentilesse,** gentility. **26. biheeste,** promise. **33. contrarien,** act contrary to. **36. ynow,** enough.

1. Britons, Bretons. **3. Rymeyed,** composed in rhyme. **4. songe,** sung. **5. redden,** read. **8. burel,** ignorant. **11. retorike,** rhetoric.

I sleep nevere in the Mount of Parnaso,°
Ne lerned Marcus Tullius Scithero;°
Colours ne knowe I noon, withouten drede,°
But swiche colours as growen in the mede,°
Or elles swiche as men dye or painte;
Colours of retorike been too quainte:°
My spirit feeleth nat of swich matere.
But if you list, my tale shul ye heere.

The Tale

In Armorik, that called is Britaine,°
Ther was a knight that loved and dide his paine°
To serve a lady in his beste wise;
And many a labour, many a greet emprise°
He for his lady wroughte er she were wonne,
For she was oon° the faireste under sonne,
And eek therto come of so heigh kinrede°
That wel unnethes° dorste this knight for drede
Telle hire his wo, his paine, and his distresse.
But atte laste she for his worthinesse,
And namely for his meeke obeisaunce,°
Hath swich a pitee caught of his penaunce°
That prively she fil of° his accord
To taken him for hir housbonde and hir lord,
Of swich lordshipe as men han over hir wives.
And for to lede the more in blisse hir lives,
Of his free wil he swoor hire as a knight
That nevere in al his lif he day ne night
Ne sholde upon him take no maistrye°

13. sleep, slept; **Parnaso,** Parnassus, home of the Muses. **14. Scithero,** Cicero. **15. colours,** i.e., rhetorical figures; **drede,** doubt. **16. mede,** meadow. **18. quainte,** unfamiliar. **21. Armorik,** Armorica; **Britaine,** Brittany. **22. dide paine,** i.e., made every effort, **24. emprise,** enterprise. **26. oon,** i.e., one of. **27. kinrede,** kindred. **28. unnethes,** with difficulty. **31. obeisaunce,** obedience. **32. penaunce,** suffering. **33. fil of,** i.e., fell in. **39. maistrye,** dominion.

Again hir wil, ne kithe° hire jalousye,
But hire obeye and folwe hir wil in al,
As any lovere to his lady shal°—
Save that the name of sovereinetee°,
That wolde he have, for shame of° his degree.
  She thanked him, and with ful greet humblesse
She saide, "Sire, sith of youre gentilesse
Ye profre me to have so large° a reine,
Ne wolde nevere God bitwixe us twaine,
As in my gilt, were outher werre° or strif.
Sire, I wol be your humble, trewe wif—
Have heer my trouthe—til that myn herte breste."°
Thus been they bothe in quiete and in reste.
  For oo thing, sires, saufly° dar I saye:
That freendes° everich other moot obeye,
If they wol longe holden compaignye.
Love wol nat be constrained by maistrye:
Whan maistrye comth, the God of Love anoon
Beteth his winges and farewel, he is goon!
Love is a thing as any spirit free;
Wommen of kinde° desiren libertee,
And nat to been constrained as a thral°—
And so doon men, if I sooth sayen shal.
Looke who that is most pacient in love,
He is at his avantage al above.
Pacience is an heigh vertu, certain,
For it venquissheth°, as thise clerkes sayn,
Thinges that rigour sholde nevere attaine°.
For every word men may nat chide or plaine:°
Lerneth to suffre, or elles, so mote I goon°,
Ye shul it lerne, wherso° ye wol or noon.

40. kithe, show. **42. shal,** ought. **43. sovereinetee,** sovereignty. **44. for . . . of,** out of respect for. **47. large,** i.e., free. **49. As in,** as a result of; **outher,** either; **werre,** war. **51. trouthe,** troth, word of honor; **breste,** break. **53. saufly,** safely. **54. freendes,** lovers. **60. of kinde,** by nature. **61. thral,** slave. **66. venquissheth,** vanquishes. **67. attaine,** i.e., overcome. **68. For,** at; **plaine,** complain. **69. so . . . goon,** so may I walk. **70. wherso,** whether.

For in this world, certain, ther no wight is
That he ne dooth or saith somtime amis:
Ire, siknesse, or constellacioun,°
Win, wo, or chaunging of complexioun°
Causeth ful ofte to doon amis or speken.
On every wrong a man may nat be wreken:°
After the time moste be temperaunce
To every wight that can on governaunce.°
And therfore hath this wise worthy knight
To live in ese suffrance hire bihight,°
And she to him ful wisly gan to swere
That nevere sholde ther be defaute° in here.
  Here may men seen an humble wis accord:
Thus hath she take hir servant and hir lord—
Servant in love and lord in mariage.
Thanne was he bothe in lordshipe and servage.°
Servage? Nay, but in lordshipe above,
Sith he hath bothe his lady and his love;
His lady, certes, and his wif also,
The which that° lawe of love accordeth to.
And whan he was in this prosperitee,
Hoom with his wif he gooth to his contree,
Nat fer fro Pedmark° ther his dwelling was,
Wher as he liveth in blisse and in solas.°
  Who coude telle but he hadde wedded be
The joye, the ese, and the prosperitee
That is bitwixe an housbonde and his wif?
A yeer and more lasted this blisful lif,
Til that the knight of which I speke of thus,
That of Kairrud° was cleped Arveragus,
Shoop him° to goon and dwelle a yeer or twaine
In Engelond, that cleped was eek Britaine,

73. constellacioun, i.e., planetary influences. **74. complexioun,** the balance of humors in the body. **76. wreken,** avenged. **78. can . . . governaunce,** is capable of self-control. **80. suffrance,** toleration; **bihight,** promised. **82. defaute,** defect. **86. servage,** position of a servant. **90. The . . . that,** as. **93. Pedmark,** Penmarch in Brittany. **94. solas,** delight. **100. Kairrud,** Kerru, a town in Brittany. **101. Shoop him,** prepared.

To seeke in armes worshipe and honour—
For al his lust° he sette in swich labour—
And dwelled ther two yeer, the book saith thus.
  Now wol I stinte° of this Arveragus,
And speke I wol of Dorigen his wif,
That loveth hir housbonde as hir hertes lif.
For his absence weepeth she and siketh,°
As doon thise noble wives whan hem liketh.°
She moorneth, waketh, waileth, fasteth, plaineth;°
Desir of his presence hire so distraineth°
That al this wide world she sette° at nought.
Hir freendes, whiche that knewe hir hevy thought,
Conforten hire in al that evere they may:
They prechen hire, they telle hire night and day
That causelees she sleeth° hirself, allas;
And every confort possible in this cas
They doon to hire with al hir bisinesse,°
Al for to make hire leve hir hevinesse.
  By proces,° as ye knowen everichoon,
Men may so longe graven° in a stoon
Til som figure therinne emprinted be:
So longe han they conforted hire til she
Received hath, by hope and by resoun,
The emprinting of hir consolacioun,
Thurgh which hir grete sorwe gan assuage:
She may nat alway duren in swich rage.°
  And eek Arveragus in al this care
Hath sent hir lettres hoom of his welfare,
And that he wol come hastily again—
Or elles hadde this sorwe hir herte slain.
Hir freendes sawe hir sorwe gan to slake,°
And prayed hire on knees, for Goddes sake,
To come and romen hire in compaignye,

104. lust, pleasure. **106. stinte,** cease. **109. siketh,** sighs. **110. liketh,** it pleases. **111. plaineth,** complains. **112. distraineth,** afflicts. **113. sette,** i.e., valued. **117. sleeth,** slays. **119. bisinesse,** assiduousness. **121. proces,** course of time. **122. graven,** engrave. **128. duren,** remain; **rage,** passion. **133. slake,** diminish.

Away to drive hir derke fantasye,
And finally she graunted that requeste:
For wel she saw that it was for the beste.
  Now stood hir castel faste by the see,
And often with hir freendes walketh she,
Hire to disporte upon the bank an heigh,
Wher as she many a ship and barge seigh,°
Sailing hir cours wher as hem liste go—
But thanne was that a parcel° of hir wo,
For of hirself ful ofte, "Allas!" saith she,
"Is ther no ship of so manye as I see
Wol bringen hoom my lord? Thanne were myn herte
Al warisshed° of his bittre paines smerte."
  Another time ther wolde she sitte and thinke,
And caste hir yën downward fro the brinke;
But whan she sawgh the grisly rokkes blake,
For verray fere so wolde hir herte quake
That on hir feet she mighte hire nat sustene:°
Thanne wolde she sitte adown upon the greene
And pitously into the see biholde,
And sayn right thus, with sorweful sikes colde:°
  "Eterne God that thurgh thy purveyaunce°
Ledest the world by certain governaunce,
In idel,° as men sayn, ye nothing make:
But Lord, thise grisly feendly° rokkes blake,
That seemen rather a foul confusioun
Of werk, than any fair creacioun
Of swich a parfit wis God and a stable,
Why han ye wrought this werk unresonable?
For by this werk south, north, ne west ne eest,
Ther nis yfostred man ne brid° ne beest:
It dooth no good, to my wit, but anoyeth.
See ye nat, Lord, how mankinde it destroyeth?

142. barge, vessel; **seigh,** saw. **144. parcel,** component. **148. warisshed,** recovered. **153. sustene,** sustain. **156. sikes,** sighs; **colde,** i.e., grievous. **157. purveyaunce,** providence. **159. In idel,** i.e., without purpose. **160. feendly,** hostile. **166. yfostred,** fed; **brid,** bird.

An hundred thousand bodies of mankinde
Han rokkes slain, al be they nat in minde:
Which mankinde is so fair part of thy werk
That thou it madest lik to thyn owene merk;°
Thanne seemed it ye hadde a greet cheertee°
Toward mankinde. But how thanne may it be
That ye swiche menes° make it to destroyen?—
Whiche menes do no good, but evere anoyen.
I woot wel clerkes wol sayn as hem leste,°
By arguments, that al is for the beste,
Though I ne can the causes nat yknowe.
But thilke God that made wind to blowe,
As keepe my lord! This° my conclusioun.
To clerkes lete I al disputisoun,°
But wolde God that alle thise rokkes blake
Were sonken° into helle for his sake!
Thise rokkes slain myn herte for the fere."
Thus wolde she sayn with many a pitous tere.
  Hir freendes sawe that it was no disport
To romen by the see, but disconfort,
And shopen° for to playen somwher elles:
They leden hire by rivers and by welles,°
And eek in othere places delitables;°
They dauncen and they playen at ches and tables.°
  So on a day, right in the morwetide,°
Unto a gardin that was ther biside,
In which that they hadde maad hir ordinaunce°
Of vitaile and of other purveyaunce,°
They goon and playe hem al the longe day.
And this was on the sixte morwe° of May,
Which May had painted with his softe showres
This gardin ful of leves and of flowres;

172. **merk,** mark, i.e., image. 173. **cheertee,** affection. 175. **menes,** means. 177. **leste,** may please. 181. **This,** i.e., this is. 182. **lete,** leave; **disputisoun,** disputation. 184. **sonken,** sunken. 189. **shopen,** arranged. 190. **welles,** springs. 191. **delitables,** delightful. 192. **tables,** backgammon. 193. **morwetide,** morning. 195. **ordinaunce,** arrangements. 196. **vitaile,** food; **purveyaunce,** provisions. 198. **morwe,** morning.

And craft of mannes hand so curiously
Arrayed hadde this gardin trewely
That nevere was ther gardin of swich pris,
But if it were the verray Paradis.
The odour of flowres and the fresshe sighte
Wolde han maked any herte lighte
That evere was born, but if too greet siknesse,
Or too greet sorwe heeld it in distresse,
So ful it was of beautee with plesaunce.
At after-diner gonne they to daunce,
And singe also, save Dorigen allone,
Which made alway hir complainte and hir mone,
For she ne sawgh him on the daunce go
That was hir housbonde and hir love also.
But nathelees she moste a time abide,
And with good hope lete hir sorwe slide.
Upon this daunce, amonges othere men,
Daunced a squier bifore Dorigen
That fressher was and jolier of array,
As to my doom, than is the month of May.
He singeth, daunceth, passing any man
That is or was sith that the world bigan.
Therwith he was, if men him sholde descrive,
Oon of the beste-faring man on live:
Yong, strong, right vertuous, and riche and wis,
And wel-biloved, and holden in greet pris.
And shortly, if the soothe I tellen shal,
Unwiting of this Dorigen at al,
This lusty squier, servant to Venus,
Which that ycleped was Aurelius,
Hadde loved hire best of any creature
Two yeer and more, as was his aventure,
But nevere dorste he tellen hire his grevaunce:
Withouten coppe he drank al his penaunce.

201. curiously, skilfully. **203. pris,** excellence. **212. mone,** moan. **219. jolier,** gayer. **220. doom,** judgment. **221. passing,** surpassing. **223. descrive,** describe. **224. beste-faring,** handsomest. **226. pris,** repute. **228. Unwiting of,** unknown to. **234. coppe,** cup; **penaunce,** suffering: i.e., he suffered in silence.

He was despaired, no thing dorste he saye—
Save in his songes somwhat wolde he wraye
His wo, as in a general complaining:
He saide he loved and was biloved no thing;
Of which matere made he manye layes,
Songes, complaintes, roundels, virelayes,
How that he dorste nat his sorwe telle,
But languissheth as a furye dooth in helle;
And die he moste, he saide, as dide Ekko
For Narcisus that dorste nat telle hir wo.
In other manere than ye heere me saye
Ne dorste he nat to hire his wo biwraye,
Save that paraventure som time at daunces,
Ther yonge folk keepen hir observaunces,
It may wel be he looked on hir face
In swich a wise as man that asketh grace;
But no thing wiste she of his entente.
Nathelees it happed, er they thennes wente,
By cause that he was hir neighebour,
And was a man of worshipe and honour,
And hadde yknowen him of time yore,
They fille in speeche, and forth more and more
Unto his purpos drow Aurelius,
And whan he sawgh his time, he saide thus:
  "Madame," quod he, "by God that this world made,
So that I wiste it mighte youre herte glade,
I wolde that day that youre Arveragus
Wente over the see that I, Aurelius,
Hadde went ther nevere I sholde have come again.
For wel I woot my service is in vain:
My gerdon is but bresting of myn herte.
Madame, reweth upon my paines smerte,

236. wraye, disclose. **238. no thing,** not at all. **243–44.** Echo was unable to communicate her love for Narcissus and eventually died in despair. **246. biwraye,** disclose. **247. paraventure,** perchance. **248. keepen . . . observaunces,** carry on their rituals. **252. thennes,** thence. **255. hadde,** i.e., she had; **yore,** long past. **256. fille,** fell. **257. drow,** drew. **260. wiste,** knew; **glade,** gladden. **265. gerdon,** reward; **bresting,** breaking. **266. reweth,** have pity on.

For with a word ye may me slee° or save.
Here at youre feet God wolde that I were grave!°
I ne have as now no leiser more to saye:
Have mercy, sweete, or ye wol do° me deye."
  She gan to looke upon Aurelius:
"Is this youre wil?" quod she, "and saye ye thus?
Nevere erst,"° quod she, "ne wiste I what ye mente.
But now, Aurelie, I knowe youre entente,
By thilke God that yaf me soule and lif,
Ne shal I nevere been untrewe wif,
In word ne werk, as fer as I have wit.
I wol be his to whom that I am knit:°
Take this for final answere as of me."
But after that in play thus saide she:
  "Aurelie," quod she, "by hye God above,
Yit wolde I graunte you to been youre love,
Sin I you see so pitously complaine,
Looke what day that endelong° Britaine
Ye remeve° alle the rokkes, stoon by stoon,
That they ne lette ship ne boot° to goon.
I saye, whan ye han maad the coost so clene
Of rokkes that ther nis no stoon yseene,
Thanne wol I love you best of any man—
Have heer my trouthe—in al that evere I can.
For wel I woot that it shal nevere bitide.
Lat swiche folies out of youre herte slide!
What daintee° sholde a man han by his lif
For to love another mannes wif,
That hath hir body whan so that him liketh?"°
  Aurelius ful ofte sore siketh:°
  "Is ther noon other grace in you?" quod he.
  "No, by that Lord," quod she, "that maked me."
Wo was Aurelie whan that he this herde,
And with a sorweful herte he thus answerde.

267. slee, slay. **268. grave,** buried. **270. do,** make. **273. erst,** before. **278. knit,** joined. **284. endelong,** along. **285. remeve,** remove. **286. lette,** hinder; **boot,** boat. **293. daintee,** delight. **295. liketh,** it pleases. **296. siketh,** sighs.

"Madame," quod he, "this were an impossible.
Thanne moot I die of sodein deeth horrible."
And with that word he turned him anoon.
Tho come hir othere freendes many oon,
And in the aleyes° romeden up and down,
And no thing wiste of this conclusioun,
But sodeinly bigonne revel newe,
Til that the brighte sonne loste his hewe,
For th'orisonte hath reft° the sonne his light—
This is as muche to saye as it was night.
And hoom they goon in joye and in solas,°
Save only wrecche° Aurelius, allas.
He to his hous is goon with sorweful herte;
He seeth he may nat from his deeth asterte;°
Him seemed that he felte his herte colde;
Up to the hevene his handes he gan holde,
And on his knees bare he sette him down,
And in his raving saide his orisoun.
For verray wo out of his wit he braide;°
He niste° what he spak, but thus he saide;
With pitous herte his plainte° hath he bigonne
Unto the goddes, and first unto the sonne:
He saide, "Appollo, god and governour
Of every plaunte, herbe, tree, and flowr,
That yivest after thy declinacioun°
To eech of hem his time and his sesoun,
As thyn herberwe° chaungeth, lowe or hye;
Lord Phebus, cast thy merciable° yë
On wrecche Aurelie which that am but lorn.°
Lo, lord, my lady hath my deeth ysworn
Withouten gilt, but° thy benignitee
Upon my deedly herte have som pitee;

305. aleyes, paths. **309. orisonte,** horizon; **reft,** deprived of. **311. solas,** delight. **312. wrecche,** wretched. **314. asterte,** escape. **319. braide,** went. **320. niste,** knew not. **321. plainte,** lament. **325. after,** according to; **declinacioun,** i.e., position in the sky. **327. herberwe,** lodging, i.e., the astrological houses in which the planets reside in alternation. **328. merciable,** merciful. **329. lorn,** lost. **331. but,** unless.

For wel I woot, lord Phebus, if you lest,
Ye may me helpen, save my lady, best.
Now voucheth sauf that I may you devise
How that I may been holpe, and in what wise:
  Youre blisful suster, Lucina the sheene,
That of the see is chief goddesse and queene—
Though Neptunus have deitee in the see,
Yit emperisse aboven him is she—
Ye knowen wel, lord, that right as hir desir
Is to be quiked and lighted of youre fir,
For which she folweth you ful bisily,
Right so the see desireth naturelly
To folwen hire, as she that is goddesse
Bothe in the see and rivers more and lesse;
Wherfore, lord Phebus, this is my requeste:
Do this miracle—or do myn herte breste—
That now next at this opposicioun,
Which in the signe shal be of the Leoun,
As prayeth hire so greet a flood to bringe
That five fadme at the leeste it overspringe
The hyeste rok in Armorik Britaine;
And lat this flood endure yeres twaine:
Thanne certes to my lady may I saye,
'Holdeth youre heeste, the rokkes been awaye.'
  Lord Phebus, dooth this miracle for me!
Praye hire she go no faster cours than ye—
I saye this, prayeth youre suster that she go
No faster cours than ye thise yeres two:
Thanne shal she been evene at the fulle alway,
And spring-flood lasten bothe night and day.
And but she vouche sauf in swich manere

333. **lest,** it pleases. 334. Except for my lady, you may help me best. 335. **devise,** describe. 336. **holpe,** helped. 337. **Lucina,** i.e., Diana, the moon; **sheene,** bright. 340. **emperisse,** empress. 342. **quiked,** quickened. 343. **bisily,** constantly. 348. **do,** make; **breste,** break. 349. **opposicioun,** the position of the sun and moon when they are at a 180° angle from one another as seen from the earth. 352. **fadme,** fathoms; **overspringe,** overrun. 356. **heeste,** promise. 363. **but,** unless.

To graunte me my soverein lady dere,
Praye hire to sinken every rok adown
Into hir owene derke regioun
Under the ground ther Pluto dwelleth inne,
Or nevere mo shal I my lady winne.
Thy temple in Delphos wol I barefoot seeke.
Lord Phebus, see the teres on my cheeke,
And of my paine have som compassioun."
And with that word in swoune he fil adown,
And longe time he lay forth in a traunce.
His brother, which that knew of his penaunce,
Up caughte him, and to bedde he hath him brought.
Despaired in this torment and this thought
Lete I this woful creature lie—
Chese he for me wher he wol live or die.
Arveragus with hele and greet honour,
As he that was of chivalrye the flowr,
Is comen hoom, and othere worthy men:
O, blisful artou now, thou Dorigen,
That hast thy lusty housbonde in thine armes,
The fresshe knight, the worthy man of armes,
That loveth thee as his owene hertes lif.
No thing list him to been imaginatif
If any wight hadde spoke whil he was oute
To hire of love; he ne hadde of it no doute:
He nought entendeth to no swich matere,
But daunceth, justeth, maketh hire good cheere.
And thus in joye and blisse I lete hem dwelle,
And of the sike Aurelius wol I telle.
In langour and in torment furious
Two yeer and more lay wrecche Aurelius,
Er any foot he mighte on erthe goon,
Ne confort in this time hadde he noon,
Save of his brother, which that was a clerk:

365. hire, i.e., Diana in her capacity as goddess of the underworld. **369. Delphos,** Delphi. **372. swoune,** swoon; **fil,** fell. **374. penaunce,** pain. **377. Lete,** leave. **378. Chese,** let him choose; **wher,** whether. **379. hele,** prosperity. **389. entendeth,** pays attention. **390. justeth,** jousts.

He knew of al this wo and al this werk,
For to noon other creature, certain,
Of this matere he dorste no word sayn.
Under his brest he bar it more secree
Than evere dide Pamphilus for Galathee.
His brest was hool withoute for to seene,
But in his herte ay was the arwe keene;
And wel ye knowe that of a sursanure
In surgerye is perilous the cure,
But men mighte touche the arwe or come therby.
His brother weep and wailed prively,
Til at the laste him fil in remembrance
That whiles he was at Orliens in France,
As yonge clerkes that been likerous
To reden artes that been curious,
Seeken in every halke and every herne
Particuler sciences for to lerne,
He him remembred that, upon a day,
At Orliens in studye a book he sey
Of magik naturel, which his felawe,
That was that time a bacheler of lawe—
Al were he ther to lerne another craft—
Hadde prively upon his desk ylaft:
Which book spak muchel of the operaciouns
Touching the eighte and twenty mansiouns
That longen to the moone—and swich folye
As in oure dayes is nat worth a flye,
For holy chirches faith in oure bileve
Ne suffreth noon illusion us to greve.
And whan this book was in his remembraunce,

401. secree, secret. **402.** Pamphilus and Galataea are the lovers in the medieval Latin *Pamphilus de Amore*. **403. withoute,** outwardly. **405. sursanure,** superficially healed wound. **407. But,** unless. **408. weep,** wept. **409. him . . . remembraunce,** i.e., he happened to remember. **410. Orliens,** Orleans. **411. likerous,** desirous. **412. reden artes,** study subjects; **curious,** occult. **413. every . . . herne,** every nook and cranny. **414. Particuler,** out of the way. **416. sey,** saw. **417. naturel,** natural magic employs astrological knowledge rather than spirits. **419. Al . . . he,** although he was. **420. ylaft,** left. **422. mansiouns,** i.e., daily positions. **423. longen,** belong. **425. bileve,** creed.

Anoon for joye his herte gan to daunce,
And to himself he saide prively,
"My brother shal be warisshed° hastily,
For I am siker° that ther be sciences
By whiche men make diverse apparences,°
Swiche as thise subtile tregettoures° playe;
For ofte at feestes have I wel herd saye
That tregettours withinne an halle large
Have maad come in a water and a barge,°
And in the halle rowen up and down;
Som time hath seemed come a grim leoun;
Som time flowres springe° as in a mede;
Som time a vine and grapes white and rede;
Som time a castel al of lim° and stoon—
And whan hem liked voided° it anoon:
Thus seemed it to every mannes sighte.
  Now thanne conclude I thus: that if I mighte
At Orliens som old felawe yfinde
That hadde thise moones mansions in minde,
Or other magik naturel above,
He sholde wel make my brother han his love.
For with an apparence a clerk may make
To mannes sighte that alle the rokkes blake
Of Britaine were yvoided everichoon,
And shippes by the brinke comen and goon,
And in swich forme enduren a day or two:
Thanne were my brother warisshed° of his wo;
Thanne moste she needes holden hir biheeste,°
Or elles he shal shame hire at the leeste."
  What sholde I make a lenger tale of this?
Unto his brotheres bed he comen is,
And swich confort he yaf him for to goon
To Orliens, that up he sterte° anoon,
And on his way forthward thanne is he fare,

430. warisshed, cured. **431. siker,** sure. **432. apparences,** apparitions. **433. tregettoures,** magicians. **436. barge,** ship. **439. springe,** grow. **441. lim,** lime. **442. voided,** caused to disappear. **454. warisshed,** cured. **455. biheeste,** promise. **460. sterte,** started.

In hope for to been lissed° of his care.
  Whan they were come almost to that citee,
But if it were a two furlong or three,
A yong clerk roming by himself they mette,
Which that in Latin thriftily hem grette,°
And after that he saide a wonder thing:
"I knowe," quod he, "the cause of your coming."
And er they ferther any foote wente,
He tolde hem al that was in hir entente.
  This Briton clerk him axed° of felawes,
The whiche that he hadde knowe in olde dawes,°
And he answerde him that they dede° were;
For which he weep° ful ofte many a tere.
  Down of his hors Aurelius lighte anoon,
And with this magicien forth is he goon
Hoom to his hous, and maden hem wel at ese:
Hem lakked no vitaile that mighte hem plese;
So wel arrayed hous as ther was oon
Aurelius in his lif saw nevere noon.
  He shewed him er he wente to soper
Forestes, parkes ful of wilde deer:
Ther saw he hertes° with hir hornes hye,
The gretteste° that evere were seen with yë;
He sawgh of hem an hundred slain with houndes,
And some with arwes bledde of bittre woundes.
  He saw, when voided° were thise wilde deer,
Thise fauconers° upon a fair river,
That with hir hawkes han the heron slain.
  Tho sawgh he knightes justing° in a plain.
And after this he dide him this plesaunce,
That he him shewed his lady on a daunce—
On which himself he daunced, as him thoughte.
And whan this maister that this magik wroughte

462. lissed, assuaged. **466. thriftily,** properly; **greete,** greeted. **471. axed,** asked. **472. dawes,** days. **473. dede,** dead. **474. weep,** wept. **483. hertes,** harts. **484. gretteste,** greatest. **487. voided,** made to disappear. **488 fauconers,** falconers. **490. justing,** jousting.

Sawgh it was time, he clapte his handes two,
And farewel, al oure revel was ago.
And yit remeved they nevere out of the hous
Whil they sawe al this sighte merveilous,
But in his studye, ther as his bookes be,
They sitten stille, and no wight but they three.
To him this maister called his squier
And saide him thus, "Is redy oure soper?
Almost an houre it is, I undertake,
Sith I you bad oure soper for to make,
Whan that thise worthy men wenten with me
Into my studye, ther as my bookes be."
"Sire," quod this squier, "whan it liketh you,
It is al redy, though ye wol right now."
"Go we thanne soupe," quod he, "as for the beste:
This amorous folk som time mote han hir reste."
At after-soper fille they in tretee
What somme sholde this maistres gerdon be
To remeven alle the rokkes of Britaine,
And eek from Gerounde to the mouth of Seine:
He made it straunge, and swoor, so God him save,
Lasse than a thousand pound he wolde nat have,
Ne gladly for that somme he wolde nat goon.
Aurelius with blisful herte anoon
Answerde thus, "Fy on a thousand pound!
This wide world, which that men saye is round,
I wolde it yive, if I were lord of it.
This bargain is ful drive, for we been knit.
Ye shal be payed trewely, by my trouthe.
But looketh now, for no necligence or slouthe,
Ye tarye us heer no lenger than tomorwe."
"Nay," quod this clerk, "have heer my faith to borwe."
To bedde is goon Aurelius whan him leste,

497. remeved, moved. **511. fille,** fell; **tretee,** negotiation. **512. somme,** sum; **gerdon,** reward. **514. Gerounde,** the Gironde river. **515. it straunge,** i.e., difficulties. **516. Lasse,** less. **522. ful drive,** fully made; **knit,** i.e., at accord. **524. slouthe,** sloth. **526. to borwe,** as a pledge.

And wel neigh al that night he hadde his reste:
What for his labour and his hope of blisse,
His woful herte of penance hadde a lisse.°
  Upon the morwe, whan that it was day,
To Britaine tooke they the righte° way,
Aurelius and this magicien biside,
And been descended ther they wolde abide;
And this was, as thise bookes me remembre,°
The colde frosty seson of Decembre.
  Phebus wax old, and hewed lik latoun,°
That in his hote declinacioun°
Shoon as the burned gold with stremes° brighte;
But now in Capricorn° adown he lighte,
Wher as he shoon ful pale, I dar wel sayn:
The bittre frostes with the sleet and rain
Destroyed hath the greene in every yeerd.°
Janus sit° by the fir with double beerd,
And drinketh of his bugle horn° the win;
Biforn him stant brawn° of the tusked swin,
And "Nowel!" crieth every lusty man.
  Aurelius in al that evere he can
Dooth to this maister cheere and reverence,
And prayeth him to doon his diligence
To bringen him out of his paines smerte,
Or with a swerd that he wolde slitte his herte.°
  This subtil clerk swich routhe° hadde of this man
That night and day he spedde him° that he can
To waiten a time of his conclusioun°—
This is to sayn, to make illusioun
By swich an apparence or jogelrye°

530. penaunce, suffering; **lisse,** alleviation. **532. righte,** direct. **535. remembre,** recall to. **537. wax,** grew; **hewed,** colored; **latoun,** brass. **538. declinacioun,** i.e., celestial position. **539. burned,** burnished; **stremes,** beams. **540. Capricorn,** the House of the Goat. **543. yeerd,** yard. **544. Janus,** the two-headed god who looks both back and forward, perpetuated in the name January; **sit,** sits. **545. bugle horn,** wild ox horn. **546. stant,** stands; **brawn** flesh. **552. slitte . . . herte,** i.e., stab his own heart. **553. routhe,** pity. **554. spedde him,** hurried. **555.** To watch for a time for his astrological operation. **557. apparence,** apparition; **jogelrye,** optical illusion.

(I ne can no termes of astrologye)
That she and every wight sholde weene and saye
That of Britaine the rokkes were awaye,
Or elles they were sonken under grounde.
So at the laste he hath his time yfounde
To maken his japes and his wrecchednesse
Of swich a supersticious cursednesse.
His tables tolletanes forth hath he brought,
Ful wel corrected; ne ther lakked nought,
Neither his collect ne his expans yeres,
Ne his rootes, ne his othere geres,
As been his centres and his arguments,
And his proporcionels convenients,
For his equacions in every thing;
And by his eighte spere in his werking
He knew ful wel how fer Alnath was shove
Fro the heed of thilke fixe Aries above
That in the ninte spere considered is:
Ful subtilly he calculed al this.
  When he hadde founde his firste mansioun,
He knew the remenant by proporcioun,
And knew the arising of his moone weel,
And in whos face and terme and every deel,
And knew ful wel the moones mansioun

558. can, know. **563. japes,** tricks; **wrecchednesse,** miserable performance. **564. cursednesse,** wickedness. **565. tables tolletanes,** astronomical tables based on the latitude of Toledo. **567.** Neither his table of collect years nor his table of expanse years: the former recorded planetary movements for long periods such as twenty years, the latter for short periods of a year. **568. rootes,** tables for making astrological propositions concerning planetary position, degrees of influence, etc.; **geres,** paraphernalia. **569. centres, arguments,** astronomical instruments for determining the positions of planets in relation to fixed stars. **570. proporcionels convenients,** fitting proportionals, i.e., special tables for scaling down more general planetary motions to the most particular. **572. spere,** sphere: i.e., the sphere of the fixed stars; **werking,** operation. **573. Alnath,** the star Arietes; **was shove,** had moved. **574–75.** From the head of that fixed star Aries which is considered to be above, in the ninth sphere. **576. calculed,** calculated. **577. firste mansioun,** the first position of the moon. **578. remenant,** rest of the positions; **proporcioun,** the use of proportion. **580. face, terme,** sectors of the signs of the zodiac.

Accordant to his operacioun,
And knew also his othere observaunces
For swiche illusions and swiche meschaunces
As hethen folk useden in thilke dayes;
For which no lenger maked he delayes,
But, thurgh his magik, for a wike or twaye
It seemed that alle the rokkes were awaye.
  Aurelius, which that yit despaired is
Wher he shal han his love or fare amis,
Awaiteth night and day on this miracle;
And whan he knew that there was noon obstacle,
That voided were thise rokkes everichoon,
Down to his maistres feet he fil anoon,
And saide, "I, woful wrecche Aurelius,
Thanke you, lord, and lady myn Venus,
That me han holpen fro my cares colde."
And to the temple his way forth hath he holde,
Wher as he knew he sholde his lady see.
And whan he saw his time, anoon right he,
With dredful herte and with ful humble cheere,
Salued hath his soverein lady dere.
  "My righte lady," quod this woful man,
"Whom I most drede and love as best I can,
And lothest were of al this world displese,
Nere it that I for you have swich disese
That I moste dien heer at youre foot anoon,
Nought wolde I telle how me is wo-bigoon.
But certes, outher moste I die or plaine:
Ye sleen me giltelees for verray paine;
But of my deeth though that ye have no routhe,
Aviseth you er that ye breke youre trouthe.
Repenteth you, for thilke God above,
Er ye me sleen by cause that I you love.

582. Accordant, i.e., to be conformable. **583. observaunces,** rules. **587. wike,** week. **590. Wher,** whether. **594. fil,** fell. **597. holpen,** helped. **601. dredful,** fear-struck. **603. righte,** own true. **606. Nere it,** were it not. **609. outher,** either; **plaine,** complain. **610. sleen,** slay. **611. routhe,** pity. **612. Aviseth you,** consider.

For Madame, wel ye woot what ye han hight—
Not that I chalenge any thing of right
Of you, my soverein lady, but youre grace:
But in a gardin yond at swich a place,
Ye woot right wel what ye bihighten me,
And in myn hand youre trouthe plighten ye
To love me best. God woot ye saiden so,
Al be that I unworthy am therto.
Madame, I speke it for the honour of you
More than to save myn hertes lif right now.
I have do so as ye comanded me,
And if ye vouche sauf, ye may go see.
Dooth as you list, have youre biheeste in minde,
For quik or deed right ther ye shal me finde.
In you lith al to do me live or deye:
But wel I woot the rokkes been awaye."
  He taketh his leve and she astoned stood:
In al hir face nas a drope of blood;
She wende nevere have come in swich a trappe.
"Allas," quod she, "that evere this sholde happe!
For wende I nevere by possibilitee
That swich a monstre or merveile mighte be;
It is agains the proces of nature."
And hoom she gooth a sorweful creature.
For verray fere unnethe may she go.
She weepeth, waileth al a day or two,
And swouneth that it routhe was to see.
But why it was to no wight tolde she,
For out of town was goon Arveragus.
But to hirself she spak and saide thus,
With face pale and with ful sorweful cheere,
In hir complainte, as ye shal after heere:

615. hight, promised. **616. chalenge,** claim. **619. bihighten,** promised. **627. biheeste,** promise. **629. lith,** lies; **do,** cause. **631. astoned,** astonished. **633. wende,** thought. **636. monstre,** wonder. **637. proces,** due course. **639. unnethe,** scarcely; **go,** walk. **641. swouneth,** swoons. **645. cheere,** countenance.

"Allas," quod she, "on thee, Fortune, I plaine,°
That unwar wrapped hast me in thy chaine,
For which t'escape woot I no socour°—
Save only deeth or dishonour:
Oon of thise two bihoveth me to chese.°
But nathelees yit have I levere to lese°
My lif, than of my body to have a shame,
Or knowen myselven fals or lese my name,
And with my deeth I may be quit,° ywis.
Hath ther nat many a noble wif er this,
And many a maide, yslain hirself, allas,
Rather than with hir body doon trespas?°
Yis, certes, lo, thise stories beren witnesse:
Whan thritty tyrants ful of cursednesse°
Hadde slain Phidon° in Atthenes atte feeste,
They comanded his doughtren for t'arreste,
And bringen hem biforn hem in despit°
Al naked, to fulfille hir foule delit,
And in hir fadres blood they made hem daunce
Upon the pavement—God yive hem meschaunce!
For which thise woful maidens, ful of drede,
Rather than they wolde lese hir maidenhede,
They prively been stert° into a welle,
And dreinte° hemselven, as the bookes telle.
They of Messene lete enquere and seeke°
Of Lacedomye° fifty maidens eke,
On whiche they wolden doon hir lecherye;
But ther was noon of al that compaignye
That she nas slain, and with a good entente
Chees° rather for to die than assente
To been oppressed° of hir maidenhede:

647. plaine, complain. **649. socour,** help. **651. chese,** choose. **652. lese,** lose. **655. quit,** freed from dilemma. **658. trespas,** sin. **660. cursednesse,** wickedness. **661. Phidon,** the story of Phidon's daughters and the thirty tyrants, as well as all the following stories, are from St. Jerome's tract against Jovinian. **663. despit,** scorn. **669. been stert,** have jumped. **670. dreinte,** drowned. **671. lete . . . seeke,** had inquiries and searches made. **672. Lacedomye,** Lacedaemonia. **676. Chees,** chose. **677. oppressed,** ravished.

Why sholde I thanne to die been in drede?
  Lo, eek, the tyrant Aristoclides
That loved a maiden highte Stymphalides,°
Whan that hir fader slain was on a night,
Unto Dianes temple gooth she aright,
And hente° the image in hir handes two;
Fro which image wolde she nevere go:
No wight ne mighte hir handes of it arace,°
Til she was slain right in the selve place.
Now sith that maidens hadden swich despit°
To been defouled with mannes foul delit,
Wel oughte a wif rather hirselven slee°
Than be defouled, as it thinketh me.
  What shal I sayn of Hasdrubales wif
That at Cartage birafte° hirself hir lif?
For whan she saw that Romains wan the town,
She took hir children alle and skipte adown
Into the fir, and chees rather to die
Than any Romain dide hire vilainye.
  Hath nat Lucrece yslain hirself, allas,
At Rome whan that she oppressed was
Of Tarquin, for hire thoughte it was a shame
To liven whan that she hadde lost hir name?
  The sevene maidens of Milesie° also
Han slain hemself for verray drede and wo
Rather than folk of Gaule hem sholde oppresse:
Mo than a thousand stories, as I gesse,
Coude I now telle as touching this matere.
  Whan Habradate° was slain, his wif so dere
Hirselven slow,° and leet hir blood to glide
In Habradates woundes deepe and wide,
And saide, 'My body at the leeste way
Ther shal no wight defoulen, if I may.'°

680. Stymphalides, Stymphalis. **683. hente,** seized. **685. arace,** tear. **687. despit,** indignation. **689. slee,** slay. **692. birafte,** deprived: Hasdrubal was king of Carthage when it was destroyed by the Romans. **701. Milesie,** Miletus. **706. Habradate,** Abradates. **707. slow,** slew. **710. if I may,** if I can help it.

What sholde I mo ensamples° herof sayn?
Sith that so manye han hemselven slain
Wel rather than they wolde defouled be,
I wol conclude that it is bet° for me
To sleen myself than been defouled thus:
I wol be trewe unto Arveragus,
Or rather slee myself in som manere—
As dide Demociones° doughter dere,
By cause that she wolde nat defouled be.
O Cedasus,° it is ful greet pitee
To reden how thy doughtren deide, allas,
That slowe hemself for swich manere cas.
As greet a pitee was it, or wel moor,
The Theban maiden that for Nichanor°
Hirselven slow right for swich manere wo.
Another Theban maiden dide right so:
For oon of Macedonie hadde hire oppressed,
She with hir deeth hir maidenhede redressed.°
What shal I sayn of Nicerates wif
That for swich caas birafte hirself hir lif?
How trewe eek was to Alcebiades°
His love, that rather for to dien chees°
Than for to suffre his body unburied be.
Lo, which a wif was Alceste,"° quod she.
"What saith Omer° of goode Penolopee?
Al Greece knoweth of hir chastitee.
Pardee, of Laodomia° is writen thus,
That whan at Troye was slain Protheselaus,
No lenger wolde she live after his day.

711. ensamples, examples. **714. bet,** better. **718. Demociones,** Demotion's. **720. Cedasus,** Scedasus. **724. for,** i.e., for fear of; **Nichanor,** Nicanor. **728. redressed,** made amends for. **731. Alcebiades,** Alcibiades' mistress risked death by burying his body after he had been decapitated by the Spartan Lysander; she did not, however, lose her life as a result. **732. chees,** chose. **734. Alceste,** Alcestis, the proposed heroine of Chaucer's *Legend of Good Women,* died in her husband's place. **735. Omer,** Homer, who relates Odysseus' return from Troy to his faithful wife Penelope. **737. Laodamia** followed her dead husband Protesilaus to the underworld.

The same of noble Porcia telle I may:
Withoute Brutus coude she nat live,
To whom she hadde al hool hir herte yive.
The parfit wifhood of Arthemesie
Honoured is thurgh al the Barbarye.
O Teuta queene, thy wifly chastitee
To alle wives may a mirour be!
The same thing I saye of Biliea,
Of Rodogone, and eek Valeria."
Thus plained Dorigen a day or twaye,
Purposing evere that she wolde deye.
But nathelees upon the thridde night
Hoom cam Arveragus, this worthy knight,
And axed hire why that she weep so sore,
And she gan weepen evere lenger the more.
"Allas," quod she, "that evere I was born:
Thus have I said," quod she; "thus have I sworn—"
And tolde him al as ye han herd bifore:
It needeth nat reherce it you namore.
This housbonde with glad cheere in freendly wise
Answerde and saide as I shal you devise:
"Is there ought elles, Dorigen, but this?"
"Nay, nay," quod she, "God help me so as wis,
This is too muche, and it were Goddes wille."
"Ye, wif," quod he, "lat sleepen that is stille.
It may be wel paraunter yit today.
Ye shul youre trouthe holden, by my fay,
For God so wisly have mercy upon me,

740. Porcia, Portia swallowed burning coals on learning of Brutus' death. **742. hool,** whole. **743. Arthemesie,** Artemisia built for her husband King Mausolus the famous tomb called the Mausoleum. **745. Teuta,** Queen of Illyria, according to Jerome, owed her long reign to her chastity. **747. Biliea,** Bilia's prowess seems to have consisted in enduring her husband's bad breath in uncomplaining silence. **748. Rodogone,** Rhodogune slew her nurse who suggested that she remarry; **Valeria** refused to marry again. **749. plained,** lamented. **753. weep,** wept. **754. evere . . . more,** always more and more. **759. cheere,** manner. **762. wis,** surely. **763. and,** if. **764. that,** what. **765. paraunter,** perhaps. **766. trouthe,** pledged word; **fay,** faith. **767. wisly,** surely.

I hadde wel levere ystiked for to be,
For verray love which that I to you have,
But if ye sholde youre trouthe keepe and save:
Trouthe is the hyeste thing that man may keepe."
But with that word he brast anoon to weepe,
And saide, "I you forbede, up paine of deeth,
That nevere whil thee lasteth lif ne breeth,
To no wight tel thou of this aventure.
As I may best I wol my wo endure,
Ne make no countenance of hevinesse,
That folk of you may deemen harm or gesse."
  And forth he cleped a squier and a maide:
"Go forth anoon with Dorigen," he saide,
"And bringeth hire to swich a place anoon."
They tooke hir leve and on hir way they goon,
But they ne wiste why they thider wente:
He nolde no wight tellen his entente.
  Paraventure an heep of you, ywis,
Wol holden him a lewed man in this,
That he wol putte his wif in jupartye.
Herkneth the tale er ye upon hire crye:
She may have bettre fortune than you seemeth,
And whan that ye han herd the tale, deemeth.
  This squier which that highte Aurelius,
On Dorigen that was so amorous,
Of aventure happed hire to meete
Amidde the town, right in the quikkest streete,
As she was boun to goon the way forth right
Toward the gardin ther as she hadde hight;
And he was to the gardinward also,
For wel he spied whan she wolde go
Out of hir hous to any manere place.
But thus they meete of aventure or grace,

768. ystiked, stabbed. **770. But if,** unless. **771. thing,** legal bond. **772. brast,** burst. **773. up,** upon. **778. deemen,** suspect. **783. wiste,** knew. **786. lewed,** stupid. **787. jupartye,** jeopardy. **789. seemeth,** it seems. **790. deemeth,** judge. **793. Of aventure,** by chance; **happed,** happened. **794. quikkest,** busiest. **795. boun,** prepared; **right,** direct. **796. hight,** promised.

And he salueth° hire with glad entente,
And axed of hire whiderward she wente.
  And she answerde half as she were mad,
"Unto the gardin as myn housbonde bad,°
My trouthe for to holde, allas, allas!"
  Aurelius gan wondren on this cas,
And in his herte hadde greet compassioun
Of hire and of hir lamentacioun,
And of Arveragus, the worthy knight,
That bad hire holden al that she hadde hight,
So loth him was his wif sholde breke hir trouthe;
And in his herte he caughte of this greet routhe,°
Considering the beste on every side
That fro his lust yit were him levere abide°
Than doon so heigh a cherlissh wrecchednesse°
Agains franchise° and alle gentilesse;
For which in fewe wordes saide he thus:
  "Madame, sayeth to youre lord Arveragus
That sith I see his grete gentilesse
To you, and eek I see wel youre distresse,
That him were levere han shame—and that were routhe—
Than ye to me sholde breke thus youre trouthe,
I have wel levere° evere to suffre wo
Than I departe° the love bitwixe you two.
I you releesse, Madame, into youre hond,
Quit every serement° and every bond
That ye han maad to me as herbiforn,
Sith thilke time which that ye were born.
My trouthe I plighte, I shal you nevere repreve°
Of no biheeste.° And here I take my leve,
As of the treweste and the beste wif
That evere yit I knew in al my lif.
But every wif be war of hir biheeste:
On Dorigen remembreth at the leeste.

801. salueth, greets. **804. bad,** bade. **812. routhe,** pity. **814. lust,** pleasure; **abide,** i.e., abstain. **715. cherlissh,** i.e., low-born; **wrecchednesse,** miserable act. **816. franchise,** generosity. **823. have . . . levere,** had much rather. **824. departe,** divide. **826. serement,** oath. **829. repreve,** reproach. **830. biheeste,** promise.

Thus can a squier doon a gentil deede
As wel as can a knight, withouten drede."°
She thanketh him upon hir knees al bare,
And hoom unto hir housbonde is she fare,
And tolde him al as ye han herd me said.
And be ye siker, he was so wel apaid°
That it were impossible me to write.
What sholde I lenger of this caas endite?
  Arveragus and Dorigen his wif
In soverein blisse leden forth hir lif.
Nevere eft° ne was ther angre hem bitweene:
He cherisseth hire as though she were a queene,
And she was to him trewe for everemore.
Of thise two folk ye gete of me namore.
  Aurelius, that his cost hath al forlorn,°
Curseth the time that evere he was born.
"Allas," quod he, "allas that I bihighte°
Of pured gold a thousand pound of wighte°
Unto this philosophre. How shall I do?
I see namore but that I am fordo.°
Myn heritage moot I needes selle
And been a beggere. Here may I nat dwelle,
And shamen al my kinrede° in this place,
But° I of him may gete bettre grace.
But nathelees I wol of him assaye
At certain dayes yeer by yere to paye,
And thanke him of his grete curteisye:
My trouthe wol I keepe, I nil nat lie."
  With herte soor he gooth unto his cofre,
And broughte gold unto this philosophre
The value of five hundred pound, I gesse,
And him biseecheth of his gentilesse
To graunten him dayes of the remenaunt,°
And saide, "Maister, I dar wel make avaunt°

836. drede, doubt. **840. siker,** sure; **apaid,** pleased. **845. eft,** again. **849. forlorn,** lost. **851. bihighte,** promised. **852. pured,** refined; **wighte,** weight. **854. fordo,** ruined. **857. kinrede,** kindred. **858. But,** unless. **867. dayes,** i.e., extended terms; **remenaunt,** remainder. **868. avaunt,** boast.

I failed nevere of my trouthe as yit,
For sikerly my dette shal be quit
Towardes you, how evere that I fare,
To goon abegged in my kirtel bare.
But wolde ye vouche sauf upon suretee
Two yeer or three for to respiten me,
Thanne were I wel, for elles moot I selle
Myn heritage: ther is namore to telle."
  This philosophre sobrely answerde,
And saide thus, whan he thise wordes herde,
"Have I nat holden covenant unto thee?"
  "Yis, certes, wel and trewely," quod he.
  "Hastou nat had thy lady as thee liketh?"
  "No, no," quod he and sorwefully he siketh.
  "What was the cause? Tel me if thou can."
  Aurelius his tale anoon bigan,
And tolde him al as ye han herd bifore:
It needeth nat to you reherce it more.
  He saide, "Arveragus, of gentilesse,
Hadde levere die in sorwe and in distresse
Than that his wif were of hir trouthe fals."
The sorwe of Dorigen he tolde him als,
How loth hire was to been a wikked wif,
And that she levere hadde lost that day hir lif,
And that hir trouthe she swoor thurgh innocence:
She nevere erst hadde herd speke of apparence.
"That made me han of hire so greet pitee;
And right as freely as he sente hire me,
As freely sente I hire to him again:
This al and som, ther is namore to sayn."
  This philosophre answerde, "Leve brother,
Everich of you dide gentilly to other.
Thou art a squier, and he is a knight:

872. abegged, abegging; **kirtel,** undergarment. **873. suretee,** security. **874. respiten,** give respite. **881. liketh,** it pleases. **882. siketh,** sighs. **890. als,** also. **894. erst,** before; **apparence,** illusion. **896. freely,** generously. **898. This . . . som,** this is all there is to it. **899. Leve,** dear.

But God forbede, for his blisful might,
But if a clerk coude doon a gentil deede
As wel as any of you, it is no drede.°
  Sire, I releesse thee thy thousand pound,
As thou right now were cropen° out of the ground,
Ne nevere er° now ne haddest knowen me.
For sire, I wol nat take a peny of thee,
For al my craft° ne nought for my travaile.
Thou hast ypayed wel for my vitaile:°
It is ynough. And farewel, have good day."
And took his hors and forth he gooth his way.
  Lordinges, this question thanne wol I axe now:
Which was the moste free,° as thinketh you?
Now telleth me, er that ye ferther wende.
I can namore: my tale is at an ende.

THE PHYSICIAN'S TALE

  Ther was, as telleth Titus Livius,°
A knight that called was Virginius,
Fulfild° of honour and of worthinesse,
And strong of freendes, and of greet richesse.
  This knight a doughter hadde by his wif:
Ne children hadde he mo° in al his lif.
Fair was this maide in excellent beautee
Aboven every wight that man may see,
For Nature hath with sovereín diligence
Yformed hire in so greet excellence
As though she wolde sayn, "Lo I, Nature,
Thus can I forme and painte a creature
Whan that me liste. Who can me countrefete?°

904. drede, doubt. **906. were cropen,** had crept. **907. er,** before. **909. craft,** art. **910. vitaile,** food. **914. free,** generous.

1. Livius, Livy, a Roman historian. **3. Fulfild,** filled full. **6. mo,** others. **13. me liste,** I please; **countrefete,** imitate.

Pygmalion nought, though he ay forge and bete,
Or grave, or painte, for I dar wel sayn
Appelles, Zanzis sholde werche in vain
Outher to grave or painte or forge or bete
If they presumeden me to countrefete.
For he that is the formere principal
Hath maked me his vicaire general
To forme and painten erthely creatures
Right as me list; and eech thing in my cure is
Under the moone that may wane and waxe.
And for my werk right no thing wol I axe:
My lord and I been ful of oon accord.
I made hire to the worshipe of my lord;
So do I alle mine othere creatures,
What colour that they han, or what figures."
Thus seemeth me that Nature wolde saye.
  This maide of age twelve yeer was and twaye
In which that Nature hadde swich delit.
For right as she can painte a lilye whit,
And reed a rose, right with swich painture
She painted hath this noble creature,
Er she were born, upon hir limes free
Wher as by right swiche colours sholden be;
And Phebus dyed hath hir tresses grete
Lik to the stremes of his burned hete.
And if that excellent was hir beautee,
A thousandfold more vertuous was she:
In hire ne lakked no condicioun
That is to praise as by discrecioun.
As wel in goost as body chast was she,
For which she flowred in virginitee,
With al humilitee and abstinence,

14. **Pygmalion,** a legendary Greek sculptor; **bete,** hammer. 15. **grave,** carve. 16. **Appelles,** Apelles, said to have built the marvelous tomb of Darius; **Zanzis,** Zeuxis, a legendary painter. 17. **Outher,** either. 19. **formere,** i.e., creator. 20. **vicaire general,** deputy. 22. **cure,** care. 24. **axe,** ask. 25. **ful of oon,** fully of the same. 30. **twaye,** two. 33. **reed,** red. 35. **free,** beautiful. 37. **Phebus,** Phoebus, the sun. 38. **stremes,** beams; **burned,** burnished. 43. **goost,** spirit.

With al attemperaunce and pacience,
With mesure eek of bering and array.
Discreet she was in answering alway
Though she were wis as Pallas, dar I sayn—
Hir facound eek ful wommanly and plain.
No countrefeted termes hadde she
To seeme wis, but after hir degree
She spak, and alle hir wordes, more and lesse,
Souning in vertu and in gentilesse.
Shamefast she was in maidens shamefastnesse,
Constant in herte and evere in bisinesse
To drive hire out of idel slogardye.
Baccus hadde of hir mouth right no maistrye,
For win and youthe dooth Venus encreesse,
As men in fir wol casten oile or greesse;
And of hir owene vertu, unconstrained,
She hath ful ofte time sik hire feined,
For that she wolde fleen the compaignye
Wher likly was to treten of folye,
As is at feestes, revels, and at daunces,
That been occasions of daliaunces.
Swiche thinges maken children for to be
Too soone ripe and bold, as men may see,
Which is ful perilous and hath been yore:
For al too soone may they lerne lore
Of boldnesse whan she woxe is a wif.
And ye, maistresses, in youre olde lif
That lordes doughters han in governaunce,
Ne taketh of my wordes no displesaunce;
Thinketh that ye been set in governinges
Of lordes doughters only for two thinges:

47. mesure, moderation; **bering,** bearing. **49. Pallas,** Pallas Athena, goddess of wisdom. **50. facound,** manner of speaking. **51. countrefeted,** artificial. **54. souning,** resounding. **57. slogardye,** sluggardliness. **58. maistrye,** domination. **59. dooth,** causes; **Venus,** i.e., sexual love. **62. feined,** pretended. **64. treten of,** i.e., involve. **66. daliaunces,** flirtations. **68. ripe,** mature. **69. yore,** long, i.e., always. **71. woxe is,** has become. **72. maistresses,** governesses.

Outher for ye han kept youre honestee,
Or elles ye han falle in freletee
And knowen wel ynough the olde daunce,
And han forsaken fully swich meschaunce
For everemo. Therfore, for Cristes sake,
To teche hem vertu looke that ye ne slake.
A theef of venison that hath forlaft
His likerousnesse and al his olde craft
Can keepe a forest best of any man.
Now keepeth wel, for if ye wol ye can.
Looke wel that ye unto no vice assente,
Lest ye be dampned for youre wikke entente,
For whoso dooth, a traitour is, certain.
And taketh keep of that that I shal sayn:
Of alle treson, soverein pestilence
Is whan a wight bitraiseth innocence.
Ye fadres and ye modres eek also,
Though ye han children, be it oon or mo,
Youre is the charge of al hir surveaunce
Whil that they been under youre governaunce.
Beeth ware if by ensample of your living,
Or by youre necligence in chastising,
That they perisse, for I dar wel saye,
If that they doon, ye shul it dere abeye.
Under a shepherde softe and necligent
The wolf hath many a sheep and ram torent.
Suffiseth oon ensample now as here,
For I moot turne again to my matere.
This maide of which I telle this tale expresse
So kepte hireself hire needed no maistresse;

77. **Outher,** either. 78. **freletee,** frailty. 81. **mo,** more. 82. **slake,** slack. 83. **forlaft,** given up. 84. **likerousnesse,** appetite (for venison). 88. **wikke,** wicked. 90. **keep,** heed. 91. The greatest plague of all treason. 92. **bitraiseth,** betrays. 95. **charge,** responsibility; **surveaunce,** surveillance. 97. **ensample,** example. 99. **perisse,** go to ruin. 100. **dere abeye,** pay for it dearly. 102. **torent,** torn apart. 104. **moot,** must. 105. **expresse,** specifically. 106. **hire,** i.e., that she.

For in hir living maidens mighten rede
As in a book every good word or deede
That longeth to a maiden vertuous,
She was so prudent and so bountevous.
For which the fame out sprang on every side
Bothe of hir beautee and hir bountee wide,
That thurgh that land they praised hire eechone
That loved vertu, save Envye allone
That sory is of other mennes wele,
And glad is of his sorwe and his unhele
(The Doctour maketh this descripcioun).
  This maide upon a day wente in the town
Toward a temple with hir moder dere,
As is of yonge maidens the manere.
Now was ther thanne a justice in that town
That governour was of that regioun,
And so bifel this juge his yën caste
Upon this maide, avising him ful faste
As she cam forby ther as this juge stood.
Anoon his herte chaunged and his mood,
So was he caught with beautee of this maide.
And to himself ful prively he saide,
"The maide shal be myn, for any man."
Anoon the Feend into his herte ran
And taughte him sodeinly that he by slighte
This maiden to his purpos winne mighte:
For certes, by no force ne by no meede
Him thoughte he was nat able for to speede,
For she was strong of freendes, and eek she
Confirmed was in swich soverein bountee
That wel he wiste he mighte hire nevere winne,
As for to make hire with hir body sinne.

109. longeth, is appropriate to. **110. bountevous,** bountiful. **112. bountee,** goodness. **115. wele,** welfare. **116. unhele,** misfortune. **117. Doctour,** not the Physician, apparently, but St. Augustine, who speaks thus of envy. **124. avising him . . . faste,** considering intently. **125. forby ther,** past where. **129. for,** despite. **131. slighte,** trickery. **133. meede,** i.e., offer of money. **134. speede,** succeed. **136. bountee,** goodness. **137. wiste,** knew.

For which, by greet deliberacioun,
He sente after a cherl, was in the town,
Which that he knew for subtil and for bold.
This juge unto this cherl his tale hath told
In secree wise, and made him to ensure
He sholde telle it to no creature,
And if he dide, he sholde lese his heed.
Whan that assented was this cursed reed,
Glad was this juge, and maked him greet cheere,
And yaf him yiftes preciouse and dere.
Whan shapen was al hir conspiracye
Fro point to point how that his lecherye
Parfourned sholde been ful subtilly—
As ye shul heere it after openly—
Hoom gooth the cherl that highte Claudius.
This false juge that highte Apius—
So was his name, for this is no fable
But knowen for historial thing notable:
The sentence of it sooth is, out of doute—
This false juge gooth now faste aboute
To hasten his delit al that he may.
And so bifel soone after on a day
This false juge, as telleth us the storye,
As he was wont, sat in his consistorye
And yaf his doomes upon sondry cas;
This false cherl cam forth a ful greet pas
And saide, "Lord, if that it be youre wille,
As dooth me right upon this pitous bille
In which I plaine upon Virginius.
And if that he wol sayn it is nat thus,
I wol it preve and finde good witnesse
That sooth is that my bille wol expresse."

143. ensure, promise. **145. lese,** lose; **heed,** head. **146. assented,** agreed upon; **reed,** plan. **149. shapen,** arranged. **151. Parfourned,** fulfilled. **153. highte,** was named. **157. sentence,** general content. **162. consistorye,** court of justice. **163. doomes,** judgments; **cas,** cases. **164. a . . . pas,** in a great hurry. **166. bille,** legal petition. **167. plaine,** complain. **169. preve,** prove. **170. that,** what.

This juge answerde, "Of this in his absence
I may nat yive definitif sentence.
Lat him do calle, and I wol gladly heere:
Thou shalt have al right and no wrong here."
Virginius cam to wite the juges wille,
And right anoon was rad this cursed bille.
The sentence of it was as ye shul heere:
"To you, my lord sire Apius so dere,
Sheweth youre poore servant Claudius
How that a knight called Virginius
Agains the lawe, agains al equitee,
Holdeth, expres again the wil of me,
My servant, which that is my thral by right,
Which fro myn hous was stole upon a night
Whil that she was ful yong: this wol I preve
By witnesse, lord, so that it nat you greve.
She nis his doughter nat, what so he saye.
Wherfore to you, my lord the juge, I praye,
Yeelde me my thral, if that it be youre wille."
Lo, this was al the sentence of his bille.
Virginius gan upon the cherl biholde;
But hastily, er he his tale tolde,
(And wolde have preved it as sholde a knight,
And eek by witnessing of many a wight,
That al was fals that saide this adversarye),
This cursed juge wolde no thing tarye,
Ne heere a word more of Virginius,
But yaf his juggement and saide thus:
"I deeme anoon this cherl his servant have.
Thou shalt no lenger in thyn hous hire save.
Go bringe hire forth and put hire in oure warde.
The cherl shal han his thral: this I awarde."

172. sentence, judgment. **173. Lat . . . calle,** have him called. **175. wite,** learn. **176. rad,** read. **177. sentence,** purport. **179. Sheweth,** alleges. **182. expres,** expressly. **183. thral,** slave. **185. preve,** prove. **187. so,** ever. **192. he,** i.e., Virginius; **tolde,** might tell. **199. deeme,** rule. **200. save,** keep. **201. warde,** keeping.

And whan this worthy knight Virginius,
Thurgh sentence of this justice Apius,
Moste° by force his dere doughter yiven
Unto the juge in lecherye to liven,
He gooth him hoom and sette him in his halle,
And leet anoon his dere doughter calle;
And with a face deed° as asshen colde,
Upon hir humble face he gan biholde,
With fadres pitee stiking thurgh his herte,
Al wolde he from his purpos nat converte.°
"Doughter," quod he, "Virginia by thy name:
Ther been two wayes, outher° deeth or shame
That thou most suffre. Allas, that I was bore,°
For nevere thou deservedest wherfore
To dien with a swerd or with a knif.
O dere doughter, endere of my lif,
Which I have fostered up with swich plesaunce
That thou were nevere out of my remembraunce,
O doughter, which that art my laste wo,
And in my lif my laste joye also,
O gemme of chastitee, in pacience
Taak thou thy deeth, for this is my sentence.
For love and nat for hate thou most° be deed:
My pitous hand moot° smiten of thyn heed.
Allas, that evere Apius thee sey!°
Thus hath he falsly juged thee today—"
And tolde hire al the cas, as ye bifore
Han herd: nat needeth for to telle it more.
"O, mercy, dere fader," quod this maide.
And with that word she bothe hir armes laide
Aboute his nekke, as she was wont to do.
The teres borste° out of hir yën two.
And saide, "Goode fader, shal I die?
Is ther no grace? Is there no remedye?"

205. Moste, must. **209. deed,** dead. **212. Al,** although; **converte,** turn aside. **214. outher,** either. **215. most,** must; **bore,** born. **225. most,** must. **226. moot,** must. **227. sey,** saw. **234. borste,** burst.

"No, certes, dere doughter myn," quod he.
"Thanne yif me leiser,° fader myn," quod she,
"My deeth for to complaine a litel space.
For pardee, Jepte° yaf his doughter grace
For to complaine er he hire slow,° allas,
And, God it woot, no thing was hir trespas°
But for° she ran hir fader for to see,
To welcome him with greet solempnitee."
And with that word she fel aswoune anoon,
And after, whan hir swouning is agoon,
She riseth up and to hir fader saide,
"Blessed be God that I shal die a maide!
Yive me my deeth er that I have a shame;
Dooth with youre child youre wil, a° Goddes name."
And with that word she prayed him ful ofte
That with his swerd he wolde smite softe;
And with that word aswoune down she fil.°
Hir fader with ful sorweful herte and wil
Hir heed of smoot, and by the top it hente,°
And to the juge he gan it to presente,
As he sat yit in doom° in consistorye.
And whan the juge it saw, as saith the storye,
He bad to take him and anhange° him faste.
But right anoon a thousand peple in thraste°
To save the knight, for routhe° and for pitee,
For knowen was the false iniquitee.
The peple anoon had suspect° in this thing
By manere of the cherles chalanging
That it was by assent of Apius:
They wisten° wel that he was lecherous.
For which unto this Apius they goon
And caste him in a prison right anoon,

238. leiser, i.e., time. **240. Jepte:** for the story of Jephtha and his daughter, see Judges XI 37–38. **241. slow,** slew. **242. woot,** knows; **trespas,** offense. **243. But for,** except that. **250. a,** in. **253. fil,** fell. **255. heed,** head; **of,** off; **hente,** seized. **257. doom,** judgment. **259. anhange,** hang. **260. thraste,** burst. **261. routhe,** sorrow. **263. suspect,** suspicion. **266. wisten,** knew.

Ther as he slow himself; and Claudius,
That servant was unto this Apius,
Was deemed for to hange upon a tree,
But that Virginius, of his pitee,
So prayed for him that he was exiled,
And elles, certes, he hadde been bigiled.
The remenant were anhanged, more and lesse,
That were consentant of this cursednesse.
  Here may men seen how sinne hath his merite:
Beeth war, for no man woot whom God wol smite,
In no degree and in no manere wise.
The worm of conscience may agrise
Of wikked lif, though it so privee be
That no man woot therof but God and he.
For be he lewed man or elles lered,
He noot how soone that he shal been afered.
Therfore I rede you this conseil take:
Forsaketh sinne, er sinne you forsake.

THE PARDONER'S PROLOGUE

The Introduction

Oure Hoste gan to swere as he were wood;
"Harrow," quod he, "by nailes and by blood,
This was a fals cherl and a fals justise.
As shameful deeth as herte may devise
Come to thise juges and hir advocats.

269. slow, slew. **271. deemed,** sentenced. **274. bigiled,** i.e., destroyed. **275. remenant,** remaining ones. **276. consentant of,** conniving in. **277. merite,** just deserts. **278. woot,** knows. **280. agrise,** become terrified. **281. privee,** private. **283. lewed,** ignorant; **lered,** learned. **284. noot,** doesn't know; **afered,** terrified. **285. rede,** advise.

1. wood, insane. **2. Harrow,** help; **nailes,** i.e., God's nails.

Algate this sely maide is slain, allas!
Allas, too dere boughte she beautee!
Wherfore I saye alday that men may see
The yiftes of Fortune and of Nature
Been cause of deeth to many a creature.
As bothe yiftes that I speke of now,
Men han ful ofte more for harm than prow.
  But trewely, myn owene maister dere,
This is a pitous tale for to heere.
But nathelees, passe over, is no fors:
I praye to God so save thy gentil cors,
And eek thine urinals and thy jurdones,
Thyn ipocras and eek thy galiones,
And every boiste ful of thy letuarye—
God blesse hem, and oure lady Sainte Marye.
So mote I theen, thou art a propre man,
And lik a prelat, by Saint Ronian!
Saide I nat wel? I can nat speke in terme.
But wel I woot, thou doost myn herte to erme
That I almost have caught a cardinacle.
By corpus bones, but if I have triacle,
Or elles a draughte of moiste and corny ale,
Or but I heere anoon a merye tale,
Myn herte is lost for pitee of this maide.
  Thou bel ami, thou Pardoner," he saide,
"Tel us som mirthe or japes right anoon."
  "It shal be doon," quod he, "by Saint Ronion.

6. **Algate,** at any rate; **sely,** innocent. 8. **alday,** always. 12. **prow,** benefit. 15. **is no fors,** i.e., never mind. 16. **cors,** body. 17. **jurdones,** jordans: the Host is somewhat confused in his endeavor to use technical medical terms. 18. **ipocras,** a medicinal drink named after Hippocrates; **galiones,** a medicine, probably invented on the spot by the Host, named after Galen. 19. **boiste,** box; **letuarye,** medicine. 21. **So . . . theen,** so might I thrive. 22 **Ronian,** St. Ronan or St. Ninian, with a possible play on runnion, sexual organ. 23. **in terme,** in technical idiom. 24. **doost,** make; **erme,** grieve. 25. **cardinacle,** apparently a cardiac condition, confused in the Host's mind with a cardinal. 26. **corpus bones,** an illiterate oath, mixing God's bones with *corpus Dei;* **triacle,** medicine. 27. **moiste . . . corny,** fresh and malty. 30. **bel ami,** fair friend. 31. **japes,** joke.

But first," quod he, "here at this ale-stake°
I wol bothe drinke and eten of a cake."
  And right anoon thise gentils gan to crye,
"Nay, lat him telle us of no ribaudye.°
Tel us som moral thing that we may lere,°
Som wit,° and thanne wol we gladly heere."
  "I graunte, ywis," quod he, "but I moot thinke
Upon som honeste° thing whil that I drinke."

The Prologue

Lordinges—quod he—in chirches whan I preche,
I paine me to han an hautein° speeche,
And ringe it out as round as gooth a belle,
For I can al by rote° that I telle.
My theme is alway oon,° and evere was:
Radix malorum est cupiditas.°
First I pronounce whennes° that I come,
And thanne my bulles shewe I alle and some.°
Oure lige lordes seel on my patente,°
That shewe I first, my body to warente,°
That no man be so bold, ne preest ne clerk,
Me to destourbe of Cristes holy werk.
And after that thanne telle I forth my tales°—
Bulles of popes and of cardinales,
Of patriarkes and bisshopes I shewe,
And in Latin I speke a wordes fewe,

33. **ale-stake,** sign of a tavern. 36. **ribaudye,** ribaldry. 37. **lere,** learn. 38. **Som wit,** i.e., something with significance. 40. **honeste,** decent.

2. **paine me,** take pains; **hautein,** loud. 4. **can . . . rote,** know by heart. 5. **oon,** i.e., the same. 6. Avarice is the root of evil. 7. **whennes,** whence. 8. **bulles,** episcopal mandates; **alle . . . some,** each and every one. 9. **lige lordes,** liege lord's, i.e., the Pope's; **seel,** seal; **patente,** papal license. 10. **warente,** keep safe. 13. **telle . . . tales,** I go on with my yarn.

To saffron with my predicacioun,°
And for to stire hem to devocioun.
  Thanne shewe I forth my longe crystal stones,°
Ycrammed ful of cloutes° and of bones—
Relikes been they, as weenen° they eechoon.
Thanne have I in laton° a shulder-boon
Which that was of an holy Jewes sheep.
"Goode men," I saye, "take of my wordes keep:°
If that this boon be wasshe in any welle,
If cow, or calf, or sheep, or oxe swelle,
That any worm hath ete or worm ystonge,°
Take water of that welle and wassh his tonge,
And it is hool° anoon. And ferthermoor,
Of pokkes and of scabbe and every soor°
Shal every sheep be hool that of this welle
Drinketh a draughte. Take keep eek that I telle:
If that the goode man that the beestes oweth°
Wol every wike,° er that the cok him croweth,
Fasting drinken of this welle a draughte—
As thilke° holy Jew oure eldres taughte—
His beestes and his stoor° shal multiplye.
  And sire, also it heleth jalousye:
For though a man be falle in jalous rage,
Lat maken with this water his potage,°
And nevere shal he more his wif mistriste,°
Though he the soothe of hir defaute wiste,°
Al hadde she° taken preestes two or three.
  Here is a mitein° eek that ye may see:
He that his hand wol putte in this mitein
He shal have multiplying of his grain,
Whan he hath sowen, be it whete or otes—
So that he offre pens or elles grotes.°

17. **saffron,** add spice to; **predicacioun,** preaching. 19. **stones,** jars. 20. **cloutes,** rags. 21. **weenen,** suppose. 22. **laton,** zinc. 24. **keep,** notice. 27. That has eaten or been bitten by any worm. 29. **hool,** i.e., sound. 30. **pokkes,** pox; **soor,** sore. 33. **oweth,** owns. 34. **wike,** week. 36. **thilke,** that same. 37. **stoor,** stock. 40. **potage,** soup. 41. **mistriste,** mistrust. 42. **defaute,** infidelity; **wiste,** knew. 43. **Al . . . she,** even if she had. 44. **mitein,** mitten. 48. **pens, grotes,** pennies, groats, coins.

Goode men and wommen, oo thing warne I you:
If any wight be in this chirche now
That hath doon sinne horrible, that he
Dar nat for shame of it yshriven be,
Or any womman, be she yong or old,
That hath ymaked hir housbonde cokewold,
Swich folk shal have no power ne no grace
To offren to my relikes in this place;
And whoso findeth him out of swich blame,
He wol come up and offre in Goddes name,
And I assoile him by the auctoritee
Which that by bulle ygraunted was to me."
By this gaude have I wonne, yeer by yeer,
An hundred mark sith I was pardoner.
I stonde lik a clerk in my pulpet,
And whan the lewed peple is down yset,
I preche so as ye han herd bifore,
And telle an hundred false japes more.
Thanne paine I me to strecche forth the nekke,
And eest and west upon the peple I bekke
As dooth a douve, sitting on a berne;
Mine handes and my tonge goon so yerne
That it is joye to see my bisinesse.
Of avarice and of swich cursednesse
Is al my preching, for to make hem free
To yiven hir pens, and namely unto me,
For myn entente is nat but for to winne,
And no thing for correccion of sinne:
I rekke nevere whan that they been beried
Though that hir soules goon a-blakeberied.
For certes, many a predicacioun
Comth ofte time of yvel entencioun:

54. cokewold, cuckold. **56. offren to,** make gifts in reverence of. **59. assoile,** absolve. **61. gaude,** trick. **62. mark,** marks, pecuniary units. **64. lewed,** ignorant. **66. japes,** tricks. **67. paine . . . me,** I take pains. **68. bekke,** i.e., shake my head. **69. douve,** dove; **berne,** barn. **70 yerne,** fast. **72. cursednesse,** sin. **73. free,** generous. **74. namely,** especially. **75. nat but,** only. **77. rekke,** care; **beried,** buried. **78. goon a-blakeberied,** go blackberrying, i.e., to hell. **79. predicacioun,** sermon.

Som for plesance of folk and flaterye,
To been avaunced by ypocrisye,
And som for vaine glorye, and som for hate;
For whan I dar noon otherways debate,
Thanne wol I stinge him with my tonge smerte
In preching, so that he shal nat asterte
To been defamed falsly, if that he
Hath trespassed to my bretheren or to me.
For though I telle nought his propre name,
Men shal wel knowe that it is the same
By signes and by othere circumstaunces.
Thus quite I folk that doon us displesaunces;
Thus spete I out my venim under hewe
Of holinesse, to seeme holy and trewe.
But shortly myn entente I wol devise:
I preche of no thing but for coveitise;
Therfore my theme is yit and evere was
Radix malorum est cupiditas.
  Thus can I preche again that same vice
Which that I use, and that is avarice.
But though myself be gilty in that sinne,
Yit can I make other folk to twinne
From avarice, and sore to repente—
But that is nat my principal entente:
I preche no thing but for coveitise.
Of this matere it oughte ynough suffise.
  Thanne telle I hem ensamples many oon
Of olde stories longe time agoon,
For lewed peple loven tales olde—
Swiche thinges can they wel reporte and holde.
What, trowe ye that whiles I may preche,
And winne gold and silver for I teche,

82. avaunced, promoted. **84. debate,** i.e., fight verbally against the object of my hate. **86. asterte,** escape. **88. trespassed to,** injured. **92. quite,** pay back; **displesaunces,** discourtesies. **93. spete,** spit; **hewe,** color. **95. devise,** describe. **102. twinne,** separate. **107. ensamples,** exempla, stories illustrating moral principles. **109. lewed,** ignorant. **110. reporte . . . holde,** repeat and remember. **111. trowe,** believe. **112. for,** because.

That I wol live in poverte wilfully?
Nay, nay, I thoughte it nevere, trewely,
For I wol preche and begge in sondry landes;
I wol nat do no labour with mine handes,
Ne make baskettes and live therby,
By cause I wol nat beggen idelly.
I wol none of the Apostles countrefete:
I wol have moneye, wolle, cheese, and whete,
Al were it yiven of the pooreste page,
Or of the pooreste widwe in a village—
Al sholde hir children sterve for famine.
Nay, I wol drinke licour of the vine
And have a joly wenche in every town.
But herkneth, lordinges, in conclusioun,
Youre liking is that I shal telle a tale:
Now have I dronke a draughte of corny ale,
By God, I hope I shal you telle a thing
That shal by reson been at youre liking;
For though myself be a ful vicious man,
A moral tale yit I you telle can,
Which I am wont to preche for to winne.
Now holde youre pees, my tale I wol biginne.

THE PARDONER'S TALE

In Flandres whilom was a compaignye
Of yonge folk that haunteden folye—
As riot, hasard, stewes, and tavernes,
Wher as with harpes, lutes, and g释ernes
They daunce and playen at dees bothe day and night,

114. thoughte, intended. **118. idelly,** i.e., without profit. **119. countrefete,** imitate. **120. wolle,** wool. **121. Al . . . it,** even though it were. **123. Al . . . sterve,** even though her children should die. **127. liking,** pleasure. **135. whilom,** once. **136. haunteden,** practiced. **137. riot,** wild parties; **hasard,** gambling; **stewes,** brothels. **138. giternes,** guitars. **139. dees,** dice.

And ete also and drinke over hir might,°
Thurgh which they doon the devel sacrifise
Withinne that develes temple in cursed wise
By superfluitee° abhominable.
Hir othes been so grete and so dampnable
That it is grisly for to heere hem swere:
Oure blessed Lordes body they totere°—
Hem thoughte that Jewes rente° him nought ynough.
And eech of hem at otheres sinne lough.°
And right anoon thanne comen tombesteres,°
Fetis and smale, and yonge frutesteres,°
Singeres with harpes, bawdes, wafereres°—
Whiche been the verray develes officeres,
To kindle and blowe the fir of lecherye
That is annexed unto glotonye:°
The Holy Writ take I to my witnesse
That luxure° is in win and dronkenesse.
Lo, how that dronken Lot unkindely°
Lay by his doughtres two unwitingly:
So dronke he was he niste° what he wroughte.
Herodes, who so wel the stories soughte,
Whan he of win was repleet at his feeste,
Right at his owene table he yaf his heeste°
To sleen° the Baptist John, ful giltelees.
  Senek saith a good word doutelees:
He saith he can no difference finde
Bitwixe a man that is out of his minde
And a man which that is dronkelewe,°
But that woodnesse, yfallen in a shrewe,°
Persevereth lenger than dooth dronkenesse.

140. over hir might, beyond their capacity. **143. superfluitee,** overindulgence. **146. totere,** tear apart, i.e., by swearing by its members. **147. rente,** tore. **148. lough,** laughed. **149. tombesteres,** dancing girls. **150. Fetis . . . smale,** shapely and neat; **frutesteres,** female fruit vendors. **151. wafereres,** cake vendors. **154. annexed,** i.e., closely related; **glotonye,** gluttony. **156. luxure,** lechery. **157. unkindely,** unnaturally. **159. niste,** didn't know. **162. heeste,** command. **163. sleen,** slay. **167. dronkelewe,** drunken. **168.** But that madness occurring in a wicked man.

O glotonye, ful of cursednesse!°
O cause first of oure confusioun!°
O original of oure dampnacioun,°
Til Crist hadde bought° us with his blood again!
Lo, how dere, shortly for to sayn,
Abought° was thilke cursed vilainye;
Corrupt was al this world for glotonye:
Adam oure fader and his wif also
Fro Paradis to labour and to wo
Were driven for that vice, it is no drede.°
For whil that Adam fasted, as I rede,
He was in Paradis; and whan that he
Eet of the fruit defended° on a tree,
Anoon he was out cast to wo and paine.
O glotonye, on thee wel oughte us plaine!°
O, wiste a man° how manye maladies
Folwen of excesse and of glotonies,
He wolde been the more mesurable°
Of his diete, sitting at his table.
Allas, the shorte throte, the tendre mouth,
Maketh that eest and west and north and south,
In erthe, in air, in water, men to swinke,°
To gete a gloton daintee mete and drinke.
Of this matere, O Paul, wel canstou trete:
"Mete unto wombe, and wombe° eek unto mete,
Shal God destroyen bothe," as Paulus saith.
Allas, a foul thing is it, by my faith,
To saye this word, and fouler is the deede
Whan man so drinketh of the white and rede°
That of his throte he maketh his privee°
Thurgh thilke cursed superfluitee.°

170. cursednesse, wickedness. **171. confusioun,** downfall. **172. dampnacioun,** damnation. **173. bought,** redeemed. **175. Abought,** paid for. **179. drede,** doubt. **182. Eet,** ate; **defended,** forbidden. **184. plaine,** complain. **185. wiste a man,** if a man knew. **187. mesurable,** moderate. **191. swinke,** work. **194. wombe,** belly. **198. white, rede,** i.e., wines. **199. privee,** privy. **200. superfluitee,** over-eating and -drinking.

The Apostle weeping saith ful pitously,
"Ther walken manye of which you told have I—
I saye it now weeping with pitous vois—
They been enemies of Cristes crois,
Of whiche the ende is deeth—wombe is hir god!"
O wombe, O bely, O stinking cod,
Fulfilled of dong and of corrupcioun!
At either ende of thee foul is the soun.
How greet labour and cost is thee to finde!
Thise cookes, how they stampe and straine and grinde,
And turnen substance into accident
To fulfillen al thy likerous talent!
Out of the harde bones knokke they
The mary, for they caste nought away
That may go thurgh the golet softe and soote.
Of spicerye of leef and bark and roote
Shal been his sauce ymaked by delit,
To make him yit a newer appetit.
But certes, he that haunteth swiche delices
Is deed whil that he liveth in tho vices.
A lecherous thing is win, and dronkenesse
Is ful of striving and of wrecchednesse.
O dronke man, disfigured is thy face!
Sour is thy breeth, foul artou to embrace!
And thurgh thy dronke nose seemeth the soun
As though thou saidest ay "Sampsoun, Sampsoun."
And yit, God woot, Sampson drank nevere win.
Thou fallest as it were a stiked swin;
Thy tonge is lost, and al thyn honeste cure,
For dronkenesse is verray sepulture

201. The Apostle, i.e., St. Paul. **204. crois,** cross. **206. cod,** bag. **207. Fulfilled,** filled full; **dong,** dung. **208. soun,** sound. **209. finde,** provide for. **210. stampe,** pound. **211.** A philosophic joke, depending on the distinction between inner reality (substance) and outward appearance (accident). **212. likerous talent,** dainty appetite. **214. mary,** marrow. **215. golet,** gullet; **soote,** sweetly. **216. spicerye,** spices. **219. delices,** pleasures. **220. deed,** dead. **222. striving,** quarreling. **227. woot,** knows. **228. stiked swin,** stuck pig. **229. honeste cure,** i.e., care for self-respect. **230. sepulture,** burial.

Of mannes wit and his discrecioun.
In whom that drinke hath dominacioun
He can no conseil keepe, it is no drede.
Now keepe you fro the white and fro the rede—
And namely fro the white win of Lepe
That is to selle in Fisshstreete or in Chepe:
The win of Spaine creepeth subtilly
In othere wines growing faste by,
Of which ther riseth swich fumositee
That whan a man hath dronken draughtes three
And weeneth that he be at hoom in Chepe,
He is in Spaine, right at the town of Lepe,
Nat at The Rochele ne at Burdeux town;
And thanne wol he sayn "Sampsoun, Sampsoun."
  But herkneth, lordinges, oo word I you praye,
That alle the soverein actes, dar I saye,
Of victories in the Olde Testament,
Thurgh verray God that is omnipotent,
Were doon in abstinence and in prayere:
Looketh the Bible and ther ye may it lere.
  Looke Attilla, the grete conquerour,
Deide in his sleep with shame and dishonour,
Bleeding at his nose in dronkenesse:
A capitain sholde live in sobrenesse.
  And overal this, aviseth you right wel
What was comanded unto Lamuel—
Nat Samuel, but Lamuel, saye I—
Redeth the Bible and finde it expresly,
Of win-yiving to hem that han justise:
Namore of this, for it may wel suffise.

233. conseil, secrets; **drede,** doubt. **235. namely,** particularly; **Lepe,** a town in Spain. **236.** Fishstreet and Cheapside are London localities. **237ff.** The Pardoner is joking at the illegal custom of adulterating fine wines of Bordeaux and La Rochelle with strong Spanish wine. **238. faste,** close. **239. fumositee,** heady fumes. **241.weeneth,** supposes. **246. soverein actes,** distinguished deeds. **250. Looketh,** behold; **lere,** learn. **255. aviseth you,** consider. **256.** Lemuel's mother told him that kings should not drink. **259. win-yiving,** wine-serving; **han,** i.e., administer.

And now that I have spoken of glotonye,
Now wol I you defende hasardrye:°
Hasard is verray moder of lesinges,°
And of deceite and cursed forsweringes,
Blaspheme of Crist, manslaughtre, and wast also
Of catel° and of time; and ferthermo,
It is repreve° and contrarye of honour
For to been holden a commune hasardour,°
And evere the hyer he is of estat
The more is he holden desolat.°
If that a prince useth hasardrye,
In alle governance and policye
He is, as by commune opinioun,
Yholde the lasse° in reputacioun.
Stilbon, that was a wis embassadour,
Was sent to Corinthe in ful greet honour
Fro Lacedomye° to make hir alliaunce,
And whan he cam him happede° parchaunce
That alle the gretteste° that were of that lond
Playing at the hasard he hem foond,°
For which as soone as it mighte be
He stal him° hoom again to his contree,
And saide, "Ther wol I nat lese° my name,
N'I wol nat take on me so greet defame°
You to allye unto none hasardours:
Sendeth othere wise embassadours,
For by my trouthe, me were levere° die
Than I you sholde to hasardours allye.
For ye that been so glorious in honours
Shal nat allye you with hasardours
As by my wil, ne as by my tretee."°
This wise philosophre, thus saide he.

262. **defende,** prohibit; **hasardrye,** gambling. 263. **moder,** mother; **lesinges,** lies. 266. **catel,** property. 267. **repreve,** disgrace. 268. **hasardour,** gambler. 270. **desolat,** i.e., dissolute. 274. **lasse,** less. 277. **Lacedomye,** Sparta. 278. **happede,** it happened. 279. **gretteste,** greatest. 280. **foond,** found. 282. **stal him,** stole away. 283. **lese,** lose. 284. **defame,** dishonour. 287. **me . . . levere,** I had rather. 291. **tretee,** treaty.

Looke eek that to the king Demetrius
The King of Parthes, as the book saith us,
Sente him a paire of dees of gold in scorn,
For he hadde used hasard therbiforn,
For which he heeld his glorye or his renown
At no value or reputacioun.
Lordes may finden other manere play
Honeste ynough to drive the day away.
Now wol I speke of othes false and grete
A word or two, as olde bookes trete:
Greet swering is a thing abhominable,
And fals swering is yit more reprevable.
The hye God forbad swering at al—
Witnesse on Mathew. But in special
Of swering saith the holy Jeremie,
"Thou shalt swere sooth thine othes and nat lie,
And swere in doom and eek in rightwisnesse,
But idel swering is a cursednesse."
Biholde and see that in the firste Table
Of hye Goddes heestes honorable
How that the seconde heeste of him is this:
"Take nat my name in idel or amis."
Lo, rather he forbedeth swich swering
Than homicide, or many a cursed thing.
I saye that as by ordre thus it stondeth—
This knoweth that his heestes understondeth
How that the seconde heeste of God is that.
And fertherover, I wol thee telle al plat
That vengeance shal nat parten from his hous
That of his othes is too outrageous.
"By Goddes precious herte!" and "By his nailes!"

294. Parthes, Parthians. **295. dees,** dice. **300. Honeste,** honorable. **304. reprevable,** reprehensible. **307. Jeremie,** Jeremiah. **309. doom,** equity; **rightwisnesse,** righteousness. **310. cursednesse,** wickedness. **311. firste Table,** the first four commandments. **312. heestes,** commandments. **315. rather,** sooner. **318. that,** i.e., he that. **320. fertherover,** moreover; **plat,** flat. **323. nailes,** fingernails.

And "By the blood of Crist that is in Hailes,
Sevene is my chaunce, and thyn is cink and traye!"
"By Goddes armes, if thou falsly playe
This daggere shal thurghout thyn herte go!"
This fruit cometh of the bicche bones two—
Forswering, ire, falsnesse, homicide.
Now for the love of Crist that for us dyde,
Lete youre othes bothe grete and smale.
But sires, now wol I telle forth my tale.
  Thise riotoures three of whiche I telle,
Longe erst er prime ronge of any belle,
Were set hem in a taverne to drinke,
And as they sat they herde a belle clinke
Biforn a cors was caried to his grave.
That oon of hem gan callen to his knave:
"Go bet," quod he, "and axe redily
What cors is this that passeth heer forby,
And looke that thou reporte his name weel."
  "Sire," quod this boy, "it needeth neveradeel:
It was me told er ye cam heer two houres.
He was, pardee, an old felawe of youres,
And sodeinly he was yslain tonight,
Fordronke as he sat on his bench upright;
Ther cam a privee thief men clepeth Deeth,
That in this contree al the peple sleeth,
And with his spere he smoot his herte atwo,
And wente his way withouten wordes mo.
He hath a thousand slain this pestilence.
And maister, er ye come in his presence,
Me thinketh that it were necessarye
For to be war of swich an adversarye;

324. Hailes, an abbey in Gloucestershire supposed to possess some of Christ's blood. **325. cink . . . traye,** five and three. **328. bicche bones,** i.e., damned dice. **331. Lete,** leave. **333. riotoures,** revelers. **334. erst er,** before; **prime,** 9 A.M. **337. cors,** corpse. **338. knave,** servant. **339. bet,** better, i.e., quick; **axe,** ask; **redily,** promptly. **341. looke,** be sure; **weel,** well. **345. tonight,** last night. **346. Fordronke,** very drunk. **347. privee,** stealthy. **348. sleeth,** slays. **351. this,** during this.

Beeth redy for to meete him everemore:
Thus taughte me my dame. I saye namore."
"By Sainte Marye," saide this taverner,
"The child saith sooth, for he hath slain this yeer,
Henne° over a mile, within a greet village,
Bothe man and womman, child and hine° and page.
I trowe his habitacion be there.
To been avised° greet wisdom it were
Er that he dide a man a dishonour."
"Ye, Goddes armes," quod this riotour,
"Is it swich peril with him for to meete?
I shal him seeke by way and eek by streete,°
I make avow to Goddes digne° bones.
Herkneth, felawes, we three been alle ones:°
Lat eech of us holde up his hand to other
And eech of us bicome otheres brother,
And we wol sleen this false traitour Deeth.
He shal be slain, he that so manye sleeth,
By Goddes dignitee, er it be night."
Togidres han thise three hir trouthes° plight
To live and dien eech of hem with other,
As though he were his owene ybore° brother.
And up they sterte,° al dronken in this rage,
And forth they goon towardes that village
Of which the taverner hadde spoke biforn.
And many a grisly ooth thanne han they sworn,
And Cristes blessed body they torente:°
Deeth shal be deed if that they may him hente.°
Whan they han goon nat fully half a mile,
Right as they wolde han treden° over a stile,
An old man and a poore with hem mette;
This olde man ful mekely hem grette,°

359. Henne, hence. **360. hine,** farm laborer. **362. avised,** wary. **366. by . . . streete,** by highway and by-way. **367. digne,** worthy. **368. ones,** of one mind. **374. trouthes,** words of honour. **376. ybore,** born. **377. sterte,** started. **381. torente,** tore apart. **382. deed,** dead; **hente,** catch. **384. treden,** stepped. **386. grette,** greeted.

And saide thus, "Now lordes, God you see."°
  The pruddeste° of thise riotoures three
Answerde again, "What, carl° with sory grace,
Why artou al forwrapped° save thy face?
Why livestou so longe in so greet age?"
  This olde man gan looke in his visage,
And saide thus, "For° I ne can nat finde
A man, though that I walked into Inde,
Neither in citee ne in no village,
That wolde chaunge his youthe for myn age;
And therfore moot I han myn age stille,
As longe time as it is Goddes wille.
  Ne Deeth, allas, ne wol nat have my lif.
Thus walke I lik a restelees caitif,°
And on the ground which is my modres° gate
I knokke with my staf bothe erly and late,
And saye, 'Leve° moder, leet me in:
Lo, how I vanisshe, flessh and blood and skin.
Allas, whan shal my bones been at reste?
Moder, with you wolde I chaunge my cheste°
That in my chambre longe time hath be,
Ye, for an haire-clout° to wrappe me.'
But yit to me she wol nat do that grace,
For which ful pale and welked° is my face.
But sires, to you it is no curteisye
To speken to an old man vilainye,°
But he trespasse° in word or elles in deede.
In Holy Writ ye may yourself wel rede,
'Agains° an old man, hoor upon his heed,
Ye shal arise.' Wherfore I yive you reed,°
Ne dooth unto an old man noon harm now,

387. God you see, may God protect you. **388. pruddeste,** proudest. **389. carl,** churl. **390. forwrapped,** wrapped up. **393. For,** because. **400. caitif,** captive. **401. modres,** mother's. **403. Leve,** dear. **406. chaunge,** exchange; **cheste,** the property chest, used as the symbol for life, or perhaps a coffin. **408. haire-clout,** haircloth, used as a winding sheet. **410. welked,** withered. **412. vilainye,** rudeness. **413. But,** unless; **trespasse,** offend. **415. Agains,** in the presence of. **416. reed,** advice.

Namore than that ye wolde men dide to you
In age, if that ye so longe abide.
And God be with you wher ye go° or ride:
I moot go thider as I have to go."
"Nay, olde cherl, by God thou shalt nat so,"
Saide this other hasardour anoon.
"Thou partest nat so lightly,° by Saint John!
Thou speke° right now of thilke traitour Deeth,
That in this contree alle oure freendes sleeth:
Have here my trouthe, as thou art his espye,
Tel wher he is, or thou shalt it abye,°
By God and by the holy sacrament!
For soothly thou art oon of his assent°
To sleen us yonge folk, thou false thief."
"Now sires," quod he, "if that ye be so lief°
To finde Deeth, turne up this crooked way,
For in that grove I lafte him, by my fay,°
Under a tree, and ther he wol abide:
Nat for youre boost° he wol him no thing hide.
See ye that ook? Right ther ye shal him finde.
God save you, that boughte again° mankinde,
And you amende." Thus saide this olde man.
And everich of thise riotoures ran
Til he cam to that tree, and ther they founde
Of florins° fine of gold ycoined rounde
Wel neigh an eighte busshels as hem thoughte—
Ne lenger thanne after Deeth they soughte,
But eech of hem so glad was of the sighte,
For that the florins been so faire and brighte,
That down they sette hem by this precious hoord.
The worste of hem he spak the firste word:
"Bretheren," quod he, "take keep° what that I saye:
My wit is greet though that I bourde° and playe.

420. go, walk. **424. lightly,** easily. **425. speke,** spoke. **428. abye,** pay for. **430. assent,** i.e., party. **432. lief,** anxious. **434. lafte,** left; **fay,** faith. **436. boost,** boast. **438. boughte again,** redeemed. **442. florins,** coins. **449. keep,** heed. **450. bourde,** joke.

This tresor hath Fortune unto us yiven
In mirthe and jolitee oure lif to liven,
And lightly° as it cometh so wol we spende.
Ey, Goddes precious dignitee, who wende°
Today that we sholde han so fair a grace?
But mighte this gold be caried fro this place
Hoom to myn hous—or elles unto youres—
For wel ye woot that al this gold is oures—
Thanne were we in heigh felicitee.
But trewely, by daye it mighte nat be:
Men wolde sayn that we were theves stronge,°
And for oure owene tresor doon us honge.°
This tresor moste ycaried be by nighte,
As wisely and as slyly as it mighte.
Therfore I rede that cut amonges us alle
Be drawe, and lat see wher the cut wol falle;
And he that hath the cut with herte blithe
Shal renne to the town, and that ful swithe,°
And bringe us breed and win ful prively;
And two of us shal keepen° subtilly
This tresor wel, and if he wol nat tarye,
Whan it is night we wol this tresor carye
By oon assent wher as us thinketh best."
That oon of hem the cut broughte in his fest°
And bad hem drawe and looke wher it wol falle;
And it fil° on the yongeste of hem alle,
And forth toward the town he wente anoon.
And also soone as that he was agoon,°
That oon of hem spak thus unto that other:
"Thou knowest wel thou art my sworen brother;
Thy profit wol I telle thee anoon:
Thou woost wel that oure felawe is agoon,
And here is gold, and that ful greet plentee,
That shal departed° been among us three.

453. **lightly,** easily. 454. **wende,** would have supposed. 461. **stronge,** flagrant. 462. **doon . . . honge,** have us hanged. 465. **rede,** advise; **cut,** lots. 468. **renne,** run; **swithe,** quickly.. 470. **keepen,** guard. 474. **fest,** fist. 476. **fil,** fell. 478. **also,** as; **agoon,** gone away. 484. **departed,** divided.

But nathelees, if I can shape° it so
That it departed were among us two,
Hadde I nat doon a freendes turn to thee?"
  That other answerde, "I noot° how that may be:
He woot that the gold is with us twaye.
What shal we doon? What shal we to him saye?"
  "Shal it be conseil?" saide the firste shrewe.°
"And I shal telle in a wordes fewe
What we shul doon, and bringe it wel aboute."
  "I graunte," quod that other, "out of doute,
That by my trouthe I wol thee nat biwraye."°
  "Now," quod the firste, "thou woost wel we be twaye,
And two of us shal strenger° be than oon:
Looke whan that he is set that right anoon
Aris as though thou woldest with him playe,
And I shal rive° him thurgh the sides twaye,
Whil that thou strugelest with him as in game,
And with thy daggere looke thou do the same;
And thanne shal al this gold departed be,
My dere freend, bitwixe thee and me.
Thanne we may bothe oure lustes° al fulfille,
And playe at dees° right at oure owene wille."
And thus accorded been thise shrewes twaye
To sleen the thridde, as ye han herd me saye.
  This yongeste, which that wente to the town,
Ful ofte in herte he rolleth up and down
The beautee of thise florins newe and brighte.
"O Lord," quod he, "if so were that I mighte
Have al this tresor to myself allone,
Ther is no man that liveth under the trone°
Of God that sholde live so merye as I."
And at the laste the feend oure enemy
Putte in his thought that he sholde poison beye,°
With which he mighte sleen his felawes twaye—

485. **shape,** arrange. 488. **noot,** don't know. 491. **conseil,** a secret; **shrewe,** vilain. 495. **biwraye,** expose. 497. **strenger,** stronger. 500. **rive,** pierce. 505. **lustes,** desires. 506. **dees,** dice. 514. **trone,** throne. 517. **beye,** buy.

Forwhy the feend foond° him in swich livinge
That he hadde leve° him to sorwe bringe:
For this was outrely° his fulle entente,
To sleen hem bothe, and nevere to repente.
  And forth he gooth—no lenger wolde he tarye—
Into the town unto a pothecarye,°
And prayed him that he him wolde selle
Som poison that he mighte his rattes quelle,°
And eek ther was a polcat in his hawe°
That, as he saide, his capons hadde yslawe,°
And fain he wolde wreke him° if he mighte
On vermin that destroyed him by nighte.
  The pothecarye answerde, "And thou shalt have
A thing that, also° God my soule save,
In al this world ther is no creature
That ete or dronke hath of this confiture°—
Nat but the mountance of a corn° of whete—
That he ne shal his lif anoon forlete.°
Ye, sterve he shal, and that in lasse° while
Than thou wolt goon a paas° nat but a mile,
The poison is so strong and violent."
This cursed man hath in his hand yhent°
This poison in a box and sith he ran
Into the nexte streete unto a man
And borwed of him large botels three,
And in the two his poison poured he—
The thridde he kepte clene for his drinke,
For al the night he shoop him for to swinke°
In carying of the gold out of that place.
And whan this riotour with sory grace
Hadde filled with win his grete botels three,
To his felawes again repaireth he.
  What needeth it to sermone of it more?

519. Forwhy, because; **foond,** found. **520. leve,** permission. **521. outrely,** plainly. **524. pothecarye,** apothecary. **526. quelle,** kill. **527. hawe,** yard. **528. yslawe,** slain. **529. fain,** gladly; **wreke him,** avenge himself. **532. also,** as. **534. confiture,** mixture. **535. mountance,** amount; **corn,** grain. **536. forlete,** lose. **537. sterve,** die; **lasse,** less. **538. goon . . . paas,** take a walk. **540. yhent,** taken. **546. shoop him,** was preparing; **swinke,** work.

For right as they had cast° his deeth bifore,
Right so they han him slain, and that anoon.
And whan that this was doon, thus spak that oon:
"Now lat us sitte and drinke and make us merye,
And afterward we wol his body berye."°
And with that word it happed him par cas°
To take the botel ther the poison was,
And drank, and yaf his felawe drinke also,
For which anoon they storven° bothe two.
  But certes I suppose that Avicen°
Wroot nevere in no canon ne in no *fen*
Mo wonder signes of empoisoning
Than hadde thise wrecches two er hir ending:
Thus ended been thise homicides two,
And eek the false empoisonere also.
  O cursed sinne of alle cursednesse!
O traitours homicide, O wikkednesse!
O glotonye, luxure,° and hasardrye!
Thou blasphemour of Crist with vilainye
And othes grete of usage° and of pride!
Allas, mankinde, how may it bitide
That to thy Creatour which that thee wroughte,
And with his precious herte blood thee boughte,°
Thou art so fals and so unkinde, allas?
  Now goode men, God foryive you youre trespas,
And ware° you fro the sinne of avarice:
Myn holy pardon may you alle warice°—
So that ye offre nobles or sterlinges,°
Or elles silver brooches, spoones, ringes.
Boweth your heed under this holy bulle!
Cometh up, ye wives, offreth of youre wolle!°
Youre name I entre here in my rolle: anoon
Into the blisse of hevene shul ye goon.
I you assoile° by myn heigh power—

552. **cast,** plotted. 556. **berye,** bury. 557. **par cas,** by chance. 560. **storven,** died. 561f. Avicenna's *Canon of Medicine* was divided into sections called fens. 569. **luxure,** lechery. 571. **usage,** habit. 574. **boughte,** redeemed. 577. **ware,** guard. 578. **warice,** save. 579. **nobles, sterlinges,** valuable coins. 582. **wolle,** wool. 585. **assoile,** absolve.

Ye that wol offre—as clene and eek as cleer
As ye were born.—And lo, sires, thus I preche.
And Jesu Crist that is oure soules leeche°
So graunte you his pardon to receive,
For that is best—I wol you nat deceive.

The Epilogue

"But sires, oo word forgat I in my tale:
I have relikes and pardon in my male°
As faire as any man in Engelond,
Whiche were me yiven by the Popes hond.
If any of you wol of devocioun
Offren and han myn absolucioun,
Come forth anoon, and kneeleth here adown,
And mekely receiveth my pardoun,
Or elles taketh pardon as ye wende,
Al newe and fressh at every miles ende—
So that ye offre alway newe and newe°
Nobles or pens whiche that be goode and trewe.
It is an honour to everich that is heer
That ye mowe have a suffisant° pardoner
T'assoile you in contrees as ye ride,
For aventures whiche that may bitide:
Paraventure ther may falle oon or two
Down of his hors and breke his nekke atwo;
Looke which a suretee° is it to you alle
That I am in youre felaweshipe yfalle
That may assoile you, bothe more and lasse,
Whan that the soule shal fro the body passe.
I rede° that oure Hoste shal biginne,
For he is most envoluped° in sinne.
Com forth, sire Host, and offre first anoon,

588. **leeche,** physician. 592. **male,** bag. 601. **newe . . . newe,** over and over. 604. **suffisant,** competent. 609. **suretee,** safeguard. 613. **rede,** advise. 614. **envoluped,** involved.

And thou shalt kisse the relikes everichoon,
Ye, for a grote: unbokele° anoon thy purs."
"Nay, nay," quod he, "thanne have I Cristes curs!
Lat be," quod he, "it shal nat be, so theech!°
Thou woldest make me kisse thyn olde breech°
And swere it were a relik of a saint,
Though it were with thy fundament depeint.°
But, by the crois which that Sainte Elaine foond,°
I wolde I hadde thy coilons° in myn hond,
In stede of relikes or of saintuarye.°
Lat cutte hem of: I wol thee helpe hem carye.
They shal be shrined in an hogges tord."°
This Pardoner answerde nat a word:
So wroth he was no word ne wolde he saye.
"Now," quod oure Host, "I wol no lenger playe
With thee, ne with noon other angry man."
But right anoon the worthy Knight bigan,
Whan that he sawgh that al the peple lough,°
"Namore of this, for it is right ynough.
Sire Pardoner, be glad and merye of cheere,
And ye, sire Host that been to me so dere,
I praye you that ye kisse the Pardoner,
And Pardoner, I praye thee, draw thee neer,
And as we diden lat us laughe and playe."
Anoon they kiste and riden forth hir waye.

617. unbokele, unbuckle. **619. theech,** may I thrive. **620. breech,** breeches. **622. depeint,** stained. **623. crois,** cross; **foond,** found. **624. coilons,** testicles. **625. saintuarye,** relic-box. **627. tord,** turd. **633. lough,** laughed.

THE SHIPMAN'S TALE

A marchant whilom° dwelled at Saint Denis
That riche was, for which men heelde him wis.
A wif he hadde of excellent beautee,
And compaignable and revelous° was she,
Which is a thing that causeth more dispence°
Than worth is al the cheere and reverence
That men hem doon at feestes and at daunces—
Swich salutacions and countenaunces°
Passen as dooth a shadwe upon the wal.
But wo is him that payen moot for al!
The sely housbonde algate° he moot paye:
He moot us clothe, and he moot us° arraye,
Al for his owene worshipe, richely—
In which array we daunçen jolily;
And if that he nought may, paraventure,°
Or elles list° no swich dispence endure,
But thinketh it is wasted and ylost,
Thanne moot another payen for oure cost,
Or lene° us gold—and that is perilous.
  This noble marchant heeld a worthy hous,
For which he hadde alday so greet repair,°
For his largesse, and for° his wif was fair,
That wonder is. But herkneth to my tale.
  Amonges alle his gestes° grete and smale
Ther was a monk, a fair man and a bold—
I trowe a thritty° winter he was old—
That evere in oon was drawing to° that place.

1. **whilom,** once upon a time. 4. **compaignable,** gregarious; **revelous,** party-loving. 5. **dispence,** expense. 8. **countenaunces,** polite behavior. 11. **sely,** "poor, innocent"; **algate,** always. 12. **us:** apparently the tale was originally written for a woman, doubtless the Wife of Bath. 15. **paraventure,** by chance. 16. **list,** desires. 19. **lene,** lend. 21. **alday,** constantly; **repair,** i.e., throngs of visitors. 22. **for** (2), because. 24. **gestes,** guests. 26. **thritty,** thirty. 27. **in oon,** continually; **drawing to,** visiting.

This yonge monk that was so fair of face
Aquainted was so with the goode man
Sith that hir firste knowliche° bigan,
That in his hous as familier was he
As it is possible any freend to be;
And for as muchel as this goode man,
And eek this monk of which that I bigan,
Were bothe two yborn in oo village,
The monk him claimeth as for cosinage,°
And he again,° he saith nat ones nay,
But was as glad therof as fowl of day;
For to his herte it was a greet plesaunce.
Thus been they knit° with eterne alliaunce,
And eech of hem gan other for t'assure
Of bretherhede whil that hir lif may dure.°
  Free was daun John and manly of dispence°—
As in that hous—and ful of diligence
To doon plesance and also greet costage:°
He nat forgat to yive the leeste page
In al that hous, but after hir degree
He yaf the lord and sithe al his meinee,°
Whan that he cam, som manere honeste° thing—
For which they were as glad of his coming
As fowl is fain whan that the sonne up riseth.
Namore of this as now, for it suffiseth.
  But so bifel, this marchant on a day
Shoop him° to make redy his array
Toward the town of Brugges° for to fare,
To byen there a porcion of ware;°
For which he hath to Paris sente anoon
A messager, and prayed hath daun John
That he sholde come to Saint Denis and playe

30. knowliche, acquaintance. **36. cosinage,** i.e., his distant kinsman. **37. again,** i.e., in reply to this. **40. knit,** joined. **42. bretherhede,** brotherhood; **dure,** last. **43. Free, manly,** generous; **dispence,** expenditure. **45. doon costage,** suffer expense. **48. sithe,** afterwards; **meinee,** household. **49. honeste,** appropriate. **54. Shoop him,** planned. **55. Brugges,** Bruges in Flanders. **56. porcion . . . ware,** part of the stock in an enterprise.

With him and with his wif a day or twaye,
Er he to Brugges wente, in alle wise.°
This noble monk of which I you devise
Hath of his abbot as him list licence,°
By cause he was a man of heigh prudence,
And eek an officer,° out for to ride
To seen hir granges and hir bernes wide;°
And unto Saint Denis he comth anoon.
Who was so welcome as my lord daun John,
Oure dere cosin, ful of curteisye?
With him broughte he a jubbe of Malvesye,°
And eek another ful of fin vernage,°
And volatil, as ay was his usage;°
And thus I lete hem ete and drinke and playe,
This marchant and this monk, a day or twaye.
The thridde day this marchant up ariseth,
And on his needes sadly him aviseth,°
And up into his countour-hous° gooth he
To rekene with himselve, wel may be,
Of thilke° yeer how that it with him stood,
And how that he dispended hadde his good,
And if that he encreessed° were or noon:
His bookes and his bagges many oon
He laith bifore him on his counting-boord;
Ful riche was his tresor and his hoord,
For which ful faste his countour-dore he shette°—
And eek he nolde that no man sholde him lette°
Of his accountes for the mene time;
And thus he sit til it was passed prime.°
Daun John was risen in the morwe° also
And in the gardin walketh to and fro,
And hath his thinges° said ful curteisly.

61. **in . . . wise,** at all costs. 63. **licence,** permission. 65. **officer,** administrative officer of the monastery. 66. **seen,** inspect; **granges,** outlying farms; **bernes,** barns; **wide,** i.e., a considerable distance away from the abbey. 70. **jubbe,** jug; **Malvesye,** malmsy. 71. **vernage,** white wine. 72. **volatil,** fowls for eating; **usage,** custom. 76. **sadly,** soberly; **him aviseth,** deliberates. 77. **contour-hous,** counting house. 79. **thilke,** that same. 81. **encreessed,** i.e., richer. 85. **shette,** shut. 86. **nolde,** didn't wish; **lette,** disturb. 88. **prime,** 9 A.M. 89. **morwe,** morning. 91. **thinges,** devotions.

This goode wif cam walking prively
Into the gardin ther he walketh softe,
And him salueth° as she hath doon ofte.
A maide child cam in hir compaignye,
Which as hire list she may governe and gie,°
For yit under the yerde° was the maide.
"O dere cosin myn, daun John," she saide,
"What aileth you so rathe° for to rise?"
"Nece;" quod he, "it oughte ynough suffise
Five houres for to sleepe upon a night,
But it were for an old appalled° wight—
As been thise wedded men that lie and dare,°
As in a forme° sit a wery hare
Were al forstraught° with houndes grete and smale.
But dere nece, why be ye so pale?
I trowe,° certes, that oure goode man
Hath you laboured sith the night bigan,
That you were neede to resten hastily."
And with that word he lough° ful merily,
And of his owene thought he weex al reed.°
This faire wif gan for to shake hir heed,°
And saide thus, "Ye, God woot al," quod she.
"Nay, cosin myn, it stant° nat so with me,
For by that God that yaf me soule and lif,
In al the reaume° of France is ther no wif
That lasse lust° hath to that sory play;
For I may singe allas and wailaway
That I was born. But to no wight," quod she,
"Dar I nat telle how that it stant with me.
Wherfore I thinke out of this land to wende,
Or elles of myself to make an ende,
So ful am I of drede and eek of care."
This monk bigan upon this wif to stare,

94. **salueth,** salutes. 96. **gie,** guide. 97. **yerde,** rod, i.e., her mother's control. 99. **rathe,** early. 102. **But,** unless; **appalled,** languid. 103. **dare,** cower. 104. **forme,** lair. 105. **forstraught,** distracted. 107. **trowe,** believe. 110. **lough,** laughed. 111. **weex,** grew; **reed,** red. 112. **heed,** head. 114. **stant,** stands. 116. **reaume,** realm. 117. **lasse,** less; **lust,** desire.

And saide, "Allas, my nece, God forbede
That ye for any sorwe or any drede
Fordo youreself. But telleth me youre grief:
Paraventure I may in youre meschief
Conseile or helpe, and therfore telleth me
Al youre anoy, for it shal been secree.
For on my portehors I make an ooth
That nevere in my lif, for lief or loth,
Ne shal I of no conseil you biwraye."
"The same again to you," quod she, "I saye:
By God and by this portehors I swere,
Though men me wolde al into peces tere,
Ne shal I nevere, for to goon to helle,
Biwraye a word of thing that ye me telle—
Nat for no cosinage or alliaunce,
But verraily for love and affiaunce."
Thus been they sworn, and herupon they kiste,
And eech of hem tolde other what hem liste.
"Cosin," quod she, "if that I hadde space,
As I have noon, and namely in this place,
Thanne wolde I telle a legende of my lif—
What I have suffred sith I was a wif
With myn housbonde, al be he youre cosin."
"Nay," quod this monk, "by God and Saint Martin,
He is namore cosin unto me
Than is this leef that hangeth on the tree.
I clepe him so, by Saint Denis of France,
To han the more cause of aquaintance
Of you, which I have loved specially,
Aboven alle wommen, sikerly:
This swere I you on my professioun.
Telleth youre grief, lest that he come adown,
And hasteth you, and gooth away anoon."

127. Fordo, destroy. **130. anoy,** trouble; **secree,** secret. **131. portehors,** breviary. **132. for . . . loth,** i.e., for love or hate. **133. conseil,** secret; **biwraye,** reveal. **139. alliaunce,** relationship. **140. affiaunce,** mutual trust. **143. space,** time. **144. namely,** especially. **147. al . . . he,** even though he is. **151. clepe,** call. **154. sikerly,** certainly. **155. professioun,** monastic oath.

"My dere love," quod she, "O my daun John,
Ful lief were me this conseil° for to hide,
But oute it moot, I may namore abide:
Myn housbonde is to me the worste man
That evere was sith that the world bigan;
But sith I am a wif it sit° nat me
To tellen no wight of oure privetee—
Neither abedde ne in noon other place.
God shilde° I sholde it tellen, for his grace!
A wif ne shal nat sayn of hir housbonde
But al honour, as I can understonde—
Save unto you this muche I tellen shal:
As help me God, he is nat worth at al
In no degree the value of a flye!
But yit me greveth most his nigardye;°
And wel ye woot that wommen naturelly
Desiren thinges sixe as wel as I:
They wolde that hir housbondes sholde be
Hardy and wise and riche and therto free,°
And buxom° unto his wif, and fressh abedde.
But by that ilke Lord that for us bledde,
For his honour myself for to arraye
A° Sonday next I moste needes paye
An hundred frankes, or elles I am lorn.°
Yit were me levere° that I were unborn
Than me were doon a sclaundre or vilainye.°
And if myn housbonde eek mighte it espye,
I nere but° lost. And therfore I you praye,
Lene me this somme, or elles moot I deye.°
Daun John, I saye lene me thise hundred frankes.
Pardee, I wil nought faile you my thankes,
If that you list to doon that I you praye,
For at a certain day I wol you paye,

159. **lief,** dear, i.e., preferable; **conseil,** private matter. 163. **sit,** is suitable for. 166. **shilde,** forbid. 172. **nigardye,** miserliness. 176. **free,** generous. 177. **buxom,** obedient. 180. **A,** on. 181. **lorn,** lost. 182. **me . . . levere,** I had rather. 183. **sclaundre,** slander; **vilainye,** rude report. 185. **nere but,** would be nothing else but. 186. **Lene,** lend; **somme,** sum; **deye,** die.

And doon to you what plesance and servise
That I may doon, right as you list devise.
And but I do, God take on me vengeance
As foul as evere hadde Genelon° of France."
  This gentil monk answerde in this manere,
"Now trewely, myn owene lady dere,
I have," quod he, "on you so greet a routhe°
That I you swere and plighte you my trouthe°
That whan youre housbonde is to Flandres fare°
I wol delivere you out of this care;
For I wol bringe you an hundred frankes."
And with that word he caughte hire by the flankes,
And hire embraceth harde, and kiste hire ofte.
"Gooth now youre way," quod he, "al stille and softe,
And lat us dine as soone as that ye may,
For by my chilindre° it is prime of day.
Gooth now, and beeth as trewe as I shal be."
  "Now elles God forbede, sire," quod she;
And forth she gooth as jolif as a pie,°
And bad the cookes that they sholde hem hie°
So that men mighte dine, and that anoon.
Up to hir housbonde is this wif ygoon,
And knokketh at his countour boldely.
  "Qui la?"° quod he. "Peter, it am I,"
Quod she. "What, sire, how longe wol ye faste?
How longe time wol ye rekene and caste°
Youre sommes and youre bookes and youre thinges?°
The devel have part on alle swiche rekeninges!
Ye have ynough, pardee, of Goddes sonde.°
Come down today, and lat youre bagges stonde:
Ne be ye nat ashamed that daun John
Shal fasting al this day elenge° goon?
What, lat us heere a masse and go we dine."

194. **Genelon,** Ganelon, the betrayer of Roland in the Charlemagne legend. 197. **routhe,** pity. 198. **trouthe,** troth, oath. 199. **fare,** gone. 206. **chilindre,** pocket sundial. 209. **jolif,** gay; **pie,** magpie. 210. **hie,** hasten. 214. **Qui la,** who's there. 216. **caste,** calculate. 217. **sommes,** sums; **thinges,** investments. 219. **sonde,** sending, gift. 222. **elenge,** wretched.

"Wif," quod this man, "litel canstou divine
The curious bisinesse that we have.
For of us chapmen, also° God me save,
And by that lord that cleped is Saint Ive,
Scarsly amonges twelve twaine shal thrive
Continuelly, lasting unto oure age.
We may wel make cheere and good visage,°
And drive forth° the world as it may be,
And keepen oure estaat in privetee
Til we be deed, or elles that we playe°
A pilgrimage, or goon out of the waye.°
And therfore have I greet necessitee
Upon this quainte world t'avise me;°
For everemore we mote stonde in drede
Of hap and fortune in oure chapmanhede.°
To Flandres wol I go tomorwe at day,
And come again as soone as evere I may;
For which, my dere wif, I thee biseeke°
As be to every wight buxom° and meeke,
And for to keepe oure good be curious,°
And honestly° governe wel oure hous:
Thou hast ynough in every manere wise
That to a thrifty houshold may suffise;
Thee lakketh noon array ne no vitaile;°
Of silver in thy purs shaltou nat faile."
And with that word his countour-dore he shette,°
And down he gooth, no lenger wolde he lette,°
But hastily a masse was ther said,
And speedily the tables were ylaid,
And to the diner faste they hem spedde,
And richely this monk the chapman fedde.
At after-diner daun John sobrely

226. chapmen, merchants; **also,** as. **230. make good visage,** put on a good front. **231. drive forth,** endure. **233. playe,** i.e., pretend: to go on a pilgrimage was a means merchants used to avoid paying their debts on time. **234. goon . . . waye,** keep out of sight. **236. avise me,** consider. **238. hap,** accident; **chapmanhede,** trade. **241. biseeke,** beseech. **242. buxom,** courteous. **243. curious,** careful. **244. honestly,** honorably. **247. vitaile,** foodstuffs. **249. shette,** shut. **250. lette,** delay.

This chapman took apart, and prively
He saide him thus, "Cosin, it standeth so
That wel I see to Brugges wol ye go.
God and Saint Austin speede you and gide!
I praye you, cosin, wisely that ye ride.
Governeth you also of youre diete
Attemprely, and namely in this hete.
Bitwixe us two needeth no straunge fare:
Farewel, cosin, God shilde you fro care.
And if that any thing by day or night,
If it lie in my power and my might,
That ye me wol comande in any wise,
It shal be doon right as ye wol devise.
  Oo thing er that ye goon, if it may be:
I wolde praye you for to lene me
An hundred frankes for a wike or twaye,
For certain beestes that I moste beye,
To store with a place that is oures.
God help me so, I wolde it were youres!
I shal nat faile surely of my day—
Nat for a thousand frankes, a mile way.
But lat this thing be secree, I you praye;
For yit tonight thise beestes moot I beye.
And fare now wel, myn owene cosin dere;
Graunt mercy of youre cost and of youre cheere."
  This noble marchant gentilly anoon
Answerde and saide, "O cosin myn, daun John,
Now sikerly this is a smal requeste:
My gold is youres whan that it you leste;
And nat only my gold, but my chaffare—
Take what you list, God shilde that ye spare.
But oo thing is, ye knowe it wel ynough,
Of chapman that hir moneye is hir plough:

262. Attemprely, moderately; **namely,** especially; **hete,** heat. **263. straunge fare,** i.e., formal manners. **264. shilde,** defend. **270. lene,** lend. **271. wike,** week. **272. beestes,** cattle. **273. To . . . with,** with which to store. **276. a . . . way,** not by a mile. **280. Graunt mercy,** many thanks. **283. sikerly,** certainly. **284. leste,** may please. **285. chaffare,** merchandise. **286. shilde,** forbid.

We may creance whil we han a name,
But goldlees for to been, it is no game.
Paye it again whan it lith in youre ese:
After my might ful fain wolde I you plese."
  Thise hundred frankes he fette forth anoon,
And privelу he took hem to daun John.
No wight in al this world wiste of this lone,
Saving this marchant and daun John allone.
They drinke and speke and rome a while and playe,
Til that daun John rideth to his abbeye.
  The morwe cam and forth this marchant rideth
To Flandresward: his prentis wel him gideth
Til he cam into Brugges merily.
Now gooth this marchant faste and bisily
Aboute his neede, and byeth and creaunceth:
He neither playeth at the dees ne daunceth,
But as a marchant, shortly for to telle,
He let his lif; and ther I lete him dwelle.
  The Sonday next the marchant was agoon,
To Saint Denis ycomen is daun John,
With crowne and beerd al fresshe and newe shave;
In al the hous ther nas so litel a knave,
Ne no wight elles, that he nas ful fain
That my lord daun John was come again.
And shortly to the point right for to goon,
This faire wif accorded with daun John
That for thise hundred frankes he sholde al night
Have hire in his armes bolt upright.
And this accord parfourned was in deede:
In mirthe al night a bisy lif they lede,
Til it was day that daun John wente his way,
And bad the meinee "Farewel, have good day,"
For noon of hem, ne no wight in the town,

289. creance, deal on credit; **name,** reputation. **291. lith,** lies. **292. fain,** gladly. **293. fette,** fetched. **299. morwe,** morning. **300. prentis,** apprentice. **304. dees,** dice. **306. let,** leads. **307. next,** i.e., next after; **agoon,** gone away. **310. knave,** houseboy. **311. fain,** glad. **316. bolt upright,** stretched flat. **317. parfourned,** performed. **320. meinee,** members of the household.

Hath of daun John right no suspecioun.
And forth he rideth hoom til his abbeye,
Or where him list: namore of him I saye.
  This marchant, whan that ended was the faire,°
To Saint Denis he gan for to repaire,
And with his wif he maketh feeste and cheere
And telleth hire that chaffare° is so dere
That needes moste he make a chevissaunce:°
For he was bounden in a reconissaunce°
To paye twenty thousand sheeld° anoon;
For which this marchant is to Paris goon
To borwe of certaine freendes that he hadde
A certain frankes, and some with him he ladde;°
And whan that he was come into the town,
For greet cheertee° and greet affeccioun
Unto daun John he first gooth, him to playe—
Nat for to axe° or borwe of him moneye,
But for to wite° and seen of his welfare,
And for to tellen him of his chaffare,
As freendes doon whan they been met yfere.°
Daun John him maketh feeste and merye cheere,
And he him tolde again ful specially
How he hadde wel ybought and graciously—
Thanked be God—al hool° his marchandise,
Save that he moste, in alle manere wise,
Maken a chevissance as for his beste,°
And thanne he sholde been in joye and reste.
  Daun John answerde, "Certes, I am fain
That ye in hele° ar comen hoom again;
And if that I were riche, as have I blisse,
Of twenty thousand sheeld sholde ye nat misse,
For ye so kindely this other day
Lente me gold; and as I can and may,

325. **faire,** i.e., the business deal. 328. **chaffare,** merchandise. 329. **chevissaunce,** arrangement to borrow. 330. **in a reconissaunce,** i.e., by a note. 331. **sheeld,** shields, coins. 334. **certain,** certain number of; **ladde,** led, took. 336. **cheertee,** fondness. 338. **axe,** ask. 339. **wite,** know. 341. **yfere,** together. 345. **hool,** whole. 347. **beste,** i.e., profit. 350. **hele,** health.

I thanke you, by God and by Saint Jame.
But nathelees, I took° unto oure dame,
Youre wif at hoom, the same gold again
Upon youre bench—she woot it wel, certain,
By certain toknes° that I can you telle.
Now by youre leve I may no lenger dwelle:
Oure abbot wol out of this town anoon,
And in his compaignye moot I goon.
Greete wel oure dame, myn owene nece° sweete,
And farewel, dere cosin, til we meete."
This marchant which that was ful war and wis
Creanced° hath and paid eek in Paris
To certain Lumbardes redy in hir hond°
The somme of gold, and gat of hem his bond,
And hoom he gooth, merye as a papinjay,
For wel he knew he stood in swich array°
That needes moste he winne in that viage°
A thousand frankes aboven al his costage.°
His wif ful redy mette him at the gate,
As she was wont of old usage algate,°
And al that night in mirthe they bisette,°
For he was riche and cleerly out of dette.
When it was day this marchant gan embrace
His wif al newe, and kiste hire on hir face,
And up he gooth and maketh it ful tough.
"Namore," quod she, "by God, ye have ynough."
And wantounly again with him she playde,
Til at the laste that this marchant saide:
"By God," quod he, "I am a litel wroth
With you, my wif, although it be me loth.°
And woot ye why? By God, as that I gesse,
That ye han maad a manere straungenesse°
Bitwixen me and my cosin daun John.

356. **took,** gave. 359. **toknes,** signs. 363. **nece,** niece. 366. **Creanced,** borrowed on credit. 367. **Lumbardes,** many money-lenders were Lombards; **redy . . . hond,** i.e., cash in hand. 370. **array,** condition. 371. **viage,** trip. 372. **costage,** expense. 374. **algate,** always. 375. **bisette,** employed. 384. **it . . . loth,** I don't like to be. 386. **straungenesse,** alienation.

Ye sholde han warned me er I hadde goon
That he you hadde an hundred frankes paid
By redy tokne; and heeld him yvele apaid
For that I to him spak of chevissaunce—
Me seemed so as by his countenaunce.
But nathelees, by God oure hevene king,
I thoughte nat to axe of him no thing.
I praye thee, wif, ne do namore so:
Tel me alway er that I fro thee go
If any dettour hath in myn absence
Ypayed thee, lest thurgh thy necligence
I mighte him axe a thing that he hath paid."
This wif was nat afered ne afraid,
But boldely she saide, and that anoon,
"Marie, I defye the false monk daun John!
I keepe nat of his toknes neveradeel.
He took me certain gold, this woot I weel.
What, yvel theedam on his monkes snoute!
For God it woot, I wende withouten doute
That he hadde yive it me by cause of you,
To doon therwith myn honour and my prow,
For cosinage and eek for bele cheere
That he hath had ful ofte times here.
But sith I see it stant in this disjoint,
I wol answere you shortly to the point:
Ye han mo slakker dettours than am I;
For I wol paye you wel and redily
Fro day to day, and if so be I faile,
I am youre wif: score it upon my taile.
And I shal paye as soone as evere I may,
For by my trouthe I have on myn array,
And nat in wast, bistowed every deel.

390. **By . . . tokne,** in ready cash; **heeld . . . apaid,** he felt himself ill-treated. 391. **chevissaunce,** borrowing. 394. **thoughte,** intended; **axe,** ask. 397. **dettour,** debtor. 400. **afered,** frightened. 403. **keepe,** care. 404. **took,** gave. 405. **yvel theedam,** ill prosperity. 406. **wende,** supposed. 408. **prow,** benefit. 409. **bele cheere,** i.e., the good treatment. 411. **stant,** stands; **disjoint,** predicament. 413. **slakker,** slower. 416. **score . . . taile,** charge it to my account (tally): there is a pun with "tail."

And for I have bistowed it so weel°
For your honour, for Goddes sake, I saye,
As be nat wroth, but lat us laughe and playe.
Ye shal my joly body han to wedde.°
By God, I wol nought paye you but abedde.
Forgive it me, myn owene spouse dere:
Turne hiderward and maketh bettre cheere."
  This marchant sawgh ther was no remedye,
And for to chide it nere° but folye.
"Sith that the thing may nat amended be,
Now wif," he saide, "and I foryive it thee.
But by thy lif, ne be namore so large:°
Keep bet° my good, this yive I thee in charge."
Thus endeth now my tale, and God us sende
Tailing° ynough unto oure lives ende.

THE PRIORESS' TALE

The Introduction

"Wel said, by corpus dominus,"° quod oure Host.
"Now longe mote thou saile by the coost,°
Sire gentil maister, gentil mariner.
God yive the monk a thousand last quaad yeer!°
Aha, felawes, beeth war of swich a jape!°
The monk putte in the mannes hood an ape,°
And in his wives eek, by Saint Austin:
Draweth no monkes more into youre in.°
  But now passe over, and lat us seeke aboute:

420. **weel,** well. 423. **to wedde,** as security for the debt. 428. **nere,** it would not be. 431. **large,** spendthrift. 432. **bet,** better. 434. **Tailing,** another pun as above, l. 416.

1. **corpus dominus,** the Host's corrupt Latin for "God's body." 2. **coost,** coast. 4. **a . . . yeer,** a thousand cartloads of bad years. 5. **jape,** trick. 6. To put an ape in some one's hood is to make a fool of him. 8. **Draweth,** i.e., invite; **in,** dwelling.

Who shal now telle first of al this route°
Another tale?" And with that word he saide,
As curteisly as it hadde been a maide,
"My lady Prioresse, by youre leve,°
So° that I wiste I sholde you nat greve,
I wolde deemen that ye telle sholde
A tale next, if so were that ye wolde.
Now wol ye vouche sauf, my lady dere?"
"Gladly," quod she, and saide as ye shal heere.

The Prologue

O Lord, oure Lord, thy name how merveilous
Is in this large world ysprad°—quod she—
For nat only thy laude° precious
Parfourned° is by men of dignitee,
But by the mouth of children thy bountee°
Parfourned is, for on the brest soukinge°
Somtime shewen they thyn heryinge.°

Wherfore in laude, as I best can or may,
Of thee and of the white lilye flowr
Which that thee bar,° and is a maide alway,
To telle a storye I wol do my labour—
Nat that I may encreessen hir honour,
For she hirself is honour, and the roote
Of bountee, next hir sone, and soules boote.°

O moder maide, O maide moder free!°
O bussh unbrent, brenning° in Moises sighte!
That ravisshedest down fro the deitee,
Thurgh thyn humblesse, the gost° that in th'alighte,

10. **route,** group. 13. **leve,** permission. 14. **So,** provided.

2. **ysprad,** spread. 3. **laude,** praise. 4. **Parfourned,** performed. 5. **bountee,** goodness. 6. **soukinge,** sucking. 7. **heryinge,** praise. 10. **bar,** bore. 14. **boote,** remedy. 15. **moder,** mother; **free,** noble. 16. **unbrent,** unburnt; **brenning,** burning. 18. **gost,** i.e., the Holy Ghost.

Of whos vertu whan he thyn herte lighte,°
Conceived was the Fadres sapience:°
Help me to telle it in thy reverence.

Lady, thy bountee, thy magnificence,°
Thy vertu and thy grete humilitee
Ther may no tonge expresse in no science;°
For somtime, lady, er men praye to thee,
Thou goost biforn° of thy benignitee,
And getest us the light of° thy prayere,
To giden us unto thy Sone so dere.

My conning is so waik,° O blisful Queene,
For to declare thy grete worthinesse,
That I ne may the weighte nat sustene,°
But as a child of twelfmonth old or lesse,
That can unnethe° any word expresse,
Right so fare I, and therfore I you praye:
Gideth my song that I shal of you saye.

The Tale

Ther was in Asie in a greet citee
Amonges Cristen folk a Jewerye,°
Sustened by a lord of that contree
For foul usure and lucre of vilainye,°
Hateful to Crist and to his compaignye;
And thurgh the streete men mighte ride and wende,
For it was free and open at either ende.

19. vertu, power; **lighte,** illuminated. **20. Fadres sapience,** one of the common terms for Christ is the Wisdom of God the Father. **22. bountee,** generosity; **magnificence,** magnanimity. **24. science,** i.e., degree of knowledge. **26. goost biforn,** anticipate. **27. getest us,** procure for us; **of,** by. **29. conning,** ability; **waik,** weak. **31. sustene,** sustain. **33. unnethe,** scarcely. **37. Jewerye,** i.e., a ghetto. **39. usure,** usury; **lucre . . . vilainye,** i.e., filthy lucre.

A litel scole of Cristen folk ther stood
Down at the ferther ende, in which ther were
Children an heep,° ycomen of Cristen blood,
That lerned in that scole yeer by yere
Swich manere doctrine as men used there—
This is to sayn, to singen and to rede,
As smale children doon in her childhede.

Among thise children was a widwes sone,
A litel clergeon° seven yeer of age,
That day by day to scole was his wone,°
And eek also, wher as he sawgh th'image
Of Cristes moder, hadde he in usage,
As him was taught, to kneele adown and saye
His Ave Marie as he gooth by the waye.

Thus hath this widwe hir litel sone ytaught
Oure blisful Lady, Cristes moder dere,
To worshipe ay, and he forgat it naught,
For sely child wol alday soone lere.°
But ay whan I remembre on this matere,
Saint Nicholas stant° evere in my presence,
For he so young to Crist dide reverence.°

This litel child his litel book lerninge,
As he sat in the scole at his Primer,
He *Alma redemptoris*° herde singe,
As children lerned hir antiphoner;°
And as he dorste, he drow him neer and neer,°
And herkned ay the wordes and the note,
Til he the firste vers coude° al by rote.

45. **Children . . . heep,** a number of children. 51. **clergeon,** diminutive of clerk. 52. **to . . . wone,** his custom was to go to school. 60. **sely,** innocent; **alday,** always; **soone,** quickly; **lere,** learn. 62. **stant,** stands. 63. It is told of St. Nicholas that even when he was at the breast he fasted on fast days. 66. **Alma redemptoris (mater),** the anthem "Gracious Mother of the Redeemer." 67. **antiphoner,** anthem-books. 68. **drow,** drew; **neer,** nearer. 70. **vers,** i.e., line; **coude,** knew.

Nat wiste he what this Latin was to saye,°
For he so yong and tendre was of age,
But on a day his felawe gan he praye
T'expounden him this song in his langage,
Or telle him why this song was in usage:
This prayde he him to construe° and declare,
Ful often time upon his knees bare.

His felawe, which that elder was than he,
Answerde him thus, "This song, I have herd saye,
Was maked of oure blisful Lady free,
Hire to salue,° and eek hire for to praye
To been oure help and socour whan we deye.°
I can namore expounde in this matere:
I lerne song, I can but smal gramere."°

"And is this song maked in reverence
Of Cristes moder?" saide this innocent.
"Now certes I wol do my diligence
To conne° it al er Cristemasse is went—
Though that I for my Primer shal be shent,°
And shal be beten° thries in an houre,
I wol it conne oure Lady for to honoure."

His felawe taughte him hoomward° prively,
Fro day to day, til he coude° it by rote;
And thanne he soong° it wel and boldely,
Fro word to word, according with the note:
Twies a day it passed thurgh his throte—
To scoleward and hoomward whan he wente.
On Cristes moder set was his entente.°

As I have said, thurghout the Jewerye
This litel child, as he cam to and fro,

71. **saye,** i.e., mean. 76. **construe,** explain. 81. **salue,** greet. 82. **socour,** succor; **deye,** die. 84. **can,** know; **gramere,** i.e., Latin. 88. **conne,** learn. 89. **for . . . Primer,** i.e., for neglecting my Primer; **shent,** punished. 90. **beten,** beaten. 92. **hoomward,** i.e., on the way home. 93. **coude,** knew. 94. **soong,** sang. 98. **entente,** heart.

Ful merily thanne wolde he singe and crye
O alma redemptoris evere mo;
The swetnesse hath his herte perced so
Of Cristes moder, that to hire to praye
He can nat stinte of° singing by the waye.

Oure firste fo, the serpent Satanas,
That hath in Jewes herte his waspes nest,
Up swal° and saide, "O Hebraic peple, allas,
Is this to you a thing that is honest,°
That swich a boy shal walken as him lest,°
In youre despit, and singe of swich sentence,°
Which is agains oure lawes reverence?"

Fro thennes forth the Jewes han conspired
This innocent out of this world to chace:
An homicide therto han they hired
That in an aleye hadde a privee place;
And as the child gan forby for to pace,°
This cursed Jew him hente° and heeld him faste,
And kitte° his throte and in a pit him caste.

I saye that in a wardrobe° they him threwe,
Wher as thise Jewes purgen hir entraile.
O cursed folk of Herodes° al newe,
What may youre yvel entente you availe?
Mordre° wol out, certain it wol nat faile,
And namely° ther th'honour of God shal sprede:
The blood out cryeth on youre cursed deede.

O martyr souded to° virginitee,
Now maistou singen, folwing evere in oon°

105. **stinte of,** cease. 108. **swal,** swelled, i.e., reared. 109. **honest,** honorable. 110. **lest,** it pleases. 111. **sentence,** i.e., teaching. 117. **gan . . . pace,** did pass by. 118. **hente,** seized. 119. **kitte,** cut. 120. **wardrobe,** privy. 122. **Herodes,** Herod, who at Christ's birth ordered all new-born children slain. 124. **Mordre,** murder. 125. **namely,** especially. 127. **souded to,** enlisted in the service of. 128. **evere in oon,** constantly.

The White Lamb celestial—quod she—
Of which the grete Evangelist Saint John
In Pathmos wroot, which saith that they that goon
Biforn this Lamb and singe a song al newe,
That nevere flesshly womman they ne knewe.

This poore widwe awaiteth al that night
After hir litel child, but he cam nought;
For which, as soone as it was dayes light,
With face pale of drede and bisy thought
She hath at scole and elleswhere him sought,
Til finally she gan so fer espye
That he last seen was in the Jewerye.

With modres pitee in hir brest enclosed,
She gooth, as she were half out of hir minde,
To every place wher as she hath supposed
By liklihede hir litel child to finde.
And evere on Cristes moder meeke and kinde
She cride, and at the laste thus she wroughte,
Among the cursed Jewes she him soughte.

She fraineth and she prayeth pitously
To every Jew that dwelte in thilke place
To telle hire if hir child wente ought forby.
They saide nay, but Jesu of his grace
Yaf in hir thought inwith a litel space
That in that place after hir sone she cride
Wher he was casten in a pit biside.

O grete God, that parfournest thy laude
By mouth of innocents, lo, here thy might!
This gemme of chastitee, this emeraude,

131. **Pathmos,** Patmos, where St. John the Divine wrote the Biblical Book of Revelation. 137. **bisy,** anxious. 139. **gan . . . espye,** i.e., discovered. 148. **fraineth,** questions. 149. **thilke,** that same. 150. **wente . . . forby,** i.e., had passed by. 152. **inwith,** within; **space,** time. 155. **parfournest,** perform; **laude,** praise. 156. **here,** i.e., here is an example of. 157. **emeraude,** emerald.

And eek of martyrdom the ruby bright,
Ther he with throte ycorven lay upright,
He *Alma redemptoris* gan to singe,
So loude that al the place gan to ringe.

The Cristen folk that thurgh the streete wente
In comen for to wondre upon this thing,
And hastily they for the provost sente.
He cam anoon, withouten tarying,
And herieth Crist that is of hevene king,
And eek his moder, honour of mankinde:
And after that the Jewes leet he binde.

This child with pitous lamentacioun
Up taken was, singing his song alway,
And with honour of greet processioun
They caryen him unto the nexte abbey.
His moder swouning by his beere lay—
Unnethe mighte the peple that was there
This newe Rachel bringen fro his beere.

With torment and with shameful deeth eechoon
The provost dooth thise Jewes for to sterve
That of this mordre wiste, and that anoon:
He nolde no swich cursednesse observe.
Yvel shal have that yvel wol deserve—
Therfore with wilde hors he dide hem drawe,
And after that he heeng hem by the lawe.

Upon his beere ay lith this innocent
Biforn the chief auter, whil the masse laste,

159. **ycorven,** cut; **upright,** supine. 164. **provost,** chief magistrate of the city. 166. **herieth,** praises. 168. **leet . . . binde,** he caused to be bound. 173. **swouning,** swooning; **beere,** bier. 174. **Unnethe,** scarcely. 175. **Rachel,** mentioned in the Gospel of St. Matthew as the type of the mother whose child was slain by Herod's command. 176. **torment,** torture. 177. **dooth,** causes; **sterve,** die. 179. **cursednesse,** wickedness; **observe,** defer to. 181. **dide . . . drawe,** had them drawn. 182. **heeng,** hanged. 183. **lith,** lies. 184. **auter,** altar.

And after that the abbot with his covent°
Han sped hem for to buryen him ful faste;
And whan they holy water on him caste,
Yit spak this child when spreind° was holy water,
And soong° *O alma redemptoris mater.*

This abbot which that was an holy man
As monkes been, or elles oughten be,
This yonge child to conjure° he bigan,
And saide, "O dere child, I halse° thee,
In vertu° of the Holy Trinitee,
Tel me what is thy cause for to singe,
Sith that thy throte is cut to my seeminge."

"My throte is cut unto my nekke-boon,"
Saide this child, "and as by way of kinde°
I sholde have died, ye, longe time agoon;
But Jesu Crist, as ye in bookes finde,
Wol° that his glorye laste and be in minde;
And for the worshipe of his moder dere
Yit may I singe *O alma* loude and clere.

This welle° of mercy, Cristes moder sweete,
I loved alway as after my conninge;°
And whan that I my lif sholde forlete,°
To me she cam, and bad me for to singe
This antheme verraily in my dyinge,
As ye han herd; and whan that I hadde songe,°
Me thoughte she laide a grain° upon my tonge.

Wherfore I singe and singe moot, certain,
In honour of that blisful maiden free,
Til fro my tonge of° taken is the grain;
And after that thus saide she to me,

185. covent, convent, fellow-monks. **188. spreind,** sprinkled. **189. Soong,** sang. **192. conjure,** make a solemn appeal to. **193. halse,** beseech. **194. vertu,** power. **198. kinde,** nature. **201. Wol,** wills. **204. welle,** source. **205. conninge,** knowledge. **206. forlete,** leave. **209. songe,** sung. **210. grain,** seed. **213. of,** off.

'My litel child, now wil I fecche thee
Whan that the grain is fro thy tonge ytake:
Be nat agast, I wol thee nat forsake.' "

This holy monk, this abbot, him mene I,
His tonge out caughte° and took away the grain,
And he yaf up the gost° ful softely;
And whan this abbot hadde this wonder sein,°
His salte teres trikled down as rain,
And gruf he fil al plat° upon the grounde,
And stille he lay as he hadde been ybounde.

The covent eek lay on the pavement,
Weeping, and herien° Cristes moder dere;
And after that they rise and forth been went,
And took away this martyr from his beere,
And in a tombe of marbelstones clere°
Enclosen they his litel body sweete,
Ther he is now: God leve° us for to meete!

O yonge Hugh° of Lincoln, slain also
With cursed Jewes, as it is notable—
For it is but a litel while ago—
Praye eek for us, we sinful folk unstable,
That of his mercy God so merciable°
On us his grete mercy multiplye,
For reverence of his moder Marie.

Amen.

THE TALE OF SIR THOPAS

The Introduction

Whan said was al this miracle, every man
As sobre was that wonder was to see,

219. caughte, pulled. **220. yaf,** gave; **gost,** spirit. **221. sein,** seen. **223. gruf, plat,** flat; **fil,** fell. **226. herien,** praise. **229. clere,** bright. **231. leve,** i.e., grant. **232. Hugh,** another child supposedly murdered by the Jews in 1255. **236. merciable,** merciful.

Til that oure Hoste japen he bigan,
And thanne at erst he looked upon me,
And saide thus, "What man artou?" quod he.
"Thou lookest as thou woldest finde an hare,
For evere upon the ground I see thee stare.

Approche neer and looke up merily.
Now ware you, sires, and lat this man have place:
He in the wast is shape as wel as I—
This were a popet in an arm t'enbrace,
For any womman, smal and fair of face;
He seemeth elvissh by his countenaunce,
For unto no wight dooth he daliaunce.

Say now somwhat, sin other folk han said.
Tel us a tale of mirthe, and that anoon."
"Hoste," quod I, "ne beeth nat yvele apaid,
For other tale, certes, can I noon,
But of a rym I lerned longe agoon."
"Ye, that is good," quod he. "Now shul we heere
Som daintee thing, me thinketh by his cheere."

The Tale

Listeth, lordes, in good entent,
And I wil telle verrayment
  Of mirthe and of solas:
Al of a knight was fair and gent
In bataile and in tournament—
  His name was Sir Thopas.

Yborn he was in fer contree,
In Flandres al biyonde the see—

3. **japen,** joke. 4. **at erst,** for the first time. 11. **popet,** doll, i.e., little fellow. 14. **dooth daliaunce,** makes conversation. 17. **yvele apaid,** ill-pleased. 18. **can,** know. 21. **daintee,** delightful; **cheere,** face.

1. **Listeth,** listen. 2. **verrayment,** truly. 3. **solas,** delight. 4. **gent,** noble, pretty. 7. **fer,** far.

At Popering° in the place.
His fader was a man ful free,°
And lord he was of that contree,
As it was Goddes grace.

Sir Thopas wax° a doughty swain:
Whit was his face as paindemain,°
His lippes rede as rose;
His rode is lik scarlet in grain,°
And I you telle in good certain
He hadde a semely nose.

His heer, his beerd, was lik saffroun,°
That to his girdel raughte° adown,
His shoon of cordewane;°
Of Brugges were his hosen° brown,
His robe was of siklatoun,°
That coste many a jane.°

He coude hunte at wilde deer,
And ride an-hawking for river,°
With grey goshawk on honde.
Therto he was a good archer,
Of wrastling was ther noon his peer,°
Ther any ram shal stonde.°

Ful many a maide bright in bowr
They moorne for him paramour,°
Whan hem were bet° to sleepe.
But he was chast, and no lechour,
And sweete as is the brambel flowr
That bereth the rede hepe.°

9. **Popering,** Poperinghe. 10. **free,** noble. 13. **wax,** grew into. 14. **paindemain,** fine white bread. 16. **rode,** complexion; **in grain,** i.e., deep-dyed. 19. **saffroun,** saffron, an orange-red spice. 20. **girdel,** belt; **raughte,** reached. 21. His shoes of Cordovan leather. 22. **Brugges,** Bruges; **hosen,** stockings. 23. **siklatoun,** cloth of gold. 24. **jane,** a small coin, i.e., cent. 26. **river,** hawking was generally practiced near a river. 29. **peer,** equal. 30. **ram,** prize for wrestling match; **stonde,** i.e., be offered. 32. **paramour,** i.e., for love. 33. **bet,** better. 36. **hepe,** roseberry.

And so bifel upon a day—
Forsoothe as I you telle may—
  Sir Thopas wolde out ride:
He worth upon his steede grey,
And in his hand a launcegay,
  A long swerd by his side.

He priketh thurgh a fair forest—
Therinne is many a wilde beest:
  Ye, bothe bukke and hare;
And as he priketh north and eest,
I telle it you, him hadde almeest
  Bitid a sory care.

There springen herbes grete and smale—
The licoris and setewale,
  And many a clowe-gilofre.
And notemuge to putte in ale,
Wheither it be moiste or stale,
  Or for to laye in cofre.

The briddes singe, it is no nay,
The sperhawk and the popinjay,
  That joye it was to heere;
The thrustelcok made eek his lay,
The wodedouve upon the spray,
  She soong ful loude and clere.

Sir Thopas fil in love-longinge,
Al whan he herde the thrustel singe,
  And priked as he were wood.
His faire steede in his prikinge

40. **worth,** mounted. 41. **launcegay,** lance. 43. **priketh,** rides. 47. **almeest,** almost. 50. **setewale,** setwall. 51. **clowe-gilofre,** clove. 52. **notemuge,** nutmeg. 53. **moiste,** fresh. 54. **cofre,** chest. 55. **nay,** i.e., denial. 56. **sperhawk,** sparrowhawk; **popinjay,** parrot. 58. **thrustelcok,** male thrush. 59. **wodedouve,** wooddove. 61. **fil,** fell; **love-longinge,** love-sickness. 63. **wood,** insane.

So swatte that men mighte him wringe—
His sides were al blood.

Sir Thopas eek so wery was
For priking on the softe gras—
So fiers was his corage—
That down he laide him in the plas,
To make his steede som solas,
And yaf him good forage.

"O Sainte Marye, bencite,
What aileth this love at me
To binde me so sore?
Me dremed al this night, pardee,
An elf-queene shal my lemman be,
And sleepe under my gore.

And elf-queene wol I have, ywis,
For in this world no womman is
Worthy to be my make
In towne:
Alle othere wommen I forsake,
And to an elf-queene I me take,
By dale and eek by downe."

Into his sadel he clomb anoon,
And priketh over stile and stoon,
And elf-queene for t'espye;
Til he so longe hath riden and goon,
That he foond in a privee woon
The contree of fairye,
So wild-e:
For in that contree was ther noon

65. **swatte,** sweated. 69. **corage,** spirit. 70. **plas,** place. 71. **solas,** i.e., rest. 73. **bencite,** for **benedicite,** bless me. 74. What cause of dissatisfaction has love with me? 77. **lemman,** mistress. 78. **gore,** skirt. 81. **make,** mate. 84. **me take,** i.e., devote myself. 86. **clomb,** climbed. 90. **foond,** found; **woon,** dwelling place.

That to him dorste ride or goon—
  Neither wif ne child-e.

Til that ther cam a greet geaunt—
His name was sire Oliphaunt,°
  A perilous° man of deede.
He saide, "Child, by Termagaunt,°
But if thou prike out of myn haunt,°
  Anoon I slee° thy steede
            With mace.
Here is the Queene of Fairye,
With harpe and pipe and symphonye,°
  Dwelling in this place."

The child saide, "Also mote I thee,°
Tomorwe wil I meete thee,
  Whan I have myn armoure.
And yit I hope, par ma fay,°
That thou shalt with this launcegay
  Abyen it ful sowre:°
            Thy mawe
Shal I percen if I may,
Er it be fully prime° of day,
  For here shaltou been slawe."°

Sire Thopas drow° abak ful faste—
This geaunt at him stones caste
  Out of a fel staf-slinge.°
But faire escapeth child° Thopas,
And al it was thurgh Goddes gras,°
  And thurgh his fair beringe.°

Yit listeth, lordes, to my tale,
Merier than the nightingale,

97. **Oliphaunt,** Elephant. 98. **perilous,** dangerous. 99. **Termagaunt,** a heathen idol. 100. **haunt,** territory. 101. **slee,** slay. 104. **symphonye,** orchestral music. 106. **Also . . . thee,** so may I thrive. 109. **par . . . fay,** by my faith. 111. **Abyen,** pay for; **sowre,** i.e., bitterly. 114. **prime,** 9 A.M. 115. **slawe,** slain. 116. **drow,** drew. 118. **fel,** dreadful; **staf-slinge,** slingshot. 119. **child,** knight. 120. **gras,** grace. 121. **beringe,** i.e., conduct.

For now I wol you roune°
How Sire Thopas with sides smale,°
Priking over hil and dale,
Is come again to towne.

His merye men comanded he
To make him bothe game and glee,°
For needes moste he fighte
With a geaunt with hevedes° three—
For paramour and jolitee°
Of oon that shoon ful brighte.

"Do come,"° he saide, "my minstrales
And geestours° for to tellen tales,
Anoon in myn arminge,
Of romances that been royales—
Of popes and of cardinales,
And eek of love-likinge."°

They fette° him first the sweete win,
And meede eek in a maselin,°
And royal spicerye,°
And gingebreed that was ful fin,
And licoris and eek comin,°
With sugre that is trye.°

He dide next his white leer,°
Of cloth of lake fin and cleer,°
A breech and eek a sherte;°
And next his sherte an aketoun,°
And over that an haubergeoun,°
For° percing of his herte;

124. **roune,** whisper, inform. 125. **sides smale,** dainty waist. 129. **glee,** music. 131. **hevedes,** heads. 132. **paramour,** true love; **jolitee,** pleasure. 134. **Do come,** have come. 135. **geestours,** tale-tellers. 139. **love-likinge,** love-pleasures. 140. **fette,** fetched. 141. **maselin,** wooden bowl. 142. **spicerye,** variety of spices. 144. **comin,** cummin, a spice. 145. **trye,** good. 146. **dide,** i.e., donned; **leer,** flanks. 147. **lake,** linen; **cleer,** bright. 148. **breech,** pair of pants; **sherte,** shirt. 149. **aketoun,** undertunic. 150. **haubergeoun,** shirt of mail. 151. **For,** i.e., to prevent.

And over that a fin hauberk—
Was al ywrought of Jewes werk—
Ful strong it was of plate;
And over that his cote-armour,
As whit as is a lilye flowr,
In which he wol debate.

His sheeld was al of gold so reed,
And therinne was a bores heed,
A charbocle by his side.
And there he swoor on ale and breed
How that the geaunt shal be deed—
Bitide what bitide.

His jambeux were of quirboily,
His swerdes sheethe of ivory,
His helm of laton bright;
His sadel was of rewel boon,
His bridel as the sonne shoon—
Or as the moone light.

His spere was of fin cypres,
That bodeth werre and nothing pees—
The heed ful sharpe ygrounde;
His steede was al dappel grey—
It gooth an ambel in the way,
Ful softely and rounde,
In londe.
Lo, lordes mine, here is a fit:
If ye wol any more of it,
To telle it wol I fonde.

152. **hauberk,** coat of mail. **153.** i.e., which was finely wrought. **155. cote-armour,** coat of arms, i.e., the cloth jacket on which the knight's heraldic bearings would be woven: Sir Topaze's was a boar's head and a **charbocle,** carbuncle, a ruby shooting forth large rays. **161. swoor,** swore. **162. deed,** dead. **164.** His leg-armor was of shaped leather. **166. laton,** brassy metal. **167. rewel boon,** ivory. **171. bodeth,** presages; **werre,** war. **174. ambel,** amble, easy pace. **175. rounde,** in a circle. **176. londe,** i.e., the country. **177. fit,** division of a poem. **179. fonde,** try.

THE SECOND FIT

Now holde youre mouth, par charitee,
Bothe knight and lady free,°
And herkneth to my spelle:°
Of bataile, and of chivalry,
And of ladies love-drury,°
Anoon I wol you telle.

Men speken of romances of pris,°
Of Horn Child and of Ypotis,°
Of Beves and Sir Gy,
Of Sir Libeux and Pleindamour—
But sire Thopas, he bereth the flowr
Of royal chivalry.

His goode steede al he bistrood,
And forth upon his way he glood,°
As sparcle out of the bronde.°
Upon his creest he bar° a towr—
And therinne stiked a lilye flowr—
God shilde his cors fro shonde!°

And for he was a knight auntrous,°
He nolde sleepen in noon hous,
But liggen° in his hoode;
His brighte helm was his wonger,°
And by him baiteth his dextrer,°
Of herbes fine and goode.

181. free, noble. **182. spelle,** song, tale. **184. love-drury,** love-making. **186. pris,** reputation. **187–9.** The romances of *Horn Child, Bevis of Southampton, Guy of Warwick,* and *The Fair Unknown* (*Li Beux Desconus*), as well as *Sir Percival of Wales* (l. 205) were popular in Chaucer's time; *Pleindamour* (the "love-filled") has not survived if it ever existed, and the only known *Ypotis* is a theological debate. **193. glood,** glided. **194.** Like a spark from the brand. **195. creest,** crest; **bar,** bore. **197.** God defend his body from harm. **198. for,** because; **auntrous,** in search of adventure. **200. liggen,** lie. **201. wonger,** pillow. **202.** And beside him grazes his horse.

Himself drank water of the wel,°
As dide the knight Sire Percivel,
  So worly under weede;°
Til on a day—

THE HOST INTERRUPTS

"Namore of this, for Goddes dignitee!"
Quod oure Hoste, "for thou makest me
So wery of thy verray lewednesse,°
That also wisly° God my soule blesse,
Mine eres aken of thy drasty° speeche.
Now swich a rym the devel I biteche!°
This may wel be rym dogerel," quod he.
  "Why so?" quod I. "Why wiltou lette° me
More of my tale than another man,
Sin that it is the beste rym I can?"°
  "By God," quod he, "for plainly, at oo word,
Thy drasty ryming is nat worth a tord!°
Thou doost nought elles but dispendest time:
Sire, at oo word, thou shalt no lenger ryme.
Lat see wher thou canst tellen ought in geeste,°
Or tel in prose somwhat at the leeste,
In which ther be som mirthe or som doctrine."
  "Gladly," quod I, "by Goddes sweete pine,°
I wol you telle a litel thing in prose,
That oughte like° you, as I suppose;
Or elles, certes, ye be too daungerous:°
It is a moral tale vertuous,
Al be it told somtime in sondry wise,
Of sondry folk, as I shal you devise.

205. Percival lived by a spring in the woods. 206. **worly,** worthy; **weede,** clothing. 210. **lewednesse,** ignorance. 211. **also wisly,** as surely as. 212. **drasty,** rubbishy. 213. **biteche,** commit to. 215. **lette,** hinder. 217. **can,** know. 219. **tord,** turd. 222. **geeste,** ? in couplets as opposed to tail rhyme. 225. **pine,** suffering. 227. **like,** please. 228. **daungerous,** hard to please.

As thus: ye woot° that every Evangelist
That telleth us the paine of Jesu Crist
Ne saith nat al thing as his felawe dooth;
But nathelees hir sentence° is al sooth,
And alle accorden° as in hir sentence,
Al be ther in hir telling difference.
For some of hem sayn more and some sayn lesse
When they his pitous passion° expresse—
I mene of Mark and Mathew, Luk, and John—
But doutelees hir sentence is al oon.°
Therfore, lordinges° alle, I you biseeche,
If that you thinke I varye as in my speeche—
As thus, though that I telle somwhat more
Of proverbes than ye han herd bifore
Comprehended in this litel tretis° here,
To enforce with th'effect° of my matere;
And though I nat the same wordes saye
As ye han herd—yit to you alle I praye
Blameth me nat, for as in my sentence
Shul ye nowher finden difference
Fro the sentence of this tretis lite°
After the which this merye tale I write.°
And therfore herkneth what that I shal saye—
And lat me tellen al my tale, I praye."

232. **woot,** know. 235. **sentence,** meaning. 236. **accorden,** agree. 239. **passion,** suffering. 241. **oon,** i.e., the same. 242. **lordinges,** gentlemen. 246. **Comprehended,** included; **tretis,** tract. 247. **effect,** point. 252. **lite,** little. 253. **After,** according to; **write,** compose.

THE MONK'S TALE

The Introduction

[Chaucer has been allowed to finish his long story of Melibeus, who was eventually persuaded by his wife Prudence not to take vengeance on his enemies but to forgive them their wrong-doings.]

Whan ended was my tale of Melibee,
And of Prudence and hir benignitee,
Oure Hoste saide, "As I am faithful man,
And by that precious corpus Madrian,°
I hadde levere° than a barel ale
That goode lief° my wif hadde herd this tale:
She nis no thing of swich pacience
As was this Melibeus wif Prudence.
By Goddes bones, whan I bete my knaves,
She bringeth me the grete clobbed° staves,
And cryeth, 'Slee° the dogges everichoon,
And breke hem bothe bak and every boon!'°
And if that any neighebor of mine
Wol nat in chirche to my wif encline,°
Or be so hardy to hire to trespace,°
Whan she comth hoom she rampeth° in my face,
And cryeth, 'False coward, wreek° thy wif!
By corpus bones,° I wol have thy knif
And thou shalt have my distaf and go spinne!'
Fro day to night right thus she wol biginne:
'Allas,' she saith, 'that evere that I was shape°
To wedden a milksop or a coward ape,
That wol been overlad° of every wight.

4. corpus Madrian, body of St. Madrian, who is unidentified. **5. levere,** rather. **6. goode lief,** good friend. **10. clobbed,** knobbed. **11. Slee,** slay. **12. boon,** bone. **14. encline,** bow. **15. trespace,** do offense. **16. rampeth,** storms. **17. wreek,** avenge. **18. corpus bones,** God's body and bones (an illiterate oath). **21. shape,** destined. **23. overlad,** overled, i.e., pushed around.

Thou darst nat stonden by thy wives right.'
This is my lif but if that I wol fighte;
And out at dore anoon I moot me dighte,
Or elles I am but lost but if that I
Be lik a wilde leon foolhardy.
I woot wel she wol do me slee somday
Som neighebor and thanne go my way—
For I am perilous with knif in honde,
Al be it that I dar nat hire withstonde,
For she is big in armes, by my faith:
That shal he finde that hire mis dooth or saith.
But lat us passe away fro this matere.
  My lord the Monk," quod he, "be merye of cheere,
For ye shal telle a tale trewely.
Lo, Rouchestre stant here faste by.
Ride forth, myn owene lord, breke nat oure game.
But by my trouthe, I knowe nat youre name:
Wher shal I calle you my lord daun John,
Or daun Thomas, or elles daun Albon?
Of what hous be ye, by youre fader kin?
I vowe to God, thou hast a ful fair skin:
It is a gentil pasture ther thou goost;
Thou art nat lik a penant or a gost.
Upon my faith, thou art som officer,
Som worthy sextein, or som celerer;
For by my fader soule, as to my doom,
Thou art a maister whan thou art at hoom,
No poore cloisterer ne no novis,
But a governour, wily and wis,
And therwithal of brawnes and of bones
A wel-faring persone for the nones.
I praye God yive him confusioun

25. **but if,** unless. 26. **moot me dighte,** must betake myself. 29. **woot,** know; **do . . . slee,** cause me to slay. 30. **go . . . way,** i.e., flee. 33. **big,** strong. 34. **mis,** amiss. 38. **Rouchestre,** Rochester; **stant,** stands. 41. **Wher,** whether; omitted in modern English; **daun,** master. 43. **hous,** i.e., monastery. 46. **penant,** one undergoing penance. 48. **sextein,** sexton; **celerer,** keeper of the wine cellar. 49. **doom,** judgment. 51. **novis,** novice. 54. **wel-faring,** handsome.

That first thee broughte unto religioun:°
Thou woldest han been a tredefowl° aright.
Haddestou as greet a leve° as thou hast might
To parfourne° al thy lust in engendrure,
Thou haddest bigeten ful many a creature.
Allas, why werestou so wid a cope?
God yive me sorwe but, and I were pope,
Nat only thou, but every mighty man,
Though he were shore ful hye upon his pan,°
Sholde have a wif, for al the world is lorn:°
Religion hath take up al the corn
Of treding, and we burel° men been shrimpes.
Of fieble trees ther comen wrecched impes:°
This maketh that oure heires been so sclendre°
And fieble that they may nat wel engendre;
This maketh that oure wives wol assaye
Religious° folk, for ye mowe bettre paye
Of Venus payements than mowe we—
God woot, no lussheburghes° payen ye!
But be nat wroth, my lord, though that I playe:
Ful ofte in game a sooth I have herd saye."
  This worthy Monk took al in pacience,
And saide, "I wol doon al my diligence—
As fer as souneth into honestee°—
To telle you a tale or two or three;
And if you list to herkne hiderward,
I wol you sayn the lif of Saint Edward;
Or elles first tragedies wol I telle,
Of whiche I have an hundred in my celle.
Tragedye is to sayn a certain storye
(As olde bookes maken us memorye)
Of him that stood in greet prosperitee,
And is yfallen out of heigh degree

56. **religioun,** i.e., monasticism. 57. **tredefowl,** breeding fowl. 58. **leve,** license. 59. **parfourne,** perform. 64. **shore,** shorn; **pan,** skull. 65. **lorn,** lost. 67. **treding,** i.e., breeding; **burel,** ignorant. 68. **impes,** saplings. 69. **sclendre,** puny. 72. **religious,** monastic. 74. **lussheburghes,** counterfeit coins. 79. **souneth . . . honestee,** i.e., accords with dignity.

Into miserye, and endeth wrecchedly.
And they been versified communely
Of sixe feet whiche men clepen exametron;
In prose eek been endited many oon,
And eek in metre in many a sondry wise.
Lo, this declaring oughte ynough suffise.
  Now herkneth if you liketh for to heere:
But first I you biseeke in this matere,
Though I by ordre telle nat thise thinges,
Be it of popes, emperours, or kinges,
After hir ages as men writen finde,
But telle hem som bifore and som bihinde,
As it now cometh unto my remembraunce:
Have me excused of myn ignoraunce."

The Tale

I wol biwaile in manere of tragedye
The harm of hem that stoode in heigh degree,
And fillen so that ther nas no remedye
To bringe hem out of hir adversitee.
For certain, whan that Fortune list to flee,
Ther may no man the cours of hire withholde:
Lat no man truste on blind prosperitee;
Beeth war by thise ensamples trewe and olde.

LUCIFER

At Lucifer, though he an angel were
And nat a man, at him I wol biginne;
For though Fortune may noon angel dere,
From heigh degree yit fil he for his sinne
Down into helle wher as he yit is inne.

91. **exametron,** hexameter. 96. **biseeke,** beseech.
3. **fillen,** fell. 5. **list,** desires. 6. **hire,** her; **withholde,** withstand. 8. **ensamples,** examples. 11. **dere,** harm. 12. **fil,** fell.

O Lucifer, brightest of angels alle,
Now artou Satanas, that maist nat twinne°
Out of miserye, in which that thou art falle.

ADAM

Lo, Adam in the feeld of Damissene°
With Goddes owene finger wrought was he,
And nat bigeten of mannes sperme unclene,
And welte° al Paradis, saving oo tree.
Hadde nevere worldly man so heigh degree
As Adam, til he for misgovernaunce
Was driven out of his heigh prosperitee
To labour, and to helle, and to meschaunce.

SAMSON

Lo Sampson, which that was annunciat°
By the angel, longe er his nativitee,
And was to God Almighty consecrat,
And stood in noblesse whil he mighte see—
Was nevere swich another as was he,
To speke of strengthe and therwith hardinesse.
But to his wives tolde he his secree,
Thurgh which he slow° himself for wrecchednesse.

Sampson, this noble almighty champioun,
Withouten wepne save his handes twaye°
He slow and al torente° the leoun,
Towardes his wedding walking by the waye.
His false wif coude him so plese and praye
Til she his conseil° knew, and she, untrewe,
Unto his foes his conseil gan biwraye,°
And him forsook, and took another newe.

15. twinne, depart. **17. Damissene,** Damascus. **20. welte,** controlled. **25. annunciat,** foretold. **32. slow,** slew: for the story of Sampson, see Judges XIII–XVI. **34. twaye,** two. **35. torente,** tore apart. **38. conseil,** secrets. **39. biwraye,** betray.

Three hundred foxes took Sampson for ire,
And alle hir tailes he togidre boond,
And sette the foxes tailes alle on fire;
For he on every tail hadde knit a brond,
And they brende alle the cornes in that lond,
And alle hir olivers and vines eke.
A thousand men he slow eek with his hond,
And hadde no wepne but an asses cheeke.

Whan they were slain, so thirsted him that he
Was wel neigh lorn, for which he gan to praye
That God wolde on his paine have som pitee,
And sende him drinke, or elles moste he deye,
And of this asses cheeke that was dreye,
Out of a wangtooth sprang anoon a welle,
Of which he drank ynough, shortly to saye:
Thus heelp him God, as *Judicum* can telle.

By verray force at Gazan on a night,
Maugree Philistians of that citee,
The gates of the town he hath up plight,
And on his bak ycaried hem hath he
Hye on an hil wher as men mighte hem see.
O noble, almighty Sampson, lief and dere,
Hadde thou nat told to wommen thy secree,
In al this world ne hadde been thy peere.

This Sampson nevere ciser drank ne win,
Ne on his heed cam rasour noon ne shere,
By precept of the messager divin,
For alle his strengthes in his heres were.
And fully twenty winter, yeer by yere,

42. **boond,** bound. 44. **knit,** fastened; **brond,** torch. 45. **brende,** burned; **cornes,** grain. 46. **olivers,** olive trees. 48. **cheeke,** jawbone. 50. **lorn,** lost. 52. **moste,** must; **deye,** die. 54. **wangtooth,** molar tooth. 56. **heelp,** helped; **Judicum,** the Book of Judges. 57. **Gazan,** Gaza. 58. **Maugree,** despite. 59. **plight,** pulled. 62. **lief,** beloved. 65. **ciser,** cider. 66. **heed,** head. 68. **heres,** hairs.

He hadde of Israel the governaunce.
But soone shal he weepe many a tere,
For wommen shul him bringen to meschaunce.

Unto his lemman Dalida he tolde
That in his heres al his strengthe lay,
And falsly to his fomen she him solde;
And, sleeping in hir barm upon a day,
She made to clippe or shere his heer away,
And made his fomen al this craft espyen.
And when that they him foond in this array,
They bounde him faste and putten out his yën.

But er his heer was clipped or yshave
There was no bond with which men mighte him binde.
But now is he in prison in a cave
Wher as they made him at the querne grinde.
O noble Sampson, strengest of mankinde,
O whilom juge in glorye and in richesse,
Now maist thou weepen with thine yën blinde,
Sith thou fro wele art falle in wrecchednesse.

Th'ende of this caitif was as I shal saye:
His fomen made a feeste upon a day,
And made him as hir fool bifore hem playe;
And this was in a temple of greet array.
But atte laste he made a foul affray,
For he two pilers shook and made hem falle,
And down fel temple and al, and there it lay,
And slow himself, and eek his fomen alle.

This is to sayn, the princes everichoon,
And eek three thousand bodies were there slain

73. **lemman,** mistress; **Dalida,** Delilah. 76. **barm,** lap. 77. **shere,** shear. 79. **foond,** found. 84. **querne,** mill. 85. **strengest,** strongest. 86. **whilom,** formerly. 88. **Sith,** since; **wele,** welfare. 89. **caitif,** captive wretch. 93. **affray,** disturbance.

With falling of the grete temple of stoon.
Of Sampson now wol I namore sayn:
Beeth war by this ensample old and plain
That no men telle hir conseil to hir wives
Of swich thing as they wolde han secree fain,
If that it touche hir limes or hir lives.

HERCULES

Of Hercules, the soverein conquerour,
Singen his werkes laude and heigh renown,
For in his time of strengthe he was the flowr:
He slow and rafte the skin fro the leoun;
He of Centauros laide the boost adown;
He Arpies slow, the cruel briddes felle;
He golden apples rafte of the dragoun;
He drow out Cerberus, the hound of helle.

He slow the cruel tyrant Busirus
And made his hors to frete him, flesh and boon;
He slow the firy serpent venimous;
Of Achilois two hornes he brak oon;
And he slow Cacus in a cave of stoon;
He slow the geant Anteus the stronge;
He slow the grisly boor, and that anoon,
And bar the hevene on his nekke longe.

101. ensample, example. **103. han,** keep; **fain,** gladly. **104. touche,** concern. **106.** His works sing laud and high renown. **108. rafte,** stripped; **leoun,** the invulnerable Nemean lion. **109. Centauros,** the Centaurs, whom Hercules put to rout on one occasion, while on another he killed the Centaur Nessus; **boost,** boast. **110. Arpies,** Harpies, wrongly identified with the Stymphalian birds. **111. rafte,** took away; **dragoun,** Ladon, guard of the tree where the apples of the Hesperides grew. **112. drow,** dragged; **Cerberus,** the three-headed dog that prevented any one from leaving hell. **113. Busirus,** Busiris, king of Egypt. **114. frete,** eat. **115. serpent,** the Lernean hydra. **116. Achilois,** Achelous, a horned sea-god from whom Hercules won his wife Dejanira; **brak,** broke. **117. Cacus,** a giant who stole from Hercules some of the oxen of Geryones. **118. Anteus,** Antaeus, another giant whom Hercules killed by holding up from the ground whence he derived his strength. **119. boor,** the Erymanthian boar. **120. bar,** bore; **longe,** for a long time: Hercules took Atlas' place as upholder of the sky while Atlas went to get the apples of the Hesperides.

Was nevere wight sith that this world bigan
That slow so manye monstres as dide he.
Thurghout this wide world his name ran,
What for his strengthe and for his hye bountee.
And every reaume wente he for to see.
He was so strong that no man mighte him lette.
At bothe the worldes endes, saith Trophee,
In stede of boundes he a piler sette.

A lemman hadde this noble champioun
That highte Dianira, fressh as May;
And as thise clerkes maken mencioun,
She hath him sent a sherte, fressh and gay:
Allas, this sherte, allas and wailaway,
Envenimed was so subtilly withalle
That er that he hadde wered it half a day
It made his flessh al from his bones falle.

But nathelees some clerkes hire excusen
By oon that highte Nessus that it maked.
Be as be may, I wol hire nought accusen,
But on his bak this sherte he wered al naked
Til that his flessh was for the venim blaked;
And whan he saw noon other remedye
In hote coles he hath himselven raked,
For with no venim deined him to die.

Thus starf this worthy, mighty Hercules.
Lo, who may truste on Fortune any throwe?
For him that folweth al this world of prees,
Er he be war, is ofte ylaid ful lowe.

121. sith, since. **124. bountee,** excellence. **125. reaume,** realm. **126. lette,** stop. **127. Trophee,** an unidentified author, perhaps the historian Guido delle Colonne. **128. boundes,** boundary stones; **piler,** pillar: Gibraltar was believed to be one of Hercules' pillars. **129. lemman,** mistress. **130. highte,** was called. **133. wailaway,** woe. **134. Envenimed,** poisoned. **135. wered,** worn. **138. Nessus,** mortally wounded by Hercules, gave the poison (his own blood) to Dejanira, assuring her it would keep Hercules faithful. **141. venim,** poison; **blaked,** blackened. **143. raked,** i.e., covered. **145. starf,** died. **146. throwe,** time. **147.** For he who follows all this busy world.

Ful wis is he that can himselven knowe.
Beeth war, for whan that Fortune list to glose,°
Thanne waiteth she hir man to overthrowe
By swich a way as he wolde leest suppose.

NEBUCHADNEZZAR

The mighty trone,° the precious tresor,
The glorious sceptre and royal majestee
That hadde the king Nabugodonosor
With tonge unnethe may descrived° be.
He twies wan° Jerusalem the citee;
The vessel of the temple he with him ladde.°
At Babyloigne was his soverein see,°
In which his glorye and his delit he hadde.

The faireste children of the blood royal,
Of Israel he leet do gelde° anoon
And maked eech of hem to be his thral.°
Amonges othere Daniel was oon,
That was the wiseste child of everichoon,
For he the dremes of the king expouned,
Ther as in Chaldeye° clerk ne was ther noon
That wiste to what fin his dremes souned.°

This proude king leet make° a statue of gold
Sixty cubites long and sevene in brede,°
To which image bothe yonge and olde
Comanded he to loute° and have in drede,
Or in a furnais° ful of flambes rede
He shal be brent° that wolde nought obeye.

150. list to glose, wishes to fool. **153. trone,** throne: for the story of Nebuchadnezzar see Daniel I–IV. **156. unnethe,** scarcely; **descrived,** described. **157. twies,** twice; **wan,** won. **158. vessel,** i.e., drinking vessels; **ladde,** took. **159. see,** seat. **162. leet do gelde,** had gelded. **163. thral,** slave. **167. Chaldeye,** Chaldea. **168. wiste,** knew; **fin,** end; **souned,** tended. **169. leet make,** had made. **170. brede,** breadth. **172. loute,** bow. **173. furnais,** furnace. **174. brent,** burned.

But nevere wolde assente to that deede
Daniel ne his yonge felawes twaye.

This king of kinges proud was and elat:°
He wende that God, that sit° in majestee,
Ne mighte him nat bireve° of his estat.
But sodeinly he loste his dignitee
And lik a beest him seemed for to be,
And eet hay as an oxe, and lay theroute
In rain; with wilde beestes walked he
Til certain time was ycome aboute.

And lik an egles fetheres weex° his heres;
His nailes lik a briddes° clawes were,
Til God releessed him a certain° yeres,
And yaf him wit; and thanne, with many a tere,
He thanked God, and evere his lif in fere°
Was he to doon amis or more trespace:°
And til that time he laid was on his beere°
He knew that God was ful of might and grace.

BELSHAZZAR

His sone, which that highte° Balthasar,
That heeld the regne after his fader day,
He by his fader coude nat be war,
For proud he was of herte and of array,
And eek an idolastre was he ay.°
His hye estaat assured° him in pride,
But Fortune caste him down—and ther he lay—
And sodeinly his regne gan divide.

177. elat, elated. **178. wende,** supposed; **sit,** sits. **179. bireve,** deprive. **185. weex,** grew. **186. briddes,** bird's. **187. releessed,** canceled for; **certain,** certain number of. **189. evere,** i.e., for all; **fere,** fear. **190. trespace,** to sin. **191. beere,** bier. **193. highte,** was named: for his story, see Daniel V. **197. idolastre,** idolater; **ay,** always. **198. assured,** made confident.

A feeste he made unto his lordes alle
Upon a time, and made hem blithe be;
And thanne his officeres gan he calle:
"Gooth, bringeth forth the vesseles," quod he,
"Which that my fader, in his prosperitee,
Out of the temple of Jerusalem birafte.
And to oure hye goddes thanke we
Of honour that oure eldres with us lafte."

His wif, his lordes, and his concubines
Ay dronken, whil hir appetites laste,
Out of thise noble vessels sondry wines.
And on a wal this king his yën caste
And saw an hand, armlees, that wroot ful faste,
For fere of which he quook and siked sore.
This hand that Balthasar so sore agaste
Wroot MANE, TECHEL, PHARES, and namore.

In al that land magicien was noon
That coude expounde what this lettre mente,
But Daniel expouned it anoon
And saide, "King, God to thy fader sente
Glorye and honour, regne, tresor, rente,
And he was proud and no thing God ne dradde;
And therfore God greet wreche upon him sente,
And him birefte the regne that he hadde.

He was out cast of mannes compaignye;
With asses was his habitacioun,
And eet hay as a beest in weet and drye
Til that he knew, by grace and by resoun,
That God of hevene hath dominacioun
Over every regne and every creature.

206. **birafte,** took away. 208. **lafte,** left. 214. **quook,** quaked; **siked,** sighed. 215. **agaste,** frightened. 216. Wrote MENE, TEKEL, UPHARSIN, and no more. 221. **rente,** income. 222. **dradde,** dread. 223. **wreche,** vengeance.

And thanne hadde God of him compassioun
And him restored his regne and his figure.

Eek thou that art his sone art proud also,
And knowest alle thise thinges verraily,
And art rebel to God and art his fo.
Thou drank eek of his vessel boldely;
Thy wif eek and thy wenches sinfully
Dronke of the same vessels sondry wines;
And heriest false goddes cursedly:
Therfore to thee yshapen ful greet pine is.

This hand was sent fro God that on the wal
Wroot MANE, TECHEL, PHARES—truste me:
Thy regne is doon, thou weyest nought at al;
Divided is thy regne, and it shal be
To Medes and to Perses yiven," quod he.
And thilke same night this king was slawe,
And Darius occupieth his degree,
Though he therto hadde neither right ne lawe.

Lordinges, ensample herby may ye take
How that in lordshipe is no sikernesse,
For whan Fortune wol a man forsake,
She bereth away his regne and his richesse,
And eek his freendes bothe more and lesse—
For what man that hath freendes thurgh Fortune,
Mishap wol make hem enemies, I gesse.
This proverbe is ful sooth and ful commune.

ZENOBIA

Zenobia, of Palymerye queene,

232. figure, i.e., human bearing. **239. heriest,** you praise. **240. yshapen,** destined; **pine,** torment. **243. weyest,** weigh. **245. Perses,** Persians. **247. thilke,** that very; **slawe,** slain. **247. degree,** rank. **248. lawe,** i.e., legal claim. **249. ensample,** example. **250. sikernesse,** security. **255. Mishap,** misfortune. **256. commune,** i.e., generally applicable. **257. Palymerye,** Palmyra.

As writen Persians of hir noblesse,
So worthy was in armes and so keene
That no wight passed hire in hardinesse,
Ne in linage, n'in other gentilesse.
Of kinges blood of Perce is she descended.
I saye nat that she hadde most fairnesse,
But of hir shap she mighte nat been amended.

From hir childhede I finde that she fledde
Office of wommen, and to wode she wente,
And many a wilde hertes blood she shedde
With arwes brode that she to hem sente.
She was so swift that she anoon hem hente.
And whan that she was elder, she wolde kille
Leons, leopardes, and beres al torente,
And in hir armes weelde hem at hir wille.

She dorste wilde beestes dennes seeke,
And rennen in the montaignes al the night,
And sleepen under the bussh; and she coude eke
Wrastlen by verray force and verray might
With any yong man, were he nevere so wight:
Ther mighte no thing in hir armes stonde.
She kepte hir maidenhede from every wight:
To no man deined hire for to be bonde.

But atte laste hir freendes han hire maried
To Odenake, a prince of that contree,
Al were it so that she hem longe taried.
And ye shal understande how that he
Nadde swiche fantasies as hadde she.
But nathelees whan they were knit in fere

262. **Perce,** Persia. 266. **Office,** functions. 269. **hente,** caught. 271. **torente,** pulled apart. 272. **weelde,** manage. 274. **rennen,** run. 277. **wight,** active. 278. **stonde,** i.e., remain standing. 280. **bonde,** bound. 282. **Odenake,** Odenathus. 283. **Al,** although; **taried,** delayed. 285. **Nadde,** didn't have; **fantasies,** desires. 286. **knit in fere,** joined together.

They lived in joye and in felicitee,
For eech of hem hadde other lief and dere.

Save oo thing, that she wolde nevere assente
By no way that he sholde by hire lie
But ones, for it was hir plein entente
To have a child, this world to multiplye.
And also soone as that she mighte espye
That she was nat with childe with that deede,
Thanne wolde she suffren him doon his fantasye
Eftsoone, and nought but ones, out of drede.

And if she were with childe at thilke cast,
Namore sholde he playen thilke game
Til fully fourty wikes weren past:
Thanne wolde she ones suffre him do the same.
Al were this Odenake wilde or tame,
He gat namore of hire, for thus she saide,
It was to wives lecherye and shame
In other caas if that men with hem playde.

Two sones by this Odenake hadde she
The which she kepte in vertu and lettrure.
But now unto oure tale turne we:
I saye so worshipful a creature,
And wis therwith, and large with mesure,
So penible in the werre and curteis eke,
Ne more labour mighte in werre endure
Was noon, though al this world men sholde seeke.

Hir riche array ne mighte nat be told,
As wel in vessel as in hir clothing;
She was al clad in perree and in gold,

288. hadde, held; **lief,** beloved. **291. plein,** full. **293. also,** as. **296. Eftsoone,** again; **drede,** doubt. **297. thilke,** that same; **cast,** i.e., act. **299. wikes,** weeks. **306. lettrure,** learning. **309. large,** generous; **mesure,** moderation. **310. penible,** indefatigable; **werre,** war. **315. vessel,** tableware. **315. perree,** jewelry.

And eek she lefte nought, for noon hunting,
To have of sondry tonges ful knowing,
Whan that she leiser hadde; and for t'entende
To lerne bookes was al hir liking—
How she in vertu mighte hir lif dispende.

And shortly of this storye for to trete,
So doughty was hir housbonde and eek she,
That they conquered manye regnes grete
In th'orient, with many a fair citee
Appertenant unto the majestee
Of Rome, and with strong hand heeld hem ful faste.
Ne nevere mighte hir fomen doon hem flee
Ay whil that Odenakes dayes laste.

Hir batailes, whoso list hem for to rede,
Again Sapor the king and othere mo,
And how that al this proces fel in deede—
Why she conquered, and what title hadde therto,
And after of hir meschief and hir wo,
How that she was biseged and ytake,
Lat him unto my maister Petrak go
That writ ynough of this, I undertake.

When Odenake was deed, she mightily
The regnes heeld and with hir propre hond
Agains hir foes she fought so cruelly
That ther nas king ne prince in al that lond
That he nas glad if that he grace foond
That she ne wolde upon his land werreye:
With hire they made alliance by bond
To been in pees, and lete hire ride and playe.

317. tonges, languages. **319. liking,** pleasure. **325. Appertenant,** belonging. **327. doon,** make. **328. Ay,** ever. **329. list,** pleases, **330. Sapor,** king of Persia; **mo,** more. **331. proces,** story; **fel,** occurred; **deede,** fact. **332. title,** claim. **335. Petrak,** Petrarch: the source is actually Boccaccio. **336. writ,** writes. **338. propre,** own. **341. foond,** found. **342. werreye,** make war.

The emperour of Rome, Claudius,
Ne him biforn, the Romain Galien,
Ne dorsten nevere been so courageous—
Ne noon Ermin,° no noon Egypcien,
No Surrian,° ne noon Arabien,
Within the feeld° that dorste with hire fighte,
Lest that she wolde hem with hir handes sleen,°
Or with hir meinee° putten hem to flighte.

In kinges habit wenten hir sones two,
As heires of hir fadres regnes alle,
And Hermanno and Thymalao
Hir names were, as Persians hem calle.
But ay Fortune hath in hir hony galle:
This mighty queene may no while endure;
Fortune out of hir regne made hire falle
To wrecchednesse and to misaventure.

Aurelian, whan that the governaunce
Of Rome cam into his handes twaye,
He shoop° upon this queene to doon vengeaunce,
And with his legions he took his waye
Toward Zenobie, and shortly for to saye,
He made hire flee, and atte laste hire hente,°
And fettred hire and eek hir children twaye,
And wan° the land, and hoom to Rome he wente.

Amonges othere thinges that he wan,
Hir chaar, that was with gold wrought and perree,°
This grete Romain, this Aurelian,
Hath with him lad° for that men sholde it see.
And biforn his triumphe walketh she,
With gilte chaines on hir nekke hanging;

348. Ermin, Armenian. **349. Surrian,** Syrian. **350. Within . . . feeld,** i.e., in a tournament. **351. sleen,** slay. **352. meinee,** troops. **363. shoop,** planned. **366. hente,** seized. **368. wan,** won. **370. chaar,** chariot; **perree,** jewelry. **372. lad,** brought.

Crowned was she as after hir degree,
And ful of perree charged hir clothing.

Allas, Fortune, that she that whilom was
Dredful to kinges and to emperoures,
Now gaureth al the peple on hire, allas!
And she that helmed was in starke stoures,
And wan by force townes strong and towres,
Shal on hir heed now were a vitremite;
And she that bar the sceptre ful of flowres,
Shal bere a distaf, hir cost for to quite.

NERO

Although that Nero were as vicious
As any feend that lith ful lowe adown,
Yit he, as telleth us Suetonius,
This wide world hadde in subjeccioun,
Bothe Eest and West, South and Septemtrioun.
Of rubies, saphires, and of perles white
Were alle his clothes brouded up and down,
For he in gemmes greetly gan delite.

More delicat, more pompous of array,
More proud was nevere emperour than he.
That ilke cloth that he hadde wered oo day
After that time he nolde it nevere see.
Nettes of gold threed hadde he greet plentee
To fisshe in Tiber whan him liste playe;
His lustes were al lawe in his decree,
For Fortune as his freend him wolde obeye.

He Rome brende for his delicacye;
The senatoures he slow upon a day

376. charged, loaded. **386. lith,** lies. **387. Suetonius:** see line 642 below. **389. Septemtrioun,** north. **391. brouded,** embroidered. **392. gan,** did. **393. delicat,** luxurious; **pompous,** festive. **395. ilke,** same; **wered,** worn. **398. liste,** pleased. **401. brende,** burnt; **delicacye,** amusement. **402. slow,** slew.

To heere how that men wolde weepe and crye;
And slow his brother, and by his suster lay.
His moder made he in pitous array:
For he hir wombe slitte to biholde
Where he conceived was—so wailaway,
That he so litel of his moder tolde.

No tere out of his yën for that sighte
Ne cam, but saide, "A fair womman was she."
Greet wonder is how that he coude or mighte
Be doomesman of hir deede beautee.
The win to bringen him comanded he
And drank anoon—noon other wo he made.
Whan might is joined unto crueltee,
Allas, too deepe wol the venim wade.

In youthe a maister hadde this emperour
To teche him lettrure and curteisye,
For of moralitee he was the flowr,
As in his time, but if bookes lie.
And whil this maister hadde of him maistrye
He maked him so lowely and so souple
That longe time it was er tyrannye
Or any vice dorste in him uncouple.

This Seneca of which that I devise,
By cause Nero hadde of him swich drede,
For he fro vices wolde him ay chastise
Discreetly, as by word and nat by deede—
"Sire," wolde he sayn, "an emperour moot neede
Be vertuous and hate tyrannye."—
For which he in a bath made him to bleede
On bothe his armes til he moste die.

407. wailaway, alas. **408. tolde,** accounted. **412. deede,** dead. **416. venim,** poison; **wade,** sink. **418. lettrure,** literature. **420. but if,** unless. **422. souple,** pliant. **424. uncouple,** break loose. **425. devise,** speak. **427. ay,** ever. **429. moot,** must. **432. moste,** must.

This Nero hadde eek of acustomaunce
In youthe agains his maister for to rise,
Which afterward him thoughte a greet grevaunce:
Therefore he made him dien in this wise.
But nathelees this Seneca the wise
Chees in a bath to die in this manere,
Rather than han another tormentrise.
And thus hath Nero slain his maister dere.

Now fel it so that Fortune liste no lenger
The hye pride of Nero to cherice,
For though that he was strong, yit was she strenger.
She thoughte thus: "By God, I am too nice
To sette a man that is fulfild of vice
In heigh degree and emperour him calle;
By God, out of his sete I wol him trice:
Whan he leest weeneth soonest shal he falle."

The peple roos upon him on a night
For his defaute, and whan he it espied,
Out of his dores anoon he hath him dight
Allone, and there he wende han been allied
He knokked faste; and ay the more he cried,
The faster shette they the dores alle.
Tho wiste he wel he hadde himself misgyed,
And wente his way—no lenger dorste he calle.

The peple cried and rumbled up and down,
That with his eres herde he how they saide,
"Where is this false tyrant, this Neroun?"
For fere almost out of his wit he braide,
And to his goddes pitously he prayde

433. **of acustomaunce,** customarily. 434. **agains,** in the presence of. 438. **Chees,** chose. 439. **tormentrise,** torment. 441. **liste,** pleased. 443. **strenger,** stronger. 444. **nice,** foolish. 445. **fulfild,** filled full. 447. **trice,** pull. 448. **weeneth,** expects. 450. **defaute,** wickedness. 451. **dight,** gone. 452. **wende,** thought to. 454. **shette,** shut. 455. **Tho,** then; **wiste,** knew; **misgyed,** misguided. 460. **braide,** i.e., went.

For sucour, but it mighte nought bitide.
For drede of this him thoughte that he deide,
And ran into a gardin him to hide.

And in this gardin foond he cherles twaye
That seten by a fire greet and reed,
And to thise cherles two he gan to praye
To sleen him and to girden of his heed,
That to his body, whan that he were deed,
Were no despit ydoon for his defame.
Himself he slow—he coude no bettre reed,
Of which Fortune lough and hadde a game.

HOLOFERNES

Was nevere capitain under a king
That regnes mo putte in subjeccioun,
Ne strenger was in feeld of alle thing
As in his time, ne gretter of renown,
Ne more pompous in heigh presumpcioun
Than Oloferne, which Fortune ay kiste
So likerously, and ladde him up and down
Til that his heed was of er that he wiste.

Nat only that this world hadde him in awe
For lesing of richesse or libertee,
But he made every man renayen his lawe:
"Nabugodonosor was god," saide he:
Noon other god sholde adored be.
Agains his heeste no wight dorste trespace,
Save in Bethulia, a strong citee,
Where Eliachim a preest was of that place.

465. foond, found. **466. reed,** red. **468. sleen,** slay; **girden,** strike. **469. deed,** dead. **470. defame,** dishonor. **471. coude,** knew; **reed,** counsel. **472. lough,** laughed. **474. mo,** more. **475. feeld,** battlefield. **477. pompous,** stately. **479. likerously,** wantonly; **ladde,** led. **480. heed,** head; **of,** off; **wiste,** knew. **482. For lesing,** for fear of losing. **483. renayen,** renounce. **484. Nabugodonosor,** Nebuchadnezzar. **486. heeste,** command. **488. Eliachim;** for all references in this passage, see the Book of Judith.

But taak keep° of the deeth of Oloferne:
Amidde his host he dronke lay a night
Within his tente, large as is a berne;°
And yit for al his pompe and al his might,
Judith, a woman, as he lay upright,°
Sleeping, his heed of smoot, and from his tente
Ful prively she stal° from every wight,
And with his heed unto hir town she wente.

KING ANTIOCHUS

What needeth it of king Antiochus
To telle his hye royal majestee,
His hye pride, his werkes venimous?°
For swich another was ther noon as he.
Rede which that he was in *Machabee*,°
And rede the proude wordes that he saide,
And why he fel fro heigh prosperitee,
And in° an hil how wrecchedly he deide.

Fortune him hadde enchaunted so in pride
That verraily he wende° he mighte attaine
Unto the sterres° upon every side,
And in a balaunce° weyen eech montaine,
And alle the floodes of the see restraine.
And Goddes peple hadde he most in hate:
Hem wolde he sleen° in torment and in paine,
Weening° that God ne mighte his pride abate.

And for that Nichanore and Timothee°
Of° Jewes weren venquisshed mightily,
Unto the Jewes swich an hate hadde he
That he bad graithe his chaar° ful hastily,

489. **keep,** heed. 491. **berne,** barn. 493. **upright,** supine. 495. **stal,** stole away. 499. **venimous,** malicious. 501. **which,** what; **Machabee;** for the story of Antiochus, see II Maccabees IX. 504. **in,** on. 506. **wende,** thought. 507. **sterres,** stars. 508. **balaunce,** scale; **weyen,** weigh. 511. **sleen,** slay. 512. **Weening,** supposing. 513. Nicanor and Timotheus were generals. 514. **Of,** by. 516. **graithe,** prepare; **chaar,** chariot.

And swoor and saide ful despitously
Unto Jerusalem he wolde eftsoone,°
To wreken his ire on it ful cruelly.
But of his purpos he was let° ful soone:

God for his manace° him so sore smoot
With invisible wounde, ay incurable,
That in his guttes carf it, and so boot°
That his paines weren inportable.°
And certainly the wreche° was resonable,
For many a mannes guttes dide he paine.
But from his purpos, cursed and dampnable,
For al his smert he wolde him nat restraine,

But bad anoon apparailen° his host,
And sodeinly, er he was of it war,
God daunted al his pride and al his boost,°
For he so sore fel out of his chaar,°
That it his limes and his skin totar,°
So that he neither mighte go° ne ride,
But in a chayer men aboute him bar,°
Al forbrused° bothe bak and side.

The wreche of God him smoot so cruelly
That thurgh his body wikked wormes crepte;
And therwithal he stank so horribly
That noon of al his meinee that him kepte,°
Wheither so he wook or elles slepte,
Ne mighte nought for stink of him endure.
In this meschief he wailed and eek wepte,
And knew° God lord of every creature.

518. **eftsoone,** go soon again. **520. let,** stopped. **521. manace,** threat. **523. carf,** cut; **boot,** bit. **524. inportable,** intolerable. **525. wreche,** vengeance. **529. apparailen,** prepare. **531. boost,** boast. **532. chaar,** chariot. **533. totar,** tore apart. **534. go,** walk. **535. chayer,** litter; **bar,** bore. **536. forbrused,** bruised. **540. meinee,** household; **kepte,** took care of. **544. knew,** recognized.

To al his host and to himself also
Ful wlatsom was the stink of his careine:
No man ne mighte him bere to ne fro.
And in this stink and this horrible paine
He starf ful wrecchedly in a montaine.
Thus hath this robbour and this homicide,
That many a man hath maad to weepe and plaine,
Swich guerdon as belongeth unto pride.

ALEXANDER

The storye of Alexandre is so commune
That every wight that hath discrecioun
Hath herd somwhat or al of his fortune.
This wide world, as in conclusioun,
He wan by strengthe or for his hye renown:
They were glad for pees unto him sende.
The pride of man and beest he laide adown
Wherso he cam, unto the worldes ende.

Comparisoun mighte nevere yit been maked
Bitwixe him and another conquerour,
For al this world for drede of him hath quaked.
He was of knighthood and of freedom flowr;
Fortune him made the heir of hir honour.
Save win and wommen no thing mighte assuage
His hye entente in armes and labour,
So was he ful of leonin corage.

What pris were it to him though I you tolde
Of Darius and an hundred thousand mo
Of kinges, princes, dukes, erles bolde,
Which he conquered and broughte hem into wo?

546. wlatsom, disgusting; **careine,** flesh. **549. starf,** died. **550. homicide,** murderer. **552. guerdon,** reward. **557. wan,** won. **564. freedom,** nobility. **566. assuage,** diminish. **569. pris,** value. **570. mo,** more.

I saye, as fer as man may ride or go
The world was his: what sholde I more devise?
For though I write or tolde you everemo
Of his knighthood, it mighte nat suffise.

Twelf yeer he regned, as saith *Machabee;*
Philippes sone of Macedoine he was,
That first was king in Greece, the contree.
O worthy, gentil Alisandre, allas
That evere sholde fallen swich a cas:
Empoisoned of thyn owene folk thou were.
Thy *sis* Fortune hath turned into *as,*
And for thee ne weep she nevere a tere.

Who shal me yive teres to complaine
The deeth of gentilesse and of franchise,
That al the world weelded in his demeine?
And yit him thoughte it mighte nat suffise,
So ful was his corage of heigh emprise.
Allas, who shal me helpe to endite
False Fortune and poison to despise?—
The whiche two of al this wo I wite.

JULIUS CAESAR

By wisdom, manhede, and by greet labour
From humble bed to royal majestee,
Up roos he, Julius the conquerour,
That wan al th'occident by land and see,
By strengthe of hand or elles by tretee,
And unto Rome made hem tributarye;
And sith of Rome the emperour was he,
Til that Fortune weex his adversarye.

573. fer, far; **go,** walk. **574. what,** why. **577. Machabee,** the Book of Machabees. **578. Macedoine,** Macedon. **583. sis,** six; **as,** ace: the terms are from dicing. **584. weep,** wept. **586. franchise,** magnanimity. **587. demeine,** control. **589. corage,** heart; **emprise,** enterprise. **590. endite,** indict. **592. wite,** blame. **596. wan,** won. **597. tretee,** treaty. **599. sith,** afterwards. **600. weex,** became.

O mighty Cesar, that in Thessalye
Again Pompeus,° fader thyn in lawe,
That of th'orient hadde al the chivalrye°
As fer as that the day biginneth dawe,°
Thou thurgh thy knighthood hast hem take and slawe,°
Save fewe folk that with Pompeus fledde,
Thurgh which thou puttest al th'orient in awe,
Thanke Fortune that so wel thee spedde.°

But now a litel while I wol biwaile
This Pompeus, this noble governour
Of Rome, which that fleigh° at this bataile.
I saye, oon of his men, a fals traitour,
His heed of° smoot, to winnen him favour
Of Julius, and him the heed he broughte.
Allas, Pompey, of th'orient conquerour,
That Fortune unto swich a fin° thee broughte.

To Rome again repaireth° Julius
With his triumphe lauriat° ful hye.
But on a time Brutus Cassius,
That evere hadde of his hye estaat envye,
Ful prively hath maad conspiracye
Agains this Julius in subtil wise,
And caste° the place in which he sholde die
With boidekins,° as I shal you devise.

This Julius to the Capitolye wente
Upon a day, as he was wont° to goon,
And in the Capitolye anoon him hente°
This false Brutus and his othere foon,
And stikked him with boidekins anoon
With many a wounde; and thus they lete him lie.

602. Pompeus, Pompey. **603. hadde,** i.e., controlled; **chivalrye,** knighthood. **604. fer,** far; **dawe,** dawn. **605. slawe,** slain. **608. spedde,** helped succeed. **611. fleigh,** fled. **613. heed,** head; **of,** off. **616. fin,** end. **617. repaireth,** returns. **618. lauriat,** crowned with laurel. **623. caste,** planned. **624. boidekins,** daggers. **626. wont,** accustomed. **627. hente,** seized.

But nevere gronte he at no strook but oon,
Or elles at two, but if his storye lie.

So manly was this Julius of herte,
And so wel loved estaatly honestee,
That though his deedly woundes sore smerte,
His mantel over his hippes caste he,
For no man sholde seen his privetee.
And as he lay of dying in a traunce,
And wiste verraily that deed was he,
Of honestee yit hadde he remembraunce.

Lucan, to thee this storye I recomende,
And to Sueton, and to Valerius also,
That of this storye writen word and ende,
How that to thise grete conqueroures two
Fortune was first freend and sitthe foo.
No man ne truste upon hir favour longe,
But have hire in await for everemo:
Witnesse on alle thise conqueroures stronge.

CROESUS

This riche Cresus, whilom king of Lyde,
Of which Cresus Cyrus sore him dradde,
Yit was he caught amiddes al his pride,
And to be brent men to the fir him ladde;
But swich a rain down fro the welkne shadde,
That slow the fir and made him to escape:

631. gronte, groaned. **632. but if,** unless. **634. estaatly,** dignified; **honestee,** honorable conduct. **635. deedly,** deadly; **smerte,** smarted. **639. wiste,** knew. **641. Lucan,** author of *Pharsalia,* a poem on the war between Caesar and Pompey; **recomende,** commit. **642. Sueton,** Suetonius, author of the *Lives of the Twelve Caesars;* **Valerius,** Valerius Maximus, author of a book telling some stories about Caesar. **643. word,** beginning. **645. sitthe,** afterwards. **647. have . . . await,** keep watch on her. **649. whilom,** once; **Lyde,** Lydia. **650.** Which Croesus Cyrus dreaded sore. **652. brent,** burned; **ladde,** led. **653. welkne,** sky; **shadde,** fell. **654. slow,** slew, put out.

But to be war no grace yit he hadde,
Til Fortune on the galwes made him gape.°

Whan he escaped was, he can nat stente°
For to biginne a newe werre° again;
He wende° wel for that Fortune him sente
Swich hap that he escaped thurgh the rain,
That of his foes he mighte nat be slain;
And eek a swevene upon a night he mette,°
Of which he was so proud and eek so fain,°
That in vengeance he al his herte sette.

Upon a tree he was, as that him thoughte,
Ther Juppiter him wessh° bothe bak and side,
And Phebus eek a fair towaile° him broughte
To drye him with; and therfore wax° his pride,
And to his doughter that stood him biside,
Which that he knew in heigh sentence habounde,°
He bad hire telle him what it signifide,
And she his dreem bigan right thus expounde:

"The tree," quod she, "the galwes is to mene,
And Juppiter bitokneth snow and rain,
And Phebus with his towaile so clene,
Tho been the sonnes stremes° for to sayn:
Thou shalt anhanged° be, fader, certain;
Rain shal thee wasshe, and sonne shal thee drye."
Thus him warned ful plat° and ful plain
His doughter, which that called was Phanye.

Anhanged was Cresus the proude king:
His royal trone° mighte him nat availe.

656. galwes, gallows; **gape,** gasp. **657. stente,** restrain himself. **658. werre,** war. **659. wende,** thought. **662. swevene,** dream; **mette,** dreamt. **663. fain,** glad. **666. wessh,** washed. **667. towaile,** towel. **668. wax,** increased. **670. sentence,** wisdom; **habounde,** abound. **676. Tho,** those; **stremes,** beams. **677. anhanged,** hanged. **679. plat,** flatly. **682. trone,** throne.

Tragedies noon other manere thing°
Ne can in singing crye ne biwaile,
But that Fortune alway wol assaile
With unwar° strook the regnes that been proude;
For whan men trusteth hire, thanne wol she faile,
And covere hir brighte face with a cloude.

PETER, KING OF SPAIN

O noble, o worthy Petro,° glorye of Spaine,
Whom Fortune heeld so hye in majestee,
Wel oughten men thy pitous deeth complaine.
Out of thy land thy brother made thee flee,
And after, at a sege,° by subtiltee
Thou were bitraised and lad° unto his tente,
Wher as he with his owene hand slow° thee,
Succeeding in thy regne and in thy rente.°

The feeld of snow with th'egle of blak therinne,°
Caught with the lymrod colored as the gleede,
He brew this cursednesse° and al this sinne.
The wikked nest° was werkere of this neede:
Nought Charles Oliver° that took ay heede
Of trouthe and honour, but of Armorike°
Geniloun Oliver, corrupt for meede,°
Broughte this worthy king in swich a brike.°

683–85. I.e., in their recital of events, tragedies can lament and bewail only the fact that Fortune will always assail, etc. **686. unwar,** unexpected. **689. Petro,** Peter (the Cruel) was king of Castile and Leon, the father of John of Gaunt's second wife; he was murdered in 1369. **693. sege,** siege. **694. bitraised,** betrayed; **lad,** led. **695. slow,** slew. **696. rente,** income. **697–98.** The lines describe the coat of arms of Bertrand Du Guesclin, which showed on a silver field a black eagle seemingly caught by a red lime-rod, a rod covered with sticky lime to trap small birds. **699. brew,** brewed: Du Guesclin brought Peter to his brother's tent; **cursednesse,** wickedness. **700. wikked nest,** a translation of French *mau ni,* "bad nest," referring to Oliver Mauny, who assisted in the murder. **701. Charles Oliver,** Charlemagne's Oliver, a faithful retainer. **702. Armorike,** Armorica, Brittany. **703. Genelon Oliver,** Genelon-Oliver, one like Ganelon who betrayed Charlemagne; **meede,** bribery. **704. brike,** trap.

PETER, KING OF CYPRUS

O worthy Petro,° king of Cypre also,
That Alisaundre wan° by heigh maistrye,
Ful many an hethen wroughtestou ful wo,
Of which thine owene liges° hadde envye,
And for no thing but for thy chivalrye
They in thy bed han slain thee by the morwe:°
Thus can Fortune hir wheel governe and gye,°
And out of joye bringe men to sorwe.

BARNABO OF LOMBARDY

Of Milan grete Barnabo Viscounte,°
God of delit and scourge of Lombardye,
Why sholde I nat thyn infortune acounte°
Sith in estaat thou clombe were° so hye.
Thy brother sone, that was thy double allye,
For he thy nevew was and sone-in-lawe,
Within his prison made thee to die—
But why ne how noot I that thou were slawe.°

UGOLINO, COUNT OF PISA

Of the Erl Hugelin of Pise the langour°
Ther may no tonge tellen for pitee;
But litel out of Pise stant° a towr,
In which towr in prison put was he,
And with him been his litel children three:
The eldeste scarsly fif yeer was of age.
Allas, Fortune, it was greet crueltee
Swiche briddes° for to putte in swich a cage.

705. Petro, Pierre de Lusignan, one of the most celebrated knights of the fourteenth century, was murdered in 1369. **706. Alisaundre wan,** captured Alexandria. **708. liges,** liegemen. **710. by,** in; **morwe,** morning. **711. gye,** guide. **713. Viscounte,** Visconti: Barnabo died in prison in 1385. **715. infortune,** misfortune; **acounte,** consider. **716. Sith,** since; **clombe were,** had climbed. **720. noot,** know not; **slawe,** slain. **721. langour,** suffering. **723. stant,** stands. **728. briddes,** birds.

Dampned he was to dien in that prisoun,
For Roger, which that bisshop was of Pise,
Hadde on him maad a fals suggestioun,
Thurgh which the peple gan upon him rise
And putten him to prison in swich wise
As ye han herd; and mete and drinke he hadde,
So smal that wel unnethe it may suffise,
And therwithal it was ful poore and badde.

And on a day bifel that in that hour
Whan that his mete wont was to be brought,
The gailer shette the dores of the towr:
He herde it wel, but he spak right nought,
And in his herte anoon ther fil a thought
That they for hunger wolde doon him dien.
"Allas," quod he, "allas that I was wrought!"
Therwith the teres fillen from his yën.

His yonge sone that three yeer was of age
Unto him saide, "Fader, why do ye weepe?
Whan wol the gailer bringen oure potage?
Is ther no morsel breed that ye do keepe?
I am so hungry that I may nat sleepe.
Now wolde God that I mighte sleepen evere:
Thanne sholde nought hunger in my wombe creepe.
Ther is no thing but breed that me were levere."

Thus day by day the child bigan to crye,
Til in his fadres barm adown it lay
And saide, "Farewel, Fader, I moot die,"
And kiste his fader and deide the same day.
And whan the woful fader deed it say,
For wo his armes two he gan to bite,

729. dampned, condemned. **730. Roger,** Ruggiero. **731. suggestioun,** accusation. **735. unnethe,** hardly. **739. shette,** shut. **741. fil,** fell, occurred. **742. doon,** cause. **744. fillen,** fell. **747. potage,** soup. **748. breed,** bread. **751. wombe,** stomach. **752. me . . . levere,** I would rather have. **754. barm,** lap. **757. deed,** dead; **say,** saw.

And saide, "Allas, Fortune, and wailaway!
Thy false wheel my wo al may I wite."°

His children wende that it for hunger was
That he his armes gnow,° and nat for wo,
And saiden, "Fader, do nat so, allas,
But rather ete the flessh upon us two.
Oure flessh thou yeve:° taak oure flessh us fro,
And ete ynough." Right thus they to him saide.
And after that withinne a day or two
They laide hem in his lappe adown and deide.

Himself despaired eek for hunger starf.°
Thus ended is this mighty Erl of Pise:
From heigh estaat Fortune away him carf.°
Of this tragedye it oughte ynough suffise.
Whoso wol heere it in a lenger wise,
Redeth the grete poete of Itaile
That highte Dant, for he can al devise°
Fro point to point: nat oo word wol he faile.°

THE NUN'S PRIEST'S TALE

The Introduction

"Ho!" quod the Knight, "good sire, namore of this:
That ye han said is right ynough, ywis,
And muchel more, for litel hevinesse
Is right ynough to muche folk I gesse:

760. wite, blame. **762. gnow,** gnawed. **765. yeve,** gave. **769. starf,** died. **771. carf,** carved, cut. **775. Dant,** Dante; **devise,** describe. **776. faile,** i.e., leave out.

I saye for me it is a greet disese,°
Wher as men han been in greet welthe and ese,
To heeren of hir sodein fal, allas;
And the contrarye is joye and greet solas,°
As whan a man hath been in poore estat,
And climbeth up and wexeth° fortunat,
And there abideth in prosperitee:
Swich thing is gladsom, as it thinketh me,
And of swich thing were goodly for to telle."
"Ye," quod oure Host, "by Sainte Poules° belle,
Ye saye right sooth: this Monk he clappeth° loude.
He spak how Fortune covered with a cloude—
I noot nevere what. And als° of a tragedye
Right now ye herde, and pardee, no remedye
It is for to biwaile ne complaine
That that is doon, and als it is a paine,
As ye° han said, to heere of hevinesse.
Sire Monk, namore of this, so God you blesse:
Youre tale anoyeth al this compaignye;
Swich talking is nat worth a boterflye,°
For therinne is ther no disport ne game.
Wherfore, sire Monk, or daun Piers by youre name,
I praye you hertely telle us somwhat elles:
For sikerly, nere° clinking of youre belles,
That on youre bridel hange on every side,
By hevene king that for us alle dyde,
I sholde er this have fallen down for sleep,
Although the slough hadde nevere been so deep.
Thanne hadde youre tale al be told in vain;
For certainly, as that thise clerkes sayn,
Wher as a man may have noon audience,
Nought helpeth it to tellen his sentence;°
And wel I woot the substance° is in me,
If any thing shal wel reported be.

5. **disese,** i.e., discomfort. 8. **solas,** delight. 10. **wexeth,** grows. 14. **Poules,** Paul's. 15. **clappeth,** chatters. 17. **noot,** don't know; **als,** also. 21. **ye,** i.e., the Knight. 24. **boterflye,** butterfly. 28. **sikerly,** certainly; **nere,** were it not for. 36. **sentence,** i.e., what he has to say. 37. **substance,** i.e., innate power to respond.

Sire, saye somwhat of hunting, I you praye."
"Nay," quod this Monk, "I have no lust° to playe.
Now lat another telle, as I have told."
Thanne spak oure Host with rude speeche and bold,
And saide unto the Nonnes Preest anoon,
"Com neer, thou Preest, com hider, thou sire John:
Tel us swich thing as may oure hertes glade.°
Be blithe, though thou ride upon a jade!°
What though thyn hors be bothe foul and lene?
If he wol serve thee, rekke nat a bene.°
Looke that thyn herte be merye everemo."
"Yis, sire," quod he, "yis, Host, so mote I go,
But I be merye, ywis, I wol be blamed."
And right anoon his tale he hath attamed,°
And thus he saide unto us everichoon,
This sweete Preest, this goodly man sire John.

The Tale

A poore widwe somdeel stape° in age
Was whilom dwelling in a narwe° cotage,
Biside a grove, stonding in a dale:
This widwe of which I telle you my tale,
Sin thilke° day that she was last a wif,
In pacience ladde° a ful simple lif.
For litel was hir catel and hir rente,°
By housbondrye° of swich as God hire sente
She foond° hirself and eek hir doughtren two.
Three large sowes hadde she and namo,
Three kin,° and eek a sheep that highte Malle.
Ful sooty was hir bowr and eek hir halle,

40. **lust,** desire. 45. **glade,** gladden. 46. **jade,** nag. 48. **rekke . . . bene,** don't care a bean. 52. **attamed,** broached.

1. **stape,** advanced. 2. **whilom,** once upon a time; **narwe,** i.e., small. 5. **thilke,** that same. 6. **ladde,** led. 7. **For,** because; **catel,** property; **rente,** income. 8. **housbondrye,** economy. 9. **foond,** provided for. 11. **kin,** cows.

In which she eet ful many a sclendre° meel;
Of poinant° sauce hire needed neveradeel:
No daintee morsel passed thurgh hir throte—
Hir diete was accordant to hir cote.°
Repleccioun° ne made hire nevere sik:
Attempre diete was al hir physik,°
And exercise and hertes suffisaunce.°
The goute lette hire nothing for to daunce,°
N'apoplexye shente nat hir heed.°
No win ne drank she, neither whit ne reed:°
Hir boord was served most with whit and blak,°
Milk and brown breed, in which she foond no lak;°
Seind bacon, and somtime an ey° or twaye,
For she was as it were a manere daye.°
A yeerd° she hadde, enclosed al withoute
With stikkes, and a drye dich aboute,
In which she hadde a cok heet° Chauntecleer:
In al the land of crowing nas his peer.
His vois was merier than the merye orgon
On massedayes that in the chirche goon;°
Wel sikerer was his crowing in his logge°
Than is a clok or an abbeye orlogge;°
By nature he knew eech ascensioun
Of th'equinoxial° in thilke town:
For whan degrees fifteene were ascended,
Thanne crew he that it mighte nat been amended.°
His comb was redder than the fin coral,
And batailed as it were a castel wal;
His bile was blak, and as the jeet° it shoon;

13. **sclendre,** scanty. 14. **poinant,** pungent. 16. **cote,** cottage. 17. **Repleccioun,** overeating. 18. **Attempre,** moderate; **physik,** medicine. 19. **suffisaunce,** contentment. 20. **lette . . . daunce,** didn't hinder her at all from dancing. 21. **shente,** hurt; **heed,** head. 22. **reed,** red. 23. **boord,** table; **whit . . . blak,** i.e., milk and bread. 24. **foond,** found; **lak,** fault. 25. **Seind,** scorched, i.e., broiled; **ey,** egg. 26. **daye,** dairymaid. 27. **yeerd,** yard. 29. **heet,** named. 32. **goon,** i.e., is played. 33. **sikerer,** more reliable; **logge,** dwelling. 34. **orlogge,** timepiece. 35–36. **ascensioun . . . equinoxial,** i.e., step in the progression of the celestial equator. 38. **crew,** crowed; **amended,** improved. 40. **batailed,** battlemented. 41. **bile,** bill; **jeet,** jet.

Like asure were his legges and his toon;°
His nailes whitter° than the lilye flowr,
And lik the burned° gold was his colour.
This gentil cok hadde in his governaunce
Sevene hennes for to doon al his plesaunce,°
Whiche were his sustres and his paramours,°
And wonder like to him as of colours;
Of whiche the faireste hewed° on hir throte
Was cleped faire damoisele Pertelote:
Curteis she was, discreet, and debonaire,°
And compaignable, and bar° hirself so faire,
Sin thilke day that she was seven night old,
That trewely she hath the herte in hold
Of Chauntecleer, loken in every lith.°
He loved hire so that wel was him therwith.
But swich a joye was it to heere hem singe,
Whan that the brighte sonne gan to springe,
In sweete accord "My Lief is Faren in Londe"°—
For thilke time, as I have understonde,
Beestes and briddes couden speke and singe.
  And so bifel that in a daweninge,
As Chauntecleer among his wives alle
Sat on his perche that was in the halle,
And next him sat this faire Pertelote,
This Chauntecleer gan gronen in his throte,
As man that in his dreem is drecched° sore.
  And whan that Pertelote thus herde him rore,
She was agast, and saide, "Herte dere,
What aileth you to grone in this manere?
Ye been a verray slepere,° fy, for shame!"
  And he answerde and saide thus, "Madame,
I praye you that ye take it nat agrief.°
By God, me mette° I was in swich meschief

42. **asure,** lapis lazuli; **toon,** toes. 43. **whitter,** whiter. 44. **burned,** burnished. 46. **plesaunce,** pleasure. 47. **sustres,** sisters; **paramours,** mistresses. 49. **hewed,** colored. 51. **debonaire,** meek. 52. **compaignable,** companionable; **bar,** bore. 55. **loken,** locked; **lith,** limb. 59. **My . . . Londe,** my love has gone away (apparently a popular song). 67. **drecched,** troubled. 71. **slepere,** sleeper. 73. **agrief,** amiss. 74. **me mette,** I dreamed.

Right now, that yit myn herte is sore afright.
Now God," quod he, "my swevene recche aright,°
And keepe my body out of foul prisoun!
Me mette how that I romed up and down
Within oure yeerd, wher as I sawgh a beest,
Was lik an hound and wolde han maad arrest°
Upon my body, and han had me deed.°
His colour was bitwixe yelow and reed,
And tipped was his tail and bothe his eres
With blak, unlik the remenant of his heres;°
His snoute smal, with glowing yën twaye.
Yit of his look for fere almost I deye:°
This caused me my groning, doutelees."
"Avoi," quod she, "fy on you, hertelees!°
Allas," quod she, "for by that God above,
Now han ye lost myn herte and al my love!
I can nat love a coward, by my faith.
For certes, what so any womman saith,
We alle desiren, if it mighte be,
To han housbondes hardy, wise, and free,°
And secree,° and no nigard, ne no fool,
Ne him that is agast of every tool,
Ne noon avauntour.° By that God above,
How dorste ye sayn for shame unto youre love
That any thing mighte make you aferd?
Have ye no mannes herte and han a beerd?
Allas, and conne ye been agast of swevenes?°
No thing, God woot, but vanitee° in swevene is!
Swevenes engendren of replexiouns,°
And ofte of fume and of complexiouns,°
Whan humours been too habundant in a wight.
Certes, this dreem which ye han met° tonight

76. swevene, dream; **recche aright,** interpret correctly, i.e., in an auspicious manner. **80. maad arrest,** laid hold. **81. had . . . deed,** i.e., killed me. **84. heres,** hairs. **86. deye,** die. **88. Avoi,** fie; **hertelees,** coward. **94. free,** generous. **95. secree,** discreet. **96. tool,** weapon. **97. avauntour,** boaster. **101. swevenes,** dreams. **102. vanitee,** i.e., empty illusion. **103.** Dreams have their origin in overeating. **104. fume,** gas; **complexiouns,** bodily humors. **106. met,** dreamed.

Comth of the grete superfluitee
Of youre rede colera,° pardee,
Which causeth folk to dreden in hir dremes
Of arwes, and of fir with rede lemes,°
Of rede beestes, that they wol hem bite,
Of contek, and of whelpes grete and lite°—
Right as the humour of malencolye°
Causeth ful many a man in sleep to crye
For fere of blake beres or boles° blake,
Or elles blake develes wol hem take.
Of othere humours coude I telle also
That werken many a man in sleep ful wo,
But I wol passe as lightly° as I can.
Lo, Caton,° which that was so wis a man,
Saide he nat thus? 'Ne do no fors of° dremes.'
Now, sire," quod she, "whan we flee fro the bemes,°
For Goddes love, as take som laxatif.
Up° peril of my soule and of my lif,
I conseile you the beste, I wol nat lie,
That bothe of colere and of malencolye
Ye purge you; and for° ye shal nat tarye,
Though in this town is noon apothecarye,
I shal myself to herbes techen you,
That shal been for youre hele and for youre prow,°
And in oure yeerd tho herbes shal I finde,
The whiche han of hir propretee by kinde°
To purge you binethe and eek above.
Foryet° nat this, for Goddes owene love.
Ye been ful colerik° of complexioun;
Ware° the sonne in his ascencioun
Ne finde you nat repleet of humours hote;°
And if it do, I dar wel laye° a grote

108. **rede colera,** red bile. 110. **arwes,** arrows; **lemes,** flames. 112. **contek,** strife; **whelpes,** dogs; **lite,** little. 113. **right,** just; **malencolye,** i.e., black bile. 115. **beres,** bears; **boles,** bulls. 119. **lightly,** quickly. 120. **Caton,** Dionysius Cato, supposed author of a book of maxims used in elementary education. 121. **Ne . . . of,** pay no attention to. 122. **flee,** fly; **bemes,** rafters. 124. **Up,** upon. 127. **for,** in order that. 130. **hele,** health; **prow,** benefit. 132. **kinde,** nature. 134. **Foryet,** forget. 135. **colerik,** bilious. 136. **Ware,** beware that. 137. **repleet,** filled; **hote,** hot. 138. **laye,** bet.

That ye shul have a fevere terciane,°
Or an agu that may be youre bane.°
A day or two ye shul han digestives
Of wormes, er ye take youre laxatives
Of lauriol, centaure, and fumetere,°
Or elles of ellebor° that groweth there,
Of catapuce, or of gaitres beries,°
Of herbe-ive growing in oure yeerd ther merye is.°
Pekke hem right up as they growe and ete hem in.
Be merye, housbonde, for youre fader kin!
Dredeth no dreem: I can saye you namore."
"Madame," quod he, "graunt mercy of youre lore.°
But nathelees, as touching daun Catoun,
That hath of wisdom swich a greet renown,
Though that he bad no dremes for to drede,
By God, men may in olde bookes rede
Of many a man more of auctoritee°
Than evere Caton was, so mote I thee,°
That al the revers sayn of his sentence,°
And han wel founden by experience
That dremes been significaciouns
As wel of joye as tribulaciouns
That folk enduren in this lif present.
Ther needeth make of this noon argument:
The verray preve° sheweth it in deede.
Oon of the gretteste auctour° that men rede
Saith thus, that whilom two felawes wente
On pilgrimage in a ful good entente,
And happed so they comen in a town,
Wher as ther was swich congregacioun
Of peple, and eek so strait of herbergage,°
That they ne founde as muche as oo cotage

139. **terciane,** tertian, recurring every other day. **140. bane,** death. **143.** Of laureole, centaury, and fumitory. **144. ellebor,** hellebore. **145.** Of caper berry or of gaiter berry. **146. herbe-ive,** herb ivy; **ther merye is,** where it is pleasant. **150. graunt . . . of,** many thanks for; **lore,** instruction. **155. auctoritee,** authority. **156. thee,** thrive. **157. sentence,** opinion. **163. verray preve,** actual experience. **164. auctour,** i.e., authors. **169. so . . . herbergage,** such shortage of lodging.

In which they bothe mighte ylogged be;
Wherfore they mosten of necessitee
As for that night departe compaignye.
And eech of hem gooth to his hostelrye,
And took his logging as it wolde falle:
That oon of hem was logged in a stalle,
Fer in a yeerd, with oxen of the plough;
That other man was logged wel ynough,
As was his aventure or his fortune,
That us governeth alle as in commune.
And so bifel that longe er it were day,
This man mette in his bed, ther as he lay,
How that his felawe gan upon him calle,
And saide, 'Allas, for in an oxes stalle
This night I shal be mordred ther I lie!
Now help me, dere brother, or I die!
In alle haste com to me,' he saide.
  This man out of his sleep for fere abraide,
But whan that he was wakened of his sleep,
He turned him and took of this no keep:
Him thoughte his dreem nas but a vanitee.
Thus twies in his sleeping dremed he,
And atte thridde time yit his felawe
Cam, as him thoughte, and saide, 'I am now slawe:
Bihold my bloody woundes deepe and wide.
Aris up erly in the morwe tide
And atte west gate of the town,' quod he,
'A carte ful of dong ther shaltou see,
In which my body is hid ful prively:
Do thilke carte arresten boldely.
My gold caused my mordre, sooth to sayn'—
And tolde him every point how he was slain,
With a ful pitous face, pale of hewe.
And truste wel, his dreem he foond ful trewe,

172. mosten, must. **173. departe,** part. **175. falle,** befall. **177. Fer,** far away. **182. mette,** dreamed. **185. mordred,** murdered. **188. abraide,** started up. **190. keep,** heed. **194. slawe,** slain. **196. morwe tide,** morning. **198. dong,** dung. **200. Do arresten,** have stopped. **204. foond,** found.

For on the morwe as soone as it was day,
To his felawes in he took the way,
And whan that he cam to this oxes stalle,
After his felawe he bigan to calle.
  The hostiler answerde him anoon,
And saide, 'Sire, youre felawe is agoon:
As soone as day he wente out of the town.'
  This man gan fallen in suspecioun,
Remembring on his dremes that he mette;
And forth he gooth, no lenger wolde he lette,
Unto the west gate of the town, and foond
A dong carte, wente as it were to donge lond,
That was arrayed in that same wise
As ye han herd the dede man devise;
And with an hardy herte he gan to crye,
'Vengeance and justice of this felonye!
My felawe mordred is this same night,
And in this carte he lith gaping upright!
I crye out on the ministres,' quod he,
'That sholde keepe and rulen this citee.
Harrow, allas, here lith my felawe slain!'
What sholde I more unto this tale sayn?
The peple up sterte and caste the carte to grounde,
And in the middel of the dong they founde
The dede man that mordred was al newe.
  O blisful God that art so just and trewe,
Lo, how that thou biwrayest mordre alway!
Mordre wol out, that see we day by day:
Mordre is so wlatsom and abhominable
To God that is so just and resonable,
That he ne wol nat suffre it heled be,
Though it abide a yeer or two or three.
Mordre wol out: this my conclusioun.
And right anoon ministres of that town

205. **morwe,** morning. 206. **in,** lodging. 209. **hostiler,** innkeeper. 210. **agoon,** gone away. 213. **mette,** dreamed. 214. **lette,** tarry. 216. **donge,** put manure on. 218. **dede,** dead. 222. **lith,** lies; **upright,** supine. 227. **sterte,** started. 229. **al newe,** recently. 231. **biwrayest,** disclose. 233. **wlatsom,** loathsome. 235. **heled,** concealed.

Han hent the cartere and so sore him pined,
And eek the hostiler so sore engined,
That they biknewe hir wikkednesse anoon,
And were anhanged by the nekke boon.
Here may men seen that dremes been to drede.
And certes, in the same book I rede—
Right in the nexte chapitre after this—
I gabbe nat, so have I joye or blis—
Two men that wolde han passed over see
For certain cause into a fer contree,
If that the wind ne hadde been contrarye
That made hem in a citee for to tarye,
That stood ful merye upon an haven side—
But on a day again the even tide
The wind gan chaunge, and blewe right as hem leste:
Jolif and glad they wenten unto reste,
And casten hem ful erly for to saile.
But to that oo man fil a greet mervaile;
That oon of hem, in sleeping as he lay,
Him mette a wonder dreem again the day:
Him thoughte a man stood by his beddes side,
And him comanded that he sholde abide,
And saide him thus, 'If thou tomorwe wende,
Thou shalt be dreint: my tale is at an ende.'
He wook and tolde his felawe what he mette,
And prayed him his viage to lette;
As for that day he prayed him to bide.
His felawe that lay by his beddes side
Gan for to laughe, and scorned him ful faste.
'No dreem,' quod he, 'may so myn herte agaste
That I wol lette for to do my thinges.
I sette nat a straw by thy dreminges,

239. **hent,** seized; **pined,** tortured. 240. **engined,** racked. 241. **biknewe,** confessed. 242. **anhanged,** hanged. 243. **to drede,** worthy of being feared. 246. **gabbe,** lie. 251. **haven,** harbor's. 252. **again,** toward. 253. **leste,** pleased. 254. **Jolif,** merry. 255. **casten hem,** determined. 256. **fil,** befell. 258. **Him mette,** he dreamed. 262. **dreint,** drowned. 264. **viage,** voyage; **lette,** delay. 268. **agaste,** terrify. 269. **lette,** delay; **thinges,** business. 270. **sette . . . by,** don't care a straw for.

For swevenes been but vanitees and japes.
Men dreme alday of owles or of apes,
And of many a maze therwithal—
Men dreme of thing that nevere was ne shal.
But sith I see that thou wolt here abide,
And thus forsleuthen wilfully thy tide,
Good woot, it reweth me, and have good day.'
And thus he took his leve and wente his way.
But er that he hadde half his cours ysailed—
Noot I nat why ne what meschaunce it ailed—
But casuelly the shippes botme rente,
And ship and man under the water wente,
In sighte of othere shippes it biside,
That with hem sailed at the same tide.
And therfore, faire Pertelote so dere,
By swiche ensamples olde maistou lere
That no man sholde been too recchelees
Of dremes, for I saye thee doutelees
That many a dreem ful sore is for to drede.

Lo, in the lif of Saint Kenelm I rede—
That was Kenulphus sone, the noble king
Of Mercenrike—how Kenelm mette a thing
A lite er he was mordred on a day.
His mordre in his avision he sey.
His norice him expounded everydeel
His swevene, and bad him for to keepe him weel
For traison, but he nas but seven yeer old,
And therfore litel tale hath he told
Of any dreem, so holy was his herte.
By God, I hadde levere than my sherte

271. swevenes, dreams; **vanitees,** illusions; **japes,** frauds. **272. alday,** constantly; **owles, apes,** i.e., absurdities. **273. maze,** delusion. **274. shal,** i.e., shall be. **276. forsleuthen,** waste. **277. it . . . me,** I'm sorry. **280.** I don't know why nor what was the trouble with it. **281. casuelly,** accidentally; **botme,** bottom; **rente,** split. **286. lere,** learn. **287. recchelees,** careless. **290. Kenelm** succeeded his father as king of Mercia at the age of seven but was slain by his sister. **292. Mercenrike,** Mercia; **mette,** dreamed. **293. lite,** little. **294. avision,** dream; **sey,** saw. **295. norice,** nurse. **296. keepe him,** guard himself. **298–99. litel . . . of,** has set little store by. **300.** i.e., I'd give my shirt.

That ye hadde rad° his legende as have I.
  Dame Pertelote, I saye you trewely,
Macrobeus,° that writ the Avisioun
In Affrike of the worthy Scipioun,
Affermeth° dremes, and saith that they been
Warning of thinges that men after seen.
  And ferthermore, I praye you looketh wel
In the Olde Testament of Daniel,
If he heeld° dremes any vanitee.
  Rede eek of Joseph and ther shul ye see
Wher° dremes be somtime—I saye nat alle—
Warning of thinges that shul after falle.
  Looke of Egypte the king daun Pharao,
His bakere and his botelere° also,
Wher they ne felte noon effect in dremes.
Whoso wol seeke actes of sondry remes°
May rede of dremes many a wonder thing.
  Lo Cresus, which that was of Lyde° king,
Mette° he nat that he sat upon a tree,
Which signified he sholde anhanged° be?
  Lo here Andromacha, Ectores° wif,
That day that Ector sholde lese° his lif,
She dremed on the same night biforn
How that the lif of Ector sholde be lorn,°
If thilke day he wente into bataile;
She warned him, but it mighte nat availe:°
He wente for to fighte nathelees,
But he was slain anoon of Achilles.
But thilke tale is al too long to telle,
And eek it is neigh day, I may nat dwelle.
Shortly I saye, as for conclusioun,
That I shal han of this avisioun°

301. rad, read. **303. Macrobeus,** Macrobius wrote a famous commentary on Cicero's *Dream of Scipio,* full of dream lore. **305. Affermeth** confirms. **309. heeld,** considered. **311. Wher,** whether. **314. botelere,** butler. **316. remes,** realms. **318. Lyde,** Lydia. **319. Mette,** dreamed. **320. anhanged,** hanged. **321. Ectores,** Hector's. **322. lese,** lose. **324. lorn,** lost. **326. availe,** do any good. 332. **avisioun,** divinely inspired dream.

Adversitee, and I saye ferthermoor
That I ne telle of laxatives no stoor,
For they been venimes, I woot it weel:
I hem defye, I love hem neveradeel.
  Now lat us speke of mirthe and stinte al this.
Madame Pertelote, so have I blis,
Of oo thing God hath sente me large grace:
For whan I see the beautee of youre face—
Ye been so scarlet reed aboute youre yën—
It maketh al my drede for to dien.
For also siker as *In principio*,
Mulier est hominis confusio.
Madame, the sentence of this Latin is,
'Womman is mannes joye and al his blis.'
For whan I feele anight youre softe side—
Al be it that I may nat on you ride,
For that oure perche is maad so narwe, allas—
I am so ful of joye and of solas
That I defye bothe swevene and dreem."
And with that word he fleigh down fro the beem,
For it was day, and eek his hennes alle,
And with a "chuk" he gan hem for to calle,
For he hadde founde a corn lay in the yeerd.
Real he was, he was namore aferd:
He fethered Pertelote twenty time,
And trad hire as ofte er it was prime.
He looketh as it were a grim leoun,
And on his toes he rometh up and down:
Him deined nat to sette his foot to grounde.
He chukketh whan he hath a corn yfounde,
And to him rennen thanne his wives alle.
Thus royal, as a prince is in his halle,

334. **telle of,** set by. 335. **venimes,** poisons. 337. **stinte,** stop. 341. **reed,** red. 343. **siker,** certain; **In principio,** a tag from the Gospel of St. John which gives the essential premises of Christianity: In the beginning was the Word. 344. Woman is man's ruination. 345. **sentence,** meaning. 350. **solas,** delight. 352. **fleigh,** flew. 356. **Real,** regal; **aferd,** afraid. 357. **fethered,** i.e., embraced. 358. **trad,** trod, copulated with; **prime,** 9 A.M. 361. **Him deined,** he deigned. 363. **rennen,** run.

Leve I this Chauntecleer in his pasture,
And after wol I telle his aventure.
  Whan that the month in which the world bigan,
That highte March, whan God first maked man,
Was compleet, and passed were also,
Sin March biran,° thritty days and two,
Bifel that Chauntecleer in al his pride,
His sevene wives walking him biside,
Caste up his yën to the brighte sonne,
That in the signe of Taurus hadde yronne
Twenty degrees and oon and somwhat more,
And knew by kinde,° and by noon other lore,
That it was prime, and crew with blisful stevene.°
"The sonne," he saide, "is clomben° up on hevene
Fourty degrees and oon and more, ywis.
Madame Pertelote, my worldes blis,
Herkneth thise blisful briddes° how they singe,
And see the fresshe flowres how they springe:
Ful is myn herte of revel and solas."
But sodeinly him fil a sorweful cas,°
For evere the latter ende of joye is wo—
God woot that worldly joye is soone ago,
And if a rethor° coude faire endite,
He in a cronicle saufly° mighte it write,
As for a soverein notabilitee.
Now every wis man lat him herkne me:
This storye is also° trewe, I undertake,
As is the book of Launcelot de Lake,
That wommen holde in ful greet reverence.
Now wol I turne again to my sentence.°
  A colfox° ful of sly iniquitee,
That in the grove hadde woned yeres three,

370. biran, passed: the date is the recurrent one of May 3. **376. kinde,** nature. **377. crew,** crowed; **stevene,** voice. **378. is clomben,** has climbed. **381. briddes,** birds. **384. fil,** befell; **cas,** chance. **387. rethor,** rhetorician. **388. saufly,** safely. **391. also,** as. **394. sentence,** main point. **395. colfox,** fox with black markings. **396. woned,** dwelled.

By heigh imaginacion forncast,
The same night thurghout the hegges brast
Into the yeerd ther Chauntecleer the faire
Was wont, and eek his wives, to repaire;
And in a bed of wortes stille he lay
Til it was passed undren of the day,
Waiting his time on Chauntecleer to falle,
As gladly doon thise homicides alle,
That in await liggen to mordre men.
O false mordrour, lurking in thy den!
O newe Scariot! Newe Geniloun!
False dissimilour! O Greek Sinoun,
That broughtest Troye al outrely to sorwe!
O Chauntecleer, accursed be that morwe
That thou into the yeerd flaugh fro the bemes!
Thou were ful wel ywarned by thy dremes
That thilke day was perilous to thee;
But what that God forwoot moot needes be,
After the opinion of certain clerkes:
Witnesse on him that any parfit clerk is
That in scole is greet altercacioun
In this matere, and greet disputisoun,
And hath been of an hundred thousand men.
But I ne can nat bulte it to the bren,
As can the holy doctour Augustin,
Or Boece, or the bisshop Bradwardin—
Wheither that Goddes worthy forwiting
Straineth me nedely for to doon a thing
("Nedely" clepe I simple necessitee),

397. I.e., foretold by Chauntecleer's dream. **398. hegges,** hedges; **brast,** burst. **401. wortes,** cabbages. **402 undren,** mid-morning. **405. liggen,** lie; **await,** ambush; **mordre,** murder. **407. Scariot,** Judas Iscariot; **Geniloun,** Ganelon, betrayer of Roland. **408. dissimilour,** dissembler; **Sinoun,** Sinon, who was responsible for the Trojan horse. **409. outrely,** utterly. **410. morwe,** morning. **411. flaugh,** flew. **414. forwoot,** foreknows; **moot,** must. **416. parfit,** perfect. **418. disputisoun,** disputation. **420. bulte,** sift; **bren,** husks. **421–22.** St. Augustine, Boethius, and Thomas Bradwardine were all occupied with the interrelationship between man's free will and God's foreknowledge. **423. forwiting,** foreknowledge. **424. Straineth,** constrains; **nedely,** necessarily.

Or elles if free chois be graunted me
To do that same thing or do it nought,
Though God forwoot it er that I was wrought;
Or if his witing straineth neveradeel,
But by necessitee condicionel—
I wol nat han to do of swich matere:
My tale is of a cok, as ye may heere,
That took his conseil of his wif with sorwe,
To walken in the yeerd upon that morwe
That he hadde met the dreem that I you tolde.
Wommenes conseils been ful ofte colde;
Wommanes conseil broughte us first to wo,
And made Adam fro Paradis to go,
Ther as he was ful merye and wel at ese.
But for I noot to whom it mighte displese
If I conseil of wommen wolde blame,
Passe over, for I saide it in my game—
Rede auctours where they trete of swich matere,
And what they sayn of wommen ye may heere—
Thise been the cokkes wordes and nat mine:
I can noon harm of no womman divine.
Faire in the sond to bathe hire merily
Lith Pertelote, and alle hir sustres by,
Again the sonne, and Chauntecleer so free
Soong merier than the mermaide in the see—
For Physiologus saith sikerly
How that they singen wel and merily.
And so bifel that as he caste his yë
Among the wortes on a boterflye,
He was war of this fox that lay ful lowe.
No thing ne liste him thanne for to crowe,
But cride anoon "Cok cok!" and up he sterte,

428. forwoot, foreknew. **429. witing,** knowledge. **430. condicionel,** Boethius' conditional necessity permitted a large measure of free will. **435. met,** dreamed. **436. colde,** i.e., baneful. **440. noot,** don't know. **442. game,** sport. **446. divine,** guess. **447. sond,** sand. **448. Lith,** lies. **449. Again,** in; **free,** noble. **450. Soong,** sang. **451. Physiologus,** supposed author of a bestiary, a book of moralized zoology. **454. boterflye,** butterfly. **456. liste him,** he wished. **457. sterte,** started.

As man that was affrayed in his herte—
For naturelly a beest desireth flee
Fro his contrarye° if he may it see,
Though he nevere erst° hadde seen it with his yë.
This Chauntecleer, whan he gan him espye,
He wolde han fled, but that the fox anoon
Saide, "Gentil sire, allas, wher wol ye goon?
Be ye afraid of me that am youre freend?
Now certes, I were worse than a feend
If I to you wolde° harm or vilainye.
I am nat come youre conseil° for t'espye,
But trewely the cause of my cominge
Was only for to herkne how that ye singe:
For trewely, ye han as merye a stevene°
As any angel hath that is in hevene.
Therwith ye han in musik more feelinge
Than hadde Boece,° or any that can singe.
My lord your fader—God his soule blesse!—
And eek youre moder, of hir gentilesse,°
Han in myn hous ybeen, to my grete ese.
And certes sire, ful fain° wolde I you plese.
But for men speke of singing, I wol saye,
So mote I brouke° wel mine yën twaye,
Save ye, I herde nevere man so singe
As dide youre fader in the morweninge.
Certes, it was of herte al that he soong.°
And for to make his vois the more strong,
He wolde so paine him° that with bothe his yën
He moste° winke, so loude wolde he cryen;
And stonden on his tiptoon therwithal,
And strecche forth his nekke long and smal;
And eek he was of swich discrecioun
That ther nas no man in no regioun

460. contrarye, i.e., natural enemy. **461. erst,** before. **467. wolde,** meant. **468. conseil,** secrets. **471. stevene,** voice. **474. Boece,** Boethius who wrote a treatise on music. **476. gentilesse,** gentility. **478. fain,** gladly. **480. mote,** might; **brouke,** enjoy the use of. **483. of herte,** heartfelt; **soong,** sang. **485. paine him,** take pains. **486. moste,** must.

That him in song or wisdom mighte passe.
I have wel rad in Daun Burnel the Asse°
Among his vers how that ther was a cok,
For° a preestes sone yaf him a knok
Upon his leg whil he was yong and nice,°
He made him for to lese° his benefice.
But certain, ther nis no comparisoun
Bitwixe the wisdom and discrecioun
Of youre fader and of his subtiltee.
Now singeth, sire, for sainte° charitee!
Lat see, conne ye youre fader countrefete?"°
  This Chauntecleer his winges gan to bete,
As man that coude his traison nat espye,
So was he ravisshed with his flaterye.
  Allas, ye lordes, many a fals flatour°
Is in youre court, and many a losengeour,°
That plesen you wel more, by my faith,
Than he that soothfastnesse° unto you saith!
Redeth Ecclesiaste° of flaterye.
Beeth war, ye lordes, of hir trecherye.
  This Chauntecleer stood hye upon his toos,
Strecching his nekke, and heeld his yën cloos,
And gan to crowe loude for the nones;
And daun Russel the fox sterte° up atones,
And by the gargat hente° Chauntecleer,
And on his bak toward the wode him beer,°
For yit ne was ther no man that him sued.°
  O destinee that maist nat been eschued!°
Allas that Chauntecleer fleigh° fro the bemes!
Allas his wif ne roughte nat of° dremes!

492. **rad**, read; **Daun . . . Asse**, Master Brunellus, a discontented donkey, was the hero of a 12th-century satirical poem by Nigel Wireker. 494. **For**, because. 495. **nice**, foolish. 496. **lese**, lose: the offended cock neglected to crow so that his master overslept, both missing his ordination and losing his benefice. 500. **sainte**, holy. 501. **conne**, can; **countrefete**, imitate. 505. **flatour**, flatterer. 506. **losengeour**, deceiver. 508. **soothfastnesse**, truth. 509. **Ecclesiaste**, the Book of Ecclesiasticus. 514. **sterte**, jumped. 515. **gargat**, throat; **hente**, seized. 516. **beer**, bore. 517. **sued**, followed. 518. **eschued**, eschewed. 519. **fleigh**, flew. 520. **roughte of**, cared for.

And on a Friday fil° al this meschaunce!
O Venus that art goddesse of plesaunce,
Sin that thy servant was this Chauntecleer,
And in thy service dide al his power—
More for delit than world° to multiplye—
Why woldestou suffre him on thy day to die?°
O Gaufred,° dere maister soverein,
That, whan thy worthy king Richard was slain
With shot,° complainedest his deeth so sore,
Why ne hadde I now thy sentence and thy lore,°
The Friday for to chide as diden ye?
For on a Friday soothly slain was he.
Thanne wolde I shewe you how that I coude plaine°
For Chauntecleres drede and for his paine.
Certes, swich cry ne lamentacioun
Was nevere of ladies maad whan Ilioun°
Was wonne, and Pyrrus with his straite° swerd,
Whan he hadde hent° King Priam by the beerd
And slain him, as saith us Eneidos,°
As maden alle the hennes in the cloos,°
Whan they hadde seen of Chauntecleer the sighte.
But sovereinly Dame Pertelote shrighte°
Ful louder than dide Hasdrubales wif
Whan that hir housbonde hadde lost his lif,
And that the Romains hadden brend Cartage:°
She was so ful of torment and of rage
That wilfully unto the fir she sterte,°
And brende hirselven with a stedefast herte.
O woful hennes, right so criden ye
As, whan that Nero brende the citee

521. fil, befell. **525. world,** i.e., population. **526.** Friday is Venus' day. **527. Gaufred,** Geoffrey of Vinsauf, a famous medieval rhetorician who wrote a lament on the death of Richard I, scolding Friday, the day on which the king died. **529. shot,** i.e., a missile. **530. sentence,** wisdom; **lore,** learning. **533. plaine,** lament. **536. Ilioun,** Ilion, Troy. **537. Pyrrus,** Pyrrhus was the Greek who slew Priam, King of Troy; **straite,** rigorous, unsparing. **538. hent,** seized. **539. Eneidos,** the *Aeneid.* **540. cloos,** yard. **542. sovereinly,** splendidly; **shrighte,** shrieked. **545. brend,** burned; **Cartage,** Hasdrubal was king of Carthage when it was destroyed by the Romans. **547. sterte,** jumped.

Of Rome, criden senatoures wives
For that hir housbondes losten alle hir lives:
Withouten gilt this Nero hath hem slain.
Now wol I turne to my tale again.
  The sely widwe and eek hir doughtres two
Herden thise hennes crye and maken wo,
And out at dores sterten they anoon,
And sien the fox toward the grove goon,
And bar upon his bak the cok away,
And criden, "Out, harrow, and wailaway,
Ha, ha, the fox," and after him they ran,
And eek with staves many another man;
Ran Colle oure dogge, and Talbot and Gerland,
And Malkin with a distaf in hir hand,
Ran cow and calf, and eek the verray hogges,
Sore aferd for berking of the dogges
And shouting of the men and wommen eke.
They ronne so hem thoughte hir herte breke;
They yelleden as feendes doon in helle;
The dokes criden as men wolde hem quelle;
The gees for fere flowen over the trees;
Out of the hive cam the swarm of bees;
So hidous was the noise, a, benedicite,
Certes, he Jakke Straw and his meinee
Ne made nevere shoutes half so shrille
Whan that they wolden any Fleming kille,
As thilke day was maad upon the fox:
Of bras they broughten bemes and of box,
Of horn, of boon, in whiche they blewe and pouped,
And therwithal they skriked and they houped—
It seemed as that hevene sholde falle.

553. According to the legend, Nero not only set fire to Rome but put many senators to death. 555. **sely,** innocent. 557. **sterten,** leapt. 558. **sien,** saw. 563. **Talbot, Gerland,** names of dogs. 566. **aferd,** frightened. 568. **ronne,** ran: **breke,** would break. 570. **dokes,** ducks; **quelle,** kill. 571. **flowen,** flew. 574. **Jakke Straw,** one of the leaders of the Peasants' Revolt of 1381, which was partly directed against the Flemings living in London; **meinee,** company. 578. **bemes,** trumpets; **box,** boxwood. 579. **boon,** bone; **pouped,** tooted. 580. **shriked,** shrieked; **houped,** whooped.

Now goode men, I praye you herkneth alle:
Lo, how Fortune turneth sodeinly
The hope and pride eek of hir enemy.
This cok that lay upon the foxes bak,
In al his drede unto the fox he spak,
And saide, "Sire, if that I were as ye,
Yit sholde I sayn, as wis God helpe me,
'Turneth ayain, ye proude cherles alle!
A verray pestilence upon you falle!
Now am I come unto this wodes side,
Maugree your heed, the cok shal here abide.
I wol him ete, in faith, and that anoon.' "
The fox answerde, "In faith, it shal be doon."
And as he spak that word, al sodeinly
The cok brak from his mouth deliverly,
And hye upon a tree he fleigh anoon.
And whan the fox sawgh that he was agoon,
"Allas," quod he, "O Chauntecleer, allas!
I have to you," quod he, "ydoon trespas,
In as muche as I maked you aferd
Whan I you hente and broughte out of the yeerd.
But sire, I dide it in no wikke entente:
Come down, and I shal telle you what I mente.
I shal saye sooth to you, God help me so."
"Nay thanne," quod he, "I shrewe us bothe two:
But first I shrewe myself, bothe blood and bones,
If thou bigile me ofter than ones;
Thou shalt namore thurgh thy flaterye
Do me to singe and winken with myn yë.
For he that winketh whan he sholde see,
Al wilfully, God lat him nevere thee."
"Nay," quod the fox, "but God yive him meschaunce
That is so undiscreet of governaunce
That jangleth whan he sholde holde his pees."

583. **turneth,** reverses, overturns. 588. **wis,** surely. 592. **Maugree . . . heed,** despite your head, i.e., despite anything you can do. 596. **deliverly,** nimbly. 597. **fleigh,** flew. 602. **hente,** seized. 603. **wikke,** wicked. 606. **shrewe,** curse. 610. **Do,** cause. 612. **thee,** thrive. 615. **jangleth,** chatters.

Lo, swich it is for to be recchelees°
And necligent and truste on flaterye.
But ye that holden this tale a folye
As of a fox, or of a cok and hen,
Taketh the moralitee, goode men.
For Saint Paul saith that al that writen is
To oure doctrine° it is ywrit, ywis:
Taketh the fruit, and lat the chaf° be stille.
Now goode God, if that it be thy wille,
As saith my lord, so make us alle goode men,
And bringe us to his hye blisse. Amen.

The Epilogue

"Sire Nonnes Preest," oure Hoste saide anoon,
"Yblessed be thy breech° and every stoon:
This was a merye tale of Chauntecleer.
But by my trouthe, if thou were seculer°
Thou woldest been a tredefowl° aright:
For if thou have corage° as thou hast might
Thee were neede of hennes, as I weene,°
Ye, mo than sevene times seventeene.
See whiche brawnes hath this gentil preest—
So greet a nekke and swich a large breest.
He looketh as a sperhawk° with his yën;
Him needeth nat his colour for to dyen
With brasil ne with grain of Portingale.°
Now sire, faire falle° you for youre tale."
And after that he with ful merye cheere
Saide unto another as ye shul heere.

616. **recchelees,** careless. 622. **doctrine,** instruction. 623. **fruit,** corn; **chaf,** husks. 628. **breech,** thighs. 630. **seculer,** i.e., a layman. 631. **tredefowl,** fowl raised for breeding purposes. 632. **corage,** desire. 633. **weene,** suppose. 637. **sperhawk,** sparrowhawk. 639. **brasil,** red powder; **grain,** dye; **Portingale,** Portugal. 640. **falle,** may it befall.

THE SECOND NUN'S TALE

The Prologue

The ministre and the norice unto vices,
Which that men clepeth in Englissh idelnesse,
That porter at the gate is of delices,
To eschewen and by hir contrarye hire oppresse—
That is to sayn, by leveful bisinesse—
Wel oughte we to doon al oure entente,
Lest that the feend thurgh idelnesse us hente.

For he that with his thousand cordes slye
Continuelly us waiteth to biclappe,
Whan he may man in idelnesse espye,
He can so lightly cacche him in his trappe,
Til that a man be hent right by the lappe
He nis nat war the feend hath him in honde:
Wel oughte us werche and idelnesse withstonde.

And though men dradden nevere for to die,
Yit seen men wel by reson, doutelees,
That idelnesse is roten slogardye,
Of which ther nevere comth no good n'encrees;
And seen that Slouthe hire holdeth on a lees,
Only for to sleepe and ete and drinken,
And to devouren al that othere swinken.

1. ministre, servant; **norice,** nurse: these nouns are the direct objects of *eschew* in l. 4. **2. clepeth,** call. **3. porter:** in the *Romance of the Rose* Lady Idleness is the porter of the gate to the garden in which the action takes place; **delices,** worldly delights. **4. contrarye,** opposite; **oppresse,** overcome. **5. leveful,** lawful. **6. doon . . . entente,** devote all our energy. **7. hente,** seize. **9. biclappe,** catch. **11. lightly,** readily. **12. lappe,** fold of a garment. **14. Wel . . . werche,** i.e., for good reason we ought to work. **15. dradden,** dreaded. **17. roten,** rotten; **slogardye,** sluggishness. **18. encrees,** profit. **19. seen,** i.e., men see; **Slouthe,** Sloth; **hire . . . lees,** holds her (Idleness) in bondage. **21. swinken,** earn by labor.

And for to putte us from swich idelnesse
That cause is of so greet confusioun,
I have here doon my faithful bisinesse,
After the legende, in translacioun
Right of thy glorious lif and passioun—
Thou with thy gerland wrought of gold and lilye:
Thee mene I, maide and martyr Sainte Cecilie.

And thou, that flowr of virgines art alle,
Of whom that Bernard list so wel to write,
To thee at my biginning first I calle:
Thou confort of us wrecches, do m'endite
Thy maidens deeth, that wan thurgh hir merite
The eternel lif, and of the feend victorye,
As man may after reden in hir storye.

Thou maide and moder, doughter of thy sone;
Thou welle of mercy, sinful soules cure,
In whom that God for bountee chees to wone;
Thou humble and heigh over every creature,
Thou nobledest so ferforth oure nature,
That no desdain the Makere hadde of kinde,
His sone in blood and flessh to clothe and winde.

Within the cloistre blisful of thy sides
Took mannes shap th'eternal Love and Pees,
That of the trine compas lord and gide is,
Whom erthe and see and hevene out of relees
Ay herien; and thou, virgine wemmelees,
Bar of thy body—and dweltest maide pure—
The creatour of every creature.

23. **confusioun,** destruction. 30. **Bernard,** St. Bernard of Clairvaux, particularly as portrayed in Dante's *Paradiso*. 32. **do,** cause. 33. **deeth,** death; **wan,** won. 37. **welle,** spring. 38. **bountee,** goodness; **chees,** chose; **wone,** dwell. 40. **nobledest,** ennobled; **so ferforth,** to such an extent. 41. **kinde,** nature. 44. The eternal Love and Peace (i.e., Christ) took man's shape. 45. **trine compas,** ? threefold world—i.e., earth, water, air. 46. **out . . . relees,** unceasingly. 47. **herien,** praise; **wemmelees,** spotless. 48. **Bar,** bore; **dweltest,** remained.

Assembled is in thee magnificence,
With mercy, goodnesse, and swich pitee,
That thou, that art the sonne of excellence,
Nat only helpest hem that prayen thee,
But ofte time of thy benignitee
Ful freely, er that men thyn help biseeche,
Thou goost biforn and art hir lives leeche.

Now help, thou meeke and blisful faire maide,
Me, flemed wrecche, in this desert of galle;
Think on the womman Cananee that saide
That whelpes eten some of the crommes alle
That from hir lordes table been yfalle;
And though that I, unworthy sone of Eve,
Be sinful, yit accepte my bileve.

And for that faith is deed withouten werkes,
So for to werken yif me wit and space,
That I be quit from thennes that most derk is.
O thou, that art so fair and ful of grace,
Be myn advocat in that hye place,
Ther as withouten ende is songe Osanne—
Thou Cristes moder, doughter dere of Anne.

And of thy light my soule in prison lighte,
That troubled is by the contagioun
Of my body, and also by the wighte
Of erthely lust and fals affeccioun:
O haven of refut, O savacioun
Of hem that been in sorwe and in distresse,
Now help, for to my werk I wol me dresse.

50. magnificence, magnanimity. **52. sonne,** sun. **56. goost biforn,** i.e., come into their hearts before they pray; **leeche,** physician. **58. flemed,** banished; **galle,** bitterness. **59. Cananee,** of Canaan. **60. whelpes,** dogs; **crommes,** crumbs. **63. bileve,** trust. **64. deed,** dead. **65. yif,** give; **space,** time. **66. quit,** i.e., saved; **thennes,** thence; **derk,** dark. **69. Osanne,** Hosanna. **70. moder,** mother. **71. lighte,** illuminate. **73. wighte,** weight. **75. refut,** refuge. **77. dresse,** turn.

Yit praye ich° you that reden that I write,
Foryive me that I do no diligence°
This ilke storye subtilly t'endite;
For bothe have I the wordes and sentence°
Of him° that at the saintes reverence
The storye wroot, and folwen hir° legende,
And praye you that ye wol my werk amende.

The Tale

ST. CECILIA'S NAME

First wolde I you the name of Sainte Cecilie
Expounde, as men may in hir storye see.
It is to sayn on Englissh "hevenes lilye,"°
For pure chastnesse of virginitee,
Or for she whitnesse hadde of honestee,°
And greene° of conscience, and of good fame
The swoote° savour, lilye was hir name.

Or Cecile is to sayn "the way° to blinde,"
For she ensample was by good techinge;
Or elles Cecile, as I writen finde,
Is joined by a manere conjoininge°
Of *hevene* and *Lia,* and here in figuringe°
The *hevene* is set for thought of holinesse,
And *Lia* for hir lasting bisinesse.

78. ich, I. **79. do no diligence,** make no effort. **81. sentence,** thought. **82. him,** Jacobus de Voragine, compiler of the Golden Legend. **83. hir,** her, i.e., St. Cecilia's.

3. hevenes lilye, the name Cecilia is here analyzed as containing the Latin words *caeli lilia,* "lilies of heaven." **5. for,** because; **honestee,** honor. **6. greene,** i.e., greenness, vigor. **7. swoote,** sweet. **8. way,** etc.: this translates the Latin *caecis via.* **11. manere conjoininge,** kind of combination. **12. Lia,** Leah: Jacob's first wife, considered a model of the active life of virtue; **in figuringe,** i.e., symbolically.

Cecile may eek be said in this manere,
"Wanting of blindnesse," for hir grete light°
Of sapience, and for hir thewes clere.°
Or elles, lo, this maidenes name bright
Of *hevene* and *leos*° comth, for which by right
Men mighte hire wel the "hevene of peple" calle,
Ensample° of goode and wise werkes alle.

For *leos* "peple" in Englissh is to saye;
And right as men may in the hevene see
The sonne and moone and sterres° every waye,
Right so men gostly in this maiden free°
Seyen° of faith the magnanimitee,
And eek the cleernesse hool° of sapience,
And sondry werkes brighte of excellence.

And right so as thise philosophres write
That hevene is swift and round and eek brenninge,°
Right so was faire Cecilie the white
Ful swift and bisy evere in good werkinge,
And round and hool in good perseveringe,
And brenning evere in charitee ful brighte:
Now have I you declared what she highte.°

ST. CECILIA'S LEGEND

This maide bright Cecilie, as hir lif saith,
Was come of Romains and of noble kinde,°
And from hir cradel up fostred in the faith
Of Crist, and bar° his gospel in hir minde.
She nevere ceessed, as I writen finde,
Of hir prayere, and God to love and drede,
Biseeking him to keepe hir maidenhede.°

16. Latin *Caecilia,* "blind woman," is interpreted by topsy-turvy logic as "lacking in blindness." **17. thewes,** virtues; **clere,** bright. **19. leos,** "people" in Greek. **21. ensample,** example. **24. sterres,** stars. **25. gostly,** spiritually; **free,** noble. **26. Seyen,** saw. **27. cleernesse,** brightness; **hool,** entire. **30. brenninge,** burning. **35. highte,** was called. **37. kinde,** stock. **39. bar,** bore. **42. maidenhede,** maidenhood.

And whan this maiden sholde until a man
Ywedded be, that was ful yong of age,
Which that ycleped° was Valerian,
And day was comen of hir mariage,
She ful devout and humble in hir corage,°
Under hir robe of gold that sat° ful faire,
Hadde next hir flessh yclad hire in an haire.°

And whil the organs maden melodye,
To God allone in hir herte thus soong she:
"O Lord, my soule and eek my body gie°
Unwemmed,° lest that I confounded be."
And for his love that deide upon a tree
Every seconde and thridde day she faste,°
Ay bidding in hir orisons ful faste.

The night cam and to bedde moste° she goon
With hir housbonde, as ofte is the manere,
And prively to him she saide anoon,
"O sweete and wel biloved spouse dere,
Ther is a conseil, and° ye wolde it heere,
Which that right fain° I wolde unto you saye,
So that ye swere ye shul it nat biwraye."°

Valerian gan faste unto hir swere
That for no caas ne thing that mighte be
He sholde nevere mo biwrayen here,°
And thanne at erst° to him thus saide she,
"I have an angel which that loveth me,
That with greet love, wher so° I wake or sleepe,
Is redy ay my body for to keepe.

And if that he may feelen, out of drede,°
That ye me touche or love in vilainye,°

45. **ycleped,** called. 47. **corage,** spirit. 48. **sat,** i.e., became her. 49. **haire,** hair-shirt. 52. **gie,** direct. 53. **Unwemmed,** unspotted. 55. **faste,** fasted. 57. **moste,** must. 61. **conseil,** secret; **and,** if. 62. **fain,** gladly. 63. **biwraye,** disclose. 66. **here,** her. 67. **at erst,** finally. 69. **wher so,** whether. 71. **drede,** doubt. 72. **vilainye,** rudeness.

He right anoon wol sleen° you with the deede,
And in youre youthe thus ye shullen die;
And if that ye in clene love me gie;°
He wol you love as me for youre clennesse,
And shewe to you his joye and his brightnesse."

This Valerian, corrected as God wolde,
Answerde again, "If I shal trusten thee,
Lat me that angel seen and him biholde;
And if that it a verray° angel be,
Thanne wol I doon as thou hast prayed me;
And if thou love another man, forsoothe,
Right with this swerd thanne wol I slee you bothe."

Cecile answerde anoonright in this wise:
"If that you list the angel shal ye see—
So that ye trowe° on Crist and you baptise.
Gooth forth to Via Apia," quod she,
"That fro this town ne stant° but miles three,
And to the poore folkes that ther dwellen
Saye hem right thus as that I shal you tellen.

Telle hem that I, Cecile, you to hem sente
To shewen you the goode Urban the olde,
For secree needes and for good entente;°
And whan that ye Saint Urban han biholde,
Telle him the wordes whiche I to you tolde;
And whan that he hath purged you fro sinne,
Thanne shal ye seen that angel er we twinne."°

This Valerian is to the place goon,
And right as him was taught by his lerninge°
He foond° this holy olde Urban anoon,
Among the saintes buriels lotinge;°

73. **sleen,** slay. 75. **gie,** govern. 81. **verray,** true. 87. **So,** provided; **trowe,** believe. 89. **stant,** stands. 94. **entente,** intention. 98. **twinne,** separate. 100. **lerninge,** i.e., instructions. 101. **foond,** found. 102. **buriels,** burial places, i.e., the Catacombs; **lotinge,** lingering.

And he anoon withouten taryinge
Dide° his message; and whan that he it tolde,
Urban for joye his handes gan upholde.

The teres from his yën leet° he falle.
"Almighty Lord, O Jesu Crist," quod he,
"Sowere of chast conseil, hierde° of us alle,
The fruit of thilke seed of chastitee
That thou hast sowe in Cecilie, taak to thee:
Lo, lik a bisy bee withouten gile
Thee serveth ay thyn owene thral° Cecile.

For thilke spouse that she took but now,
Ful lik a fiers leon, she sendeth here
As meeke as evere was any lamb to you."
And with that word anoon ther gan appere
An old man clad in white clothes clere°
That hadde a book with lettre of gold in honde,
And gan biforn Valerian to stonde.

Valerian as deed fil down for drede
Whan he him sawgh, and he up hente° him tho,
And on his book right thus he gan to rede:
"Oo° Lord, oo faith, oo God withouten mo,
Oo Cristendom, and fader of alle also,
Aboven alle and overal everywhere."
Thise wordes al with gold ywriten were.

Whan this was rad° thanne saide this olde man,
"Levestou this thing or no? Say ye° or nay."
"I leve al this thing," quod Valerian,
"For soother° thing than this, I dar wel say,
Under the hevene no wight thinke may."
Thanne vanisshed this olde man, he niste° where,
And Pope Urban him cristned right there.

104. Dide, performed. **106. leet,** let. **108. hierde,** shepherd. **112. thral,** servant. **117. clere,** bright. **121. hente,** took. **123. Oo,** one. **127. rad,** read. **128. Levestou,** do you believe; **ye,** yea. **130. soother,** truer. **132. niste,** knew not.

Valerian gooth hoom and fint° Cecilie
Inwith° his chambre with an angel stonde:
This angel hadde of roses and of lilye
Corownes° two, the whiche he bar in honde;
And first to Cecile, as I understonde,
He yaf that oon, and after gan he take°
That other to Valerian hir make.°

"With body clene and with unwemmed° thought
Keepeth ay wel thise corownes," quod he.
"Fro Paradis to you have I hem brought,
Ne nevere mo ne shal they roten° be,
Ne lese hir swoote° savour, trusteth me;
Ne nevere wight shal seen hem with his yë
But° he be chast and hate vilainye.

And thou, Valerian, for thou so soone
Assentedest to good conseil also,
Say what thee list, and thou shalt han thy boone."
"I have a brother," quod Valerian tho,
"That in this world I love no man so:
I praye you that my brother may han grace
To knowe the trouthe—as I do—in this place."

The angel saide, "God liketh thy requeste,
And bothe with the palm of martyrdoom
Ye shullen come unto his blisful feeste."°
And with that word Tiburce his brother coom;°
And whan that he the savour undernoom°
Which that the roses and the lilies caste,
Withinne his herte he gan to wondre faste,

And saide, "I wondre, this time of the yere,
Whennes that swoote savour cometh so
Of rose and lilies that I smelle here?

134. fint, finds. **135. Inwith**, within. **137. Corownes**, crowns. **139. take**, give. **140. make**, mate. **141. unwemmed**, unspotted. **144. roten**, withered. **145. lese**, lose; **swoote**, sweet. **147. But**, unless. **157. feeste**, feast. **158. coom**, came. **159. undernoom**, perceived.

For though I hadde hem in mine handes two,
The savour mighte in me no depper° go.
The sweete smel that in myn herte I finde
Hath chaunged me al in another kinde."°

Valerian saide, "Two corownes han we,
Snow-white and rose-rede° that shinen clere,
Whiche that thine yën han no might to see.
And as thou smellest hem thurgh my prayere,
So shaltou seen hem, leve° brother dere,
If it be so thou wolt withouten slouthe°
Bileve aright and knowen° verray trouthe."

Tiburce answerde, "Saistou this to me
In soothnesse,° or in dreem I herkne this?"
"In dremes," quod Valerian, "han we be
Unto this time, my brother myn, ywis.°
But now at erst° in trouthe oure dwelling is."
"How woostou° this?" quod Tiburce. "In what wise?"
Quod Valerian, "That shal I thee devise:°

The angel of God hath me the trouthe ytaught
Which thou shalt seen if that thou wolt renaye°
The idoles and be clene, and elles° naught."
(And of the miracle of thise corownes twaye
Saint Ambrose in his preface list° to saye;
Solempnely this noble doctour dere
Commendeth it, and saith in this manere:

"The palm of martyrdom for to receive
Sainte Cecile, fulfild° of Goddes yifte,
The world and eek hir chambre gan she waive°—

166. **depper,** more deeply. 168. **al . . . kinde,** into something entirely different. 170. **rede,** red. 173. **leve,** beloved. 174. **slouthe,** i.e., tarrying. 175. **knowen,** acknowledge. 177. **soothnesse,** reality. 179. **ywis,** indeed. 180. **at erst,** finally for the first time. 181. **woostou,** do you know. 182. **devise,** describe. 184. **renaye,** renounce. 185. **elles,** otherwise. 187. **preface,** a prayer, ascribed to St. Ambrose, in the mass celebrated on St. Cecilia's Day; **list,** i.e., takes care. 191. **fulfild,** filled full. 192. **gan . . . waive,** she turned away from.

Witnesse Tiburces and Valerians shrifte,°
To whiche God of his bountee wolde shifte°
Corownes two of flowres wel smellinge,
And made his angel hem the corownes bringe.

The maide hath brought men to blisse above:
The world hath wist° what it was worth, certain,
Devocioun of chastitee to love.")°
Tho shewed him Cecile al open and plain
That alle idoles nis but a thing in vain,
For they been dombe and therto they been deve,°
And charged him his idoles for to leve.°

"Whoso that troweth nat this, a beest° he is,"
Quod tho Tiburce, "if that I shal nat lie."
And she gan kisse his brest, that herde this,
And was ful glad he coude trouthe espye.°
"This day I take thee for myn allye,"
Saide this blisful faire maide dere,
And after that she saide as ye may heere:

"Lo, right so as the love of Crist," quod she,
"Made me thy brotheres wif, right in that wise
Anoon for myn allye here take I thee,
Sin that thou wolt thine idoles despise.
Go with thy brother now and thee baptise,
And make thee clene so that thou mowe° biholde
The angeles face of which thy brother tolde."

Tiburce answerde and saide, "Brother dere,
First tel me whider I shal° and to what man?
To whom?" quod he. "Com forth with right good cheere:
I wol thee lede unto the Pope Urban."
"Til Urban? Brother myn Valerian,"

193. shrifte, i.e., conversion. **194. shifte,** assign. **198. wist,** learned. **198–99. what . . . love,** i.e., what devotion to chastity is capable of effecting in terms of love. **202. deve,** deaf. **203. leve,** abandon. **204. beest,** beast. **207. espye,** perceive. **216. mowe,** may. **219. shal,** i.e., shall go.

Quod tho Tiburce, "woltou me thider lede?
Me thinketh that it were a wonder deede:

Ne menestou nat Urban,"° quod he tho,
"That is so ofte dampned to be deed,°
And woneth in halkes° alwey to and fro,
And dar nat ones putte forth his heed?°
Men sholde hym brennen in a fir so reed°
If he were founde or that men mighte him spye—
And we also, to bere him compaignye.

And whil we seeken thilke divinitee
That is yhid in hevene prively,
Algate ybrend° in this world shul we be."
To whom Cecile answerde boldely,
"Men mighte dreden wel and skilfully°
This lif to lese,° myn owene dere brother,
If this were living only, and noon other;

But ther is bettre lif in other place
That nevere shal be lost, ne drede thee nought,
Which Goddes sone us tolde thurgh his grace;
That fadres sone hath alle thinges wrought;
And al that wrought is with a skilful thought,°
The gost° that fro the fader gan proceede
Hath souled hem, withouten any drede.°

By word and by miracle, he, Goddes sone,
Whan he was in this world declared here
That ther was other lif ther men may wone."°
To whom answerde Tiburce, "O suster dere,
Ne saidestou right now in this manere:

225. Ne . . . nat, you don't mean. **226. dampned,** condemned; **deed,** dead. **227. woneth,** lives; **halkes,** hiding-places. **228. heed,** head. **229. brennen,** burn; **reed,** red. **234. Algate,** nevertheless; **ybrend,** burnt. **236. skilfully,** with reason. **237. lese,** lose. **243. skilful thought,** a reasonable mind. **244. gost,** spirit. **245. souled,** endowed with souls; **drede,** doubt. **248. lif ther,** i.e., place where; **wone,** live.

'Ther nis but oo° God, Lord in soothfastnesse'?
And now of three how maistou bere witnesse?"

"That shal I telle," quod she, "er I go.
Right as a man hath sapiences° three,
Memorye, engin,° and intellect also,
So in oo being of divinitee
Three persones may ther right wel be."
Tho gan she him ful bisily to preche
Of Cristes come,° and of his paines teche;

And manye pointes of his passioun—
How Goddes sone in this world was withholde°
To doon mankinde plein° remissioun,
That was ybounde in sinne and cares colde:
Al this thing she unto Tiburce tolde.
And after this Tiburce in good entente
With Valerian to Pope Urban he wente,

That thanked God, and with glad herte and light°
He cristned him and made him in that place
Parfit° in his lerninge, Goddes knight.
And after this Tiburce gat swich grace
That every day he sawgh in time and space
The angel of God, and every manere boone
That he God axed, it was sped° ful soone.

It were ful hard by ordre for to sayn
How manye wondres Jesus for hem wroughte,
But at the laste, to tellen short and plain,
The sergeants of the town of Rome hem soughte,
And hem biforn Almache the Prefect broughte,
Which hem opposed° and knew al hir entente;
And to the image of Jupiter hem sente,

251. oo, one. **254. sapiences,** i.e., kinds of intelligence. **255. engin,** intuition. **259. come,** coming. **261. was withholde,** i.e., employed himself. **262. plein,** full. **267. light,** adj. **269. Parfit,** perfect. **273. axed,** asked of; **sped,** i.e., granted. **279. opposed,** examined.

And saide, "Whoso wol nat sacrifise,
Swap of his heed: this is my sentence heer."
Anoon thise martyrs that I you devise
Oon Maximus, that was an officer
Of the prefectes and his corniculer,
Hem hente, and whan he forth the saintes ladde,
Himself he weep for pitee that he hadde.

Whan Maximus hadde herd the saintes lore,
He gat him of the tormentoures leve,
And ladde hem to his hous withoute more;
And with hir preching er that it were eve
They gonnen fro the tormentours to reve,
And fro Maxime, and fro his folk eechone,
The false faith, to trowe in God allone.

Cecile cam, whan it was woxen night,
With preestes that hem cristned alle yfere;
And afterward, whan day was woxen light,
Cecile hem saide with a ful stedefast cheere,
"Now Cristes owene knightes, leve and dere,
Caste al away the werkes of derknesse,
And armeth you in armour of brightnesse.

Ye han forsoothe ydoon a greet bataile,
Youre cours is doon, youre faith han ye conserved:
Gooth to the crowne of lif that may nat faile—
The rightful juge which that ye han served
Shal yive it you as ye han it deserved."
And whan this thing was said as I devise,
Men ledde hem forth to doon the sacrifise.

But whan they weren to the place brought,
To tellen shortly the conclusioun,

282. **Swap,** strike; **heed,** head. 283. **devise,** describe. 285. **prefectes,** prefect's; **corniculer,** assistant. 286. **hente,** seized; **ladde,** led. 287. **weep,** wept. 288. **lore,** teaching. 289. **tormentoures,** executioners; **leve,** permission. 290. **ladde,** led. 292. **reve,** tear away. 294. **to,** in order to. 295. **woxen,** become. 296. **yfere,** together. 298. **cheere,** manner. 299. **leve,** beloved. 302. **ydoon,** finished. 303. **cours,** race; **conserved,** kept.

They nolde encense ne sacrifice right nought,
But on hir knees they setten hem adown,
With humble herte and sad devocioun,
And losten bothe hir hevedes in the place:
Hir soules wenten to the king of grace.

This Maximus, that sawgh this thing bitide,
With pitous teres tolde it anoonright
That he hir soules sawgh to hevene glide,
With angels ful of cleernesse and of light,
And with his word converted many a wight:
For which Almachius dide him so bete
With whippe of leed til he his lif gan lete.

Cecile him took and buried him anoon
By Tiburce and Valerian softely,
Withinne hir burying place under the stoon;
And after this Almachius hastily
Bad his ministres fecchen openly
Cecile, so that she mighte in his presense
Doon sacrifice and Jupiter encense.

But they, converted at hir wise lore,
Wepten ful sore and yaven ful credence
Unto hir word, and criden more and more,
"Crist, Goddes sone withouten difference,
Is verray God—this is al oure sentence—
That hath so good a servant him to serve:
This with oo vois we trowen though we sterve."

Almachius, that herde of this doinge,
Bad fecchen Cecile that he mighte hire see;
And alderfirst, lo, this was his axinge:

311. **encense,** burn incense. 313. **sad,** steadfast. 314. **hevedes,** heads. 319. **cleernesse,** brightness. 321. **dide . . . bete,** had him so beaten. 322. **leed,** lead; **gan lete,** did leave. 324. **softely,** surreptitiously. 325. **hir,** their. 330. **lore,** teaching. 333. **difference,** i.e., distinction between Father and Son. 334. **sentence,** belief. 335. **That,** who, i.e., God. 336. **oo,** one; **trowen,** i.e., acknowledge; **sterve,** die. 339. **alderfirst,** first of all; **axinge,** i.e., question.

"What manere womman artou?" tho quod he.
"I am a gentil womman born," quod she.
"I axe thee," quod he, "though it thee greve,
Of thy religion and of thy bileve."°

"Ye han bigonne youre question folily,"°
Quod she, "that wolden two answeres conclude°
In oo demande. Ye axed lewedly."°
Almache answerde unto that similitude,°
"Of whennes comth thyn answering so rude?"
"Of whennes?" quod she whan that she was frained.°
"Of conscience and of good faith unfeined."°

Almachius saide, "Ne takestou noon heede
Of my power?" And she answerde him this:
"Youre might," quod she, "ful litel is to drede,°
For every mortal mannes power nis
But lik a bladdre ful of wind, ywis:°
For with a needles point whan it is blowe°
May al the boost° of it be laid ful lowe."

"Ful wrongfully bigonne thou," quod he,
"And yit in wrong is al thy perseveraunce.
Woostou nat how oure mighty princes free°
Han thus comanded and maad ordinaunce
That every Cristen wight shal han penaunce°
But if that he his Cristendom withsaye,°
And goon al quit if he wol it renaye?"°

"Youre princes erren as youre nobleye° dooth,"
Quod tho Cecile, "and with a wood° sentence
Ye make us gilty; and it is nat sooth:

343. **bileve,** creed. 344. **folily,** foolishly. 345. **conclude,** i.e., include the possibility of. 346. **lewedly,** ignorantly. 347. **similitude,** statement. 349. **frained,** questioned. 350. **unfeined,** unfeigning. 353. **to drede,** to be feared. 355. **ywis,** indeed. 356. **it,** i.e., the bladder; **blowe,** inflated. 357. **boost,** boast. 360. **Woostou,** do you know; **free,** generous. 362. **penaunce,** torture. 363. **But if,** unless; **withsaye,** deny. 364. **quit,** absolved; **renaye,** renounce. 365. **nobleye,** nobility. 366. **wood,** insane.

For ye, that knowen wel oure innocence,
For as muche as we doon a reverence
To Crist, and for we bere a Cristen name,
Ye putte on us a crime and eek a blame.

But we that knowen thilke name so
For vertuous, we may it nat withsaye."
Almache answerde, "Chees oon of thise two:
Do sacrifice or Cristendom renaye,
That thou mowe now escapen by that waye."
At which this holy blisful faire maide
Gan for to laughe, and to the juge she saide:

"O juge, confus in thy nicetee,
Woltou that I renaye innocence
To maken me a wikked wight?" quod she.
"Lo, he dissimuleth here in audience;
He stareth and woodeth in his advertence."
To whom Almachius, "Unsely wrecche,
Ne woostou nat how fer my might may strecche?

Han nat oure mighty princes to me yiven,
Ye, bothe power and auctoritee
To maken folk to dien or to liven?
Why spekestou so proudly thanne to me?"
"I speke nought but stedefastly," quod she,
"Nat proudly, for I saye, as for my side,
We haten deedly thilke vice of pride.

And if thou drede nat a sooth to heere,
Thanne wol I shewe al openly by right
That thou hast maad a ful greet lesing here:
Thou saist thy princes han thee yiven might
Bothe for to sleen and for to quiken a wight—

372. **name,** i.e., of Christianity. 374. **Chees,** choose. 376. **mowe,** may. 379. **nicetee,** folly. 382. **dissimuleth,** i.e., says what he cannot mean; **audience,** public. 383. **woodeth,** raves; **advertence,** i.e., intellectual control. 384. **Unsely,** unhappy. 385. **fer,** far. 387. **Ye,** yea. 392. **deedly,** deadly. 395. **lesing,** lie. 397. **sleen,** slay; **quiken,** bring to life.

Thou that ne maist but only lif bireve;°
Thou hast noon other power ne no leve.°

But thou maist sayn thy princes han thee maked
Ministre of deeth;° for if thou speke of mo,
Thou liest, for thy power is ful naked."°
"Do way thy boldnesse," saide Almachius tho,
"And sacrifice to oure goddes er thou go:
I recche° nat what wrong that thou me profre,
For I can suffre it as a philosphre;

But thilke wronges may I nat endure
That thou spekest of oure goddes here," quod he.
Cecile answerde, "O nice° creature,
Thou saidest no word sin thou spake to me
That I ne knew therwith thy nicetee;°
And that thou were in every manere wise
A lewed officer, a vain° justise.

Ther lakketh no thing to thine outter yën
That thou nart blind;° for thing that we seen alle,
That is a stoon that men may wel espyen,
That ilke stoon a god thou wolt it calle.
I rede° thee, lat thyn hand upon it falle,
And taste° it wel, and stoon thou shalt it finde—
Sin that thou seest nat with thine yën blinde.

It is a shame that the peple shal
So scornen thee and laughe at thy folye,
For communly men woot it wel overal
That mighty God is in his hevenes hye;
And thise images wel thou maist espye
To thee ne to hemself mowe° nought profite,
For in effect they be nat worth a mite."

398. bireve, take away. **399. leve,** permission. **401. deeth,** death. **402. naked,** i.e., weak. **405. recche,** care. **409. nice,** foolish. **411. nicetee,** foolishness. **413. lewed,** ignorant; **vain,** foolish. **414–15. Ther . . . blind,** i.e., in every respect you are physically blind. **418. rede,** advise. **419. taste,** feel. **426. mowe,** may.

Thise wordes and swiche othere saide she,
And he weex wroth and bad men sholde hire lede
Hoom til hir hous; "And in hir hous," quod he,
Bren hire right in a bath of flaumbes rede."
And as he bad, right so was doon the deede,
For in a bath they gonne hire faste shetten,
And night and day greet fir they under betten.

The longe night and eek a day also
For al the fir and eek the bathes hete
She sat al cold and feelede no wo:
It made hire nat oo drope for to swete;
But in that bath hir lif she moste lete,
For he Almachius, with ful wikke entente,
To sleen hire in the bath his sonde sente.

Three strokes in the nekke he smoot hire tho,
The tormentour, but for no manere chaunce
He mighte nat smite al hir nekke atwo.
And for ther was that time an ordinaunce
That no man sholde doon man swich penaunce
The ferthe strook to smiten, softe or sore,
This tormentour ne dorste do namore–

But half deed, with hir nekke ycorven, there
He lefte hire lie, and on his way he went.
The Cristen folk whiche that aboute hire were
With sheetes han the blood ful faire yhent.
Three dayes lived she in this torment,
And nevere ceessed hem the faith to teche
That she hadde fostered; hem she gan to preche,

And hem she yaf hir moebles and hir thing,
And to the Pope Urban bitook hem so,

431. **Bren,** burn; **flaumbes,** flames. 433. **shetten,** shut. 434. **betten,** built. 436. **hete,** heat. 438. **swete,** sweat. 439. **moste lete,** must leave. 440. **wikke,** wicked. 441. **sonde,** message. 442. **smoot,** smote. 446. **doon,** cause; **penaunce,** suffering. 447. **ferthe,** fourth; **softe or sore,** gently or harshly. 449. **deed,** dead; **ycorven,** cut open. 452. **yhent,** taken. 456. **moebles,** furniture; **thing,** possessions. 457. **bitook,** entrusted.

And saide, "I axed° this of hevene king
To han respit three dayes and namo,
To recomende to you er that I go
Thise soules, lo, and that I mighte do wirche°
Here of myn hous perpetuelly a chirche."

Saint Urban with his deknes° prively
The body fette,° and buried it by nighte,
Among his othere saintes honestly.°
Hir hous the Chirche of Sainte Cecile highte:
Saint Urban halwed° it as he wel mighte,
In which into this day in noble wise
Men doon to Crist and to his sainte servise.

THE CANON'S YEOMAN'S TALE

The Introduction

Whan ended was the lif of Sainte Cecile,
Er we hadde riden fully five mile,
At Boughton-under-Blee us gan atake°
A man that clothed was in clothes blake,
And under that he hadde a whit surplis.°
His hakeney, that was al pomely gris,°
So swette° that it wonder was to see:
It seemed he hadde priked° miles three.
The hors eek that his Yeman° rood upon
So swette that unnethe° mighte he goon:
Aboute the peitrel° stood the foom ful hye.
He was of foom al flekked as a pie.°
A male twayfold on his croper° lay.

458. **axed,** asked. 461. **do wirche,** have made. 463. **deknes,** deacons. 464. **fette,** fetched. 465. **honestly,** honorably. 467. **halwed,** consecrated.

3. **atake,** catch up with. 5. **surplis,** surplice. 6. **pomely gris,** dappled grey. 7. **swette,** sweated. 8. **priked,** ridden fast. 9. **Yeman,** yeoman, servant. 10. **unnethe,** scarcely. 11. **peitrel,** horsecollar. 12. **pie,** magpie. 13. **male,** pouch; **twayfold,** double; **croper,** crupper.

It seemed that he caried lite array:°
Al light for somer° rood this worthy man.
And in myn herte wondren I bigan
What that he was, til that I understood
How that his cloke was sowed to his hood,
For which, whan I longe hadde avised me,°
I deemed him som Chanon° for to be.
His hat heeng at his bak down by a las,°
For he hadde riden more than trot or pas:°
He hadde ay priked lik as he were wood.°
A clote-leef° he hadde under his hood
For swoot,° and for to keepe his heed fro hete—
But it was joye for to seen him swete!
His forheed dropped as a stillatorye°
Were ful of plantaine and of peritorye.°
And whan that he was come he gan to crye,
"God save," quod he, "this joly compaignye!
Faste have I priked," quod he, "for youre sake,
By cause that I wolde you overtake,
To riden in this merye compaignye."
His Yeman eek was ful of curteisye
And saide, "Sires, now in the morwetide°
Out of youre hostelrye I sawgh you ride,
And warned heer my lord and my soverein,°
Which that to ride with you is ful fain°
For his disport—he loveth daliaunce."°
"Freend, for thy warning God yive thee good chaunce,"
Saide oure Hoste. "Certes, it wolde seeme
Thy lord were wis, and so I may wel deeme.
He is ful jocunde also, dar I laye.°
Can he ought telle a merye tale or twaye,
With which he glade° may this compaignye?"

14. **lite**, little; **array**, clothing. 15. **somer**, summer. 19. **avised me**, pondered, 20. **Chanon**, canon, member of a religious order. 21. **heeng**, hung; **las**, strap. 22. **more**, faster; **pas**, i.e., a walking gait. 23. **wood**, mad. 24. **clote-leef**, aster leaf. 25. **For swoot**, against sweat. 27. **stillatorye**, still. 28. **peritorye**, pellitory: this and plantain are herbs commonly distilled to produce medicines. 35. **morwetide**, morning time. 37. **soverein**, master. 38. **fain**, glad. 39. **daliaunce**, social chitchat. 43. **laye**, wager. 45. **glade**, gladden.

"Who, sire? My lord? Ye, ye, withoute lie,
He can° of mirthe and eek of jolitee
Nought but ynough. Also, sire, trusteth me,
And° ye him knewe as wel as do I,
Ye wolde wondre how wel and craftily
He coude werke, and that in sondry wise.
He hath take on him many greet emprise°
Which were ful hard for any that is here
To bringe aboute, but they of him it lere.°
As hoomly as he rit° amonges you,
If ye him knewe, it wolde be youre prow:°
Ye wolde nat forgoon his aquaintaunce
For muchel good, I dar laye in balaunce°
Al that I have in my possessioun.
He is a man of heigh discrecioun:
I warne you wel, he is a passing° man."
"Wel," quod oure Host, "I praye thee, tel me than,
Is he a clerk or noon? Tel what he is."
"Nay, he is gretter° than a clerk, ywis,"
Saide the Yeman, "and in wordes fewe,
Host, of his craft somwhat I wol you shewe.
I saye my lord can° swich a subtiltee—
But al his craft ye may nat wite at° me,
And somwhat helpe I yit to his werkinge—
That al this ground which we been on ridinge
Til that we come to Canterbury town
He coude al clene turne upsodown,°
And pave it al of silver and of gold!"
And whan this Yeman hadde thus ytold
Unto oure Host, he saide, "Benedicite!°
This thing is wonder merveilous to me,
Sith that thy lord is of so heigh prudence,
By cause of which men sholde him reverence,
That of his worshipe rekketh he so lite:°

47. can, knows. **49. And,** if. **52. emprise,** enterprise. **54. lere,** learn. **55. hoomly,** informally; **rit,** rides. **56. prow,** profit. **58. laye . . . balaunce,** i.e., bet. **61. passing,** i.e., superior. **64. gretter,** greater. **67. can,** is capable of. **68. wite at,** know from. **72. upsodown,** upside-down. **75. Benedicite,** bless me. **79. rekketh,** cares; **lite,** little.

His oversloppe° nis nat worth a mite
As in effect to him, so mote I go—
It is al bawdy and totore° also.
Why is thy lord so sluttish,° I thee praye,
And is of power bettre clothes to beye,°
If that his deede accorde with thy speeche?
Tel me that, and that I thee biseeche."
"Why?" quod this Yeman. "Wherto axe ye me?"
"God helpe me so, for he shal nevere thee.°
But I wol nat avowe that° I saye,
And therfore keepe it secree,° I you praye.
He is too wis, in faith, as I bileve:
That that is overdoon, it nil nat preve,°
And right as clerkes sayn, it is a vice.
Wherfore in that I holde him lewed and nice,°
For whan a man hath over-greet a wit,
Ful ofte him happeth to misusen it.
So dooth my lord, and that me greveth sore.
God it amende—I can saye now namore."
"Therof no fors,° goode Yeman," quod oure Host:
"Sith of the conning of thy lord thou woost,°
Tel how he dooth, I praye thee hertely,
Sith that he is so crafty and so sly.°
Wher dwellen ye, if it to telle be?"
"In the suburbes of a town," quod he,
"Lurking in hernes° and in lanes blinde,
Wher as thise robbers and thise theves by kinde°
Holden hir privee fereful residence,
As they that dar nat shewen hir presence:
So fare we, if I shal saye the soothe."
"Yit," quod oure Hoste, "lat me talke to thee:
Why art thou discoloured on thy face?"
"Peter," quod he, "God yive it harde grace!

80. **oversloppe,** surplice. 82. **bawdy,** dirty; **totore,** tattered. 83. **sluttish,** slovenly. 84. **beye,** buy. 88. **thee,** prosper. 89. **avowe,** admit; **that,** what. 90. **secree,** secret. 92. **preve,** prove, i.e., turn out well. 94. **lewed,** ignorant; **nice,** foolish. 99. **fors,** matter. 100. **conning,** ability; **woost,** know. 102. **crafty,** skilled; **sly,** clever. 105. **hernes,** corners. 106. **by kinde,** naturally.

I am so used in the fir to blowe
That it hath chaunged my colour, as I trowe;
I am nat wont in no mirour to prye,
But swinke sore and lerne to multiplye.
We blondren evere and pouren in the fir,
And for al that we failen of oure desir,
For evere we lakken oure conclusioun.
To muche folk we doon illusioun,
And borwe gold, be it a pound or two,
Or ten or twelve, or manye sommes mo,
And make hem weenen at the leeste waye
That of a pound we coude make twaye.
Yit is it fals, and ay we han good hope
It for to doon, and after it we grope.
But that science is so fer us biforn,
We mowe nat, although we hadde it sworn,
It overtake, it slit away so faste:
It wol us maken beggeres atte laste."
 Whil this Yeman was thus in this talking,
This Chanon drow him neer and herde al thing
Which that this Yeman spak, for suspecioun
Of mennes speeche evere hadde this Chanoun:
For Caton saith he that gilty is
Deemeth alle thing be spoke of him, ywis.
By cause of that he gan so neigh to drawe
To his Yeman that he herde al his sawe,
And thus he saide unto his Yeman tho:
"Hold now thy pees and speek no wordes mo,
For if thou doost thou shalt it dere abye:
Thou sclaundrest me heer in this compaignye,
And eek discoverest that thou sholdest hide."
 "Ye," quod oure Host, "tel on what so bitide:
Of al this threting rekke thee nat a mite."

114. trowe, believe. **115. prye,** peer. **116. swinke,** work; **multiplye,** the technical term for the alchemical process of turning baser metals into gold. **117. blondren,** blunder. **119. lakken . . . conclusioun,** fail of our purpose. **122. sommes,** sums. **129. slit,** slides. **132. drow,** drew. **135. Caton,** the primer ascribed to Dionysius Cato. **138. sawe,** saying. **141. abye,** pay for. **142. sclaundrest,** slander. **143. discoverest,** disclose. **145. rekke,** care.

"In faith," quod he, "namore I do but lite."°
 And whan this Chanon sawgh it wolde nat be,
But his Yeman wolde telle his privetee,
He fledde away for verray sorwe and shame.
 "A," quod the Yeman, "here shal arise game.
Al that I can° anoon now wol I telle,
Sin he is goon: the foule feend him quelle!°
For nevere heerafter wol I with him meete,
For peny ne for pound, I you bihete.°
He that me broughte first unto that game,
Er that he die, sorwe have he and shame—
For it is ernest° to me, by my faith:
That feele I wel, what so any man saith.
And yit for al my smert, and al my grief,
For al my sorwe, labour, and meschief,
I coude nevere leve° it in no wise.
Now wolde God my wit mighte suffise
To tellen al that longeth° to that art.
But nathelees, yit wol I telle you part:
Sith that my lord is goon I wol nat spare;
Swich thing as I knowe I wol declare."

The Prologue

 With this Chanoun I dwelt have sevene yeer,
And of his science am I nevere the neer.°
Al that I hadde I have ylost therby,
And God woot, so hath manye mo° than I.
Ther I was wont° to be right fressh and gay
Of clothing and of other good array,
Now may I were an hose° upon myn heed;

146. lite, little. **151. can,** know. **152. quelle,** kill. **154. bihete,** promise. **157. ernest,** there is a wordplay with **game**—i.e., alchemy—in. l. 155. **161. leve,** abandon. **163. longeth,** pertains.

2. of, i.e., to; **neer,** nearer. **4. woot,** knows; **mo,** more. **5. wont,** accustomed. **7. hose,** stocking.

And where my colour was bothe fressh and reed,
Now is it wan and of a leden hewe.°
Whoso it useth, sore shal he rewe.°
And of my swink° yit blered is myn yë:
Lo which avauntage is to multiplye!°
That sliding° science hath me maad so bare
That I have no good wher that evere I fare.
And yit I am endetted° so therby
Of gold that I have borwed, trewely,
That whil I live I shal it quite° nevere.
Lat every man be war by me for evere.
What manere man that casteth him° therto,
If he continue, I holde his thrift ydo.°
For s'helpe me God, therby shal he nat winne,
But empte his purs, and make his wittes thinne.
And whan he thurgh his madnesse and folye
Hath lost his owene good thurgh jeupartye,°
Than he exciteth other folk therto
To lese° hire good as he himself hath do.
For unto shrewes joye it is and ese°
To have hir felawes in paine and disese.°
Thus was I ones lerned of a clerk—
Of that no charge:° I wol speke of oure werk.
Whan we been ther as we shul exercise
Oure elvisshe° craft, we seemen wonder wise:
Oure termes been so clergial° and so quainte.
I blowe the fir til that myn herte fainte.—
  What° sholde I tellen eech proporcion
Of thinges whiche that we werke upon,
As on five or sixe ounces, wel may be,
Of silver—or som other quantitee—
And bisye me to telle you the names

9. hewe, hue. **10. it,** i.e., alchemy; **rewe,** rue. **11. swink,** work. **12. multiplye,** practice alchemy. **13. sliding,** slippery. **15. endetted,** indebted. **17. quite,** repay. **19. casteth him,** applies himself. **20. thrift ydo,** prosperity finished. **24. jeupardye,** i.e., jeopardizing it. **26. lese,** lose. **27. shrewes,** scoundrels; **ese,** comfort. **28. disese,** discomfort **30. charge,** matter. **32. elvisshe,** mysterious. **33. clergial,** pedantic. **35. What,** why.

Of orpiment, brent bones, iren squames
That into powdre grounden been ful smal?
And in an erthen pot how put is al,
And salt yput in, and also paper
Biforn thise powdres that I speke of heer,
And wel ycovered with a lampe of glas,
And of muche other thing which that ther was,
And of the pot and glasses enluting
That of the air mighte passe out no thing,
And of the esy fir, and smert also,
Which that was maad, and of the care and wo
That we hadde in oure materes subliming,
And in amalgaming and calcining
Of quiksilver, yclept mercurye crude.
For alle oure sleightes we can nat conclude:
Oure orpiment and sublimed mercurye,
Oure grounden litarge eek on the porfurye—
Of eech of thise of ounces a certain—
Nought helpeth us—oure labour is in vain.
Ne eek oure spirites ascensioun,
Ne oure materes that lie al fix adown,
Mowe in oure werking no thing us availe,
For lost is al oure labour and travaile,
And al the cost—a twenty devel waye!—
Is lost also which we upon it laye.
  Ther is also ful many another thing
That is unto oure craft apertening,
Though I by ordre hem nat reherce can
By cause that I am a lewed man;
Yit wol I telle hem as they come to minde—

40. orpiment, yellow arsenic; **brent,** burned; **squames,** scalings. **45. lampe,** thin plate. **47. enluting,** smearing with clay. **49. esy,** gentle; **smert,** brisk. **51. materes subliming,** vaporizing materials. **52. amalgaming,** alloying with mercury; **calcining,** reducing to the purest state. **53. yclept,** called. **54. sleightes,** skills; **conclude,** succeed. **56. litarge,** melted lead treated with a current of air; **porfurye,** i.e., a slab of the hard rock porphyry. **57. certain,** measured amount. **59. spirites,** vapors; **ascensioun,** rising. **61. Mowe,** may. **63. a . . . waye,** an exasperated oath. **66. apertening,** belonging. **68. lewed,** ignorant.

Though I ne can nat sette hem in hir kinde—
As bole armoniak, verdegrees, boras,
And sondry vessels maad of erthe and glas:
Oure urinals and oure descensories,
Violes, crosselets, and sublimatories,
Cucurbites, and alembikes eek,
And othere swiche, dere ynough a leek.
Nat needeth it for to reherce hem alle—
Watres rubifying and boles galle,
Arsenik, sal armoniak, and brimstoon,
And herbes coude I telle eek many oon,
As egremoine, valerian, and lunarye,
And othere swiche, if that me liste tarye—
Oure lampes brenning bothe night and day
To bringe aboute oure purpos if we may,
Oure furnais eek of calcinacioun
And of watres albificacioun,
Unslekked lim, chalk, and glaire of an ey,
Powdres diverse, asshes, dong, pisse and clay,
Cered pokets, sal peter, vitriole,
And diverse fires maad of wode and cole,
Sal tartre, alkali, and sal preparat,
And combust materes and coagulat;
Clay maad with hors or mannes heer, and oile
Of tartre, alum glas, berm, wort, argoile,

70. Though I can't arrange them according to their nature. **71.** Such as Armenian bole (earth), green copper-rust, borax. **73. descensories,** distilling vessels with the apertures at the bottom. **74.** Vials, crucibles, and subliming pots. **75. cucurbites,** gourd-shaped retorts; **alembikes,** alembics, the caps of the cucurbits through which the distilled matter passed. **76. dere ynough,** i.e., not worth. **78. rubifying,** reddening; **boles galle,** bull's bile. **79. sal armoniak,** Salt of Ammon; **brimstoon,** sulphur. **81.** As agrimony, valerian, and moon-wort. **82. liste,** pleased. **83. brenning,** burning. **85. furnais,** furnace. **86. albificacioun,** turning white. **87.** Unslaked lime, chalk, and white of an egg. **88. dong,** dung. **89–92.** Bags sealed with wax, saltpeter, sulphuric acid, And various fires made of wood and coal, Salt of tartar, alkali, especially prepared salt, And burnt and clotted materials. **93. hors,** horse's; **heer,** hair. **94. glas,** i.e., crystalized; **berm,** yeast, **wort,** unfermented beer; **argoile,** crude tartar.

Resalgar, and oure materes embibing,
And eek of oure materes encorporing,
And of oure silver citrinacioun,
Oure cementing and fermentacioun,
Oure ingotes, testes, and manye mo.
I wol you telle as me was taught also
The foure spirits and the bodies sevene
By ordre, as ofte I herde my lord hem nevene:
The firste spirit quiksilver called is,
The seconde orpiment, the thridde, ywis,
Sal armoniak, and the ferthe brimstoon.
The bodies sevene eek, lo, hem heere anoon:
Sol gold is, and Luna silver we threpe;
Mars iren, Mercurye quiksilver we clepe;
Saturnus leed, and Jupiter is tin,
And Venus coper, by my fader kin!
This cursed craft whoso wol exercise
He shal no good han that him may suffise,
For al the good he spendeth theraboute
He lese shal, therof have I no doute.
Whoso that listeth outen his folye
Lat him come forth and lerne multiplye,
And every man that ought hath in his cofre,
Lat him appere and waxe a philosophre.
Ascaunce that craft is so light to lere?
Nay, nay, God woot, al be he monk or frere,
Preest or chanoun, or any other wight,
Though he sitte at his book bothe day and night
In lerning of this elvissh, nice lore,

95–99. Red Arsenic, and absorption of our materials, And also of the incorporation of our materials, And of the turning to citron color of our silver, Our combining of solids and fermentation, Our ingots, vessels for assaying metals, and many others. **102. nevene,** name. **104. ywis,** indeed. **106. heere,** hear. **107. Sol,** the sun; **Luna,** the moon; **threpe,** maintain to be. **108. clepe,** call. **109. leed,** lead. **114. lese,** lose. **115. listeth,** pleases; **outen,** demonstrate. **116. multiplye,** to practice alchemy. **117. ought,** anything. **118. waxe,** grow into. **119. Ascaunce,** i.e., perhaps you think; **light,** easy; **lere,** learn. **120. al be he,** even though he is. **123. nice,** foolish.

Al is in vain, and, pardee, muchel more
To lerne a lewed man this subtiltee—
Fy, speke nat therof, for it wol nat be.
Al conne he lettrure, or conne he noon,
As in effect he shal finde it al oon.
For bothe two, by my savacioun,
Concluden in multiplicacioun
Ylike wel, whan they han al ydo—
This is to sayn, they failen, bothe two.
  Yit forgat I to maken rehersaile
Of watres corosif, or of limaile,
And of bodies mollificacioun,
And also of hir induracioun,
Oiles, ablucions, and metal fusible—
To tellen al wolde passen any Bible
That owher is; wherfore, as for the beste,
Of alle thise names now wol I me reste,
For as I trowe, I have you told ynowe
To raise a feend, al looke he nevere so rowe.
  A, nay, lat be, the philosophres stoon—
Elixir clept—we seeken faste eechoon,
For hadde we him, thanne were we siker ynow.
But unto God of hevene I make avow,
For al oure craft, when we han al ydo,
And al oure sleighte, he wol nat come us to.
He hath ymaad us spende muchel good,
For sorwe of which almost we waxen wood—
But that good hope creepeth in oure herte,
Supposing evere, though we sore smerte,
To be releved by him afterward.
Swich supposing and hope is sharp and hard—

125. lerne, teach; **lewed,** ignorant. **127. Al conne he,** whether he knows; **lettrure,** book-lore. **128. oon,** the same. **129. savacioun,** salvation. **130. Concluden,** succeed. **134. corosif,** corrosive; **limaile,** filings. **135. mollificacioun,** softening. **136. induracioun,** hardening. **137. ablucions,** washings; **fusible,** capable of being fused. **138. passen,** outdo. **139. owher,** anywhere. **141. trowe,** believe. **142. al,** although; **rowe,** rough. **144. Elixir clept,** called Elixir. **145. him,** i.e., Elixir; **siker,** secure. **148. sleighte,** cunning. **150. waxen wood,** go mad. **154. sharp,** painful.

I warne you wel, it is to seeken evere.
That futur temps hath maad men to dissevere—
In trust therof—from al that evere they hadde.
Yit of that art they can nat waxen sadde,
For unto hem it is a bittre-sweete—
So seemeth it, for nadde they but a sheete
Which that they mighte wrappe hem in at night,
And a brat to walke in by daylight,
They wolde hem selle and spenden on this craft:
They can nat stinte til nothing be laft.
And everemore wher that evere they goon
Men may hem knowe by smel of brimstoon:
For al the world they stinken as a goot;
Hir savor is so rammish and so hoot
That though a man a mile from hem be,
The savor wol infecte him, trusteth me.
Lo, thus by smelling and threedbare array,
If that men liste, this folk they knowe may.
And if a man wol aske hem prively
Why they been clothed so unthriftily,
They right anoon wol rounen in his ere
And sayn that if that they espied were
Men wolde hem slee by cause of hir science.
Lo, thus this folk bitrayen innocence.
  Passe over this: I go my tale unto:
Er that the pot be on the fir ydo
Of metals with a certain quantitee—
My lord hem tempreth, and no man but he
(Now he is goon I dar saye boldely),
For as men sayn, he can doon craftily—
Algate I woot wel he hath swich a name.

155. to seeken, i.e., to be sought. **156. temps,** tense. **158. waxen sadde,** i.e., have enough. **160. nadde they but,** if they had only. **162. brat,** cloak. **164. stinte,** stop; **laft,** left. **167. goot,** goat. **168. rammish,** ram-like, fetid; **hoot,** hot. **172. liste,** please; **knowe,** recognize. **174. unthriftily,** poorly. **175. rounen,** whisper. **176. espied,** discovered. **177. slee,** slay. **180. ydo,** placed. **185. Algate,** at any rate; **woot,** know; **name,** reputation.

And yit ful ofte he renneth in a blame,
And wite ye how? Ful ofte it happeth so
The pot tobreketh, and farewel, al is go:
Thise metals been of so greet violence
Oure walles mowe nat make hem resistence,
But if they weren wrought of lim and stoon;
They percen so and thurgh the wal they goon,
And some of hem sinke into the ground.
Thus han we lost by times many a pound.
And some are scatered al the floor aboute;
Some lepe into the roof. Withouten doute,
Though that the Feend nat in oure sighte him shewe
I trowe he be with us, that ilke shrewe:
In helle wher that he is lord and sire
Nis ther more wo ne more rancor and ire
Whan that oure pot is broke, as I have said:
Every man chit and halt him yvele apaid.
  Some saide it was long on the fir-making;
Some saide nay, it was on the blowing
(Thanne was I fered, for that was myn office).
  "Straw," quod the thridde, "ye been lewed and nice.
It was nat tempred as it oughte be."
  "Nay," quod the ferthe, "stinte and herkne me:
By cause oure fir ne was nat maad of beech,
That is the cause, and other noon, so theech."
I can nat telle wher on it was long,
But wel I woot, greet strif is us among.
  "What," quod my lord, "ther is namore to doone.
Of thise perils I wol be war eftsoone.
I am right siker that the pot was crased.

186. renneth in, encounters. **187. wite,** know. **188. tobreketh,** breaks into pieces. **190. mowe,** may. **191. But if,** unless. **194. by,** at. **197. him,** himself. **198. trowe,** believe; **ilke shrewe,** same scoundrel. **202.** Every man chides and holds himself badly requited. **203. long on,** due to. **205. fered,** afraid; **office,** job. **206. lewed,** ignorant; **nice,** foolish. **208. stinte,** cease. **210. theech,** may I thrive. **212. woot,** know. **214. eftsoone,** an other time. **215. siker,** sure; **crased,** cracked.

Be as be may, be ye no thing amased.
As usage is, lat sweepe the floor as swithe:°
Plukke up youre hertes and beeth glad and blithe."
  The mullok° on an heep ysweeped was,
And on the floor ycast a canevas,°
And al this mullok in a sive° ythrowe,
And sifted and ypikked many a throwe.°
  "Pardee," quod oon, "somwhat of oure metal
Yit is ther here, though that we han nat al.
And though this thing mishapped have as now,
Another time it may be wel ynow.
Us moste° putte oure good in aventure:
A marchant, pardee, may nat ay° endure,
Trusteth me wel, in his prosperitee;
Som time his good is drowned in the see,
And som time comth it sauf° unto the londe."
  "Pees," quod my lord, "the nexte time I wol fonde°
To bringe oure craft al in another plite,°
And but I do, sires, lat me han the wite.°
Ther was defaute in somwhat, wel I woot."
  Another saide the fir was over-hoot,
But be it hoot or cold, I dar saye this,
That we concluden everemore amis.
We faile of that which that we wolden have,
And in oure madnesse everemore we rave.
And whan we been togideres everichoon,°
Every man seemeth a Salomon.
But al thing which that shineth as the gold
Nis nat gold, as that I have herd told,
Ne every apple that is fair at yë
Ne is nat good, what so men clappe° or crye.
  Right so, lo, fareth it amonges us:
He that seemeth the wiseste, by Jesus,

217. swithe, quickly. **219. mullok,** debris. **220. canevas,** canvas. **221. sive,** sieve. **222. throwe,** time. **227. Us moste,** we must. **228. ay,** always. **231. sauf,** safe. **232. fonde,** try. **233. plite,** condition. **234. but,** unless; **wite,** blame. **241. everichoon,** all. **246. clappe,** chatter.

Is most fool whan it cometh to the preef;
And he that seemeth trewest is a theef.
That shul ye knowe er that I fro you wende,
By that I of my tale have maad an ende.

The Tale

Ther is a chanon of religioun
Amonges us, wolde infecte al a town,
Though it as greet were as was Ninevee,
Rome, Alisaundre, Troye, and othere three:
His sleightes and his infinite falsnesse
Ther coude no man writen, as I gesse,
Though that he mighte live a thousand yeer.
In al this world of falshede nis his peer,
For in his termes he wol so him winde,
And speke his wordes in so sly a kinde,
Whan he commune shal with any wight,
That he wol make him doten anoon right,
But it a feend be, as himselven is.
Ful many a man he hath bigiled er this,
And wol, if that he live may a while;
And yit men ride and goon ful many a mile
Him for to seeke and have his aquaintaunce,
Nought knowing of his false governaunce.
And if you list to yive me audience
I wol it tellen here in youre presence.
But worshipful chanouns religious,
Ne deemeth nat that I sclaundre youre hous,
Although my tale of a chanon be:

249. preef, proof. **252. that,** the time that.

1. chanon of religioun, canon in religious orders. **4. Alisaundre,** Alexandria. **5. sleightes,** tricks. **9. winde,** conceal. **12. doten,** become foolish. **13. But,** unless. **16. goon,** walk. **19. list,** please. **22. sclaundre,** slander.

Of every ordre som shrewe is, pardee,
And God forbede that al a compaignye
Sholde rewe oo singuler mannes folye.
To sclaundren you is nothing myn entente,
But to correcten that is mis I mente.
This tale was nat only told for you,
But eek for othere more. Ye woot wel how
That among Cristes aposteles twelve
Ther was no traitour but Judas himselve.
Thanne why sholde the remenant have a blame
That giltelees were? By you I saye the same,
Save only this, if ye wol herkne me:
If any Judas in youre covent be
Remeveth him bitimes, I you rede,
If shame or los may cause him any drede.
And beeth no thing displesed, I you praye,
But in this cas herkeneth what I shal saye.
In London was a preest, an annueler,
That therin dwelled hadde many a yeer,
Which was so plesant and so servisable
Unto the wif wher as he was at table,
That she wolde suffre him nothing for to paye
For boord ne clothing, wente he nevere so gaye;
And spending silver hadde he right ynow—
Therof, no fors: I wol proceede as now
To telle forth my tale of the chanoun
That broughte this preest to confusioun.
This false chanon cam upon a day
Unto this preestes chambre wher he lay,
Biseeching him to lene him a certain
Of gold, and he wolde quite it him again.

24. I.e., There is some member of every order who is a scoundrel. **26. rewe,** i.e., suffer for. **28. mis,** wrong; **mente,** intended. **33. remenant,** rest. **36. covent,** body. **37. Remeveth,** remove; **bitimes,** at once; **rede,** advise. **41. annueler,** a priest whose only task was to say annual masses for the souls of the dead. **44. was at table,** i.e., boarded. **46. gaye,** gaily. **48. fors,** matter. **50. confusioun,** ruin. **53. lene,** lend; **certain,** certain amount. **54. quite,** repay.

"Lene me a mark," quod he, "but dayes three,
And at my day I wol it quite thee.
And if so be that thou me finde fals,
Another day do hange me by the hals."
This preest him took a mark and that as swithe,
And this chanoun him thanked ofte sithe,
And took his leve, and wente forth his waye,
And at the thridde day broughte his moneye,
And to the preest he took his gold again,
Wherof this preest was wonder glad and fain.
"Certes," quod he, "nothing anoyeth me
To lene a man a noble or two or three,
Or what thing were in my possessioun
Whan he so trewe is of condicioun
That in no wise he breke wol his day.
To swich a man I can nevere saye nay."
"What," quod this chanon, "sholde I be untrewe?
Nay, that were thing yfallen al of newe.
Trouthe is a thing that I wol evere keepe
Unto that day in which that I shal creepe
Into my grave, and elles God forbede.
Bileveth this as siker as the Crede.
God thanke I—and in good time be it said—
That ther was nevere man yit yvele apaid
For gold ne silver that he to me lente,
Ne nevere falshede in myn herte I mente.
And, sire," quod he, "now of my privetee,
Sin ye so goodlich han been unto me
And kithed to me so greet gentilesse,
Somwhat to quite you with youre kindenesse,
I wol you shewe—and, if you list to lere,

55. mark, about two-thirds of a pound. **58. do . . . hals,** have me hanged by the neck. **59. took,** gave; **as swithe,** at once. **60. sithe,** time. **64. fain,** pleased. **65. anoyeth,** harms. **66. noble,** half a mark. **72. were,** would be; **yfallen,** happening; **of newe,** recently. **76. siker,** sure; **Crede,** Creed. **78. yvele apaid,** badly repaid. **80. mente,** intended. **81. privetee,** secrets. **82. Sin,** since. **83. kithed,** showed. **84. quite you with,** repay you for. **85. lere,** learn.

I wol you teche—pleinly° the manere
How I can werken in philosophye.°
Taketh good heede, ye shul wel seen at yë
That I wol doon a maistrye° er I go."
"Ye," quod the preest, "ye, sire, and wol ye so?
Marye, therof I praye you hertely."
"At youre commandement, sire, trewely,"
Quod the chanoun, "and elles God forbede."
Lo how this theef coude his servise bede.°
Ful sooth it is that swich profred servise
Stinketh, as witnessen thise olde wise.
And that ful soone I wol it verifye
In this chanoun, roote of al trecherye,
That evere more delit hath and gladnesse,
Swiche feendly thoughtes in his herte impresse,°
How Cristes peple he may to meschief bringe—
God keepe us from his false dissimulinge!°
Nought wiste° this preest with whom that he delte,
Ne of his harm coming he nothing felte.
O sely preest! O sely° innocent!
With coveitise anoon thou shalt be blent.°
O gracelees, ful blind is thy conceit!°
No thing artou war of the deceit
Which that this fox yshapen° hath to thee.
His wily wrenches° thou ne maist nat flee:
Wherfore to go to the conclusioun
That refereth to thy confusioun,°
Unhappy man, anoon I wol me hie°
To tellen thyn unwit° and thy folye,
And eek the falsnesse of that other wrecche
As ferforth° as my conning wol strecche.
—This chanon was my lord, ye wolden weene?°

86. pleinly, fully. **87. philosophye,** i.e., alchemy. **89. maistrye,** masterly operation. **94. bede,** proffer. **100. feendly,** fiendish; **impresse,** throng. **102. dissimulinge,** pretenses. **103. wiste,** knew. **105. sely,** simple. **106. coveitise,** avarice; **blent,** deceived. **107. conceit,** fancy. **109. yshapen,** worked up. **110. wrenches,** dodges. **112. confusioun,** downfall. **113. hie,** hasten. **114. unwit,** stupidity. **116. ferforth,** far. **117. weene,** suppose.

Sire Hoost, in faith and by the hevenes queene,
It was another chanon and nat he,
That can an hundredfold more subtiltee:
He hath bitrayed folkes many time;
Of his falsnesse it dulleth me to rime;
Evere whan I speke of his falshede
For shame of him my cheekes waxen rede—
Algates they biginnen for to glowe,
For reednesse have I noon, right wel I knowe,
In my visage, for fumes diverse
Of metals which ye han herd me reherse
Consumed and wasted han my reednesse.
Now taak heede of this chanons cursednesse:
"Sire," quod he to the preest, "lat youre man goon
For quiksilver, that we it hadde anoon.
And lat him bringen ounces two or three,
And whan he comth, as faste shul ye see
A wonder thing which ye saw nevere er this."
"Sire," quod the preest, "it shal be doon, ywis."
He bad his servant fecchen him this thing,
And he al redy was at his bidding,
And wente him forth, and cam anoon again
With this quiksilver, shortly for to sayn,
And took thise ounces three to the chanoun.
And he hem laide faire and wel adown,
And bad the servant coles for to bringe
That he anoon mighte go to his werkinge.
The coles right anoon weren yfet,
And this chanoun took out a crosselet
Of his bosom, and shewed it the preest.
"This instrument," quod he, "which that thou seest,
Taak in thyn hand and put thyself therinne
Of this quiksilver an ounce, and here biginne,
In name of Crist, to waxe a philosophre.

120. can, knows. **124. waxen,** grow. **125. Algates,** at any rate. **132. that we hadde,** so that we might have. **136. ywis,** indeed. **141. took,** gave. **145. yfet,** fetched. **146. crosselet,** crucible. **147. Of,** from. **151. waxe,** become; **philosophre,** alchemist.

Ther been ful fewe whiche that I wolde profre
To shewen hem thus muche of my science,
For ye shul seen here by experience
That this quiksilver I wol mortifye°
Right in youre sighte anoon, withouten lie,
And make it as good silver and as fin°
As ther is any in youre purs or myn
Or elleswhere, and make it malliable,°
Or elles holdeth me fals and unable°
Amonges folk for evere to appere.
I have a powdre here that coste me dere,
Shal make al good, for it is cause of al
My conning,° which that I you shewen shal.
Voideth° youre man and lat him be theroute,
And shette° the dore whiles we been aboute
Oure privetee,° that no man us espye
Whiles that we werke in this philosophye."
  Al as he bad fulfilled was in deede:
This ilke servant anoonright out yede°
And his maister shette the dore anoon,
And to hir labour speedily they goon.
  This preest at this chanouns cursed bidding
Upon the fir anoon sette this thing,
And blew the fir, and bisied him ful faste,
And this chanoun into the crosselet caste
A powdre—noot I° wherof that it was
Ymaad—outher° of chalk outher of glas
Or somwhat elles—was nat worth a flye—
To blinde with this preest, and bad him hie°
The coles for to couchen° al above
The crosselet. "For in tokening° I thee love,"

155. mortifye, rigidify, i.e., turn to real silver. **157. fin,** fine. **159. malliable,** malleable, subject to being worked on by a hammer. **160. unable,** incapable. **164. conning,** skill. **165. Voideth,** send out. **166. shette,** shut. **167. privetee,** secret business. **170. ilke,** same; **yede,** went. **177. noot I,** I don't know. **178. outher,** either, or. **180. blinde,** deceive; **hie,** hurry. **181. couchen,** bank. **182. in tokening,** as a sign that.

Quod this chanoun, "Thine owene handes two
Shul werke al thing which that shal here be do."
  "Graunt mercy," quod the preest, and was ful glad,
And couched coles as the chanon bad.
And whil he bisy was, this feendly wrecche,
This false chanoun—the foule Feend him fecche!—
Out of his bosom took a beechen cole
In which ful subtilly was maad an hole,
And therinne put was of silver limaile
An ounce, and stopped was withouten faile
This hole with wex, to keepe the limaile in.
And understondeth that this false gin
Was nat maad there, but it was maad bifore—
And othere thinges I shal telle more
Herafterward which that he with him broughte:
Er he cam there, him to bigile he thoughte.
And so he dide er that they wente atwinne:
Til he hadde terved him coude he nat blinne.
It dulleth me whan that I of him speke;
Of his falshede fain wolde I me wreke
If I wiste how—but he is here and there;
He is so variant he abit nowhere.
  But taketh heede now, sires, for Goddes love:
He took his cole of which I spak above
And in his hand he bar it prively,
And whiles that the preest couched bisily
The coles, as I tolde you er this,
This chanon saide, "Freend, ye doon amis:
This is nat couched as it oughte be.
But soone I shal amenden it," quod he.
"Now lat me medle therwith but a while,
For of you have I pitee, by Saint Gile.
Ye been right hoot—I see wel how ye swete.

185. Graunt mercy, many thanks. **187. feendly,** fiendish. **189. beechen cole,** coal of beech wood. **191. limaile,** shavings. **193. wex,** wax. **194. gin,** device. **198. thoughte,** planned. **199. atwinne,** apart. **200. terved,** skinned; **blinne,** stop. **202. fain,** gladly; **wreke,** avenge. **203. wiste,** knew. **204. variant,** changeable; **abit,** abides. **207. bar,** bore. **215. hoot,** hot.

Have here a cloth and wipe away the wete."
And whiles that the preest wiped his face,
This chanon took his cole—with sory grace!—
And laide it above, upon the middeward°
Of the crosselet, and blew wel afterward
Til that the coles gonne faste brenne.°
"Now yive us drinke," quod the chanon thenne.
"As swithe° al shal be wel, I undertake.°
Sitte we down, and lat us mirye make."
And whan that this chanounes beechen cole
Was brent,° al the lemaile out of the hole
Into the crosselet fel anoon adown.
And so it moste° needes by resoun,
Sin° it so evene aboven couched° was.
But therof wiste° the preest nothing, allas:
He deemed alle the coles yliche good,
For of the sleighte° he nothing understood.
And whan this alcamystre° saw his time,
"Rise up," quod he, "sire preest, and stondeth by me.
And for I woot° wel ingot have ye noon,
Gooth walketh forth and bringeth a chalk stoon,
For I wol make it of the same shap
That is an ingot, if I may han hap.°
And bringeth eek with you a bolle° or panne
Ful of water, and ye shul see wel thanne
How that oure bisinesse shal thrive and preve.°
And yit, for° ye shul han no misbileve
Ne wrong conceite° of me in youre absence,
I ne wol nat been out of youre presence,
But go with you and come with you again."
The chamber dore, shortly for to sayn,
They opened and shette and wente hir waye,

219. middeward, middle part, i.e., at the center of the cross. **221. brenne,** burn. **223. As swithe,** straightway; **undertake,** guarantee. **226. brent,** burned. **228. moste,** must. **229. Sin,** since; **couched,** placed. **230. wiste,** knew. **232. sleighte,** trick. **233. alcamystre,** alchemist. **235. woot,** know. **238. hap,** luck. **239. bolle,** bowl. **241. preve,** succeed. **242. for,** in order that. **243. conceite,** idea.

And forth with hem they carieden the keye,
And come again withouten any delay.
What sholde I taryen al the longe day?
He took the chalk and shoop it in the wise
Of an ingot, as I shal you devise:
I saye he took out of his owene sleeve
A teine of silver—yvele mote he cheve!—
Which that ne was nat but an ounce of weighte—
And taketh heede now of his cursed sleighte:
He shoop his ingot in lengthe and in brede
Of this teine, withouten any drede,
So slyly that the preest it nat espide,
And in his sleeve again he gan it hide,
And fro the fir he took up his matere
And in th'ingot putte it with mirye cheere,
And in the water vessel he it caste
Whan that him liste, and bad the preest as faste,
"Looke what ther is—put in thyn hand and grope.
Thou finde shalt there silver, as I hope."
(What, devel of helle, sholde it elles be?
Shaving of silver silver is, pardee.)
He putte his hand in and took up a teine
Of silver fin, and glad in every veine
Was this preest whan he saw it was so.
"Goddes blessing and his modres also
And alle halwes have ye, sire chanoun,"
Saide the preest, "and I hir malisoun
But, and ye vouche sauf to techen me
This noble craft and this subtilitee,
I wol be youre in al that evere I may."
  Quod the chanoun, "Yit wol I make assay
The seconde time, that ye may taken heede
And been expert of this, and in youre neede

250. What, why. **251. shoop,** fashioned; **wise,** shape. **252. devise,** describe. **254. teine,** small bar; **yvele . . . cheve,** may he come to a bad end. **257. brede,** breadth. **258. drede,** doubt. **261. matere,** material. **264. liste,** pleased. **273. halwes,** saints. **274. malisoun,** curse. **275. and,** if. **277. youre,** yours. **278. assay,** trial.

Another day assaye in myn absence
This discipline and this crafty science.
Lat take another ounce," quod he tho,
"Of quiksilver withouten wordes mo,°
And do therwith as ye han doon er this
With that other which now silver is."
This preest him bisieth in al that he can
To doon as this chanoun, this cursed man,
Comanded him, and faste blew the fir
For to come to th'effect° of his desir.
And this chanoun right in the mene while
Al redy was this preest eft° to bigile,
And for a countenance in his hand he bar°
A holwe stikke—taak keep° and be war—
In th'ende of which an ounce and namore
Of silver limaile put was as bifore
Was in his cole; and stopped with wex weel°
For to keepe in his limaile every deel,°
And whil this preest was in his bisinesse
This chanon with his stikke gan him dresse°
To hien° anoon, and his powdre caste in
As he dide er—the Devel out of his skin
Him terve,° I praye to God, for his falshede,
For he was evere fals in thought and deede—
And with his stikke above the crosselet
That was ordained with that false jet°
He stired the coles til relente° gan
The wex again° the fir, as every man,
But it a fool be, woot wel it moot° neede.
And al that in the stikke was out yede°
And in the crosselet hastiliche it fel.
Now, goode sires, what wol ye bet° than wel?

284. **mo,** more. 290. **effect,** principal end. 292. **eft,** again. 293. **a countenance,** i.e., to appear natural; **bar,** bore. 294. **keep,** heed. 297. **weel,** well. 298. **deel,** bit. 300. **dresse,** prepare. 301. **hien,** hurry. 303. **terve,** strip. 306. **jet,** device. 307. **relente,** soften. 308. **again,** i.e., in the heat of. 309. **But,** unless; **woot,** knows; **moot,** must. 310. **yede,** gone. 312. **bet,** better.

Whan that this preest thus was bigiled again,
Supposing° nought but trouthe, sooth to sayn,
He was so glad that I can nat expresse
In no manere his mirthe and his gladnesse.
And to the chanon he profred eftsoone°
Body and good. "Ye," quod the chanon soone,
"Though poore I be, crafty thou shalt me finde.
I warne thee, yit is ther more bihinde.°
Is ther any coper herinne?" saide he.
"Ye," quod the preest, "sire, I trowe° wel ther be."
"Elles go bye us som, and that as swithe.°
Now goode sire, go forth thy way and hie° thee."
He wente his way and with this coper cam,
And this chanoun it in his handes nam,°
And of that coper weyed° out but an ounce.
(Al too simple is my tonge to pronounce,
As ministre of my wit, the doublenesse°
Of this chanoun, roote of al cursednesse.
He seemed freendly to hem that knewe him nought,
But he was feendly° bothe in werk and thought.
It werieth° me to telle of his falsnesse,
And nathelees yit wol I it expresse
To th'entente that men may be war therby,
And for noon other cause, trewely.)
He putte this ounce of coper in the crosselet,
And on the fir as swithe° he hath it set,
And caste in powdre, and made the preest to blowe,
And in his werking for to stoupe lowe
As he dide er, and al nas but a jape:°
Right as him liste, the preest he made his ape.°
And afterward in th'ingot he it caste,
And in the panne putte it at the laste
Of water, and in he putte his owene hond,

314. Supposing, suspecting. **317. eftsoone,** again. **320. bihinde,** i.e., to come. **322. trowe,** think. **323. as swithe,** at once.. **324. hie,** hasten. **326. nam,** took. **327. weyed,** weighed. **329. ministre,** agent; **doublenesse,** duplicity. **332. feendly,** fiendish. **333. werieth,** wearies. **338. as swithe,** as quickly. **341. jape,** trick. **342. liste,** pleased; **ape,** i.e., dupe.

And in his sleeve, as ye biforenhond
Herde me telle, he hadde a silver teine:
He slyly took it out, this cursed heine,
Unwiting this preest of his false craft,
And in the pannes botme he hath it laft,
And in the water rumbled to and fro,
And wonder prively took up also
The coper teine, nought knowing this preest,
And hidde it, and him hente by the breest,
And to him spak, and thus saide in his game,
"Stoupeth adown! By God, ye been to blame:
Helpeth me now, as I dide you whil er.
Putte in youre hand, and looketh what is ther."
This preest took up this silver teine anoon,
And thanne saide the chanon, "Lat us goon
With thise three teines which that we han wrought
To som goldsmith and wite if they been ought.
For by my faith, I nolde for myn hood
But if they were of silver fin and good,
And that as swithe preved shal it be."
Unto the goldsmith with thise teines three
They wente, and putte thise teines in assay
To fir and hamer: mighte no man saye nay
But that they weren as hem oughte be.
This sotted preest, who was gladder than he?
Was never brid gladder again the day,
Ne nightingale in the seson of May
Was nevere noon that liste bet to singe,
Ne lady lustier in carolinge,
Or, for to speke of love and wommanhede,
Ne knight in armes to doon an hardy deede

347. teine, bar. **348. heine,** wretch. **349. Unwiting this preest,** with this priest not knowing. **350. laft,** left. **351. rumbled,** fumbled. **352. prively,** secretly. **354. hente,** took. **357. whil er,** a while ago. **362. wite,** learn; **ought,** i.e., of any value. **363–64. I nolde . . . if,** i.e., I'd be willing to lose my hood unless. **365. preved,** proved. **370. sotted,** bedoted. **371. brid,** bird; **again,** at the coming of. **373. liste,** pleased; **bet,** better. **374. lustier,** more delighted.

To stonde in grace of his lady dere,
Than hadde this preest this sorye craft to lere.
And to the chanon thus he spak and saide,
"For love of God that for us alle deide,
And as I may deserve it unto you,
What shal this receit coste? Telleth now."
"By oure lady," quod this chanoun, "it is dere,
I warne you wel, for save I and a frere,
In Engelond ther can no man it make."
"No fors," quod he, "now, sire, for Goddes sake,
What shal I paye? Telleth me, I praye."
"Ywis," quod he, "it is ful dere, I saye.
Sire, at oo word, if that thee list it have,
Ye shul paye fourty pound, so God me save;
And nere the freendshipe that ye dide er this
To me, ye sholde paye more, ywis."
This preest the somme of fourty pound anoon
Of nobles fette, and took hem everichoon
To this chanoun for this ilke receit:
Al his werking nas but fraude and deceit.
"Sire preest," he saide, "I keepe han no los
Of my craft, for I wolde it kept were clos.
And as ye love me, keepeth it secree,
For, and men knewen al my subtiltee,
By God, they wolden han so greet envye
To me by cause of my philosophye,
I sholde be deed—ther were noon other waye."
"God it forbede," quod the preest, "what saye ye?
Yit hadde I levere spenden al the good
Which that I have, or elles waxe I wood,
Than that ye sholden falle in swich meschief."
"For youre good wil, sire, have ye right good preef,"
Quod the chanoun, "and farewel, graunt mercy."

378. hadde, i.e., was; **lere,** learn. **381. deserve,** requite. **382. receit,** formula. **386. fors,** matter. **388. Ywis,** indeed. **389. list,** please. **391. nere,** were it not for. **394. fette,** fetched; **took,** gave. **397. keepe,** care to; **los,** fame. **400. and,** if. **403. deed,** i.e., murdered; **were,** would be. **406. waxe I wood,** may I go mad. **408. preef,** success. **409. graunt mercy,** many thanks.

He wente his way and nevere the preest him sy°
After that day. And whan that this preest sholde
Maken assay at swich time as he wolde
Of this receit, farewel, it wolde nat be.
Lo, thus bijaped and bigiled was he;
Thus maketh he° his introduccioun
To bringe folk to hir destruccioun.

Considereth, sires, how that in eech estaat
Bitwixe men and gold ther is debaat
So ferforth that unnethes is ther noon.°
This multiplying blent° so many oon
That, in good faith, I trowe° that it be
The cause grettest of swich scarsetee.
Philosophres speken so mistily
In this craft that men can nat come therby,
For° any wit that men han nowadayes.
They mowe wel chiteren° as doon thise jayes,
And in hir termes sette hir lust and paine,°
But to hir purpos shul they nevere attaine.
A man may lightly lerne—if he have ought°—
To multiplye—and bringe his good to nought.
Lo, swich a lucre is in this lusty° game,
A mannes mirthe it wol turne into grame,°
And empten also grete and hevy purses,
And maken folk for to purchasen curses
Of hem that han hir good therto ylent.
O fy, for shame, they that han been brent,°
Allas, can they nat flee the fires hete!
Ye that it use, I rede ye it lete°
Lest ye lese al, for bet° than nevere is late:
Nevere to thrive were too long° a date.

410. sy, saw. **415. he,** i.e., the canon. **419.** To such an extent that there is scarcely any left. **420. blent,** deceives. **421. trowe,** think. **425. For,** despite. **426. mowe,** may; **chiteren,** chatter. **427. sette . . . paine,** devote their heart and energy. **429. lightly,** easily; **ought,** any possessions. **431. lucre,** profit; **lusty,** pleasing. **432. grame,** grief. **436. brent,** burned. **438. rede,** advise; **lete,** give up. **439. lese,** lose; **bet,** better. **440. were,** would be; **long,** i.e., far.

Though ye prolle ay,° ye shul it nevere finde.
Ye been as bold as is Bayard° the blinde
That blundreth forth and peril casteth° noon:
He is as bold to renne° against a stoon
As for to goon bisides° in the waye.
So faren ye that multiplye, I saye:
If that youre yën can nat seen aright,
Looke that youre minde lakke nought his sight,
For though ye looke nevere so brode° and stare,
Ye shul nothing winne on that chaffare,°
But wasten al that ye may rape and renne.°
Withdrawe the fir lest it too faste brenne;°
Medleth namore with that art, I mene,
For if ye doon, youre thrift° is goon ful clene.
And right as swithe° I wol you tellen here
What philosophres sayn in this matere:
  Lo, thus saith Arnold of the Newe Town,°
As his *Rosarye* maketh mencioun—
He saith right thus, withouten any lie:
"Ther may no man Mercurye mortifye°
But it be with his brother knowleching."°
How be° he which that firste saide this thing
Of philosophres fader was, Hermes.°
He saith how that the dragon, doutelees,
Ne dieth nat but if that he be slain
With his brother, and that is for to sayn,
By the dragon Mercurye and noon other
He understood, and brimstoon by his brother,
That out of Sol and Luna° were ydrawe.

441. prolle, search; **ay,** ever. **442. Bayard,** a horse. **443. casteth,** i.e., expects. **444. renne,** run. **445. bisides,** from side to side. **449. brode,** broadly. **450. chaffare,** merchandise. **451. rape and renne,** grab and handle. **452. brenne,** burn. **454. thrift,** prosperity. **455. as swithe,** at once. **457. Arnold . . . Town,** Arnoldus de Villa Nova, author of an alchemical tract called the *Rosarium Philosophorum.* **460. mortifye,** rigidify. **461.** Unless it is with the knowledge of his (Mercury's) brother: it appears from line 468 that the brother is sulphur. **462. How be,** however. **463.** Was the father of philosophers, Hermes: Hermes Trismegistus was the supposed inventor of alchemy, and a number of alchemical works were ascribed to him. **469. Sol,** the sun or gold; **Luna,** the moon, or silver.

And therfore saide he—taak heede to my sawe°—
"Lat no man bisye him this art for to seeche
But if° that he th'entencion and the speeche
Of philosophres understonde can;
And if he do, he is a lewed° man.
For this science and this conning," quod he,
"Is of the secree of secretes, pardee."
  Also ther was a disciple of Plato
That on a time saide his maister to
(As his book *Senior*° wol bere witnesse),
And this was his demande in soothfastnesse,
"Tel me the name of the privee° stoon."
  And Plato answerde unto him anoon,
"Take the stoon that Titanos men name."
"Which is that?" quod he. "Magnasia is the same,"
Saide Plato. "Ye, sire, and is it thus?
This is *ignotum per ignotius*.°
What is Magnasia, good sire, I you praye?"
  "It is a water that is maad, I saye,
Of elementes foure," quod Plato.
  "Tel me the roote, good sire," quod he tho,°
"Of that water, if it be youre wille."
  "Nay, nay," quod Plato, "certain, that I nil.°
The philosophres sworn were everichoon
That they sholde discovere it unto noon,
Ne in no book it write in no manere.
For unto Crist it is so lief° and dere
That he ne wol nat that it discovered be
But where it liketh° to his deitee
Men for t'inspire, and eek for to defende°
Whom that him liketh. Lo, this is the ende."
  Thanne conclude I thus: sith° that God of hevene
Ne wol nat that the philosophres nevene°

470. sawe, saying. **472. But if,** unless. **474. lewed,** stupid. **479. Senior,** a book on alchemy. **481. privee,** secret, i.e., philosopher's. **486.** This is to explain the unknown by something more unknown. **490. tho,** then. **492. nil,** will not. **496. lief,** precious. **498. liketh,** pleases. **499. defende,** forbid. **501. sith,** since. **502. nevene,** name.

How that a man shal come unto this stoon,
I rede as for the beste, lat it goon.
For whoso maketh God his adversarye
As for to werken any thing contrarye
Of his wil, certes, nevere shal he thrive
Though that he multiplye terme of his live.
And there a point, for ended is my tale;
God sende every trewe man boote of his bale.

THE MANCIPLE'S TALE

The Introduction

Woot ye nat wher ther stant a litel town
Which that cleped is Bobbe-Up-and-Down,
Under the Blee, in Canterbury waye?
Ther gan oure Hoste for to jape and playe,
And saide, "Sires, what, Dun is in the mire!
Is ther no man for prayere ne for hire
That wol awake oure felawe al bihinde?
A thief mighte him ful lightly robbe and binde.
See how he nappeth! See how, for cokkes bones,
That he wol falle fro his hors atones!
Is that a Cook of London, with meschaunce?
Do him come forth: he knoweth his penaunce,
For he shal telle a tale, by my fay,
Although it be nat worth a botel hay.
Awaak, thou Cook!" quod he. "God yive thee sorwe!
What aileth thee to sleepe by the morwe?

504. rede, advise. **508. terme,** i.e., the whole time. **509. point,** period. **510. boote,** remedy; **bale,** evil.

3. Blee, the Blean forest. **4. jape,** joke. **5. Dun . . . mire,** things are at a standstill: Dun is a traditional name for a horse. **8. lightly,** easily. **12. Do,** have. **13. fay,** faith. **14. botel,** i.e., bundle of. **16. by . . . morwe,** in the morning.

Hastou had fleen° al night? Or artou dronke?
Or hastou with som quene° al night yswonke,°
So that thou maist nat holden up thyn heed?"°
  This Cook that was ful pale and nothing reed°
Saide to oure Host, "So God my soule blesse,
As ther is falle on me swich hevinesse—
Noot I nat why—that me were levere sleepe
Than the beste galon win in Chepe."°
  "Wel," quod the Manciple, "if it may doon ese
To thee, sire Cook, and to no wight displese
Which that heer rideth in this compaignye,
And that oure Host wol of his curteisye,
I wol as now excuse thee of thy tale.
For in good faith, thy visage is ful pale,
Thine yën daswen° eek, as that me thinketh,
And wel I woot thy breeth ful soure stinketh:
That sheweth wel thou art nat wel-disposed.°
Of me, certain, thou shalt nat been yglosed:°
See how he ganeth,° lo, this dronken wight,
As though he wolde swolwe° us anoonright!
Hold cloos thy mouth, man, by thy fader kin!
The devel of helle sette his foot therin:
Thy cursed breeth infecte wol us alle.
Fy, stinking swin, fy! Foule mote thee falle!
A, taketh heede, sires, of this lusty man!
Now, sweete sire, wol ye justen atte fan?°
Therto me thinketh ye been wel yshape.°
I trowe that ye dronken han win-ape,°
And that is whan men playen with a straw."
And with his speeche the Cook wax wroth and wraw,°
And on the Manciple gan he nodde faste

17. **fleen,** fleas. 18. **quene,** prostitute; **yswonke,** labored. 19. **heed,** head. 20. **reed,** red. 24. **Chepe,** Cheapside in London. 31. **daswen,** are dim. 33. **wel-disposed,** in good health. 34. **yglosed,** flattered. 35. **ganeth,** yawns. 36. **swolwe,** swallow. 42. **justen . . . fan,** joust against a winnowing wan. 43. **yshape,** prepared. 44. **win-ape,** ape-wine: the Cook is at the third stage of drunkenness in the series lamb-drunk, lion-drunk, ape-drunk, pig-drunk: apes presumably play with straws. 46. **wraw,** angry.

For lak of speeche, and down the hors him caste,
Wher as he lay til that men up him took—
This was a fair chivachee of a Cook!
Allas, he nadde yholde him by his ladel!
And er that he again were in his sadel,
Ther was greet shouving bothe to and fro,
To lifte him up, and muchel care and wo,
So unweeldy was this sory palled gost.
And to the Manciple thanne spak oure Host:
"By cause drinke hath dominacioun
Upon this man, by my savacioun,
I trowe he lewedly telle wolde his tale.
For were it win, or old or moisty ale
That he hath dronke, he speketh in his nose,
And fneseth faste, and eek he hath the pose.
He hath also to do more than ynough
To keepen him and his capil out of the slough.
And if he falle from his capil eftsoone,
Thanne shal we alle have ynough to doone
In lifting up his hevy dronken cors.
Tel on thy tale! Of him I make no fors.
But yit, Manciple, in faith, thou art too nice
Thus openly repreve him of his vice:
Another day he wol, paraventure,
Reclaime thee and bringe thee to the lure.
I mene, he speke wol of smale thinges,
As for to pinchen at thy rekeninges:
That were nat honeste, if it cam to preef."
"No," quod the Manciple, "that were a greet meschief!
So mighte he lightly bringe me in the snare.
Yit hadde I levere payen for the mare

50. chivachee, cavalry expedition. **53. shouving,** shoving. **55. palled,** weak. **59. lewedly,** ignorantly, i.e., badly. **60. moisty,** new. **62. fneseth,** snorts; **the pose,** a cold. **64. capil,** horse. **65. eftsoone,** again. **67. cors,** body. **68. fors,** matter. **69. nice,** fastidious and foolish. **70. repreve,** to reprove. **72. Reclaime,** tame; **bringe . . . lure,** get you under control; both verbs are borrowed from the idiom of falconry. **74. pinchen,** find fault with. **75. were,** would be; **honeste,** creditable to you; **preef,** proof.

Which he rit on than he sholde with me strive.
I wol nat wratthe him, also mote I thrive.
That that I spak, I saide it in my bourde.
And wite ye what I have heer in a gourde?
A draughte of win, ye, of a ripe grape,
And right anoon ye shul seen a good jape:
This Cook shal drinke therof if I may;
Up paine of deeth, he wol nat saye me nay."
  And certainly, to tellen as it was,
Of this vessel the Cook drank faste, allas!
What needed it? He drank ynough biforn.
And whan he hadde pouped in this horn,
To the Manciple he took the gourde again,
And of that drinke the Cook was wonder fain,
And thanked him in swich wise as he coude.
  Thanne gan oure Host to laughen wonder loude,
And saide, "I see wel it is necessarye
Wher that we goon good drinke we with us carye,
For that wol turne rancour and disese
T'accord and love, and many a wrong appese.
  O Bacus, yblessed be thy name,
That so canst turnen ernest into game!
Worshipe and thank be to thy deitee.
Of that matere ye gete namore of me.
Tel on thy tale, Manciple, I thee praye."
  "Wel sire," quod he, "now herkneth what I saye."

The Tale

  Whan Phebus dwelled here in this erthe adown,
As olde bookes maken mencioun,
He was the moste lusty bacheler

79. **rit,** rides. 80. **wratthe,** anger; **also,** so. 81. **bourde,** joking. 82. **wite,** know. 83. **ripe,** mellow. 86. **Up,** upon. 90. **pouped,** tooted. 91. **took,** gave. 92. **fain,** glad. 97. **disese,** ill-feeling. 99. **Bacus,** Bacchus.
3. **lusty,** vigorous; **bacheler,** young knight.

In al this world, and eek the beste archer:
He slow° Python the serpent as he lay
Sleeping again° the sonne upon a day;
And many another noble worthy deede
He with his bowe wroughte, as men may rede.
  Playen he coude on every minstralcye,°
And singen that it was a melodye
To heeren of his clere vois the soun.
Certes, the king of Thebes, Amphioun,°
That with his singing walled that citee
Coude nevere singen half so wel as he.
Therto he was the seemlieste man
That is or was sith° that the world bigan.
What needeth it his fetures to descrive?°
For in this world was noon so fair on live.
He was therwith fulfild° of gentilesse,
Of honour, and of parfit° worthinesse.
  This Phebus that was flowr of bachelrye,°
As wel in freedom as in chivalrye°
For his disport°—in signe eek of victorye
Of Python, so as telleth us the storye—
Was wont° to beren in his hand a bowe.
  Now hadde this Phebus in his hous a crowe
Which in a cage he fostred many a day
And taughte it speke, as men teche a jay.
Whit was this crowe as is a snow-whit swan,
And countrefete° the speeche of every man
He coude whan he sholde telle a tale.
Therwith in al this world no nightingale
Ne coude by an hundred thousand deel°
Singen so wonder mirily and weel.°

5. **slow,** slew. 6. **again,** i.e., in. 9. **minstralcye,** musical instrument. 12. **Amphioun,** Amphion, the king who helped build Thebes by his magical music. 16. **sith,** since. 17. **descrive,** describe. 19. **fulfild,** filled full. 20. **parfit,** perfect. 21. **bachelrye,** young knighthood. 22. As well when he was not under arms as when he was. 23. **disport,** pleasure. 25. **wont,** accustomed. 30. **countrefete,** imitate. 33. **thousand deel,** thousandth part. 34. **weel,** well.

Now hadde this Phebus in his hous a wif
Which that he lovede more than his lif,
And night and day dide evere his diligence
Hire for to plese and doon hire reverence—
Save only, that the soothe if I shal sayn,
Jalous he was, and wolde have kept hire fain,°
For him were loth bijaped° for to be.
And so is every wight in swich degree,°
But al for nought, for it availeth nought:
A good wif that is clene of werk and thought
Sholde nat be kept in noon await,° certain;
And trewely the labour is in vain
To keep a shrewe,° for it wol nat be.
This holde I for a verray nicetee,°
To spille° labour for to keepe wives:
Thus writen° olde clerkes in hir lives.
But now to purpos as I first bigan:
This worthy Phebus dooth al that he can
To plesen hire, weening° by swich plesaunce,
And for his manhood and his governaunce,
That no man sholde han put him from hir grace.
But God it woot,° ther may no man embrace°
As to destraine° a thing which that Nature
Hath naturelly set in a creature.
Take any brid and put it in a cage,
And do al thyn entente and thy corage°
To fostre it tendrely with mete and drinke
Of alle daintees that thou canst bithinke,
And keepe it al so clenely as thou may,
Although his cage of gold be nevere so gay,
Yit hath this brid by twenty thousand fold°
Levere in a forest that is wilde and cold
Goon ete wormes and swich wrecchednesse.

40. kept, guarded; **fain,** gladly. **41. bijaped,** tricked. **42. degree,** situation. **45. in await,** under watch. **47. shrewe,** bad one. **48. verray nicetee,** true bit of foolishness. **49. spille,** waste. **50. writen,** wrote. **53. weening,** supposing. **56. woot,** knows; **embrace,** i.e., succeed. **57. destraine,** constrain. **60.** And devote your heart and mind. **65. fold,** i.e., times.

For evere this brid wol doon his bisinesse
T'escape out of his cage, if he may:
His libertee this brid desireth ay.°
  Lat take a cat and fostre him wel with milk
And tendre flessh, and make his couche of silk;
And lat him seen a mous go by the wal,
Anoon he waiveth° milk and flessh and al,
And every daintee that is in the hous,
Swich appetit hath he to ete a mous.
Lo, here hath lust° his dominacioun,
And appetit flemeth° discrecioun.
  A she-wolf also hath a vilains kinde:°
The lewedeste° wolf that she may finde,
Or leest of reputacion, that wol she take
In time whan hire lust° to han a make.°
  Alle thise ensamples speke I by thise men
That been untrewe, and nothing by wommen;
For men han evere a likerous° appetit
On lower thing to parfournen hir delit
Than on hir wives, be they nevere so faire,
Ne nevere so trewe, ne so debonaire.°
Flessh is so newefangel° (with meschaunce!)°
That we ne conne in nothing have plesaunce
That souneth into° vertu, any while.
  This Phebus which that thoughte upon no gile
Deceived was for al his jolitee,°
For under him another hadde she,
A man of litel reputacioun,
Nought worth to Phebus, in comparisoun.
The more harm is, it happeth ofte so,
Of which ther cometh muchel harm and wo.
  And so bifel whan Phebus was absent,

70. ay, always. **74. waiveth,** forsakes. **77. lust,** desire. **78. flemeth,** banishes. **79. kinde,** nature. **80. lewedeste,** most disreputable. **82. lust,** pleases; **make,** mate. **85. likerous,** lecherous. **88. debonaire,** meek. **89. newefangel,** fond of novelty; **with meschaunce,** i.e., a curse on it. **91. souneth into,** is consistent with. **93. jolitee,** companionableness.

His wif anoon hath for hir lemman sent—
Hir lemman? certes, this is a knavissh speeche:
Foryiveth it me, and that I you biseeche.
The wise Plato saith, as ye may rede,
The word moot neede accorde with the deede;
If men shal telle proprely a thing
The word moot cosin be to the werking.
I am a boistous man, right thus saye I:
Ther nis no difference, trewely,
Bitwixe a wif that is of heigh degree,
If of hir body dishoneste she be,
And a poore wenche, other than this
(If it so be they werke bothe amis):
But that the gentile in estaat above
She shal be cleped his lady as in love,
And for that other is poore womman,
She shal be cleped his wenche or his lemman.
But God it woot, myn owene dere brother,
Men layn that oon as lowe as lith that other.
Right so bitwixe a titlelees tyraunt
And an outlawe or a theef erraunt
The same I saye—ther is no difference.
To Alisandre was told this sentence
That, for the tyrant is of gretter might
By force of meinee for to sleen downright
And brennen hous and hoom and make al plain,
Lo, therfore is he cleped a capitain.
And for the outlawe hath but smal meinee,
And may nat doon so greet an harm as he,
Ne bringe a contree to so greet meschief,
Men clepen him an outlawe or a theef.
But for I am a man nat textuel
I wol nat telle of textes nevere a deel:

100. lemman, lover. **104. moot,** must. **106. werking,** action. **107. boistous,** blunt. **114. cleped,** called. **115. for,** because. **116. lemman,** mistress. **118. lith** lies. **119. titlelees,** usurping. **120. theef erraunt,** common thief. **122. Alisandre,** Alexander the Great; **sentence,** opinion. **124. meinee,** his retinue; **sleen,** slay. **125. brennen,** burn; **plain,** level. **132. deel,** bit.

I wol go to my tale as I bigan:
  Whan Phebus wif hadde sent for hir lemman
Anoon they wroughte al hir lust volage.
The white crowe that heeng ay in the cage
Biheeld hir werk and saide nevere a word.
And whan that hoom was come Phebus the lord
This crowe sang, "Cokkou! cokkou! cokkou!"
  "What, brid," quod Phebus, "what song singestou?
Ne were thou wont so mirily to singe
That to myn herte it was a rejoisinge
To heere thy vois? Allas, what song is this?"
  "By God," quod he, "I singe nat amis.
Phebus," quod he, "for al thy worthinesse,
For al thy beautee and thy gentilesse,
For al thy song and al thy minstralcye,
For al thy waiting, blered is thyn yë
With oon of litel reputacioun,
Nat worth to thee, as in comparisoun,
The mountance of a gnat, so mote I thrive:
For in thy bed thy wif I saw him swive."
  What wol ye more? The crowe anoon him tolde
By sadde tokenes and by wordes bolde
How that his wif hadde doon hir lecherye,
Him to greet shame and to greet vilainye,
And tolde him ofte he saw it with his yën.
  This Phebus gan awayward for to wryen:
Him thoughte his sorweful herte brast atwo.
His bowe he bente and sette therinne a flo,
And in his ire his wif thanne hath he slain.
This is th'effect, ther nis namore to sayn.
For sorwe of which he brak his minstralcye,
Bothe harpe and lute and giterne and sautrye,

135. volage, flighty. **136. heeng,** hung; **ay,** ever. **141. wont,** accustomed. **148. waiting,** watching; **blered . . . yë,** i.e., you have been deceived. **149. With,** by. **151. mountance,** value; **mote,** may. **152. swive,** copulate with. **154. sadde,** firm. **158. wryen,** turn. **159. brast,** was breaking. **160. flo,** arrow. **163. brak,** broke; **minstralcye,** musical instruments. **164. giterne,** guitar; **sautrye,** psaltery, a kind of harp.

And eek he brak his arwes and his bowe.
And after that thus spak he to the crowe:
  "Traitour," quod he, "with tonge of scorpioun,
Thou hast me brought to my confusioun.°
Allas that I was wrought! Why nere I deed?°
O dere wif, o gemme of lustiheed,°
That were to me so sad° and eek so trewe,
Now listou° deed with face pale of hewe,
Ful giltelees, that dorste I swere, ywis.°
O rakel° hand, to doon so foule amis!
O trouble° wit, o ire recchelees,°
That unavised° smitest gilteless!
O wantrust,° ful of fals suspecioun!
Where was thy wit and thy discrecioun?
O every man, be war of rakelnesse;°
Ne trowe° nothing withouten strong witnesse;
Smit nat too soone, er that ye witen° why,
And beeth avised wel and sobrely
Er ye doon any execucioun
Upon° youre ire for suspecioun.
Allas, a thousand folk hath rakel ire
Fully fordoon,° or brought hem in the mire.
Allas, for sorwe I wol myselven slee."°
  And to the crowe, "O false theef!" saide he,
"I wol thee quite° anoon thy false tale:
Thou songe whilom° lik a nightingale;
Now shaltou, false theef, thy song forgoon,
And eek thy white fetheres everichoon,
Ne nevere in al thy lif ne shaltou speke.
Thus shal men on a traitour been awreke.°
Thou and thyn ofspring evere shul be blake,

168. confusioun, downfall. **169. nere I deed,** hadn't I died. **170. lustiheed,** delight. **171. sad,** constant. **172. listou,** you lie. **173. ywis,** indeed. **174. rakel,** rash. **175. trouble,** disturbed; **recchelees,** reckless. **176. unavised,** without taking thought. **177. wantrust,** distrust. **179. rakelnesse,** rashness. **180. trowe,** believe. **181. er,** before; **witen,** know. **184. Upon,** i.e., motivated by. **186. fordoon,** destroyed. **187. slee,** slay. **189. quite,** repay. **190. whilom,** once. **194. awreke,** avenged.

Ne nevere sweete noise shul ye make,
But ever crye again° tempest and rain,
In tokening that thurgh thee my wif is slain."
And to the crowe he sterte° and that anoon
And pulled his white fetheres everichoon,
And made him blak, and refte° him al his song,
And eek his speeche, and out at dore him slong°
Unto the Devel, which I him bitake.°
And for this caas been alle crowes blake.
  Lordinges, by this ensample,° I you praye,
Beeth war and taketh keep° what that I saye.
Ne telleth nevere no man in youre lif
How that another man hath dight° his wif:
He wol you haten mortally, certain.
Daun Salomon, as wise clerkes sayn,
Techeth a man to keepe his tonge wel—
But as I saide, I am nat textuel.
But nathelees, thus taughte me my dame:°
"My sone, think on the crowe, a° Goddes name;
My sone, keep wel thy tonge and keep thy freend.
A wikked tonge is worse than a feend:
My sone, from a feend men may hem blesse.°
My sone, God of his endelees goodnesse
Walled a tonge with teeth and lippes eke,
For man sholde him avise° what he speke.
My sone, ful ofte for too muche speeche
Hath many a man been spilt,° as clerkes teche,
But for litel speeche, avisely,°
Is no man shent,° to speke generally.
My sone, thy tonge sholdestou restraine
At alle times but whan thou doost thy paine°
To speke of God in honour and prayere.

197. again, at the approach of. **199. sterte,** started. **201. refte,** took from. **202. slong,** slung. **203. him bitake,** intrust him to. **205. ensample,** example. **206. keep,** heed. **208. dight,** lain with. **213. dame,** mother. **214. a,** in. **217. blesse,** protect by making the sign of the cross. **220. For,** in order that; **him avise,** take thought. **222. spilt,** ruined. **223. avisely,** seriously. **224. shent,** shamed. **226. but,** except; **doost thy paine,** take care.

The firste vertu, sone, if thou wolt lere,
Is to restraine and keepe wel thy tonge:
Thus lernen children whan that they been yonge.
My sone, of muchel speking yvele avised,
Ther lesse speking hadde ynough suffised,
Comth muchel harm: thus was me told and taught.
In muchel speeche sinne wanteth naught.
Woostou wherof a rakel tonge serveth?
Right as a swerd forcutteth and forkerveth
An arm atwo, my dere sone, right so
A tonge cutteth freendshipe al atwo.
A janglere is to God abhominable:
Rede Salomon so wis and honorable;
Rede David in his psalmes; rede Senekke.
My sone, speek nought but with thyn heed thou bekke—
Dissimule as thou were deef—if that thou heere
A janglere speke of perilous matere.
The Fleming saith—and lerne it if thee leste—
That 'litel jangling causeth muchel reste.'
My sone, if thou no wikked word hast said
Thee thar nat drede for to be biwraid;
But he that hath missaid, I dar wel sayn,
He may by no way clepe his word again:
Thing that is said is said, and forth it gooth,
Though him repente or be him nevere so loth.
He is his thral to whom that he hath said
A tale of which he is now yvele apaid.
My sone, be war, and be no auctor newe
Of tidinges, wheither they been false or trewe.
Wherso thou come, amonges hye or lowe,
Keep wel thy tonge, and think upon the crowe."

228. lere, learn. **231. yvele,** badly. **234. wanteth,** is lacking. **235. Woostou,** do you know; **rakel,** rash. **236. forkerveth,** slices. **239. janglere,** blabbermouth. **241. Senekke,** Seneca. **242. heed,** head. **273. Dissimule,** pretend. **275. leste,** please. **278. thar,** need; **biwraid,** betrayed. **280. clepe,** call. **283. thral,** slave. **284. yvele apaid,** ill-pleased. **285. auctor newe,** i.e., first author.

THE PARSON'S TALE

The Introduction

By that the Manciple hadde his tale al ended,
The sonne fro the south line was descended
So lowe, that he nas nat to my sighte
Degrees nine and twenty as in highte.
Four of the clokke it was, so as I gesse,
For elevene foot, or litel more or lesse,
My shadwe was at thilke time as there,
Of swich feet as my lengthe parted were
In sixe feet equal of proporcioun.
Therwith the moones exaltacioun—
I mene Libra—alway gan ascende,
As we were entring at a thropes ende.
For which oure Host, as he was wont to gie
As in this caas oure joly compaignye,
Saide in this wise, "Lordinges everichoon,
Now lakketh us no tales mo than oon:
Fulfild is my sentence and my decree;
I trowe that we han herd of eech degree;
Almost fulfild is al myn ordinaunce.
I praye to God, so yive him right good chaunce
That telleth this tale to us lustily.
Sire preest," quod he, "artou a vicary,
Or arte a Person? Say sooth, by thy fay.
Be what thou be, ne breek thou nat oure play,
For every man save thou hath told his tale.
Unbokele and shew us what is in thy male!
For trewely, me thinketh by thy cheere
Thou sholdest knitte up wel a greet matere.

1. By that, by the time that. **2. south line,** i.e., the line that runs parallel to the celestial equator to its south and some 28 degrees from it. **8. as,** as if; **parted,** divided. **10. exaltacioun,** position of dominant influence. **11. Libra,** the Scales. **12. thropes,** village's. **13. gie,** lead. **17. sentence,** purpose. **18. trowe,** believe. **22. vicary,** vicar. **23. fay,** faith. **24. breek,** break. **26. male,** bag. **27. cheere,** expression.

Tel us a fable anoon, for cokkes bones!"
  This Person answerde al atones,
"Thou getest fable noon ytold for me,
For Paul, that writeth unto Timothee,
Repreveth hem that waiven soothfastnesse,
And tellen fables and swich wrecchednesse.
Why sholde I sowen draf out of my fest,
Whan I may sowen whete if that me lest?
For which I saye that if you list to heere
Moralitee and vertuous matere,
And thanne that ye wol yive me audience,
I wol ful fain, at Cristes reverence,
Do you plesance leveful as I can.
But trusteth wel, I am a southren man:
I can nat geeste Rum-Ram-Ruf by lettre—
Ne, God woot, rym holde I but litel bettre.
And therfore, if you list, I wol nat glose;
I wol you telle a merye tale in prose,
To knitte up al this feeste and make an ende.
And Jesu for his grace wit me sende
To shewe you the way in this viage
Of thilke parfit glorious pilgrimage
That highte Jerusalem celestial.
And if ye vouche sauf, anoon I shal
Biginne upon my tale, for which I praye
Telle youre avis: I can no bettre saye.
But nathelees, this meditacioun
I putte it ay under correccioun
Of clerkes, for I am nat textuel:
I take but the sentence, trusteth wel.
Therfore I make protestacioun
That I wol stonde to correccioun."

32. **Timothee,** Timothy. 33. **Repreveth,** reproves; **waiven,** depart from; **soothfastnesse,** truth. 35. **draf,** chaff; **fest,** fist. 40. **fain,** gladly. 41. **leveful,** lawful. 43. **geeste,** tell stories; **Rum-Ram-Ruf . . . lettre,** i.e., in the alliterative measure without rhyme. 44. **holde,** consider. 45. **glose,** i.e., speak in order to please. 49. **viage,** journey. 54. **avis,** opinion. 57. **textuel,** literal, faithful to the letter. 58. **sentence,** meaning. 59. **protestacioun,** public acknowledgment.

Upon this word we han assented soone,
For, as it seemed, it was for to doone
To enden in som vertuous sentence,°
And for to yive him space and audience;
And bede° oure Host he sholde to him saye
That alle we to telle his tale him praye.
Oure Hoste hadde the wordes for us alle:
"Sire preest," quod he, "now faire you bifalle:
Telleth," quod he, "youre meditacioun.
But hasteth you, the sonne wol adown.
Beeth fructuous, and that in litel space,°
And to do wel God sende you his grace.
Saye what you list, and we wol gladly heere."
And with that word he saide in this manere.

From THE PARSON'S TALE

The Beginning: The Pilgrimage-Way to the Heavenly City

Oure sweete Lord God of Hevene, that no man wol perisse° but wol that we comen alle to the knowliche of him and to the blisful lif that is perdurable, amonesteth° us by the prophete Jeremie° that saith in this wise: "Stondeth upon the wayes and seeth and axeth° of olde pathes (that is to sayn, of olde sentences)° which is the goode way, and walketh in that way, and ye shul finde refresshing for youre soules."

Manye been the wayes espirituels° that leden folk to oure Lord Jesu Crist and to the regne of glorye: of whiche wayes

63. **sentence,** doctrine. 65. **bede,** i.e., we bade. 71. **fructuous,** fruitful; **space,** time.

1. **that . . . perisse,** who wishes no man to perish. 3. **perdurable,** eternal; **amonesteth,** admonishes. 4. **Jeremie,** see Jeremiah VI.16. 5. **axeth,** ask. 6. **sentences,** opinions. 8. **espirituels,** spiritual.

ther is a ful noble way and a ful covenable which may nat faile to man ne to womman that thurgh sinne hath misgoon fro the righte way of Jerusalem celestial; and this way is cleped Penitence. . . .

The Remedy for the Sin of Lechery

Now cometh the remedye agains Lecherye, and that is generally Chastitee and Continence that restraineth alle the desordainee mevinges that comen of flesshly talents. And evere the gretter merite shal he han that most restraineth the wikkede eschaufinges of the ardure of this sinne. And this is in two maneres: that is to sayn, chastitee in mariage and chastitee of widwehood.

Now shaltou understonde that matrimoine is leeful assembling of man and of womman that receiven by vertu of the sacrement the bond thurgh which they may nat be departed in al hir life—that is to sayn, whil that they liven bothe. This, as saith the book, is a ful greet sacrement: God maked it, as I have said, in Paradis, and wolde himself be born in mariage. And for to halwen mariage, he was at a wedding where as he turned water into win, which was the firste miracle that he wroughte in erthe biforn his disciples. Trewe effect of mariage clenseth fornicacion and replenisseth Holy Chirche of good linage (for that is the ende of mariage), and it chaungeth deedly sinne into venial sinne bitwixe hem that been ywedded, and maketh the hertes al oon of hem that been ywedded, as wel as the bodies.

This is verray mariage that was establissed by God er that sinne bigan, whan naturel lawe was in his right point in Par-

10. convenable, appropriate. **13. cleped,** called.

3. desordainee mevinges, inordinate impulses; **talents,** desires. **5 eschaufinges,** blazings; **ardure,** fire. **8. leeful,** licit. **10. departed,** separated. **14. halwen,** sanctify. **18. linage,** i.e., progeny. **20. al oon,** in unity. **23. was . . . point,** i.e., exercised proper control.

adis; and it was ordained that oo man sholde have but oo womman, and oo womman but oo man (as saith Saint Augustine) by manye resons: First, for mariage is figured bitwixe Crist and Holy Chirche; and that other is for a man is heved of a womman—algate, by ordinance it sholde be so. For if a womman hadde mo men than oon, thanne sholde she have mo hevedes than oon, and that were an horrible thing biforn God; and eek a womman ne mighte nat plese to many folk at ones. And also ther ne sholde nevere be pees ne reste amonges hem, for everich wolde axen his owene thing. And fortherover, no man sholde knowe his owene engendrure, ne who sholde have his heritage, and the womman sholde been the lesse biloved fro the time that she were conjoint to manye men.

Now cometh how that a man sholde bere him with his wif, and namely in two thinges, that is to sayn, in suffrance and in reverence, as shewed Crist whan he made first womman. For he ne made hire nat of the heved of Adam for she sholde nat claime too greet lorshipe: for ther as womman hath the maistrye she maketh too greet desray (ther needen none ensamples of this: the experience of day by day oughte suffise). Also, certes, God ne made nat womman of the foot of Adam, for she ne sholde nat be holden too lowe, for she can nat paciently suffre. But God made womman of the rib of Adam for womman sholde be felawe unto man. Man sholde bere him to his wif in faith, in trouthe, and in love, as saith Sainte Paul, that a man sholde loven his wif as Crist loved Holy Chirche, that loved it so wel that he deide for it. So sholde a man for his wif, if it were neede.

Now how that a womman sholde be subjet to hir housbonde, that telleth Sainte Peter: First, in obedience. And eek, as saith the decree, a womman that is a wif, as longe as she is a wif, she hath noon auctoritee to swere ne to bere witnesse withoute leve of hir housbonde that is hir lord—algate,

26. **by,** i.e., for; **figured,** symbolized as. 27. **heved,** head. 28. **algate,** at any rate. 29. **mo,** more. 34. **fortherover,** furthermore; **his . . . engendrure,** i.e., whom he had engendered. 38. **bere him,** behave. 39. **namely,** especially. 43. **desray,** disorder.

he sholde be so by reson. She sholde eek serven him in alle honestee, and been attempree of hir array; I woot wel that they sholde setten hir entente to plesen hir housbondes, but nat by hir quaintise of array: Saint Jerome saith that wives that been apparailed in silk and in precious purpre ne mowe nat clothen hem in Jesu Crist. What saith Saint John eek in this matere? Saint Gregorye eek saith that no wight seeketh precious array but only for vaine glorye to been honoured the more biforn the peple. It is a greet folye a womman to have a fair array outward and in hireself be foul inward. A wif sholde eek be mesurable in looking and in bering and in laughing, and discreet in alle hir wordes and hir deedes. And aboven alle worldly thinges she sholde loven hir housbonde with al hir herte, and to him be trewe of hir body (so sholde an housbonde eek be to his wif): for sith that al the body is the housbondes, so sholde hir herte been, or elles ther is bitwixe hem two as in that no parfit mariage.

Thanne shul men understonde that for three thinges a man and his wif flesshly mowen assemble. The firste is in entente of engendrure of children to the service of God: for certes, that is the cause final of matrimoine. Another cause is to yeelden everich of hem to other the dette of hir bodies, for neither of hem hath power of his owene body. The thridde is for to eschewe lecherye and vilainye. The ferthe is, for soothe, deedly sinne. As to the firste, it is meritorye; the seconde also, for, as saith the decree, that she hath merite of chastitee that yeeldeth to hir housbonde the dette of hir body, ye, though it be again hir liking and the lust of hir herte. The thridde manere is venial sinne—and, trewely, scarsly may any of thise be withoute venial sinne, for the corrupcion and for the delit. The ferthe manere is for to understonde if they assemble only for amorous love and for noon of the forsaide causes, but for to accomplice thilke brenning delit—they rekke nevere how

59. attempree, moderate. **60. setten hir entente,** do their best. **61. quaintise,** flamboyance. **62. precious,** expensive; **purpre,** scarlet. **68. mesurable,** modest. **72. sith,** since. **76. mowen,** may. **77. engendrure,** engendering. **79. everich,** each. **82. meritorye,** meritorious. **85. again,** against. **90. thilke brenning,** that same burning; **rekke,** care.

ofte—soothly, it is deedly sinne. And yit with sorwe some folk wol painen hem more to doon than to hir appetit suffiseth. . . .

Another remedye agains lecherye is specially to withdrawen swiche thinges as yive occasion to thilke vilainye, as ese, eting, and drinking: for certes, whan the pot boileth strongly, the beste remedye is to withdrawe the fir. Sleeping longe in greet quiete is eek a greet norice to lecherye. Another remedye agains lecherye is that a man or a womman eschewe the compaignye of hem by whiche he douteth to be tempted: for al be it so that the deede be withstonden, yit is ther greet temptacion. Soothly, a whit wal, although it ne brenne nought fully by stiking of a candele, yit is the wal blak of the leit. Ful ofte time I rede that no man truste in his owene perfeccion but he be stronger than Sampson, holier than David, and wiser than Salomon.

CHAUCER'S RETRACTION

Here Taketh the Makere of This Book His Leve

Now praye I to hem alle that herkne this litel tretis or rede, that if ther be any thing in it that liketh hem, that therof they thanken oure Lord Jesu Crist, of whom proceedeth al wit and al goodnesse. And if ther be any thing that displese hem, I praye hem also that they arrette it to the defaute of myn unconning, and nat to my wil, that wolde ful fain have said bettre if I hadde had conning. For oure book saith, "Al that is writen is writen for oure doctrine," and that is myn entente. Wherfore I biseeke you mekely, for the

92. painen hem, exert themselves. **96. ese,** ease. **98. norice,** nurse. **100. douteth,** fears. **103. brenne,** burn. **104. leit,** flame. **105. but,** unless.

1. tretis, treatise. **2. liketh,** pleases. **5. arrette,** ascribe. **6. defaute,** defect; **unconning,** lack of skill. **7. fain,** gladly. **9. biseeke,** beseech.

mercy of God, that ye praye for me that Crist have mercy on me and foryive me my giltes, and namely of my translacions and enditinges of worldly vanitees, the whiche I revoke in my retraccions: as is the book of Troilus; the book also of Fame; the book of the five and twenty Ladies;° the book of the Duchesse; the book of Saint Valentines Day of the Parlement of Briddes; the tales of Canterbury, thilke° that sounen into° sinne; the book of the Leon;° and many another book, if they were in my remembrance, and many a song and many a leccherous lay: that Crist for his grete mercy foryive me the sinne. But of the translacion of Boece° *de Consolatione,* and othere bookes of legendes of saintes, and omelies,° and moralitee, and devocion, that thanke I oure Lord Jesu Crist and his blisful Moder and alle the saintes of hevene, biseeking hem that they from hennes° forth unto my lives ende sende me grace to biwaile my giltes and to studye to the salvacion of my soule, and graunte me grace of verray penitence, confession, and satisfaccion to doon in this present lif, thurgh the benigne grace of him that is king of kinges and preest over alle preestes, that boughte° us with the precious blood of his herte, so that I may been oon of hem at the day of doom that shulle be saved. *Qui cum patre et Spiritu Sancto vivis et regnas Deus per omnia saecula. Amen.*

14. **Ladies,** i.e., the Legend of Good Women. 16. **thilke,** those; **sounen into,** tend toward. 17. **Leon,** the Book of the Lion has not been preserved. 20. **Boece,** Boethius. 21. **omelies,** homilies. 24. **hennes,** hence. 29. **boughte,** redeemed.

Minor Poems

THE BOOK OF THE DUCHESS

I have greet wonder, by this light,
How that I live, for day ne night
I may nat sleepe wel neigh nought.
I have so many an idel thought
Purely for defaute of sleep
That, by my trouthe, I take no keep
Of no thing, how it cometh or gooth,
Ne me nis no thing lief ne loth:
Al is yliche good to me,
Joye or sorwe, wherso it be,
For I have feeling in no thing,
But as it were a mazed thing,
Alway in point to falle adown;
For sorweful imaginacioun
Is alway hoolly in my minde;
And wel ye woot againes Kinde
It were to liven in this wise,
For Nature wolde nat suffise
To noon erthely creature

5. **defaute,** lack. 6. **take no keep,** pay no attention. 8. **lief ne loth,** welcome or hateful. 9. **yliche,** alike. 12. **mazed,** dazed. 13. **in point,** about. 15. **hoolly,** wholly. 16. **Kinde,** Nature.

Nat longe time to endure
Withoute sleep, and be in sorwe.
And I ne may, ne night ne morwe,
Sleepe, and this malencolye
And drede I have for to die.
Defaute of sleep and hevinesse
Hath slain my spirit of quiknesse,°
That I have lost al lustiheed;°
Swiche fantasies been in myn heed°
So I noot° what is best to do.
But men mighte axe° me why so
I may nat sleepe, and what me is.°
But nathelees, who axe this
Leseth his axing° trewely:
Myselven can nat telle why
The soothe; but trewely, as I gesse,
I holde it be a siknesse
That I have suffred this eighte yeer;
And yit my boote° is nevere the neer,°
For ther is physicien but oon
That may me hele. But that is doon;
Passe we over until eft:°
That wil nat be moot° needes be left.
Oure firste matere is good to° keepe.°
  So whan I saw I mighte nat sleepe
Til now late this other night,
Upon my bed I sat upright
And bad oon reche° me a book,
A romance, and he it me took,°
To rede and drive the night away,
For me thoughte it bettre play°
Than playe either at ches or tables.°
And in this book were writen fables

26. **quiknesse,** vitality. 27. **lustiheed,** enthusiasm. 28. **heed,** head. 29. **noot,** don't know. 30. **axe,** ask. 31. **what me is,** what's the matter with me. 33. **Leseth his axing,** wastes his question. 38. **boote,** cure; **neer,** nearer. 41. **eft,** i.e., another time. 42. **moot,** most. 43. **is . . . keepe,** is good to adhere to. 47. **reche,** hand. 48. **took,** gave. 50. **play,** sport. 51. **tables,** backgammon.

That clerkes hadde in olde time—
And othere poetes—put in ryme,
To rede and for to be in minde,
Whil men loved the lawe of Kinde.
This book ne spak but of swiche thinges,
Of queenes lives and of kinges,
And manye othere thinges smale.
Among al this I foond a tale
That me thoughte a wonder thing.
This was the tale: Ther was a king
That highte Ceys, and hadde a wif,
The beste that mighte bere lif,
And this queene highte Alcyone.
So it bifel, therafter soone,
This king wol wenden over see;
To tellen shortly, whan that he
Was in the see, thus in this wise,
Swich a tempest gan to rise
That brak hir mast and made it falle,
And clefte hir ship and dreinte hem alle,
That nevere was founde, as it telles,
Boord ne man ne no thing elles:
Right thus this king Ceys loste his lif.
  Now for to speke of his wif:
This lady that was left at hoom
Hath wonder that the king ne coom
Hoom, for it was a longe terme.
Anoon hir herte bigan to erme,
And for that hire thoughte everemo
It was nat wel—hire thoughte so—
She longed so after the king,
That certes it were a pitous thing
To telle hir hertely sorweful lif,
That she hadde, this noble wif,

56. lawe of Kinde, law of Nature, which appears to have been considered the characteristic religion of pre-Christian times. **60. foond,** found. **63. Ceys,** Ceyx: the story of Ceyx and Alcyone is in Ovid's *Metamorphoses*. **71. hir,** their, i.e., the king's sailors'. **72. dreinte,** drowned. **78. coom,** came. **80. erme,** grieve. **85. hertely,** heartfelt.

For him, allas, she loved alderbest.
Anoon she sente bothe eest and west
To seeke him, but they founde nought.
"Allas," quod she, "that I was wrought!
And wher my lord, my love, be deed?
Certes, I wil nevere ete breed—
I make avow to my God here—
But I mowe of my lord heere."
Swich sorwe this lady to hire took
That trewely I, which made this book,
Hadde swich pitee and swich routhe
To rede hir sorwe, that by my trouthe,
I ferde the worse al the morwe
After, to thenken on hir sorwe.
So whan this lady coude heere no word
That no man mighte finde hir lord,
Ful ofte she swouned and saide, "Allas."
For sorwe ful neigh wood she was;
Ne she coude no reed but oon,
But down on knees she sat anoon
And wepte, that pitee was to heere.
"A, mercy, sweete lady dere,"
Quod she to Juno hir goddesse,
"Helpe me out of this distresse,
And yive me grace my lord to see
Soone, or wite wher so he be,
Or how he fareth, or in what wise,
And I shal make you sacrifise,
And hoolly youres bicome I shal
With good wil, body, herte and al.
And but thou wilt this, lady sweete,
Sende me grace to sleepe and mete
In my sleep som certain swevene,

87. alderbest, best of all. **91. wher,** whether: omitted in translation. **92. breed,** bread. **94. But I mowe,** unless I may. **97. routhe,** compassion. **99. ferde,** fared, felt. **104. wood,** mad. **105. coude,** knew; **reed,** plan of action. **112. wite,** learn. **117. but,** unless. **118. mete,** dream. **119. swevene,** dream.

Wherthurgh that I may knowe evene°
Whether my lord be quik or deed."
With that word she heeng° down the heed
And fil aswoune° as cold as stoon:
Hir wommen caughte hire up anoon,
And broughten hire in bed al naked,
And she, forweeped and forwaked,°
Was wery, and thus the dede sleep
Fil on hire er she tooke keep,°
Thurgh Juno that hadde herd hir boone,°
That made hire to sleepe soone.
For as she prayde, right so was doon
In deede: for Juno right anoon
Called thus hir messager
To do hir errand, and he cam neer.
Whan he was come, she bad him thus:
"Go bet,"° quod Juno, "to Morpheus—
Thou knowest him wel, the god of sleep;
Now understond wel and taak keep:
Say thus on my half that he
Go faste into the Grete See,°
And bid him that, on° alle thing,
He take up Ceys body the king,
That lieth ful pale and no thing rody.°
Bid him creepe into the body
And do° it goon to Alcyone
The queene, ther she lith° allone,
And shewe hire shortly, it is no nay,
How it was dreint° this other day;
And do° the body speke right so
Right as it was woned° to do
The whiles that it was alive.

120. **evene,** for sure. 122. **heeng,** hung. 123. **fil aswoune,** fell in a swoon. 126. **forweeped and forwaked,** worn out with weeping and waking. 128. **Fil,** fell; **keep,** heed. 129. **boone,** prayer. 136. **bet,** i.e., quickly. 140. **Grete See,** Mediterranean. 141. **on,** i.e., above. 143. **rody,** ruddy. 145. **do,** make. 146. **lith,** lies. 148. **dreint,** drowned. 149. **do,** make. 150. **woned,** accustomed.

Go now faste and hie thee blive."
  This messager took leve and wente
Upon his way, and nevere ne stente
Til he cam to the derke valeye
That stant bitwixe rokkes twaye,
Ther nevere yit grew corn ne gras,
Ne tree, ne nought that on live was—
Beest ne man ne nothing elles—
Save that ther were a fewe welles
Come renning fro the clives adown,
That made a deedly sleeping soun,
And ronnen down right by a cave
That was under a rok ygrave
Amidde the valeye, wonder deepe,
Ther thise goddes lay and sleepe:
Morpheus and Eclympasteir,
That was the god of sleepes heir,
That sleep and dide noon other werk.
This cave was also as derk
As helle-pit overal aboute.
They hadde good leiser for to route,
To envye who mighte sleepe best;
Some heenge hir chin upon hir brest
And slepte upright, hir heed yhed,
And some lay naked in hir bed,
And sleepe whiles the dayes laste.
  This messager cam fleeing faste,
And cried, "O ho, awake anoon!"
It was for nought, ther herde him noon.
"Awake," quod he. "Who is lith there?"
And blew his horn right in hir ere,
And cried "Awaketh!" wonder hye.

152. **hie,** hasten; **blive,** quickly. 154. **stente,** stopped. 156. **stant,** stands. 160. **welles,** springs. 161. **renning,** running; **clives,** cliffs. 162. **deedly,** deadly. 164. **ygrave,** carved out. 166. **sleepe,** slept. 167. **Eclympasteir,** a god of sleep found only here and in Chaucer's immediate source, Froissart. 169. **sleep,** slept. 172. **route,** snore. 173. **envye,** compete with each other. 174. **heenge,** hung. 175. **upright,** stretched flat; **heed,** head; **yhed,** hidden, covered. 178. **fleeing,** flying. 181. **is lith,** is it that lies.

This god of sleep with his oon yë
Caste up and axed, "Who clepeth° ther?"
"It am I," quod this messager.
"Juno bad thou sholdest goon—"
And tolde him what he sholde doon,
As I have told you hertofore:
It is no neede reherce it more;
And wente his way whan he hadde sayed.
Anoon this god of sleep abrayed°
Out of his sleep, and gan to goon,
And dide as he hadde bede° him doon:
Took up the dreinte° body soone,
And bar° it forth to Alcyone,
His wif the queene, ther as she lay,
Right evene a quarter bifore day;°
And stood right at hir beddes feet,
And called hire right as she heet°
By name, and saide, "My sweete wif,
Awake, lat be youre sorweful lif,
For in youre sorwe ther lith no reed;°
For certes, sweete, I am but deed:°
Ye shul me nevere on live ysee.
But goode sweete herte, that ye°
Burye my body, for swich a tide°
Ye mowe° it finde the see biside.
And farewel, sweete, my worldes blisse:
I praye God youre sorwe lisse°—
Too litel while oure blisse lasteth."
With that hir yën up she casteth
And saw nought. "Allas," quod she for sorwe,
And deide within the thridde morwe.°
But what she saide more in that swow°
I may nat telle you as now:

185. **Caste,** i.e., looked; **clepeth,** calls. 192. **abrayed,** started up. 194. **bede,** bidden. 195. **dreinte,** drowned. 196. **bar,** bore. 198. **quarter . . . day,** in the last quarter of the night. 200. **heet,** was named. 203. **lith no reed,** is no help. 204. **deed,** dead. 206. **that ye,** i.e., do you. 207. **tide,** time. 208. **mowe,** may. 210. **lisse,** assuage. 214. **morwe,** morning. 215. **swow,** faint.

It were too longe for to dwelle;
My firste matere I wol you telle,
Wherfore I have told this thing
Of Alcyone and Ceys the king.
For thus muche dar I saye weel:
I hadde be dolven everydeel,
And deed, right thurgh defaute of sleep,
If I ne hadde red and take keep
Of this tale next bifore.
And I wol telle you wherfore:
For I ne mighte, for boote ne bale,
Sleepe er I hadde red this tale
Of this dreinte Ceys the king,
And of the goddes of sleeping.
  Whan I hadde red this tale weel,
And overlooked it everydeel,
Me thoughte wonder if it were so:
For I hadde nevere herd speke er tho
Of no goddes that coude make
Men to sleepe ne for to wake,
For I ne knew nevere God but oon.
And in my game I saide anoon—
And yit me liste right yvele to playe—
Rather than that I sholde deye
Thurgh defaute of sleeping thus,
I wolde yive thilke Morpheus,
Or his goddesse dame Juno,
Or som wight elles, I ne roughte who,
To make me sleepe and have som reste—
"I wil yive him the alderbeste
Yifte that evere he abood his live,
And here onward, right now as blive,
If he wol make me sleepe a lite:

222. **dolven,** buried. 223. **defaute,** lack. 224. **red,** read; **keep,** heed. 227. **boote ne bale,** good nor evil. 234. **er tho,** before them. 238. **in my game,** playfully. 239. And yet I felt little like joking. 240. **deye,** die. 242. **thilke,** the same. 244. **roughte,** cared. 246. **alderbeste,** best of all. 247. Gift that he ever expected to get in his life. 248. **onward,** in advance; **as blive,** at once. 249. **lite,** little.

Of downe of pure douves white
I wol yive him a feder bed,
Rayed with gold and right wel cled
In fin blak satin doutremer,
And many a pilwe, and every beer
Of cloth of Reines, to sleepe softe:
Him thar nat neede to turnen ofte.
And I wol yive him al that falles
To a chambre, and alle his halles
I wol do painte with pure gold,
And tapite hem ful many fold
Of oo sute. This shal he have—
If I wiste wher were his cave—
If he can make me sleepe soone,
As dide the goddesse queene Alcyone.
And thus this ilke god Morpheus
May winne of me mo fees thus
Than evere he wan; and to Juno,
That is his goddesse, I shal so do
I trowe that she shal holde hire paid."
  I hadde unnethe that word ysaid,
Right thus as I have told it you,
That sodeinly, I niste how,
Swich a lust anoon me took
To sleepe, that right upon my book
I fil asleepe; and therwith evene
Me mette so inly sweete a swevene,
So wonderful, that nevere yit
I trowe no man hadde the wit
To conne wel my swevene rede—
No, not Joseph, withoute drede,

250. **douves,** doves. 252. **Rayed,** striped; **cled,** clad, covered. 253. **doutremer,** from over the sea, i.e., imported. 254. **beer,** pillow-case. 255. **cloth of Reines,** linen made in Rennes. 256. **Him thar,** he need. 257. **falles,** is appropriate to. 259. **do painte,** have painted. 260. **tapite,** hang with tapestry. 261. **Of oo sute,** i.e., designed to match. 267. **wan,** earned before. 269. **paid,** pleased. 270. **unnethe,** scarcely. 272. **niste,** didn't know. 273. **lust,** desire. 275. **fil,** fell. 276. **Me mette,** I dreamed; **inly,** extremely; **swevene,** dream. 279. **conne,** be able; **rede,** interpret.

Of Egypte, he that redde so
The kinges meting Pharao,
No more than coude the leeste of us;
Ne nat scarsly Macrobeus—
He that wroot al th'avisioun
That he mette, king Scipioun,
The noble man, the Affrican
(Swiche mervailes fortuned than) —
I trowe arede my dremes evene.
Lo, thus it was, this was my swevene;
Me thoughte thus: That it was May,
And in the dawening I lay—
Me mette thus—in my bed al naked,
And looked forth, for I was waked
With smale fowles a greet heep,
That hadde affrayed me out of my sleep,
Thurgh noise and swetnesse of hir song.
And as me mette, they sat among
Upon my chambre roof withoute,
Upon the tiles overal aboute,
And soong everich in his wise
The moste solempne servise
By note, that evere man I trowe
Hadde herd; for some of them soonge lowe,
Some hye, and alle of oon accord.
To telle shortly at oo word,
Was nevere herd so sweete a stevene,
But it hadde be a thing of hevene,
So merye a soun, so sweete entunes,
That certes, for the town of Tunis,

281. redde, interpreted. **282. meting,** dream. **284.** Macrobius' commentary on Cicero's *Dream of Scipio* was the source of much medieval dream-lore. **285. avisioun,** significant dream. **288. fortuned,** happened. **289.** Could, I believe, interpret my dreams properly. **293. Me mette,** I dreamed. **295. With,** by; **heep,** number. **296. affrayed,** startled. **298. among,** here and there. **301. soong,** sang. **302. solempne,** splendid. **303. trowe,** believe. **307. stevene,** chorus. **308. But,** unless. **309. entunes,** tunes. **310–11.:** i.e., I would have given the town of Tunis not to have missed hearing them sing.

I nolde but I hadde herd hem singe;
For al my chambre gan to ringe
Thurgh singing of hir armonye;
For instrument nor melodye
Was nowher herd yit half so sweete,
Nor of accord half so meete;°
For ther was noon of hem that feined°
To singe, for eech of hem him pained°
To finde out merye crafty° notes:
They ne spared nat hir throtes.
And sooth to sayn, my chambre was
Ful wel depainted,° and with glas
Were alle the windowes wel yglased°
Ful clere, and nat an hole ycrased,°
That to biholde it was greet joye.
For hoolly al the storye of Troye
Was in the glasing ywrought thus—
Of Ector and king Priamus,°
Of Achilles and king Lamedon,
And eek of Medea and Jason,
Of Paris, Elaine, and of Lavine;
And alle the walles with colours fine
Were painted, bothe text and glose,°
Of al the Romance of the Rose.°
My windowes were shet° eechoon,
And thurgh the glas the sonne shoon
Upon my bed, with brighte bemes,
With manye glade gilde stremes;°
And eek the welken° was so fair—
Blew, bright, clere was the air—

316. meete, i.e., harmonious. **317. feined,** shirked. **318. him pained,** took pains. **319. crafty,** artistic. **322. depainted,** furnished with murals. **323. yglased,** glassed. **324. ycrased,** broken. **328 ff.** The names were all associated with the Troy legend in the Middle Ages: Hector, Priam, Achilles, Paris, and Helen with the Trojan war itself; Laomedon and Jason and Medea with its antecedent causes; and Lavinia, the Italian princess whom the Trojan Aeneas eventually married, with its historical consequences. **333. glose,** gloss. **334. Romance of the Rose,** the 13th-century French poem which is one of Chaucer's principal sources. **335. shet,** shut. **338. gilde,** gilt; **stremes,** rays. **339. welken,** sky.

And ful attempre forsoothe it was,
For nother too cold nor hoot it nas,
Ne in al the welken was a cloude.
  And as I lay thus, wonder loude
Me thoughte I herde an hunte blowe
T'assaye his horn, and for to knowe
Whether it were cleer or hoors of soun.
And I herde going bothe up and down
Men, hors, houndes, and other thing,
And alle men speke of hunting—
How they wolde slee the hert with stengthe,
And how the hert hadde upon lengthe
So muche embosed—I noot now what.
Anoon right whan I herde that—
How that they wolde on hunting goon—
I was right glad, and up anoon
Took my hors, and forth I wente
Out of my chambre; I nevere stente
Til I cam to the feeld withoute.
Ther overtook I a greet route
Of huntes and eek of foresteres,
With manye relayes and limeres,
And hied hem to the forest faste,
And I with hem. So at the laste
I asked oon, ladde a limere:
  "Say, felawe, who shal hunte here?"
Quod I, and he answerde agen:
  "Sire, th'emperour Octovien,"
Quod he, "and is here faste by."
  "A Goddes half, in good time," quod I,
"Go we faste," and gan to ride.
Whan we come to the forest side
Every man dide right anoon

341. **attempre,** temperate. 342. **nother,** neither. 345. **hunte,** huntsman. 346. **assaye,** test. 349. **hors,** horses. 352–53. **hadde . . . embosed,** i.e., how much in length its antlers had grown. 358. **stente,** stopped. 360. **route,** company. 361. **huntes,** hunters. 362. **relayes,** hounds kept in reserve; **limeres,** tracking hounds. 363. **And hied,** i.e., and they hastened. 365. **ladde,** i.e., who led. 370. **A . . . half,** for God's sake.

As to hunting fil to doon:
The maister hunte, anoon foot-hoot,
With a greet horn blew three moot
At the uncoupling of his houndes;
Within a while the hert founde is,
Yhalowed, and rechased faste
Longe time; and so at the laste
This hert rused and stal away
Fro alle the houndes a privee way:
The houndes hadde overshote him alle,
And were upon a defaute falle.
Therwith the hunte, wonder faste,
Blew a forloin at the laste.
I was go walked fro my tree,
And as I wente ther cam by me
A whelpe, that fawned me as I stood,
That hadde yfolwed and coude no good.
It cam and crepte to me as lowe
Right as it hadde me yknowe,
Heeld down his heed and joined his eres,
And laide al smoothe down his heres.
I wolde have caught it, and anoon
It fledde and was fro me goon,
And I him folwed, and it forth wente
Down by a flowry greene wente,
Ful thikke of gras, ful softe and sweete,
With flowres fele faire under feete,
And litel used—it seemed thus;
For bothe Flora and Zephyrus,
They two that make flowres growe,
Hadde maad hir dwelling ther, I trowe,
For it was, on to biholde,
As though th'erthe envye wolde

374. fil, i.e., it was appropriate. **375. anoon foot-hoot,** with the greatest haste. **376. moot,** notes. **378. hert,** hart. **379. Yhalowed,** i.e., brought to the hounds' attention with shouting; **rechased,** pursued. **381. rused,** changed his course; **stal,** stole. **384.** i.e., and had lost the scent. **386. forloin,** recall. **390. coude no good,** didn't know what to do. **393. heed,** head. **398. wente,** path. **400. fele,** many. **406. envye,** strive in rivalry.

To be gayer than the hevene,
To have mo flowres, swiche sevene°
As in the welken sterres° be:
It hadde forgete the povertee
That winter, thurgh his colde morwes,°
Hadde maad it suffre, and his sorwes—
Al was forgeten, and that was seene,°
For al the wode was waxen° greene;
Swetnesse of dewe hadde maad it waxe.
It is no neede eek for to axe°
Wher ther were many greene greves,°
Or thikke of trees, so ful of leves,
And every tree stood by himselve
Fro other wel ten feet or twelve—
So grete trees, so huge of strengthe,
Of fourty or fifty fadme° lengthe,
Clene withoute bough or stikke,
With croppes° brode and eek as thikke:
They° were nat an inche asonder,
That it was shadwe overal under.
And many an hert and many an hinde
Was bothe bifore me and bihinde;
Of fawnes, sowres,° bukkes, does
Was ful the wode, and manye roes,
And manye squireles that sete°
Ful hye upon the trees and ete,°
And in hir manere made feestes.
Shortly, it was so ful of beestes,
That though Argus, the noble contour,°
Sete to rekene in his countour,°
And rekene with his figures ten°—

408. swiche sevene, seven times as many. **409. sterres,** stars. **411. morwes,** mornings. **413. seene,** i.e., evident. **414. waxen,** grown. **416. axe,** ask. **417. Wher,** whether; **greves,** thickets. **422. fadme,** fathoms. **424. croppes,** i.e., foliage. **425. They,** i.e., the tips of the branches of the individual trees. **429. sowres,** sorrels, three-year-old male deer. **431. sete,** sat. **432. ete,** ate. **435. Argus,** Algus, an Arabian mathematician; **contour,** calculator. **436. countour,** counting-house. **437. figures ten,** i.e., Arabic numerals as opposed to the Roman numerals still widely used.

For by tho figures mowe al ken,
If they be crafty, rekene and nombre,
And telle of every thing the nombre—
Yit sholde he faile to rekene evene
The wondres me mette in my swevene.
  But forth I romed right wonder faste
Down the wode. So at the laste
I was war of a man in blak
That sat, and hadde yturned his bak
To an ook, an huge tree.
"Lord," thoughte I, "who may that be?
What aileth him to sitten heer?"
Anoon right I wente neer:
Thanne foond I sitte evene upright
A wonder wel-faringe knight—
By the manere me thoughte so—
Of good muchel, and right yong therto,
Of the age of four and twenty yeer:
Upon his beerd but litel heer;
And he was clothed al in blak.
I stalked evene unto his bak,
And ther I stood as stille as ought,
That, sooth to saye, he saw me nought,
Forwhy he heeng his heed adown.
And with a deedly sorweful soun
He made of rym ten vers or twelve
Of a complainte to himselve—
The moste pitee, the moste routhe,
That evere I herde, for by my trouthe,
It was greet wonder that Nature
Mighte suffre any creature
To have swich sorwe and be nat deed.
Ful pitous pale and no thing reed,
He saide a lay, a manere song,

438. **ken,** kin, mankind. 441. **evene,** accurately. 442. **me mette,** I dreamed. 451. **foond,** found. 452. **wel-faringe,** distinguished. 454. **muchel,** size. 459. **ought,** anything. 461. **Forwhy,** because; **heeng,** hung. 462. **deedly,** deadly. 465. **routhe,** sorrow. 470. **reed,** red.

Withoute note, withoute song,°
And was this, for ful wel I can
Reherce it right; thus it bigan:

"I have of sorwe so greet woon°
That joye gete I nevere noon,
Now that I see my lady bright,
Which I have loved with al my might,
Is fro me deed, and is agoon.°

Allas, deeth, what aileth thee,
That thou noldest have taken me,
Whan thou tooke my lady sweete,
That was so fair, so fressh, so free,°
So good that men may wel see
Of al goodnesse she hadde no meete?"°

Whan he hadde maad thus his complainte
His sorweful herte gan faste fainte,
And his spirites wexen dede;°
The blood was fled, for pure drede,
Down to his herte to make him warm—
For wel it feeled the herte hadde harm—
To wite eek why it was adrad,°
By kinde,° and for to make it glad;
For it is membre principal
Of the body, and that made al
His hewe chaunge and waxe greene
And pale, for ther no blood is seene
In no manere lim° of his.
Anoon therwith whan I sawgh this,
He ferde thus yvele ther he seet,°
I wente and stood right at his feet
And grette° him; but he spak nought,

472. **song,** music. 475. **woon,** plenty. 479. **deed,** dead; **agoon,** gone away. 483. **free,** noble. 485. **meete,** equal. 488. **wexen dede,** grew dead. 492. **wite,** learn; **adrad,** full of dread. 493. **kinde,** nature. 498. **lim,** limb. 500. He fared so badly where he sat. 502. **grette,** greeted.

But argued with his owene thought,
And in his wit disputed faste
Why and how his lif mighte laste,
Him thoughte his sorwes were so smerte,
And lay so cold upon his herte.
So thurgh his sorwe and hevy thought
Made him that he herde me nought:
For he hadde wel neigh lost his minde,
Though Pan, that men clepe god of Kinde,
Were for his sorwes nevere so wroth.
But at the laste, to sayn right sooth,
He was war of me, how I stood
Bifore him and dide of myn hood,
And hadde ygret him as I best coude,
Debonairly and no thing loude.
He saide, "I praye thee, be nat wroth;
I herde thee nat, to sayn thee sooth,
Ne I sawgh thee nat, sire, trewely."
"A, goode sire, no fors," quod I,
"I am right sory if I have ought
Destroubled you out of youre thought.
Foryive me if I have mistake."
"Yis, th'amendes is light to make,"
Quod he, "for ther lith noon therto.
Ther is no thing mis said nor do."
Lo, how goodly spak this knight,
As it hadde be another wight:
He made it nouther tough ne quainte.
And I saw that and gan m'aquainte
With him, and foond him so tretable,
Right wonder skilful and resonable,
As me thoughte, for al his bale,
Anoon right I gan finde a tale

511. Kinde, Nature. **515. of,** off. **516. ygret,** greeted. **517. Debonairly,** modestly. **521. fors,** matter. **522. ought,** at all. **523. Destroubled,** disturbed. **525. light,** easy. **526. lith,** i.e., is required. **527. mis,** amiss. **530.** i.e., He didn't make it hard for me. **531. m'aquainte,** get acquainted. **532. foond,** found; **tretable,** affable. **533. skilful,** sensible. **534. bale,** grief. **535. finde a tale,** devise something to say.

To him, to looke wher I mighte ought
Have more knowing of his thought.
  "Sire," quod I, "this game is doon;
I holde that this hert be goon:
Thise huntes conne him nowher see."
  "I do no fors therof," quod he.
"My thought is theron nevere a deel."
  "By oure Lord," quod I, "I trowe you weel.
Right so me thenketh by youre cheere.
But sire, oo thing wol ye heere?
Me thinketh in greet sorwe I you see:
But certes, sire, if that ye
Wolde ought discure me youre wo,
I wolde, as wis God helpe me so,
Amende it, if I can or may.
Ye mowe preve it by assay.
For by my trouthe, to make you hool
I wol do al my power hool;
And telleth me of youre sorwes smerte:
Paraunter it may ese youre herte,
That seemeth ful sik under youre side."
  With that he looked on me aside,
As who saith, "Nay, that wol nat be."
  "Graunt mercy, goode freend," quod he.
"I thanke thee that thou woldest so,
But it may nevere the rather be do:
No man may my sorwe glade;
That maketh myn hewe to falle and fade,
And hath myn understonding lorn,
That me is wo that I was born.
May nought make my sorwes slide,
Nat alle the remedies of Ovide,

536. wher, whether. **538. game,** i.e., hunt. **540. huntes,** huntsmen. **541. do fors,** care. **544. cheere,** manner. **548. discure,** disclose. **549. wis,** surely. **551.** You may make trial of it. **552. hool,** whole. **555. Paraunter,** perhaps. **559. Graunt mercy,** many thanks. **561. rather,** sooner. **562. glade,** gladden. **563. hewe,** color. **564. lorn,** impaired. **566. slide,** i.e., disappear. **567. Ovide,** Ovid wrote a poetic *Remedy of Love.*

Ne Orpheus, god of melodye,
Ne Dedalus with his playes slye;
Ne hele me may no physicien,
Nat Ipocras ne Galien.
Me is wo that I live houres twelve.
But who so wol assaye himselve
Whether his herte can have pitee
Of any sorwe, lat him see me–
I, wrecche that deeth hath maad al naked
Of al the blis that evere was maked,
Yworthe worst of alle wightes,
That hate my dayes and my nightes.
My lif, my lustes be me lothe,
For al welfare and I be wrothe.
The pure deeth is so ful my fo
That I wolde die, it wil nat so:
For whan I folwe it, it wol flee;
I wolde have him, it nil have me.
This is my paine, withoute reed,
Alway dying and be nat deed,
That Tesiphus that lith in helle
May nat of more sorwe telle.
And who so wiste al, by my trouthe,
My sorwe, but he hadde routhe
And pitee of my sorwes smerte,
That man hath a feendly herte.
For who so seeth me first on morwe
May sayn he hath met with sorwe,
For I am sorwe and sorwe is I.
  Allas, and I wol telle thee why
My song is turned to plaininge,

568. **Orpheus,** whose harping was capable of soothing all pain. 569. **Dedalus,** Daedalus, builder of the Cretan Labyrinth and inventor of wings that enabled him to fly; **playes slye,** clever diversions. 571. **Ipocras, Galien,** Hippocrates and Galen, legendary physicians. 578. **Yworthe,** become. 580. **lustes,** pleasures. 581. **wrothe,** i.e., angry with each other. 586. **reed,** remedy. 588. **Tesiphus,** Sisyphus or Tityus, both of whom had horrible punishments in the Underworld; **lith,** lies. 590. **wiste,** knew. 591. **but,** unless; **routhe,** pity. 593. **feendly,** fiendish. 598. **plaininge,** complaint.

And al my laughter to weepinge,
My glade thoughtes to hevinesse;
In travaile° is myn idelnesse
And eek my reste; my wele° is wo,
My good is harm; and everemo
In wratthe is turned my playinge,
And my delit into sorwinge;
Myn hele° is turned into siknesse,
In drede is al my sikernesse;°
To derk is turned al my light,
My wit is folye, my day is night,
My love is hate, my sleep wakinge,
My mirthe and meles is fastinge;
My countenance is nicetee,°
And al abawed,° wher so I be;
My pees in pleding and in werre.°
Allas, how mighte I fare werre?°
My boldnesse is turned to shame,
For fals Fortune hath played a game
At the ches with me, allas the while!
The traitresse fals and ful of gile,
That al bihoteth and nothing halt,°
She gooth upright, yit is she halt,°
That baggeth° foule and looketh faire,
The despitouse debonaire°
That scorneth many a creature:
An idole of fals portraiture
Is she, for she wol soone wrien;°
She is the monstres heed ywrien,°
As filthe over-ystrawed° with flowres;
Hir moste worshipe and hir flowr° is
To lien, for that is hir nature,

601. **travaile,** labor. 602. **wele,** welfare. 606. **hele,** health. 607. **sikernesse,** certainty. 612. **countenance,** i.e., decorum; **nicetee,** foolishness. 613. **abawed,** amazed. 614. **pleding,** contention; **werre,** war. 615. **werre,** worse. 620. **bihoteth,** promises; **halt,** holds. 621. **gooth,** walks; **halt,** lame. 622. **baggeth,** squints. 623. The cruel meek one. 626. **wrien,** turn away. 627. **heed,** head; **ywrien,** concealed. 628. **over-ystrawed,** overstrewn. 629. **flowr,** i.e., best quality.

Withoute faith, lawe, or mesure;
She is fals and evere laughinge
With oon yë, and that other weepinge;
That is brought up, she set al down;
I likne hire to the scorpioun,
That is a fals flateringe beeste,
For with his heed he maketh feeste,
But al amidde his flateringe,
With his taile it wol stinge
And envenime, and so wol she;
She is th'enviouse charitee,
That is ay fals and seemeth weel;
So turneth she hir false wheel
Aboute, for it is nothing stable—
Now by the fir, now atte table,
For many oon hath she thus yblent;
She is play of enchauntement,
That seemeth oon and is nat so.
The false theef, what hath she do,
Trowest thou? By oure Lord, I wol thee saye:
At the ches with me she gan to playe;
With hir false draughtes divers
She stal on me and took my fers:
And whan I sawgh my fers awaye,
Allas, I couthe no lenger playe,
But saide, 'Fare wel, sweete, ywis,
And fare wel al that evere ther is.'
Therwith Fortune saide, 'Chek here!'—
And maat in the midpoint of the chekkere,
With a poune errant! Allas,
Ful craftier to playe she was
Than Athalus that made the game

631. **mesure**, moderation. 634. **That**, what; **set**, sets. 635. **likne**, liken. 637. **maketh feeste**, i.e., pretends to be friendly. 640. **envenime**, poison. 642. **weel**, well. 646. **yblent**, deceived. 647. **play**, illusion. 648. **oon**, stable. 650. **Trowest**, believe. 652. **draughtes**, moves. 653. **stal on**, stole up on; **fers**, queen. 655. **couthe**, could. 659. **maat**, checkmate; **chekkere**, board. 660. **poune errant**, stray pawn. 662. **Athalus**, Attalus, supposed inventor of chess; **made**, invented.

First of the ches—so was his name.
But God wolde I hadde ones or twies
Ycoud and knowe the juparties
That coude the Greek Pyctagores—
I sholde have played the bet at ches,
And kept my fers the bet therby.
And though wherto? For trewely,
I holde that wissh nat worth a stree:
It hadde be nevere the bet for me;
For Fortune can so many a wile,
Ther be but fewe can hire bigile.
And eek she is the lasse to blame—
Myself I wolde have do the same,
Bifore God, hadde I be as she:
She oughte the more excused be.
For this I saye yit more therto:
Hadde I be God and mighte have do
My wille, whan she my fers caughte,
I wolde have drawe the same draughte,
For also wis God yive me reste,
I dar wel swere she took the beste.
But thurgh that draughte I have lorn
My blisse. Allas that I was born!
For everemore I trowe trewely,
For al my wil, my lust hoolly
Is turned. But yit what to doone?
By oure Lord, it is to die soone.
For nothing I leve it nought
To live and die right in this thought:
For ther nis planete in firmament,
Ne in air ne in erthe noon element,

665. **Ycoud,** been familiar with; **juparties,** mathematical chances. **666. coude,** knew; **Pyctagores,** Pythagoras, Greek philosopher and mathematician. **670. stree,** straw. **672. can,** knows. **674. lasse,** less. **680. caughte,** i.e., took. **681.** I would have made the same move. **682. also wis,** as surely as. **684. draughte,** move; **lorn,** lost. **686. trowe,** think. **687. For,** despite; **lust,** pleasure; **hoolly,** wholly. **688. turned,** i.e., frustrated. **690. leve it,** give it up. **691. thought,** state of mind.

That they ne yive me a yifte eechone
Of weeping whan I am allone.
For whan that I avise me weel,
And bithenke me everydeel,
How that ther lith in rekening
In my sorwe for nothing,
And how ther liveth no gladnesse
May glade me of my distresse,
And how I have lost suffisaunce,
And therto I have no plesaunce,
Thanne may I saye I have right nought.
And whan al this falleth in my thought,
Allas, thanne am I overcome,
For that is doon is nat to come.
I have more sorwe than Tantale."
 And whan I herde him telle this tale
Thus pitously, as I you telle,
Unnethe mighte I lenger dwelle,
It dide myn herte so muche wo.
 "A, goode sire," quod I, "saye nat so.
Have som pitee on youre nature
That formed you to creature.
Remembre you of Socrates,
For he ne counted nat three strees
Of nought that Fortune coude do."
 "No," quod he, "I can nat so."
 "Why so, goode sire? Yis, pardee," quod I.
"Ne saye nought so, for trewely,
Though ye hadde lost the ferses twelve,
And ye for sorwe mordred yourselve,
Ye sholde be dampned in this cas
By as good right as Medea was,

696. **avise me,** consider. 697. i.e., And ponder all aspects of my situation. 698–99. How that there remains nothing to be paid me for my sorrow. 701. **glade,** gladden. 702. **suffisaunce,** satisfaction. 705. **falleth,** occurs. 707. **that,** what. 708. **Tantale,** Tantalus, one of the Underworld's chief sufferers. 711. **Unnethe,** scarcely. 717. **strees,** straws. 722. **ferses,** queens. 723. **mordred,** murdered. 724. **dampned,** damned.

That slow hir children for Jason;
And Phyllis also for Demophon
Heeng hirself, so wailaway,
For he hadde broke his terme day
To come to hire; another rage
Hadde Dido eek the queene of Cartage,
That slow hirself for Eneas
Was fals. Which a fool she was!
And Eccho died for Narcisus
Nolde nat love hire, and right thus
Hath many another folye doon.
And for Dalida died Samson,
That slow himself with a piler.
But ther is no man alive heer
Wolde for a fers make this wo."
"Why so?" quod he. "It is nat so.
Thou woost ful litel what thou menest:
I have lost more than thou weenest."
"Lo, sire, that may be," quod I.
"Goode sire, telle me al hoolly
In what wise, how, why, and wherfore
That ye have thus youre blisse lore."
"Blithely," quod he. "Com sitte adown:
I telle thee up a condicioun
That thou shal hoolly, with al thy wit,
Do thyn entente to herkne it."
"Yis, sire." "Sweer thy trouthe therto."
"Gladly." "Do thanne holde herto."
"I shal right blithely, so God me save,
Hoolly, with al the wit I have,
Heere you as wel as I can."
"A Goddes half," quod he and bigan.
"Sire," quod he, "sith first I couthe

726. **slow,** slew. 728. **Heeng,** hanged. 729. **terme, day,** promised day of return. 731. **Cartage,** Carthage. 733. **Which,** what. 734. **for,** because. 737. **Dalida,** Delilah. 740. **fers,** queen. 742. **woost,** know. 743. **weenest,** suppose. 747. **lore,** lost. 749. **up,** upon. 751. **thyn entente,** i.e., your best. 757. **A,** on. 758. **couthe,** could.

Have any manere wit fro youthe,
Or kindely understonding
To comprehende in any thing
What love was, in myn owene wit,
Dredelees, I have evere yit
Be tributarye and yive rente
To Love hoolly with good entente,
And thurgh plesance become his thral,
With good wil, body, herte, and al:
Al this I putte in his servage,
As to my lord, and dide homage,
And ful devoutly I prayde him to
He sholde bisette myn herte so
That it plesance to him were,
And worshipe to my lady dere.
And this was longe and many a yeer
Er that myn herte was set owheer,
That I dide this, and niste why:
I trowe it cam me kindely;
Paraunter I was therto most able,
As a whit wal or a table,
For it is redy to cacche and take
Alle that men wol therinne make,
Whether so men wol portraye or painte,
Be the werkes nevere so quainte.
And thilke time I ferde right so.
I was able to have lerned tho,
And to have coud, as wel or better,
Paraunter other art or letter;
But for love cam first in my thought,
Therfore I forgat it nought.
I chees love to my firste craft:
Therfore it is with me laft;

760. **kindely,** natural. 762. **wit,** mind. 763. **Dredelees,** doubtless. 764. **tributarye,** a subject; **rente,** payment. 765. **hoolly,** wholly. 768. **servage,** service. 771. **bisette,** dispose. 775. **owheer,** anywhere. 776. **niste,** knew not. 777. **trowe,** think; **kindely,** naturally. 778. **Paraunter,** perhaps; **able,** adapted. 779. **table,** tablet. 784. **ferde,** behaved. 785. **tho,** then. 786. **coud,** learned. 787. **letter,** study. 790. **chees,** chose. 791. **laft,** left.

Forwhy° I took it of so yong age,
That malice hadde my corage°
Nat that time turned to nothing
Thurgh too muchel knowleching.°
For that time Youthe, my maistresse,
Governed me in idelnesse,
For it was in my firste youthe,
And tho ful litel good I couthe;°
For alle my werkes were flittinge°
That time, and al my thought varyinge:°
Alle were to me yliche° good
That I knew tho; but thus it stood:
  It happed that I cam, on a day,
Into a place ther that I sey°
Trewely the fairest compaignye
Of ladies that evere man with yë
Hadde seen togidre in oo place.
Shal I clepe it hap other° grace
That broughte me ther? Nay, but Fortune,
That is to lien ful commune,°
The false traiteresse pervers—
God wolde I coude clepe hire wers,°
For now she wercheth° me ful wo,
And I wol telle soone why so.
  Among thise ladies thus eechoon,
Sooth to sayne, I sawgh oon
That was lik noon of the route:°
For I dar swere, withoute doute,
That as the someres sonne bright
Is fairer, clerer, and hath more light
Than any other planete in hevene—
The moone, or the sterres° sevene—
For al the world so hadde she

792. **Forwhy,** because. 793. **corage,** heart. 795. **knowleching,** knowledge. 799. **good,** i.e., what was best; **couthe,** knew. 800. **flittinge,** fleeting. 801. **varyinge,** fickle. 802. **yliche,** alike. 805. **sey,** saw. 809. **clepe,** call; **hap,** luck; **other,** or. 811. **commune,** i.e., accustomed. 813. **wers,** worse. 814. **wercheth,** works. 818. **route,** group. 823. **sterres,** stars.

Surmounted hem alle of beautee,
Of manere and of comelinesse,
Of stature and of wel-set gladnesse,
Of goodlihede, and so wel biseye—
Shortly, what shal I more saye?
By God and his halwes twelve,
It was my sweete, right as hirselve.
She had so stedefast countenaunce,
So noble port and maintenaunce,
And Love, that hadde wel herd my boone,
Hadde espied me thus soone,
That she ful soone in my thought,
As helpe me God, so was ycought
So sodeinly, that I ne took
No manere conseil but at hir look
And at myn herte; forwhy hir yën
So gladly, I trowe, myn herte sien,
That purely tho myn owene thought
Saide it were better serve hire for nought
Than with another to be weel.
And it was sooth, for everydeel
I wol anoon right telle thee why:
I sawgh hire daunce so comely,
Carole and singe so sweetely,
Laughe and playe so wommanly,
And looke so debonairly,
So goodly speke and so freendly,
That certes I trowe that everemoor
Nas seen so blisful a tresor.
For every heer on hir heed,
Sooth to sayn, it was nat reed,
Ne neither yelow ne brown it nas—
Me thoughte most lik gold it was.

827. **wel-set,** well-disposed. 828. **wel biseye,** fair to see. 830. **halwes,** saints, i.e., apostles. 832. **countenaunce,** appearance. 833. **port,** bearing; **maintenaunce,** demeanor. 834. **boone,** prayer. 837. **ycought,** caught. 840. **forwhy,** because. 841. **trowe,** think; **sien,** saw. 842. **purely,** i.e., categorically. 844. **weel,** well. 845. **everydeel,** every bit. 850. **debonairly,** demurely. 853. **tresor,** treasure. 854. **heer,** hair; **heed,** head.

And whiche° yën my lady hadde!
Debonaire, goode, glade, and sadde,°
Simple, of good muchel,° nought too wide.
Therto hir look nas nat aside,
Ne overthwart, but biset so weel,°
It drew and took up everydeel°
Alle that on hire gan biholde.
Hir yën seemed anoon she wolde
Have mercy—fooles wenden so,
But it was nevere the rather do.°
It nas no countrefeted° thing:
It was hir owne pure° looking,
That the goddesse, Dame Nature,
Hadde maad hem open by mesure,°
And cloos; for were she nevere so glad,
Hir looking was nat foly sprad,°
Ne wildely, though that she playde.
But evere me thoughte hir yën saide,
'By God, my wratthe is al foryive.'
Therwith hire liste so wel to live°
That dulnesse was of hire adrad;°
She nas too sobre ne too glad:
In alle thinges more mesure°
Hadde nevere, I trowe, creature.
But many oon with hir look she herte,°
And that sat° hire ful litel at herte,
For she knew nothing of hir° thought;
But whether she knew or knew it nought,
Algate she ne roughte of hem a stree.°
To gete hir love no neer° was he
That woned at hoom than he in Inde:°

858. whiche, what. **859. Debonaire,** modest; **sadde,** unwavering. **860. Simple,** sincere; **muchel,** size. **862. overthwart,** askance; **biset,** disposed; **weel,** well. **863. everydeel,** entirely. **866. wenden,** thought. **867. rather,** sooner; **do,** done. **868. countrefeted,** imitated. **869. hir owne pure,** her very own. **871. hem,** i.e., her eyes; **by mesure,** i.e., exactly right. **873. foly,** foolishly; **sprad,** dispensed. **877. liste . . . live,** she took such pleasure in life. **878. adrad,** in dread. **880. mesure,** moderation. **882. herte,** hurt. **883. sat,** i.e., affected. **884. hir,** their. **886. Algate,** at any rate; **roughte,** cared; **stree,** straw. **887. neer,** nearer. **888. woned,** dwelled; **Inde,** India.

The formeest° was alway bihinde.
But goode folk over alle other
She loved as man may do his brother;
Of which love she was wonder large,°
In skilful places that bere charge.°
  But which° a visage she hadde therto!
Allas, myn herte is wonder wo°
That I ne can descriven it:
Me lakketh bothe Englissh and wit
For to undo° it at the fulle;
And eek my spirites be so dulle,
So greet a thing for to devise.°
I have no wit that can suffise
To comprehende° hir beautee:
But thus muche dar I sayn, that she
Was rody, fressh, and lively hewed,°
And every day hir beautee newed,°
And neigh hir face was alderbest:°
For certes Nature hadde swich lest°
To make that fair, that trewely she
Was hir chief patrone° of beautee,
And chief ensample° of al hir werk,
And moustre;° for be it nevere so derk,
Me thinketh I see hire everemo.
And yit moreover, though alle tho°
That evere lived were now alive,
Ne sholde han founde to descrive°
In al hir face a wikked° signe,
For it was sad, simple° and benigne.
  And which a goodly, softe speeche
Hadde that sweete, my lives leeche!°

889. formeest, foremost. **892. large,** generous. **893.** In reasonable places that might bear the responsibility. **894. which,** what. **895. wo,** i.e., woeful. **898. undo,** i.e., reveal. **900. greet,** great; **devise,** describe. **902. comprehende,** i.e., express completely. **904. rody,** ruddy, i.e., pink and white; **hewed,** colored. **905. newed,** was renewed. **906. neigh,** almost; **alderbest,** best of all. **907. lest,** pleasure. **909. patrone,** beneficiary. **910. ensample,** example. **911. moustre,** pattern. **913. tho,** those. **915.** i.e., One should not have found any one to describe. **916. wikked,** evil. **917. sad,** steadfast; **simple,** sincere. **919. leeche,** physician.

So freendly and so wel ygrounded,
Up al reson so wel yfounded,
And so tretable to alle goode,
That I dar swere wel, by the roode,
Of eloquence was nevere founde
So sweete a souninge facounde,
Ne trewer tonged, ne scorned lasse,
Ne bet coude hele, that, by the masse,
I dorste swere, though the Pope it songe,
That ther was nevere yit thurgh hir tonge
Man ne womman greetly harmed:
As for hire, was al harm hid;
Ne lasse flatering in hir word,
That purely hir simple record
Was founde as trewe as any bond
Or trouthe of any mannes hond;
Ne chide she coude nevere a deel—
That knoweth al the world ful weel.
  But swich a fairnesse of a nekke
Hadde that sweete, that boon nor brekke
Nas ther noon seene that missat:
It was smoothe, straight, and pure flat
Withouten hole—or canel-boon,
As by seeming, she hadde noon.
Hir throte, as I have now memoire,
Seemed a round towr of ivoire
Of good greetnesse, and nought too greet.
And goode, faire Whit she heet:
That was my lady name right;
She was bothe fair and bright:
She hadde nat hir name wrong.

920. **ygrounded,** based. 921. **Up,** upon. 922. **tretable,** affable; **goode,** i.e., good people. 923. **roode,** cross. 925. **souninge,** sounding; **facounde,** manner of speaking. 926. **lasse,** less. 927. **bet,** better. 928. **songe,** sang. 930. **greetly,** greatly. 931. **was . . . hid,** i.e., slander was unthought of. 933. **purely,** merely; **record,** statement. 936. **chide,** scold; **deel,** bit. 937. **weel,** well. 939. **boon,** bone; **brekke,** flaw. 940. **missat,** was ill-becoming. 941. **pure,** entirely. 942. **canel-boon,** collar-bone. 944. **memoire,** memory. 946. **greetnesse,** i.e., size; **greet,** large. 947. **Whit,** i.e., Blanche; **heet,** was named.

Right faire shuldres and body long
She hadde, and armes—every lith°
Fattish,° flesshy, nat greet therwith;
Right white handes and nailes rede;
Rounde brestes; and of good brede°
Hir hippes were; a straight flat bak.
I knew on hire noon other lak°
That alle hir limes nere pure sewinge°
In as fer° as I hadde knowinge.
   Therto she coude so wel playe,
Whan that hire liste,° that I dar saye
That she was lik to torche bright,
That every man may take of light
Ynough, and it hath nevere the lesse.
Of manere and of comelinesse
Right so ferde° my lady dere,
For every wight of hir manere
Mighte cacche ynough, if that he wolde,
If he hadde yën hire to biholde.
For I dar swere wel if that she
Hadde among ten thousand be,
She wolde have be, at the leeste,
A chief mirour° of al the feeste—
Though they° hadde stonde in a rowe—
To mennes yën that coude have knowe.°
For wher so men hadde played or waked,°
Me thoughte the felaweshipe° as naked
Withouten hire, that I sawgh ones,
As a corowne withoute stones.
Trewely she was to myn yë
The soleine Phenix° of Arabye:
For ther liveth nevere but oon,

952. **lith,** limb. 953. **Fattish,** plump. 955. **brede,** breadth. 957. **lak,** flaw. 958. i.e., So that all her limbs were perfectly matched. 959. **fer,** far. 961. **liste,** it pleased. 966. **ferde,** fared. 973. **mirour,** i.e., point of focus. 974. **they,** i.e., all the ladies. 975. **coude have knowe,** i.e., were capable of discrimination. 976. **waked,** i.e., stayed up late. 977. **felaweshipe,** gathering. 981. **soleine,** solitary; **Phenix,** Phoenix, a legendary bird of which there is said to be but one.

Ne swich as she ne knowe I noon.
  To speke of goodnesse, trewely she
Hadde as muche debonairtee°
As evere hadde Hester° in the Bible,
And more, if more were possible.
And sooth to sayne, therwithal
She hadde a wit so general,°
So hoole° enclined to alle goode,
That al hir wit was set, by the roode,
Withoute malice upon gladnesse.
And therto I sawgh nevere yit a lesse
Harmful than she was in doinge:
I saye nat that she ne hadde knowinge
What harm was, or elles she
Hadde coud° no good, so thinketh me.
  And trewely, for to speke of trouthe,°
But she hadde had, it hadde be routhe.°
Therof she hadde so muche hir deel°—
And I dar sayn and swere it weel—
That Trouthe himself, over al and al,°
Had chose his maner° principal
In hire, that was his resting place.
Therto she hadde the moste grace
To have stedefast perseveraunce,
And esy attempre governaunce,°
That evere I knew or wiste° yit;
So pure suffrant was hir wit,°
And reson gladly she understood,
It folwed wel she coude good:°
She used gladly to do weel.
  Thise were hir maneres every deel:°
Therwith she loved so wel right,

985. debonairtee, modesty. **986. Hester,** Esther, a model of womanly qualities. **989. wit,** mind; **general,** broad. **990. hoole,** wholly. **997. coud,** known. **998. trouthe,** integrity. **999. But,** unless; **had,** i.e., had it (integrity); **routhe,** a pity. **1000. deel,** share. **1002. al . . . al,** all others. **1003. maner,** manor. **1007. attempre,** gentle; **governaunce,** conduct. **1008. wiste,** i.e., had experienced. **1009. pure suffrant,** entirely tolerant; **wit,** mind. **1011. coude good,** knew what was best. **1013. deel,** part.

She wrong do wolde to no wight—
No wight mighte do hire no shame,
She loved so wel hir owene name.
Hire luste to holde no wight in honde,
Ne, be thou siker, she wolde nat fonde
To holde no wight in balaunce
By half word ne by countenaunce,
But if men wolde upon hire lie;
Ne sende men into Walakye,
To Pruce and into Tartarye,
To Alisandre, ne into Turkye,
And bidde him faste anoon that he
Go hoodless into the Drye See,
And come hoom by the Carrenar,
And saye, 'Sire, be now right war
That I may of you heere sayn
Worshipe er that ye come again.'
She ne used no swiche knakkes smale.
  But wherfore that I telle my tale?
Right on this same, as I have said,
Was hoolly al my love laid.
For certes she was, that sweete wif,
My suffisance, my lust, my lif,
Myn hap, myn hele, and al my blesse,
My worldes welfare, and my goddesse,
And I hoolly hires and everydeel."
  "By oure Lord," quod I, "I trowe you weel.
Hardily youre love was wel biset:
I noot how ye mighte have do bet."

1016. **do . . . shame,** i.e., accuse her of anything shameful. **1017. name,** reputation. **1018.** She did not wish to deal with any one disingenuously. **1019. siker,** certain; **fonde,** try. **1020. in balaunce,** i.e., on tenterhooks. **1021.** By ambiguous word or look. **1022. But if,** unless. **1023. Walakye,** Wallachia in Rumania. **1024. Pruce,** Prussia. **1025. Alisandre,** Alexandria in Egypt. **1027. Drye See,** Gobi Desert. **1028. Carrenar,** the lake Kara Nor, beside the Gobi Desert. **1030. sayn,** i.e., spoken. **1032. knakkes smale,** petty tricks. **1035. hoolly,** wholly. **1036. wif,** woman. **1037. suffisance,** satisfaction; **lust,** pleasure. **1038. hap,** happiness; **hele,** health; **blesse,** bliss. **1040. hires,** hers. **1041. weel,** well. **1042. Hardily,** certainly; **biset,** placed.

"Bet! ne no wight so wel!" quod he.
"I trowe it, sire," quod I, "pardee."
"Nay, leve it wel!" "Sire, so do I:
I leve you wel that trewely
You thoughte that she was the beste,
And to biholde the alderfaireste,
Who so hadde looked hire with youre yën."
"With mine? Nay, alle that hire sien
Saide and swore it was so.
And though they ne hadde, I wolde tho
Have loved best my lady free.
Though I hadde had al the beautee
That evere hadde Alcipiades,
And al the strengthe of Ercules,
And therto hadde the worthinesse
Of Alisander, and al the richesse
That evere was in Babyloine,
In Cartage or in Macedoine,
Or in Rome, or in Ninevee;
And therto also hardy be
As was Ector, so have I joye,
That Achilles slow at Troye—
And therfore was he slain also
In a temple, for bothe two
Were slain, he and Antilegius
(And so saith Dares Phrygius),
For love of Polyxena—
Or been as wis as Minerva,
I wolde evere, withoute drede,

1046. **leve,** believe. 1049. **alderfaireste,** fairest of all. 1051. **sien,** saw. 1056. **Alcipiades,** Alcibiades, an Athenian famous for his attractiveness. 1057. **Ercules,** Hercules. 1059. **Alisander,** Alexander the Great. 1060. **Babyloine,** Babylon. 1061. **Cartage,** Carthage; **Macedoine,** Macedonia, Alexander's kingdom. 1062. **Ninevee,** Nineveh. 1064. **Ector,** Hector, the Trojan hero. 1065. **slow,** slew. 1068. **Antilegius,** Antilochus for Archilochus: having killed Hector, the Greek Achilles fell in love with Hector's sister Polyxena, and when he and his companion Archilochus tried to obtain Polyxena they were both slain. 1069. **Dares Phrygius,** Dares the Trojan, presumed author of a first-hand account of the Trojan war. 1071. **Minerva,** Roman goddess of wisdom. 1072. **drede,** doubt.

Have loved hire, for I moste neede.
Neede? Nay, trewely, I gabbe now:
Nought neede, and I wol telle how.
For of good wil myn herte it wolde,
And eek to love hire I was holde,
As for the faireste and the beste.
She was so good, so have I reste,
As evere was Penolopee of Greece;
Or as the noble wif Lucrece,
That was the beste (he telleth thus
The Romain Titus Livius),
She was as good, and nothing lik,
Though hir stories be autentik:
Algate she was as trewe as she.
  But wherfore that I telle thee?
Whan I first my lady sey,
I was right yong, sooth to say,
And ful greet neede I hadde to lerne.
Whan myn herte wolde yerne
To love, it was a greet emprise.
But as my wit coude best suffise,
After my yonge, childly wit,
Withoute drede, I bisette it
To love hire in my beste wise,
To do hire worshipe and the servise
That I coude tho, by my trouthe,
Withoute feining outher slouthe:
For wonder fain I wolde hire see:
So muchel it amended me,
That whan I sawgh hire first amorwe
I was warisshed of al my sorwe
Of al day after til it were eve:

1074. **gabbe,** rave. 1077. **holde,** obligated. 1080. **Penolopee,** Penelope, the long-suffering, virtuous wife of Odysseus. 1081. **Lucrece,** whose famous rape and suicide are told by Roman historian Livy. 1085. **hir,** i.e., Lucrece's; **autentik,** authentic. 1086. **Algate,** at any rate. 1088. **sey,** saw. 1092. **emprise,** undertaking. 1094. **childly,** childish. 1095. **drede,** doubt; **bisette,** applied. 1099. Without shirking or negligence. 1100. **fain,** gladly. 1102. **amorwe,** in the morning. 1103. **warisshed,** cured.

Me thoughte nothing mighte me greve,
Were my sorwes nevere so smerte.
And yit she sit so in myn herte
That, by my trouthe, I nolde nought
For al this world out of my thought
Leve my lady. No, trewely."
"Now, by my trouthe, sire," quod I,
"Me thinketh ye have swich a chaunce
As shrifte withoute repentaunce."
"Repentaunce! Nay, fy," quod he.
"Sholde I now repente me
To love? Nay, certes, thanne were I wel
Wers than was Achitofel,
Or Antenor, so have I joye,
The traitor that bitraised Troye,
Or the false Geneloun,
He that purchased the tresoun
Of Rowland and of Oliver.
Nay, whil I am alive heer
I nil forgete hire neveremo."
"Now, goode sire," quod I tho,
"Ye han wel told me herbifore—
It is no neede to reherce more—
How ye saw hire first and where:
But wolde ye telle me the manere
To hire which was youre firste speeche,
Therof I wolde you biseeche;
And how she knew first youre thought—
Whether ye loved hire or nought;
And telleth me eek what ye have lore—
I herde you telle herbifore."
"Ye," saide he, "thou noost what thou menest:

1107. sit, sits, remains. **1110. Leve,** leave. **1112. chaunce,** i.e., good luck. **1113.** As to be absolved without having repented, i.e., to receive a blessing without having suffered for it. **1117. Wers,** worse; **Achitofel,** who stirred up David's son Absalom to revolt against his father. **1119. bitraised,** betrayed. **1120. Geneloun,** Ganelon, who betrayed Roland and Oliver in the Charlemagne legend. **1121. purchased the tresoun,** procured the betrayal. **1134. lore,** lost.

I have lost more than thou weenest."
  "What los is that?" quod I tho.
"Nil she nat love you? Is it so?
Or have ye ought doon amis
That she hath left you? Is it this?
For Goddes love, telle me al."
  "Bifore God," quod he, "and I shal.
I saye right as I have said:
On hire was al my love laid,
And yit she niste it nat, nevere a deel,
Nought longe time, leve it weel.
For be right siker, I dorste nought,
For al this world, telle hire my thought;
Ne I wolde have wratthed hire, trewely.
For woostou why? She was lady
Of the body—she hadde the herte,
And who hath that may nat asterte.
But for to keepe me fro idelnesse,
Trewely, I dide my bisinesse
To make songes as I best coude;
And ofte time I soong hem loude,
And made songes thus a greet deel—
Although I coude nat make so weel
Songes, ne knowe the art al
As coude Lamekes sone Tubal,
That foond out first the art of song:
For as his brothers hamers roong
Upon his anvelt up and down,
Therof he took the firste soun;
But Greekes sayn Pyctagoras,
That he the firste finder was

1146. niste, knew not; **deel,** bit. **1147. leve,** believe. **1148. siker,** certain. **1150. wratthed,** angered. **1151. woostou,** do you know. **1152. Of the,** i.e., who controlled my. **1153.** And if some one has that, the victim may not escape. **1161. Lamekes,** Lamech's: according to the Bible, Jubal invented instrumental music and his brother Tubalcain devised metal-working. **1162. foond out,** invented. **1163. hamers,** hammers; **roong,** rang. **1164. anvelt,** anvil. **1165. soun,** i.e., melody. **1166. Pyctagoras,** Pythagoras. **1167. finder,** inventor.

Of the art—Aurora telleth so.
But therof no fors of hem two:
Algates songes thus I made
Of my feeling, myn herte to glade.
And lo, this was alderferst—
I noot wher it were the werst:
  'Lord, it maketh myn herte light,
Whan I thenke on that sweete wight,
That is so seemely on to see;
And wisshe to God it mighte so be
That she wolde holde me for hir knight,
My lady that is so fair and bright.'
  Now have I told thee, sooth to say,
My firste song. Upon a day
I bithoughte me what wo
And sorwe that I suffred tho
For hire, and yit she wiste it nought,
Ne telle hire dorste I nat my thought.
'Allas,' thoughte I, 'I can no reed,
And but I telle hire, I am but deed;
And if I telle hire, to saye right sooth,
I am adrad she wol be wroth.
Allas, what shal I thanne do?'
  In this debaat I was so wo
Me thoughte myn herte braste atwain.
So at the laste, sooth to sayn,
I bithoughte me that Nature
Ne formed nevere in creature
So muche beautee, trewely,
And bountee, withoute mercy.
In hope of that my tale I tolde,
With sorwe, as that I nevere sholde.

1168. Aurora, Peter of Riga's twelfth-century versification of the Bible. **1169. fors,** matter. **1170. Algates,** at any rate. **1171. glade,** gladden. **1172. alderferst,** first of all. **1173. noot,** know not; **wher,** whether. **1184. wiste,** knew. **1186. can no reed,** know no remedy. **1187. but,** unless; **deed,** dead. **1191. wo,** woeful. **1192. braste,** would break; **atwain,** in two. **1197. bountee,** excellence. **1199. as that,** i.e., in a way that.

For needes, and maugree myn heed,
I moste have told hire or be deed!
I noot wel how that I bigan—
Ful yvele reherce it I can;
And eek, as helpe me God withal,
I trowe it was in the dismal—
That was the ten woundes of Egypte.
For many a word I overskipte
In my tale, for pure fere
Lest my wordes misset were;
With sorweful herte and woundes dede,
Softe and quaking for pure drede
And shame, and stinting in my tale,
For ferde, and myn hewe al pale:
Ful ofte I weex bothe pale and reed;
Bowing to hire, I heeng the heed;
I dorste nat ones looke hire on,
For wit, manere, and al was goon.
I saide 'Mercy,' and no more:
It was no game, it sat me sore.
  So at the laste, sooth to sayn,
Whan that myn herte was come again—
To telle shortly al my speeche—
With hool herte I gan hire biseeche
That she wolde be my lady sweete,
And swoor and gan hire hertely hete
Evere to be stedefast and trewe,
And love hire alway fresshly newe,
And nevere other lady have,
And al hir worshipe for to save

1200. maugree, despite; **heed,** head. **1201. moste,** must. **1202. noot,** know not. **1203. yvele,** badly. **1205. dismal,** evil days. **1206.** The evil days (Latin *dies mali*) of the year, which were thought to arrive periodically, are here associated with the Ten Plagues visited upon the Egyptians (Old French *dix mals*). **1209. misset were,** should be misconstrued. **1210. dede,** deadly. **1212. stinting,** halting. **1213. For ferde,** terrified. **1214. weex,** grew; **reed,** red. **1215. heeng,** hung. **1219. sat,** i.e., afflicted. **1225. swoor,** swore; **hertely,** sincerely; **hete,** promise. **1229. worshipe,** reputation for womanly virtue.

As I best coude—I swoor hire this.
'For youres is al that evere ther is
For everemore, myn herte sweete,
And nevere to false you, but I mete,°
I nil, as wis° God helpe me so.'
And whan I hadde my tale ydo,
God woot, she accounted nat a stree°
Of al my tale—so thoughte me.
To telle shortly right as it is,
Trewely hir answere it was this;
I can nat now wel countrefete°
Hir wordes, but this was the grete°
Of hir answere: she saide nay
Al outrely.° Allas, that day
The sorwe I suffred and the wo,
That trewely Cassandra,° that so
Biwailed the destruccioun
Of Troye and of Ilioun,°
Hadde nevere swich sorwe as I tho.
I dorste namore saye therto
For pure fere, but stal° away.
And thus I lived ful many a day,
That trewely I hadde no neede
Ferther than my beddes hede°
Nevere a day to seeche° sorwe:
I foond° it redy every morwe,
Forwhy I loved hire in no gere.°
So it bifel another yere
I thoughte ones I wolde fonde°
To do hire knowe° and understonde
My wo, and she wel understood

1233. **false,** betray; **but I mete,** unless I'm dreaming. **1234. wis,** surely. **1236. stree,** straw. **1240. countrefete,** imitate. **1241. grete,** substance. **1243. Al outrely,** absolutely. **1245. Cassandra,** one of Priam's daughters who foresaw the destruction of her father's city. **1247. Ilioun,** the citadel of Troy. **1250. stal,** stole. **1253. hede,** head. **1254. seeche,** seek. **1255. foond,** found. **1256. Forwhy,** because; **in no gere,** i.e., with no possibility of changing. **1258. fonde,** try. **1259. do hire knowe,** make her realize.

That I ne wilned no thing but good
And worshipe, and to keepe hir name
Over alle thinges, and drede hir shame,
And was so bisy hire to serve,
And pitee were I sholde sterve,
Sith that I wilned noon harm, ywis—
So whan my lady knew al this,
My lady yaf me al hoolly
The noble yifte of hir mercy,
Saving hir worshipe, by alle wayes—
Dredelees I mene none othere wayes—
And therwith she yaf me a ring,
I trowe it was the firste thing.
But if myn herte was ywaxe
Glad, that is no neede to axe.
As helpe me God, I was as blive
Raised, as fro deeth to live;
Of alle happes the alderbeste,
The gladdest and the moste at reste.
For trewely that sweete wight,
Whan I hadde wrong and she the right,
She wolde alway so goodly
Foryive me, so debonairly—
In al my youthe, in al chaunce,
She took me in hir governaunce.
Therwith she was alway so trewe
Oure joye was evere yliche newe;
Oure hertes weren so evene a paire
That nevere nas that oon contraire
To that other for no wo;
Forsoothe yliche they suffred tho
Oo blisse and eek oo sorwe bothe;
Yliche they were bothe glade and wrothe;

1261. **wilned,** desired. 1263. **drede,** fear for. 1265. **sterve,** die. 1270. **Saving hir worshipe,** keeping her honor safe. 1271. **Dredelees,** doubtless. 1274. **ywaxe,** grown. 1275. **axe,** ask. 1276. **blive,** quickly. 1278. **happes,** happinesses; **alderbeste,** best of all. 1279. **moste at reste,** i.e., most satisfying. 1283. **debonairly,** modestly. 1287. **yliche,** alike. 1291. **tho,** then.

Al was us oon, withoute were;
And thus we lived ful many a yere
So wel I can nat telle how."
"Sire," quod I, "wher is she now?"
"Now?" quod he, and stinte anoon.
Therwith he weex as deed as stoon,
And saide, "Allas that I was bore,
That was the los that herbifore
I tolde thee that I hadde lorn.
Bithenke how I saide herbiforn,
'Thou woost ful litel what thou menest:
I have lost more than thou weenest.'
God woot, allas, right that was she."
"Allas, sire, how? What may that be?"
"She is deed." "Nay!" "Yis, by my trouthe."
"Is that your los? By God, it is routhe."
And with that word right anoon
They gan to strake forth; al was doon
For that time the hert-hunting.
With that me thoughte that this king
Gan hoomwardes for to ride
Unto a place was ther biside,
Which was from us but a lite,
A *long castel* with walles *white,*
By saint *Johan,* on a *riche hil,*
As me mette; but thus it fil;
Right thus me mette, as I you telle,
That in the castel ther was a belle,
As it hadde smite houres twelve;
Therwith I awook myselve,
And foond me lying in my bed;
And the book that I hadde red

1294. were, doubt. **1298. stinte,** stopped. **1299. weex,** grew; **deed,** dead. **1300. bore,** born. **1302. lorn,** lost. **1303. Bithenke,** remember. **1309. routhe,** pity. **1311. strake forth,** announce with the horn the hunt's successful end. **1316. lite,** little. **1317. long castel, white,** the latter stands for Blanche, the former for Lancaster (Long-Caster); Blanche was Duchess of Lancaster. **1318. Johan, riche hil,** for John of Richmond (Rich-Mount), John of Gaunt's original title. **1319. me mette,** I dreamed; **fil,** befell. **1324. foond,** found.

Of Alcyone and Ceys the king,
And of the goddes of sleeping,
I foond it in myn hand ful evene.
Thoughte I, "This is so quainte a swevene,°
That I wol, by proces° of time,
Fonde° to putte this swevene in ryme,
As I can best, and that anoon."
This was my swevene; now it is doon.

1329. swevene, dream. **1330. by proces,** in due course. **1331. Fonde,** try.

THE HOUSE OF FAME

Book One

PROEM

God turne us every dreem to goode:
For it is wonder, by the roode,°
To my wit, what causeth swevenes,°
Either on morwes° or on evenes,
And why th'effect° folweth of some,
And of some it shal nevere come;
Why that is an avisioun,°
And why this a revelacioun,°
Why this a dreem, why that a swevene,°
And nought to every man lich evene;°
Why this a fantome, why thise oracles,°
I noot,° but who so of thise miracles
The causes knoweth bet° than I,
Divine he,° for I certainly
Ne can° hem nought, ne nevere thinke
Too bisily my wit to swinke°
To knowe of hir signifiaunce,
The gendres,° neither the distaunce°
Of times of hem, ne the causes,
Or why this is more than that cause is—
As if folkes complexiouns°
Make hem dreme of reflexiouns,°
Or elles thus, as othere sayn,

2. **roode,** cross. 3. **swevenes,** dreams. 4. **morwes,** mornings. 5. **effect,** anticipated result. 7–8. **avisioun, revelacioun,** apparently dreams of supernatural origin. 9. **dreem, swevene,** these are hard to distinguish. 10. **lich evene,** exactly the same. 11. **fantome,** deceitful dream; **oracles,** prophetic dreams. 12. **noot,** don't know. 13. **bet,** better. 14. **Divine he,** let him guess. 15. **can,** know. 16. **swinke,** belabor. 18. **gendres,** kinds; **distaunce,** interval. 21. **complexiouns,** temperaments. 22. **reflexiouns,** reflections of waking events.

For too greet feblenesse of hir brain,
By abstinence or by siknesse,
Prison, stewe, or greet distresse,
Or elles by disordinaunce
Of naturel acustomaunce,
That som man is too curious
In studye, or malencolious,
Or thus, so inly ful of drede
That no man may him boote bede;
Or elles that devocioun
Of some, and contemplacioun
Causeth swiche dremes ofte,
Or that the cruel lif unsofte
Which thise ilke loveres leden,
That hopen overmuche or dreden,
That purely hir impressiouns
Causeth hem avisiouns;
Or if that spirits have the might
To make folk to dreme anight;
Or if the soule of propre kinde
Be so parfit, as men finde,
That it forwoot that is to come,
And that it warneth al and some
Of everich of hir aventures
By avisions or by figures,
But that oure flessh ne hath no might
To understonde it aright,
For it is warned too derkly;
But why the cause is, nought woot I.
Wel worthe of this thing grete clerkes
That trete of this and othere werkes,
For I of noon opinioun
Nil as now make mencioun,

27–28. Or else through disordering of their natural routine. **29. som,** one; **curious,** painstaking. **30. malencolious,** bilious. **32. boote bede,** offer help. **39–40.** That their dominant thoughts alone cause prophetic dreams. **43. propre kinde,** its own nature. **44. parfit,** perfect. **45. forwoot,** foreknows. **46. al and some,** each and every one. **48. figures,** symbols. **52. woot,** know. **53.** Good luck to great scholars in this matter.

But only that the holy roode
Turne us every dreem to goode;
For nevere sith that I was born,
Ne no man elles me biforn,
Mette, I trowe stedefastly,
So wonderful a dreem as I,
The tenthe day now of Decembre,
The which as I can now remembre
I wol you telle everydeel.

INVOCATION

But at my ginning, trusteth weel,
I wol make invocacioun,
With special devocioun,
Unto the God of Sleep anoon,
That dwelleth in a cave of stoon,
Upon a streem that cometh fro Lete,
That is a flood of helle unsweete;
Biside a folk men clepeth Cimerie,
Ther sleepeth ay this god unmerye,
With his sleepy thousand sones
That alway for to sleepe hir wone is;
That to this god that I of rede
Praye I that he wolde me speede
My swevene for to telle aright,
If every dreem stonde in his might;
And he that mevere is of al
That is, and was, and evere shal,
So yive hem joye that it heere
Of alle that they dreme toyere,
And for to stonde alle in grace
Of hir loves, or in what place
That hem were levest for to stonde,

61. **Mette,** dreamed. 66. **ginning,** beginning. 71. **Lete,** Lethe. 73. **clepeth,** call; **Cimerie,** the Cimmerians, who lived in a perpetually clouded land. 75. **sones,** sons. 76. **wone,** custom. 77. **of rede,** speak of. 81. **mevere,** mover, i.e., God. 84. **toyere,** this year. 87. **hem were levest,** they most preferred.

And shilde° hem fro poverte and shonde,°
And fro unhap° and eech disese,
And sende hem al that may hem plese
That take it wel and scorne it nought,
Ne it misdeeme° in hir thought
Thurgh malicious entencioun;
And whoso thurgh presumpsioun,
Or hate, or scorn, or thurgh envye,
Despit, or jape,° or vilainye,
Misdeeme it, praye I Jesus God,
That dreme he barefoot, dreme he shod,
That every harm that any man
Hath had sith the world bigan
Bifalle him therof er he sterve,°
And graunte he mote° it ful deserve,
Lo, with swich a conclusioun
As hadde of his avisioun
Cresus that was king of Lyde,°
That hye upon a gebet° dyde.°
This prayere shal he have of me:
I am no bet° in charitee.
Now herkneth, as I have you sayed,
What that I mette° er I abrayed.°

THE STORY

[The narrator dreams that he is inside a wonderful temple of glass, on the walls of which is portrayed the story of Virgil's *Aeneid.* The description of this occupies 370 lines.]

Whan I out at the dores cam,
I faste aboute me biheeld;
Thanne sawgh I but a large feeld,
As fer as that I mighte see,

88. shilde, defend; **shonde,** harm. **89. unhap,** misfortune. **92. misdeeme,** i.e., willfully misjudge. **96. jape,** levity. **101. sterve,** die. **102. mote,** may. **105.** For the story of Croesus of Lydia, see the Monk's Tale, ll. 81–120. **106. gebet,** gallows; **dyde,** died. **108. bet,** better. **110. mette,** dreamed; **abrayed,** awoke.

Withouten town, or hous, or tree,
Or bussh, or gras, or ered° lond.
For al the feeld nas but of sond,°
As smal° as man may see yit lie
In the desert of Libye.°
Ne I no manere creature
That is yformed by nature
Ne sawgh, me to rede or wisse.°
"O Crist," thoughte I, "that art in blisse,
Fro fantome and illusioun
Me save!" And with devocioun
Mine yën to the hevene I caste.
Tho was I war, lo, at the laste
That faste by the sonne, as hye
As kenne° mighte I with myn yë,
Me thoughte I sawgh an egle sore,°
But that it seemed muche more°
Than I hadde any egle sein.°
But this as sooth as deeth, certain,
It was of gold and shoon so brighte
That nevere saw men swich a sighte,
But if the hevene hadde ywonne°
Al newe of gold another sonne:
So shoon the egles fetheres brighte,
And somwhat downward gan it lighte.

Book Two

PROEM

Now herkneth, every manere man
That Englissh understonde can,
And listneth of my dreem to lere,°
For now at erst° shul ye heere

116. **ered,** plowed. 117. **sond,** sand. 118. **smal,** fine. 119. **Libye,** Libya. 122. **rede,** advise; **wisse,** direct. 129. **kenne,** i.e., see. 130. **sore,** soar. 131. **more,** larger. 132. **sein,** seen. 136. **But if,** unless; **ywonne,** gained.
3. **lere,** learn. 4. **at erst,** for the first time.

So sely an avisioun
That Isaie ne Scipioun,
Ne king Nabugodonosor,
Pharao, Turnus, ne Elcanor,
Ne mette swich a dreem as this.
Now faire, blisful, O Cypris,
So be my favour at this time;
And ye me to endite and ryme
Helpeth, that on Parnaso dwelle,
By Elicon, the clere welle.
O Thought, that wroot al that I mette,
And in the tresorye it shette
Of my brain, now shal men see
If any vertu in thee be
To telle al my dreem aright:
Now kithe thyn engin and thy might.

THE STORY

This egle of which I have you told,
That shoon with fetheres as of gold,
Which that so hye gan to sore,
I gan biholde more and more,
To see the beautee and the wonder;
But nevere was ther dint of thonder,
Ne that thing that men calle foudre—
That smoot somtime a towr to powdre
And in his swifte coming brende—
That so swithe gan descende
As this fowl, whan it biheeld

5. **sely,** auspicious. 6. **Isaie,** Isaiah, whose prophecy is framed in a vision; **Scipioun,** Scipio, whose dream is narrated by Cicero. 7. **Nabugodonosor,** Nebuchadnezzar, whose dreams were interpreted by Daniel. 8. **Pharao,** Pharaoh, whose dream was interpreted by Joseph; **Turnus,** which of several dream-like apparitions to Aeneas' antagonist is meant is not clear. **Elcanor,** identification uncertain. 9. **mette,** dreamed. 10. **Cypris,** Venus. 13–14. **that . . . Elicon,** i.e., the Muses associated with Parnassus and Helicon. 16. **shette,** shut. 18. **vertu,** power. 20. **kithe,** make known; **engin,** ingenuity. 26. **dint,** bolt. 27. **foudre,** lightning. 28. **smoot,** smote. 29. **his,** its; **brende,** burnt. 30. **swithe,** swiftly.

That I aroume was in the feeld.
And with his grimme pawes stronge,
Within his sharpe nailes longe,
Me fleeing in a swap he hente,
And with his sours ayain up wente,
Me carying in his clawes starke,
As lightly as I were a larke,
How hye I can nat telle you;
For I cam up, I niste how;
For so astonied and asweved
Was every vertu in my heved—
What with his sours and with my drede—
That al my feeling gan to dede,
Forwhy it was too greet affray.
  Thus I longe in his clawes lay
Til at the laste he to me spak
In mannes vois, and saide "Awak!
And be nat agast, for shame,"
And called me tho by my name;
And for I sholde the bet abraide,
Me mette, "Awak!" to me he saide
Right in the same vois and stevene
That useth oon that I coude nevene.
And with that vois, sooth for to sayn,
My minde cam to me again,
For it was goodly said to me:
So was it nevere wont to be.
And herwithal I gan to stere,
And he me in his feet to bere,
Til that he felte that I hadde hete,
And felte eek that myn herte bete,
And tho gan he me to disporte,

32. **aroume,** at large. 33. **pawes,** i.e., talons. 35. **Flying, he seized me with a swish.** 36. **sours,** upward flight. 37. **starke,** powerful. 40. **niste,** didn't know. 41. **astonied,** stunned; **asweved,** dazed. 42. **vertu,** i.e., sense; **heved,** head. 44. **dede,** deaden. 45. **Forwhy,** because; **affray,** fright. 51. **abraide,** come to my senses. 53. **stevene,** tone. 54. **nevene,** name. 58. **wont,** accustomed. 59. **stere,** stir. 61. **hete,** heat, life. 63. **tho,** then; **disporte,** cheer up.

And with wordes to conforte,
And saide twies, "Sainte Marye,
Thou art noyous for to carye!
And nothing needeth it, pardee;
For also wis God helpe me,
As thou noon harm shalt have of this;
And this caas that bitid thee is
Is for thy lore and for thy prow.
Lat see, darst thou yit looke now?
Be ful assured, boldely,
I am thy freend." And therwith I
Gan for to wondren in my minde.
"O God," thoughte I, "that madest kinde,
Shal I noon other wayes die?
Wher Joves wol me stellifye?
Or what thing may this signifye?
I neither am Ennoc ne Elie,
Ne Romulus ne Ganymede,
That was ybore up, as men rede,
To hevene with daun Jupiter,
And maad the goddes boteler."
Lo, this was tho my fantasye.
But he that bar me gan espye
That I so thoughte, and saide this:
"Thou deemest of thyself amis.
For Joves is nat theraboute—
I dar wel putte thee out of doute—
To make of thee as yit a sterre;
But er I bere thee muche ferre,
I wol thee telle what I am,
And whider thou shalt, and why I cam
To do this, so that thou take

66. **noyous,** hard. 68. **also wis,** just as surely as. 70. **bitid thee is,** has happened to you. 71. **lore,** instruction; **prow,** benefit. 76. **kinde,** nature. 78. Will Jupiter turn me into a star. 80. **Ennoc,** Enoch, of whom it is said that God took him—presumably up to heaven; **Elie,** Elijah, who rode to heaven in a chariot. 81. **Romulus,** who was carried to heaven by Mars. 82. **ybore,** carried. 83. **daun,** lord. 84. **boteler,** butler. 89. **Joves,** Jupiter; **theraboute,** i.e., engaged in that. 91. **sterre,** star. 92. **ferre,** farther.

Good herte, and nat for fere quake."
"Gladly," quod I. "Now, wel," quod he,
"First, I that in my feet have thee—
Of which thou hast a fere and wonder—
Am dwelling with the god of thonder,
Which that men callen Jupiter,
That dooth me flee ful ofte fer
To do al his comandement.
And for this cause he hath me sent
To thee; now herke, by thy trouthe:
Certain, he hath of thee routhe
That thou so longe, trewely,
Hast served so ententifly
His blinde nevew Cupido,
And faire Venus also,
Withoute guerdon evere yit,
And neverethelesse hast set thy wit—
Although that in thyn heed ful lite is—
To make bookes, songes, dites,
In rym, or elles in cadence,
As thou best canst, in reverence
Of Love, and of his servants eke,
That have his service sought and seeke;
And painest thee to praise his art,
Although thou haddest nevere part.
Wherfore, also God me blesse,
Joves halt it greet humblesse
And vertu eek, that thou wolt make
Anight ful ofte thyn heed to ake,
In thy studye so thou writest,
And everemo of Love enditest,
In honour of him, and in praisinges,
And in his folkes fortheringes;
And in hir matere al devisest,

102. **dooth me flee,** makes me fly. 106. **routhe,** pity. 108. **ententifly,** diligently. 109. **nevew,** nephew. 111. **guerdon,** reward. 113. **heed,** head; **lite,** little. 115. **cadence,** ? rhythm. 119. **painest thee,** take pains. 120. **part,** share. 121. **also,** so. 122. **Joves,** Jupiter; **halt,** holds. 128. And in furthering his folk.

And nought him nor his folk despisest,
Although thou maist go in the daunce
Of hem that him list nat avaunce.°
Wherfore as I saide, ywis,
Jupiter considereth this,
And also, beau sire,° othere thinges:
That is, that thou hast no tidinges
Of Loves folk, if they be glade,
Ne of nought elles that God made;
And nought only fro fer contree
That ther no tiding cometh to thee,
But of thy verray neighebores,
That dwelle almost at thy dores,
Thou heerest neither that nor this:
For whan thy labour doon al is,
And hast maad alle thy rekeninges,
In stede of reste and newe thinges,
Thou goost hoom to thy hous anoon,
And also dombe as any stoon,
Thou sittest at another book,
Til fully daswed° is thy look;
And livest thus as an heremite,°
Although thyn abstinence is lite.°
And therfore Joves, thurgh his grace,
Wol° that I bere thee to a place
Which that highte the Hous of Fame,
To do thee som disport and game,
In som recompensacioun
Of labour and devocioun
That thou hast had, lo, causelees,
To Cupido the recchelees.°
And thus this god, thurgh his merite,
Wol with som manere thing thee quite,°
So that thou wolt be of good cheere.
For trust wel that thou shalt yheere,

132. Of those whom he does not wish to prosper. **135. beau sire,** fair sir. **150. daswed,** dazed. **151. heremite,** hermit. **152. lite,** little. **154. Wol,** wills. **160. recchelees,** careless. **162. quite,** requite.

Whan we be come ther I saye,
Mo wonder thinges, dar I laye,°
Of Loves folkes mo tidinges,
Bothe soothe sawes and lesinges,°
And mo loves newe bigonne,
And longe yserved loves wonne,°
And mo loves casuelly
That bitide,° no man woot why,
But as a blind man stert° an hare;
And more jolitee and fare°
Whil that they finde love of steel,
As thinketh hem, and overal weel;°
Mo discordes, mo jalousies,
Mo murmures and mo novelries,°
And mo dissimulaciouns,
And feined reparaciouns,°
And mo berdes in two houres,
Withoute rasour or sisoures,
Ymaad, than graines be of sondes;°
And eek mo holding in hondes,°
And also mo renovelaunces°
Of olde forleten° aquaintaunces;
Mo love-dayes and accordes
Than on instruments be cordes;
And eek of loves mo eschaunges°
Than evere cornes were in graunges.°
Unnethe maistou trowen° this?"
Quod he. "No, helpe me God so wis,"°
Quod I. "No, why?" quod he. "For it
Were impossible to my wit,

166. wonder, wondrous; **laye,** bet. **168.** Both true sayings and lies. **170. yserved,** worked for; **wonne,** won. **171–72. loves . . . bitide,** loves that occur accidentally. **173. stert,** starts. **174. fare,** activity. **176. weel,** well. **178. murmures,** complaints; **novelries,** i.e., new loves. **180.** And pretend reconciliations. **181–83.** And more beards made in two hours without razor or scissors than there are grains of sand; i.e., more deceptions. **184. holding in hondes,** keeping in suspense. **185. renovelaunces,** renewals. **186. forleten,** abandoned. **189. eschaunges,** exchanges. **190. cornes,** kernels; **graunges,** barns. **191. Unnethe,** hardly; **trowen,** believe. **192. wis,** surely.

Though that Fame hadde alle the pies
In al a realme, and alle the spies,
How that yit she sholde heere al this,
Or they espye it." "O, yis, yis,"
Quod he to me, "that can I preve
By reson worthy for to leve,
So that thou yive thyn advertence
To understonde my sentence.
First shalt thou heere wher she dwelleth,
And so thyn owene book it telleth:
Hir palais stant, as I shal saye,
Right evene in middes of the waye
Bitwixen hevene and erthe and see,
That whatsoevere in al thise three
Is spoken, either privee or apert,
The air therto is so overt,
And stant eek in so just a place,
That every soun moot to it pace;
Or what so cometh fro any tonge
Be it rouned, red, or songe,
Or spoke in suretee or in drede,
Certain it moste thider neede.
Now herkne wel, forwhy I wil
Tellen thee a propre skil,
And worth a demonstracioun,
In myn imaginacioun.
  Geffrey, thou woost right wel this,
That every kindely thing that is
Hath a kindely stede ther he
May best in it conserved be,
Unto which place every thing,
Thurgh his kindely enclining,

195. pies, magpies, birds that were commonly reputed to be spreaders of rumors. **199. preve,** prove. **220. leve,** believe. **201. advertence,** attention. **202. sentence,** meaning. **205. stant,** stands. **209. privee or apert,** privately or publicly. **210. overt,** unobstructed. **212. moot,** must; **pace,** pass. **214. rouned,** whispered; **red,** read. **215. suretee,** confidence. **216. moste,** must; **thider,** i.e., go thither. **217. forwhy,** because. **218. skil,** reason. **222. kindely,** natural. **223. kindely stede,** natural place.

Meveth° for to come to
Whan that it is away therfro;
As thus: lo, thou maist alday° see
That any thing that hevy be,
As stoon, or leed, or thing of wighte°—
And bere it nevere so hye on highte,
Lat go thyn hand, it falleth down.
Right so saye I by fir or soun,
Or smoke or othere thinges lighte;
Alway they seeke upward on highte
Whil eech of hem is at his large:
Light thing upward and downward charge.°
And for this cause maist thou see
That every river to the see
Enclined is to go by kinde;°
And by thise skiles,° as I finde,
Hath fissh dwelling in flood and see,
And trees eek in erthe be;
Thus every thing, by this resoun,
Hath his propre mansioun°
To which he seeketh to repaire,
As ther it sholde nat apaire.°
Lo, this sentence is knowen couth°
Of every philosophres mouth,
As Aristotle and daun° Platon,
And othere clerkes many oon;
And to conferme my resoun,
Thou woost wel this, that speeche is soun,
Or elles no man mighte it heere.
Now herke what I wol thee lere:°
Soun is nought but air ybroken;
And every speeche that is spoken,
Loud or privee, foul or fair,
In his substance is but air.

227. **Meveth,** moves. 229. **alday,** constantly. 231. **leed,** lead; **wighte,** weight. 238. **charge,** heavy thing. 241. **kinde,** nature. 242. **skiles,** reasons. 246. **mansioun,** dwelling place. 248. **apaire,** deteriorate. 249. **sentence,** i.e., fact; **knowen couth,** well-known. 251. **daun,** master. 256. **lere,** teach.

For as flaumbe is but lighted smoke,
Right so soun is air ybroke.
But this may be in many wise,
Of which I wil thee two devise:
Of soun that cometh of pipe or harpe.
For whan a pipe is blowen sharpe,
The air is twist with violence
And rent—lo, this is my sentence.
Eek whan men harpe stringes smite,
Whether it be muche or lite,
Lo, with the strook the air tobreketh:
And right so breketh it whan men speketh.
Thus woost thou wel what thing is speeche.
Now hennesforth I wol thee teche
How every speeche, or noise, or soun,
Thurgh his multiplicacioun,
Though it were piped of a mous,
Moot neede come to Fames hous.
I preve it thus—taak heede now—
By experience, for if that thou
Throwe on water now a stoon,
Wel woost thou it wol make anoon
A litel roundel as a cercle,
Paraunter brood as a covercle;
And right anoon thou shalt see weel
That wheel wol cause another wheel,
And that the thridde, and so forth, brother,
Every cercle causing other,
Widder than himselve was;
And thus fro roundel to compas,
Eech aboute other goinge,
Caused of otheres steringe,
And multiplying everemo,

261. flaumbe, flame. **268. sentence,** point. **271. strook,** stroke; **tobreketh,** shatters. **273. woost,** know. **276. his,** its. **277. of,** by. **278. Moot,** must. **279. preve,** prove. **283. roundel,** ring. **284. Paraunter,** perhaps; **covercle,** pot-lid. **285. weel,** well. **289. Widder,** wider. **290.** i.e., And thus from a little ring to the full circumference. **292. steringe,** stirring.

Til that it be so fer° ygo,
Til it at bothe brinkes be:
Although thou mowe° it nat ysee
Above, it gooth yit alway under,
Although thou thenke it a greet wonder.
And who so saith of trouthe I varye,
Bid him preven° the contrarye.
And right thus every word, ywis,
That loude or pryvee spoken is,
Meveth° first an air aboute,
And of this meving, out of doute,
Another air anoon is meved;
As I have of the water preved
That every cercle causeth other,
Right so of air, my leve° brother:
Everich air another stereth°
More and more, and speeche upbereth,
Of vois, or noise, or word, or soun,
Ay thurgh multiplicacioun,
Til it be atte° Hous of Fame:
Taak it in ernest or in game.
  Now have I told, if thou have minde,
How speeche or soun, of pure kinde,°
Enclined is upward to meve—
This maist thou feele wel I preve—
And that same stede, ywis,
That every thing enclined to is
Hath his kindeliche stede;°
That sheweth it, withouten drede,°
That kindely° the mansioun
Of every speeche, of every soun,
Be it either foul or fair,
Hath his kinde° place in air.
And sin that every thing that is

294. **fer,** far. 296. **mowe,** may. 300. **preven,** prove. 303. **Meveth,** moves. 308. **leve,** dear. 309. **stereth,** stirs. 313. **atte,** at the. 316. **of pure kinde,** by their very nature. 319–21. ? And that every location, indeed, to which each thing is inclined, has *its* proper location. 322. **drede,** doubt. 323. **kindely,** naturally. 326. **kinde,** natural.

Out of his kinde place, ywis,
Meveth thider for to go,
If it awaye be therfro—
As I have bifore preved thee—
It sueth,° every soun, pardee,
Moveth kindely to pace°
Al up into his kindely° place.
And this place of which I telle,
Ther as Fame list° to dwelle,
Is set amiddes of thise three:
Hevene, erthe, and eek the see,
As most conservatif° the soun.
Thanne is this the conclusioun:
That every speeche of every man,
As I thee telle first bigan,
Meveth up on heigh to pace
Kindely to Fames place.
Tel me this now faithfully,
Have I nat preved thus simply,
Without any subtiltee
Of speeche, or greet prolixitee
Of termes of philosophye,
Of figures of poetrye,
Or colours of retorike?
Pardee, it oughte thee to like.°
For hard langage and hard matere
Is encumbrous° for to heere
Atones. Woost° thou nat wel this?"
And I answerde and saide, "Yis."
"Aha," quod he, "lo, so I can
Lewedly to a lewed° man
Speke, and shewe him swiche skiles°
That he may shake hem by the biles,°
So palpable they sholden be.

332. **sueth,** follows. 333. **kindely,** naturally; **pace,** pass. 334. **kindely,** natural. 336. **list,** it pleases. 339. **conservatif,** retentive of. 352. **like,** please. 354. **encumbrous,** bothersome. 355. **Woost,** know. 358. **Lewedly,** in layman's language; **lewed,** uneducated. 359. **skiles,** reasons. 360. **biles,** bills, beaks.

But tel me this, now praye I thee,
How thenketh thee my conclusioun?"
Quod he. "A good persuasioun,"
Quod I, "it is, and like to be
Right so as thou hast preved° me."
"By God," quod he, "and as I leve,°
Thou shalt have yit, er it be eve,
Of every word of this sentence
A preve° by experience;
And with thine eres heeren weel,°
Top and tail and everydeel,
That every word that spoken is
Cometh into Fames hous, ywis,
As I have said. What wilt thou more?"
And with this word upper to sore°
He gan, and saide, "By saint Jame,
Now wil we speke al of game.°
How farest thou?" quod he to me.
"Wel," quod I. "Now see," quod he,
"By thy trouthe, yond adown,
Wher° that thou knowest any town
Or hous or any other thing?
And whan thou hast of ought knowing,
Looke that thou warne me,
And I anoon shal telle thee
How fer° that thou art now therfro."
And I adown to° looken tho,
And biholde feeldes and plaines,
And now hilles and now mountaines,
Now valeyes, now forestes,
And now unnethes° grete beestes,
Now riveres, now citees,
Now townes, and now grete trees,
Now shippes sailing in the see.
But thus soone in a while he

366. **preved,** proved. 367. **leve,** believe. 370. **preve,** proof. 371. **weel,** well. 376. **sore,** soar. 378. **game,** pleasure. 382. **Wher,** whether. 387. **fer,** far. 388. **to,** i.e., began to. 392. **unnethes,** with difficulty.

Was flowen fro the ground so hye
That al the world, as to myn yë,
No more seemed than a prikke,
Or elles was the air so thikke
That I ne mighte nat discerne.
With that he spak to me as yerne,
And saide, "Seest thou any token
Of ought that in the world is spoken?"
I saide, "Nay." "No wonder nis,"
Quod he, "for half so heigh as this
Nas Alexander Macedo,
Ne the king daun Scipio,
That saw in dreem at point devis
Helle and erthe and paradis,
Ne eek the wrecche Dedalus,
Ne his child nice Icarus,
That fleegh so hye that the hete
His winges malte, and he fil wete
In mid the see, and ther he dreinte,
For whom was maked muche complainte.
Now turn upward," quod he, "thy face,
And bihold this large place,
This air, but looke thou ne be
Adrad of hem that thou shalt see.
For in this region, certain,
Dwelleth many a citezein,
Of which that speketh daun Plato:
Thise been the airissh beestes, lo!"
And so saw I al that meinee,
Bothe goon and also flee.

399. **prikke,** pin-prick. **402. yerne,** eagerly. **407. Macedo,** the Macedonian: Alexander was taken high in the air in a chariot drawn by griffins. 408. **Scipio,** see p. 651, ll. 31 ff. **409. at point devis,** perfectly. **411. Dedalus,** Daedalus, who invented wings with which he and his son Icarus could fly; but Icarus flew so near the sun that the wax with which the wings were fixed to him melted and he fell in the sea. **412. nice,** foolish. **413. fleegh,** flew. **414. malte,** melted; **fil,** fell. **415. dreinte,** drowned. **420. Adrad,** afraid. 423. **daun,** master. 425. **meinee,** company. 426. Both walking and also flying.

"Now," quod he, "cast up thyn yë;
See yonder, lo, the galaxye,
Which men clepeth the Milky Way
For it is whit (and some, parfay,
Callen it Watlinge Streete),
That ones was ybrent with hete
Whan the sonnes sone the rede,
That highte Pheton, wolde lede
Algate his fader carte and gie.
The carte hors gonne wel espye
That he coude no governaunce,
And gan for to lepe and launce,
And beren him now up, now down,
Til that he saw the Scorpioun–
Which that in hevene a signe is yit–
And he forfered lost his wit
Of that, and leet the reines goon
Of his hors, and they anoon
Gonne up to mounten and down descende,
Til bothe the air and erthe brende,
Til Jupiter, lo, at the laste,
Him slow and fro the carte caste.
Lo, is it nat a muchel meschaunce
To lete a fool han governaunce
Of thing that he can nat demeine?"
And with this word, sooth for to sayne,
He gan upper alway to sore,
And gladded me ay more and more,
So faithfully to me spak he.
Tho gan I to looken under me,
And biheeld the airissh beestes,
Cloudes, mistes, and tempestes,

430. whit, white; **parfay,** by my faith. **431. Watlinge Streete,** a famous road in England. **432. ybrent,** burned. **433.** When the son of the red sun. **434. highte,** was named; **Pheton,** Phaeton, who tried to drive the chariot of the sun his father with disastrous results. **435. Algate,** at all costs; **gie,** guide. **436. hors,** horses. **437.** That he had not learned control. **438. launce,** rear. **442. forfered,** terrified. **446. brende,** burnt. **448. slow,** slew. **451. demeine,** handle.

Snowes, hailes, raines, windes,
And th'engendring in hir kindes,°
Al the way thurgh which I cam.
"O God," quod I, "that made Adam,
Muche is thy might and thy noblesse."°
And tho° thoughte I upon Boece°
That writ, "A thought may flee° so hye
With fetheres of philosophye,
To passen everich element,
And whan he hath so fer° ywent,
Thanne may be seen bihinde his bak
Cloude, erthe,"—and al that I of spak.
Tho gan I waxen in a were°
And saide, "I woot° wel I am here,
But wher° in body or in gost
I noot,° ywis, but God, thou woost.
For more cleer entendement°
Nas me nevere yit ysent."
And thanne thoughte I on Marcian,°
And eek on Anteclaudian,°
That sooth was hir descripsioun
Of al the hevenes regioun,
As fer as that I saw the preve:°
Therfore I can hem now bileve.
With that this egle bigan to crye,
"Lat be," quod he, "thy fantasye.
Wilt thou lere of sterres ought?"°
"Nay, certainly," quod I, "right nought."
"And why?" "For I am now too old."
"Elles I wolde thee have told,"
Quod he, "the sterres names, lo,

460. i.e., And the various causes of each of them. **463. noblesse,** grandeur. **464. tho,** then; **Boece,** Boethius. **465. writ,** writes; **flee,** fly. **468. fer,** far. **471.** Then I began to come into doubt. **472. woot,** know. **473. wher,** whether. **474. noot,** don't know. **475. entendement,** comprehension. **477. Marcian,** Martianus Capella, who wrote about the heavens. **478. Anteclaudian,** the *Anticlaudianus* of Alanus de Insulis, which includes passages on the heavens. **481. preve,** proof. **485. lere,** learn; **sterres,** stars; **ought,** anything.

And alle the hevenes signes therto,
And which they been." "No fors,"° quod I.
"Yis, pardee," quod he. "Woostou° why?
For whan thou redest poetrye,
How goddes gonne stellifye°
Briddes, Fissh, Beest,° or him or here,
As the Raven or either Bere,°
Or Ariones Harpe fin,°
Castor, Pollux, or Delphin,°
Or Atalantes Doughtres° sevene—
How alle thise arn set in hevene.
For though thou have hem ofte on honde,°
Yit noostou° nat wher that they stonde."
"No fors,"° quod I, "it is no neede.
I leve° as wel, so God me speede,
Hem that write of this matere,
As though° I knewe hir places here;
And eek they shinen here so brighte
It sholde shenden° al my sighte
To looke on hem." "That may well be,"
Quod he, and so forth bar° he me
A while, and thanne he gan to crye
That nevere herde I thing so hye,
"Now up the heed,° for al is weel!
Saint Julian, lo, bon hostel!°
See heer the House of Fame, lo!
Maistou nat heeren that I do?"
"What?" quod I. "The grete soun,"
Quod he, "that rumbleth up and down

491. fors, matter. **492. Woostou,** do you know. **494. stellifye,** create constellations. **495. Briddes, Fissh, Beest,** apparently the constellations Aquila, Pisces, and Taurus; **here,** her. **496. Raven,** the constellation Corvus; **either Bere,** Ursa Minor and Ursa Major. **497. Ariones Harpe,** Arion's Harp, the constellation Lyra; **fin,** delicate. **498.** Castor and Pollux are the constellation Gemini; **Delphin,** the constellation Delphinus. **499. Atalantes Doughtres,** Atlas' daughters, the Pleiades. **501. have . . . honde,** often have to do with them. **502. noostou,** you don't know. **503. fors,** matter. **504. leve,** believe. **506. As though,** i.e., as if. **508. shenden,** ruin. **510. bar,** bore. **513. heed,** head. **514. Julian,** patron saint of hospitality; **bon hostel,** good hostelry.

In Fames hous, ful of tidinges,
Bothe of fair speeche and chidinges,
And of fals and sooth° compouned:°
Herke wel, it is nat rouned.°
Heerestou nat the grete swough?"°
"Yis, pardee," quod I, "wel ynough."
"And what soun is it lik?" quod he.
"Peter, beting of the see,"
Quod I, "ayain the rokkes holwe,°
Whan tempest dooth° the shippes swolwe;°
And lat a man stonde, out of doute,
A mile thennes and heere it route;°
Or elles lik the laste humblinge,°
After a clappe of oo thondringe,
Whan Joves° hath the air ybete.
But it dooth° me for fere swete."°
"Nay, dreed thee nat therof," quod he,
"It is no thing wol biten thee.
Thou shalt noon harm have, trewely."
And with this word bothe he and I
As neigh the place arrived were
As men may casten with a spere.
I niste° how, but in a streete
He sette me faire on my feete
And saide, "Walke forth a paas
And taak thyn aventure or caas°
That thou shalt finde in Fames place."
"Now," quod I, "whil we han space
To speke er that I go fro thee,
For the love of God, tel me—
In sooth that wol I of thee lere°—
If this noise that I heere
Be, as I have herd thee tellen,
Of folk that down in erthe dwellen,

521. **sooth,** true; **compouned,** mixed. 522. **rouned,** whispered. 523. **swough,** murmuring sound. 527. **holwe,** hollow. 528. **dooth,** causes; **swolwe,** swallow, founder. 530. **route,** roar. 531. **humblinge,** rumbling. 533. **Joves,** Jupiter. 534. **dooth,** makes; **swete,** sweat. 541. **niste,** didn't know. 544. **caas,** chance. 549. **lere,** learn.

And cometh heer in the same wise
As I thee herde er this devise?
That ther lives° body nis
In al that house that yonder is
That maketh al this loude fare?"°
"No," quod he," by sainte Clare,
And also wis God rede me;°
But oo thing I wil warne thee,
Of the which thou wolt have wonder:
Lo, to the Hous of Fame yonder—
Thou woost now how—cometh every speeche—
It needeth nought eft° thee to teche—
But understond now right wel this:
Whan any speeche ycomen is
Up to the palais, anoonright
It waxeth° like the same wight
Which that the word in erthe spak,
Be it clothed reed° or blak,
And so wereth° his liknesse
That spak the word, that thou wilt gesse
That it the same body be,
Man or womman, he or she.
And is nat this a wonder thing?"
"Yis," quod I tho,° "by hevene king."
And with this word, "Farewel," quod he,
"And here I wol abiden thee.
And God of hevene sende thee grace
Som good to lerne in this place."
And I of him took leve anoon,
And gan forth to the palais goon.

555. **lives,** living. 557. **fare,** bustle. 559. And as surely as God counsel me. 564. **eft,** again. 568. **waxeth,** becomes. 570. **reed,** red. 571. **wereth,** wears. 576. **tho,** then.

THE PARLIAMENT OF FOWLS

The lif so short, the craft so long to lerne,
Th'assay° so sharp, so hard the conqueringe,
The dredful joye alway that slit so yerne,°
Al this mene I by Love, that my feelinge
Astonieth° with his wonderful werkinge
So sore, ywis, that whan I on him thinke,
Nat woot I wel wher that I flete° or sinke.

For al be that I knowe nat Love in deede,
Ne woot how that he quiteth folk hir hire,°
Yit happeth me ful ofte in bookes rede
Of his miracles and his cruel ire;
That rede I wel, he wol be lord and sire:
I dar nat sayn—his strokes been so sore—
But° "God save swich a lord!"—I saye namore.

Of usage, what for lust and what for lore,°
On bookes rede I ofte, as I you tolde;
But wherfore that I speke al this: nat yore°
Agoon it happed me for to biholde
Upon a book, was write with lettres olde;
And therupon, a certain thing to lerne,
The longe day ful faste I redde and yerne.°

For out of olde feeldes, as men saith,
Cometh al this newe corn from yeer to yere;
And out of olde bookes, in good faith,
Cometh al this newe science that men lere.°
But now to purpos as of this matere:

2. **assay,** attempt. 3. **slit,** slides, slips away; **yerne,** quickly. 5. **Astonieth,** is astonished. 7. **woot,** know; **wher,** whether; **flete,** float. 9. **quiteth,** pays; **hire,** wages. 14. **But,** i.e., anything but. 15. **usage,** habit; **lust,** pleasure; **lore,** instruction. 17. **yore,** long. 21. **yerne,** eagerly. 25. **lere,** learn.

To rede forth so gan me to delite
That al that day me thoughte but a lite.

This book of which I make of mencioun
Entitled was al thus, as I shal telle:
"Tullius of the Dreem of Scipioun."
Chapitres sevene it hadde, of hevene and helle
And erthe, and soules that therinne dwelle;
Of which as shortly as I can it trete,
Of his sentence I wol you sayn the grete:

First telleth it when Scipion was come
In Affrike, how he meeteth Massinisse,
That him for joye in armes hath ynome;
Thanne telleth he hir speeche, and of the blisse
That was bitwixe hem til that day gan misse;
And how his auncestre African so dere
Gan in his sleep that night to him appere.

Thanne telleth it that from a sterry place
How African hath him Cartage shewed,
And warned him biforn of al his grace,
And saide what man, lered other lewed,
That loved commune profit, wel ythewed,
He sholde into a blisful place wende,
Ther as joye is that last withouten ende.

Thanne axed he if folk that now been dede
Han lif and dwelling in another place;
And African saide, "Ye, withouten drede,
And that oure present worldes lives space
Nis but a manere deeth, what way we trace.

28. lite, i.e., little while. **31.** i.e., Macrobius' edition of Marcus Tullius Cicero on the Dream of Scipio. **35. his sentence,** its story; **grete,** substance. **37. Massinisse,** Masinissa. **38. ynome,** taken. **40. misse,** come to an end. **41. African,** Scipio Africanus Major, the famous antagonist of Hannibal. **43. sterry,** starry. **44. Cartage,** Carthage. **46. lered,** learned; **other,** or; **lewed,** uneducated. **47. ythewed,** behaved. **49. last,** lasts. **50. axed,** asked; **dede,** dead. **52. drede,** doubt. **54.** Is nothing but a kind of death, whatever path we follow.

And rightful folk shul goon after they die
To hevene"; and shewed him the Galaxye.

Thanne shewed he him the litel erthe that here is,
At regard of the hevenes quantitee;
And after shewed he him the nine speres;
And after that the melodye herde he
That cometh of thilke speres thries three,
That welle is of musik and melodye
In this world here, and cause of armonye.

Thanne bad he him, sin erthe was so lite,
And deceivable, and ful of harde grace,
That he ne sholde him in the world delite.
Thanne tolde he him in certain yeres space
That every sterre sholde come into his place,
Ther it was first, and al sholde out of minde
That in this world is doon of al mankinde.

Thanne prayed him Scipion to telle him al
The way to come into that hevene blisse;
And he saide, "Know thyself first immortal,
And looke ay bisily thou werke and wisse
To commune profit, and thou shalt nat misse
To comen swiftly to this place dere,
That ful of blisse is, and of soules clere.

But brekeres of the lawe, sooth to sayne,
And likerous folk, after that they been dede
Shul whirle aboute th'erthe alway in paine,
Til many a world be passed, out of drede,
And that foryiven is hir wikked deede:
Thanne shal they comen into this blisful place,
To which to comen, God sende thee his grace."

58. **At regard of,** in comparison to; **quantitee,** size. 59. **speres,** spheres. 61. **thilke,** those same. 62. **welle,** source. 63. **armonye,** harmony. 64. **lite,** little. 65. **deceivable,** deceitful. 74. **wisse,** teach. 79. **likerous,** lecherous; **dede,** dead. 81. **drede,** doubt. 82. **that,** i.e., until.

The day gan folwen and the derke night,
That reveth beestes from hir bisinesse,°
Birafte me my book for lak of light,
And to my bed I gan me for to dresse,°
Fulfild of thought and bisy° hevinesse:
For bothe I hadde thing which that I nolde,
And eek I ne hadde that thing that I wolde.

But finally my spirit at the laste,
Forwery° of my labour al the day,
Took reste, that made me to sleepe faste;
And in my sleep I mette,° as that I lay,
How Affrican, right in the same array
That Scipion him saw bifore that tide,°
Was come, and stood right at my beddes side.

The wery hunter, sleeping in his bed,
To wode ayain his minde gooth anoon;
The juge dremeth how his plees been sped;
The cartere dremeth how his carte is goon;
The riche, of gold; the knight fight with his foon;°
The sike met he drinketh of the tonne;°
The lovere met he hath his lady wonne.

Can I nat sayn if that the cause were
For I hadde red of Affrican biforn,
That made me to mete° that he stood there:
But thus saide he: "Thou hast thee so wel born°
In looking of myn olde book totorn,°
Of which Macrobie roughte nat a lite,°
That somdeel of thy labour wolde I quite."°

86. **reveth,** takes away; **bisinesse,** anxiety. 88. **dresse,** prepare. 89. **Fulfild,** filled; **bisy,** anxious. 93. **Forwery,** tired out. 95. **mette,** dreamed. 97. **tide,** time. 103. **fight,** fights; **foon,** foes. 104. **met,** dreams; **tonne,** tun, i.e., vessel of medicinal liquid. 108. **mete,** dream. 109. **born,** behaved. 110. **totorn,** tattered. 111. **Macrobie,** Macrobius, editor of Cicero's *Dream of Scipio* in the form Chaucer knew it; **roughte,** cared; **lite,** little. 112. **quite,** repay.

Cytherea, thou blisful lady sweete,
That with thy firbrand dauntest whom thee lest,
And madest me this swevene for to mete,
Be thou myn help in this, for thou maist best;
As wisly as I sawgh thee north-north-west
Whan I bigan my swevene for to write,
So yif me might to ryme and eek t'endite.

This forsaide Affrican me hente anoon,
And forth with him unto a gate broughte,
Right of a park walled with greene stoon,
And over the gates with lettres large ywroughte
Ther were vers ywriten, as me thoughte,
On either side, of ful greet difference,
Of which I shal now sayn the plein sentence:

"Thurgh me men goon into that blisful place
Of hertes hele and deedly woundes cure;
Thurgh me men goon unto the welle of grace,
Ther greene and lusty May shal evere endure:
This is the way to al good aventure;
Be glad, thou redere, and thy sorwe of-caste;
Al open am I: passe in, and speed thee faste."

"Thurgh me men goon," thanne spak that other side,
"Unto the mortal strokes of the spere
Of which Desdain and Daunger is the gide,
That nevere yit shal fruit ne leves bere;
This streem you ledeth to the sorweful were
Ther as the fissh in prison is al drye:
Th'eschewing is only the remedye."

Thise vers of gold and blak ywriten were,
Of whiche I gan astonied to biholde,

113. **Cytherea,** Venus. 114. **lest,** it pleases. 115. **swevene,** dream. 117. **wisly,** surely. 119. **yif,** give. 120. **hente,** took. 126. **plein,** full; **sentence,** meaning. 128. **hele,** healing. 129. **welle,** spring. 132. **redere,** reader; **of-caste,** cast off. 136. **Daunger,** haughtiness. 138. **were,** weir. 140. **eschewing,** avoidance. 142. **astonied,** astonished.

Forwhy that oon encreessed ay my fere,
And with that other gan myn herte bolde.
That oon me hette, that other dide me colde:
No wit hadde I, for errour, for to chese
To entre or fleen, or me to save or lese.

Right as bitwixen adamantes two
Of evene might, a pece of iren set
Ne hath no might to meve to ne fro—
For what that oon may hale, that other let—
Ferde I, that niste whether me was bet
To entre or leve, til Affrican my gide
Me hente, and shoof in at the gates wide,

And saide, "It stant writen in thy face
Thyn errour, though thou telle it nat to me;
But dreed thee nat to come into this place,
For this writing nis no thing ment by thee,
Ne by noon but he Loves servant be;
For thou of love hast lost thy tast, I gesse,
As sik man hath of sweete and bitternesse.

But nathelees, although that thou be dul,
Yit that thou canst nat do, yit maist thou see;
For many a man that may nat stonde a pul,
It liketh him at wrastling for to be,
And deemen yit wher he do bet or he.
And ther, if thou haddest conning for t'endite,
I shal thee shewe matere for to write."

With that myn hand he took in his anoon,
Of which I confort caughte, and that as faste;

143. **Forwhy,** because. 144. **bolde,** become bold. 145. **hette,** inflamed; **dide me colde,** caused me to cool. 146. **wit,** i.e., power to come to a decision; **errour,** bewilderment; **chese,** choose. 147. **lese,** bring to ruin. 148. **adamantes,** magnets. 150. **meve,** move. 151. **hale,** pull; **let,** prevents. 152. **Ferde,** fared; **niste,** knew not. 154. **hente,** seized; **shoof,** shoved. 155. **stant,** stands. 159. **but,** unless. 164. **stonde a pul,** i.e., engage in wrestling. 166. **deemen,** judge; **wher,** whether.

But Lord, so I was glad and wel bigoon,
For overal wher that I mine yën caste
Were trees clad with leves that ay shal laste,
Eech in his kinde, of colour fressh and greene
As emeraude, that joye was to seene.

The bildere ook, and eek the hardy assh;
The pilere elm, the cofre unto caraine;
The boxtree pipere; holm to whippes lassh;
The sailing firre; the cypres, deeth to plaine;
The shetere ew; the asp for shaftes plaine;
The olive of pees; and eek the dronke vine;
The victour palm; the laurer to divine.

A gardin saw I ful of blosmy boughes
Upon a river in a greene mede,
Ther as the swetnesse everemore ynough is,
With flowres white, blewe, and yelowe, and rede,
And colde welle-stremes no thing dede,
That swimmen ful of smale fisshes lighte,
With finnes rede, and scales silver-brighte.

On every bough the briddes herde I singe
With vois of angel in hir armonye;
Some bisied hem hir briddes forth to bringe.
The litel conies to hir play gonne hie;
And ferther al aboute I gan espye
The dredful ro, the buk, the hert, the hinde,
Squireles, and beestes smale of gentil kinde.

Of instruments of stringes in accord
Herde I so playe a ravisshing swetnesse

171. wel bigoon, joyous. **176. bildere,** i.e., for building. **177. pilere,** for pillars; **cofre,** box; **caraine,** dead bodies. **178. pipere,** i.e., for musical pipes. **179. deeth,** death; **plaine,** complain. **180. shetere,** shooter, i.e., for bows; **asp,** aspen; **plaine,** smooth. **181. dronke,** drunken, since wine-producing. **182. divine,** augur: the laurel was used in consulting of oracles. **187. dede,** i.e., stagnant. **190. briddes,** birds. **193. conies,** rabbits. **195. dredful,** frightened.

That God, that Makere is of al and Lord,
Ne herde nevere bettre, as I gesse.
Therwith a wind, unnethe it mighte be lesse,
Made in the leves greene a noise softe
Accordant to the briddes song alofte.

The air of that place so attempre was
That nevere was grevance of hoot ne cold;
Ther weex eek every hoolsom spice and gras:
No man may there waxe sik ne old.
Yit was ther joye more than a thousandfold
Than man can telle; ne nevere wolde it nighte,
But ay cleer day to any mannes sighte.

Under a tree biside a welle I sey
Cupide oure lord his arwes forge and file;
And at his feet his bowe al redy lay,
And Wil his doughter tempered al this while
The hevedes in the welle, and with hir wile
She couched hem after they sholde serve,
Some for to slee, and some to wounde and kerve.

Tho was I war of Plesance anoon right,
And of Array, and Lust, and Curteisye,
And of the Craft that can and hath the might
To doon by force a wight to doon folye:
Disfigurat was she, I nil nat lie.
And by hemself under an ook, I gesse,
Saw I Delit that stood by Gentilesse.

I saw Beautee withouten any attir,
And Youthe ful of game and jolitee,
Foolhardinesse, and Flaterye, and Desir,

201. **unnethe,** scarcely. 203. **Accordant to,** in tune with. 204. **attempre,** temperate. 205. **hoot,** hot. 206. **weex,** grew. 209. **nighte,** become night. 211. **welle,** spring; **sey,** saw. 215. **hevedes,** (arrow)heads; **wile,** skill. 216. **couched,** laid down; **after,** i.e., arranged according to how. 217. **slee,** slay; **kerve,** cut. 219. **Lust,** desire. 221. **doon,** cause.

Messagerye, and Meede, and othere three—
Hir names shal nat here be told for me;
And upon pileres grete of jasper longe
I saw a temple of bras yfounded stronge.

Aboute that temple daunceden alway
Wommen ynowe, of whiche some ther were
Faire of hemself, and some of hem were gay;
In kirteles al dischevele wente they there:
That was hir office alway, yeer by yere.
And on the temple of douves white and faire
Saw I sittinge many an hundred paire.

Bifore the temple-dore ful sobrely
Dame Pees sat with a curtin in hir hond,
And by hir side, wonder discreetly,
Dame Pacience sitting ther I foond,
With face pale, upon an hil of sond;
And aldernext withinne and eek withoute
Biheeste and Art, and of hir folk a route.

Within the temple of sikes hote as fir
I herde a swough that gan aboute renne,
Whiche sikes were engendred with desir,
That maden every auter for to brenne
Of newe flaumbe; and wel espied I thenne
That al the cause of sorwes that they drie
Cometh of the bittre goddesse Jalousye.

The god Priapus saw I, as I wente,
Within the temple in soverein place stonde,

228. **Messagerye,** the allegorical figure which represents go-betweens; **Meede,** cash-payment; **othere three,** i.e., a number of others. **229. for,** by. **233. ynowe,** enough. **235. dischevele,** with hair loose. **236. office,** duty. **237. douves,** doves. **240. curtin,** curtain. **242. foond,** found. **243. sond,** sand. **244. aldernext,** next of all. **245. Biheeste,** Promise; **Art,** Subtlety; **route,** number. **246. sikes,** sighs. **247. swough,** murmuring sound; **renne,** run. **249. auter,** altar; **brenne,** burn. **250. flaumbe,** flame. **251. drie,** endure. **253. Priapus,** a Roman fertility god.

In swich array as whan the asse him shente°
With cry by night, and with his sceptre in honde;
Ful bisily men gonne assaye and fonde°
Upon his heed° to sette, of sondry hewe,
Gerlandes ful of flowres fresshe and newe.

And in a privee corner in disport
Foond° I Venus and hir porter Richesse,
That was ful noble and hautain of hir port;°
Derk was the place, but afterward lightnesse
I saw a lite—unnethe° it mighte be lesse;
And on a bed of gold she lay to reste,
Til that the hote sonne gan to weste.°

Hire gilte heres with a golden threed°
Ybounden were, untressed° as she lay;
And naked from the brest up to the heed
Men mighte hire seen; and soothly for to say,
The remenant was wel covered to my pay°
Right with a subtil coverchief of Valence:
Ther nas no thikker cloth of no defence.°

The place yaf a thousand savours soote,°
And Bacus,° god of win, sat hire biside,
And Ceres next that dooth of hunger boote,°
And as I saide, amiddes lay Cypride,°
To whom on knees two yonge folk ther cride
To been hir° help; but thus I leet hire lie,
And ferther in the temple I gan espye,

That, in despit of Diane the chaste,
Ful many a bowe ybroke heeng° on the wal,

255. **shente,** abashed: Priapus' plot against the chastity of a certain virgin nymph was frustrated when she was awakened by the cry of an ass. 257. **assaye and fonde,** endeavor and strive. 258. **heed,** head. 261. **Foond,** found. 262. **hautain,** haughty; **port,** bearing. 264. **lite,** little; **unnethe,** scarcely. 266. **weste,** go west. 267. **threed,** thread. 268. **untressed,** unbraided. 271. **pay,** pleasure. 273. i.e., There was no thicker cloth (than the thin Valence kerchief) to defend her from sight. 274. **soote,** sweet. 275. **Bacus,** Bacchus. 276. **dooth boote of,** allays. 277. **Cypride,** Venus. 279. **hir,** their. 282. **heeng,** hung.

Of maidenes swiche as gonne hir times waste
In hir service; and painted overal
Ful many a storye, of which I touche shal
A fewe, as of Caliste and Atalante,
And many a maide of which the name I wante.

Semiramis, Candace, and Ercules,
Biblis, Dido, Thisbe, and Pyramus,
Tristam, Isoude, Paris, and Achilles,
Elaine, Cleopatre, and Troilus,
Sylla, and eek the moder of Romulus:
Alle thise were painted on that other side,
And al hir love, and in what plit they dyde.

Whan I was come ayain unto the place
That I of spak, that was so soote and greene,
Forth welk I tho myselven to solace;
Tho was I war wher that ther sat a queene,
That as of light the someres sonne sheene
Passeth the sterre, right so over mesure
She fairer was than any creature.

And in a launde upon an hil of flowres
Was set this noble goddesse Nature;
Of braunches were hir halles and hir bowres,
Ywrought after hir cast and hir mesure;
Ne was ther fowl that cometh of engendrure
That they ne were alle prest in hir presence
To take hir doom, and yive hire audience.

For this was on Saint Valentines day,
Whan every brid cometh ther to chese his make,

286. Callisto and Atalanta, like the others named in this stanza, were famous lovers. **287. wante,** lack. **288. Candace,** who enchanted Alexander the Great; **Ercules,** Hercules. **290. Isoude,** Isolde. **291. Elaine,** Helen of Troy. **292. Sylla,** Scylla; **moder,** mother, i.e., Rhea Silvia. **294. plit,** circumstances. **297. welk,** walked; **tho,** then. **299. sheene,** bright. **300. Passeth,** surpasses; **sterre,** star; **over,** beyond. **302. launde,** meadow. **305. cast,** contrivance. **307. prest,** ready. **310. brid,** bird; **chese,** choose; **make,** mate.

Of every kinde that men thinke may;
And that so huge a noise gan they make,
That erthe and air and tree and every lake
So ful was that unnethe° was ther space
For me to stonde, so ful was al the place.

And right as Alain° in the "Plainte of Kinde"
Deviseth° Nature in array and face,
In swich array men mighte hire there finde.
This noble emperesse,° ful of grace,
Bad every fowl to take his owene place,
As they were wont alway, from yeer to yere,
Saint Valentines Day, to stonden there.

That is to sayn, the fowles of ravine°
Were hyest set, and thanne the fowles smale
That eten as hem Nature wolde encline.
As worm, or thing of which I telle no tale;
And waterfowl sat lowest in the dale;
But fowl that liveth by seed sat on the greene,
And that so fele° that wonder was to seene.

Ther mighte men the royal egle finde,
That with his sharpe look perceth° the sonne;
And othere egles of a lower kinde
Of whiche that clerkes wel devise conne;
Ther was the tyrant with his fetheres donne°
And greye—I mene the goshawk—that dooth pine°
To briddes for his outrageous ravine.°

The gentil faucon that with his feet distraineth°
The kinges hand; the hardy sperhawk° eke,
The quailes fo; the merlion that paineth°

314. unnethe, hardly. **316. Alain,** Alanus de Insulis, whose *Complaint of Nature* personifies Nature much as Chaucer does. **317. Deviseth,** describes. **319. emperesse,** empress. **323. ravine,** prey. **329. fele,** many. **331. perceth,** pierces. **334. donne,** dun. **335. pine,** hurt. **336. ravine,** voracity. **337. distraineth,** takes hold on: falcons being royal birds are often pictured perched on the hands of kings. **338. sperhawk,** sparrowhawk. **339. merlion,** merlin; **paineth,** takes pains.

Himself ful ofte the larke for to seeke;
Ther was the douve with hir yën meeke;
The jalous swan, ayains his deeth that singeth;
The owle eek that of deeth the bode bringeth;

The crane, geant with his trompes soun;
The theef, the chough, and eek the jangling pie;
The scorning jay; the eeles fo, heroun;
The false lapwing, ful of trecherye;
The starling that the conseil can biwrye;
The tame rodok, and the coward kite;
The cok, that orlogge is of thropes lite;

The sparwe, Venus sone; the nightingale,
That clepeth forth the greene leves newe;
The swalwe, mortherere of the fowles smale
That maken hony of flowres fresshe of hewe;
The wedded turtel, with hir herte trewe;
The pecok, with his angeles clothes brighte;
The fesant, scornere of the cok by nighte;

The wakere goos; the cokkou evere unkinde;
The popinjay ful of delicasye;
The drake, stroyere of his owene kinde;
The stork, the wrekere of avouterye;
The hote cormerant of glotonye;

342. ayains, at the coming of. **343. bode,** warning. **344. geant,** giant; **trompes,** trumpet's. **345. chough,** a kind of crow; **jangling,** chattering; **pie,** magpie. **348. conseil,** secret; **biwrye,** disclose. **349. rodok,** ruddock, European robin. **350. orlogge,** timepiece; **thropes,** villages; **lite,** little. **353. swalwe,** swallow; **mortherere,** murderer; **fowles smale,** i.e., bees. **355. turtel,** turtledove. **357.** The pheasant scorns the rooster perhaps because the pheasant is supposed to be capable of mating with domestic hens. **358. wakere,** wakener: geese are reputed to have awakened Rome against a stealthy barbarian attack; **unkinde,** unnatural: the cuckoo deposits its eggs in the nests of other birds. **359. delicasye,** daintiness. **360. stroyere,** destroyer: drakes sometimes kill their young. **361. wrekere of avouterye,** avenger of adultery: storks were supposed to kill their adulterous mates. **362. hote,** hot: the ravenous cormorant is thought of as burning from its own gluttony.

The raven wis; the crowe with vois of care;
The throstel old; the frosty feeldefare.

What sholde I sayn? Of fowles every kinde
That in this world hath fetheres and stature,
Men mighten in that place assembled finde,
Bifore the noble goddesse Nature;
And everich of hem dide his bisy cure
Benignely to chese or for to take,
By hir accord, his formel or his make.

But to the point: Nature heeld on hir hond
A formel egle, of shap the gentileste
That evere she among hir werkes foond,
The most benigne and the goodlieste:
In hire was every vertu at his reste,
So ferforth that Nature hirself hadde blisse
To looke on hire, and ofte hir beek to kisse.

Nature, vicarye of the Almighty Lord
That hoot, cold, hevy, light, and moist and dreye
Hath knit with evene nombres of accord,
In esy vois gan for to speke and saye,
"Fowles, take heede of my sentence, I praye;
And for youre ese, in forthering of youre neede,
As faste as I may speke, I wol you speede.

Ye knowe wel how, Saint Valentines Day,
By my statut and thurgh my governaunce,
Ye come for to chese—and flee youre way—
Youre makes as I prike you with plesaunce.
But nathelees, my rightful ordinaunce
May I nat breke, for al this world to winne,
That he that most is worthy shal biginne.

364. **throstel,** thrush; **feeldefare,** fieldfare, another kind of thrush. 366. **stature,** standing. 369. **dide . . . cure,** acted with anxious care. 370. **chese,** choose. 371. **formel,** female eagle or hawk; **make,** mate. 374. **foond,** found. 376. **at his reste,** i.e., at home. 377. **so ferforth,** to such an extent. 379. **vicarye,** vicar. 380. **dreye,** dry. 381. **knit,** joined. 388. **flee,** fly. 389. **makes,** mates; **prike,** prick, inspire.

The tercelet egle, as that ye knowe ful weel,
The fowl royal aboven every degree,
The wise and worthy, secree, trewe as steel,
Which I have formed, as ye may wel see,
In every part as it best liketh me—
It needeth nat his shap you to devise—
He shal first chese and speken in his gise.

And after him by ordre shul ye chese,
After youre kinde, everich as you liketh,
And as youre hap is shul ye winne or lese—
But which of you that love most entriketh,
God sende him hire that sorest for him siketh."
And therwithal the tercel gan she calle,
And saide, "My sone, the chois is to you falle.

But nathelees, in this condicioun
Moot be the chois of everich that is here:
That she agree to his eleccioun,
What so he be that sholde be hir fere.
This is oure usage alway, from yeer to yere:
And who so may at this time have his grace,
In blisful time he cam into this place."

With heed enclined and with humble cheere
This royal tercel spak and taried nought:
"Unto my soverein lady, and nat my fere,
I chese, and chese with wil and herte and thought,
The formel on your hand, so wel ywrought,
Whos I am al, and evere wil hire serve,
Do what hire list to do me live or sterve;

Biseeking hire of mercy and of grace,
As she that is my lady sovereine—
Or lat me die present in this place:

393. tercelet, male. **399. chese,** choose; **gise,** manner. **402. lese,** lose. **403. entriketh,** entraps. **404. siketh,** sighs. **405. tercel,** male eagle. **408. Moot,** must. **410. fere,** mate. **420. do,** cause; **sterve,** die.

For certes, longe I may nat live in paine,
For in myn herte is corven every veine;
And having reward only to my trouthe,
My dere herte, have of my wo som routhe.

And if that I to hire be founde untrewe,
Disobeisant, or wilful necligent,
Avauntour, or in proces love a newe,
I praye to you, this be my juggement:
That with thise fowles be I al torent
That ilke day that evere she me finde
To hire untrewe, or in my gilt unkinde.

And sin that hire loveth noon so wel as I—
Al be that she me nevere of love bihette—
Thanne oughte she be myn thurgh hir mercy,
For other bond can I noon on hire knette;
Ne nevere for no wo ne shal I lette
To serven hire, how fer so that she wende;
Saye what you list: my tale is at an ende."

Right as the fresshe, rede rose newe
Ayain the somer sonne coloured is,
Right so for shame al waxen gan the hewe
Of this formel, whan she herde al this.
She neither answerde wel, ne saide amis,
So sore abasshed was she, til that Nature
Saide, "Doughter, drede you nought, I you assure."

Another tercel egle spak anoon,
Of lower kinde, and saide, "That shal nat be!
I love hire bet than ye doon, by saint John,
Or at the leeste I love as wel as ye,
And lenger have served hire in my degree:

425. **corven,** cut. 426. **reward,** regard. 427. **routhe,** pity. 429. **Disobeisant,** disobedient. 430. **Avauntour,** boaster; **proces,** time. 432. **torent,** torn apart. 436. **bihette,** promised. 438. **knette,** fasten. 439. **lette,** stop. 443. **Ayain,** i.e., in the light of. 444. **waxen,** increase. 451. **bet,** better.

And if she sholde have loved for long loving,
To me ful longe hadde be the guerdoning.

I dar eek sayn, if she me finde fals,
Unkinde, or janglere, or rebel in any wise,
Or jalous, do me hangen by the hals;
And but I bere me in hir servise
As wel as that my wit can me suffise,
From point to point, hir honour for to save,
Take ye my lif, and al the good I have."

The thridde tercel egle answerde tho:
"Now, sires, ye seen the litel leiser here,
For every fowl crieth out to been ago
Forth with his make, or with his lady dere;
And eek Nature hirself ne wol nat heere,
For tarying here, nat half that I wolde saye;
And but I speke, I moot for sorwe deye:

Of long service avaunte I me no thing—
But as possible is me to die today
For wo, as he that hath been languisshing
This twenty yeer; and as wel happen may
A man may serven bet, and more to pay,
In half a yeer, although it were no more,
Than som man dooth that hath served ful yore.

I saye nat this by me, for I ne can
Doon no service that may my lady plese;
But I dar sayn I am hir trewest man,
As to my doom, and fainest wolde hire ese;
At shorte wordes, til that deeth me sese,

455. **longe,** i.e., long ago; **guerdoning,** reward. 457. **janglere,** blabbermouth. 458. **do . . . hals,** have me hanged by the neck. 459. **but,** unless. 463. **thridde,** third; **tho,** then. 466. **make,** mate. 469. **but,** unless; **moot,** must. 470. **avaunte,** boast. 474. **bet,** better; **more to pay,** to greater pleasure. 480. **doom,** judgment; **fainest,** most gladly; **ese,** please. 481. **sese,** seize.

I wil been hires, whether I wake or winke,
And trewe in al that herte may bithinke."

Of al my lif, sin that day I was born,
So gentil plee in love or other thing
Ne herde nevere no man me biforn,
Who that hadde leiser and conning
For to reherce hir cheere and hir speking:
And from the morwe° gan this speeche laste,
Til downward drow the sonne wonder faste.

The noise of fowles for to been delivered
So loude roong:° "Have doon, and lat us wende!"
That wel wende I the wode hadde al toslivered.°
"Come of!" they criden, "allas, ye wole us shende.°
Whan shal youre cursed pleting° have an ende?
How sholde a juge either partye leve,°
For ye or nay, withouten other preve?"°

The goos, the cokkou, and the doke also
So cride, "Kek kek, cokkou, quek quek," hye
That thurgh mine eres the noise wente tho.
The goos saide, "Al this nis nat worth a flye!
But I can shape° herof a remedye:
And I wol saye my verdit faire and swithe°
For waterfowl, who so be wroth or blithe."

"And I for wormfowl," quod the fool cokkou.
"And I wol of myn owene auctoritee,
For commune speed,° take on me the charge now:
For to delivere us is greet charitee."
"Ye may abide a while yit, pardee,"
Quod the turtel, "if it be youre wille:
A wight may speke him were as fair been stille.°

489. morwe, morning. **492. roong,** rang. **493. wende,** thought; **toslivered,** fallen to pieces. **494. shende,** ruin. **495. pleting,** pleading. **496. leve,** believe. **497. preve,** proof. **502. shape,** arrange. **503. swithe,** quickly. **507. speed,** profit. **511.** ? A person may speak who had better have remained quiet.

I am a seedfowl, oon the unworthieste,
That woot I wel, and litel of conninge;
But bet is that a wightes tonge reste
Than entremetten him of swich doinge
Of which he neither rede can ne singe.
And who so dooth, ful foule himself accloyeth:
For office uncommitted ofte anoyeth."

Nature, which that alway hadde an ere
To murmur of the lewednesse bihinde,
With facound vois saide, "Holde youre tonges there,
And I shal soone, I hope, a conseil finde
You to delivere, and from this noise unbinde;
I jugge of every folk men shul oon calle
To sayn the verdit for you fowles alle."

Assented was to this conclusioun
The briddes alle; and fowles of ravine
Han chosen first, by plain eleccioun,
The tercelet of the faucon to diffine
Al hir sentence, as hem liste to termine;
And to Nature him gonne to presente,
And she accepteth him with glad entente.

The tercelet saide thanne, "In this manere
Ful hard were it to preve by resoun
Who loveth best this gentil formel here,
For everich hath swich replicacioun,
That noon by skiles may been brought adown.
I can nat see that arguments availe:
Thanne seemeth it ther moste be bataile."

512. oon, i.e., one of. **513. woot,** know. **514. bet,** better; **reste,** be quiet. **515. entremetten him of,** interfere in. **516. rede,** advise. **517. accloyeth,** overloads. **518. office uncommitted,** i.e., a task not delegated to one. **520. murmur . . . lewednesse,** i.e., the complaining of the unsophisticated birds. **521. facound,** eloquent. **527. ravine,** prey. **529–530. diffine . . . sentence,** present their opinion. **530. liste,** it pleased; **termine,** decide. **534. preve,** prove. **536. replicacioun,** ability to reply. **537. skiles,** reasons. **539. moste,** must.

"Al redy," quod thise egles tercels tho.°
"Nay, sires," quod he, "if that I dorste it saye,
Ye doon me wrong, my tale is nat ydo.
For sires, ne taketh nat agrief,° I praye,
It may nat goon as ye wolde in this waye:
Oure° is the vois that han the charge° on honde,
And to the juges doom ye moten stonde.

And therfore, pees; I saye, as to my wit,
Me wolde thinke° how that the worthieste
Of knighthood, and° lengest hath used it,
Most of estaat, of blood the gentileste,
Were sittingest° for hire, if that hire leste;
And of thise three she woot hirself, I trowe,
Which that he be, for hire is light° to knowe."

The waterfowles han hir hedes laid
Togidre; and of a short avisement,°
Whan everich hadde his large golee° said,
They saiden soothly, alle by oon assent,
How that the goos, with hir facounde gent,°
"That so desireth to pronounce oure neede
Shal telle oure tale," and prayed God hire speede.

As for thise waterfowles tho bigan
The goos to speke, and in hir cakelinge
She saide, "Pees, now take keep,° every man,
And herkneth which° a reson I shal bringe:
My wit is sharp, I love no taryinge.
I saye, I rede° him, though he were my brother,
But° she wil love him, lat him take another."

540. tho, then. **543. agrief,** amiss. **545. Oure,** ours; **charge,** responsibility. **548. Me wolde thinke,** it would seem to me. **549. and,** and the one who. **551. sittingest,** most suitable. **553. hire is light,** it is easy for her. **555. avisement,** deliberation. **556. golee,** mouthful. **558. facounde gent,** gentle eloquence. **563. keep,** heed. **564. which,** what. **566. rede,** advise. **567. But,** unless.

"Lo, here a parfit reson of a goos,"
Quod the sperhawk. "Nevere mote she thee!
Lo, swich it is to have a tonge loos!
Now pardee, fool, now were it bet for thee
Han holde thy pees than shewe thy nicetee.
It lith nat in his might ne in his wille,
But sooth is said, a fool can nat be stille."

The laughtre aroos of gentil fowles alle,
And right anoon the seedfowl chosen hadde
The turtel trewe, and gonne hire to hem calle,
And prayed hire for to sayn the soothe sadde
Of this matere, and axed what she radde:
And she answerde that plainly hir entente
She wolde it shewe, and soothly what she mente.

"Nay, God forbede a lovere sholde chaunge,"
The turtel saide, and weex for shame al reed.
"Though that his lady everemore be straunge,
Yit lat him serve hire til that he be deed.
Forsoothe, I praise nat the gooses reed.
'For though she dyde, I wolde noon other make:
I wil been hires til that the deeth me take.' "

"Wel bourded," quod the doke, "by myn hat!
That men shal loven alway causelees—
Who can a reson finde or wit in that?
Daunceth he merye that is mirthelees?
What sholde I rekke of him that is recchelees?
Ye, queke," yit said the doke, ful wel and faire:
"Ther been mo sterres, God woot, than a paire."

568. **parfit,** perfect. 569. **thee,** thrive. 571. **bet,** better. 572. **nicetee,** foolishness. 573. **lith,** lies. 578. **sadde,** earnestly. 579. **axed,** asked; **radde,** advised. 583. **weex,** grew. 584. **straunge,** hostile. 586. **reed,** advice. 587. **wolde,** would want; **make,** mate. 588. **hires,** hers. 589. **bourded,** joked. 593. **rekke,** care; **is recchelees,** doesn't care. 594. **queke,** quack. 595. **sterres,** stars.

"Now fy, cherl," quod the gentil tercelet:
"Out of the donghil cam that word ful right.
Thou canst nat seen what thing is wel biset;
Thou farest by love as owles doon by light:
The day hem blent, but wel they seen by night.
Thy kinde is of so lowe a wrecchednesse
That what love is thou canst nat seen ne gesse."

Tho gan the cokkou putte him forth in prees
For fowl that eteth worm, and saide blive,
"So I," quod he, "may have my make in pees,
I recche nat how longe that ye strive.
Lat eech of him be solein al hir live,
This is my reed, sin they may nat accorde:
This shorte lesson needeth nat recorde."

"Ye, have the gloton fild ynough his paunche,
Thanne are we wel," saide thanne a merlioun.
"Thou mortherere of the haysoge on the braunche
That broughte thee forth, thou reweful glotoun,
Live thou solein, wormes corrupcioun,
For no fors is of lak of thy nature:
Go, lewed be thou whil that the world may dure."

"Now pees," quod Nature, "I comande heer,
For I have herd al youre opinioun,
And in effect yit be we nevere the neer.
But finally, this is my conclusioun:
That she hirself shal han the eleccioun
Of whom hire list; and who be wroth or blithe,
Him that she cheseth he shal hire have as swithe.

598. **wel biset,** i.e., in good condition. 599. **farest,** behave. 600. **blent,** blinds. 603. **prees,** public. 604. **blive,** straightway. 606. **recche,** care. 607. **solein,** single. 608. **reed,** advice. 609. **recorde,** i.e., to be recorded. 611. **merlioun,** merlin. 612. **mortherere,** murderer; **haysoge,** hedge-sparrow. 613. **broughte thee forth,** since the egg from which the cuckoo hatched was placed in its nest; **reweful,** pitiful. 614. **solein,** single. 615. i.e., For it doesn't matter if your line dies out. 616. **lewed,** ignorant; **dure,** endure. 619. **neer,** nearer. 623. **cheseth,** chooses; **as swithe,** at once.

For sin it may nat here discussed be
Who loveth hire best, as saith the tercelet,
Thanne wol I doon hire this favour, that she
Shal have right him on whom hir herte is set,
And he hire that his herte hath on hire knet.
Thus jugge I, Nature, for I may nat lie:
To noon estaat have I noon other yë.

But as for conseil for to chese a make,
If I were Reson, certes thanne wolde I
Conseile you the royal tercel take–
As saide the tercelet ful skilfully–
As for the gentileste and most worthy,
Which I have wrought so wel to my plesaunce
That to you oughte it been a suffisaunce."

With dredful vois the formel tho answerde,
"Myn rightful lady, goddesse of Nature,
Sooth is that I am evere under youre yerde,
As is another lives creature,
And moot been youre whil that my lif may dure;
And therfore, graunteth me my firste boone,
And myn entente you wol I sayn wel soone."

"I graunte it you," quod she. And right anoon
This formel egle spak in this degree:
"Almighty queene, unto this yeer be goon,
I axe respit for to avise me,
And after that to have my chois al free:
This al and som that I wol speke and saye;
Ye gete namore although ye do me deye.

I wol nat serve Venus ne Cupide
Forsoothe, as yit, by no manere waye."

628. knet, fastened. **630.** i.e., I take no other considerations into account. **637.** i.e., That it ought to be enough for you. **640. yerde,** rod. **641. another lives,** i.e., any other living. **642. moot,** must; **youre,** yours. **643. boone,** prayer. **647. unto,** until. **648. axe,** ask; **avise me,** think it over. **651. do me deye,** put me to death.

"Now, sin it may noon otherwise bitide,"
Quod tho Nature, "here is namore to saye.
Thanne wolde I that thise fowles were awaye,
Eech with his make, for tarying lenger here,"
And saide hem thus, as ye shul after heere.

"To you speke I, you tercelets," quod Nature.
"Beeth of good herte, and serveth alle three:
A yeer is nat so longe to endure,
And eech of you paine him in his degree
For to do wel; for God woot, quit is she
Fro you this yeer, what after so bifalle:
This entremes is dressed for you alle."

And whan this werk al brought was to an ende,
To every fowl Nature yaf his make
By evene accord, and on hir way they wende.
But Lord, the blisse and joye that they make,
For eech gan other in his winges take,
And with hir nekkes eech gan other winde,
Thanking alway the noble queene of Kinde.

But first were chosen fowles for to singe—
As yeer by yere was alway the usaunce—
To singe a roundel at hir departinge,
To doon to Nature honour and plesaunce.
The note, I trowe, ymaked was in Fraunce;
The wordes were swiche as ye may here finde
The nexte vers, as I now have in minde.

"Now welcome, somer, with thy sonne softe,
That hast thise wintres wedres overshake,
And driven away the large nightes blake.

657. make, mate; **for,** i.e., to prevent. **662. paine him,** take pains. **663. quit,** delivered. **665. entremes,** intermission; **dressed,** ordained. **672. Kinde,** Nature. **674. usaunce,** custom. **681. wedres,** storms; **overshake,** dispelled.

Saint Valentin, that art ful heigh on lofte,
Thus singen smale fowles for thy sake:
Now welcome, somer, with thy sonne softe,
That hast thise wintres wedres overshake,
And driven away the large nightes blake.

Wel han they cause for to gladen ofte,
Sith eech of hem recovered hath his make;
Ful blisful mowe they singe whan they wake:
Now welcome, somer, with thy sonne softe,
That hast thise wintres wedres overshake,
And driven away the large nightes blake."

And with the shouting, whan the song was do,
That fowles maden at hir flight away,
I wook, and othere bookes took me to
To rede upon, and yit I rede alway,
In hope, ywis, to rede so somday,
That I shal mete somthing for to fare
The bet, and thus to rede I nil nat spare.

690. mowe, may. **699. mete,** dream. **700. bet,** better.

THE PROLOGUE TO THE LEGEND OF GOOD WOMEN

A thousand sithes have I herd men telle
That ther is joye in hevene and paine in helle,
And I accorde wel that it be so:
But nathelees, this woot I wel also,
That ther n'is noon that dwelleth in this contree
That either hath in helle or hevene ybe,
Ne may of it none othere wayes witen
But as he hath herd said, or founde it writen;
For by assay ther may no man it preve.
But Goddes forbode but men sholde leve
Wel more thing than men han seen with yë:
Men shal nat weenen every thing a lie
For that he sawgh it nat of yore ago;
God woot a thing is nevere the lasse so
Though every wight ne may it nat ysee:
Bernard the monk ne sawgh nat al, pardee.
Thanne moten we, to bookes that we finde,
Thurgh whiche that olde thinges been in minde,
And to the doctrine of thise olde wise
Yiven credence in every skilful wise,
And trowen on thise olde appreved stories
Of holinesse, of regnes, of victories,
Of love, of hate, of othere sondry thinges,
Of whiche I may nat make rehercinges.
And if that olde bookes weren awaye,
Yloren were of remembrance the keye.

1. sithes, times. **3. accorde,** agree. **4. woot,** know. **7. witen,** know. **9. assay,** actual experience; **preve,** prove. **10. Goddes forbode,** God forbid; **leve,** believe. **12. weenen,** suppose. **13. of yore,** i.e., long. **16. Bernard:** ? St. Bernard of Clairvaux, a learned theologian. **17. moten,** must. **20. skilful,** reasonable. **21. trowen on,** put trust in; **appreved,** well-established. **24. rehercinges,** enumeration. **26. Yloren,** lost.

Wel oughte us thanne on olde bookes leve,°
Ther as ther is noon other assay by preve.
  And as for me, though that my wit be lite,
On bookes for to rede I me delite,
And in myn herte have hem in reverence,
And to hem yive swich lust° and swich credence
That ther is wel unnethe° game noon
That from my bookes maketh me to goon,
But it be other° upon the haliday,
Or elles in the joly time of May,
Whan that I heere the smale fowles singe,
And that the flowres ginne for to springe—
Farewel my studye, as lasting that sesoun.
  Now have I therto this condicioun,
That of alle the flowres in the mede
Thanne love I most thise flowres white and rede,
Swiche as men calle daisies in oure town:
To hem have I so greet affeccioun,
As I saide erst,° whan comen is the May,
That in my bed ther daweth° me no day
That I n'am up and walking in the mede
To seen thise flowres again the sonne sprede°
Whan it upriseth by the morwe sheene°—
The longe day thus walking in the greene.
And whan the sonne ginneth for to weste°
Thanne closeth it and draweth it to reste,
So sore it is afered° of the night,
Til on the morwe that it is dayes light.
This dayes-yë, of alle flowres flowr,
Fulfild of vertu and of al honour,
And evere ylike fair and fressh of hewe,
As wel in winter as in somer newe,
Fain° wolde I praisen if I coude aright:
But wo is me, it lith° nat in my might:

27. **leve,** believe. 32. **lust,** pleasure. 33. **wel unnethe,** scarcely. 35. **other,** either. 45. **erst,** before. 46. **daweth,** dawns. 48. **again,** i.e., in the light of; **sprede,** spread, open. 49. **morwe,** morning; **sheene,** bright. 51. **weste,** sink west. 53. **afered,** afraid. 59. **Fain,** gladly. 60. **lith,** lies.

For wel I woot that folk han herbiforn
Of making ropen, and lad away the corn;
And I come after, glening here and there,
And am ful glad if I may finde an ere
Of any goodly word that they han left.
And if it happe me reherce eft
That they han in hir fresshe songes said,
I hope that they wol nat been yvele apaid,
Sith it is said in forthring and honour
Of hem that either serven leef or flowr;
For trusteth wel, I n'have nat undertake
As of the leef again the flowr to make,
Ne of the flowr to make again the leef,
No more than of the corn again the sheef;
For, as to me, is levere noon ne lother:
I am withholde yit with nevere nother;
I noot who serveth leef ne who the flowr—
That nis nothing th'entente of my labour;
For this werk is al of another tonne,
Of olde storye, er swich strif was bigonne.
  But wherfore that I spak to yive credence
To bookes olde, and doon hem reverence,
Is for men sholde auctoritees bileve,
Ther as ther lith noon other assay by preve;
For myn entente is, er I fro you fare,
The naked text in Englissh to declare
Of many a storye or elles of many a geste,
As auctors sayn: leveth hem if you leste.
  Whan passed was almost the month of May,
And I hadde romed al the someres day
The greene medowe, of which that I you tolde,

62. Reaped (the field) in poetry of this sort and taken away the wheat. **63. glening,** gleaning. **64. ere,** ear of grain. **66. eft,** again. **68. yvele apaid,** ill-pleased. **69. forthring,** furtherance. **70. leef or flowr,** apparently a reference to a popular game of the period in which courtiers divided into two groups in order to make good the claim of the Leaf or the Flower as a symbol of love. **72. make,** write. 75. For to me neither is better or worse than the other. **76. withholde,** attached to the service of; **nother,** neither. **77. noot,** don't know. **79. tonne,** tun, i.e., kind. **84. lith,** lies; **assay by preve,** test by experience. **87. geste,** tale. **88. leveth,** believe.

Upon the fresshe daisye to biholde,
And that the sonne out of the south gan weste°,
And closed was the flowr and goon to reste—
For derknesse of the night of which she dredde—
Hoom to my hous ful swiftly I me spedde,
And in a litel erber° that I have,
Ybenched newe with turves fresshe ygrave°,
I bad men sholde me my couche make,
For daintee of° the newe someres sake;
I bad hem strowe flowres on my bed.
Whan I was laid and hadde mine yën hed°,
I fil° asleepe within an houre or two.
Me mette how I was in the medowe tho°,
And that I romed in that same gise°
To seen that flowr, as ye han herd devise.
Fair was this medowe, as thoughte me, overal;
With flowres soote embrouded° was it al;
As for to speke of gomme°, or erbe, or tree,
Comparison may noon ymaked be,
For it surmounted pleinly° alle odoures,
And of riche beautee alle flowres.
Forgeten hadde the erthe his poore estaat
Of winter, that him naked made and maat°,
And with his swerd° of cold so sore hadde greved:
Now hadde th'attempre° sonne al that releved,
And clothed him in greene al newe again.
The smale fowles, of the seson fain°,
That from the panter and the net been scaped°,
Upon the fowlere that hem made awhaped°
In winter, and destroyed hadde hir brood,
In his despit it thoughte° it dide hem good

93. weste, move west. **97. erber,** garden. **98. Ybenched,** furnished with benches; **turves,** sods; **fresshe ygrave,** freshly dug. **100. daintee of,** delight in. **102. hed,** hid, shut. **103. fil,** fell. **104. Me mette,** I dreamed; **tho,** then. **105. gise,** fashion. **108. soote,** sweet; **embrouded,** embroidered. **109. gomme,** gum. **111. pleinly,** fully. **114. maat,** (check)mate, i.e., powerless. **115. swerd,** sword. **116. attempre,** temperate. **118. fain,** glad. **119. panter,** snare; **scaped,** escaped. **120. awhaped,** terrified. **122. it thoughte,** i.e., it seemed to them that.

To singe of him, and in hir song despise
The foule cherl that for his coveitise°
Hadde hem betrayed with his sophistrye.
This was hir song: "The fowlere we defye."
And some songen on the braunches clere
Layes of love, that joye it was to heere,
In worshipe and in praising of hir make°,
And of the newe, blisful someres sake;
And songen, "Blissed be Saint Valentin!
At his day I chees° you to be myn,
Withoute repenting, myn herte sweete."
And therwithal hir bekes gonne meete,
Yeelding honour and humble obeisaunces°,
And after diden othere observaunces
Right longing on° to Love and to Nature,
The which shoop° eech of hem to creature.
This song to herknen I dide al myn entente,
Forwhy I mette I wiste° what they mente,
Til at the laste a larke soong° above:
"I see," quod she, "the mighty God of Love:
Lo, yond he cometh! I see his winges sprede."
Tho gan I looke endelong the mede°
And saw him come, and in his hand a queene
Clothed in royal habit al of greene:
A fret° of gold she hadde next hir heer,
And upon that a whit corowne she beer°,
With manye flowres; and I shal nat lie,
For al the world right as the dayesye
Ycorowned is with white leves lite°,
Swiche were the flowres of hir corowne white;
For of oo perle fin° oriental
Hir white corowne was ymaked al;
For which the white corowne above the greene

124. coveitise, avarice. **129. make,** mate. **132. chees,** chose. **135. obeisaunces,** courtesies. **137. Right . . . on,** appropriate. **138. shoop,** created. **140. Forwhy,** because; **mette,** dreamed; **wiste,** knew. **141. soong,** sang. **144. Tho,** then; **endelong,** toward the end of; **mede,** meadow. **147. fret,** net. **148. beer,** bore. **151. lite,** little. **153. perle fin,** fine pearl.

Made hire lik a daisye for to seene,°
Considered° eek the fret of gold above.
Yclothed was this mighty God of Love
Of silk ybrouded ful of greene greves,°
A gerland on his heed of rose leves
Stiked° al with lilye flowres newe—
But of his face I can nat sayn the hewe,
For sikerly° his face shoon so brighte
That with the gleem astoned° was the sighte:
A furlong way I mighte him nat biholde.°
But at the laste in hand I saw him holde
Two firy dartes as the gleedes° rede,
And angelliche° his winges gan he sprede;
And al be that men sayn that blind is he,
Algate° me thoughte he mighte wel ysee,
For sternely on me he gan biholde,
So that his looking dooth myn herte colde;°
And by the hand he heeld the noble queene
Corowned with whit and clothed al in greene,
So wommanly, so benigne, and so meeke,
That in this world though that men wolde seeke,
Half hir beautee sholde men nat finde
In creature that formed is by Kinde.°
Hir name was Alceste the debonaire:°
I praye to God that evere falle° she faire,
For n'hadde confort been of hir presence,
I hadde be deed withouten any defence,
For drede of Loves wordes and his cheere,°
As whan time is, herafter ye shal heere.
  Bihinde this God of Love upon this greene
I saw coming of ladies nineteene,
In royal habit, a ful esy paas,°

156. **for to seene,** to behold. 157. **Considered,** considering. 159. **ybrouded,** embroidered; **greves,** i.e., branchlike figures. 161. **Stiked,** stuck full. 163. **sikerly,** certainly. 164. **astoned,** stunned. 165. **biholde,** i.e., bear to look at. 167. **gleedes,** hot coals. 168. **angelliche,** like an angel. 170. **Algate,** at any rate. 172. **dooth . . . colde,** makes my heart freeze. 178. **Kinde,** nature. 179. **debonaire,** meek. 180. **falle,** befall, i.e., fare. 183. **cheere,** manner. 187. **esy paas,** leisurely gait.

And after hem cam of wommen swich a traas,
That, sin that God Adam hadde maad of erthe,
The thridde part of wommen, ne the ferthe,
Ne wende I nat by possibilitee
Hadden evere in this wide world ybe—
And trewe of love thise wommen were eechoon.
Now whether was that a wonder thing or noon,
That right anoon as that they gonne espye
The flowr which that I clepe the dayesye,
Ful sodeinly they stinten alle at ones,
And kneeled adown, as it were for the nones,
And after that they wenten in compas,
Dauncing aboute this flowr an esy pas,
And songen as it were in carole wise
The balade which that I shal you devise:

The Balade

Hid, Absolon, thy gilte tresses clere;
Ester, lay thou thy mekenesse al adown;
Hid, Jonathas, al thy freendly manere;
Penolopee and Marcia Catoun,
Make of youre wifhood no comparisoun;
Hide ye youre beautees, Isoude and Elaine:
Alceste is here, that al that may distaine.

188. traas, train. **190. ferthe,** fourth. **191. wende,** thought. **196. clepe,** call. **197. stinten,** stopped. **198. for the nones,** for the purpose, i.e., as a result of seeing the daisy. **199. compas,** circle. **201. songen,** sang; **carole wise,** i.e., both singing and dancing. **203. Absolon,** Absalom, the rebellious son of David and a prototype of physical beauty; **gilte,** golden. **204. Ester,** Esther, who as Ahasuerus' queen promoted the fortunes of her kinsman Mordecai and of her people the Jews. **205. Jonathas,** Jonathan, Saul's son and David's friend, a prototype of fidelity. **206. Penolopee,** Penelope, wife of Ulysses, whose fidelity during his long absence was proverbial; **Marcia Catoun,** Marcia the wife of Cato the Younger, a model of steadfastness in women. **207. wifhood,** womanhood. **208. Isoude,** Isolt, Tristram's beloved in the medieval legend; **Elaine,** Helen of Troy. **209. Alceste,** Alcestis, the wife of Admetus the Thessalian, for whom she offered to die; **distaine,** make dim.

Thy faire body, lat it nat appere,
Lavine; and thou, Lucrece of Rome town,
And Polyxene, that boughte love so dere;
Eek Cleopatre, with al thy passioun,
Hide ye youre trouthe in love and youre renown;
And thou, Thisbe, that hast for love swich paine:
Alceste is here, that al that may distaine.

Hero, Dido, Ladomia alle in fere;
Eek Phyllis hanging for thy Demophoun;
And Canace, espied by thy cheere,
Ysipyle betrayed with Jasoun,
Make of youre trouthe in love no boost ne soun;
Nor Ypermestre or Adriane ne plaine:
Alceste is here, that al that may distaine.

Whan that this balade al ysongen was,
Upon the softe and soote greene gras
They setten hem ful softely adown,
By ordre, alle in compas environ:
First sat the God of Love, and thanne his queene,
With the white corowne, clad in greene,
And sitthen al the remenant by and by,
As they were of degree, ful curteisly;
Ne nat a word was spoken in that place

211. **Lavine,** Lavinia, Aeneas' Italian wife; **Lucrece,** victim of Tarquin's rape, who committed suicide. 212. **Polyxene,** Polyxena, Priam's daughter, slain that the dead Achilles might be reunited with her. 213. **Cleopatre,** Cleopatra, Queen of Egypt and Mark Antony's mistress; **passioun,** suffering. 215. **Thisbe,** Pyramus' beloved, who committed suicide after he had killed himself. 217. **Hero** committed suicide after her lover Leander was drowned; **Dido** killed herself when Aeneas abandoned her; **Ladomia,** Laodamia, who killed herself in order to rejoin her dead husband Protesilaus; **in fere,** together. 218. **Phyllis** hanged herself when Demophon abandoned her. 219. **Canace** was punished for loving her brother; **espied,** recognized; **cheere,** appearance. 220. **Ysipyle,** Hypsipyle, who remained faithful to her false lover Jason; **with,** by. 221. **boost,** boast. 222. **Ypermestre,** Hypermnestra, who was punished for refusing to kill her husband Lynceus; **Adriane,** Ariadne, who enabled Theseus to slay the Minotaur and was subsequently abandoned by him; **ne plaine,** make no complaint. 225. **soote,** sweet. 227. **in compas environ,** in a circle. 230. **sitthen,** afterwards; **by and by,** side by side.

The mountance of a furlong way of space.
I, lening faste by under a bente,
Abood to knowe what this peple mente,
As stille as any stoon, til at the laste
The God of Love on me his yë caste,
And saide, "Who resteth there?" And I answerde
Unto his axing, whan that I him herde,
And saide, "Sire, it am I," and cam him neer
And salued him. Quod he, "What doost thou heer
In my presence, and that so boldely?
For it were bettre worthy trewely
A worm to come in my sighte than thou."
"And why, sire," quod I, "and it like you?"
"For thou," quod he, "art therto nothing able:
My servants been alle wise and honourable.
Thou art my mortal fo and me werreyest,
And of mine olde servants thou missayest,
And hinderest hem with thy translacioun,
And lettest folk to han devocioun
To serven me, and holdest it folye
To truste on me: thou maist it nat denye,
For in plein text—it needeth nat to glose—
Thou hast translated the Romance of the Rose,
That is an heresye agains my lawe;
And makest wise folk fro me withdrawe,
And thinkest in thy wit, that is ful cool,
That he nis but a verray propre fool
That loveth paramours too harde and hote.
Wel woot I therby thou biginnest dote,
As olde fooles, whan hir spirit faileth,
Thanne blame they folk, and wite nat what hem aileth.
Hast thou nat maad in Englissh eek the book

233. The time taken to walk a furlong. **234. bente,** slope. **235. Abood,** abided. **239. axing,** question. **241. salued,** saluted. **243. bettre,** more. **245. and,** if; **like,** please. **246. able,** worthy. **248. werreyest,** make war on. **249. missayest,** speak slanderously. **251. lettest . . . han,** prevent people from having. **254. plein,** full; glose, i.e., speak circumspectly. **260. paramours,** mistresses. **261. woot,** know. **263. wite,** blame.

How that Criseide Troilus forsook,
In shewing how that wommen han doon mis?°
But nathelees, answere me now to this:
Why noldest thou as wel have said goodnesse
Of wommen, as thou hast said wikkednesse?
Was ther no good matere in thy minde,
N'in alle thy bookes ne coudest thou nat finde
Som storye of wommen that were goode and trewe?
Yis, God woot, sixty bookes olde and newe
Hast thou thyself, alle ful of stories grete
That bothe Romains and eek Greekes trete
Of sondry wommen, which lif that they ladde,
And evere an hundred goode again° oon badde:
This knoweth God and alle clerkes eke
That usen° swiche materes for to seeke.
What saith Valerie, Titus, or Claudian?°
What saith Jerome agains Jovinian?°
How clene maidenes and how trewe wives,
How stedefaste widwes during alle hir lives
Telleth Jerome, and that nat of a fewe,
But I dar sayn an hundred on a rewe,°
That it is pitee for to rede, and routhe,
The wo that they endure for hir trouthe:
For to hir love were they so trewe
That, rather than they wolde take a newe,
They chose to be deed in sondry wise,
And deiden° as the storye wol devise.
And some were brend, and some were cut the hals,°
And some dreinte° for they wolden nat be fals:
For alle keeped they hir maidenhede,
Or elles wedlok, or hir widwehede;

266. mis, offense. **277. again,** against. **279. usen,** are accustomed. **280. Valerie,** ? Valerius Maximus, who praises various women; **Titus,** Titus Livy, who tells the story of Lucrece; **Claudian,** the poet who told of Proserpina's rape by Pluto. **281.** The relatively few good women that St. Jerome mentions in his tract against Jovinian appear in Dorigen's lament in the Franklin's Tale, lines 659–748. **285. rewe,** row. **290. deed,** dead. **291. deiden,** died. **292. brend,** burnt; **were . . . hals,** had their throats cut. **293. dreinte,** drowned.

And this thing was nat kept for holinesse,
But al for verray vertu and clennesse,
And for men sholde sette on hem no lak—
And yit they were hethene, al the pak,
That were so sore ydrad of alle shame.
Thise olde wommen kepte so hir name
That in this world I trowe men shal nat finde
A man that coude be so trewe and kinde
As was the leeste womman in that tide.
What saith also the pistel of Ovide
Of trewe wives and of hir labour?
What Vincent in his Storial Mirour?
Eek al the world of auctours maistou heere,
Cristene and hethene, trete of swich matere:
It needeth nat al day thus for t'endite.
But yit I saye, what aileth thee to write
The draf of stories, and forgete the corn?
By Sainte Venus, of whom that I was born,
Although thou reneyed hast my lay,
As othere olde fooles many a day,
Thou shalt repente so that it shal be seene."
  Thanne spak Alceste, the worthieste queene,
And saide, "God, right of youre curteisye
Ye moten herknen if he can replye
Agains thise pointes that ye han to him meved:
A god ne sholde nat thus been agreved,
But of his deitee he shal be stable,
And therto rightful and eek merciable;
He shal nat rightfully his ire wreke
Er he have herd the other partye speke.
Al nis nat gospel that is to you plained:

298. And in order that no one should ascribe blame to them. **300. ydrad,** afraid. **302. trowe,** believe. **304. tide,** time. **305. pistel of Ovide,** Ovid's epistle, i.e., the Heroides, a series of complaints by famous women. **306. labour,** suffering. **307. Vincent,** author of an encyclopedia, one section of which he calls the Mirror of History ("Historiale"). **312. draf,** husks; **corn,** kernel. **314. reneyed,** rejected; **lay,** law. **319. moten,** must. **320. to him meved,** i.e., urged against him. **321. agreved,** angry. **323. merciable,** merciful. **324. wreke,** avenge. **326. plained,** complained.

The God of Love heereth many a tale yfeined;
For in youre court is many a losengeour,
And many a quainte totelere accusour,
That tabouren in youre eres many a thing
For hate or for jalous imagining,
And for to han with you som daliaunce.
Envye—I praye to God yive hire meschaunce—
Is lavender in the grete court alway,
For she ne parteth neither night ne day
Out of the hous of Cesar—thus saith Dante:
Who so that gooth, alway she wol nat wante.
This man to you may wrongly been accused,
Ther as by right him oughte been excused;
Or elles, sire, for that this man is nice,
He may translate a thing in no malice,
But for he useth bookes for to make,
And taketh noon heede of what matere he take:
Therfore he wroot the Rose and eek Criseide
Of innocence, and niste what he saide;
Or him was boden make thilke twaye
Of som persone, and dorste it nat withsaye,
For he hath write many a book er this;
He n'hath nat doon so grevously amis
To translate that olde clerkes write,
As though that he of malice wolde endite
Despit of love, and hadde himself ywrought.
This sholde a rightwis lord han in his thought,
And nat been lik tyrants of Lumbardye,
That usen wilfulhede and tyrannye.
For he that king or lord is naturel,
Him oughte nat be tyrant and cruel
As is a fermour, to doon the harm he can:

327. yfeined, i.e., false. **328. losengeour,** flatterer. **329.** And many a crafty tale-telling accuser. **330. tabouren,** drum. **332. daliaunce,** conversation. **334. lavender,** laundress. **337. she . . . wante,** won't be missing. **340. nice,** foolish. **342. useth,** is accustomed. **345. niste,** didn't know. **346. boden,** bidden. **347. withsaye,** refuse. **352. Despit,** contempt. **354. Lumbardye,** Lombardy. **355. usen wilfulhede,** employ wilfulness. **356. naturel,** by birth. **358. fermour,** tax-collector.

He moste thinke it is his lige man,
And that him oughte, of verray duetee,
Shewen his peple plein benignitee,
And wel to heeren hir excusaciouns,
And hir complaintes and peticiouns
In due time, whan they shal it profre.
This is the sentence of the philosophre:
A king to keepe his liges in justice,
Withouten doute that is his office,
And therto is king ful deepe ysworn
Ful many an hundred winter herbiforn;
And for to keepe his lordes hir degree,
As it is right and skilful that they be
Enhaunsed and honoured and most dere,
For they been half-goddes in this world here.
This shal he doon bothe to poore and riche—
Al be that hir estaat be nat yliche—
And han of poore folk compassioun.
For lo, the gentil kinde of the leoun:
For whan a flye offendeth him or biteth,
He with his tail away the flye smiteth
Al esily, for of his genterye
Him deineth nat to wreke him on a flye,
As dooth a curre or elles another beest.
In noble corage oughte been arrest,
And weyen everything by equitee,
And evere han reward to his owene degree.
For sire, it is no maistrye for a lord
To dampne a man withoute answere or word,
And for a lord that is wel foul to use.
And if so be he may him nat excuse,

359. **moste,** must; **lige,** liege. 360. **duetee,** duty. 362. **excusaciouns,** excuses. 365. **sentence,** opinion. 370. **his lordes,** for his lords. 371. **skilful,** reasonable. 372. **Enhaunsed,** advanced. 375. **yliche,** alike. 377. **kinde,** nature. 380. **esily,** gently; **genterye,** nobility. 381. **wreke him,** avenge himself. 383. **corage,** heart; **arrest,** restraint. 384. **weyen,** i.e., the noble heart should weigh. 385. **reward,** regard. 386. **maistrye,** i.e., proper use of power. 387. **dampne,** condemn. 388. **foul to use,** i.e., a foul practice.

But axeth mercy with a sorweful herte
And profreth him right in his bare sherte
To been right at youre owene juggement,
Thanne oughte a god by short avisement
Considere his owene honour and his trespas:
For sith no cause of deeth lith in this cas,
You oughte been the lightere merciable.
Leteth youre ire and beeth somwhat tretable:
The man hath served you of his conning,
And forthered youre lawe with his making;
Whil he was yong he kepte youre estat—
I noot wher he be now a renegat,
But wel I woot with that he can endite,
He hath maked lewed folk to delite
To serven yow, in praising of youre name.
He made the book that highte the Hous of Fame,
And eek the Deeth of Blaunche the Duchesse,
And the Parlement of Fowles as I gesse,
And al the love of Palamon and Arcite
Of Thebes, though the storye is knowe lite,
And many an ympne for youre halidayes,
That highten balades, roundels, virelayes;
And for to speke of other bisinesse,
He hath in prose translated Boece,
And of the Wrecched Engendring of Mankinde,
As man may in Pope Innocent yfinde;
And made the lif also of Sainte Cecile;
He made also, goon is a greet while,
Origenes upon the Maudelaine:

390. **axeth,** asks. 391. i.e., Presents himself for trial without defense. 393. **avisement,** deliberation. 395. **deeth,** death; **lith,** lies. 396. **lightere,** more readily; **merciable,** merciful. 397. **Leteth,** leave; **tretable,** tractable. 398. **of his conning,** i.e., as best he can. 399. **making,** poetry. 401. **noot,** know not; **wher,** whether; **renegat,** renegade. 402. **with that,** i.e., as well as. 403. **lewed,** uneducated. 408. **Palamon and Arcite:** i.e., the Knight's Tale. 409. **lite,** little. 410. **ympne,** hymn. 413. **Boece:** i.e., Boethius' "The Consolation of Philosophy." 414–15. Chaucer's translation of Innocent III's "Wretched Engendering of Mankind" has not survived. 416. **made,** wrote; **Sainte Cecile:** i.e., the Second Nun's Tale. 418. Chaucer's translation of Origen's homily "Mary Magdalene" has not survived.

Him oughte now to have the lesse paine;
He hath maad many a lay and many a thing.
Now as ye been a god and eek a king,
I, youre Alceste, whilom queene of Thrace,
I axe you this man right of youre grace
That ye him nevere hurte in al his live;
And he shal swere to you, and that as blive,
He shal no more agilten in this wise,
But he shal maken as ye wol devise
Of wommen trewe in loving al hir live,
Wher so ye wol of maiden or of wive,
And fortheren you as muche as he missaide
Or in the Rose or elles in Criseide."
 The God of Love answerde hire thus anoon:
"Madame," quod he, "it is so longe agoon
That I you knew so charitable and trewe,
That nevere yit sith that the world was newe
To me ne foond I nevere noon bettre than thee,
That if that I wole save my degree
I may n'I wil nat werne youre requeste:
Al lith in you, dooth with him what you leste;
I al foryive withoute lenger space;
For who so yiveth a yifte or dooth a grace,
Do it betime, his thank is wel the more.
And deemeth ye what he shal doon therfore.
 Go thanke now my lady here," quod he.
 I roos and down I sette me on my knee,
And saide thus: "Madame, the God above
Foryeelde you that ye the God of Love
Han maked me his wratthe to foryive,
And yive me grace so longe for to live
That I may knowe soothly what ye be
That han me holpen and put me in swich degree.
But trewely, I wende as in this cas

422. **whilom,** once. 423. **axe,** ask. 425. **blive,** quickly. 426. **agilten,** offend. 429. **Wher,** whether. 436. **foond,** found. 437. **save my degree,** preserve my dignity. 438. **werne,** refuse. 439. **lith,** lies; **leste,** it please. 442. **betime,** quickly. 447. **Foryeelde,** repay. 448. **me,** i.e., against me; **forgive,** give up. 451. **holpen,** helped. 452. **wende,** thought.

Nought have agilt, ne doon to love trespas,
Forwhy a trewe man, withoute drede,
Hath nat to parte with a theves deede,
Ne a trewe lovere oughte me nat blame
Though that I speke a fals lovere som shame:
They oughte rather with me for to holde
For that I of Criseide wroot or tolde,
Or of the Rose. What so myn auctor mente,
Algate, God woot, it was myn entente
To forthere trouthe in love and it cherice,
And to be war from falsnesse and from vice
By swich ensample: this was my meninge."
  And she answerde, "Lat be thyn arguinge,
For Love ne wol nat countrepleted be
In right ne wrong, and lerne this at me.
Thou hast thy grace, and hold thee right therto;
Now wol I sayn what penance thou shalt do
For thy trespas, and understond it here:
Thou shalt, whil that thou livest, yeer by yere,
The moste partye of thy time spende
In making of a glorious legende
Of goode wommen, maidenes and wives
That were trewe in loving al hir lives,
And telle of false men that hem betrayen,
That al hir lif ne doon nought but assayen
How manye wommen they may doon a shame:
For in youre world that is now holden game.
And though thee listeth nat a lovere be,
Speek wel of love; this penance yive I thee,
And to the God of Love I shal so praye
That he shal charge his servants by any waye
To fortheren thee and wel thy labour quite.
Go now thy way, thy penance is but lite."

453. Nought have agilt, not to have offended in any way. **454. Forwhy,** because; **drede,** doubt. **455. parte with,** i.e., share in the blame for. **461. Algate,** at any rate. **462. cherice,** cherish. **463. to be war,** i.e., to put people on their guard. **465. Lat,** let. **466. countrepleted,** argued against. **472. partye,** part. **479. game,** sport. **480. listeth,** it pleases. **484. quite,** requite. **485. lite,** little.

The God of Love gan smile, and thanne he saide,
"Woostou," quod he, "wher° this be wif or maide,
Or queene or countesse, or of what degree,
That has so litel penance yiven thee,
That hast deserved sorer° for to smerte?
But pitee renneth° soone in gentil herte:
That maist thou seen; she kitheth° what she is."
And I answerde, "Nay, sire, so have I blis,
No more but that I see wel she is good."
"That is a trewe tale, by myn hood,"
Quod Love, "and that thou knowest wel, pardee,
If it be so that thou avise thee.°
Hast thou nat in a book, lith° in thy cheste,
The grete goodnesse of the queene Alceste,
That turned was into a dayesye?—
She that for hir housbonde chees° to die,
And eek to goon to helle rather than he;
And Ercules° rescued hire, pardee,
And broughte hire out of helle again to blis?"
And I answerde again and saide, "Yis,
Now knowe I hire. And is this goode Alceste
The dayesye, and myn owene hertes reste?
Now feele I wel the goodnesse of this wif,
That bothe after hir deeth and in hir lif
Hir grete bountee° doubleth hir renown.
Wel hath she quit° me myn affeccioun
That I have to hir flowr the dayesye:
No wonder is though Jove hire stellifye,°
As telleth Agathon,° for hir goodnesse.
Hir white corowne bereth of it witnesse,
For also manye vertues hath she
As smale flowres in hir corowne be.

487. Woostou, do you know; **wher,** whether. **490. sorer,** more sorely. **491. renneth,** runs, i.e., wells up. **492. kitheth,** makes known. **497. avise thee,** think it over. **498. lith,** that lies. **501. chees,** chose. **503. Ercules,** Hercules, who went down and brought Alcestis back from hell where she had gone in the place of her husband. **510. bountee,** generosity. **511. quit,** repaid. **513. stellifye,** turn her into a star. **514. Agathon,** i.e., *Agatho's Feast,* as Plato's *Symposium* was called, which related the story of Alcestis.

In remembrance of hire and in honour
Cybella made the daisye, and the flowr
Ycorowned al with whit, as men may see;
And Mars yaf to hir corowne reed, pardee,
In stede of rubies, set among the white."
Therwith this queene weex reed for shame a lite
Whan she was praised so in hir presence.
"Thanne," saide Love, "a ful greet necligence
Was it to thee to write unstedfastnesse
Of wommen, sith thou knowest hir goodnesse
By preve and eek by stories here biforn.
Lat be the chaf and writ wel of the corn.
Why noldest thou han writen of Alceste,
And leten Criseide been asleepe and reste?
For of Alceste sholde thy writing be,
Sin that thou woost that kalender is she
Of goodnesse, for she taughte of fin lovinge,
And namely of wifhood the livinge,
And alle the boundes that she oughte keepe:
Thy litel wit was thilke time asleepe.
But now I charge thee upon thy lif
That in thy legende thou make of this wif
Whan thou hast othere smale maad bifore;
And fare now wel, I charge thee namore.
At Cleopatre I wol that thou biginne,
And so forth, and my love so shaltou winne."
And with that word of sleep I gan awake,
And right thus on my legende gan I make.

519. **Cybella,** Cybele, goddess of nature. 521. **reed,** red. 523. **weex,** grew. 528. **preve,** experience. 529. **chaf,** husks; **corn,** kernel. 533. **woost,** know; **kalender,** model. 534. **fin,** fine. 539. **make,** write. 540. **smale,** i.e., less important ones. 542. **wol,** will.

AN ALPHABETICAL HYMN TO THE VIRGIN MARY

*A*lmighty and al merciable° queene
To whom that al this world fleeth for socour,°
To have relees of sinne, of sorwe and teene:°
Glorious virgine, of alle flowres flowr,
To thee I flee, confounded in errour;°
Help and releve, thou mighty debonaire;°
Have mercy on my perilous langour:°
Venquisshed me hath my cruel adversaire.

*B*ountee so fixed hath in thyn herte his tente
That wel I woot thou wolt my socour be;
Thou canst nat werne° him that with good entente
Axeth thyn help; thyn herte is ay so free,°
Thou art largesse of plein° felicitee;
Haven of refut,° of quiete and of reste,
Lo, how that theves sevene° chasen me:
Help, lady bright, er that my ship tobreste.°

*C*onfort is noon but in you, lady dere,
For lo, my sinne and my confusioun,
Which oughten nat in thy presence appere,
Han take on me a grevous accioun,°
Of verray right and desperacioun;°
And as by right they mighten wel sustene°
That I were worthy my dampnacioun,°
Nere° mercy of you, blisful hevene queene.

1. **merciable,** merciful. 2. **fleeth,** flees; **socour,** succor. 3. **teene,** distress. 5. **errour,** bewilderment. 6. **debonaire,** meek (one). 7. **langour,** weakness. 11. **werne,** refuse. 12. **Axeth,** asks; **free,** generous. 13. **largesse,** liberality; **plein,** full. 14. **refut,** refuge. 15. **theves sevene,** i.e., the seven deadly sins. 16. **tobreste,** break apart. 20. Have initiated a grievous lawsuit against me. 21. **verray,** true; **desperacioun,** i.e., because of my despair. 22. **sustene,** sustain, prove. 23. **dampnacioun,** damnation. 24. **Nere,** were it not for.

*D*oute is ther noon, thou queene of misericorde,
That thou nart cause of grace and mercy here;
God vouched sauf thurgh thee with us t'accorde;
For certes, Cristes blisful moder dere,
Were now the bowe bent in swich manere
As it was first, of justice and of ire,
The rightful God nolde of no mercy heere:
But thurgh thee han we grace as we desire.

*E*vere hath myn hope of refut been in thee,
For herbiforn ful ofte, in many a wise,
Hast thou to misericorde received me;
But, mercy, lady, at the grete assise;
Whan we shul come bifore the hye justise,
So litel fruit shal thanne in me be founde
That but thou er that day correcte me,
Of verray right my werk me wol confounde.

*F*leeing I flee for socour to thy tente,
Me for to hide from tempest ful of drede,
Biseeching you that ye you nat absente;
Though I be wikke, O help yit at this neede;
Al have I been a beest in wil and deede,
Yit, lady, thou me clothe with thy grace:
Thyn enemy and myn—lady, taak heede—
Unto my deeth in point is me to chace.

*G*lorious maide and moder, which that nevere
Were bittre, neither in erthe nor in see,
But ful of swetnesse and of mercy evere,
Help that my fader be nat wroth with me.
Speek thou, for I ne dar nat him ysee,
So have I doon in erthe, allas the while.
But certes, but if thou my sucour be,
To stink eterne he wol my gost exile.

25. **misericorde,** mercy. 27. **accorde,** become reconciled. 33. **refut,** refuge. 36. **assise,** inquest, i.e., the Last Judgment. 44. **wikke,** wicked. 45. **Al have I,** although I have. 48. **in point is,** is about to. 55. **but if,** unless. 56. **gost,** spirit.

*H*e vouched sauf, tel him, as was his wille,
Bicomen a man to have oure alliaunce,
And with his precious blood he wroot the bille
Upon the crois as general acquitaunce
To every penitent in ful creaunce;
And therfore, lady bright, thou for us praye;
Thanne shalt thou bothe stinte al his grevaunce,
And make oure fo to failen of his preye.

I woot it wel, thou wolt been oure socour,
Thou art so ful of bountee, in certain;
For whan a soule falleth in errour,
Thy pitee gooth and haleth him ayain;
Thanne makest thou his pees with his soverein,
And bringest him out of the crooked streete:
Who so thee loveth, he shal nat love in vain;
That shal he finde as he the lif shal lete.

*K*alenderes enlumined been they
That in this world been lighted with thy name;
And who so gooth to you the righte way,
Him thar nat drede in soule to be lame.
Now, queene of confort, sith thou art that same
To whom I seeke for my medicine,
Lat nat my fo namore my wounde entame:
Myn hele into thyn hand al I resine.

*L*ady, thy sorwe can I nat portraye
Under the crois, ne his grevous penaunce;
But for youre bothes paines I you praye,
Lat nat oure alder fo make his bobaunce
That he hath in his listes of meschaunce
Convict that ye bothe have bought so dere;

58. **Bicomen,** to become; **oure alliaunce,** i.e., kinship with us. 59. **bille,** legal contract. 60. **acquitaunce,** legal discharge. 61. **creaunce,** faith. 63. **stinte,** put a stop to. 68. **haleth,** pulls back. 72. **lete,** leave. 73. **enlumined,** made bright. 76. **thar,** need. 79. **entame,** reopen. 80. **hele,** health; **resine,** consign. 82. **his,** i.e., Christ's. 84. **oure . . . fo,** the foe of us all; **bobaunce,** boast. 85. **listes,** i.e., arena. 86. **Convict,** overcome; **that,** i.e., those whom.

As I saide erst, thou ground of oure substaunce,
Continue on us thy pitous yën clere.

*M*oises, that sawgh the bussh with flaumbes rede
Brenning, of which ther nevere a stikke brende,
Was signe of thyn unwemmed maidenhede:
Thou art the bussh on which ther gan descende
The Holy Gost, the which that Moises wende
Hadde been afir, and this was in figure;
Now, lady, from the fir thou us defende,
Which that in helle eternally shal dure.

*N*oble princesse, that nevere haddest peere,
Certes, if any confort in us be,
That cometh of thee, thou Cristes moder dere;
We han noon other melodye or glee
Us to rejoice in our adversitee,
Ne advocat noon that wol and dar so praye
For us, and that for litel hire as ye,
That helpen for an Ave-Marie or twaye.

O verray light of yën that been blinde,
O verray lust of labour and distresse,
O tresorere of bountee to mankinde,
Thee whom God chees to moder for humblesse;
From his ancille he made thee maistresse
Of hevene and erthe, oure bille up for to bede:
This world awaiteth evere on thy goodnesse,
For thou ne failest nevere wight at neede.

*P*urpos I have somtime for to enquere
Wherfore and why the Holy Gost thee soughte,

87. erst, before. **89. Moises,** Moses: see the Book of Exodus III; **flaumbes,** flames. **90. Brenning,** burning; **brende,** burnt. **91. unwemmed,** unspotted. **93. wende,** supposed. **94. in figure,** i.e., symbolic. **96. dure,** endure. **106. lust,** desire, object. **107. tresorere,** treasurer, dispenser. **108. chees,** chose; **to moder,** as his mother. **109. ancille,** handmaiden. **110. oure . . . bede,** to offer up our petition. **113. enquere,** inquire.

Whan Gabrielles vois cam to thyn ere:
He nat to werre us swich a wonder wroughte,
But for to save us that he sitthen boughte;
Thanne needeth us no wepne us for to save,
But only ther we diden nat as us oughte
Do penitence, and mercy axe and have.

Queene of confort, yit whan I me bithinke
That I agilt have bothe him and thee,
And that my soule is worthy for to sinke,
Allas, I caitif, whider may I flee?
Who shal unto thy sone my mene be?
Who but thyself, that art of pitee welle?
Thou hast more routhe on oure adversitee
Than in this world mighte any tonge telle.

Redresse me, moder, and me chastise,
For certainly my fadres chastisinge
That dar I nought biden in no wise,
So hidous is his rightful rekeninge.
Moder, of whom oure mercy gan to springe,
Beeth ye my juge, and eek my soules leeche,
For evere in you is pitee haboundinge
To eech that wol of pitee you biseeche.

Sooth is that God ne graunteth no pitee
Withoute thee, for God of his goodnesse
Foryiveth noon but it like unto thee:
He hath thee maked vicare and maistresse
Of al the world, and eek gouvernouresse
Of hevene, and he represseth his justise
After thy wil; and therfore in witnesse
He hath thee corowned in so royal wise.

116. werre, make war on. **117. sitthen,** afterwards. **119. ther,** i.e., in cases where. **120. axe,** ask. **122. agilt,** offended. **124. caitif,** captive. **125. mene,** intermediary. **127. routhe,** pity. **129. Redresse,** correct. **134. leeche,** physician. **135. haboundinge,** abounding. **139. but,** unless; **like,** please.

*T*emple devout, ther God hath his woninge,°
Fro which thise misbilevedᵒ deprived been,
To you my soule penitent I bringe:
Receive me, I can no ferther fleen;
With thornes venimous, O hevene queen,
For which the erthe accursed was ful yore,
I am so wounded as ye may wel seen,
That I am lost almost, it smert° so sore.

*V*irgine, that art so noble of apparaile,°
And ledest us into the hye towr
Of Paradis, thou me wisse° and conseile
How I may have thy grace and thy socour:
Al° have I been in filthe and in errour,
Lady, unto thy court thou me ajourne,°
That cleped° is thy bench, O fresshe flowr,
Ther as that mercy evere shal sojourne.

*X*ristus° thy sone, that in this world alighte
Upon the crois to suffre his passioun,
And eek that Longius his herte pighte,°
And made his herte blood to renne° adown—
And al was this for my savacioun,
And I to him am fals and eek unkinde,
And yit he wol° nat my dampnacioun:
This thanke I you, socour of al mankinde.

*Y*saac was figure° of his deeth, certain,
That so fer forth° his fader wolde obeye
That him ne roughte no thing to be slain:°

145. woninge, dwelling. **146. misbilevèd,** misbelieving (ones), i.e., heretics and pagans. **152. smert,** smarts. **153. apparaile,** i.e., person. **155. wisse,** direct. **157. Al,** although. **158. ajourne,** summon. **159. cleped,** called. **161. Xristus:** the chi (χ) of Greek Χριστος is taken as English *X*. **163.** Longius or Longinus was the blind man who was forced to pierce Christ's side with a spear; **pighte,** pierced. **164. renne,** run. **167. wol,** desires. **169. Ysaac,** Isaac, whose father Abraham almost put him to death at God's command; **figure,** symbol. **170. so fer forth,** to such lengths. **171.** That he cared not at all that he was slain.

Right so thy sone liste as a lamb to deye.
Now, lady ful of mercy, I you praye,
Sith he his mercy mesured so large,
By ye nat scant, for alle we singe and saye
That ye been from vengeance ay oure targe.

Zacharie you clepeth the opene welle
To wasshe sinful soule out of his gilt:
Therfore this lesson oughte I wel to telle,
That nere thy tendre herte, we weren spilt.
Now lady, sith thou bothe canst and wilt
Been to the seed of Adam merciable,
Bring us to that palais that is bilt
To penitents that been to mercy able.

MERCILESS BEAUTY

I

Youre yën two wol slee me sodeinly:
I may the beautee of hem nat sustene,
So woundeth it thurghout myn herte keene.

And but youre word wol helen hastily
Myn hertes wounde, whil that it is greene,
  Youre yën two wol slee me sodeinly:
  I may the beautee of hem nat sustene.

Upon my trouthe, I saye you faithfully
That ye been of my lif and deeth the queene,
For with my deeth the trouthe shal be seene.

172. liste, pleased. **176. targe,** shield. **177. Zacharie,** Zechariah, the prophet; **clepeth,** calls; **welle,** fountain. **180. nere,** were it not for; **spilt,** destroyed. **182. merciable,** merciful. **184. able,** deserving.

1. slee, slay. **2. sustene,** withstand. **3. keene,** keenly. **4. but,** unless. **5. greene,** i.e., fresh.

Youre yën two wol slee me sodeinly:
I may the beautee of hem nat sustene,
So woundeth it thurghout myn herte keene.

II

So hath youre beautee fro youre herte chaced
Pitee, that me ne availeth nought to plaine:
For Daunger halt youre mercy in his chaine.
Giltelees my deeth thus han ye me purchaced;
I saye you sooth, me needeth nought to feine:
So hath youre beautee fro youre herte chaced
Pitee, that me ne availeth nought to plaine.

Allas, that nature hath in you compaced
So greet beautee that no man may attaine
To mercy, though he sterve for the paine.
So hath youre beautee fro youre herte chaced
Pitee, that me ne availeth nought to plaine:
For Daunger halt youre mercy in his chaine.

III

Sin I fro Love escaped am so fat,
I nevere thenke to been in his prison lene:
Sin I am free, I counte him nat a bene.

He may answere and saye right this and that;
I do no fors, I speke right as I mene:
Sin I fro Love escaped am so fat,
I nevere thenke to been in his prison lene.

Love hath my name ystrike out of his sclat,
And he is strike out of my bookes clene

15. **plaine,** complain. 16. **Daunger,** haughtiness; **halt,** holds. 17. **purchaced,** procured. 18. **feine,** dissemble. 21. **compaced,** enclosed. 23. **sterve,** die. 28. **thenke,** intend. 29. **counte him,** consider him worth; **bene,** bean. 31. **do no fors,** don't care. 34. **ystrike,** struck; **sclat,** slate.

For everemo; ther is noon other mene.
  Sin I fro Love escaped am so fat,
  I nevere thenke to been in his prison lene:
  Sin I am free, I counte him nat a bene.

TO ROSAMOND

Madame, ye been of alle beautee shrine
As fer as cercled is the mapemounde:
For as the crystal glorious ye shine,
And like ruby been youre cheekes rounde.
Therwith ye been so merye and so jocounde
That at a revel whan that I see you daunce
It is an oinement unto my wounde,
Though ye to me ne do no daliaunce.

For though I weepe of teres ful a tine,
Yit may that wo myn herte nat confounde;
Youre semy vois, that ye so smal outtwine,
Maketh my thought in joye and blis habounde:
So curteisly I go with love bounde
That to myself I saye in my penaunce,
"Suffiseth me to love you, Rosemounde,
Though ye to me ne do no daliaunce."

Was nevere pik walwed in galauntine
As I in love am walwed and ywounde,
For which ful ofte I of myself divine
That I am trewe Tristam the secounde;

36. mene, solution.

2. i.e., To the farthest circumference of the map of the world. **8. me . . . daliaunce,** i.e., show me no encouragement. **9. tine,** tub. **11. semy,** small; **smal,** delicately; **outtwine,** spin out. **12. habounde,** abound. **14. penaunce,** i.e., pangs of unrequited love. **17. pik,** pike; **walwed in galauntine,** rolled in galantine sauce. **20. Tristam,** the famous lover of Isolt in medieval legend, renowned for his constancy.

My love may not refreide nor affounde;
I brenne ay in amorous plesaunce:
Do what you list, I wol youre thral be founde,
Though ye to me ne do no daliaunce.

COMPLAINT TO HIS PURSE

To you, my purs, and to noon other wight,
Complaine I, for ye be my lady dere.
I am so sory, now that ye be light,
For certes, but if ye make me hevy cheere,
Me were as lief be laid upon my beere;
For which unto youre mercy thus I crye:
Beeth hevy again, or elles moot I die.

Now voucheth sauf this day er it be night
That I of you the blisful soun may heere,
Or see youre colour, lik the sonne bright,
That of yelownesse hadde nevere peere.
Ye be my lif, ye be myn hertes steere,
Queene of confort and of good compaignye:
Beeth hevy again, or elles moot I die.

Ye purs, that been to me my lives light
And saviour, as in this world down here,
Out of this tonne helpe me thurgh your might,
Sith that ye wol nat be my tresorere;
For I am shave as neigh as any frere.
But yit I praye unto youre curteisye:
Beeth hevy again, or elles moot I die.

21. refreide nor affounde, cool nor freeze. **22. brenne,** burn. **23. list,** it pleases; **thral,** slave.

4. but if, unless. **5. Me . . . lief,** I'd just as soon; **beere,** bier. **7. moot,** must. **12. steere,** rudder, guide. **17. tonne,** tun, ? predicament. **18. tresorere,** disburser. **19. neigh,** close; **frere,** friar.

Envoy to Henry IV

O conquerour of Brutus Albioun,°
Which that by line and free eleccioun
Been verray king, this song to you I sende:
And ye, that mowen° alle oure harmes amende,
Have minde upon my supplicacioun.

TO HIS SCRIBE ADAM

Adam scrivain,° if evere it thee bifalle
Boece° or Troilus for to writen newe,
Under thy longe lokkes thou moste have the scalle,°
But after my making thou write more trewe,°
So ofte a day I moot° thy werk renewe,
It to correcte, and eek to rubbe and scrape:
And al is thurgh thy necligence and rape.°

ENVOY TO BUKTON

My maister Bukton, whan of Crist oure king
Was axed,° "What is trouthe or soothfastnesse?"
He nat a word answerde to that axing,°
As who saith, "No man is al trewe, I gesse."
And therfore though I highte° to expresse
The sorwe and wo that is in mariage,
I dar nat writen of it no wikkednesse,
Lest I myself falle eft in swich dotage.°

22. **Brutus Albioun,** Britain (Albion) was supposed to have been founded by Brutus, the grandson of Aeneas who founded Rome. 25. **mowen,** may.

1. **scrivain,** scribe. 2. **Boece,** i.e., Chaucer's translation of Boethius. 3. **thou moste,** i.e., may you; **scalle,** scurf. 4. Unless you write more accurately what I've composed. 5. **moot,** must. 7. **rape,** haste.

2. **axed,** asked. 3. **axing,** question. 5. **highte,** promised. 8. **eft,** again; **dotage,** stupidity.

I wol nat sayn how that it is the chaine
Of Satanas, on which he gnaweth evere;
But I dar sayn, were he out of his paine,
As by his wil he wolde be bounde nevere:
But thilke doted fool that eft hath levere
Ychained be, than out of prison creepe,
God lete him nevere fro his wo dissevere,
Ne no man him biwaile though he weepe.

But yit, lest thou do worse, taak a wif:
Bet is to wedde than brenne in worse wise.
But thou shalt have sorwe on thy flessh thy lif,
And been thy wives thral, as sayn thise wise.
And if that Holy Writ may nat suffise,
Experience shal thee teche, so may happe,
That thee were levere to be take in Frise,
Than eft falle of wedding in the trappe.

This litel writ, proverbes, or figure,
I sende you: taak keep of it, I rede.
Unwis is he that can no wele endure:
If thou be siker, put thee nat in drede.
The Wif of Bathe I praye you that ye rede
Of this matere that we have on honde:
God graunte you youre lif freely to lede
In freedom, for ful hard is to be bonde.

ENVOY TO SCOGAN

Tobroken been the statuts hye in hevene
That creat were eternally to dure,

10. Satanas, Satan. **13. hath levere,** would prefer to. **18. Bet,** better; **brenne,** burn. **19. thy** (2), i.e., during your. **23. take in Frise,** captured in Friesland. **24. eft,** again. **25. figure,** illustration. **26. keep,** heed; **rede,** advise. **27. wele,** prosperity. **28. siker,** secure. **32. bonde,** bound.

1. Tobroken, shattered. **2. creat,** created; **dure,** endure.

Sin that I see the brighte goddes sevene
Mowe weepe and waile and passioun endure,
As may in erthe a mortal creature.
Allas, from whennes may this thing proceede?—
Of which errour I die almost for drede.

By word eterne whilom was it shape
That from the fifthe cercle, in no manere,
Ne mighte a drope of teres down escape,
But now so weepeth Venus in hir spere
That with hir teres she wol drenche us here.
Allas, Scogan, this is for thyn offence:
Thou causest this diluge of pestilence.

Hast thou nat said, in blaspheme of the goddes,
Thurgh pride and thurgh thy grete reccheleesnesse,
Swich thing as in the lawe of love forbode is—
That for thy lady saw nat thy distresse,
Therfore thou yave hire up at Michelmesse?
Allas, Scogan, of olde folk ne yonge,
Was nevere erst Scogan blamed for his tonge.

Thow drowe in scorn Cupide eek to record
Of thilke rebel word that thou hast spoken,
For which he wol no lenger be thy lord;
And though his bowe, Scogan, be nat broken,
He wol nat with his arwes been ywroken
On thee, ne me, ne noon of oure figure:
We shal of him have neither hurt ne cure.

Now certes, freend, I drede of thyn unhap,
Lest for thy gilt the wreche of love proceede

3. **goddes,** planets. 4. **passioun,** suffering. 7. **errour,** bewildering circumstance. 8. **whilom,** once; **shape,** decreed. 9. **fifthe cercle,** the orbit of Venus. 11. **spere,** sphere. 12. **drenche,** drown. 14. **diluge,** deluge. 16. **reccheleesnesse,** recklessness. 17. **forbode,** forbidden. 18. **for,** because. 21. **erst,** before. 22. You also scornfully called Cupid to witness. 23. **thilke,** that same. 26. **ywroken,** avenged. 29. **unhap,** misfortune. 30. **wreche,** vengeance.

On alle hem that been hore and rounde of shap,
That been so likly folk in love to speede;
Thanne shal we for oure labour han no meede.
But wel I woot thou wolt answere and saye,
"Lo, olde grisel list to ryme and playe."

Nay, Scogan, say nat so, for I m'excuse;
God helpe me so, in no rym, doutelees,
Ne thinke I nevere of sleep to wake my muse
That rusteth in my sheethe stille in pees.
Whil I was yong, I putte it forth in prees;
But al shal passen that men prose or ryme:
Take every man his turn, as for his time.

Scogan, that kneelest at the welles heed
Of grace, of al honour and worthinesse,
In th'ende of which streem I am dul as deed,
Forgete in solitarye wildernesse,
Yit, Scogan, think on Tullius kindenesse:
Minne thy freend ther it may fructifye;
Farewel, and looke thou nevere eft Love defye.

LACK OF STEADFASTNESS

Somtime this world was so stedefast and stable
That mannes word was holde obligacioun,
And now it is so fals and deceivable
That word and werk, as in conclusioun,
Be nothing oon, for turned up-so-down
Is al this world by wikked wilfulnesse,
That al is lost thurgh lak of stedfastnesse.

31. **hore,** hoary. 32. **likly,** able; **speede,** help. 33. **meede,** reward. 35. The old gray horse feels like rhyming and playing. 40. **prees,** public. 43. **welles heed,** stream's head, probably the royal court at Windsor. 45. **ende,** probably Greenwich, where Chaucer lived for a time. 46. **Forgete,** forgotten. 47. **Tullius,** Cicero, who wrote a treatise on friendship. 48. **Minne,** remember. 49. **eft,** again.

3. **deceivable,** deceitful. 5. **oon,** i.e., the same; **up-so-down,** upside down.

What maketh this world to be so variable
But lust that folkes have in dissencioun?
For nowadayes a man is holde unable
But if he can, by som collusioun,
Do his neighebor wrong or oppressioun.
What causeth this but wilful wrecchednesse,
That al is lost for lak of stedfastnesse?

Trouthe is put down, reson is holden fable,
Vertu hath now no dominacioun;
Pitee exiled, no man is merciable;
Thurgh coveitise is blent discrecioun;
The world hath maad a permutacioun
From right to wrong, from trouthe to fikelnesse,
That al is lost for lak of stedfastnesse.

Envoy to Richard II

O Prince, desire for to be honourable;
Cherisse thy folk, and hate extorcioun;
Suffre no thing that may be reprevable
To thyn estaat doon in thy regioun.
Shew forth thy swerd of castigacioun:
Dreed God, do lawe, love trouthe and worthinesse,
And drive thy peple again to stedfastnesse.

GENTILESSE

The firste fader and findere of gentilesse,
What man desireth gentil for to be
Moste folwe his traas, and alle his wittes dresse
Vertu to sue, and vices for to flee:

9. **lust,** pleasure. 10. **unable,** incompetent. 15. **fable,** fiction. 17. **merciable,** merciful. 18. **coveitise,** avarice; **blent,** blinded. 24. **be reprevable,** bring reproof. 25. **doon,** to be done. 27. **do,** execute.

1. **findere,** founder. 3. **traas,** path; **dresse,** prepare. 4. **sue,** follow.

For unto vertu longeth dignitee,
And nought the revers, saufly dar I deeme,
Al were he mitre, crowne, or diademe.

This firste stok was ground of rightwisnesse,
Trewe of his word, sobre, pietous, and free,
Clene of his gost, and loved bisinesse
Against the vice of slouthe, in honestee;
And but his heir love vertu as dide he,
He is nat gentil, though he riche seeme,
Al were he mitre, crowne, or diademe.

Vice may wel be heir to old richesse,
But ther may no man, as ye may wel see,
Biquethe his heir his vertuous noblesse:
That is appropred unto no degree
But to the firste fader in majestee,
That maketh his heir him that wol him queme,
Al were he mitre, crowne, or diademe.

TRUTH

Flee fro the prees and dwelle with soothfastnesse;
Suffise unto thy thing, though it be smal;
For hoord hath hate, and climbing tikelnesse;
Prees hath envye, and wele blent overal.
Savoure no more than thee bihoove shal;
Rule wel thyself that other folk canst rede:
And Trouthe shal delivere, it is no drede.

5. **longeth,** belongs. 6. **saufly,** safely. 7. **Al were he,** even if he wear. 8. **rightwisnesse,** righteousness. 9. **pietous,** merciful; **free,** generous. 10. **gost,** spirit. 11. **slouthe,** sloth. 13. **riche,** noble. 18. **appropred,** exclusively assigned. 20. **queme,** please.

1. **prees,** crowd. 2. **Suffise . . . thing,** i.e., be content with what you have. 3. **hoord,** hoarding; **hath,** i.e., causes; **tikelnesse,** insecurity. 4. **wele,** prosperity; **blent,** blinds. 5. **Savoure,** relish. 6. **rede,** advise.

Tempest thee nought al crooked to redresse°
In trust of hire° that turneth as a bal;
Muche wele stant in litel bisinesse;°
Be war therfore to spurne ayains an al.°
Strive nat as dooth the crokke with the wal.
Daunte° thyself that dauntest otheres deede:
And Trouthe shal delivere, it is no drede.

That thee is sent, receive in buxomnesse;°
The wrastling for the world axeth° a fal;
Here is noon hoom, here nis but wildernesse:
Forth, pilgrim, forth! Forth, beest, out of thy stal!
Know thy contree, looke up, thank God of al.
Hold the heigh way and lat thy gost° thee lede:
And Trouthe shal delivere, it is no drede.

Therfore, thou Vache,° leve thyn olde wrecchednesse
Unto the world; leve° now to be thral.
Crye him mercy that of his heigh goodnesse
Made thee of nought, and in especial
Draw unto him, and pray in general,
For thee and eek for othere, hevenelich meede:°
And Trouthe shal delivere, it is no drede.

8. Do not disturb yourself to straighten all that's crooked. **9. hire,** Fortune, who is like a ball in that she is always turning a different aspect to men. **10. wele,** peace of mind; **stant,** stands; **bisinesse,** anxiety. **11. spurne . . . al,** i.e., kick against the pricks. **13. Daunte,** master. **15. buxomnesse,** obedience. **16. axeth,** asks for. **20. gost,** spirit. **22. Vache,** probably Sir Philip de la Vache, with a pun on the French word for "cow." **23. leve,** i.e., cease. **27. meede,** reward.

Troilus and Criseide

BOOK ONE

The Prologue

The double sorwe of Troilus to tellen,
That was the king Priamus sone of Troye,
In loving how his aventures fellen
Fro wo to wele, and after out of joye,
My purpos is, er that I parte fro ye:
Tesiphone, thou help me for t'endite
Thise woful vers that weepen as I write.

To thee clepe I, thou goddesse of torment,
Thou cruel furye, sorwing evere in paine:
Help me, that am the sorweful instrument
That helpeth loveres as I can, to plaine;
For wel sit it, the soothe for to sayne,
A woful wight to han a drery fere,
And to a sorweful tale a sory cheere.

2. **Priamus,** Priam's: Priam was King of Troy at the time of the Greek siege. 4. **wele,** happiness. 6. **Tesiphone,** Tisiphone, one of the classic furies. 7. **vers that,** verses which. 8. **clepe,** call. 11. **plaine,** complain. 12. **sit it,** it is suiting. 13. **fere,** companion. 14. **cheere,** manner.

For I, that God of Loves servants serve,
Ne dar to Love for myn unliklinesse
Prayen for speed, al sholde I therfore sterve,
So fer am I from his help in derknesse;
But nathelees, if this may doon gladnesse
To any lovere, and his cause availe,
Have he my thank, and myn be this travaile.

But ye loveres that bathen in gladnesse,
If any drope of pitee in you be,
Remembreth you on passed hevinesse
That ye han felt, and on the adversitee
Of othere folk, and thinketh how that ye
Han felt that Love dorste you displese,
Or ye han wonne him with too greet an ese.

And prayeth for hem that been in the cas
Of Troilus, as ye may after heere,
That Love hem bringe in hevene to solas;
And eek for me, prayeth to God so dere
That I have might to shewe in som manere
Swich paine and wo as Loves folk endure,
In Troilus unsely aventure.

And biddeth eek for hem that been despaired
In love, that nevere nil recovered be;
And eek for hem that falsly been apaired
Thurgh wikked tonges, be it he or she:
Thus biddeth God, for his benignitee,
To graunte hem soone out of this world to pace
That been despaired out of Loves grace.

And biddeth eek for hem that been at ese,
That God hem graunte ay good perseveraunce,

17. **speed,** success; **al,** although; **sterve,** die. 18. **fer,** far. 21. **travaile,** work. 24. **passed,** by-gone. 28. **Or,** or else. 35. **unsely,** unhappy. 36. **biddeth,** pray. 37. **recovered,** cured. 38. **apaired,** slandered. 41. **pace,** pass. 44. **perseveraunce,** continuance.

And sende hem might hir ladies so to plese
That it to Love be worshipe and plesaunce;
For so hope I my soule best avaunce,
To praye for hem that Loves servants be,
And write hir wo, and live in charitee;

And for to have of hem compassioun,
As though I were hir owene brother dere.
Now herkneth with a good entencioun,
For now wil I goon straight to my matere,
In which ye may the double sorwes heere
Of Troilus, in loving of Criseide,
And how that she forsook him er she deide.

The Story

It is wel wist how that the Greekes stronge
In armes with a thousand shippes wente
To Troyewardes, and the citee longe
Assegeden—neigh ten yeer er they stente—
In divers wise and in oon entente:
The ravisshing to wreken of Elaine,
By Paris doon, they wroughten al hir paine.

Now fil it so that in the town ther was
Dwelling a lord of greet auctoritee,
A greet divin that cleped was Calcas,
That in science so expert was that he
Knew wel that Troye sholde destroyed be,
By answere of his god that highte thus:
Daun Phebus or Appollo Delphicus.

47. **avaunce,** to make prosper. 56. **deide,** died. 57. **wist,** known. 59. **To Troyewardes,** towards Troy. 60. **Assegeden,** besieged; **stente,** stopped. 62. **wreken,** avenge; **Elaine,** Helen, the Grecian queen whose kidnapping by Troilus' brother Paris caused the Trojan war. 63. **wroughten,** i.e., undertook; **paine,** trouble. 64. **fil,** befell. 66. **divin,** seer; **cleped,** called; **Calcas,** Calchas. 69. **answere,** i.e., oracle. 70. Lord Phoebus or Apollo of Delphi.

So whan this Calcas knew by calculinge,
And eek by answere of this Appollo,
That Greekes sholden swich a peple bringe
Thurgh which that Troye moste been fordo,
He caste anoon out of the town to go,
For wel wiste he by sort that Troye sholde
Destroyed been—ye, wolde who so nolde.

For which, for to departen softely
Took purpos ful this forknowinge wise,
And to the Greekes host ful prively
He stal anoon, and they in curteis wise
Him diden bothe worshipe and servise,
In trust that he hath conning hem to rede
In every peril which that is to drede.

The noise up roos, whan it was first espied,
Thurgh al the town, and generally was spoken
That Calcas traitour fled was and allied
With hem of Greece; and casten to be wroken
On him that falsly hadde his faith so broken,
And saiden, "He and al his kin atones
Been worthy for to brennen, fel and bones."

Now hadde Calcas lefte in this meschaunce,
Al unwist of this false and wikked deede,
His doughter, which that was in greet penaunce,
For of hir lif she was ful sore in drede,
As she that niste what was best to rede;
For bothe a widwe was she, and allone
Of any freend to whom she dorste mone.

71. **calculinge,** forecast. 74. **fordo,** destroyed. 75. **caste,** plotted. 76. **wiste,** knew; **sort,** lot, i.e., divination. 77. **wolde who so nolde,** whoever desired or did not desire it. 78. **softely,** quietly. 79. **wise,** wise man. 81. **stal,** stole. 83. **conning,** skill; **rede,** advise. 85. **espied,** discovered. 88. **casten,** i.e., the people planned; **wroken,** avenged. 91. **brennen,** burn; **fel,** skin. 93. **unwist,** unknowing. 94. **penaunce,** sorrow. 96. **niste,** knew not; **rede,** i.e., do. 98. **mone,** complain.

Criseide was this lady name aright:
As to my doom° in al Troyes citee
Nas noon so fair, for passing° every wight,
So angelik was hir natif beautee,
That lik a thing immortal seemed she,
As dooth an hevenissh parfit° creature
That down were sent in scorning of nature.

This lady, which that alday herde at ere
Hir fadres shame, his falsnesse and tresoun,
Wel neigh out of hir wit for sorwe and fere,
In widwes habit large, of samit° brown,
On knees she fil biforn Ector° adown:
With pitous vois and tendrely weeping,
His mercy bad,° hirselven excusing.

Now was this Ector pitous of nature,
And sawgh that she was sorwefully bigoon,°
And that she was so fair a creature;
Of his goodnesse he gladed° hire anoon,
And saide, "Lat youre fadres tresoun goon
Forth with meschaunce,° and ye yourself in joye
Dwelleth with us whil you good list° in Troye.

And al th'honour that men may doon you° have,
As ferforth as° youre fader dwelled here,
Ye shul have, and youre body shal men save,°
As fer° as I may ought enquere or heere."
And she him thanked with ful humble cheere,
And ofter wolde, and° it hadde been his wille,
And took hir leve, and hoom,° and heeld hire stille.

100. doom, judgment. **101. passing,** surpassing. **104. parfit,** perfect. **109. large,** full; **samit,** samite, a heavy silk. **110. fil,** fell; **Ector,** Hector, the chief of Priam's sons. **112. bad,** asked. **114. bigoon,** situated. **116. gladed,** gladdened. **118. Forth . . . meschaunce,** i.e., to the devil. **119. list,** please. **120. doon you,** cause you to. **121. ferforth as,** much as when. **122. save,** keep safe. **123. fer,** far. **125. ofter,** more often; **wolde,** i.e., would have thanked him; **and,** if. **126. hoom,** i.e., went home.

And in hir hous she abood with swich meinee
As til hir honour neede was to holde,
And whil she was dwelling in that citee
Kepte hir estaat, and bothe of yonge and olde
Ful wel biloved, and wel men of hire tolde—
But whether that she children hadde or noon,
I rede it nought, therfore I late it goon.

The thinges fellen as they doon of werre
Bitwixen hem of Troye and Greekes ofte,
For som day boughten they of Troye it derre,
And eft the Greekes founden no thing softe
The folk of Troye; and thus Fortune on lofte,
Now up, now down, gan hem to wheelen bothe
After hir cours, ay whil that they were wrothe.

But how this town cam to destruccioun
Ne falleth nought to purpos me to telle,
For it were here a long digressioun
Fro my matere, and you too longe to dwelle:
But the Troyan geestes as they felle,
In Omer or in Dares or in Dite
Who so that can may reden hem as they write.

But though the Greekes hem of Troye shetten
And hir citee biseged al aboute,
Hir olde usage nolde they nat letten,
As for to honoure hir goddes ful devoute;
But aldermost in honour, out of doute,
They hadde a relik heet Palladion,
That was hir trist aboven everichoon.

127. **abood,** abided; **meinee,** company. 128. **til,** to. 134. **fellen,** befell; **werre,** war. 136. **som,** one; **derre,** more dearly. 137. **eft,** again. 139. **wheelen,** turn on her wheel. 140. **After hir,** according to her. 144. **dwelle,** make remain. 145. **geestes,** stories; **felle,** happened. 146. **Omer,** Homer; **Dares,** Dares of Troy, supposed author of an account of the Trojan war; **Dite,** Dictys of Crete, supposed author of a diary recounting the siege of Troy. 148. **shetten,** shut, i.e., shut in. 150. **letten,** forgo. 152. **aldermost,** most of all. 153. **heet,** called; **Palladion,** a statue of Athena. 154. **trist,** trust.

And so bifel, whan comen was the time
Of Aperil, whan clothed is the mede°
With newe greene of lusty Veer the prime,°
And swoote° smellen flowres white and rede,
In sondry wises shewed,° as I rede,
The folk of Troye hir observances olde,
Palladiones feeste for to holde.

And to the temple in al hir beste wise
In general ther wente many a wight,
To herknen of Palladion the servise;
And namely,° so many a lusty knight,
So many a lady fressh and maiden bright,
Ful wel arrayed, bothe the moste and leeste,°
Ye, bothe for the seson and the feeste.°

Among thise othere folk was Criseida,
In widwes habit blak, but nathelees,
Right as oure firste lettre is now an *A*,
In beautee first so stood she makelees:°
Hir goodly looking gladed al the prees.°
Nas nevere yit seen thing to been praised derre,°
Nor under cloude blak so bright a sterre,°

As was Criseide, as folk saide everichone
That hire biheelden in hir blake weede.
And yit she stood ful lowe and stille allone,
Bihinden othere folk, in litel brede,°
And neigh the dore, ay under shames drede:
Simple of attir and debonaire of cheere,°
With ful assured looking and manere.

This Troilus, as he was wont to gide
His yonge knightes, ladde hem up and down

156. mede, meadow. **157. Veer,** springtime; **prime,** beginning. **158. swoote,** sweet. **159. shewed,** i.e., they showed. **165. namely,** especially. **167. moste and leeste,** i.e., proud and humble. **168. Ye,** yea; **feeste,** festival. **172. makeless,** matchless. **173. gladed,** gladdened; **prees,** throng. **174. derre,** more dearly. **175. sterre,** star. **179. in litel brede,** a little apart. **181. attir,** dress; **debonaire,** meek; **cheere,** manner.

In thilke large temple on every side,
Biholding ay the ladies of the town,
Now here, now there, for no devocioun
Hadde he to noon, to reven° him his reste,
But gan to praisen and lakken whom him leste.°

And in his walk ful faste he gan to waiten°
If knight or squier of his compaignye
Gan for to sike, or lete his yën baiten°
On any womman that he coude espye:
He wolde smile and holden it folye,
And saide him thus, "God woot, she sleepeth softe
For love of thee whan thou turnest ful ofte.

I have herd told, pardieux, of youre living,
Ye loveres, and youre lewed° observaunces,
And which° a labour folk han in winning
Of love, and in the keeping whiche doutaunces;°
And whan youre prey is lost, wo and penaunces!
O verray fooles, nice° and blinde be ye:
Ther nis nat oon can war by other be."

And with that word he gan caste up the browe
Ascances,° "Lo, is this nought wisely spoken?"
At which the God of Love gan looken rowe,°
Right for despit, and shoop for to been wroken:°
He kidde° anoon his bowe nas nought broken,
For sodeinly he hitte him atte fulle°—
And yit as proud a pecok can he pulle.°

O blinde world, O blinde entencioun,
How often falleth al the effect contraire
Of surquidrye° and foul presumpcioun;

188. reven, take away from. **189. lakken,** find fault with; **leste,** pleased. **190. faste,** hard; **waiten,** watch. **192. sike,** sigh; **baiten,** feed. **198. lewed,** stupid. **199. which,** what. **200. doutaunces,** perplexities. **202. nice,** silly. **205. Ascances,** as if to say. **206. rowe,** roughly. **207. despit,** contempt; **shoop,** planned; **wroken,** avenged. **208. kidde,** made known. **209. atte fulle,** i.e., squarely. **210. pulle,** pluck. **213. surquidrye,** pride.

For caught is proud, and caught is debonaire:
This Troilus is clomben on the staire,
And litel weeneth that he moste descenden—
But alday faileth thing that fooles wenden.

As proude Bayard ginneth for to skippe
Out of the way, so prikketh him his corn,
Til he a lassh have of the longe whippe,
Thanne thinketh he, "Though I praunce al biforn,
First in the trais ful fat and newe shorn,
Yit am I but an hors, and horses lawe
I moot endure, and with my feres drawe."

So ferde it by this fierse and proude knight:
Though he a worthy kinges sone were,
And wende no thing hadde had swich might
Ayains his wille that sholde his herte stere,
Yit with a look his herte weex afere,
That he that now was most in pride above,
Weex sodeinly most subjet unto love.

Forthy ensample taketh of this man,
Ye wise, proude, and worthy folkes alle,
To scornen Love, which that so soone can
The freedom of youre hertes to him thralle—
For evere it was, and evere it shal bifalle,
That Love is he that alle thing may binde,
For may no man fordoon the lawe of Kinde.

That this be sooth hath preved and dooth yit,
For this trowe I ye knowen alle or some;

214. **debonaire,** humble. 215. **is clomben,** has climbed. 216. **weeneth,** thinks; **moste,** must. 217. **alday,** constantly; **wenden,** thought to be the case. 218. **Bayard,** typical name for a horse. 219. **prikketh . . . corn,** i.e., he feels his oats. 222. **trais,** wagon trace; **newe shorn,** recently sheared. 224. **feres,** mates. 225. **ferde,** fared, happened. 227. **wende,** supposed. 228. **stere,** disturb. 229. **weex afere,** waxed afire. 231. **Weex,** grew. 232. **ensample,** example. 234. **To,** i.e., not to. 235. **thralle,** enthrall. 238. **fordoon,** undo; **Kinde,** nature. 239. **preved,** proved itself. 240. **trowe,** believe; **alle or some,** one or all.

Men reden nat that folk han gretter° wit
Than they that han be most with love ynome,°
And strengest folk been therwith overcome,
The worthieste and gretteste of degree—
This was and is and yit men shal it see.

And trewelich, it sit wel° to be so,
For alderwiseste° han therwith been plesed,
And they that han been aldermost° in wo
With love han been conforted most and esed;
And ofte it hath the cruel herte apesed,
And worthy folk maad worthier of name,
And causeth most to dreden vice and shame.

And sith it may nat goodly been withstonde,°
And is a thing so vertuous in kinde,°
Refuseth nat to Love for to been bonde,°
Sin as himselven list° he may you binde:
The yerde is bet that bowen wol and winde°
Than that that brest, and therfore I you rede°
To folwen him that so wel can you lede.

But for to tellen forth in special
As of this kinges sone of which I tolde,
And leten othere thinges collateral,°
Of him thenke I my tale forth to holde,
Bothe of his joye and of his cares colde,
And al his werk as touching this matere:
For I it gan, I wol therto refere.°

Within the temple he wente him forth playing,
This Troilus, of every wight aboute
On this lady and now on that looking,

241. **gretter,** greater. 242. **ynome,** overtaken. 246. **sit wel,** is most suitable. 247. **alderwiseste,** the wisest of all. 248. **aldermost,** most of all. 253. **goodly,** properly; **withstonde,** withstood. 254. **kinde,** nature. 255. **bonde,** bound. 256. **list,** it pleases. 257. **yerde,** rod; **bet,** better; **winde,** bend. 258. **brest,** breaks; **rede,** advise. 262. **leten,** leave; **collateral,** subordinate. 266. **For,** because; **refere,** return.

Wher so she were of town or of withoute,
And upon caas bifel that thurgh a route
His yë perced, and so deepe it wente,
Til on Criseide it smoot, and ther it stente.

And sodeinly he weex therwith astoned,
And gan hire bet biholde in thrifty wise.
"O mercy God," thoughte he, "wher hastou woned,
That art so fair and goodly to devise?"
Therwith his herte gan to sprede and rise,
And softe siked lest men mighte him heere,
And caughte ayain his firste playing cheere.

She nas nat with the leeste of hir stature,
But alle hir limes so wel answeringe
Weren to wommanhood, that creature
Was nevere lasse mannissh in seeminge;
And eek the pure wise of hir mevinge
Shewed wel that men mighte in hire gesse
Honour, estaat, and wommanly noblesse.

To Troilus right wonder wel withalle
Gan for to like hir meving and hir cheere,
Which somdeel deinous was, for she leet falle
Hir look a lite aside in swich manere
Ascances, "What, may I nat stonden here?"
And after that hir looking gan she lighte,
That nevere thoughte him seen so good a sighte.

And of hir look in him ther gan to quiken
So greet desir and swich affeccioun,

270. **Wher,** whether. 271. **route,** crowd. 273. **smoot,** fell; **stente,** stopped. 274. **weex,** grew; **astoned,** astounded. 275. **bet,** better; **thrifty,** decorous. 276. **woned,** dwelt. 277. **devise,** describe. 278. **sprede,** unfold. 279. **siked,** he sighed. 280. **playing cheere,** facetious manner. 281. **leeste,** smallest; **of,** in. 282. **limes,** limbs. 284. **lasse,** less; **mannissh,** masculine. 285. **mevinge,** movement. 289. **like,** please; **cheere,** appearance. 290. **deinous,** disdainful. 291. **lite,** little. 292. **Ascances,** as if to say. 293. **lighte,** brighten.

That in his herte botme° gan to stiken
Of hire his fixe° and deepe impressioun;
And though he erst hadde poured° up and down,
He was tho glad his hornes in to shrinke:°
Unnethes wiste he how to looke or winke.°

Lo, he that leet° himselven so conninge,
And scorned hem that Loves paines drien,°
Was ful unwar that Love hadde his dwellinge
Within the subtile stremes° of hir yën;
That sodeinly him thoughte he felte dien,
Right with hir look, the spirit in his herte—
Blissed be love that can thus folk converte!

She, this in blak, liking° to Troilus
Over alle thing, he stood for to biholde,
Ne his desir, ne wherfor he stood thus,
He neither cheere made° ne word tolde,
But from afer, his manere for to holde,°
On othere thinges his look somtime he caste—
And ofte on hire, whil that the service laste.°

And after this, nat fulliche al awhaped,°
Out of the temple al esiliche° he wente,
Repenting him that he hadde evere yjaped°
Of Loves folk, lest fully the descente
Of scorn fille° on himself; but what he mente,
Lest it were wist° on any manere side,
His wo he gan dissimulen° and hide.

Whan he was fro the temple thus departed,
He straight anoon unto his palais turneth,

297. **herte botme,** heart's bottom. 298. **fixe,** fixed. 299. **erst,** before; **poured,** gazed. 300. **tho,** then; **shrinke,** i.e., pull. 301. **Unnethes,** hardly; **wiste,** knew; **winke,** blink. 302. **leet,** thought. 303. **drien,** suffer. 305. **stremes,** beams. 309. **liking,** pleasing. 312. **cheere made,** i.e., revealed by his face. 313. **afer,** afar; **holde,** preserve. 315. **laste,** lasted. 316. **awhaped,** astounded. 317. **esiliche,** nonchalantly. 318. **yjaped,** made fun. 320. **fille,** should fall. 321. **wist,** known. 322. **dissimulen,** dissemble.

Right with hir look thurgh-shoten° and thurgh-darted—
Al feineth he in lust° that he sojurneth;
And al his cheere and speeche also he burneth,°
And ay of Loves servants every while,
Himself to wrye,° at hem he gan to smile,

And saide, "Lord, so ye live alle in lest,°
Ye loveres, for the conningeste° of you
That serven most ententifliche° and best,
Him tit as often harm therof as prow:°
Youre hire is quit ayain, ye, God woot° how,
Nought wel for wel, but scorn for good servise:
In faith, youre ordre is ruled in good wise.

In nouncertain been alle youre observaunces,°
But it a fewe, sely° pointes be;
Ne no thing axeth° so grete attendaunces
As dooth your lay,° and that knowe alle ye.
But that is nat the worste, as mote I thee,°
But tolde I you the worste point, I leve,°
Al saide I sooth, ye wolden at me greve.

But take this: that ye loveres ofte eschue,°
Or elles doon of good entencioun,
Ful ofte thy lady wol it misconstrue,
And deeme it harm in hir opinioun;
And yit if she for other enchesoun°
Be wroth, thanne shaltou have a groin° anoon:
Lord, wel is him that may of you been oon!"

325. **thurgh-shoten,** shot through. 326. **Al feineth,** even though he pretends; **lust,** pleasure. 327. **burneth,** smooths. 329. **wrye,** cover. 330. **lest,** pleasure. 331. **conningeste,** cleverest. 332. **ententifliche,** attentively. 333. **Him tit,** there happens to him; **prow,** profit. 334. **hire,** i.e., wage; **quit,** paid; **woot,** knows. 337. **nouncertain,** uncertainty; **observaunces,** duties. 338. **But,** unless; **sely,** lucky. 339. **axeth,** requires. 340. **lay,** law. 341. **as . . . thee,** so may I thrive. 342. **tolde I,** if I told; **leve,** believe. 343. **Al,** although. 344. **that,** what; **eschue,** avoid. 348. **enchesoun,** reason. 349. **groin,** complaint.

But for al this, whan that he saw his time,
He heeld his pees, noon other boote him gained,
For Love bigan his fetheres so to lime
That wel unnethe until his folk he feined
That othere bisy needes him distrained;
For wo was him that what to doon he niste,
But bad his folk to goon wher that hem liste.

And whan that he in chambre was allone,
He down upon his beddes feet him sette,
And first he gan to sike, and eft to grone,
And thoughte ay on hire so withouten lette,
That as he sat and wook, his spirit mette
That he hire sawgh, and temple, and al the wise
Right of hir look, and gan it newe avise.

Thus gan he make a mirour of his minde,
In which he sawgh al hoolly hir figure,
And that he wel coude in his herte finde
It was to him a right good aventure
To love swich oon, and if he dide his cure
To serven hire, yit mighte he falle in grace,
Or elles for oon of hir servants pace;

Imagining that travaile nor grame
Ne mighte for so goodly oon be lorn
As she, ne him for his desir no shame,
Al were it wist, but in pris and upborn
Of alle loveres wel more than biforn—
Thus argumented he in his ginning,
Ful unavised of his wo coming.

352. **boote,** remedy; **gained,** availed. 353. **lime,** smear with birdlime, i.e., clip his wings. 354. **unnethe,** with difficulty; **until,** to; **feined,** pretended. 355. **bisy,** exacting. 356. **niste,** knew not. 357. **bad,** bade; **liste,** it pleased. 360. **sike,** sigh; **eft,** again. 361. **lette,** ceasing. 362. **mette,** dreamed. 364. **avise,** consider. 369. **cure,** care, i.e., best. 370. **in,** into. 371. **pace,** pass. 372. **grame,** grief. 373. **lorn,** lost, i.e., wasted. 374. **him,** i.e., he would have. 375. **Al . . . wist,** although it were known; **pris,** praise; **upborn,** exalted. 377. **ginning,** beginning.

Thus took he purpos Loves craft to sewe,°
And thoughte he wolde werken prively,
First to hiden his desir in mewe,°
From every wight yborn al outrely,°
But he mighte ought° recovered be therby;
Remembring him that love too wide yblowe°
Yelt° bittre fruit, though sweete seed be sowe.

And over al this, yit muchel more he thoughte,
What for to speke, and what to holden inne;
And what to arten° hire to love he soughte;
And on a song anoon right to biginne,
And gan loude on his sorwe for to winne,°
For with good hope he gan fully assente
Criseide for to love, and nought repente.

And of his song nought only the sentence°
(As writ myn auctour called Lollius)°,
But pleinly,° save oure tonges difference,
I dar wel sayn, in al that Troilus
Saide in his song—lo, every word, right thus
As I shal sayn; and whoso list° it heere,
Lo, next this vers he may it finde here:

"If no love is, O God, what feele I so?
And if love is, what thing and which is he?
If love be good, from whennes cometh my wo?
If it be wikke, a wonder thinketh° me,
Whan every torment and adversitee
That cometh of him may to me savory thinke,°
For ay thurste I, the more that ich° it drinke.

379. sewe, pursue. **381. mewe,** closet. **382. wight yborn,** born man; **outrely,** utterly. **383. But,** unless; **ought,** in any way. **384. yblowe,** i.e., publicized. **385. Yelt,** yields. **388. arten,** entice. **390. winne,** triumph. **393. sentence,** general meaning. **394. writ,** writes; **Lollius,** supposed author of the poem Chaucer pretends he is translating. **395. pleinly,** fully. **398. list,** pleases. **403. wikke,** wrong; **thinketh,** it seems to. **405. savory,** pleasant; **thinke,** seem. **406. ich,** I.

And if that at myn owene lust I brenne,°
From whennes cometh my wailing and my plainte?°
If harm agree me, wherto plaine° I thenne?—
I noot, ne why unwery° that I fainte.
O quikke deeth, O sweete harm so quainte,°
How may of thee in me swich quantitee,
But if° that I consente that it be?

And if that I consente, I wrongfully
Complaine: ywis, thus possed° to and fro,
Al stereless within a boot° am I
Amidde the see, bitwixen windes two,
That in contrarye stonden everemo.
Allas, what is this wonder maladye?
For hoot° of cold, for cold of hoot I die."

And to the God of Love thus saide he
With pitous vois, "O Lord, now youres is
My spirit which that oughte youres be.
You thanke I, lord, that han me brought to this.
But whether goddesse or womman, ywis,
She be, I noot, which that ye do° me serve:
But as hir man I wol ay live and sterve.°

Ye stonden in hir yën mightily,
As in a place unto youre vertu digne;°
Wherfore, lord, if my service or I
May liken° you, so beeth to me benigne;
For myn estaat royal I here resigne
Into hir hand, and with ful humble cheere
Bicome hir man, as to my lady dere."

407. **lust,** pleasure; **brenne,** burn. 408. **whennes,** whence; **plainte,** complaint. 409. **agree,** agree with; **plaine,** complain. 410. **noot,** know not; **unwery,** i.e., though untired. 411. **quikke,** living; **quainte,** strange. 413. **But if,** unless. 415. **possed,** pushed. 416. **sterelees,** rudderless; **boot,** boat. 420. **hoot,** hot. 426. **do,** make. 427. **sterve,** die. 429. **digne,** worthy. 431. **liken,** please.

In him ne deined° spare blood royal
The fir of love, the wherfro God me blesse,°
Ne him forbar° in no degree, for al
His vertu or his excellent prowesse,
But heeld him as his thral lowe in distresse,
And brende° him so in sondry wise al newe,
That sixty time a day he loste his hewe.

So muche day by day his owene thought
For lust to hire gan quiken and encreesse,°
That every other charge° he sette at nought.
Forthy ful ofte, his hote fir to ceesse,°
To seen hir goodly look he gan to preesse,°
For thereby to been esed wel he wende:°
And ay the neer he was, the more he brende.°

For ay the neer the fir, the hotter is—
This trowe° I knoweth al this compaignye.
But were he fer or neer, I dar saye this:
By night or day, for wisdom or folye,
His herte, which that is his brestes yë,
Was ay on hire that fairer was to seene
Than evere were Elaine or Polyxene.°

Eek of the day ther passed nought an houre
That to himself a thousand time he saide,
"Good goodly, to whom serve I and laboure
As I best can, now wolde God, Criseide,
Ye wolden on me rewe° er that I deide!
My dere herte, allas, myn hele° and hewe
And lif is lost, but° ye wol on me rewe."

435. **deined,** (the fire of love) did not deign to. **436. the . . . blesse,** from which God shield me. **437. forbar,** spared. **440. brende,** burned. **443. lust to,** desire for; **encreesse,** swell. **444. charge,** business. **445. Forthy,** therefore; **ceesse,** assuage. **446. preesse,** press. **447. esed,** comforted; **wende,** thought. **448. neer,** nearer; **brende,** burned. **450. trowe,** believe. **455. Polyxene,** Polyxena, one of Troilus' sisters, with whom the ghost of Achilles became enamored. **460. rewe,** have pity. **461. hele,** health. **462. but,** unless.

Alle othere dredes weren from him fledde,
Bothe of th'assege° and his savacioun,
N'in him desir none othere fawnes° bredde
But argumentes to his conclusioun,°
That she of him wolde han compassioun,
And he to been hir man whil he may dure,°
Lo, here° his lif, and from the deeth his cure.

The sharpe shoures felle of armes preve,°
That Ector or his othere bretheren diden,
Ne made him only therfore ones meve;°
And yit was he, wher so men wente° or riden,
Founde oon the beste, and lengest° time abiden
Ther peril was, and dide eek swich travaile
In armes, that to thenke it was merveile.

But for noon hate he to the Greekes hadde,
Ne also for the rescous° of the town,
Ne made him thus in armes for to madde,°
But only, lo, for this conclusioun,
To liken hire the bet° for his renown;
Fro day to day in armes so he spedde
That the Greekes as the deeth° him dredde.

And fro this forth tho refte° him Love his sleep,
And made his mete his fo, and eek his sorwe
Gan multiplye that, whoso took keep,°
It shewed in his hewe bothe eve and morwe;°
Therfore a title he gan him for to borwe°
Of other siknesse, lest men of him wende°
That the hote fir of Love him brende;°

464. **assege,** siege. 465. **fawnes,** i.e., progeny. 466. **conclusioun,** determination. 468. **dure,** live. 469. **here,** her. 470. **shoures,** attacks; **felle,** fierce; **armes preve,** deeds of arms. 472. **only,** i.e., a single time; **meve,** move. 473. **wente,** walked. 474. **oon,** one of; **lengest,** i.e., he could the longest. 478. **rescous,** relief. 479. **madde,** rage. 481. **liken,** please; **bet,** better. 483. **deeth,** plague. 484. **tho,** then; **refte,** deprived. 486. **keep,** heed. 487. **hewe,** color; **morwe,** morning. 488. **title,** i.e., pretense; **borwe,** borrow. 489. **wende,** supposed. 490. **brende,** burned.

And saide he hadde a fevere and ferde° amis.
But how it was certain I can nat saye,
If that his lady understood nat this
Or feined hire she niste°—oon of the twaye.
But wel I rede that by no manere waye
Ne seemed it as that she of him roughte,°
Or of his paine, or whatsoevere he thoughte.

But thanne felte this Troilus swich wo
That he was wel neigh wood,° for ay his drede
Was this, that she som wight hadde loved so
That nevere of him she wolde han taken heede;
For which him thoughte he felte his herte bleede;
Ne of his wo ne dorste he nat biginne
To tellen hire, for al this world to winne.

But whan he hadde a space from his care,
Thus to himself ful ofte he gan to plaine;°
He saide, "O fool, now artou in the snare,
That whilom japedest° at loves paine!
Now artou hent,° now gnaw thyn owene chaine:
Thou were ay wont eech lovere reprehende°
Of thing fro which thou canst thee nat defende.

What wol now every lovere sayn of thee,
If this be wist,° but evere in thyn absence
Laughen in scorn, and sayn, 'Lo, ther gooth he
That is the man of so greet sapience,
And heeld us loveres leest in reverence!
Now thanked God, he may goon in the daunce
Of hem that Love list fiebly° for t'avaunce.'

But O, thou woful Troilus, God wolde,
Sith thou most° loven thurgh thy destinee,

491. **ferde,** fared. 494. **feined hire,** pretended; **niste,** knew not. 496. **roughte,** cared. 499. **wood,** mad. 506. **plaine,** complain. 508. **whilom,** once; **japedest,** joked. 509. **hent,** caught. 510. **reprehende,** rebuke. 513. **wist,** known. 518. **list,** pleases; **fiebly,** weakly. 520. **most,** must.

That thou biset° were on swich oon that sholde
Knowe al thy wo, al lakked hire° pitee.
But also° cold in love towardes thee
Thy lady is as frost in winter moone,
And thou fordoon° as snow in fir is soone.

God wolde I were arrived in the port
Of deeth, to which my sorwe wol me lede.
A, Lord, to me it were a greet confort—
Thanne were I quit of languisshing in drede;
For be myn hidde sorwe yblowe on brede,°
I shal bijaped° been a thousand time
More than that fool of whos folye men ryme.

But now, help God and ye, sweete for whom
I plaine,° ycaught, nevere the wight° so faste—
O mercy, dere herte, and help me from
The deeth, for I, whil that my lif may laste,
More than myself wol love you to the laste;
And with som freendly look gladeth° me, sweete,
Though nevere more thing ye me bihete."°

Thise wordes and ful many another too
He spak, and called evere in his complainte
Hir name, for to tellen hire his wo,
Til neigh that he in salte teres dreinte:°
Al was for nought, she herde nat his plainte.°
And whan that he bithoughte on that folye,
A thousandfold his wo gan multiplye.

Biwailing in his chambre thus allone,
A freend of his that called was Pandare
Cam ones in unwar° and herde him grone,

521. **biset,** i.e., decided. 522. **al lakked hire,** although she lacked. 523. **also,** as. 525. **fordoon,** destroyed. 530. **hidde,** hidden; **yblowe,** blown; **on brede,** far and wide. 531. **bijaped,** mocked. 534. **plaine,** complain; **the wight,** a man. 538. **gladeth,** gladden. 539. **bihete,** promise. 543. **dreinte,** drowned. 544. **plainte,** complaint. 549. **unwar,** unexpectedly.

And saw his freend in swich distresse and care:
"Allas," quod he, "what causeth al this fare?
O mercy God, what unhap may this mene?
Han now thus soone Greekes maad you lene?

Or hastou som remors of conscience,
And art now falle in som devocioun,
And wailest for thy sinne and thyn offence,
And hast forfered caught attricioun?
God save hem that biseged han oure town,
That so can laye oure jolitee on presse,
And bringe oure lusty folk to holinesse."

Thise wordes saide he for the nones alle,
That with swich thing he mighte him angry maken,
And with angre doon his wo to falle,
As for the time, and his corage awaken.
But wel he wiste, as fer as tonges spaken,
Ther nas a man of gretter hardinesse
Than he, ne more desired worthinesse.

"What caas," quod Troilus, "and what aventure
Hath gided thee to seen me languisshing,
That am refus of every creature?
But, for the love of God, at my praying,
Go hennes away, for certes my dying
Wol thee disese, and I moot needes deye.
Therfore go way, ther is namore to saye.

But if thou weene I be thus sik for drede,
It is nought so, and therfore scorne nought.
Ther is another thing I take of heede
Wel more than ought the Greekes han yit wrought,

551. fare, fuss. **552. unhap,** misfortune. **553. lene,** lean, emaciated. **557. forfered,** terrified; **attricioun,** i.e., an attack of contrition. **559. lay on presse,** i.e., spoil. **561. nones,** immediate purpose. **563. doon,** make. **565. wiste,** knew; **fer,** far. **567. ne,** i.e., nor one who. **568. caas,** chance; **aventure,** fortune. **570. refus,** rejected. **573. disese,** distress; **moot,** must. **575. weene,** suppose.

Which cause is of my deeth for sorwe and thought.
But though that I now telle it thee ne leste,°
Be thou nought wroth, I hide it for the beste."

This Pandare that neigh malt for wo and routhe°
Ful ofte saide, "Allas, what may this be?
Now, freend," quod he, "if evere love or trouthe
Hath been or is bitwixen thee and me,
Ne do thou nevere swich a crueltee
To hiden fro thy freend so greet a care:
Wistou° nought wel that it am I, Pandare?

I wol parten° with thee al thy paine,
If it be so I do thee no confort,
As it is freendes right, sooth for to sayne,
To entreparten° wo as glad disport.
I have and shal, for trewe or fals report,
In wrong and right, yloved thee al my live—
Hid nat thy wo fro me, but tel it blive."°

Thanne gan this sorweful Troilus to sike,°
And saide him thus, "God leve° it be my beste
To telle it thee, for sith it may thee like,°
Yit wol I telle it though myn herte breste°—
And wel woot° I thou maist do me no reste.
But lest thou deeme I triste° nat to thee,
Now herke, freend, for thus it stant° with me:

Love, ayains the which who so defendeth
Himselven most, him alderleest° availeth,
With desespair° so sorwefully me offendeth,
That straight unto the deeth myn herte faileth;
Therto desir so brenningly° me assaileth,

580. **leste,** wish. 582. **malt,** melted; **routhe,** pity. 588. **Wistou,** know you. 589. **parten,** share. 592. **entreparten,** share. 595. **Hid,** hide; **blive,** at once. 596. **sike,** sigh. 597. **leve,** grant. 598. **like,** please. 599. **breste,** break. 600. **woot,** know. 601. **deeme,** suspect; **triste,** trust. 602. **stant,** stands. 604. **alderleest,** least of all. 605. **desespair,** hopelessness. 607. **brenningly,** burningly.

That to been slain it were a gretter joye
To me than king of Greece been and Troye.

Sufficeth this, my fulle freend Pandare,
That I have said, for now woostou my wo.
And for the love of God, my colde care
So hid it wel, I tolde it nevere to mo;
For harmes mighten fallen mo than two
If it were wist; but be thou in gladnesse,
And lat me sterve unknowe of my distresse."

"How hastou thus unkindely and longe
Hid this fro me, thou fool?" quod Pandarus.
"Paraunter thou might after swich oon longe
That myn avis anoon may helpen us."
"This were a wonder thing," quod Troilus.
"Thou coudest nevere in love thyselven wisse:
How devel maistou bringe me to blisse?"

"Ye, Troilus, now herke," quod Pandare,
"Though I be nice, it happeth often so
That oon that excesse dooth ful yvele fare,
By good conseil can keepe his freend therfro.
I have myself eek seen a blind man go,
Ther as he fel that coude looken wide:
A fool may eek a wis man ofte gide.

A whestoon is no kerving instrument,
But yit it maketh sharpe kerving tooles.
And ther thou woost that I have ought miswent,
Eschew thou that, for swich thing to thee scole is;
Thus often wise men been war by fooles.

610. Sufficeth, it suffices. **611. woostou,** you know. **613. mo,** others. **614. mo,** more. **615. wist,** known. **616. sterve,** die. **619. Paraunter,** perhaps. **620. avis,** advice. **622. wisse,** guide. **623. How devel,** how the devil. **625. nice,** foolish. **626. excesse,** too much emotion; **dooth,** makes; **yvele,** badly. **631. whestoon,** whetstone; **kerving,** carving. **633. woost,** know; **ought,** in any way. **634. Eschew,** avoid; **scole,** school, i.e., example.

If thou do so, thy wit is wel bewared:°
By his contrarye is every thing declared.°

For how mighte evere swetnesse han been knowe
To him that nevere tasted bitternesse?
Ne no man may been inly° glad, I trowe,
That nevere was in sorwe or som distresse.
Eek whit by blak, by shame eek worthinesse—
Eech, set by other, more for other seemeth,
As men may see, and so the wise it deemeth.°

Sith thus of two contraries is oo lore,°
I, that have in love so ofte assayed,
Grevances oughte conne,° and wel the more
Conseilen thee of that thou art amayed;°
Eek thee ne oughte nat been yvele apayed°
Though I desire with thee for to bere
Thyn hevy charge: it shal thee lasse dere.°

I woot wel that it fareth thus by me
As to thy brother Paris, an hierdesse°
(Which that ycleped° was Oënone)
Wroot in a complainte of hir hevinesse.
Ye sawgh the lettre that she wroot, I gesse?"
"Nay, nevere yit, ywis," quod Troilus.
"Now," quod Pandare, "herkne, it was thus:

'Phebus, that first foond° art of medicine,'
Quod she, 'and coude° in every wightes care
Remedye and reed by herbes he knew fine,°
Yit to himself his conning was ful bare,°
For Love hadde him so bounden in a snare,

636. **bewared,** put on guard. 637. **declared,** made known. 640. **inly,** entirely. 644. **deemeth,** judges. 645. **lore,** lesson. 647. **Grevances . . . conne,** ought to be able to recognize causes of grief. 648. **amayed,** perplexed. 649. **yvele apayed,** ill-pleased. 651. **charge,** load; **lasse,** less; **dere,** hurt. 653. **hierdesse,** shepherdess. 654. **ycleped,** called. 659. **Phebus,** Apollo; **foond,** invented. 660. **coude,** i.e., prescribed. 661. **reed,** corrective; **fine,** ingeniously. 662. **bare,** i.e., useless.

Al for the doughter of the king Amete,
That al his craft ne coude his sorwes bete.'

Right so fare I, unhappily for me:
I love oon best, and that me smerteth sore;
And yit paraunter can I reden thee,
And nat myselve; repreve me namore:
I have no cause, I woot wel, for to sore
As dooth an hawk that listeth for to playe,
But to thyn help yit somwhat can I saye.

And of oo thing right siker maistou be:
That certain, for to dien in the paine,
That I shal neveremo discoveren thee;
Ne by my trouthe, I keepe nat restraine
Thee fro thy love, though that it were Elaine,
That is thy brother wif, if ich it wiste:
Be what she be, and love hire as thee liste.

Therfore as freend fulliche in me assure.
But tel me plat now, what is th'enchesoun
And final cause of wo that ye endure?
For douteth no thing, myn entencioun
Nis nat to you of reprehencioun
To speke as now, for no wight may bireve
A man to love, til that him list to leve.

And witeth wel that bothe two been vices:
Mistrusten alle, or elles alle leve.
But wel I woot the mene of it no vice is:
For to trusten som wight is a preve

664. **Amete,** Admetus: Apollo's love for his daughter is a medieval invention. 665. **bete,** improve. 667. **me smerteth,** causes me to smart. 668. **paraunter,** perhaps; **reden,** advise. 669. **repreve,** reproach. 670. **sore,** soar. 673. **siker,** certain. 674. **the paine,** torture. 675. **discoveren,** reveal. 676. **keepe,** care. 678. **ich,** I; **wiste,** knew. 680. **assure,** have confidence. 681. **plat,** flatly; **enchesoun,** reason. 685. **bireve,** i.e., stop. 686. **list,** it please; **leve,** leave off. 687. **witeth,** know. 688. **leve,** believe. 689. **mene,** mean. 690. **preve,** proof.

Of trouthe, and forthy wolde I fain remeve
Thy wronge conceite, and do thee som wight triste,
Thy wo to telle; and tel me if thee liste.

The wise saith, 'Wo him that is allone,
For, and he falle, he hath noon help to rise.'
And sith thou hast a felawe, tel thy mone;
For this nis nought certain the nexte wise
To winne love—as techen us the wise—
To walwe and weepe as Niobe the queene,
Whos teres yit in marbel been yseene.

Lat be thy weeping and thy drerinesse,
And lat us lissen wo with other speeche.
So may thy woful time seeme lesse.
Delite nat in wo thy wo to seeche,
As doon thise fooles that hir sorwes eche
With sorwe whan they han misaventure,
And listen nought to seeche hem other cure.

Men sayn, 'To wrecche is consolacioun
To have another felawe in his paine.'
That oughte wel been oure opinioun,
For bothe thou and I of love we plaine:
So ful of sorwe am I, sooth for to sayne,
That certainly namore harde grace
May sitte on me, forwhy ther is no space.

If God wol, thou art nat agast of me,
Lest I wolde of thy lady thee begile:
Thou woost thyself whom that I love, pardee,
As I best can, goon sitthen longe while.

691. **forthy,** therefore; **remeve,** remove. 692. **conceite,** idea; **triste,** trust. 695. **and,** if. 696. **mone,** complaint. 697. **nexte,** nearest. 699. **walwe,** turn; **Niobe,** although turned to stone, continued to weep for the death of her children. 702. **lissen,** assuage. 704. **seeche,** seek. 705. **eche,** increase. 707. **listen,** desire. 711. **plaine,** complain. 714. **forwhy,** because. 717. **woost,** know. 718. **goon sitthen,** i.e., for.

And sith thou woost I do it for no wile,
And sith I am he that thou trustest most,
Tel me somwhat, sin al my wo thou woost."

Yit Troilus for al this no word saide,
But longe he lay as stille as he deed were;
And after this with siking he abraide,
And to Pandarus vois he lente his ere,
And up his yën caste, that in fere
Was Pandarus, lest that in frenesye
He sholde falle, or elles soone die,

And cried "Awaak" ful wonderliche and sharpe.
"What, slomberestou as in a litargye?
Or artou lik an asse to the harpe,
That heereth soun whan men the stringes playe,
But in his minde of that no melodye
May sinken, him to gladen, for that he
So dul is of his bestialitee?"

And with that Pandare of his wordes stente,
And Troilus yit him no thing answerde,
Forwhy to tellen nas nat his entente
To nevere no man for whom that he so ferde:
For it is said, "Man maketh ofte a yerde
With which the makere is himself ybeten
In sondry manere, as thise wise treten."

And nameliche in his conseil tellinge
That toucheth love, that oughte been secree,
For of himself it wol ynough out springe,
But if that it the bet governed be;
Eek somtime it is craft to seeme flee

719. **wile,** trick. 724. **siking,** sighing; **abraide,** started up. 726. **fere,** fear. 727. **frenesye,** frenzy. 730. **slomberestou,** do you slumber; **litargye,** lethargy. 736. **stente,** ceased. 738. **Forwhy,** because. 739. **ferde,** behaved. 740. **yerde,** rod. 742. **treten,** say. 743. **nameliche,** especially; **conseil,** secrets. 744. **secree,** secret. 746. **But if,** unless; **bet,** better.

Fro thing which in effect men hunte faste—
Al this gan Troilus in his herte caste.

But nathelees, whan he hadde herd him crye
"Awaak," he gan to siken wonder sore,
And saide, "Freend, though that I stille lie,
I am nat deef; now pees, and crye namore,
For I have herd thy wordes and thy lore.
But suffre me my meschief to biwaile,
For thy proverbes may me nought availe,

Nor other cure canstou noon for me.
Eek I nil nat been cured; I wol deye.
What knowe I of the queene Niobe?
Lat be thine olde ensamples, I thee praye."
"No," quod Pandarus, "therfore I saye,
Swich is delit of fooles to biweepe
Hir wo, but seeken boote they ne keepe.

Now knowe I that ther reson in thee faileth.
But tel me, if I wiste what she were,
For whom that thee al this misaunter aileth,
Dorst thou that I tolde in hir ere
Thy wo, sith thou darst nought thyself for fere,
And hire bisoughte on thee to han som routhe?"
"Why, nay," quod he, "by God and by my trouthe."

"What, nat as bisily," quod Pandarus,
"As though myn owene lif lay on this neede?"
"No, certes, brother," quod this Troilus.
"And why?" "For that thou sholdest nevere speede."
"Woostou that wel?" "Ye, that is out drede,"
Quod Troilus; "for al that evere ye conne,
She nil to noon swich wrecche as I been wonne."

749. **caste,** consider. 751. **siken,** sigh. 757. **canstou,** do you know. 760. **ensamples,** examples. 763. **boote,** remedy; **keepe,** care. 765. **wiste,** knew. 766. **misaunter,** unhappiness. 769. **routhe,** pity. 771. **bisily,** assiduously. 775. **drede,** doubt. 776. **conne,** can do. 777. **nil,** will not.

Quod Pandarus, "Allas, what may this be,
That thou despaired art thus causelees?
What, liveth nat thy lady, benedicite?°
How woostou so that thou art gracelees?°
Swich yvel is nat alway bootelees.°
Why, put° nat impossible thus thy cure,
Sin thing to come is ofte in aventure.°

I graunte wel that thou endurest wo
As sharp as dooth he Ticyus° in helle,
Whos stomak fowles tiren° everemo,
That highten vultures, as bookes telle;
But I may nat endure that thou dwelle
In so unskilful° an opinioun
That of thy wo is no curacioun.°

But ones niltou for° thy coward herte,
And for thyn ire and foolissh wilfulnesse,
For wantrust,° tellen of thy sorwes smerte,
Ne to thyn owene help doon bisinesse,
As muche as speke a reson more or lesse?
But list as he that lest of no thing recche°—
What womman coude loven swich a wrecche?

What may she deemen other of thy deeth,
If thou thus die and she noot° why it is,
But that for fere is yolden° up thy breeth,
For° Greekes han biseged us, ywis?
Lord, which° a thank thanne shaltou han of this!
Thus wol she sayn, and al the town at ones:
'The wrecche is deed, the devel have his bones!'

780. benedicite, bless me. **781. gracelees,** without favor. **782. yvel,** evil; **bootelees,** without remedy. **783. put,** i.e., assume. **784. in aventure,** i.e., a matter of chance. **786. Ticyus,** Tityus. **787. tiren,** tear. **790. unskilful,** unreasonable. **791. curacioun,** cure. **792. for,** i.e., despite. **794. wantrust,** lack of trust. **797. list,** lie flat; **lest,** desires; **recche,** to care. **800. noot,** knows not. **801. yolden,** yielded. **802. For,** because. **803. which,** what.

Thou maist allone here weepe and crye and kneele,
But love a womman that° she woot it nought,
And she wol quite° that thou shalt nat feele:
Unknowe unkist, and lost that° is unsought.
What, many a man hath love ful dere abought,
Twenty winter that his lady wiste,°
That nevere yit his lady mouth he kiste.

What° sholde he therfore fallen in despair,
Or be recreant for his owene teene,°
Or sleen himself, al° be his lady fair?
Nay, nay, but evere in oon be fressh and greene°
To serve and love his dere hertes queene,
And thinke it is a guerdon° hire to serve
A thousandfold more than he can deserve."

And of that word took heede Troilus,
And thoughte anoon what folye he was inne,
And how that sooth him saide Pandarus,
That for to sleen himself mighte he nat winne,
But bothe doon unmanhood and a sinne,
And of his deeth his lady nought to wite,°
For of his wo, God woot, she knew ful lite.°

And with that thought he gan ful sore sike°
And saide, "Allas, what is me best to do?"
To whom Pandare answerde, "If thee like,
The beste is that thou telle me al thy wo.
And have my trouthe, but° thou it finde so
I be thy boote° er that it be ful longe,
To peces do me drawe and sitthen honge."°

807. that, in such a way that. **808. quite,** repay. **808, 809. that,** what. **811.** i.e., Whose lady knew of his love for twenty years. **813. What,** why. **814. recreant,** cowardly; **teene,** distress. **815. sleen,** slay; **al,** although. **816. greene,** eager. **818. guerdon,** reward. **825. wite,** blame. **826. woot,** knows; **lite,** little. **827. sike,** sigh. **831. but,** unless. **832. boote,** help. **833. do me drawe,** have me drawn; **honge,** hanged.

"Ye, so thou saist," quod Troilus tho, "allas,
But God woot it is nought the rather so.
Ful hard were it to helpen in this cas.
For wel finde I that Fortune is my fo,
Ne alle the men that riden can or go
May of hir cruel wheel the harm withstonde,
For as hire list she playeth with free and bonde."

Quod Pandarus, "Thanne blamestou Fortune
For thou art wroth? ye, now at erst I see.
Woost thou nat wel that Fortune is commune
To every manere wight in som degree?
And yit thou hast this confort, lo, pardee,
That as hir joyes moten overgoon,
So mote hir sorwes passen everichoon.

For if hir wheel stinte any thing to turne,
Than ceessed she Fortune anoon to be.
Now, sith hir wheel by no way may sojurne,
What woostou if hir mutabilitee
Right as thyselven list wol doon by thee,
Or that she be nought fer fro thyn helpinge?
Paraunter thou hast cause for to singe.

And therfore woostou what I thee biseeche?
Lat be thy wo and turning to the grounde,
For whoso list have heling of his leeche,
To him bihooveth first unwree his wounde.
To Cerberus in helle ay be I bounde,
Were it for my suster al thy sorwe,
By my wil she sholde be al thyn tomorwe.

835. **rather,** sooner. 838. **go,** walk. 840. **bonde,** serf. 842. **wroth,** angry; **erst,** last. 846. **moten,** must; **overgoon,** pass away. 848. **stinte,** ceased. 850. **sojurne,** stop. 851. **woostou,** do you know. 852. **list,** it pleases. 853. **fer,** far; **thyn helpinge,** i.e., helping you. 854. **Paraunter,** perhaps. 857. **leeche,** doctor. 858. **unwree,** disclose. 859. **Cerberus,** the three-headed dog that guards the entrance to the classical hell.

Looke up, I saye, and tel me what she is
Anoon, that I may goon aboute thy neede.
Knowe ich hire ought? for my love, tel me this:
Thanne wolde I hopen rather for to speede."
Tho gan the veine of Troilus to bleede,
For he was hit and weex al reed for shame.
"Aha," quod Pandare, "here biginneth game."

And with that word he gan him for to shake,
And saide, "Thief, thou shalt hire name telle."
But tho gan sely Troilus for to quake
As though men sholde han led him into helle,
And saide, "Allas, of al my wo the welle,
Thanne is my sweete fo called Criseide,"
And wel neigh with the word for fere he deide.

And whan that Pandare herde hir name nevene,
Lord, he was glad, and saide, "Freend so dere,
Now fare aright, for Joves name in hevene:
Love hath biset thee wel, be of good cheere,
For of good name and wisdom and manere
She hath ynough, and eek of gentilesse—
If she be fair, thou woost thyself, I gesse.

Ne nevere sawgh a more bountevous
Of hir estaat, ne gladder, ne of speeche
A frendlier n'a more gracious
For to do wel, ne lasse hadde neede seeche
What for to doon; and al this bet to eche,
In honour too as fer as she may strecche:
A kinges herte seemeth by hires a wrecche.

And forthy looke of good confort thou be,
For certainly, the firste point is this

864. ich, I; **ought,** at all. **865. rather,** sooner. **867. weex,** grew; **reed,** red. **871. tho,** then; **sely,** poor. **873. welle,** source. **876. nevene,** to be named. **879. biset,** placed. **883. bountevous,** magnanimous. **886. seeche,** to seek. **887. bet,** better; **eche,** augment. **888. as fer,** i.e., she is as far. **890. forthy,** therefore.

Of noble corage and wel ordainee,
A man to have pees with himself, ywis;
So oughtest thou, for nought but good it is
To loven wel, and in a worthy place:
Thee oughte nat to clepe it hap but grace.

And also think and therwith glade thee,
That sith thy lady vertuous is in al,
So folweth it that ther is som pitee
Amonges alle thise othere in general;
And forthy see that thou in special
Requere nought that is ayains hir name—
For vertu streccheth nought himself to shame.

But wel is me that evere that I was born
That thou biset art in so good a place,
For, by my trouthe, in love I dorste have sworn
Thee sholde nevere han tid thus fair a grace.
And woostow why? for thou were wont to chace
At Love in scorn, and for despit him calle
Saint Idiot, lord of thise fooles alle.

How often hastou maad thy nice japes,
And said that Loves servants everichone
Of nicetee been verray Goddes apes;
And some wolde mucche hir mete allone,
Ligging abedde, and make hem for to grone;
And som thou saidest hadde a blanche fevere,
And prayedest God he sholde nevere kevere.

And som of hem took on him for the cold
More than ynough, so saidestou ful ofte;
And some han feined ofte time and told

892. corage, heart; **ordainee,** governed. **896. clepe,** call; **hap,** luck; **grace,** i.e., special favor. **897. glade thee,** be glad. **902. Requere,** demand. **905. biset,** situated. **907. tid,** happened. **908. chace,** i.e., badger. **911. nice japes,** foolish jokes. **913. nicetee,** folly. **914. mucche,** munch; **mete,** dinner. **915. Ligging,** lying. **916. som,** one; **blanche fevere,** white fever, i.e., puppy love. **917. kevere,** recover. **920. feined,** pretended.

How that they waken whan they sleepen softe:
And thus they wolde han brought hemself alofte,
And nathelees were under at the laste—
Thus saidestou, and japedest ful faste.

Yit saidestou that for the more part
Thise loveres wolden speke in general,
And thoughten that it was a siker° art
For failing for t'assayen over al.°
Now may I jape of thee if that I shal.
But nathelees, though that I sholde deye,
That thou art noon of tho° I dorste saye.

Now beet thy brest and say to God of Love,
'Thy grace, lord, for now I me repente
If I misspak, for now myself I love.'
Thus say with al thyn herte in good entente."
Quod Troilus, "A, lord, I me consente,
And praye to thee my japes° thou foryive,
And I shal nevere more whil I live."

"Thou saist wel," quod Pandare, "and now I hope
That thou the goddes wratthe hast al apesed.
And sitthen thou hast wopen° many a drope,
And said swich thing wherwith thy god is plesed,
Now wolde nevere God but thou were esed;°
And think wel she of whom rist° al thy wo
Herafter may thy confort be also.

For thilke ground that bereth the weedes wikke°
Bereth eek thise hoolsom° herbes as ful ofte;
Next the foule netle rough and thikke
The rose waxeth swoote° and smoothe and softe;
And next the valeye is the hil alofte;

927. siker, sure. **928. For,** against; **over al,** everywhere. **931. tho,** those. **937. japes,** jokes. **941. wopen,** wept. **943. esed,** comforted. **944. rist,** rises. **946. wikke,** troublesome. **947. hoolsom,** wholesome. **949. swoote,** sweet.

And next the derke night, the glade morwe—
And also joye is next the fin of sorwe.

Now looke that attempre be thy bridel,
And for the beste ay suffre to the tide,
Or elles al oure labour is on idel:
He hasteth wel that wisely can abide.
Be diligent and trewe, and ay wel hide;
Be lusty, free, persevere in thy servise—
And al is wel if thou werke in this wise.

But he that parted is in every place
Is nowher hool, as writen clerkes wise.
What wonder is though swich oon have no grace?
Eek woostou how it fareth of som servise—
As plaunte a tree or herbe in sondry wise,
And on the morwe pulle it up as blive,
No wonder is though it may nevere thrive.

And sith that God of Love hath thee bistowed
In place digne unto thy worthinesse,
Stond faste, for to good port hastou rowed.
And of thyself, for any hevinesse,
Hope alway wel, for but if drerinesse
Or overhaste oure bothe labour shende,
I hope of this to maken a good ende.

And woostou why I am the lasse afered
Of this matere with my nece trete?
For this I have herd said of wise lered:
Was nevere man or womman yit bigete
That was unapt to suffren loves hete—

952. **fin,** end. 953. **attempre,** well in control; **bridel,** bridle. 954. **suffre,** i.e., be patient; **tide,** time. 955. **on idel,** in vain. 958. **free,** generous. 960. **parted,** divided. 963. **of som servise,** with some lovers. 965. **as blive,** at once. 968. **digne,** worthy. 970. **for,** despite. 971. **but if,** unless. 972. **oure . . . labour,** the labor of both of us; **shende,** spoil. 974. **lasse,** less. 975. **nece,** niece; **trete,** to discuss. 976. **lered,** learned (men). 977. **bigete,** begotten. 978. **hete,** heat.

Celestial, or elles love of kinde:°
Forthy° som grace I hope in hire to finde.

And for to speke of hire in special,
Hir beautee to bithinken° and hir youthe,
It sit° it nought to been celestial
As yit, though that hire liste bothe and couthe.°
But trewely, it sate hire wel right nouthe°
A worthy knight to loven and cherice—
And but she do, I holde it for a vice.

Wherfore I am and wol been ay redy
To paine me° to do you this servise;
For bothe you° to plese thus hope I
Herafterward, for ye been bothe wise,
And conne it conseil° keepe in swich a wise
That no man shal the wiser of it be—
And so we may been gladded alle three.

And, by my trouthe, I have right now of thee
A good conceite° in my wit as I gesse,
And what it is I wol now that thou see:
I thenke, sith that Love of his goodnesse
Hath thee converted out of wikkednesse,
That thou shalt been the beste post, I leve,°
Of al his lay,° and most his foes greve.

Ensample° why, see now thise wise clerkes
That erren aldermost ayain° a lawe,
And been converted from hir wikked werkes,
Thurgh grace of God that list° hem to him drawe,
Thanne arn thise folk that han most God in awe,

979. Celestial, i.e., spiritual love; **of kinde,** natural, i.e., love between the sexes. **980. Forthy,** therefore. **982. bithinken,** consider. **983. sit,** suits. **984. liste,** pleased; **couthe,** she could. **985. sate,** would suit; **nouthe,** now. **989. paine me,** take pains. **990. bothe you,** both of you. **992. conne,** can; **conseil,** secret. **996. conceite,** idea. **1000. post,** pillar; **leve,** believe. **1001. lay,** law. **1002. Ensample,** example. **1003. aldermost,** most of all; **ayain,** against. **1005. list,** it pleases.

And strengest faithed° been, I understonde,
And conne an errour alderbest° withstonde."

Whan Troilus hadde herd Pandare assented
To been his help in loving of Criseide,
Weex of his wo, as who° saith, untormented;
But hotter weex his love, and thus he saide,
With sobre cheere, although his herte playde:°
"Now blisful Venus, help er that I sterve!°
Of thee, Pandare, I mowe som thank deserve.°

But dere freend, how shal my wo be lesse
Til this be doon? And goode, eek tel me this:
How wiltou sayn of me and my distresse
Lest she be wroth—this drede I most, ywis—
Or nil nat heere or trowen° how it is?
Al this drede I, and eek for the manere
Of thee, hir eem,° she nil no swich thing heere."

Quod Pandarus, "Thou hast a ful greet care
Lest that the cherl may falle out of the moone.
Why lord, I hate of thee thy nice fare.°
Why, entremette of that thou hast to doone!°
For Goddes love, I bidde thee a boone:°
So lat m'allone, and it shal be thy beste."
"Why, freend," quod he, "now do right as thee leste.°

But herke, Pandare, oo word, for I nolde
That thou in me wendest° so greet folye
That to my lady I desiren sholde
That toucheth harm or any vilainye.°

1007. **strengest faithed,** most strongly faithful. **1008. alderbest,** best of all. **1011. Weex,** he grew; **who,** one. **1013. playde,** was light. **1014. sterve,** die. 1015. **Of,** for; **mowe,** may; **thank deserve,** incur gratitude. **1020. trowen,** believe. **1022. eem,** uncle. **1025. nice fare,** foolish fuss. **1026.** i.e., Why, confine your meddling to what you have to do. **1027. bidde,** ask; **boone,** favor. **1029. leste,** it may please. **1031. wendest,** i.e., suspected. **1033. That,** what; **toucheth,** i.e., involves; **vilainye,** vulgarity.

For dredelees,° me were levere die,
Than she of me ought elles understoode
But that that mighte sounen into° goode."

Tho lough° this Pandare and anoon answerde,
"And I thy borwe;° fy, no wight dooth but so.
I roughte° nought though that she stoode and herde
How that thou saist. But farewel, I wol go.
Adieu, be glad, God speede us bothe two.
Yif me this labour and this bisinesse,
And of my speed° be thyn al that swetnesse."

Tho Troilus gan down on knees to falle,
And Pandare in his armes hente° faste,
And saide, "Now fy on the Greekes alle!
Yit Pandare, God shal helpe us atte laste,
And dredelees, if that my lif may laste,
And God toforn,° lo, some of hem shal smerte;
And yit m'athenketh that this avaunt me sterte.°

Now Pandarus, I can namore saye,
But thou wis,° thou woost, thou maist, thou art al;
My lif, my deeth, hoole° in thyn hand I laye:
Help now!" Quod he, "Yis, by my trouthe, I shal."
"God yeelde thee, freend, and this in special,"
Quod Troilus, "that thou me recomande°
To hire that to the deeth me may comande."

This Pandarus, tho° desirous to serve
His fulle freend, thanne saide in this manere:
"Farewel, and thenk I wol thy thank deserve,
Have here my trouthe, and that thou shalt wel heere,"
And wente his way, thenking on this matere,

1034. dredelees, doubtless. **1036. sounen into,** tend toward. **1037. Tho,** then; **lough,** laughed. **1038. borwe,** security. **1039. roughte,** would care. **1043. speed,** success. **1045. hente,** took. **1049. God toforn,** before God. **1050. m'athenketh,** I repent; **avaunt,** boast; **me sterte,** i.e., escaped from my mouth. **1052. wis,** ? lead. **1053. hoole,** wholly. **1056. recomande,** commend. **1058. tho,** then.

And how he best mighte hire biseeche of grace,
And finde a time therto, and a place.

For every wight that hath an hous to founde
Ne renneth nought the werk for to biginne
With rakel hand, but he wol bide a stounde,
And sende his hertes line out fro withinne,
Alderfirst his purpos for to winne.
Al this Pandare in his herte thoughte,
And caste his werk ful wisely er he wroughte.

But Troilus lay tho no lenger down,
But up anoon upon his steede bay,
And in the feeld he played the leoun.
Wo was that Greek that with him mette aday!
And in the town his manere tho forth ay
So goodly was, and gat him so in grace,
That eech him loved that looked on his face.

For he bicam the frendlieste wight,
The gentileste, and eek the moste free,
The thriftieste, and oon the beste knight
That in his time was or mighte be:
Dede were his japes and his crueltee,
His hye port, and his manere straunge—
And eech of tho gan for a vertu chaunge.

Now lat us stinte of Troilus a stounde,
That fareth lik a man that hurt is sore,
And is somdeel of aking of his wounde
Ylissed wel, but heled no deel more;
And as an esy pacient the lore

1065. **founde,** build. 1066. **renneth,** runs. 1067. **rakel,** rash; **stounde,** while. 1069. **Alderfirst,** first of all; **purpos . . . winne,** attain his intent. 1071. **caste,** considered. 1073. **bay,** brown. 1077. **gat,** got, i.e., brought. 1080. **free,** generous. 1081. **thriftieste,** best-behaved; **oon,** one of. 1083. **japes,** jokes. 1084. **hye port,** arrogant bearing; **straunge,** unfriendly. 1085. **tho,** those. 1086. **stinte,** cease; **stounde,** while. 1089. **Ylissed,** relieved. 1090. **lore,** treatment.

Abit of him that gooth aboute his cure,
And thus he drieth forth his aventure.

BOOK TWO

The Prologue

Out of thise blake wawes for to saile,
O wind, O wind, the weder ginneth clere,
For in this see the boot hath swich travaile
Of my conning that unnethe I it steere:
This see clepe I the tempestous matere
Of desespair that Troilus was inne—
But now of hope the kalendes biginne.

O lady myn, that called art Cleo,
Thou be my speed fro this forth, and my muse,
To ryme wel this book til I have do:
Me needeth here noon other art to use,
Forwhy to every lovere I me excuse
That of no sentement I this endite,
But out of Latin in my tonge it write.

Wherfore I nil have neither thank ne blame
Of al this werk, but praye you mekely,
Disblameth me if any word be lame,
For as myn auctour saide so saye I;
Eek though I speke of love unfeelingly,

1091. Abit, i.e., undergoes. **1092. drieth forth,** endures; **aventure,** fortune.
1. wawes, waves. **3. boot,** boat; **travaile,** trouble. **4. conning,** steersmanship; **unnethe,** with difficulty. **5. clepe,** call. **6. desespair,** despair. **7. kalendes,** first days. **8. Cleo,** Clio, the Muse of history. **9. speed,** help. **12. Forwhy,** because. **13. of,** with. **17. Disblameth,** excuse.

No wonder is, for it no thing of newe is:
A blind man can nat juggen wel in hewes.

Ye knowe eek that in forme of speeche is chaunge
Within a thousand yeer, and wordes tho°
That hadden pris° now wonder nice° and straunge
Us thenketh hem, and yit they spake hem so,
And spedde as wel in love as men now do;
Eek for to winnen love in sondry ages
In sondry landes sondry been usages.

And forthy° if it happe in any wise
That here be any lovere in this place,
That herkneth as the storye can devise,
How Troilus cam to his lady grace,
And thenketh, "So nolde I nat love purchace,"°
Or wondreth on his speeche or his doinge,
I noot,° but it is me no wonderinge.

For every wight which that to Rome went°
Halt° nat oo path or alway oo manere;
Eek in som land were al the game shent°
If that they ferde° in love as men doon here,
As thus: in open doing, or in cheere,°
In visiting, in forme, or saide hir sawes;°
Forthy men sayn, "Eech contree hath his lawes."

Eek scarsly been ther in this place three
That have in love saide lik and doon in al,
For to thy purpos this may liken° thee,
And thee right nought; yit al is said or shal.°
Eek some men grave in tree,° some in stoon wal,
As it bitit.° But sin I have bigonne,
Myn auctour shal I folwen if I conne.°

23. **tho,** then. 24. **pris,** value; **nice,** foolish. 29. **forthy,** therefore. 33. **purchace,** procure. 35. **noot,** know not. 36. **went,** wends. 37. **Halt,** holds. 38. **shent,** spoiled. 39. **ferde,** behaved. 40. **open,** unsecretive; **or,** either; **cheere,** appearance. 41. **or . . . sawes,** or in speaking their speeches. 45. **liken,** please. 46. **shal,** i.e., will be. 47. **grave,** carve; **tree,** wood. 48. **bitit,** happens. 49. **conne,** can.

The Story

In May, that moder is of monthes glade,
That fresshe flowres blewe and white and rede
Been quike again, that winter dede made,
And ful of baume is fleting every mede,°
Whan Phebus dooth his brighte bemes sprede
Right in the White Bole, it so bitidde,°
As I shal singe, on Mayes day the thridde,°

That Pandarus, for al his wise speeche,
Felte eek his part of loves shottes keene,
That coude he nevere so wel of loving preche,
It made his hewe aday ful ofte greene;
So shoop it that him fil that day a teene°
In love, for which in wo to bed he wente,
And made er it was day ful many a wente.°

The swalwe Proigne° with a sorweful lay
Whan morwen cam gan make hir waymentinge°
Why she forshapen° was, and evere lay
Pandare abedde, half in a slomberinge,
Til she so neigh him made hir chateringe,
How Tereus gan forth hir suster take,
That with the noise of hire he gan awake,

And gan to calle and dresse him° up to rise,
Remembring him his erand was to doone
From Troilus, and eek his grete emprise;°

53. **baume,** balm; **fleting,** floating; **mede,** meadow. 55. **White Bole,** White Bull, Taurus, the sign of the zodiac that the sun is in during late April and early May; **bitidde,** happened. 56. **thridde,** third. 61. **So shoop it,** it was so ordained; **fil,** there befell; **teene,** feeling of distress. 63. **wente,** turn. 64. **Proigne,** Procne, who was turned into a swallow after she had helped avenge her sister Philomela's rape by her husband Tereus. 65. **morwen,** morning; **waymentinge,** lamentation. 66. **forshapen,** transformed. 71. **dresse him,** prepare. 73. **emprise,** undertaking.

And caste, and knew in good plit was the moone
To doon viage, and took his way ful soone
Unto his neces palais ther biside—
Now Janus, god of entree, thou him gide!

Whan he was come into his neces place,
"Wher is my lady?" to hir folk quod he.
And they him tolde, and he forth in gan pace,
And foond two othere ladies sete and she
Within a paved parlour, and they three
Herden a maiden reden hem the geste
Of the sege of Thebes whil hem leste.

Quod Pandarus, "Madame, God you see,
With al your book and al the compaignye."
"Ey, uncle myn, welcome, ywis," quod she.
And up she roos, and by the hand in hie
She took him faste, and saide, "This night thrie—
To goode mote it turne—of you I mette."
And with that word she down on benche him sette.

"Ye, nece, ye shal faren wel the bet,
If God wol, al this yeer," quod Pandarus.
"But I am sory that I have you let
To herknen of youre book ye praisen thus.
For Goddes love, what saith it? Telle it us.
Is it of love? O, som good ye me lere."
"Uncle," quod she, "youre maistresse is nat here."

With that they gonnen laughe, and tho she saide,
"This romance is of Thebes that we rede.
And we han herd how that King Laius deide

74. caste, i.e., considered what the astrological situation foretold; **plit,** position. **75. doon viage,** i.e., begin an undertaking. **77. Janus,** the Roman god of beginnings and of doors. **80. pace,** pass. **81. foond,** found that; **sete,** were sitting. **82. paved,** tiled. **83. geste,** story. **84. leste,** it pleased. **85. see,** watch over. **88. hie,** haste. **89. This night thrie,** the night before last. **90. mote,** may; **mette,** dreamed. **92. bet,** better. **94. let,** prevented. **97. lere,** teach. **99. tho,** then.

Thurgh Edippus his sone, and al that deede.
And here we stinten at thise lettres rede,
How that the bisshop, as the book can telle,
Amphiorax fil thurgh the ground to helle."

Quod Pandarus, "Al this knowe I myselve,
And al th'assege of Thebes and the care,
For herof been ther maked bookes twelve.
But lat be this, and telle me how ye fare.
Do way youre barbe and shew youre face bare.
Do way youre book, rise up, and lat us daunce,
And lat us doon to May som observaunce."

"I? God forbede," quod she. "Be ye mad?
Is that a widwes lif, so God you save?
By God, ye maken me right sore adrad.
Ye been so wilde, it seemeth as ye rave.
It satte me wel bet ay in a cave
To bidde and rede on holy saintes lives.
Lat maidens goon to daunce, and yonge wives."

"As evere thrive I," quod this Pandarus,
"Yit coude I telle a thing to doon you playe."
"Now, uncle dere," quod she, "telle it us,
For Goddes love. Is thanne th'assege awaye?
I am of Greekes so fered that I deye."
"Nay, nay," quod he, "as evere mote I thrive,
It is a thing wel bet than swiche five."

"Ye, holy God," quod she, "what thing is that?
What, bet than swiche five? I, nay, ywis.

102. Edippus, Oedipus, the son of the King of Thebes, who, as was foretold at his birth, eventually killed his father Laius. **103. stinten,** stop; **lettres rede,** red letters, indicating a new chapter. **104. bisshop,** i.e., priest, seer. **105. Amphiorax,** Amphiaraus, one of those who undertook the siege of Thebes and, as he had foretold, perished there when the earth opened and swallowed him; **fil,** fell. **107. assege,** siege. **110. barbe,** veil. **117. satte,** would suit; **bet,** better. **118. bidde,** pray. **121. doon,** make. **124. fered,** afraid. **125. mote,** may. **126.** It's five times better than that. **128. I,** oh.

For al this world ne can I reden what
It sholde been. Som jape I trowe is this.
And but youreselven telle us what it is,
My wit is for t'arede it al too lene.
As helpe me God, I noot nat what ye mene."

"And I thy borwe, ne nevere shal for me
This thing be told to you, as mote I thrive."
"And why so, uncle myn, why so?" quod she.
"By God," quod he, "that wol I telle as blive:
For prouder womman is ther noon on live,
And ye it wiste, in al the town of Troye.
I jape nought, as evere have I joye."

Tho gan she wondren more than biforn
A thousandfold, and down hir yën caste;
For nevere sith the time that she was born
To knowe thing desired she so faste;
And with a sik she saide him atte laste,
"Now, uncle myn, I nil you nought displese,
Nor axen more that may do you disese."

So after this, with many wordes glade
And freendly tales and with merye cheere,
Of this and that they played and gonnen wade
In many an uncouthe glad and deep matere,
As freendes doon whan they been met yfere,
Til she gan axen him how Ector ferde,
That was the townes wal and Greekes yerde.

"Ful wel, I thanke it God," quod Pandarus,
"Save in his arm he hath a litel wounde—
And eek his fresshe brother Troilus,

129. **reden,** say. 130. **jape,** practical joke; **trowe,** believe. 131. **but,** unless. 132. **arede,** interpret. 133. **noot,** don't know. 134. **I thy borwe,** i.e., I'll guarantee it. 137. **as blive,** at once. 139. **And,** if; **wiste,** knew. 140. **jape,** joke. 145. **sik,** sigh. 147. **axen,** ask; **disese,** embarrassment. 151. **uncouthe,** uncommonly. 152. **yfere,** together. 153. **ferde,** fared. 154. **wal,** i.e., defense; **yerde,** rod, i.e., scourge.

The wise, worthy Ector the secounde,
In whom that alle vertu list habounde,°
As alle trouthe and alle gentilesse,
Wisdom, honour, freedom,° and worthinesse."

"In good faith, eem," quod she, "that liketh° me:
They faren wel, God save hem bothe two.
For treweliche, I holde it greet daintee°
A kinges sone in armes wel to do,
And been of goode condicions° therto:
For greet power and moral vertu here
Is selde yseen in oo persone yfere."°

"In good faith, that is sooth," quod Pandarus.
"But by my trouthe, the king has sones twaye—
That is to mene, Ector and Troilus—
That certainly, though that I sholde deye,
They been as voide° of vices, dar I saye,
As any men that liven under the sonne:
Hir might is wide yknowe, and what they conne.°

Of Ector needeth namore for to telle:
In al this world ther nis a bettre knight
Than he that is of worthinesse welle,°
And he wel more vertu hath than might—
This knoweth many a wis and worthy wight.
The same pris° of Troilus I saye:
God helpe me so, I knowe nat swiche twaye."

"By God," quod she, "of Ector that is sooth.
Of Troilus the same thing trowe° I;
For dredelees° men tellen that he dooth
In armes day by day so worthily,

159. **list habounde,** pleases to abound. 161. **freedom,** generosity. 162. **eem,** uncle; **liketh,** pleases. 164. **holde,** consider; **greet daintee,** i.e., a most pleasing thing. 166. **condicions,** i.e., character. 168. **selde,** seldom; **yfere,** together. 173. **voide,** empty. 175. **conne,** can do. 178. **welle,** source. 181. **pris,** praise. 184. **trowe,** believe. 185. **dredelees,** doubtless.

And bereth him here at home so gentilly
To every wight, that alle pris hath he
Of hem that me were levest praised be."

"Ye saye right sooth, ywis," quod Pandarus,
"For yesterday, who so hadde with him been,
He mighte han wondred upon Troilus,
For nevere yit so thikke a swarm of been
Ne fleigh as Greekes for him gonne fleen;
And thurgh the feeld in every wightes ere
Ther nas no cry but 'Troilus is there!'

Now heer, now ther, he hunted hem so faste
Ther nas but Greekes blood, and Troilus;
Now hem he hurte, and hem alle down he caste;
Ay wher he wente it was arrayed thus:
He was hir deeth, and sheeld and lif for us,
That as that day ther dorste noon withstonde,
Whil that he heeld his bloody swerd in honde.

Therto he is the frendlieste man
Of greet estaat that evere I sawgh my live,
And wher him list best felaweshipe can
To swich as him thinketh able for to thrive."
And with that word tho Pandarus as blive
He took his leve and saide, "I wol goon henne."
"Nay, blame have I, myn uncle," quod she thenne.

"What aileth you to be thus wery soone,
And nameliche of wommen? Wol ye so?
Nay, sitteth down. By God, I have to doone
With you, to speke of wisdom er ye go."
And every wight that was aboute hem tho,

189. Of those that I should most like to be praised by. **190. ywis,** indeed. **193. been,** bees. **194. fleigh,** flew. **200. arrayed,** disposed. **205. my,** i.e., in my. **206. list,** it pleases; **felaweshipe can,** shows friendliness. **207. able,** worthy. **208. tho,** then; **as blive,** straightway. **209. henne,** hence. **212. nameliche,** especially. **213. to doone,** i.e., business. **214. wisdom,** i.e., something serious.

That herde that, gan fer away to stonde,
Whil they two hadde al that hem liste in honde.

Whan that hir tale al brought was to an ende
Of hir estaat and of hir governaunce,
Quod Pandarus, "Now is it time I wende.
But yit I saye, ariseth, lat us daunce,
And cast youre widwes habit to meschaunce.
What list you thus youreself to disfigure,
Sith you is tid thus fair an aventure?"

"A, wel bithought, for love of God," quod she,
"Shal I nat witen what ye mene of this?"
"No, this thing axeth leiser," tho quod he,
"And eek me wolde muche greve, ywis,
If I it tolde and ye it tooke amis.
Yit were it bet my tonge for to stille
Than saye a sooth that were ayains youre wille.

For nece, by the goddesse Minerve,
And Jupiter that maketh the thonder ringe,
And by the blisful Venus that I serve,
Ye been the womman in this world livinge–
Withouten paramour, to my witinge–
That I best love, and lothest am to greve;
And that ye witen wel youreself, I leve."

"Ywis, myn uncle," quod she, "graunt mercy.
Youre frendshipe have I founden evere yit.
I am to no man holden, trewely,
So muche as you, and have so litel quit.
And with the grace of God, emforth my wit,

217. **hadde . . . honde,** i.e., discussed whatever business they pleased. 218. **tale,** conversation. 219. **governaunce,** management. 223. **What,** why; **disfigure,** deface. 224. **you is tid,** there has happened to you. 226. **witen,** discover. 227. **axeth,** requires. 230. **bet,** better; **stille,** hold in silence. 236. **paramour,** lover; **witinge,** knowledge. 238. **leve,** believe. 239. **graunt mercy,** many thanks. 240. **founden,** i.e., found true. 241. **holden,** beholden. 242. **quit,** repaid. 243. **emforth,** in proportion to.

As in my gilt I shal you nevere offende;
And if I have er this, I wol amende.

But for the love of God I you biseeche,
As ye been he that I love most and triste,
Lat be to me youre fremde manere speeche,
And saye to me, youre nece, what you liste."
And with that word hir uncle anoon hire kiste,
And saide, "Gladly, leve nece dere:
Take it for goode that I shal saye you here."

With that she gan hir yën down to caste,
And Pandarus to coughe gan a lite,
And saide, "Nece, alway, lo, to the laste,
How so it be that some men hem delite
With subtil art hir tales for to endite,
Yit for al that, in hir entencioun
Hir tale is al for som conclusioun.

And sitthen th'ende is every tales strengthe,
And this matere is so bihovely,
What sholde I pointe, or drawen it on lengthe
To you, that been my freend so faithfully?"
And with that word he gan right inwardly
Biholden hire, and looken on hir face,
And saide, "On swich a mirour, goode grace."

Thanne thoughte he thus, "If I my tale endite
Ought hard, or make a proces any while,
She shal no savour have therinne but lite,
And trowe I wolde hire in my wil bigile;
For tendre wittes weenen al be wile

247. **triste,** trust. 248. **fremde,** strange, unnatural. 251. **leve,** beloved. 254. **lite,** little. 259. **for som conclusion,** directed toward a certain end. 261. **bihovely,** relevant. 262. **What,** why; **pointe,** i.e., expatiate. 264. **inwardly,** intimately. 268. **Ought,** in any way; **proces,** argument. 269. **savour,** pleasure; **lite,** little. 270. **trowe,** i.e., she will believe. 271. **weenen,** suppose; **wile,** guile.

Ther as they can nought pleinly° understonde:
Forthy hir wit to serven wol I fonde."°

And looked on hire in a bisy° wise,
And she was war that he biheeld hire so,
And saide, "Lord, so faste ye m'avise!°
Sey° ye me nevere er now? What, saye ye no?"
"Yis, yis," quod he, "and bet° wol er I go.
But by my trouthe, I thoughte° now if ye
Be fortunat, for now men shal it see.

For every wight som goodly aventure
Som time is shape,° if he it can receiven.
But if that he wol take of it no cure°
Whan that it cometh, but wilfully it waiven,°
Lo, neither caas° ne fortune him deceiven,
But right his verray slouthe° and wrecchednesse,
And swich a wight is for to blame, I gesse.

Good aventure, O bele° nece, have ye
Ful lightly founden, and° ye conne it take.
And for the love of God, and eek of me,
Cacche it anoon, lest aventure slake.°
What sholde I lenger proces° of it make?
Yif me youre hand, for in this world is noon—
If that you liste—a wight so wel bigoon.°

And sith I speke of good entencioun,
As I to you have told wel herbiforn,
And love as wel youre honour and renown
As creature in al this world yborn,

272. **pleinly,** fully. 273. **Forthy,** therefore; **serven,** adjust to; **fonde,** try. 274. **bisy,** attentive. 276. **avise,** consider. 277. **Sey,** saw. 278. **bet,** better. 279. **thoughte,** i.e., wondered. 282. **shape,** destined. 283. **cure,** care. 284. **waiven,** forgo. 285. **caas,** chance. 286. **right,** just; **slouthe,** indolence. 288. **bele,** fair. 289. **lightly,** easily; **and,** if. 291. **aventure,** fortune; **slake,** slacken. 292. **proces,** argument. 294. **wel bigoon,** well-off, lucky.

By alle tho° othes that I have you sworn,
And ye be wroth therfore, or weene° I lie,
Ne shal I nevere seen you eft° with yë.

Beeth nought agast, ne quaketh nought. Wherto?
Ne chaungeth nought for fere so youre hewe.
For hardily,° the werste of this is do,°
And though my tale as now be to you newe,
Yit trist° alway ye shal me finde trewe;
And were it thing that me thoughte unsittinge,°
To you wolde I no swiche tales bringe."

"And, goode eem, for Goddes love, I praye,"
Quod she, "come of,° and telle me what it is.
For bothe I am agast what ye wol saye,
And eek me longeth it to wite,° ywis.
For whether it be wel or be amis,
Saye on, lat me nat in this fere dwelle."
"So wol I doon; now herkeneth, I shal telle:

Now, nece myn, the kinges dere sone,
The goode, wise, worthy, fresshe and free,°
Which alway for to doon wel is his wone,°
The noble Troilus, so loveth thee,
That but° ye helpe, it wol his bane° be.
Lo, here is al—what sholde I more saye?
Dooth what you list to make him live or deye.

But if ye lete him die, I wol sterve.°
Have here my trouthe, nece, I nil nat lien,
Al° sholde I with this knif my throte kerve."°
With that the teres breste° out of his yën,
And saide, "If that ye doon° us bothe dien

299. **tho,** those. 300. **And,** if; **weene,** think. 301. **eft,** again. 304. **hardily,** assuredly; **do,** done. 306. **trist,** trust. 307. **unsittinge,** unsuitable. 310. **come of,** be done. 312. **wite,** know. 317. **free,** generous. 318. **wone,** habit. 320. **but,** unless; **bane,** destruction. 323. **sterve,** die. 325. **Al,** although; **kerve,** cut. 326. **breste,** burst. 327. **doon,** cause.

Thus giltelees, thanne have ye fisshed faire.
What mende ye though that we bothe apaire?°

Allas, he which that is my lord so dere,
That trewe man, that noble, gentil knight,
That nought desireth but youre freendly cheere,°
I see him dien ther he gooth° upright,
And hasteth him with al his fulle might
For to be slain, if his fortune assente.
Allas, that God you swich a beautee sente!

If it be so that ye so cruel be
That of his deeth you listeth nought to recche,°
That is so trewe and worthy as ye see,
Namore than of a japer° or a wrecche,
If ye be swich, youre beautee may nat strecche°
To make amendes of so cruel a deede:
Avisement is good bifore the neede.°

Wo worth the faire gemme vertulees!°
Wo worth that herbe also that dooth no boote!°
Wo worth that beautee that is routhelees!°
Wo worth that wight that tret eech° under foote!
And ye that been of beautee crop° and roote,
If therwithal in you ne be no routhe,
Thanne is it harm ye liven, by my trouthe.

And also, think wel that this is no gaude,°
For me were levere thou and I and he
Were hanged, than I sholde been his bawde,°
As heigh as men mighte on us alle ysee.°

329. **What mende ye,** how are you bettered; **apaire,** perish. 332. **cheere,** manner. 333. **gooth,** walks. 338. **listeth,** it pleases; **recche,** care. 340. **japer,** fraud. 341. **strecche,** i.e., prove adequate. 343. It is good to take thought before the event requires it. 344. **Wo worth,** i.e., bad end to; **vertulees,** powerless, i.e., without the defensive and medicinal properties the Middle Ages ascribed to jewels. 345. **boote,** remedy. 346. **routhelees,** ruthless. 347. **tret,** treads; **eech,** every one. 348. **crop,** top. 351. **gaude,** trick. 353. **bawde,** pimp. 354. **ysee,** look.

I am thyn eem,° the shame were to me
As wel as thee, if that I sholde assente
Thurgh myn abet that he thyn honour shente.°

Now understonde, for I you nought requere°
To binde you to him thurgh no biheeste,°
But only that ye make him bettre cheere
Than ye han doon er this, and more feeste,°
So that his lif be saved atte leeste.
This al and som, and pleinly° oure entente:
God helpe me so, I nevere other mente.

Lo, this requeste is nought but skile,° ywis,
Ne doute° of reson, pardee, is ther noon.
I sette° the worste that ye dredden this:
Men wolde wondren seen° him come or goon.
Ther ayeins answere I thus anoon,
That every wight, but he be fool of kinde,°
Wol deeme it love of frendshipe in his minde.

What, who wolde deemen° though he see a man
To temple go, that he th'images eteth?
Thenk eek how wel and wisely that he can
Governe himself, that he no thing foryeteth,°
That wher he cometh he pris° and thank him geteth.
And eek therto he shal come here so selde,
What fors° were it though al the town biheelde?

Swich love of freendes regneth° al this town—
And wrie° you in that mantel everemo.
And God so wis° be my savacioun,
As I have said, youre best is to do so.

355. **eem,** uncle. 357. **abet,** abetting, assistance; **shente,** ruined. 358. **requere,** require. 359. **biheeste,** promise. 361. **more feeste,** i.e., better welcome. 363. **This . . . som,** i.e., this is the short and long; **pleinly,** fully. 365. **skile,** reason. 366. **doute,** fear. 367. **sette,** assume. 368. **seen,** to see. 370. **but,** unless; **of kinde,** by nature. 372. **deemen,** suspect. 375. **foryeteth,** forgets. 376. **pris,** praise. 378. **fors,** matter. 379. **regneth,** prevails in. 380. **wrie,** cover. 381. **wis,** surely.

But alway, goode nece, to stinte his wo,
So lat youre daunger sucred been a lite,
That of his deeth ye be nought for to wite."

Criseide, which that herde him in this wise,
Thoughte, "I shal feelen what he meneth, ywis."
"Now, eem," quod she, "what wolde ye devise?
What is youre reed I sholde doon of this?"
"That is wel said," quod he. "Certain, best is
That ye him love ayain for his lovinge,
As love for love is skilful guerdoninge.

Thenk eek how elde wasteth every houre
In eech of you a partye of beautee,
And therfore er that age thee devoure,
Go love, for old ther wil no wight of thee.
Lat this proverbe a lore unto you be:
'Too late ywar,' quod Beautee whan it paste;
And elde daunteth daunger at the laste.

The kinges fool is wont to cryen loude,
Whan that him thinketh a womman berth hire hye,
'So longe mote ye live, and alle proude,
Til crowes feet be growen under youre yë;
And sende you thanne a mirour in to prye,
In which that ye may see youre face amorwe.'
Nece, I bidde, wisshe you namore sorwe."

With this he stinte and caste adown the heed,
And she bigan to breste aweepe anoon,

383. **stinte,** stop. 384. **daunger,** i.e., reluctance and suspicion; **sucred,** sweetened; **lite,** little. 385. **wite,** blame. 389. **reed,** advice. 392. **skilful,** reasonable; **guerdoninge,** reward. 393. **elde,** age. 394. **partye,** part. 396. **old . . . thee,** no one will want you when you're old. 397. **lore,** lesson. 398. **ywar,** aware; **paste,** passed. 399. **daunteth,** subdues. 401. **berth hire hye,** behaves arrogantly. 402. **mote,** may. 404. **prye,** peer. 405. **amorwe,** in the morning. 406. **bidde,** pray. 407. **stinte,** paused. 408. **breste aweepe,** break into weeping.

And saide, "Allas for wo, why nere I deed,°
For of this world the faith is al agoon!
Allas, what sholde straunge° to me doon,
Whan he that for my beste freend I wende°
Ret me to love, and sholde it me defende!°

Allas, I wolde han trusted, doutelees,
That if that I thurgh my disaventure°
Hadde loved outher° him or Achilles,
Ector, or any mannes creature,
Ye nolde han had no mercy ne mesure°
On me, but alway had me in repreve.°
This false world, allas, who may it leve?°

What, is this al the joye and al the feeste?
Is this youre reed? Is this my blisful cas?°
Is this the verray meede of youre biheeste?°
Is al this painted proces° said, allas?
Right for this, fy! O lady myn Pallas,
Thou in this dredful caas for me purveye,°
For so astoned° am I that I deye."

With that she gan ful sorwefully to sike.°
"A, may it be no bet?"° quod Pandarus.
"By God, I shal namore come here this wike,°
And God aforn,° that am mistrusted thus.
I see ful wel that ye sette lite° of us,
Or of oure deeth. Allas, I, woful wrecche!
Mighte he yit live, of me is nought to recche.°

O cruel god, O despitouse Marte!°
O furies three of helle, on you I crye!

409. deed, dead. **411. straunge,** strangers. **412. wende,** i.e., took. **413. Ret,** advises; **defende,** prohibit. **415. disaventure,** bad luck. **416. outher,** either. **418. mesure,** moderation. **419. repreve,** reproach. **420. leve,** trust. **422. reed,** advice; **cas,** chance. **423. verray meede,** i.e., true value; **biheeste,** promise. **424. painted proces,** specious argument. **426. purveye,** provide. **427. astoned,** stunned. **428. sike,** sigh. **429. bet,** better. **430. wike,** week. **431. aforn,** before. **432. sette lite,** care little. **434. recche,** care. **435. despitouse,** merciless; **Marte,** Mars.

So lat me nevere out of this hous departe,
If that I mente harm or vilainye.
But sith I see my lord moot needes die,
And I with him, here I me shrive and saye
That wikkedly ye doon us bothe deye.

But sith it liketh you that I be deed,
By Neptunus that god is of the see,
Fro this forth I shal nevere eten breed,
Til I myn owene herte blood may see.
For certain I wol die as soone as he."
And up he sterte and on his way he raughte,
Til she again him by the lappe caughte.

Criseide, which that wel neigh starf for fere,
So as she was the ferefulleste wight
That mighte be, and herde eek with hir ere,
And sawgh the sorweful ernest of the knight,
And in his prayere eek sawgh noon unright,
And for the harm that mighte eek fallen more,
She gan to rewe and dredde hire wonder sore.

And thoughte thus: "Unhappes fallen thikke
Alday for love, and in swich manere cas
As men been cruel in hemself and wikke;
And if this man slee here himself, allas,
In my presence, it wol be no solas.
What men wolde of it deeme I can nat saye:
It needeth me ful slyly for to playe."

And with a sorweful sik she saide thrie,
"A, lord, what me is tid a sory chaunce!
For myn estaat lith now in jupartye,

438. **vilainye,** i.e., anything vulgar. 439. **moot,** must. 441. **doon,** cause. 447. **raughte,** reached, went. 448. **lappe,** fold in a garment. 449. **starf,** died. 454. **fallen,** happen. 455. **rewe,** feel remorse. 456. **Unhappes,** misfortunes. 457. **Alday,** constantly. 458. **wikke,** perverse. 459. **slee,** slay. 460. **solas,** comfort. 463. **sik,** sigh; **thrie,** thrice. 464. **is tid,** has befallen. 465. **lith,** lies; **jupartye,** jeopardy.

And eek myn eemes lif is in balaunce.
But nathelees, with Goddes governaunce,
I shal so doon, myn honour shal I keepe,
And eek his lif"—and stinte for to weepe.

"Of harmes two the lesse is for to chese:
Yit have I levere maken him good cheere
In honour, than myn eemes lif to lese.
Ye sayn ye nothing elles me requere?"
"No, wis," quod he, "myn owene nece dere."
"Now, wel," quod she, "and I wol doon my paine:
I shal myn herte ayains my lust constraine.

But that I nil nat holden him in honde,
Ne love a man ne can I nought ne may
Ayains my wil, but elles wol I fonde,
Myn honour sauf, plesen him fro day to day.
Therto nolde I nat ones han said nay,
But that I dredde as in my fantasye:
But ceesse cause, ay ceesseth maladye.

But here I make a protestacioun
That in this proces if ye depper go,
That certainly, for no savacioun
Of you, though that ye sterven bothe two,
Though al the world on oo day be my fo,
Ne shal I nevere of him han other routhe."
"I graunte wel," quod Pandare, "by my trouthe.

But may I truste wel therto?" quod he;
"That of this thing that ye han hight me here,
Ye wol it holden trewely unto me?"

466. eemes, uncle's. **469. stinte,** ceased. **470. for to chese,** the one to choose. **472. lese,** lose. **474. wis,** indeed. **475. paine,** i.e., best. **476. lust,** desire. **477. But,** except; **holden . . . honde,** keep him in false hope. **479. fonde,** try. **480. sauf,** safe. **482. fantasye,** imagination. **483. ceesse cause,** if the cause cease. **484. protestacioun,** avowal. **485. proces,** business; **depper,** more deeply. **487. sterven,** die. **489. routhe,** pity. **492. hight,** promised.

"Ye, doutelees," quod she, "myn uncle dere."
"Ne that I shal han cause in this matere,"
Quod he, "to plaine,° or after you to preche?"
"Why no, pardee." What needeth more speeche?

Tho fillen they in othere tales° glade,
Til at the laste, "O goode eem," quod she tho,
"For his love which that us bothe made,
Tel me how first ye wisten° of his wo?
Woot° noon of it but ye?" He saide, "No."
"Can he wel speke of love?" quod she. "I praye,
Tel me, for I the bet me shal purveye."°

Tho Pandarus a litel gan to smile,
And saide, "By my trouthe, I shal you telle.
This other day nought goon ful longe while,
Inwith the palais gardin by a welle°
Gan he and I wel half a day to dwelle,
Right for to speken of an ordinaunce,°
How we the Greekes mighten disavaunce.°

Soone after that bigonne we to lepe
And casten with oure dartes to and fro,
Til at the laste he saide he wolde sleepe,
And on the gras adown he laide him tho,
And I after gan romen to and fro,
Til that I herde, as that I welk° allone,
How he bigan ful wofully to grone.

Tho gan I stalke him softely bihinde;
And sikerly,° the soothe for to sayne,
As I can clepe° ayain now to my minde,
Right thus to Love he gan him for to plaine:°
He saide, 'Lord, have routhe upon my paine.

496. **plaine,** complain. 498. **Tho,** then; **fillen,** fell; **tales,** i.e., conversation. 501. **wisten,** learned. 502. **Woot,** knows. 504. **purveye,** prepare. 508. **Inwith,** within; **welle,** spring. 510. **ordinaunce,** plan. 511. **disavaunce,** set back. 517. **welk,** walked. 520. **sikerly,** certainly. 521. **clepe,** call. 522. **plaine,** complain.

Al° have I been rebel in myn entente,
Now, *mea culpa*,° lord, I me repente.

O god, that at thy disposicioun
Ledest the fin by juste purveyaunce°
Of every wight, my lowe° confessioun
Accepte in gree,° and sende me swich penaunce
As liketh thee, but from desesperaunce,°
That may my gost departe° away fro thee,
Thou be my sheeld, for thy benignitee.

For certes, lord, so sore hath she me wounded,
That stood in blak, with looking of hir yën,
That to myn hertes botme it is ysounded,°
Thurgh which I woot that I moot needes dien.
This is the werste, I dar me nat biwryen,°
And wel the hotter been the gleedes rede
That men hem wrien with asshen° pale and dede.'

With that he smoot° his heed adown anoon,
And gan to mottre, I noot° what, trewely.
And I with that gan stille away to goon,
And leet ther of as no thing wist° hadde I;
And cam ayain anoon, and stood him by,
And saide, 'Awake, ye sleepen al too longe.
It seemeth nat that Love dooth you longe,°

That sleepen so that no man may you wake.
Who sey° evere er this so dul a man?'
'Ye, freend,' quod he, 'do° ye youre hedes ake
For Love, and lat me liven as I can.'
But though that he for wo was pale and wan,

524. Al, although. **525. mea culpa,** I confess that the blame is mine. **527. Ledest the fin,** accomplishes the end; **purveyaunce,** foresight. **528. lowe,** humble. **529. gree,** favor. **530. desesperaunce,** despair. **531. gost,** spirit; **departe,** separate. **535. botme,** bottom; **ysounded,** plunged. **537. biwryen,** reveal. **539. wrien,** cover; **asshen,** ashes. **540. smoot,** smote. **541. mottre,** mutter; **noot,** don't know. **543. leet,** acted; **wist,** known. **546. dooth you longe,** causes you to long. **548. sey,** saw. **549. do,** make.

Yit made he tho as fressh a countenaunce
As though he sholde have led the newe daunce.

This passed forth til now this other day
It fil° that I cam roming al allone
Into his chambre, and foond° how that he lay
Upon his bed, but man so sore grone
Ne herde I nevere, and what that was his mone°
Ne wiste I nought, for as I was cominge
Al sodeinly he lefte his complaininge.

Of which I took somwhat suspecioun,
And neer I cam, and foond he wepte sore;
And God so wis° be my savacioun,
As nevere of thing hadde I no routhe° more,
For neither with engines ne with lore°
Unnethes° mighte I fro the deeth him keepe,
That yit I feele myn herte for him weepe.

And God woot, nevere sith that I was born
Was I so bisy no man for to preche,
Ne nevere was to wight so deepe ysworn,
Er he me tolde who mighte been his leeche°.
But now to you rehercen al his speeche,
Or alle his woful wordes for to soune°,
Ne bidde me nought, but ye wol see me swoune°.

But for to save his lif, and elles nought,
And to noon harm of you, thus am I driven.
And for the love of God that us hath wrought,
Swich cheere him dooth that he and I may liven.
Now have I plat to you myn herte shriven°,
And sith ye woot° that myn entente is clene,
Take heede therof, for I noon yvel° mene.

555. **fil,** happened. 556. **foond,** found. 558. **mone,** i.e., cause of complaint. 563. **wis,** surely. 564. **routhe,** pity. 565. **engines,** tricks; **lore,** i.e., experience. 566. **Unnethes,** hardly. 571. **leeche,** doctor. 573. **soune,** speak. 574. **but,** unless; **swoune,** faint. 579. **plat,** flatly; **shriven,** confessed. 580. **woot,** know. 581. **yvel,** evil.

And right good thrift I praye to God have ye,
That han swich oon ycaught withouten net.
And be ye wis as ye be fair to see,
Wel in the ring thanne is the rubye set.
Ther were nevere two so wel ymet,
Whan ye been his al hool as he is youre.
Ther mighty God graunte us to see that houre!"

"Nay, therof spak I nought, ha ha," quod she:
"As helpe me God, ye shenden every deel."
"O, mercy, dere nece," anoon quod he,
"What so I spak, I mente nought but weel.
By Mars the god that helmed is of steel,
Now beeth nought wroth, my blood, my nece dere."
"Now, wel," quod she, "foryiven be it here."

With this he took his leve, and hoom he wente,
And Lord, so was he glad and wel bigoon.
Criseide aroos, no lenger she ne stente,
But straight into hir closet wente anoon,
And sette hire down as stille as any stoon,
And every word gan up and down to winde
That he hadde said, as it cam hire to minde,

And was somdeel astoned in hir thought
Right for the newe caas, but whan that she
Was ful avised, tho foond she right nought
Of peril why she oughte afered be.
For man may love of possibilitee
A womman so his herte may tobreste,
And she nought love ayain but if hire leste.

But as she sat allone and thoughte thus,
Ascry aroos at scarmuche al withoute,

582. **thrift**, success. 587. **hool**, whole; **youre**, yours. 588. **Ther**, i.e., may. 589. **ha**, oh. 590. **shenden**, spoil; **deel**, bit. 592. **weel**, well. 597. **bigoon**, i.e., pleased. 598. **stente**, lingered. 599. **closet**, private room. 603. **astoned**, astonished. 604. **caas**, chance. 605. **Was ful avised**, had considered fully; **foond**, found. 608. **tobreste**, break. 609. **but if**, unless; **leste**, it please. 611. **Ascry**, outcry; **scarmuche**, skirmish.

And men criden in the streete, "See Troilus
Hath right now put to flight the Greekes route!"
With that gan al hir meinee for to shoute,
"A, go we see! Caste up the latis wide,
For thurgh this streete he moot to palais ride.

For other way is to the gate noon
Of Dardanus, ther open is the chaine."
With that cam he and al his folk anoon,
An esy paas riding in routes twaine,
Right as his happy day was, sooth to sayne.
For which men sayn, "May nought disturbed be
That shal bitiden of necessitee."

This Troilus sat on his baye steede
Al armed, save his heed, ful richely,
And wounded was his hors and gan to bleede,
On which he rood a paas ful softely.
But swich a knightly sighte trewely
As was on him, was nought, withouten faile,
To looke on Mars that god is of bataile.

So lik a man of armes and a knight
He was to seen, fulfilled of heigh prowesse;
For bothe he hadde a body and a might
To doon that thing, as wel as hardinesse;
And eek to seen him in his gere him dresse,
So fressh, so yong, so weeldy seemed he,
It was an hevene upon him for to see.

His helme tohewen was in twenty places,
That by a tissu heeng his bak bihinde;
His sheeld todasshed was with swerdes and maces,
In which men mighte many an arwe finde,

613. route, mob. **614. meinee,** household. **615. latis,** lattice window. **616. moot,** must. **620. esy paas,** slow gait; **routes,** groups. **624. baye,** brown. **625. heed,** head. **627. paas,** gait. **629. withouten faile,** i.e., to be sure. **636. weeldy,** vigorous. **638. tohewen,** hacked. **639. tissu,** band; **heeng,** hung. **640. todasshed,** battered. **641. arwe,** arrow.

That thirled hadde horn and nerf and rinde;
And ay the peple cride, "Here cometh oure joye,
And, next his brother, holder up of Troye."

For which he weex a litel reed for shame,
Whan he the peple upon him herde cryen,
That to biholde it was a noble game
How sobreliche he caste down his yën.
Criseida gan al his cheere espyen,
And leet it so softe in hir herte sinke,
That to hirself she saide, "Who yaf me drinke?"

For of hir owene thought she weex al reed,
Remembring hire right thus, "Lo, this is he
Which that myn uncle swereth he moot be deed,
But I on him have mercy and pitee."
And with that thought for pure ashamed she
Gan in hir heed to pulle, and that as faste,
Whil he and al the peple forby paste;

And gan to caste and rollen up and down
Within hir thought his excellent prowesse,
And his estaat, and also his renown,
His wit, his shap, and eek his gentilesse.
But most hir favour was for his distresse
Was al for hire, and thoughte it was a routhe
To sleen swich oon, if that he mente trouthe.

Now mighte som envious jangle thus:
"This was a sodein love. How mighte it be
That she so lightly loved Troilus,
Right for the firste sighte? Ye, pardee!"
Now who so saith so, mote he nevere ythee,

642. i.e., That had pierced the bone and sinew and skin of which the shield was made. **645. weex,** grew; **reed,** red. **649. cheere,** appearance. **654. deed,** dead. **655. But,** unless. **658. forby paste,** passed by. **659. caste,** consider. **663. for,** because. **664. routhe,** pity. **665. sleen,** slay. **667. sodein,** sudden. **668. lightly,** readily. **670. mote,** may; **ythee,** thrive.

For every thing a ginning hath it neede
Er al be wrought, withouten any drede.

For I saye nought that she so sodeinly
Yaf him hir love, but that she gan encline
To like him first, and I have told you why.
And after that his manhood and his pine°
Made love withinne hir herte for to mine,
For which by proces and by good servise
He gat hir love, and in no sodein wise.

And also, blisful Venus wel arrayed°
Sat in hir seventhe hous° of hevene tho,
Disposed wel, and with aspectes payed°
To helpe sely° Troilus of his wo.
And sooth to sayn, she was not al a fo
To Troilus in his nativetee:
God woot that wel the sonner spedde° he.

Now lat us stinte of Troilus a throwe,°
That rideth forth, and lat us turne faste
Unto Criseide, that heeng° hir heed ful lowe
Ther as she sat allone, and gan to caste°
Wheron she wolde appointe hire° atte laste,
If it so were hir eem ne wolde ceesse
For Troilus upon hire for to preesse.°

And Lord, so she gan in hir thought argue
In this matere of which I have you told,
And what to doon best were, and what eschue,°
That plited° she ful ofte in many a fold;

676. **pine,** suffering. 680. **arrayed,** disposed. 681. **seventhe hous,** i.e., most propitious position. 682. **with aspectes payed,** i.e., with her rays shining at such an angle as to seem pleased. 683. **sely,** poor. 686. **sonner,** sooner; **spedde,** succeeded. 687. **stinte,** cease; **throwe,** moment. 689. **heeng,** hung. 690. **caste,** consider. 691. **Wheron . . . hire,** what course she would follow. 693. **preesse,** press. 696. **eschue,** avoid. 697. **plited,** pleated, i.e., thought over.

Now was hir herte warm, now was it cold;
And what she thoughte somwhat shal I write,
As to myn auctour listeth for t'endite.

She thoughte wel that Troilus persone
She knew by sighte, and eek his gentilesse,
And thus she saide, "Al were it nat to doone
To graunte him love, yit for his worthinesse
It were honour with play and with gladnesse
In honestee with swich a lord to dele,
For myn estaat, and also for his hele.

Eek wel woot I my kinges sone is he,
And sith he hath to see me swich delit,
If I wolde outreliche his sighte flee,
Paraunter he mighte have me in despit:
Thurgh which I mighte stonde in worse plit.
Now were I wis me hate to purchace,
Withouten neede, ther I may stonde in grace?

In every thing I woot ther lith mesure,
For though a man forbede dronkenesse,
He nought forbet that every creature
Be drinkelees for alway, as I gesse.
Eek sith I woot for me is his distresse,
I ne oughte nought for that thing him despise,
Sith it is so he meneth in good wise.

And eek I knowe of longe time agoon
His thewes goode, and that he is nat nice;
N'avauntour, saith men, certain he is noon—
Too wis is he to doon so greet a vice;
Ne als I nil him nevere so cherice

703. Al, although; **to doone,** i.e., suitable. **706. honestee,** honorable conduct. **707. hele,** health. **708. woot,** know. **710. outreliche,** entirely. **711. Paraunter,** perhaps; **despit,** contempt. **712. plit,** situation. **715. lith,** lies; **mesure,** moderation. **717. forbet,** i.e., enjoins. **723. thewes,** habits; **nice,** foolish. **724. avauntour,** boaster. **726. als,** also.

That he may make avaunt° by juste cause:
He shal me nevere binde in swich a clause.°

Now sette a caas:° the hardest is, ywis,
Men mighten deemen° that he loveth me.
What dishonour were it unto me, this?
May ich him lette° of that? Why, nay, pardee.
I knowe also, and alday heere and see,
Men loven wommen al biside hir leve,°
And whan hem list namore, lat hem leve.°

I thenke eek how he able° is for to have
Of al this noble town the thriftieste°
To been his love, so she hir honour save;
For oute and oute° he is the worthieste,
Save only Ector, which that is the beste.
And yit his lif al lith now in my cure;°
But swich is love, and eek myn aventure.

Ne me to love a wonder is it nought,
For wel woot I myself, so God me speede
(Al° wolde I that noon wiste of this thought),
I am oon the faireste, out of drede,°
And goodlieste, who that taketh heede;
And so men sayn in al the town of Troye:
What wonder is though he of me have joye?

I am myn owene womman, wel at ese—
I thanke it God—as after myn estat,
Right yong, and stonde untied in lusty lese,°
Withouten jalousye or swich debat.
Shal noon housbonde sayn to me 'Chek-mat!'

727. avaunt, boast. **728. clause,** article. **729. sette a caas,** assume a situation. **730. deemen,** suspect. **732. ich,** I; **lette,** hinder. **734. biside,** without; **hir leve,** the ladies' permission. **735. list,** it pleases; **leve,** leave off. **736. able,** worthy. **737. thriftieste,** best-conducted woman. **739. oute . . . oute,** by far and away. **741. lith,** lies; **cure,** care. **745. Al,** although. **746. oon,** one of; **drede,** doubt. **752. lusty lese,** i.e., love's leash.

For either they been ful of jalousye,
Or maisterful, or loven novelrye.

What shal I doon? To what fin live I thus?
Shal I nat love in caas if that me leste?
What, pardeux, I am nat religious.
And though that I myn herte sette at reste
Upon this knight, that is the worthieste,
And keepe alway myn honour and my name,
By alle right it may do me no shame."

But right as whan the sonne shineth brighte
In March, that chaungeth ofte time his face,
And that a cloude is put with wind to flighte,
Which oversprat the sonne as for a space,
A cloudy thought gan thurgh hir soule pace,
That overspradde hir brighte thoughtes alle,
So that for fere almost she gan to falle.

That thought was this: "Allas, sin I am free,
Sholde I now love, and putte in jupartye
My sikernesse, and thrallen libertee?
Allas, how dorste I thenken that folye?
May I nought wel in other folk espye
Hir dredful joye, hir constrainte, and hir paine?
Ther loveth noon that she nath why to plaine.

For love is yit the moste stormy lif,
Right of himself, that evere was bigonne;
For evere som mistrust and nice strif
Ther is in love; som cloude is over that sonne.
Therto we wrecched wommen nothing conne,

755. **they,** i.e., husbands. 756. **maisterful,** domineering; **novelrye,** novelty. 757. **fin,** end. 758. **leste,** it please. 759. **religious,** i.e., a nun. 767. **oversprat,** overspreads. 768. **pace,** pass. 772. **jupartye,** jeopardy. 773. **sikernesse,** security; **thrallen,** enslave. 776. **dredful,** timorous. 777. **that . . . plaine,** who has not some reason to complain. 779. **himself,** itself. 780. **nice,** foolish. 782. **conne,** can do.

Whan us is wo, but weepe and sitte and thinke;
Oure wreche° is this, oure owene wo to drinke.

Also thise wikked tonges been so prest°
To speke us harm; eek men been so untrewe,
That right anoon as ceessed is hir lest,°
So ceesseth love, and forth to love a newe;
But harm ydoon is doon, who so it rewe:°
For though thise men for love hem first torende,°
Ful sharp biginning breketh ofte at ende.

How ofte time hath it yknowen be
The treson that to wommen hath been do;
To what fin° is swich love I can nat see,
Or wher bicometh° it whan it is ago—
Ther is no wight that woot, I trowe° so,
Wher it bicomth; lo, no wight on it spurneth!°
That erst° was nothing into nought it turneth.

How bisy, if I love, eek moste° I be
To plesen hem that jangle of love and dremen,°
And coye° hem that they saye noon harm of me;
For though ther be no cause, yit hem seemen
Al be for harm that folk hir freendes quemen;°
And who may stoppen every wikked tonge,
Or soun of belles, whil that they been ronge?"

And after that hir thought gan for to clere,°
And saide, "He which that nothing undertaketh
Nothing n'acheveth, be him loth or dere."°
And with another thought hir herte quaketh;
Thanne sleepeth hope, and after drede awaketh:

784. wreche, vengeance. **785. prest,** quick. **787. lest,** lust. **789. rewe,** regret. **790. torende,** tear apart. **794. fin,** end. **795. wher bicometh,** what becomes of. **796. trowe,** believe. **797. spurneth,** trips. **798. erst,** first. **799. moste,** must. **800. jangle,** gossip; **dremen,** imagine things. **801. coye,** cajole. **802–03. yit . . . quemen,** ? yet it seems to them that it is all for harm that people please their friends. **806. clere,** brighten. **808. be . . . dere,** whether he like it or not.

Now hoot, now cold, but thus bitwixen twaye,
She rist hire up, and wente hire for to playe.

Adown the staire anoonright tho she wente
Into the gardin with hir neces three,
And up and down ther made many a wente—
Flexippe, and she, Tharbe, and Antigone—
To playen that it joye was to see;
And othere of hir wommen a greet route
Hire folweden in the gardin al aboute.

This yeerd was large and railed alle th'aleyes,
And shadwed wel with blosmy bowes greene,
And benched newe, and sonded alle the wayes,
In which she walketh arm in arm bitweene,
Til at the laste Antigone the sheene
Gan on a Troyan song to singen clere,
That it an hevene was hir vois to heere.

She saide, "O Love, to whom I have and shal
Been humble subjet, trewe in myn entente,
As I best can, to you, lord, yive ich al,
For everemo myn hertes lust to rente;
For nevere yit thy grace no wight sente
So blisful cause as me, my lif to lede
In alle joye and suretee out of drede.

Ye, blisful god, han me so wel biset
In love, ywis, that alle that bereth lif
Imaginen ne coude how to be bet.
For lord, withouten jalousye or strif,
I love oon which that most is ententif
To serven wel, unwery or unfeined,
That evere was, and leest with harm distained.

811. hoot, hot. **812. rist,** rises. **815. wente,** turn. **818. route,** throng. **820. yeerd,** yard; **railed,** fenced; **aleyes,** paths. **822. benched,** provided with benches of turf; **sonded,** sanded. **824. sheene,** fair. **830. lust,** desire; **to rente,** as tribute. **833. suretee,** security. **834. biset,** placed. **836. bet,** better. **838. ententif,** attentive. **839. unfeined,** unshirking. **840. harm,** reproach; **distained,** stained.

As he that is the welle° of worthinesse,
Of trouthe ground, mirour of goodliheed,°
Of wit Appollo, stoon of sikernesse,°
Of vertu roote, of lust findere and heed,°
Thurgh which is alle sorwe fro me deed°—
Ywis, I love him best, so dooth he me:
Now good thrift° have he, wher so that he be!

Whom sholde I thanken but you, God of Love,
Of al this blisse in which to bathe I ginne?
And thanked be ye, lord, for that I love:
This is the righte lif that I am inne,
To flemen° alle manere vice and sinne;
This dooth me so to vertu for t'entende,°
That day by day I in my wille amende.

And who so saith that for to love is vice,
Or thraldom, though he feele it in distresse,
He outher is envious or right nice,°
Or is unmighty for his shrewednesse°
To loven; for swich manere folk, I gesse,
Defamen love as nothing of it knowe:
They speken, but they benten nevere his bowe.

What is the sonne wers of kinde right,°
Though that a man for fieblesse° of his yën
May nought endure on it to see for bright,°
Or love the wers, though wrecches on it cryen?
No wele is worth that may no sorwe drien;°
And forthy who that hath an heed of verre,°
Fro cast of stones ware him in the werre.°

841. welle, source. **842. goodliheed,** goodliness. **843. of wit Appollo,** i.e., god of intelligence; **sikernesse,** reliability. **844. lust,** pleasure; **findere,** deviser; **heed,** head. **845. deed,** dead. **847. thrift,** success. **852. flemen,** banish. **853. dooth,** makes; **entende,** strive. **857. outher,** either; **nice,** foolish. **858. shrewednesse,** wickedness. **862. of kinde right,** in its nature. **863. fieblesse,** feebleness. **864. see,** look; **bright,** i.e., brightness. **866. wele,** happiness; **worth,** worthy; **drien,** suffer. **867. forthy,** therefore; **heed,** head; **verre,** glass. **868. ware him,** let him beware; **werre,** war.

But I with al myn herte and al my might,
As I have said, wol love unto my laste
My dere herte and al myn owene knight,
In which myn herte growen is so faste,
And his in me, that it shal evere laste:
Al° dredde I first to love him to biginne,
Now woot I wel ther is no peril inne."

And of hir song right with that word she stente,°
And therwithal, "Now, nece," quod Criseide,
"Who made this song now with so good entente?"
Antigone answerde anoon and saide,
"Madame, ywis, the goodlieste maide
Of greet estaat in al the town of Troye,
And let° hir lif in most honour and joye."

"Forsoothe, so it seemeth by hir song,"
Quod tho Criseide, and gan therwith to sike,°
And saide, "Lord, is ther swich blisse among
Thise loveres as they conne faire endite?"°
"Ye, wis,"° quod fressh Antigone the white,
"For al the folk that han or been on live
Ne conne wel the blisse of love descrive.

But weene° ye that every wrecche woot
The parfite° blisse of love? Why, nay, ywis.
They weenen al be love if oon be hoot.°
Do way, do way, they woot nothing of this.
Men moste axe° at saintes if it is
Ought° fair in hevene. Why? For they can telle.
And axen feendes is it foul in helle."

Criseide unto that purpos nought answerde,
But saide, "Ywis, it wil be night as faste."

874. **Al,** although. 876. **stente,** stopped. 882. **And let,** and one who leads. 884. **sike,** sigh. 886. **endite,** describe. 887. **wis,** indeed. 890. **weene,** suppose. 891. **parfite,** perfect. 892. **hoot,** hot. 894. **moste,** must; **axe,** ask. 895. **Ought,** at all.

But every word which that she of hire herde,
She gan to prenten° in hir herte faste,
And ay gan love lesse hire for t'agaste°
Than it dide erst,° and sinken in hir herte,
That she weex somwhat able to converte.°

The dayes honour and the hevenes yë,
The nightes fo—al this clepe I the sonne—
Gan westren faste, and downward for to wrye,°
As he that hadde his dayes cours yronne,
And white thinges wexen dimme and donne°
For lak of light, and sterres° for t'appere,
That she and al hir folk in wente yfere.°

So whan it liked hire to go to reste,
And voided° weren they that voiden oughte,
She saide that to sleepen wel hire leste;°
Hir wommen soone til° hir bed hire broughte.
Whan al was hust,° thanne lay she stille and thoughte
Of al this thing the manere and the wise:
Reherce it needeth nought, for ye been wise.

A nightingale upon a cedre greene,
Under the chambre wal ther as she lay,
Ful loude soong ayain the moone sheene°
Paraunter° in his briddes wise a lay
Of love, that made hir herte fressh and gay,
That herkned she so longe in good entente,
That at the laste the dede sleep hire hente.°

And as she sleep, anoonright tho hire mette°
How that an egle, fethered whit as boon,°

900. prenten, imprint. **901. agaste,** terrify. **902. erst,** before. **903. converte,** to be converted. **906. westren,** sink west; **wrye,** turn. **908. wexen,** grew; **donne,** dun. **909. sterres,** stars. **910. yfere,** together. **912. voided,** departed. **913. leste,** it pleased. **914. til,** to. **915. hust,** hushed. **920. soong,** sang; **ayain,** i.e., to; **sheene,** bright. **921. Paraunter,** perhaps. **924. dede,** dead; **hente,** seized. **925. sleep,** slept; **hire mette,** she dreamed. **926. boon,** bone.

Under hir brest his longe clawes sette,
And out hir herte he rente, and that anoon,
And dide° his herte into hir brest to goon—
Of which she nought agroos ne nothing smerte°—
And forth he fleigh° with herte left for herte.

Now lat hire sleepe, and we oure tales holde
Of Troilus, that is to palais riden
Fro the scarmuche° of the which I tolde,
And in his chambre sit° and hath abiden,
Til two or three of his messages yeden°
For Pandarus, and soughten him ful faste,
Til they him founde and broughte him at the laste.

This Pandarus cam leping in atones,
And saide thus, "Who hath been wel ybete°
Today with swerdes and with slinge-stones,
But Troilus, that hath caught him an hete?"°
And gan to jape, and saide, "Lord, so ye swete!°
But ris and lat us soupe° and go to reste."
And he answerde him, "Do we as thee leste."

With al the haste goodly that they mighte
They spedde hem fro the soper unto bedde;
And every wight out at the dore him dighte,°
And wher him liste upon his way he spedde.
But Troilus, that thoughte his herte bledde
For wo til that he herde som tidinge,
He saide, "Freend, shal I now weepe or singe?"

Quod Pandarus, "Ly stille and lat me sleepe,
And doon thyn hood. Thy needes spedde° be,
And chees° if thou wolt singe or daunce or lepe.

929. **dide,** made. 930. **agroos,** feared; **smerte,** felt hurt. 931. **fleigh,** flew. 934. **scarmuche,** skirmish. 935. **sit,** sits. 936. **messages,** messengers; **yeden,** went. 940. **ybete,** beaten. 942. **hete,** heat, fever. 943. **jape,** joke; **swete,** sweat. 944. **soupe,** sup. 948. **him dighte,** i.e., went. 954. **doon,** put on; **spedde,** expedited. 955. **chees,** choose.

At shorte wordes, thou shalt trowen° me:
Sire, my nece wol do wel by thee,
And love thee best, by God and by my trouthe,
But lak of pursuit make it in thy slouthe.°

For thus ferforth° I have thy werk bigonne
Fro day to day, til this day by the morwe°
Hir love of frendshipe have I to thee wonne,
And also hath she laid hir faith to borwe:°
Algate a foot is hameled° of thy sorwe."
What sholde I lenger sermon of it holde?
As ye han herd bifore, al he him tolde.

But right as flowres, thurgh the cold of night
Yclosed, stoupen° on hir stalkes lowe,
Redressen hem ayain° the sonne bright,
And spreden on hir kinde cours° by rowe,
Right so gan tho his yën up to throwe
This Troilus, and saide, "O Venus dere,
Thy might, thy grace, yheried° be it here."

And to Pandare he heeld up bothe his hondes,
And saide, "Lord, al thyn be that I have,
For I am hool, and brosten° been my bondes.
A thousand Troyes who so that me yave,
Eech after other, God so wis° me save,
Ne mighte me so gladen. Lo, myn herte,
It spredeth so for joye it wol tosterte.°

But lord, how shal I doon? How shal I liven?
Whan shal I next my dere herte see?
How shal this longe time away be driven

956. **trowen,** trust. 959. **But,** unless; **make,** cause; **slouthe,** sloth, i.e., negligence. 960. **ferforth,** far. 961. **by the morwe,** in the morning. 963. **to borwe,** as a pledge. 964. **Algate,** at any rate; **a,** one; **hameled,** lamed. 968. **stoupen,** droop. 969. **Redressen hem,** stand up again; **ayain,** in. 970. **spreden,** open; **on . . . cours,** in their natural course. 973. **yheried,** praised. 976. **hool,** i.e, cured; **brosten,** broken. 978. **wis,** surely. 980. **tosterte,** leap out.

Til that thou be ayain at hire fro me?
Thou maist answere, 'Abid, abid,' but he
That hangeth by the nekke, sooth to sayne,
In greet disese° abideth for the paine."

"Al esily, now for the love of Marte,"°
Quod Pandarus, "for every thing hath time.
So longe abid til that the night departe,
For also siker as thou list° here by me,
And God toforn, I wil be ther at prime,°
And for thee werke somwhat as I shal saye—
Or on som other wight this charge° laye.

For pardee, God woot I have evere yit
Been redy thee to serve, and to this night
Have I nought feined, but emforth° my wit
Doon al thy lust,° and shal with al my might.
Do now as I shal sayn, and fare aright.
And if thou nilt, wite° al thyself thy care:
On me is nought along thyn yvel fare.°

I woot wel that thou wiser art than I
A thousandfold, but if I were as thou,
God helpe me so, as I wolde outrely°
Of myn owene hand write hire right now
A lettre, in which I wolde hire tellen how
I ferde amis, and hire biseeche of routhe.°
Now help thyself, and leve it nought for slouthe.°

And I myself wol therwith to hire goon,
And whan thou woost° that I am with hire there,
Worth° thou upon a courser right anoon—
Ye, hardily, right in thy beste gere—

987. disese, distress. **988. Marte,** Mars. **991. siker,** sure; **list,** lie. **992. prime,** 9 A.M. **994. charge,** responsibility. **997. feined,** shirked; **emforth,** according to. **998. lust,** pleasure. **1000. wite,** blame. **1001.** I am not responsible for your faring badly. **1004. outrely,** absolutely. **1007. ferde,** fared; **routhe,** pity. **1008. leve,** leave; **slouthe,** negligence. **1010. woost,** know. **1011. Worth,** mount.

And rid forth by the place as nought it were,
And thou shalt finde us, if I may, sittinge
At som windowe into the streete lookinge.

And if thee list, thanne may thou us salue,°
And upon me make thou thy countenaunce.°
But by thy lif, be war, and faste eschue°
To taryen ought—God shilde° us fro meschaunce!
Rid forth thy way, and hold thy governaunce,°
And we shal speke of thee somwhat, I trowe,°
Whan thou art goon, to doon° thine eres glowe.

Touching thy lettre, thou art wis ynough:
I woot thou nilt it digneliche° endite,
As make it with thise argumentes tough,
Ne scrivenissh or craftily° thou it write.
Biblotte it with thy teres eek a lite;°
And if thou write a goodly word al softe,
Though it be good, reherce it nought too ofte.

For though the beste harpour upon live
Wolde on the beste-souned joly harpe
That evere was, with alle his fingres five
Touche ay oo string, or ay oo warble° harpe,
Were his nailes pointed nevere so sharpe,
It sholde maken every wight to dulle°
To heere his glee, and of his strokes fulle.°

Ne jompre eek no discordant thing yfere,°
As thus, to usen termes of physik;
In loves termes hold of thy matere
The forme alway, and do that it be lik.°

1016. **salue,** greet. 1017. **countenaunce,** i.e., greeting. 1018. **eschue,** avoid. 1019. **shilde,** defend. 1020. **governaunce,** self-control. 1021. **trowe,** trust. 1022. **doon,** make. 1024. **digneliche,** disdainfully. 1026. **scrivenissh,** legalistic; **craftily,** pedantically. 1027. **Biblotte,** blot; **lite,** little. 1033. **warble,** chord. 1035. **dulle,** become bored. 1036. **glee,** music; **fulle,** satiated. 1037. **jompre,** jumble; **yfere,** together. 1040. **do,** see; **lik,** apt.

For if a paintour wolde painte a pik
With asses feet, and hede it as an ape,
It cordeth nought, so were it but a jape."

This conseil liked wel unto Troilus,
But as a dredful lovere he saide this,
"Allas, my dere brother Pandarus,
I am ashamed for to write, ywis,
Lest of myn innocence I saide amis,
Or that she nolde it for despit receive.
Thanne were I deed: ther mighte it nothing waive."

To that Pandare answerde, "If thee lest,
Do that I saye, and lat me therwith goon.
For by that Lord that formed eest and west,
I hope of it to bringe answere anoon
Of hir hand, and if that thou nilt noon,
Lat be, and sory mote he been his live
Ayains thy lust that helpeth thee to thrive."

Quod Troilus, "Depardeux, ich assente;
Sith that thee list I wil arise and write—
And blisful God praye ich with good entente
The viage and the lettre I shal endite,
So speede it, and thou Minerva the white,
Yif thou me wit my lettre to devise."
And sette him down and wroot right in this wise:

First he gan hire his righte lady calle,
His hertes lif, his lust, his sorwes leeche,
His blisse, and eek thise othere termes alle,
That in swich caas thise loveres alle seeche;
And in ful humble wise as in his speeche

1041. pik, pike. **1042. hede,** put a head on. **1043. cordeth,** is not suitable; **jape,** joke. **1049. despit,** scorn. **1050. deed,** dead; **waive,** avoid. **1051. lest,** it pleases. **1056. mote,** may; **his,** i.e., during his. **1057. lust,** wish. **1061. viage,** enterprise. **1066. lust,** desire; **leeche,** cure. **1068. seeche,** seek.

He gan him recomande unto hir grace:
To telle al how, it axeth muchel space.

And after this ful lowely he hire prayde
To be nought wroth, though he of his folye
So hardy was to hire to write, and saide
That love it made, or elles moste he die;
And pitously gan mercy for to crye;
And after that he saide—and leigh ful loude—
Himself was litel worth, and lesse he coude;

And that she sholde han his conning excused,
That litel was; and eek he dredde hire so,
And his unworthinesse ay he accused;
And after that thanne gan he telle his wo—
But that was endelees, withouten ho—
And saide he wolde in trouthe alway him holde;
And redde it over, and gan the lettre folde.

And with his salte teres gan he bathe
The rubye in his signet, and it sette
Upon the wex deliverliche and rathe.
Therwith a thousand times er he lette
He kiste tho the lettre that he shette,
And saide, "Lettre, a blisful destinee
Thee shapen is: my lady shal thee see."

This Pandare took the lettre, and that bitime
Amorwe, and to his neces palais sterte;
And faste he swoor that it was passed prime,
And gan to jape, and saide, "Ywis, myn herte
So fressh it is, although it sore smerte,

1074. hardy, bold. **1075. moste,** must. **1077. leigh,** lied. **1078. and . . . coude,** i.e., and he was less able than worthy. **1079. conning,** ability. **1081. accused,** blamed. **1083. ho,** halt! **1088. wex,** wax; **deliverliche,** quickly; **rathe,** soon. **1089. lette,** stopped. **1090. shette,** closed. **1092. shapen,** fated. **1093. bitime,** early. **1094. Amorwe,** in the morning; **sterte,** started. **1095. prime,** 9 A.M. **1096. jape,** joke.

I may nought sleepe nevere a Mayes morwe:
I have a joly wo, a lusty sorwe."

Criseide, whan that she hir uncle herde,
With dredful herte, and desirous to heere
The cause of his coming, thus answerde,
"Now, by youre fay, myn uncle," quod she, "dere,
What manere windes gideth you now here?
Telle us youre joly wo and youre penaunce,
How ferforth be ye put in loves daunce."

"By God," quod he, "I hoppe alway bihinde."
And she to laughe, it thoughte hir herte breste.
Quod Pandarus, "Looke alway that ye finde
Game in myn hood, but herkneth if you leste:
Ther is right now come into town a geste,
A Greek espye, and telleth newe thinges,
For which I come to telle you newe tidinges.

Into the gardin go we and ye shal heere
Al prively of this a long sermoun."
With that they wenten arm in arm yfere
Into the gardin from the chambre down.
And whan that he so fer was that the soun
Of that he spak no man heeren mighte,
He saide hire thus, and out the lettre pighte:

"Lo, he that is al hoolly youres free,
Him recomandeth lowely to youre grace,
And sente you this lettre here by me.
Aviseth you on it whan you have space,
And of som goodly answere you purchace,
Or helpe me God, so plainly for to sayne,
He may nat longe liven for his paine."

1103. fay, faith. **1105. penaunce,** suffering. **1106. ferforth,** far. **1108. thoughte,** seemed; **breste,** would break. **1110. Game . . . hood,** i.e., reason to make fun of me. **1111. geste,** stranger. **1116. yfere,** together. **1120. pighte,** plucked. **1121. hoolly,** wholly. **1124. Aviseth you,** consider. **1125. purchace,** provide.

Ful dredfully tho gan she stonden stille,
And took it nought, but al hir humble cheere
Gan for to chaunge, and saide, "Scrit ne bille,
For love of God, that toucheth swich matere,
Ne bringe me noon; and also, uncle dere,
To myn estaat have more reward, I praye,
Than to his lust. What sholde I more saye?

And looketh now if this be resonable–
And letteth nought, for favor ne for slouthe,
To sayn a sooth: now were it convenable
To myn estaat, by God and by youre trouthe,
To taken it, or to han of him routhe,
In harming of myself, or in repreve?
Bere it ayain, for him that ye on leve."

This Pandarus gan on hire for to stare,
And saide, "Now is this the grettest wonder
That evere I sawgh. Lat be this nice fare!
To deeth moot I ysmiten be with thonder,
If for the citee which that stondeth yonder
Wolde I a lettre unto you bringe or take
To harm of you. What list you thus it make?

But thus ye faren wel neigh alle and some,
That he that most desireth you to serve,
On him ye recche leest wher he bicome,
And whether that he live or elles sterve.
But for al that that evere I may deserve,
Refuse nought," quod he, and hente hire faste,
And in hir bosom the lettre down he thraste,

1130. Scrit, script; **bille,** petition. **1133. reward,** regard. **1134. lust,** wish. **1136. letteth,** delay; **slouthe,** negligence. **1137. convenable,** suitable. **1139. routhe,** pity. **1140. repreve,** reproach. **1141. on leve,** believe in. **1144. nice fare,** foolish fuss. **1145. moot,** may. **1148. What,** why; **list,** does it please. **1149. alle and some,** one and all. **1151. recche,** care; **wher he bicome,** what becomes of him. **1152. sterve,** die. **1154. hente,** seized. **1155. thraste,** thrust.

And saide hire, "Now caste it away anoon,
That folk may seen and gauren on us twaye."
Quod she, "I can abide til they be goon,"
And gan to smile, and saide him, "Eem, I praye,
Swich answere as you list youreself purveye,
For trewely I nil no lettre write."
"No? Thanne wol I," quod he, "so ye endite."

Therwith she lough and saide, "Go we dine."
And he gan at himself to jape faste,
And saide, "Nece, I have so greet a pine
For love, that everich other day I faste."
And gan his beste japes forth to caste,
And made hire so to laughe at his folye,
That she for laughter wende for to die.

And whan that she was comen into halle,
"Now, eem," quod she, "we wol go dine anoon."
And gan some of hir wommen to hire calle,
And straight into hir chambre gan she goon.
But of hir bisinesses this was oon—
Amonges othere thinges, out of drede—
Ful prively this lettre for to rede;

Avised word by word in every line,
And foond no lak: she thoughte he coude good;
And up it putte, and wente hire into dine;
But Pandarus, that in a studye stood,
Er he was war she took him by the hood,
And saide, "Ye were caught er that ye wiste."
"I vouche sauf," quod he. "Do what you liste."

Tho wesshen they and sette hem down and ete,
And after noon ful slyly Pandarus

1157. gauren, stare. **1159. Eem,** uncle. **1160. purveye,** provide. **1162. so,** provided that; **endite,** compose, i.e., dictate. **1163. lough,** laughed. **1165. pine,** torment. **1169. wende,** thought. **1175. drede,** doubt. **1177. Avised,** considered. **1178. foond,** found; **lak,** fault; **coude good,** knew what to do. **1182. wiste,** knew. **1184. wesshen,** washed; **ete,** ate.

Gan drawe him to the windowe next the streete,
And saide, "Nece, who hath arrayed thus
The yonder hous that stant aforyain° us?"
"Which hous?" quod she, and gan for to biholde,
And knew it wel, and whos it was him tolde.

And fillen° forth in speeche of thinges smale,
And seten° in the windowe bothe twaye;
Whan Pandarus sawgh time unto his tale,
And sawgh wel that hir folk weren alle awaye,
"Now, nece myn, telle on," quod he, "I saye
How liketh you the lettre that ye woot?°
Can he theron? For by my trouthe, I noot."°

Therwith al rosy-hewed tho weex° she,
And gan to homme,° and saide, "So I trowe."°
"Acquite° him well, for Goddes love," quod he.
"Myself to meedes wol the lettre sowe,"°
And heeld his handes up, and sat on knowe.°
"Now, goode nece, be it nevere so lite,
Yive me the labour it to sowe and plite."°

"Ye, for I can so writen," quod she tho,
"And eek I noot what I sholde to him saye."
"Nay, nece," quod Pandare, "saye nat so.
Yit at the leeste thanketh him, I praye,
Of his goode wille, and dooth° him nat to deye.
Now for the love of me, my nece dere,
Refuseth nat at this time my prayere."

"Depardeux," quod she, "God leve al be weel!°
God helpe me so, this is the firste lettre
That evere I wroot, ye, al or any deel."°

1188. **stant,** stands; **aforyain,** opposite. 1191. **fillen,** they fell. 1192. **seten,** sat. 1196. **woot,** know. 1197. **Can he,** has he ability; **noot,** don't know. 1198. **weex,** grew. 1199. **homme,** hum; **trowe,** believe. 1200. **Acquite,** repay. 1201. **to meedes,** as a reward; **sowe,** the sheets forming the letter were sewed together by the writer. 1202. **knowe,** knee. 1204. **plite,** fold. 1209. **dooth,** make. 1212. **leve,** grant; **weel,** well. 1214. **deel,** part.

And into a closet for t'avise hire bettre
She wente allone, and gan hir herte unfettre
Out of desdaines prison but a lite,
And sette hire down, and gan a letter write.

Of which to telle in short is myn entente
Th'effect, as fer as I can understonde:
She thanked him of al that he wel mente
Towardes hire; but holden him in honde
She nolde nought, ne make hirselven bonde
In love; but as his suster, him to plese,
She wolde fain to doon his herte an ese.

She shette it, and into Pandare gan goon
Ther as he sat and looked into streete,
And down she sette hire by him on a stoon
Of jaspre, upon a quisshin gold-ybete,
And saide, "As wisly helpe me God the grete,
I nevere dide thing with more paine
Than writen this, to which ye me constraine,"

And took it him. He thanked hire and saide,
"God woot, of thing ful often loth bigonne
Cometh ende good; and nece myn, Criseide,
That ye to him of hard now been ywonne
Oughte he be glad, by God and yonder sonne.
Forwhy men saith, 'Impressiones lighte
Ful lightly been ay redy to the flighte.'

But ye han played tyrant neigh too longe,
And hard was it youre herte for to grave.
Now stinte, that ye no lenger on it honge,

1215. closet, private chamber; **avise hire,** consider. **1217. lite,** little. **1222. holden . . . honde,** keep him in false hope. **1223. bonde,** slave. **1224. suster,** sister. **1225. fain,** gladly. **1226. shette,** closed. **1229. quisshin,** cushion; **gold-ybete,** gold-embroidered. **1230. wisly,** surely. **1233. took,** gave. **1234. loth,** i.e., reluctantly. **1236. of hard,** i.e., from harshness. **1238. Forwhy,** therefore. **1239. lightly,** quickly. **1241. grave,** impress. **1242. stinte,** stop; **honge,** hang.

Al wolde ye the forme of daunger save.
But hasteth you to doon him joye have;
For trusteth wel, too longe ydoon hardnesse
Causeth despit ful often for distresse."

And right as they declamed this matere,
Lo, Troilus, right at the streetes ende,
Cam riding with his tenthe some yfere,
Al softely, and thiderward gan bende
Ther as they sete, as was his way to wende
To palaisward; and Pandarus him espide
And saide, "Nece, ysee who comth here ride.

O flee nought in—he seeth us, I suppose—
Lest he may thinken that ye him eschue."
"Nay, nay," quod she, and weex as reed as rose.
With that he gan hire humbly to salue
With dredful cheere, and ofte his hewes mue,
And up his look debonairly he caste,
And bekked on Pandare, and forth he paste.

God woot if he sat on his hors aright,
Or goodly was biseen that ilke day;
God woot wher he was lik a manly knight!
What sholde I drecche, or telle of his array?
Criseide, which that alle thise thinges sey,
To telle in short, hire liked alle in fere,
His persone, his array, his look, his cheere,

His goodly manere and his gentilesse,
So wel that nevere sith that she was born

1243. Though you would preserve a show of reluctance. **1244. doon,** let. **1245. ydoon,** maintained. **1246. despit,** contempt. **1247. declamed,** discussed. **1249. his tenthe some,** i.e., nine others of his retinue; **yfere,** together. **1250. bende,** turn. **1251. sete,** sat. **1255. eschue,** avoid. **1256. weex,** grew. **1257. salue,** salute. **1258. mue,** change. **1259. debonairly,** meekly. **1260. bekked on,** nodded to; **paste,** passed. **1262. biseen,** i.e., appearing. **1263. wher,** whether. **1264. What,** why; **drecche,** take time. **1265. sey,** saw. **1266. liked,** pleased; **in fere,** together.

Ne hadde she swich routhe of his distresse;
And how so she hath hard been heerbiforn,
To God hope I she hath now caught a thorn,
She shal nat pulle it out this nexte wike—
God sende me swiche thornes on to pike!

Pandare, which that stood hire faste by,
Felte iren hoot, and he bigan to smite,
And saide, "Nece, I praye you hertely,
Telle me that I shal axen you a lite:
A womman that were of his deeth to wite,
Withouten his gilt, but for hire lakked routhe,
Were it wel doon?" Quod she, "Nay, by my trouthe."

"God helpe me so," quod he, "ye saye me sooth.
Ye feelen wel youreself that I nought lie.
Lo, yond he rit." Quod she, "Ye, so he dooth."
"Wel," quod Pandare, "as I have told you thrie,
Lat be youre nice shame and youre folye,
And speke with him in esing of his herte:
Lat nicetee nat do you bothe smerte."

But theron was to heven and to doone;
Considered alle thing, it may nat be.
And why? For shame, and it were eek too soone
To graunten him so greet a libertee;
For pleinly hir entente, as saide she,
Was for to love him unwist if she mighte,
And guerdone him with nothing but with sighte.

But Pandarus thoughte, "It shal nought be so;
If that I may, this nice opinioun
Shal nought be holden fully yeres two."

1273. wike, week. **1274. pike,** pick. **1276. hoot,** hot. **1277. hertely,** sincerely. **1278. axen,** ask. **1279. wite,** blame. **1280. for,** because; **routhe,** pity. **1284. rit,** rides. **1285. thrie,** thrice. **1286. nice,** silly; **shame,** modesty. **1288. nicetee,** foolishness; **do,** make. **1289. heven,** heave; **doone,** i.e., work. **1293. pleinly,** fully. **1294. unwist,** unknown. **1295. guerdone,** reward.

What sholde I make of this a long sermoun?
He moste assente on that conclusioun,
As for the time; and whan that it was eve,
And al was wel, he roos and took his leve.

And on his way ful faste hoomward he spedde,
And right for joye he felte his herte daunce;
And Troilus he foond allone abedde,
That lay as do thise loveres in a traunce,
Bitwixen hope and derk desesperaunce.
But Pandarus, right at his in-cominge,
He soong, as who saith, "Somwhat I bringe,"

And saide, "Who is in his bed so soone
Yburied thus?" "It am I, freend," quod he.
"Who, Troilus? Nay, helpe me so the moone,"
Quod Pandarus, "thou shalt arise and see
A charme that was sent right now to thee,
The which can helen thee of thyn accesse,
If thou do forth with al thy bisinesse."

"Ye, thurgh the might of God," quod Troilus.
And Pandarus gan him the lettre take,
And saide, "Pardee, God hath holpen us.
Have here a light, and looke on al this blake."
But ofte gan the herte glade and quake
Of Troilus, whil that he gan it rede,
So as the wordes yave him hope or drede.

But finally he took al for the beste
That she him wroot, for somwhat he biheeld
On which him thoughte he mighte his herte reste,
Al covered she tho wordes under sheeld.
Thus to the more worthy part he heeld,

1305. **foond,** found. 1307. **desesperaunce,** despair. 1309. **soong,** sang. 1315. **accesse,** fever. 1319. **holpen,** helped. 1320. **blake,** black. 1321. **glade,** gladden. 1327. **Al,** although; **tho,** those.

That what for hope and Pandarus biheeste,
His grete wo foryede he at the leeste.

But as we may alday oureselven see,
Thurgh more wode or cole the more fir,
Right so encrees of hope, of what it be,
Therwith ful ofte encreesseth eek desir;
Or as an ook comth of a litel spir,
So thurgh his lettre which that she him sente
Encreessen gan desir, of which he brente.

Wherfore I saye alway that day and night
This Troilus gan to desiren more
Than he dide erst, thurgh hope, and dide his might
To preessen on as by Pandarus lore,
And writen to hire of his sorwes sore:
Fro day to day he leet it nought refreide,
That by Pandare he wroot somwhat or saide;

And dide also his othere observaunces,
That til a lovere longeth in this cas;
And after that thise dees turned on chaunces,
So was he outher glad or saide allas,
And heeld after his gistes ay his pas.
And after swiche answeres as he hadde,
So were his dayes sory outher gladde.

But to Pandare alway was his recours,
And pitously gan ay to him to plaine,
And him bisoughte of reed and som socours;
And Pandarus, that sawgh his woode paine,
Weex wel neigh deed for routhe, sooth to sayne,

1329. biheeste, promise. **1330. foryede,** forwent. **1333. of . . . be,** i.e., whatever the hope is for. **1335. spir,** shoot. **1337. brente,** burned. **1340. erst,** before. **1341. preessen,** press; **lore,** instruction. **1343. refreide,** cool. **1346. til,** to; **longeth,** it is proper. **1347. after that,** according as; **dees,** dice; **on chaunces,** on throws. **1348. outher,** either. **1349. gistes,** stages of a journey. **1353. plaine,** complain. **1354. reed,** advice; **socours,** help. **1355. woode,** mad. **1356. Weex,** grew; **deed,** dead.

And bisily with al his herte caste°
Som of his wo to sleen,° and that as faste;

And saide, "Lord, and freend, and brother dere,
God woot that thy disese dooth me wo,
But wiltou stinten° al this woful cheere,
And by my trouthe, er it be dayes two,
And God toforn, yit shal I shape° it so
That thou shalt come into a certain place
Ther as thou maist thyself hire praye of grace.

And certainly—I noot if thou it woost,
But tho that been expert in love it saye—
It is oon of the thinges forthereth most,
A man to han a leiser for to praye,
And siker place his wo for to biwraye;°
For in good herte it moot° som routhe impresse
To heere and see the giltelees in distresse.

Paraunter° thinkestou: 'Though it be so
That kinde wolde doon° hire to biginne
To have a manere routhe upon my wo,
Saith daunger,° "Nay, thou shalt me nevere winne."
So ruleth hire hir hertes gost° withinne
That though she bende, yit she stant° on roote.
What in effect is this unto my boote?'°

Thenk heerayains whan that the sturdy ook,
On which men hakketh ofte for the nones,°
Received hath the happy falling strook,°
The grete sweigh dooth° it come al atones,
As doon thise rokkes or thise milnestones;°

1357. caste, planned. **1358. sleen,** slay. **1361. stinten,** stop. **1363. toforn,** before; **shape,** arrange. **1370. siker,** secure; **biwraye,** reveal. **1371. moot,** must. **1373. Paraunter,** perhaps. **1374. kinde,** nature; **doon,** make. **1376. daunger,** modesty. **1377. gost,** spirit. **1378. stant,** stands. **1379. boote,** cure. **1381. nones,** purpose. **1382. falling strook,** stroke that fells it. **1383. sweigh,** sway; **dooth,** makes. **1384. milnestones,** millstones.

For swifter cours comth thing that is of wighte,
Whan it descendeth, than doon thinges lighte.

And reed that boweth down for every blast,
Ful lightly, ceesse wind, it wol arise;
But so nil nought an ook whan it is cast.
It needeth me nought thee longe to forbise:
Men shal rejoicen of a greet emprise
Acheved wel, and stant withouten doute,
Al han men been the lenger theraboute.

But Troilus, yit tel me if thee lest
A thing now which that I shal axen thee:
Which is thy brother that thou lovest best,
As in thy verray hertes privetee?"
"Ywis, my brother Deiphebus," quod he.
"Now," quod Pandare, "er houres twies twelve,
He shal thee ese, unwist of it himselve.

Now lat m'allone and werken as I may,"
Quod he. And to Deiphebus wente he tho,
Which hadde his lord and grete freend been ay—
Save Troilus, no man he loved so.
To telle in short withouten wordes mo,
Quod Pandarus, "I praye you that ye be
Freend to a cause which that toucheth me."

"Yis, pardee," quod Deiphebus, "wel thou woost,
In al that evere I may, and God tofore,
Al nere it but for man I love most,
My brother Troilus; but say wherfore
It is, for sith that day that I was bore,

1385. wighte, weight. **1389. cast,** thrown down. **1390. forbise,** give examples. **1391. emprise,** enterprise. **1392. stant,** one that stands. **1393. Al,** although. **1394. lest,** it pleases. **1395. axen,** ask. **1400. unwist,** unknowing. **1409. tofore,** before. **1410.** i.e., ? Unless it involved my opposing the man I love most. **1412. bore,** born.

I nas, ne neveremo to been I thinke,
Ayains a thing that mighte thee forthinke."

Pandare gan him thanke, and to him saide,
"Lo, sire, I have a lady in this town
That is my nece, and called is Criseide,
Which some men wolden doon oppressioun,
And wrongfully han hir possessioun;
Wherfore I of youre lordshipe you biseeche
To been oure freend, withouten more speeche."

Deiphebus him answerde, "O, is nat this,
That thou spekest of to me thus straungely,
Criseide, my freend?" Pandare he saide, "Sire, yis."
"Thanne needeth," quod Deiphebus, "hardily
Namore to speke, for trusteth wel that I
Wol be hir champion with spore and yerde:
I roughte nought though alle hir foes it herde.

But tel me thou, that woost al this matere,
How I mighte best availen?" "Now, lat see,"
Quod Pandarus; "if ye, my lord so dere,
Wolden as now do this honour to me,
To prayen hire tomorwe, lo, that she
Come unto you, hir plaintes to devise,
Hir adversaries wolde of it agrise.

And if I more dorste praye you as now,
And chargen you to han so greet travaile,
To han some of youre bretheren here with you,
That mighten of hir cause bet availe;
Thanne woot I wel she mighte nevere faile
For to been holpen, what at youre instaunce,
What with hir othere freendes governaunce."

1413. thinke, intend. **1414.** Against a thing so that it might displease you. **1418. Which,** to whom; **oppressioun,** violence. **1425. hardily,** assuredly. **1427. spore,** spur; **yerde,** rod, i.e., weapon. **1428. roughte,** would care. **1434. plaintes,** complaints; **devise,** describe. **1435. agrise,** be frightened. **1439. bet,** better. **1441. holpen,** helped. **1442. governaunce,** management.

Deiphebus, which that comen was of kinde°
To al honour and bountee° to consente,
Answerde, "It shal be doon, and I can finde
Yit gretter help to this in myn entente.
What wiltou sayn if I for Elaine sente
To speke of this? I trowe it be the beste,
For she may leden Paris as hire leste.°

Of Ector, which that is my lord my brother,
It needeth nought to praye him freend to be,
For I have herd him oo time and eek other
Speke of Criseide swich honour that he
May sayn no bet, swich hap to him° hath she:
It needeth nought his helpes for to crave;
He shal be swich right as we wol him have.

Speek thou thyself also to Troilus
On my bihalve, and praye him with us dine."
"Sire, al this shal be doon," quod Pandarus;
And took his leve, and nevere gan to fine,°
But to his neces hous as straight as line
He cam, and foond hire fro the mete° arise,
And sette him down, and spak right in this wise.

He saide, "O verray God, so have I ronne!°
Lo, nece myn, see ye nought how I swete?°
I noot wher ye the more thank me conne.°
Be ye nought war how false Polyphete
Is now aboute eftsoones for to plete,°
And bringe on you advocacies° newe?"
"I? no," quod she, and chaunged al hir hewe.

"What is he more aboute me to drecche,°
And doon me wrong? What shal I doon, allas?

1443. of kinde, by nature. **1444. bountee,** generosity. **1449. leste,** it please. **1454. hap to him,** good luck as far as he is concerned. **1460. fine,** stop. **1462. foond,** found; **mete,** dinner. **1464. ronne,** run. **1465. swete,** sweat. **1466. wher,** whether; **conne,** show. **1468. eftsoones,** again; **plete,** go to law. **1469. advocacies,** lawsuits. **1471. What,** why; **drecche,** harass.

Yit of himself no thing ne wolde I recche,
Nere it for Antenor and Eneas,
That been his freendes in swich manere cas.
But for the love of God, myn uncle dere,
No fors of that: lat him han al yfere.

Withouten that I have ynough for us."
"Nay," quod Pandare, "it shal no thing be so,
For I have been right now at Deiphebus,
At Ector, and mine othere lordes mo,
And shortly maked eech of hem his fo,
That, by my thrift, he shal it nevere winne,
For ought he can, whan that so he biginne."

And as they casten what was best to doone,
Deiphebus, of his owene curteisye,
Cam hire to praye in his propre persone
To holde him on the morwe compaignye
At diner, which she nolde nought denye,
But goodly gan to his prayere obeye:
He thanked hire, and wente upon his waye.

Whan this was doon, this Pandare up anoon—
To telle in short—and forth gan for to wende
To Troilus, as stille as any stoon;
And al this thing he tolde him, word and ende,
And how that he Deiphebus gan to blende,
And saide him, "Now is time, if that thou conne,
To bere thee wel tomorwe, and al is wonne.

Now speek, now pray, now pitously complaine;
Lat nought for nice shame or drede or slouthe:
Somtime a man moot telle his owene paine;
Bileve it, and she shal han on thee routhe.

1473. recche, care. **1474. Nere it,** were it not for; **Eneas,** Aeneas. **1477. fors,** matter; **yfere,** together. **1485. casten,** considered. **1487. propre,** own. **1495. word and ende,** beginning and end. **1496. blende,** deceive. **1500. Lat nought,** i.e., leave nothing undone; **nice,** foolish; **slouthe,** negligence. **1501. moot,** must.

Thou shalt be saved, by thy faith, in trouthe.
But wel woot I that thou art now in drede,
And what it is I laye I can arede.

Thou thinkest, 'Now, how sholde I doon al this?
For by my cheeres mosten folk espye
That for hir love is that I fare amis:
Yit hadde I levere unwist for sorwe die.'
Now think nat so, for thou doost greet folye,
For I right now have founden oo manere
Of sleighte, for to coveren al thy cheere.

Thou shalt goon overnight, and that bilive,
Unto Deiphebus hous as thee to playe,
Thy maladye away the bet to drive—
Forwhy thou seemest sik, sooth for to saye;
And after that down in thy bed thee laye,
And saye thou maist no lenger up endure,
And lie right ther, and bide thyn aventure.

Say that thy fevere is wont thee for to take
The same time, and lasten til amorwe;
And lat see now how wel thou canst it make;
For, pardee, sik is he that is in sorwe.
Go now, farewel, and Venus here to borwe,
I hope, and thou this purpos holde ferme,
Thy grace she shal fully thee conferme."

Quod Troilus, "Ywis, thou needelees
Conseilest me that siklich I me feine,
For I am sik in ernest, doutelees,
So that wel neigh I sterve for the paine."
Quod Pandarus, "Thou shal the bettre plaine,

1505. **laye,** bet; **arede,** guess. 1507. **cheeres,** appearance; **mosten,** must. 1509. **unwist,** undetected. 1512. **sleighte,** trickery; **coveren,** i.e., make a plausible explanation for; **cheere,** behavior. 1513. **bilive,** at once. 1516. **Forwhy,** because. 1521. **amorwe,** tomorrow. 1524. **borwe,** as a pledge. 1528. **siklich . . . feine,** pretend to be sick. 1530. **sterve,** die. 1531. **plaine,** complain.

And hast the lesse neede to countrefete:
For him men deemen hoot that men seen swete.°

Lo, hold thee at thy tryste° cloos, and I
Shal wel the deer unto thy bowe drive."
Therwith he took his leve al softely,
And Troilus to palais wente blive:°
So glad ne was he nevere in al his live,
And to Pandarus reed° gan al assente,
And to Deiphebus hous at night he wente.

What needeth you to tellen al the cheere
That Deiphebus unto his brother made,
Or his accesse,° or his siklich manere—
How men gan him with clothes for to lade°
Whan he was laid, and how men wolde him glade?°
But al for nought: he heeld forth ay the wise
That ye han herd Pandare er this devise.

But certain is, er Troilus him laide,
Deiphebus hadde him prayed over night
To been a freend and helping to Criseide.
God woot that he it graunted anoon right,
To been hir fulle freend with al his might:
But swich a neede was to praye him thenne,
As for to bidde a wood man for to renne!°

The morwen cam, and neighen gan the time
Of meeltide,° that the faire queene Elaine
Shoop hire to been, an houre after the prime,°
With Deiphebus, to whom she nolde feine;°
But as his suster hoomly,° sooth to sayne,

1533. **swete,** sweat. 1534. **tryste,** hunting blind. 1537. **blive,** at once. 1539. **reed,** advice. 1543. **accesse,** fever. 1544. **clothes,** covers; **lade,** load. 1545. **laid,** i.e., bedded; **glade,** gladden. 1554. **wood,** mad; **renne,** run. 1556. **meeltide,** mealtime. 1557. **Shoop hire,** arranged; **prime,** 9 A.M. 1558. **feine,** i.e., refuse her presence. 1559. **suster,** i.e., sister-in-law; **hoomly,** familiarly.

She cam to diner in hir plaine entente–
But God and Pandare wiste al what this mente.

Cam eek Criseide, al innocent of this;
Antigone, hir suster Tarbe also.
But flee we now prolixitee best is,
For love of God, and lat us faste go
Right to th'effect, withouten tales mo,
Why al this folk assembled in this place,
And lat us of hir saluinges pace.

Greet honour dide hem Deiphebus certain,
And fedde hem wel with al that mighte like,
But everemore allas was his refrain,
"My goode brother Troilus the sike
Lith yit," and therwith gan to sike;
And after that he pained him to glade
Hem as he mighte, and cheere good he made.

Complained eek Elaine of his siknesse
So faithfully that pitee was to heere;
And every wight gan waxen for accesse
A leeche anoon, and saide, "In this manere
Men curen folk: this charme I wol you lere."
But ther sat oon, al liste hire nought to teche,
That thoughte, "Best coude I yit been his leeche."

After complainte, him gonnen they to praise,
As folk doon yit whan som wight hath bigonne
To praise a man, and up with praise him raise
A thousandfold yit hyer than the sonne:
"He is–he can that fewe lordes conne."

1560. in . . . entente, open-heartedly. **1561. But,** only. **1568. saluinges,** greetings; **pace,** pass by. **1570. like,** be pleasing. **1572. sike,** sick. **1573. Lith,** lies; **sike,** sigh. **1574. pained him,** took pains; **glade,** cheer. **1577. faithfully,** loyally. **1578. waxen,** become; **for accesse,** against fever. **1579. leeche,** doctor. **1580. lere,** teach. **1581. al list hire,** although she did not please. **1587. can,** can do.

And Pandarus of that they wolde afferme,
He nought forgat hir praising to conferme.

Herde al this thing Criseide wel ynough,
And every word gan for to notifye,
For which with sobre cheere hir herte lough:
For who is that ne wolde hire glorifye
To mowen swich a knight doon live or die?
But al pace I, lest ye too longe dwelle,
For for oo fin is al that evere I telle.

The time cam fro diner for to rise,
And as hem oughte arisen everichoon,
And gonne a while of this and that devise;
But Pandarus brak al that speeche anoon,
And saide to Deiphebus, "Wol ye goon,
If youre wille be, as I you prayde,
To speke here of the needes of Criseide?"

Elaine, which that by the hand hire heeld,
Took first the tale and saide, "Go we blive."
And goodly on Criseide she biheeld,
And saide, "Joves lat him nevere thrive
That dooth you harm, and bringe him soone of live;
And yive me sorwe, but he shal it rewe,
If that I may, and alle folk be trewe."

"Tel thou thy neces caas," quod Deiphebus
To Pandarus, "for thou canst best it telle."
"My lordes and my ladies, it stant thus—
What sholde I lenger," quod he, "do you dwelle?"
He roong hem out a proces lik a belle

1591. notifye, take note of. **1592. lough,** laughed. **1594. mowen,** be able; **doon,** make. **1595. pace,** pass. **1596. for oo fin,** for one purpose. **1598. as hem oughte,** i.e., with due precedence. **1599. devise,** converse. **1600. brak,** interrupted. **1605. blive,** at once. **1607. Joves,** Jove. **1608. of live,** from life. **1609. but,** unless; **rewe,** regret. **1610. and,** if. **1613. stant,** stands. **1614. What,** why; **do . . . dwelle,** make you wait. **1615. roong,** rang; **proces,** argument.

Upon hir fo that highte Polyphete,
So heinous that men mighte on it spete.

Answerde of this eech worse of hem than other,
And Polyphete they gonnen thus to warien,
"Anhonged be swich oon, were he my brother—
And so he shal, for it ne may nought varyen."
What sholde I lenger in this tale taryen?
Pleinliche alle atones they hire highten
To been hir help in al that evere they mighten.

Spak thanne Elaine, and saide, "Pandarus,
Woot ought my lord my brother this matere?
I mene Ector; or woot it Troilus?"
He saide, "Ye, but wol ye now me heere?
Me thinketh this, sith that Troilus is here,
It were good, if that ye wolde assente,
She tolde hirself him al this er she wente.

For he wol have the more hir grief at herte,
By cause, lo, that she a lady is.
And by youre leve, I wol but in right sterte
And do you wite, and that anoon, ywis,
If that he sleepe, or wol ought heere of this."
And in he lepte, and saide him in his ere,
"God have thy soule: ybrought have I thy beere."

To smilen of this gan tho Troilus,
And Pandarus, withouten rekeninge,
Out wente anoon to Elaine and Deiphebus,
And saide hem, "So ther be no taryinge,
Ne more prees, he wol wel that ye bringe
Criseida my lady that is here,
And as he may enduren he wol heere.

1616. highte, was named. **1617. spete,** spit. **1619. warien,** curse. **1620. Anhonged,** hanged. **1621. varyen,** be otherwise. **1623. Pleinliche,** fully; **highten,** promised. **1634. but . . . sterte,** i.e., just look in. **1635. do you wite,** let you know. **1638. beere,** bier. **1640. rekeninge,** i.e., further calculation. **1642. So,** provided that. **1643. more prees,** larger group.

But wel ye woot the chambre is but lite,
And fewe folk may lightly make it warm.
Now looketh ye—for I wol have no wite
To bringe in prees that mighte doon him harm,
Or him disesen, for my bettre arm—
Wher it be bet she bide til eftsoones?
Now looketh ye that knowen what to doon is.

I saye for me, best is as I can knowe,
That no wight in ne wente but ye twaye,
But it were I, for I can in a throwe
Reherce hir caas unlik that she can saye.
And after this she may him ones praye
To been good lord in short, and take hir leve:
This may nought muchel of his reste him reve.

And eek for she is straunge, he wol forbere
His ese, which that him thar nought for you.
Eek other thing that toucheth nought to here
He wol me telle—I woot it wel right now—
That secret is, and for the townes prow."
And they that nothing knewe of his entente,
Withouten more, to Troilus in they wente.

Elaine, in al hir goodly softe wise,
Gan him salue, and wommanly to playe,
And saide, "Ywis, ye moste alwayes arise.
Now faire brother, beeth al hool, I praye,"
And gan hir arm right over his shulder laye,
And him with al hir wit to reconforte;
As she best coude, she gan him to disporte.

1647. **lightly,** easily. 1648. **wite,** blame. 1649. **prees,** i.e., a crowd. 1650. **disesen,** disturb; **for . . . arm,** i.e., for anything. 1651. **Wher it be,** might it be; **eftsoones,** later. 1655. **But,** unless; **throwe,** moment. 1656. **unlik,** different from, i.e., better than; **that,** what. 1659. **reve,** deprive. 1660. **for,** because; **straunge,** a stranger; **forbere,** forgo. 1661. **thar,** need. 1662. **toucheth nought,** is not relevant; **here,** her. 1664. **prow,** profit. 1668. **salue,** greet. 1669. **Ywis,** indeed; **alwayes,** by all means; **arise,** i.e., get well. 1670. **hool,** well.

So after this, quod she, "We you biseeke,
My dere brother Deiphebus and I,
For love of God—and so dooth Pandare eke—
To been good lord and freend right hertely
Unto Criseide, which that certainly
Receiveth wrong, as woot wel here Pandare,
That can hir caas wel bet than I declare."

This Pandarus gan newe his tonge affile,
And al hir caas reherce, and that anoon.
Whan it was said, soone after in a while,
Quod Troilus, "As soone as I may goon,
I wol right fain with all my might been oon—
Have God my trouthe—hir cause to sustene."
"Good thrift have ye," quod Elaine the queene.

Quod Pandarus, "And it youre wille be
That she may take hir leve er that she go—
Or elles God forbede it tho," quod he—
"If that she vouche sauf for to do so."
And with that word quod Troilus, "Ye two,
Deiphebus and my suster lief and dere,
To you have I to speke of oo matere,

To been avised by youre reed the bettre."
And foond as hap was at his beddes heed
The copye of a tretis and a lettre
That Ector hadde him sent to axen reed
If swich a man was worthy to been deed—
Woot I nought who—but in a grisly wise
He prayed hem anoon on it avise.

Deiphebus gan this lettre for t'unfolde
In ernest greet; so dide Elaine the queene,

1681. **affile,** sharpen. 1684. **goon,** walk. 1685. **fain,** gladly. 1686. **sustene,** sustain. 1687. **thrift,** luck. 1688. **And,** if. 1693. **lief,** beloved. 1695. **reed,** counsel. 1696. **foond,** found; **hap,** chance. 1697. **tretis,** document. 1698. **axen reed,** ask advice. 1699. **deed,** put to death. 1701. **avise,** consider. 1703. **greet,** great.

And roming outward faste it gonne biholde,
Downward a staire into an herber° greene.
This ilke thing they redden hem bitweene,
And largely, the mountance° of an houre,
They gonne on it to reden and to poure.

Now lat hem rede, and turne we anoon
To Pandarus, that gan ful faste prye°
That al was wel, and out he gan to goon
Into the grete chambre, and that in hie,°
And saide, "God save al this compaignye.
Come, nece myn, my lady queene Elaine
Abideth you, and eek my lordes twaine.

Rise, take with you youre nece Antigone,
Or whom you list—or no fors, hardily,°
The lesse prees° the bet—come forth with me,
And looke that ye thanken humblely
Hem alle three; and whan ye may goodly
Youre time see, taketh of hem youre leve,
Lest we too longe his restes him bireve."°

Al innocent of Pandarus entente
Quod tho Criseide, "Go we, uncle dere."
And arm in arm inward with him she wente,
Avised° wel hir wordes and hir cheere.
And Pandarus, in ernestful manere,
Saide, "Alle folk, for Goddes love I praye,
Stinteth° right here, and softely you playe.

Aviseth you what folk been here withinne,
And in what plit° oon is, God him amende,
And inward thus ful softely biginne.
Nece, I conjure and heighly you defende,°

1705. **herber,** garden. 1707. **mountance,** extent. 1710. **prye,** spy. 1712. **hie,** haste. 1717. **fors,** matter; **hardily,** surely. 1718. **prees,** crowd. 1722. **bireve,** deprive of. 1726. **Avised,** having considered. 1729. **Stinteth,** stop. 1731. **plit,** situation. 1733. **defende,** prohibit.

On his half which that soule us alle sende,
And in the vertu of the corownes twaine,
Slee nought this man that hath for you this paine.

Fy on the devel! Think which oon he is,
And in what plit he lith. Com of anoon!
Think al swich taried tide but lost it nis:
That wol ye bothe sayn whan ye been oon.
Secoundely ther yit divineth noon
Upon you two. Com of now, if ye conne:
Whil folk is blent, lo, al the time is wonne.

In titering and pursuit and delayes,
The folk divinen at wagging of a stree;
And though ye wolde han after merye dayes,
Thanne dare ye nought. And why? For she and she
Spak swich a word—thus looked he and he.
Lest time ylost, I dar nought with you dele:
Com of therfore, and bringeth him to hele."

But now to you, ye loveres that been here,
Was Troilus nought in a kankedort,
That lay and mighte whispring of hem heere,
And thoughte, "O lord, right now renneth my sort
Fully to die or han anoon confort,"
And was the firste time he sholde hire praye
Of love? O mighty God, what shal he saye?

1734. **sende,** has sent. 1735. **corownes twaine,** two crowns, ? those of martyrdom and purity. 1736. **Slee,** slay. 1738. **lith,** lies. 1739. **taried tide,** time spent in delay. 1741. **divineth,** guesses. 1743. **blent,** deceived. 1744. **titering,** hesitating. 1745. **stree,** straw. 1746. **wolde,** would want to; **after,** afterwards. 1749. **Lest time ylost,** i.e., lest time were lost; **dele,** i.e., entreat. 1750. **hele,** health. 1752. **kankedort,** ? dilemma. 1754. **renneth,** runs; **sort,** lot.

BOOK THREE

The Prologue

O blisful light of which the bemes clere
Adorneth al the thridde hevene faire,
O sonnes lief, O Joves doughter dere,
Plesance of love, O goodly debonaire,
In gentil hertes ay redy to repaire,
O verray cause of hele and of gladnesse:
Yheried be thy might and thy goodnesse.

In hevene and helle, in erthe and salte see
Is felt thy might, if that I wel discerne:
As man, brid, beest, fissh, herbe and greene tree
Thee feele in times with vapour eterne.
God loveth, and to love wol nat werne,
And in this world no lives creature
Withouten love is worth, or may endure.

Ye Joves first to thilke affectes glade,
Thurgh which that thinges liven alle and be,
Commeveden, and amorous him made
On mortal thing, and as you list ay ye
Yive him in love ese or adversitee,
And in a thousand formes down him sente
For love in erthe, and whom you liste he hente.

1. **light,** i.e., Venus; **clere,** bright. 2. **thridde hevene,** third sphere, considered Venus'. 3. **sonnes lief,** sun's beloved. 4. **debonaire,** meek one. 6. **hele,** welfare. 7. **Yheried,** praised. 11. **times,** seasons; **vapour,** exhalation. 12. **werne,** refuse. 13. **lives,** living. 14. **worth,** worthy. 15. **Joves,** Jove (object of *Commeveden*). 17. **Commeveden,** excited. 18. **list,** it pleases. 20. **formes,** the shapes Jupiter assumed in his wooing of mortal women. 21. **liste,** it pleased; **hente,** possessed.

Ye fierse Mars apaisen of his ire,
And as you list ye maken hertes digne:
Algates hem that ye wol sette afire,
They dreden shame, and vices they resigne;
Ye do hem curteis be, fresshe and benigne;
And heigh or lowe after a wight entendeth,
The joyes that he hath, youre might him sendeth.

Ye holden regne and hous in unitee;
Ye soothfast cause of frendshipe been also;
Ye knowe al thilke covered qualitee
Of thinges which that folk on wondren so,
Whan they can nought construe how it may jo
She loveth him, or why he loveth here—
As why this fissh and nought that comth to were.

Ye folk a lawe han set in universe,
And this knowe I by hem that loveres be,
That who so striveth with you hath the werse.
Now, lady bright, for thy benignitee,
At reverence of hem that serven thee,
Whos clerk I am, so techeth me devise
Som joye of that is felt in thy servise.

Ye in my naked herte sentement
Inheelde, and do me shewe of thy swetnesse.
Caliope, thy vois be now present,
For now is neede: seestou nought my distresse,
How I moot telle anoonright the gladnesse
Of Troilus to Venus heryinge?—
To which gladnesse who neede hath God him bringe!

22. **apaisen,** pacify. 23. **digne,** worthy. 24. **Algates,** always. 26. **do,** make. 27. **after,** according as; **entendeth,** aims. 29. **regne,** realm. 31. **covered,** secret. 33. **jo,** come to pass. 34. **here,** her. 35. **were,** wier. 36. **folk,** i.e., for folk. 40. **At,** in. 41. **devise,** describe. 42. **that,** that which. 43. **naked,** i.e., barren. 44. **Inheelde,** infuse; **do,** make. 45. **Caliope,** Calliope, the Muse of epic poetry and of eloquence. 47. **moot,** must. 48. **to Venus heryinge,** in Venus' praise.

The Story

Lay al this mene while Troilus,
Recording° his lesson in this manere:
"Ma fay,"° thoughte he, "thus wol I saye and thus.
Thus wol I plaine° unto my lady dere.
That word is good, and this shal be my cheere.°
This nil I nought foryeten° in no wise."
God leve° him werken as he can devise!

And Lord, so that his herte gan to quappe,°
Heering hire come, and shorte for to sike;°
And Pandarus, that ledde hire by the lappe,°
Cam neer and gan in at the curtin pike,°
And saide, "God do boote on alle sike!°
See who is here you comen to visite:
Lo, here is she that is youre deeth to wite."°

Therwith it seemed as he wepte almost.
"Aha," quod Troilus so rewefully,°
"Wher be me wo, almighty God thou woost!°
Who is al ther? I see nought, trewely."
"Sire," quod Criseide, "it is Pandare and I."
"Ye, sweete herte! Allas, I may nought rise
To kneele and do you honour in som wise."

And dressed him upward, and she right tho°
Gan bothe hir handes softe upon him laye.
"O, for the love of God, do ye nought so
To me," quod she. "I,° what is this to saye?

51. **Recording,** memorizing. 52. **Ma fay,** my faith. 53. **plaine,** complain. 54. **cheere,** manner. 55. **foryeten,** forget. 56. **leve,** let. 57. **quappe,** beat. 58. **sike,** sigh. 59. **lappe,** fold in a garment. 60. **pike,** peek. 61. **do boote on,** give relief to; **sike,** sick persons. 63. **wite,** blame for. 65. **rewefully,** pitifully. 66. **Wher,** whether; **woost,** know. 71. **dressed,** raised; **tho,** then. 74. **I,** oh.

Sire, comen am I to you for causes twaye:
First you to thanke, and of youre lordshipe° eke
Continuance I wolde you biseeke."°

This Troilus, that herde his lady praye
Of lordshipe him, weex neither quik ne deed,°
Ne mighte oo word for shame to it saye,
Although men sholde smiten of his heed.
But Lord, so he weex sodeinliche reed.
And sire, his lesson that he wende conne°
To prayen hire is thurgh his wit yronne.°

Criseide al this espied wel ynough,
For she was wis, and loved him nevere the lasse,°
Al nere he malapert or made it tough,°
Or was too bold to singe a fool a masse.°
But whan his shame gan somwhat to passe,
His resons,° as I may my rymes holde,
I you wol telle as techen bookes olde.

In chaunged vois, right for his verray drede,
Which vois eek quook,° and therto his manere
Goodly abaist, and now his hewes rede,°
Now pale, unto Criseide his lady dere,
With look down cast and humble yyolden cheere,°
Lo, the alderfirste word that him asterte°
Was twies, "Mercy, mercy, sweete herte,"

And stinte° a while, and whan he mighte out bringe,
The nexte word was, "God woot, for I have,
As faithfully as I have had conninge,
Been youres al, so God my soule save,

76. **lordshipe,** protection. 77. **biseeke,** beseech. 79. **weex,** became; **deed,** dead. 83. **wende conne,** thought he knew. 84. **yronne,** run out. 86. **lasse,** less. 87. Even if he was not forward and did not behave brashly. 88. **Or,** i.e., nor; **singe . . . masse,** i.e., speak fulsomely. 90. **resons,** speeches. 93. **quook,** quaked. 94. **abaist,** abashed; **rede,** red. 96. **yyolden cheere,** submissive look. 97. **alderfirste word,** first word of all; **aserte,** escaped. 99. **stinte,** paused.

And shal til that I, woful wight, be grave;°
And though I dar ne can unto you plaine,°
Ywis, I suffre nought the lasse paine.

Thus muche as now, O wommanliche wif,
I may out bringe, and if this you displese,
That shal I wreke° upon myn owene lif,
Right soone, I trowe,° and do youre herte an ese,
If with my deeth youre herte may apese.°
But sin that ye han herd me somwhat saye,
Now recche° I nevere how soone that I deye."

Therwith his manly sorwe to biholde
It mighte han maad an herte of stoon to rewe,°
And Pandare weep as he to water wolde,°
And poked evere his nece newe and newe,°
And saide, "Wo-bigoon been hertes trewe!
For love of God, make of this thing an ende,
Or slee° us bothe at ones er that ye wende."

"I, what?" quod she. "By God and by my trouthe,
I noot nat what ye wilne° that I saye."
"I, what?" quod he. "That ye han on him routhe,°
For Goddes love, and dooth° him nought to deye."
"Now thanne," thus quod she, "I wolde him praye
To telle me the fin° of his entente:
Yit wiste° I nevere wel what that he mente."

"What that I mene, O sweete herte dere?"
Quod Troilus. "O goodly fresshe free,°
That with the stremes° of youre yën clere
Ye wolde somtime freendly on me see,°
And thanne agreen that I may been he,

103. **shal,** shall be; **grave,** buried. 104. **dar,** i.e., neither dare; **plaine,** complain. 108. **wreke,** avenge. 109. **trowe,** believe. 110. **apese,** be pacified. 112. **recche,** care. 114. **stoon,** stone; **rewe,** feel pity. 115. **weep,** wept; **wolde,** i.e., would turn. 116. **newe,** again. 119. **slee,** slay. 121. **wilne,** wish. 122. **routhe,** pity. 123. **dooth,** cause. 125. **fin,** end. 126. **wiste,** knew. 128. **free,** noble one. 129. **stremes,** beams. 130. **see,** look.

Withouten braunche of vice in any wise,
In trouthe alway to doon you my servise,

As to my lady right and chief resort,
With al my wit and al my diligence;
And I to han right as you list confort,
Under youre yerde egal to myn offence:
As deeth, if that I breke youre defence;
And that ye deine me so muche honour
Me to comanden ought in any hour.

And I to been youre verray, humble, trewe,
Secret, and in my paines pacient,
And everemo desiren fresshly newe
To serven and been ay ylike diligent;
And with good herte al hoolly youre talent
Receiven wel, how sore that me smerte.
Lo, this mene I, myn owene sweete herte."

Quod Pandarus, "Lo, here an hard requeste,
And resonable a lady for to werne!
Now nece myn, by natal Joves feeste,
Were I a god, ye sholden sterve as yerne,
That heeren wel this man wol no thing yerne
But youre honour, and seen him almost sterve,
And been so loth to suffren him you serve."

With that she gan hir yën on him caste
Ful esily and ful debonairly,
Avising hire, and hied nought too faste
With nevere a word, but saide him softely,
"Myn honour sauf, I wol wel trewely,

134. **resort,** i.e., refuge. 137. **yerde,** rod, rule; **egal,** equal. 138. **defence,** prohibition. 139. **deine,** condescend. 140. **ought,** anything at all. 141. **youre,** yours. 145. **hoolly,** wholly; **talent,** desire. 146. **me smerte,** I smart. 149. **werne,** refuse. 151. **sterve,** die; **yerne,** quickly. 152. **yerne,** desire. 156. **debonairly,** gently. 157. **Avising hire,** pondering; **hied,** hastened. 159. **sauf,** safe.

And in swich forme as he gan now devise,
Receiven him fully to my servise;

Biseeching him for Goddes love that he
Wolde in honour of trouthe and gentilesse,
As I wel mene, eek menen wel to me;
And myn honour with wit and bisinesse°
Ay keepe; and if I may doon him gladnesse,
From hennesforth, ywis, I nil nought feine:°
Now beeth al hool; no lenger ye ne plaine.°

But nathelees this warne I you," quod she.
"A kinges sone although ye be, ywis,
Ye shal namore han sovereinetee
Of me in love than right in that caas is;
N'I nil forbere, if that ye doon amis,
To wratthe° you; and whil that ye me serve,
Cherissen you right after° ye deserve.

And shortly, dere herte and al my knight,
Beeth glad, and draweth you to lustinesse;
And I shal trewely with al my might
Youre bittre turnen al into swetnesse:
If I be she that may you do gladnesse,
For every wo ye shal recovere a blisse,"
And him in armes took and gan him kisse.

Fil° Pandarus on knees and up his yën
To hevene threw, and heeld his handes hye:
"Immortal god," quod he, "that maist nought dien,
Cupide I mene, of this maist glorifye:
And Venus, thou maist maken melodye:
Withouten hand° me seemeth that in the towne
For this merveile ich heere eech belle soune.°

165. bisinesse, carefulness. **167. hennesforth,** henceforth; **feine,** shirk. **168. hool,** i.e., well; **plaine,** complain. **174. wratthe,** anger. **175. Cherissen,** cherish; **after,** according as. **183. Fil,** fell. **188. Withouten hand,** spontaneously. **189. soune,** sound.

But ho, namore as now of this matere,
Forwhy° this folk wol comen up anoon,
That han the lettre red—lo, I hem heere.
But I conjure thee, Criseide, and oon,
And two, thou Troilus, whan thou maist goon,°
That at myn hous ye been at my warninge,°
For I ful wel shal shape° youre cominge.

And eseth ther youre hertes right ynough,
And lat see which of you shal bere the belle°
To speke of love aright"—therwith he lough°—
"For ther have ye a leiser for to telle."
Quod Troilus, "How longe shal I dwelle
Er this be doon?" Quod he, "Whan thou maist rise,
This thing shal be right as I you devise."°

With that Elaine and also Deiphebus
Tho comen upward right at the staires ende,
And Lord, so thanne gan gronen Troilus,
His brother and his suster for to blende.°
Quod Pandarus, "It time is that we wende:
Take, nece myn, youre leve at alle three,
And lat hem speke and cometh forth with me."

She took hir leve at hem ful thriftily,°
As she wel coude, and they hire reverence
Unto the fulle diden hardily,°
And wonder wel speken in hir absence
Of hire, in praising of hir excellence—
Hir governance,° hir wit, and hir manere
Comendede that joye was to heere.

Now lat hire wende into hir owene place,
And turne we to Troilus ayain,

191. Forwhy, because. **194. goon,** walk. **195. warninge,** i.e., call. **196. shape,** arrange. **198. bere the belle,** win the prize. **199. lough,** laughed. **203. devise,** describe. **207. blende,** deceive. **211. thriftily,** decorously. **213. hardily,** frankly. **216. governance,** behavior.

That gan ful lightly of the lettre pace,°
That Deiphebus hadde in the gardin sein;°
And of Elaine and him he wolde fain°
Delivered been, and saide that him leste
To sleepe, and after tales° han a reste.

Elaine him kiste and took hir leve blive,°
Deiphebus eek, and hoom wente every wight;
And Pandarus, as faste as he may drive,
To Troilus tho cam as line right,°
And on a pailet° al that glade night
By Troilus he lay with merye cheere
To tale, and wel was hem they were yfere.°

Whan every wight was voided° but they two,
And alle the dores weren faste yshette,°
To telle in short withouten wordes mo,
This Pandarus, withouten any lette,°
Up roos and on his beddes side him sette,
And gan to speken in a sobre wise
To Troilus, as I shal you devise.

"Myn alderlevest° lord and brother dere,
God woot, and thou, that it sat me so sore°
Whan I thee sawgh so languisshing toyere°
For love, of which thy wo weex° alway more,
That I with al my might and al my lore
Have evere sitthen° doon my bisinesse
To bringe thee to joye out of distresse;

And have it brought to swich plit as thou woost,°
So that thurgh me thou stondest now in waye

220. **lightly,** quickly; **of pace,** pass over. 221. **sein,** seen. 222. **fain,** gladly. 224. **tales,** conversation. 225. **blive,** straightway. 228. **right,** straight. 229. **pailet,** cot. 231. **To tale,** for conversation; **yfere,** together. 232. **was voided,** had withdrawn. 233. **yshette,** shut. 235. **lette,** delay. 239. **alderlevest,** dearest of all. 240. **sat,** i.e., affected; **sore,** badly. 241. **toyere,** this year. 242. **weex,** grew. 244. **sitthen,** since. 246. **plit,** condition; **woost,** know.

To faren wel. I saye it for no boost:
And woostou why? For shame it is to saye,
For thee have I bigonne a gamen playe
Which that I nevere do shal eft for other,
Although he were a thousandfold my brother.

That is to saye, for thee am I bicomen,
Bitwixen game and ernest, swich a mene
As maken wommen unto men to comen—
Al saye I nought, thou woost wel what I mene:
For thee have I my nece, of vices clene,
So fully maad thy gentilesse triste,
That al been shal right as thyselven liste.

But God that al woot take I to witnesse,
That nevere I this for coveitise wroughte,
But only for t'abregge that distresse,
For which wel neigh thou deidest, as me thoughte.
But goode brother, do now as thee oughte,
For Goddes love, and keep hire out of blame,
Sin thou art wis, and save alway hir name.

For wel thou woost the name as yit of here
Among the peple, as who saith, halwed is,
For that man is unbore, I dar wel swere,
That evere wiste that she dide amis.
But wo is me that I, that cause al this,
May thinken that she is my nece dere,
And I hir eem and traitour eek yfere.

And were it wist that I thurgh myn engin
Hadde in my nece yput this fantasye
To doon thy lust and hoolly to be thyn,

248. **boost**, boast. 249. **woostou**, do you know. 251. **eft**, again. 254. **mene**, instrument. 256. **Al . . . nought**, although I don't say it. 258. **triste**, trust. 259. **liste**, may please. 261. **coveitise**, avarice. 262. **abregge**, lessen. 263. **deidest**, died. 267. **here**, her. 268. **halwed**, sacred. 269. **unbore**, unborn. 270. **wiste**, knew. 273. **eem**, uncle; **yfere**, together. 274. **engin**, devising. 275. **fantasye**, idea. 276. **lust**, pleasure.

Why, al the world upon it wolde crye,
And sayn that I the werste trecherye
Dide in this caas that evere was bigonne,
And she forlost, and thou right nought ywonne.

Wherfore er I wol ferther goon a paas,
Yit eft I thee biseeche and fully saye
That privetee go with us in this caas—
That is to sayn, that thou us nevere wraye.
And be nought wroth though I thee ofte praye
To holden secree swich an heigh matere,
For skilful is, thou woost wel, my prayere.

And think what wo ther hath bitid er this
For making of avauntes, as men rede,
And what meschaunce in this world yit there is,
Fro day to day, right for that wikked deede;
For which thise wise clerkes that been dede
Han evere thus proverbed to us yonge
That first vertu is to keepe tonge.

And nere it that I wilne as now t'abregge
Diffusion of speeche, I coude almost
A thousand olde stories thee allegge
Of wommen lost thurgh fals and fooles boost.
Proverbes canst thyself ynowe and woost
Ayains that vice for to been a labbe,
Al saide men sooth as often as they gabbe.

O tonge, allas, so often here biforn
Hastou maad many a lady bright of hewe
Said, 'Wailaway the day that I was born!'
And many a maides sorwe for to newe;

280. forlost, utterly lost; **ywonne,** won. **281. goon a paas,** proceed. **282. eft,** again. **284. wraye,** reveal. **287. skilful,** reasonable. **288. bitid,** happened. **289. avauntes,** boasts. **292. dede,** dead. **294. keepe tonge,** keep quiet. **295. nere it,** if it were not; **abregge,** cut short. **297. allegge,** adduce. **298. fooles,** fools'; **boost,** boast. **299. canst,** know; **ynowe,** enough. **300. labbe,** blabbermouth. **301. Al,** even if; **gabbe,** lie. **305. newe,** renew.

And for the more part al is untrewe
That men of yelpe, and it were brought to preve:
Of kinde noon avauntour is to leve.°

Avauntour and a liere al is oon;
As thus: I pose° a womman graunte me
Hir love, and saith that other wol° she noon,
And I am sworn to holden it secree,
And after I go telle it two or three—
Ywis, I am avauntour at the leeste,
And a liere, for I breke my biheeste.°

Now looke thanne if they be nought to blame,
Swich manere folk—what shal I clepe° hem, what?—
That hem avaunte° of wommen, and by name,
That yit bihighte° hem nevere this ne that,
Ne knewe hem more than myn olde hat.
No wonder is, so God me sende hele,°
Though wommen dreden with us men to dele.

I saye nought this for no mistrust of you,
Ne for no wis man, but for fooles nice,°
And for the harm that in the world is now,
As wel for folye ofte as for malice;
For wel woot I in wise folk that vice
No womman drat,° if she be wel avised,
For wise been by fooles harm chastised.

But now to purpos, leve° brother dere:
Have al this thing that I have said in minde,
And keep thee cloos;° and be now of good cheere,
For at thy day thou shalt me trewe finde:
I shal the proces sette° in swich a kinde,

307. of yelpe, boast of; **and,** if; **preve,** proof. **308.** In the nature of things no boaster is to be believed. **310. pose,** make the assumption that. **311. wol,** wants. **315. biheeste,** promise. **317. clepe,** call. **318. hem avaunte,** boast. **319. bihighte,** promised. **321. hele,** salvation. **324. nice,** silly. **328. drat,** dreads. **330. leve,** beloved. **332. cloos,** close-mouthed. **334. proces,** business; **sette,** arrange.

And God toforn, that it shal thee suffise,
For it shal be right as thou wolt devise.

For wel I woot thou menest wel, pardee,
Therfore I dar this fully undertake.
Thou woost eek what thy lady graunted thee,
And day is set the chartres up to make.
Have now good night, I may no lenger wake;
And bid for me, sin thou art now in blisse,
That God me sende deeth or soone lisse."

Who mighte telle half the joye or feeste
Which that the soule of Troilus tho felte,
Heering th'effect of Pandarus biheeste?
His olde wo, that made his herte swelte,
Gan tho for joye wasten and tomelte,
And al the richesse of his sikes sore
At ones fledde, he felte of hem namore.

But right so as thise holtes and thise hayes,
That han in winter dede been and dreye,
Revesten hem in greene whan that May is,
Whan every lusty liketh best to playe,
Right in that selve wise, sooth for to saye,
Weex sodeinliche his herte ful of joye,
That gladder was ther nevere man in Troye;

And gan his look on Pandarus up caste,
Ful sobrely and freendly for to see,
And saide, "Freend, in Aperil the laste,
As wel thou woost, if it remembre thee,
How neigh the deeth for wo thou founde me,

340. **the chartres . . . make,** to put it down in legal form, i.e., to render it operative. 342. **bid,** pray. 343. **lisse,** comfort. 346. **biheeste,** promise. 347. **swelte,** faint. 348. **tomelte,** dissolve. 349. **richesse,** i.e., profusion; **sikes,** sighs. 351. **holtes,** groves; **hayes,** hedges. 352. **dede,** dead; **dreye,** dry. 353. **Revesten,** reclothe. 354. **lusty,** i.e., lusty person. 356. **Weex,** grew.

And how thou didest al thy bisinesse
To knowe of me the cause of my distresse;

Thou woost how longe ich it forbar to saye
To thee, that art the man that I best triste;
And peril noon was it to thee biwraye—
That wiste I wel; but tel me, if thee liste,
Sith I so loth was that thyself it wiste,
How dorste I mo tellen of this matere,
That quake now, and no wight may us heere?

But nathelees, by that God I thee swere,
That as him list may al this world governe,
And if I lie, Achilles with his spere
Myn herte cleve, al were my lif eterne
As I am mortal, if I late or yerne
Wolde it biwraye, or dorste, or sholde conne,
For al the good that God made under sonne:

That rather die I wolde and determine,
As thinketh me, now stokked in prisoun,
In wrecchednesse, in filthe, and in vermine,
Caitif to cruel king Agamenoun:
And this in alle the temples of this town
Upon the goddes alle, I wol thee swere
Tomorwe day, if that it liketh thee heere.

And that thou hast so muche ydo for me,
That I ne may it nevere more deserve,
This knowe I wel, al mighte I now for thee
A thousand times on a morwe sterve:
I can namore, but that I wol thee serve

365. **forbar,** forbore. 366. **triste,** trust. 367. **biwraye,** disclose. 369. **wiste,** should know. 370. **dorste,** should I dare; **mo,** others. 375. **al,** although. 376. **yerne,** soon. 377. **dorste,** should dare; **conne,** be able to. 379. **determine,** come to end. 380. **stokked,** put in the stocks. 382. **Caitif,** captive; **Agamenoun,** Agamemnon, leader of the Greek expedition against Troy. 387. **deserve,** requite. 388. **al,** even though. 389. **morwe,** i.e., day; **sterve,** die.

Right as thy sclave, whider so thou wende,
For everemore unto my lives ende.

But here, with al myn herte, I thee biseeche
That nevere in me thou deeme swich folye
As I shal sayn: me thoughte by thy speeche
That this which thou me doost for compaignye,
I sholde weene it were a bawderye—
I am nought wood, al if I lewed be:
It is nought so, that woot I wel, pardee.

But he that gooth for gold or for richesse
On swich message, calle him what thee list;
And this that thou doost, calle it gentilesse,
Compassion, and felaweshipe, and trist.
Depart it so, for widewher is wist
How that ther is diversitee requered
Bitwixen thinges like, as I have lered.

And that thou knowe I thinke nought ne weene
That this service a shame be or jape,
I have my faire suster Polyxene,
Cassandre, Elaine, or any of the frape:
Be she nevere so fair or wel yshape,
Tel me which thou wilt of everichone
To han for thyn, and lat me thanne allone.

But sith that thou hast doon me this servise
My lif to save, and for noon hope of meede,
So for the love of God, this grete emprise,
Parfourne it oute, for now is most neede;
For heigh and lowe, withouten any drede,

394. **deeme,** suspect. 396. **compaignye,** companionship. 397. **weene,** suppose; **a bawderye,** the act of a pimp. 398. **wood,** mad; **lewed,** ignorant. 401. **message,** errand. 403. **trist,** trust. 404. **Depart it so,** make this distinction; **widewher,** far and wide; **wist,** known. 405. **diversitee,** distinction; **requered,** needed. 406. **lered,** learned. 408. **jape,** joke. 410. **frape,** group. 415. **meede,** reward. 416. **emprise,** enterprise. 417. **Parfourne,** perform. 418. **drede,** doubt.

I wol alway thine heestes° alle keepe:
Have now good night, and lat us bothe sleepe."

Thus heeld him eech of other wel apayed,°
That al the world ne mighte it bet amende;°
And on the morwe whan they were arrayed
Eech to his owene needes gan entende:°
But Troilus, though as the fir he brende°
For sharp desir of hope and of plesaunce,
He nought forgat his goode governaunce,°

But in himself with manhood gan restraine
Eech racle deede and eech unbridled cheere,°
That alle tho° that liven, sooth to sayne,
Ne sholde han wist° by word or by manere
What that he mente as touching this matere:
From every wight as fer° as is the cloude
He was, so wel dissimulen° he coude.

And al the while which that I you devise
This was his lif: with al his fulle might
By day he was in Martes° heigh servise—
This is to sayn, in armes as a knight;
And for the more part the longe night
He lay and thoughte how that he mighte serve
His lady best, hir thank° for to deserve.

Nil I nought swere, although he laye softe,
That in his thought he nas somwhat disesed,°
Ne that he turned on his pilwes ofte,
And wolde of that him missed han been sesed.°
But in swich caas man is nought alway plesed,

419. **heestes,** commands. 421. **apayed,** pleased. 422. **bet amende,** improve. 424. **entende,** attend. 425. **brende,** burned. 427. **governaunce,** behavior. 429. **racle,** rash; **cheere,** look. 430. **tho,** those. 431. **wist,** known. 433. **fer,** far. 434. **dissimulen,** dissemble. 437. **Martes,** Mars's. 441. **thank,** gratitude. 443. **disesed,** troubled. 445. **sesed,** possessed.

For ought I woot, namore than was he:
That can I deeme of possibilitee.°

But certain is, to purpos for to go,
That in this while, as writen is in geste,°
He sawgh his lady somtime, and also
She with him spak whan that she dorste or leste;
And by hir bothe avis,° as was the beste,
Appointeden ful warly° in this neede,
So as they dorste, how they wolde proceede.

But it was spoken in so short a wise,
In swich await° alway, and in swich fere,
Lest any wight divinen or devise°
Wolde of hem two, or to it laye an ere,
That al this world so lief° to hem ne were
As that Cupide wolde hem grace sende
To make of hir speeche aright an ende.

But thilke litel that they spake or wroughte,
His wise gost° took ay of al swich heede,
It seemed hire he wiste what she thoughte
Withouten word, so that it was no neede
To bidde him ought to doon, or ought forbede:°
For which hire thoughte that love, al° come it late,
Of alle joye hadde opened hire the yate.°

And shortly of this proces for to pace,°
So wel his werk and wordes he bisette,°
That he so ful stood in his lady° grace,
That twenty thousand times er she lette°
She thanked God that evere she with him mette:

448. i.e., I can see how that is possible. **450. geste,** story. **453. hir bothe avis,** mutual consent. **454. Appointeden,** arranged; **warly,** cautiously. **457. await,** watchfulness. **458. divinen,** guess; **devise,** imagine. **460. lief,** dear. **464. gost,** spirit. **467. forbede,** forbid. **468. al,** although. **469. yate,** gate. **470. proces,** business; **pace,** pass. **471. bisette,** applied. **472. lady,** lady's. **473. lette,** stopped.

So coude he him governe in swich servise,
That al the world ne mighte it bet avise;

Forwhy she foond him so discreet in al,
So secret and of swich obeisaunce,
That wel she felte he was to hire a wal
Of steel, and sheeld from every displeasaunce,
That to been in his goode governaunce,
So wis he was, she was namore afered—
I mene as fer as oughte been requered.

And Pandarus to quike alway the fir
Was evere ylike prest and diligent:
To ese his freend was set al his desir;
He shoof ay on, he to and fro was sent,
He lettres bar whan Troilus was absent,
That nevere man as in his freendes neede
Ne bar him bet than he, withouten drede.

But now paraunter som man waiten wolde
That every word, or soonde, or look, or cheere
Of Troilus that I rehercen sholde,
In al this while unto his lady dere:
I trowe it were a long thing for to heere,
Or of what wight that stant in swich disjointe
His wordes alle, or every look to pointe.

Forsoothe I have nought herd it doon er this
In storye noon, ne no man here, I weene.
And though I wolde, I coude nought, ywis,
For ther was som epistel hem bitweene
That wolde, as saith myn auctour, wel contene

476. **avise,** devise. 477. **Forwhy,** inasmuch as; **foond,** found. 478. **obeisaunce,** courtesy. 481. **governaunce,** control. 483. **requered,** necessary. 484. **quike,** quicken. 485. **prest,** prompt. 487. **shoof,** pushed. 488. **bar,** bore. 490. **him,** himself; **drede,** doubt. 491. **paraunter,** perhaps; **waiten,** expect. 492. **soonde,** message; **cheere,** i.e., action. 495. **trowe,** believe. 496. **stant,** stands; **disjointe,** situation. 497. **pointe,** list. 502. **contene,** contain.

Neigh half this book, of which him liste nought write.
How sholde I thanne a line of it endite?

But to the grete effect: thanne saye I thus,
That stonding in concord and in quiete
Thise ilke two, Criseide and Troilus,
As I have said, and in this time sweete—
Save only often mighte they nought meete,
Ne leiser have hir speeches to fulfelle—
That it bifel right as I shal you telle,

That Pandarus, that evere dide his might
Right for the fin that I shal speke of here,
As for to bringen to his hous som night
His faire nece and Troilus yfere,
Wher as at leiser al this heigh matere
Touching hir love were at the fulle up bounde,
Hadde out of doute a time to it founde.

For he with greet deliberacioun
Hadde every thing that herto mighte availe
Forncast and put in execucioun,
And neither left for cost nor for travaile:
Come if hem liste, hem sholde no thing faile;
And for to been in ought espied there,
That wiste he wel an impossible were.

Dredelees it cleer was in the wind
From every pie and every lette-game:
Now al is wel, for al the world is blind
In this matere, bothe fremed and tame.
This timber is al ready up to frame:

510. **fulfelle,** fulfill. 513. **fin,** end. 515. **yfere,** together. 517. **were,** should be; **up bounde,** i.e., made fast. 518. **out of doute,** beyond fear. 519. **greet,** great. 521. **Forncast,** arranged in advance. 522. **left,** i.e., left anything undone. 524. **in ought,** in any way. 525. **impossible,** impossibility. 526. **Dredelees,** doubtless; **cleer,** free. 527. **pie,** magpie, chatterbox; **lette-game,** spoilsport. 529. **fremed,** wild. 530. **up to frame,** to put up.

Us lakketh nought but that we witen wolde
A certain hour in which she comen sholde.

And Troilus, that al this purveyaunce
Knew at the fulle and waited on it ay,
Hadde herupon eek maad greet ordinaunce,
And founde his cause and therto his array,
If that he were missed night or day
Ther whil he was aboute this servise,
That he was goon to doon his sacrifise;

And moste at swich a temple allone wake,
Answered of Appollo for to be,
And first to seen the holy laurer quake,
Er that Appollo spak out of the tree,
To telle him next whan Greekes sholde flee—
And forthy lette him no man, God forbede,
But praye Appollo helpen in this neede.

Now is ther litel more for to doone,
But Pandare up, and shortly for to sayne,
Right soone upon the chaunging of the moone,
Whan lightlees is the world a night or twaine,
And that the welken shoop him for to raine,
He straight amorwe unto his nece wente—
Ye han wel herd the fin of his entente.

Whan he was come, he gan anoon to playe,
As he was wont, and of himself to jape;
And finally he swoor and gan hire saye,
By this and that, she sholde nought escape,
Ne lenger doon him after hire to cape,

531. **witen**, learn. 533. **purveyaunce**, preparation. 535. **ordinaunce**, arrangements. 536. **cause**, i.e., excuse; **array**, manner of acting. 540. **moste**, must. 542. **laurer**, laurel; **quake**, shake: that is, in giving the answer of Apollo. 545. **forthy**, therefore; **lette**, hinder. 548. **up**, i.e., went into action. 551. **welken**, sky; **shoop him**, was getting ready. 552. **amorwe**, in the morning. 553. **fin**, end. 555. **jape**, joke. 558. **doon**, make; **cape**, gape.

But certainly she moste, by hir leve,
Come soupen° in his hous with him at eve.

At which she lough° and gan hire faste excuse,
And saide, "It raineth. Lo, how sholde I goon?"
"Lat be," quod he, "ne stonde nought thus to muse.
This moot be doon. Ye shal be ther anoon."
So at the laste herof they fille at oon,°
Or elles, softe he swoor hire in hir ere,
He nolde nevere comen ther she were.

Soone after this she to him gan to roune,°
And axed° him if Troilus were there:
He swoor hire nay, for he was out of towne,
And saide, "Nece, I pose° that he were:
You tharste° nevere han the more fere,
For rather than men mighte him ther espye,
Me were levere a thousandfold to die."

Nought list° myn auctour fully to declare
What that she thoughte whan that he saide so,
That Troilus was out of towne yfare,
As if he saide therof sooth or no;
But that withouten await° with him to go
She graunted him, sith he hire that bisoughte,
And as his nece obeyed as hire oughte.

But nathelees yit gan she him biseeche,
Although with him to goon it was no fere,
For to been war of goosissh° peples speeche,
That dremen thinges whiche as nevere were,
And wel avise him whom he broughte there;
And saide him, "Eem, sin I moste on you triste,°
Looke al be wel, and do now as you liste."

560. **soupen,** sup. 561. **lough,** laughed. 565. **fille at oon,** i.e., agreed. 568. **roune,** whisper. 569. **axed,** asked. 571. **I pose,** i.e., supposing. 572. **You tharste,** you would need. 575. **list,** it pleases. 579. **await,** watchfulness. 584. **goosissh,** gooselike, silly. 587. **Eem,** uncle; **moste,** must; **triste,** trust.

He swoor hire yis by stokkes° and by stones,
And by the goddes that in hevene dwelle,
Or elles were him levere, soule and bones,
With Pluto° king as deepe been in helle
As Tantalus.° What sholde I more telle?
Whan al was wel he roos and took his leve,
And she to soper cam, whan it was eve,

With a certain° of hir owene men,
And with hir faire nece Antigone,
And othere of hir wommen nine or ten.
But who was glad now? Who, as trowe° ye,
But Troilus, that stood and mighte it see
Thurghout a litel window in a stewe,°
Ther he bishet sin midnight was in mewe,°

Unwist° of every wight but of Pandare.
But to the point: now whan that she was come,
With alle joye and alle freendes fare°
Hir eem anoon in armes hath hire nome,°
And after to the soper alle and some,°
Whan time was, ful softe they hem sette—
God woot ther was no daintee for to fette.°

And after soper gonnen they to rise
At ese wel, with hertes fresshe and glade;
And wel was him that coude best devise°
To liken° hire, or that hire laughen made:
He soong, she playde, he tolde tale of Wade.°
But at the laste, as every thing hath ende,
She took hir leve, and needes wolde wende.

589. **yis,** yes; **stokkes,** stumps. 592. **Pluto,** king of the classic Hades. 593. **Tantalus,** whose wickedness earned him a particularly horrible punishment in Hades. 596. **certain,** certain number. 599. **trowe,** may believe. 601. **stewe,** closet. 602. **bishet,** shut up; **in mewe,** i.e., as in a coop. 603. **Unwist,** unknown. 605. **fare,** ceremony. 606. **nome,** taken. 607. **alle and some,** all and sundry. 609. **to fette,** to fetch, i.e., lacking. 612. **devise,** contrive. 613. **liken,** please. 614. **soong,** sang; **Wade,** a legendary hero.

But O Fortune, executrice of wierdes!
O influences of thise hevenes hye!
Sooth is that under God ye been oure hierdes,
Though to us beestes been the causes wrie.
This mene I now: for she gan hoomward hie,
But execut was al biside hir leve
The goddes wil, for which she moste bleve.

The bente moone with hir hornes pale,
Saturne, and Jove in Cancro joined were,
That swich a rain from hevene gan avale,
That every manere womman that was there
Hadde of that smoky rain a verray fere:
At which Pandare tho lough, and saide thenne,
"Now were it time a lady to go henne!

But, goode nece, if I mighte evere plese
You any thing, thanne praye ich you," quod he,
"To doon myn herte as now so greet an ese
As for to dwelle here al this night with me,
Forwhy this is youre owene hous, pardee.
For by my trouthe, I saye it nought agame,
To wende as now it were to me a shame."

Criseide, which that coude as muche good
As half a world, took heede of his prayere;
And sin it roon, and al was on a flood,
She thoughte, "As good chepe may I dwellen here,
And graunte it gladly with a freendes cheere,
And have a thank, as grucche and thanne abide—
For hoom to goon, it may nought wel bitide."

617. **wierdes,** i.e., individual destinies. 619. **hierdes,** herdsmen. 620. **wrie,** hidden. 621. **hie,** hasten. 622. **execut,** executed. 623. **moste bleve,** must remain. 624. **bente,** crescent. 625. The conjunction in the house of the Crab (Cancer) of the Moon, Saturn, and Jupiter is a relatively infrequent astrological event and one which was thought to cause rain. 626. **avale,** fall. 628. **smoky,** misty. 629. **lough,** laughed. 630. **henne,** hence. 635. **Forwhy,** because. 636. **agame,** in joking. 638. **coude,** knew. 640. **roon,** rained. 641. **good chepe,** easily. 642. **cheere,** manner. 643. **grucche,** complain.

"I wol," quod she, "myn uncle lief and dere;
Sin that you list, it skile is to be so.
I am right glad with you to dwellen here:
I saide but agame I wolde go."
"Ywis, graunt mercy, nece," quod he tho,
"Were it agame or no, sooth for to telle,
Now am I glad sin that you list to dwelle."

Thus al is wel. But tho bigan aright
The newe joye and al the feeste again.
But Pandarus, if goodly hadde he might,
He wolde han hied hire to bedde fain,
And saide, "Lord, this is an huge rain:
This were a weder for to sleepen inne—
And that I rede us soone to biginne.

And nece, woot ye wher I wol you laye,
For that we shul nat liggen fer asonder,
And for ye neither shullen, dar I saye,
Heeren noise of raines ne of thonder?
By God, right in my litel closet yonder.
And I wol in that outer hous allone
Be wardein of youre wommen everichone.

And in this middel chambre that ye see
Shul youre wommen sleepen wel and softe;
And ther I saide shal youre selven be:
And if ye liggen wel tonight, come ofte,
And careth nought what weder is alofte.
The win anoon, and whan so that you leste,
So go we sleepe: I trowe it be the beste."

Ther nis namore, but herafter soone
They voidee dronke and travers drawe anoon.

645. **lief**, beloved. 646. **skile**, reason. 649. **graunt mercy**, many thanks. 653. **newe**, renewed. 655. **hied**, hastened; **fain**, gladly. 657. **weder**, weather. 658. **rede**, advise. 660. **liggen**, lie; **fer**, far. 661. **for**, in order that. 664. **hous**, i.e., compartment. 665. **wardein**, guardian. 671. **The win**, i.e., bring the wine; **leste**, it please. 674. **voidee**, loving-cup; **travers**, curtains.

Gan every wight that hadde nought to doone
More in the place out of the chambre goon.
And everemo so sterneliche it roon,
And blew therwith so wonderliche loude,
That wel neigh no man heeren other coude.

Tho Pandarus, hir eem, right as him oughte,
With wommen swiche as were hire most aboute,
Ful glad unto hir beddes side hire broughte,
And took his leve, and gan ful lowe loute,
And saide, "Here at this closet dore withoute,
Right overthwart, youre wommen liggen alle,
That whom you list of hem ye may hire calle."

So whan that she was in the closet laid,
And alle hir wommen forth by ordinaunce
Abedde weren ther as I have said,
Ther was namore to skippen nor to traunce,
But boden go to bedde with meschaunce
If any wight were stiring anywhere,
And lat hem sleepen that abedde were.

But Pandarus, that wel coude eech a deel
The olde daunce, and every point therinne,
Whan that he sawgh that alle thing was weel,
He thoughte he wolde upon his werk biginne,
And gan the stewe dore al softe unpinne,
And stille as stoon, withouten lenger lette,
By Troilus adown right he him sette,

And shortly to the point right for to goon,
Of al this werk he tolde him word and ende,

677. **sterneliche**, violently; **roon**, rained. 683. **loute**, bow. 685. **overthwart**, opposite; **liggen**, lie. 686. **list**, it pleases. 688. **ordinaunce**, order. 690. **traunce**, tramp about. 691. **boden**, i.e., any person was commanded. 694. **coude**, knew; **deel**, part. 695. **olde daunce**, dance of love. 696. **weel**, well. 698. **stewe**, closet; **unpinne**, open. 699. **lette**, delay. 702. **word**, beginning.

And saide, "Make thee redy right anoon,
For thou shalt into hevene blisse wende."
"Now blisful Venus, thou me grace sende,"
Quod Troilus, "for nevere yit no neede
Hadde ich er now, ne halvendeel° the drede."

Quod Pandarus, "Ne dreed thee nevere a deel;°
For it shal be right as thou wolt desire.
So thrive I, this night shal I make it weel,
Or casten al the gruel in the fire."
"Yit, blisful Venus, this night thou me inspire,"
Quod Troilus, "as wis° as I thee serve,
And evere bet and bet shal til I sterve.

And if ich hadde, O Venus ful of mirthe,
Aspectes° badde of Mars or of Saturne,
Or thou combust or let° were in my birthe,
Thy fader pray al thilke harm disturne°
Of grace, and that I glad ayain may turne,
For love of him thou lovedest in the shawe°—
I mene Adoon, that with the boor was slawe.°

O Jove eek, for the love of faire Europe,
The which in forme of bole away thou fette;°
Now help! O Mars, thou with thy bloody cope,
For love of Cypris, thou me nought ne lette!°
O Phebus, thenk whan Dane hirselven shette°
Under the bark, and laurer weex° for drede;
Yit for hir love, O help now at this neede!

707. **halvendeel,** half. 708. **dreed.** dread; **deel,** bit. 713. **wis,** surely. 716. **aspectes,** i.e., planetary influences: Mars and Saturn were the most baleful of the planets. 717. **thou,** i.e., your influence; **combust,** quenched; **let,** hindered. 718. **disturne,** turn aside. 720. **shawe,** wood. 721. **Adoon,** Adonis, Venus' lover; **boor,** boar; **slawe,** slain. 723. **bole,** bull; **fette,** fetched: Jupiter took the form of a bull in order to carry away the fair Europa. 725. **Cypris,** Venus, whom Mars loved; **lette,** hinder. 726. **Phebus,** Phoebus Apollo; **Dane,** Daphne; **shette,** shut. 727. **laurer,** laurel; **weex,** became: Daphne was rescued from the amorous Apollo when she was turned into a laurel tree.

Mercurye, for the love of Hierse eke,
For which Pallas was with Aglauros wroth,
Now help! and eek Diane I thee biseeke
That this viage be nought to thee loth!
O fatal sustren which, er any cloth
Me shapen was, my destinee me sponne,
So helpeth to this werk that is bigonne."

Quod Pandarus, "Thou wrecched mouses herte,
Artou agast so that she wol thee bite?
Why, doon this furred cloke upon thy sherte,
And folwe me, for I wol have the wite.
But bid, and lat me goon bifore a lite."
And with that word he gan undoon a trappe,
And Troilus he broughte in by the lappe.

The sterne wind so loude gan to route
That no wight other noise mighte heere,
And they that layen at the dore withoute
Ful sikerly they slepten alle yfere;
And Pandarus, with a ful sobre cheere,
Gooth to the dore anoon withouten lette
Ther as they laye, and softely it shette.

And as he cam ayainward prively,
His nece awook and axed, "Who gooth there?"
"My dere nece," quod he, "it am I.
Ne wondreth nought, ne have of it no fere."
And neer he cam and saide hire in hir ere,
"No word, for love of God I you biseeche:
Lat no wight risen and heeren of oure speeche."

729. **Hierse,** Herse, who had been entrusted with a secret by Pallas Athena which Herse's sister Aglauros revealed, thereby incurring Athena's wrath; Herse was later loved by Mercury. 731. **Diane,** Diana, goddess of chastity. 732. **viage,** project. 733. **fatal sustren,** the three Fates. 734. **sponne,** spun. 738. **doon,** don. 739. **wite,** blame. 740. **bid,** wait; **lite,** little. 741. **trappe,** trapdoor. 742. **lappe,** fold in a garment. 743. **route,** howl. 746. **sikerly,** undisturbed; **yfere,** together. 747. **cheere,** face. 748. **lette,** delay. 749. **shette,** shut. 750. **ayainward,** i.e., up to her. 751. **axed,** asked.

"What, which way be ye comen, benedicite,"
Quod she, "and how thus unwist of hem alle?"
"Here at this secree trappe dore," quod he.
Quod tho Criseide, "Lat me som wight calle."
"I, God forbede that it sholde falle,"
Quod Pandarus, "that ye swich folye wroughte:
They mighte deemen thing they nevere er thoughte.

It is nought good a sleeping hound to wake,
Ne yive a wight a cause to divine:
Youre wommen sleepen alle, I undertake,
So that for hem the hous men mighte mine,
And sleepen wolen til the sonne shine;
And whan my tale brought is to an ende,
Unwist right as I cam so wol I wende.

Now nece myn, ye shul wel understonde,"
Quod he, "so as ye wommen deemen alle,
That for to holde in love a man in honde,
And him hir lief and dere herte calle,
And maken him an houve above an calle—
I mene as love another in this mene while—
She dooth hirself a shame and him a gile.

Now wherby that I telle you al this:
Ye woot youreself as wel as any wight
How that youre love al fully graunted is
To Troilus, the worthieste knight
Oon of this world, and therto trouthe yplight
That, but it were on him along, ye nolde
Him nevere falsen whil ye liven sholde.

757. **benedicite,** bless me. 758. **unwist,** unknown. 761. **falle,** happen. 763. **deemen,** suspect. 765. **divine,** guess. 766. **undertake,** warrant. 772. **deemen,** think. 773. i.e., That to pretend to love a man. 774. **lief,** beloved. 775. **maken . . . calle,** make him a hood over a cap, i.e., deceive him. 777. **gile,** trick. 782. **Oon . . . world,** i.e., unique; **yplight,** i.e., you have promised. 783. **but,** unless; **on him along,** through his fault. 784. **falsen,** play false to.

Now stant° it thus, that sith I fro you wente,
This Troilus, right platly° for to sayn,
Is thurgh a goter by a privee wente°
Into my chambre come in al this rain,
Unwist° of every manere wight, certain,
Save of myself, as wisly° have I joye,
And by the faith I shal° Priam of Troye.

And he is come in swich paine and distresse,
That but he be al fully wood° by this,
He sodeinly moot falle into woodnesse,°
But if° God helpe; and cause why is this:
He saith him told is of a freend of his
How that ye sholden love oon hatte° Horaste,
For sorwe of which this night shal been his laste."

Criseide, which that al this wonder herde,
Gan sodeinly aboute hir herte colde,°
And with a sik° she sorwefully answerde,
"Allas, I wende,° who so tales tolde,
My dere herte wolde me nought holde
So lightly fals. Allas, conceites° wronge,
What harm they doon! For now live I too longe.

Horaste, allas, and falsen Troilus!
I knowe him nought, God helpe me so," quod she.
"Allas, what wikked spirit tolde him thus?
Now certes, eem, tomorwe and° I him see,
I shal therof as ful excusen me,
As evere dide womman, if him like."
And with that word she gan ful sore sike.°

785. **stant,** stands. 786. **platly,** flatly. 787. **goter,** gutter; **wente,** passage. 789. **Unwist,** unknown. 790. **wisly,** surely. 791. **shal,** owe. 793. **but,** unless; **wood,** mad. 794. **moot,** must; **woodnesse,** insanity. 795. **But if,** unless. 797. **hatte,** named. 800. **colde,** grow cold. 801. **sik,** sigh. 802. **wende,** thought. 804. **lightly,** readily; **conceites,** imaginings. 809. **and,** if. 812. **sike,** sigh.

"O God," quod she, "so worldly selinesse,
Which clerkes callen fals felicitee,
Ymedled is with many a bitternesse!
Ful anguisshous thanne is, God woot," quod she,
"Condicioun of vain prosperitee:
For either joyes comen nought yfere,
Or elles no wight hath hem alway here.

O brotel wele of mannes joye unstable,
With what wight so thou be or how thou playe,
Either he woot that thou, joye, art muable,
Or woot it nought: it moot been oon of twaye.
Now if he woot it nought, how may he saye
That he hath verray joye and selinesse,
That is of ignorance ay in derknesse?

Now if he woot that joye is transitorye,
As every joye of worldly thing moot flee,
Thanne every time he that hath in memorye,
The drede of lesing maketh him that he
May in no parfit selinesse be.
And if to lese his joye he sette a mite,
Thanne seemeth it that joye is worth but lite.

Wherfore I wol diffine in this matere
That trewely, for ought I can espye,
Ther is no verray wele in this world here.
But O thou wikked serpent jalousye,
Thou misbileved and envious folye,
Why hastou Troilus maad to me untriste,
That nevere yit agilte him that I wiste?"

813. **selinesse,** happiness. 815. **Ymedled,** mingled. 816. **anguisshous,** anguished. 818. **yfere,** together. 820. **brotel,** brittle; **wele,** prosperity. 822. **muable,** mutable. 823. **moot,** must. 830. **lesing,** losing. 831. **parfit,** perfect. 832. **lese,** lose; **sette,** i.e., cares. 833. **lite,** little. 834. **diffine,** conclude. 838. **misbileved,** misbelieving. 839. **untriste,** distrustful. 840. **agilte,** wronged; **wiste,** knew.

Quod Pandarus, "Thus fallen is the cas."
"Why, uncle myn," quod she, "who tolde him this?
Why dooth my dere herte thus, allas?"
"Ye woot, ye nece myn," quod he, "what is.
I hope al shal be wel that is amis,
For ye may quenche al this if that you leste°—
And dooth right so, for I holde it the beste."

"So shal I do tomorwe, ywis," quod she,
"And God toforn, so that it shal suffise."
"Tomorwe? Allas, that were a fair,"° quod he.
"Nay, nay, it may nat stonden in this wise:
For nece myn, thus writen clerkes wise,
That peril is with drecching in ydrawe°—
Nay, swiche abodes been nought worth an hawe.°

Nece, alle thing hath time, I dar avowe;
For whan a chambre afire is or an halle,
Wel more neede is sodeinly rescowe,°
Than to disputen and axe° amonges alle
How the candel in the straw is falle.
A, benedicite, for al among that fare°
The harm is doon, and farewel, feeldefare!°

And nece myn, ne take it nought agrief:°
If that ye suffre him al night in this wo,
God helpe me so, ye hadde him nevere lief,°
That dar I sayn. Now ther is but we two—
But wel I woot that ye wol nat do so—
Ye been too wis to doon so greet folye,
To putte his lif al night in jupertye."°

846. leste, it please. **850. a fair,** i.e., a fine thing. **853.** That danger is increased by procrastination. **854. abodes,** delays; **hawe,** hawthorn berry. **857. sodeinly,** straightway; **rescowe,** bring help. **858. axe,** ask. **860. fare,** procedure. **861. farewel, feeldefare,** goodby, bird, i.e., the bird has flown. **862. agrief,** amiss. **864. hadde,** held; **lief,** dear. **868. jupertye,** jeopardy.

"Hadde I him nevere lief? By God, I weene
Ye hadde nevere thing so lief," quod she.
"Now by my thrift," quod he, "that shal be seene,
For sin ye make this ensample of me,
If ich al night wolde him in sorwe see
For al the tresor in the town of Troye,
I bidde God I nevere mote have joye.

Now looke thanne, if ye that been his love
Shul putte his lif al night in jupertye,
For thing of nought, now by that God above,
Nought only this delay comth of folye,
But of malice, if that I shal nought lie:
What, platly, and ye suffre him in distresse,
Ye neither bountee doon ne gentilesse."

Quod tho Criseide, "Wol ye doon oo thing?
And ye therwith shal stinte al his disese.
Have here and bereth him this blewe ring,
For ther is no thing mighte him bettre plese,
Save I myself, ne more his herte apese;
And saye my dere herte that his sorwe
Is causelees: that shal be seen tomorwe."

"A ring!" quod he. "Ye, haselwodes shaken!
Ye, nece myn, that ring moste han a stoon
That mighte dede men alive maken,
And swich a ring trowe I that ye have noon:
Discrecion out of youre heed is goon—
That feele I now," quod he, "and that is routhe:
O time ylost, wel maistou cursen slouthe!

869. weene, think. **871. thrift,** welfare. **875. bidde,** pray; **mote,** may. **881. platly,** flatly; **and,** if. **882. bountee,** generous action. **884. stinte,** stop; **disese,** distress. **885. blewe,** blue. **887. apese,** comfort. **890. haselwodes,** hazel woods. **891. moste,** must. **894. heed,** head. **895. routhe,** pity. **896. slouthe,** negligence.

Woot ye nat wel that noble and heigh corage°
Ne sorweth nought—ne stinteth eek—for lite?°
But if a fool were in a jalous rage,
I nolde setten at° his sorwe a mite,
But feffe him with a fewe wordes white°
Another day, whan that I mighte him finde.
But this thing stant° al in another kinde:

This is so gentil and so tendre of herte
That with his deeth he wol his sorwes wreke;°
For trusteth wel, how sore that him smerte,
He wol to you no jalous wordes speke.
And forthy,° nece, er that his herte breke,
So speke youreself to him of this matere—
For with a word ye may his herte steere.°

Now have I told what peril he is inne,
And his coming unwist° is to every wight,
Ne, pardee, harm may ther be noon ne sinne—
I wol myself be with you al this night;
Ye knowe eek how it is youre owene knight,
And that by right ye moste upon him triste°—
And I al prest° to fecchen him whan you liste."

This accident° so pitous was to heere,
And eek so lik a sooth at prime face,°
And Troilus hir knight to hire so dere,
His privee coming and the siker° place,
That though that she dide him as thanne a grace,
Considered alle thinges as they stoode,
No wonder is, sin she dide al for goode.

Criseide answerde, "As wisly° God at reste
My soule bringe, as me is for him wo!

897. corage, heart. **898. stinteth,** stops; **lite,** little. **900. setten at,** value. **901. feffe,** endow; **white,** i.e., plausible. **903. stant,** stands. **905. wreke,** banish. **908. forthy,** therefore. **910. steere,** control. **912. unwist,** unknown. **916. moste,** must; **triste,** trust. **917. prest,** ready. **918. accident,** incident. **919. prime face,** first appearance. **921. siker,** safe. **925. wisly,** surely.

And eem, ywis, fain° wolde I doon the beste,
If that ich hadde a grace to do so;
But whether that ye dwelle° or for him go,
I am til God me bettre minde sende
At dulcarnoun,° right at my wittes ende."

Quod Pandarus, "Ye, nece, wol ye heere?
Dulcarnoun called is Fleming of Wrecches:°
It seemeth hard, for wrecches wol nought lere°
For verray slouthe or othere wilful tecches;°
This is said by hem that been nought worth two fecches,°
But ye been wis, and that we han on honde
Nis neither hard, ne skilful° to withstonde."

"Thanne, eem," quod she, "dooth herof as you list.
But er he come I wol first up arise.
And for the love of God, sin al my trist°
Is on you two, and ye been bothe wise,
So werketh now in so discreet a wise
That I may have honour and he plesaunce:
For I am here al in youre governaunce."

"That is wel said," quod he, "my nece dere,
Ther good thrift° on that wise gentil herte!
But liggeth° stille, and taketh him right here—
It needeth nought no ferther for him sterte.°
And eech of you eseth otheres sorwes smerte,
For love of God. And Venus, I thee herye,°
For soone hope I we shul been alle merye."

This Troilus ful soone on knees him sette,
Ful sobrely, right by hir beddes heed,

927. **fain,** gladly. 929. **dwelle,** stay here. 931. **At dulcarnoun,** at an impasse. 933. **Fleming of Wrecches,** router of dunces: the name of a difficult proposition in geometry; cf. *pons asinorum.* 934. **lere,** learn. 935. **slouthe,** negligence; **tecches,** faults. 936. **fecches,** beans. 938. **skilful,** reasonable. 941. **trist,** trust. 947. **Ther good thrift,** i.e., may prosperity be. 948. **liggeth,** lie. 949. **sterte,** move. 951. **herye,** praise.

And in his beste wise his lady grette.
But Lord, so she weex sodeinliche reed;
Ne though men sholden smiten of hir heed,
She coude nought a word aright out bringe
So sodeinly, for his sodein cominge.

But Pandarus, that so wel coude feele
In every thing, to playe anoon bigan,
And saide, "Nece, see how this lord can kneele.
Now for youre trouthe, see this gentil man."
And with that word he for a quisshen ran,
And saide, "Kneeleth now whil that you leste,
Ther God youre hertes bringe soone at reste."

Can I nought sayn, for she bad him nought rise,
If sorwe it putte out of hir remembraunce,
Or elles that she took it in the wise
Of duetee, as for his observaunce;
But wel finde I she dide him this plesaunce
That she him kiste, although she siked sore,
And bad him sitte adown withouten more.

Quod Pandarus, "Now wol ye wel biginne,
Now dooth him sitte, goode nece dere,
Upon youre beddes side al ther withinne,
That eech of you the bet may other heere."
And with that word he drow him to the fere,
And took a light, and foond his countenaunce
As for to looke upon an old romaunce.

Criseide, that was Troilus lady right,
And clere stood on a grounde of sikernesse,
Al thoughte she hir servant and hir knight

955. **grette,** greeted. 956. **weex,** grew; **reed,** red. 957. **of,** off; **heed,** head. 964. **quisshen,** cushion. 965. **leste,** it please. 966. **Ther,** i.e., may. 970. **duetee,** duty. 972. **siked,** sighed. 975. **dooth,** make. 977. **bet,** better. 978. **drow him,** withdrew; **fere,** fireplace. 979. **foond his countenaunce,** assumed an attitude. 982. **sikernesse,** security. 983. **Al,** although.

Ne sholde of right noon untrouthe° in hire gesse,
Yit nathelees, considered° his distresse,
And that love is in cause of swich folye,
Thus to him spak she of his jalousye:

"Lo, herte myn, as wolde the excellence
Of Love, ayains the which that no man may—
Ne oughte eek—goodly° make resistence,
And eek by cause I felte wel and sey°
Youre grete trouthe and servise every day,
And that youre herte al myn was, sooth to sayne,
This droof me for to rewe° upon youre paine.

And youre goodnesse have I founden alway yit,
Of which, my dere herte and al my knight,
I thanke it you as fer° as I have wit,
Al° can I nought as muche as it were right;
And I emforth° my conning and my might
Have and ay shal, how sore that me smerte,
Been to you trewe and hool° with al myn herte:

And dredelees° that shal be founde at preve.°
But herte myn, what al this is to sayne
Shal wel be told, so that ye nought you greve
Though I to you right on youreself complaine;
For therwith mene I finally the paine,
That halt° youre herte and myn in hevinesse,
Fully to sleen,° and every wrong redresse.

My goode myn, noot° I for why ne how
That jalousye, allas, that wikked wivere,°
Thus causelees is cropen° into you,
The harm of which I wolde fain° delivere.

984. untrouthe, infidelity. **985. considered,** considering. **990. goodly,** properly. **991. sey,** saw. **994. droof,** drove; **rewe,** have pity. **997. fer,** far. **998. Al,** although. **999. emforth,** according to. **1001. hool,** whole. **1002. dredelees,** doubtless; **preve,** experience. **1007. halt,** holds. **1008. sleen,** slay. **1009. My . . . myn,** i.e., my own good love; **noot,** know not. **1010. wivere,** serpent. **1011. cropen,** crept. **1012. fain,** gladly.

Allas that he al hool or of him slivere
Sholde han his refut in so digne a place—
Ther Jove him soone out of youre herte arace.

But O, thou Jove, O auctour of Nature,
Is this an honour to thy deitee,
That folk ungiltif suffren hir injure,
And who that giltif is al quit gooth he?
O were it leful for to plaine on thee,
That undeserved suffrest jalousye,
Of that I wolde upon thee plaine and crye.

Eek al my wo is this, that folk now usen
To sayn right thus, that jalousye is love;
And wolde a busshel venim al excusen,
For that oo grain of love is on it shove.
But that woot hye God that sit above,
If it be likker love or hate or grame—
And after that it oughte bere his name.

But certain is, som manere jalousye
Is excusable more than som, ywis,
As whan cause is, and som swich fantasye
With pietee so wel repressed is
That it unnethe dooth or saith amis,
But goodly drinketh up al his distresse—
And that excuse I for the gentilesse;

And som so ful of furye is and despit
That it surmounteth his repressioun.
But herte myn, ye been nat in that plit,

1013. **hool,** entire; **slivere,** part. 1014. **réfut,** refuge; **digne,** honorable. 1015. **Ther,** i.e., may; **arace,** pluck. 1018. **ungiltif,** guiltless; **injure,** injury. 1019. **quit,** unpunished. 1020. **leful,** lawful; **plaine,** complain. 1021. That permit unwarranted jealousy. 1025. **venim,** of poison. 1026. **shove,** i.e., placed. 1027. **sit,** sits. 1028. **likker,** more like; **grame,** wrath. 1029. **his,** its. 1032. **fantasye,** wild idea. 1033. **pietee,** pity. 1034. **unnethe,** hardly. 1035. **drinketh up,** i.e., consumes inwardly. 1037. **despit,** malice. 1039. **plit,** plight.

That thanke I God, for which youre passioun,
I wol nought calle it but illusioun
Of habundance of love and bisy cure,
That dooth youre herte this disese endure,

Of which I am right sory but nought wroth.
But for my devoir and youre hertes reste,
Wher so you list by ordal or by ooth,
By sort or in what wise so you leste,
For love of God, lat preve it for the beste:
And if I be giltif, do me deye.
Allas, what mighte I more doon or saye?"

With that a fewe brighte teres newe
Out of hir yën fille, and thus she saide,
"Now God, thou woost, in thought ne deede, untrewe
To Troilus was nevere yit Criseide."
With that hir heed down in the bed she laide,
And with the sheete it wreigh and sighte sore,
And heeld hir pees: nought oo word spak she more.

But now helpe God to quenchen al this sorwe:
So hope I that he shal, for he best may.
For I have seen of a ful misty morwe
Folwen ful ofte a merye someres day;
And after winter folweth greene May;
Men seen alday, and reden eek in stories,
That after sharpe showres been victories.

This Troilus, whan he hir wordes herde,
Have ye no care, him liste nought to sleepe;
For it thoughte him no strokes of a yerde

1040. **passioun,** attack of jealousy. 1042. **habundance,** abundance; **bisy cure,** anxious care. 1043. **dooth,** makes; **disese,** distress. 1044. **wroth** angry. 1045. **devoir,** duty. 1046. **Wher so,** whichever; **ordal,** ordeal. 1047. **sort,** lot; **leste,** it may please. 1048. **preve,** test. 1049. **giltif,** guilty; **do me deye,** put me to death. 1052. **fille,** fell. 1055. **heed,** head. 1056. **wreigh,** covered; **sighte,** sighed. 1060. **morwe,** morning. 1063. **alday,** constantly. 1064. **showres,** battles. 1067. **thoughte,** seemed to; **yerde,** rod.

To heere or seen Criseide his lady weepe;
But wel he felte aboute his herte creepe,
For every tere which that Criseide asterte,°
The crampe of deeth to straine° him by the herte.

And in his minde he gan the time accurse
That he come there, and that that he was born,
For now is wikked° turned into worse:
And al that labour he hath doon biforn
He wende it lost, he thoughte he nas but lorn;°
"O Pandarus," thoughte he, "allas, thy wile
Serveth of nought, so wailaway the while."

And therwithal he heeng adown the heed,°
And fil on knees, and sorwefully he sighte.°
What mighte he sayn? He felte he nas but deed,
For wroth was she that sholde his sorwes lighte.°
But nathelees, whan that he speken mighte,
Than saide he thus, "God woot that of this game,
Whan al is wist,° thanne am I nought to blame."

Therwith the sorwe so his herte shette°
That from his yën fil ther nought a tere,
And every spirit his vigour in knette,°
So they astoned° or oppressed were;
The feeling of his sorwe or of his fere,
Or of ought elles, fled was out of towne,
And down he fil al sodeinly aswoune.°

This was no litel sorwe for to see,
But al was hust,° and Pandare up as faste:
"O nece, pees, or we be lost," quod he.
"Beeth nought agast." But certain, at the laste,

1070. asterte, escaped. **1071. deeth,** death; **straine,** constrain. **1074. wikked,** bad. **1076. wende,** thought; **lorn,** lost. **1079. heeng,** hung; **heed,** head. **1080. fil,** fell; **sighte,** sighed. **1082. lighte,** lighten. **1085. wist,** known. **1086. shette,** closed off. **1088.** i.e., And each of his bodily functions lost its power. **1089. astoned,** stunned. **1092. aswoune,** in a swoon. **1094. hust,** hushed.

For this or that he into bed him caste,
And saide, "O thief, is this a mannes herte?"
And of he rente al to his bare sherte,

And saide, "Nece, but ye helpe us now,
Allas, youre owene Troilus is lorn."
"Ywis, so wolde I and I wiste how,
Ful fain," quod she. "Allas that I was born!"
"Ye, nece, wol ye pullen out the thorn
That stiketh in his herte?" quod Pandare.
"Saye 'Al foryive,' and stinte al this fare."

"Ye, that to me," quod she, "ful levere were
Than al the good the sonne aboute gooth."
And therwithal she swoor him in his ere,
"Ywis, my dere herte, I am nought wroth,
Have here my trouthe and many another ooth.
Now speke to me, for it am I, Criseide"—
But al for nought: yit mighte he nought abraide.

Therwith his pous and paumes of his hondes
They gan to frote, and wete his temples twaine;
And to deliveren him fro bittre bondes
She ofte him kiste. And shortly for to sayne,
Him to revoken she dide al hir paine:
And at the laste he gan his breeth to drawe,
And of his swough soone after that adawe,

And gan bet minde and reson to him take.
But wonder sore he was abaist, ywis,
And with a sik whan he gan bet awake,
He saide, "O mercy, God, what thing is this?"
"Why do ye with youreselven thus amis?"

1099. of, off; **rente,** tore. **1100. but,** unless. **1101. lorn,** lost. **1102. and,** if; **wiste,** knew. **1103. fain,** gladly. **1106. stinte,** put an end to; **fare,** fuss. **1113. abraide,** come to his senses. **1114. pous,** pulse; **paumes,** palms. **1115. frote,** rub. **1118. revoken,** bring to his senses; **paine,** i.e., best. **1120. swough,** swoon; **adawe,** to awake. **1121. bet,** better. **1122. abaist,** abashed. **1123. sik,** sigh.

Quod tho Criseide. "Is this a mannes game?
What, Troilus, wol ye do thus for shame?"

And therwithal hir arm over him she laide,
And al foryaf, and ofte time him keste.°
He thanked hire, and to hire spak and saide
As fil° to purpos for his herte reste,
And she to that answerde him as hire leste,°
And with hir goodly wordes him disporte°
She gan, and ofte his sorwes to conforte.

Quod Pandarus, "For ought I can espyen,
This light nor I ne serven here of nought:
Light is nought good for sike° folkes yën.
But for the love of God, sin ye been brought
In thus good plit,° lat now no hevy thought
Been hanging in the hertes of you twaye"—
And bar the candel to the chimineye.°

Soone after this, though it no neede were,
Whan she swiche othes as hire liste devise
Hadde of him take, hire thoughte tho no fere,
Ne cause eek noon, to bidde him thennes rise.
Yit lasse° thing than othes may suffise
In many a caas; for every wight, I gesse,
That loveth wel meneth but gentilesse.

But in effect she wolde wite° anoon
Of what man and eek wher and also why
He jalous was, sin ther was cause noon;
And eek the signe that he took° it by,
She bad him that to telle hire bisily,
Or elles, certain, she bar him on honde°
That this was doon of malice, hire to fonde.°

1129. keste, kissed. **1131. fil,** fell. **1132. leste,** it pleased. **1133. disporte,** to cheer. **1137. sike,** sick. **1139. plit,** situation. **1141. bar,** bore; **chimineye,** fireplace. **1146. lasse,** smaller. **1149. wite,** learn. **1152. took,** i.e., understood. **1154. bar . . . honde,** accused him. **1155. fonde,** test.

Withouten more, shortly for to sayne,
He moste obeye unto his lady heeste,°
And for the lasse harm he moste feine:°
He saide hire whan she was at swich a feeste,
She mighte on him han looked at the leeste—
Noot I nought what: al dere ynough a risshe,°
As he that needes moste a cause fisshe.°

And she answerde, "Sweete, al° were it so,
What harm was that, sin I noon yvel° mene?
For by that God that boughte° us bothe two,
In alle thing is myn entente clene.
Swiche arguments ne been nought worth a bene.
Wol ye the childissh jalous countrefete?°
Now were it worthy that ye were ybete."°

Tho Troilus gan sorwefully for to sike:°
Lest she be wroth him thoughte his herte deide,
And saide, "Allas, upon my sorwes sike°
Have mercy, sweete herte myn Criseide.
And if that in tho° wordes that I saide
Be any wrong, I wol namore trespace.
Dooth what you list: I am al in youre grace."

And she answerde, "Of gilt misericorde.°
That is to sayn that I foryive al this;
And evere more on this night you recorde,°
And beeth wel war ye do namore amis."
"Nay, dere herte myn," quod he, "ywis."
"And now," quod she, "that I have doon° you smerte,
Foryive it me, myn owene sweete herte."

1157. heeste, command. **1158. feine,** pretend. **1161. al . . . risshe,** all worth a rush, i.e., of no importance. **1162. cause,** excuse; **fisshe,** fish up. **1163. al,** although. **1164. yvel,** evil. **1165. boughte,** redeemed. **1168. countrefete,** imitate. **1169. ybete,** beaten. **1170. sike,** sigh. **1172. sike,** sickly. **1174. tho,** those. **1177. Of gilt misericorde,** mercy for offense. **1179. you recorde,** remember. **1182. doon,** made.

This Troilus, with blisse of that supprised,
Putte al in Goddes hand, as he that mente
No thing but wel, and sodeinly avised,
He hire in armes faste to him hente;
And Pandarus, with a ful good entente,
Laide him to sleepe and saide, "If ye be wise,
Swouneth nought now, lest more folk arise."

What mighte or may the sely larke saye
Whan that the sperhawk hath him in his foot?
I can namore, but of thise ilke twaye,
To whom this tale sucre be or swoot,
Though that I tarye a yeer, som time I moot
After myn auctour tellen hir gladnesse,
As wel as I have told hir hevinesse.

Criseide, which that felte hire thus ytake—
As writen clerkes in hir bookes olde—
Right as an aspes leef she gan to quake,
Whan she him felte hire in his armes folde.
But Troilus, al hool of cares colde,
Gan thanken tho the blisful goddes sevene:
Thus sondry paines bringen folk to hevene.

This Troilus in armes gan hire straine,
And saide, "O sweete, as evere mote I goon,
Now be ye caught, now is ther but we twaine.
Now yeeldeth you, for other boote is noon."
To that Criseide answerde thus anoon,
"Ne hadde I er now, my sweete herte dere,
Been yolde, ywis, I were now nought here."

O sooth is said, that heled for to be
As of a fevre or other greet siknesse,

1186. **avised,** i.e., with his wits about him. 1187. **hente,** took. 1190. **Swouneth,** swoon. 1191. **sely,** innocent. 1192. **sperhawk,** sparrowhawk. 1194. **sucre,** sugar; **swoot,** sweet. 1195. **moot,** must. 1200. **aspes,** aspen. 1202. **hool,** well. 1205. **straine,** press. 1206. **mote,** may; **goon,** walk. 1208. **boote,** i.e., alternative. 1211. **yolde,** yielded.

Men moste drinke, as men may ofte see,
Ful bittre drinke; and for to han gladnesse
Men drinken ofte paine and greet distresse:
I mene it here as for this aventure
That thurgh a paine hath founden al his cure.

And now swetnesse seemeth more sweete
That bitternesse was assayed biforn;
For out of wo in blisse now they flete;°
Noon swich they felten sin they were born.
Now is this bet than bothe two be lorn:°
For love of God, take every womman heede
To werken thus, if it comth to the neede.

Criseide, al quit from every drede and teene,°
As she that juste cause hadde him to triste,°
Made him swich feeste it joye was to seene,
Whan she his trouthe and clene entente wiste;°
And as aboute a tree, with many a twiste,
Bitrent and writh° the sweete wodebinde,
Gan eech of hem in armes other winde.

And as the newe abaised° nightingale,
That stinteth° first whan she biginneth singe,
Whan that she heereth any hierde tale,°
Or in the hegges any wight stiringe,
And after siker dooth° hir vois out ringe,
Right so Criseide, whan she hir drede stente,°
Opened hir herte and tolde him hir entente.

And right as he that seeth his deeth yshapen,°
And dien moot° in ought that he may gesse,

1221. flete, float. **1223. bet,** better; **lorn,** lost. **1226. quit,** freed; **teene,** grief. **1227. triste,** trust. **1229. wiste,** knew. **1231. Bitrent,** encircles; **writh,** twines. **1233. newe abaised,** recently frightened. **1234. stinteth,** pauses. **1235. hierde tale,** shepherd talk. **1237. siker,** confident; **dooth,** makes. **1238. stente,** ended. **1240. yshapen,** prepared. **1241. moot,** must.

And sodeinly rescous dooth him escapen,
And from his deeth is brought in sikernesse,
For al this world in swich present gladnesse
Was Troilus, and hath his lady sweete.
With worse hap God lat us nevere meete!

Hir armes smale, hir straighte bak and softe,
Hir sides longe, flesshly, smoothe, and white,
He gan to stroke, and good thrift bad ful ofte
Hir snowissh throte, hir brestes rounde and lite.
Thus in this hevene he gan him to delite;
And therwithal a thousand time hire kiste,
That what to doon for joye unnethe he wiste.

Thanne saide he thus: "O Love, O Charitee,
Thy moder eek, Cytherea the sweete,
After thyselve next heried be she—
Venus mene I, the wel-willy planete;
And next that, Ymeneus, I thee greete:
For nevere man was to you goddes holde
As I, which ye han brought fro cares colde.

Benigne Love, thou holy bond of thinges,
Who so wol grace and list thee nought honouren,
Lo, his desir wol flee withouten winges;
For noldestou of bountee hem socouren
That serven best and most alway labouren,
Yit were al lost, that dar I wel sayn, certes,
But if thy grace passed oure desertes.

And for thou me, that coude leest deserve
Of hem that nombred been unto thy grace,

1242. **sodeinly,** unexpectedly; **rescous,** rescue; **dooth,** i.e., lets. **1243. sikernesse,** security. **1246. hap,** luck. **1249. good thrift bad,** i.e., blessed. **1250. lite,** small. **1253. unnethe,** hardly; **wiste,** knew. **1255. Cytherea,** Venus. **1256. heried,** praised. **1257. wel-willy,** benevolent. **1258. Ymeneus,** Hymen, god of nuptials. **1259. holde,** beholden. **1262. wol,** desires; **list,** wishes. **1264. noldestou,** if you did not wish; **bountee,** generosity; **socouren,** aid. **1267. But if,** unless; **passed,** exceeded.

Hast holpen, ther I likly was to sterve,
And me bistowed in so heigh a place
That thilke boundes may no blisse pace,
I can namore, but laude and reverence
Be to thy bountee and thyn excellence."

And therwithal Criseide anoon he kiste,
Of which, certain, she felte no disese,
And thus saide he, "Now wolde God I wiste,
Myn herte sweete, how I you mighte plese.
What man," quod he, "was evere thus at ese
As I, on which the faireste and the beste
That evere I sawgh deineth hir herte reste?

Here may men seen that mercy passeth right:
Th'experience of that is felt in me,
That am unworthy to so sweete a wight.
But herte myn, of youre benignitee,
So thinketh, though that I unworthy be,
Yit moot I neede amenden in som wise
Right thurgh the vertu of youre heigh servise.

And for the love of God, my lady dere,
Sin God hath wrought me for I shal you serve,
As thus I mene, he wol ye be my steere,
To do me live—if that you liste—or sterve,
So techeth me how that I may deserve
Youre thank, so that I thurgh myn ignoraunce
Ne do no thing that you be displesaunce.

For certes, fresshe wommanliche wif,
This dar I saye, that trouthe and diligence,
That shal ye finden in me al my lif;
N'I wol nat, certain, breke youre defence:

1270. **holpen,** helped; **sterve,** die. 1272. **pace,** pass. 1276. **disese,** displeasure. 1281. **deineth,** condescends. 1282. **passeth,** surpasses. 1287. **moot,** must. 1291. **wol,** desires that; **steere,** guide. 1292. **do,** make; **sterve,** die. 1299. **defence,** prohibition.

And if I do, present or in absence,
For love of God, lat slee° me with the deede,
If that it like° unto youre wommanhede."

"Ywis," quod she, "myn owene hertes lust,°
My ground of ese, and al myn herte dere,
Gramercy,° for on that is al my trust.
But lat us falle away fro this matere,
For it suffiseth this that said is here.
And at oo word, withouten repentaunce,
Welcome, my knight, my pees, my suffisaunce."°

Of hir delit or joyes oon the leeste°
Were impossible to my wit to saye,
But juggeth, ye that han been at the feeste
Of swich gladnesse, if that hem liste playe.
I can namore, but thus thise ilke twaye
That night, bitwixen drede and sikernesse,°
Felten in love the grete worthinesse.

O blisful night, of hem so longe ysought,
How blithe unto hem bothe two thou were!
Why n'hadde I swich oon with my soule ybought,
Ye, or the leeste joye that was there?
Away, thou foule daunger° and thou fere,
And lat hem in this hevene blisse dwelle,
That is so heigh that al ne can I telle.

But sooth is, though I can nat tellen al,
As can myn auctour of his excellence,
Yit have I said—and God toforn°—and shal
In every thing al hoolly his sentence;°
And if that ich, at Loves reverence,

1301. slee, slay. **1302. like,** please. **1303. lust,** desire. **1305. Gramercy,** many thanks. **1309. suffisaunce,** satisfaction. **1310. oon the leeste,** the least one. **1315. sikernesse,** confidence. **1321. daunger,** disdain. **1326. toforn,** before. **1327. hoolly,** wholly; **sentence,** general meaning.

Have any word in eeched for the beste,
Dooth therwithal right as youreselven leste.

For mine wordes, here and every part,
I speke hem alle under correccioun
Of you that feeling have in loves art,
And putte it al in youre discrecioun
T'encreesse or maken diminucioun
Of my langage, and that I you biseeche.
But now to purpos of my rather speeche:

Thise ilke two that been in armes laft,
So loth to hem asonder goon it were,
That eech from other wende been biraft,
Or elles, lo, this was hir moste fere:
That al this thing but nice dremes were;
For which ful ofte eech of hem saide, "O sweete,
Clippe ich you thus, or elles I it mete?"

And Lord, so he gan goodly on hire see,
And nevere his look ne bleinte from hir face,
And saide, "O dere herte, may it be
That it be sooth that ye been in this place?"
"Ye, herte myn, God thanke I of his grace,"
Quod tho Criseide, and therwithal him kiste,
That wher his spirit was for joye he niste.

This Troilus ful ofte hir yën two
Gan for to kisse, and saide, "O yën clere,
It weren ye that wroughte me swich wo,
Ye humble nettes of my lady dere.
Though ther be mercy writen in youre cheere,
God woot the text ful hard is, sooth, to finde:
How coude ye withouten bond me binde?"

1329. **in eeched,** added. 1330. **leste,** it please. 1337. **rather,** earlier; **speeche,** subject. 1338. **laft,** left. 1340. **wende,** thought to; **biraft,** separated. 1342. **nice,** foolish. 1344. **Clippe,** embrace; **mete,** am dreaming. 1345. **see,** look. 1346. **bleinte,** turned aside. 1351. **niste,** knew not. 1356. **cheere,** expression.

Therwith he gan hir faste in armes take,
And wel an hundred times gan he sike—
Nought swiche sorweful sikes as men make
For wo, or elles whan that folk been sike,
But esy sikes swiche as been to like,
That shewed his affeccion withinne:
Of swiche sikes coude he nought bilinne.

Soone after this they spake of sondry thinges,
As fil to purpos of this aventure,
And playing entrechaungeden hir ringes,
Of whiche I can nought tellen no scripture;
But wel I woot a brooch, gold and azure,
In which a rubye set was lik an herte,
Criseide him yaf, and stak it on his sherte.

Lord, trowe ye a covetous or a wrecche,
That blameth love and halt of it despit,
That of tho pans that he can mokre and crecche
Was evere yit yyiven him swich delit
As is in love, in oon point in som plit?
Nay doutelees, for also God me save,
So parfit joye may no nigard have.

They wol sayn "Yis," but Lord, so that they lie,
Tho bisy wrecches ful of wo and drede;
They callen love a woodnesse or folye,
But it shal falle hem as I shal you rede:
They shal forgoon the white and eek the rede,
And live in wo, ther God yive hem meschaunce,
And every lovere in his trouthe avaunce.

1360. sike, to sigh. **1362. sike,** sick. **1363. to like,** pleasing. **1365. bilinne,** cease. **1368. entrechaungeden,** exchanged. **1369. scripture,** i.e., motto. **1370. azure,** lapis lazuli. **1372. stak,** pinned. **1373. trowe,** believe; **covetous,** miser. **1374. halt,** holds. **1375. tho pans,** those pennies; **mokre,** hoard; **crecche,** amass. **1377.** i.e., As is in a single point of some circumstances of love. **1378. also,** so. **1379. parfit,** perfect. **1382. woodnesse,** madness. **1383. falle,** happen to; **rede,** tell. **1384. rede,** i.e., red wine.

As wolde God tho wrecches that despise
Servise of love hadde eres also longe
As hadde Mida, ful of coveitise,
And therto dronken hadde as hoot and stronge
As Crassus dide for his affectes wronge,
To techen hem that they been in the vice,
And loveres nought, although they holde hem nice.

Thise ilke two of whom that I you saye,
Whan that hir hertes wel assured were,
Tho gonne they to speken and to playe,
And eek rehercen how and whan and where
They knewe hem first, and every wo or fere
That passed was; but al swich hevinesse,
I thanke it God, was turned to gladnesse.

And evermo whan that hem fil to speke
Of any thing of swich a time agoon,
With kissing al that tale sholde breke,
And fallen in a newe joye anoon,
And diden al hir might, sin they were oon,
For to recoveren blisse and been at ese,
And passed wo with joye contrepese.

Reson wol nought that I speke of sleep,
For it accordeth nought to my matere:
Good woot they tooke of that ful litel keep;
But lest this night, that was to hem so dere,
Ne sholde in vain escape in no manere,
It was biset in joye and bisinesse
Of al that souneth into gentilesse.

1387. tho, those. **1389. Mida,** Midas: for a favor he had done to a god he was given the power to turn to gold whatever he touched; at another time for an offense to a god he was inflicted with a pair of ass's ears. **1391. affectes,** desires: after slaying the Roman general Crassus in battle, the Parthian king poured molten gold into his mouth. **1393. nice,** foolish. **1398. hem,** i.e., each other. **1401. hem fil,** they happened. **1402. agoon,** gone by. **1403. breke,** interrupt. **1407. contrepese,** to counterbalance. **1408. wol,** desires. **1410. keep,** heed. **1413. biset,** employed. **1414. souneth into,** relates to.

But whan the cok, commune astrologer,
Gan on his brest to bete and after crowe,
And Lucifer, the dayes messager,
Gan for to rise and out hir bemes throwe,
And eestward roos—to him that coude it knowe—
Fortuna Major, that anoon Criseide,
With herte soor, to Troilus thus saide:

"Myn hertes lif, my trust, al my plesaunce,
That I was born, allas, what me is wo,
That day of us moot make disseveraunce,
For time it is to rise and hennes go,
Or elles I am lost for everemo.
O night, allas, why niltou over us hove
As longe as whan Almena lay by Jove?

O blake night, as folk in bookes rede,
That shapen art by God this world to hide
At certain times with thy derke weede,
That under that men mighte in reste abide,
Wel oughten beestes plaine and folk thee chide,
That ther as day with labour wolde us breste,
That thou thus fleest, and deinest us nought reste.

Thou doost, allas, too shortly thyn office,
Thou rakle night, ther God, Makere of Kinde,
Thee for thyn haste and unkinde vice
So faste ay to oure hemisperie binde
That neveremore under the grounde thou winde:
For now for thou so hiest out of Troye
Have I forgoon thus hastily my joye."

1417. Lucifer, the planet Venus seen as the morning star. **1420. Fortuna Major,** ? a constellation. **1424. moot,** must; **disseveraunce,** separation. **1425. hennes,** hence. **1427. hove,** linger. **1428. Almena,** Alcmena: Jupiter caused the night to be extended to three times its normal length when he lay with Alcmena, the betrothed of Amphitryon, and begot Hercules on her. **1430. shapen,** created. **1431. weede,** i.e., cloak. **1433. plaine,** complain. **1434. breste,** afflict. **1435. deinest,** condescend to permit. **1436. office,** task. **1437. rakle,** impetuous; **ther,** may; **Kinde,** nature. **1439. hemisperie,** hemisphere. **1440. winde,** revolve. **1441. hiest,** hasten.

This Troilus, that with tho wordes felte,
As thoughte him tho, for pietous distresse
The bloody teres from his herte melte,
As he that nevere yit swich hevinesse
Assayed hadde out of so greet gladnesse,
Gan therwithal Criseide his lady dere
In armes straine, and saide in this manere:

"O cruel day, accusour of the joye
That night and love han stole and faste ywrien,
Accursed be thy coming into Troye,
For every bore hath oon of thy brighte yën.
Envious day, what list thee so to spyen?
What hastou lost? What seekest thou this place?—
Ther God thy light so quenche for his grace!

Allas, what have thise loveres thee agilt?
Despitous day, thyn be the paine of helle,
For many a lovere hastou slain and wilt:
Thy pouring in wol nowher late hem dwelle.
What proferestou thy light here for to selle?
Go selle it hem that smale seles grave—
We wol thee nought: us needeth no day have."

And eek the sonne Titan wolde he chide,
And saide, "O fool, wel may men thee despise,
That hast the dawing al night by thy side,
And suffrest hire so soone up fro thee rise,
For to disese loveres in this wise.
What, holde youre bed ther, thou and eek thy morwe:
I bidde God so yive you bothe sorwe."

Therwith ful sore he sighte and thus he saide,
"My lady right, and of my wele or wo

1444. pietous, piteous. **1447. Assayed,** experienced. **1449. straine,** press. **1450. accusour,** betrayer. **1451. ywrien,** hidden. **1453. bore,** chink. **1457.. agilt,** offended. **1458. Despitous,** malicious. **1460. late,** let. **1461. What,** why. **1462. seles,** seals; **grave,** engrave. **1466. dawing,** dawn. **1468. disese,** disturb. **1469. morwe,** morning. **1471. sighte,** sighed.

The welle and roote, O goodly myn Criseide,
And shal I rise, allas, and shal I so?
Now feele I that myn herte moot atwo,
For how sholde I my lif an houre save,
Sin that with you is al the lif ich have?

What shal I doon? for certes I noot how
Ne whan, allas, I shal the time see
That in this plit I may been eft with you;
And of my lif God woot how that shal be,
Sin that desir right now so biteth me
That I am deed anoon but I returne:
How sholde I longe, allas, fro you sojurne?

But nathelees, myn owene lady bright,
Yit were it so that I wiste outrely
That I, youre humble servant and youre knight,
Were in youre herte yset so fermely
As ye in myn—the which thing, trewely,
Me levere were than thise worldes twaine—
Yit sholde I bet enduren al my paine."

To that Criseide answerde right anoon,
And with a sik she saide, "O herte dere,
The game, ywis, so ferforth now is goon
That first shal Phebus fallen fro his spere,
And everich egle been the douves fere,
And everich rok out of his place sterte,
Er Troilus out of Creseides herte.

Ye been so deepe inwith myn herte grave
That, though I wolde it turne out of my thought,
As wisly verray God my soule save,

1473. welle, source. **1475. moot,** i.e., must break. **1480. plit,** situation. **1483. but,** unless. **1486. wiste,** knew; **outrely,** absolutely. **1491. bet,** better. **1493. sik,** sigh. **1494. ferforth,** far. **1495. Phebus,** Phoebus, the sun; **spere,** sphere. **1496. douves,** dove's; **fere,** mate. **1497. sterte,** start. **1499. inwith,** within; **grave,** buried. **1501. wisly,** surely.

To dien in the paine I coude nought;
And for the love of God that us hath wrought,
Lat in youre brain noon other fantasye
So creepe that it cause me to die.

And that ye me wolde han as faste in minde
As I have you, that wolde I you biseeche;
And if I wiste soothly that to finde,
God mighte nought a point my joyes eeche.
But herte myn, withouten more speeche,
Beeth to me trewe, or elles were it routhe,
For I am thyn, by God and by my trouthe.

Beeth glad forthy and live in sikernesse:
Thus saide I nevere er this, ne shal to mo;
And if to you it were a greet gladnesse
To turne ayain soone after that ye go,
As fain wolde I as ye that it were so,
As wisly God myn herte bringe to reste,"
And him in armes took and ofte keste.

Agains his wil, sith it moot needes be,
This Troilus up roos and faste him cledde,
And in his armes took his lady free
An hundred time, and on his way him spedde,
And with swiche wordes as his herte bledde
He saide, "Farewel, my dere herte sweete,
Ther God us graunte sounde and soone meete."

To which no word for sorwe she answerde,
So sore gan his parting hire distraine.
And Troilus unto his palais ferde,
As wo-bigoon as she was, sooth to sayne,

1502. **the paine,** i.e., torture. 1509. **eeche,** increase. 1511. **routhe,** pity. 1513. **forthy,** therefore; **sikernesse,** confidence. 1514. **mo,** others. 1515. **greet,** great. 1517. **fain,** glad. 1518. **wisly,** surely. 1519. **keste,** kissed. 1520. **moot,** must. 1521. **cledde,** clad. 1526. **Ther,** i.e., may; **sounde, in** health. 1528. **distraine,** distress. 1529. **ferde,** went.

So harde him wroong of sharp desir the paine,
For to been eft ther he was in plesaunce,
That it may nevere oute of his remembraunce.

Returned to his royal palais soone,
He softe into his bed gan for to slinke,
To sleepe longe, as he was wont to doone,
But al for nought—he may wel ligge and winke,
But sleep ne may ther in his herte sinke,
Thinking how she, for whom desir him brende,
A thousandfold was worth more than he wende;

And in his thought gan up and down to winde
Hir wordes alle, and every countenaunce,
And fermely empreessen in his minde
The leeste point that to him was plesaunce;
And verrailiche of thilke remembraunce
Desir al newe him brende, and lust to breede
Gan more than erst, and yit took he noọn heede.

Criseide also, right in the same wise
Of Troilus, gan in hir herte shette
His worthinesse, his lust, his deedes wise,
His gentilesse, and how she with him mette,
Thanking Love he so wel hire bisette,
Desiring ofte to han hir herte dere
In swich a plit she dorste make him cheere.

Pandare, amorwe which that comen was
Unto his nece and gan hire faire greete,
Saide, "Al this night so rained it, allas,
That al my drede is that ye, nece sweete,
Han litel leiser had to sleepe and mete.

1531. wroong, wrung. **1537. ligge,** lie. **1540. wende,** supposed. **1541. winde,** revolve. **1545. verrailiche,** verily. **1546. lust,** desire; **breede,** grow. **1547. erst,** before. **1549. shette,** enclose. **1550. lust,** vigor. **1552. bisette,** placed. **1554. plit,** situation. **1555. amorwe,** in the morning. **1559. mete,** dream.

Al night," quod he, "hath rain so do° me wake,
That some of us I trowe hir hedes ake."

And neer he cam and saide, "How stant° it now?
This merye morwe, nece, how can° ye fare?"
Criseide answerde, "Nevere the bet for you,
Fox that ye been. God yive youre herte care!
God helpe me so, ye caused al this fare.°
Trowe I," quod she, "for alle youre wordes white,°
O who so seeth you knoweth you ful lite."°

With that she gan hir face for to wrye°
With the sheete, and weex for shame al reed,°
And Pandarus gan under for to prye,
And saide, "Nece, if that I shal be deed,°
Have here a swerd and smiteth of myn heed."
With that his arm al sodeinly he thriste°
Under hir nekke, and at the laste hire kiste.

I passe al that which chargeth nought° to saye:
What, God foryaf his deeth, and she also
Foryaf, and with hir uncle gan to playe,
For other cause was ther noon but so.
But of this thing right to th'effect to go,
Whan time was hoom to hir hous she wente,
And Pandarus hath fully his entente.

Now turne we ayain to Troilus,
That restelees ful longe abedde lay,
And privily sente after Pandarus
To him to come in al the haste he may;
He cam anoon, nought ones saide he nay,
And Troilus ful sobrely he grette,°
And down upon the beddes side him sette.

1560. **do,** made. 1562. **stant,** stands. 1563. **can,** do. 1566. **fare,** business. 1567. **Trowe,** believe; **white,** i.e., plausible. 1568. **lite,** little. 1569. **wrye,** cover. 1570. **weex,** grew; **reed,** red. 1572. **deed,** dead. 1574. **thriste,** thrust. 1576. **chargeth nought,** is of no importance. 1588. **grette,** greeted.

This Troilus, with al th'affeccioun
Of freendes love that herte may devise,
To Pandarus on knees fil adown,
And er that he wolde of the place arise,
He gan him thanken in his beste wise:
An hundred sithe he gan the time blesse
That he was born to bringe him fro distresse.

He saide, "O freend, of freendes the alderbeste
That evere was, the soothe for to telle,
Thou hast in hevene ybrought my soule at reste
Fro Flegeton, the firy flood of helle;
That though I mighte a thousand times selle
Upon a day my lif in thy servise,
It mighte nought a mote in that suffise.

The sonne, which that al the world may see,
Sawgh nevere yit my lif, that dar I laye,
So inly fair and goodly as is she,
Whos I am al and shal til that I deye.
And that I am hires, dar I saye,
That thanked be the hye worthinesse
Of Love, and eek thy kinde bisinesse.

Thus hastou me no litel thing yyive,
For which to thee obliged be for ay
My lif; and why? for thurgh thyn help I live,
Or elles deed hadde I been many a day."
And with that word down in his bed he lay,
And Pandarus ful sobrely him herde,
Til al was said, and thanne he him answerde:

"My dere freend, if I have doon for thee
In any caas, God woot it is me lief,

1595. **sithe,** times. **1597. alderbeste,** best of all. **1600. Flegeton,** one of the rivers of Hades. **1603.** i.e., It could not in any way suffice as repayment. **1605. my,** i.e., in my; **laye,** wager. **1606. inly,** superlatively. **1610. bisinesse,** activity. **1619. lief,** i.e., pleasing.

And am as glad as man may of it be,
God helpe me so. But take now nat agrief°
That I shal sayn: be war of this meschief,
That ther as thou now brought art in thy blisse,
That thou thyself ne cause it nat to misse.°

For of Fortunes sharp adversitee
The worste kinde of infortune° is this:
A man to han been in prosperitee,
And it remembren whan it passed is.
Th'art wis ynough, forthy° do nat amis;
Be nought too rakel° though thou sitte warme,
For if thou be, certain it wol thee harme.

Thou art at ese, and hold thee wel therinne.
For also sur as reed° is every fir,
As greet a craft° is keepe wel as winne:
Bridle alway wel thy speeche and thy desir,
For worldly joye halt nought but by a wir.°
That preveth wel—it brest alday° so ofte—
Forthy neede is to werken with it softe."°

Quod Troilus, "I hope, and God toforn,
My dere freend, that I shal so me bere,°
That in my gilt ther shal no thing be lorn,°
N'I nil nought rakle as for to greven here.°
It needeth nought this matere ofte stere,°
For wistestou° myn herte wel, Pandare,
God woot of this thou woldest litel care."°

Tho gan he telle him of his glade night,
And wherof first his herte drede and how,
And saide, "Freend, as I am trewe knight,

1621. **agrief,** amiss. 1624. **misse,** i.e., disappear. 1626. **infortune,** misfortune. 1629. **forthy,** therefore. 1630. **rakel,** rash. 1633. **reed,** red. 1634. **craft,** art. 1636. **halt,** holds; **wir,** wire. 1637. **preveth,** is proved; **brest,** breaks; **alday,** constantly. 1638. **softe,** gently. 1640. **me bere,** behave. 1641. **lorn,** lost. 1642. **rakle,** behave rashly; **here,** her. 1643. **stere,** bring up. 1644. **wistestou,** if you knew. 1645. **care,** worry.

And by that faith I shal to God and you,
I hadde it nevere half so hote as now,
And ay the more that desir me biteth,
To love hire best the more it me deliteth.

I noot myself nought wisly what it is,
But now I feele a newe qualitee,
Ye, al another than I dide er this."
Pandare answerde and saide thus, that "He
That ones may in hevenes blisse be,
He feeleth otherwayes, dar I laye,
Than thilke time he first herde of it saye."

This is a word for al, that Troilus
Was nevere ful to speke of this matere,
And for to praisen unto Pandarus
The bountee of his righte lady dere,
And Pandarus to thanke and maken cheere;
This tale ay was spanne-newe to biginne,
Til that the night departed hem atwinne.

Soone after this, for that Fortune it wolde,
Ycomen was the blisful time sweete
That Troilus was warned that he sholde
There he was erst Criseide his lady meete,
For which he felte his herte in joye flete,
And faithfully gan alle the goddes herye—
And lat see now if that he can be merye.

And holden was the forme and al the wise
Of hir coming and of his also
As it was erst, which needeth nought devise.
But plainly to th'effect right for to go,
In joye and suretee Pandarus hem two

1649. shal, owe. **1650. hote,** hot. **1653. wisly,** surely. **1658. laye,** wager. **1661. ful,** too full. **1663. bountee,** virtues. **1665. spanne-newe,** brand-new. **1666. departed hem atwinne,** separated them. **1670. erst,** before. **1671. flete,** float. **1672. herye,** praise. **1676. devise,** describe. **1678. suretee,** security.

Abedde broughte whan that hem bothe leste;
And thus they been in quiete and in reste.

Nought it needeth you, sin they been met,
To axe° at me if that they blithe were,
For if it erst was wel, tho was it bet°
A thousandfold: this needeth nought enquere.°
Ago° was every sorwe and every fere,
And bothe ywis they hadde—and so they wende°—
As muche joye as herte may comprehende.

This is no litel thing of for to saye;
This passeth every wit for to devise,°
For eech of hem gan otheres lust° obeye;
Felicitee, which that thise clerkes wise
Comenden so, ne may nought here suffise;
This joye may nought ywriten be with inke;
This passeth al that herte may bithinke.

But cruel day, so wailaway the stounde,°
Gan for t'approche, as they by signes knewe,
For which hem thoughte feelen deethes wounde;
So wo was hem that chaungen gan hir hewe,°
And day they gonnen to despise al newe,
Calling it traitour, envious, and worse,
And bitterly the dayes light they curse.

Quod Troilus, "Allas, now am I war
That Pyros° and tho swifte steedes three,
Whiche that drawen forth the sonnes char,°
Han goon som bipath° in despit of me:
This maketh it so soone day to be,

1682. axe, ask. **1683. bet,** better. **1684. enquere,** to ask. **1685. Ago,** passed by. **1686. wende,** thought. **1689. passeth,** surpasses; **devise,** describe. **1690. lust,** desire. **1695. wailaway,** alas; **stounde,** time. **1698. hewe,** color. **1703. Pyros,** Pyrois, one of the four horses drawing the chariot of the sun. **1704. char,** chariot. **1705. bipath,** short-cut.

And for the sonne him hasteth thus to rise,
Ne shal I nevere doon him sacrifise."

But needes day departe hem moste soone,
And whan hir speeche doon was and hir cheere,
They twinne anoon as they were wont to doone,
And setten time of meeting eft yfere.
And many a night they wroughte in this manere.
And thus Fortune a time ledde in joye
Criseide and eek this kinges sone of Troye.

In suffisance, in blisse, and in singinges,
This Troilus gan al his lif to lede:
He spendeth, justeth, maketh festeyinges;
He yiveth freely ofte and chaungeth weede,
And heeld aboute him alway, out of drede,
A world of folk as cam him wel by kinde,
The fressheste and the beste he coude finde,

That swich a vois was of him and a stevene,
Thurghout the world, of honour and largesse,
That it up roong unto the gates of hevene;
And as in love he was in swich gladnesse
That in his herte he deemed, as I gesse,
That ther nis lovere in this world at ese
So wel as he, and thus gan love him plese.

The goodlihede or beautee which that kinde
In any other lady hadde yset,
Can nought the mountance of a knotte unbinde
Aboute his herte of al Criseides net;
He was so narwe ymasked and yknet

1709. departe, separate; **moste,** must. **1711. twinne,** part. **1712. eft,** again; **yfere,** together. **1718. justeth,** jousts; **festeyinges,** feasts. **1719. freely,** generously; **weede,** clothing. **1720. drede,** doubt. **1721. cam,** became; **by kinde,** naturally. **1723. stevene,** report. **1725. roong,** rang. **1730. kinde,** nature. **1732. mountance,** extent. **1734. ymasked and yknet,** enmeshed and snared.

That it undoon on any manere side,
That nil nought been, for ought that may bitide.

And by the hand ful ofte he wolde take
This Pandarus, and into gardin lede,
And swich a feeste and swich a proces make
Him of Criseide and of hir wommanhede,
And of hir beautee, that, withouten drede,
It was an hevene his wordes for to heere;
And thanne he wolde singe in this manere:

Troilus' Song

"Love, that of erthe and see hath governaunce;
Love, that his heestes hath in hevene hye;
Love, that with an hoolsom alliaunce
Halt peples joined as him list hem gie;
Love, that knitteth lawe of compaignye,
And couples dooth in vertu for to dwelle:
Bind this accord that I have told and telle.

That that the world with faith which that is stable
Diverseth so his stoundes concordinge;
That elements that been so discordable
Holden a bond perpetuelly duringe;
That Phebus moot his rosy day forth bringe,
And that the moone hath lordshipe over the nightes—
Al this dooth Love, ay heried be his mightes.

That that the see, that greedy is to flowen,
Constraineth to a certain ende so
His floodes, that so fiersly they ne growen

1739. **feeste,** rejoicing; **proces,** wonderful story. **1741. drede,** doubt. **1745. heestes,** commands. **1746. hoolsom,** wholesome. **1747. Halt,** holds; **list,** it pleases; **gie,** govern. **1748. knitteth,** weaves. **1749. dooth,** makes. **1751. That that,** the fact that. 1752. Varies so its harmonious seasons. **1753–54.** The fact that elements so discordant share a perpetually enduring relationship. 1755. **moot,** must. 1757. **dooth,** causes; **heried,** praised. **1758. greedy,** desirous; **flowen,** i.e., overflow.

To drenchen erthe and al for everemo;
And if that Love ought° lete his bridel go,
Alle that now loveth asonder sholde lepe,
And lost were al that Love halt now tohepe.°

So wolde God, that Auctour is of Kinde,°
That with his bond Love of his vertu liste°
To cerclen° hertes alle and faste binde,
That from his bond no wight the way out wiste;°
And hertes colde, hem wolde I that he twiste°
To maken hem love, and that him liste ay rewe°
On hertes sore, and keepe hem that been trewe."

In alle needes for the townes werre°
He was, and ay the firste in armes dight;°
And certainly, but if° that bookes erre,
Save Ector, most ydred of any wight;
And this encrees of hardinesse and might
Cam him of love, his lady° thank to winne,
That altered his spirit so withinne.

In time of trewe° on hawking wolde he ride,
Or elles hunte boor, bere,° or leoun—
The smale beestes leet he goon biside.°
And whan that he cam riding into town,
Ful ofte his lady from hir window down,
As fressh as faucon comen out of mewe,°
Ful redy was him goodly to salewe.°

And most of love and vertu was his speeche,
And in despit hadde alle wrecchednesse;°

1762. **ought**, in any way. 1764. **halt**, holds; **tohepe**, together in harmony. 1765. **Kinde**, nature. 1766. That, out of his virtue, it might please Love with his bond. 1767. **cerclen**, encircle. 1768. **wiste**, knew. 1769. **twiste**, would twist. 1770. **liste**, it would please; **rewe**, have pity. 1772. **werre**, war. 1773. **dight**, prepared. 1774. **but if**, unless. 1777. **lady**, lady's. 1779. **trewe**, truce. 1780. **boor**, boar; **bere**, bear. 1781. **goon biside**, escape. 1784. **mewe**, coop. 1785. **salewe**, greet. 1787. **wrecchednesse**, ill-behavior.

And doutelees, no neede was him biseeche
To honouren hem that hadde worthinesse,
And esen hem that weren in distresse;
And glad he was if any wight wel ferde,
That lovere was, whan he it wiste or herde.

For sooth to sayne, he lost heeld every wight
But if he were in Loves heigh servise—
I mene folk that oughte it been of right;
And over al this, so wel coude he devise
Of sentement, and in so uncouth wise,
Al his array, that every lovere thoughte
That al was wel, what so he saide or wroughte.

And though that he be come of blood royal,
Him liste of pride at no wight for to chace;
Benigne he was to eech in general,
For which he gat him thank in every place.
Thus wolde Love—yheried be his grace—
That pride and ire, envye and avarice,
He gan to flee, and everich other vice.

Thou lady bright, the doughter to Dione,
Thy blinde and winged sone eek, daun Cupide,
Ye sustren nine eek that by Elicone
In hil Parnaso listen for t'abide,
That ye thus fer han deined me to gide—
I can namore, but sin that ye wol wende,
Ye heried been for ay withouten ende.

Thurgh you have I said fully in my song
Th'effect and joye of Troilus servise,

1790. esen, comfort. **1791. ferde,** fared. **1792. wiste,** knew. **1794. But if,** unless. **1795. it,** i.e., in the service of love. **1796–98. coude . . . array,** ? he could make all his outward appearance conform with his inward feeling, and in so striking a manner. **1801. chace,** harass. **1803. gat,** got. **1804. yheried,** praised. **1807. Dione,** Venus' mother. **1809. sustren,** sisters, i.e., the Muses; **Elicone,** Helicon. **1810. Parnaso,** Parnassus; **listen,** are pleased. **1811. fer,** far. **1813. heried,** praised.

Al be that ther was some disese among,°
As to myn auctour listeth° to devise.
My thridde° book now ende ich in this wise,
And Troilus, in lust° and in quiete,
Is with Criseide, his owene herte sweete.

BOOK FOUR

The Prologue

But al too litel, wailaway° the while,
Lasteth swich joye, ythanked be Fortune,
That seemeth trewest whan she wol bigile,
And can to fooles so hir song entune°
That she hem hent and blent,° traitour commune:
And whan a wight is from hir wheel ythrowe,
Thanne laugheth she, and maketh him the mowe.°

From Troilus she gan hir brighte face
Away to writhe,° and took of him noon heede,
But caste him clene out of his lady° grace;
And on hir wheel she sette up Diomede;
For which myn herte right now ginneth bleede,
And now my penne, allas, with which I write,
Quaketh for drede of that I moste° endite.

For how Criseide Troilus forsook—
Or at the leeste how that she was unkinde—
Moot° hennesforth been matere of my book,
As writen folk thurgh which it is in minde:

1816. Al, although; **disese,** distress; **among,** as well. **1817. listeth, it** pleases. **1818. thridde,** third. **1819. lust,** pleasure.

1. wailaway, alas. **4. entune,** intone. **5. hent,** seizes; **blent,** blinds. **7. maketh . . . mowe,** makes a face at him. **9. writhe,** turn. **10. lady,** lady's. **14. that,** what; **moste,** must. **17. Moot,** must.

Allas that they sholde evere cause finde
To speke hire harm—and if they on hire lie,
Ywis, hemself sholde han the vilainye.

O ye Erines, Nightes doughtren three,
That endelees complainen evere in pine,
Megera, Alete, and eek Tesiphone;
Thou cruel Mars eek, fader to Quirine,
This ilke ferthe book me helpeth fine,
So that the los of lif and love yfere
Of Troilus be fully shewed here.

The Story

Ligging in host, as I have said er this,
The Greekes stronge aboute Troye town,
Bifel that whan that Phebus shining is
Upon the brest of Ercules leoun,
That Ector, with ful many a bold baroun,
Caste on a day with Greekes for to fighte,
As he was wont to greve hem what he mighte.

Noot I how long or short it was bitweene
This purpos and that day they fighten mente,
But on a day, wel armed bright and sheene,
Ector and many a worthy wight out wente,
With spere in hande and bigge bowes bente,
And in the beerd, withouten lenger lette,
Hir fomen in the feeld anoon hem mette.

22. **Erines,** Erinyes, Furies. 24. Megaera, Alecto, and also Tisiphone. 25. **Quirine,** Quirinus, Romulus. 26. **ferthe,** fourth; **fine,** finish. 27. **yfere,** together. 29. **Ligging,** lying. 31–2. It happened that when the sun is shining in the Sign of the Lion (the zodiacal sign is here identified with the Nemean lion that Hercules slew). 34. **Caste,** planned. 36. **Noot,** know not. 38. **sheene,** shining. 41. **in the beerd,** i.e., face to face; **lette,** delay.

The longe day with speres sharpe ygrounde,
With arwes, dartes, swerdes, maces felle,
They fighten and bringen hors and man to grounde,
And with hir axes out the braines quelle;
But in the laste showr, sooth for to telle,
The folk of Troye hemselven so misledden
That with the worse at night hoomward they fledden.

At which day was taken Antenor,
Maugree Polydamas or Monesteo,
Santippe, Sarpedon, Polynestor,
Polyte, or eek the Trojan daun Rupheo,
And othere lasse folk as Phebuseo,
So that for harm that day the folk of Troye
Dredden to lese a greet part of hir joye.

Of Priamus was yive at Greek requeste
A time of trewe, and tho they gonnen trete,
Hir prisoners to chaungen, meste and leeste,
And for the surplus yiven sommes grete:
This thing anoon was couth in every streete,
Bothe in th'assege, in town, and every where,
And with the firste it cam to Calcas ere.

Whan Calcas knew thise tretis sholde holde,
In consistorye among the Greekes soone
He gan in thringe forth with lordes olde,
And sette him there as he was wont to doone;
And with a chaunged face hem bad a boone,
For love of God, so doon that reverence
To stinte noise and yive him audience.

43. **ygrounde,** whetted. 44. **felle,** fell, cruel. 46. **quelle,** smite. 47. **showr,** onslaught. 48. **misledden,** misconducted. 51. **Maugree,** despite; **Polydamas,** etc., most of these Trojans were apparently not captured, but are mentioned merely as attempting to rescue Antenor. 53. **daun,** lord. 54. **lasse,** lesser. 56. **lese,** lose. 58. **trewe,** truce; **tho,** then. 59. **meste,** greatest. 60. **sommes,** sums. 61. **couth,** known. 62. **assege,** siege, i.e., Greek camp. 63. **ere,** ear. 64. **tretis,** terms of truce. 65. **consistorye,** assembly. 66. **in thringe,** press in. 68. **hem bad,** he asked them. 70. **stinte,** put an end to.

Thanne saide he thus: "Lo, lordes mine, ich was
Troyan, as it is knowen out of drede;
And if that you remembre, I am Calcas
That alderfirst yaf confort to youre neede,
And tolde wel how that ye sholden speede—
For dredelees thurgh you shal in a stounde
Been Troye ybrend and beten down to grounde.

And in what forme or in what manere wise
This town to shende and al youre lust t'acheve,
Ye han er this wel herd it me devise:
This knowe ye, my lordes, as I leve.
And for the Greekes weren me so leve,
I cam myself, in my propre persone,
To teche in this how you was best to doone,

Having unto my tresor ne my rente
Right no resport to respect of youre ese;
Thus al my good I lefte and to you wente,
Weening in this you lordes for to plese.
But al this los ne dooth me no disese—
I vouche sauf, as wisly have I joye,
For you to lese al that I have in Troye,

Save of a doughter that I lefte, allas,
Sleeping at hoom whan out of Troye I sterte.
O sterne, O cruel fader that I was,
How mighte I have in that so hard an herte?
Allas I ne hadde ybrought hire in hir sherte!
For sorwe of which I wol nought live tomorwe,
But if ye lordes rewe upon my sorwe.

72. **drede,** doubt. 74. **alderfirst,** first of all. 75. **speede,** succeed. 76. **dredelees,** doubtless; **stounde,** while. 77. **ybrend,** burnt. 79. **shende,** destroy; **lust,** desire. 81. **leve,** believe. 82. **for,** because; **leve,** dear. 84. **propre,** own. 85. **rente,** income. 86. **resport,** regard; **to respect of,** i.e., in comparison with my regard for. 88. **Weening,** supposing. 89. **disese,** distress. 90. **wisly,** surely. 91. **lese,** lose. 93. **sterte,** stole. 96. **sherte,** shift. 98. **But if,** unless; **rewe,** have pity.

For by that cause I sawgh no time er now
Hire to deliveren, ich holden have my pees;
But now or nevere, if that it like you,
I may hire have right soone, doutelees.
O, help and grace amonges al this prees!°
Rewe on this olde caitif in distresse,
Sin I thurgh you have al this hevinesse.

Ye have now caught and fettred in prisoun
Troyans ynowe, and if youre willes be,
My child with oon may have redempcioun;
Now for the love of God, and of bountee,°
Oon of so fele,° allas, so yive him me:
What neede were it this prayere for to werne,°
Sin ye shul bothe have folk and town as yerne?°

On peril of my lif, I shal nat lie,
Appollo hath me told it faithfully;
I have eek founde it by astronomye,°
By sort,° and by augurye eek trewely;
And dar wel saye the time is faste by
That fir and flaumbe on al the town shal sprede,
And thus shal Troye turne to asshen dede.°

For certain Phebus and Neptunus bothe,
That makeden the walles of the town,
Been with the folk of Troye alway so wrothe,
That they wol bringe it to confusioun,
Right in despit of King Lameadoun:°
By cause he nolde payen hem hir hire,°
The town of Troye shal been set on fire."

103. **prees,** throng. 109. **bountee,** generosity. 110. **fele,** many. 111. **werne,** refuse. 112. **as yerne,** at once. 115. **astronomye,** astrology. 116. **sort,** divination. 119. **dede,** dead. 124. **Lameadoun,** Laomedon, the founder of Troy; his offense to Phoebus Apollo and Neptune was one of the causes of the city's fall. 125. **hire,** i.e., the wages due them for their services to Laomedon.

Telling his tale, alway this olde greye,
Humble in his speeche and in his looking eke,
The salte teres from his yën twaye
Ful faste ronnen down by either cheeke;
So longe he gan of socour hem biseeke,
That, for to hele him of his sorwes sore,
They yave him Antenor withouten more.

But who was glad ynough but Calkas tho?
And of this thing ful soone his needes laide
On hem that sholden for the tretis go;
And hem for Antenor ful ofte prayde
To bringen hoom king Troas and Criseide;
And whan Priam his save-garde sente,
Th'embassadours to Troye straight they wente.

The cause ytold of hir coming, the olde
Priam the king ful soone in general
Leet herupon his parlement to holde,
Of which th'effect rehercen you I shal;
Th'embassadours been answerd for final:
Th'eschaunge of prisoners and al this neede
Hem liketh wel, and forth in they proceede

This Troilus was present in the place
Whan axed was for Antenor Criseide,
For which ful soone chaungen gan his face,
As he that with tho wordes wel neigh deide;
But nathelees he no word to it saide:
Lest men sholde his affeccion espye,
With mannes herte he gan his sorwe drie,

And ful of anguissh and of grisly drede
Abood what lordes wolde unto it saye;
And if they wolde graunte—as God forbede!—

130. ronnen, ran. **131. biseeke,** beseech. **135. needes,** requirements. **136. tretis,** treaty. **139. save-garde,** safe-conduct. **147. liketh,** pleases. **149. axed,** asked. **154. drie,** endure. **156. Abood,** i.e., waited to see.

Th'eschaunge of hire, thanne thoughte he thinges twaye:
First how to save hir honour, and what waye
He mighte best th'eschaunge of hire withstonde;
Ful faste he caste how al this mighte stonde.

Love him made al prest to doon hire bide,
And rather dien than she sholde go;
But Reson saide him on that other side,
"Withouten assent of hire ne do nat so,
Lest for thy werk she wolde be thy fo,
And sayn that thurgh thy medling is yblowe
Youre bother love ther it was erst unknowe."

For which he gan deliberen for the beste
That, though the lordes wolde that she wente,
He wolde late hem graunte what hem leste,
And telle his lady first what that they mente;
And whan that she hadde said him hir entente,
Therafter wolde he werken also blive,
Though al the world ayain it wolde strive.

Ector, which that wel the Greekes herde
For Antenor how they wolde han Criseide,
Gan it withstonde, and sobrely answerde:
"Sires, she nis no prisoner," he saide.
"I noot on you who that this charge laide,
But on my part ye may eftsoones hem telle
We usen here no womman for to selle."

The noise of peple up sterte thanne at ones,
As breme as blase of straw yset on fire—
For infortune it wolde for the nones

161. caste, considered. **162. prest,** eager; **doon,** make. **165. hire,** her. **167. yblowe,** made public. **168. Youre bother love,** the love of you both; **erst,** before. **169. deliberen,** deliberate. **171. leste,** it pleased. **174. also blive,** at once. **180. noot,** know not. **181. eftsoones,** in response. **182. usen,** are accustomed. **184. breme,** fierce. **185. infortune,** bad luck; **for the nones,** on this occasion.

They sholden hir confusion° desire.
"Ector," quod they, "what gost° may you inspire
This womman thus to shilde, and doon° us lese
Daun Antenor? A wrong way now ye chese!°

That is so wis and eek so bold baroun,
And we han neede to folk,° as men may see:
He is eek oon the grettest° of this town.
O Ector, lat tho fantasies be!
O king Priam," quod they, "thus segge° we,
That al oure vois is to forgoon° Criseide,"
And to deliveren Antenor they prayde.

O Juvenal° lord, trewe is thy sentence,
That litel witen folk what is to yerne,°
That° they ne finde in hir desir offence,
For cloude of errour let° hem to discerne
What best is; and lo, here ensample as yerne:°
This folk desiren now deliveraunce
Of Antenor, that broughte hem to meschaunce.

For he was after traitour to the town
Of Troye. Allas, they quite him out too rathe!°
O nice° world, lo, thy discrecioun!
Criseide, which that nevere dide hem scathe,°
Shal now no lenger in hir blisse bathe;
But Antenor, he shal come hoom to towne,
And she shal out: thus saide here and houne.°

For which delibered° was by parlement
For Antenor to yeelden out Criseide,

186. **hir,** i.e., their own; **confusion,** ruin. 187. **gost,** spirit, i.e., mad idea. 188. **shilde,** defend; **doon,** make; **lese,** lose. 189. **Daun,** lord; **chese,** choose. 191. **to folk,** i.e., of warriors. 192. **oon the grettest,** one of the greatest. 194. **segge,** say. 195. **forgoon,** give up. 197. **Juvenal,** Roman satirist, known to the Middle Ages for his moralizations. 198. **witen,** know; **is to yerne,** ought to be desired. 199. **That,** so that. 200. **let,** impedes. 201. **as yerne,** i.e., at hand. 205. **quite,** redeem; **rathe,** soon. 206. **nice,** foolish. 207. **scathe,** harm. 210. **here and houne,** ? high and low. 211. **delibered,** decided.

And it pronounced° by the president,
Although that Ector "Nay," ful ofte prayde.
And finally, what wight that it withsaide,
It was for nought: it moste° been and sholde,
For substance° of the parlement it wolde.

Departed out of parlement eechone,
This Troilus, withouten wordes mo,
Unto his chambre spedde him faste allone,
But if° it were a man of his or two,
The whiche he bad out faste for to go,
By cause he wolde sleepen, as he saide:
And hastily upon his bed him laide.

And as in winter leves been biraft,°
Eech after other, til the tree be bare,
So that ther nis but bark and braunche ylaft,°
Lith Troilus biraft° of eech welfare,
Ybounden in the blake bark of care,
Disposed wood out of his wit to braide,°
So sore him sat the chaunging° of Criseide.

He rist him up and every dore he shette,°
And window eek, and tho this sorweful man
Upon his beddes side adown him sette,
Ful lik a deed image,° pale and wan;
And in his brest the heped° wo bigan
Out breste,° and he to werken in this wise
In his woodnesse,° as I shal you devise.

Right as the wilde bole° biginneth springe,
Now here, now ther, ydarted° to the herte,
And of his deeth roreth in complaininge,

213. **pronounced,** decreed. 216. **moste,** must. 217. **substance,** majority. 221. **But if,** unless. 225. **biraft,** removed. 227. **ylaft,** left. 228. **Lith,** lies; **biraft,** deprived. 230. **wood,** mad; **braide,** go. 231. **sat,** i.e., affected; **chaunging,** exchange. 232. **rist,** rises; **shette,** shut. 235. **deed,** dead; **image,** statue. 236. **heped,** piled up. 237. **breste,** burst. 238. **woodnesse,** madness. 239. **bole,** bull. 240. **ydarted,** pierced.

Right so gan he aboute the chambre sterte,°
Smiting his brest ay with his fistes smerte;°
His heed° to the wal, his body to the grounde,
Ful ofte he swapped, himselven to confounde.°

His yën two, for pietee° of herte,
Out stremeden as swifte welles° twaye;
The hye sobbes of his sorwes smerte
His speeche him refte—unnethes° mighte he saye,
"O deeth, allas, why niltou do° me deye?
Accursed be that day which that Nature
Shoop me to been a lives° creature."

But after, whan the furye and al the rage,
Which that his herte twiste and faste threste,°
By lengthe of time somwhat gan assuage,
Upon his bed he laide him down to reste;
But tho bigonne his teres more out breste,°
That wonder is the body may suffise°
To half this wo which that I you devise.°

Thanne saide he thus: "Fortune, allas the while,
What have I doon? what have I thus agilt?°
How mightestou for routhe° me bigile?
Is ther no grace, and shal I thus be spilt?°
Shal thus Criseide away for that° thou wilt?
Allas, how maistou in thyn herte finde
To been to me thus cruel and unkinde?

Have I thee nought honoured al my live,
As thou wel woost,° above the goddes alle?
Why wiltou me fro joye thus deprive?

242. **sterte,** pace. 243. **smerte,** hard. 244. **heed,** head. 245. **swapped,** dashed; **confounde,** i.e., kill. 246. **pietee,** pity. 247. **welles,** springs. 249. **him refte,** took away from him; **unnethes,** with difficulty. 250. **do,** make. 252. **Shoop,** created; **lives,** living. 254. **twiste,** twisted; **threste,** constricted. 257. **breste,** burst. 258. **suffise,** be strong enough. 259. **devise,** describe. 261. **agilt,** offended. 262. **routhe,** pity. 263. **spilt,** ruined. 264. **for that,** because. 268. **woost,** know.

O Troilus, what may men now thee calle
But wrecche of wrecches, out of honour falle
Into miserye, in which I wol biwaile
Criseide, allas, til that the breeth me faile.

Allas, Fortune, if that my lif in joye
Displesed hadde unto thy foule envye,
Why ne haddestou my fader, king of Troye,
Biraft the lif, or doon° my bretheren die,
Or slain myself that thus complaine and crye?—
I, combre-world,° that may of no thing serve,
But evere die, and nevere fully sterve.°

If that Criseide allone were me laft,°
Nought roughte I° whider thou woldest me steere.
And hire,° allas, thanne hastou me biraft?
But everemore, lo, this is thy manere,
To reve a wight that° most is to him dere,
To preve in that thy geerful° violence:
Thus am I lost; ther helpeth no defence.

O verray lord of love, O God, allas,
That knowest best myn herte and al my thought,
What shal my sorweful lif doon in this cas,
If I forgo that I so dere have bought?
Sin ye Criseide and me han fully brought
Into youre grace, and bothe oure hertes seled,°
How may ye suffre, allas, it be repeled?°

What may I doon? I shal, whil I may dure°
On live in torment and in cruel paine,
This infortune or this disaventure°
Allone as I was born, ywis, complaine;

277. **Biraft,** taken away; **doon,** made. 279. **combre-world,** world-cumberer. 280. **sterve,** perish. 281. **me laft,** left to me. 282. **roughte I,** I would not care. 283. **hire,** her. 285. **reve,** take from; **that,** what. 286. **preve,** prove; **geerful,** changing. 293. **seled,** sealed. 294. **repeled,** nullified. 295. **dure,** endure. 297. **infortune,** misfortune; **disaventure,** misadventure.

Ne nevere wol I seen it shine or raine,
But ende I wol, as Edippe in derknesse,
My sorweful lif, and dien in distresse.

O wery gost, that errest to and fro,
Why niltou fleen out of the wofuleste
Body that evere mighte on grounde go?
O soule lurking in this wo unneste,
Flee forth out of myn herte, and lat it breste,
And folwe alway Criseide, thy lady dere:
Thy righte place is now no lenger here.

O woful yën two, sin youre disport
Was al to seen Criseides yën brighte,
What shul ye doon but for my disconfort
Stonden for nought and weepen out youre sighte,
Sin she is queint that wont was you to lighte?
In vain fro this forth have ich yën twaye
Yformed, sin youre vertu is awaye.

O my Criseide, O lady sovereine
Of this woful soule that thus crieth,
Who shal now yiven confort to thy paine?
Allas, no wight; but whan myn herte dieth,
My spirit, which that so unto you hieth,
Receive in gree, for that shal ay you serve:
Forthy no fors is though the body sterve.

O ye loveres, that heigh upon the wheel
Been set of Fortune in good aventure,
God leve that ye finde ay love of steel,
And longe mote youre lif in joye endure!
But whan ye comen by my sepulture,

300. **Edippe,** Oedipus, who died blind. 302. **gost,** spirit; **errest,** wander. 303. **fleen,** fly. 305. **unneste,** deprived of nesting place. 306. **breste,** break. 312. **Stonden . . . nought,** exist for no purpose. 313. **queint,** quenched. 315. **Yformed,** i.e., provided me. 320. **hieth,** hastens. 321. **gree,** favor. 322. **Forthy,** therefore; **fors,** matter; **sterve,** die. 325. **leve,** permit. 326. **mote,** may. 327. **sepulture,** sepulchre.

Remembreth that youre felawe resteth there—
For I loved eek, though ich unworthy were.

O olde, unhoolsom, and mislived man,
Calcas I mene, allas, what ailed thee
To been a Greek, sin thou art born Troyan?
O Calcas, which that wolt my bane be,
In cursed time was thou born for me!
As wolde blisful Jove for his joye
That I thee hadde wher I wolde in Troye!"

A thousand sikes hotter than the gleede
Out of his brest eech after other wente,
Medled with plaintes newe his wo to feede,
For which his woful teres nevere stente;
And shortly, so his paines him torente,
And weex so maat, that joye or penaunce
He feeleth noon, but lith forth in a traunce.

Pandare, which that in the parlement
Hadde herd what every lord and burgeis saide,
And how ful graunted was by oon assent
For Antenor to yeelden so Criseide,
Gan wel neigh wood out of his wit to braide,
So that for wo he niste what he mente,
But in a rees to Troilus he wente.

A certain knight, that for the time kepte
The chambre dore, undide it him anoon;
And Pandare, that ful tendreliche wepte,
Into the derke chambre, as stille as stoon,
Toward the bed gan softely to goon,
So confus that he niste what to saye:
For verray wo his wit was neigh awaye.

330. unhoolsom, unhealthy; **mislived,** bad-living. **333. bane,** destruction. **337. sikes,** sighs. **339. Medled,** mingled; **plaintes,** complaints. **340. stente,** ceased. **341. torente,** tore apart. **342. weex,** he grew; **maat,** exhausted; **penaunce,** sorrow. **343. lith,** lies. **348. wood,** mad; **braide,** go. **349. niste,** knew not. **350. rees,** rush. **351 kepte,** guarded.

And with his cheere and looking al totorn°
For sorwe of this, and with his armes folden,
He stood this woful Troilus biforn,
And on his pitous face he gan biholden.
But Lord, so ofte gan his herte colden,
Seeing his freend in wo, whos hevinesse
His herte slow,° as thoughte him, for distresse.

This woful wight, this Troilus, that felte
His freend Pandare ycomen him to see,
Gan as the snow ayain° the sonne melte;
For which this sorweful Pandare of pitee
Gan for to weepe as tendreliche as he.
And spechelees thus been thise ilke twaye,
That neither mighte oo word for sorwe saye.

But at the laste this woful Troilus,
Neigh deed for smert, gan bresten° out to rore,
And with a sorweful noise he saide thus,
Among his sobbes and his sikes° sore:
"Lo, Pandare, I am deed° withouten more.
Hastou nat herd at parlement," he saide,
"For Antenor how lost is my Criseide?"

This Pandarus, ful deed and pale of hewe,
Ful pitously answerde and saide, "Yis,
As wisly° were it fals as it is trewe,
That I have herd, and woot° al how it is.
O mercy God, who wolde have trowed° this?
Who wolde have wend that in so litel a throwe°
Fortune oure joye wolde han overthrowe?

For in this world ther is no creature,
As to my doom,° that evere saw ruine

358. **cheere,** manner; **totorn,** ravaged. 364. **slow,** slew. 367. **ayain,** i.e., in. 373. **deed,** dead; **smert,** pain; **bresten,** burst. 375. **sikes,** sighs. 379. **deed,** deadly. 381. **wisly,** surely. 382. **woot,** know. 383. **trowed,** believed. 384. **wend,** thought; **throwe,** space. 387. **doom,** judgment.

Straunger than this thurgh caas° or aventure.
But who may al eschewe or al divine?°
Swich is this world. Forthy I thus define:°
Ne truste no wight to finden in Fortune
Ay propretee;° hir yiftes been commune.

But tel me this: why thou art now so mad
To sorwen thus? Why listou° in this wise,
Sin thy desir al hoolly hastou had,
So that by right it oughte ynough suffise?
But I, that nevere felte in my servise
A freendly cheere or looking of an yë,
Lat me thus weepe and wailen til I die.

And over al this, as thou wel woost thyselve,
This town is ful of ladies al aboute,
And to my doom fairer than swiche twelve°
As evere she was shal I finde in som route,°
Ye, oon or two, withouten any doute.
Forthy be glad, myn owene dere brother:
If she be lost, we shal recovere another.

What, God forbede alway that eech plesaunce
In oo thing were and in noon other wight:
If oon can singe, another can wel daunce;
If this be goodly, she is glad and light;
And this is fair, and that can good aright:°
Eech for his vertu holden is for dere,
Bothe heroner and faucoun for rivere.°

And eek, as writ Zanzis° that was ful wis,
The newe love out chaseth ofte the olde,

388. **caas,** chance. 389. i.e., But who can avoid every pitfall or foresee everything? 390. **Forthy,** therefore; **define,** conclude. 392. **Ay propretee,** i.e., what always conforms to your wish. 394. **listou,** do you lie. 402. **fairer . . . twelve,** twelve times fairer. 403. **route,** throng. 411. **can good aright,** knows how to handle herself. 413. **heroner,** heron-hawk; **faucon,** falcon; **rivere,** i.e., hawking ground. 414. **writ,** writes; **Zanzis,** a supposed writer.

And upon newe caas lith newe avis.°
Thenk eek thy lif to saven artou holde.°
Swich fir by proces shal of kinde colde:°
For sin it is but casuel plesaunce,
Som caas° shal putte it out of remembraunce.

For also sur as day comth after night,
The newe love, labour, or other wo,
Or elles selde-seeing° of a wight,
Doon olde affeccions alle overgo.°
And for thy part thou shalt have oon of tho
T'abregge° with thy bittre paines smerte:
Absence of hire shal drive hire out of herte."

Thise wordes saide he for the nones° alle,
To helpe his freend, lest he for sorwe deide.
For doutelees, to doon his wo to falle,°
He roughte nought what unthrift° that he saide.
But Troilus, that neigh for sorwe deide,
Took litel heede of al that evere he mente:
Oon ere it herde, at other out it wente.

But at the laste he answerde and saide, "Freend,
This leechecraft,° or heled thus to be,
Were wel sitting° if that I were a feend—
To traisen° a wight that trewe is unto me.
I praye God lat this conseil nevere ythee,°
But do me rather sterve° anoonright here,
Er I thus do as thou me woldest lere.°

She that I serve, ywis, what so thou saye,
To whom myn herte inhabit is° by right,

416. i.e., And new circumstances require new attitudes. 417. **holde,** bound. 418. **by proces,** in due course; **of kinde,** by nature; **colde,** cool. 420. **caas,** i.e., new situation. 423. **selde-seeing,** seldom-seeing. 424. **Doon,** make; **overgo,** pass away. 426. **abregge,** assuage. 428. **nones,** occasion. 430. **doon,** make; **falle,** decrease. 431. **roughte,** cared; **unthrift,** nonsense. 436. **leechecraft,** medicine. 437. **sitting,** suitable. 438. **traisen,** betray. 439. **ythee,** succeed. 440. **do,** make; **sterve,** die. 441. **lere,** teach. 443. **inhabit is,** i.e., is given.

Shal han me hoolly hires til that I deye.
For Pandarus, sin I have trouthe hire hight,
I wol nat been untrewe for no wight,
But as hir man I wol ay live and sterve,
And nevere other creature serve.

And ther thou saist thou shalt as faire finde
As she, lat be make no comparisoun
To creature yformed here by kinde.
O leve Pandare, in conclusioun,
I wol nat been of thyn opinioun
Touching al this; for which I thee biseeche,
So hold thy pees: thou sleest me with thy speeche.

Thou biddest me I sholde love another
Al fresshly newe, and late Criseide go:
It lith nat in my power, leve brother;
And though I mighte, I wolde nat do so.
But canstou playen raket, to and fro,
Netle in, doke out, now this, now that, Pandare?
Now foule falle hire that for thy wo that care!

Thou farest eek by me, thou Pandarus,
As he that, whan a wight is wo-bigoon,
He cometh to him a paas and saith right thus:
'Think nat on smert and thou shalt feele noon.'
Thou moost me first transmewen in a stoon,
And reve me my passiounes alle,
Er thou so lightly do my wo to falle.

The deeth may wel out of my brest departe
The lif, so longe may this sorwe mine;

444. hoolly, altogether; **hires,** hers. **445. hight,** promised. **447. sterve,** die. **451. kinde,** nature. **452. leve,** dear. **455. sleest,** slay. **458. lith,** lies. **460. raket,** rackets, a game not unlike tennis. **461. Netle, doke,** nettle, dock: Troilus is quoting a charm said when curing nettle-rash by the use of dockweed. **462. falle,** befall; **hire,** her; **care,** would feel any pity. **463. farest,** behave. **465. a paas,** strolling. **467. moost,** must; **transmewen,** transform. **468. reve me,** take away from me. **469. do,** cause. **470. departe,** separate. **471. mine,** i.e., subvert me.

But fro my soule shal Criseides darte
Out neveremo, but down with Proserpine
Whan I am deed I wol go wone in pine,
And ther I wol eternally complaine
My wo, and how that twinned be we twaine.

Thou hast here maad an argument for fin,
How that it sholde lasse paine be
Criseide to forgoon for she was myn,
And lived in ese and in felicitee—
Why gabbestou, that saidest unto me
That 'Him is worse that is fro wele ythrowe,
Than he hadde erst noon of that wele yknowe'?

But tel me now, sin that thee thinketh so light
To chaungen so in love ay to and fro,
Why hastou nat doon bisily thy might
To chaungen hire that dooth thee al thy wo?
Why niltou lete hire fro thyn herte go?
Why niltou love another lady sweete,
That may thyn herte sette in quiete?

If thou hast had in love ay swich meschaunce,
And canst it nought yit fro thyn herte drive,
I, that lived in lust and in plesaunce
With hire as muche as creature on live,
How sholde I that foryete, and that as blive?
O where hastou been hid so longe in mue
That canst so wel and formally argue?

Nay, Pandarus, nought worth is al thy reed.
But doutelees, for ought that may bifalle,
Withoute wordes mo, I wol be deed.

473. **Proserpine,** Queen of the Underworld. 474. **wone,** dwell; **pine,** torment. 476. **twinned,** divided. 477. **for fin,** to the conclusion. 478. **lasse,** less. 479. **for,** because. 481. **gabbestou,** do you talk nonsense. 482. **wele,** prosperity. 483. **erst,** before. 484. **light,** easy. 487. **dooth,** causes. 493. **lust,** pleasure. 495. **foryete,** forget; **as blive,** quickly. 496. **mue,** cage. 498. **reed,** advice.

O deeth, that endere art of sorwes alle,
Com now, sin so ofte after thee I calle,
For sely is that deeth, sooth for to sayne,
That, ofte ycleped, comth and endeth paine.

Wel woot I, whil my lif was in quiete,
Er deeth me slowe I wolde have yiven hire;
But now thy coming is to me so sweete,
That in this world I nothing so desire:
O deeth, sin with this sorwe I am on fire,
Thou oughte me anoon in teres drenche,
Or with thy colde strook myn hete quenche.

Sin that thou sleest so fele in sondry wise,
Ayains hir wille, unprayed day and night,
Do me at my requeste this servise:
Delivere now the world—thanne doost thou right—
Of me, that am the wofuleste wight
That evere was; for time is that I sterve,
Sin in this world of nothing may I serve."

This Troilus in teres gan distille,
As licour out of a lambek ful faste,
And Pandarus gan holde his tonge stille,
And to the ground his yën down he caste;
But nathelees thus thoughte he at the laste,
"What, pardee, rather than my felawe deye,
Yit shal I somwhat more unto him saye,"

And saide, "Freend, sin thou hast swich distresse,
And sin thee list mine arguments to blame,
Why nilt thyselven helpe to doon redresse,
And with thy manhede letten al this grame?
Go ravisshe hire, ne canstou nat, for shame?

503. **sely,** happy. 504. **ycleped,** called. 505. **woot,** know. 506. **slowe,** slew; **hire,** pay. 510. **drenche,** drown. 512. **sleest,** slay; **fele,** many. 517. **sterve,** die. 520. **lambek,** alembic. 527. **list,** it pleases. 529. **letten,** stop; **grame,** harm. 530. **ravisshe,** abduct.

And outher° lat hire out of towne fare,
Or hold hire stille and leef this nice care.°

Artou in Troye and hast noon hardiment°
To take a womman which that loveth thee,
And wolde hirselven been of thyn assent?
Now is this nat a nice vanitee?°
Ris up anoon, and lat this weeping be,
And kith° thou art a man: for in this houre
I wol been deed, or she shal bleven oure."°

To this answerde him Troilus ful softe,
And saide, "Pardee, leve° brother dere,
Al this have I myself yit thought ful ofte,
And more thing than thou devisest here.
But why this thing is laft° thou shalt wel heere,
And whan thou me hast yive an audience,
Therafter maistou telle al thy sentence.°

First, sin thou woost this town hath al this werre°
For ravisshing of wommen so by might,
It sholde nought be suffred me to erre,
As it stant° now, ne doon so greet unright:
I sholde han also blame of every wight
My fadres graunt if that I so withstood,
Sin she is chaunged° for the townes good.

I have eek thought, so it were hir assent,
To axe° hire at my fader of his grace:
Than thinke I this were hir accusement°—
Sin wel I woot I may hire nought purchace:°
For sin my fader, in so heigh a place

531. **outher,** either. 532. **leef,** desist from; **nice care,** foolish behavior. 533. **hardiment,** courage. 536. **vanitee,** futility. 538. **kith,** show. 539. **bleven,** remain; **oure,** ours. 541. **leve,** beloved. 544. **laft,** i.e., left undone. 546. **sentence,** opinion. 547. **werre,** war. 550. **stant,** stands. 553. **chaunged,** exchanged. 555. **axe,** ask for. 556. **hir accusement,** an accusation of her. 557. **purchace,** obtain.

As parlement, hath hir eschaunge enseled,
He nil for me his lettre be repeled.

Yit drede I most hir herte to perturbe
With violence, if I do swich a game;
For if I wolde it openly disturbe,
It moste be disclaundre to hir name.
And me were levere deed than hire diffame—
As nolde God, but if I sholde have
Hir honour levere than my lif to save.

Thus am I lost, for ought that I can see.
For certain is, sin that I am hir knight,
I moste hir honour levere han than me
In every caas, as lovere oughte of right.
Thus am I with desir and reson twight:
Desir for to disturben hire me redeth,
And reson nil nat, so myn herte dredeth."

Thus weeping that he coude nevere ceesse,
He saide, "Allas, how shal I, wrecche, fare?
For wel feele I alway my love encreesse,
And hope is lasse and lasse alway, Pandare.
Encreessen eek the causes of my care:
So wailaway, why nil myn herte breste?
For as in love ther is but litel reste."

Pandare answerde, "Freend, thou maist for me
Doon as thee list, but hadde ich it so hote,
And thyn estaat, she sholde go with me,
Though al this town cride on this thing by note:
I nolde sette at al that noise a grote,

559. **enseled,** ratified. 560. **repeled,** revoked. 564. **moste,** must; **disclaundre,** slander. 565. **me . . . deed,** I should rather die; **diffame,** bring into disrepute. 566. **As . . . God,** i.e., God forbid. 567. **levere,** dearer. 570. I must hold her honor dearer than myself. 572. **twight,** pulled. 573. **redeth,** advises. 578. **lasse,** less. 580. **breste,** break. 583. **list,** it pleases; **hote,** hot. 585. **by note,** i.e., in one voice. 586. **sette at,** i.e., care for; **grote,** groat, penny.

For whan men han wel cried, thanne wol they roune;
Eek wonder last but nine night nevere in towne.

Divine nat in reson ay so deepe,
Ne curteisly, but help thyselve anoon:
Bet is that othere than thyselven weepe;
And namely, sin ye two been al oon,
Ris up, for by myn heed, she shal nat goon;
And rather be in blame a lite yfounde,
Than sterve here as a gnat withouten wounde.

It is no shame unto you, ne no vice,
Hire to withholden that ye love most:
Paraunter she mighte holde thee for nice
To laten hire go thus to the Greekes host.
Thenk eek Fortune, as wel thyselven woost,
Helpeth hardy man to his emprise—
And waiveth wrecches for hir cowardise.

And though thy lady wolde a lite hire greve,
Thou shalt thyself thy pees herafter make.
But as for me, certain I can nat leve
That she wolde it as now for yvel take.
Why sholde thanne of-fered thyn herte quake?
Thenk eek how Paris hath—that is thy brother—
A love, and why shaltou nat have another?

And Troilus, oo thing I dar thee swere:
That if Criseide, which that is thy lief,
Now loveth thee as wel as thou doost here,
God helpe me so, she nil nat take agrief
Though thou do boote anoon in this meschief;

587. **roune,** whisper, get tired of crying. 588. **last,** lasts; **but,** i.e., more than. 589. **Divine,** ponder. 591. **Bet,** better. 592. **namely,** especially. 593. **heed,** head. 594. **lite,** little. 595. **sterve,** die. 598. **Paraunter,** perhaps; **nice,** foolish. 599. **laten,** let. 600. **woost,** know. 601. **emprise,** undertaking. 602. **waiveth,** neglects. 605. **leve,** believe. 606. **for yvel,** ill. 607. **of-fered,** terrified. 609. **another,** i.e., one too. 611. **lief,** beloved. 612. **here,** her. 613. **agrief,** amiss. 614. **do boote,** find remedy.

And if she wilneth fro thee for to passe,
Thanne is she fals, so love hire wel the lasse.°

Forthy taak herte and think right as a knight:
Thurgh love is broken alday° every lawe.
Kith° now somwhat thy corage and thy might;
Have mercy on thyself for° any awe;
Lat nat this wrecched wo thyn herte gnawe,
But manly set the world on sixe and sevene,
And if thou die a martyr, go to hevene.

I wol myself been with thee at this deede,
Though ich and al my kin upon a stounde°
Shulle in a streete as dogges liggen° dede,
Thurghgirt° with many a wid and bloody wounde.
In every caas I wol a freend be founde.
And if thee list here sterven° as a wrecche,
Adieu: the devil speede him that recche."°

This Troilus gan with tho wordes quiken,°
And saide, "Freend, graunt mercy,° ich assente;
But certainly thou maist nat so me priken,
Ne paine noon ne may me so tormente,
That for no caas it is nat myn entente,
At shorte wordes, though I dien sholde,
To ravisshen hire but if° hirself it wolde."

"Why, so mene I," quod Pandarus, "al this day.
But tel me thanne: hastou hir wil assayed,
That sorwest thus?" And he answerde him, "Nay."
"Wherof artou," quod Pandare, "thanne amayed,°
That noost nat that she wol been yvele apayed°

616. **lasse,** less. 618. **alday,** constantly. 619. **Kith,** make known. 620. **for,** despite. 625. **upon a stounde,** in a moment. 626. **liggen,** lie. 627. **Thurghgirt,** pierced. 629. **list,** it pleases; **sterven,** die. 630. **speede,** prosper; **recche,** may care. 631. **quiken,** revive. 632. **graunt mercy,** many thanks. 637. **but if,** unless. 641. **amayed,** dismayed. 642. **noost,** know not; **yvele apayed,** badly pleased.

To ravisshen hire, sin thou hast nought been there,
But if that Jove tolde it in thyn ere?

Forthy ris up as nought ne were, anoon,
And wassh thy face, and to the king thou wende,
Or he may wondren whider thou art goon:
Thou moost with wisdom him and othere blende
Or upon caas he may after thee sende,
Er thou be war. And shortly, brother dere,
Be glad, and lat me werke in this matere:

For I wol shape it so that sikerly
Thou shalt this night somtime in som manere
Come speken with thy lady prively,
And by hir wordes eek as by hir cheere
Thou shalt ful soone aperceive and wel heere
Al hir entente, and in this caas the beste.
And fare now wel, for in this point I reste."

The swifte fame, which that false thinges
Egal reporteth lik the thinges trewe,
Was thurghout Troye yfled with preste winges,
Fro man to man, and made this tale al newe:
How Calcas doughter, with hir brighte hewe,
At parlement, withouten wordes moor,
Ygraunted was in chaunge of Antenor.

The whiche tale anoonright as Criseide
Hadde herd, she which that of hir fader roughte
As in this caas right nought, ne whan he deide,
Ful bisily to Jupiter bisoughte
Yive hem meschaunce that this tretis broughte;
But shortly, lest thise tales soothe were,
She dorste at no wight asken it for fere;

644. But if, unless. **645. Forthy,** therefore. **648. moost,** must; **blende,** deceive. **652. shape,** arrange; **sikerly,** certainly. **660. Egal,** equally. **661. preste,** rapid. **667. roughte,** cared. **670. tretis,** treaty.

As she that hadde hir herte and al hir minde
On Troilus yset so wonder faste,
That al this world ne mighte hir love unbinde,
Ne Troilus out of hir herte caste:
She wol been his whil that hir lif may laste.
And thus she brenneth° bothe in love and drede,
So that she niste what was best to rede.°

But as men seen in town and al aboute
That wommen usen° freendes to visite,
So to Criseide of wommen cam a route,°
For pitous joye, and wenden° hire delite;
And with hir tales, dere ynough a mite,°
Thise wommen, which that in the citee dwelle,
They sette hem down and saide as I shal telle.

Quod first that oon: "I am glad, trewely,
By cause of you, that shal youre fader see."
Another saide, "Ywis, so nam nat I,
For al too litel hath she with us be."
Quod tho the thridde,° "I hope, ywis, that she
Shal bringen us the pees on every side,
That when she gooth, almighty God hire gide."

Tho° wordes and tho wommanisshe thinges,
She herde hem right as though she thennes were;
For God it woot, hir herte on other thing is;
Although the body sate among hem there,
Hir advertence° is alway elleswhere:
For Troilus ful faste hir soule soughte;
Withouten word on him alway she thoughte.

Thise wommen, that thus wenden° hire to plese,
Aboute nought gonne alle hir tales° spende:

678. brenneth, burns. **679. niste,** knew not; **rede,** i.e., do. **681. usen,** are accustomed. **682. route,** number. **683. wenden,** thought to. **684. dere . . . mite,** worth no more than a mite. **691. thridde,** third. **694. Tho,** those. **698. advertence,** attention. **701. wenden,** thought. **702. Aboute nought,** to no purpose; **tales,** conversation.

Swich vanitee ne can doon hire noon ese,
As she that al this mene while brende
Of other passion than that they wende,
So that she felte almost hir herte die,
For wo and wery of that compaignye.

For which no lenger mighte she restraine
Hir teres, so they gonnen up to welle,
That yaven signes of the bittre paine
In which hir spirit was and moste dwelle,
Remembering hire from hevene into which helle
She fallen was, sin she forgooth the sighte
Of Troilus; and sorwefully she sighte.

And thilke fooles sitting hire aboute
Wenden that she wepte and siked sore
By cause that she sholde out of that route
Departen, and nevere playe with hem more.
And they that hadde yknowen hire of yore
Sawgh hire so weepe and thoughte it kindenesse,
And eech of hem wepte eek for hir distresse.

And bisily they gonnen hire conforte
Of thing, God woot, on which she litel thoughte;
And with hir tales wenden hire disporte,
And to be glad they ofte hire bisoughte:
But swich an ese therwith they hire wroughte,
Right as a man is esed for to feele,
For ache of heed, to clawen him on his heele.

But after al this nice vanitee
They tooke hir leve and hoom they wenten alle.
Criseide, ful of sorweful pietee,
Into hir chambre up wente out of the halle,
And on hir bed she gan for deed to falle,

704. **brende,** burned. 707. **wery,** i.e., weariness. 711. **moste,** must. 714. **sighte,** sighed. 716. **siked,** sighed. 728. **heed,** head; **clawen,** scratch. 729. **nice,** foolish. 731. **pietee,** pity. 733. **deed,** dead.

In purpos nevere thennes for to rise.
And thus she wroughte as I shal you devise:

Hir ounded heer that sonnish was of hewe
She rente, and eek hir fingres longe and smale
She wroong ful ofte, and bad God on hire rewe,
And with the deeth to doon boote on hir bale;
Hir hewe, whilom bright that tho was pale,
Bar witnesse of hir wo and hir constrainte;
And thus she spak, sobbing in hir complainte:

"Allas," quod she, "out of this regioun,
I, woful wrecche and infortuned wight,
And born in cursed constellacioun,
Moot goon, and thus departen from my knight!
Wo worth, allas, that ilke dayes light
On which I sawgh him first with yën twaine,
That causeth me—and ich him—al this paine."

Therwith the teres from hir yën two
Down falle as showr in Aperil as swithe;
Hir white brest she beet, and for the wo
After the deeth she cried a thousand sithe,
Sin he that wont hir wo was for to lithe,
She moot forgoon; for which disaventure
She heeld hirself a forlost creature.

She saide, "How shal he doon, and ich also?
How sholde I live if that I from him twinne?
O dere herte, eek that I love so,
Who shal that sorwe sleen that ye been inne?
O Calcas fader, thyn be al this sinne!

736. ounded, wavy; **heer,** hair; **sonnish,** sunny. **737. rente,** tore; **smale,** delicate. **738. wroong,** wrung; **rewe,** pity. **739. doon . . . bale,** remedy her harm. **740. whilom,** formerly. **744. infortuned,** unfortunate. **746. Moot,** must. **747. worth,** be to. **751. swithe,** quickly. **752. beet,** beat. **753. sithe,** times. **754. lithe,** cure. **756. forlost,** utterly lost. **758. twinne,** separate. **760. sleen,** slay.

A, moder myn that cleped° were Argive,
Wo worth that day that thou me bere° on live!

To what fin° sholde I live and sorwen thus?
How sholde a fissh withouten water dure?°
What is Criseide worth from Troilus?
How sholde a plaunte or lives° creature
Live withouten his kinde noriture?°
For which ful ofte a byword° here I saye,
That rootelees moot greene° soone deye.

I shal doon thus, sin neither swerd ne darte
Dar I noon handle for the crueltee:
That ilke day that I from you departe—
If sorwe of that nil nat my bane° be—
Thanne shal no mete ne drinke come in me
Til I my soule out of my brest unsheethe;°
And thus myselven wol I doon to deethe.

And, Troilus, my clothes everichoon
Shul blake been, in tokening, herte sweete,
That I am as out of this world agoon,
That wont was you to setten in quiete.
And of myn ordre,° ay til deeth me meete,
The observance° evere in youre absence
Shal sorwe been, complainte, and abstinence.

Myn herte and eek the woful gost° therinne
Biquethe I with youre spirit to complaine
Eternally, for they shal nevere twinne;°
For though in erthe ytwinned be we twaine,
Yit in the feeld of pitee out of paine

762. **moder,** mother; **cleped,** called. 763. **worth,** be to; **bere,** gave birth to. 764. **fin,** end. 765. **dure,** last. 767. **lives,** living. 768. **kinde,** natural; **noriture,** sustenance. 769. **byword,** proverb. 770. **moot,** must; **greene,** i.e., a plant. 774. **bane,** destruction. 776. **unsheethe,** i.e., draw. 782. **ordre,** condition of life. 783. **observance,** usage. 785. **gost,** spirit. 787. **twinne,** separate.

That highte Elysos shal we been yfere,
As Orpheus and Erudice his fere.

Thus, herte myn, for Antenor, allas,
I soone shal be chaunged, as I weene.
But how shal ye doon in this sorweful cas?
How shal youre tendre herte this sustene?
But, herte myn, foryete this sorwe and teene,
And me also—for soothly for to saye,
So ye wel fare, I recche nought to deye."

How mighte it evere yred been or ysonge,
The plainte that she made in hir distresse—
I noot; but as for me, my litel tonge,
If I descriven wolde hir hevinesse,
It sholde make hir sorwe seeme lesse
Than that it was, and childisshly deface
Hir heigh complainte, and therfore ich it pace.

Pandare, which that sent from Troilus
Was to Criseide, as ye han herd devise,
That for the best it was accorded thus—
And he ful glad to doon him that servise—
Unto Criseide in a ful secree wise,
Ther as she lay in torment and in rage,
Cam hire to telle al hoolly his message,

And foond that she hirselven gan to trete
Ful pitously, for with hir salte teres
Hir brest, hir face ybathed was al wete:
The mighty tresses of hir sonnishe heres
Unbroiden hangen al aboute hir eres,

790. highte, is called; **Elysos,** Elysium, the Elysian fields, the heaven of the classic world; **yfere,** together. **791. Erudice,** Eurydice, Orpheus' wife whom he once tried to rescue from the Underworld; **fere,** mate. **793. chaunged,** exchanged. **795. sustene,** sustain, bear. **796. teene,** grief. **798. So,** provided; **recche,** care; **to,** i.e., if I. **799. yred,** narrated. **800. plainte,** complaint. **801. noot,** know not; **litel,** i.e., inadequate. **805. pace,** pass over. **811. rage,** frenzy. **812. hoolly,** wholly. **813. foond,** found. **816. sonnishe,** sunny. **817. Unbroiden,** unbraided.

Which yaf him verray signal of martyre°
Of deeth, which that hir herte gan desire.

Whan she him sawgh, she gan for sorwe anoon
Hir tery° face atwixe hir armes hide,
For which this Pandare is so wo-bigoon
That in the hous he mighte unnethe° abide,
As he that pitee felte on every side:
For if Criseide had erst° complained sore,
Tho gan she plaine° a thousand times more;

And in hir aspre° plainte thus she saide:
"Pandare first of joyes mo than two
Was cause causing unto me, Criseide,°
That now transmued° been in cruel wo.
Wher° shal I saye to you welcome or no,
That alderfirst° me broughte unto servise
Of Love, allas, that endeth in swich wise?

Endeth thanne love in wo? Ye, or men lieth!
And alle worldly blisse, as thinketh me,
The ende of blisse ay sorwe it occupieth,°
And who so troweth° nat that it so be,
Lat him upon me, woful wrecche, ysee,°
That myself hate and ay my birthe accurse,
Feeling alway fro wikke° I go to worse.

Whoso me seeth, he seeth sorwe al atones,
Paine, torment, plainte, wo, distresse;
Out of my woful body harm ther noon is,
As anguissh, langour,° cruel bitternesse,
Anoy,° smert, drede, furye, and eek siknesse:

818. martyre, martyrdom. **821. tery,** teary. **823. unnethe,** scarcely. **825. erst,** before. **826. plaine,** complain. **827. aspre,** bitter. **828–9.** i.e., Pandar was the agent that first caused me, Criseide, more joys than merely two. **830. transmued,** transformed. **831. Wher,** whether. **832. alderfirst,** first of all. **836.** i.e., Sorrow always replaces bliss in the end. **837. troweth,** believes. **838. ysee,** look. **840. wikke,** bad. **844. langour,** sickness. **845. Anoy,** injury.

I trowe, ywis, from hevene teres raine
For pitee of myn aspre and cruel paine."

"And thou, my suster ful of disconfort,"
Quod Pandarus, "what thinkestou to do?
Why nastou to thyselven som resport?
Why wiltou thus thyself, allas, fordo?
Leef al this werk and taak now heede to
That I shal sayn, and herkne of good entente
This that by me thy Troilus thee sente."

Turnede hire tho Criseide, a wo makinge
So greet that it a deeth was for to see.
"Allas," quod she, "what wordes may ye bringe?
What wol my dere herte sayn to me,
Which that I drede neveremo to see?
Wol he han plainte or teres er I wende?
I have ynowe, if he therafter sende."

She was right swich to seen in hir visage
As is that wight that men on beere binde:
Hir face, lik of Paradis the image,
Was al ychaunged in another kinde;
The play, the laughter men was wont to finde
On hire, and eek hir joyes everichone
Been fled, and thus lith now Criseide allone.

Aboute hir yën two a purpre ring
Bitrent, in soothfast tokening of hir paine,
That to biholde it was a deedly thing;
For which Pandare mighte nat restraine
The teres from his yën for to raine;
But nathelees, as he best mighte, he saide
From Troilus thise wordes to Criseide:

847. **aspre,** bitter. 848. **suster,** sister. 850. **nastou,** have you not; **resport,** regard. 851. **fordo,** destroy. 852. **Leef,** leave. 856. **greet,** great. 861. **ynowe,** enough. 863. **beere,** bier. 868. **lith,** lies. 869. **purpre,** purple. 870. **Bitrent,** encircles. 871. **deedly,** deadly.

"Lo, nece, I trowe ye han herd al how
The king, with othere lordes, for the beste
Hath maad eschaunge of Antenor and you,
That cause is of this sorwe and this unreste.
But how this caas dooth Troilus moleste,
That may noon erthely mannes tonge saye:
For verray wo his wit is al awaye.

For which we han so sorwed, he and I,
That into litel bothe it hadde us slawe;
But thurgh my conseil this day finally
He somwhat is fro weeping now withdrawe,
And seemeth me that he desireth fawe
With you to been al night, for to devise
Remedye in this, if ther were any wise.

This, short and plain, th'effect of my message,
As ferforth as my wit can comprehende:
For ye that been of torment in swich rage
May to no long prologe as now entende.
And herupon ye may answere him sende–
And for the love of God, my nece dere,
So leve this wo er Troilus be here."

"Greet is my wo," quod she, and sighte sore
As she that feeleth deedly sharp distresse;
"But yit to me his sorwe is muchel more,
That love him bet than he himself, I gesse.
Allas, for me hath he swich hevinesse?
Can he for me so pitously complaine?
Ywis, this sorwe doubleth al my paine.

Grevous to me, God woot, is for to twinne,"
Quod she, "but yit it harder is to me
To seen the sorwe which that he is inne,

876. **trowe,** believe. 878. **eschaunge,** exchange. 880. **moleste,** distress. 884. **into litel,** i.e., nearly; **slawe,** slain. 887. **fawe,** gladly. 891. **ferforth,** far. 893. **entende,** attend. 896. **leve,** leave. 897. **Greet,** great; **sighte,** sighed. 900. **bet,** better. 904. **twinne,** separate.

For wel woot I it wol my bane° be,
And die I wolde in certain," tho quod she.
"But bid him come er deeth, that thus me threteth,°
Drive out that gost which in myn herte beteth."°

Thise wordes said, she on hir armes two
Fil gruf,° and gan to weepen pitously.
Quod Pandarus, "Allas, why do ye so,
Sin wel ye woot° the time is faste by
That he shal come? Arise up hastily,
That he you nat biwopen° thus ne finde—
But ye wol have him wood° out of his minde.

For wiste he that ye ferde° in this manere,
He wolde himselven slee. And if I wende°
To han this fare,° he sholde nat come here,
For al the good that Priam may dispende.
For to what fin he wolde anoon pretende,°
That knowe ich wel; and forthy° yit I saye,
So leve this sorwe, or platly,° he wol deye.

And shapeth you his sorwe for t'abregge,°
And nought encreesse, leve° nece sweete;
Beeth rather to him cause of flat than egge,°
And with som wisdom ye his sorwes bete.°
What helpeth it to weepen ful a streete,
Or though ye bothe in salte teres dreinte?°
Bet is a time of cure ay than of plainte.°

I mene thus: whan ich him hider bringe,
Sin ye been wise and bothe of oon assent,

907. **bane,** destruction. 909. **threteth,** threatens. 910. **gost,** spirit; **beteth,** i.e., lives. 912. **gruf,** prone. 914. **woot,** know. 916. **biwopen,** i.e., tear-stained. 917. **But,** unless; **wood,** mad. 918. **wiste he,** if he knew; **ferde,** behaved. 919. **slee,** slay; **wende,** thought. 920. **fare,** fuss. 922. **fin,** end; **pretende,** aim. 923. **forthy,** therefore. 924. **leve,** cease; **platly,** flatly. 925. **shapeth you,** arrange; **abregge,** curtail. 926. **leve,** dear. 927. **flat,** i.e., the flat of a sword, in legend sometimes endowed with healing power; **egge,** edge. 928. **bete,** mend. 930. **dreinte,** drowned. 931. It's better to spend time finding remedy than complaining.

So shapeth you how disturbe youre goinge,
Or come ayain soone after ye be went;
Wommen been wise in short avisement:
And lat seen how youre wit shal now availe,
And what that I may helpe, it shal nat faile."

"Go," quod Criseide, "and uncle, trewely,
I shal doon al my might me to restraine
From weeping in his sighte, and bisily
Him for to glade I shal doon al my paine,
And in myn herte seeken every veine,
If to this soor ther may be founden salve—
It shal nat lakke, certain, on my halve."

Gooth Pandarus and Troilus he soughte,
Til in a temple he foond him al allone,
As he that of his lif no lenger roughte;
But to the pitous goddes everichone
Ful tendrely he prayde and made his mone,
To doon him soone out of the world to pace—
For wel he thoughte ther was noon other grace.

And shortly, al the soothe for to saye,
He was so fallen in despair that day,
That outrely he shoop him for to deye,
For right thus was his argument alway:
He saide he nas but lorn, "So wailaway,
For al that comth, comth by necessitee:
Thus to been lorn, it is my destinee.

For certainly this woot I wel," he saide,
"That forsighte of divine purveyaunce
Hath seen alway me to forgoon Criseide,

934. Find a way to hinder your departure. **936. in . . . avisement,** upon short deliberation. **942. glade,** gladden. **944. soor,** sore. **947. foond,** found. **948. roughte,** cared. **950. mone,** moan. **951. doon,** cause; **pace,** pass. **955. outrely,** solely; **shoop him,** planned. **957. nas but lorn,** was no more than lost. **961–2.** That the foresight of the Divine Providence has always seen that I should lose Criseide.

Sin God seeth every thing, out of doutaunce,
And hem disponeth, thurgh his ordinaunce,
In hir merites soothly for to be,
As they shul comen by predestinee.

But nathelees, allas, whom shal I leve?
For ther been grete clerkes, many oon,
That destinee thurgh argumentes preve;
And some men sayn that needely ther is noon,
But that free chois is yiven us everichoon.
O wailaway, so slye arn clerkes olde
That I noot whos opinion I may holde.

For some men sayn, if God seeth al biforn—
Ne God may nat deceived been, pardee—
Thanne moot it fallen though men hadde it sworn,
That purveyance hath seen bifore to be.
Wherfore I saye that, from eterne if he
Hath wist biforn oure thought eek as oure deede,
We han no free chois as thise clerkes rede.

For other thought ne other deede also
Mighte nevere been, but swich as purveyaunce,
Which may nat been deceived neveremo,
Hath feeled biforn, withouten ignoraunce.
For if ther mighte been a variaunce
To writhen out fro Goddes purveyinge,
Ther nere no prescience of thing cominge.

But it were rather an opinioun
Uncertain, and no stedefast forseeinge;

963. **doutaunce,** doubt. 964. **disponeth,** disposes. 965. **In,** according to; **merites,** rewards. 966. i.e., In the way that has been preordained for them. 967. **leve,** believe. 969. **preve,** prove. 970. **needely,** of necessity. 972. **slye,** clever. 973. **noot,** know not. 976. **moot,** must; **fallen,** happen; **it** (2), i.e., the opposite. 977. **purveyance,** providence. 978. **eterne,** eternity. 979. **wist,** known. 980. **rede,** say. 984. **feeled,** sensed. 985. **variaunce,** variation. 986. **writhen,** twist; **purveyinge,** foresight.

And, certes, that were an abusioun
That God sholde han no parfit cleer witinge
More than we men that han doutous weeninge:
But swich an error upon God to gesse
Were fals and foul and wikked cursednesse.

Eek this is an opinion of some
That han hir top ful heigh and smoothe yshore—
They sayn right thus: that thing is nat to come
For that the prescience hath seen bifore
That it shal come, but they sayn that therfore
That it shal come, therfore the purveyaunce
Woot it bifore, withouten ignoraunce.

And in this manere this necessitee
Returneth in his part contrarye again:
For needfully bihoveth it nat to be
That thilke thinges fallen in certain
That been purveyed, but needely, as they sayn,
Bihoveth it that thinges whiche that falle,
That they in certain been purveyed alle.

I mene as though I laboured me in this:
To enqueren which thing cause of which thing be—
As wheither that the prèscience of God is
The certain cause of the necessitee
Of thinges that to comen be, pardee;
Or if necessitee of thing cominge
Be cause certain of the purveyinge.

But now n'enforce I me nat in shewinge
How the ordre of causes stant; but wel woot I

990. abusioun, slander. **991. parfit cleer,** perfectly clear; **witinge,** knowledge. **992. doutous,** dubious; **weeninge,** guessing. **994. cursednesse,** malice. **996. top,** crown; **yshore,** shorn. **998. For that,** because. **999. therfore,** i.e., because. **1003. Returneth,** devolves; **his,** its. **1004. bihoveth it,** it is necessary. **1005. fallen,** occur; **in,** i.e., for. **1006. purveyed,** foreseen. **1010. enqueren,** inquire. **1016. enforce I me,** I try. **1017. stant,** stands.

That it bihoveth that the bifallinge
Of thinges wist bifore, certainly,
Be necessarye, al seeme it nat therby
That prescience putte falling necessaire
To thing to come, al falle it foule or faire.

For if ther sitte a man yond on a see,
Thanne by necessitee bihoveth it
That, certes, thyn opinion sooth be
That weenest or conjectest that he sit;
And ferther over now ayainward yit,
Lo, right so is it of the part contrarye,
As thus—now herkne, for I wol nat tarye:

I saye that if the opinion of thee
Be sooth for that he sit, thanne saye I this,
That he moot sitten by necessitee;
And thus necessitee in either is:
For in him neede of sitting is, ywis,
And in thee neede of sooth; and thus, forsoothe,
Ther moot necessitee been in you bothe.

But thou maist sayn the man sit nat therfore
That thyn opinion of his sitting sooth is,
But rather, for the man sit therbifore,
Therfore is thyn opinion sooth, ywis.
And I saye though the cause of sooth of this
Comth of his sitting, yit necessitee
Is entrechaunged bothe in him and thee.

Thus in the same wise, out of doutaunce,
I may wel maken, as it seemeth me,

1018. bifallinge, occurrence. **1019. wist,** known. **1020. al seeme it,** although it seem. **1021. putte,** i.e., makes; **falling,** occurring. **1022. al falle it,** i.e., whether it occur. **1023. see,** seat. **1026. weenest,** think; **conjectest,** conjecture; **sit,** sits. **1027. ferther over,** moreover; **ayainward,** on the other hand. **1028. part contrarye,** opposite point. **1031. for that,** because. **1032. moot,** must. **1037–38. therfore That,** i.e., because. **1039. for,** because; **therbifore,** i.e., before being seen. **1043. entrechaunged,** mingled. **1044. doutaunce,** doubt.

My resoning of Goddes purveyaunce,
And of the thinges that to comen be.
By which reson men may wel ysee
That thilke thinges that in erthe falle,
That by necessitee they comen alle.

For although that for thing shal come, ywis,
Therfore it is purveyed certainly—
Nat that it comth for it purveyed is—
Yit, nathelees, bihoveth it needfully
That thing to come be purveyed trewely,
Or elles thinges that purveyed be,
That they bitiden by necessitee.

And this suffiseth right ynough, certain,
For to destroye oure free chois everydeel.
But now is this abusion to sayn
That falling of the thinges temporel
Is cause of Goddes prescience eternel:
Now, trewely, that is a fals sentence,
That thing to come sholde cause his prescience.

What mighte I weene, and I hadde swich a thought,
But that God purveyeth thing that is to come
For that it is to come, and elles nought?
So mighte I weene that thinges, alle and some,
That whilom been bifalle and overcome,
Been cause of thilke soverein purveyaunce
That forwoot al withouten ignoraunce.

And over al this, yit saye I more herto:
That, right as whan I woot ther is a thing,
Ywis, that thing moot needfully be so;

1049. falle, occur. **1051. that for,** because. **1053. for,** because. **1059. everydeel,** every bit. **1060. abusion,** slander. **1061. falling,** occurrence. **1063. sentence,** opinion. **1065. weene,** suppose; **and,** if. **1067. For that,** because. **1068. alle and some,** one and all. **1069. whilom,** formerly; **overcome,** gone by. **1070. soverein,** supreme. **1071. forwoot,** foreknows. **1074. moot,** must.

Eek right so, whan I woot a thing coming,
So moot it come; and thus the bifalling
Of thinges that been wist bifore the tide,
They mowe nat been eschewed on no side."

Thanne saide he thus, "Almighty Jove in trone,
That woost of al this thing the soothfastnesse,
Rewe on my sorwe, or do me dien soone,
Or bring Criseide and me fro this distresse!"
And whil he was in al this hevinesse,
Disputing with himself in this matere,
Cam Pandare in, and saide as ye may heere:

"O mighty God," quod Pandarus, "in trone,
I, who sawgh evere a wis man faren so?
Why, Troilus, what thinkestou to doone?
Hastou swich lust to been thyn owene fo?
What, pardee, yit is nat Criseide ago!
Why lust thee so thyself fordoon for drede,
That in thyn heed thine yën seemen dede?

Hastou nat lived many a yeer biforn
Withouten hire, and ferd ful wel at ese?
Artou for hire and for noon other born?
Hath kinde thee wrought al only hire to plese?
Lat be and think right thus in thy disese,
That in the dees right as ther fallen chaunces,
Right so in love ther come and goon plesaunces.

And yit is this a wonder most of alle,
Why thou thus sorwest, sin thou noost nat yit,
Touching hir going, how that it shal falle,
Ne if she can hirself disturben it:

1077. wist, known; **tide,** time. **1078. mowe,** may; **side,** i.e., account. **1079. trone,** throne. **1080. woost,** know. **1081. Rewe,** have pity; **do,** make. **1087. I,** oh; **faren,** behave. **1089. lust,** pleasure. **1091. lust,** does it please; **fordoon,** destroy. **1092. heed,** head; **dede,** dead. **1094. hire,** her; **ferd,** fared. **1096. kinde,** nature; **al only,** exclusively. **1097. disese,** distress. **1098. dees,** dice. **1101. noost,** know not. **1103. disturben,** hinder.

Thou hast nat yit assayed al hir wit.
A man may al bitime his nekke bede
Whan it shal of, and sorwen at the neede.

Forthy taak heede of that I shal thee saye:
I have with hire yspoke and longe ybe,
So as accorded was bitwixe us twaye,
And everemo me thinketh thus, that she
Hath somwhat in hir hertes privetee
Wherwith she can, if I shal right arede,
Disturben al this of which thou art in drede.

For which my conseil is, whan it is night
Thou to hire go and make of this an ende.
And blisful Juno thurgh hir grete might
Shal, as I hope, hir grace unto us sende:
Myn herte saith, 'Certain she shal nat wende.'
And forthy put thyn herte a while in reste,
And hold this purpos, for it is the beste."

This Troilus answerde and sighte sore:
"Thou saist right wel, and I wol doon right so,"
And what him liste he saide unto it more.
And whan that it was time for to go,
Ful prively himself, withouten mo,
Unto hire cam as he was wont to doone.
And how they wroughte I shal you tellen soone.

Sooth is that whan they gonnen first to meete,
So gan the paine hir hertes for to twiste
That neither of hem other mighte greete,
But hem in armes tooke, and after kiste.
The lasse woful of hem bothe niste
Wher that he was, ne mighte oo word out bringe,
As I saide erst, for wo and for sobbinge.

1105. **al bitime,** i.e., soon enough; **bede,** offer. 1106. **of,** i.e., be cut off. 1107. **Forthy,** therefore. 1112. **arede,** guess. 1121. **sighte,** sighed. 1123. **liste,** it pleased. 1125. **mo,** others. 1132. **lasse,** less; **niste,** knew not. 1134. **erst,** before.

The woful teres that they leten falle
As bittre weren, out of teres kinde,
For paine, as in ligne aloes or galle:
So bittre teres weep nought, as I finde,
The woful Myrra thurgh the bark and rinde;
That in this world ther nis so hard an herte,
That nolde han rewed on hir paines smerte.

But whan hir woful wery gostes twaine
Returned been ther as hem oughte to dwelle,
And that somwhat to waiken gan the paine
By lengthe of plainte, and ebben gan the welle
Of hir teres, and the herte unswelle,
With broken vois, al hoors forshright, Criseide
To Troilus thise ilke wordes saide:

"O Jove, I die, and mercy I biseeche!
Help, Troilus!" and therwithal hir face
Upon his brest she laide, and loste speeche,
Hir woful spirit from his propre place,
Right with the word, alway o point to pace:
And thus she lith with hewes pale and greene,
That whilom fressh and fairest was to seene.

This Troilus, that on hir gan biholde,
Cleping hir name—and she lay as for deed—
Withouten answere, and felte hir limes colde,
Hir yën throwen upward to hir heed,
This sorweful man can now noon other reed,
But ofte time hir colde mouth he kiste:
Wher him was wo God and himself it wiste.

1136. **kinde,** nature. 1137. **ligne aloes,** lignaloes, a bitter drug; **galle,** bile. 1138. **weep,** wept. 1139. **Myrra,** Myrrha, who was turned into a tree as a consequence of her incestuous love for her father. 1141. **rewed,** had pity. 1142. **gostes,** spirits. 1144. **waiken,** weaken. 1145. **welle,** fountain. 1147. **hoors,** hoarse; **forshright,** i.e., for shrieking. 1153. **o,** on; **pace,** pass away. 1154. **lith,** lies. 1155. **whilom,** formerly. 1157. **Cleping,** calling; **deed,** dead. 1158. **limes,** limbs. 1159. **throwen,** i.e., rolled; **heed,** head. 1160. **can,** knows; **reed,** remedy. 1162. **Wher,** whether; **wiste,** knew.

He rist him up and long straight he hire laide,
For signe of lif, for ought he can or may,
Can he noon finde in no caas on Criseide;
For which his song ful ofte is wailaway.
But whan he sawgh that spechelees she lay,
With sorweful vois and herte of blisse al bare,
He saide how she was fro this world yfare.

So after that he longe hadde hire complained,
His handes wronge, and said that was to saye,
And with his teres salte hir brest birained,
He gan tho teres wipen of ful dreye,
And pitously gan for the soule praye,
And saide, "O Lord that set art in thy trone,
Rewe eek on me, for I shal folwe hire soone."

She cold was and withouten sentement,
For ought he woot, for breeth ne felte he noon;
And this was him a pregnant argument
That she was forth out of this world agoon.
And whan he sawgh ther was noon other woon,
He gan hir limes dresse in swich manere
As men doon hem that shal been laid on beere.

And after this, with sterne and cruel herte
His swerd anoon out of his sheethe he twighte,
Himself to sleen, how sore that him smerte,
So that his soule hir soule folwen mighte,
Ther as the doom of Minos wolde it dighte,
Sin Love and cruel Fortune it ne wolde
That in this world he lenger liven sholde.

Thanne saide he thus: "Fulfild of heigh desdain,
O cruel Jove, and thou, Fortune adverse,

1163. rist, rises; **long straight,** stretched out. **1164. ought,** anything. **1171. wronge,** wrung. **1172. birained,** moistened. **1173. dreye,** dry. **1175. trone,** throne. **1177. sentement,** feeling. **1181. woon,** resource. **1182. dresse,** arrange. **1183. beere,** bier. **1185. twighte,** pulled. **1186. sleen,** slay. **1188. Minos,** judge of the Underworld; **dighte,** dispose.

This al and som,° that falsly have ye slain
Criseide; and sin ye may do me no werse,
Fy on youre might and werkes so diverse!
Thus cowardly ye shal me nevere winne:°
Ther shal no deeth me fro my lady twinne.°

For I this world, sin ye have slain hire thus,
Wol lete,° and folwe hir spirit lowe or hye.
Shal nevere lovere sayn that Troilus
Dar nat for fere with his lady die.
For certain I wol bere hire compainye:
But sin ye wol nat suffren us liven here,
Yit suffreth that oure soules been yfere.°

And thou, citee, which that I leve in wo;
And thou, Priam, and bretheren alle yfere;
And thou, my moder, farewel, for I go:
And Atropos, maak redy thou my beere.°
And thou, Criseide, O sweete herte dere,
Receive now my spirit," wolde he saye,
With swerd at herte, al redy for to deye.

But as God wolde, of swough therwith sh'abraide,°
And gan to sike,° and "Troilus!" she cride.
And he answerde, "Lady myn Criseide,
Live ye yit?" and leet his swerd down glide.
"Ye, herte myn, that thanked be Cupide,"
Quod she; and therwithal she sore sighte,°
And he bigan to glade hire as he mighte;

Took hire in armes two and kiste hire ofte,
And hire to glade° he dide al his entente;
For which hir gost, that flikered ay on lofte,
Into hir woful herte ayain it wente.

1193. This . . . som, i.e., this is the whole fact. **1196. winne,** triumph over. **1197. twinne,** separate. **1199. lete,** leave. **1204. yfere,** together. **1208. Atropos,** the third of the Fates, who cuts the thread of man's life; **beere,** bier. **1212. swough,** swoon; **abraide,** started up. **1213. sike,** sigh. **1217. sighte,** sighed. **1218. glade,** gladden.

But at the laste, as hir yë glente
Aside, anoon she gan his swerd espye,
As it lay bare, and gan for fere crye,

And axed him why he it hadde out drawe.
And Troilus anoon the cause hire tolde,
And how himself therwith he wolde han slawe;
For which Criseide upon him gan biholde,
And gan him in hir armes faste folde,
And saide, "O mercy God, lo, which a deede!
Allas, how neigh we weren bothe dede!

Thanne if I nadde spoken, as grace was,
Ye wolde han slain youreself anoon?" quod she.
"Ye, doutelees." And she answerde "Allas,
For by that ilke Lord that made me,
I nolde a furlong way on live have be
After youre deeth, to han been crowned queene
Of al that land the sonne on shineth sheene;

But with this selve swerd which that here is
Myselve I wolde han slawe," quod she tho.
"But ho, for we han right ynough of this,
And lat us rise, and straight to bedde go,
And there lat us speken of oure wo—
For by the morter which that I see brenne
Knowe I ful wel that day is nat fer henne."

Whan they were in hir bed, in armes folde,
Nought was it lik tho nightes herbiforn,
For pitously eech other gan biholde,
As they that hadden al hir blisse ylorn,
Biwailing ay the day that they were born;

1223. glente, glanced. **1226. axed,** asked. **1228. slawe,** slain. **1237. a furlong** way, i.e., the time it takes to travel a furlong. **1239. sheene,** brightly. **1241. slawe,** slain. **1245. morter,** mortar, a thick candle serving as a chamber-light; **brenne,** burn. **1246. fer henne,** far hence. **1250. ylorn,** lost.

Til at the laste this sorweful wight Criseide
To Troilus thise ilke wordes saide.

"Lo, herte myn, wel woot ye this," quod she,
"That if a wight alway his wo complaine,
And seeketh nought how holpen for to be,
It nis but folye and encrees of paine;
And sin that here assembled be we twaine
To finde boote of wo that we been inne,
It were al time soone to biginne.

I am a womman, as ful wel ye woot,
And as I am avised sodeinly,
So wol I telle you, whil it is hoot:
Me thinketh thus, that nouther ye nor I
Oughte half this wo to maken skilfully,
For ther is art ynough for to redresse
That yit is mis, and sleen this hevinesse.

Sooth is, the wo the which that we been inne,
For ought I woot, for no thing elles is
But for the cause that we sholden twinne:
Considered al, ther nis namore amis.
But what is thanne a remedye unto this,
But that we shape us soone for to meete?
This al and som, my dere herte sweete.

Now that I shal wel bringen it aboute
To come ayain soone after that I go,
Therfore am I no manere thing in doute;
For dredelees, within a wike or two
I shal been here, and that it may be so,
By alle right and in a wordes fewe
I shal you wel an heep of wayes shewe.

1256. holpen, helped. **1257. encrees,** increase. **1259. boote,** remedy. **1262.** i.e., And as I am capable of finding expedients quickly. **1263. hoot,** hot. **1264. nouther,** neither. **1265. skilfully,** reasonably. **1267. mis,** amiss; **sleen,** destroy. **1270. twinne,** separate. **1273. shape us,** arrange. **1274. This . . . som,** i.e., this is all there is to it. **1278. dredelees,** doubtless; **wike,** week.

For which I wol nat make long sermoun—
For time ylost may nat recovered be—
But I wol goon to my conclusioun,
And to the beste, in ought that I can see.
And, for the love of God, foryive it me
If I speke ought ayains youre hertes reste,
For, trewely, I speke it for the beste,

Making alway a protestacioun
That now thise wordes, which that I shal saye,
Nis but to shewen you my mocioun
To finde unto oure help the beste waye;
And taketh it noon other wise, I praye:
For in effect what so ye may comaunde
That wol I doon, for that is no demaunde.

Now herkneth. This ye han wel understonde:
My going graunted is by parlement
So ferforth that it may nat be withstonde
For al this world, as by my juggement;
And sin ther helpeth noon avisement
To letten it, lat it passe out of minde,
And lat us shape a bettre way to finde.

The soothe is, the twinning of us twaine
Wol us disese and cruelliche anoye;
But him bihoveth som time han a paine
That serveth Love, if that he wol han joye.
And sin I shal no ferther out of Troye
Than I may riden ayain on half a morwe,
It oughte lesse causen us to sorwe,

So as I shal nat so been hid in mewe,
That day by day, myn owene herte dere—

1285. ought, anything. **1289. protestacioun,** declaration. **1291. mocioun,** desire. **1295. demaunde,** question. **1298. ferforth,** far. **1300. avisement,** plan. **1301. letten,** prevent. **1302. shape,** arrange. **1303. twinning,** separation. **1304. disese,** distress; **anoye,** hurt. **1308. morwe,** morning. **1310. mewe,** cage.

Sin wel ye woot that it is now a trewe—
Ye shal ful wel al myn estaat yheere;
And er that trewe is doon, I shal been here.
And thanne have ye bothe Antenor ywonne,
And me also: beeth glad now, if ye conne.

And thenk right thus: Criseide is now agoon;
But what, she shal come hastiliche ayain.
And whan, allas? By God, lo, right anoon,
Er dayes ten, this dar I saufly sayn.
And thanne at erste shal we be so fain,
So as we shal togideres evere dwelle,
That al this world ne mighte oure blisse telle.

I see that ofte time, ther as we been now,
That for the beste, oure conseil for to hide,
Ye speke nat with me, nor I with you,
In fourtenight, ne see you go ne ride.
May ye nought ten dayes thanne abide
For myn honour? In swich an aventure,
Ywis, ye mowen elles lite endure.

Ye knowe eek how that al my kin is here,
But if that onliche it my fader be;
And eek mine othere thinges alle yfere,
And nameliche, my dere herte, ye,
Whom that I nolde leven for to see
For al this world, as wid as it hath space—
Or elles see ich nevere Joves face.

Why trowe ye my fader in this wise
Coveiteth to see me, but for drede
Lest in this town that folkes me despise,

1312. **trewe,** truce. 1313. **al myn estaat,** i.e., all about me. 1315. **ywonne,** gained. 1320. **saufly,** safely. 1321. **erste,** last; **fain,** glad. 1325. **conseil,** secrets. 1330. **mowen,** may; **lite,** little. 1332. **But if,** unless; **onliche,** only. 1333. **yfere,** together. 1334. **nameliche,** especially. 1335. **leven,** cease.

By cause of him, for his unhappy deede?
What woot my fader what lif that I lede?
For if he wiste in Troye how wel I fare,
Us needeth for my wending nought to care.

Ye seen that every day, eek more and more,
Men trete of pees, and it supposed is
That men the queene Elaine shal restore,
And Greekes us restoren that is mis;
So though ther nere confort noon but this,
That men purposen pees on every side,
Ye may the bettre at ese of herte abide.

For if that it be pees, myn herte dere,
The nature of the pees moot needes drive
That men moste entrecommunen yfere,
And to and fro eek ride and goon as blive,
Alday as thikke as been fleen from an hive,
And every wight han libertee to bleve
Wher as him liste the bet, withouten leve.

And though so be that pees ther may be noon,
Yit hider, though ther nevere pees ne were,
I moste come, for whider sholde I goon,
Or how, meschaunce, sholde I dwellen there,
Among tho men of armes evere in fere?
For which, as wisly God my soule rede,
I can not seen wherof ye sholden drede.

Have here another way: if it so be
That al this thing ne may you nat suffise,
My fader, as ye knowen wel, pardee,

1348. mis, amiss. **1353. moot,** must; **drive,** bring it about. **1354. moste,** must; **entrecommunen,** intermingle. **1355. goon,** walk; **as blive,** quickly. **1356. Alday,** constantly; **been,** bees; **fleen,** fly. **1357. bleve,** remain. **1358. liste,** it may please; **bet,** better; **leve,** permission. **1362. meschaunce,** i.e., by ill luck. **1363. in fere,** together. **1364. wisly,** surely; **rede,** provide for.

Is old, and elde is full of coveitise,°
And I right now have founden al the gise°
Withouten net wherwith I shal him hente,°
And herkneth now, if that ye wol assente:

Lo, Troilus, men sayn that hard it is
The wolf ful and the wether hool° to have;
This is to sayn that men ful ofte, ywis,
Mote spenden part, the remenant for to save;
For ay with gold men may the herte grave°
Of him that set is upon coveitise;
And how I mene I shal it you devise:

The moeble° which that I have in this town
Unto my fader shal I take, and saye
That right for trust and for savacioun°
It sent is fro a freend of his or twaye;
The whiche freendes ferventliche him praye
To senden after more, and that in hie,°
Whil that this town stant thus in jupartye.°

And that shal been an huge quantitee—
Thus shal I sayn—but lest it folk espide,
This may be sent by no wight but by me.
I shal eek shewen him, if pees bitide,
What freendes that I have on every side
Toward the court, to doon the wratthe pace°
Of Priamus, and doon him stonde in grace.

So what for oo thing and for other, sweete,
I shal him so enchaunte with my sawes,°
That right in hevene his soule is shal he mete;°
For° al Appollo, or his clerkes lawes,

1369. elde, old age; **coveitise,** avarice. **1370. gise,** manner. **1371. hente,** catch. **1374. wether,** ram; **hool,** whole. **1377. grave,** engrave. **1380. moeble,** possessions. **1382. savacioun,** preservation. **1385. hie,** haste. **1386. stant,** stands; **jupartye,** jeopardy. **1392. Toward,** i.e., associated with; **doon,** make; **pace,** pass away. **1395. sawes,** stories. **1396. mete,** dream. **1397. For,** despite.

Or calculing, availeth nat three hawes:
Desir of gold shal so his soule blende
That as me list I shal wel make an ende.

And if he wolde ought by his sort it preve
If that I lie, in certain I shal fonde
Disturben him and plukke him by the sleeve,
Making his sort, or beren him on honde
He hath nat wel the goddes understonde—
For goddes speken in amphilogies,
And for oo sooth they tellen twenty lies.

Eek drede foond first goddes, I suppose—
Thus shal I sayn—and eek his coward herte
Made him amis the goddes text to glose,
Whan he forfered out of Delphos sterte.
And but I make him soone to converte,
And doon my reed within a day or twaye,
I wol to you oblige me to deye."

And treweliche, as writen wel I finde
That al this thing was said of good entente,
And that hir herte trewe was and kinde
Towardes him, and spak right as she mente;
And that she starf for wo neigh whan she wente,
And was in purpos evere to be trewe:
Thus writen they that of hir werkes knewe.

This Troilus, with herte and eres spradde,
Herde al this thing devisen to and fro;
And verrailiche it seemed that he hadde

1398. calculing, divination; **hawes,** hawthorn berries. **1399. blende,** deceive. **1401. ought,** in any way; **sort,** augury; **preve,** test. **1402. fonde,** try. **1404. beren him on honde,** persuade him. **1406. amphilogies,** ambiguities. **1408. foond,** invented. **1410. glose,** interpret. **1411. forfered,** terrified; **Delphos,** Delphi, where the oracle of Apollo first warned Calchas of the impending doom of Troy; **sterte,** started. **1412.** And unless I make him change his mind soon. **1413. reed,** advice. **1414. oblige me,** obligate myself. **1419. starf,** died. **1422. spradde,** opened. **1423. devisen,** i.e., described.

The selve wit;° but yit to late hire go,
His herte misforyaf° him everemo.
But finally he gan his herte wreste°
To trusten hire, and took it for the beste.

For which the grete furye of his penaunce°
Was queint° with hope, and therwith hem bitweene
Bigan for joye th'amorouse daunce;
And as the briddes, whan the sonne is sheene,°
Deliten in hir song in leves greene,
Right so the wordes that they spake yfere°
Delited hem and made hir hertes clere.

But nathelees, the wending of Criseide
For al this world may nat out of his minde;
For which ful ofte he pitously hire prayde
That of hir heeste° he mighte hire trewe finde,
And saide hire, "Certes, if ye be unkinde,
And but ye come at day set° into Troye,
Ne shal I nevere have hele,° honour, ne joye.

For also sooth as sonne uprist o morwe,°
And God so wisly° thou me, woful wrecche,
To reste bringe out of this cruel sorwe,
I wol myselven slee if that ye drecche.°
But of my deeth though litel be to recche,°
Yit er that ye me causen so to smerte,
Dwelle rather here, myn owene sweete herte.

For trewely, myn owene lady dere,
Tho sleightes yit that I have herd you stere°
Ful shaply been to failen alle yfere.°

1425. **selve wit,** same idea. 1426. **misforyaf,** misgave. 1427. **wreste,** turn. 1429. **penaunce,** suffering. 1430. **queint,** quenched. 1432. **sheene,** bright. 1434. **yfere,** together. 1439. **heeste,** promise. 1441. **but,** unless; **set,** appointed. 1442. **hele,** health. 1443. **also,** as; **uprist,** rises up; **o morwe,** in morning. 1444. **wisly,** surely. 1446. **slee,** slay; **drecche,** delay. 1447. **recche,** care. 1451. **sleightes,** tricks; **stere,** i.e., devise. 1452. **shaply,** likely; **yfere,** together.

For thus men saith: 'That oon thenketh the bere,
But al another thenketh his ledere.'
Youre sire is wis, and said is, out of drede,
'Men may the wise atrenne and nought atrede.'

It is ful hard to halten unespied
Bifore a crepel, for he can the craft.
Youre fader is in sleighte as Argus yëd;
For al be that his moeble is him biraft,
His olde sleighte is yit with him laft:
Ye shal nat blende him for youre wommanhede,
Ne feine aright, and that is al my drede.

I noot if pees shal everemo bitide,
But pees or no, for ernest ne for game,
I woot sin Calcas on the Greekes side
Hath ones been, and lost so foule his name,
He dar namore come here ayain for shame:
For which that way, for ought I can espye,
To trusten on nis but a fantasye.

Ye shal eek seen youre fader shal you glose
To been a wif; and as he can wel preche,
He shal som Greek so praise and wel alose
That ravisshen he shal you with his speeche,
Or do you doon by force as he shal teche;
And Troilus, of whom ye nil han routhe,
Shal causelees so sterven in his trouthe.

And over al this, youre fader shal despise
Us alle, and sayn this citee nis but lorn,

1453. **bere,** bear. 1454. **ledere,** leader, keeper. 1455. **drede,** doubt. 1456. **atrenne,** outrun; **atrede,** outthink. 1457. **halten,** limp. 1458. **crepel,** cripple; **can,** knows; **craft,** art. 1459. **sleighte,** trickery; **as Argus yëd,** eyed like Argus, who had a hundred eyes. 1460. **moeble,** possessions; **him biraft,** removed from him. 1461. **laft,** left. 1462. **blende,** trick. 1463. **feine,** pretend. 1471. **glose,** flatter. 1473. **alose,** praise. 1475. **do,** make. 1476. **routhe,** pity. 1477. **causelees,** i.e., guiltless; **sterven,** die. 1479. **nis but lorn,** is no better than lost.

And that th'assege nevere shal arise,
Forwhy the Greekes han it alle sworn,
Til we be slain and down oure walles torn.
And thus he shal you with his wordes fere,
That ay drede I that ye wol bleven there.

Ye shal eek seen so many a lusty knight
Among the Greekes, ful of worthinesse,
And eech of hem with herte, wit, and might,
To plesen you doon al his bisinesse,
That ye shal dullen of the rudenesse
Of us sely Troyans, but if routhe
Remorde you, or vertu of youre trouthe.

And this to me so grevous is to thinke
That fro my brest it wol my soule rende;
Ne, dredelees, in me ther may nat sinke
A good opinion if that ye wende,
Forwhy youre fadres sleighte wol us shende:
And if ye goon, as I have told you yore,
So thenk I nam but deed, withoute more;

For which with humble, trewe, and pitous herte,
A thousand times mercy I you praye;
So reweth on mine aspre paines smerte,
And dooth somwhat as that I shal you saye,
And lat us stele away bitwixe us twaye.
And think that folye is whan man may chese
For accident his substaunce ay to lese.

I mene thus, that sin we mowe er day
Wel stele away and been togidre so,

1480. **arise,** i.e., be raised. 1481. **Forwhy,** because. 1483. **fere,** frighten. 1484. **bleven,** remain. 1489. **dullen,** become bored. 1490. **sely,** poor; **but if,** unless; **routhe,** pity. 1491. **Remorde,** cause remorse to; **vertu,** power. 1494. **dredelees,** doubtless; **sinke,** i.e., take hold. 1495. **opinion,** expectation. 1496. **Forwhy,** because; **shende,** ruin. 1498. **deed,** dead. 1501. **reweth,** have pity; **aspre,** bitter. 1504. **chese,** choose. 1505. To lose forever the inner worth because of the outward aspect. 1506. **mowe,** may.

What wit were it to putten in assay,°
In caas ye sholden to youre fader go,
If that ye mighten come ayain or no?
Thus mene I, that it were a greet folye
To putte that sikernesse in jupartye.°

And vulgarly to speken of substaunce,°
Of tresor may we bothe with us lede
Ynough to live in honour and plesaunce,
Til into time that we shul been dede:
And thus we may eschewen al this drede.
For everich other way ye can recorde,°
Myn herte, ywis, may therwith nought accorde.

And hardily,° ne dredeth no poverte,
For I have kin and freendes elleswhere,
That though we comen in oure bare sherte
Us sholde neither lakken gold ne gere,°
But been honoured whil we dwelten there:
And go we anoon, for as in myn entente,
This is the beste, if that ye wol assente."

Criseide with a sik° right in this wise
Answerde, "Ywis, my dere herte trewe,
We may wel stele away as ye devise,
And finden swich unthrifty° wayes newe;
But afterward ful sore it wol us rewe.°
And helpe me God so at my moste neede,
As causelees ye suffren al this drede.

For thilke day that I, for cherissinge
Or drede of fader or any other wight,
Or for estaat, delit, or for weddinge,
Be fals to you, my Troilus, my knight,

1508. wit, sense; **in assay,** to the test. **1512. sikernesse,** security; **jupartye,** jeopardy. **1513. substaunce,** money. **1518. recorde,** devise. **1520. hardily,** assuredly. **1523. gere,** possessions. **1527. sik,** sigh. **1530. unthrifty,** profitless. **1531. rewe,** rue.

Saturnes doughter Juno, thurgh hir might,
As wood as Atthamante do me dwelle
Eternalliche in Styx, the pit of helle.

And thus on every god celestial
I swere it you, and eek on eech goddesse,
On every nymphe and deitee infernal,
On satyry and fauny, more and lesse,
That halve-goddes been of wildernesse;
And Atropos my threed of lif tobreste,
If I be fals: now trowe me if you leste.

And thou, Simois, that as an arwe clere
Thurgh Troye rennest ay downward to the see,
Beer witnesse of this word that said is here,
That thilke day that ich untrewe be
To Troilus, myn owene herte free,
That thou returne bakward to thy welle,
And I with body and soule sinke in helle.

But that ye speke away thus for to go
And leten alle youre freendes, God forbede
For any womman that ye sholden so,
And namely sin Troye hath now swich neede
Of help. And eek of oo thing taketh heede:
If this were wist, my lif laye in balaunce,
And youre honour. God shilde us fro meschaunce!

And if so be that pees herafter take,
As alday happeth after anger game,
Why, lord, the sorwe and wo ye wolden make,
That ye ne dorste come ayain for shame;

1539. wood, mad; **Atthamante,** Athamas, whom the Furies drove mad at Juno's request; **do,** make. **1544. satyry,** the satyrs; **fauny,** the fauns. **1545. halve-,** demi-. **1546. tobreste,** break. **1547. trowe,** believe; **leste,** it please. **1548. Simois,** river of Troy; **arwe clere,** bright arrow. **1549. rennest,** run. **1552. free,** noble. **1553. welle,** source. **1558. namely,** especially. **1560. wist,** known. **1561. shilde,** defend. **1562. take,** i.e., is made. **1563. alday,** constantly; **game,** pleasure.

And er that ye juperten so youre name,
Beeth nought too hastif in this hote fare—
For hastif man ne wanteth nevere care.

What trowe ye the peple eek al aboute
Wolde of it saye? It is ful light t'arede:
They wolde saye and swere it out of doute,
That love ne droof you nought to doon this deede,
But lust voluptuous and coward drede.
Thus were al lost, ywis, myn herte dere,
Your honour which that now shineth so clere.

And also thinketh on myn honestee,
That flowreth yit, how foule I sholde it shende,
And with what filthe it spotted sholde be,
If in this forme I sholde with you wende;
Ne though I lived unto the worldes ende,
My name sholde I nevere ayainward winne:
Thus were I lost, and that were routhe and sinne.

And forthy slee with reson al this hete.
Men sayn the suffrant overcometh, pardee;
Eek whoso wol han lief, he lief moot lete.
Thus maketh vertu of necessitee
By pacience, and think that lord is he
Of Fortune ay that nought wol of hire recche,
And she ne daunteth no wight but a wrecche.

And trusteth this, that certes, herte sweete,
Er Phebus suster, Lucina the sheene,
The Leon passe out of this Ariete,
I wol been here withouten any weene:

1566. **juperten,** jeopardize. 1567. **hastif,** hasty. 1570. **light,** easy; **arede,** tell. 1572. **droof,** drove. 1577. **shende,** spoil. 1581. **ayainward,** back again. 1582. **routhe,** pity. 1583. **slee,** slay; **hete,** heat. 1584. **suffrant,** patient one; **overcometh,** triumphs. 1585. **lief,** what is dear; **moot,** must; **lete,** leave. 1588. **recche,** care. 1591. **Lucina,** the moon; **sheene,** bright. 1592. i.e., Pass out of its present House of the Ram and beyond the Lion. 1593. **weene,** doubt.

I mene, as helpe me Juno hevenes queene,
The tenthe day, but if° that deeth m'assaile,
I wol you seen withouten any faile."

"And now, so this be sooth," quod Troilus,
"I shal wel suffre unto the tenthe day,
Sin that I see that neede it moot be thus.
But for the love of God, if it be may,
So lat us stelen priveliche away:
For evere in oon,° as for to live in reste,
Myn herte saith that it wol be the beste."

"O mercy God, what lif is this?" quod she.
"Allas, ye slee me thus for verray teene!°
I see wel now that ye mistrusten me,
For by youre wordes it is wel yseene.
Now for the love of Cynthia the sheene,
Mistruste me nought thus causelees for routhe,
Sin to be trewe I have you plight my trouthe.

And thinketh wel that som time it is wit
To spende a time, a time for to winne;
Ne pardee, lorn° am I nought fro you yit,
Though that we been a day or two atwinne.°
Drive out tho fantasies you withinne,
And trusteth me, and leveth° eek youre sorwe,
Or, here my trouthe, I wol nought live til morwe.

For if ye wiste how sore it dooth° me smerte,
Ye wolde ceesse of this; for God, thou woost
The pure spirit weepeth in myn herte
To see you weepen that I love most,
And that I moot goon to the Greekes host.
Ye, nere it that I wiste remedye
To come ayain, right here I wolde die.

1595. **but if,** unless. 1602. **in oon,** constantly. 1605. **slee,** slay; **teene,** vexation. 1613. **lorn,** lost. 1614. **atwinne,** apart. 1616. **leveth,** leave. 1618. **wiste,** knew; **dooth,** makes.

But certes I am nought so nice a wight
That I ne can imaginen a way
To come ayain that day that I have hight,
For who may holde a thing that wol away?
My fader nought, for al his quainte play.
And by my thrift, my wending out of Troye
Another day shal turne us alle to joye.

Forthy with al myn herte I you biseeke,
If that you list doon ought for my prayere,
And for that love which that I love you eke,
That ere that I departe fro you here,
That of so good a confort and a cheere
I may you seen, that ye may bringe at reste
Myn herte, which that is o point to breste.

And over al this I praye you," quod she tho,
"Myn owene hertes soothfast suffisaunce,
Sin I am thyn al hool, withouten mo,
That whil that I am absent, no plesaunce
Of other do me fro youre remembraunce:
For I am evere agast, forwhy men rede
That love is thing ay ful of bisy drede.

For in this world ther liveth lady noon,
If that ye were untrewe—as God defende—
That so bitraised were or wo-bigoon
As I, that alle trouthe in you entende.
And doutelees, if that ich other wende,
I nere but deed: and er ye cause finde,
For Goddes love, so beeth me nought unkinde."

1625. **nice,** foolish. 1627. **hight,** promised. 1629. **nought,** i.e., cannot; **quainte,** clever; **play,** i.e., ability. 1630. **thrift,** prosperity. 1632. **Forthy,** therefore; **biseeke,** beseech. 1638. **o,** on; **breste,** break. 1640. **suffisaunce,** sufficiency. 1641. **hool,** whole. 1643. **do,** i.e., put. 1644. **forwhy,** because. 1645. **bisy,** anxious. 1647. **defende,** forbid. 1648. **bitraised,** betrayed; **were,** would be. 1649. **entende,** i.e., believe to be. 1650. **wende,** thought. 1651. **deed,** dead.

To this answerde Troilus and saide,
"Now God, to whom there nis no cause ywrye,
Me glade, as wis I nevere unto Criseide,
Sin thilke day I sawgh hire first with yë,
Was fals ne nevere shal til that I die:
At shorte wordes, wel ye may me leve.
I can namore: it shal be founde at preve."

"Graunt mercy, goode myn, ywis," quod she,
"And blisful Venus lat me nevere sterve
Er I may stonde of plesance in degree,
To quite him wel that so wel can deserve;
And whil that God my wit wol me conserve,
I shal so doon; so trewe I have you founde,
That ay honour to meward shal rebounde.

For trusteth wel that youre estaat royal,
Ne vain delit, nor only worthinesse
Of you in werre or torney marcial,
Ne pompe, array, nobleye, or eek richesse,
Ne made me to rewe on youre distresse,
But moral vertu, grounded upon trouthe—
That was the cause I first hadde on you routhe.

Eek gentil herte and manhood that ye hadde,
And that ye hadde, as me thoughte, in despit
Every thing that souned into badde,
As rudenesse and peplissh appetit,
And that youre reson bridled youre delit:
This made aboven every creature
That I was youre, and shal whil I may dure.

1654. ywrye, hidden. **1655. glade,** gladden; **wis,** sure. **1658. leve,** believe. **1659. preve,** proof. **1660. Graunt mercy,** many thanks. **1662. degree,** condition. **1663. quite,** repay. **1666. to meward,** toward me. **1668. only,** merely. **1669. werre,** war; **torney marcial,** martial tournament. **1670. nobleye,** aristocracy. **1671. rewe,** have pity. **1673. routhe,** pity. **1675. hadde,** held. **1676. souned,** tended. **1677. peplissh,** vulgar; **appetit,** desires. **1680. youre,** yours; **dure,** live.

And this may lengthe of yeres nought fordo,
Ne remuable Fortune deface;
But Juppiter, that of his might may do
The sorweful to be glad, so yive us grace
Er nightes ten to meeten in this place,
So that it may youre herte and myn suffise:
And fareth now wel, for time is that ye rise."

And after that they longe yplained hadde,
And ofte ykist and straite in armes folde,
The day gan rise, and Troilus him cladde,
And rewefulliche his lady gan biholde,
As he that felte deethes cares colde;
And to hire grace he gan him recomaunde:
Wher he was wo, this holde I no demaunde.

For mannes heed imaginen ne can,
N'entendement considere, ne tonge telle
The cruel paines of this sorweful man,
That passen every torment down in helle.
For whan he sawgh that she ne mighte dwelle,
Which that his soule out of his herte rente,
Withouten more out of the chambre he wente.

BOOK FIVE

The Prologue

Approchen gan the fatal destinee
That Joves hath in disposicioun,
And to you, angry Parcas, sustren three,

1681. **fordo,** corrupt. 1682. **remuable,** mutable. 1683. **do,** cause. 1688. **yplained,** lamented. 1689. **straite,** closely. 1693. **recomaunde,** commend. 1694. **Wher,** whether; **demaunde,** question. 1695. **heed,** head. 1696. **entendement,** attentiveness.

3. **Parcas,** Parcae, the three Fates.

Committeth to doon execucioun:
For which Criseide moste out of the town,
And Troilus shal dwellen forth in pine,
Til Lachesis his threed no lenger twine.

The Story

The gold-ytressed Phebus heigh on lofte
Thries hadde alle with his bemes clene
The snowes molte, and Zephyrus as ofte
Ybrought ayain the tendre leves greene,
Sin that the sone of Ecuba the queene
Bigan to love hire first, for whom his sorwe
Was al that she departe sholde amorwe.

Ful redy was at prime Diomede
Criseide unto the Greekes host to lede,
For sorwe of which she felte hir herte bleede,
As she that niste what was best to rede.
And trewely, as men in bookes rede,
Men wiste nevere womman han the care,
Ne was so loth out of a town to fare.

This Troilus, withouten reed or lore,
As man that hath his joyes eek forlore,
Was waiting on his lady everemore,
As she that was the soothfast crop and more
Of al his lust or joyes heretofore:
But Troilus, now farewel al thy joye,
For shaltou nevere seen hire eft in Troye.

6. pine, pain. **7. Lachesis,** the second Fate, who spun the thread of human lives. **10. molte,** melted; **Zephyrus,** the west wind. **12. Ecuba,** Hecuba, Troilus' mother. **14. amorwe,** in the morning. **15. prime,** 9 A.M. **18. niste,** knew not; **best to rede,** the best thing to do. **22. reed,** plan; **lore,** i.e., idea. **23. forlore,** lost. **25. crop and more,** branch and root. **26. lust,** pleasure. **28. eft,** again.

Sooth is that whil he bood° in this manere,
He gan his wo ful manly for to hide,
That wel unnethe° it seene was in his cheere;
But at the yate° ther she sholde out ride
With certain folk he hoved,° hire t'abide,
So wo-bigoon, al wolde he nought him plaine,°
That on his hors unnethe° he sat for paine.

For ire he quook,° so gan his herte gnawe
Whan Diomede on hors gan him to dresse,°
And saide to himself this ilke sawe,°
"Allas," quod he, "thus foul a wrecchednesse,
Why suffre ich it? Why nil ich it redresse?
Were it nat bet° atones for to die
Than everemore in langour° thus to crye?

Why nil I make atones riche and poore
To have ynough to doone er that she go?
Why nil I bringe al Troye upon a rore?°
Why nil I sleen° this Diomede also?
Why nil I rather with a man or two
Stele hire away? Why wol I this endure?
Why nil I helpen to myn owne cure?"

But why he nolde doon so fel° a deede
That shal I sayn, and why him liste it spare:°
He hadde in herte alwayes a manere drede
Lest that Criseide, in rumour of this fare,°
Sholde han been slain—lo, this was al his care,
And elles certain, as I saide yore,
He hadde it doon withouten wordes more.

29. **bood,** waited. 31. **unnethe,** hardly. 32. **yate,** gate. 33. **hoved,** lingered. 34. **al wolde he,** although he would; **him plaine,** complain. 35. **unnethe,** with difficulty. 36. **quook,** quaked. 37. **dresse,** mount. 38. **sawe,** speech. 41. **bet,** better. 42. **langour,** sickness. 45. **upon a rore,** into uproar. 46. **sleen,** slay. 50. **fel,** fierce. 51. **liste,** it pleased; **spare,** refrain from. 53. **rumour . . . fare,** uproar of this act.

Criseide whan she redy was to ride,
Ful sorwefully she sighte and saide allas;
But forth she moot, for ought that may bitide,
And forth she rit ful sorwefully a pas—
Ther is noon other remedye in this cas.
What wonder is though that hire sore smerte,
Whan she forgooth hir owene sweete herte?

This Troilus, in wise of curteisye,
With hawk on hande and with an huge route
Of knightes, rood and dide hire compaignye,
Passing al the valeye fer withoute,
And ferther wolde han riden out of doute
Ful fain, and wo was him to goon so soone:
But turne he moste, and it was eek to doone.

And right with that was Antenor ycome
Out of the Greekes host, and every wight
Was of it glad, and saide he was welcome.
And Troilus, al nere his herte light,
He pained him with al his fulle might
Him to withholde of weeping atte leeste,
And Antenor he kiste and made feeste.

And therwithal he moste his leve take,
And caste his yë upon hire pitously,
And neer he rood, his cause for to make,
To take hire by the hand al sobrely.
And Lord, so she gan weepen tendrely,
And he ful softe and slyly gan hire saye,
"Now holde youre day, and do me nat to deye."

With that his courser turned he aboute,
With face pale, and unto Diomede

58. **sighte,** sighed. 59. **moot,** i.e., must go. 60. **rit,** rides; **a pas,** at a walk. 64. **wise,** manner. 65. **route,** company. 66. **rood,** rode. 67. **fer,** far. 69. **fain,** gladly. 70. **moste,** must. 74. **al,** although. 75. **pained him,** took pains. 77. **feeste,** i.e., welcome. 80. **make,** i.e., plead. 83. **slyly,** stealthily. 84. **do,** cause.

No word he spak, ne noon of al his route:
Of which the sone of Tydeus took heede,
As he that coude more than the creede
In swich a craft, and by the reine hire hente.
And Troilus to Troye hoomward he wente.

This Diomede that ledde hire by the bridel,
Whan that he sawgh the folk of Troye awaye,
Thoughte, "Al my labour shal nat been on idel
If that I may, for somwhat shal I saye;
For at the worste it may yit shorte oure waye:
I have herd said eek times twies twelve,
'He is a fool that wol foryete himselve.' "

But nathelees, this thoughte he wel ynough:
That "Certainliche, I am aboute nought
If that I speke of love or make it tough,
For doutelees, if she have in hir thought
Him that I gesse, he may nat been ybrought
So soone away. But I shal finde a mene
That she nought wite as yit shal what I mene."

This Diomede, as he that coude his good,
Whan this was doon, gan fallen forth in speeche
Of this and that, and axed why she stood
In swich disese, and gan hire eek biseeche,
That if that he encreesse mighte or eeche
With any thing hir ese, that she sholde
Comande it him, and saide he doon it wolde.

For treweliche he swoor hire as a knight
That ther nas thing with which he mighte hire plese,
That he nolde doon his paine and al his might
To doon it, for to doon hir herte an ese;

88. **Tydeus,** Diomede's father. 89. **coude,** knew. 90. **hente,** took. 94. **on idel,** in vain. 96. **shorte,** shorten. 100. **I . . . nought,** i.e., I'm wasting my time. 101. **tough,** hard. 104. **mene,** means. 105. **wite,** know. 106. **coude . . . good,** knew what was good for him. 108. **axed,** asked. 109. **disese,** distress. 110. **eeche,** augment. 113. **swoor,** swore. 115. **paine,** i.e., best.

And prayde hire she wolde hir sorwe apese,
And saide, "Ywis, we Greekes can have joye
To honouren you as wel as folk of Troye."

He saide eek thus: "I woot you thinketh straunge—
No wonder is, for it is to you newe—
The aquaintance of thise Troyans to chaunge
For folk of Greece that ye nevere knewe.
But wolde nevere God but if as trewe
A Greek ye sholde among us alle finde
As any Troyan is, and eek as kinde.

And by the cause I swere you right, lo, now,
To been youre freend and helply to my might;
And for that more aquaintance eek of you
Have ich had than another straunger wight,
So fro this forth I praye you day and night,
Comandeth me, how sore that me smerte,
To doon al that may like unto youre herte;

And that ye me wolde as youre brother trete,
And taketh nought my frendshipe in despit;
And though youre sorwes be for thinges grete,
Noot I nat why, but out of more respit
Myn herte hath for t'amende it greet delit:
And if I may youre harmes nat redresse,
I am right sory for youre hevinesse,

For though ye Troyans with us Greekes wrothe
Han many a day been, alway yit, pardee,
Oo god of love in sooth we serven bothe:
And for the love of God, my lady free,
Whom so ye hate, as beeth nat wroth with me:
For trewely, ther can no wight you serve
That half so loth youre wratthe wolde deserve.

127. by . . . cause, therefore. **128. helply,** helpful; **to,** to the extent of. **133. like,** please. **135. despit,** scorn. **137. out . . . respit,** without further delay. **138. greet,** great. **147.** That would be half so loath to earn your anger.

And nere it° that we been so neigh the tente
Of Calcas, which that seen us bothe may,
I wolde of this you telle al myn entente.
But this enseled° til another day,
Yive me youre hand: I am and shal been ay—
God helpe me so—whil that my lif may dure,°
Youre owene aboven every creature.

Thus saide I nevere er now to womman born,
For God myn herte as wisly glade° so,
I loved nevere womman herebiforn
As paramours,° ne nevere shal no mo.°
And for the love of God, beeth nat my fo,
Al° can I nought to you, my lady dere,
Complaine aright, for I am yit to lere.°

And wondreth nought, myn owene lady bright,
Though that I speke of love to you thus blive;°
For I have herd er this of many a wight
Hath loved thing he nevere sawgh his live:°
Eek I am nat of power for to strive
Ayains the God of Love, but him obeye
I wol alway, and mercy I you praye.

Ther been so worthy knightes in this place,
And ye so fair, that everich of hem alle
Wol painen him° to stonden in youre grace:
But mighte me so fair a grace falle°
That ye me for youre servant wolde calle,
So lowely° ne so trewely you serve
Nil noon of hem as I shal til I sterve."°

Criseide unto that purpos lite° answerde,
As she that was with sorwe oppressed so

148. nere it, were it not. **151. this enseled,** i.e., with this sealed up. **153. dure,** last. **156. wisly,** surely; **glade,** gladden. **158. paramours,** true love; **mo,** others. **160. Al,** although. **161. lere,** be taught. **163. blive,** quickly. **165. his live,** i.e., before in his life. **171. painen him,** do his best. **172. falle,** befall. **174. lowely,** humbly. **175. sterve,** die. **176. lite,** little.

That in effect she nought his tales herde,
But here and ther, now here a word or two.
Hire thoughte hir sorweful herte brast atwo,
For whan she gan hir fader fer espye,
Wel neigh down of hir hors she gan to sie.

But nathelees she thanketh Diomede
Of al his travaile and his goode cheere,
And that him liste his frendshipe hire to bede,
And she accepteth it in good manere,
And wol do fain that is him lief and dere,
And trusten him she wolde, and wel she mighte,
As saide she; and from hir hors sh'alighte.

Hir fader hath hire in his armes nome,
And twenty time he kiste his doughter sweete,
And saide, "O dere doughter myn, welcome."
She saide eek she was fain with him to meete,
And stood forth muwet, milde, and mansuete.
But here I leve hire with hir fader dwelle,
And forth I wol of Troilus you telle.

To Troye is come this woful Troilus
In sorwe aboven alle sorwes smerte,
With felon look and face despitous;
Tho sodeinly down fro his hors he sterte,
And thurgh his palais with a swollen herte
To chambre he wente: of nothing took he heede,
Ne noon to him dar speke a word for drede.

And ther his sorwes that he spared hadde
He yaf an issue large, and "Deeth!" he cride.
And in his throwes frenetik and madde
He curseth Jove, Appollo, and eek Cupide;

178. tales, words. **180. brast,** broke. **181. fer,** afar. **182. sie,** sink. **184. travaile,** pains. **185. liste,** it pleased; **bede,** offer. **187. fain,** gladly; **that,** what; **lief,** agreeable. **190. nome,** taken. **194. muwet,** mute; **mansuete,** gentle. **199. felon,** murderous; **despitous,** cruel. **206. throwes,** throes.

He curseth Ceres, Bacus, and Cypride,°
His birthe, himself, his fate, and eek nature,
And, save his lady, every creature.

To bedde he gooth and wheeleth° ther and turneth
In furye as dooth he Ixion° in helle,
And in this wise he neigh til day sojurneth.
But tho bigan his herte a lite° unswelle,
Thurgh teres which that gonnen up to welle,
And pitously he cride upon Criseide,
And to himself right thus he spak and saide:

"Wher is myn owene lady lief° and dere?
Wher is hir white brest, wher is it, where?
Wher been hir armes and hir yën clere,
That yesternight this time with me were?
Now may I weepe allone many a tere,
And graspe aboute I may, but in this place,
Save a pilwe,° I finde nought t'enbrace.

How shal I do whan she shal come ayain?
I noot, allas. Why leet ich hire to go?
As wolde God ich hadde as tho been slain!
O herte myn, Criseide, O sweete fo,
O lady myn that I love and na mo,
To whom for everemore myn herte I dowe,°
See how I die—ye nil me nat rescowe.°

Who seeth you now, my righte lode sterre?°
Who sit right now, or stant° in youre presence?
Who can conforten now youre hertes werre?°
Now I am goon, whom yive ye audience?
Who speketh for me right now in myn absence?

208. **Bacus,** Bacchus; **Cypride,** i.e., Venus. 211. **wheeleth,** revolves. 212. **Ixion,** whose doom in the Underworld was to be turned endlessly on a wheel. 214. **lite,** little. 218. **lief,** beloved. 224. **pilwe,** pillow. 230. **dowe,** give. 231. **rescowe,** rescue. 232. **righte . . . sterre,** true loadstar. 233. **sit,** sits; **stant,** stands. 234. **werre,** war.

Allas, no wight, and that is al my care,
For wel woot I as yvele° as I ye fare.

How sholde I thus ten dayes ful endure,
Whan I the firste night have al this teene?°
How shal she doon eek, sorweful creature?
For tendernesse how shal she thus sustene°
Swich wo for me? O pitous, pale, and greene
Shal been youre fresshe wommanliche face
For langour, er ye turne° unto this place."

And whan he fil° in any slomberinges,
Anoon biginne he sholde for to grone,
And dremen of the dredfulleste thinges
That mighte been, as mete° he were allone,
In place horrible making ay his mone;
Or meten that he was amonges alle
His enemies, and in hir handes falle.

And therwithal his body sholde sterte,
And with the stert al sodeinliche awake,
And swich a tremor feele aboute his herte
That of the fere his body sholde quake;
And therwithal he sholde a noise make,
And seeme as though he sholde falle deepe
From heigh o lofte,° and thanne he wolde weepe,

And rewen on° himself so pitously
That wonder was to heere his fantasye.
Another time he sholde mightily
Conforte himself, and sayn it was folye
So causelees swich drede for to drie;°
And eft biginne his aspre° sorwes newe,
That every man mighte on his sorwes rewe.

238. **yvele,** badly. **240. teene,** grief. **242. sustene,** sustain. **245. langour,** heart-sickness; **turne,** return. **246. fil,** fell. **249. mete,** dream. 259. **o lofte,** aloft. **260. rewen on,** feel pity for. **264. drie,** suffer. **265. eft,** again; **aspre,** bitter.

Who coude telle aright or ful descrive
His wo, his plainte, his langour, and his pine?—
Nought alle the men that han or been on live.
Thou redere maist thyself ful wel divine
That swich a wo my wit can nat define:
On idel for to write it sholde I swinke,
Whan that my wit is wery it to thinke.

On hevene yit the sterres weren seene,
Although ful pale ywoxen was the moone,
And whiten gan the orisonte sheene
Al eestward, as it wont is for to doone;
And Phebus with his rosy carte soone
Gan after that to dresse him up to fare,
Whan Troilus hath sent after Pandare.

This Pandare, that of al the day bifore
Ne mighte han comen Troilus to see,
Although he on his heed it hadde swore—
For with the king Priam al day was he,
So that it lay nought in his libertee
Nowher to goon—but on the morwe he wente
To Troilus, whan that he for him sente.

For in his herte he coude wel divine
That Troilus al night for sorwe wook,
And that he wolde telle him of his pine:
This knew he wel ynough withoute book.
For which to chambre straight the way he took,
And Troilus tho sobreliche he grette,
And on the bed ful soone he gan him sette.

"My Pandarus," quod Troilus, "the sorwe
Which that I drie I may nat longe endure—

268. **pine,** pain. 270. **redere,** reader. 272. **On idel,** in vain; **swinke,** toil. 274. **sterres,** stars. 275. **ywoxen,** grown. 276. **orisonte,** horizon; **sheene,** brightly. 279. **dresse him,** prepare. 283. **heed,** head. 289. **wook,** lay awake. 290. **pine,** suffering. 291. **book,** i.e., being told. 293. **grette,** greeted. 296. **drie,** suffer.

I trowe I shal nat liven til tomorwe:
For which I wolde always on aventure
To thee devisen of my sepulture
The forme, and of my moeble thou dispone
Right as thee seemeth best is for to doone.

But of the fir and flaumbe funeral
In which my body brennen shal to gleede,
And of the feeste and playes palestral
At my vigile, I praye thee take good heede
That al be wel, and offre Mars my steede,
My swerd, myn helm; and, leve brother dere,
My sheeld to Pallas yif, that shineth clere.

The powdre in which myn herte ybrend shal turne,
That praye I thee thou take and it conserve
In a vessel that men clepeth an urne
Of gold, and to my lady that I serve,
For love of whom thus pitousliche I sterve,
So yive it hire, and do me this plesaunce,
To prayen hire keepe it for a remembraunce.

For wel I feele by my maladye,
And by my dremes now and yore ago,
Al certainly that I moot needes die:
The owle which that highte Escaphilo
Hath after me shright al thise nightes two.
And god Mercurye, of me now, woful wrecche,
The soule gide, and whan thee liste it fecche."

Pandare answerde and saide, "Troilus,
My dere freend, as I have told thee yore

297. trowe, believe. **298. always on aventure,** i.e., in case I should die. **299. devisen,** arrange; **sepulture,** burial. **300. moeble,** possessions; **dispone,** dispose. **303. brennen,** burn. **304. playes,** games; **palestral,** athletic. **305. vigile,** wake. **307. leve,** beloved. **308. yif,** give. **309. ybrend,** burned. **311. clepeth,** call. **313. sterve,** die. **319. Escaphilo,** Ascalaphus, turned into an owl by Proserpina, queen of the realms of death. **320. shright,** shrieked. **322. liste,** it please.

That it is folye for to sorwen thus,
And causelees, for which I can namore:
But who so wol nought trowen reed ne lore,
I can nat seen in him no remedye,
But lat him worthen with his fantasye.

But Troilus, I praye thee, tel me now
If that thou trowe er this that any wight
Hath loved paramours as wel as thou—
Ye, God woot, and fro many a worthy knight
Hath his lady goon a fourtenight,
And he nat yit maad halvendeel the fare.
What neede is thee to maken al this care?—

Sin day by day thou maist thyselven see
That from his love or elles from his wif
A man moot twinnen of necessitee—
Ye, though he love hire as his owene lif:
Yit nil he with himself thus maken strif.
For wel thou woost, my leve brother dere,
That alway freendes may nat been yfere.

How doon thise folk that seen hir loves wedded
By freendes might, as it bitit ful ofte,
And seen hem in hir spouses bed ybedded?
God woot they take it wisely, faire, and softe,
Forwhy good hope halt up hir herte o lofte,
And for they can a time of sorwe endure:
As time hem hurt, a time dooth hem cure.

So sholdestou endure and laten slide
The time, and fonde to been glad and light:
Ten dayes nis so longe nought t'abide.
And sin she thee to comen hath bihight,

327. **reed,** advice. 329. **worthen,** i.e., be. 332. **paramours,** i.e., a mistress. 335. **halvendeel,** half; **fare,** fuss. 339. **twinnen,** separate. 345. **By . . . might,** i.e., through the arrangements of family friends; **bitit,** happens. 348. **Forwhy,** because; **halt,** holds. 350. **hurt,** hurts. 351. **laten,** let. 352. **fonde,** try. 354. **bihight,** promised.

She nil hir heeste breken for no wight:
For dreed thee nat that she nil finden waye
To come ayain—my lif that dorste I laye.

Thy swevenes eek, and al swich fantasye,
Drif out and lat hem faren to meschaunce;
For they proceede of thy malencolye,
That dooth thee feele in sleep al this penaunce.
A straw for alle swevenes signifiaunce!
God helpe me so, I counte hem nought a bene:
Ther woot no man aright what dremes mene.

For preestes of the temple tellen this,
That dremes been the revelaciouns
Of goddes, and as wel they telle, ywis,
That they been infernals illusiouns;
And leeches sayn that of complexiouns
Proceeden they, or fast or glotonye—
Who woot in sooth thus what they signifye?

Eek othere sayn that thurgh impressiouns,
As if a wight hath faste a thing in minde,
That therof cometh swiche avisiouns;
And othere sayn, as they in bookes finde,
That after times of the yeer by kinde
Men dreme, and that th'effect gooth by the moone—
But leef no dreem, for it is nought to doone.

Wel worthe of dremes ay thise olde wives!
And, treweliche, eek augurye of thise fowles—
For fere of which men weenen lese hir lives—
As ravenes qualm or shriching of thise owles,

355. **heeste,** promise. 357. **laye,** wager. 358. **swevenes,** dreams. 359. **Drif,** drive. 360. **malencolye,** black humor. 361. **dooth,** makes; **penaunce,** suffering. 363. **counte,** value. 368. **infernals,** hellish. 369. **leeches,** physicians; **complexiouns,** combinations of humors. 374. **avisiouns,** dreams. 376. **by kinde,** naturally. 378. **leef,** believe. 379. i.e., Let old women do what they can with dreams. 381. **weenen,** think; **lese,** to lose. 382. **qualm,** croak; **shriching,** screeching.

To trowen on it bothe fals and foul is.
Allas, allas, so noble a creature
As is a man shal dreden swich ordure!

For which with al myn herte I thee biseeche
Unto thyself that al this thou foryive.
And ris up now, withouten more speeche,
And lat us caste how forth may best be drive
The time, and eek how fresshly we may live
Whan that she comth, the which shal be right soone:
God helpe me so, the beste is thus to doone.

Ris, lat us speke of lusty lif in Troye
That we han led, and forth the time drive;
And eek of time coming us rejoye,
That bringen shal oure blisse now so blive.
And langour of thise twies dayes five–
We shal therwith so foryete oure oppresse,
That wel unnethe it doon us shal duresse.

This town is ful of lordes al aboute,
And trewes lasten al this mene while:
Go we playe us in som lusty route–
To Sarpedon, nat hennes but a mile.
And thus thou shalt the time wel bigile,
And drive it forth unto that blisful morwe
That thou hire see that cause is of thy sorwe.

Now ris, my dere brother Troilus,
For certes it noon honour is to thee
To weepe and in thy bed to jouken thus;
For treweliche, of oo thing trust to me:
If thou thus ligge a day or two or three,

383. trowen, believe. **385. ordure,** filthy stuff. **387. foryive,** give up. **389. caste,** arrange; **drive,** passed. **395. rejoye,** rejoice. **396. blive,** soon. **398. oppresse,** grief. **399. unnethe,** scarcely; **duresse,** hardship. **401. trewes,** truces. **402. route,** throng. **404. bigile,** while away. **409. jouken,** roost. **411. ligge,** lie.

The folk wol weene that thou for cowardise
Thee feinest sik, and that thou darst nat rise."

This Troilus answerde, "O brother dere,
This knowen folk that han ysuffred paine:
That though he weepe and make sorweful cheere
That feeleth harm and smert in every veine,
No wonder is, and though ich evere plaine
Or alway weepe, I am no thing to blame,
Sin I have lost the cause of al my game.

But sin of fin force I moot arise,
I shal arise as soone as evere I may—
And God, to whom myn herte I sacrifise,
So sende us hastily the tenthe day:
For ther was nevere fowl so fain of May
As I shal been whan that she comth in Troye
That cause is of my torment and my joye.

But whider is thy reed," quod Troilus,
"That we may playe us best in al this town?"
"By God, my conseil is," quod Pandarus,
"To ride and playe us with king Sarpedoun."
So longe of this they speken up and down,
Til Troilus gan at the laste assente
To rise, and forth to Sarpedon they wente.

This Sarpedon, as he that honorable
Was evere his live, and ful of heigh prowesse,
With al that mighte yserved been on table
That daintee was, al coste it greet richesse,
He fedde hem day by day, that swich noblesse,
As saiden bothe the moste and eek the leeste,
Was nevere er that day wist at any feeste.

412. weene, think. **413. feinest,** feign. **418. plaine,** complain. **420. game,** joy. **421. fin,** sheer. **425. fain,** glad. **428. reed,** advice. **436. evere his live,** all his life. **438. al,** although. **441. wist,** known.

Nor in this world ther is noon instrument
Delicious, thurgh wind or touche of corde,
As fer as any wight hath evere ywent
That tonge telle or herte may recorde,
That at that feeste it nas wel herd accorde;
Ne of ladies eek so fair a compaignye
On daunce, er tho, was nevere yseen with yë.

But what availeth this to Troilus,
That for his sorwe nothing of it roughte?
For evere in oon his herte pietous
Ful bisily Criseide his lady soughte:
On hire was evere al that his herte thoughte—
Now this, now that, so faste imagininge,
That glade, ywis, can him no festeyinge.

Thise ladies eek that at this feeste been,
Sin that he sawgh his lady was awaye,
It was his sorwe upon hem for to seen,
Or for to heere on instrumentes to playe:
For she that of his herte berth the keye
Was absent, lo, this was his fantasye—
That no wight sholde maken melodye!

Nor ther nas houre in al the day or night,
Whan he was there as no wight mighte him heere,
That he ne saide, "O lufsom lady bright,
How have ye faren sin that ye were there?
Welcome, ywis, myn owene lady dere."
But wailaway, al this nas but a maze:
Fortune his houve entended bet to glaze.

The lettres eek that she of olde time
Hadde him ysent he wolde allone rede,

443. **Delicious,** delightful. 444. **fer,** far. 445. **recorde,** recall. 446. **accorde,** i.e., played. 448. **tho,** then. 450. **roughte,** cared. 451. **pietous,** pitiful. 455. **glade,** gladden; **festeyinge,** feasting. 460. **For,** because; **berth.** bears. 465. **lufsom,** lovely. 469. **houve,** hood: to glaze one's hood is to beguile one.

An hundred sithe atwixen noon and prime,
Refiguring hir shap, hir wommanhede
Within his herte, and every word or deede
That passed was; and thus he droof t'an ende
The ferthe day, and saide he wolde wende,

And saide, "Leve brother Pandarus,
Entendestou that we shal here bileve
Til Sarpedon wol forth congeyen us?
Yit were it fairer that we tooke oure leve:
For Goddes love, lat us now soone at eve
Our leve take, and hoomward lat us turne;
For treweliche, I nil nat thus sojurne."

Pandare answerde, "Be we comen hider
To fecchen fir and rennen hoom ayain?
God helpe me so, I can nat tellen whider
We mighte goon, if I shal soothly sayn,
Ther any wight is of us more fain
Than Sarpedon; and if we hennes hie
Thus sodeinly, I holde it vilainye,

Sin that we saiden that we wolde bileve
With him a wike, and now thus sodeinly,
The ferthe day to take of him oure leve:
He wolde wondren on it, trewely.
Lat us holden forth oure purpos fermely,
And sin that ye bihighten him to bide,
Holde forward now, and after lat us ride."

This Pandarus with alle paine and wo
Made him to dwelle, and at the wikes ende
Of Sarpedon they tooke hir leve tho,
And on hir way they spedden hem to wende.

472. **sithe,** times. 473. **Refiguring,** recalling to mind. 475. **droof,** drove, made pass. 476. **ferthe,** fourth. 477. **Leve,** dear. 478. **bileve,** remain. 479. **congeyen,** dismiss. 485. **rennen,** run. 489. **hie,** hasten. 490. **vilainye,** rudeness. 491. **bileve,** stay. 492. **wike,** week. 496. **bihighten,** promised. 497. **forward,** agreement.

Quod Troilus, "Now Lord me grace sende
That I may finde at my hoom-cominge
Criseide comen," and therwith gan he singe.

"Ye, haselwode,"° thoughte this Pandare,
And to himself ful softeliche he saide,
"God woot, refreiden may this hote fare°
Er Calcas sende Troilus Criseide."
But nathelees he japed° thus and saide,
And swoor, ywis, his herte him wel bihighte°
She wolde come as soone as evere she mighte.

Whan they unto the palais were ycomen
Of Troilus, they down of hors alighte,
And to the chambre hir way thanne han they nomen,°
And into time that it gan to nighte
They spaken of Criseide the brighte;
And after this whan that hem bothe leste,°
They spedde hem fro the soper unto reste.

On morwe as soone as day bigan to clere,°
This Troilus gan of his sleep t'abraide,°
And to Pandare, his owene brother dere,
"For love of God," ful pitously he saide,
"As go we seen the palais of Criseide:
For sin we yit may have namore feeste,°
So lat us seen hir palais atte leeste."

And therwithal, his meinee for to blende,°
A cause he foond° in towne for to go,
And to Criseides hous they gonnen wende.
But Lord, this sely° Troilus was wo:
Him thoughte his sorweful herte braste° atwo,

505. haselwode, hazelwood: ? an expression of doubt. **507. refreiden,** turn cold; **fare,** behavior. **509. japed,** joked. **510. bihighte,** promised. **514. nomen,** taken. **517. leste,** it pleased. **519. clere,** brighten. **520. abraide,** awake. **524. feeste,** i.e., pleasure. **526. meinee,** retinue; **blende,** deceive. **527. foond,** invented. **529. sely,** innocent. **530. braste,** would break.

For whan he sawgh hir dores spered alle,
Wel neigh for sorwe adown he gan to falle.

Therwith whan he was war and gan biholde
How shet was every window of the place,
As frost him thoughte his herte gan to colde;
For which with chaunged deedlich pale face,
Withouten word he forthby gan to pace,
And as God wolde, he gan so faste ride
That no wight of his countenance espide.

Thanne saide he thus: "O palais desolat,
O hous of houses, whilom best ylight,
O palais empty and disconsolat,
O thou lanterne of which queint is the light,
O palais whilom day, that now art night,
Wel oughtestou to falle, and I to die,
Sin she is went that wont was us to gie.

O palais whilom crowne of palais alle,
Enlumined with sonne of alle blisse,
O ring fro which the rubye is out falle,
O cause of wo, that cause hast been of blisse,
Yit sin I may no bet, fain wolde I kisse
Thy colde dores, dorste I for this route:
And farewel, shrine of which the saint is oute."

Therwith he caste on Pandarus his yë
With chaunged face, and pitous to biholde,
And as he mighte his time aright espye,
Ay as he rood to Pandarus he tolde
His newe sorwe and eek his joyes olde,
So pitously, and with so deed an hewe,
That every wight mighte on his sorwe rewe.

531. spered, barred. **534. shet,** shut. **535. colde,** chill. **536. deedlich,** deadly. **537. forthby,** by; **pace,** pass. **541. whilom,** formerly; **ylight,** illuminated. **543. queint,** quenched. **546. gie,** govern. **551. bet,** better; **fain,** gladly. **552. route,** throng. **557. rood,** rode. **559. deed,** dead. **560. rewe,** have pity.

Fro thennesforth he rideth up and down,
And every thing cam him to remembraunce,
As he rood forby° places of the town
In which he whilom hadde al his plesaunce.
"Lo, yonder sawgh ich myn owene lady daunce,
And in that temple, with hir yën clere°
Me caughte first my righte° lady dere.

And yonder have I herd ful lustily
My dere herte laughe, and yonder playe
Sawgh ich hire ones eek ful blisfully;
And yonder ones to me gan she saye,
'Now goode sweete, love me wel, I praye.'
And yond so goodly gan she me biholde
That to the deeth myn herte is to hir holde.°

And at that corner in the yonder hous
Herde I myn alderlevest° lady dere,
So wommanly with vois melodious,
Singen so wel, so goodly and so clere,
That in my soule yit me thinketh ich heere
The blisful soun.° And in that yonder place
My lady first me took unto hir grace."

Thanne thoughte he thus: "O blisful lord Cupide,
Whan I the proces have in my memorye
How thou me hast werreyed° on every side,
Men mighte a book make of it lik a storye.°
What neede is thee to seeke on me victorye,
Sin I am thyn and hoolly° at thy wille?
What joye hastou thyn owene folk to spille?°

Wel hastou, lord, ywroke° on me thyn ire,
Thou mighty god and dredful for to greve.°

563. **forby,** past. 566. **clere,** bright. 567. **righte,** i.e., own true. 574. **holde,** obligated. 576. **alderlevest,** dearest of all. 580. **soun,** sound. 584. **werreyed,** made war on. 585. **storye,** history. 587. **hoolly,** wholly. 588. **spille,** bring to ruin. 589. **ywroke,** avenged. 590. **greve,** offend.

Now mercy, lord! thou woost wel I desire
Thy grace most of alle lustes leve,
And live and die I wol in thy bileve:
For which I n'axe in guerdoun but a boone—
That thou Criseide ayain me sende soone.

Distraine hir herte as faste to returne
As thou doost myn to longen hire to see:
Thanne woot I wel that she nil nought sojurne.
Now blisful lord, so cruel thou ne be
Unto the blood of Troye, I praye thee,
As Juno was unto the blood Thebane,
For which the folk of Thebes caughte hir bane."

And after this he to the yates wente,
Ther as Criseide out rood, a ful good pas,
And up and down ther made he many a wente,
And to himself ful ofte he saide, "Allas,
Fro hennes rood my blisse and my solas;
As wolde blisful God now for his joye
I mighte hire seen ayain come into Troye.

And to the yonder hil I gan hire gide,
Allas, and ther I took of hire my leve;
And yond I sawgh hire to hir fader ride,
For sorwe of which myn herte shal tocleve;
And hider hoom I cam whan it was eve,
And here I dwelle, out cast from alle joye,
And shal, til I may seen hire eft in Troye."

And of himself imagined he ofte
To been defeet, and pale, and waxen lesse
Than he was wont, and that men saiden softe,
"What may it be? Who can the soothe gesse

592. lustes leve, dear desires. **593. bileve,** creed. **594. axe,** ask; **guerdoun,** reward. **596. Distraine,** constrain. **602. bane,** destruction: for the story of Thebes, see below, line 1486. **605. wente,** turn. **607. solas,** delight. **613. tocleve,** break apart. **616. eft,** again. **618. defeet,** disfigured; **waxen,** grown.

Why Troilus hath al this hevinesse?"
And al this nas but his malencolye
That he hadde of himself swich fantasye.

Another time imaginen he wolde
That every wight that wente by the waye
Hadde of him routhe, and that they sayn sholde,
"I am right sory Troilus wol deye."
And thus he droof a day yit forth or twaye,
As ye have herd. Swich lif right gan he lede,
As he that stood bitwixen hope and drede.

For which him liked in his songes shewe
Th'encheson of his wo, as he best mighte;
And made a song of wordes but a fewe,
Somwhat his woful herte for to lighte;
And whan he was from every mannes sighte,
With softe vois he of his lady dere,
That absent was, gan singe as ye may heere:

Troilus' Song

"O sterre of which I lost have al the light,
With herte soor wel oughte I to biwaile
That evere derk in torment, night by night,
Toward my deeth with wind in steere I saile;
For which the tenthe night if that I faile
The giding of thy bemes bright an houre,
My ship and me Carybdis wol devoure."

This song whan he thus songen hadde, soone
He fil ayain into his sikes olde.
And every night, as was his wone to doone,

621. **hevinesse,** despondency. 626. **routhe,** pity. 628. **droof,** passed. 632. **encheson,** reason. 634. **lighte,** lighten. 638. **sterre,** star. 641. **steere,** control. 642. **faile,** miss. 644. **Carybdis,** Charybdis, the famous whirlpool. 646. **fil,** fell; **sikes,** sighs. 647. **wone,** custom.

He stood the brighte moone to biholde,
And al his sorwe he to the moone tolde,
And saide, "Ywis, whan thou art horned newe,
I shal be glad, if al the world be trewe.

I sawgh thine hornes olde eek by the morwe
Whan hennes rood my righte lady dere,
That cause is of my torment and my sorwe;
For which, O brighte Latona the clere,
For love of God, ren faste aboute thy spere:
For whan thine hornes newe ginnen springe,
Thanne shal she come that may my blisse bringe."

The dayes more, and lenger every night,
Than they been wont to be, him thoughte tho,
And that the sonne wente his cours unright,
By lenger way than it was wont to do;
And saide, "Ywis, me dredeth everemo
The sonnes sone, Phaton, be on live,
And that his fader carte amis he drive."

Upon the walles faste eek wolde he walke,
And on the Greekes host he wolde see;
And to himself right thus he wolde talke,
"Lo, yonder is my owene lady free,
Or elles yonder ther tho tentes be,
And thennes comth this air that is so soote
That in my soule I feele it dooth me boote.

And hardily, this wind that more and more
Thus stoundemele encreesseth in my face,
Is of my ladies deepe sikes sore;
I preve it thus: for in noon other place

655. **Latona,** ? error for Lucina, Latona's daughter and one of the names of Diana in her capacity as moon goddess. 656. **ren,** run; **spere,** sphere. 664. **Phaton,** Phaeton, whose attempt to drive the sun-chariot of his father Phoebus ended in disaster. 671. **soote,** sweet. 672. **boote,** i.e., good. 673. **hardily,** assuredly. 674. **stoundemele,** gradually. 675. **sikes,** sighs. 676. **preve,** prove.

Of al this town, save onliche° in this space,
Feele I no wind that souneth so lik paine;
It saith, 'Allas, why twinned° be we twaine?' "

This longe time he driveth forth° right thus,
Til fully passed was the ninthe night;
And ay biside him was this Pandarus,
That bisily dide al his fulle might
Him to conforte and make his herte light,
Yiving him hope alway the tenthe morwe
That she shal come and stinten° al his sorwe.

Upon that other side eek was Criseide
With wommen fewe among the Greekes stronge;
For which ful ofte a day, "Allas," she saide,
"That I was born! Wel may myn herte longe
After my deeth, for now live I too longe!
Allas, and I ne may it nat amende,
For now is wors than evere yit I wende:°

My fader nil for nothing do me grace
To goon ayain, for nought I can him queme;°
And if so be that I my terme pace,°
My Troilus shal in his herte deeme
That I am fals, and so it may wel seeme:
Thus shal ich have unthank° on every side—
That I was born so wailaway the tide!°

And if that I me putte in jupartye°
To stele away by night, and it bifalle
That I be caught, I shal be holde a spye;
Or elles, lo, this drede I most of alle,
If in the handes of som wrecche I falle,
I nam but lost, al be myn herte trewe—
Now mighty God, thou on my sorwe rewe!"°

677. onliche, only. **679. twinned,** separated. **680. driveth forth,** i.e., makes go by. **686. stinten,** put an end to. **693. wende,** would have believed. **695. queme,** gratify. **696. pace,** pass. **699. unthank,** ill will. **700. tide,** time. **701. jupartye,** jeopardy. **707. rewe,** have pity.

Ful pale ywaxen° was hir brighte face,
Hir limes° lene, as she that al the day
Stood, whan she dorste, and looked on the place
Ther she was born, and ther she dwelt hadde ay;
And al the night weeping, allas, she lay.
And thus despaired out of alle cure,
She ladde° hir lif, this woful creature.

Ful ofte a day she sighte° eek for distresse,
And in hirself she wente ay portrayinge
Of Troilus the grete worthinesse,
And alle his goodly wordes recordinge,°
Sin first that day hir love bigan to springe:
And thus she sette hir woful herte afire
Thurgh remembrance of that she gan desire.

In al this world ther nis so cruel herte
That hire hadde herd complainen in hir sorwe,
That nolde han weepen° for hir paines smerte;
So tendrely she wepte bothe eve and morwe,
Hire needed none teres for to borwe.°
And this was yit the worste of al hir paine:
Ther was no wight to whom she dorste hire plaine.°

Ful rewefully she looked upon Troye,
Biheeld the towres hye and eek the halles;
"Allas," quod she, "the plesance and the joye,
The which that now al turned into galle° is,
Have ich had ofte within the yonder walles.
O Troilus, what doostou now?" she saide.
"Lord, whether° thou yit thenke upon Criseide?

Allas I ne hadde trowed on youre lore,°
And went with you, as ye me redde° er this.

708. **ywaxen,** grown. 709. **limes,** limbs. 714. **ladde,** led. 715. **sighte,** sighed. 718. **recordinge,** recalling. 724. **weepen,** wept. 726. **borwe,** borrow. 728. **hire plaine,** complain. 732. **galle,** bitterness. 735. **whether,** i.e., I ask whether or not. 736. **I . . . trowed,** that I did not trust; **lore,** i.e., plan. 737. **redde,** advised.

Thanne hadde I now nat siked° half so sore.
Who mighte have said that I hadde doon amis
To stele away with swich oon as he is?
But al too late comth the letuarye°
Whan men the cors° unto the grave carye.

Too late is now to speke of that matere;
Prudence, allas, oon of thine yën three
Me lakked alway er that I cam here:
On time ypassed wel remembred me,
And present time eek coude ich wel ysee,
But futur time, er I was in the snare,
Coude I nat seen—that causeth al my care.

But nathelees, bitide what bitide,
I shal tomorwe at night, by eest or west,
Out of this host stele on som manere side,
And goon with Troilus wher as him lest:
This purpos wol ich holde, and this is best.
No fors of wikked tonges janglerye,°
For evere on love have wrecches had envye.

For whoso wol of every word take heede,
Or rulen him by every wightes wit,
Ne shal he nevere thriven, out of drede:°
For that that some men blamen evere yit,
Lo, other manere folk comenden it.
And as for me, for al swich variaunce,
Felicitee clepe I my suffisaunce.°

For which, withouten any wordes mo,
To Troye I wol, as for conclusioun."
But God it woot, er fully monthes two
She was ful fer° fro that entencioun:
For bothe Troilus and Troye town

738. siked, sighed. **741. letuarye,** medicine. **742. cors,** body. **755. fors,** matter; **janglerye,** babbling. **759. drede,** doubt. **763. clepe,** call; **suffisaunce,** contentment. **767. fer,** far.

Shal knottelees thurghout hir herte slide—
For she wol take a purpos for t'abide.

This Diomede, of whom you telle I gan,
Gooth now within himself ay arguinge,
With al the sleighte and al that evere he can,
How he may best, with shortest taryinge,
Into his net Criseides herte bringe;
To this entente he coude nevere fine:
To fisshen hire he laide out hook and line.

But nathelees wel in his herte he thoughte
That she was nat withoute a love in Troye,
For evere sitthen he hire thennes broughte
Ne coude he seen hire laughe or maken joye.
He niste how best hir herte for t'acoye:
"But for t'assaye," he saide, "nought it ne greveth,
For he that nought n'assayeth nought n'acheveth."

Yit saide he to himself upon a night,
"Now am I nat a fool, that woot wel how
Hir wo for love is of another wight,
And herupon to goon assaye hire now?
I may wel wite it nil nat been my prow:
For wise folk in bookes it expresse,
'Men shal nat wowe a wight in hevinesse.'

But whoso mighte winnen swich a flowr
From him for whom she moorneth night and day,
He mighte sayn he were a conquerour."
And right anoon, as he that bold was ay,
Thoughte in his herte, "Happe how happe may,
Al sholde I die, I wol hir herte seeche:
I shal namore lesen but my speeche."

769. knottelees, knotless, i.e., like a thread without knots. **773. sleighte,** trickery; **can,** knows. **776. fine,** put an end. **782. niste,** knew not; **acoye,** tame. **789. wite,** know; **prow,** profit. **791. wowe,** woo. **797. Al,** although; **seeche,** seek. **798. lesen,** lose.

This Diomede, as bookes us declare,
Was in his needes prest° and corageous,
With sterne vois and mighty limes square,°
Hardy, testif,° strong, and chivalrous
Of deedes, lik his fader Tydeus;
And some men sayn he was of tonge large;°
And heir he was of Calydoine and Arge.°

Criseide mene° was of hir stature,
Therto of shap, of face, and eek of cheere,
Ther mighte been no fairer creature;
And ofte times this was hir manere:
To goon ytressed with hir heres clere
Down by hir coler at hir bak bihinde,°
Which with a threed of gold she wolde binde;

And, save hir browes joineden yfere,°
Ther nas no lak° in ought I can espyen;
But for to speken of hir yën clere,
Lo, trewely they writen that hire sien°
That Paradis stood formed in hir yën;
And with hir riche beautee everemore
Stroof° love in hire ay which of hem was more.

She sobre was, eek simple° and wis withal,
The beste ynorisshed° eek that mighte be,
And goodly of hir speeche in general;
Charitable, estaatlich, lusty, free,°
Ne nevere mo ne lakked hire pitee:
Tendre-herted, sliding of corage°—
But trewely I can nat telle hir age.

800. **needes,** personal actions; **prest,** quick. 801. **square,** strong. 802. **testif,** headstrong. 804. **large,** lax. 805. **Calydoine,** Calydon; **Arge,** Argos. 806. **mene,** middling. 810–11. To go about with her bright hair braided and hanging down over her collar behind. 813. **yfere,** together. 814. **lak,** blemish. 816. **sien,** saw. 819. **Stroof,** strove. 820. **simple,** sincere. 821. **ynorisshed,** brought up. 823. **estaatlich,** dignified; **lusty,** lively; **free,** generous. 825. **corage,** heart.

And Troilus wel waxen was in highte,
And compleet formed by proporcioun,
So wel that kinde it nought amenden mighte;
Yong, fressh, strong, and hardy as leoun,
Trewe as steel in eech condicioun,
Oon of the best entecched creature
That is or shal whil that the world may dure.

And certainly in storye it is founde
That Troilus was nevere unto no wight,
As in his time, in no degree secounde
In durring doon that longeth to a knight;
Al mighte a geant passen him of might,
His herte ay with the firste and with the beste
Stood paregal, to durre doon that him leste.

But for to tellen forth of Diomede:
It fil that after on the tenthe day
Sin that Criseide out of the citee yede,
This Diomede, as fressh as braunche in May,
Cam to the tente ther as Calcas lay,
And feined him with Calcas han to doone:
But what he mente I shal you tellen soone.

Criseide, at shorte wordes for to telle,
Welcomed him and down him by hire sette—
And he was ethe ynough to maken dwelle.
And after this, withouten longe lette,
The spices and the win men forth hem fette,
And forth they speke of this and that yfere,
As freendes doon, of which som shal ye heere.

828. **compleet,** without any defect. 829. **kinde,** nature. 832. **entecched,** endowed with good qualities. 833. **dure,** last. 837. **durring doon,** daring to do; **longeth to,** is appropriate for. 838. **Al,** although; **geant,** giant; **passen,** be superior to. 840. **paregal,** on equal terms; **durre,** dare. 842. **fil,** befell. 843. **yede,** went. 846. **feined him,** pretended; **han to doone,** to have business. 850. **ethe,** easy; **dwelle,** remain. 851. **lette,** delay. 852. **fette,** fetched. 853. **yfere,** together.

He gan first fallen of the werre° in speeche
Bitwixen hem and the folk of Troye town,
And of th'assege° he gan hire eek biseeche
To tellen him what was hir opinioun;
Fro that demande he so descendeth down
To axen° hire if that hire straunge thoughte
The Greekes gise° and werkes that they wroughte;

And why hir fader tarieth so longe
To wedden hire unto some worthy wight.
Criseide, that was in hir paines stronge
For love of Troilus hir owene knight,
As fer forth as she conning° hadde or might
Answerde him tho, but as of his entente
It seemed nat she wiste° what he mente.

But nathelees this ilke Diomede
Gan in himself assure,° and thus he saide,
"If ich aright have taken of you heede,
Me thinketh thus, O lady myn Criseide,
That sin I first hand on youre bridel laide,
Whan ye out come of Troye by the morwe,
Ne coude I nevere seen you but in sorwe.

Can I nat sayn what may the cause be
But if° for love of som Troyan it were,
The which right sore wolde athinken° me
That ye for any wight that dwelleth there
Sholden spille a quarter of a tere,
Or pitously youreselven so bigile—
For dredelees,° it is nought worth the while.

The folk of Troye, as who saith, alle and some°
In prison been, as ye yourselven see;

855. **werre,** war. 857. **assege,** siege. 860. **axen,** ask. 861. **gise,** manners. 866. **fer,** far; **conning,** ability. 868. **wiste,** knew. 870. **assure,** take confidence. 877. **But if,** unless. 878. **athinken,** displease. 882. **dredelees,** without doubt. 883. **alle and some,** one and all.

For thennes shal nat oon alive come
For al the gold atwixen sonne and see.
Trusteth wel and understondeth me:
Ther shal nat oon to mercy goon on live,
Al were he lord of worldes twies five.

Swich wreche on hem for fecching of Elaine
Ther shal been take, er that we hennes wende,
That Manes, whiche that goddes been of paine,
Shal been agast that Greekes wol hem shende;
And men shul drede unto the worldes ende
From hennesforth to ravisshen any queene,
So cruel shal oure wreche on hem be seene.

And but if Calcas lede us with ambages—
That is to sayn, with doubles wordes slye,
Swich as men clepen a word with two visages—
Ye shal wel knowen that I nought ne lie,
And al this thing right seen it with youre yë,
And that anoon, ye nil nat trowe how soone:
Now taketh heede, for it is for to doone.

What weene ye youre wise fader wolde
Han yiven Antenor for you anoon,
If he ne wiste that the citee sholde
Destroyed been? Why nay, so mote I goon:
He knew ful wel ther shal nat scapen oon
That Troyan is, and for the grete fere
He dorste nat ye dwelte lenger there.

What wol ye more, lufsom lady dere?
Lat Troye and Troyan fro youre herte pace.
Drive out that bittre hope, and make good cheere,
And clepe ayain the beautee of youre face,

889. Al, although. **890. wreche,** vengeance. **892. Manes,** spirits of the dead. **893. shende,** put to shame. **897. ambages,** ambiguities. **899. clepen,** call. **902. trowe,** believe. **904. weene,** suppose. **907. mote,** might. **908. scapen,** escape. **911. lufsom,** lovesome. **912. pace,** pass. **914. clepe,** call.

That ye with salte teres so deface:
For Troye is brought in swich a jupartye
That it to save is now no remedye.

And thenketh wel ye shal in Greekes finde
A more parfit love er it be night
Than any Troÿan is, and more kinde,
And bet to serven you wol doon his might:
And if ye vouche sauf, my lady bright,
I wol been he to serven you myselve,
Ye, levere than be lord of Greeces twelve."

And with that word he gan to waxen reed,
And in his speeche a litel wight he quook,
And caste aside a litel wight his heed,
And stinte a while, and afterward he wook,
And sobreliche on hire he threw his look,
And saide, "I am, al be it you no joye,
As gentil man as any wight in Troye.

For if my fader Tydeus," he saide,
"Ylived hadde, ich hadde been er this
Of Calydoine and Arge a king, Criseide;
And so hope I that I shall yit, ywis.
But he was slain, allas, the more harm is,
Unhappily at Thebes al too rathe,
Polymite and many a man to scathe.

But herte myn, sin that I am youre man,
And been the first of whom I seeche grace,
To serve you as hertely as I can—
And evere shal, whil I to live have space—

916. **jupartye,** jeopardy. 919. **parfit,** perfect. 924. **levere,** rather. 925. **reed,** red. 926. **wight,** bit; **quook,** quaked. 928. **stinte,** stopped; **wook,** i.e., woke from silence. 934. **Calydoine,** Calydon; **Arge,** Argos. 937. **rathe,** soon. 938. To the harm of Polynices and many a man: Tydeus was slain while fighting for Polynices' claim to the throne of Thebes. 940. **seeche,** seek. 941. **hertely,** devoutly.

So er that I departe out of this place,
Ye wol me graunte that I may tomorwe,
At bettre leiser, tellen you my sorwe."

What sholde I telle his wordes that he saide?
He spak ynough for oo day at the meeste.
It preveth wel: he spak so that Criseide
Graunted on the morwe, at his requeste,
For to speken with him at the leeste—
So that he nolde speke of swich matere.
And thus to him she saide as ye mowe heere,

As she that hadde hir herte on Troilus
So faste that ther may it noon arace;
And straungely she spak, and saide thus:
"O Diomede, I love that ilke place
Ther I was born, and Joves, for his grace,
Delivere it soone of al that dooth it care:
God, for thy might, so leve it wel to fare.

The Greekes wolde hir wratthe on Troye wreke,
If that they mighte—I knowe it wel, ywis;
But it shal nought bifallen as ye speke,
And God toforn, and ferther over this,
I woot my fader wis and redy is;
And that he me hath bought, as ye me tolde,
So dere, I am the more unto him holde.

That Greekes been of heigh condicioun
I woot eek wel; but certain, men shal finde
As worthy folk withinne Troye town,
As conning, and as parfit, and as kinde,
As been bitwixen Orcades and Inde;

946. What, why. **947. meeste,** most. **948. preveth,** proves. **952. mowe,** may. **954. arace,** tear away. **955. straungely,** distantly. **958. dooth,** causes. **959. leve** i.e., grant. **960. wreke,** wreak. **963. toforn,** before; **ferther over,** beyond. **966. holde,** obligated. **970. conning,** able; **parfit,** perfect. **971. Orcades,** the Orkneys; **Inde,** India.

And that ye coude wel youre lady serve,
I trowe eek wel, hir thank for to deserve.

But as to speke of love, ywis," she saide,
"I hadde a lord to whom I wedded was,
The whos myn herte al was til that he deide;
And other love, as helpe me now Pallas,
Ther in myn herte nis ne nevere was—
And that ye been of noble and heigh kinrede,
I have wel herd it tellen, out of drede;

And that dooth me to han so greet a wonder
That ye wol scornen any womman so;
Eek God woot love and I been fer asonder:
I am disposed bet, so mote I go,
Unto my deeth to plainen and maken wo.
What I shal after doon I can nat saye,
But treweliche, as yit me list nat playe.

Myn herte is now in tribulacioun,
And ye in armes bisy day by day;
Herafter, whan ye wonnen han the town,
Paraunter thanne so it happen may,
That whan I see that nevere er I sey,
Thanne wol I werke that I nevere wroughte:
This word to you ynough suffisen oughte.

Tomorwe eek wol I speken with you fain—
So that ye touchen nought of this matere;
And whan you list, ye may come here ayain;
And er ye goon, thus muche I saye you here:
As helpe me Pallas with hir heres clere,
If that I sholde of any Greek han routhe,
It sholde be youreselven, by my trouthe.

973. **trowe,** believe. 979. **kinrede,** kindred. 980. **drede,** doubt. 981. **dooth,** causes. 983. **fer,** far. 984. **bet,** i.e., rather; **mote,** may. 985. **plainen,** lament. 987. **list,** it pleases. 991. **Paraunter,** perhaps. 992. **that,** what; **sey,** saw. 995. **fain,** gladly. 999. **heres clere,** bright hair. 1000 **routhe,** pity.

I saye nat therfore that I wol you love,
N'I saye nat nay; but in conclusioun,
I mene wel, by God that sit° above."
And therwithal she caste hir yën down,
And gan to sike,° and saide, "O Troye town,
Yit bidde° I God in quiete and in reste
I may you seen, or do myn herte breste."°

But in effect, and shortly for to saye,
This Diomede al fresshly newe ayain
Gan preessen° on, and faste hir mercy praye;
And after this, the soothe for to sayn,
Hir glove he took, of which he was ful fain;
And finally, whan it was waxen° eve,
And al was wel, he roos and took his leve.

The brighte Venus folwed and ay taughte°
The way ther brode Phebus° down alighte;
And Cynthia hir charhors overraughte,°
To whirle out of the Leon° if she mighte;
And Signifer° his candeles sheweth brighte,
Whan that Criseide unto hir bedde wente,
Inwith° hir fadres faire brighte tente;

Returning° in hir soule ay up and down
The wordes of this sodein° Diomede,
His grete estaat, and peril of the town,
And that she was allone and hadde neede
Of freendes help: and thus bigan to breede
The cause why—the soothe for to telle—
That she took fully purpos for to dwelle.°

1004. sit, sits. **1006. sike,** sigh. **1007. bidde,** pray. **1008. do,** make; **breste,** break. **1011. preessen,** press. **1014. waxen,** grown. **1016. Venus,** i.e., the evening star; **taughte,** i.e., indicated. **1017. Phebus,** i.e., the sun. **1018.** Cynthia, the moon, strained over her chariot horses. **1019. Leo,** the sign of the Lion. **1020. Signifer,** the Zodiac. **1022. Inwith,** within. **1023. Returning,** revolving. **1024. sodein,** sudden. **1029. dwelle,** remain.

The morwen cam, and gostly for to speke,
This Diomede is come unto Criseide;
And shortly, lest that ye my tale breke,
So wel he for himselven spak and saide
That alle hir sikes sore adown he laide;
And finally, the soothe for to sayne,
He refte hire of the grete of al hir paine.

And after this the storye telleth us
That she him yaf the faire baye steede,
The which he ones wan of Troilus;
And eek a brooch—and that was litel neede—
That Troilus was, she yaf this Diomede;
And eek, the bet from sorwe him to releve,
She made him were a pencel of hir sleeve.

I finde eek in stories elleswhere,
Whan thurgh the body hurt was Diomede
Of Troilus, tho wepte she many a tere
Whan that she sawgh his wide woundes bleede;
And that she took to keepen him good heede,
And for to helen him of his sorwes smerte:
Men sayn—I noot—that she yaf him hir herte.

But trewely, the storye telleth us
Ther made nevere womman more wo
Than she, whan that she falsed Troilus:
She saide, "Allas, for now is clene ago
My name of trouthe in love for everemo,
For I have falsed oon the gentileste
That evere was, and oon the worthieste.

Allas, of me unto the worldes ende
Shal neither been ywriten nor ysonge

1030. gostly, i.e., the gospel truth. **1032. breke,** interrupt. **1034. sikes,** sighs. **1036. refte,** relieved; **grete,** the greater part. **1038. yaf,** gave; **baye steede,** a brown horse Diomede had first given to Criseide. **1039. wan,** won. **1042. bet,** better. **1043. pencel,** strip. **1048. keepen,** tend. **1050. noot,** know not. **1053. falsed,** betrayed. **1056. oon,** i.e., one of.

No good word, for thise bookes wol me shende.
O, rolled shal I been on many a tonge;
Thurghout the world my belle shal be ronge;
And wommen most wol haten me of alle—
Allas that swich a caas me sholde falle!

They wol sayn in as muche as in me is
I have hem doon dishonour, wailaway!
Al be I nat the first that dide amis,
What helpeth that to doon my blame away?
But sin I see ther is no bettre way,
And that too late is now for me to rewe,
To Diomede, algate, I wol be trewe.

But Troilus, sin I no bettre may,
And sin that thus departen ye and I,
Yit praye I God so yive you right good day,
As for the gentileste, trewely,
That evere I sawgh to serven faithfully,
And best can ay his lady honour keepe."—
And with that word she brast anoon to weepe.

"And certes, you ne haten shal I nevere,
And freendes love, that shal ye han of me,
And my good word, al sholde I liven evere.
And, trewely, I wolde sory be
For to seen you in adversitee;
And giltelees I woot wel I you leve—
But al shal passe, and thus I take my leve."

But trewely, how longe it was bitweene
That she forsook him for this Diomede,
Ther is noon auctour telleth it, I weene.
Take every man now to his bookes heede:

1060. shende, disgrace. **1064. falle,** happen. **1068. doon,** put. **1070. rewe,** regret. **1071. algate,** at any rate. **1073. departen,** part. **1077. lady,** lady's. **1078. brast,** burst. **1081. al,** although. **1088. weene,** suppose.

He shal no terme finden, out of drede;
For though that he bigan to wowe hire soone,
Er he hire wan yit was ther more to doone.

Ne me ne list this sely womman chide
Ferther than the storye wol devise:
Hir name, allas, is punisshed so wide,
That for hir gilt it oughte ynough suffise;
And if I mighte excuse hire any wise,
For she so sory was for hir untrouthe,
Ywis, I wolde excuse hire yit for routhe.

This Troilus, as I bifore have told,
Thus driveth forth as wel as he hath might,
But ofte was his herte hoot and cold;
And namely that ilke ninthe night,
Which on the morwe she hadde him bihight
To come ayain, God woot ful litel reste
Hadde he that night—nothing to sleepe him leste.

The laurer-crowned Phebus with his hete
Gan in his cours, ay upward as he wente,
To warmen of the Eest See the wawes wete;
And Nisus doughter soong with fressh entente,
Whan Troilus his Pandare after sente,
And on the walles of the town they playde,
To looke if they can seen ought of Criseide.

Til it was noon they stooden for to see
Who that ther come, and every manere wight
That cam fro fer, they saiden it was she—
Til that they coude knowen him aright.
Now was his herte dul, now was it light,

1090. terme, stated interval; **drede,** doubt. **1091. wowe,** woo. **1092.** wan, won. **1093. sely,** poor. **1098. untrouthe,** infidelity. **1099. routhe,** pity. **1101. driveth,** i.e., endures. **1103. namely,** especially. **1104. bihight,** promised. **1106. leste,** it pleased. **1107. laurer,** laurel. **1109. wawes,** waves. **1110. Nisus,** whose daughter betrayed her father and was turned into a lark; **soong,** sang. **1116. fer,** far.

And thus bijaped stonden for to stare,
Aboute nought, this Troilus and Pandare.

To Pandarus this Troilus tho saide,
"For ought I woot, bifore noon sikerly
Into this town ne comth nat here Criseide;
She hath ynough to doone, hardily,
To winnen from hir fader, so trowe I:
Hir olde fader wol yit make hir dine
Er that she go—God yive his herte pine!"

Pandare answerde, "It may wel be, certain.
And forthy lat us dine, I thee biseeche.
And after noon thanne maistou come ayain."
And hoom they go withoute more speeche,
And comen ayain—but longe may they seeche
Er that they finde that they after cape:
Fortune hem bothe thenketh for to jape.

Quod Troilus, "I see wel now that she
Is taried with hir olde fader so
That, er she come, it wol neigh even be.
Com, forth I wol unto the yate go:
Thise porters been unconning everemo,
And I wol doon hem holden up the yate,
As nought ne were, although she come late."

The day gooth faste, and after that cam eve,
And yit cam nought to Troilus Criseide.
He looketh forth by hegge, by tree, by greve,
And fer his heed over the wal he laide;
And at the laste he turned him and saide,
"By God, I woot hir mening now, Pandare—
Almost, ywis, al newe was my care.

1119. bijaped, tricked. **1120. Aboute nought,** to no purpose. **1122. sikerly,** surely. **1124. hardily,** assuredly. **1125. trowe,** believe. **1127. pine,** torment. **1129. forthy,** therefore. **1132. seeche,** seek. **1133. cape,** gape. **1134. jape,** fool. **1137. even,** evening. **1138. yate,** gate. **1139. unconning,** stupid. **1140. doon,** make. **1144. greve,** thicket. **1145. fer,** far.

Now doutelees this lady can hir good:
I woot she meneth riden prively.
I comende hir wisdom, by myn hood:
She wol nat maken peple nicely
Gaure on hire whan she comth, but softely,
By night, into the town she thinketh ride.
And dere brother, think nat longe t'abide:

We han nought elles for to doon, ywis.
And Pandarus, now woltou trowen me?
Have here my trouthe, I see hire, yond she is!
Heve up thine yën, man, maistou nat see?"
Pandare answerde, "Nay, so mote I thee.
Al wrong, by God! What saistou, man, where arte?
That I see yond nis but a fare carte."

"Allas, thou saist right sooth," quod Troilus.
"But hardily, it is nought al for nought
That in myn herte I now rejoice thus;
It is ayains som good, I have a thought–
Noot I nat how, but sin that I was wrought
Ne felte I swich a confort, dar I saye:
She comth tonight, my lif that dorste I laye."

Pandare answerde, "It may be wel ynough,"
And heeld with him of al that evere he saide;
But in his herte he thoughte, and softe lough,
And to himself ful sobreliche he saide,
"From haselwode, ther joly Robin playde,
Shal come al that thou abidest here:
Ye, farewel al the snow of ferne yere."

1149. can . . . good, knows what is best for her. **1152. nicely,** foolishly. **1153. Gaure,** stare. **1159. Heve,** raise. **1160. mote,** may; **thee,** thrive. **1162. fare carte,** ? road wagon. **1164. hardily,** assuredly. **1166. ayains,** i.e., in consequence of the coming of. **1169. laye,** wager. **1171. heeld,** i.e., agreed. **1172. lough,** laughed. **1174. haselwode,** hazelwood; **Robin,** Robin Hood. **1176. ferne,** past.

The wardein of the yates gan to calle
The folk which that withoute the yates were,
And bad hem driven in hir beestes alle,
Or al the night they moste bleven there;
And fer withinne the night, with many a tere,
This Troilus gan hoomward for to ride,
For wel he seeth it helpeth nought t'abide.

But nathelees he gladed him in this:
He thoughte he misaccounted hadde his day,
And saide, "I understonde have al amis,
For thilke night I last Criseide sey,
She saide, 'I shal been here, if that I may,
Er that the moone, O dere herte sweete,
The Leon passe out of this Ariete.'

For which she may yit holde al hir biheeste."
And on the morwe unto the yate he wente,
And up and down, by weste and eek by eeste,
Upon the walles made he many a wente—
But al for nought: his hope alway him blente.
For which at night, in sorwe and sikes sore,
He wente him hoom withouten any more.

His hope al clene out of his herte fledde;
He nath wheron now lenger for to honge;
But for the paine him thoughte his herte bledde,
So were his throwes sharpe and wonder stronge:
For whan he sawgh that she abood so longe,
He niste what he juggen of it mighte,
Sin she hath broken that she him bihighte.

The thridde, ferthe, fifthe, sixte day,
After tho dayes ten of which I tolde,

1177. wardein, guardian. **1180. bleven,** remain. **1187. sey,** saw. **1190.** i.e., starting from the Ram pass beyond the Lion. **1191. biheeste,** promise. **1194. wente,** turn. **1195. blente,** blinded. **1196. sikes,** sighs. **1199. honge,** hang. **1201. throwes,** throes. **1202. abood,** abided. **1203. niste,** knew not. **1204. bihighte,** promised.

Bitwixen hope and drede his herte lay,
Yit somwhat trusting on hir heestes olde:
But whan he sawgh she nolde hir terme holde,
He can now seen noon other remedye
But for to shape him soone for to die.

Therwith the wikked spirit—God us blesse—
Which that men clepeth the woode jalousye,
Gan in him creepe in al this hevinesse;
For which, by cause he wolde soone die,
He ne eet ne drank for his malencolye,
And eek from every compaignye he fledde:
This was the lif that al the time he ledde.

He so defeet was that no manere man
Unnethe him mighte knowen ther he wente;
So was he lene, and therto pale and wan,
And fieble that he walked by potente;
And with his ire he thus himselve shente;
And whoso axed him wherof he smerte,
He saide his harm was al aboute his herte.

Priam ful ofte, and eek his moder dere,
His bretheren and his sustren, gan him fraine
Why he sorweful was in al his cheere,
And what thing was the cause of al his paine—
But al for nought: he nolde his cause plaine,
But saide he felte a grevous maladye
Aboute his herte, and fain he wolde die.

So on a day he laide him down to sleepe,
And so bifel that in his sleep he thoughte
That in a forest faste he welk to weepe,
For love of hire that him this paine wroughte,

1208. heestes, promises. **1211. shape,** prepare. **1213. men,** one; **woode,** raging. **1219. defeet,** disfigured. **1220. Unnethe,** hardly. **1222. potente,** crutch. **1223. shente,** harmed. **1227. fraine,** question. **1230. plaine,** lament. **1232. fain,** gladly. **1235. welk,** walked.

And up and down as he the forest soughte,°
Him mette he saw a boor° with tuskes grete,
That sleep ayain° the brighte sonnes hete.

And by this boor, faste in hir armes folde,
Lay kissing ay his lady bright Criseide—
For sorwe of which whan he it gan biholde,
And for despit, out of his sleep he braide,°
And loude he cride on Pandarus and saide,
"O Pandarus, now knowe I crop° and roote—
I nam but deed: ther nis noon other boote.°

My lady brighte Criseide hath me bitrayed,
In whom I trusted most of any wight;
She elleswhere hath now hir herte apayed:°
The blisful goddes, thurgh hir grete might,
Han in my dreem yshewed it ful right;
Thus in my dreem Criseide have I biholde."
And al this thing to Pandarus he tolde.

"O my Criseide, allas, what subtiltee,
What newe lust,° what beautee, what science,
What wratthe of juste cause han ye to me?
What gilt of me, what fel° experience,
Hath from me reft, allas, thyn advertence?°
O trust, O faith, O deepe assuraunce!
Who hath me reft, Criseide, al my plesaunce?

Allas, why leet I you from hennes go,
For which wel neigh out of my wit I braide?°
Who shal now trowe° on othes any mo?
God woot I wende,° O lady brighte Criseide,
That every word was gospel that ye saide:

1237. **soughte,** searched. 1238. **mette,** dreamed; **boor,** boar. 1239. **ayain,** in. 1243. **despit,** indignation; **braide,** started. 1245. **crop,** i.e., branch. 1246. **boote,** help. 1249. **apayed,** satisfied. 1255. **lust,** pleasure. 1257. **fel,** dire. 1258. **reft,** taken; **advertence,** i.e., mind. 1262. **braide,** i.e., go. 1263. **trowe,** trust. 1264. **wende,** supposed.

But who may bet bigile, if that him liste,°
Than he on whom men weeneth best to triste?°

What shal I doon, my Pandarus? Allas,
I feele now so sharp a newe paine,
Sin that ther lith° no remedye in this cas,
That bet were it I with mine handes twaine
Myselven slowe, than alway thus to plaine:°
For thurgh the deeth my wo sholde have an ende,
Ther every day with lif myselve I shende."°

Pandare answerde and saide, "Allas the while
That I was born! Have I nat said er this
That dremes many a manere man bigile?
And why? For folk expounden hem amis.
How darstou sayn that fals thy lady is,
For any dreem, right for thyn owene drede?
Lat be this thought: thou canst no dremes rede.°

Paraunter° ther thou dremest of this boor,
It may be so that it may signifye
Hir fader, which that old is and eek hoor,
Ayain the sonne lith o point° to die,
And she for sorwe ginneth weepe and crye,
And kisseth him ther he lith on the grounde:
Thus sholdestou thy dreem aright expounde."

"How mighte I thanne doon," quod Troilus,
"To knowe of this, ye, were it nevere so lite?"°
"Now saistou wisely," quod this Pandarus;
"My reed° is this: sin thou canst wel endite,
That hastily a lettre thou hire write,
Thurgh which thou shalt wel bringen it aboute
To knowe a sooth of that thou art in doute.

1266. bet, better; **liste,** it please. **1267. triste,** trust. **1270. lith,** lies. **1272. slowe,** slew; **plaine,** mourn. **1274. shende,** hurt. **1281. rede,** interpret. **1282. Paraunter,** perhaps. **1285. Ayain,** i.e., in; **lith,** lies; **o point,** about. **1290. lite,** little. **1292. reed,** advice.

And see now why: for this I dar wel sayn,
That if so is that she untrewe be,
I can nat trowen that she wol write ayain;
And if she write, thou shalt ful soone ysee
As wheither she hath any libertee
To come ayain; or elles, in som clause,
If she be let,° she wol assigne a cause.

Thou hast nat writen hire sin that she wente,
Nor she to thee; and this I dorste laye:°
Ther may swich cause been in hir entente
That, hardily,° thou wolt thyselven saye
That hir abood° the beste is for you twaye.
Now writ hire thanne, and thou shalt feele soone
A sooth of al. Ther is namore to doone."

Accorded been to this conclusioun,
And that anoon, thise ilke lordes two;
And hastily sit Troilus adown,
And rolleth in his herte to and fro
How he may best descriven hire his wo;
And to Criseide, his owene lady dere,
He wroot right thus, and saide as ye may heere:

Troilus' Letter

"Right fresshe flowr, whos I been have and shal,
Withouten part of elleswhere servise,°
With herte, body, lif, lust,° thought, and al,
I, woful wight, in everich humble wise
That tonge telle or herte may devise,
As ofte as matere occupieth place,
Me recomande° unto youre noble grace.

1302. let, hindered. **1304. laye,** wager. **1306. hardily,** certainly. **1307. abood,** delay. **1318.** i.e., Without sharing my service elsewhere. **1319. lust,** desire. **1323. recomande,** commend.

Liketh you to witen,° sweete herte,
As ye wel knowe, how longe time agoon
That ye me lefte in aspre° paines smerte,
Whan that ye wente; of which boote° noon
Have I noon had, but evere wors-bigoon°
Fro day to day am I, and so moot° dwelle,
Whil it you list, of wele and wo my welle.°

For which to you with dredful herte trewe
I write, as he that sorwe drifth° to write,
My wo, that everich houre encreesseth newe,
Complaining as I dar or can endite;
And that defaced is, that may ye wite°
The teres whiche that fro mine yën raine,
That wolden speke, if that they coude, and plaine.°

You first biseeche I that youre yën clere
To looke on this defouled ye nat holde;°
And over al this that ye, my lady dere,
Wol vouche sauf this lettre to biholde;
And by the cause eek of my cares colde
That sleeth my wit, if ought amis m'asterte,°
Foryive it me, myn owene sweete herte.

If any servant dorste or oughte of right
Upon his lady pitously complaine,
Thanne weene° I that ich oughte be that wight,
Considered° this, that ye thise monthes twaine
Han taried ther ye saiden, sooth to sayne,
But dayes ten ye nolde in host sojurne—
But in two monthes yit ye nat returne.

But for as muche as me moot needes like°
Al that you liste, I dar nat plaine more,

1324. **Liketh,** may it please; **witen,** know. 1326. **aspre,** bitter. 1327. **boote,** remedy. 1328. **wors-bigoon,** worse off. 1329. **moot,** must. 1330. **wele,** happiness; **welle,** source. 1332. **drifth,** drives. 1335. **that** (1), what; **wite,** blame upon. 1337. **plaine,** complain. 1339. **defouled,** abused; **holde,** consider. 1343. **sleeth,** slays; **m'asterte,** escape me. 1347. **weene,** think. 1348. **Considered,** considering. 1352. **like,** please.

But humblely, with sorweful sikes sike,
You write ich mine unresty sorwes sore,
Fro day to day desiring everemore
To knowen fully, if youre wille it were,
How ye han ferd and doon whil ye be there;

The whos welfare and hele eek God encreesse
In honour, swich that upward in degree
It growe alway, so that it nevere ceesse;
Right as youre herte ay can, my lady free,
Devise, I praye to God, so mote it be,
And graunte it that ye soone upon me rewe,
As wisly as in al I am you trewe.

And if you liketh knowen of the fare
Of me, whos wo ther may no wit descrive,
I can namore, but cheste of every care,
At writing of this lettre I was on live,
Al redy out my woful gost to drive,
Which I delaye, and holde him yit in honde
Upon the sighte of matere of youre sonde.

Mine yën two, in vain with whiche I see,
Of sorweful teres salte are waxen welles;
My song in plainte of myn adversitee,
Myn good in harm, myn ese eek waxen helle is;
My joye in wo; I can saye you nought elles,
But turned is—for which my lif I warye—
Everich joye or ese in his contrarye;

Which with youre coming hoom ayain to Troye
Ye may redresse, and more a thousand sithe
Than evere ich hadde encreessen in me joye:

1354. sikes sike, sickly sighs. **1355. unresty,** unabating. **1358. ferd,** fared. **1359. hele,** health. **1363. mote,** may. **1364. rewe,** rue. **1365. wisly,** surely. **1368. cheste,** receptacle. **1370. gost,** spirit. **1372. Upon,** in expectation of; **sonde,** sending. **1374. waxen,** become. **1378. warye,** curse, **1381. sithe,** times.

For was ther nevere herte yit so blithe
To han his lif, as I shal been as swithe
As I you see; and though no manere routhe
Commeve you, yit thinketh on youre trouthe.

And if so be my gilt hath deeth deserved,
Or if you list namore upon me see,
In guerdon yit of that I have you served,
Biseeche I you, myn owene lady free,
That herupon ye wolden write me,
For love of God, my righte lode sterre—
Ther deeth may make an ende of al my werre;

If other cause ought dooth you for to dwelle,
That with youre lettre ye me reconforte,
For though to me youre absence is an helle,
With pacience I wol my wo comporte,
And with youre lettre of hope I wol disporte:
Now writeth, sweete, and lat me thus nat plaine—
With hope or deeth delivereth me fro paine.

Ywis, myn owene dere herte trewe,
I woot that whan ye next upon me see,
So lost have I myn hele and eek myn hewe,
Criseide shal nought conne knowen me.
Ywis, myn hertes day, my lady free,
So thursteth ay myn herte to biholde
Youre beautee, that my lif unnethe I holde.

I saye namore, al have I for to saye
To you wel more than I telle may;
But wheither that ye do me live or deye,
Yit praye I God so yive you right good day;

1384. **swithe,** soon. 1385. **routhe,** compassion. 1386. **Commeve,** incite. 1389. **guerdon,** reward. 1390. **free,** generous. 1392. **righte . . . sterre,** true lodestar. 1393. **werre,** war. 1394. **dooth,** makes. 1397. **comporte,** endure. 1403. **hele,** health. 1404. **conne knowen,** be able to recognize. 1407. **unnethe,** with difficulty. 1408. **al,** although. 1410. **do,** make.

And fareth wel, goodly, faire, fresshe may,
As ye that lif or deeth may me comaunde;
And to youre trouthe ay I me recomaunde,

With hele swich, that but ye yiven me
The same hele, I shal noon hele have:
In you lith, whan you liste that it so be,
The day in which me clothen shal my grave;
In you my lif, in you might for to save
Me fro disese of alle paines smerte;
And fare now wel, myn owene sweete herte."

This lettre forth was sent unto Criseide;
Of which hir answere in effect was this:
Ful pitously she wroot ayain and saide
That also soone as that she mighte, ywis,
She wolde come and mende al that was mis;
And finally she wroot and saide him than,
She wolde come, ye, but she niste whan.

But in hir lettre made she swiche feestes
That wonder was, and swerth she loveth him best—
Of which he foond but botmelees biheestes.
But Troilus, thou maist now, eest or west,
Pipe in an ivy leef, if that thee lest.
Thus gooth the world: God shilde us fro meschaunce,
And every wight that meneth trouthe avaunce.

Encreessen gan the wo fro day to night
Of Troilus for tarying of Criseide,
And lessen gan his hope and eek his might.
For which al down he in his bed him laide;
He ne eet, ne drank, ne sleep, ne word ne saide,

1412. may, maid. **1415. hele,** health: used both literally and as the salutation of the letter. **1417. lith,** it lies. **1420. disese,** distress. **1425. also,** as. **1426. mis,** amiss. **1427. than,** then. **1428. ye,** yea; **niste,** knew not. **1429. feestes,** endearments. **1430. swerth,** swears. **1431. foond,** found; **botmelees biheestes,** baseless promises. **1433. Pipe . . . leef,** i.e., whistle futilely. **1434. shilde,** defend. **1435. avaunce,** prosper. **1440. eet,** ate; **sleep,** slept.

Imagining ay that she was unkinde,
For which wel neigh he weex out of his minde.

This dreem, of which I told have eek biforn,
May nevere come out of his remembraunce:
He thoughte ay wel he hadde his lady lorn,
And that Joves, of his purveyaunce,
Him shewed hadde in sleep the signifiaunce
Of hir untrouthe, and his disaventure,
And that the boor was shewed him in figure.

For which he for Sibylle his suster sente,
That called was Cassandre eek al aboute,
And al his dreem he tolde hire er he stente,
And hire bisoughte assoilen him the doute
Of the stronge boor with tuskes stoute;
And finally, withinne a litel stounde,
Cassandre him gan right thus his dreem expounde.

She gan first smile, and saide, "O brother dere,
If thou a sooth of this desirest knowe,
Thou moost a fewe of olde stories heere,
To purpos how that Fortune overthrowe
Hath lordes olde, thurgh which withinne a throwe
Thou wel this boor shalt knowe, and of what kinde
He comen is, as men in bookes finde.

Diane, which that wroth was and in ire
For Greekes nolde doon hire sacrifise,
Ne encens upon hir auter sette afire,
She, for that Greekes gonne hire so despise,
Wrak hire in a wonder cruel wise;
For with a boor, as greet as oxe in stalle,
She made up frete hir corn and vines alle.

1442. weex, i.e., went. **1445. lorn,** lost. **1446. purveyaunce,** providence. **1448. untrouthe,** unfidelity. **1449. boor,** boar; **in figure,** symbolically. **1452. stente,** stopped. **1453. assoilen,** to resolve. **1455. stounde,** while. **1459. moost,** must. **1461. throwe,** little time. **1462. kinde,** family. **1464. Diane,** Diana. **1465. For,** because. **1466. encens,** incense; **auter,** altar. **1468. Wrak hire,** avenged herself. **1470. up frete,** be eaten up.

To slee° this boor was al the contree raised;
Amonges which ther cam this boor to see
A maide, oon of this world the beste ypraised;
And Meleagre, lord of that contree,
He loved so this fresshe maiden free,
That with his manhood er he wolde stente°
The boor he slow, and hire the heed° he sente.

Of which, as olde bookes tellen us,
Ther roos a contek° and a greet envye;
And of this lord descended Tydeus
By line, or elles olde bookes lie;
But how this Meleagre gan to die
Thurgh his moder wol I you nought telle,
For al too longe it were for to dwelle."

She tolde eek how Tydeus, er she stente,°
Unto the stronge citee of Thebes,°
To claimen kingdom of the citee wente
For his felawe, daun Polymites,
Of which the brother daun Ethiocles

1471. slee, slay. **1476. stente,** finish. **1477. slow,** slew; **heed,** head. **1479. contek,** strife: Meleager's uncles resented his presentation of the boar's head to the maiden Atalanta, whereupon Meleager slew them, thus bringing on his own death through the agency of his mother. **1485. stente,** stopped. **1486. citee of Thebes:** in the following lines Cassandra gives a rapid summary of the legend of Thebes, as it is told by Statius. Upon the deposition of Oedipus, king of Thebes, his two sons Polynices (*Polymites*) and Eteocles (*Ethiocles*) agreed to rule the kingdom alternately for a year at a time. But after the first year Eteocles refused to yield the government to Polynices, who then prevailed upon his father-in-law Adrastus, king of Argos, to attack the city. Adrastus organized the famous expedition of the Seven against Thebes. All the seven generals except Adrastus were fated to lose their lives in the war. Cassandra mentions Amphiaraus (*Amphiorax*) as being swallowed up by the earth, the drowning of Hippomedon, Capaneus' destruction by a thunderbolt, and the deaths of Archemorus (*Archimoris*), Parthenopaeus (*Parthenope*), and Tydeus, the father of Diomede, and a descendant of Meleager. The expedition ended in failure when the sixth doomed general, Polynices, and his alienated brother, Eteocles, killed each other. Among other details of the story, Cassandra mentions how the son of Haemon (*Hemonides*) escaped death when Tydeus slew fifty other Theban knights.

Ful wrongfully of Thebes heeld the strengthe—
This tolde she by proces, al by lengthe.

She tolde eek how Hemonides asterte
Whan Tydeus slow fifty knightes stoute;
She tolde eek alle the prophecies by herte,
And how that sevene kinges with hir route
Bisegeden the citee al aboute;
And of the holy serpent, and the welle,
And of the furies, al she gan him telle;

Of Archimoris burying and the playes,
And how Amphiorax fil thurgh the grounde;
How Tydeus was slain, lord of Argeyes,
And how Ipomedon in litel stounde
Was dreint, and deed Parthenope of wounde;
And also how Capaneus the proude
With thonder dint was slain, that cride loude.

She gan eek telle him how that either brother,
Ethiocles and Polymite, also
At a scarmuche eech of hem slow other,
And of Argives weeping and hir wo;
And how the town was brent she tolde eek tho,
And so descendeth down from gestes olde
To Diomede, and thus she spak and tolde.

"This ilke boor bitokneth Diomede,
Tydeus sone, that down descended is
Fro Meleagre, that made the boor to bleede;
And thy lady, wherso she be, ywis,
This Diomede hir herte hath and she his—
Weep if thou wolt, or leef, for out of doute,
This Diomede is inne and thou art oute."

1492. asterte, escaped. **1493. slow,** slew. **1495. route,** company. **1499. playes,** funeral games. **1500. fil,** fell. **1501. Argeyes,** Argives. **1502. in litel stounde,** in a little while. **1503. dreint,** drowned; **deed,** dead. **1505. dint,** bolt. **1508. scarmuche,** skirmish. **1510. brent,** burned. **1511. gestes,** stories. **1513. boor,** boar. **1518. leef,** leave off.

"Thou saist nat sooth," quod he, "thou sorceresse!
With al thy false gost of prophecye,
Thou weenest been a greet divineresse!
Now seestou nat this fool of fantasye
Paineth hire on ladies for to lie?
Away," quod he, "ther Joves yive thee sorwe!
Thou shalt be fals paraunter yit tomorwe.

As wel thou mightest lien on Alceste,
That was of creatures, but men lie,
That evere weren, kindest and the beste:
For whan hir housbonde was in jupartye
To die himself, but if she wolde die,
She chees for him to die and goon to helle,
And starf anoon, as us the bookes telle."

Cassandre gooth, and he with cruel herte
Foryat his wo for angre of hir speeche;
And from his bed al sodeinly he sterte,
As though al hool him hadde ymaad a leeche;
And day by day he gan enquere and seeche
A sooth of this with al his fulle cure—
And thus he drieth forth his aventure.

Fortune, which that permutacioun
Of thinges hath, as it is hire committed
Thurgh purveyance and disposicioun
Of hye Jove, as regnes shal be flitted
Fro folk in folk, or whan they shal be smitted,
Gan pulle away the fetheres brighte of Troye
Fro day to day, til they been bare of joye.

1521. **gost,** spirit. 1522. **weenest,** think; **been,** i.e., that you are; **divineresse,** seeress. 1524. **Paineth hire,** takes pains. 1528. **but,** unless. 1530. **jupartye,** jeopardy. 1531. **but if,** unless. 1532. **chees,** chose. 1533. **starf,** died. 1536. **sterte,** leapt. 1537. **hool,** whole; **leeche,** physician. 1538. **enquere,** inquire; **seeche,** seek. 1539. **cure,** care. 1540. **drieth,** endures. 1543. **purveyance,** foresight. 1544. **regnes,** kingdoms; **flitted,** shifted. 1545. **smitted,** struck down.

Among al this the fin of the parodye°
Of Ector gan approchen wonder blive:°
The Fate wolde his soule sholde unbodye,
And shapen hadde a mene° it out to drive;
Ayains which Fate him helpeth nat to strive,
But on a day to fighten gan he wende,
At which, allas, he caughte his lives ende.

For which me thinketh every manere wight
That haunteth° armes oughte to biwaile
The deeth of him that was so noble a knight,
For as he drow a king by th'aventaile,°
Unwar of this, Achilles thurgh the maile
And thurgh the body gan him for to rive:
And thus the worthy knight was brought of live.°

For whom, as olde bookes tellen us,
Was maad swich wo that tonge it may nat telle,
And namely° the sorwe of Troilus,
That next him was of worthinesse welle;°
And in this wo gan Troilus to dwelle,
That what for sorwe, and love, and for unreste,
Ful ofte a day he bad his herte breste.°

But nathelees, though he gan him despaire
And dradde° ay that his lady was untrewe,
Yit ay on hire his herte gan repaire,
And as thise loveres doon, he soughte ay newe
To gete ayain Criseide, bright of hewe;
And in his herte he wente hire excusinge
That Calcas caused al hir taryinge.

And ofte time he was in purpos grete°
Himselve lik a pilgrim to disgise,

1548. **fin,** end; **parodye,** period. 1549. **blive,** quickly. 1551. **shapen,** arranged; **mene,** means. 1556. **haunteth,** practices. 1558. **drow,** dragged; **aventaile,** mouthpiece of a helmet. 1561. **of live,** out of life. 1564. **namely,** especially. 1565. **welle,** source. 1568. **breste,** break. 1570. **dradde,** dreaded. 1576. **grete,** i.e., firmly.

To seen hire; but he may nat contrefete
To been unknowen of folk that weren wise,
Ne finde excuse aright that may suffise,
If he among the Greekes knowen were:
For which he weep ful ofte and many a tere.

To hire he wroot yit ofte time al newe,
Ful pitously—he lefte it nought for slouthe—
Biseeching hire that sin that he was trewe,
That she wol come ayain, and holde hir trouthe;
For which Criseide upon a day for routhe—
I take it so—touching al this matere
Wroot him ayain, and saide as ye may heere:

Criseide's Letter

"Cupides sone, ensample of goodlihede,
O swerd of knighthood, sours of gentilesse,
How mighte a wight in torment and in drede,
And helelees, you sende as yit gladnesse?
I hertelees, I sik, I in distresse,
Sin ye with me nor I with you may dele,
You neither sende ich herte may nor hele.

Youre lettres ful, the papir al yplainted,
Conceived hath myn hertes pietee;
I have eek seen with teres al depainted
Youre lettre, and how that ye requeren me
To come ayain, which yit ne may nat be;
But why, lest that this lettre founden were,
No mencion ne make I now, for fere.

1578. **contrefete,** i.e., so change appearance. 1581. **knowen,** recognized. 1582. **weep,** wept. 1583. **wroot,** wrote. 1584. **slouthe,** negligence. 1587. **routhe,** pity. 1590. **ensample,** model. 1593. **helelees,** without health. 1597. **yplainted,** i.e., covered with complaint. 1598. **Conceived,** comprehended; **pietee,** pity (subject of *Conceived hath*). 1599. **depainted,** i.e., stained. 1600. **requeren,** entreat.

Grevous to me, God woot, is youre unreste,
Youre haste, and that the goddes ordinaunce
It seemeth nat ye take it for the beste;
Nor other thing nis in youre remembraunce,
As thinketh me, but only youre plesaunce;
And beeth nat wroth, and that I you biseeche:
For that I tarye is al for wikked speeche.

For I have herd wel more than I wende
Touching us two how thinges han ystonde,
Which I shal with dissimuling amende;
And—beeth nat wroth—I have eek understonde
How ye ne do but holden me in honde;
But now no fors—I can nat in you gesse
But alle trouthe and alle gentilesse.

Come I wol, but yit in swich disjointe
I stonde as now, that what yeer or what day
That this shal be, that can I nought appointe;
But in effect I praye you as I may
Of youre good word and of youre frendshipe ay:
For, trewely, whil that my lif may dure,
As for a freend ye may in me assure.

Yit praye ich you in yvel ye ne take
That it is short which that I to you write:
I dar nat ther I am wel lettres make,
Ne nevere yit ne coude I wel endite;
Eek greet effect men write in place lite:
Th'entente is al, and nat the lettres space.
And fareth now wel: God have you in his grace."

This Troilus this lettre thoughte al straunge
Whan he it sawgh, and sorwefulliche he sighte;

1610. For, i.e., the reason; **wikked,** slanderous. **1611. wende,** supposed. **1613. dissimuling,** dissembling. **1615.** How you are only toying with me. **1616. fors,** matter. **1618. disjointe,** predicament. **1623. dure,** last. **1624. assure,** have confidence. **1625. in yvel,** amiss. **1629. lite,** small. **1633. sighte,** sighed.

Him thoughte it lik a kalendes of a chaunge,
But finally, he ful ne trowen mighte
That she ne wolde him holden that she highte:
For with ful yvel wil list him to leve
That loveth wel, in swich caas, though him greve.

But nathelees men sayn that at the laste,
For any thing, men shal the soothe see;
And swich a caas bitidde, and that as faste,
That Troilus wel understood that she
Nas nought so kinde as that hire oughte be;
And finally he woot now out of doute
That al is lost that he hath been aboute.

Stood on a day in his malencolye
This Troilus, and in suspecioun
Of hire for whom he wende for to die,
And so bifel that thurghout Troye town,
As was the gise, yborn was up and down
A manere cote-armour, as saith the storye,
Biforn Deiphebe in signe of his victorye.

The whiche cote, as telleth Lollius,
Deiphebe it hadde rent fro Diomede
The same day; and whan this Troilus
It sawgh, he gan to taken of it heede,
Avising of the lengthe and of the brede,
And al the werk; but as he gan biholde,
Ful sodeinly his herte gan to colde;

As he that on the coler foond withinne
A brooch that he Criseide yaf that morwe
That she from Troye moste needes twinne,

1634. **kalendes,** beginning. **1635. trowen,** believe. **1636. that,** what; **highte,** promised. **1637.** i.e., For he is most reluctant to believe. **1648. wende,** thought. **1653. Lollius,** the imaginary Latin author of the work Chaucer pretends to be translating. **1654. rent,** torn. **1657. Avising of,** considering; **brede,** breadth. **1659. colde,** grow cold. **1660. coler,** collar; **foond,** found. **1662. twinne,** depart.

In remembrance of him and of his sorwe—
And she him laide ayain hir faith to borwe°
To keepe it ay; but now ful wel he wiste
His lady nas no lenger on to triste.

He gooth him hoom and gan ful soone sende
For Pandarus, and al this newe chaunce,
And of this brooch, he tolde him word° and ende,
Complaining of hir hertes variaunce,°
His longe love, his trouthe, and his penaunce;°
And after deeth, withouten wordes more,
Ful faste he cride, his reste him to restore.

Thanne spak he thus, "O lady myn Criseide,
Where is youre faith, and where is youre biheeste?°
Where is youre love? Where is youre trouthe?" he saide.
"Of Diomede have ye now al this feeste?°
Allas, I wolde han trowed° atte leeste
That sin ye nolde in trouthe to me stonde,
That ye thus nolde han holden me in honde.°

Who shal now trowe on any othes mo?
Allas, I nevere wolde han wend° er this
That ye Criseide coude han chaunged so;
Ne but I hadde agilt° and doon amis,
So cruel wende I nought youre herte, ywis,
To slee° me thus. Allas, youre name of trouthe
Is now fordoon, and that is al my routhe.°

Was ther noon other brooch you liste lete,°
To feffe° with youre newe love?" quod he,
"But thilke brooch that I, with teres wete,
You yaf as for a remembrance of me?

1664. to borwe, as a pledge. **1669. word,** beginning. **1670. variaunce,** fickleness. **1671. penaunce,** suffering. **1675. biheeste,** promise. **1677. feeste,** i.e., joy. **1678. trowed,** believed. **1680. holden . . . honde,** i.e., pretended to love me. **1682. wend,** thought. **1684. but,** unless; **agilt,** offended. **1686. slee,** slay. **1687. fordoon,** ruined; **routhe,** pity. **1688. liste,** it pleased; **lete,** let go. **1689. feffe,** endow.

Noon other cause, allas, ne hadde ye,
But for despit,° and eek for that ye mente,
Al outrely,° to shewen youre entente.

Thurgh which I see that clene out of youre minde
Ye han me cast—and I ne can nor may,
For al this world, withinne myn herte finde
To unloven you a quarter of a day.
In cursed time I born was, wailaway,
That you, that doon° me al this wo endure,
Yit love I best of any creature.

Now God," quod he, "me sende yit the grace
That I may meeten with this Diomede;
And trewely, if I have might and space
Yit shal I make, I hope, his sides bleede.
O God," quod he, "that oughtest taken heede
To forthren trouthe and wronges to punice,°
Why niltou doon a vengeance of this vice?°

O Pandare, that in dremes for to triste°
Me blamed hast, and wont art ofte upbraide,
Now maistou see thyself, if that thee liste,
How trewe is now thy nece, bright Criseide.
In sondry formes, God it woot," he saide,
"The goddes shewen bothe joye and teene°
In sleep, and by my dreem it is now seene.

And certainly, withouten more speeche,
From hennesforth as ferforth° as I may,
Myn owene deeth in armes wol I seeche:°
I recche° nat how soone be the day.
But trewely, Criseide, sweete may,°
Whom I have ay with al my might yserved,
That ye thus doon, I have it nat deserved."

1693. despit, spitefulness. **1694. outrely,** outwardly. **1700. doon,** make. **1707. forthren,** further; **punice,** punish. **1708. vice,** wrong. **1709. triste,** trust. **1714. teene,** sorrow. **1717. ferforth,** far. **1718. seeche,** seek. **1719. recche,** care. **1720. may,** maid.

This Pandarus, that alle thise thinges herde,
And wiste wel he saide a sooth of this,
He nought a word ayain to him answerde,
For sory of his freendes sorwe he is,
And shamed for his nece hath doon amis;
And stant astoned° of thise causes twaye,
As stille as stoon—a word ne coude he saye.

But at the laste thus he spak and saide:
"My brother dere, I may do thee namore.
What sholde I sayn? I hate, ywis, Criseide,
And God woot I wol hate hire everemore.
And that thou me bisoughtest doon of yore,
Having unto myn honour ne my reste°
Right no reward, I dide al that thee leste.°

If I dide ought that mighte liken° thee,
It is me lief;° and of this treson now,
God woot that it a sorwe is unto me;
And dredelees,° for hertes ese of you,
Right fain I wolde amende it, wiste I° how.
And fro this world almighty God I praye
Delivere hire soone: I can namore saye."

Greet was the sorwe and plainte° of Troilus:
But forth hir cours Fortune ay gan to holde;
Criseide loveth the sone of Tydeus,
And Troilus moot° weepe in cares colde—
Swich is this world, whoso it can biholde:
In eech estaat is litel hertes reste—
God leve° us for to take it for the beste!

In many cruel bataile, out of drede,°
Of Troilus, this ilke noble knight,

1728. **stant,** stands; **astoned,** stunned. 1735. **reste,** peace of mind. 1736. **reward,** regard; **leste,** it pleased. 1737. **liken,** please. 1738. **It . . . lief,** I am glad of it. 1740. **dredelees,** doubtless. 1741. **fain,** gladly; **wiste I,** if I knew. 1744. **Greet,** great; **plainte,** lamentation. 1747. **moot,** must. 1750. **leve,** grant. 1751. **drede,** doubt.

As men may in thise olde bookes rede,
Was seen his knighthood and his grete might;
And dredelees, his ire day and night
Ful cruelly the Greekes ay aboughte,°
And alway most this Diomede he soughte.

And ofte time I finde that they mette
With bloody strokes and with wordes grete,
Assaying how hir speres weren whette,
And God it woot, with many a cruel hete°
Gan Troilus upon his helm to bete:
But nathelees, Fortune it nought ne wolde
Of otheres hand that either dien sholde.

And if I hadde ytaken° for to write
The armes of this ilke worthy man,
Thanne wolde ich of his batailes endite;
But for that I to writen first bigan
Of his love, I have said as I can:
His worthy deedes, whoso list hem heere,
Rede Dares—he can telle hem alle yfere;°

Biseeching every lady bright of hewe,
And every gentil womman what she be,
That al be that Criseide was untrewe,
That for that gilt she nat be wroth with me:
Ye may hir giltes in othere bookes see,
And gladlier I wol write, if you leste,°
Penolopees° trouthe and good Alceste.

N'I saye nat this al only for thise men,
But most for wommen that bitraised° be
Thurgh false folk—God yive hem sorwe, amen!—
That with hir grete wit and subtiltee

1756. aboughte, paid for. **1761. hete,** rage. **1765. ytaken,** undertaken. **1771. Dares,** supposed author of a late account of the Trojan war; **yfere,** together. **1777. leste,** it please. **1778. Penolopees,** Penelope's. **1780. bitraised,** betrayed.

Bitraise you; and this commeveth° me
To speke, and in effect you alle I praye,
Beeth war of men, and herkneth what I saye.

Go litel book, go litel myn tragedye,
Ther° God thy makere yit, er that he die,
So sende might to make° in som comedye;
But litel book, no making° thou n'envye,
But subjet be to alle poesye,
And kis the steppes wher as thou seest pace°
Virgile, Ovide, Omer, Lucan, and Stace.°

And for ther is so greet diversitee
In Englissh, and in writing of oure tonge,
So praye I God that noon miswrite thee,
Ne thee mismetre for defaute of tonge;°
And red° wherso thou be, or elles songe,
That thou be understonde, God I biseeche—
But yit to purpos of my rather° speeche.

The wratthe, as I bigan you for to saye,
Of Troilus the Greekes boughten dere,
For thousandes his handes maden deye,
As he that was withouten any pere,°
Save Ector, in his time, as I can heere:
But wailaway, save only Goddes wille:
Despitously him slow° the fierse Achille.

And whan that he was slain in this manere,
His lighte gost° ful blisfully is went
Up to the holwenesse of the eighte spere,°
In convers leting everich element;°
And ther he sawgh, with ful avisement,°

1783. **commeveth,** moves. 1787. **Ther,** i.e., may. 1788. **make,** write. 1789. **making,** poetry. 1791. **pace,** pass. 1792. **Omer,** Homer; **Lucan,** Roman poet; **Stace,** Statius, late Latin author of an epic concerning Thebes. 1796. **mismetre,** misscan; **defaute,** deficiency; **tonge,** speech. 1797. **red,** read. 1799. **rather,** earlier. 1803. **pere,** peer. 1806. **slow,** slew. 1808. **gost,** spirit. 1809. **holwenesse,** i.e., concavity; **spere,** sphere. 1810. Leaving behind all the elements. 1811. **avisement,** deliberation.

The erratik sterres herkning armonye,
With sounes ful of hevenissh melodye.

And down from thennes faste he gan avise
This litel spot of erthe, that with the see
Embraced is, and fully gan despise
This wrecched world, and heeld al vanitee
To respect of the plein felicitee
That is in hevene above; and at the laste,
Ther he was slain his looking down he caste,

And in himself he lough right at the wo
Of hem that wepten for his deeth so faste,
And dampned al oure werk that folweth so
The blinde lust, the which that may nat laste,
And sholden al oure herte on hevene caste;
And forth he wente, shortly for to telle,
Ther as Mercurye sorted him to dwelle.

Swich fin hath, lo, this Troilus for love;
Swich fin hath al his grete worthinesse;
Swich fin hath his estaat real above;
Swich fin his lust, swich fin hath his noblesse;
Swich fin hath false worldes brotelnesse:
And thus bigan his loving of Criseide,
As I have told, and in this wise he deide.

O yonge fresshe folkes, he or she,
In which that love up groweth with youre age,
Repaireth hoom fro worldly vanitee,
And of youre herte up casteth the visage
To thilke God that after his image
You made; and thinketh al nis but a faire,
This world that passeth soone as flowres faire;

1812. erratik, wandering; **armonye,** the music of the spheres. **1813. sounes,** sounds. **1814. avise,** contemplate. **1818. To respect of,** in comparison with; **plein,** full. **1821. lough,** laughed. **1823. dampned,** condemned. **1824. lust,** desire. **1827. Mercurye,** the agent who assigns souls to their final homes; **sorted,** allotted. **1828. fin,** end. **1830. real,** royal. **1832. brotelnesse,** brittleness.

And loveth him, the which that right for love
Upon a crois, oure soules for to beye,
First starf, and roos, and sit in hevene above;
For he nil falsen no wight, dar I saye,
That wol his herte al hoolly on him laye:
And sin he best to love is and most meeke,
What needeth feined loves for to seeke?

Lo, here of payens cursed olde rites;
Lo, here what alle hir goddes may availe;
Lo, here thise wrecched worldes appetites;
Lo, here the fin and guerdon for travaile
Of Jove, Appollo, of Mars, of swich rascaile;
Lo, here the forme of olde clerkes speeche
In poetrye, if ye hir bookes seeche.

O moral Gower, this book I directe
To thee, and to thee, philosophical Strode,
To vouchen sauf, ther neede is, to correcte,
Of youre benignitees and zeles goode;
And to that soothfast Crist that starf on roode,
With al myn herte of mercy evere I praye;
And to the Lord right thus I speke and saye:

Thou oon and two and three eterne on live,
That regnest ay in three and two and oon,
Uncircumscript and al maist circumscrive,
Us from visible and invisible foon
Defende, and to thy mercy everichoon
So make us, Jesus, for thy mercy digne,
For love of Maide and Moder thyn benigne.

1843. **crois,** cross; **beye,** redeem. 1844. **starf,** died; **roos,** rose; **sit,** sits. 1845. **falsen,** betray. 1846. **hoolly,** wholly. 1848. **feined,** feigned, shirked. 1849. **payens,** pagans'. 1852. **fin,** end; **guerdon,** reward; **travaile,** i.e., the works. 1853. **rascaile,** mob. 1855. **seeche,** seek. 1856. **Gower,** Chaucer's friend, the poet. 1857. **Strode,** probably Ralph Strode, a philosopher. 1860. **starf,** died; **roode,** cross. 1863. **eterne,** eternal. 1865. **Uncircumscript,** uncircumscribed. 1866. **foon,** foes. 1868. **digne,** worthy.

Part II
COMMENTARY

CHAUCER'S LANGUAGE

CHAUCER WROTE in the dialect of the city of London, where he resided during most of his life. Medieval or Middle English, unlike Modern English, was not a single highly standardized speech, but consisted of a number of regional dialects each of which possessed its own idiosyncrasies; even in any one regional dialect there were apt to be differentiated subdivisions. Thus the dialect of London was in most respects similar to the regional dialect known as East Midland, but London's location in the extreme south of this dialect area caused it to admit into its own speech certain Southern as well as Kentish peculiarities; furthermore, the cosmopolitan nature of London's population tended to soften resistance to the intrusion of idiosyncrasies from remoter dialect areas. The dialect of London actually became the ancestor of Modern Standard English (and of Modern Standard American), and this has resulted in making Chaucer one of the easiest of the Middle English poets for us to read today. Even so, Middle English—the term applied to the conglomerated dialects spoken between the Norman Conquest and the year 1500—differs in at least two distinctive ways from English speech today. The first of these differences is in the pronunciation of the long vowels and dipththongs, the second in the fact that Middle English preserved to a far greater extent than Modern English the inflectional system of pre-Conquest Old English (Anglo-Saxon).

THE SOUNDS OF MIDDLE ENGLISH

VOWELS

ME (Middle English) makes a clear distinction between long vowels and short vowels. ModE (Modern English) often tends to blur this distinction. Modern American particularly tends to prolong short vowels and either to shorten long vowels or to draw them out in diphthongs. Furthermore, the whole system of ME long vowels has been altered in ModE by the process known as the Great Vowel Shift, as a result of which the long vowels lost their original phonetic values and took on others.

Short vowels

The system of short vowels has suffered very little alteration:

ME short *a* (as in ME *sat*) is pronounced like the *o* in American *hot*

ME short *e* (as in ME *bed*) is pronounced like the *e* in ModE *bed*

ME short *i* (as in ME *his*) is pronounced like the *i* in ModE *his*

ME short *o* (as in ME *fox*) is pronounced like the *o* in Modern British *fox*

ME short *u* (as in ME *ful*) is pronounced like the *u* in ModE *full*

Short i. In ME, as in ModE, there is no distinction between the sounds of *i* and vocalic *y*, so that the descriptions of *i* apply equally to *y*.

Short o. In American speech original short *o* is frequently unrounded to such an extent that it approximates the sound of the ME short *a*. The original ME sound of short *o* is, however, preserved in Modern British speech. In American terms the sound is perhaps best described as that of *aw* in *law* spoken quickly, without prolongation.

Short u. ME short *u* is frequently spelled *o* (see below, p. 846). ModE short *u* has several distinct sounds (*cut, hurt, full*), but ME short *u* had only one.

General. Students who have had French should be on guard *not* to nasalize the pronunciation of the vowels plus *m* or *n* as in French *enfant*, etc. They should also be on guard *not* to lengthen short *i* to the sound of *i* in *machine*.

Long vowels

The system of long vowels is, for the reasons given above, complicated. In general, ModE long *a* has taken over one of the two original sounds of ME long *e;* ModE long *e* has taken over the original sound of ME long *i;* one of the two original sounds of ME long *o* has taken over the other, which has in turn taken over the original sound of ME long *u;* ME long *i* and *u* have become diphthongized in ModE.

ME long *a* (as in ME *name*) is pronounced like the *a* in ModE *father*

ME long open ę (as in ME *deel*) is pronounced like the *ea* in ModE *swear*

ME long close *e* (as in ME *feet*) is pronounced like the *a* in ModE *name*

ME long *i* (as in ME *whit*) is pronounced like the *ee* in ModE *feet*

ME long open ǫ (as in ME *holy*) is pronounced like the *aw* in ModE *law*

ME long close *o* (as in ME *roote*) is pronounced like the *o* in ModE *holy*

ME long *u* spelled *ou, ow* (as in ME *aboute, town*) is pronounced like the *oo* in ModE *root*

ME long *u* spelled *u* (as in ME *vertu*) is pronounced like the *ew* in ModE *curfew*

Long a. The actual sound was probably more fronted and flatter than the *a* in ModE *father,* but is difficult for American students to reproduce.

Long e, open and close. The distinction in sound between original long open ę (indicated by a subscript hook) and long close *e* in ME has generally disappeared in ModE, in which words with original ME open ę like *meat, wheat* have the same sound as words with original ME close *e* like *teeth, sheep;* only a few words with original open ę like *steak, break, great* still reflect the old distinction. The distinction was retained in early ModE; in the fifteenth century the two sounds began to be differentiated in spelling, long open ę being represented by the digraph *ea* and long close *e* by *ee* or *e*. In Chaucer's time, however, both sounds were spelled either *e* or *ee.* In order to determine whether one is dealing in Chaucer with open or close long *e* it is necessary, therefore, to consult the ModE equivalent, if one exists. Thus the following ME words spelled with *ea* in their ModE equivalents have long open ę: *bęęm,* beam; *ęte,* eat; *gręęt/ gręte,* great; *hęte,* heat; *hęęth,* heath; *lęęf,* leaf; *lępe,* leap; *pęęs,* peace; *plęse,* please; *sęę,* sea; *spęke,* speak; *yęęr/yęre,* year; and, with ModE vowel shortening: *bręęth,* breath; *dęęth,* death; *dęęd/ dęde,* dead. On the other hand, the following words spelled with *ee* or *e* in their ModE equivalents have long close *e: be,* be, been; *deeme,* deem; *greete,* greet; *knee,* knee; *see,* see; *sheep,* sheep; *sweete,* sweet; *teeth,* teeth. There are a few exceptions to this normal development: for instance, ModE *hear* and *dear* represent ME long close *e,* while ModE *speech* represents long open ę. Chaucer sometimes either rhymes inaccurately or exploits dialectal variations to make what seem to be rhymes of open and close *e,* as in the pair *sęę-be,* sea-be.

Long o, open and close. While the distinction between long open *ǫ* (also indicated here by a hook) and long close *o* is not represented by ME spelling, which has *o* or *oo* for both sounds, it is reflected both by ModE pronunciation and, in general, by ModE spelling. ME long open *ǫ* results in the ModE spelling *oa* or *o* with the pronunciation of *o* in ModE *holy: bǫǫt,* boat; *cǫte,* coat; *fǫ,* foe; *gǫ,* go; *hǫǫm,* home; *tǫ,* toe. ME long close *o* results in the ModE spelling *oo* or *o* with the pronunciation of *oo* in ModE *food,* or, with modern vowel shortening, of *oo* in ModE *good: cook,* cook; *do,* do; *foot,* foot; *looke,* look; *roote,* root; *to,* to, too. Exceptional in both spelling and pronunciation are ModE *brother, other, mother* (ME *moder*), which in ME had long close *o.* As with the two sounds of *e,* Chaucer occasionally rhymes the two sounds of *o*: *gǫ-do.*

Long u. The distinction between the two sounds of long *u* is preserved in both ME and ModE spelling. For an original Old English long *u,* ME adopted the spelling *ou, ow,* which is still retained today: *about, town.* The original ME sound has been generally diphthongized in ModE (though not in the pronoun *you*). Long *u* in words introduced into ME from French and Latin was and is generally spelled *u,* and the sound has not been diphthongized in ModE: *virtue.* But because in ME both the spelling *ou, ow,* and the spelling *u* can represent other sounds than ME long *u,* it is necessary to consult the ModE equivalent to determine the ME pronunciation (see above, *Short Vowels,* and below, *Diphthongs*).

Diphthongs

The ME system of diphthongs is fairly easy in essentials, though difficult in details:

ME *ai, ay, ei, ey* (as in ME *day*) may be pronounced like the *ay* in ModE *day*

ME *au, aw* (as in ME *chaunge, saw*) may be pronounced like the *ou* in ModE *out*

ME *eu, ew* (as in ME *newe*) may be pronounced like the *ew* in ModE *curfew*

ME *oi, oy* (as in ME *joye*) may be pronounced like the *oy* in ModE *joy*

ME *ou, ow* (as in ME *thoughte*) may be pronounced like the *ou* in ModE *thought*

ai, ay, ei, ey. The actual sound of the diphthong lay halfway between the *ay* of ModE *day* and the *ai* of ModE *aisle,* but most Americans have difficulty reproducing the sound.

eu, ew. There were actually two distinct sounds for this diphthong, but the one given includes the great majority of cases. A few words, notably *fewe, shrewe, lewed,* were sounded *ę* plus *u,* rather than the *i* plus *u* of *curfew.*

ou, ow. This diphthong occurs only in ME words whose ModE equivalents have either the sound of *ou* in ModE *thought* or the sound of *ow* in ModE *show.* Note that ME *soule* and the three common words *routhe, slouthe,* and *trouthe* contain the diphthong, but that *cours, ynough,* and *you* represent ME long *u* despite irregular development in ModE pronunciation. The actual sound of the diphthong was probably more prolonged than ModE *thought,* nearer to *aw* plus *oo.*

Unstressed vowels

ME probably tended to reduce all unstressed vowels, whether long or short in origin, to the neutral sound of the final *a* in ModE *sofa.* But in syllabic poetry which, like Chaucer's, makes a good deal of use of secondary stress there was probably a countertendency at work to keep the length of secondarily stressed vowels and even at times to lengthen those vowels that speech habit had tended to shorten. This lengthening tendency would operate particularly in polysyllabic borrowings from French and Latin. Thus such a word as *abhominable* (abominable) necessarily would receive two metrical stresses because of its length: *abhómináble*; and it is likely that the stress upon the *a* in *-able* would cause the vowel to be pronounced as a long ME *a* rather than as the neutral sound to which it would be ordinarily reduced in conversation. The problem of the length of secondarily stressed vowels does not arise much in native English words because such words had generally been reduced to three or fewer syllables in the course of time, and the vast majority are of one or two syllables only.

By far the most common unstressed syllable is final *e,* pronounced, as has been said above, like the *a* in ModE *sofa.* This neutral vowel sound was also probably kept in the terminations *ed, en, es,* and *eth,* though occasional rhymes suggest the raising of the sound to *i* in the terminations *ed, es,* and *eth.*

Distinction in spelling between long and short vowels

ME had no very consistent system for distinguishing between long and short vowels, and the reader will be constantly forced to consult ModE equivalents. The following are the few principles that may be safely applied in this edition.

a, e, o. 1. A doubling of any of these vowels will always indicate that it is long: *caas,* case; *maad,* made; *beem,* beam; *feet; goon,* go, gone; *roote,* root.

2. Any of these vowels appearing singly in a stressed open syllable of a two-syllable word will be long: *name, make, mete* (meat), *stele* (steal), *holy, nose, brother.* Note that an open syllable is one whose vowel is followed by a single consonant or *th* between it and the vowel of the next syllable, and that the pronounced final *e* of ME words makes two syllables where today we have but one.

3. Any of these vowels appearing in a stressed open syllable which is the first of a three-syllable or longer word will ordinarily be short: *carye,* carry (where the *y* and *e* count as two syllables), *hevenes,* heavens.

4. Any of these vowels appearing in a monosyllable before a single consonant ending the word will be short: *hat, men, God.*

5. Any of these vowels appearing before a doubled consonant will be short: *dradde,* dreaded; *sette,* set; *pottes,* pots.

i (y). Because of certain developments of phonology, the principles governing *a, e,* and *o* do not apply to *i* (*y*). The letter was seldom doubled to indicate length (never in this edition). In an open syllable as described under (2) above, *i* might be short or long: thus *wite* represents both the verb *to know* with short *i* and the verb *to blame* with long *i.* In a monosyllable ending in a single consonant (4), *i* might also be short or long: *wit,* wit; *whit,* white. Indeed, only (5) applies with any consistency: *sitte,* sit.

u. The *u* also represents an exception to the principles listed for *a, e, o* above, only (5) applying with any regularity. The problem is simplified, however, by the fact that long *u* from Old English was always written *ou, ow.* To distinguish short *u* from long *u* in borrowed words it is necessary to consult the ModE equivalent (see above, *Long Vowels,* Long *u*).

In a number of words short *u* is arbitrarily spelled *o: sone,* son; *sonne,* sun; *love, above, come, some,* and so on. In ME handwriting *m* was represented by three unconnected downstrokes or minims; *n* was represented by two such strokes; and *u* and *v*, which were identical, were also represented in noninitial positions by two downstrokes. This meant that the combination *um* would be represented by five downstrokes and the combinations *un* and *uv* by four; *umm* by eight, and *unn* by six. Such groups of downstrokes were hard to read: should *s* plus four downstrokes plus *e* be read as *suve,* or *snue,* or (since *i* was made by a single dotted downstroke) *sinie,* or *sime,* or *smie,* or *sune*? And *tune* would be read as *tuve* or *time, luve* as *lune* or *linie.* In order to simplify interpretation, French-trained scribes arbitrarily assumed the habit of writing in such combinations *o* for short *u,* since in the dialect of central France the two sounds were closely related. Unlike the practice of writing *y* for *i* (also adopted in order to prevent confusion in minim combinations), the writing of *o* for short *u* has persisted in ModE, so that today we still have many words like *son, love, come* which are actually pronounced with their original short *u,* though spelled with *o.* Once again, the reader of Chaucer will be forced to consult ModE equivalents, though here he must remember to think of pronunciation rather than of spelling.

CONSONANTS

The consonants of ME are pronounced like their ModE correspondents, though the following peculiarities should be noted:

gg: Either hard as in ModE *dagger* (ME *daggere*) or soft as in ModE *bridge* (ME *brigge*)

gh: Not silent as in ModE, but pronounced like the *ch* in German *ich* or *nach*

gn: Both consonants pronounced at the beginning of a word such as *gnawe*; *g* silent when the combination occurs in noninitial positions, as in *signe*

kn: Both consonants pronounced, as in *knight, knowe*

h: At the beginning of short English words and words borrowed from French not pronounced: *his, him, hem, humble*

l: Pronounced in combinations where it is now silent: *folk, half*

wr: Both consonants pronounced in words like *write, wringe*

gh. This sound has been completely lost from ModE, so that no modern equivalents can be given for English. After *e, i,* or *ei,* *gh* has the sound of *ch* in German *ich;* after *a, o, u,* or any combination of them, *gh* has the sound of *ch* in German *Nacht.*

Doubled consonants. It is possible but not certain that both members of a pair of doubled consonants were pronounced: *cat-tes,* cat's; *fet-te,* fetched; *wit-tes,* wits; *pot-tes,* pots; *son-nes,* sun's.

A NOTE ON SPELLING IN THIS EDITION

As has been explained in the Preface, the spelling of this text has aimed at internal consistency, and wherever possible the forms of individual ME words have been assimilated to the forms of their ModE descendants. Assimilation to ModE spelling has not been carried out where it would falsify phonology. For instance, *caas* cannot be written *case:* a final *e* in ME times often had syllabic value. Nor can *ridden* be written for the past participle *riden* (with short *i*), since it is possible that in Chaucer's speech both members of a "long" (doubled) consonant were sounded separately. The diphthongs *ay* or *ai* can be used in words like *saye, saide,* even though many of the words now spelled with *a* were almost invariably spelled by the scribes of Chaucer's dialect with *e: seye, seide.* The scribal practice was based on an older etymological distinction which had no real value in Chaucer's time, when *ei* (*ey*) and *ai* (*ay*) had the same sound, and the *a*-spellings were common to Chaucer's more northerly contemporaries and were indeed increasing even in the London area. The ME scribal practice of writing *y* for *i* in juxtaposition with *m, n,* and *u* (*v*) was, as explained above, purely formal, so that it is as sensible to sacrifice whatever "flavor" the word *smyle* may have to the clarity of *smile* as it is to write *th* for the old letter thorn or to set down *live* and *use* where the scribes put *liue* and *vse.* These latter assimilations to modern spelling have long been made by even the most conservative editors of Chaucer.

If it is impossible to attain internal consistency in the representation of individual sounds, it is at least possible to follow ME practice in distinguishing between long and short *a, e,* and *o.* These vowels are long in open syllables and short when followed by two consonants, conditions which have in general been inherited by ModE. When they are long in a closed syllable the length is indicated by a double vowel: *caas, seen, boon* ("bone"). Long *e* and *o* in open syllables have been doubled when the doubling occurs also in the ModE descendant: *cheere, roote.* When long *e* and *o* are terminal, the spelling of the modern equivalent has been followed: *see* but *be.* The reader may find some exceptions to these principles, but none that will impair his comprehension. Nothing has been done to distinguish between long and short *i:* the scribal practice of representing long *i* by doubling is rare in itself and impossible in modern spelling, and, as was explained above, short *i* may not be indicated by arbitrarily doubling the following consonant. Long *u* in native words is indicated by either *ou* or *ow* according to modern spelling, even though a ME spelling such as *flowr* is very rare. There is no way to differentiate long *u* in loanwords from short *u.*

No way exists of distinguishing between long open and long close *e* and *o,* since *ea* and *oa* for the open sound are of early ModE origin. In any case, the system would often be foreign to ModE, which not only uses at times a single *e* or *o* for both the open and the close sounds, but also—especially with open *e*—misrepresents the Chaucerian value.

THE PARTS OF SPEECH IN MIDDLE ENGLISH

NOUNS

Nouns form the plural and the possessive by adding *es* if they end in a consonant, *s* if they end in a vowel: *knight, knightes* (knights, knight's, knights'); *roote, rootes* (roots, root's, roots'). The *es* is generally pronounced as an additional syllable, but if the meter requires it may be reduced to *s* as in ModE.

Some nouns, notably *lady,* do not inflect for the genitive singular: *his lady grace,* his lady's grace. A few nouns like *hors, deer,* fail to add *es* for the plural; a few others, notably *yë,* eye, form the plural with *n: yën.* Especially with cardinal numbers, a number of nouns fail to add *es* for the plural: *twenty yeer, thousand pound, hundred sithe* (a hundred times).

Note that short-voweled monosyllabic nouns ending in a single consonant double the consonant on adding *es—cat: cattes, bed: beddes, wit: wittes, God: Goddes.*

Inflection of nouns for other cases besides the possessive, a characteristic of Old English, had apparently ceased by Chaucer's time. His language contains, however, a number of so-called "petrified" datives: *bed,* but *to bedde; child,* but *with childe; town,* but *to towne.*

PRONOUNS

Personal

SINGULAR			PLURAL		
Subjective	*Possessive*	*Objective*	*Subjective*	*Possessive*	*Objective*
I, ich	my(n), mine	me	we	oure	us
thou	thy(n), thine	thee	ye	youre	you
he	his	him			
she	hir	hire	they	hir	hem
it	his	it			

Note that Chaucer does not use *them* but *hem,* not *their* but *hir.* The second person plural was used for the second person singular in polite address, but the singular forms were still widely used. Note that the second person plural *you* was still limited to the objective, the subjective form being *ye.* The neuter singular possessive *its* had not yet become current, and Chaucer still uses *his* for "its" as well as "his."

The spellings *hire* for the feminine objective and *hir* for the feminine singular possessive and for the plural possessive are arbitrary editorial choices from a number of possibilities.

Demonstrative

SINGULAR: this, that   PLURAL: thise, tho (these, those)

Relative

Subjective: that, which, the which, which that (who, which, that)
Possessive: whos (whose)
Objective: that, which, the which, which that (whom, which, that); whom (whom)

Note that *who* in Chaucer's speech is not a relative pronoun, but an interrogative or indefinite meaning *whoever.*

ADJECTIVES

Inflection of adjectives, which has disappeared from ModE, still appeared in ME, although it was in general limited to monosyllabic adjectives ending in a consonant: *good, yong, old, long,* etc. These add *e* in the weak declension; that is, when they stand before the noun they modify but follow (1) the definite article *the,* (2) the demonstratives *this* and *that,* (3) possessive pronouns such as *my, youre, his,* etc., or (4) a noun in the possessive: *the goode man, this olde hors, his yonge sone, the loveres fresshe maide,* but *a good man, an old hors, a yong sone, a fressh maide.* They also add *e* when modifying a noun in the vocative: *O goode God, O yonge man!* and this use tends to be extended so that the *e* appears on adjectives modifying proper names regardless of the case: *olde Saturne spak.* Finally, these adjectives add *e* when they stand next to a plural noun they modify: *longe nightes, bookes olde.* The *e* may be omitted when the adjective is in the predicate or otherwise removed from the plural noun: *tales that been olde* or *old.* Note that with adjectives of two or more syllables ending in a consonant, inflection is sporadic at best, and in Chaucer depends mainly on metrical considerations.

As with nouns, inflection of adjectives for other cases than those discussed had ceased, though a few petrifactions remain: *a long swerd,* but *longe time,* for a long time.

Unlike nouns, monosyllabic adjectives ending in a single consonant rarely double the consonant on adding *e,* and the vowel of the inflected form, if it is *a, e,* or *o,* therefore lengthens: *a blăk hors* but *rokkes blāke.*

Adjectives are in general compared as in ModE by the addition of *er(e)* for the comparative, *est(e)* for the superlative. Sometimes the long vowel of an adjective will be shortened in the comparative and superlative forms: *sweete, swettere, swetteste; greet/grete, grettere, gretteste.*

In Chaucer's times adjectives were still being formed from nouns by the addition of *ly* or *lich* (cf. ModE *goodly, lovely*).

ADVERBS

Adverbs could be formed from adjectives either by the addition of *ly* or *liche* or by the addition of a final *e.* Thus the adjective *fair* may be converted into the adverb *fairly, fairliche, faire,* fairly. An adjective already ending in *e* may be an adverb as it stands: *sweete,* sweet or sweetly. In loose syntax it is often difficult to discriminate between adjectives and adverbs of the type of *sweete.*

VERBS

In both ModE and ME verbs are weak or strong. Weak verbs, which are by far the more common, are in general distinguishable by two characteristics: (1) they form their preterites and past participles with a *d* or *t* suffix; (2) and they usually have the same vowel in both the present and in the preterite, though a long vowel of the present may be shortened in the preterite: ModE *love, loved; hear, heard; meet, met.* Strong verbs do not use a *t* or *d* suffix to form the preterite but have a different vowel in the preterite and frequently in the past participle: ModE *begin, began, begun; find, found, found; take, took, taken.*

Except in the preterite indicative and imperative singular the inflectional endings of strong and weak verbs in ME are the same. In the following paradigms *heeren,* to hear, and *loven,* to love, serve as the models for weak verbs; *taken,* to take, and *ginnen,* to begin, for strong.

Present Indicative

I *heere, love, take, ginne*
thou *heerest, lovest, takest, ginnest*
he (she, it) *heereth, loveth, taketh, ginneth*
we (ye, they) *heere (n), love (n), take (n), ginne (n)*

Present Subjunctive

I, thou, he, etc., *heere, love, take, ginne*
we, ye, they *heere (n), love (n), take (n), ginne (n)*

Preterite Indicative Weak

I *herde,* I *loved (e)*
thou *herdest, lovedest*
he (she, it) *herde, loved (e)*
we (ye, they) *herde (n), loved (e)* or *loveden*

Note that in weak preterites when inflectional *e* or *en* results in a form of three or more syllables, there is a tendency, especially in iambic poetry, to omit one or the other of the lightly stressed syllables. Chaucer's scribes generally write *he loved* rather than *he lovede*; it is possible that Chaucer intended the pronunciation *he lovde:* intersyllabic *e* in all verb forms is frequently elided.

Preterite Indicative Strong

I *took, gan*
thou *tooke, gonne* or *gan*
he (she, it) *took, gan*
we (ye, they) *tooke (n), gonne (n)* or *gan*

Note that in many strong verbs, of which *ginnen* is one type, the vowel of the preterite singular first and third person differs from that of the plural and second person singular. In the ModE of these verbs one vowel has dominated the other, and the simplification was already occurring in Chaucer's time, so that he often writes *they gan,* using the singular for the plural without inflectional ending.

Preterite Subjunctive

I, thou, he etc., *herde, lovede, tooke, gonne*
we, ye, they *herde (n), lovede (n), tooke (n), gonne (n)*

Note that in verbs like *ginnen* with two vowels for the preterite indicative, it is that of the plural which appears in the subjunctive.

Imperative: Weak	Strong
(thou) *heer, love*	(thou) *taak, gin*
(ye) *heere (th), love (th)*	(ye) *take (th), ginne (th)*

Note that the only difference between weak and strong in the imperative is that some weak verbs take *e* in the singular.

Infinitive

heere (n), love (n), take (n), ginne (n)

Past Participle: Weak	Strong
(*y*) *herd,* (*y*) *loved*	(*y*) *take (n),* (*y*) *gonne (n)*

Note that the weak past participle ends in *d* or in *t* (*ymet,* met) while the strong ends in *e* or *n.* The prefix *y* is used sporadically.

A few verbs are irregularly inflected. Important are:

doon, to do.	Present: *I do, thou doost, he dooth, we do (on).* Preterite: *dide* (weak). Past participle: (*y*) *do (on).*
goon, to go.	Present: *I go, thou goost, he gooth, we go (on).* Preterite: *wente* (weak). Past participle: (*y*) *go (on).*
connen, to be able.	Present: *I can, thou canst, he can, we conne (n)* or *can.* Preterite: *coude* (weak). Past participle: *coud.*
been, to be.	Present: *I am, thou art, he is, we be (en)* or *are (n).* Preterite: *I was, thou were, he was, we were (n).* Past participle: (*y*) *be (en).*

Impersonal verbs

The following are the commonest of the many verbs which are either personal or not represented in ModE, but were impersonal in ME (forms given are present indicative): *liketh,* it pleases;

list (*lest, lust*), it pleases; *oughte,* it is necessary; *thinketh* (*thenketh*), it seems. Examples: *me list go,* I want to go; *us oughte be war,* we ought to be careful; *as me thinketh,* as I think.

A general note on verbs

The number of alternate forms for ME verbs both strong and weak, as well as the number of verb forms no longer in use, is far too great to be treated here. In this edition all forms which may give trouble to the reader are explained at the foot of the page, and unusual or irregular principal parts are listed in the Glossary.

In general, it may be said that strong verbs have a tendency to become weak, and many that were strong in Chaucer's time are now either weak or in the process of becoming so, for instance: *abide, carve, climb, glide, help, let, melt, quake, shave, yield.* Others had already developed weak forms by Chaucer's time: thus *weepen* and *sleepen* both have strong preterites, *weep* and *sleep,* as well as weak, *wepte* and *slepte,* and the instances might be multiplied indefinitely. One of the few verbs that has reversed the normal process and gone from weak to strong is *wear:* Chaucer's preterite, *wered(e),* wore, is weak.

CONJUNCTIONS

There are some differences both in form and in meaning between ME and ModE conjunctions. The following list includes the more common ME conjunctions that have disappeared from ModE, along with obsolete meanings of conjunctions still in use. Although conjunctions that have survived in general had in ME the same range of meaning they have now, only the archaic meanings are given here.

al plus subjunctive verb plus subject, although, even if: *al speke he,* even if he speaks
al be (*that*), although
als, as
also, as: *also God my soule blesse,* as God may bless my soul
as, as: untranslatable when used to reinforce *ther* and *wher* (see below); standing before a verb in the imperative it may have the sense of an unemphatic *please*
but, unless: *but ye do, I shal be deed,* unless you do, I shall die
but if (*that*), unless
eek, eke, also

er, before

for (that), because: *for she was vertuous, she wolde have noon,* because she was, etc.

forthy, therefore, because

forwhy, because

sin, since

sith, sit (t) hen, since

ther (as), where: *the chapel belle ther as this lord was,* the chapel bell where this lord was [Note that *ther* generally appears where ModE would have *where.*]

wher, whether: untranslatable when introducing a double direct question: *wher shal I love or no?,* shall I love or not?

wher (as), where: generally replaced by *ther (as)* [Note that the ModE meaning *whereas* is very rare.]

PREPOSITIONS

The following is a list of obsolete forms and meanings of prepositions. In general, prepositions that have survived had the same range of meanings in ME as in ModE, though these are not given here.

after, after, according to

again(s), ayain(s), against, exposed to, opposite, to meet: *ayains the sonne,* in (exposed to) the sun; *he cam ayains me,* he came to meet me

at, at, of, from: *axeth at me,* ask of me; *ye shal nat wite at me,* you will not learn from me

for, for: particularly common are the senses "despite" and "for the sake of avoiding": *for al hir bountee,* despite all her excellence; *for swoot,* to avoid the perspiration

for to, to

fro, from

in, in, on: *liggen in the floor,* lie on the floor

inwith, within

maugree, despite

of (1), of: often used meaning "by" in an expression of personal agent; *slain of Mars,* slain by Mars; (2) off

toward(es), toward: prefix and suffix often surround the object; *to Romeward,* toward Rome

thurgh, through

til, to

up, upon

with, with, by: often used in agent expressions; *bismotered with his habergeoun,* stained by his hauberk; *betrayed with Jasoun,* betrayed by Jason

NEGATIVES

ME has the same negatives as ModE, plus three forms for not, *nat, nought,* and the particle *ne* (*ne . . . ne,* neither . . . nor). Negatives are far more frequent in ME than in ModE, since a multiplicity of them does not result in canceling out but in intensification: *He* nevere *yit* no *vilainye* ne *saide in al his lif unto* no *manere wight.*

CHAUCER'S VERSIFICATION

THE PENTAMETER LINE

The great majority of Chaucer's poems are written in the iambic pentameter line; that is, a line ideally consisting of ten syllables divided into five feet of two syllables each with stress on the second syllable.

| In Soúth|werk át | the Tá|bard ás | I laý |

An additional unstressed syllable may be added to the end of the line without affecting its rhythm. Because many ME words ended in a final *e* that was still pronounced, the eleventh syllable is particularly common in Chaucer's pentameter.

| The hó|ly blís|ful már|tyr fór | to seé|ke

Some readers prefer not to pronounce final *e* at the end of the line, but Chaucer's carefulness in not rhyming words that normally have *e* with those that do not suggests that he himself sounded it.

Final e

Final *e* within the line is of great importance to the meter of Chaucer, since it often supplies the alternate unstressed syllables of his line, and to fail to pronounce it where it is required by the rhythm is to spoil the line. In the following examples pronounced *e* is indicated by a dieresis (*ë*).

| To tél|lë yoú | ál the | condí|cioún |
| That fró | the tí|më thát | he fírst | bigán |

Potentially every final *e* is pronounceable, but actually there are countless instances where it is suppressed. Some of the typical situations are:

1. When it precedes a word beginning with a vowel. Suppressed *e* is indicated by a dot beneath it (*ẹ*).

| Wel nínẹ | and twén|ty ín | a cóm|paignný|ë

2. When it precedes a short common word beginning with an *h*, such as *he, his, him, hir*(*e*), *hath, have, hadde.*

| For sóothẹ | he wás | a wór|thy mán | withál|lë

3. When it represents the inflectional ending of a common auxiliary verb such as *have, hadde, coude, mighte, wolde, sholde,* etc.

| This íl|kë wór|thy Knýght | hadde beén | alsó |

4. In general, when it appears at the end of one of the very common words in English speech such as *thanne,* (*n*) *evere, hire,* etc.

| Thánne lóng|en fólk | to goón | on píl|grimá|gës

[*Note.* The exceptions to all these generalizations are numerous in the extreme.

| Swich ár|rogán|cë ís | nat wórth | an hén |
| Yit hád|dë hé | but lí|tel góld | in cóf|rë
| He coú|dë sóng|es mákẹ | and wél | endí|të]

5. In the greatest number of cases in which final *e* is suppressed there is probably no other reason than the demands of the meter.

| For hé | was lá|të cómẹ | from hís | viá|gë
| In hópẹ | to stón|den ín | his lá|dy grá|cë
| Hir nósẹ | tretís, | hir ý|ën gréyẹ | as glás |

In the last analysis, perhaps the most that can be said about final *e* is that it is pronounced or silent according to the demands of the meter.

Treatment of syllables

Certain final unstressed syllables of two or three letters tend to lose syllabic value when the meter demands it. These include syllables formed with *e,* such as *ed, el* (*e*) , *en, er* (*e*) , *es, eth,* and occasional syllables formed with other vowels.

| He wáitẹd | áfter | no pómpẹ | and ré|verén|cë
| That tréw|ë lóvẹ | was évẹrẹ | so ývẹlẹ | bisét |
| For hé | haddẹ gétẹn | him yít | no bé|nëfí|cë
| And wón|derlý | delívẹrẹ, | and óf | greet stréng|thë
| And pál|mërẹs fór | to seé|ken straúng|ë strón|dës

Notice that (*n*)*evere* is frequently reduced to a monosyllable, perhaps pronounced (*n*)*e'er.*

Terminal –*y*(*e*) and –*we* may become consonantal before a word beginning with a vowel and thus lose syllabic value.

| At má|n–ya nó|blẹ arí|vee háddẹ | he bé |
| Wel coúdẹ | she cá|r–yea mór|sel ańd | wel keé|pë
| Ató|nes ín | this hér|ber–weás | is nów |

As in ModE speech, medial unstressed syllables, especially *e,* are very often elided.

| So háddẹ | I spó|ken wíth | hem é|v'richoón |
| To Cán|terb'rý | with fúl | devoút | corág|ë

Certain adjacent syllables that have coalesced in ModE are ordinarily pronounced separately in Chaucer's verse.

| The cré|atoúr | of év|ẹry cré|atú|rë

The suffixes *ion, ioun* are almost always dissyllabic.

| To tél|lë yoú | al thé | condí|ci–oún |
| And Í | saidẹ hís | opí|ni–ón | was goód |

Metrical variations

No good verse is ever exactly regular, and Chaucer permits himself a number of variations from the strict pattern. The most important of these are:

1. In the first foot of the line the stress is sometimes reversed; that is, a trochee (′ –) is substituted for the expected iamb (– ′).

| Bóld was | hir fácẹ | and faír | and reéd | of heẃ|ë

Because of the number of words, especially those derived from French, in which alternate stress was possible in ME, it is not always possible surely to identify trochaic substitution. For instance, at the beginning of the line, *curteis* might conceivably be either iambic or trochaic. In case of doubt it is best to do whatever comes naturally.

2. Chaucer more often achieves the effect of an initial trochee by omitting the first syllable of the line entirely, and writing what is actually a nine-syllable (or, if it ends in final *e,* a ten-syllable) line.

| *x* Gíng|len ín | a whíst|ling wínd | as clé|rë
| *x* Nów | Pandárẹ | I cán | namó|rë saý|ë
| *x* Àt | which boók | he loúgh | alwaý | ful fás|të
| *x* Ànd | with wór|thy wóm|men óf | the toẃn |

In the first two examples the effect is entirely natural, but when the stress falls on a preposition or a conjunction, as it does in the last two examples, modern readers may not be pleased. Nevertheless, Chaucer seems to have written a great many lines of this sort.

3. Reversals of stress may occur in the second, third, or fourth foot of the line as well as in the first.

| Ful sé|mëlý | áfter | hir métẹ | she raúght|ë

The possibility of alternate stress in words derived from the French and the possibility that certain English suffixes which are now invariably unstressed may in ME have been capable of stress often make it difficult to identify stress reversal within the line.

4. Occasionally an extra syllable occurs within the line. If this is a final *e,* the general practice is to omit it (see above, *Final e,* [5]), but when the syllable forms a separate word, it seems necessary to sound it.

| With a thréd|barẹ cópẹ, | as ís | a poórẹ | scolér

This so-called anapestic substitution (– – – for – –́) may be used to account for some but not all of the cases dealt with above, under *Treatment of Syllables.*

THE TETRAMETER LINE

Three of Chaucer's earlier works, his translation of the *Romance of the Rose* (not included in this text), his *Book of the Duchess,* and his *House of Fame,* are written in an eight-syllable line of four feet, in general iambic.

I hávẹ	greet wón	der bý	this líght
Hoẃ that	I lívẹ	for daý	ne níght
I maý	nat sleé	pë wél	neigh noúght.

All the possibilities for variation, suppression, and so forth, that have been mentioned in connection with the pentameter line obtain here also, with the difference that irregularities of all sorts are far more common in the shorter line. Whether this is because the copyists have been unusually careless or because of Chaucer's artlessness—or art—is not determinable. In any case it is virtually impossible to read these earlier poems smoothly without a good deal of study. Even so, occasional lines seem to admit of no metrical resolution.

RHYME SCHEMES

All Chaucer's poetry in the tetrameter line and much of it in the pentameter line rhymes in couplets. The rhyme royal stanza, seven lines of iambic pentameter rhyming *ababbcc,* he used in a number of poems, apparently to achieve a somewhat more contemplative tone than the simple heroic couplet would permit. His poems in rhyme royal are the *Parliament of Fowls, Troilus,* and the Man of Law's, Clerk's, Prioress', and Second Nun's Tales. *The Monk's Tale* is in a variant pentameter stanza of eight lines rhyming *ababbcbc. The Tale of Sir Thopas* is in an imitation of the common ME romance form known as tail rhyme. The basic unit is a six-line stanza rhyming *aabaab,* the *a*-lines containing four stresses and the *b*-lines three. There are, however, variations both elegant and inelegant: shortage of rhyme may produce the pattern *aabccb,* and a line of one stress occasionally forms a bridge to a three-line supplement to the basic stanza.

Chaucer's short poems show wide experimentation with stanzaic patterns, mostly based on French models.

CHAUCER'S LIFE

CHAUCER WAS BORN about the year 1344—though this date, like so much else in his life, is based only upon inference, and he may have been born a few years earlier. His father was a prosperous London wine merchant named John Chaucer, and the poet was probably born in John's house in the wine-marketing area of London, the Vintry, a short distance from the bank of the Thames. How he spent his youth and what sort of education he received we do not know. It has been conjectured, partly on the basis of an old anecdote, that he studied law at the Inner Temple, and certainly his father was rich enough to pay for such an education. All we can be sure of is that he was, for his time, well educated.

For prominent members of the bourgeoisie like John Chaucer to place their sons in the households of great princes was a common enough practice in the later Middle Ages, and it is no special distinction to the poet that his name appears—for the first time anywhere—in the records of the Countess of Ulster, wife of the Prince Lionel of Antwerp, third son of the reigning monarch Edward III. In the spring of 1357, when the poet was probably about thirteen, it is recorded that the Countess paid out seven shillings to purchase a cloak, a pair of breeches, and a pair of shoes for Geoffrey Chaucer, one of her retainers. Later in the same year she allowed two more small sums of money for his maintenance. What service he performed in the household of the Prince and Countess is not known, but he is generally supposed to have been a page, a lad who would fulfill duties partly menial, partly ceremonial, and partly social. The great princes of the Middle Ages were always on the move from manor to manor or to and from the royal court; as a member of the Prince's retinue Chaucer probably got to see a good deal of England. In 1357, for instance, he might have visited London, Windsor, Woodstock, Doncaster, and doubtless did visit Hatfield in Yorkshire, where the household often resided and where he might first have heard the dialect, laughable to a southern man, that Alan and John speak in *The Reeve's Tale.*

Two years later, in 1359, Chaucer appears again in the records, this time as a result of having participated in one of the intermittent military campaigns in Edward III's endless war against the French. (For a youth in his middle teens to accompany his master to war was not unusual.) The poet suffered the indignity of being captured by the enemy, and the King contributed sixteen pounds (a pound might be valued at about $75 in today's currency) for his ransom. Capture by the enemy in the Middle Ages, while it may have been something of a fiasco, was in no sense a disaster; the opposing warriers, when not actually fighting, often enjoyed pleasant social relations. Chaucer's participation in actual warfare was probably short, for he seems to have been taken prisoner near the beginning of the campaign—perhaps near Rheims—and to have been released shortly before its conclusion. He could thus return safely to England, though how long he remained in the service of Lionel and the Countess is not known.

Indeed, nothing is known of Chaucer's life during the seven years following March 1, 1360, when the ransom was paid. The silence that enfolds him is broken in June 1367, when Edward III granted an annuity of twenty pounds to his beloved *vallectus* Geoffrey Chaucer. A *vallectus* meant literally a valet of the chamber of the King, but probably by Chaucer's time any menial services that he had to perform were purely ceremonial. Doubtless the valet—which may be rendered also *yeoman* or *esquire*—was employed for whatever services he was particularly adept at performing, whether clerical, military, or diplomatic: Chaucer's forte seems to have been that of a trusted messenger, a minor diplomat.

At what point in the interval between 1360 and 1367 Chaucer joined the royal household has not been discovered. During the same interval he probably took a wife and, perhaps through her, began his association with John of Gaunt, the fourth son of Edward III, who was to become a formidably powerful figure after the accession to the throne of Gaunt's young nephew, Richard II. Chaucer's wife, Philippa, was originally a lady of the chamber of Edward's queen, also named Philippa, and it is in this capacity that she was granted a royal annuity of ten marks (a mark is two thirds of a pound) in September, 1366. At the time she is referred to by her maiden name, but since women generally retained their maiden names after marriage, this does not necessarily mean that she was not already married to Geoffrey. The two are not spoken of as man and wife until 1374, when John of Gaunt granted an annuity of ten pounds to Chaucer as a reward for his own services and for the services his wife Philippa had rendered to John's mother Queen Philippa and to his second wife, Constance of Castile. Philippa's employment with the Queen ended when the Queen died in 1369, within a short time of the death of John's first wife, Blanche of Lancaster. Philippa Chaucer's sister, Katherine Swynford, was married to one of John's retainers, and this may have facilitated Philippa Chaucer's employment in the household when John married Constance in 1371. In any case, in August, 1372, Philippa received from John an annuity of ten pounds a year. Chaucer's *Book of the Duchess,* which must have been written shortly after the death of Blanche —whom it laments—testifies to his own close connection with John of Gaunt by the late sixties. But whether he owed this connection to his own qualities or to his wife and sister-in-law Katherine (who, left a widow in 1372, became John's mistress and, in 1396, his third wife) is not clear. It is curious that while there is a good deal to suggest that John of Gaunt acted as the poet's patron, it cannot be proved that Chaucer was ever in his service. But it is certain that the joint annuity Philippa and he derived from John, added to Philippa's independent annuity and many gifts from the same source, made the connection a valuable one.

From 1367, the year Chaucer is first mentioned as a member of the royal household, to 1386, the poet seems to have prospered greatly. He was frequently called upon to make trips abroad in the service of the King, and we have records of the sums he received for these expeditions. He seems to have made trips in 1368, 1369, and 1370, but little is known about them. In 1372 he was sent to Genoa as part of a commission that was to deal with the Genoese on a matter of facilitating trade with England. It appears that while on this journey he visited the great cultural center of Florence, and it is often supposed that his Italian travels first brought him into acquaintance with the works of the Italian writers Boccaccio, Petrarch, and Dante, the first of whom was to become Chaucer's favorite source. There is speculation that he may actually have met Petrarch, but there is no firm evidence for this belief and much against it. In any case, the first Italian journey provided Chaucer the opportunity, if he needed it, to widen his literary horizons.

In the year 1374 Chaucer was made Controller of the Customs and Subsidies on Wool for the port of London. The duties were those of a highly responsible accountant (Chaucer was required to keep the accounts in his own hand) who checked on the collections made by the two Collectors of the Customs. Despite the responsibility it required, the position paid the relatively low salary of ten pounds a year. But Chaucer enjoyed as well both the pensions he had accumulated and those of his wife. Furthermore, the Customs seems to have offered opportunities for enrichment beyond the actual salary. He may have received income from fees, and he at least once received a very large sum as the value of a shipment of wool that had been confiscated when its handlers tried to dispose of it without acquiring a license or paying the duty. Chaucer also received annual bonuses for performing his duties well, and in the year he took the position, the King had augmented his emoluments by granting him a daily pitcher of wine—a not insignificant gift, whether the wine was consumed or commuted into cash. The Court was mindful of him in other ways, too, for he was several times assigned the legal guardianship of heirs in their minority, and, whatever his duties, they were well rewarded.

Nor did the King consider Chaucer's duties at the port as disqualifying him from being sent abroad on royal business. He seems to have made a trip in 1376 and two in 1377. According to unofficial reports which do not accord with the official ones, he visited France in 1377 as part of a commission which was to seek Princess Marie of France as a wife for the English heir-apparent Richard, a union which it was hoped would put an end to the interminable hostilities between the French and English. But while Chaucer was in France, Princess Marie died, and before he had returned to England, Edward III was also dead and Richard, at the age of ten, had assumed the throne. Among the records of Richard's official acts that we retain are his renewal of Chaucer's appointment in the Customs, his confirmation of the poet's royal annuity, and his commutation of the daily pitcher of wine into an annuity of twenty marks. In 1378 the new King, following his grandfather's practice, once again sent Chaucer abroad, this time on a mission to Milan. The lord with whom the English commission was to negotiate was Bernabo Visconti, whose subsequent murder is lamented in *The Monk's Tale.* The brief lament betrays, however, no hint of Chaucer's personal relationship with Bernabo.

All we know about Chaucer's personal life during these years is that he resided in a house situated on the city wall at Aldgate, which he had leased rent-free (another benefit) the year he had entered the Customs. Presumably he led the life of a family man, but Philippa continues to exist only as a name in the official records, not as a personality—unless it is she whose tone of voice in waking him in the morning the poet unfavorably compares with the eagle's gentler technique in the *House of Fame.* An Elizabeth Chaucy, whose name survives in records, may have been his daughter, and the Thomas Chaucer who was a prominent person in the next generation was probably his son. But, except for reporting that he did accounts by day and read at night, Chaucer's poetry is uninformative about this phase of his life—indeed, from what he says about himself one would get the impression that he was a bachelor. Almost the only document not relating to his official life or his finances is worse than useless as a clue to his personal life: it is a deed, dated 1380, in which a woman named Cecily Chaumpaigne releases Geoffrey Chaucer from every sort of liability having to do with her *raptus.* What this scandalous-sounding document really means is uncertain: there is good reason not to take it at face value, but we must suspend final judgment until the legal historians have further studied the evidence.

Chaucer continued in the Customs until 1386. By that time he was actually filling two positions, since he had been appointed Controller of the Petty Customs on wines and other merchandise in 1382. But the work may have begun to weary him. For two periods, during 1383 and 1384, he was allowed to be absent from the position on personal business, and in 1385 he was given leave to exercise his responsibilities through a deputy. New interests, which required his residence in the County of Kent, were apparently engaging him. In October 1385 he was appointed a Justice of Peace for Kent, and he was one of Kent's representatives—a Knight of the Shire—to the session of Parliament held in 1386. In October of that year he gave up his rent-free dwelling at Aldgate, and in December he was replaced in the Customs by two other appointees. Presumably he was now residing at Greenwich, on the pilgrim road to Canterbury.

The two-and-a-half-year period beginning with his departure from the Customs has been seen by some scholars as the nadir of his otherwise successful official career, and the waning of John of Gaunt's influence at Court—Gaunt, absent from England, was replaced by his youngest brother, Thomas of Gloucester, as the virtual regent of England—has been invoked as a reason for Chaucer's retirement. But in view of the little evidence there is for supposing that John of Gaunt was Chaucer's chief protector, it may be that Chaucer's retirement was voluntary: most scholars date the beginning of the *Canterbury Tales* to these years, and perhaps the poet thought that he was now sufficiently well off to devote his time to his principal interest, poetry. If so, like many another man who has retired relatively early, he miscalculated. In 1387 his wife's annuities ceased, presumably because of her death. This may have been a double disaster. In any case the records suggest that in the following year Chaucer was badly in debt, and in May of the same year his royal annuity was transferred to another person. The transfer was made at Chaucer's request, so that it is possible that he sold it for a sum of ready cash—a rather more drastic way of raising money than borrowing on one's life insurance, but not entirely dissimilar.

His retirement, whether voluntary or enforced, came to an end in mid-1389 when Richard II, who had now made himself independent of his powerful uncles, appointed Chaucer Clerk of the King's Works for a large number of royal properties in and about London. The salary was good, but the work was proportionately demanding. In order to provide for the maintenance and repair of the King's sundry castles, manors, and lodges, the poet had to keep track of a mass of detail and constantly to be on the move from one estate to another. Since he paid the laborers before the Treasury paid him, he had to keep dunning the latter for sums expended out of his own pocket. In 1390 he was held up and robbed several times within a few days—doubtless the penalty he had to pay for being known to handle substantial sums of money. Two years of this work was apparently enough, for he seems to have taken the first opportunity to find more congenial employment. In June 1391 he gave up the clerkship and five days later he was appointed a deputy forester of one of the King's parks (i.e., forests) in Somerset. We know neither his salary in this post nor much about the exact nature of the duties he actually performed. Certainly the work was largely executive, and may have permitted him to continue to reside at Greenwich. In 1393 the King expressed his pleasure with Chaucer by giving him ten pounds, and in 1394 a new royal annuity of twenty pounds was granted him. Despite these evidences of prosperity, the records show that Chaucer was a good deal in debt during the nineties, but whether this was because he lived too expensively or because he had trouble collecting from the Treasury money due him in his various capacities is not clear. In any case, in the autumn of 1398, after his commission as deputy forester was renewed, we find him entreating the King to grant him a butt of wine annually: the petition is couched in terms calculated to make him seem a virtual pauper, but all such petitioners, regardless of their real prosperity, made themselves sound like paupers in order to give the King an excuse for a further draft on the Treasury. Chaucer got his butt of wine.

In 1399 Richard II was removed from the throne by his cousin Henry of Lancaster, Henry IV, and this son of John of Gaunt and the Duchess Blanche after some delay granted Chaucer an annuity of forty marks, as well as confirming the existent royal pension of twenty pounds a year and the poet's right to the annual butt of wine. But if his financial troubles were over, so, almost, was his life. In December 1399 he leased, for fifty-three years, a house in the garden of Westminster Abbey, and in June of 1400 his pension was collected for the last time. According to the old inscription on his tomb in Westminster Abbey, erected a century and a half after the event it commemorates, he died on October 25, 1400.

Historical records describe Chaucer as a successful man of affairs who, so far as the records themselves are concerned, might never have written a line of poetry in his whole life. Indeed, it is theoretically—though not practically—possible that there were two Geoffrey Chaucers, one a businessman whose career may be reconstructed, the other a poet about whom nothing is known beyond the scattered references to him in the works of other poets, John Gower, Thomas Hoccleve, and the Frenchman Eustache Deschamps (who calls him a "great translator"). The separation dramatizes the danger implicit in trying to perceive any very significant relation between a poet's work and his life, for if one were to proceed backward, reconstructing Chaucer from his works, one would most likely arrive at something quite different from what has been summarized above.

Nevertheless, given the data of his life, one is able to perceive more clearly and even to explain certain characteristics of his work. The strong, practical cast of mind in the man is something that we should not be surprised to find in the author of the poetry. And if the vast sophistication requisite to a man who flourished under three very different monarchs is not at all what we should have expected from the naïve innocent who figures as the first person singular of many of his works, the sophistication and the innocence are historically explicable. The naïveté, of course, is a literary pose (see the discussion of the pilgrim Chaucer below). But from the biography we know that the poet was a bourgeois who passed his life among important aristocrats, men proud, knowing, impatient, arrogant. In such a situation he had to devise some means tactfully to reveal his own superior sensitivity. The naïve narrator has the effect of removing the poet from his own work, so that his poetry seems spoken not by but through him—as if he were its innocent victim. Chaucer's life suggests why he became the most tactful poet that ever wrote.

Few of Chaucer's poems can be dated with any certainty, but by combining the topical references some of them contain—for instance, the Nun's Priest's reference to Jack Straw of the Peasant's Revolt of 1381—with what we know of his life and of the history of the time, by heeding what he himself tells of his own work in the *Legend of Good Women,* and by making admittedly subjective distinctions between mature and immature works, it is possible to give him a literary chronology that seems satisfactory even if it is only approximate. The following represents, for his chief works, a modification of the widely accepted scheme which allows the poet three successive periods of productivity—the so-called French, Italian, and English periods.

I. Before 1372: period of poetic apprenticeship, largely under French influence

Translation of the *Roman de la Rose*
Book of the Duchess (between Blanche's death in 1368—until recently thought to be 1369—and Gaunt's remarriage in 1371)

II. 1372–80: period of early maturity, largely under Italian influence

House of Fame
Second Nun's Tale (probably called the *Life of St. Cecilia*)
Some of the Monk's tragedies

III. 1380–85: period of middle maturity; Italian influence continuing, influence of Boethius strong

Translation of Boethius' *Consolation of Philosophy* (prose)
Knight's Tale (perhaps a stanzaic version called *Palamon and Arcite*)
Parliament of Fowls
Troilus and Criseide
Legend of Good Women

IV. 1386–1400: period of full maturity; various influences, all well assimilated

Canterbury Tales (the framework and most of the tales, though many feel that the two prose stories, *Melibeus* and the Parson's, as well as the Man of Law's, Physician's, and Manciple's, in addition to those named above, are earlier)

There is a partial relationship between Chaucer's verse forms and the chronology of his works. The poems that are considered his earliest, the translation of the *Roman,* the *Book of the Duchess,* and the *House of Fame,* are all written in octosyllabic couplets, the popular form for French poetry of the time. In his middle periods, his chief poems were in stanzaic form with the pentameter line: the Monk's tragedies in an eight-line stanza, and the *Second Nun's Tale,* the *Parliament of Fowls,* and *Troilus* in rhyme royal. In the final period the majority of the poems are in pentameter couplets. But the fact that Chaucer employed rhyme royal for the Man of Law's, Clerk's and Prioress' Tales is not sufficient reason for excluding them from his last period. The choice between couplets and rhyme royal is obviously an artistic one.

THE CANTERBURY TALES

According to Chaucer's original plan, the completed *Canterbury Tales* would have included about one hundred and twenty tales, for the Host's suggestion, to which the pilgrims agree, is that each of them shall tell two tales on the way to Canterbury and two on the journey back to London; the Prologue enumerates thirty pilgrims, not counting the Host or the narrator. If Chaucer had finished his work, it would undoubtedly have been the longest poem in the English language. But he seems not to have formulated the idea until the latter 1380's, perhaps 1386, when he had no more than fourteen years to live, and at his death in 1400 only the Prologue and twenty-four tales (two of them, the Cook's and Squire's, unfinished) had taken shape. And he had already become restive beneath the rigorousness of his original design, for one of the tales, the Canon's Yeoman's, is related by a newcomer to the group of pilgrims that assembled at Southwark. Chaucer was not a poet who would risk stunting his development in order to adhere to a preconceived plan, and apparently his plan expanded as he wrote. While one may lament that he did not live longer and produce more, it is probable that a life indefinitely extended would not have seen the completion of the work. Men of large genius often entertain aspirations that assume that they will live forever.

The *Canterbury Tales* have come down to us complete or substantially complete in some fifty-five handwritten manuscripts, mostly of the fifteenth century; another thirty early manuscripts contain one or more tales from the Canterbury group. Since the text of any one manuscript varies more or less widely from the text of any other, what is presented in a modern edition such as this is an end-product (though only a temporary one) of the labors of generations of scholars who have analyzed the vast amount of surviving data. In the reading of many lines this edition differs from its predecessors just as succeeding editions will differ from this: it is doubtful, indeed, that we shall ever arrive at a totally definitive text of Chaucer's works. Among the most difficult outstanding problems is that of the order of the *Canterbury Tales.* In general the manuscripts give us the tales in ten blocks, or "fragments," but the order of the fragments varies wildly. The order adopted in this edition is that of the famous Ellesmere manuscript, which is as follows: The first fragment contains the *General Prologue* and the tales of the Knight, Miller, Reeve, and Cook (unfinished). The second contains the *Man of Law's Tale*; the third, the *Wife of Bath's Prologue and Tale* and the Friar's and Summoner's tales; the fourth, the Clerk's and Merchant's; the fifth, which is actually joined to the fourth, the Squire's and Franklin's; the sixth, the Physician's and the *Pardoner's Prologue and Tale*; the seventh and longest, the Shipman's, Prioress', *Sir Thopas, Melibeus* (omitted here), Monk's, and Nun's Priest's; the eighth, the Second Nun's and the Canon's Yeoman's; the ninth, the Manciple's; and the tenth, the Parson's (omitted). This order has recently been vigorously challenged, largely because it makes the town of Sittingbourne (*Wife of Bath's Prologue,* line 853) appear before Rochester (introduction to the *Monk's Tale,* line 38), when in fact Sittingbourne is some ten miles further from London than Rochester on the road to Canterbury. Despite this geographical anomaly, the editor prefers the Ellesmere order, which seems better accredited and has the advantage that the tales of the seventh fragment provide a climax to the student reading the *Canterbury Tales* for the first time.

The so-called framing-tale which, as in the *Canterbury Tales,* gives the unity of a single tale to a collection was popular in the fourteenth century. Gower, for instance, had used it in his *Confessio Amantis* (*Lover's Confession*), and Chaucer's *Monk's Tale* and *Legend of Good Women* depend on a similarly simple framing device. A closer analogy to the *Canterbury Tales* is provided by Giovanni Boccaccio's *Decameron,* the third of three instances in his works of framed tales: in the *Decameron* a group of ten young Florentines leave their city during an epidemic and travel from one country villa to another; they spend their leisure hours in telling, by turn, ten tales a day for a period of ten days. Another Italian, Giovanni Sercambi, had used the more lively device of a journey on horseback shortly before Chaucer hit upon his pilgrimage. In Sercambi, a group of persons avoid a plague at Lucca by touring Italy, during which trip their elected leader entertains them with stories. Chaucer's scheme might have been a modification of any of these (though there is no evidence that he knew Sercambi's work or Boccaccio's *Decameron*), but he may well have thought of it independently; pilgrims were, after all, known to be prodigious storytellers, and Chaucer had lived for a time in Greenwich, along the pilgrimage route from London to Canterbury. In any case, Chaucer's is perhaps the best of the framing devices in conception and certainly the best in execution. He exploits to the full the scope it affords for dramatic action and the dramatic development of character—in the portraits of the Prologue, in the links between the tales, and in the self-revelation of the narrators. For him the pilgrimage is a kind of pattern and image of man's uncertain but lively progress through an infinitely various world toward a destination which would be presumed the same for every Christian traveler.

The shrine which Canterbury Cathedral contained was the most popular of the many hallowed sites of fourteenth-century England. It was here, in the year 1170, that Archbishop Thomas à Becket had been brutally murdered by retainers of King Henry II. The blood that flowed from the wounds of the martyr was preserved by his associates who had witnessed his death, and this blood soon revealed its miracle-working power by healing the sick and injured to whom it was applied. The victim of so dramatic an end was canonized within three years and the scene of his murder became at once an object of pilgrimage. Every spring, as the roads of England became once more passable, pilgrims from all over the country descended upon his shrine in throngs.

Canterbury, situated in the county of Kent, lies some fifty-five miles east-southeast of London by the modern road. Its geographical location is such that travelers from everywhere in England except Kent itself and the extreme southern counties made their way there via London. Such inns as the Tabard in Southwark, on the south side of the Thames across from the old City of London, were assembly places for pilgrims to Canterbury. Chaucer's Host is evidently used to putting up large numbers of them, and probably during the warm months they were his chief customers. (In this connection it should be observed that an inn called the Tabard existed in Southwark in Chaucer's time and that the records concerning Southwark also mention a Harry Bailly, innkeeper.) The journey from Southwark to the shrine might be hurriedly accomplished on horseback in two days; most pilgrims, operating under no urgency to fulfill their mission and return home, took three days or three and a half. In his completed version of the *Canterbury Tales* Chaucer may have planned to identify the towns where his pilgrims passed the nights en route. But in the present form of the poem there are only isolated references to places on the road, and the pilgrimage does not even arrive at its destination. If this is to be regretted, we can at least console ourselves in finding a kind of eternity in the unfinished journey, which when last mentioned in the Parson's prologue is hastening through the lengthening shadows toward a little village that must forever remain unidentified.

THE GENERAL PROLOGUE

The *General Prologue* to the *Canterbury Tales* is Chaucer's best-known and probably best-loved poetic achievement, despite its being largely static: the pictures are profoundly vital, though they have no chance to come down off the wall and participate in the dramatic action implicit in them. The design is, indeed, characteristically medieval. No modern writer would dream of characterizing his *dramatis personae* in a group before they could reveal themselves through significant action. For a medieval man Chaucer was curiously sensitive to the vices of medieval literature, and in the Prologue he shows himself aware of the dangers offered by the static portraiture he has chosen to employ, for he does everything he can to ward off tedium. Thus he arranges the order of the portraits in such a way as to permit a number of highly suggestive juxtapositions (examples are given in the discussions of the characters). He enlivens the portraits and their significance with the comedy that arises from the simplicity of the narrator. He makes bold variations in the length of the descriptions—sixty-two lines for the Friar, thirteen for the Plowman. And, of course, he also varies his descriptive technique, sometimes giving us the body top to toe, sometimes emphasizing past experience, sometimes habitual action; even more striking, the Five Gildsmen are melted into a single image of the thriving *petit bourgeois,* and the Manciple is epitomized as an exclamation mark punctuating his talent for cheating his masters.

The extraordinary quality of the portraits is their vitality, the illusion that each gives the reader that the character being described is not a fiction but a person, so that it seems as if the poet has not created but merely recorded. How Chaucer accomplishes this illusion is difficult to analyze, and even to give a proper descriptive name to its literary effect is not easy. Most of the characters are standard types; yet the adjective *typical,* with its connotations of the general as opposed to the particular, fails to do justice to such characterization. On the other hand, the word *real,* with its modern connotation of the individual existing as a unique entity, is equally inadequate, since it tends to exclude the typical which lends the characters much of their meaning.

Of the two, *real,* with certain important limitations, is surely the better, for the characters make their chief appeal to the reader's innate sense of reality. This kind of realism is not at all the same thing as naturalism, which requires that things be not merely possible but probable. Chaucer does, indeed, use naturalism to a limited extent in order to achieve the verisimilitude the absence of which would alienate most readers, but he departs from it whenever it serves his larger purpose to do so. The number of the Knight's campaigns and of the Wife of Bath's pilgrimages is, for instance, highly improbable if not totally impossible; yet they are significant factors in making up the reality of the Knight and the Wife. Indeed, while any one or several of the characters might possibly have the superlative qualities assigned them, twenty-nine superlatives are altogether improbable. Nor does Chaucer scruple at using all sorts of nonnaturalistic techniques. His narrator knows more about the states of mind and the previous history of the pilgrims than even the most prying of observers could learn in months of inquiry—he even knows the state of mind of the Gildsmen's wives, who are not present on the pilgrimage, and he can describe the close-mouthed Reeve's dwelling in far-off Norfolk. For the reader to worry about these matters would be as foolish as for him to fear that the sound of the horses' hooves would drown out the Prioress as she tells her tale.

Nor does Chaucer's true realism lie in his meticulous detail. The Prioress' table manners and the Miller's wart have their own strongly individualizing effect that pleases us, but if taken merely as picturesque details they lose their significance. People are, indeed, made up of a number of such bits and pieces, but in literature they must be made up into some sort of a whole. That is, reality as we know it consists largely of an infinite number of uncorrelated *minutiae* which the great poet knows how to combine into something we recognize as more real than anything we could ourselves perceive. The Prioress' table manners are far more than a charming accidental detail: actually they convey the very essence of the courteous, misdirected lady. And the Miller's wart helps similarly to make up the sum of what the Miller is: ugly and crude, yet unabashed and vital. These details are not atoms falling in chaos; they are part of Chaucer's cosmos.

It is a tribute to Chaucer's "realism" that scholars have made valiant attempts to search the records of late fourteenth-century England for the originals of his pilgrims. This kind of exercise, while it provides much historical matter that serves to illustrate the life medieval Englishmen led, inevitably undervalues Chaucer's true genius. It is almost as if the scholars suspected that no poet could create such characters unless the Creator had in turn provided him with models. Of course Chaucer had to know people in order to create the Canterbury pilgrims. But he did not have to know these very pilgrims. Most of them, indeed, have literary ancestry; they derive from contemporary satirical portraits of types. Chaucer's genius was not to see that types are individuals and individuals types—though that is not a mean perception in itself—but to be able to combine the two so that his characters are at once perfect types and perfect individuals.

The *General Prologue* begins with a long rhetorical sentence that, while introducing the pilgrimage, develops one of the poet's characteristic paradoxes. Stripped to its essentials all this eighteen-line sentence says is that in spring, when all nature begins to revive, people want to go on pilgrimages. But the logic of Chaucer's sentence is not so arrow-straight. Appealing to classic mythology, Chaucer tells us of the generative influence of Zephyrus, the west wind, which brings back to life the earth deadened by the drought of March. (It is a comment on Chaucer's "naturalism" that England suffers no drought in March; Chaucer's drought is a metaphorical one, taken from a rhetorical tradition that goes back to classic literature, and to the Mediterranean countries where March is a dry month.) The wind's regenerative effect is felt by field and forest—and by birds, whom it renders sleepless for love. Now the sentence reaches what is supposed to be its true point: *then* men long to go on pilgrimages. But the force of the word *pilgrimage*—a journey for a spiritual end—is not permitted to become dominant: first we have to hear about palmers, those professional pilgrims who travel all over the known world far more for travel's sake than for religion's. It is not until the last lines of the sentence that we are allowed to think of the holy martyr whose shrine is at Canterbury and whose homage is the goal of the pilgrimage.

Of course, Chaucer is presenting the spiritual act of pilgrimage as one manifestation of a vast urge toward regeneration (which is what Christianity is), but there is a wonderful illogic in the way the great urge has been qualified by love-sick birds (who are juxtaposed to pilgrimage-bent people) and in the way that tourism has got into the pilgrimage. What the complete sentence has succeeded in saying is that the spring, which engenders thoughts of love, makes people want to go on pilgrimages, during which they will see the world, in order to perform an act of piety. Too many disparate elements have entered the motivation, but the poet recognizes that, given man's nature and this world, they always do. A stern moralist—there were many such who expressed themselves on the subject of pilgrimages during Chaucer's later life—might well say that if people are sincere in making a pilgrimage, love of the kind connoted by birds, *wanderlust,* and even spring ought to have nothing to do with it. But in his poetry Chaucer rarely suggests that he would agree with such a statement. He does, of course, perceive the tension among the diverse motivations, and he is exploiting it brilliantly. But this confusion in the mind of man, this inability to sort out motives with a clear recognition of the spiritual and worldly, is nowhere condemned—though it is often laughed at—in Chaucer's poetry. (The austere *Parson's Tale,* which is not poetry, is another matter.) What Chaucer believed, or what his poetry "teaches" on the subject, it would not be wise to try to assert in prose. But the possibility revealed in the first sentence of the *Canterbury Tales* is often implicit in his poetry. It is that the divine love that revives the dead world annually is large enough to countenance the whole paradox of man's nature.

THE PILGRIMS

CHAUCER THE PILGRIM

Chaucer composed the *Canterbury Tales,* as he composed most of his poems, as if he were going to read them aloud to an audience. Before the invention of printing, when a writer's work was available only in the autograph version or in expensive manuscript copies that had a very limited circulation, the poet was traditionally not only the composer but also the performer of his works. It is only natural that this personal relationship to an audience should have caused heightened self-consciousness in the poet, particularly since the audience was likely to consist of members of the court circle, into which the poet—like Chaucer—had made his entry through talent rather than birth. Under these circumstances the poetry had to convey the deference as well as the dignity of the poet. Deference and dignity are subsumed under diplomacy, and fortunately Chaucer was sufficiently diplomatic that not only was he called upon officially to serve as a diplomat, but also he was able to solve at once the artistic and social problem in writing and presenting his poetry. The solution he hit upon—as early as the *Book of the Duchess*—was one which involved the submergence of his own personality into the personality of a fictional substitute, who speaks for or instead of the poet and who resembles the poet in many ways and even bears his name. Since this fictional Chaucer speaks in the first person, the reader who—as we must—first encounters Chaucer's poetry in print naturally assumes that the speaker is the poet Chaucer. Yet actually the enormous difference between the poet and the speaker in his poetry is the area in which Chaucer's poetic vision is broadest and most manifold.

If one imagines Chaucer himself reading the *Canterbury Tales* at court—as it is likely that he did—one can begin to see some of the elements that make up this complex poetic vision. In the first place, Chaucer obviously exploits his physical personality—that of a pleasingly plump, cheerful, perhaps unimpressive little man—for such humor as it will afford: he assigns this personality to his fictional representative in such a way that when it is mentioned within the poem the audience will laugh at it as they probably never would at the actual Chaucer. But the physical similarity between the two Chaucers is ultimately less important than the temperamental similarity which it is meant to suggest—the affability, the air of deference, of eagerness to please, of naïveté, all of them somehow exaggerated when the man they belong to puts them into his fictional surrogate. The temperamental similarity is in turn chiefly important as a device that serves to bring out the more significant mental dissimilarity between Chaucer the poet and Chaucer the narrator. It is here that the latter takes leave of the former, for while the narrator is almost unfailingly simple-minded, the poet who has created him and has found a place for his simplicity in the poem—indeed, has sometimes made the meaning depend on it—is anything but simple-minded. The intellectual difference between the two can and often does constitute a philosophical commentary on the poem. One must, however, arrive at this commentary through a process of gradual awareness. We ought, therefore, to inquire into the character of this pleasingly plump, affable, simple narrator of the *Canterbury Tales* before we can hope to comprehend the more inclusive vision of the equally plump, equally affable, but assuredly not simple poet.

The pilgrim Chaucer is, in his own unpretentious way, a seeker after truth. He is even related (and the reader would be expected to recognize this) to that most distinguished of medieval pilgrims, Dante, the narrator of the *Divine Comedy*. But our pilgrim's way of proceeding on his quest reveals from the very beginning a fatal overconfidence in his ability to see things as they are merely by looking at them hard. To be sure, he is energetic, does not trust to luck, and makes a valiant show of braving experience. It is with a distinct hint of pride that he reports on his success in interviewing all nine and twenty of his fellow pilgrims before sunset; it is with rugged determination that he promises to relate all he knows concerning every single one of them. But he never stops to consider whether the intentions of a conscientious reporter are enough to insure an accurate presentation of reality. The inevitable result is that in evaluating the other pilgrims, the pilgrim Chaucer constantly falls a victim to his faith in a simple one-to-one correspondence between the various facets of reality. He is impressed by prowess in the Knight, and assumes that therefore self-assertive virility must be equally laudable in the Monk; he finds the Shipman pleasant company, and concludes that a scrupulous conscience is not, after all, a necessary criterion for approval. He can, indeed, respond admiringly to more than ordinary goodness, but as a result is apt to be equally dazzled by superlative qualities of any description, even those as inconsequential as the size of the Miller's mouth, or as sinister as the hypocritical Friar's aptitude for "fair language." This confusion over values manifests itself first and last in his inability to distinguish between the properties of words and things. Not only is he taken in by the assertive oratorical powers of several of his fellows; he is betrayed, against his own principles, into practicing specious oratory himself and believing it to be effective. This happens especially at moments of emotional intensity, when the speaker is particularly anxious to establish praise or blame. He takes it for granted that repeated insistence on the adverb *ful* (equivalent of the modern *very*) will infallibly establish the excellence of the Prioress, whereas the actual effect is rather to convey her hypnotic power over him. He is under the impression, likewise, that explicit condemnation of the Summoner's irreverent attitude in matters of excommunication will suffice to clear his own Christian conscience, but his condoning of far worse offenses by the Summoner casts suspicion on his profundity, if not his sincerity. The simple equations by means of which the pilgrim Chaucer is attempting to keep a record of his memorable experiences on the way to Canterbury are constantly breaking down.

The break-down occurs, of course, on a larger scale as well, and it is in this way that the ironic role of Chaucer the pilgrim is amplified in proportion as his control over his material decreases. In the context of the Prologue, whole portraits get out of hand, and can be read upside down, as it were. The Monk's is an excellent example: almost everything that is said in praise of him as a manly man can reflect unfavorably on his supposedly chosen vocation as a monk. In the context of the entire poem, the pilgrim Chaucer's own tale of Sir Thopas gets out of hand, and is publicly censored as unworthy of continuation. We, who in the absence of evidence to the contrary had originally extended to the fictional "I" the willing suspension of our own disbelief, must learn to look for guidance to the poet Chaucer, trusting that he and the pilgrim are not by any means identical in all respects.

Apart from humor, and an implied compliment to the sophisticated intelligence of the audience, what has been gained, one may ask, by the poet's considered refusal to speak directly, in his own person? The way of indirection is generally the way of irony, and allows for a pervasive suggestiveness to which the reader is then free to assign any number of meanings. Irony, moreover, provides in both tone and content for the possibility of a sustained paradox. Medieval literature abounds in satire, not infrequently full of savage condemnation. Chaucer's satire, by and large, is far funnier than the rest, and yet partly for this reason perhaps more telling. The narrator's failure to see what is wrong emphasizes the wrong; irony, of which this is a complex kind, always heightens. Yet a satiric portrait, while intellectually telling, need not, thanks to the narrator's good nature, be emotionally scathing. This is not the only way to write successful satire, but it was clearly Chaucer's intention to write satire of a rather special kind; to present both halves of the human paradox and to retain both without allowing the positive and negative values to cancel each other out. The Monk as monk is a failure who must surely be condemned by discriminating men. As a man, the Monk is one of the most impressive of God's creatures and his manliness, although irrelevant to his vocation, commands the appreciation of men. The narrator's undiscriminating attitude ironically condemns, literally appreciates.

And Chaucer the poet, on whom not only Chaucer the pilgrim, but also the Host and the Parson depend for insight? He, too, is a pilgrim, and exemplifies yet another aspect of man's search for truth. His vision of human reality postulates the simultaneous existence of at first sight mutually exclusive opposites, and is almost perfectly contained in Pope's famous couplet on man:

> Sole judge of Truth, in endless Error hurled:
> The glory, jest, and riddle of the world.

THE KNIGHT

The medieval chivalric ideal combined, perhaps more explicitly than any other to which men might aspire, the spiritual with the secular aspects of human life. By beginning his portraits with the ideal knight's, Chaucer sets up a pattern of perfection against which all the other pilgrims may be measured. At the same time he is beginning with the dominant figure of his own age, which was still the Age of Chivalry however degenerate actual knighthood may have become. At its best, as in Chaucer's Knight, chivalry consisted in an active dedication to the principle of upholding by arms a good higher than one's own. In feudal terms a knight owed fealty, generally through several intermediate overlords, to his King, the leader of knighthood in any one nation. The King in turn was considered God's earthly representative, interpreting and enforcing God's will on earth, so that through his King a knight owed a fealty to God far more exacting than the worship expected of the average layman. In the Middle Ages God was often spoken of as the King of Kings who among His first creative acts brought into being the chivalric orders of angels, and the Crucifixion was sometimes represented as a tournament in which the Christ-Knight jousted with the Enemy.

While the spiritual associations of chivalry were thus of great importance, a knight by his profession of arms was wholeheartedly concerned with the world—with the physical fight against tangible evil and with the imposition upon society of an order that would in some measure reflect the divine order. In practice, of course, it often happened that personal or political interpretations of God's will were made by individual overlords in the chivalric hierarchy and that these interpretations were at variance with one another and with any conceivable higher order. For instance, during much of the fourteenth century the Kings of England and France were engaged with one another in a futile war in which God's will was interpreted according to the political motives of each nation. If he were a historical person, Chaucer's Knight would have been involved in this war. But Chaucer is careful to mention only his participation in such wars as were, in a sense, holy wars, fought in defense of Christendom against the pagan incursions into Europe: campaigns against the Moors in the Spanish kingdom of Granada, in Morocco, and in Algeria; against the Moslems at Alexandria in Egypt, in Turkey, and in Armenia; against the northern barbarians in Prussia, Lithuania, and Russia. The names of these campaigns must have had for the contemporary reader the same proud ring that such names as Normandy, El Alamein, and Iwo Jima have today—great battles which momentarily united much of the civilized world against a common enemy. Indeed, when we are told that the Knight was "full worthy in his lord's war," it almost seems as if we are to understand not his earthly overlord but God.

Just as the wars in which he has fought are not political but religious, so his personality as it appears in the Prologue is less that of an experienced veteran than that of a perfect knight. In him the inward qualities of *trouthe* and *freedom,* fidelity to an ideal and largeness of spirit, find expression in *honour* and *curteisye,* honorable deeds and generous behavior. For Chaucer such a man also resolves one of the oldest antitheses in Western thought, the one that is supposed to exist between the valiant warrior and the sage counselor. The Knight is both at once, "for though that he were worthy [i.e., brave], he was wis." Of all the pilgrims the Knight (with the Parson) seems most aware of the real purpose of the pilgrimage. Having just returned from his latest campaign, he proceeds at once in his travel-stained clothing to offer thanks to the saint who has protected him.

THE SQUIRE

While the Knight has ascribed to him the more august attributes of chivalry, his son the Squire retains the more human and perhaps more endearing ones. His youthful campaigns have been against the French, and his primary interest is in winning the love of his lady, whom he has hoped to impress by his military exploits. The chivalric ideal—which was never unworldly—exacted devotion to one's lady just as it did devotion to one's lord and to God. There is therefore nothing unknightly in the Squire's preoccupation with love. Nor is there in his other accomplishments, such as composition of music and verse, sketching, and penmanship. These are as much chivalric accomplishments as prowess in arms, and the division of qualities in Chaucer's portraits of the Knight and the Squire should not be taken as prejudicial to the latter. What the Squire is, the Knight once was, and what the Knight is, the Squire may yet be. But the Squire is not yet fully developed. As a squire he is either in the final stage of apprenticeship to knighthood or else a newly made knight who must still serve under the banner of one more widely experienced. By actions such as that of carving his father's meat the Squire disciplines himself in the humility in which the Knight is perfect.

THE YEOMAN

The Knight's single servant, the Yeoman, resembles in military rank and in character a seasoned sergeant in a modern army—neat, orderly, efficient, and extremely scrupulous in the care of his weapons and equipment. Trained as a woodsman, he carries the mighty longbow whose deadly effect was revolutionizing warfare during Chaucer's lifetime. The portrait of the Yeoman carries into the lower-class milieu the sense of purposeful order that we associate with the Knight he serves.

THE PRIORESS

The Prioress, who may be the Superior of the Convent at Stratford-at-the-Bow where she learned French, is an amiable, polite, pretty, and sentimental lady—a very human mixture of benevolence and weakness. The true vocation of a nun, a powerful impulse to devote one's life to the worship of God, was probably rarer in the Middle Ages than the large number of nunneries would suggest. Convents were often the refuge of well-born women whose fathers were too poor to provide the dowry without which no woman was considered marriageable. The ideal to which a nun subscribed was no less elevated than it is today, but there were inevitably a good many nuns whose dedication to the ideal was not entirely voluntary, even though such nuns were not often overtly rebellious.

Chaucer's Prioress seems to belong with those not wholly dedicated. She is a complex of qualities that make a most attractive woman but do not make a woman into a nun. Her elegant if not very authentic French, her fine table manners, her devotion to courtly behavior, her spoiled little dogs, her sympathy for the small and helpless, her fashionable clothing, pretty face, and good figure—these are the qualities of a lady of the world. The poet, indeed, describes her in terms borrowed from the stock descriptions of heroines of medieval romance—soft red mouth, gray eyes, well-proportioned nose, and broad forehead—and makes her, inevitably, sincere and demure, "simple and coy." Such a woman naturally appeals to a man, and the narrator's enthusiasm for her is aroused to so superlative a degree that a superlative modifies almost every one of her qualities.

Of course he never does get around to speaking about her conscience. He starts to do so when he calls her charitable, but the Prioress' charity—a word that in Chaucer's time connoted the whole range of Christian love—gets lost among dogs and mice, while conscience is dissipated among tears and prettiness.

The narrator's failure to get down to the matter of her conscience implies no criticism of her on his part. It does, however, evoke in the reader some concern for the ideal that the Prioress in her preoccupation with what is easy and agreeable seems not fully to recognize. Although this ideal is never mentioned, it lies just beneath the surface, at the same time hidden and revealed by the narrator's enthusiasm for qualities irrelevant to it. The reiteration in the very first line, "a Nun, a Prioress," suggests a worship of God more profound than subsequently appears. Moreover, historians tell us that much of what the Prioress occupies herself with was forbidden to fourteenth-century nuns—dogs, brooches, pleated headdresses, even pilgrimages. Such details as these, the significance of which the narrator fails to recognize, raise questions about the Prioress that are not open to a final answer.

The most interesting question is how the Prioress would interpret the ambiguous motto on her brooch. "Love conquers all" had originally referred only to earthly love, but it had long since been taken to refer to the love that Christ brought to earth. For which love was the Prioress intended? The question is perhaps echoed in her mild oath, "By Saint Loy!" It is related that when the parents of the maiden Godeberta were discussing the possibility of her marriage, St. Loy suddenly placed upon her finger a ring which he declared made her forever a bride of Christ. He thus made it possible for her to become a saint, but her wishes do not seem to have been consulted before her dedication. The question receives a kind of answer in the naïve enthusiasm the narrator feels for the Prioress. While it provides a point of vantage for a satire that might be caustic, it seems to suggest also that the love of God is broad enough to encompass the gentle, well-intentioned, misdirected Prioress.

The Prioress is accompanied by the Second Nun, who serves as her secretary, and by three priests. Since historical records suggest that an actual prioress would travel with but one priest, and since Chaucer speaks later of but one priest, it has been suggested that line 164 was left unfinished by Chaucer and finished by a scribe. But there is no evidence for this, and the reader may make what he will of the three priests.

THE MONK

With the Monk, satire becomes sharper even while it remains oblique. The monastic ideal is specifically a rejection of the world in favor of eternity, but the Monk is described entirely in terms of this world. He is a fine figure of a man, whose flesh no monastic fasting or vigil have mortified. Indeed, he has a superabundant vitality that reminds one of the fine horses he owns and the fine fat beasts he loves to hunt. His masterful personality quite overwhelms the narrator, just as, in a different way, the Prioress' charming femininity had done. But brute force is less attractive than charm, and the poet subjects it to more emphatic satire. We are never sure that the Prioress fully knows what she ought to be doing, but the Monk knows and even boasts about his failure to behave as a monk should. He indignantly refuses to obey St. Augustine's command that monks should perform manual labor. How shall the world be served? he asks, no doubt encouraged by the narrator's approval of his common sense. The question asserts, though negatively, the essential premise of monasticism: the world is not to be served. With his strange logic the narrator then explains that *therefore* the Monk was a *prikasour* or hard-rider, as if hard riding were the ultimate in worldly service. As a rider the Monk shares something of chivalry (French *cheval,* horse), and just as the Knight from the time he first began "to riden out he loved chivalrye," so the Monk was "an outridere that loved venerye." The echoing of the first line by the second makes a tacit contrast between the two men.

THE FRIAR

All four orders of friars—Franciscan, Dominican, Carmelite, and Augustinian—derived their ideal ultimately from St. Francis of Assisi, who began his preaching and teaching in the first decade of the thirteenth century. The ideal was simple. St. Francis enjoined his followers to obey Christ's precepts given to his disciples and to those "who would be perfect." Forsaking possessions and all other worldly connections, friars were to go forth, without money or spare clothing or baggage, to preach and minister to all God's creatures, particularly to the homeless, the beggars, and the lepers, who were the untouchables of medieval Europe. No provision was made for the friars' food and lodging. They were to take what God provided, living cheerfully and humbly in the poverty of the least of those to whom they preached. The great nobility of this ideal made the friars' failure to live up to it appear even more deplorable than a similar degeneration among the monastic orders. It was the deterioration of the latter that had stimulated St. Francis to found his own spiritual order. The work of the friars at the beginning was of extraordinary benefit to Europe, and many friars performed their mission devotedly throughout the Middle Ages. Yet within a century and a half of their founding the figure of the greedy friar was to become commoner and more harshly treated in satirical literature than the older figure of the worldly monk.

Chaucer's Friar, like Chaucer's Monk, is a classic of his type. The practice of begging, which in the beginning had been only a kind of occasional accident in a friar's life, had become organized so that friars like Hubert would pay rent for the exclusive right to beg in a certain area. The Christlike ideal of absolute poverty was thus perverted to serve the end of greed, and greed overturned every ideal, stated or implied, of St. Francis. In Chaucer's Friar, service to the poor has been exchanged for service to the rich, in whose favor Hubert probably helps to adjudicate lawsuits on "love-days," days set aside for settling cases out of court. Humility has become an arrogance and pride of life that refuses to have anything to do with the destitute. The cheerfulness of spirit associated with St. Francis has become the gaiety of an accomplished ballad-singer and flirt, an intimate of barmaids, and a seducer of maidens. These last, in a kind of parody of an act of charity, the Friar subsequently provides with a dowry and marries off to eligible bachelors.

But the Friar's greed subverts not only St. Francis' ideal but the very fabric of the Church as well, for the Friar is licensed to act as a confessor. To be valid, the sacrament of penance must consist not only of confession, but also of contrition and satisfaction. That is, one must persuade the confessor that one is truly sorry for one's sins before one confesses, and afterward one must perform the penance he assigns. But since Hubert accepts cash as proof of contrition and again in lieu of satisfaction, a rich man might receive the Friar's absolution for sins that he does not repent, and for which he is not penalized in any way that will actually inconvenience him. Furthermore, the proceeds of this sale of God's absolution, if they do not go directly into the Friar's pocket, go to the erection of his priory —for which, in the rule of St. Francis, there is no provision. The Friar's portrait, even more than the Monk's, contains a list of abuses which by inversion define the ideal that the Friar is violating. The gravity of the violation is in turn emphasized by the superlatives the narrator uses in describing the efficiency of the Friar's malpractices.

THE MERCHANT

Chivalry and religion are followed by commerce in the sequence of the portraits. The Merchant, who at this point is of no particular interest in himself, is interesting as a representative of what was to become one of the dominant types of our civilization, one that had already in Chaucer's time assumed great importance. The Merchant is all merchant, from his "Flanderish" beaver hat on down. England's chief trade route for its chief industry, wool, lay between its eastern ports and Flanders on the continent; hence, the interest that the man under the hat has in maintaining the seaguard between Orwell in Suffolk and Middelburgh in Flanders. Since he is an importer and exporter he naturally deals with foreign currencies, fluctuations of which he exploits profitably if illegally. His entire personality is so formed as to give him the appearance of a man of great responsibility, erect and imposing in his carriage, officious and formal in his transactions, sober and reserved in his speech—except on the subject of his profits. To inspire confidence in one's reliability was even more important for a merchant in the Middle Ages than it is today, for the merchant's person had not yet been replaced by the impersonal corporation that one now confidently invests in. Of course, in Chaucer's time the lending of money at interest was still technically forbidden, which naturally complicated a merchant's position. It did not mean, as it might seem to, that a merchant hard pressed for capital could borrow without interest; it meant in fact that he had to pay high rates of interest, and the more unsound his position the higher the rate he had to pay. If, like Shakespeare's Antonio, the merchant of Venice, he found himself in real need of cash while all his own capital was known to be tied up in merchandise still at sea, he might be unmercifully squeezed by the moneylender. In view of this a merchant would take pains always to conceal any anxieties he might be feeling and he would, like Chaucer's Merchant, be particularly careful to hide his indebtedness from a prospective lender, lest the interest rates go up. Sometimes when his ships failed to dock in time he might have to leave town suddenly, in which case a pilgrimage would offer a good excuse for his departure. Under such circumstances to preserve anonymity, as Chaucer's Merchant seems to be doing, would be highly prudent.

THE CLERK

The Clerk offers a contrast to the Merchant in what the latter—and perhaps the narrator—would consider his positively peculiar disregard for money. He also offers a contrast of a different sort with the clerks we shall meet later in the Miller's and Reeve's tales, for unlike them he is entirely absorbed in his studies at Oxford. In Chaucer's time the word *clerk* denoted either an ecclesiastic or a learned man; sometimes it meant both together, since higher education was maintained both by and for the clergy. A young man before attending a university would ordinarily have expressed his intention to enter the Church. This he did by undergoing the rite of the tonsure, during which he received the distinctive haircut worn by all the Church's enlisted servants. But the tonsure was only the first and lowest of the ecclesiastical orders; if one wanted to attain a responsible and self-supporting position in the Church one had to advance to the priesthood. Many who assumed the tonsure, however, went no further, and others who did take higher orders still stopped short of the priesthood. But as long as they retained the tonsure they could claim certain legal immunities as churchmen, even though in other respects they behaved as laymen. A good many college students seem to have belonged to this class.

Such clerks might put their learning to use by becoming either teachers or else secretaries to wealthy laymen. Chaucer's idealized clerk is not so worldly as to assume the office of secretary. On the other hand, he has not exerted himself to advance to an ecclesiastical living or benefice, which would require him to perform the pastoral duties of a priest. Rather, he is a pure scholar, entirely devoted to the study of moral philosophy and eschewing in its favor both the pleasurable and the practical aspects of life. Dominated by mind to the exclusion of body, he spends all his little income on the development of his intellect. This income, as was the case with most college students of the time, is given him by his friends as an act of charity. But unlike many of his fellows, he repays it by praying for the souls of the donors, who expected no other form of repayment. Eventually the time will come when he must provide for himself, and the last line of the portrait suggests that he will do so by teaching.

THE SERGEANT OF LAW

From the fact that the rank of Sergeant of Law in medieval England was the highest a lawyer could attain, one might infer that Chaucer's Sergeant is a devoted servant of justice. But while history records the existence of idealists of the law in the Middle Ages, literature rarely mentions them, and Chaucer's Sergeant is merely an exalted representative of a type common in satire. His royal appointment as a Justice of the Assizes, empowered to try cases of all sorts, is not to be considered the culminating event of a distinguished legal career; rather it is his reward for having outstripped his competitors in the business of making the practice of law lucrative. Despite his high judicial position the Sergeant's real interest remains centered in making money. Some of this comes in the form of fees and possibly of bribes, but more results from the investments in real estate that his legal knowledge enables him to make. In the Middle Ages land was the safest and most profitable of all investments, but its transfer from one owner to another often involved the most tortuous legal complexities. Much land was entailed—that is, it had been willed from father to son with the proviso that it should never pass from the family. The Sergeant's knowledge of precedents put him in a good position to get around entail if anyone could. Furthermore, no one would be able to find a flaw in the deed which subsequently assured the land to him. Thus all the skill that might be directed toward settling problems of right and wrong is used instead to make the Sergeant rich.

Like the Merchant, he knows how much external appearances contribute to financial success and he is careful to seem the busiest man in the world. Of course, as the narrator observes, he is not really very busy. The narrator's mild witticism suggests that all the world feels free to laugh at a lawyer—though not without a tinge of envy for his wealth.

THE FRANKLIN

By Chaucer's time the term *franklin* seems to have indicated a worthy member of the gentry, although it had originally meant *freedman* and must have applied to the lower classes. The development of the word probably reflects the history of families that over the years moved from rags to riches. In any case, Chaucer's Franklin seems to have arrived at the happy point where, having acquired considerable wealth, he is more interested in using it sociably and enjoyably than he is in acquiring more (unlike many of the other pilgrims). The emphasis that is placed on his appetite suggests that the Franklin's view of life is conditioned by deep-rooted materialism, but he nevertheless aspires to the more liberal set of values associated with the aristocracy: he may love to eat, but his generosity as a host has made him into a local St. Julian, the patron saint of hospitality. Moreover, he has some awareness of the social responsibilities that wealth brings, for like Chaucer himself he has been a Justice of the Peace and has represented his county in Parliament as a Knight of the Shire. There is no suggestion that he has held these and his other offices through self-interest. He seems to be one of the relatively few pilgrims who are capable of disinterested conduct.

THE FIVE GILDSMEN

The Gildsmen are also on the social ladder, though they are a good deal nearer its bottom than the Franklin. Since they are burghers—city men—it is possible that their rise will be more rapid than his and they may, indeed, accomplish in a generation or two what the rural Franklin and his forebears took four or five generations to do. The Gildsmen are climbing fast and the narrator joins their wives in cheering them on. The social milieu in which these tradesmen operate is the parish gild. This was a fraternity that was generally formed to honor a locally popular saint. The members celebrated the saint's feast day with appropriate religious solemnity, but since the gilds were social as well as religious, they would also celebrate the eve of the saint's day—the vigil—with a fine banquet. The Gildsmen are wearing the livery—uniform—of their gild. Their prosperity, which is the Gildsmen's chief qualification for social success, is apparent in the silver mounting of their knives. According to the law these should have been of brass, silver being deemed appropriate only to persons of superior birth. But men qualified for important positions in the city government naturally refused to hide their light under the bushel of so old-fashioned a restriction which, despite the constant interchange between the social ranks, went on pretending that no man could ever leave the rank God had assigned him at birth. And indeed no law was able to prevent the rise of the middle classes to which the Gildsmen belong.

THE COOK

The portrait of the Cook whom the Gildsmen have employed for the trip is itself a concoction of culinary superlatives. It tells us nothing of the Cook's personality except what is suggested by his knowledge of London ale. As it turns out, that is enough. For the rest, the portrait seems designed mainly as a frame for the unsavory joke about the Cook's ulcer which will make the antiseptic contemporary reader wince. The narrator seems unaware of his own joke: he is sorry about the Cook's ulcer, not disgusted by it.

THE SHIPMAN

The portrait of the Shipman, like that of the Cook, describes the occupation rather than the man. But something of the Shipman's personality is revealed if only as a kind of corollary to his excellence as a sea captain. The daring and fortitude of a good sailor do not breed regard for niceties of conscience, and the Shipman has as little of the latter as he has plenty of the former. In the absence of a regular navy, the merchant marine in wartime did duty as the defender of the seas, and in the absence of a good system of communications an individual sea captain might become somewhat vague about whether a war was going on or not and if so who was the enemy. Obviously it was safer and more profitable to fight first and ask questions later: potentially hostile witnesses could be invited to swim home. Evidently when the Shipman was on board the *Magdalene,* he had none of the awkwardness that characterizes his horseback-riding. On the other hand, being on land also deprived him of the opportunity to steal one's cargo or make one walk the plank, so one might find him a good companion. That is, if, like the narrator, one were determined to see the brighter side of things.

THE DOCTOR OF MEDICINE

In the Middle Ages physicians, like lawyers, were the constant butt of satirists, who seldom found a good word to say about them. The Doctor on the pilgrimage is unusually well treated, for he is said actually to be able to heal the sick. One feels that the narrator was never treated by the Doctor but is repeating the Doctor's own report of his medical skill.

Medieval medicine was a fusion of primitive physical science and astrology, the latter being as important to it as the former. In order to help a patient the doctor first diagnosed his disease, which was thought to be caused by an imbalance in the system of bodily humors (see gloss to ll. 416 ff). This could only be done by consulting the stars as well as the patient, in whom the particular balance of humors that normally prevailed had been determined by the position of the planets at his birth. Having diagnosed the disease, a doctor had then to consult the patient's horoscope in order to discover the time when the stars would be most propitious for working a cure. Then the doctor had to wait for the time to arrive. In order to prevent the patient's death in the meanwhile a conscientious physician like Chaucer's might take certain steps: by using talismanic images he could either counterfeit an astrological situation (ascendancy) favorable to the patient, or perhaps counterfeit—by making an image of him—a patient susceptible to benign influence from the heavens as they actually stood. If these remedies did not prove effective the doctor could console himself that he had done his best, and collect his fee from the survivors. If drugs had been administered he could also collect a percentage of their cost from his old friend the druggist—who may have recommended the doctor to the patient originally.

Business was naturally brisk for doctors in times of pestilence, when they could become very rich in a short while. Chaucer's Doctor, like his Lawyer, knows how to exploit his skill so that it will pay, and to increase his skill and its reward seems to have studied all the medical books that were ever written. These do not include the Bible, where he could have learned of an attitude toward healing the sick which is, from his point of view, highly unprofitable. Generosity is too uneconomical for his cold character. He hoards his money as he hoards his skill. The medicine known as *aurum potabile*—potable gold—is the symbol of how he practices his profession.

THE WIFE OF BATH

The Wife of Bath explains herself so brilliantly in her own Prologue that little comment on her need be made here. That she is a weaver is a fact mentioned only in the *General Prologue.* Probably for the medieval reader it established the Wife as an economically independent bourgeoise, a type that was becoming increasingly common in Chaucer's time. One ought not to forget, however, that Eve, the prototype of all women, was the weaver who spun while Adam dug the earth, and that the Wife of Bath in all respects takes after her first mother.

The Wife's independence (of both spirit and means) and her sexuality are the two qualities that the portrait chiefly develops. Their combination in her has enabled her to outlast five husbands, not to mention "other company in youth." Her clothing is elegant and extreme; elegant because, despite her rugged durability, she is intensely feminine, and extreme because she is flamboyantly unconventional. She defends with a woman's vanity and a warrior's ferocity her assumed right to be the first to make offering in Church. Since in the Middle Ages it was proverbial that a husband who allowed his wife to make pilgrimages was asking to be cuckolded, the Wife's many voyages to distant shrines emphasize her sexual aberrancy—her tendency to wander "by the way." Fittingly enough, the Wife is gap-toothed, a condition supposed to mark a person moved by both lust and *wanderlust.* As an experienced traveler she is naturally highly sociable. Though an affront to her vanity would put her out of charity, her interest in the more fleshly aspects of love never waned, for that kind of love was her real art. How the art of love as practiced by a militant devotee brought on the deafness that excites the narrator's pity we are to learn later.

THE PARSON

From the representative of fleshly love Chaucer moves to a representative of true Christian charity, the poor Parson, whose idealism equals the Knight's and, like it, offers a contrast with the base motivations of the succeeding pilgrims. The disastrous plagues that swept through England several times after the mid-fourteenth century so depopulated the country that many rural parishes could no longer support their priests. As a result, priests often rented their parishes to vicars even needier than themselves and migrated to the larger cities where money was still to be had. In London, for instance, a priest might find employment at St. Paul's in one of the numerous prayer-foundations established by wealthy persons: all he would have to do was sing a daily mass for the soul of the benefactor; for this he would be well paid. Or he might find employment with a parish gild like that of the Five Gildsmen—whose members sometimes maintained a priest to pray for their souls and supervise the gild's religious activities. Chaucer's Parson, however, did not take this easy escape from parochial duties, and he stands as a rebuke to those who did. He is the good shepherd to his flock, modeling himself on the Good Shepherd of the Gospels. He patiently endures the poverty that is his lot, content with little and reluctant to invoke the dreaded weapon of excommunication against such parishioners as are unable to pay their tithes—the tenth of their income claimed by the Church. Indeed, the Parson takes literally the injunction that it is more blessed to give than to receive. With all his kindliness, the Parson is no sentimental benefactor, however. Where his own good example fails to impress itself on a wayward member of his flock he is ready to employ plain talk. His staff symbolizes not only support but chastisement, and it is no respecter of persons. Perhaps the Parson lacks some of the warmer human traits, but if he does it is because he lets nothing not essential to his profession come between him and its exercise.

THE PLOWMAN

The depopulation caused by the great pestilences that made parish priests abandon their duties also made farm workers abandon theirs. Agricultural laborers were legally bound to the soil in Chaucer's time. That is, they were expected always to perform their labor on the estate on which they were born. But when depopulation made farm labor scarce, many surviving workers left their own areas for those offering higher pay, since, in their desperate need to get in the crops, many estate managers overlooked legal technicalities and tried to outbid their competitors for the labor market. The decrease in agricultural production was thus complicated by the higher wages paid to farm workers, and the price of food rose, seriously endangering England's economic situation. As is apt to be the case when the price of labor is high, the laborer of the late fourteenth century was generally vilified by satirists. Chaucer's Plowman is unusual in the praise he receives—though of course he is, like the Parson, even more unusual in deserving it. The Plowman has continued to obey the laws, not only the man-made ones forbidding him to leave his land, but also the moral law which envisioned the tillers of the soil as forming the great base upon which the whole structure of medieval civilization rested. Chaucer's Plowman partakes of the same Gospel simplicity as his brother the Parson. The fruits of his toil and the fruits of his spirit are one. By loving and serving both God and his neighbor he abides by the great commandments upon which hang all the Law and the Prophets. For so sympathetic a presentation Chaucer may owe something to his contemporary William Langland who, in his poem *Piers Plowman,* also portrays a simple farmer who is in many ways Christlike.

THE MILLER

Contrasting with the Parson and Plowman are five other lower-class pilgrims, all of them thoroughgoing rascals. The first of these is the Miller, a brute of vast strength whose grossness of physique has its counterpart in the grossness of the speech that belches from his huge furnace of a mouth. He pushes himself to the forefront of the pilgrimage with the same violence he uses in breaking down doors with his head, and with more noise. Millers as a class were considered notably dishonest and Chaucer's Miller is no exception. He can get away with taking three times the amount of grain that constitutes his legal fee for the service of grinding. The narrator, in accord with his custom, admires the glittering proficiency of the Miller's rascality.

THE MANCIPLE

A manciple is the steward of a club, in this case a "temple" or society of lawyers. Presumably Chaucer's Manciple gives satisfaction to his employers, but the narrator is mainly concerned with the Manciple's ability to cheat them. He makes a profit on everything he buys for the society, whether he pays cash or buys on tally—that is, on credit. Since his employers are twelve of the smartest lawyers in England, competent to manage huge sums of money (and perhaps pretty good cheats themselves), the Manciple is a kind of *ne plus ultra* of thievery. At least, as the narrator observes, he is one of the most wonderful of the Creator's works.

THE REEVE

The Reeve is a factor or agent who manages the farmlands of a rich young absentee landlord—an easier mark, perhaps, than a dozen lawyers, and a more profitable one. A slender, suspicious, irascible man, the Reeve is an excellent manager and excellently manages to have what his efficiency has saved go into his own pockets rather than his employer's. He has feathered his nest luxuriously. Moreover, his nest is not one of the little huddle of buildings that made up the "town" where the farm workers normally lived, but is handsomely situated by itself in a shady spot on the pastureland. The Reeve is as hard to cheat as he is good at cheating and no plots among his underlings escape his observation. But his own thefts are undetected, for he can make an account book look honest to any auditor. He can as easily fool his master, a man of not many brains though of good heart who rewards Oswald for lending him money that was his own in the first place. Symbolic of the close dealing and spare economy of the Reeve are his close-cropped head and beard and his skinny legs. His wit is a better instrument of self-defense than his sword, which has grown rusty in disuse. It is perhaps to avoid contact with his enemy the Miller that he rides last: we shall see this enmity develop later. On the other hand, the rear is the best position from which to watch what is going on among any band of travelers, and it may be merely because of a habitual watchfulness that the Reeve brings up the rear.

THE SUMMONER

In the Middle Ages in Europe there were two sets of law courts, the civil and the ecclesiastical. The latter exercised jurisdiction not only over clerics involved in most crimes or misdemeanors but also over laymen involved in offenses against the Church as well as in certain offenses which today we should consider properly the business of the state. Not only the layman charged with failure to pay his tithes was tried before an ecclesiastical court, but also a layman charged with a moral offense such as fornication. The ecclesiastical courts were therefore an important factor in the daily lives of the people, and the summoner, an agent of these courts, was a familiar and dreaded figure.

England was divided into dioceses, each with its own bishop; under the bishop was an official known as the archdeacon, who presided over the ecclesiastical court. The archdeacon in turn was served by a summoner, who was generally a layman, not a cleric. As the name indicates, the summoner's duty was to serve a summons on alleged offenders and to see that they appeared in court at the proper time. Summoners were not originally supposed to have any police power, but by the end of the fourteenth century they had acquired a good deal of practical power as a natural result of their connection with the courts. Not only did they summon offenders, they spied them out and reported them. Furthermore, if we can believe the literary tradition, summoners exercised their power solely for their own benefit, threatening the innocent with false charges, blackmailing the guilty, accepting bribes, taking a percentage of the fines imposed by the court, and generally conspiring in their own interest with or against the archdeacon.

Chaucer's Summoner is representative of this tradition. He is as repulsive physically as he is morally, his horribly diseased face symbolizing his diseased spirit and gross appetites. The jurisdiction of his court over fornication has enabled him to become the organizer of prostitution within the diocese. Apparently he receives a share of the money taken in by the prostitutes whom he permits to practice. Furthermore, by forcing them to give him the names of their customers, he is able to get more money by blackmailing the men. What the narrator finds admirable about the Summoner is his moderation in extortion, his fellow feeling for his victims. He is ready to forgive a good fellow's keeping a mistress for a whole year in return for a single quart of wine: after all, the sin is one he loves himself. The narrator's surprising geniality in describing this ugly character reflects the lack of moral discrimination that fear of summoners produced in the average man.

THE PARDONER

The Summoner's boon companion, the Pardoner, is another corrupter of the ecclesiastical system. According to the Church's doctrine, to give money to a charitable enterprise is an act of piety for which the Church may repay the donor by granting him some indulgence for his sins. Since this indulgence is ultimately a draft on the treasury of God's mercy, it may be awarded only by the Pope, who inherited St. Peter's keys, or in the Pope's name by such high clerics as archbishops and bishops. It may, however, be transmitted through properly qualified agents of the hierarchy. In the Middle Ages, as today, many charitable institutions depended on private gifts, and the Church tried to stimulate gifts by arranging indulgences for the donors. In this the pardoner acted as chief agent. Employed to raise money for a given charitable enterprise, he was empowered by the Church to dispense indulgences in return for donations. His prescribed function was to proceed from church to church throughout an assigned area, to explain his mission to the assembled congregation, to accept contributions, and, in the name of the Church, to dispense pardon. Canon law limited his role severely. He was not in any sense a seller of indulgence but was merely empowered to make a free gift of it to those who gave money to the institution he represented. The pardon he issued was valid only as temporal satisfaction for sins fully repented and confessed. He was generally forbidden to preach, since, if he was in clerical orders at all, he had rarely advanced far enough to be entitled to that privilege. As a result, his eloquence might not extend beyond the explanation of his mission. The gifts he collected were, of course, to be delivered to the institution that employed him. He was expected to lead a decent, sober life, avoiding the taverns. His movements were subject to regulation, and he might not enter a diocese without receiving a license from its bishop. Finally, he had to display his credentials in every parish he visited.

There may have been pardoners who acted as they should, but if they did their reward has been silence. By the end of the fourteenth century, at least in literature, a pardoner has become synonymous with a rogue. His granting of pardon is described as a wholly commercial affair in which the sum involved has ceased to be a gift and has become payment for value received. Pardoners often claim the power to forgive sins unrepented and unconfessed and advertise their remission as effective even in hell. They assert the right to preach and are thus able to play upon the emotions of the enormously impressionable medieval congregations. They are notoriously wenchers and tavern-haunters. Worse, they are very often complete frauds, employed by no institution and bearing forged licenses and forged pardons. Because of the internationalism of the Church a pardoner may plausibly say that he represents institutions located in the remotest parts of Europe—and before one can ask any questions of his supposed employers he is many miles away. Since he bears highly official-looking documents that enjoin parish priests to admit him to their churches the humble parson may consider him a dangerous man to offend, and some may know too little Latin to be able to examine his *bona fide*s with anything but superstitious awe. It is on the whole safer to admit him to one's church, hoping that he will not strip the congregation of its potential offerings for the next two months. Occasionally a strong-minded, suspicious priest may forcibly eject a pardoner, but more often he will agree to admit him for a fifty-fifty split of the proceeds.

Chaucer's Pardoner belongs to the general type. Whether he really represents the hospital of Roncesvalles or is an absolute fraud is not made clear. Roncesvalles is in Spain and, even though the hospital had a branch in London, inquiries about the Pardoner would be difficult to make. In all ascertainable matters he is as fraudulent as the relics he has acquired on his travels. The sale of these increases his already considerable income, for to the medieval mind the wonder-working power of relics was a very real thing, and the securing of a genuine relic for one's own church would be worth whatever it cost. Thus everything works to feed the Pardoner's avarice, and not the least the eloquence and wit he employs in preying upon the aspirations of his pious victims. The depth of his depravity is symbolized in his physical disability—in the fact that he is a eunuch. With this condition are associated the fine, thin hair, the high but penetrating voice, the beardlessness, and the pretense of being a gay, virile, amorous fellow. For though the narrator—and hence presumably everyone else, too—guesses his condition at once, it is the one fact about himself that he conceals in the amazingly candid confession of his viciousness. His desire to hide this one fact later becomes the means by which the seemingly triumphant evil of one who has set his heart against man and God is rendered impotent.

THE HOST

The character of the Host—whose name is later given as Harry Bailly—is only rapidly sketched, since as master of ceremonies he will have opportunity to reveal himself later. Initially we are told only of his competence as a social manager and of his great virility. We see the former in operation at once when—by what the narrator considers the most extraordinary bit of luck—the Knight somehow draws the straw that makes him the first storyteller. The Host's virility associates him with the manly Monk as it dissociates him from the effeminate Pardoner, and conditions the relationships that later develop between him and them. The comedy provided by the Host's enthusiasm and his self-confidence as a literary critic will be evident as the pilgrimage proceeds.

THE KNIGHT'S TALE

The *Knight's Tale* has been well described as a philosophical romance. Although the plot is derived from an epic, Giovanni Boccaccio's Italian poem *Il Teseida,* the tale's preoccupation with love and warfare is characteristic of the medieval chivalric romance. But the story's theme is perhaps of more significance than its form or plot. Palamon's success and Arcite's failure raise certain questions about the nature of the justice that disposes worldly events, and certain answers are suggested. The source for these is the sixth-century treatise *The Consolation of Philosophy* by the Roman philosophic writer Boethius. Boethian thought is, inevitably, somewhat modified by Chaucer in terms of the medieval chivalric ideal and of the prevailing pessimism of the late fourteenth century.

Boethius' book, one that appealed greatly to Chaucer, who translated it into English prose, was written when its author was in prison awaiting execution for crimes against the state. A man of much distinction as a public servant and a scholar, Boethius had become prominent in public affairs under the Visigothic Emperor Theodoric. But Boethius was a Roman of the classic mold, deeply concerned with preserving the traditional values of Roman government, and it was inevitable that his principles should bring him into collision with the far less scrupulous emperor. After a lifetime of service to Rome, Boethius found himself stripped of all honors and condemned to death. The consolation that he proposed for this sad predicament takes the form of a dialogue between himself and Philosophy, personified as a woman who visits him in his prison. Finding him lamenting his fate and abusing Fortune, Philosophy gradually persuades him to assume philosophical equanimity, so that by the end of the dialogue Boethius understands the nature of the world well enough to become reconciled with his lot. The book amounts, on the practical level, to a demonstration of the principle that the man who devotes himself to the values of the spirit may remain unmoved by whatever ill fortune befalls him. According to Philosophy, the world is governed, if remotely, by a deity who represents the highest good: that there is a divine plan is evident to the philosopher, even if he cannot understand the details of it. But by having confidence in its existence and by valuing only what is really good in this world—that is, what at least partakes of the highest good—a man may achieve a state of mind in which external evil is reduced to an irrelevant illusion, even the evil that befalls him. Though Boethius was a Christian and his book relies on Christian ethics, he makes no specific reference to Christianity and by avoiding the issue of the life to come places the emphasis of his thought on this world and man's deportment in it—precisely what Chaucer does in the *Knight's Tale.* It is this emphasis that makes Boethius' book and Chaucer's tale both so strongly stoic: with no promise of reward or punishment man must adjust himself to life on earth as if there were no other. If one finds it surprising that the intensely Christian Chaucer, writing in the intensely Christian Middle Ages, should in a serious philosophic poem eschew the Christian solution to the problem of earthly justice, one must bear in mind that Boethius' book, which made the same eschewal, was very popular with the Middle Ages in general.

In the *Knight's Tale* the philosophic problem is why of two young men equally worthy (or unworthy) one should live to attain happiness with the woman he loves and the other should end, through the most capricious of accidents, in his grave, "allone, withouten any compaignye." The answer given by Theseus, who is the spokesman for the poem's overt philosophy, is simply that there is no reason that man can hope to understand. Nevertheless, behind all apparent accidents it is necessary to believe that there lies the will of a benevolent deity who resides at the center of the great universe in which our world is but a remote point. And far removed as it is, our world is still controlled by the great chain that proceeds from the Prime Mover. Since man cannot know the Prime Mover's purposes, he must accept willingly what comes to him—and, in practical terms, "make a virtue of necessity." The poem's emphasis on necessity results in a statement that is rather less consoling than Boethius': fate seems to operate with a petty malignancy to frustrate to the last detail the wills of the characters, and its predominating part in everyday life becomes—as it is intended to be—oppressive. This oppressiveness undoubtedly reflects the increasing pessimism of the later Middle Ages. On the other hand, while the poem's picture of life is a dreary one in many ways, there is no tendency within it to urge on the reader the ascetic escape from life that frequently is associated with the stoic atttiude. The characters are enjoined—as Theseus enjoins Palamon and Emily —to live life as fully and as richly as destiny will permit: if Arcite's death is seemingly senseless and unjust, it at least enables him to die with his glory untarnished—and it enables Palamon to have his desire at long last. There is a practical economy about this attitude that is both Chaucerian and also characteristic of his simultaneously pessimistic and pleasure-loving era. And in the paradoxical attitude that Theseus sets forth, that man ought to maintain a suspicious and detached attitude toward a world in which he must be wholeheartedly involved, there is something peculiarly Chaucerian.

One naturally responds to a rivalry such as that between Palamon and Arcite by taking sides. Some critics have argued that Palamon is the worthier of the two; but others have sided with Arcite, considering him the more deserving. Chaucer probably expected the reader to take sides, but if he intended that one young man should be recognized as the worthier he seems to have gone about it badly. The claims of the two are equally balanced: in any one scene Palamon may be more admirable than Arcite, but in the next Arcite will behave better than Palamon. Neither of them behaves consistently better than the other up to Arcite's death, the nobility of which should cancel any doubts about Arcite's essential worthiness, just as Palamon's sincere grief at Arcite's death should cancel any doubts about Palamon's worthiness. The truth seems to be that the young men are on an even footing and that, from the earthly point of view, justice operates with equal whimsicality in bringing Arcite to death and Palamon to happiness. This is what the overt theme of the tale, presented by Theseus, makes clear.

On the other hand, it must be remembered that justice merely seems whimsical to dwellers on earth, while the divine plan must be just; and something of this higher justice appears within the poem to lend support to Theseus' postulation of the divine plan. It is undeniably fitting that Palamon, who initially mistook Emily for Venus, who dedicates himself as Venus' knight, and who prays not for victory but for Emily, should in the end get the heroine; it is equally fitting that Arcite, who worships Mars and asks for victory, should win the tournament. But on the moral plane the issues are unresolved and remain as curiously remote as the divine plan itself. It is difficult to find in Venus and Mars satisfactory allegories of the moral characters of Palamon and Arcite, as some have tried to do. Chaucer has been at pains to show Venus' temple as little more cheerful a place than Mars'; and in the effective astrological action, lest the planetary attributes of beneficent Venus should seem to symbolize the moral superiority of her knight over the servant of the maleficent Mars, Chaucer replaces Venus by the most baleful of all the planets, Saturn, and he is the direct agent of Palamon's eventual victory. Besides, one must remember that chivalry was equally a matter of love and warfare, of Venus and Mars, and a knight whose moral conduct was all Venerean or all Martian was only half a knight. In their actions Palamon and Arcite are equally the warrior and the lover. Therefore the rightness of Venus' eventual victory cannot be extended to Palamon's character; rather, it reflects a supramoral perception of the way the universe is conducted.

The tale does not show Chaucer as particularly interested in the characterization of individuals. The heroine Emily is a symbol of the loveliness life and society have to offer, but her effect is generalized: she is beautiful, therefore lovable. Palamon and Arcite are differentiated in individual scenes, but neither stands out especially from the generality of brave, lovestruck young men. Perhaps the most memorable character is Theseus, who gives the poem's theme overt expression and whose own actions are a demonstration of the stoicism which never ceases to struggle with a bad world. He sees that the world is chaotic, but with his every considered action he tries to bring to this chaos as much order as he can. Like the Almighty, his first consideration is always the imposition of order: he interrupts his homecoming in order to avenge Creon's insults to the widowed queens; he ordains that the young knights will fight it out in the lists rather than in the woods; he builds the lists in a splendidly formal fashion; he arranges the magnificent funeral for Arcite; and he, in the end, joins Palamon and Emily. That the bringing of order involves cruelty—the destruction of Thebes, the imprisonment of the heroes, even their execution—represents the practical compromise that, moral or not, medieval chivalry believed in. So chaotic a world could never be returned to a prelapsarian state. To make it livable at all the ruler could not, it was thought, be forgiving to the point of softness. Medieval chivalry would have accepted the execution of Palamon and Arcite that Theseus first ordains as something right and proper—though it was capable also of accepting the mercy the women beg him to grant as something better.

Aside from its chivalric plot, the *Knight's Tale* is admirably suited to its narrator, whose personality, not much revealed in the idealism of the portrait in the *General Prologue,* is allowed to develop within the bounds of the same idealism. Against the excesses of the plot the Knight's firm self-control is constantly reflected. He has—like Theseus—sympathy with the rash young men and their foolish actions while he recognizes their rashness and folly for what they are. At every point in the story where emotion tends to become swollen and disorderly he is quick to restrain it. For he seems to recognize and practice a principle that is a part of the Boethian system but was not much practiced by the Middle Ages, as it is not always practiced by the hotheaded Theseus—namely, that excessive emotion is an enslavement of the spirit and a threat to order. At several of the most serious moments of the poem, the Knight's humor provides an antidote to the overinvolvement of the characters in their fate. He is, after all, an old soldier who has observed that deaths in battle have no connection with any recognizable system of earthly justice and that to expect a good man to avoid an ill end is to expose oneself to paralyzing frustration. It is necessary to go on living in this uncertain world, doing the best one can, always expecting the worst to happen. As he himself puts it,

> It is ful fair a man to bere him evene,
> For alday meeteth men at unset stevene.

"It is a good thing for a man to bear himself with equanimity, for one is constantly keeping appointments one never made." Or, as Shakespeare was later to say, "The readiness is all."

THE MILLER'S TALE

The *Miller's Tale,* like the tales of the Reeve, Cook, and Shipman, belongs to the medieval literary genre known as the *fabliau.* This is a versified short story which generally involves bourgeois or lower-class personages in a comic situation that is obscene and farfetched, though the narration often shows a good deal of care for realistic detail. The plot is apt to hinge on what we should call a practical joke, though the joker, like Nicholas, usually has some more pragmatic purpose than humor alone. In a number of fabliaux, as in the Miller's and Reeve's Tales, the instigators of the chief action are students (clerks), a fact that suggests that the authors of such stories were also students, perhaps some of the "wandering scholars" who, moving from university to university in their pursuit of an education, made their precarious living by a lively, if not always decorous, use of their wits. The fabliau flourished particularly in France, but although there are a number of examples of it in the other continental vernaculars it hardly occurs in English literature outside Chaucer. Upon the development of his narrative technique the form may well have exerted a beneficent influence, for a number of his poems that are not of the genre display its characteristic high-spiritedness, gaiety, and that rapidity of action that is so opposed to the medieval practice of interminable expatiation. Chaucer's *Miller's Tale* is the highest artistic expression of the fabliau—so high a one, indeed, that the term *fabliau* scarcely does it justice. It comprises two originally separate stories, one having to do with an elaborate deception of a jealous husband who is persuaded that a world-devouring flood threatens him, the other with an ignominious kiss and the awful revenge it provokes. These plots are happily united in Chaucer (whether or not for the first time by him is not known) when Nicholas' cry for water, which is the natural conclusion of the second plot, precipitates the climax of the first.

Chaucer has gone far beyond the usual simplicity of the fabliau in his handling of the tale. In the first place he gives it a place within the dramatic framework of the pilgrimage, for it is in order to *quite,* repay, the *Knight's Tale* that the drunken Miller interrupts the orderly progress of the tale-telling, and the claim of repayment is by no means invalid. The Knight's courtly romance has described what the Miller would have considered the marvelously impractical love of two young men for a rather pallid lady; the Miller takes the same triangle and transfers it from remote Athens to contemporary Oxford, translating one young man into a highly practical college student and the other into a rather impractical parish clerk and choosing for his heroine not an aristocratic lady but a thoroughly vital country wench. While resetting the situation he retains, however, some of the conventions of the courtly romance—though, of course, he does so only to make them ridiculous. Nicholas he describes not only in terms that establish him accurately as a fourteenth-century college student with interests extending far beyond the curriculum, but also in terms that suggest that Nicholas is a worthy romance hero. He is, for instance, almost invariably *hende,* a catch-all adjective meaning something like "nice" which is almost invariably applied to the heroes of Middle English romance: but *hende* also means "clever," "handy," and "at hand," all of which, in his relations to Alison, Nicholas certainly is. The fact of his practical handiness provides a derisive commentary on his romantic niceness, as if the spiritual elevation that the usual *hende* hero pretended to was in reality only a disguise for his practical animality. That is, Nicholas' directness of purpose makes fun of the idealized but remote love of those nice young men Palamon and Arcite for a lady whom they have never met and scarcely seen. (It should be observed that Chaucer, who avoids clichés in serious verse, does not actually call Palamon and Arcite *hende,* but since that is precisely what they are, the Miller exercises the satirist's prerogative of taking the deed for the word.) Similarly the long description of Alison at the same time presents an attractive, frisky, lusty country girl and burlesques the conventional item-by-item catalogue of charms, physical and spiritual, that a heroine of romance generally receives. The immediate difference between Alison and Emily is suggested by the fact that the latter is first described largely in terms of the red and white flowers she is gathering in the walled garden, while the former is described in terms full of the activity and vitality of the barnyard. Many heroines of romance are compared to flowers, but only Alison is a *piggesnye,* a pig's eye, which, while it is a flower, has quite a different symbolic impact from—let us say—a rose.

Absolon, the third member of the quadrangle, is a rather special case. His remote namesake Absalom, son of King David, had, mainly because of his famous luxuriance of hair, been early typed as an example of great personal beauty. His good fortune was vitiated, however, by the fact that beauty is usually associated with women, and as the centuries passed Absalom found himself a prisoner in the conventional catalogues of predominantly feminine beauties: thus in Chaucer's balade in the *Legend of Good Women* (ll. 203–23) Absalom introduces a list that contains only one other man among some twenty lovely ladies. While the parish clerk of Oxford suffers from this rhetorical accident, it enables the Miller to develop his characterization of him with some of the idiom that is usually applied only to heroines of romance. Thus doomed to effeminacy, poor Absolon has not only the prettiness, but also the high voice, the delicacy of sentiment, and the fastidiousness in speech, dress, and manners of a courtly lady. At the same time, of course, the Miller presents a realistic small-town dandy, a parish clerk (not a priest) who is in love with all the fair women of the parish but seems more concerned with the ritual of hopelessly loving a girl than with winning her. In this respect, he is probably not unlike the Miller's conception of Palamon and Arcite. He is certainly unlike Nicholas, whose to-the-point wooing of Alison, while conducted in the speech of courtly love, succeeds with a precipitousness that is anything but courtly.

The jealous husband, John the carpenter, is as vivid a character as the rest, though he receives no elaborate description. He is proud of being an uneducated working man and his scorn for intellectuals enables him at first to act with supercilious superiority toward the student Nicholas. John knows better than to pry into God's secrets—until Nicholas offers him a fore-warning of the Almighty's intention to repeat Noah's flood, after which his disrespect for education disappears. Neither the poet nor the Miller invites much sympathy for John's sad fate, though his love for Alison is real enough: but the fact is that John belongs to the fictional type of the senile lover, and he has violated one of the first laws of nature by pre-empting a wife younger than himself. Once he has done this it follows inexorably that he shall be punished.

The *Miller's Tale* reflects on the Knight's not only as a sardonic commentary on courtly attitudes. The Knight used his romance plot to present what many would consider a gloomy picture of a world in which the workings of a higher justice are impenetrably obscure. The Miller's world reasserts the principle of an active love of life, and his high-spiritedness, for all its immorality, is so positive a thing that one hesitates to question its validity. Moreover, his world is distinguished by its even-handed justice. As we have seen, the senile lover gets his just deserts when he is cuckolded, injured, and ridiculed. *Hende* Nicholas, who glories in the physical reality of life, is, despite all his cleverness, punished in an appropriate manner. The effeminate Absolon, whose fastidiousness must appear to the gross Miller as a kind of mania, receives equally appropriate retribution. Justice is, however, chivalrous: to the heroine of a courtly romance no ultimate evil ever comes, and Alison escapes scot-free.

The village world of the *Miller's Tale* is realistic in detail, yet the general attitude of the story is as idealized as the Knight's, except that the idealism is comic. Nicholas' elaborate plan to accomplish a perfectly simple action presupposes a world of inordinate complexity (as well as of boundless energy). Developments show that the presupposition was correct, for in the end it appears that the Miller's world, like the Knight's, contains forces that men can set into motion but cannot thereafter control. In the *Miller's Tale,* however, these forces operate to make every joke perfect in a way the instigator did not contemplate. To achieve the ultimate hilarity, they enable Nicholas to overhear the unspoken thoughts of Absolon and cause Alison and Nicholas actually to expect that Absolon will accept a second kiss—even cause him to expect them to expect him to. In the Miller's world, the unseen forces ride roughshod over probability in order to fulfill the great conspiracy to make laughter supreme.

THE REEVE'S TALE

Although it is a wonderfully funny story told with all the poet's great technical skill, the second of Chaucer's fabliaux is perhaps of a somewhat lower order than the first. Revenge, which is its theme, seems too mean and low a thing to be raised to the level of pure sportiveness that the theme of carnal love achieves in the *Miller's Tale.* Chaucer was apparently aware that revenge does not lend itself so readily to the kind of comic idealization we have seen in the previous story, for he assigned it to the calculating, unattractive Reeve, who uses it to effect his own revenge on the Miller for the latter's fancied insult. By the tale's curious introduction Chaucer emphasizes the dark-mindedness of the Reeve, who casts the shadow of his own meanness over the story and reabsorbs into himself that tinge of meanness that the story inherently contains. Despite, however, all implications of matters more mean-spirited than light-hearted, the *Reeve's Tale* is in terms of general hilarity far closer to the Miller's than it is to even the best fabliaux in literature outside of Chaucer: were it not for the *Miller's Tale,* the Reeve's would undoubtedly be the supreme achievement in the genre.

The dominant figure in the tale is the proud miller whom we meet so high on Fortune's wheel and leave so low. His pride is based not only on his personal talents—bully, jack-of-all-trades, thief—but also on his social position. For he has married the richly-dowered, nunnery-educated daughter of the village parson, a lineage of which both man and wife are very proud. (That the parson, sworn to celibacy, could beget only illegitimate children troubles neither of them, if it ever crosses their minds.) Since the parson, rich in ecclesiastical possessions (to which he has no legal right), intends to make the miller's daughter his heir, the miller foresees an even further improvement in the family's social position. Malkin is to be kept waiting until a socially eligible man comes along, though she is already twenty and by medieval standards an old maid. To a man so firmly in control of his own and his family's destiny two students present no threat, but rather an opportunity for him to show the ease with which he manages things. Effortlessly he thwarts their plans to keep him honest while he exposes them to embarrassment and expense.

The young men who are silly enough to challenge him seem to be his natural dupes. In the first place they are students, members of a profession which as a practical man he despises. But they are even more clearly incompetent because they speak a dialect different from his own: Northern English, which the average southern man in medieval England seems to have found excruciatingly funny. (The more striking Northernisms are indicated by an asterisk in the glosses of this edition). For a time the miller's victories confirm his low opinion of the clerks—men without honor in this part of the country. But in the end the dupes undo all his jealous guarding of his wife's honor, impair the marketable value of his daughter, regain their corn, and beat him well. The impractical students have triumphed through stealth—especially the stealthy manipulation of bedroom furniture—over a far more forceful, more practical man. And while these worms are turning, the Reeve, also a man apart and like the clerks something of a northerner, takes his own sly revenge on his own more forceful antagonist.

THE COOK'S TALE

Apparently it was originally Chaucer's intention to develop a conflict between the Cook and the Host like the one between the Miller and the Reeve. The seeds of this are in the introduction to the *Cook's Tale* (which also serves as an epilogue to the *Reeve's Tale*), in which the Cook threatens to repay the Host's insults by telling of an innkeeper who is made the butt of a joke. The conflict is momentarily postponed, however, because the Cook is bursting with a story to compare with the Reeve's and Miller's Tales. The first fifty-odd lines—which are all we have of the *Cook's Tale*—introduce a promising anecdote about a rascally apprentice and his low friends, but probably Chaucer felt that a third fabliau would scarcely serve the variety that he had promised, and therefore left it unfinished. It is indicative of the imperfect state of the *Canterbury Tales* that when the Cook is reintroduced in the prologue of the *Manciple's Tale* there is no suggestion of the earlier action in which he had figured. Presumably Chaucer intended to cancel this link and the unfinished story.

THE MAN OF LAW'S TALE

This introduction to this tale is memorable chiefly for the Man of Law's discussion of the work of the poet Chaucer—who is not, apparently, the same person as the fictional first-person-singular who reports the pilgrimage. In a highly condescending way the Man of Law describes Chaucer's industriousness as a poet, but seems to think his merits are more quantitative than qualitative: Chaucer has made himself a nuisance by pre-empting all the plots the Man of Law can think of that are suited to versification. The Man of Law gives a desultory list of some of Chaucer's fictions, beginning with the story of Ceyx and Alcyone (generally believed to refer to the *Book of the Duchess*) and continuing with a number of the stories that comprise the *Legend of Good Women.* He concludes the catalogue with the consoling observation that Chaucer's stories are at least clean, since the poet eschews plots that concern incest. This remark is generally supposed to be a mocking reference to the contemporary poet—and Chaucer's friend—John Gower, who in his *Confessio Amantis* told the incestuous stories of Canace and of Apollonius, though he left out the grisly detail that the Man of Law mentions in line 85. Since Gower omitted from a later edition of the *Confessio Amantis* a passage in praise of Chaucer, it has been supposed that he took offense at Chaucer's mild mockery. There is, however, no supporting evidence for this.

In the list of stories the Man of Law credits to Chaucer there are a number that appear neither in the *Legend of Good Women* nor anywhere else in his preserved works, though they are precisely the stories of the faithful ladies that the God of Love in the *Legend* enjoins the poet to tell. Perhaps Chaucer was laughingly trying to get credit for having completed more of that poem than his evident impatience with its subject permitted him to do. On the other hand, most of these stories had already been told by Gower in his *Confessio Amantis,* and it is possible that through the Man of Law Chaucer was reflecting a confusion in a nonliterary mind between poems on the same topics by

Gower and by Chaucer. This would lend at once more humor and less sharpness to his seeming preference for Chaucer. If Chaucer was involving his friend Gower in some joke, one hopes that the latter had enough sense of humor not to take offense.

That the Man of Law announces that he will speak in prose and then proceeds to tell a tale in rhyme-royal stanzas must be accounted to a change of mind on Chaucer's part: at one time he had in mind to assign him a prose story, but then gave him the sad narrative of Custance's woes and neglected to alter the line that promises prose. The fact that the story is exceedingly—even excessively—pietistic presents a problem to the reader who expects the kind of congruence of teller with tale that he has encountered in the first four Canterbury stories: there is nothing in the description of the Man of Law in the *General Prologue*—a thorough-going, self-serving materialist if there ever was one—to lead us to expect to hear from him something so wholly non-materialistic. That Chaucer foresaw our surprise is indicated by the Man of Law's curious little prologue concerning poverty: this derives mainly from Pope Innocent III's *De Contemptu Mundi* (Of Contempt for the World), one of the gloomiest and most popular of all medieval moral books which deplores, with extraordinary enthusiasm, everything mundane. The Man of Law's borrowing from it takes, however, a most unexpected turn: after roundly deploring poverty, the Man of Law goes on to celebrate the joys of wealth, which, needless to say, Innocent deplored as energetically as he did poverty. This Prologue serves to excuse the reader who finds that the tale itself, for all its piety, has more self-conscious rhetoric than sincerely felt substance, and has, indeed, a somewhat hollow ring when compared with that other story of a long-suffering woman, the *Clerk's Tale* of Griselda.

The story of Custance, a representative of a very popular folk tale in which high-born ladies suffer dreadfully from the machinations of wicked mothers-in-law and other malignant relatives, also appears in Gower's *Confessio Amantis,* and it is possible that Chaucer had read Gower's version, though his chief source was also Gower's, the Anglo-Norman Chronicle of Nicholas

Trivet, written in the early fourteenth century. It may have been the fact of Gower's having told the story that influenced Chaucer to assign it to the Man of Law, who thus follows up the references to Gower in the introduction. While scarcely suited to the Man of Law's moral character, it seems suited to the sense of decorum that such a character might be expected to have—a conviction that stories should be historically true (as Trivet asserted Custance's was) and morally edifying, to the hearer if not to the teller: stories should, that is, have the appearance of worth. Moreover the elaborate rhetoric of the tale is such as might be expected of a courtroom lawyer who tries to influence the court by excoriating those whom he is prosecuting and inviting sympathy for those whom he is defending. Yet the tale is really moving only on the occasions of Custance's prayers as she takes ship to leave Syria and Northumberland. In general the story lacks the human profundity of the *Clerk's Tale*: Custance's faith that God will provide for her is justified through a lifetime of sad and violent events, but her passivity is such that the reader's sympathy for her is but passively engaged. She protests, perhaps, too little, and the Man of Law too much.

The short interlude that follows the tale seems designed to introduce a story of a different kind from that of Custance and probably simultaneously to develop a conflict between the teller of the new tale and the Parson. But Chaucer again seems to have changed his plan, and it is not now known who the teller was to be. A number of manuscripts read *Squier* in line 19; others read *Somnour;* and one reads *Shipman.* If one adopts *Shipman,* then the *Shipman's Tale* and the tales tied to it through the Nun's Priest's should follow the Man of Law's. But no manuscript actually juxtaposes the Man of Law's with the Shipman's, and the present editor has followed those manuscripts which postpone the *Shipman's Tale* until much later and place the Wife of Bath's after the Man of Law's. Since the Wife of Bath is not now linked to anything preceding, the editor has adopted a bold (and controversial) suggestion that line 19 of the present passage originally read *Wif of Bathe*: this gives coherence to the chosen order, though it probably does not represent Chaucer's final intention—assuming that he had one.

THE WIFE OF BATH'S PROLOGUE

The Wife of Bath, always competitive, still competes with Falstaff for the title of the greatest comic character in English literature. Her own ancestry extends back through a literary tradition of antifeminism probably as old as Western culture, though the oldest of her identifiable progenitors is the *Golden Book of Marriages,* written by the Greek Theophrastus, pupil and successor of Aristotle, about 300 B.C. While deriving something also from the Roman Juvenal's viciously antifeminist Sixth Satire, written about 50 A.D., the Wife probably owes most of her inheritance to St. Jerome's attack (written about 400) on the monk Jovinian, who had rashly undervalued the importance of chastity and hence the gravity of the peril women offer men. From later times, one can find in her certain influences of the Englishman Walter Map's witty letter to Rufinus dissuading him from matrimony (written about 1200); and she shares some characteristics of the Old Woman in the second part of the French *Romance of the Rose,* composed about 1280 by Jean de Meun, who constantly amuses himself and his audience with unflattering remarks about women. Her most recent forbear is Eustache Deschamps' *Mirror of Marriage,* a lengthy dissuasion from matrimony that was finished only a few years before the Wife of Bath came to life in Chaucer's poem.

Two salient facts should be noted about this literary ancestry: it generally sees woman at her conceivable worst, and its origin is entirely masculine. The Greek belief that only men were capable of virtue and that women distracted men from its pursuit was adopted by the late Roman stoics, who tried even more rigorously to insulate the virtuous man from the commitment to life that relations with women entail. The latter tradition was in turn adopted by the early propagandists for Christian monasticism, who tended to regard the other sex as the worst of the temptations offered by the world they had renounced. The result of this long tradition was that by Chaucer's time a notion of woman as a kind of monster enjoyed an authority and respectability which made it seem valid despite anything a man might, in his everyday life, observe to the contrary. It is this curious traditional version of the truth about woman that Chaucer decided to put to the test in his fiction.

The Wife of Bath's mission, then, is to summarize in her own personality everything that had been said against women for hundreds of years—to write *Q.E.D.* to a proposition that the centuries had been laboring on. One supposes that when he first thought of her Chaucer was possessed of the happy and mischievous idea of forcing the reader to compare the Wife, representing woman in her traditionally lecherous, traditionally avaricious, traditionally domineering, traditionally pragmatic form, with women as the reader knew them: the Wife would be placed before her ink-stained perpetuators and be allowed to say, "You made me what I am today: I hope you're satisfied." Such a plan shows the characteristic double-edge of Chaucerian satire: the creators of the tradition, and contemporary men who professed to believe it, are satirized because the character is a monstrous perversion of what experience shows; but women are satirized too, because in many of her characteristics, inextricably interwoven with the monstrosities, the Wife of Bath is precisely what experience teaches. Chaucer was able here—as so often elsewhere—to have it both ways.

But while this highly distorted concept of womanhood is superbly realized in the Wife of Bath, something better is also realized. As she goes on talking, her traditional lechery, avarice, wilfulness, and pragmatism become woven into a complex of human character that is of a different order from the comparatively negative satirical theme. Her explanations of why she felt entitled to a multiplicity of husbands and how, by deceit and shrewishness, she managed them for her own profit are—despite their grossness—the significant probings of an individual trying to live happily in a world governed by rules that even the most aware of women can only imperfectly understand. If the Wife of Bath has not wholly won the game, she has by no means capitulated. There remains for her the fun she has had in handling her men and in competing with them for the mastery—the fun she has had in life itself. It is this motif that comes to dominate her Prologue as it nears its end. The Wife ceases to be an enormously funny parody of a woman invented by woman-haters, ceases even to be a woman fascinating for her intense individuality, ceases in a way to be a woman at all, and becomes instead a high and gallant symbol of a humanity in which weakness and fortitude are inextricably mingled. In the passage in which she surveys her youth with both regret and blessing for what has passed she seems to enlarge the boundaries of human consciousness, so that mankind itself becomes more vital because of her.

If the *Wife of Bath's Prologue* were the only literature to survive between 1200 and 1600 one might say that in her character the Renaissance sprang from the Middle Ages.

THE WIFE OF BATH'S TALE

The *Wife of Bath's Tale* demonstrates the happiest aspects of her character. In what was probably a less developed form she was assigned the tale now told by the Shipman, which illustrates the supposedly basic feminine attributes of avarice and lechery. The present story illustrates a more interesting theme, her desire to dominate the male, along with the corollary—inevitable to the Wife—that female dominance brings happiness to marriage. Chaucer has adapted a popular story (which appears in contemporary romance and in a later ballad, as well as in John Gower's *Confessio Amantis*) in such a way as to heighten the Wife's thesis. In the analogues the story is handled in a different style, its real point being to demonstrate the courtesy of the hero, who weds the hag uncomplainingly and treats her as if she were the fairest lady in the land; in two versions the knight is Sir Gawain, the most courteous of Arthur's followers, who promises to marry her not in order to save his own life but his king's. The lady's transformation is thus a reward of virtue. In Chaucer the polite knight becomes a convicted rapist who keeps his vow only under duress and in the sulkiest possible manner. The reformation of such unlikely material is the ultimate tribute the Wife could pay to woman's ability to accomplish good if she is allowed to dominate.

The tale is in other respects entirely the Wife's. The wit with which she pays off the Friar, who has had the temerity to interrupt her, while at the same time getting her own story under way, is what we have learned to expect from her. So also is the digression on feminine desires and weaknesses which leads her to give the story of Midas—in which Midas' queen is substituted for the barber of the original Ovidian version. Criticism is sometimes directed against the hag's long sermon to her young husband, on the grounds that it reveals an unexpected delicacy in the Wife's character, but behind all the masculine forcefulness of the Wife's Prologue there lies a highly feminine sensitivity. Finally, it need hardly be said that there is a suggestive parallel between the hag and the Wife of Bath, both of whom wed husbands far younger than they; but the hag, of course, is able to regain her beauty. In her story the Wife is able to make the rules that govern the world, as she has not been able to do in her life. Pathos, however, must not be allowed to carry the day; the coarse vigor of the Wife's final benediction restores the full robustness of her personality. She will, one may be sure, always be as sturdily merry as before.

THE FRIAR'S TALE

The Friar, whose quarrel with the Summoner had its beginning in the Friar's interruption of the Wife of Bath, tells of the divine retribution that is visited upon a summoner who is in every respect a counterpart to the one on the pilgrimage, a dishonest rogue whose principal function is to administer for his own profit the local prostitution ring. The Friar uses a system of equivalences to accomplish his devastating satire. A summoner is, by definition, a thief and a pimp (line 54); when he meets an itinerant devil he identifies himself as a bailiff (an overseer who manages an estate for its owner), for he dared not, "for verray filthe and shame," say that he was a summoner, "for the name" (lines 93–4). The devil identifies himself as a bailiff, too, and as the two talk they begin to appear as mirror images of one another. But the summoner, who has initially concealed his true profession, fails to realize that the devil has done the same—and that the devil is, indeed, a summoner also; this is a possibility that the reader becomes aware of when the devil reveals himself as a resident of hell, a revelation which the summoner accepts with only mild surprise and a callous lack of alarm. But the devil is a far more scrupulous agent than the summoner, for he refuses to seize what is not justly due to his lord, while the summoner issues false summonses without cause. It is only after the summoner has been certified as wholly legitimate prey that the devil seizes him: first the summoner asks that he himself be snatched to hell if he ever repents of trying to extort money from the old woman, and then the old woman, with heartfelt sincerity, consigns him to hell if he doesn't repent. Thus the devil claims him justly and, with a nice sense of economy, claims also the pan that the old woman in her passion had inadvertently assigned to him.

But the Friar goes a step too far. Instead of ending his tale with the summoner's being snatched off to hell, he goes on to boast of how, if he wished, he could call upon his great learning in divinity in order to tell his listeners all about the pains of hell. And indeed, in the Middle Ages friars commonly considered themselves the upholders of book-learning, the true intellectuals of the time, a fact often given prominence in satires directed against them. Chaucer's portrait of Friar Hubert in the *General Prologue* hardly draws upon this motif, but it appears in the introduction to his tale in his patronizing remarks to the Wife of Bath about her use of "scole matere" (line 8). With the last section of his tale, his pride in his learning emerges fully, with the double result that the sharpness of his satire on the Summoner is somewhat blunted, and, worse, that the victim of his satire is shown an aspect of the Friar which he may exploit in order to turn the tables on him.

THE SUMMONER'S TALE

In his tale the Summoner turns the tables on the Friar not once but twice. Since the Friar has boasted of his knowledge of hell, the Summoner begins his rejoinder with an outrageous anecdote that explains why friars are so knowledgeable on the subject. This anecdote reverses the terms of a little story told by members of a monastic order, of how one of them, carried to heaven in a vision, saw none of his order there, but upon making inquiry about their whereabouts, had it revealed to him that they resided beneath the mantle of the Virgin Mary. Whether Chaucer was the first to give a hellish contortion to this story is not known.

The Summoner's main story is of a friar who is in all respects the image of Friar Hubert—a superbly tenacious beggar, a flirt, a fraud (with his claim to have seen his hostess' child borne to heaven), and a total hypocrite who boasts of his austere life after having ordered a roasted pig's head for dinner and whose monologue to the sick Thomas is as much devoted to the glorifying of friars as it is to the wickedness of Thomas's wrathfulness. In this monologue Chaucer gives a careful portrait of a man in love with the sound of his own words—the sound, not the sense, which constantly threatens to get out of control, as, indeed, it does when the Friar interprets one of the stories he has told in condemnation of ire as proving that one should never, for any reason, chide important people. But, like Friar Hubert, the friar unwittingly sets a trap into which he is to fall. Rebuking Thomas for giving to other orders of friars besides his own, he asks, "What is a farthing worth parted in twelve?" (line 259); and this, along with his insistence on "groping" Thomas's conscience, sets Thomas's sick head to plotting. But the outrageous gift he bestows on the friar turns out not to be the climax of the tale: instead, outrage is capped with outrage. The enraged friar goes to the lord of the village and complains of what has happened, and in the course of the conversation between the lord, the lady, and the friar, it becomes not the nature of the gift that is offensive, but the condition made upon its bestowal that all the friars in the convent should share in it equally. The issue thus appears as an intellectual problem which the Friar, as a Master of Arts in Divinity, is enraged at being unable to solve. But the lord's squire Jankin is equal to the task, and every one—except the friar—is satisfied by his solution. The solution is, to be sure, a scholastic triumph, only matched by Thomas's marvelous imaginativeness in formulating the problem in the first place.

It is significant that Chaucer lets the Summoner have the last, devastating word in the quarrel. The Friar's degradation begins when he becomes involved in a quarrel with so low a fellow as the Summoner, and it is completed when he is permitted no rebuttal to the Summoner's scurrility. This is the harshest judgment visited by the author on any pilgrim except the Pardoner.

THE CLERK'S TALE

The *Clerk's Tale* is based on a moralized version of a very old folk-story about the mating of a mortal woman with an immortal lover whose actions are controlled by forces entirely incomprehensible to her human mind. The story was retold for the

Middle Ages in rationalized form by Giovanni Boccaccio, who used it as the last of the hundred tales which make up his *Decameron* (written before 1353). His friend Petrarch, reading Boccaccio's story many years later, was much impressed with it and decided to translate it from Italian into the dignity of Latin, at the same time bringing out the moral significance he found latent in it. Petrarch's Latin version, one of the last of his many literary endeavors, became extraordinarily popular almost at once, and within a very few years translations of it into various European vernaculars were being circulated. Chaucer's poetic version (which the Clerk ascribes to Petrarch without mentioning Boccaccio) is based both on Petrarch's original Latin and on an anonymous French translation.

In a letter to Boccaccio commenting on his own revision of the story, Petrarch recounts the reactions of the first two of his friends to whom he showed it. The first, a Paduan, was so overcome by tears halfway through that he could not continue reading and had to have the remainder read to him. The author then showed it to a Veronese. This man read the tale from beginning to end unmoved, and when he had finished he handed the book back to Petrarch with the comment: "I would have wept too, for the subject certainly excites pity, and the style is well-adapted to call forth tears, and I am not hard-hearted. But I believed, and still believe, that the whole thing is an invention."

It is doubtful that Chaucer ever heard of Petrarch's experience with the Veronese, but as he read the Latin he must have perceived the essential problem that Petrarch had not wholly solved: given a tale of inhuman cruelty and of endurance equally inhuman, how can the author make it believable in human terms? Comparison of the *Clerk's Tale* with its source shows how Chaucer tried to solve the problem and to make the story appeal not only to the ready sentimentalist but also to the reader of more detached attitude. His solution involves first the complete sacrifice of Walter, who in Petrarch is treated in general as though he were a normal human being possessed of all his faculties. In Chaucer, on the other hand, the man is ruled by a dreadful obsession to test his wife, for which abnormality he deserves and gets nothing but blame: the reader is invited not to explore but merely to deplore his unbalanced character. But of course as Walter is dehumanized, Griselda is apt to be also, for it is not human to go on loving a monster. It was nevertheless Chaucer's daring plan to make Griselda credibly human despite the tremendous difficulty of the job. This he endeavored to do by increasing her vitality. In the first place the virtue he endows her with is not really the traditional patience which often suggests, as it did to Shakespeare's Viola, a kind of monumental passivity, but rather constancy. Unlike patience, which can be ascribed to a dumb animal, constancy demands that its possessor be fully aware of the cost of what he is doing even while he continues to do it. Thus Griselda is not, strictly speaking, being patient at all when—in lines added by Chaucer (796–805)—she comments on the difference in Walter as a husband and the impression he gave of himself the day that they were married; nor again when she observes that her share in her two children has been only the pain of childbirth (lines 594–95), a detail that Chaucer intentionally mistranslates from an assertion by Petrarch's Griselda that her claim to the children is nothing compared to Walter's. Nor is she dumbly animal in her acknowledgement that her daughter must die for her sake (line 504, a Chaucerian addition). On these occasions it is clear that she has counted the cost of what she is letting Walter do and is fully conscious how great it is. This same kind of awareness—a basic human quality distinguishing man from the animals—appears in Chaucer's addition to Griselda's original vow to Walter (lines 306–08): "I will never disobey you, even though the result should be death, *though I should be loath to die.*" (This is another instance of intentional mistranslation: literally rendered, the Latin reads, "Nor might you do anything, even though you ordered me put to death, which I should begrudge.") In Chaucer's version the principle of awareness is directly stated in terms of the principle of vitality, of love of life. The value Griselda places upon Walter does not blind her to the many other values of life; but of her own volition she has made constancy to him supreme.

As the tale proceeds a subtle but important development occurs. While Walter remains the visible symbol of the vow Griselda made him, it seems less Walter than the vow itself that Griselda is thinking of. The husband is increasingly unworthy of his wife's constancy, but that constancy is rather to her own promise than to her husband. Thus in Chaucer, as compared with Petrarch, the problem of exacting sympathy for a woman who continues to love a monster is diminished. It is Griselda's perfectly human integrity—her *trouthe*—that she and the reader prize above all. "Dost thou still retain thine integrity?" Job's wife asks Job. "Curse God and die." The reader of the *Clerk's Tale* may wish that Griselda would curse Walter and die. But the woman Griselda, unlike the man Job, never curses Walter, for to do so would be to give up the integrity for and through which she lives.

The *Clerk's Tale* is frequently considered, within the context of the so-called Marriage Group, as an answer to the Wife of Bath's unorthodox notions about woman's role in marriage. In view of the tale's conclusion and its Envoy, where the difference between Griselda's wifely conduct and the Wife's is emphasized, such an interpretation is valid enough. Another connection between the two tales lies in the fact that the Clerk, a member of the group traditionally hostile to women, paints a far more flattering portrait of a woman than anything the staunchest of feminists could herself devise; and it could be argued that Griselda's force of character is, in a vastly different way, as great as the Wife's. But such cross-connections should not blind one to the fact that the story itself concerns human values of a rather different order from those that concern the Wife of Bath, and that it is not really a story of marriage at all, but a story of constancy to an ideal so ably executed by Chaucer that the Petrarchan allegorical interpretation (lines 1086–1106), in which Griselda is the model for Christian constancy under the tests God makes of His creatures, comes almost as an anticlimax. Griselda's adherence to her integrity has penetrated regions of the human spirit which are perhaps beyond reach of the allegory of which Petrarch speaks. But of course Chaucer's world is full of various values, and while the idealism of the *Clerk's Tale* subordinates certain values that are inherent in its plot, it does not actually cancel them out, any more than Griselda's supreme evaluation of her oath to Walter cancels out all other values for her. Therefore in his Envoy, an uproarious *tour-de-force,* the Clerk—and Chaucer—restore the balance by reasserting those everyday values that the tale has held in subordination.

THE MERCHANT'S TALE

There is no more startling disclosure of character in the *Canterbury Tales* than the one that follows the telling of the tale of Griselda. All the Merchant's carefully guarded reserve, all the impervious countenance his profession has taught him to assume, collapses in the uncontrollably furious "No!" with which he reacts to the Clerk's portrait of a saintly wife. The dam has given away and the ugly muck that formerly lay hidden beneath the surface of the lake is exposed to the sight of all. In order to destroy what he considers the fiction of the Clerk's lovely idea of woman the Merchant is ready to destroy the fiction of his own dignity, and in trying to replace that idea with his own vile one he reveals his own vileness. Instead of the boasted profits with which he fills his conversation he discloses his real loss, not only of a wife but of all values higher than those of the market place.

While in his tale the Merchant does not tell us of his unhappy marital experience, the attitudes he assumes toward the plot and its people are conditioned by what has happened to him. His memory is full of the romantic notion of women he had before he acquired a wife, even while his heart overflows with disgust and hatred for all women because his wife did not fit that notion. This strife of before and after is a constant tension in the poem and accounts for its extraordinary ironical passages in which the narrator heaps praise on the attitudes he has come to detest. Thus May—sweet, demure, perfidious May—is lavished with the sentimental tributes of courtly love while her actions become increasingly mean, culminating in her complete degradation in the pear tree. It is May, of course, that the Merchant hates most, even though the plot accords her the triumph of a fiend, but his attitude toward January is hardly less emotional and even more complex. As one who feels himself similarly cheated in the marriage bargain, the Merchant cannot help according him occasional sympathy, but most of the time he detests and scorns his folly just as he detests and scorns himself for his own folly in ever having entertained notions like January's. If there is anyone in the story who enjoys the Merchant's approval it is Justinus, whose hardheaded and cheaply cynical counsel makes the good mercantile point that a man ought to examine goods very carefully before he buys them. But his conclusion seems to be the same as the Merchant's: the goods, if a woman, will cheat you anyhow.

Amid a great complex of bitter irony every possible change is rung on the blindness of January, the habitual self-deceiver who, regardless of the condition of his eyesight, remains, from beginning to end, *blent*—the Middle English word meaning both "blind" and "deceived." But if the symbolism has its obvious root in the old saying, "Love is blind," it also draws something from the passage in which Christ explains to his disciples why he speaks obscurely to the multitude: ". . . whosoever hath not, from him shall be taken away even that he hath. Therefore speak I to them in parables: because they seeing see not; and hearing they hear not, neither do they understand." From January, the spiritual pauper to whom love is lechery and taking a bride no different from buying a domestic animal, is taken away even what he has; seeing, he sees not, neither does he understand.

Nor does the Merchant understand either. Sharing January's basic animal attitude toward women, he feels himself superior to January because he himself is undeceived and can recognize May for what she is—a thoroughly bad bargain. The investment returns only half the expected rate of interest, for while May serves January's lechery she fails to be the faithful consort that he had wanted to comfort his old age. It no more occurs to the Merchant than it does to January that marriage involves something more on the husband's part than a transfer of funds from one commodity to another, and throughout the tale the word *love* is sadly ironical. Nevertheless, though the Merchant does not perceive it, his story suggests again and again the fatal limitation on his own and January's approach to marriage. This appears most clearly in the treatment of May, who despite her unpardonable conduct is potentially something better than a domestic animal. In the terrible passages describing old January's love-making, Chaucer subtly shifts the point of view from January to May, and allows us to imagine what even the best of women would suffer in such a marriage. Furthermore, for the *dei ex machina* that in his fabliau source were probably Christ and St. Peter, Chaucer substitutes Pluto and Proserpina, who represent the archetype of the kind of marriage depicted in the *Merchant's Tale.* As a girl Proserpina was ravished by Pluto, whose gloomy kingdom of the underworld she was henceforth compelled to share for half the year. May's hell was little better. Nothing, of course, excuses her conduct toward her ravisher, but in view of his character a kind of rough justice is established in the poem. This is perversely reflected in the Merchant's quotation of the words spoken after the creation of Adam:

> Lat us now make an help unto this man
> Lik to himself.

Chaucer was expert at the business of making a poem assume a meaning unknown to the fictional narrator, but perhaps nowhere did he succeed more brilliantly with the device than here. To express his disgust with women and marriage the Merchant constantly speaks ironically, stating the opposite of what he means—the positive for the negative. But in stating the positive even in order to disprove its existence he has nevertheless stated something better than his negative, and something to which the healthy mind will always revert. The Merchant himself is caught within the larger irony of the poem, and in the end his cynical condemnation of January and May becomes a profoundly sad commentary not only on their failure to understand, but on his own.

THE SQUIRE'S TALE

The *Squire's Tale* is a representative of a popular medieval genre, the oriental romance, full of magic and marvels and plot upon plot. How sincerely Chaucer was committed to telling the tale is not clear. It may represent a sincere artistic effort of his youth that got out of hand—or found itself going nowhere—which he later assigned to the young Squire. Certainly it reads at times as if its author had swallowed a rhetorical handbook whole but had not fully digested it. The telling is graced by a kind of youthful enthusiasm and enterprise, but ungraced by narrative discipline. The several magic objects brought to Cambiuskan and Canacee are lovingly catalogued, discussed, and stored, but it is apparent from the narrative of Canacee and the magic ring that the teller will not quickly be able to get the brass horse and the rest out of storage and into action. And Canacee's ring, which provides the motivation for Part II of the story, is potentially the least exciting of the gifts. The incident involving Canacee and the love-lorn hawk is in constant danger of falling from pathos into mere sentimentality or mere absurdity: it is hard to believe that the creator of Chantecleer and Pertelote could with a straight face describe a hawk as a "tigre" who falls on his knees to his love (lines 534–5). One suspects that at some point in the telling,

Chaucer began to parody the form—and even himself—and then decided to make the Squire the recipient of the curious production: it is possible to feel that, while he admired the Squire for being so fine an example of his type, he failed to find the type very interesting. Chaucer is surely having a joke at the Squire's expense when at the end of Part II he has him give a brief summary of the future action of the tale—an action that would have taken thousands of lines to complete at the rate the Squire is progressing. After a characteristic two-line rhetorical warm-up at the beginning of Part III, the Squire spontaneously stops or the Franklin interrupts him—it is not clear which. It is likely, however, that the Franklin, who genuinely admires the Squire, is extricating him and the company from a narrative in which they might be caught forever.

THE FRANKLIN'S TALE

The *Franklin's Tale* is generally considered a member of the Marriage Group, since its picture of a marriage based on mutual respect and toleration gives a kind of resolution to the problems treated successively by the Wife of Bath, the Clerk, and the Merchant. But while the tale does indeed answer some of the questions those tales have raised, it has its own independent and perhaps more important significance. This significance has less to do with marriage than with the virtues of *trouthe,* integrity (Griselda's virtue), and *freedom,* generosity, upon which an ideal marriage must depend.

Dorigen, the story's heroine, is one of Chaucer's most delicately drawn ladies. Young and beautiful, high-born, virtuous, idealistic, she is all that a worthy knight could desire, and so much emphasis is placed by the unfailingly sympathetic Franklin on her fine qualities that one almost neglects to notice that Dorigen is not without her crucial weaknesses. For all her excellences, she has a certain rigor, a certain impatience (against which the Franklin warns us in lines 63–78), that very nearly undo her. She tends to expect the world at large to live up to her own idealistic vision of it—that is, to comport itself according to her own high standards so that she can go on being the perfect wife without interference from outside. Her husband Arveragus, on the other hand, is, while equally idealistic, a chivalrous gentleman well aware that his profession entails both arms and love. After a long honeymoon he leaves his wife and crosses the channel to Britain in order to exercise his valor (presumably as one of King Arthur's knights). Dorigen, with a woman's immediacy, sees as the symbol of the dangers he may encounter the ugly rocks that make the coast of Brittany so hostile to mariners, and these rocks she bitterly resents. Indeed, in a delightfully feminine speech she calls the Almighty to task for having created them, since they are obviously not of the things that are for the best in the best of all possible worlds: she wishes them heartily away. Only the most rigorous of theologians would call Dorigen's address to God sinful, but it nevertheless amounts to a request that Nature should reorganize the divine creation in order to fit it to Dorigen's notions of how things ought to be.

The hitherto silent Aurelius, a courtly lover of the old immoral tradition which stipulates that love is possible only outside marriage, finally makes his passion for Dorigen known to her. Like the virtuous wife she is (and most unlike most courtly heroines), she is shocked and rebuffs him. But while she is making it clear to Aurelius that he is not living up to her ideas of how men should behave, she apparently makes an analogy between his bad behavior and nature's in allowing the ugly rocks to remain where they are. She then combines her two irritations by promising to love Aurelius on the rather cruel condition that he remove the rocks. In substance, she promises to be untrue to her own nature if Aurelius manages to rearrange creation. Thereupon we see Aurelius repeating, in effect, Dorigen's address to God, though the objects of his prayer are not Christian, but the pagan gods of nature. His prayer is no more successful than hers, and he goes into the courtly lover's typical decline.

Upon the safe return of Arveragus, Dorigen forgets all about her promise until, through the use of illusion, the rocks are made to disappear. Illusion has turned an illusory evil into a real one. The rocks were never really evil: they were, so to speak, merely performing their function as part of God's creation. But the disappearance that Dorigen has desired seems about to destroy Dorigen and her ideal marriage. By an ironic paradox Dorigen's own impractical, uncompromising idealism has brought her into a situation where she must act in direct opposition to it. For a time she luxuriates in the contemplation of suicide (which is no real solution to her dilemma). But, having proved conclusively that suicide is her only expedient, she does the sensible thing of taking the problem to Arveragus, who has been out of town.

Arveragus' insistence that Dorigen keep her pledge to Aurelius has been attacked by some critics as silly. But if we criticize Arveragus we are really making Dorigen's initial mistake, which was to assume that the world owes it to us to make us practical returns for our idealism. Arveragus knows better: an ideal has no relevance unless we are willing to sacrifice our whole world to it—and *trouthe* is "the highest contract that man may keep." Of course, Arveragus is right. Moreover, if we are prepared for the sacrifice, it may follow—as it does here—that the world will make us the practical return we had hoped for. The solution to Dorigen's dilemma is foreshadowed in the memorable passage that precedes the account of the vanishing of the rocks, the passage on "the cold and frosty season of December" when Nature seems most dead and most sterile—yet nonetheless the season of Nowel (from Latin *natalis,* birthday) when Christ came to redeem the dead world and to fulfill the Old Law with the New. For in the poem the Christian virtue of *freedom* (generosity) fulfills the Old Testament contractual law of *trouthe* (the covenant). Both virtues are important, since *trouthe* calls *freedom* into existence as the Old Testament may be said to have called into existence the New. Through generosity the evil that Dorigen has unwittingly brought into being is once more relegated to illusion, and Dorigen, we assume, has learned to distinguish the real from the unreal.

The Franklin tells us that his story is a Breton lay, a form of narrative poem that is best represented in the work of the twelfth-century French poetess Marie de France. Presumably the lays were originated by the minstrels of Brittany, the region of northern France where the *Franklin's Tale* takes place. Chaucer, however, does not seem to have been reworking any genuine lay, but rather recasting an old story found in his favorite source, Boccaccio, into the form of an idealized Breton lay. His impression of what one ought to be was probably based on a reading of one or two Middle English romances which their anonymous authors assert to be examples of the genre. From these he extracted the characteristics of many of the known lays: brevity, simplicity, concern with love and the inviolability of promises, use of the supernatural, and a predominantly optimistic spirit.

It might be said that even if there had been no genre of the Breton lay before Chaucer, the *Franklin's Tale* would have established one.

The spirit of optimism is particularly appropriate to the sanguine, generous Franklin, as are other aspects of his tale. The most obvious of these is his translation of all that is ideal in courtly love—which traditionally had its roots in adultery—into terms of a happy marriage. This splendidly illustrates bourgeois aspiration to aristocratic virtues, with inevitable redefinition—and less inevitable purification—in the context of bourgeois practicality. The possible degenerative result of such appropriation of aristocratic virtues is made fun of in *Sir Thopas,* but in the *Franklin's Tale* they lose none of their luster. His idea of marriage is a far finer thing than the immorality of courtly love, as it is also far finer than the commercial drabness of much contemporary bourgeois marriage. Thus the tale, like its teller, anticipates later social history, for the modern ideal of marriage is precisely that mixture of the aristocratic with the bourgeois which the *Franklin's Tale* shows.

Chaucer's obvious admiration for the kind of man the Franklin is does not blind him to the little quirks that are characteristic of the bourgeois, no matter how aspiring. The most amusing of these is the Franklin's most unaristocratic preoccupation with the value of money. This is at once apparent in the introduction to the tale, in which he brings to bear a financial image even while he is congratulating the aristocratic Squire on his *gentilesse* (line 11). Within the tale itself the Franklin lays stress on the size of Aurelius' debt to the magician. And it is not difficult to see something of the narrator himself in his hero Arveragus when the latter defines the virtue of *trouthe* as a *thing,* a legal contract such as was executed in any bourgeois commercial transaction, that must at all costs be kept.

THE PHYSICIAN'S TALE

The *Physician's Tale,* like the *Man of Law's Tale,* is a pious story assigned to a person of no real piety whose respect for propriety rather than sincere moral earnestness seems to lead him to speak as he does. Since Chaucer portrays such materialistic pilgrims telling such tales, it seems likely that members of Chaucer's audience no different from the tellers enjoyed hearing them told—or at least preferred them to merely entertaining stories: people self-importantly dedicated to business (and to busy-ness) may feel that while entertainment is pure waste, moral doctrine, no matter how little they apply it to themselves, may be written off as a kind of deduction from the tax on their time that they consider all non-profitable activity to be. The *Physican's Tale* has little coherent interest: Nature's monologue is agreeable, the portrait of Virginia amiable if priggish, the advice to governesses and parents good, the gory story far more absurd than in Livy's Latin version, and the concluding warning about the power of conscience a total *non-sequitur.* But there is nothing in the fabric to prove that the intent is not wholly serious: even the fact that Virginia, after comparing herself with Jephtha's daughter, rejoices that she will die a virgin, while Jephtha's daughter bewails her virginity before being put to death by her father, may be a pure accident, though a wry one. In any case, it seems a fact that stories of damsels in dreadful distress appeal to people who generally consider literature a poor substitute for the reality of everyday life.

THE PARDONER'S PROLOGUE AND EPILOGUE

The Pardoner, like the Wife of Bath, owes something to the continuation of the *Roman de la Rose,* which thus contributed both to the most vital and to the most repellently sterile of Chaucer's characters. In the French poem Jean de Meun introduces a character named False-Seeming, a professional hypocrite who pretends to a holiness that he possesses not at all. By way of making an apology for his way of life, False-Seeming explains, with the utmost candor and the greatest pride in his own cleverness, the various guises his hypocrisy assumes. This situation, in which a hypocrite attempts to justify himself by revealing the full truth, provides Chaucer with the essential framework for the Pardoner's prologue.

It also gives him the first of a series of paradoxes that are developed in the character and in his tale. Paradox in Chaucer's poetry, as in Milton's, often has two opposed functions: when applied to the mysteries of the Christian religion (the Virgin-Mother, the God-Man) it expresses the superiority of the divine to the laws that govern nature; applied to human beings it may express the animality of man's nature in its farthest remove from the divinity of his creator. This is certainly true of the Pardoner, who while he converts grace—God's great gift to man—into cash for his own pocket, simultaneously perverts the divine system of salvation in order to accomplish his own damnation. Fittingly enough, he eventually is entrapped by the paradox of his own nature. The *General Prologue* makes it clear that the Pardoner is a eunuch. To the medieval mind, which liked to find in the visible world the patterns of the invisible, this lack of manliness would suggest the barrenness of the Pardoner's spirit, and it is this condition that causes, in the visible world of the pilgrimage, the punishment that he seems to be doomed to in the world of the spirit. The Pardoner has, from his first appearance, presented himself as a virile, gay lad, a jolly good fellow, an accomplished wencher. When he enters the scene in the *General Prologue* he is singing a love song—though an ironically wistful one; he has the temerity to interrupt the Wife of Bath, that great proponent of sexual love, in order to publicize his virility; when the Host, addressing the Physician, swears by Saint Runnion—apparently a reference to sexuality—the Pardoner must needs repeat the oath; he seems pleased, in the same passage, to be called *bel ami,* a phrase that still means "lover" in Modern French; and finally, he boasts that he will have a jolly wench in every town. In view of the evident facts of the case, all this is the rankest hypocrisy. As the only hypocrisy that survives the candor of the Pardoner's self-revelation it probably is the explanation for his candor, for men often believe that they can best keep a shameful secret by seeming to reveal the whole truth about themselves.

But the Pardoner's secret is, of course, a secret only to himself: at any rate Chaucer the pilgrim guessed it at once. But as long as the secret remains unspoken the Pardoner dwells securely in his own delusion, so that the secret remains valid for him. Yet at the end of his frightening story he wantonly imperils—and destroys—the fragile structure on which his self-confidence depends. Whatever his reasons—avarice, good-fellowship, humor—he concludes his sermon with an offer to sell his pardon to the pilgrims even after all he has told about his own fraudulence. Ironically he picks the worst possible victim, that rough, manly man who might be supposed to have a natural antipathy for the unmasculine Pardoner. The insult to the Host's intelligence is the first and last failure of the Pardoner's intelligence, for the Host's violently obscene reaction reveals the Pardoner's secret. Thereupon the man whose clever tongue has seemed to give him control of every situation is reduced to furious silence.

THE PARDONER'S TALE

The *Pardoner's Tale* is a sample of the sermons with which the Pardoner frightens his congregations into the Christian generosity that makes him rich. Although the story proper (lines 333 ff) illustrates his accustomed text, "Avarice is the root of evil," the introductory lines are a highly emotive discussion of drunkenness, gluttony, swearing, and gambling (with a few glances at lechery). These latter are, to be sure, sins practiced by the young men whom avarice is in the story ultimately to destroy, but the Pardoner's choice of them for his rhetoric doubtless depends on the fact that they are the sins that can be made to sound most exciting. Since the sermon was one of the main sources of entertainment for the Middle Ages, the preacher generally entertained while he taught, and nothing is easier to dramatize successfully to an uneducated audience than riotous living. Furthermore, it is characteristic of the riotous-living Pardoner's sense of irony that he should here too, as with avarice, inveigh against the vices he himself practices. He privately delights in his own experience with these vices: there is something gloatingly cynical in his description of a drunken dice-game, so knowingly graphic as to exceed the limits of art. But while the Pardoner may be having his secret laugh, he does not cease to work upon his audience's emotions with every lurid detail that a morbid imagination can provide.

The story itself is one of the most impressive ventures into the supernatural that English literature affords. It is a very old story indeed, probably having its origin in the primitive animism of the East, although in the Pardoner's mouth it becomes an anecdote of contemporary Europe. The plot in which three revelers who set out to find Death find him in the gold that has made them forget the object of their search gives Chaucer ample opportunity for grim irony. This develops mostly through the speeches of the participants in the story, who are constantly saying far more than they think they are. The naturalism of the dialogue increases by contrast the terror of the supernatural forces that are effortlessly accomplishing their end. For instance, in the monologue of the strange old man who directs the youths to their death, the ultimate mysteries of human life are treated with the familiarity we accord homely, everyday things. And Death in the end turns out to be someone who, if not a rural bully dwelling in the next village, is equally close at hand. Out of the miasma that hangs invisible just above the heads of the revelers, Death reaches with sure hand to claim those who had so arrogantly started out to slay him. Nevertheless, despite the strong aura of the supernatural, the entire action is restricted to a purely natural sequence of events.

The ending Chaucer has assigned to the Pardoner himself makes his exemplum even more brilliant. The man who, like the revelers in his story, seems so firmly in control of his destiny, has in his sermon eloquently demonstrated that avenging powers dwell close to a man's own home. If it is not the supernatural, it is at least an ironic destiny working through his own nature that impels the Pardoner to provoke his own social destruction among the pilgrims.

THE SHIPMAN'S TALE

The *Shipman's Tale* was evidently intended originally for the Wife of Bath, for the editorial comments in lines 11–19 require a feminine narrator and the theme illustrates one of the basic motifs in the Wife's character, her preoccupation with the possibility of exploiting physical charms for financial gain. As Chaucer continued to think about—and perhaps to add to—the Wife's character, however, this particular motif seems to have become less important to him than the larger issue of sovereignty, and in the end he assigned her the more relevant and attractive story of the ugly crone and the sulky knight. He then reassigned the Wife's original story to the Shipman, whose intellectually rather undefined character the tale neither entirely fits nor entirely fails to fit. The retention of the lines which mark the speaker as a woman is characteristic of the unfinished state in which Chaucer left the *Canterbury Tales.*

The story is a very old folk-tale known as "The Lover's Gift Regained," which appears in many languages and in many versions. While it is a fabliau like the Miller's and Reeve's tales and a brilliantly told one, it has little of the direct appeal to the sense of humor—little of the hilarity—that these have, and is marked rather by the cold brilliance, at once effective and repulsive, that one finds in the *Merchant's Tale.* The reduction of all human values to commercial ones is accomplished with almost mathematical precision: the merchant is rich, "for which men held him wise"; his wife attractive, "which is a thing that causes more expense" than it is worth; and the monk is popular because of the elegance of his gifts and the size of his tips. The central issue, of course, is the sum of one hundred franks which becomes on two occasions the value of the fair wife's sexual compliance, first to the monk, later to her husband. This motif is brilliantly emphasized by such a rhyme as *frankes–flankes* (lines 201–2), by the series of possible *doubles-entendres* in the dialogue between monk and merchant when the former is borrowing the money, and finally by the pun on *taille* which is used twice at the end of the story (lines 416, 434): "talley," a notched stick on which was recorded the amount due on merchandise purchased on credit, and "tail" in the obscene sense. The second use of this pun, by the narrator in his closing benediction, serves as formal notification that a mathematical proposition has been proved.

Chaucer's transfer of the tale away from the Wife of Bath is understandable. From the enthusiastic partiality that is a part of her fully developed humanity we should expect some of the rich personal interpretation she gives to the tale later assigned her, and for her to expend her enthusiasm on so sordid and sterile a situation as this would necessarily diminish her. Aside from the joke it makes—which is, of course, more than sufficient on one level of reading—the story demonstrates that the vision of life as a purely mercantile arrangement sterilizes those who hold it so that all human values disappear, including that of human awareness. Within the tale neither the cheating nor the cheated perceive any significance in their actions beyond the immediate financial gain or loss that is incurred, and since there is no real financial loss, the events hardly cause a ripple on the surface of their lives. Sensitivity to other values besides cash has been submitted to appraisal and, having been found nonconvertible, has been thrown away. With characteristic Chaucerian irony, this point is reinforced by the insensitivity of the narrator, who sees nothing in the story beyond a clever trick and a smart evasion. However unorthodox the Wife of Bath's values may be, they are not inhuman, and her awareness is far too great to content itself with mere cleverness (besides, she could hardly approve of the wife's letting herself be tricked by the monk). By reassigning the tale to a neutral figure whose unawareness enhances its theme, Chaucer lets his carefully worked-out equations perform their own cold demonstration.

THE PRIORESS' TALE

The *Prioress' Tale* is of a very common medieval type known as a Miracle of the Virgin. This particular story (which resembles but is not to be confused with the story of Hugh of Lincoln that the Prioress mentions in line 232) exists in many versions in the later Middle Ages. It illustrates a most important aspect of medieval Christianity, the belief that God occasionally violates the rules of nature as we know them in order to work His own ends. Here the miracle celebrates the glory of God's mother and also, perhaps incidentally, accomplishes the punishment of those who are taken to be her enemies. Since the emphasis in any story of a miracle is on the wonder-working power of God, it generally will not deal with the subtleties of human nature, and the narrator of a miracle must exploit other areas of interest than the problematical, with which more intellectual poetry is usually concerned.

The *Prioress' Tale* is a strange mixture of delicacy and horror, so that it is capable of producing two entirely different impacts. From one side it is all delicacy and piety. The prologue is Chaucer's most splendid prayer, exemplifying his ability to employ conventional symbols (for instance, the paradox of the Virgin-Mother revealed as the bush which burnt unconsumed in Moses' sight) in such a way as to achieve a great and fresh sincerity. At the same time it remains the Prioress' prayer, for her own innocence, as well as that of the conventional suppliant, seems to appear in the final lines in which she compares herself to a year-old child. Having read her portrait in the *General Prologue,* we are aware that there are facets to this innocence which do not entirely suit an ideal nun, but the touching humility of her prologue dispels for the moment all but her spiritual innocence. The human frailty is still there—as a matter of fact, we have just been reminded of it by the Host's exaggerated politeness in calling upon her—but it seems now to have been purified. And, of course, the little martyr and his widowed mother are treated with a tender-heartedness that is more truly Christian than the sentimentality with which the Prioress reacts to dogs and mice.

But on the other surface of the coin is the harsh, un-Christian attitude to the Jews, and the preoccupation with vengeance that ill accords with a tone of tender piety: the Prioress is responsible for these, too. As for the vengeance, the society of the fourteenth century was in many respects very primitive and in it, as Huizinga has said, one is constantly aware of the mingled odor of blood and roses. Emotionalism that excludes the intellect—as it does in the *Prioress' Tale*—can be a dangerous thing, for the psychological transition from exquisite sensibility to bloodshed is an easy one. Whatever else, the exquisite Prioress is a creature of her age—and also, unhappily, of its more ignorant side. This explains her blind hatred of the Jews, whom many in the Middle Ages condemned as the bitterest enemies of Christianity, quite forgetting both Christ's charity and the significance of the fact that He was Himself a Jew. But the Church of which the Prioress was a nun harbored no such hatred as the Prioress displays, and indeed did everything it could to make clear the un-Christianness of an attitude like hers. Chaucer was, of course, aware of this, and the objectivity of his treatment of the *Prioress' Tale* should prevent us from identifying her views with his. While as an artist and medieval Christian he committed himself to the story of the miracle, he could not have believed that such a story represented the supreme form of Christian narrative. Indeed, for him or for us to see in the *Prioress' Tale* the epitome of medieval Christianity would be fatally to undervalue the greatness of medieval religious thought. In its delicacy and devotional quality and as a response to the injunction that men must become as little children, the *Prioress' Tale* is valid. Apparently the narrowly limited Prioress can find no better way to express her religion than this. But Chaucer, an intelligent man and a great poet, is in no way limited. He made the *Prioress' Tale* in some ways as pretty as her own brooch, but it is the failure of her character, not his, which makes the poem so imperfect an expression of the motto *Amor Vincit Omnia.*

THE TALE OF SIR THOPAS

In *Sir Thopas* Chaucer makes one of his best jokes, and a complex joke at that. The poem is in itself a brilliant burlesque of a common type of Middle English romance, but it is even more delightful for the action it provides within the dramatic framework of the *Canterbury Tales.*

In its function as a burlesque *Sir Thopas* exploits the historical fact that many French romances written for aristocratic audiences in the twelfth century were translated into English for bourgeois audiences in the fourteenth. The Old French romance writers generally treated their chivalric material—love and warfare—in terms of a highly artificial code of conduct that was as important to the audience as the plot itself: while the knightly hero took part in a number of exciting battles (and love affairs), his adventures were significant only if he was able to maintain throughout them a careful conformity to the idealized code of chivalric behavior. Chaucer and his own aristocratic audience were entirely capable of reading French romances in the original, and the poet was sufficiently interested in them to attempt a French type of romance in the *Squire's Tale.* But the English middle classes, who were increasing in size and importance, did not as a rule read French, and their appetite for narrative literature created a demand for romances in their own tongue. This demand was partly supplied by anonymous adapters of the earlier French stories, probably professional minstrels who earned their living by reciting poems at the well-laden tables of the prosperous bourgeoisie. Either because they did not recognize the elaborate conventions of behavior that permeated French romance or because they realized that their English audience would not care for them, the minstrels generally reproduced in English only the bare bones of the original story—the plot. Stripped of its courtly sentiment—which is the only intellectual nourishment it has to offer—the average romance is reduced to a crude series of rather absurd events which can satisfy nothing more than the most primitive craving for action. This is apparently what the bourgeois audience wanted. Furthermore, since every reader wants to identify himself with the hero of a story, and since a twelfth-century French knight was not easily identifiable with a fourteenth-century English bourgeois, the minstrel-adapters naturally remade the hero in the image of their auditors, as does many a historical novelist today. This is legitimate enough; but to the reader who knows both the culture that is being adapted and the culture it is being adapted to, the result may seem hilarious.

The hero of Chaucer's burlesque goes through some of the motions of a twelfth-century knight-errant, but at heart he is the drabbest sort of late fourteenth-century burgher. Since the Flemings who had come to England in connection with the wool trade seem to have been considered the acme (or nadir) of bourgeois manners and morals, Chaucer has made his hero Flemish. Sir Thopas' nationality enhances his lack of chivalric qualities—of aristocratic bearing. He excels at the unknightly sports of wrestling and archery; he swears by the bourgeois staples ale and bread; he climbs onto his horse (there are several Middle English verbs for getting a knight on a horse, but *climb* is too reminiscent of the stepladder to be one of them); and his horse seems built for comfort rather than derring-do. The hero's notable chastity (perhaps symbolized in his name, Topaze, the stone of chastity) is unusual if not absolutely impossible in a knight of popular romance, and with a cruelty that has little to do with his being a bourgeois, Chaucer has exploited this chastity to make it seem downright effeminacy. Sir Thopas is also a most reluctant hero, dominated by prudence to the exclusion of valor, for he refuses in a most unknightly way to fight unarmed, and when he prepares for battle he dons an extraordinary amount of defensive armor.

But Chaucer's burlesque is not only of plot but also of style. The minstrel romances of Middle English are not much distinguished for their poetic technique. Oral delivery, predominantly dependent on memory, demands first of all a dogtrot rhythm, and secondly, a useful store of formulas to fit every occasion, including those occasions when the poet needs a rhyme and cannot think of a revelant one. Chaucer's tale is full of the clichés of the poorer romances—*it is no nay, forsoothe as I you telle may, by dale and eek by downe,* and a host of others. Misuse of these clichés is mainly responsible for Sir Thopas' effeminacy: in Middle English romance certain attributes, and certain terms for their expression, are arbitrarily assigned to the heroes, others to the heroines. Chaucer in *Sir Thopas*—as he did in describing Absolon in the *Miller's Tale*—uses some of the female terms for the male, giving his knight the *sides smale* and pink-and-white complexion of a lady. This kind of verbal criticism is extended to so small a thing as the final *-e:* the minstrel poets did not ordinarily pronounce the letter upon which Chaucer's own beautifully manipulated syllabic verse largely depends, and Chaucer dutifully writes in *Sir Thopas* such rhymes as *grace/gras* (grass), impossible in his own system. Meanwhile all the action—or inaction—of the story is told in the most horrendously emphatic meter, which lays as much stress on the hero's seemly nose as it could have laid upon his slaughter of the three-headed giant—had Thopas not so prudently retired. The meter is one that marches martially on through thick and thin with the sense of great deeds being done while Sir Thopas himself is sometimes moving backwards, sometimes listening to romances of popes and cardinals, sometimes merely lying down on the soft grass to dream about an elf-queen.

But the poem involves a larger effect. It must be remembered that within the fiction of the *Canterbury Tales* the pilgrim Chaucer is telling what is for him the best rhyme he knows, and that there is, from his point of view, nothing funny about it—just as there is nothing funny about it to the Host who so rudely interrupts him: it is for both of them a serious endeavor of art, though the Host does not find it a successful one. But when we recall that for the real Chaucer's audience, the pilgrim Chaucer and the poet occupied the same body and could at any time become the same person, *Sir Thopas* seems a joke on a far larger scale: the creator of the whole pilgrimage, including all its stories and their tellers, faced in his fictional form with the necessity of creating a story, takes refuge in the most primitive kind of imaginative construction. The relation between the creator and the created that the situation implies is revealed by a mind almost godlike in the breadth and humility of its ironic vision. G. K. Chesterton has reminded us of the best analogue to *Sir Thopas* that occurs in English literature: Bottom's play of Pyramus and Thisbe in the *Midsummer Night's Dream,* Shakespeare's most Chaucerian work. In Theseus' comment on the ludicrous performance being given by the solemn artisans, there seems an overt statement of what Chaucer implies when he assigns his fictional representative the romance of *Sir Thopas:* "The best in this kind are but shadows."

EPILOGUE TO THE TALE OF SIR THOPAS

(Chaucer's Tale of Melibeus)

Having displeased the Host by his attempt to give a tale in verse, Chaucer the Pilgrim takes the advice given him and delivers a story in prose. This concerns Melibeus who desires to avenge himself for the injuries his enemies have dealt him but is argued into peaceful demeanor by the counsels of his wife Prudence. While for the Host to permit Chaucer to finish this tale may seem strange to the reader reduced to stupefaction by Prudence's interminable good advice, the story (or sermon) was nevertheless a very popular one in the Middle Ages when readers did not entirely distinguish between pleasure in literature and pleasure in being edified. Chaucer himself probably did distinguish between these pleasures—but he also probably felt more pleasure in being edified than we are apt to. Hence it is not strictly correct to say that the *Tale of Melibeus* is Chaucer's revenge for having been interrupted in *Sir Thopas:* that is, the tale is in no way meant to be treated as an elaborate hoax. On the other hand, while the story's good advice must be taken seriously, its lack of literary qualities and of any real imagination are nicely suited to the demonstrated capabilities of the pilgrim Chaucer.

THE MONK'S TALE

The *Monk's Tale* presents a series of short histories of famous men and women who suffered sad downfalls—that is, it is a series of medieval "tragedies." Tragedy as it was generally defined in the Middle Ages lacked almost all the elements that make Greek or Shakespearean tragedy one of the most profound of literary forms. Medieval tragedy is centered in the concept of the goddess Fortune—Fortuna in Roman antiquity. According to the usual metaphor, Fortune governs a great wheel (rather like a Ferris wheel) upon which human beings ride during their lifetime. The motion that Fortune imparts to the wheel is uncertain and changeable, so that riders may have small ups and downs or may even remain in one place, high or low, for considerable periods. But it is characteristic of the "tragic" figure that he should achieve the highest position in the circuit, remain there for a time, and then be hurled precipitously to the bottom, where he generally ends his days in misery. Fully stated, as it is in Boethius and the Boethian *Knight's Tale,* the concept of Fortune has two essential aspects: from the point of view of finite fallen man, the goddess seems merely whimsical; but from the philosophic point of view, she executes the divine will—whose reasons none may know—and teaches man not to trust to the things of this earth, since their essence is instability. Unfortunately for its literary effect, the typical medieval statement of the idea, which we see in the *Monk's Tale,* dealt only with the first aspect, assuming that if one kept hammering on the wretched end of all human aspirations one would teach one's readers to beware of the world. The result is not only monotony, but a kind of inversion of the basic doctrine. God disappears entirely; Fortune appears to exercise full control, and exercises it malignantly. The Christian generalization that humanity is fatally flawed is expressed in such a way that in a series of tragedies no discrimination is apt to be made between virtue and vice: the former seems as futile as the latter, and the "tragic flaw" of more mature tragedy is not permitted development. The inversion of the basic concept of Fortune becomes complete when a narrative designed to make men distrust the world begins to suggest, as the *Monk's Tale* sometimes does, that the only good in life is the period, however short, that one is allowed at the top of the wheel.

Whether this misleading impression of the doctrine of Fortune is to be blamed on the general assumption that any audience knew and would bear firmly in mind the more important aspect of the doctrine, or whether it represents an actual misunderstanding of the doctrine, is a matter difficult to settle. Considered as a thing in itself, as in the last analysis every poem must be, the *Monk's Tale* does, however, seem to represent a genuine misunderstanding. It seems infected with a real pessimism, a despairing disgust with life, that amounts to a kind of morbid parody of the monastic ideal. The dedicated monk renounces the world, not because he finds it disagreeable, but because he believes that the spiritual values implicit in asceticism are of a higher order than worldly values: while it may seem that he is running away from something, his impulse is ideally carrying him toward something better. The pessimist, on the other hand, recognizes no positive pole: he is renouncing something that he finds disagreeable for no other reason than that it is disagreeable.

Futhermore, it is characteristic of the pessimist that he does not really reject the values of the world at all: his strictures apply only to the disagreeable aspects of life, and when life offers him pleasures he seizes them eagerly. Thus he is constantly oscillating—as men in the later Middle Ages seem always to have been doing—between frenzied rapture and frenzied despair. In this despair, moreover, he seems to find a dismal pleasure—hence, one supposes, the popularity in the pessimistic Middle Ages of such stories as those told by Chaucer's Monk. It cannot be denied that the negative attitudes of disillusionment and disappointment were often exploited by the propagandists of monasticism—significantly the Monk has a hundred tragedies in his cell—but to confuse the religious ascetic ideal with mere pessimism is to disparage medieval Christianity, which did not forget, as the pessimist does, that a seemingly chaotic world does not imply a chaotic and unguided universe.

It is ironic that the worldly Monk should recite a series of stories that teach hatred of the world. This is certainly not what we should have expected of him; nor is it what the Host expected. It is, indeed, the Host's expectation of something truer to the Monk's real nature that makes the Monk choose the subject he does: Harry is so exhilarated by the Monk's worldliness—apparent in his triumphant virility—that he presumes to make rude jokes about him, and so puts the Monk on his dignity. To offset this imputation of worldliness he recalls the tragedies he had probably been required to read when he first entered his order. Their recitation restores his injured dignity. At the same time their nature suggests a vital defect in the Monk's conception of what rejection of the world really involves.

It seems evident both from the brusque interruption of the Monk (Chaucer's revenge on his own pompous creation) and from the witty reflections on tragedy in the *Nun's Priest's Tale* that Chaucer was aware of the fatal flaw in the series. But this is not to admit that he had composed them in any spirit of levity. The most important of his numerous sources was Boccaccio's *Falls of Illustrious Men and Women,* a similar though far longer compilation of which the Italian writer was much prouder than he was of the works for which he is now better known. Undoubtedly Chaucer wrote his own series (in his youth, one likes to think) with the utmost seriousness. In their present context Chaucer again succeeds in having it both ways. If the tragedies are to be read at all they must be read seriously, but the reader is at liberty to accept the Knight's and Host's opinion as authoritative, and skip them.

Most of the tragedies are conventional enough and need no commentary. It should be observed that the Monk, aware that at least some of them ought to present examples of a human failing, sometimes clutches rather desperately for a moral. Thus Hercules and Samson, according to him, illustrate the dire results of trusting women, and Nero, while said to be punished for his viciousness, is punished no worse than his own highly virtuous teacher Seneca: Fortune is so haphazard that life is reduced to moral chaos. The monk, a "manly man," has particular admiration for military heroes—Alexander, Caesar, Pompey, the two Peters; the only woman to receive his praise is Zenobia, a notable virago. Perhaps the tragedy of Ugolino is of greatest interest, for its source is one of the most terrifying of the encounters with damned souls that Dante records in the *Inferno*. Chaucer's version suffers badly by comparison. Dante's Ugolino is a man of vast strength of mind, as powerful and self-controlled as he is wicked, and his account of his own ending carries all the pity and terror of Greek tragedy. In Chaucer we feel only pity for a tender father suffering wrongfully and not very bravely, and the emotional force of the narrative is weakened by the emphasis laid on the pathetic little boys. In the *Inferno* Ugolino (discovered gnawing on the skull of his enemy the Archbishop) prefaces his account by prophesying that his hearer will weep, but he himself weeps neither within his tale nor in the telling of it, and Dante's reader is moved too profoundly for tears. In Chaucer the floodgates are opened. Nothing could better demonstrate the besetting vices of medieval tragedy than Chaucer's handling of this short narrative.

THE NUN'S PRIEST'S TALE

It is the nature of the beast fable, of which the *Nun's Priest's Tale* is an example, to make fun of human attitudes by assigning them to the lower animals. Perhaps no other form of satire has proved so charming throughout literary history. From Aesop's fables through the medieval French mock-epic *Reynard the Fox* (upon a version of which the *Nun's Priest's Tale* relies for its slight plot), down to La Fontaine and Br'er Rabbit, the beast who acts like a man has enjoyed general popularity. In the *Nun's Priest's Tale* one of the most charming of poets has given the genre a superbly comic expression. Yet much of the tale's humor lies neither in its plot nor in the equivalence of man and beast, but in the extraordinary dilation of the telling. For while Chaucer was endowing his feathered hero and heroine with many of the qualities of a courtly lover and his lady, he was also embellishing his tale with an ample selection of the rhetorical commonplaces of Western civilization. To analyze the effect these have on the story it is necessary to investigate briefly what rhetoric is.

The art of expressive speech and writing or, more narrowly, of persuasive speech is a fair enough definition of rhetoric. But considered as a set of formulas for expressing a recurrent idea or situation, rhetoric may amount to little more than cliché. It is also possible to think of rhetoric, as one frequently does today, as a kind of cosmetic art—that of adorning bare facts. Yet something is lacking here. The rhetorical mode of expression may be said to consist in using language in such a way as to bring about certain preferred interpretations. Compare, for example, an apparently bare statement, "The sun sets," with the rhetorical statement, "The Sun drove his chariot beyond the waters of the western seas." To the ancient mind the last statement would suggest a particular kind of order and meaning in the universe—in other words, a cosmos. This piece of rhetoric was the ancient man's way of reassuring himself that chaos would not come again with the setting of the sun. Today we probably prefer the simplicity of the first statement. Yet "The sun sets" has its residue of rhetoric: we know that the sun does not set but only seems to. We accept this inaccurate and quite rhetorical statement because we are reluctant, even when we know better, to displace ourselves from our inherited position at the center of creation. Rhetoric still stands between us and the fear of something which, even if it is not chaos, is disconcerting.

It follows that rhetoric in this sense is something more than language of adornment. It is, in fact, a powerful weapon of survival in a vast and alien universe. In our own time, as in the Middle Ages and in the Age of Homer, rhetoric has served to satisfy man's need for security and to provide a sense of the importance of his own existence and of the whole human enterprise.

It is true that rhetoric, as it operates for persuasion and self-persuasion, may become merely an instrument of deception, a matter of clichés and of superficial and contradictory thinking. One finds examples in advertising and political slogans and in the mutually inconsistent wisdom of proverbs. The excesses of rhetoric invite satire; regarded satirically, rhetoric may be taken as a kind of inadequate defense that man erects against an inscrutable reality. It is in this way that Chaucer is viewing it in the *Nun's Priest's Tale.* Most noticeably, of course, he employs the standard rhetoric of heroic poetry in order to give the utmost mock-significance to each of Chantecleer's actions. Even the best of epic heroes suffers from the handicap of being only one of an untold number of people who have lived on earth, and the fact that Achilles and Hector still have significance (if a fading one) is due to the gigantic rhetorical effort of Homer, who persuades his reader that these were the very best in their kind who ever lived. By a similar technique Chantecleer is made the best rooster that ever lived, so that his death amid the teeth of Dan Russel—if it had occurred—could have provided a tragic episode every bit as significant to mankind as the death of Hector. Or so the Nun's Priest would have us believe, what with his epic manner and his full-dress similes, his references to the fall of Troy, the burning of Rome, the destruction of Carthage, to Sinon, Ganelon, and Judas Iscariot, to the awful problems of free will and foreordination. And, if this were not sufficient to persuade us of the importance of Chantecleer to the scheme of things, the divine powers take the trouble to send the rooster a monitory dream concerning his impending fate. The logic of the comedy is unexceptionable: these are the devices that made Hector and Achilles, and hence all men in their persons, significant; will not the devices do the same for Chantecleer?

While he deals largely in the rhetorical commonplaces appropriate to epic heroes, the Nun's Priest does not ignore commonplaces less exalted. The discussion of the significance of dreams reflects one of man's most enduring attempts to enhance his importance, and the basic disagreement between the cock and the hen regarding dreams is an embarrassing instance of the rhetorical tradition's having produced two entirely antipathetic answers to the same problem. Similarly, the age-old question of woman is answered—in one breath, as it were—by two equally valid if mutually exclusive commonplaces: woman is man's ruination and woman is all man's bliss. Especially prominent is the rhetoric of "authority," by which poets assure themselves that what they are doing is unexceptionable: when the rooster's singing is compared with the singing of mermaids, the expert on mermaids' singing is named—Physiologus, whose authority presumably makes the simile respectable. It is inevitable that the Friday on which Chantecleer's near-tragedy occurs should be castigated in the terms set by that most formidable and dullest of medieval rhetoricians, Geoffrey of Vinsauf, who carried almost to its ultimate point formalization of expression and stultification of thought.

The *Nun's Priest's Tale* is full of what seem to be backward references to the preceding tales, so that it is sometimes taken as a parody-summary of all that has gone before. The reason for this is probably less that Chaucer had the other tales in mind as he wrote (indeed, he could have written the *Nun's Priest's Tale* without having any thought of the others) than that in it he employs comically all the rhetorical devices that were a part of his own poetical inheritance. But with the *Monk's Tale,* which immediately precedes, the Nun's Priest's does seem to have a more organic connection. The Monk had pitilessly labored the emasculated notion of tragedy current in the Middle Ages, with all its emphasis on the dominance of Fortune, viewed apart from human responsibility. In taking by turns the attitude toward Chantecleer of the Monk ("Oh destiny that mayst not be eschewed") and the more ethical attitude that the cock was fondly overcome by female charm (he "took his counsel of his wife, with sorrow"), Chaucer is comically exploiting a paradox the two ends of which are played against the poor narrator, caught in the middle and not knowing whether to blame fate or rooster and compromising by doing both by turns. Yet this elusive interaction between man's nature and his destiny is one of the concomitants of a far more profound kind of tragedy than anything the Monk's definition could produce: Macbeth also had his fatal influences and his deliberate wrongdoings. As a work of the intellect, even though it is wholly comic, the Nun's Priest's Tale is far more serious and mature than the Monk's. Its author might well have produced a Shakespearean tragedy—provided he could have stopped laughing.

The man who is able to maintain a satiric view toward rhetoric—the sum of the ideas by which people are helped to preserve their self-respect—is not apt to be popular with his victims. Inevitably, they will search him out to discover the pretensions under which he subsists. Aware that in the personality of the satirist will always exist grounds for rebutting the satire, Chaucer carefully gives us nothing to work on in the character of the Nun's Priest: there is no portrait of him in the *General Prologue,* and the introduction to his tale reveals only the most inoffensive of men. But in one important respect he is very like his creator: he can survey the world as if he were no part of it, as if he were situated comfortably on the moon looking at a human race whom he knew and loved wholeheartedly but whose ills he was immune from. This is the same godlike detachment that characterizes the incident of the telling of *Sir Thopas* and also, in another way, *Troilus.* It is almost as if the Creator were watching with loving sympathy and humorous appreciation the solemn endeavors of His creatures to understand the situation in which He has placed them.

THE SECOND NUN'S TALE

The *Second Nun's Tale* does not show the poet at his characteristic Chaucerian best; yet it is probably the best-told example in Middle English poetry of a saint's life. Saints' lives were an extremely popular and important form of medieval literature, typically represented in the vast compilation called the Golden Legend, from which Chaucer took the account of the martyrdom of Cecilia, following his source closely. As he says himself, he exerted no diligence to retell the story subtly, but devoted all his poetic skill to the versification of the rhyme-royal stanzas.

Medieval saints' characters vary little from one another. All possess alike an absolute confidence in the rectitude of their own beliefs and a rather ill-mannered contempt for any one who believes differently. The godly seem to require no other traits but godliness, while those who have other traits must have derived them from the devil. Lest the wicked should prove more interesting than the good they are generally presented as being as monotonously bad as the good are good. There is something at least potentially interesting about Almachius, but the potential is destroyed when he (rather arbitrarily, it seems) devises the horrible torture in which the saint meets her end. Complexity naturally disappears when everything is represented as either hell-doomed or heaven-directed, and the reader is left to admire only the technical proficiency with which the tale is told. It is when he deserts hagiography for pure fiction, as in the *Clerk's Tale,* that Chaucer is able to render the complex suffering of a saintly person.

THE CANON'S YEOMAN'S TALE

Chaucer refused to become a slave to any convention, even the self-imposed one of working within the cast of characters he established in the *General Prologue.* Before the majority of the pilgrims had been assigned even one of their proposed four tales the poet broke the pattern in order to introduce the Canon's Yeoman and, very briefly, the Canon himself. As Chaucer approached the end of his literary activity his interests apparently became increasingly dramatic, a tendency that is itself dramatized by this disruption of the symmetry of the original plan. Nothing prevented him from assigning the *Canon's Yeoman's Tale* to one of the pilgrims already introduced; but he must have felt that the vitality of the pilgrimage would be increased —as it is—by the headlong incursion of the two figures and by their sudden quarrel. At the same time, the incident lends urgency to the Yeoman's story, for the breathlessness of his arrival remains throughout his explosive description of the fraud—and the attraction—inherent in alchemy.

The Yeoman is introduced at the moment of a great crisis in his life. For many years he has served the fraudulent cleric who devotes his energies to trying to transmute baser metals into gold, and he has apparently been a docile and compliant servant. Indeed, his first words, which advertise his master's extraordinary powers, seem to be laying the foundation for some fraud to be practiced upon the pilgrims. Yet while he is in the very act of praising the Canon, something occurs that turns his praise into abuse. Just what causes the revulsion is not entirely clear. Probably it is his sudden awareness, stimulated by the Host's pointed questions, of the contrast between the brilliantly accomplished man he is praising and the dirty, sweating Canon to whom the praise is supposed to apply. Certainly his revulsion must be partly due to the Host's comment about his own complexion, the discoloration of which is the only genuine transmutation that years of alchemic experimentation have been able to effect. In any case, he turns from lies to candor, and the Canon, seeing that the game is up, rides off as hastily as he has come.

In the first part of the *Canon's Yeoman's Tale,* here called the Prologue, the speaker makes a long list of some of the many and diverse supplies required in alchemical experiments, gives a brief sampling of the esoteric terminology alchemists use, and then describes a typical experiment in which the pot containing the metals to be transmuted blows up: this accident introduces an amusing scene in which the experimenters gather up the remains of their metals, give various explanations for what went wrong, and vow to proceed more warily the next time. Chaucer always took a peculiar pleasure in rendering catalogues in rhymed verse—whether of famous doctors in the *General Prologue* or of astronomical instruments in the *Franklin's Tale*—and the catalogue in the Yeoman's tale is a masterpiece of virtuosity. One wonders, of course, where Chaucer got his seemingly detailed knowledge of alchemical terminology. That he had a strong scientific interest is shown by his preoccupation throughout his works with astronomy and by his *Treatise on the Astrolable,* which explains how one uses that astronomical implement. But whether his knowledge of alchemy came from the laboratory or the library has not been determined, though it seems as if he knew a good deal more about alchemy than he would need to know in order to write a simple satire of alchemists.

The Yeoman's tale proper is a meticulously detailed account of how a Canon (not, the Yeoman assures the Host, *his* Canon) cheats a chantry priest out of a large sum of money after allowing the priest to participate in three experiments in which baser metals—quicksilver in the first two, copper in the third—are apparently turned into silver: each transmutation depends on a different feat of sleight-of-hand. The narration is constantly interrupted—and salted—by the Yeoman's irrepressible indignation at the Canon's wickedness. But even though the Yeoman concludes that alchemy is a science the secret of which will never be found, one still feels that not all the failure and all the fraud in the world will quite overcome its fascination for him, and that in a few weeks he will be faithfully serving another dishonest alchemist. The tension in him between disgust and hope is apparent in everything he says. He is like the confirmed gambler who, while aware that he can never really win, even suspecting that the whole game is crooked in the first place, still hopes someday to make a fortune.

THE MANCIPLE'S TALE

The incident that occurs in the Introduction to the *Manciple's Tale,* like the breathless arrival of the Canon and his Yeoman before the preceding tale, attests to the poet's increasing interest in the dramatic potentialities of his design for the *Canterbury Tales.* The quarrel between the supercilious Manciple and the drunken Cook is a variation on the quarrels between the Miller and Reeve and the Friar and Summoner. In this case the incident may have failed to produce a recriminatory tale from the Cook because the point of the *Manciple's Tale* is directed against himself. His story of the tell-tale bird comes ultimately from Ovid's *Metamorphoses,* though Chaucer was also familiar with it in one or another of its medieval vernacular versions, including, probably, the *Ovide Moralisé*; this work renders Ovid's stories respectable by moralizing them, sometimes with a deadly earnest that deprives them of all life. In the present case, the moral that one ought to keep one's mouth closed about other people's misbehavior is precisely what at the end of the introduction to the tale the Host tells the Manciple and the Manciple freely admits, and he pounds the lesson home in his tale. The fact that the moral is not in any very real sense moral also suits the Manciple's character: the story represents purely prudential wisdom, giving instruction on how to get along in the world; and this the Manciple does very well with the lawyers whom he so successfully cheats.

THE INTRODUCTION TO THE PARSON'S TALE; CHAUCER'S RETRACTION

(The Parson's Tale)

On December 4, 1399, Chaucer leased (for a period of 53 years!) a house situated in the garden of Westminster Abbey in London. On June 5, 1400, he drew his pension for the last time—or at least it is under that date that his name appears for the last time in the appropriate records. And, according to the tomb that was later erected for him in the Abbey, on October 25, 1400, Chaucer died. Perhaps no entirely certain inference can be drawn from these data, but it is convenient to believe what they seem to tell us, that the poet passed the last months of his life close to the monks of Westminster. If this is true, then it is almost necessary to suppose that the *Introduction to the Parson's Tale* and *Chaucer's Retraction*—though not the *Parson's Tale* itself—were composed within the same period.

The tale with which the Parson "knits up all the feast" certainly answers to specification as a virtuous one. It is an enormously long discussion in prose of the sacrament of penance and of the seven deadly sins, apparently translated by Chaucer from the Latin of some manual directed at helping priests in the performance of their spiritual duties. Its piety does not, however, raise it into the realm of literature, and although it has moments of imaginative art it remains on the whole a tract of rather specialized interest. Scholars generally agree that the translation was made at an earlier stage in Chaucer's career, since it seems to be the source for a number of passages in the other tales. It is possible that the aging poet, aware of the imminence of his death, introduced it without revision into the *Canterbury Tales,* lest time should not be given him to produce a virtuous tale of a more poetic kind. In any case, the *Parson's Tale* would be good for the poet's and the reader's soul, and that, rather than esthetic pleasure, was the important thing.

From the literary point of view, the Parson's introduction is more exciting than his tale. To the medieval mind the allegorical implications of a pilgrimage were obvious, so that again and again the reader of medieval literature encounters the commonplace that this life is but a pilgrimage—from birth to death or from earth to heaven, the Celestial City to which every Christian soul aspires. To some of Chaucer's contemporaries his avoidance throughout most of the *Canterbury Tales* of the expected implications of the pilgrimage must have come as a surprise. It is not until they read the Parson's introduction that they would have found the journey taking on the metaphorical connotations that were hitherto lacking. Gone is the illusion of everyday reality that we have been accustomed to, replaced by a kind of spiritual realism that is for the moment far more significant. Although the Manciple began his brief story early in the morning, when he finishes it has somehow got to be four o'clock in the afternoon. The time scheme has been altered in such a way as to refer to the pilgrimage that Geoffrey Chaucer has been making for the last fifty-odd years. That pilgrimage is hastening to an end and the poet's spirit—doubtless guided by the monks of Westminster—is concerned more and more urgently with the Celestial City to which, as a good Christian despite his many sins and sinful stories, he aspires.

Over the fictional pilgrimage, which has for many years been the reflection of his own mind and which now becomes its reflection in a more personal sense, there comes something of the chill and urgency of late afternoon. There is hardly time for the telling of one more tale. The shadows are lengthening and the sun has but twenty-nine degrees to sink before darkness falls on the nine-and-twenty pilgrims. Libra, the Scales that symbolize God's justice, is ascending in the skies. Already a kind of darkness that makes recognition difficult seems to have come over the pilgrims. Where are they? At the end of a little nameless village that is surely neither on the road to Canterbury nor on the road back, but on a road that leads to a city far from England. The Host speaks to the Parson as if he had never seen him before, recognizing only the priest and knowing nothing of the man. In this suddenly alien and lonely world we must hurry to get in the last, virtuous tale. Why is it the last? Not because the grand plan that Chaucer devised has been brought close to completion, but because a grander one of a greater Creator is hurrying to its end. And so the introduction (perhaps hastily revised) concludes with the Host's injunction for haste:

> "Telleth," quod he, "youre meditacioun.
> But hasteth you, the sonne wol adown.
> Beeth fructuous, and that in litel space,
> And to do wel God sende you his grace."

These may have been the last lines of verse that Chaucer wrote.

The *Parson's Tale* is followed by *Chaucer's Retraction,* in which he specifies the sinful poems that he repents having composed. These include most of his greatest works. Many modern readers, faced by the poet's rejection of what we like best, are made acutely uncomfortable by the retraction, and attempts have been made to vitiate its force by calling it a merely conventional act of piety. But this is to defend the poet by questioning the man's integrity, and is hardly legitimate. The retraction must be taken as heartfelt. The poet was about to die and he feared for his soul. There is no doubt that from the strictest point of view—that of a medieval monk—much of what he had written was sinful. Is it not a Christian's duty to use the talents God had given him in serving the glory of God, and had Chaucer not written much that has no explicit Christian reference? (Indeed, the inclusion of such harmless poems as the *Book of the Duchess* among those Chaucer repents can only be accounted for by its failure to invoke conventional Christian consolation.) It had certainly often occurred to Chaucer that there are other ways of celebrating God's glory than through direct praise of Him, but at the close of the poet's life the voice of authority was on the other side. Logical as ever, he did what was best for his soul.

Even at the end, however, the artist in him did not entirely disappear. The retraction is a part of the *Parson's Tale* to which its first sentence refers, as does also Chaucer's prayer for the grace of true repentance. And the *Parson's Tale* is in turn a part of the literary creation known as the *Canterbury Tales* whose underlying fiction, the pilgrimage, becomes at the end a symbol of the reality of Chaucer's own life. Many of the tales he had come to deplore, but it is within their framework that he chose to make his farewell to the world. Apparently he felt that the fiction he had created was an essential—perhaps *the* essential—part of the total reality that God had created in the person of Geoffrey Chaucer.

MINOR POEMS

THE BOOK OF THE DUCHESS

Blanche, Duchess of Lancaster, the mother of the formidable prince who in the last year of Chaucer's life became King Henry IV, died of the plague in 1368. Whether Chaucer was at that time a member of the household of Blanche and her husband John of Gaunt is not entirely certain, but in any case the poet seems to have been well enough acquainted with the amiable Duchess and her husband to undertake the task of writing a poem that would both praise the dead and offer consolation to the living. In order to be at once tactful and relevant in an age when important people remarried with what now seems like indecent haste, Chaucer's poem must have been written shortly after the Duchess' death—certainly by the middle of 1370. It is thus one of his few works that can be dated with any certainty, and is probably also one of the earliest of his poems that have survived.

Based in its details on a number of French models and hence in some respects the least original of Chaucer's poems, the *Book of the Duchess* nevertheless gives an effect that is strikingly original—almost, indeed, to the point of eccentricity. The form is the highly conventional one of the dream vision and many of the incidents, and even lines, are taken directly from the works of Chaucer's French contemporaries, Froissart, Machaut, and Deschamps. But none of the many sources is in any sense a true elegy nor does any of them show the great delicacy and sensitivity of Chaucer's poem. Despite certain difficulties it offers, almost no reader will fail to sense the poem's unusual charm, and a little study will reveal the great skill of its relatively youthful author.

Either because John of Gaunt was not the sort of man who would respond favorably to a more orthodox consolation or because Chaucer felt that his imagination operated more productively outside the limits of traditional Christian theology, the poet chose to set his poem in a dream world where the mythology of the pagan past exists side by side with fourteenth-century courtly behavior. All the diverse elements that make up this dream world are bound together by a principle of universal sympathy, the symbol of which is the once-mentioned Pan, the god of Nature. The numbed, distressful, lovesick state of the Dreamer makes him sympathize naturally with the mourning Knight. Ovid's story of Ceyx and Alcyone, which arouses the Dreamer's pity and brings him indirectly the blessing of sleep, is a mirror image of the Knight's own story and an echo of the Dreamer's own sense of privation. The bright loveliness of nature on a May morning is at once a contrast to and a potential antidote for both the Knight's and the Dreamer's sorrow. The chief of the several agents that brings the Dreamer to the Knight's aid is a little dog, perhaps to us the most pleasing symbol of the sympathy that pervades Chaucer's dream world: our instinctive reaction to the bewildered puppy is, like the Dreamer's, a release of affection, an opening of the heart. In such a world the very blood of the Black Knight's body is animated by sympathy and rushes to his heart to learn the cause of his grief. And Pan, the universal god of Nature, is himself disturbed by the magnitude of the Knight's sorrow.

The Dreamer is perhaps Chaucer's first experiment with the device of the fictional narrator. It is a remarkably successful one even though the character is not, from the psychological point of view, a wholly understandable entity. He seems at times almost too stupid to be true: though he has initially overheard the Knight lament his lady's death, he keeps pestering the mourner to reveal the cause of his grief; he is so literal-minded that he is unable to penetrate the meaning of the Knight's transparent metaphor—that in a game of chess Fortune has captured the Knight's queen; when he finally extracts the truth from the Knight the Dreamer has nothing to offer except the spare comment, "It's a pity." Nevertheless, this stupid character accomplishes his mission of consolation, and that is what he is intended to do. His very density forces the Knight to sing the praises of his lady ever louder and louder, and his literalism makes the Knight eventually bow to the fact of her death. In the process the Knight has done what every bereaved person must: he has progressed from negative resistance to positive acceptance. Chaucer was, of course, far too tactful to point up a lesson in textbook style, but the Knight's speeches progressively demonstrate the fact, if not the Knight's realization of it, that despite his loss he has had much to rejoice for; and his ultimate words, "She is dead," mark a new and more positive stage in a mourner's evaluation of his experience.

Regardless of what we may think of the Dreamer's intelligence, then, he has at least caused the fictional Knight to escape the paralysis imposed upon him by his grief. That Nature, like the pagan god Pan, abhors the paralysis of grief and does everything it can to cure it is the underlying and unifying theme of the poem. If the Dreamer is stupid it is because he is an actor in a drama written by Nature and in Nature stupidity can at times have a supreme efficacy. The Dreamer opens the heart of the grieving Knight with a naïve sympathy that is not unlike the little dog's, and given release, the grief in turn releases the griever. In his handling of the Dreamer—as frequently elsewhere—Chaucer's interest is in something more significant than the verisimilitude of his fiction. He is not, after all, writing a poem about how Chaucer consoled John of Gaunt, but trying to console John of Gaunt (and readers generally) by writing a poem in which an encounter between two fictional characters reveals a profound truth about human sorrow.

When one considers that John of Gaunt was a prince of the realm, the fourth son of the reigning monarch Edward III, and that Chaucer was a young bourgeois, one must admire the adroitness of the poet. By speaking in the first person he achieves emotional immediacy, yet at the same time the consolation is achieved by almost complete self-effacement. It is not he who praises the dead lady but the fictional representative of her husband, nor is it he who presumes to offer consolation, but the sympathetic world in which he finds himself, an actor in Nature's play. It is interesting to observe that this notion of himself as a bewildered, slightly comic creature in a world manipulated by a higher power was, as time went on, to become his characteristic pose.

THE HOUSE OF FAME

The *House of Fame* is Chaucer's most curious and elusive poem, and its unfinished state suggests that Chaucer abandoned it because it got out of hand. After the mock-solemn discussion of dreams in the prologue, the narrator tells us in Book I that on a December night he dreamed he was in a wonderful temple of glass on the walls of which was depicted the whole story of Virgil's *Aeneid*. There follows a résumé of the Latin epic, recounted in such a way that the emphasis falls on the tragic love between Aeneas and Dido. After some four hundred lines of description the narrator withdraws from the temple to find himself in the middle of a vast desert. While he is wondering what he should do he sees an eagle soaring down toward him. Here Book I ends.

Book II, which is reproduced in this volume, reports the narrator's journey with the eagle up to the House of Fame, an incident whose humor enables it to stand alone. In Book III, the narrator, having arrived at his destination in mid-air, visits the Temple of Fame and discovers by what principles (or lack of them) men become famous in history. The Temple of Fame is another very ornate structure, filled with the statues of all the famous poets and historians of the past. There the goddess is enthroned and men appear before her to establish their claims in regard to fame. The goddess' dispensations are wildly whimsical. Some who have deserved and desire good fame are granted it; others equally worthy are given ill fame; others receive oblivion. Some who have deserved ill fame receive good fame, and so on. Throughout, the goddess maintains an attitude of righteous virtue, regardless of how wrong her judgments may be. After a time the narrator, aided by another bystander and by the eagle, makes his way to the nearby House of Rumor. This is an extraordinary structure of wicker, of great length, which constantly whirls about. Within the House of Rumor is a vast congregation of people exchanging gossip. The bits of information and of misinformation that they relay to one another eventually take physical shape and fly from the wicker palace to the House of Fame, where the goddess labels them, assigns them terms of life, and dispatches them to earth. In escaping from their house true and false rumors compete for priority, and the narrator observes that sometimes the true and the false join into one physical body. The narrator's observations are suddenly interrupted by a great rush of people to one corner of the room. He joins them and sees a man "of great authority" who is about to speak. Here the poem abruptly ends.

The eagle's promise that Chaucer will learn some new "love-tidings," combined with the love-story of Book I and the general consideration of rumor and fame in Book III, has led scholars to suppose that the poem is an elaborate prelude to the revelation of some fact of interest to Chaucer's circle, perhaps a royal betrothal. It is difficult, however, to see how any revelation could be other than a small tail on a large dog. Perhaps no interpretation will ever succeed in making complete sense of the poem's amorphous structure, but certain aspects of the work show a preoccupation with the problem of the relative validity of recorded history and direct experience. In Book II the narrator appears as a man entirely persuaded of the truth of old books. These suffice him and he does not feel the need of any direct experience of the things of which he reads. When the eagle, representing the empirical attitude, offers him direct experience and—indeed—imposes it on him, the narrator rejects it insofar as his helpless condition will permit, and he seems positively resentful of what he cannot reject: apparently he would much prefer to read about such exciting experiences rather than have to endure them. He behaves as if he were afraid that too much reality would force him to change the comfortable attitude he has assumed toward life. Chaucer reverts to the problem of the different versions of reality given by history and experience in his *Troilus,* and indeed, the problem is one that is reflected in many of his poems. If Chaucer intended this to be the central problem of the *House of Fame,* however, he failed to express it in entirely comprehensible terms.

THE PARLIAMENT OF FOWLS

The *Parliament of Fowls* is a poem about love that is both lyric and philosophical. The lyric aspect is provided chiefly by the figure of the unloved narrator, hopelessly seeking some kind of fulfilment in books and not discovering it even in dreams. In an old book—Macrobius' fourth-century commentary on Cicero's "Dream of Scipio"—the narrator finds a description of a universe animated by divine love. But love of this sort is not what he seeks, and the book leaves him filled with the tortured yearning of unfulfilled desire. He sleeps, and in a dream the protagonist of the book appears to him and escorts him to the garden of romantic love. To the average man this garden offers at once the greatest pleasure and the greatest pain life can give. But to the dreamer it can offer nothing, for his guide assures him that he cannot suffer either of the alternatives. Frustrated—if perhaps also coldly comforted—he enters Venus' garden and beholds all the loveliness and ugliness of carnal love. Adjoining this garden is another, presided over by Nature, a goddess also concerned with love, but in its procreative rather than romantic aspects, since she is responsible to God for life's continuance on earth. It is St. Valentine's Day, on which all the birds assemble before Nature to receive their mates. Their business is, however, impeded by a dispute among three male eagles who love the same female. The eagles' debate spreads to the lower orders of birds whose mating cannot be accomplished until the eagles' debate is settled. The lower orders express themselves as sentimentally sympathetic with or harshly hostile to the courtly-love issues involved. Finally Nature defers the settlement of the eagles' problem for a year and the other birds receive their mates. A song is sung in praise of St. Valentine. The poet wakes and vows to go on reading, in hope some time to fare the better: to him the dream has brought no satisfaction.

Philosophically the poem has surveyed love in all its wonderful variety: the divine love that animates the universe; passion, which produces the most intense joy and sorrow man is capable of; love as the procreative faculty by which God peoples the earth; and love as a unifying or disrupting social force. The treatment accorded these visions does not seem to exalt one above the other. It is not a matter of choosing either *A* or *B* or *C,* but of seeing *A* and *B* and *C* all as emanations of the mysterious force that everyone—except the narrator—seems to experience and to think he understands. For the narrator it remains incomprehensible, because he cannot feel, even though he can see, its many guises and the many attitudes—courtly, carnal, sentimental, scientific, practical, and divine—with which men approach it. He can only describe the multiform mystery. Yet it is the sense of his privation, so urgently expressed in the opening stanzas, that defines the real and great value of the principle that the poem celebrates. St. Valentine's Day symbolizes the return of spring—and love—to earth, but to the wintry narrator that spring will never come.

THE LEGEND OF GOOD WOMEN

In the fiction of the prologue to the *Legend of Good Women* Chaucer is probably giving a poetic version of an incident in his own life. According to the charge that the God of Love lays against him, Chaucer has offended the law of love—and slandered womankind—by translating the antifeminist *Romance of the Rose* and by writing of Criseide's unfaithfulness. It is reasonable to suppose that among the most influential of the women who might be offended by Chaucer's slanders was Anne of Bohemia, the attractive young wife of the reigning monarch of England, Richard II. The Queen was, of course, in a position to exact an apology from the poet, and she probably ordered him to correct the injustice he had done her sex—specifically, by devoting his time to a series of stories about good (i.e., faithful) women. It is easy to recognize in the Alceste of the prologue a symbol for Queen Anne, to whom the poem is thus an extremely tactful tribute. That in the fiction the Queen becomes the poet's defender rather than accuser is a poetic license always permitted eulogistic poetry.

The whole incident is recounted with an obliquity so subtle that the reader may easily fail to notice some of the comic ironies involved. Chaucer begins with a disquisition on credibility, establishing the principle that we must believe far more than we may verify by experience. Personally, he informs us, he loves old books which report all sorts of truths that his own experience fails to corroborate. Then, before we know what the relevance of all this is, the poet is off worshiping daisies. Indeed, the relevance of the initial discussion is never made explicit: Chaucer later returns to it only to remark that he intends to tell some old stories which we can believe or not. For the time being we are left with the daisy, which he describes as having many of the nobler attributes of a woman but which, in the poet's waking life, is nothing more than a daisy. And then, of course, within the dream the daisy turns into a woman and, indeed, a woman worthy of worship—Alceste, who according to legend offered to die in the place of her husband. This marvelously faithful woman is now a queen, and Queen Anne would be less than human if she failed to recognize herself in the heroine of so courtly a poem.

The narrator's unfailing stupidity prevents him from realizing, until the God of Love informs him, that the daisy he has been worshiping is, symbolically at least, Queen Alceste. His stupidity also is the keynote of Alceste's defense of the poet: apparently it is sufficient to enable him to translate books without knowing what they mean. All this amounts to a fine mixture of flattery, self-deprecation, and, when one comes to think of it, a brilliantly comic refusal on the poet's part to yield an inch in the estimate of the generality of womankind that is reflected in his handling of Criseide. It is not until we have finished the prologue that we understand the relevance of Chaucer's opening remarks on the credibility of old books. Old books describe faithful women and he is perfectly willing to believe old books, but personally he has never met a faithful woman and is astounded by the thousands that follow the God of Love. He has himself always preferred daisies to women—and if his daisy turns out to be the faithful woman Queen Anne, then she is the one and only exception that he has ever known: and she is a dream.

The prologue has been preserved in two forms, of which the one reproduced in this volume is generally—but not unanimously—thought to be a revision of the other. It omits Alceste's injunction to the poet that he present the completed *Legend* to the Queen at Eltham or Sheen, and the best explanation for this omission is the death of Anne in 1394, which so distressed her emotional husband that he actually ordered the destruction of the palace at Sheen where she died. (The objection that within Chaucer's dream Alceste could not symbolize Anne because Alceste's injunction mentions Anne as a distinct person is based on a mistaken notion of the consistency required by medieval allegory: within the fiction Anne and Alceste may be one and the same, but this does not preclude Anne's having, outside of the poem, a real existence which the poem recognizes.) Regardless of the priority of the two prologues, it is generally agreed that the one reproduced here has the tighter structure, although it lacks some of the charm of the other; it has been preferred largely because it gives a longer and more comic account of Chaucer's literary career.

Of the many good women that he was commanded to write about, Chaucer completed only the stories of Cleopatra, Thisbe, Dido, Hypsipyle and Medea (treated in one section, since they were both betrayed by Jason), Lucrece, Ariadne, Philomela, Phyllis, and Hypermnestra (not quite concluded). The average length of the stories is about two hundred lines. It is evident—and becomes increasingly so as the series continues—that the subject of uniformly faithful women was not one that much interested Chaucer. In short passages, particularly in the stories of

Lucrece and Ariadne, he displays his dramatic power at its best, but in general he gives the impression that he is writing with his left hand. In a way he makes a curious virtue of the necessity under which he is working, for as the stories go on his own reluctance to tell them becomes an increasingly important factor in the telling. What is initially a rather excessive use of the old convention "to make a long story short—" turns into exasperated impatience with the monotony of it all. A delightful flippancy intrudes itself in the drawing of the "morals." The injunction to show how much better women are than men is taken more and more literally, so that by the end any man, no matter how incidental to the story, becomes a deep-dyed villain and any woman, regardless of tradition to the contrary, becomes a saint. The result is a series of melodramas now excitingly told, now leavened with the common sense of wit. The *Legend* ends abruptly just before Chaucer is to draw the moral of the sad story of Hypermnestra. Whether the termination was caused by Anne's death or by the poet's revulsion at having to vary the same old moral once again we do not know. We may safely share Chaucer's relief that the task did not have to be carried on.

SHORT POEMS

The fewer than twenty short poems that have been preserved in Chaucer's name probably represent but a small part of his total output of miscellaneous verse. A court poet would have had to compose all sorts of occasional poems of an ephemeral nature that would naturally expose them to the risk of becoming lost. Indeed, most of the extant short poems have been transmitted not in the manuscripts of Chaucer's longer works but haphazardly on odd leaves of manuscripts dealing with various non-Chaucerian matters. We have enough of his short verse to be able to admire his skill in handling a number of complex verse forms and to judge that he was as original in his short flights of fancy as he was in his long narratives—and enough also to make us glad that he did not dissipate too large a portion of his energy in such compositions. The ten poems reproduced here are among the more memorable of his miscellaneous verses.

AN ALPHABETICAL HYMN TO THE VIRGIN

The *Hymn to the Virgin* is a free translation of some lines in William Deguilleville's long French allegory, *The Pilgrimage of Human Life,* and is as superior to its original as it is independent of it. Even so, the passion of the prayer is not maintained with equal intensity through all twenty-three stanzas and a sense of strain occasionally betrays itself. According to an amiable legend, Chaucer made the translation at the request of the same Blanche of Lancaster whose death is lamented in the *Book of the Duchess,* and the poem may well be an early one; the stanza form is the same as that of the *Monk's Tale,* presumably also an early composition.

It should be noted that in medieval handwriting *i* was not distinguished from *j,* nor *u* from *v.* While *w* was a distinct letter in English, Chaucer apparently chose to consider it nothing more than a double *u* and omitted it. For *x* he substituted the Greek *chi,* which has the form of *x* but the sound of *ch* in *Christ.*

MERCILESS BEAUTY

While not certainly attributable to Chaucer, *Merciless Beauty* (which may be a group of three poems) has a characteristic Chaucerian ring and is generally accepted as his. The first two sections employ the typical imagery and extravagant emotion of the courtly-love lyric—the power of the lady's eyes to slay the lover, the struggle between her native pity and her *daunger*—her natural tendency to resist the loss of identity that love involves—and so on. The third section is a highly uncourtly if practical statement that the poet, having fallen out of love, intends to stay out. Such an attitude is unthinkable for the true courtly lover, who is expected to love his lady forever no matter how badly she treats him. The third section contains what seems to be a reference to Chaucer's plumpness.

TO ROSAMOND

To Rosamond is another variation on the courtly-love lyric. The extravagance of courtly images and attitudes is exaggerated and transferred from the realm of the ideal to the realm of the real:

the abused courtly lover might well produce a flood of tears but he would hardly measure them by the vatful, and he might be overwhelmed with love, but not like a fish served buried in sauce. The images applied to Rosamond make her perhaps a bit too crystalline and brittle. And while the convention of the hopeless lover's everlasting fidelity is maintained, the poet's presumably woeful state seems nevertheless to leave him rather comfortable, not to say downright jolly.

COMPLAINT TO HIS PURSE

Complaint to His Purse is a third variation on the courtly lover's poem in praise of his lady—in this case his purse. The imagery commonly applied to the lady is here highly confusing so far as any image of a lady is concerned but perfectly logical with regard to a purse. Ladies, like coins, should be golden, and like purses they should not be light (i.e., fickle). On the other hand, they should not be heavy either, as purses should be.

The envoy is addressed to Henry IV. In a document apparently back-dated three days after he had been accepted as king in 1399 Henry renewed and increased the pension Chaucer had received under Richard.

TO HIS SCRIBE ADAM

To Adam records in the rhyme royal of *Troilus* Chaucer's exasperation with his scribe's bad copying of that poem and of the translation of Boethius. We doubtless owe to Adam's carelessness many of the textual difficulties that we have inherited. But while medieval scribes have always enjoyed a reputation for supreme inefficiency, it might be said in Adam's defense that since none of Chaucer's works have come to us in the poet's handwriting, we cannot be sure that there was not some excuse for Adam's errors.

ENVOY TO BUKTON

The *Envoy to Bukton* is an occasional poem produced by the poet's friend's announcement of his forthcoming marriage—the kind of verse that might today be read at a bachelor dinner. Chaucer's simple advice—*Don't*—is expressed with tortuous deviousness. Behind the poem lies not only Christ's failure to reply to Pilate's question, "What is truth?"—referred to in the first two lines—but also the statement, "The truth shall make you free." The poet pretends that he has promised—i.e., has given his *trouthe*—to tell Bukton of the woe in marriage, but he cannot be true to his word, thus exemplifying what Christ's silence before Pilate was presumed to mean, that no man is entirely true. But the reason Chaucer cannot be entirely true is that, if the truth shall make you free, it follows by the laws of choplogic that you cannot be true unless you are free, and Chaucer is afraid that he himself may yet exchange his freedom for the bondage of remarriage. As a result he says that he will not describe marriage as the horrible thing which—by a comic use of the rhetorical device of *praeteritio*—he proceeds to say it is. Having presumably failed of his promise, he recommends that Bukton read what the Wife of Bath has to say on the subject.

ENVOY TO SCOGAN

The *Envoy to Scogan* is a mock-solemn chiding poem occasioned by Scogan's having renounced his lady shortly before a very rainy spell. Chaucer deduces that the rainfall represents Venus' tears at Scogan's renunciation of love, and reproaches his friend for angering her son Cupid. The latter, however, will not avenge himself by blighting Scogan's chances in love, for which both Scogan and Chaucer are too old, but by causing the failure of their poetical efforts to help other lovers. This will mean that the poets like Chaucer and Scogan will get no reward. The envoy picks up the motif of reward. Chaucer, apparently living in isolation at Greenwich on the Thames, implores Scogan, living at the royal court in Windsor on the Thames, to be mindful of his friend in such a way that it will do him some practical good.

LACK OF STEADFASTNESS

Lack of Steadfastness is an exercise in the genre of advice to kings, in this case Richard II. Chaucer should probably not be given too much credit for assuming this role of moral counselor to the monarch. Kings in the Middle Ages received a very large amount of good advice from court poets, probably as part of the poets' duties. It may be said, however, that Chaucer's poem, while not inapplicable in many reigns, was particularly relevant to Richard's.

GENTILESSE

That the virtue of *gentilesse*—in which is combined courtesy of manner with courtesy of mind—is not the inevitable adjunct of aristocratic birth though most appropriate to it is a medieval commonplace. It forms, for instance, the main theme of the old hag's sermon to her young husband in the Wife of Bath's Tale and is embodied in the person of the humbly born Griselda. The present poem with its elevated but by no means vehement tone is Chaucer's most succinct expression of the idea. It is important to observe that the doctrine, which, of course, has its origins in Christ's teaching, implies only the moral democracy of mankind and was never transferred by the Middle Ages into the political or even sociological realm. The same man who, like Chaucer, would argue for the moral equality of men, would support political and social autocracy to his dying day.

TRUTH

The story that Chaucer composed *Truth* on his deathbed is highly improbable, but it does point up the high regard the poet held for the quality of *trouthe* throughout his literary career. *Trouthe* is exalted again and again in his works, positively as the Knight's principal virtue and, in the *Franklin's Tale,* as the highest contract that men may keep, and negatively as the quality that Criseide most offends. It is difficult to give a very precise meaning to the word in Middle English, just as it is difficult to define exactly what Christ meant when He said to His disciples, "And ye shall know the truth, and the truth shall make you free"—which is the text upon which Chaucer's poem relies. Certainly any definition must include the truth of revealed Christianity, but aside from this theological significance it has the moral meaning of "integrity" and the philosophical meaning of "reality." Since these are also attributes of God—to whom Chaucer's contemporary William Langland sometimes assigns the allegorical name Truth—it is perhaps permissible to identify the quality with everything that is godlike in man.

The emphasis that Chaucer's ballade gives the term is philosophical. One must remain detached from the turmoil of this world, must be able to assume a relaxed attitude amid the complexities of existence. Earth is not reality, but a mere shadow of the great reality that resides ultimately in God, toward which the pilgrimage of life is directed. Chaucer's metaphors are characteristically homely and practical, very much of this world. And though it is not our home, wrestling and climbing, crock and awl invest it with some of the charm that Chaucer never fails to implant in his pictures of the only reality that we have experienced. The old attitude of delighted involvement in a world from which one must remain philosophically detached is reasserted. Man is an animal whose real country is elsewhere, but as an animal he is deeply implicated in the world into which he was born. This paradox is the source of some of Chaucer's best poetry. With characteristic lightness of touch he marshals his poem *Truth* in such a way that the envoy to his friend Vache reminds him that he is an animal (*vache* is French for "cow"), while it enjoins him to hold the high spiritual way.

TROILUS AND CRISEIDE

CHAUCER'S LONGEST SINGLE POEM is his greatest artistic achievement and one of the greatest in English literature. It possesses to the highest degree that quality, which characterizes most great poetry, of being always open to reinterpretation, of yielding different meanings to different generations and kinds of readers, who, no matter how they may disagree with one another on even its most important points, nevertheless agree in sharing the profoundly moving experience the poem offers them. Its highly elusive quality, which not only permits but encourages a multiplicity of interpretations, is in no way the result of incompetence on the part of the poet, but something carefully sought after as the best way of expressing a complex vision.

Chaucer is believed to have completed the work about 1385 or 1386, with some fifteen years of productivity remaining to him. Only extraordinary resourcefulness could bring it about that, having accomplished in *Troilus* what might well seem the principal work of his life, he was able to turn to other themes and other attitudes with undiminished energy and enthusiasm for experimentation. Readers occasionally wonder why romantic love—which is both a theme and an attitude—plays so little part in the *Canterbury Tales* that employed the last years of his life: the explanation lies in *Troilus*. Chaucer was apparently aware that he could not surpass his own treatment of this subject. And magnificent as the Canterbury collection is, both in the large conception and in the individual tales, *Troilus*' grandeur remains unsurpassed.

The source of the poem is one of Boccaccio's youthful works, the *Filostrato* (the Love-Stricken, according to Boccaccio's false etymology), a passionate narrative of 5700 lines in stanzaic Italian verse, completed before 1350, probably about 1340. Boccaccio's poem, in the original Italian and in a French translation, furnished Chaucer the essential plot, most of the narrative details—

though Chaucer made a number of important additions—and even with a number of lines readily adapted to translation into English. Yet the qualities of the two poems are entirely different, and Chaucer's is, artistically speaking, by far the more original. In the clear, brilliant light of the Italian work everything seems fully realized, fully understood. One reads with interest, admiration, and excitement: the mind's eye is filled. Yet there is little in the poem that does not meet the eye, and the reader does not tend to re-create what he has seen after he no longer sees it. By contrast, Chaucer's poem is mist-enshrouded: the sun does, indeed, break through at times, but things are difficult to see steadily for more than a short period, reappear in changed shape, become illusory, vanish; as the poem progresses one finds oneself groping more and more in a world where forms are indistinct but have infinite suggestiveness; the mind creates and re-creates; and at the end one has not so much beheld an experience objectively as lived it in the emotions.

As in so many of Chaucer's poems, the guise of the narrator is important to an interpretation of the work. At the outset this seems to be the familiar one of the unloved servant of the God of Love, the man whose inexperience renders him singularly ill-fitted to write a romance, but who will nevertheless perform the pious act of translating—of all things!—an unhappy love story. As in the *Parliament of Fowls,* the value of love within the poem is heightened by the narrator's exclusion from it, his yearning toward it. But this lyrical function of the narrator is in *Troilus* less important than his dual, paradoxical function as a historian whose knowledge of the story is wholly book-derived and as an invisible yet omnipresent participant in the action. It is as a historian that he first presents himself—a rather fussy, nervous scholar who has got hold of some old books, particularly one by Lollius, that tell the story of the Trojan lovers. This he means to translate, although he complains that his sources fail to give as much information as they ought. Nevertheless, they present the essentials: the sorrow Troilus suffered before he won Criseide, and how she forsook him in the end (Bk. I, 55–56). Starting out with such inadequate and unpromising data, the historian proceeds to re-create the story as if he himself were living it without knowing its outcome. His second guise, that of the participant, unlike the guise of the historian, is largely implicit, a matter of the emotional intensity and lack of objectivity with which he approaches the characters. As the poem proceeds, the tension between the two attitudes, the historian dealing with incontrovertible fact, the participant speaking from equally incontrovertible emotional experience, increases until it becomes almost unendurable. By the beginning of Book IV (lines 15–21) the narrator's love for Criseide has become such that when he finds himself forced to face the issue of her perfidy he comes close to denying the truth of his old books. *For how Criseide Troilus forsook,* he begins, forthrightly enough; but reluctance to credit the bare statement causes him to soften it:

> Or at the leeste, how that she was unkinde,
> Moot hennesforth been matere of my book,
> As writen folk thurgh which it is in minde:
> Allas that they sholde evere cause finde
> To speke hire harm–and if they on hire lie,
> Ywis, hemself sholde han the vilainye.

It is a strange historian who becomes so emotionally involved with the personages of his history that he is willing to impugn the reliability of the sources upon which his whole knowledge of those personages presumably depends.

These two divergent attitudes of the narrator come to form an image of the philosophical speculation that permeates much of the poem: is it possible in this world to maintain a single firm idea of the reality of any given human situation or character? This speculation may be best illustrated in its bearing on Criseide, upon whom so much of the emotional force of the poem centers. History records the literal fact that Criseide proved, in the end, unworthy of the love Troilus bore her. This is the flattest, most basic, and least assailable of realities. (At the time Chaucer was writing, Criseide's character may not yet have suffered the deterioration that, by Shakespeare's time, made her a kind of literary model of the unfaithful woman; nevertheless Chaucer's method of handling her is essentially what it would have been if the process had already taken place.) Despite our knowledge of the ending, the narrator's loving presentation of Criseide in the course of the poem makes us feel the powerful attraction that brought about Troilus' love; and we are even persuaded that she was worthy of it. Indeed, *Troilus* gains something of the poignancy of the elegy by the very fact that we are aware of Criseide's eventual perfidy at the same time the narrator is depicting the profound spell she casts—just as we know that Blanche, in the *Book of the Duchess,* is dead even while the Black Knight describes the charm of her vitality. History tends to pronounce judgment on the final perfidy of Criseide as effectively nullifying her positive worth as a human being; but the historical point of view does not exhaust the reality of Criseide as the heroine of the poem.

It is true that at the end of the poem we are left with two widely different versions of Criseide's reality, versions made mutually exclusive by the conventions of romance. These conventions make it impossible for a heroine worthy of love to prove faithless; and ultimately we must, of course, bow to the fact of her faithlessness. We must remember, however, that it was Chaucer's aim to make the reader suffer vicariously the experience of Troilus. The poet therefore creates in the person of Criseide one of the most alluring of heroines; and more, he persuades us that her downfall does not so much falsify our first judgment of her as compel us to see the tragic nature of reality, in which the best so often becomes the worst.

Criseide's most emphatically displayed characteristic is amiability—that is, lovability: she has almost all the qualities that men might hope to encounter in their first loves. This is perhaps the same as saying that she is above all feminine, suggesting for a young man like Troilus the compelling mystery and challenge of her sex. She is lovely in appearance, demure yet self-possessed, capable of both gaiety and gravity, glamorous in the truest sense of the word. Although she says nothing really witty, she responds to Pandarus' wit in such a way as to seem witty; her constant awareness of implications beneath the surface of the situation suggests, if it does not prove, intelligence. With her uncle and with Troilus she has the curiously endearing charm that arises from her consciousness, humorously and wryly expressed, of her own complicity in the events that befall her. The grace and tenderness with which she finally yields to Troilus (Bk. III, 1210–11) are almost magically appealing.

But Chaucer did something more than present Criseide as the completely agreeable heroine; he also suggested in her a really complex human being, filled with all sorts of latent qualities which are much more than mere enhancements of her magnetism. Chaucer's presentation, indeed, is so full as to invite his readers to find in Criseide the seeds of her eventual falseness;

but Criseide's potentialities as a human being, so brilliantly sketched as partly to justify calling *Troilus* a psychological novel, elude us in the end. Several excellent critics have purported to find in this or that one of her qualities the definitive clue to her betrayal, but others continue to feel that the mainsprings of her action lie hidden. It seems to follow that if the poet were trying to make her motivation psychologically clear, he failed badly. It is, however, certain that this was not his purpose. Instead, he meant to present in Criseide a broad range of the undefined but recognizable potentialities inherent in human nature.

Our longest and seemingly most penetrating view into Criseide's character is afforded by Book II (596 ff), when we are shown her reactions to the news her uncle brings her about Troilus' love. These reactions are filled with apparent clues to her basic character, but when analyzed they lead to ambiguous conclusions. Criseide is much concerned with Troilus' high estate as a prince of Troy, and this concern might be interpreted as indicative of opportunism; conversely, because her already precarious situation in the city might make it dangerous to refuse him, her concern might be interpreted as fearfulness. If the fact of her concern, regardless of what it springs from, is taken as an indication of an overcalculating nature, then the impression is counterbalanced by her involuntary moment of intoxication when she sees Troilus, in all his martial glory, riding homeward from battle. This incident in turn might suggest an oversensual nature; but the circumspection with which, a little later, she considers the whole affair might well reinforce an impression of her frigidity. Again, her inability to make up her mind might be taken to prove her indecisiveness and ineffectuality; on the other hand, since the problems she is facing are entirely realistic, it might be used to prove her native practicality.

The narrator is of singularly little assistance to the reader who is trying to solve the enigma. On every crucial psychological issue both he and his old books are silent. We do not know, though we may suspect, what Criseide thought when Pandarus told her Troilus was out of town the day she came to dine. We never know to what extent she was influenced by her uncle's specious, often self-contradictory, arguments. And the narrator's explanations are even worse than his silences. For instance, just after Criseide experiences the moment of intoxication mentioned above, the narrator pauses to consider the hypothetical objection of some envious person that she was falling in love too fast (Bk. II, 666 ff). With a fine show of indignation he protests that she did not fall in love immediately: she merely began to incline toward Troilus, who had to win her with long service. The effect of this kind of explanation—of which there are a number in the poem—is complex, not to say chaotic. The reader, who may never have thought that Criseide is proceeding too fast, is suddenly encouraged to think she is by the narrator's gratuitous denial. The reader is made, as it were, an involuntary critic of the action instead of a mere spectator. Moreover, he is made to judge Criseide according to a norm that the narrator's tone assumes to be well known but that is in fact undefined and totally unknown, namely, the decorous rate of speed with which a woman should fall in love. Finally, having cleared Criseide of a charge which only he has made, the narrator asserts, in the very next stanza, that it was not her fault but Troilus' destiny that she should fall in love with him so soon. Analyzed by the intellect alone, the passage seems to suggest that Criseide did fall in love too quickly. Yet it precedes the far longer one in which she considers the whole matter so carefully that some critics have accused her of proceeding too deliberately!

The fact is that we do not read poetry with the intellect alone, and that when poetry makes two contradictory statements they do not cancel each other out. Both remain as part of the essential poetic truth, which is not the same thing at all as logic. There is surely no abstract, logical, ideal course of action for a woman falling in love, but we can recognize the process as being truly represented by Criseide. Some parts of her nature are driving her forward with a speed that is utterly terrifying to the rest of her nature, and a bewildering variety of motives assert themselves in turn. But however we analyze these, in the long run we can say with assurance only that they are human. Any one of them, given a development which the poem resolutely refuses to permit, might become the reason for her eventual betrayal: mere timidity, mere opportunism, mere sensuality, mere inefficiency—even mere femininity. As it stands, however, we are emotionally no more prepared for the denouement than Troilus, though we have had one important advantage over him: we have been permitted to see, and have been disturbed by, suggestions of depths in Criseide that her lover could not have seen. Our confidence in her is less serene, particularly as a result of the narrator's reassurances. It may be that her very elusiveness makes us nervous. If so, that is as it should be, since the only possible resolution of the two realities mentioned earlier lies in the unpredictability, the instability, of even the most lovely of mortal women.

Just as in later literature Criseide was to become the type of a faithless woman, so her charming, witty, intelligent uncle Pandarus was, by a worse fate, to become the type of a pimp. In a long conversation in Book III (238–420) Pandarus and Troilus discuss, among other things, the implications of Pandarus' helping Troilus win Criseide. The conclusion they come to is less than satisfactory: Pandarus' help is not the act of a procurer because he receives no reward for it. Thereafter the matter is not one of the overt issues of the poem, though in his last speech to Troilus (Bk. V, 1734–36) Pandarus reverts to it almost as if he foresaw the deterioration of his name Pandar to pander. And while not overt, the issue once raised can never be wholly banished from the mind. Parallel to the question the poem raises about Criseide, "Is her reality that of a worthy lover or that of an unfaithful wench?" is the question it raises about Pandarus' assistance of Troilus: "Is this the action of a loyal friend or of a mere pimp?"

History—in this case later literary history—has answered the question to the detriment of Pandarus, but the answer this poem gives is less absolute. The reader is assured by everyone—by Troilus, by Pandarus himself, by the narrator—that what Pandarus does is done wholly because of his devotion to Troilus, and surely the moralist must admit that human action is qualified by the motives of the agent. Yet, just as was the case with Criseide, when we watch his character in action we seem to glimpse potentials—undefined, to be sure—that are not of a piece with the notion of a friend acting with entire altruism. In general he seems, like his niece, a person of great charm: gay, cheerful, witty, mocking and self-mocking, friendly, helpful, practical, intelligent, sympathetic, loyal—one could hardly wish for a better companion or friend. But despite these qualities, one's confidence in him does not remain altogether secure. Perhaps his pleasure in arranging this affair is too great. The brilliant comedy he performs at the lovers' bedside—a touch of the *Miller's Tale*—is perhaps suggestive of some vital flaw in his nature (and the narrator does nothing to improve the situation by failing to send Pandarus off to his own chamber). Even the delightful scene of Pandarus' visit to Criseide's bedside after Troilus has departed is not without a hint of prurience. In the long run, it may be said of the complexity of Pandarus, as of the complexity of Criseide, that it displays such a rich array of human qualities that we are at a loss in analyzing his ultimate motives and character.

Pandarus bears a relation to the problem of reality—and hence to the philosophical speculation that is carried on in the poem—in another way. He is what would generally be called today a thoroughgoing realist. Paradoxically, this seems to mean that he has no respect for reality at all. For him, things are whatever one makes them. To accomplish a given action, all one has to do is manipulate the situation so as to produce the proper pressures on the actors. It does not matter in the least if these pressures are in reality nonexistent; it only matters that the actors should think them real. In putting his philosophy to work, Pandarus becomes the master-spinner of illusions. A persecutor from whom Criseide needs protection is conjured up out of thin air. A dinner party is manipulated with excruciating attention to detail so that Criseide may be introduced to Troilus under the most respectable of circumstances. When Criseide must be induced to receive Troilus in her bedchamber, a rival lover named Horaste, whom Criseide had never smiled upon and Troilus had never felt jealous of, emerges full-blown from Pandarus' fertile mind to produce the necessary pressure. And if Pandarus cannot actually produce rain, his foreknowledge that rain will come serves the magician's purpose of insuring that his dinner guest will stay the night. The love affair itself seems to result largely from the illusions Pandarus creates for the paralyzed Troilus and the passive Criseide. One would not be surprised if he were to dictate Troilus' first letter to Criseide and then to dictate her response, so close does he come to being the author of a living fiction.

Upon the significance of all this illusion-spinning the poem makes no overt comment. It even fails to distinguish clearly between real and illusory pressures exerted on Criseide: for instance, we do not know whether Pandarus' account of his discovering Troilus' love-sicknesses (Bk. II, 505–53) is in the realm of fact or merely a charming invention with which to please Criseide. But in the poem's totality the implications of Pandarus' illusions cannot be avoided, because we know that in the end

Criseide's love for Troilus will prove to be a kind of illusion. Moreover, the dominant role the illusions play in the love affair, whether commented on or not, forces them on our consciousness, and once more we experience a sense of insecurity. This is embodied in the poem by the interchange between the lovers when their love is consummated (Bk. III, 1338–52); both of them, especially Troilus, express uncertainty whether such bliss can in fact be true.

Pandarus continues a realist and a would-be manipulator of realities until the end, when reality defeats him. His first reaction on hearing that Criseide must leave the city is that the love affair is finished. He tries to persuade Troilus to give her up (Bk. IV, 380 ff), to forget about her, and when that practical approach fails, as it is doomed to, he tries another equally practical one, equally doomed to fail: forcefully to prevent her going. When Troilus replies, with his usual integrity, that he cannot constrain Criseide against her will, Pandarus observes that if Criseide consents to leave Troy, Troilus must consider her false (Bk. IV, 610–15). With this speech—which, incidentally, is the most strikingly revealing of several of Pandarus' reflections on Criseide in the last two books—his effective role in the poem is completed. From then on all he can do is act as go-between. His efforts to rearrange reality in order to preserve the love affair are paltry and futile. After Criseide's departure from Troy we see him upholding Troilus' hopes even when he himself recognizes their futility, and while in the earlier books Pandarus' attempts to uphold illusion did not seem offensive, now they seem the work of a half-hearted trickster. It is almost as if the reality he had tortured were having its revenge on him by redefining his actions as those of a mere procurer: for Criseide, after all, becomes little better than a whore. In the end Pandarus—and Pandarus alone—accepts history's version of Criseide: by saying, in his pathetic last speech (Bk. V, 1731–43), that he hates her, he makes clear that for him any other value she may have seemed to possess has been canceled out. He submits to the ultimate reality as Troilus, who can never "unlove" Criseide, refuses to do; yet one has felt that Pandarus' love for his niece was, in its way, as great as Troilus'.

Troilus, the hero of the poem and the most important of its personages, may seem in some respects less interesting than Pandarus or Criseide. If, however, he lacks their human variety, his *trouthe,* his integrity, makes him in the long run a more fully realized person. This integrity, the quality that he will not surrender even to keep Criseide with him, is the one human value the poem leaves entirely unquestioned: it is because of it that Troilus is granted his ultimate vision. It places him, of course, in sharp contrast with Criseide and her *untrouthe,* and since one of the meanings of *trouthe* is reality, he emerges as more real than she. The sad fact that integrity does him no practical good does not in any way impair its value; indeed, its value seems enhanced by its preventing him, at least on one occasion, from attaining an apparent good. If he had been a different person—a Diomede, for instance—he might well have used force to stop Criseide's exchange. This is what Pandarus advises and what both narrator and reader momentarily find themselves hoping for. But Troilus is acutely aware of both the public and the private implications of such an act. Criseide's exchange had been legally determined by the parliament and duly ratified by King Priam, and to prevent it forcefully would be to substitute anarchy for law: the Trojan war had itself been caused by Paris' rape of Queen Helen, and to seize Criseide would be once again to risk precipitating endless violent countermeasures. Furthermore, according to the medieval conventions of courtly love, the lover was the servant of his mistress—as the word *mistress* still suggests—and for the servant to overrule the mistress was unthinkable. As it frequently does, the courtly convention here merely articulates a real factor in the relationship of civilized men and women. A lover cannot impose his will upon his love, for unless she remains at all times possessed of free will, love itself becomes meaningless and the love affair vitiated. Similarly, to seize her would be inevitably to disclose their love affair and ruin her good name, which, according to the courtly code, he was sworn to protect. In view of these matters, for Troilus to "ravish" Criseide would be for him to violate his own nature, which, as Criseide perceives, is one of moral virtue, grounded upon truth.

But if Troilus is the only unequivocally worthwhile person in the poem, why, one must ask, is he its principal sufferer? Troilus ascribes his misery to the operation of Fortune, or malevolent fate. A heavy atmosphere of fatality does, indeed, hang over the poem, so that even if the reader had not been told the outcome of the love affair he might feel it inevitable that Troilus should in the end fall, like Troy. Yet with one exception all the specific incidents, although the narrator may invoke for them the causality of the stars, seem equally attributable to the action of one of the three actors in the love tragedy. The exception is the intervention of Criseide's forgotten father Calchas, an intervention that comes from his sure foreknowledge of the city's doom and that is beyond the control of Pandarus or the lovers. Elsewhere causality is ambiguous. For instance, the narrator ascribes to astrological influences entirely remote from Criseide's control the rain which prevented Criseide's leaving her uncle's house. On the other hand, we are aware that the rain had been foreseen by Pandarus, so that what may be deemed fate in its relation to Criseide is at the same time mere machination on the part of Pandarus. Nor are we sure enough of Criseide's state of mind in accepting her uncle's invitation—the narrator has been marvelously ambiguous about that too—clearly to exonerate her from an acquiescence in a foreseen fate so prompt as to make fate's role negligible. But here as elsewhere the impression of fatal influence is not canceled out by the impression of human responsibility: both impressions remain and even unite into a single impression poetically truer than either by itself. Similarly, Troilus' failure to prevent Criseide from leaving Troy, while it is the result of his own free will, might still be ascribed to fate, for in order to have stopped her Troilus would have had to be someone other than Troilus, and this he could not be.

In a more universal and more tragic sense, the impossibility of a human being's becoming anything but what he is is one of the principal points—perhaps the principal point—that the poem makes, and it is toward this point that the poem has been steadily moving. The form, as has been said above, is that of a history, the end of which is known, being lived by personages who do not know their end, and presented at times as if neither narrator nor reader knows it. Preoccupied constantly during the presentation with the charm and delight of humanity as represented by Criseide and Pandarus, we can little more believe that things will turn out as they do than can Troilus. The fact that they turn out as they do almost seems, at times, a violation of our idea of reality; within the poem we are now and again apt to ascribe the ending to a malevolent fate which, in order to bring about what it foresees, contorts and constrains events and persons from their natural course. This is the ultimate conclusion of which Troilus is capable in his lifetime. His long soliloquy in Book IV (958–1078) on predestination and free will comes in its tortured circularity to nothing more than a statement that what God has foreseen must be—that free will does not exist. This soliloquy, of course, precedes any suspicion on his part of Criseide's infidelity, so that he is not forced to consider the problem of her free will operating evilly. When suspicions have once occurred, he is no longer able to think even as clearly as he does here, but vacillates pathetically between the two conflicting realities, Criseide's apparently true love and Criseide's faithlessness. His still relatively happy ignorance stops him in his soliloquy from going to the extreme of accusing his god of devising a plot that does not fit its characters; but this is an accusation that occasional readers have, with some reason, made against Chaucer the poet, just as Chaucer the narrator comes close to making it against his old books.

But to the profoundly medieval, profoundly Christian Chaucer there could be no other plot because there could be no other characters. According to some medieval thinkers, the whole duty of the historian was to find in recorded history the image of instability: it is in this sense that the *Monk's Tale* presents history, bad as the tale is. The premise underlying such a definition of history is that natural, fallen man is unstable. Chaucer, while surely not bound to any arbitrary point of view, presents in *Troilus and Criseide* a pattern of human instability. Criseide is its chief exponent in terms of human character; Pandarus in terms of human action. Troilus comes, because of his *trouthe,* as near to stability as man may come; but within a world where mutation is the law—and in a world in which the stability of a Christian God does not exist—it does him no good. Given Boethius or Christian doctrine, Troilus might have progressed beyond the point he does in his soliloquy on foreordination. As it is, he concludes where Boethius began in his *Consolation of Philosophy,* before Philosophy had persuaded him that he must not commit himself wholly and exclusively to this unstable world. Troilus' *trouthe* is, as has been said above, a real value; but within the terms set by the poem, it must remain only a moral value, imitating one aspect of God, who is *Trouthe,* but hopelesly limited in other respects. Despite its alternate meaning, reality, it cannot help Troilus perceive ultimate reality, which only God can perceive; conversely, it cannot defend him against illusion—the illusion of Criseide's stability, of the enduring power of human love. It cannot, in short, enable him to see that of all the conflicting realities the poem presents none is in the end real, since compared to the reality of God no earthly substance has reality.

The poem comes to its tragic conclusion by no such bald statement as the above. We have seen how in the ambiguity of the characterization of Criseide and Pandarus there has been, since the beginning, the potential of instability. One might say that in their very elusiveness, their unknowability, resides equally the image of unreality. And we have since the beginning been fully aware of where the story is leading, though our willingness to forget is the product of Chaucer's art. As the poem approaches its climax—or anticlimax—the poet so manipulates us that while we continue our intense involvement with the characters, we begin to see them increasingly in the light of historical generalization. Halfway through the fifth book this manipulation appears most brilliantly. It is the ninth night after Criseide's departure, and we are taken to the Greek camp to see how she is faring with her plots to return to Troy, as she had promised, on the tenth day (Bk. V, 686 ff). Her pathetic soliloquy, so futile, so devoid of resource, so spiritless, leaves us infinitely saddened. The narrator, seemingly in hot pursuit of his story, turns quickly to Diomede, and for a moment we enter that blunt, aggressive, unillusioned mind. Diomede's interior monologue completed, the narrator, as if suddenly recalling his own failure to characterize Diomede earlier, gives us a one-stanza pen-portrait of him. And then, by a curious afterthought, he gives a three-stanza description of Criseide and a two-stanza description of Troilus (Bk. V, 806–40). The quality of these is, contextually, strange in the extreme: they are impersonal, trivial, oversimplified—as if a historian had collected all the information there was about several persons of no special significance and were listing it, not because of its inherent interest, but because the historian's duty is to assemble and preserve any sort of scraps turned up during his research. And indeed these scraps are in a very real sense the oldest historical material relating to the story of Troilus and Criseide, the sparse material from which the full-grown story eventually sprang. Chaucer's source for the portraits is not Boccaccio, but rather a sixth-century narrative of the fall of Troy ascribed to Dares the Phrygian. This book pads out its paltry fiction with brief descriptions of important people concerned with the Trojan war, among them Diomede, Troilus, and Criseide, described just as Chaucer describes them in Book V but still some centuries removed from the relationship later writers were to give them. When, nearing the end of his poem, Chaucer saw that it was time to turn from the guise of the passionately committed participant to the guise of the objective, remote, detached historian, he did so with a vengeance. Perhaps nowhere else in the poem are the two conflicting versions of reality more boldly juxtaposed. Certainly nowhere else is the shock so great as when the historian, having listed a miscellany of Criseide's attributes, some trivial but all agreeable enough, brings the portrait to the muted conclusion:

> Tendre-herted, sliding of corage—
> But trewely I can nat telle hir age.

Sliding of corage: the simple unemphatic statement of Criseide's instability of heart is not even the climax of the portrait. From the point of view of the realistic historian, human nature is capable only of anticlimax.

The sudden re-emergence of the detached historian at this point in Book V provides a kind of foretaste of the dominant mood in which the poem concludes; but the narrator's other guise continues to reappear whenever Criseide is mentioned. Indeed, Chaucer's manipulation of the two guises, and through them of the reader, is nowhere more adroit than in his handling of Criseide's betrayal. Time and again while the narrative inexorably demonstrates the progress of her infidelity the narrator leaps to her defense, and by the very inadequacy of the defense reinforces the reader's condemnation of her. The most striking instance of this technique occurs after Diomede has visited Criseide on the eleventh day, when she has already broken her promise to Troilus. The interview she has with Diomede is not described; instead the narrator rapidly summarizes all the later history of her amorous dealings with the Greek (Bk. V, 1030–50). And then, having given to the whole history of her treachery the emotional impact of a single action committed in a day or two, he indignantly asserts that while his books are silent on this subject, all this successful wooing by Diomede must have taken a long time! As if this were not enough, he carries us back to Troy to show us Troilus, standing on the walls, still scanning the outlying roads for his beloved. Months of action have rushed by in the Greek camp, but in Troy it is still only the tenth day, the day Criseide is to return.

Thus the poem moves with mounting emotional force to its conclusion. The actual ending of the poem (Bk. V, 1765 ff)—generally though incorrectly called its epilogue—gathers up with extraordinary effectiveness the many moods and many attitudes which have alternated in the course of the narrative. There is both low and high comedy—and perhaps high truth, too—in the poet's prayer to "every lady bright of hue," that she not blame him for Criseide's faithlessness, and in his baldly illogical claim that he has told the story "not only" that men should beware of women but "mostly" that women should beware of men. There is comedy also in the poet's self-conscious fear that he has failed to make himself clear, that readers will mis-scan his lines and miss his meaning. The works of the great poets of the past with which he fears his "little book" (of more than eight thousand lines) might be compared make him nervous. His successive echoes of the first line of the *Aeneid* (1765–66) and of the first line of the *Iliad* (1800) suggest that he is afraid he ought to have written not a love poem but a martial epic—if only he were up to it. In any case, may God give him power to write a comedy.

These outbursts of nervousness—which are perhaps a kind of mocking image of man's inability to make sense of the materials his own history provides him—intrude upon the story before it is actually finished, and almost by an afterthought the poet returns to it in order to tell the end of Troilus. Inevitably enough, history does not permit Troilus to kill Diomede or to be killed by him: even that meager satisfaction is denied to our sense of the way things ought to be. Instead, Troilus is killed by Achilles. Only when he has been thus freed from his earthly misery is he rewarded for his earthly fidelity: he is admitted into heaven, a heaven that is physically pagan but theologically Christian. (It is not the first time in medieval literature that *trouthe* allows a non-Christian to enter into a Christian heaven, for according to both Langland and Dante the same quality had raised to heaven the Emperor Trajan.) From his remote sphere Troilus is granted that vision of the world he lately left which enables him to see in full perspective the pettiness and fragility to which he had committed his being: his *trouthe,* finally receiving its philosophic extension, is made whole. But Troilus' is not the ultimate vision in the poem. His could come only after his death, but to the Christian reader the vision is possible at all times during his life. In the last lines of the poem Chaucer gathers up all the flickering emotions, the flickering loves with which he has been dealing and unites them into the great harmony of the only true and perfect love. All the conflicting realities and illusions of the old story are subsumed under the one supreme reality.

Thus the conclusion asserts most solemnly the principle—toward which the poem has been steadily moving—that man's nature and his works are and must be unstable and unreal. Some readers are apt to feel, however, that the poet's final statement cancels all the human values which his own loving treatment has made real; that he is, in effect, saying either that he ought not to have written the poem or that the reader ought not to have read it. This feeling is natural enough in view of Chaucer's entirely specific condemnation of all things mortal except man's ability to love God. But it must be borne in mind that the ending is a part of the poem, and no matter how sincere a statement it is on the part of the poet, the ending combines with all the other parts of the poem to produce the poem's own ultimate meaning. As has been said before, nothing a poet writes is ever canceled out by anything else he writes, and both the haunting loveliness of the story of Troilus and Criseide and the necessity of rejecting it remain valid for the reader. And also, one may suppose, for Chaucer. For the lines in which he condemns the world—

> . . . and thinketh al nis but a faire,
> This world that passeth soone as flowres faire—

poignantly enhance the very thing that he is repudiating. It is in the quality of these lines, taken as an epitome of the quality of the whole poem, that the ultimate meaning of *Troilus* lies. The simultaneous awareness of the real validity of human values —and hence our need to commit ourselves to them—and of their inevitable transitoriness—and hence our need to remain uncommitted—represents a complex, mature, truly tragic vision of mankind. The prayer of the poem's last stanza suggests the poet's faith that his vision is also subsumed under the vision of the Author of all things.

GLOSSARY

THIS GLOSSARY includes *(1)* common words that have not been regularly glossed in the text, and *(2)* less common words that have been glossed upon their first appearance but not when they recur in the same passage. Words that have substantially the same meaning and form in ME as in ModE are included only when they illustrate certain characteristic ME word forms.

In general, when a single word may be converted by the addition of common suffixes into several related words only the basic form appears: the noun **sorwe,** sorrow, readily yields the verb **sorwen,** the adjective **sorweful,** and the adverb **sorwefully, sorwefulliche,** so that only **sorwe** is listed. The commoner ME suffixes are as follows: *(1)* For forming nouns: **-ance, -ant** (originally adjectival), **-ee** (for ModE **-y: libertee,** liberty), **-ence, -er(e)** (**make/makere**), **-esse** (no longer used: **gentil/gentilesse**), **-hęde** (now replaced by **-hood: maidenhęde,** maidenhood), **-hood, -ion,** particularly **-acion** (for ModE **-ation**), and **-nesse**; *(2)* for forming adjectives: **-able** (often with active sense: **merciable,** merciful), **-ful, -lęęs** (for ModE **-less**), **-ly** or **lich(e)**, **-ous,** and **-y**; *(3)* for forming adverbs: **-e** (**fair/faire,** fair/fairly), **-ly** or **liche.**

Weak verbs are marked *vb.,* strong verbs *st. vb.* Potentially puzzling forms for the preterite of weak verbs are listed in parentheses: **weenen,** suppose (preterite **wende**). The past participle of weak verbs is not given: it is the same as the preterite form without final *e,* or, if the preterite ends in a doubled consonant plus **e** (**hidde**), the second consonant of the pair is also dropped (**hid**). When there is authority for them in Chaucer's poetry, the principal parts of strong verbs are given in parentheses, in this manner: following the abbreviation *pret.* the preterite singular; then, following a semicolon, the preterite plural if it exists and has a different form from the singular; then the abbreviation *pp.* followed by the past participle: **riden** (*pret.* **rǫǫd; rĭden;** *pp.* **rĭden**). In listing the infinitive and preterite plural of all verbs and the past participle of strong verbs the terminal **n** is given, but it should be remembered that this **n** is often omitted in Chaucer's poetry. Similarly, the **y** prefix of the past participle, which frequently appears in the text, is not indicated in the principal parts listed. The weak past participle **hid** may appear as **yhid,** and the strong past participle **fallen** has also the potential of **yfallen, yfalle,** and **falle.**

Long open **e** and **o** are marked with a hook: **ę, ǫ** (see above, pp. 1003–4). For convenience, short *i* has sometimes been distinguished from long *i* where it appears in an open syllable or where no ModE equivalent exists to suggest the quality. The scribal spelling of *o* for a phonetic short *u* is represented by italicizing the *o*; **l*o*ve.**

abiden, *st. vb.* (*pret.* **abǫǫd;** *pp.* **abĭden**), abide, wait, wait for, remain
able, *adj.,* able, worthy, fit
accord, *n.,* accord, agreement, will; **–en,** *vb.,* agree, be suitable; **–ant,** *adj.,* according, suitable
acheven, *vb.,* achieve, fulfill, perform
adown, *adv.,* down, downward
adrad, *pp.,* adread, frightened
afer(e)d, *pp.,* afraid, anxious
affeccion, *n.,* affection, emotion, fixation
affrayed, *pp.,* afraid
after, *prep.,* after, according to
again(es), *prep. and adv.,* against, opposite, toward, again, in reply
agast, *pp.,* aghast, frightened
agǫ(ǫn), *pp.,* gone, gone away, departed
ailen, *impers. vb.,* ail, trouble
aken, *vb.,* ache
al(le), *adj. and pron.,* all
albe, *conj.,* although, whether
alday, *adv.,* constantly, always, every day
algate(s), *adv.,* at any rate, in any case, by all means, always
allas, *interj.,* alas
allǫne, *adj.,* alone
allye, *n.,* ally, kinsman; **–n,** *vb.,* ally, take as an ally or kinsman
alofte, *adv.,* aloft, on high
als, alsǫ, also, *adv. and conj.,* also, as
amenden, *vb.,* amend, make amends, improve, improve upon, heal
amidde(s), *prep.,* amid
amis, *adv.,* amiss, wrongly, wickedly, badly
among(es), *prep.,* among
amorwe, *adv.,* in the morning, the next morning
and, *conj.,* and, if
anight, *adv.,* at night
anǫǫn, *adv.,* straightway, at once
anoy, *n.,* trouble, vexation; **–en,** *vb.,* trouble, vex, injure
apesen, *vb.,* appease
apperen, *vb.,* appear
apprǫchen, *vb.,* approach
arisen, *st. vb.* (*pret.* **arǫǫs;** *pp.* **arĭsen**), arise
array, *n.,* array, condition, state, arrangement; **–en,** *vb.,* arrange, furnish, dress, disguise
arwe, *n.,* arrow
asonder, *adv.,* apart
assay, *n.,* test, attempt, assay; **–en,** *vb.,* test, try out
assent, *n.,* assent, concurrence, opinion; **–en,** agree, consent
asterte, *vb.* (*pret.* **asterte**), start out, escape from
aston(i)ed, *pp.,* astonished, bewildered, stunned
aswoune, *adv.,* in a swoon
atǫnes, *adv.,* at once, at the same time
atte, *phrase,* at the
atwixen, *prep.,* between
atwo, *adv.,* in two
auctor, *n.,* author; **–itee,** *n.,* authority
auter, *n.,* altar
avauncen, *vb.,* advance, aid, promote, enhance
avaunt, *n.,* boast
avauntage, *n.,* advantage
aventure, *n.,* adventure, chance
avis, *n.,* opinion, deliberation, plan, agreement; **–en,** *vb.,* consider, pon-

der: *generally reflexive;* **–ement,** *n.,* consideration
avow, *n.,* vow
awaken, *st. vb.* (*pret.* **awǫǫk;** *pp.* **awaken**), awaken
axen, *vb.,* ask
ay, *adv.,* always
ayain(es): *see* **again(es)**

bacheler, *n.,* bachelor, young knight
badde, *adj.,* bad
bane, *n.,* destruction, bane
bareine, *adj.,* barren
bataile, *n.,* battle
be(en), *irreg. vb.* (*pres. sing.* 1 **am,** 2 **art,** 3 **is;** *plu.* **be[en], beeth, are;** *pret. sing.* 1, 3 **was,** 2 **were;** *plu.* **were[n];** *pp.* **be[en]**), be
bęęm, *plu.* **bęmes,** *n.,* beam
bęęrd, *n.,* beard
bęęst, *n.,* beast
beggen, *vb.,* beg; **beggere,** *n.,* beggar
bęne, *n.,* bean
benedicitē, *Latin interj.,* bless (me, us)
benigne, *adj.,* amiable, tractable, demure, benign
bęren, *st. vb.* (*pret.* **bar, bęęr; baren;** *pp.* **bǫre, bǫr[e]n**), bear
berne, *n.,* barn
bet, *adj. and adv.,* better
bęten, *st. and wk. vb.* (*pret. plu.* **beten, betten;** *pp.* **bet, bęten**), beat
bettre, *adj. and adv.,* better
b(e)yen, *vb.* (*pret.* **boughte**), buy, pay for, redeem
bicomen, *st. vb.* (*see* **comen**), become
bidden, *st. vb.* (*pret.* **bad; beden;** *pp.* **bǫden**), bid, pray, command
biden, *st. vb.* (*see* **abiden**), bide, wait for
bifallen, *impers. st. vb.* (*pret.* **bifil, bifel;** *pp.* **bifallen**), befall
bifore, biforn, *prep. and adv.,* before
bigilen, *vb.,* beguile, deceive
biginnen, *st. vb.* (*pret.* **began; bigonnen;** *pp.* **bigonnen**), begin
bigǫǫn, *adj.,* (woe-)begone
bihęęste, *n.,* promise
bihinde, *prep. and adv.,* behind
bihǫlden, *st. vb.* (*pret.* **biheeld;** *pp.* **bihǫlden**), behold
bihoven, *impers. vb.,* behoove, be necessary
biknǫwen, *st. vb.* (*see* **knǫwen**), acknowledge
bileve, *n.,* creed, belief; **–n,** *vb.,* believe
binden, *st. vb.* (*pret.* **bǫǫnd;** *pp.* **bounden**), bind
binęthe, *adv.,* beneath
biręven, *vb.* (*pret.* **birafte**), bereave, deprive, take away from
biseechen, biseeken *vb.* (*pret.* **bisoughte**), beseech
bisegen, *vb.,* besiege
biside, *prep. and adv.,* beside
bisy, *adj.,* busy, assiduous; **bisily,** *adv.,* busily, carefully, assiduously; **bisinesse,** *n.,* business, care, activity
biten, *st. vb.* (*pret.* **bǫǫt;** *pp.* **bĭten**), bite
bithenken, bithinken, *vb.* (*pret.* **bithoughte**), bethink, think of, recall
bitiden, *impers. vb.* (*pret.* **bitidde**), happen, betide
bitweene, *prep. and adv.,* between
bitwixe, *prep. and adv.,* between
biyonde, *prep. and adv.,* beyond
blăk, blāke, *adj.,* black
blew, *adj.,* blue
blis(se), *n.* bliss, happiness; **blisful,** *adj.,* blessed, blissful
blīve, *adv.,* at once
blosme, *n.,* blossom
blǫwen, *st. vb.* (*pret.* **blew;** *pp.* **blǫwen**), blow, make public
bokeler, *n.,* buckler, shield
bǫǫn, *pl.* **bǫnes,** *n.,* bone
boone, *n.,* prayer, request, favor
bǫǫr, *plu.* **bǫres,** *n.,* boar
bǫǫrd, *n.,* board
bǫǫst, *n.,* boast
bǫǫt, *n.,* boat
boote, *n.,* remedy, restorative

borwe, *n.,* pledge; **to —,** as a pledge; **–n,** *vb.,* borrow
bǫthe, *adj., pron., and conj.,* both
botme, *n.,* bottom
bountee, *n.,* generosity, excellence
bowr, *n.,* bower, bedroom
brawn, *n.,* brawn; **–es,** *n. pl.,* muscles
brę̄d, *n.,* bread
brę̄th, *n.,* breath
bręken, *st. vb.* (*pret.* **brak;** *pp.* **brǫken**), break
brennen, *vb.* (*pret.* **brende;** *pp.* **brent**), burn
brest, *n.,* breast
bresten, *st. vb.* (*pret.* **brast; brosten;** *pp.* **brosten**), burst, break out
brĭd, *n.,* bird
bridel, *n.,* bridle
bringen, *vb.* (*pret.* **broughte**), bring
brǭd, brǭde, *adj.,* broad
but, *conj.,* but, unless; **but if,** unless
byen: *see* **b(e)yen**

ca(a)s, *n.,* case, chance, circumstance
cacchen, *vb.* (*pret.* **caughte**), catch
caitif, *n.* (*pl.* **caitives**), captive, wretch
cam: *see* **comen**
can: *see* **connen**
care, *n.,* care, sorrow, anxiety
caryen, *vb.,* carry
casten, *vb.* (*pret.* **caste**), cast, throw, contrive, plot, plan
catel, *n.,* property, capital
cę̄ssen, *vb.,* cease, stop, end
certes, *adv.,* certainly, surely, to be sure
chacen, *vb.,* chase, drive
chaffare, *n.,* merchandise
chapman, *n.,* merchant
charge, *n.,* charge, load, responsibility; **–n,** *vb.,* charge, enjoin
chaunce, *n.,* chance, event, luck
chaunge, *n.,* change; **–n,** *vb.,* change, exchange, alternate
cheere, *n.,* countenance, appearance, manner, behavior, cheer
cherissen, chericen, *vb.,* cherish
cherl, *n.,* churl, low-born fellow
ches, *n.,* chess
chesen, *st. vb.* (*pret.* **chę̄s; chǫsen;** *pp.* **chǫsen**), choose
chiden, *vb.* (*pret.* **chidde**), chide, scold
child, *n.,* child, knight; **with childe,** pregnant
chirche, cherche, *n.* church
chivalrye, *n.,* chivalry, the profession of knighthood
chois, *n.,* choice
clause, *n.,* clause, short space
cleer, clere, *adj.,* bright, clear; **clere,** *adv.,* brightly, clearly
clęne, *adj.,* clean
clępen, *vb.,* call, name
clerk, *n.,* clerk, cleric, student
climben, *st. vb.* (*pret.* **clamb; clomben;** *pp.* **clomben**), climb
clǫke, *n.,* cloak
clǫthen, *vb.* (*pret.* **cladde**), clothe
cofre, *n.,* coffer, chest
cokewold, *n.,* cuckold
cokkou, *n.,* cuckoo
cǫld, *adj.,* cool, cold
cǫle, *n.,* coal
coler, *n.,* collar
colour, *n.,* color, excuse
comanden, *vb.,* command
comen, *st. vb.* (*pret.* **cam, coom; comen;** *pp.* **comen**), come
comenden, *vb.,* commend, entrust
commune, *n.,* commons, common people; *adj.,* common, general
compaignye, *n.,* company
complexion, *n.,* temperament, humor, complexion
confermen, *vb.,* confirm
confort, *n.,* comfort; **–en,** *vb.,* comfort
connen, *vb.* (*pres. sing.* 1, 3 **can,** 2 **canst;** *plu.* **can, connen;** *pret.* **coude, couthe**), be able, know
conning, *n.,* skill, knowledge, cunning; *adj.,* skillful
conseil, *n.,* counsel, advice, plan, secret; **–en,** *vb.,* advise
constance, *n.,* constancy
contraire, *adj.,* contrary

contrarye, *n.,* contrary, opposite; **–n,** *vb.,* contradict
contree, *n.,* country
cǫǫst, *n.,* coast
cǫpe, *n.,* cope, cape
corage, *n.,* heart, courage, virility
corn, *n.,* corn, grain, piece of grain
c(o)rowne, *n.,* crown; **–n,** *vb.*
cor(p)s, *n.,* body, corpse
cosin, *n.,* cousin
costage, *n.,* expense
cǫte, *n.* (1), coat
cǫte, *n.* (2), cottage
coude: *see* **connen**
countenance, *n.,* countenance, appearance, manner, expression
countrefeten, *vb.,* imitate, counterfeit
cours, *n.,* course
courser, *n.,* courser, horse
coveiten, *vb.,* covet, desire, crave
coveitise, *n.,* covetousness, avarice, desire
coverchief, *n.,* kerchief
craft, *n.,* skill, art; **–y,** *adj.,* skillful, artistic
creature, *n.,* creature
creepen, *st. and wk. vb.* (*pret.* **crę̄ęp, crepte; crę̄ępen, crepte;** *pp.* **crǫpen**), creep
crois, *n.,* cross
cure, *n.,* cure, care, attention
curious, *adj.,* well-wrought, careful
curs, *n.,* curse, excommunication; **–en,** *vb.*
cursednesse, *n.,* wickedness, intractability
curteis, *adj.,* courteous, mild, gentle
curteisye, *n.,* courtesy
cutten, *vb.* (*pret.* **kitte;** *pp.* **cut**), cut

daintee, *n.,* delight; *adj.,* fine, splendid
daliance, *n.,* dalliance, conversation, friendly behavior
dampnen, *vb.,* condemn, damn; **dampnable,** *adj.* damnable; **dampnacion,** *n.,* damnation, condemnation
darren, *vb.* (*pres. sing.* 1, 3 **dar,** 2 **darst;** *plu.* **dar;** *pret. and subj.* **dorste**), dare
daun, *n.,* master
daunce, *n.,* dance; **–n,** *vb.*
daunger, *n.,* haughtiness, standoffishness; danger
dawen, *vb.,* dawn; **–ing,** *n.,* dawn
dayesye, daisye, *n.,* daisy
deba(a)t, *n.,* debate, strife, fight
debonaire, *adj.,* gracious, kindly, humble, meek
dęden, *vb.,* deaden, become deathly
dęęd, dęde, *adj.,* dead, deadly; **dęędly,** *adj.,* deadly
dęęde, deede, *n.,* deed
dęęf, *adj.,* deaf
dęęl, *n.,* part, portion, share, bit
deemen, *vb.,* deem, judge, think
dees, *n.,* dice
dęęth, *n.,* death
defaute, *n.,* lack, fault
defence, defense, *n.,* prohibition; defense
defenden, *vb.,* prohibit, defend
defyen, *vb.,* defy, distrust, denounce
degree, *n.,* degree, rank, order, state, condition
deinen, *vb.,* deign, condescend
dęlen, *vb.,* deal, treat
delit, *n.,* delight; **–able,** *adj.,* delightful, delicious; **–en,** *vb.*
delven, *st. vb.* (*pret.* **dalf;** *pp.* **dolven**), dig, bury
depainted, *pp.,* painted, depicted
depardeux, *interj.,* by heaven
departen, *vb.,* separate, depart
dere, *adj.,* dear, expensive
derk, *adj.,* dark; **–nesse,** *n.,* darkness
descriven, *vb.,* describe
desdain, *n.,* disdain; **–en,** *vb.*
deserven, *vb.,* earn, deserve
despaired, *pp.,* in despair
despit, *n.,* spite, scorn, malice, hatred, cruelty; **–ous,** *adj.,* unmerciful, spiteful, cruel
dette, *n.,* debt; **dettour,** *n.,* debtor
devel, *n.,* devil

devis, *n.,* devising, disposal; **at point devis,** perfectly, fully; **–en,** *vb.,* arrange, describe; contrive
deyen, dien, *vb.* (*pret.* **deide, dyde**), die
dide: *see* **doon**
dighten, *vb.* (*pret.* **dighte**), prepare, dress; *refl.* go
digne, *adj.,* worthy
dignitee, *n.,* dignity, honor, worthiness, position
disaventure, *n.,* misadventure, misfortune
disconfort, *n.,* discomfort, defeat
discrecion, *n.,* discretion, ability to make distinctions
disęse, *n.,* distress, trouble; disease; **–n,** *vb.*
dispence, dispense, *n.,* expense, expenditure
dispenden, *vb.,* spend, expend, waste
displęsen, *vb.,* displease; **–ance,** *n.,* displeasure, source of irritation or sorrow
disport, *n.,* sociability; playfulness, sport; delight; **–en,** *vb.,* please, delight, amuse
divinen, *vb.,* guess, divine
doke, *n.,* duck
domb, *adj.,* dumb, mute
dong, *n.,* dung
doom, *n.,* judgment, opinion; doom
doon, *vb.* (*pres. sing.* 1 **do;** 2 **doost;** 3 **dooth;** *plu.* **do[on];** *pret.* **dĭde;** *pp.* **do[on]**), do, cause, make; **it is to doon(e),** it's the right thing to do
dore, *n.,* door
doughter, *n.,* daughter
doute, *n.,* doubt, fear; **–lees,** *adv.,* doubtless
douve, *n.,* dove
draughte, *n.,* drink
drawen, *st. vb.* (*pret.* **drow;** *pp.* **drawen**), pull, draw
dręde, *n.,* dread, doubt; **–lees,** *adv.,* doubtless
dręden, *vb.* (*pret.* **dredde, dradde**), dread
dredful, *adj.,* full of dread, timid
dręęm, *pl.* **dręmes,** *n.,* dream; **dręmen,** *vb.*
drenchen, *vb.* (*pret.* **dreinte**), drown
drery, *adj.,* dreary
dressen, *vb.,* arrange, dispose, equip, dress, prepare
dr(e)ye, *adj.,* dry
drien, *vb.,* suffer, endure
drinken, *st. vb.* (*pret.* **drank; dronken;** *pp.* **dronken**), drink
driven, *st. vb.* (*pret.* **drǫǫf; drĭven;** *pp.* **drĭven**), drive, spend (time)
dronke(n), *pp.,* drunken, drunk; **dronkenesse,** *n.,* drunkenness
duc, *n.,* duke
duetee, *n.,* duty, obligation
duren, *vb.,* endure, last
dwellen, *vb.,* stay, remain, linger, dwell

ęęch, *adj. and pron.,* each; **–ǫǫn,** *pron.,* each one
ęęk, eek, ęke, eke, *adv.,* also
ęęm, *n.,* uncle
ęęst, *n.,* east
effect, *n.,* effect, main point
eft, *adv.,* again
ęgle, *n.,* eagle
elde, *n.,* old age
elles, *adv.,* else; **–wher,** elsewhere
embassadour, *n.,* ambassador
emforth, *prep.,* to the full extent of
emprenten, *vb.,* imprint, impress
emprise, *n.,* enterprise
enbracen, *vb.,* embrace
encens, *n.,* incense
enclinen, *vb.,* incline
encręęs, *n.,* increase; **–sen,** *vb.*
endelong, *prep.,* along
enditen, *vb.,* endite, write, compose
enformen, *vb.,* inform
engendrure, *n.,* engendering
enhauncen, *vb.,* enhance, magnify, advance
enqueren, *vb.,* inquire
ensample, *n.,* example, sample; exemplum
ensure, *vb.,* insure, assure
entencion, *n.,* intention
entenden, *vb.,* intend, attend, aim

entente, *n.,* intent, meaning; wish, will, desire
ęr, *adv., conj. and prep.,* before
ęre, *n.,* ear
erl, *n.,* earl
erly, *adj.,* early
ernest, *n.,* promise; earnest
ers, *n.,* rump
ęrst, *adv.,* first; **at ęrst,** at last, finally
erthe, *n.,* earth
eschaunge, *n.,* exchange
eschuen, eschewen, *vb.,* eschew, avoid
ęse, *n.,* ease, comfort; redress; security; **–n,** *vb.,* put at ease, help
espye, *n.,* spy; **–n,** *vb.,* observe, notice, find out, recognize
esta(a)t, *n.,* state, condition; **–ly,** *adj.,* deliberate, composed
ęsy, *adj.,* easy, lenient, mild
ęten, *st. vb.* (*pret.* **ęęt; ęten;** *pp.* **ęten**), eat
eterne, *adj.,* eternal
evene, *adj.,* moderate, impartial, even; *adv.,* even; exactly; right; just
evere, *adv.,* ever; **–mǫ, –mǫǫr, –mǫre,** evermore
everich, *adj. and pron.,* every, every one; **everichǫǫn,** every one
every, *adj.,* every; **–dęęl,** altogether, entirely
expres, *adj.,* express, specific; *adv.,* expressly

făder, *n.,* father
fain, *adj. and adv.,* glad, fain
fallen, *st. vb.* (*pret.* **fel, fil; fillen;** *pp.* **fallen**), fall, happen, become
fantasye, *n.,* fantasy, hallucination, whim
faren, *st. and wk. vb.* (*pret.* **ferde;** *pp.* **faren, ferd**), fare, go
far(e)wel, *vb. phrase,* farewell
faste, *adv.,* fast; close by, hard, vigorously, eagerly
faucon, *n.,* falcon
fay, *n.,* faith
fecchen, *vb.* (*pret.* **fette**), fetch
federes, *n. pl.,* feathers
feeld, *n.,* field
feend, *n.,* fiend
fęęste, *n.,* feast; joy; **–n,** *vb.,* feast, rejoice
feinen, *vb.,* feign, pretend; shirk
felawe, *n.,* fellow, companion; **–shipe,** fellowship, company
fer(re), *adj. and adv.,* far, farther
fere, *n.* (1), mate, companion; **in fere,** together
fęre, *n.* (2), fear
fęred, *pp.,* frightened
ferforth, *adv.,* far; **so —,** as far as; to the full extent that
ferme, *adj.,* firm
ferthe, *adj.,* fourth
ferther, forther, *adv.,* farther, further
fetheres, *n. pl.,* feathers
fet(t)ren, *vb.,* fetter
fi, *interj.,* fie! shame!
fieble, *adj.,* feeble
fiers, *adj.,* fierce
fighten, *st. vb.* (*pret.* **faught; foughten;** *pp.* **foughten**), fight
fin, *adj.,* fine
fīn, *n.,* end
finden, *st. vb.* (*pret.* **fǫǫnd; founden;** *pp.* **founden**), find, devise, provide
fir, *n.,* fire; **–y,** *adj.,* fiery
firre, *n.,* fir
fit, *n.,* intense experience; division of a poem
flaumbe, *n.,* flame
fleen, *st. vb.* (*pret.* **fleigh; flowen;** *pp.* **flowen**), fly
fleen, *vb.* (*pret.* **fledde**), flee
flowr, *n.,* flower
fǫ, *pl.,* **fǫes, fǫǫn,** *n.,* foes
folk, *n.,* folk, people
folwen, *vb.,* follow, pursue
folye, *n.,* folly, madness
fǫnden, *vb.,* strive, try
for, *prep.,* for, against, for fear of; *conj.,* for, because
forbeden, *st. vb.* (*pret.* **forbad;** *pp.* **forbǫden**), forbid
forbęren, *st. vb.* (*see* **beren**), forbear
forby, *adv.,* by, past

fordoon, *vb.* (*see* **doon**), spoil, ruin, kill
forgeten, foryeten, *st. vb.* (*see* **geten**), forget
forgǫǫn, *vb.* (*see* **goon**), forgo, give up, do without
forhęęd, *n.*, forehead
forlǫre, forlorn, *pp.*, forlorn, utterly lost
fors, *n.*, matter, consequence; **doon no —**, pay no attention
forsaken, *st. vb.* (*pret.* **forsook**; *pp.* **forsaken**), forsake
forsoothe, *prep. phrase*, forsooth, indeed, to be sure
forth, *adv.*, forth, along
forthren, *vb.*, further, advance
forthy, *adv.*, therefore
forwhy, *conj.*, because
foryeten: *see* **forgeten**
foryiven, *st. vb.* (*see* **yiven**), forgive
frankelain, *n.*, franklin
free, *adj.*, generous, noble, filled with magnanimity; free; **–dom**, *n.*, generosity, magnanimity
freend, *n.*, friend
fręletee, *n.*, frailty
frendshipe, *n.*, friendship
fressh, *adj.*, fresh, lively, brisk, vigorous
fręre, *n.*, friar
fro, from, *prep.*, from
ful(le), *adj.*, full, entire; **ful**, *adv.*, very
fulfillen, *vb.*, fill full, fulfill

gadren, *vb.*, gather
gailer, *n.*, jailor
gainen, *impers. vb.*, avail, gain
game, *n.*, pleasure, sport, game, jest
gan: *see* **ginnen**
geant, *n.*, giant
gęęste, geste, *n.*, story, gest
gentil, *adj.*, gentle, well-born, well-behaved; **–esse**, *n.*, gentility, gentleness, good behavior
gęre, *n.*, gear, tackle; clothing
gerland, *n.*, garland
gessen, *vb.*, guess
gest, *n.*, guest
geten, *st. vb.* (*pret.* **gat**; *pp.* **geten**), get, beget
gide, *n.*, guide
gile, *n.*, gile
gilt, *n.*, guilt
ginnen, *st. vb.* (*pret.* **gan**; **gan, gonnen**; *pp.* **gonnen**), begin; *pret. often means* did: I **gan go**, I did go
gise, *n.*, guise, manner; disposal
glad, *adj.*, glad, joyful, cheerful, bright; **–en**, *vb.*, cheer, gladden
gleede, *n.*, gleed, live coal
gliden, *st. vb.* (*pret.* **glǫǫd**, *pp.* **glĭden**), glide, slip
glǫsen, *vb.*, gloze, explain; cheat
glotoun, *n.*, glutton; **–ye**, *n.*, gluttony
gonnen: *see* **ginnen**
good, *adj.*, good; **–ly** *adj.*, pleasing; **–ly**, *adv.*, decently, properly, pleasingly
gǫǫn, *vb.* (*pres. sing.* 1 **gǫ**, 2 **gǫǫst**, 3 **gǫǫth**; *plu.* **gǫ[ǫn]**; *pret.* **wente**; *pp.* **gǫ[ǫn],went**), go, walk
gǫǫst, *n.*, spirit, ghost
gossib, *n.*, gossip, friend
governance, *n.*, control
grace, *n.*, grace, divine grace or favor, good chance, gift
gramercy, graunt mercy, *phrase*, many thanks
graunt, *n.*, grant; **–en**, *vb.*, grant, decree
graven, *st. vb.* (*pp.* **graven**), bury, dig; engrave
gręce, *n.*, grease
gręęt, gręte, *adj.*, great
greeten, *vb.* (*pret.* **grette**), greet
gretter, grettest, *comp. and super. of* **gręęt**, *adj.*
grevance, *n.*, grievance
greven, *vb.*, grieve, annoy, trouble, become angry
grevous, *adj.*, grievous
grinden, *st. vb.* (*pp.* **grounden**), grind
grǫnen, *vb.*, groan
growen, *st. and wk. vb.* (*pret.* **grew**; **growed**; *pp.* **growen**), grow

grucchen, *vb.,* complain
guerdon, *n.,* guerdon, reward, recompense
gyen, *vb.,* guide, control

half, halve, *adj.,* half; *n.,* behalf, part, half
haliday, *n.,* holiday, holy day
halt: *see* **holden**
han: *see* **haven**
hangen, *st. and wk. vb.* (*pret.* **heeng; hanged;** *pp.* **hanged**), hang
hap, *n.,* chance, happening
happen, *vb.* (*pret.* **happed**), happen
hardily, *adv.,* certainly, assuredly
harlot, *n.,* lewd fellow; **–rye,** *n.,* lewdness, indecency
harneis, *n.,* harness, equipment
harrow, *interj., a cry for help*
hasten, *vb.,* hasten
hastif, *adj.,* hasty; **hastily,** *adv.,* at once
haunt, *n.,* haunt, territory; practice; **–en,** *vb.,* practice
have(n), han, *vb.* (*pres. sing.* 1, **have,** 2 **hast,** 3 **hath;** *plu.* **have, han;** *pret.* **hadde**), have
hęęd, *plu.* **hędes,** *n.,* head
heede, *n.,* heed, attention
hęęp, *n.,* heap, number
heer, *plu.* **heres,** *n.,* hair
heer, *see* **here**
heeren, *vb.* (*pret.* **herde**), hear
hęęste, *n.,* promise
hęęth, *n.,* heath, meadowland
heigh, hye, *adj. and adv.,* high
hęle, *n.,* health, welfare, salvation; **–n,** *vb.,* heal
helpen, *st. vb.* (*pret.* **hęęlp;** *pp.* **hǫlpen**), help
hem, *obj. pron.,* them
hende, *adj.,* clever, handy, attractive, nice
henne(s), *adv.,* hence
henten, *vb.* (*pret.* **hente**), take, seize
heraud, *n.,* herald
herberwe, *n.,* harbor, lodging
here, heer, *adv.,* here; *as a prefix often* **her–**
herke, *interj.,* hark
herknen, *vb.,* hearken, listen
hert, *n.,* hart
herte, *n.,* heart; **–ly,** *adj.,* hearty, loving, sincere; *adv.,* heartily, etc.
herten, hurten, *vb.* (*pret.* **herte, hurte**), hurt
hęte, *n.,* heat
heten, *vb.* (*pret.* **highte**), promise; be called
hęthen, *adj.,* heathen
hevene, *n.,* heaven
hęvy, *adj.,* heavy, sorry; **hevinesse,** *n.,* care, sorrow, heaviness
hewe, *n.,* hue, color
hiden, *vb.* (pret. **hidde**), hide
hider, *adv.,* hither
hidous, *adj.,* hideous
hien, *vb.,* hie, hasten
hight(e): *see* **heten**
highte, *n.,* height; **on—,** on high, aloud
hir, *poss. pron.,* her, hers; their, theirs
hire, *obj. pron.,* her
his, *poss. pron.,* his, its
hǫlden, *st. vb.* (*pres. sing.* 3 **halt;** *pret.* **heeld;** *pp.* **hǫlden**), hold, consider
holwe, *adj.,* hollow
hǫnd, hand, *n.,* hand; **hath on honde,** is engaged with
honeste, *adj.,* honorable; **–tee,** *n.,* honor, dignity
hood, *n.,* hood, mantle
hǫǫl, *adj.,* whole, entire
hǫǫlsom, *adj.,* wholesome, sound
hǫǫm, *adv. and n.,* home
hǫǫr, *adj.,* hoary
hǫǫt, hǫte, *adj.,* hot
hors, *n.,* horse(s)
hǫst(e), *n.,* host, innkeeper
hostiler, *n.,* innkeeper
housbonde, *n.,* husband
how, *adv.,* how, what
humblesse, *n.,* humility
humour, *n.,* humor, condition of the body
hust, *adj.,* hushed; *interj.,* hush
hye: *see* **heigh**

I, ich, *nom. pron.,* I
idel, *adj.,* idle, vain; **in, on—,** in vain
ile, *n.,* isle
ilke, *adv.,* same
in, *n.,* dwelling, lodging
in, *prep. and adv.,* in, on
infortune, *n.,* misfortune—particularly as a result of planetary influence
inne, *adv.,* in
inwith, *prep.,* within
iren, *n.,* iron

jalous, *adj.,* jealous
janglen, *vb.,* speak foolishly, prattle
jape, *n.,* joke, jest
joly, jolif, *adj.,* jolly, pretty, trim, lusty; **jolitee,** *n.,* mirth, pleasure, enjoyment
juge, *n.,* judge
juggement, *n.,* judgment
jupartye, *n.,* jeopardy
justen, *vb.,* joust
justise, justice, *n.,* justice, judge

keep, *n.,* attention, heed; **–en,** *vb.,* watch, guard, save, take care of, care to
kemben, *vb.* (*pret.* **kempte, kembde;** *pp.* **kempt**) comb
kepere, *n.,* keeper
kinde, *n.,* kind, sort, nature; *often personified,* Nature; *adj.,* kind, natural; **–ly,** *adj.,* kindly, natural; *adv.,* naturally
kinrede, *n.,* kindred
kissen, *vb.* (*pret.* **kiste**), kiss
knave, *n.,* manservant, boy; knave
knẹden, *vb.,* knead
knitten, *vb.* (*pret.* **knitte**), fasten, tie, join
knǫwen, *st. vb.* (*pret.* **knew;** *pp.* **knǫwen**), know, recognize

lak, *n.,* fault, lack
lakken, *vb.,* blame, find fault with; *impers.* lack
langage, *n.,* language
langour, *n.,* sickness, grief, ill-health
large, *adj.,* wide, broad, large; **–ly,** *adv.,* largely, generously; **–sse,** *n.,* generosity
lasse, lesse, *adj. and adv.,* less
lasten, *vb.* (*pret.* **laste**), last, extend, endure
laten: *see* **lẹten**
laughen, *st. and wk. vb.* (*pret.* **lough; laughed;** *pp.* **laughen**), laugh, smile
laurer, *n.,* laurel
lay, *n.* (1), law
lay, *n.* (2), song, lay
layen, leggen, *vb.* (*pret.* **laide**), lay
lec(c)herye, *n.,* lechery
lec(c)hour, *n.,* lecher
lẹden, *vb.* (*pret.* **ledde, ladde**), lead, bring, take
lę̣che, *n.,* physician, leech; **— craft,** art of healing
lę̣ẹf, *pl.* **lẹves,** *n.,* leaf
lę̣ẹst(e), *adj. and adv.,* least; **at the — way,** at least
legende, *n.,* legend, biography of a saint
leiser, *n.,* leisure, opportunity
lemman, *n.,* mistress
lẹne, *adj.,* lean
lẹnen, *vb.* (*pret.* **lente**), lend, give
lenger, *adj. and adv.,* longer
leon, *n.,* lion; **–esse,** lioness
lẹpen, *st. vb.* (*pret.* **leep**), leap
lẹren, *vb.,* teach, learn
lernen, *vb.,* learn, teach
lesen, *st. and wk. vb.* (*pret.* **lę̣ẹs, loste;** *pp.* **lost, lǫr[e]n**), lose
lest(e): *see* **listen**
lẹten, laten, *st. vb.* (*pres. sing.* 3 **let;** *imperative* **lat;** *pret.* **leet; leten;** *pp.* **laten**), let, leave
letten, *vb.* (*pret.* **lette**), prevent, hinder; leave off, cease
leve, *adj.: see* **lief**
lẹve, *n.,* leave, permission
lẹven, *vb,* (*pret.* **lefte, lafte**), leave
leven, *vb.,* believe, trust in
levere, *comp. adj. and adv.,* dearer, rather
lewed, *adj.,* uneducated, ignorant
licour, *n.,* liquor, liquid

lief, leve, *adj.,* dear, beloved
lien, liggen, *st. vb.* (*pret.* **lay**; *pp.* **lain**), lie, rest
lien, *st. vb.,* lie, tell a lie; **liere,** *n.,* liar
lif, *n.,* life, body; **on live,** alive
lige, *n.,* liege
light, *adj.,* easy, light, glad
lik(e), *adj. and adv.,* like
liken, *impers. vb.,* please
likly, *adj.,* likely
liknesse, *n.,* likeness
lime, *n.,* limb
linage, *n.,* lineage
lisse, *n.,* comfort, surcease, abatement; **–n,** *vb.,* comfort, abate, assuage
listen, lesten, lusten, *impers. vb.* (*pres.* **list, lest, lust**; *pret.* **liste, leste, luste**), please
listes, *n. pl.,* lists, tournament ground
līte, *adj. and adv.,* little
lītel, *adj. and adv.,* little
lǫ, *interj.,* lo, behold
(**on**) **lofte,** *phrase,* aloft, on high
loggen, *vb.,* lodge
lǫnd, land, *n.,* land
looking, *n.,* look, regard, glance
lordinges, *n. pl.,* gentlemen, sirs
lordshipe, *n.,* lordship, dominion
lǫre, *n.,* lore, teaching; plan
lorn, *pp.,* lost, ruined
los, *n.,* loss
lǫth, *adj.,* loath, reluctant
love, *n.,* love
lǫwe, *adj.,* low, humble; **–ly,** *adj. and adv.,* humbly
lust, *n.,* desire, pleasure, wish
lust(e): *see* **listen**
lusty, *adj.,* hearty, healthy, vigorous, vital, lusty; **lustinesse,** *n.,* enthusiasm, heartiness, robustness

maidenhęde, *n.,* maidenhood, virginity
maintenen, *vb.,* maintain
maister, *n.,* master
maistresse, *n.,* mistress
maistrye, *n.,* mastery, sovereignty, dominion, main force
maken, *vb.* (*pret.* **made, maked;** *pp.* **maad, maked**), make
makere, *n.,* maker, author
malencolye, *n.,* melancholy, the humor in which the black bile is dominant
manace, *n.,* threat; **–n,** *vb.,* threaten
manciple, *n.,* manciple, steward
manere, *n.,* manner, fashion
many(e), *adj. and pron.,* many
marchant, *n.,* merchant
markis, *n.,* marquis; **–esse,** marquise
maryen, *vb.,* marry
matere, *n.,* matter
maugree, *prep.,* in spite of
męde, *n.,* mead, meadow
meede, *n.,* meed, reward, bribe
meeke, *adj.,* meek; **mekely,** *adv.*
męęl, *n.,* repast, meal
meẹte, *adj.,* meet, proper, fitting, equal
meeten, *vb.* (*pret.* **mette**), meet
męle, *n.,* grain, meal
męne, *n.,* mean, median; **–s,** means
męnen, *vb.* (*pret.* **mente**), mean, intend, have in mind
mercy, *n.,* mercy; **merciable,** *adj.,* merciful
merveile, *n.,* marvel; **–ous,** *adj.,* marvelous, extraordinary
merye, mirye, murye, *adj.,* merry, prosperous, well-off, salutary
meschaunce, *n.,* misfortune, mischance; **with —,** with bad luck
meschief, *n.,* misfortune, mischance
message, *n.,* errand, message, messenger; **–r,** messenger
mesure, *n.,* measure, moderation
męte, *n.,* meat, meal
meten, *vb.* (*pret.* **mette**), dream
meven, *vb.,* move
might, *n.,* might, power, strength
minstralcye, *n.,* minstrelsy, music
mirour, *n.,* mirror
mirthe, *n.,* mirth, joy, prosperity
misaventure, *n.,* misadventure, mishap, ill-luck
misgǫǫn, *st. vb.* (*see* **gǫǫn**), go astray, err
mistristen, mistrusten, *vb.,* mistrust

mǫ, *adj. and adv.*, more; *pron.*, others
moder, *n.*, mother
mǫne, *n.*, moan
mǫǫrnen, *vb.*, mourn, lament
moot: *see* **moten**
mordre, *n.*, murder; **–n**, *vb.*; **–re**, **mordrour**, *n.*, murderer
mǫre, **mǫǫr**, *adj., adv., and pron.*, more; **withoute more**, without further ado
morwe, *n.*, morning, morrow; **–ening**, morning
mǫst, **mǫste**, *adj. and adv.*, most
moste, *vb.*, must: *see* **moten**
moten, *irreg. vb.* (*pres. sing.* 1, 3 **moot**, 2 **moost**; *plu.* **moten**; *pret.* **moste**), must, may
mǫwen, *irreg. vb.* (*pres. sing.* 1, 3 **may**, 2 **maist**; *plu.* **may**, **mǫwen**; *pret.* **mighte**), may, can, be able
muche(l), *adj. and adv.*, much
murye: *see* **merye**
myn, **mine**, *poss. pron.*, my, mine

na, *adv.*, no; **namǫ**, *pron.*, no more; **namǫre**, *adv.*, no longer, no more
nam, *vb.*, *for* **ne am**, am not
namely, *adv.*, especially, namely
narwe, *adj.*, narrow
nas, *vb.*, *for* **ne was**, was not
nat, *adv.*, not
nathelees, *adv.*, nevertheless
naught: *see* **nought**
nay, *adv.*, nay, no; **it is no —**, **withoute —**, there's no denying it.
ne, *adv. and conj.*, no, not, nor
nece, *n.*, niece
necligence, *n.*, negligence, laziness
necligent, *adj.*, negligent, lazy
neede, *n.*, need, requirement; **–es**, *adv.*, needs; **–n**, *impers. vb.*
nęęr, *adv.*, near, nearer
neigh, **nye**, *adj. and adv.*, nigh, near
neighebor, *n.*, neighbor
nere, *vb.*, *for* **ne were**, were not
nevere, *adv.*, never; **–mǫ**, **–mǫre**, *adv.*, never more; **neveradeel**, not a bit, not at all
newe, *adj.*, new; *adv.*, newly, again
next(e), *adj. and adv.*, next, nearest
nice, *adj.*, foolish, finicky; **–tee**, *n.*, foolishness
nigard, *n.*, miser, niggard; **–ye**, miserliness
nil, *vb.*, *for* **ne wil**, will not
nilt, *vb.*, *for* **ne wilt**, wilt not
nis, *vb.*, *for* **ne is**, is not
niste, *vb.*, *for* **ne wiste**, did not know
nǫ, *adv.*, no
noblesse, *n.*, nobility, aristocracy
nolde, *vb.*, *for* **ne wolde**, would not
nombre, *n.*, number
nǫnes, *n. plu.*, occasion, purpose, nonce
nonne, *n.*, nun
nǫǫn, **nǫne**, *adj. and pron.*, no one, none
nǫǫst, *vb.*, *for* **ne woost**, knowest not
nǫǫt, *vb.*, *for* **ne woot**, know(s) not
norice, *n.*, nurse
norissen, *vb.*, nourish, bring up, nurse
note, *n.*, music, singing voice
nothing, *pron. and adv.*, nothing, no, in no way
nought, *pron. and adv.*, nothing, nought, not at all, not, in no way
now, *adv.*, now
nye: *see* **neigh**

obeisance, *n.*, obedience, subservience, compliance
obeisant, *adj.*, obedient
of, *prep. and adv.*, of, by; off
offren, *vb.*, offer, make an oblation
ofte, *adj. and adv.*, oft, often; **–n**, *adv.*, often; **–r**, oftener
oinement, *n.*, ointment
ǫld, *adj.*, old
on, *prep. and adv.*, on
ǫnes, *adv.*, once
ǫnly, *adv.*, only, merely
ǫǫk, *pl.* **ǫkes**, *n.*, oak
ǫǫ(n), *adj. and pron.*, one; **at ǫǫn**, in accord
ǫǫth, *pl.* **ǫthes**, *n.*, oath
ordinance, *n.*, decree, arrangement, disposal

orison, *n.,* orison, prayer
other(e), *adj. and pron.,* other, others; *conj.,* either, or
otherway(e)s, *adv.,* otherwise
ought, *pron. and adv.,* anything, aught; in any way
oughte, *impers. pret. vb.,* ought
oure, oures, *poss. pron.,* our, ours, of us
out(e), *adv.,* out; **out of doute,** without doubt
outher, *conj.,* either
outrely, *adv.,* utterly, entirely, solely
over, *adj. and adv.,* over; **–al,** *adv.,* in general, everywhere, throughout
owen(e), *adj.,* own

pa(a)s, *n.,* step, pace, rate
pacen, passen, *vb.,* pass, surpass
pacience, *n.,* patience, suffering
palais, *n,* palace
par, *French prep.,* by, for
paramour, *n.,* mistress, lover; romantic love; **–s,** *adv.,* with romantic love
paraventure, paraunter, *adv.,* perhaps, perchance, by chance
pardee, pardeux, *interj.,* pardie, by heaven
parfay, *interj.,* by my faith
parfit, *adj.,* perfect
parfournen, *vb.,* perform, complete
parlement, n., parliament, assembly
part, *n.,* part, share; **–en,** *vb.,* share, divide, depart
passion, *n.,* passion, suffering
pece, *n.,* piece
pęcok, *n.,* peacock
peer, *n. and adj.,* peer, equal, match
pęęs, *n.,* peace
penance, *n.,* suffering, penance
pens, *n. plu.,* pence, pennies
peple, *n.,* people, common people
percen, *vb.,* pierce
perilous, *adj.,* dangerous
perle, *n.,* pearl
permutacion, *n.,* permutation, transformation
person, *n.,* parson
persone, *n.,* person
philosophre, *n.,* philosopher, alchemist
pietee, *n.,* pity
piler, *n.,* pillar
pilwe, *n.,* pillow
pine, *n.,* pain, torture, suffering
pisse, *n.,* urine; **–n,** *vb.,* urinate
pitee, *n.,* pity; **pitous,** *adj.,* piteous, pitiful, merciful
plain, *adj.,* plain, clear, smooth, level
plainen, *vb.,* complain, lament
plainte, *n.,* plaint, complaint, lament
play, *n.,* play, recreation, sport, joking; in general any nonserious occupation; **–en,** *vb.,* play, enjoy oneself, indulge in recreation or nonserious occupation
plein, *adj.,* full: *often indistinguishable from* **plain**
plesance, *n.,* pleasure, pleasantness, joy
plesant, *adj.,* pleasant
plęsen, *vb.,* please
plighten, *vb.* (*pret.* **plighte**), promise, pledge
poore, *adj.,* poor
portrayen, *vb.,* draw, sketch, picture; **portrayour,** *n.,* artist
pouren, *vb.,* pore, gaze; pour
poverte(e), *n.,* poverty
pręchen, *vb.,* preach; **pręchour,** *n.,* preacher
pręęs, *n.,* press, crowd; **–sen,** *vb.,* press, push
preest, *n.,* priest
preve, *n.,* proof, test, experiment; **–n,** *vb.,* prove, test
priken, *vb.,* prick, stimulate, ride horseback
prime, *n.,* prime, generally about 9 A.M.
privee, *adj.,* privy, private, secret; **prively,** *adv.;* **privetee,** *n.,* privacy, secrets
proces, *n.,* proceeding, argument, course of time
profre, *n.,* proffer, offer; **–n,** *vb.,* proffer, offer, put forth
propre, *adj.,* proper, neat; one's own

prowesse, *n.,* prowess, accomplishments
pure, *adj.,* pure, unmixed; very
purpre, *adj.,* purple
purveyen, *vb.,* provide, purvey; **purveyance,** *n.,* provision, providence, foresight, foreknowledge

quaint, *adj.,* quaint, strange, sly
quaken, *st. vb.* (*pret.* **quǫǫk**), quake
queinte, *n.,* pudendum
quenchen, *vb.* (*pret.* **queinte**), quench, put out
quik(ke), *adj.,* quick, lively, living; **quiken,** *vb.,* come to life, bring to life
quīten, *vb.* (*pret.* **quitte**), pay, repay
quod, *pret. vb.,* said

rage, *n.,* rage, torment; **–n,** *vb.,* rave, behave violently or wantonly
rathe, *adv.,* early; **–r,** earlier, sooner, rather
raunsoun, *n.,* ransom
ravisshen, *vb.,* ravish, delight; seize
reaume, *n.,* realm
rebel, *adj.,* rebellious
recchen, rekken, *vb.* (*pret.* **roughte**), care, reck; **recchelees,** *adj.,* careless
ręchen, *vb.* (*pret.* **raughte**), reach, stretch
recomanden, *vb.,* recommend, entrust
reconforten, *vb.,* recomfort
recorden, *vb.,* record, recollect, remind
ręden, *vb.* (*pret.* **redde, radde**), read, interpret; advise; say
redressen, *vb.,* redress, make amends for
rędy, *adj.,* ready
ręęd, *n.,* advice, counsel; plan
ręęd, ręde, *adj.,* red
regne, *n.,* reign, kingdom; **–n,** *vb.,* reign, rule
rehercen, *vb.,* rehearse, repeat
rekenen, *vb.,* reckon, calculate, count
rekken: *see* **recchen**
relęęssen, *vb.,* release
releven, *vb.,* relieve
religion, *n.,* religion, monastic order; **religious,** *adj.,* monastic
relik, *n.,* relic
remedye, *n.,* remedy, plan of action
remenant, *n.,* remnant, remainder
remeven, *vb.,* remove
renden, *vb.* (*pret.* **rente**), rend, tear
rennen, *st. vb.* (*pret.* **ran,** *pp.* **ronnen**), run
repreve, *n.,* reproof; **–n,** *vb.,* reprove
requeren, *vb.* require
ręson, *n.,* reason, opinion
respit, *n.,* delay, breathing-space
reste, *n.,* rest, ease, peace of mind
retorike, *n.,* rhetoric
ręven, *vb.* (*pret.* **refte, rafte**), reave, bereave, deprive, take away
rewen, *vb.,* rue, regret, have pity
riche, *adj.,* rich, expensive, well-stocked; **–sse,** *n.,* wealth, richness, excellence
riden, *st. vb.* (*pret.* **rǫǫd; rĭden;** *pp.* **rĭden**), ride
right, *adv.,* exactly, very, just; **– as,** just as
right, *n.,* right, justice
right, *adj.,* straight, direct, true; *with negative expressions,* at all
rightwis, *adj.,* righteous
ringen, *st. vb.* (*pret.* **rǫǫng; rongen;** *pp.* **rongen**), ring
riot, *n.,* violent behavior; **–our,** rowdy fellow
risen, *st. vb.* (*pret.* **rǫǫs; rĭsen;** *pp.* **rĭsen**), rise
riven, *st. vb.* (*pret.* **rǫǫf**), split, pierce
rok, *n.,* rock, cliff
rǫmen, *vb.,* roam, stroll
roode, *n.,* rood, cross
rǫren, *vb.,* roar
rǫten, *adj.,* rotten
rounen, *vb.,* whisper, tell
route, *n.,* group, throng, company
routhe, *n.,* ruth, pity, regret
rym, ryme, *n.,* rhyme; **rymen,** *vb.,* rhyme

sad, sadde, *adj.,* steadfast, constant; sober, serious

sal, *pres. vb.* (*Northern*), shall
saluen, *vb.*, greet, hail, salute
sanguin, *adj.*, sanguine, dominated by the blood
sauf, *adj.*, safe; **–ly**, *adv.*, safely, without fear
savacion, *n.*, salvation
save, *prep.*, save, except
savour, *n.*, odor, taste, flavor
saw(gh): *see* **seen**
sawe, *n.*, saw, saying
say(e)n, *vb.* (*pres. sing.* 2 **saist**, 3 **saith**; *pret.* **saide**), say
scapen, *vb.*, escape
scarsly, *adv.*, scarcely, sparely
science, *n.*, knowledge, learning
sclaundre, *n.*, slander
sclave, *n.*, slave
sclendre, *adj.*, slender
scole, *n.*, school; **–r**, scholar
secree, *adj.*, secret, discreet
seculer, *adj.*, secular, not in ecclesiastical orders
sęę, *n.*, sea
seechen, **seeken**, *vb.* (*pret.* **soughte**), seek
sęęl, *n.*, seal
seemen, *impers. vb.*, seem
seene, *adj.*, seen
seen, *st. vb.* (*pret.* **saw**, **sawgh**; **sawen**; *pp.* **see[n]**), see; look after
sege, *n.*, siege
selde, **seldom**, *adv.*, seldom
self, **selve(n)**, *pron. and adj.*, self, same
sellen, *st. vb.* (*pret.* **solde**), sell
sely, *adj.*, innocent, unsophisticated, harmless, pathetic; happy, fortunate
semely, *adj. and adv.*, seemly
senden, *vb.* (*pret.* **sente**), send
sentence, *n.*, meaning, opinion, statement, proverb, main point
sermon, *n.*, sermon, conversation, statement; **–en**, *vb.*, talk at length
servage, *n.*, slavery
servant, *n.*, servant, lover
sęson, *n.*, season
setten, *vb.* (*pret.* **sette**), set
shadwe, *n.*, shadow
shaken, *st. vb.* (*pret.* **shook**; *pp.* **shaken**), shake
shal, *pl.* **shullen**, *pres. vb.*, shall
shame, *n.*, shame, sense of shame, modesty
shapen, *st. vb.* (*pret.* **shǫǫp**; *pp.* **shapen**), shape, create, arrange, decree, plan
shęęf, *n.*, sheaf
sheeld, *n.*, shield; *also*, a coin
sheene, *adj.*, shiny, bright
shęęthe, *n.*, sheath
shenden, *vb.* (*pret.* **shente**), ruin, spoil, embarrass
sherte, *n.*, shirt
shetten, *vb.* (*pret.* **shette**), shut
shewen, *vb.*, show
shinen, *st. vb.* (pret. **shǫǫn**), shine
shire, *n.*, shire, county
sho, *pl.* **shoes**, **shoon**, *n.*, shoe
sholde, *pret. vb.*, should
showr, *n.*, shower, onslaught
shrewe, *n.*, wicked person, rascal; **–dnesse**, wickness, perversity
shriven, *st. vb.*, absolve, shrive
shul, *pres. vb. pl.*, shall
shulder, *n.*, shoulder
signifiance, *n.*, significance, meaning
sīk, *adj.*, sick
sīk, *n.*, sigh; **–en**, *vb.*
sīker, *adj.*, certain, sure, secure; **–ly**, *adv.*; **–nesse**, *n.*, security, certainty
sīn, *conj.*, since
singen, *st. vb.* (*pret.* **sǫǫng**; **songen**; *pp.* **songen**), sing
sīre, *n.*, sir, sire
sīth, *conj.*, since
sīthe, *n.*, time
sit(t)hen, *adv. and conj.*, since, after
sitten, *st. vb.* (*pret.* **sat**, **sęęt**; **sat**, **sęten**; *pp.* **sęten**), sit
skīle, *n.*, reason, argument; **skilful**, *adj.*, reasonable
slęęn, *st. vb.* (*pret.* **slow**; *pp.* **slain**, **slawen**), slay
slęępen, **sleepen**, *st. and wk. vb.* (*pret.* **sleep**, **slepte**), sleep
sleigh, **slye**, *adj.*, sly, clever, stealthy, secretive

sleighte, *n.*, trick, craft, cunning
slomber, *n.*, slumber; **slombren**, *vb.*
slouthe, *n.*, sloth, laziness, idleness, negligence
smal(e), *adj.*, small, delicate, trivial
smert, *n.*, smart; *adj.*, smarting; **–en**, *vb.*, smart
smīten, *st. vb.* (*pret.* **smǫǫt**, *pp.* **smĭten**), smite, strike
socour, *n.*, aid, succor
sodein, *adj.*, sudden, impetuous; unexpected
sojurnen, *vb.*, stay, remain, linger, delay
sola(a)s, *n.*, pleasure, delight, solace
solacen, *vb.*, comfort, cheer
som(e), *adj. and pron.*, one, some; **somdęęl**, *pron.*, somewhat
somer, *n.*, summer
somme, *n.*, sum
somnour, *n.*, summoner
sǫnd, *n.*, sand
sondry, *adj.*, sundry
sone, *n.*, son
sonne, *n.*, sun
soone, *adv.*, at once, immediately
sǫǫr, *n.*, sore; **sǫǫr, sore**, *adj.*; **sǫre**, *adv.*
sooth, *adj.*, true; **the soothe**, the truth; **soothfast**, *adj.*, true
soper, *n.*, supper, the evening meal
sǫren, *vb.*, soar
sorwe, *n.*, sorrow
sǫry, *adj.*, sorry
soun, *n.*, sound; **–en**, *vb.*, sound, resound, tend
soupen, *vb.*, sup, dine
soverein, *adj.*, sovereign, principal; **–etee**, *n.*, mastery, dominion
space, *n.*, time, space
sparen, *vb.*, spare, hesitate, act with restraint
sparwe, *n.*, sparrow
spęęche, *n.*, speech
speeden, *vb.* (*pret.* **spedde**), speed, succeed, prosper, satisfy
spęken, *st. vb.* (*pret.* **spak**; **spęken**; *pp.* **spǫken**), speak
spęre, *n.*, spear
spousen, *vb.*, espouse, wed
spręden, *vb.* (*pret.* **spredde, spradde**), spread, grow
springen, *st. vb.* (*pret.* **sprǫǫng**; *pp.* **sprongen**), spring
squier, *n.*, squire
stable, *adj.*, stable, enduring, fixed
stęde, *n.*, stead, place
stedefast, *adj.*, steadfast
stęlen, *st. vb.* (*pret.* **stal**; *pp.* **stǫlen**), steal
stenten, stinten, *vb.* (*pret.* **stente, stinte, –d**), stop, leave off
sterre, *n.*, star
sterten, *vb.* (*pret.* **sterte**), start up, awake, go
sterven, *st. vb.* (*pret.* **starf**; **storven**; *pp.* **storven**), die
stiren, *vb.*, stir
stiropes, *n. plu.*, stirrups
stǫnden, *st. vb.* (*pres. sing.* 3 **stant**; *pret.* **stood**; *pp.* **stǫnden**), stand
stǫǫn, *pl.* **stǫnes**, *n.*, stone
stǫǫr, *n.*, store
stounde, *n.*, moment
stoupen, *vb.*, stoop
stout, *adj.*, strong, powerful, bold
straunge, *adj.*, foreign, alien, strange
strecchen, *vb.* (*pret.* **straughte**), stretch
stręęm, *plu.* **stręmes**, *n.*, stream, beam
strepen, *vb.*, strip
strīf, *n.*, strife, activity, striving
strǫnde, *n.*, strand
strǫǫk, *n.*, stroke
subget, subjet, *adj. and n.*, subject
substance, *n.*, property, possessions, substance
subtil, *adj.*, subtle, tenuous, thin; **–tee**, *n.*, sublety, wiliness
sufficen, suffisen, *vb.*, suffice
suffisance, *n.*, sufficiency, contentment
suffren, *vb.*, suffer, permit
sur, *adj.*, sure, certain
sustenen, *vb.*, sustain, endure
suster, *pl.* **susters, sustren**, *n.*, sister
swalwe, *n.*, swallow
swerd, *n.*, sword

swęren, *st. vb.* (*pret.* **swǫǫr; swǫren;** *pp.* **swǫren**), swear
swęten, *vb.* (*pret.* **swatte**), sweat
swetnesse, *n.*, sweetness
swevene, *n.*, dream
swich, *adj. and pron.*, such
swimmen, *st. vb.* (*pret. plu.* **swommen**), swim
swink, *n.*, toil, work
swinken, *st. vb.*, toil, work
swīthe, *adv.*, quickly; **as —**, at once
swīven, *vb.*, copulate with
swoune, *n.*, swoon; **–n**, *vb.*

taken, *st. vb.* (*pret.* **took;** *pp.* **taken**), take, give, receive
taryen, *vb.*, tarry, delay, remain
tęchen, *vb.* (*pret.* **taughte**), teach
tellen, *vb.* (*pret.* **tolde**), tell
tene, *n.*, grief, vexation
tercel(et), *n.*, male eagle
tęre, *n.*, tear
tęren, *st. vb.* (*pp.* **tǫrn**), tear, rend
terme, *n.*, term, limit, extent, appointed time
thank, *n.*, thanks, gratitude; **–en**, *vb.*, thank, feel grateful to
thanne, *adv.*, then
theef, *plu.* **theves**, *n.*, thief
theen, *vb.*, thrive
thenken, thinken, *impers. vb.* (*pret.* **thoughte**), seem
thennes, *adv.*, thence
ther(e), *adv.*, there; **therinne**, therein; **therto, therwithal**, besides, moreover, in addition
thider, *adv.*, thither
thikke, *adj.*, thick, stout, robust
thilke, *adj.*, the same, that, those
thing, *pl.* **thing, thinges**, *n.*, thing, deed, contract
thinken: *see* **thenken**
thise, *adj. and pron.*, these
thǫ, *adv.*, then
thǫ, *adj. and pron.*, those
thonder, *n.*, thunder
thręęd, *n.*, thread; **thredbare**, *adj.*, threadbare
thresshfold, *n.*, threshold
thresten, *vb.* (*pret.* **thraste**), thrust
thridde, *adj.*, third
thrīës, *adv.*, thrice
thrift, *n.*, good luck, good management, prosperity; **–y**, *adj.*, decent, proper, excellent; **–ily**, *adv.*
thritty, *adj.*, thirty
thrǫte, *n.*, throat
thrǫwen, *st. vb.* (*pret.* **threw;** *pp.* **thrǫwen**), throw
thurgh, *prep.*, through
thursten, *vb.*, thirst
thy(n), thine, *poss. pron.*, thy, thine
tide, *n.*, time, tide
tiden, *vb.* (*pret.* **tidde**), happen, betide
til, *prep.*, till, to
to, *prep.*, to, till
tǫ, *pl.* **tǫes, tǫǫn**, *n.*, toe
tofore, toforn, *prep.*, before
togidre(s), *adv.*, together
tomorwe, *adv.*, tomorrow, the next morning
tonge, *n.*, tongue
touchen, *vb.*, touch, pertain to
toward(es), *prep.*, toward, in anticipation of, in preparation for
towr, *n.*, tower
travaile, *n.*, travel, work, labor, suffering; **–n**, *vb.*, work, suffer, be in labor
trecherye, *n.*, treachery
tręden, *st. vb.* (*pret.* **trad;** *pp.* **trǫden**), tread
tręson, *n.*, treason
tręsor, *n.*, treasure
trespa(a)s, *n.*, wrong, sin; **trespacen**, *vb.*, trespass, do wrong
tręten, *vb.*, treat, speak, relate
trewe, *adj.*, true, sincere, faithful
trompe, *n.*, trumpet
trone, *n.*, throne
trouthe, *n.*, truth, integrity, fidelity
trǫwen, *vb.*, trust, believe
turnen, *vb.*, turn, return, go
twaine, twaye, *adj. and pron.*, twain, two
twīës, *adv.*, twice
twisten, *vb.* (*pret.* **twiste**), twist
two, *adj. and pron.*, two

under, *prep. and adv.,* under; **–nethe,** *adv.,* underneath
understǫnden, *st. vb.* (*see* **stonden**), understand
undertaken, *st. vb.* (*see* **taken**), undertake, vouch, guarantee
undoon, *vb.* (*see* **doon**), undo
unkinde, *adj.,* unkind, unnatural
unknǫwe, *pp.,* unknown
unlik, *adj.,* unlike
unnęthe(s), *adv.,* scarcely, hardly, with difficulty
until, *prep.,* until, unto
unto, *prep.,* unto, until
untrewe, *adj.,* false, untrue
untrouthe, *n.,* falseness, lack of constancy
unwar, *adj.,* unaware, unwary
unwist, *adj.,* unknown
up, *prep. and adv.,* up, upon
upright, *adv.,* at full length, upright
usen, *vb.,* use, employ, be accustomed to

vain, *adj.,* empty, futile, vain
valeye, *n.,* valley
vanitee, *n.,* futility, falsity
venim, *n.,* venom, poison; **–ous,** *adj.*
verray, *adj.,* true, proper; **verraily,** *adv.,* verily, truly
vers, *n.,* verse
vertu, *n.,* virtue, power, strength, capacity; **–ous,** *adj.,* virtuous, powerful, capable
viage, *n.,* voyage, trip, project
vice, *n.,* flaw, defect, vice
vilainye, *n.,* villainy, discourtesy, crudity, slander
vitaile, *n.,* victuals, foodstuff
voiden, *vb.,* void, make empty
vois, *n.,* voice
vouchen sauf, *vb. phrase,* vouchsafe, grant, guarantee, condescend

waik, *adj.,* weak
wailaway, *interj.,* woe, alas
waimenting, *n.,* noisy lament
waiten, *vb.,* wait, watch, wait an opportunity
waiven, *vb.,* avoid, withdraw
waken, *st. and wk. vb.* (*pret.* **wǫǫk;** *pp.* **waked**), wake, remain awake
wan: *see* **winnen**
wanten, *vb.,* want, lack
wantoune, *adj.,* wanton; **–sse,** *n.,* wantonness
war, *adj.,* ware, wary, aware; **–en,** *vb.,* beware, be on guard
wardein, *n.,* warden, guardian
warnen, *vb.,* warn, notify in advance
waxen, *st. vb.* (*pret.* **weex;** *pp.* **woxen**), wax, grow, become
weder, *n.,* weather, storm
we(e)l, *adv.,* well
weenen, *vb.* (*pret.* **wende**), ween, think, suppose
weepen, *st. and wk. vb.* (*pret.* **weep, wepte;** *pp.* **wopen, weepen, wept**), weep
węle, *n.,* prosperity, well-being, salvation
welle, *n.,* well, spring, source
welthe, *n.,* wealth
wenche, *n.,* wench, loose woman, servant girl
wenden, *vb.* (*pret.* **wente**), wend, go, turn
wepne, *n.,* weapon
węren, *vb.* (*pret.* **węred**), wear
werk, *n.,* work
werken, werchen, wirken, wirchen, *vb.* (*pret.* **wroughte**), work, make, conduct onself
werre, *n.,* war
wers(e), wors(e), *adj. and adv.,* worse
werst(e), worst(e), *adj. and adv.,* worst
wery, *adj.,* weary
wex, *n.,* wax
whan, *conj.,* when
what, *pron.,* what; *adv.,* why
wheither, whether, *conj.,* whether
whennes, *adv.,* whence
wher(e), *adv. and conj.,* where; **wherinne,** wherein; **–thurgh,** wherethrough
wher, *interrog. conj.,* whether

whęte, *n.,* wheat
which, *adj. and pron.,* which, what
whider, *adv.,* whither
whil(es), *conj.,* while
while, *n.,* while, time
whilom, *adv.,* once upon a time, formerly
who, *subj. pron.,* who, whoever; **whos,** *poss. pron.,* whose
who so, who that, *subj. pron. indef.,* whoso, whoever, if any one
widwe, *n.,* widow
wīf, *n.* (*pl.* **wīves**), wife, woman
wight, *n.,* creature, person; bit
wighte, *n.,* weight
wiket, *n.,* gate
wikke, *adj.,* crooked, perverse, wicked
wil(le), *n.,* will, desire
wil, *pres. vb.,* will
wile, *n.,* wile, trick
wilnen, *vb.,* desire, intend
win, *n.,* wine
winnen, *st. vb.* (*pret.* **wan**; *pp.* **wonnen**), win, triumph
wirchen, wirken: *see* **werken**
wĭs, wĭsly, *adv.,* surely
wīs, *adj.,* wise
wise, *n.,* wise, manner, way
wiste: *see* **witen**
wit, *n.,* wit, intelligence, knowledge
wĭten, *vb.* (*pres. sing.* 1, 3 **wǫǫt,** 2 **wǫǫst**; *plu.* **wǫǫt, wĭten**; *pret.* **wiste**), know
wīten, *vb.,* blame
with, *prep.,* with, by; **–al(le),** withal; **–inne,** within
withoute(n), *prep. and adv.,* without, outside
withsayn, *vb.* (*see* **sayn**), withsay, deny
withstǫnden, *st. vb.* (*see* **stonden**), withstand, resist
wǫ, *n.,* woe
wode, *n.,* wood
wol, *pres. vb.,* will; **wolt,** wilt
wolde, *pret. vb.,* would
wombe, *n.,* stomach, womb
womman, *pl.* **wommen,** *n.,* woman
wonder, *adj.,* wonderful, extraordinary; *n.,* wonder, marvel
wont, *n.,* wont, custom, habit
wood, *adj.,* mad, insane, frenzied
woot, woost: *see* **witen**
wrastlen, *vb.,* wrestle
wratthe, *n.,* wrath, anger
wrecche, *n.,* wretch; **–d,** *adj.*
wręken, *st. vb.* (*pp.* **wręken, wrǫken**), avenge
wrīten, *st. vb.* (*pret.* **wrǫǫt; wrĭten;** *pp.* **wrĭten**), write
wrǫth, *adj.,* wroth, angry
wroughte: *see* **werken**

ye, *subj. pron.,* ye, you
yë, *plu.* **yën,** *n.,* eye
ye, *interj.,* yea, yes
yeelden, *st. vb.* (*pret.* **yald;** *pp.* **yǫlden**), yield, repay
yęęr, yęre, *n.,* year
yeerd, *n.,* yard
yelow, *adj.,* yellow
yeman, *n.,* yeoman
yernen, *vb.,* yearn
yfere, *adv.,* together
yfinden, *st. vb.* (*see* **finden**), find
yheeren, *vb.* (*see* **heeren**), hear
yĭfte, *n.,* gift
yĭs, *adv.,* yes
yĭt, *adv.,* yet
yĭven, *st. vb.* (*pret.* **yaf; yaven, yęven;** *pp.* **yĭven**), give
ylīch(e), ylīk(e), *adj. and adv.,* like, alike
ynough, ynowe, *adj. and adv.,* enough
yǫk, *n.,* yoke
yond, *adv.,* yonder, yon
yong, *adj.,* young
yǫre, *adv.,* yore, long since, long ago
you, *obj. pron.,* you
youre(s), *poss. pron.,* your, yours
ypocrisie, *n.,* hypocrisy
yseen, *st. vb.* (*see* **seen**), see
yseene, *adj.,* visible
yvel, *adj.,* evil, bad, poor; **–e,** *adv.*
ywĭs, *adv.,* indeed, to be sure

BIBLIOGRAPHY

I. *Criticism: single authors*

BENNETT, H. S. *Chaucer and the Fifteenth Century.* Oxford: Clarendon Press, 1947.

BREWER, D. S. *Chaucer* (3d ed.). London: Longman, 1973.

BRONSON, B. H. *In Search of Chaucer.* Toronto: University of Toronto Press, 1960.

BURROW, J. A. *Ricardian Poetry.* London: Routledge & Kegan Paul, 1971.

CHESTERTON, G. K. *Chaucer.* London: Faber & Faber, 1932.

CLEMEN, WOLFGANG. *Chaucer's Early Poetry.* London: Methuen, 1963.

COGHILL, NEVILL. *Geoffrey Chaucer.* London: Longman, 1956.

COGHILL, NEVILL. *The Poet Chaucer.* London: Cumberlege, 1949.

CORSA, H. S. *Chaucer, Poet of Mirth and Morality.* Notre Dame: University of Notre Dame Press, 1964.

CURRY, W. C. *Chaucer and the Medieval Sciences* (2d ed.). New York: Barnes & Noble, 1960.

DONALDSON, E. T. *Speaking of Chaucer.* New York: W. W. Norton, 1970.

ELIASON, N. E. *The Language of Chaucer's Poetry* (*Anglistica* XVII). Copenhagen: Rosenkilde & Bagger, 1972.

GEROULD, G. H. *Chaucerian Essays.* Princeton: Princeton University Press, 1952.

JORDAN, R. M. *Chaucer and the Shape of Creation.* Cambridge: Harvard University Press, 1967.

KEAN, P. M. *Chaucer and the Making of English Poetry.* 2 vols. London: Routledge & Kegan Paul, 1972.

KITTREDGE, G. L. *Chaucer and His Poetry.* Cambridge: Harvard University Press, 1915.

LAWLOR, JOHN. *Chaucer.* London: Hutchinson, 1968.

LAWRENCE, W. W. *Chaucer and the Canterbury Tales.* New York: Columbia University Press, 1950.

LEGOUIS, EMILE. *Geoffrey Chaucer.* New York: E. P. Dutton, 1913.

LOWES, J. L. *Geoffrey Chaucer and the Development of His Genius.* Boston: Houghton Mifflin, 1934.

LUMIANSKY, R. M. *Of Sondry Folk.* Austin: University of Texas Press, 1955.

MALONE, KEMP. *Chapters on Chaucer.* Baltimore: The Johns Hopkins University Press, 1951.

MUSCATINE, CHARLES. *Chaucer and the French Tradition.* Berkeley: University of California Press, 1957.

PATCH, H. R. *On Rereading Chaucer.* Cambridge: Harvard University Press, 1939.

PAYNE, R. O. *The Key of Remembrance: A Study of Chaucer's Poetics.* New Haven: Yale University Press, 1963.

PRESTON, RAYMOND. *Chaucer.* New York: Sheed & Ward, 1952.

ROBERTSON, D. W., Jr. *A Preface to Chaucer.* Princeton: Princeton University Press, 1963.

ROOT, R. K. *The Poetry of Chaucer* (2d ed.). Boston: Houghton Mifflin, 1922.

RUGGIERS, P. G. *The Art of the Canterbury Tales.* Madison: University of Wisconsin Press, 1965.

SPEIRS, JOHN. *Chaucer the Maker.* London: Faber & Faber, 1951.

TATLOCK, J. S. P. *The Mind and Art of Chaucer.* Syracuse: Syracuse University Press, 1950.

II. *Criticism: collections of essays by various hands.*

BREWER, D. S., ed. *Chaucer and Chaucerians.* University, Ala.: University of Alabama Press, 1966.

BURROW, J. A., ed. *Geoffrey Chaucer.* Baltimore: Penguin Books, 1969.

CAWLEY, A. C., ed. *Chaucer's Mind and Art.* Edinburgh: Oliver & Boyd, 1969.

OWEN, C. A., Jr., ed. *Discussions of the Canterbury Tales.* Boston: Heath, 1962.

ROWLAND, BERYL, ed. *Companion to Chaucer Studies.* Toronto: Oxford University Press, 1968.

SCHOECK, R. J., and JEROME TAYLOR, eds. *Chaucer Criticism.* 2 vols.: I. *The Canterbury Tales.* II. *Troilus and Criseyde & The Minor Poems.* Notre Dame: Notre Dame University Press, 1960, 1961.

WAGENKNECHT, EDWARD, ed. *Chaucer, Modern Essays in Criticism.* New York: Oxford University Press, 1959.

III. *Life*

CHUTE, MARCHETTE. *Geoffrey Chaucer of England.* New York: E. P. Dutton, 1946.

CROW, M. M., and C. C. OLSON, eds. *Chaucer Life-Records.* Oxford: Clarendon Press, 1966.

IV. *Background*

BREWER, D. S. *Chaucer in His Time.* London: Nelson, 1963.

BOWDEN, MURIEL. *A Commentary on the General Prologue to the Canterbury Tales.* New York: Macmillan, 1948.

COULTON, G. G. *Chaucer and His England.* London: Methuen, 1908.

HUIZINGA, J. *The Waning of the Middle Ages.* Garden City: Doubleday-Anchor, 1954.

LOOMIS, R. S. *A Mirror of Chaucer's World.* Princeton: Princeton University Press, 1965.

MANLY, J. M. *Some New Light on Chaucer.* New York: Henry Holt, 1926.

RICKERT, EDITH. *Chaucer's World.* New York: Columbia University Press, 1948.

V. *Literary sources*

BRYAN, W. F., and GERMAINE DEMPSTER, eds. *Sources and Analogues of Chaucer's Canterbury Tales.* Chicago: University of Chicago Press, 1941.

GORDON, R. K., ed. *The Story of Troilus.* New York: E. P. Dutton, 1964.

VI. *Annotated editions*

BAUGH, A. C. *Chaucer's Major Poetry.* New York: Appleton-Century-Crofts, 1963.

MANLY, J. M. *Canterbury Tales.* New York: Henry Holt, 1928.

PRATT, R. A. *The Tales of Canterbury.* Boston: Houghton Mifflin, 1974.

ROBINSON, F. N. *The Complete Works of Chaucer* (2d ed.). Boston: Houghton Mifflin, 1957.

ROOT, R. K. *The Book of Troilus and Criseyde.* Princeton: Princeton University Press, 1926.

SKEAT, W. W. *The Complete Works of Geoffrey Chaucer.* 7 vols. Oxford: Clarendon Press, 1894–7.

VII. *Handbook*

FRENCH, R. D. *A Chaucer Handbook* (2d ed.). New York: Appleton-Century-Crofts, 1947.

VIII. *Bibliographies*

BAUGH, A. C. *Chaucer.* New York: Appleton-Century-Crofts, 1968.

CRAWFORD, W. R. *Bibliography of Chaucer 1954–63.* Seattle: University of Washington Press, 1967.

GRIFFITH, D. D. *Bibliography of Chaucer 1908–1953.* Seattle: University of Washington Press, 1955.

HAMMOND, E. P. *Chaucer: A Bibliographical Manual.* New York: Macmillan, 1908.

IX. *Language*

KÖKERITZ, HELGE. *A Guide to Chaucer's Pronunciation.* New York: Holt, Rinehart and Winston, 1962.

MOORE, SAMUEL. *Historical Outlines of English Sounds and Inflections,* revised by A. H. Marckwardt. Ann Arbor: George Wahr Publishing Co., 1951.